TIME WITH GOD

NEW CENTURY VERSION

WORD PUBLISHING
Dallas · London · Vancouver · Melbourne

TIME WITH GOD
The New Testament for Busy People

Library of Congress Cataloging-in-Publication Data:

Bible.   N.T.   English.   New Century.   1991
    Time with God: the New Testament for busy people: New Century Version.
      p.   cm.
    Arranged for daily readings.
    ISBN 0–8499–0923–6 (HB).
    1. Devotional calendars.   I. Word Publishing.   II. Title.
BS2095.N364   1991
22.5'208—dc20
                                       91–30799
                                          CIP

1 2 3 4 9   RRD   9 8 7 6 5 4 3 2 1

Printed in the United States of America

INTRODUCTION

*W*ould you like to know God better . . . to explore exciting Scriptural truths each day and still meet your other demands and responsibilities . . . to be challenged (at a comfortable pace) to grow deeper in your faith?

Time with God has been designed for you! In fifteen minutes a day, you can systematically explore the treasures of Scripture. You may begin any time you wish, and at the end of the year you will have read the entire New Testament and related sections from every book of the Old Testament. Plus you will have received insights from classical and contempory writers.

There's a reading for Monday, Tuesday, Wednesday, Thursday, Friday, and one for Saturday/Sunday. (We know how busy weekends can be.)

Each two-page reading begins with the New Testament passage for the day and is followed by Old Testament passages that reinforce the theme. This unique format allows you to see Scripture's truths unfold and to gain a new understanding of God's love and mercy throughout history.

If you wish, you may read thematically. Maybe you're wrestling with a problem at work, an issue of faith, or some type of suffering. Or maybe you would like to study a particular biblical theme. Whatever your need, the index on page 626 will guide you to just the right reading.

Not only is *Time with God* a valuable aid in personal growth and meditative study, it is helpful for small groups and Sunday school classes.

Time with God features the New Century Version, an accurate and readable translation that makes it well suited to devotional reading. In fact, because of its ease of reading, you may find it hard to stop at just one reading a day.

Most likely, you will recognize many of the authors' quotations we've included. Their insights—gleaned from more than one hundred seventy books—will challenge your thinking, broaden your understanding, and guide you to an even deeper relationship with God. The credits at the end of the book show the source of each quotation so you may pursue further reading.

Questions at the end of each reading will help you evaluate and apply what you've read. They are also excellent discussion starters for small group settings.

We invite you now to spend time with God and discover what He has in store for you!

Amanda and Stephen Sorenson
Editors

MONDAY:

The Savior of God's People Is Born

Matthew 1:1–25

NEW TESTAMENT READING

The Family History of Jesus

*T*his is the family history of Jesus Christ. He came from the family of David, and David came from the family of Abraham.

Abraham was the father of Isaac.

Isaac was the father of Jacob.

Jacob was the father of Judah and his brothers.

Judah was the father of Perez and Zerah. (Their mother was Tamar.)

Perez was the father of Hezron.

Hezron was the father of Ram.

Ram was the father of Amminadab.

Amminadab was the father of Nahshon.

Nahshon was the father of Salmon.

Salmon was the father of Boaz. (Boaz's mother was Rahab.)

Boaz was the father of Obed. (Obed's mother was Ruth.)

Obed was the father of Jesse.

Jesse was the father of King David.

David was the father of Solomon. (Solomon's mother had been Uriah's wife.)

Solomon was the father of Rehoboam.

Rehoboam was the father of Abijah.

Abijah was the father of Asa.

Asa was the father of Jehoshaphat.

Jehoshaphat was the father of Jehoram.

Jehoram was the ancestor of Uzziah.

Uzziah was the father of Jotham.

Jotham was the father of Ahaz.

Ahaz was the father of Hezekiah.

Hezekiah was the father of Manasseh.

Manasseh was the father of Amon.

Amon was the father of Josiah.

Josiah was the grandfather of Jehoiachin and his brothers. (This was at the time that the people were taken to Babylon.)

After they were taken to Babylon:

Jehoiachin was the father of Shealtiel.

Shealtiel was the grandfather of Zerubbabel.

Zerubbabel was the father of Abiud.

Abiud was the father of Eliakim.

Eliakim was the father of Azor.

Azor was the father of Zadok.

Zadok was the father of Akim.

Akim was the father of Eliud.

Eliud was the father of Eleazar.

Eleazar was the father of Matthan.

Matthan was the father of Jacob.

Jacob was the father of Joseph.

Joseph was the husband of Mary, and Mary was the mother of Jesus. Jesus is called the Christ.

So there were fourteen generations from Abraham to David. And there were fourteen generations from David until the people were taken to Babylon. And there were fourteen generations from the time when the people were taken to Babylon until Christ was born.

The Birth of Jesus Christ

*T*his is how the birth of Jesus Christ came about. His mother Mary was engaged to marry Joseph, but before they married, she learned she was pregnant by the power of the Holy Spirit. Because Mary's husband, Joseph, was a good man, he did not want to disgrace her in public, so he planned to divorce her secretly.

While Joseph thought about these things, an angel of the Lord came to him in a dream. The angel said, "Joseph, descendant of David, don't be afraid to take Mary as your wife, because the baby in her is from the Holy Spirit. She will give birth to a son, and you will name him Jesus, because he will save his people from their sins."

All this happened to bring about what the Lord had said through the prophet: "The virgin will be pregnant. She will have a son, and they will name him Immanuel," which means "God is with us."

When Joseph woke up, he did what the Lord's angel had told him to do. Joseph took Mary as his wife, but he did not have sexual relations with her until she gave birth to the son. And Joseph named him Jesus.

*T*hen the LORD spoke to Ahaz again, saying, "Ask for a sign from the LORD your God to prove to yourself that these things are true. It may be a sign from as deep as the place of the dead or as high as the heavens."

But Ahaz said, "I will not ask for a sign or test the LORD."

Then Isaiah said, "Ahaz, descendant of David, listen carefully! Isn't it bad enough that you wear out the patience of people? Do you also have to wear out the patience of my God? The Lord himself will give you a sign: The virgin will be pregnant. She will have a son, and she will name him Immanuel."

Isaiah 7:10–14

*W*hen Abram was ninety-nine years old, the LORD appeared to him and said, "I am God Almighty. Obey me and do what is right. I will make an agreement between us, and I will make you the ancestor of many people."

Then Abram bowed facedown on the ground. God said to him, "I am making my agreement with you: I will make you the father of many nations. I am changing your name from Abram to Abraham because I am making you a father of many nations. I will give you many descendants. New nations will be born from you, and kings will come from you. And I will make an agreement between me and you and all your descendants from now on: I will be your God and the God of all your descendants. You live in the land of Canaan now as a stranger, but I will give you and your descendants all this land forever. And I will be the God of your descendants."

Genesis 17:1–8

*T*he LORD said, "Should I tell Abraham what I am going to do now? Abraham's children will certainly become a great and powerful nation, and all nations on the earth will be blessed through him."

Genesis 18:17–18

*T*he doctrine of the virgin birth is crucial to our faith. The incarnation of the Son of God was accomplished by a creative act of the Holy Spirit in the body of Mary, a virgin. It was a special miracle performed by the third person of the Holy Trinity—the Holy Spirit—which enabled the second person of the Trinity—the eternal Son of God—to take upon Himself a genuine, although sinless, human nature. He was born of a virgin, as a man, without surrendering any aspect of His deity. . . .

. . . This may be difficult to understand, but we can understand the concept even if we can't grasp it in our minds. Jesus was fully human and fully divine. He was not just a prophet, He was God.

. . . One with us, yet one with God. He had to become man because man was the one who had sinned. He had to be God because God was the only One who could do anything about the sin of man. Humanity had tried for centuries, and the situation only got worse! The only way God could bring about the salvation of the fallen human race was to assume the form of the race He was to redeem.

God has given us the means to know the truth. Jesus is the way to the Father, because He is our Redeemer. He is the truth because He is the fulfillment of all the prophecies concerning Him. He is the life because He overcame death. . . . Jesus has the fullness of God dwelling in Him bodily forever and ever. The Son of God became the Son of man so that the sons of men might become the sons of God.

Terry Fullam

PAUSE FOR REFLECTION

*W*hat does the virgin birth of Jesus signify for all people, for King Ahaz, and for you? In what ways have all nations been blessed through the children of Abraham? How has Jesus, son of Abraham and son of God, blessed your life?

3

TUESDAY:
God Guides and Protects Us
Matthew 2:1–23

NEW TESTAMENT READING

Wise Men Come to Visit Jesus

*J*esus was born in the town of Bethlehem in Judea during the time when Herod was king. When Jesus was born, some wise men from the east came to Jerusalem. They asked, "Where is the baby who was born to be the king of the Jews? We saw his star in the east and have come to worship him."

When King Herod heard this, he was troubled, as well as all the people in Jerusalem. Herod called a meeting of all the leading priests and teachers of the law and asked them where the Christ would be born. They answered, "In the town of Bethlehem in Judea. The prophet wrote about this in the Scriptures:

'But you, Bethlehem, in the land of
  Judah,
    are important among the tribes of
  Judah.
A ruler will come from you
    who will be like a shepherd for my
      people Israel.'"   *Micah 5:2*

Then Herod had a secret meeting with the wise men and learned from them the exact time they first saw the star. He sent the wise men to Bethlehem, saying, "Look carefully for the child. When you find him, come tell me so I can worship him too."

After the wise men heard the king, they left. The star that they had seen in the east went before them until it stopped above the place where the child was. When the wise men saw the star, they were filled with joy. They came to the house where the child was and saw him with his mother, Mary, and they bowed down and worshiped him. They opened their gifts and gave him treasures of gold, frankincense, and myrrh. But God warned the wise men in a dream not to go back to Herod, so they returned to their own country by a different way.

Jesus' Parents Take Him to Egypt

*A*fter they left, an angel of the Lord came to Joseph in a dream and said, "Get up! Take the child and his mother and escape to Egypt, because Herod is starting to look for the child so he can kill him. Stay in Egypt until I tell you to return."

So Joseph got up and left for Egypt during the night with the child and his mother. And Joseph stayed in Egypt until Herod died. This happened to bring about what the Lord had said through the prophet: "I called my son out of Egypt."

Herod Kills the Baby Boys

*W*hen Herod saw that the wise men had tricked him, he was furious. So he gave an order to kill all the baby boys in Bethlehem and in the surrounding area who were two years old or younger. This was in keeping with the time he learned from the wise men. So what God had said through the prophet Jeremiah came true:

"A voice was heard in Ramah
    of painful crying and deep sadness:
Rachel crying for her children.
    She refused to be comforted,
    because her children are dead."
                    Jeremiah 31:15

Joseph and Mary Return

*A*fter Herod died, an angel of the Lord spoke to Joseph in a dream while he was in Egypt. The angel said, "Get up! Take the child and his mother and go to the land of Israel, because the people who were trying to kill the child are now dead."

So Joseph took the child and his mother and went to Israel. But he heard that Archelaus was now king in Judea since his father Herod had died. So Joseph was afraid to go there. After being warned in a dream, he went to the area of Galilee, to a town called Nazareth, and lived there. And so what God had said through the prophets came true: "He will be called a Nazarene."

OLD TESTAMENT READING

*B*e merciful to me, God; be merciful to me

4

because I come to you for protection.
Let me hide under the shadow of your wings
until the trouble has passed.

I cry out to God Most High,
to the God who does everything for me.
He sends help from heaven and saves me.
He punishes those who chase me.
Selah
God sends me his love and truth.

Enemies, like lions, are all around me;
I must lie down among them.
Their teeth are like spears and arrows,
their tongues as sharp as swords.

God is supreme over the skies;
his majesty covers the earth.

They set a trap for me.
I am very worried.
They dug a pit in my path,
but they fell into it themselves. *Selah*

My heart is steady, God; my heart is steady.
I will sing and praise you.
Wake up, my soul.
Wake up, harp and lyre!
I will wake up the dawn.
Lord, I will praise you among the nations;
I will sing songs of praise about you to all the nations.
Your great love reaches to the skies,
your truth to the clouds.
God, you are supreme above the skies.
Let your glory be over all the earth.
Psalm 57:1–11

*B*ut you, Bethlehem Ephrathah,
though you are too small to be among the army groups from Judah,
from you will come one who will rule Israel for me.
He comes from very old times,
from days long ago."

The LORD will give up his people
until the one who is having a baby gives birth;

then the rest of his relatives will return to the people of Israel.
At that time the ruler of Israel will stand and take care of his people
with the LORD's strength
and with the power of the name of the LORD his God.
The Israelites will live in safety,
because his greatness will reach all over the earth.
He will bring peace.
Micah 5:2–5a

INSIGHTS

*N*othing is clearer in the Bible than the guarantee of divine guidance to anyone who seeks it. Every day of your life can be God-planned and directed. Day by day, moment by moment, step by step.

God desires to and delights in directing your life.

God has led. This is history's testimony. Looking back over lives, we can see how beautifully, wonderfully, lovingly God has led. "As for me, the LORD has led me," testified the servant of Abraham (Genesis 24:27).

God will lead. This is the testimony of doctrine. The Scriptures teach it by precept and example throughout Old and New Testaments. The word of God declares it to be so. Looking ahead—before the need, before the crunch—we can testify that God will lead.

God is leading! This is the testimony of faith, where the rubber meets the road. God has promised to lead, and I seek to be led—an unbeatable combination. God's promise, my submission.

God has led, for which I am grateful.

I know God will lead, and for this I praise and thank Him.

God is leading! This is my confidence and joy . . . my rest.

Richard Halverson

PAUSE FOR REFLECTION

*N*ote the instances in which God protected the child Jesus and how each of those also fulfilled prophecy. What does this reveal to you about God's sovereignty and faithfulness in protecting his own?

WEDNESDAY:

Change Your Hearts and Lives

Matthew 3:1—4:11

The Work of John the Baptist

*A*bout that time John the Baptist began preaching in the desert area of Judea. John said, "Change your hearts and lives because the kingdom of heaven is near." John the Baptist is the one Isaiah the prophet was talking about when he said:

"This is a voice of one
who calls out in the desert:
'Prepare the way for the Lord.
Make the road straight for him.'"

Isaiah 40:3

John's clothes were made from camel's hair, and he wore a leather belt around his waist. For food, he ate locusts and wild honey. Many people came from Jerusalem and Judea and all the area around the Jordan River to hear John. They confessed their sins, and he baptized them in the Jordan River.

Many of the Pharisees and Sadducees came to the place where John was baptizing people. When John saw them, he said, "You are all snakes! Who warned you to run away from God's coming punishment? Do the things that show you really have changed your hearts and lives. And don't think you can say to yourselves, 'Abraham is our father.' I tell you that God could make children for Abraham from these rocks. The ax is now ready to cut down the trees, and every tree that does not produce good fruit will be cut down and thrown into the fire.

"I baptize you with water to show that your hearts and lives have changed. But there is one coming after me who is greater than I am, whose sandals I am not good enough to carry. He will baptize you with the Holy Spirit and fire. He will come ready to clean the grain, separating the good grain from the chaff. He will put the good part of the grain into his barn, but he will burn the chaff with a fire that cannot be put out."

Jesus Is Baptized by John

*A*t that time Jesus came from Galilee to the Jordan River and wanted John to baptize him. But John tried to stop him, saying, "Why do you come to me to be baptized? I need to be baptized by you!"

Jesus answered, "Let it be this way for now. We should do all things that are God's will." So John agreed to baptize Jesus.

As soon as Jesus was baptized, he came up out of the water. Then heaven opened, and he saw God's Spirit coming down on him like a dove. And a voice from heaven said, "This is my Son, whom I love, and I am very pleased with him."

The Temptation of Jesus

*T*hen the Spirit led Jesus into the desert to be tempted by the devil. Jesus ate nothing for forty days and nights. After this, he was very hungry. The devil came to Jesus to tempt him, saying, "If you are the Son of God, tell these rocks to become bread."

Jesus answered, "It is written in the Scriptures, 'A person does not live by eating only bread, but by everything God says.'"

Then the devil led Jesus to the holy city of Jerusalem and put him on a high place of the Temple. The devil said, "If you are the Son of God, jump down, because it is written in the Scriptures:

'He has put his angels in charge of you.
They will catch you in their hands
so that you will not hit your foot on a
rock.'" *Psalm 91:11–12*

Jesus answered him, "It also says in the Scriptures, 'Do not test the Lord your God.'"

Then the devil led Jesus to the top of a very high mountain and showed him all the kingdoms of the world and all their splendor. The devil said, "If you will bow down and worship me, I will give you all these things."

Jesus said to the devil, "Go away from me, Satan! It is written in the Scriptures, 'You must worship the Lord your God and serve only him.'"

So the devil left Jesus, and angels came and took care of him.

I will praise the LORD at all times;
  his praise is always on my lips.
My whole being praises the LORD.
  The poor will hear and be glad.
Glorify the LORD with me,
  and let us praise his name together.

I asked the LORD for help, and he
    answered me.
  He saved me from all that I feared.
Those who go to him for help are
    happy,
  and they are never disgraced.
This poor man called, and the LORD
    heard him
  and saved him from all his troubles.
The angel of the LORD camps around
    those who fear God,
  and he saves them.

Examine and see how good the LORD is.
  Happy is the person who trusts him.
You who belong to the LORD, fear him!
  Those who fear him will have
    everything they need.
Even lions may get weak and hungry,
  but those who look to the LORD will
    have every good thing.
Children, come and listen to me.
  I will teach you to worship the
    Lord.
You must do these things
  to enjoy life and have many happy
    days.
You must not say evil things,
  and you must not tell lies.
Stop doing evil and do good.
  Look for peace and work for it.

The LORD sees the good people
  and listens to their prayers.
But the LORD is against those who do
    evil;
  he makes the world forget them.
The LORD hears good people when they
    cry out to him,
  and he saves them from all their
    troubles.
The LORD is close to the brokenhearted,
  and he saves those whose spirits
    have been crushed.

People who do what is right may have
    many problems,
  but the LORD will solve them all.
He will protect their very bones;
  not one of them will be broken.
Evil will kill the wicked;
  those who hate good people will be
    judged guilty.
But the LORD saves his servants' lives;
  no one who trusts him will be
    judged guilty.

Psalm 34:1–22

INSIGHTS

Jean, a small shopkeeper in Bordeaux, worked long hours with virtually nothing to show for his labors. Even his best efforts to beguile the Paris tax collector left him very little for his family. His life was depressing and without purpose, until the day when a missionary entered his shop to make a purchase.

Before leaving the shop, this foreigner shared his faith with Jean, and for the first time the shopkeeper realized that there was more to life than he had ever supposed. . . .

As he grew in faith, Jean became convinced that his lifestyle must be radically altered and that he could no longer lie about how much income he was making at his little shop. When the time came to submit his tax forms, he filled them out in full and paid the required amount of taxes. The local tax clerk was stunned, and word spread like wildfire among the shopkeepers. Jean's wife was outraged, and his neighbors were convinced that he had lost his mind. When they inquired about his foolish actions, he could only explain that God had made him a different man.

Ruth Tucker

PAUSE FOR REFLECTION

What message from God did John bring to the people of his day? Was it different from the message of the Old Testament? Was it different from Jesus' message? What does it mean to have a changed heart and live a changed life today?

THURSDAY:

"Come, Follow Me"

Matthew 4:12—5:12

Jesus Begins Work in Galilee

*W*hen Jesus heard that John had been put in prison, he went back to Galilee. He left Nazareth and went to live in Capernaum, a town near Lake Galilee, in the area near Zebulun and Naphtali. Jesus did this to bring about what the prophet Isaiah had said:

"Land of Zebulun and land of Naphtali
along the sea,
beyond the Jordan River.
This is Galilee where the non-Jewish
people live.
These people who live in darkness
will see a great light.
They live in a place covered with the
shadows of death,
but a light will shine on them."

Isaiah 9:1–2

Jesus Chooses Some Followers

*F*rom that time Jesus began to preach, saying, "Change your hearts and lives, because the kingdom of heaven is near."

As Jesus was walking by Lake Galilee, he saw two brothers, Simon (called Peter) and his brother Andrew. They were throwing a net into the lake because they were fishermen. Jesus said, "Come follow me, and I will make you fish for people." So Simon and Andrew immediately left their nets and followed him.

As Jesus continued walking by Lake Galilee, he saw two other brothers, James and John, the sons of Zebedee. They were in a boat with their father Zebedee, mending their nets. Jesus told them to come with him. Immediately they left the boat and their father, and they followed Jesus.

Jesus Teaches and Heals People

*J*esus went everywhere in Galilee, teaching in the synagogues, preaching the Good News about the kingdom of heaven, and healing all the people's diseases and sicknesses.

The news about Jesus spread all over Syria, and people brought all the sick to him. They were suffering from different kinds of diseases. Some were in great pain, some had demons, some were epileptics, and some were paralyzed. Jesus healed all of them. Many people from Galilee, the Ten Towns, Jerusalem, Judea, and the land across the Jordan River followed him.

Jesus Teaches the People

*W*hen Jesus saw the crowds, he went up on a hill and sat down. His followers came to him, and he began to teach them, saying:

"Those people who know they have great
spiritual needs are happy,
because the kingdom of heaven belongs
to them.
Those who are sad now are happy,
because God will comfort them.
Those who are humble are happy,
because the earth will belong to them.
Those who want to do right more than anything else are happy,
because God will fully satisfy them.
Those who show mercy to others are happy,
because God will show mercy to them.
Those who are pure in their thinking are
happy,
because they will be with God.
Those who work to bring peace are happy,
because God will call them his children.
Those who are treated badly for doing good
are happy,
because the kingdom of heaven belongs
to them.

"People will insult you and hurt you. They will lie and say all kinds of evil things about you because you follow me. But when they do, you will be happy. Rejoice and be glad, because you have a great reward waiting for you in heaven. People did the same evil things to the prophets who lived before you."

*T*he LORD said to Abram, "Leave your country, your relatives, and your father's family, and go to the land I will show you.

I will make you a great nation,

and I will bless you.
I will make you famous,
and you will be a blessing to others.
I will bless those who bless you,
and I will place a curse on those who
harm you.
And all the people on earth
will be blessed through you."

So Abram left Haran as the LORD had told him, and Lot went with him. At this time Abram was seventy-five years old.

Genesis 12:1–4

*I*n the year that King Uzziah died, I saw the Lord sitting on a very high throne. His long robe filled the Temple. Heavenly creatures of fire stood above him. Each creature had six wings: It used two wings to cover its face, two wings to cover its feet, and two wings for flying. Each creature was calling to the others:

"Holy, holy, holy is the LORD All-
Powerful.
His glory fills the whole earth."

Their calling caused the frame around the door to shake, as the Temple filled with smoke.

I said, "Oh, no! I will be destroyed. I am not pure, and I live among people who are not pure, but I have seen the King, the LORD All-Powerful."

One of the heavenly creatures used a pair of tongs to take a hot coal from the altar. Then he flew to me with the hot coal in his hand. The creature touched my mouth with the hot coal and said, "Look, your guilt is taken away, because this hot coal has touched your lips. Your sin is taken away."

Then I heard the Lord's voice, saying, "Whom can I send? Who will go for us?"

So I said, "Here I am. Send me!"

Isaiah 6:1–8

*A*t its simplest Christ's call was 'Follow me'. He asked men and women for their personal allegiance. He invited them to learn from him, to obey his words and to identify themselves with his cause.

Now there can be no following without a previous forsaking. To follow Christ is to renounce all lesser loyalties. In the days when he lived among men on earth, this meant a literal abandonment of home and work. . . .

Today, in principle, the call of the Lord Jesus has not changed. He still says 'Follow me', and adds, 'whoever of you does not renounce all that he has cannot be my disciple'. In practice, however, this does not mean for the majority of Christians a physical departure from their home or their job. It implies rather an inner surrender of both, and a refusal to allow either family or ambition to occupy the first place in our lives.

Let me be more explicit about the forsaking which cannot be separated from the following of Jesus Christ.

First, there must be a renunciation of sin. This, in a word, is repentance. It is the first part of Christian conversion. It can in no circumstances be bypassed. Repentance and faith belong together. We cannot follow Christ without forsaking sin. . . .

Second, there must be a renunciation of self. In order to follow Christ we must not only forsake isolated sins, but renounce the very principle of self-will which lies at the root of every act of sin. To follow Christ is to surrender to him the rights over our own lives. It is to abdicate the throne of our heart and do homage to him as our King. . . .

So in order to follow Christ we have to deny ourselves, to crucify ourselves, to lose ourselves. The full, inexorable demand of Jesus Christ is now laid bare. He does not call us to a sloppy half-heartedness, but to a vigorous, absolute commitment. He calls us to make him our Lord.

John Stott

*W*hat did the men mentioned in these passages forsake in order to follow God? What have you had to forsake in order to follow Jesus? Think about what occupies first place in your life now. Pray that you will make following Jesus most important.

FRIDAY:

Take God's Light into the World

Matthew 5:13–37

You Are like Salt and Light

You are the salt of the earth. But if the salt loses its salty taste, it cannot be made salty again. It is good for nothing, except to be thrown out and walked on.

"You are the light that gives light to the world. A city that is built on a hill cannot be hidden. And people don't hide a light under a bowl. They put it on a lampstand so the light shines for all the people in the house. In the same way, you should be a light for other people. Live so that they will see the good things you do and will praise your Father in heaven.

The Importance of the Law

Don't think that I have come to destroy the law of Moses or the teaching of the prophets. I have not come to destroy them but to bring about what they said. I tell you the truth, nothing will disappear from the law until heaven and earth are gone. Not even the smallest letter or the smallest part of a letter will be lost until everything has happened. Whoever refuses to obey any command and teaches other people not to obey that command will be the least important in the kingdom of heaven. But whoever obeys the commands and teaches other people to obey them will be great in the kingdom of heaven. I tell you that if you are no more obedient than the teachers of the law and the Pharisees, you will never enter the kingdom of heaven.

Jesus Teaches About Anger

You have heard that it was said to our people long ago, 'You must not murder anyone. Anyone who murders another will be judged.' But I tell you, if you are angry with a brother or sister, you will be judged. If you say bad things to a brother or sister, you will be judged by the council. And if you call someone a fool, you will be in danger of the fire of hell.

"So when you offer your gift to God at the altar, and you remember that your brother or sister has something against you, leave your gift there at the altar. Go and make peace with that person, and then come and offer your gift.

"If your enemy is taking you to court, become friends quickly, before you go to court. Otherwise, your enemy might turn you over to the judge, and the judge might give you to a guard to put you in jail. I tell you the truth, you will not leave there until you have paid everything you owe.

Jesus Teaches About Sexual Sin

You have heard that it was said, 'You must not be guilty of adultery.' But I tell you that if anyone looks at a woman and wants to sin sexually with her, in his mind he has already done that sin with the woman. If your right eye causes you to sin, take it out and throw it away. It is better to lose one part of your body than to have your whole body thrown into hell. If your right hand causes you to sin, cut it off and throw it away. It is better to lose one part of your body than for your whole body to go into hell.

Jesus Teaches About Divorce

It was also said, 'Anyone who divorces his wife must give her a written divorce paper.' But I tell you that anyone who divorces his wife forces her to be guilty of adultery. The only reason for a man to divorce his wife is if she has sexual relations with another man. And anyone who marries that divorced woman is guilty of adultery.

Make Promises Carefully

You have heard that it was said to our people long ago, 'Don't break your promises, but keep the promises you make to the Lord.' But I tell you, never swear an oath. Don't swear an oath using the name of heaven, because heaven is God's throne. Don't swear an oath using the name of the earth, because the earth belongs to God. Don't swear an oath using the name of Jerusalem, because that is the city of the great King. Don't even swear by your own head, because you cannot make one hair on your head become white or black. Say only yes if you mean yes, and no if you mean no. If you say more than yes or no, it is from the Evil One."

OLD   TESTAMENT   READING

*A*ll of you people in faraway places, listen to me.
    Listen, all you nations far away.
    Before I was born, the Lord called me to serve him.
        The Lord named me while I was still in my mother's body.
    He made my tongue like a sharp sword.
        He hid me in the shadow of his hand.
    He made me like a sharp arrow.
        He hid me in the holder for his arrows.
    He told me, "Israel, you are my servant.
    I will show my glory through you."
    Now he told me,
    "You are an important servant to me
        to bring back the tribes of Jacob,
        to bring back the people of Israel who are left alive.
    But, more importantly, I will make you a light for all nations
        to show people all over the world the way to be saved."

Isaiah 49:1–3, 6

*T*he skies and the earth belong to you.
    You made the world and everything in it.
    You created the north and the south.
        Mount Tabor and Mount Hermon sing for joy at your name.
    Your arm has great power.
        Your hand is strong; your right hand is lifted up.
    Your kingdom is built on what is right and fair.
        Love and truth are in all you do.

Happy are the people who know how to praise you.
    Lord, let them live in the light of your presence.

Psalm 89:11–15

*P*eople who love the Lord hate evil.
    The Lord watches over those who follow him
        and frees them from the power of the wicked.
    Light shines on those who do right;
        joy belongs to those who are honest.

Psalm 97:10–11

*L*ord, you give light to my lamp.
    My God brightens the darkness around me.

Psalm 18:28

INSIGHTS

*N*owhere in the Bible are we commanded to bring non-Christians into the church to get saved. In fact, there is not one instance in the Bible of anyone who ever got converted in a church or synagogue. For instance, in Luke 19, our Lord did not ask Zaccheus to meet Him at the synagogue on the Sabbath. Instead, he went to Zaccheus' home. The misconception is that the pagan is supposed to come and hear; the Biblical mandate for the believer is to go and tell.

If we are to be salt and light in our world, we need to go where the lost are. That might mean inviting them into your home for dinner, going next door to visit with them, playing miniature golf together, or doing something else with them. The Holy Spirit will start working in their lives as they watch our lives and try to figure out why we are different.

Robert Tamasy

APPLICATION

*T*hink about what it means to be salt and light in the world today. What kind of lifestyle shines as a light to the world and shows people how to be saved? How do you need to change your life in order to be the salt and light God wants you to be?

WEEKEND:

The Wonder of God's Forgiveness

Matthew 5:38—6:15

Don't Fight Back

*Y*ou have heard that it was said, 'An eye for an eye, and a tooth for a tooth.' But I tell you, don't stand up against an evil person. If someone slaps you on the right cheek, turn to him the other cheek also. If someone wants to sue you in court and take your shirt, let him have your coat also. If someone forces you to go with him one mile, go with him two miles. If a person asks you for something, give it to him. Don't refuse to give to someone who wants to borrow from you.

Love All People

*Y*ou have heard that it was said, 'Love your neighbor and hate your enemies.' But I say to you, love your enemies. Pray for those who hurt you. If you do this, you will be true children of your Father in heaven. He causes the sun to rise on good people and on evil people, and he sends rain to those who do right and to those who do wrong. If you love only the people who love you, you will get no reward. Even the tax collectors do that. And if you are nice only to your friends, you are no better than other people. Even those who don't know God are nice to their friends. So you must be perfect, just as your Father in heaven is perfect.

Jesus Teaches About Giving

*B*e careful! When you do good things, don't do them in front of people to be seen by them. If you do that, you will have no reward from your Father in heaven.

"When you give to the poor, don't be like the hypocrites. They blow trumpets in the synagogues and on the streets so that people will see them and honor them. I tell you the truth, those hypocrites already have their full reward. So when you give to the poor, don't let anyone know what you are doing. Your giving should be done in secret. Your Father can see what is done in secret, and he will reward you.

Jesus Teaches About Prayer

*W*hen you pray, don't be like the hypocrites. They love to stand in the synagogues and on the street corners and pray so people will see them. I tell you the truth, they already have their full reward. When you pray, you should go into your room and close the door and pray to your Father who cannot be seen. Your Father can see what is done in secret, and he will reward you.

"And when you pray, don't be like those people who don't know God. They continue saying things that mean nothing, thinking that God will hear them because of their many words. Don't be like them, because your Father knows the things you need before you ask him. So when you pray, you should pray like this:

'Our Father in heaven,
may your name always be kept holy.
May your kingdom come
and what you want be done,
    here on earth as it is in heaven.
Give us the food we need for each day.
Forgive us for our sins,
    just as we have forgiven those who
        sinned against us.
And do not cause us to be tempted,
but save us from the Evil One.'

Yes, if you forgive others for their sins, your Father in heaven will also forgive you for your sins. But if you don't forgive others, your Father in heaven will not forgive your sins."

*L*ORD, I give myself to you;
    my God, I trust you.
Do not let me be disgraced;
    do not let my enemies laugh at me.
No one who trusts you will be disgraced,
    but those who sin without excuse
        will be disgraced.

LORD, tell me your ways.
    Show me how to live.

Guide me in your truth,
and teach me, my God, my Savior.
I trust you all day long.
LORD, remember your mercy and love
that you have shown since long ago.
Do not remember the sins
and wrong things I did when I was
young.
But remember to love me always
because you are good, LORD.

The LORD is good and right;
he points sinners to the right way.
He shows those who are humble how
to do right,
and he teaches them his ways.
All the LORD's ways are loving and true
for those who follow the demands of
his agreement.
For the sake of your name, LORD,
forgive my many sins.
Are there those who respect the LORD?
He will point them to the best way.
They will enjoy a good life,
and their children will inherit the
land.
The LORD tells his secrets to those who
respect him;
he tells them about his agreement.
My eyes are always looking to the LORD
for help.
He will keep me from any traps.
Turn to me and have mercy on me,
because I am lonely and hurting.
My troubles have grown larger;
free me from my problems.
Look at my suffering and troubles,
and take away all my sins.
Look at how many enemies I have!
See how much they hate me!
Protect me and save me.
I trust you, so do not let me be
disgraced.
My hope is in you,
so may goodness and honesty
guard me.
God, save Israel from all their troubles!
Psalm 25:1–22

*S*cripture *is realistic in its treatment of sin, whether in the believer or unbeliever. It* recognizes *that sin is a continuing problem, even for the believer. He is not forever done with sin when he is converted, because he never gets beyond the reach of temptation. True, he has experienced the joy of forgiveness. He revels in the assurance that his guilt has been removed, but he is nowhere promised exemption from the lure of tempation or the possibility of sinning. . . .*

. . . What lies hidden in the depths of our subconscious mind—below the level of consciousness? The Master Psychologist gave His diagnosis: "From within, out of the heart of men, proceed the evil thoughts and fornications, thefts, murders, adulteries." (Mark 7:21). Then how is it possible for a God who hates sin and requires purity, to continue having dealings with a sin-prone believer, to say nothing of permitting a deepening intimacy? The answer is that in the multifaceted death of His Son, provision is made for a cleaning so deep, so radical, so continuous that a believer can walk with God in unbroken communion and deepening fellowship. Only the pure in heart can have the vision of God, and, for that, cleansing is essential. . . .

Scripture is clear that upon believing, we are justified from all things (Acts 13:39). Our sins are forgiven and remembered no more (Heb. 8:12). Because our guilt and penalty were borne by Jesus on the cross, we will never come into judgment for them. But Christians do sin after conversion. For such sins, there is forgiveness through the blood of Christ (1 John 1:7). That forgiveness is granted in response to true repentance and confession (1:9).

J. Oswald Sanders

*I*n your own words, describe how God wants *his people to pray. Why do you think seeking God's forgiveness is an essential part of prayer? Approach God now in prayer. Make yourself pure before him and share with him all that is in your heart.*

M O N D A Y:

God Wants Us to Seek, Honor, and Trust Him

Matthew 6:16—7:6

Jesus Teaches About Worship

*W*hen you give up eating, don't put on a sad face like the hypocrites. They make their faces look sad to show people they are giving up eating. I tell you the truth, those hypocrites already have their full reward. So when you give up eating, comb your hair and wash your face. Then people will not know that you are giving up eating, but your Father, whom you cannot see, will see you. Your Father sees what is done in secret, and he will reward you.

God Is More Important than Money

*D*on't store treasures for yourselves here on earth where moths and rust will destroy them and thieves can break in and steal them. But store your treasures in heaven where they cannot be destroyed by moths or rust and where thieves cannot break in and steal them. Your heart will be where your treasure is.

"The eye is a light for the body. If your eyes are good, your whole body will be full of light. But if your eyes are evil, your whole body will be full of darkness. And if the only light you have is really darkness, then you have the worst darkness.

"No one can serve two masters. The person will hate one master and love the other, or will follow one master and refuse to follow the other. You cannot serve both God and worldly riches.

Don't Worry

*S*o I tell you, don't worry about the food or drink you need to live, or about the clothes you need for your body. Life is more than food, and the body is more than clothes. Look at the birds in the air. They don't plant or harvest or store food in barns, but your heavenly Father feeds them. And you know that you are worth much more than the birds. You cannot add any time to your life by worrying about it.

"And why do you worry about clothes? Look at how the lilies in the field grow. They don't work or make clothes for themselves. But I tell you that even Solomon with his riches was not dressed as beautifully as one of these flowers. God clothes the grass in the field, which is alive today but tomorrow is thrown into the fire. So you can be even more sure that God will clothe you. Don't have so little faith! Don't worry and say, 'What will we eat?' or 'What will we drink?' or 'What will we wear?' The people who don't know God keep trying to get these things, and your Father in heaven knows you need them. The thing you should want most is God's kingdom and doing what God wants. Then all these other things you need will be given to you. So don't worry about tomorrow, because tomorrow will have its own worries. Each day has enough trouble of its own.

Be Careful About Judging Others

*D*on't judge other people, or you will be judged. You will be judged in the same way that you judge others, and the amount you give to others will be given to you.

"Why do you notice the little piece of dust in your friend's eye, but you don't notice the big piece of wood in your own eye? How can you say to your friend, 'Let me take that little piece of dust out of your eye'? Look at yourself! You still have that big piece of wood in your own eye. You hypocrite! First, take the wood out of your own eye. Then you will see clearly to take the dust out of your friend's eye.

"Don't give holy things to dogs, and don't throw your pearls before pigs. Pigs will only trample on them, and dogs will turn to attack you."

*O*n the twenty-fourth day of that same month, the people of Israel gathered. They did not eat, and they wore rough cloth and put dust on their heads to show their sadness. Those people whose ancestors were from Israel had separated themselves from all foreigners. They stood and confessed their sins and their ancestors' sins. For a fourth of the day they stood where they were and read from the Book of the Teachings of the LORD their God. For another fourth of the day they confessed their sins and worshiped the LORD their God.

Nehemiah 9:1–3

*T*hey say, 'To honor you we had
   special days when we gave up
   eating,
but you didn't see.
We humbled ourselves to honor you,
   but you didn't notice.'"

But the LORD says, "You do what
   pleases yourselves on these
   special days,
   and you are unfair to your workers.
On these special days when you do not
   eat, you argue and fight
   and hit each other with your fists.
You cannot do these things as you do
   now
   and believe your prayers are heard
   in heaven.
This kind of special day is not what I
   want.
   This is not the way I want people to
   be sorry for what they have done.
I don't want people just to bow their
   heads like a plant
   and wear rough cloth and lie in
   ashes to show their sadness.
This is what you do on your special
   days when you do not eat,
   but do you think this is what the
   LORD wants?"

Isaiah 58:3–5

*T*he LORD says, "Even now, come back
   to me with all your heart.
   Go without food, and cry and be
   sad."

Tearing your clothes is not enough to
   show you are sad;
   let your heart be broken.
Come back to the LORD your God,
   because he is kind and shows
   mercy.
He doesn't become angry quickly,
   and he has great love.

Joel 2:12–13a

*I*n the fourth year Darius was king, on the fourth day of the ninth month, which is called Kislev, the LORD spoke his word to Zechariah. The city of Bethel sent Sharezer, Regem-Melech, and their men to ask the LORD a question. They went to the prophets and priests who were at the Temple of the LORD All-Powerful. The men said, "For years in the fifth month of each year we have shown our sadness and gone without food. Should we continue to do this?"

The LORD All-Powerful spoke his word to me, saying, "Tell the priests and the people in the land: 'For seventy years you went without food and cried in the fifth and seventh months, but that was not really for me. And when you ate and drank, it was really for yourselves.'"

Zechariah 7:1–6

INSIGHTS

*O*ur problem is that we want to test God rather than trust him. We want to experiment with him rather than rely on him. We're like the boy who tests the doubtful ice instead of skating confidently where God is leading. What is our faith worth if we don't trust completely? It is perfectly natural to trust in our own understanding, to rely on our own natural strengths, gifts, or talents (and indeed some modern prophets tell us to do so!). But it is the walk of faith to trust his teaching and direction. Give him first place and let him have precedence. This is the secret of safe guidance and peaceful progression. Simple dependence upon him, committing our all to him, obeying him implicitly—this is how to acknowledge him "in all thy ways." As St. Augustine said centuries ago, "Beware of despairing about yourself: you are commanded to put your trust in God, and not in yourself."

Al Bryant

APPLICATION

*D*escribe the kind of life that truly honors God. What are God's people to trust him to provide? In what ways do you trust and seek God on a daily basis?

TUESDAY:

There Is Wisdom and Goodness in Walking in God's Ways

Matthew 7:7—8:4

Ask God for What You Need

*A*sk, and God will give to you. Search, and you will find. Knock, and the door will open for you. Yes, everyone who asks will receive. Everyone who searches will find. And everyone who knocks will have the door opened.

"If your children ask for bread, which of you would give them a stone? Or if your children ask for a fish, would you give them a snake? Even though you are bad, you know how to give good gifts to your children. How much more your heavenly Father will give good things to those who ask him!

The Most Important Rule

*D*o to others what you want them to do to you. This is the meaning of the law of Moses and the teaching of the prophets.

The Way to Heaven Is Hard

*E*nter through the narrow gate. The gate is wide and the road is wide that leads to hell, and many people enter through that gate. But the gate is small and the road is narrow that leads to true life. Only a few people find that road.

People Know You by Your Actions

*B*e careful of false prophets. They come to you looking gentle like sheep, but they are really dangerous like wolves. You will know these people by what they do. Grapes don't come from thornbushes, and figs don't come from thorny weeds. In the same way, every good tree produces good fruit, but a bad tree produces bad fruit. A good tree cannot produce bad fruit, and a bad tree cannot produce good fruit. Every tree that does not produce good fruit is cut down and thrown into the fire. In the same way, you will know these false prophets by what they do.

"Not all those who say that I am their Lord will enter the kingdom of heaven. The only people who will enter the kingdom of heaven are those who do what my Father in heaven wants. On the last day many people will say to me, 'Lord, Lord, we spoke for you, and through you we forced out demons and did many miracles.' Then I will tell them clearly, 'Get away from me, you who do evil. I never knew you.'

Two Kinds of People

*E*veryone who hears my words and obeys them is like a wise man who built his house on rock. It rained hard, the floods came, and the winds blew and hit that house. But it did not fall, because it was built on rock. Everyone who hears my words and does not obey them is like a foolish man who built his house on sand. It rained hard, the floods came, and the winds blew and hit that house, and it fell with a big crash."

When Jesus finished saying these things, the people were amazed at his teaching, because he did not teach like their teachers of the law. He taught like a person who had authority.

Jesus Heals a Sick Man

*W*hen Jesus came down from the hill, great crowds followed him. Then a man with a skin disease came to Jesus. The man bowed down before him and said, "Lord, you can heal me if you will."

Jesus reached out his hand and touched the man and said, "I will. Be healed!" And immediately the man was healed from his disease. Then Jesus said to him, "Don't tell anyone about this. But go and show yourself to the priest and offer the gift Moses commanded for people who are made well. This will show the people what I have done."

*H*appy are those who don't listen to
    the wicked,
  who don't go where sinners go,
  who don't do what evil people do.
They love the LORD's teachings,
  and they think about those teach-
    ings day and night.

They are strong, like a tree planted by a
river.
The tree produces fruit in season,
and its leaves don't die.
Everything they do will succeed.

But wicked people are not like that.
They are like chaff that the wind
blows away.
So the wicked will not escape God's
punishment.
Sinners will not worship with God's
people.
This is because the LORD takes care of
his people,
but the wicked will be destroyed.

Psalm 1:1–6

*W*hen a person's steps follow the LORD,
God is pleased with his ways.
If he stumbles, he will not fall,
because the LORD holds his hand.

I was young, and now I am old,
but I have never seen good people
left helpless
or their children begging for food.

Psalm 37:23–25

*B*ut good people will grow like palm
trees;
they will be tall like the cedars of
Lebanon.
Like trees planted in the Temple of the
LORD,
they will grow strong in the courtyards of our God.
When they are old, they will still
produce fruit;
they will be healthy and fresh.
They will say that the LORD is good.
He is my Rock, and there is no
wrong in him.

Psalm 92:12–15

*B*ut as for you, human, your people are
talking about you by the walls and in the
doorways of houses. They say to each other:
'Come now, and hear the message from the
LORD.' So they come to you in crowds as if
they were really ready to listen. They sit in
front of you as if they were my people and
hear your words, but they will not obey
them. With their mouths they tell me they
love me, but their hearts desire their selfish profits. To your people you are nothing
more than a singer who sings love songs
and has a beautiful voice and plays a musical instrument well. They hear your words,
but they will not obey them.
"When this comes true, and it surely will
happen, then the people will know that a
prophet has been among them."

Ezekiel 33:30–33

INSIGHTS

*I*t must be admitted that, in its first stages,
the broad way is generally easy and rather
delightful. The boat launched on the flowing
stream sweeps merrily and pleasantly along
the gradient of the road slopes so as to make
walking easy, the sun shines, and the path is
filled with bright flowers. But to a life given
up to self-indulgence, there is only one end—
destruction.
There is a more excellent way, but it is too
narrow to admit the trailing garments of
passionate desire, too narrow for pride, self-
indulgence, greed, and avarice—it is the Way
of the Cross, but it leads to Life! We all want
to see life—and the remarkable thing is that
those who expect to get most out of it by self-
indulgence miss everything; whilst those who
seem to curtail their lives by following Christ,
win everything. Few find and enter this path,
is the lament of our Lord. Let us put our hand
in His, that He may lead us into the path of
life, "that shineth more and more unto the
perfect day."

F. B. Meyer

APPLICATION

*W*hat good things does God promise to those
who search for him and walk in his ways?
What kind of person makes the decision to
walk through the narrow gate and build on
the Rock? What kind of person are you? On
what path do you walk? What will be the reward of that path?

WEDNESDAY:
Jesus' Amazing Authority
Matthew 8:5–27

NEW TESTAMENT READING

Jesus Heals a Soldier's Servant

When Jesus entered the city of Capernaum, an army officer came to him, begging for help. The officer said, "Lord, my servant is at home in bed. He can't move his body and is in much pain."

Jesus said to the officer, "I will go and heal him."

The officer answered, "Lord, I am not worthy for you to come into my house. You only need to command it, and my servant will be healed. I, too, am a man under the authority of others, and I have soldiers under my command. I tell one soldier, 'Go,' and he goes. I tell another soldier, 'Come,' and he comes. I say to my servant, 'Do this,' and my servant does it.

When Jesus heard this, he was amazed. He said to those who were following him, "I tell you the truth, this is the greatest faith I have found, even in Israel. Many people will come from the east and from the west and will sit and eat with Abraham, Isaac, and Jacob in the kingdom of heaven. But those people who should be in the kingdom will be thrown outside into the darkness, where people will cry and grind their teeth with pain."

Then Jesus said to the officer, "Go home. Your servant will be healed just as you believed he would." And his servant was healed that same hour.

Jesus Heals Many People

When Jesus went to Peter's house, he saw that Peter's mother-in-law was sick in bed with a fever. Jesus touched her hand, and the fever left her. Then she stood up and began to serve Jesus.

That evening people brought to Jesus many who had demons. Jesus spoke and the demons left them, and he healed all the sick. He did these things to bring about what Isaiah the prophet had said:

"He took our suffering on him
and carried our diseases."

Isaiah 53:4

People Want to Follow Jesus

When Jesus saw the crowd around him, he told his followers to go to the other side of the lake. Then a teacher of the law came to Jesus and said, "Teacher, I will follow you any place you go."

Jesus said to him, "The foxes have holes to live in, and the birds have nests, but the Son of Man has no place to rest his head."

Another man, one of Jesus' followers, said to him, "Lord, first let me go and bury my father."

But Jesus told him, "Follow me, and let the people who are dead bury their own dead."

Jesus Calms a Storm

Jesus got into a boat, and his followers went with him. A great storm arose on the lake so that waves covered the boat, but Jesus was sleeping. His followers went to him and woke him, saying, "Lord, save us! We will drown!"

Jesus answered, "Why are you afraid? You don't have enough faith." Then Jesus got up and gave a command to the wind and the waves, and it became completely calm.

The men were amazed and said, "What kind of man is this? Even the wind and the waves obey him!"

OLD TESTAMENT READING

You answer us in amazing ways,
    God our Savior.
People everywhere on the earth
    and beyond the sea trust you.
You made the mountains by your
        strength;
    you are dressed in power.
You stopped the roaring seas,
    the roaring waves,
    and the uproar of the nations.
Even those people at the ends of the
        earth fear your miracles.
    You are praised from where the sun
        rises to where it sets.

Psalm 65:5–8

*M*y whole being, praise the LORD.
LORD my God, you are very great.
You are clothed with glory and majesty;
you wear light like a robe.
You stretch out the skies like a tent.
You build your room above the
clouds.
You make the clouds your chariot,
and you ride on the wings of the wind.
You make the winds your messengers,
and flames of fire are your servants.

You built the earth on its foundations
so it can never be moved.
You covered the earth with oceans;
the water was above the mountains.
But at your command, the water
rushed away.
When you thundered your orders, it
hurried away.
The mountains rose; the valleys sank.
The water went to the places you
made for it.
You set borders for the seas that they
cannot cross,
so water will never cover the earth
again.

LORD, you have made many things;
with your wisdom you made them
all.
The earth is full of your riches.
Look at the sea, so big and wide,
with creatures large and small that
cannot be counted.
Ships travel over the ocean,
and there is the sea monster
Leviathan,
which you made to play there.

All these things depend on you
to give them their food at the right
time.
When you give it to them,
they gather it up.
When you open your hand,
they are filled with good food.
When you turn away from them,
they become frightened.
When you take away their breath,
they die and turn to dust.
When you breathe on them,
they are created,
and you make the land new again.

May the glory of the LORD be forever.
May the LORD enjoy what he has
made.
He just looks at the earth, and it
shakes.
He touches the mountains, and they
smoke.

I will sing to the LORD all my life;
I will sing praises to my God as long
as I live.

Psalm 104:1–9, 24–33

INSIGHTS

*W*hen Jesus was on earth He displayed re-
markable powers. He raised Lazarus from the
dead and performed many other miracles. His
contemporaries noted an element of His
power that we sometimes do not—the power
of His speaking. The gospel writers reported
that Jesus did not speak like the scribes and
the Pharisees but as one "having authority"
(see Matt. 7:29). . . .

When Jesus spoke as "One having author-
ity," . . . His words were weighty. They were
not thinly disguised smoke screens. His words
were not empty. In contrast to the scribes and
Pharisees, the teaching of Jesus was full, rich,
and powerful.

Behind the authority of Jesus stood the
omnipotent power of God, the link to Jesus'
divine authority. The very word authority
hints at a connection to the word authorship.
God is the omnipotent author of His creation.
He is the omnipotent redeemer of His cre-
ation. He exercises omnipotent authority over
His creation.

The Father had given all authority on
heaven and on earth to Jesus. With those
credentials, it is no wonder that the contem-
poraries of Jesus referred to Him as One who
spoke with authority.

R. C. Sproul

PAUSE FOR REFLECTION

*I*n what ways did Jesus' followers see his
powerful authority demonstrated? In what did
the psalmist recognize his authority? What
reveals his authority to you? Is his authority
as real to you as to the army officer?

THURSDAY:

God Forgives and Saves

Matthew 8:28—9:17

NEW   TESTAMENT   READING

Jesus Heals Two Men with Demons

When Jesus arrived at the other side of the lake in the area of the Gadarene people, two men who had demons in them met him. These men lived in the burial caves and were so dangerous that people could not use the road by those caves. They shouted, "What do you want with us, Son of God? Did you come here to torture us before the right time?"

Near that place there was a large herd of pigs feeding. The demons begged Jesus, "If you make us leave these men, please send us into that herd of pigs."

Jesus said to them, "Go!" So the demons left the men and went into the pigs. Then the whole herd rushed down the hill into the lake and were drowned. The herdsmen ran away and went into town, where they told about all of this and what had happened to the men who had demons. Then the whole town went out to see Jesus. When they saw him, they begged him to leave their area.

Jesus Heals a Paralyzed Man

Jesus got into a boat and went back across the lake to his own town. Some people brought to Jesus a man who was paralyzed and lying on a mat. When Jesus saw the faith of these people, he said to the paralyzed man, "Be encouraged, young man. Your sins are forgiven."

Some of the teachers of the law said to themselves, "This man speaks as if he were God. That is blasphemy!"

Knowing their thoughts, Jesus said, "Why are you thinking evil thoughts? Which is easier: to say, 'Your sins are forgiven,' or to tell him, 'Stand up and walk'? But I will prove to you that the Son of Man has authority on earth to forgive sins." Then Jesus said to the paralyzed man, "Stand up, take your mat, and go home." And the man stood up and went home.

When the people saw this, they were amazed and praised God for giving power like this to human beings.

Jesus Chooses Matthew

When Jesus was leaving, he saw a man named Matthew sitting in the tax collector's booth. Jesus said to him, "Follow me," and he stood up and followed Jesus.

As Jesus was having dinner at Matthew's house, many tax collectors and "sinners" came and ate with Jesus and his followers. When the Pharisees saw this, they asked Jesus' followers, "Why does your teacher eat with tax collectors and sinners?"

When Jesus heard them, he said, "It is not the healthy people who need a doctor, but the sick. Go and learn what this means: 'I want kindness more than I want animal sacrifices.' I did not come to invite good people but to invite sinners."

Jesus' Followers Are Criticized

Then the followers of John came to Jesus and said, "Why do we and the Pharisees often give up eating for a certain time, but your followers don't?"

Jesus answered, "The friends of the bridegroom are not sad while he is with them. But the time will come when the bridegroom will be taken from them, and then they will give up eating.

"No one sews a patch of unshrunk cloth over a hole in an old coat. If he does, the patch will shrink and pull away from the coat, making the hole worse. Also, people never pour new wine into old leather bags. Otherwise, the bags will break, the wine will spill, and the wine bags will be ruined. But people always pour new wine into new wine bags. Then both will continue to be good."

OLD   TESTAMENT   READING

Happy is the person
    whose sins are forgiven,
    whose wrongs are pardoned.
Happy is the person
    whom the LORD does not consider
      guilty
    and in whom there is nothing false.

When I kept things to myself,
I felt weak deep inside me.
I moaned all day long.
Day and night you punished me.
My strength was gone as in the
summer heat. *Selah*
Then I confessed my sins to you
and didn't hide my guilt.
I said, "I will confess my sins to the
LORD,"
and you forgave my guilt. *Selah*

For this reason, all who obey you
should pray to you while they still
can.
When troubles rise like a flood,
they will not reach them.
You are my hiding place.
You protect me from my troubles
and fill me with songs of salvation.
Selah
Psalm 32:1–7

*T*he LORD shows mercy and is kind.
He does not become angry quickly,
and he has great love.
He will not always accuse us,
and he will not be angry forever.
He has not punished us as our sins
should be punished;
he has not repaid us for the evil we
have done.
As high as the sky is above the earth,
so great is his love for those who
respect him.
He has taken our sins away from us
as far as the east is from west.
The LORD has mercy on those who
respect him,
as a father has mercy on his
children.
Psalm 103:8–13

I, I am the One who forgives all your
sins, for my sake;
I will not remember your sins."
Isaiah 43:25

INSIGHTS

*O*ther faiths assume our ability to secure and retain God's favor by right action and give us detailed guidance as to how to do it; but Christianity has said that sin has so ruined us that we cannot do this. It is beyond our power to keep the law of God as we should; we are guilty and helpless, wholly unable to save ourselves, and so must be saved, if at all, by the action of another.

Other faiths direct us to follow the teaching of their founders—famous men long deceased; but Christianity, identifying its founder as God incarnate, who died for our sins and rose again to bestow forgiveness, proclaims him as alive and calls on us to trust him and his atoning work, making him the object of our worship and service. Redemption through the love of the Son of God, who became man, bore his Father's judgment on our sins, and rose from death to reign forever, is a theme without parallel in the world's religions.

Christianity proclaims that those who repent of sin and trust in Jesus Christ are created anew at the heart of their being by the Holy Spirit. They are united to Jesus Christ in his risen life, their inner nature is changed, so that their deepest impulse is not now to disobey God and serve self, but to deny self and obey God. Thus they are born again into a new life of fellowship with Christ, assurance, forgiveness, and sonship to God and are given unconquerable hope and joy. There is nothing like this in any other religion.

J. I. Packer

APPLICATION

*W*hy do you think Jesus offered forgiveness as well as healing to the paralyzed man? What amazes you about God's forgiveness and healing? If Jesus is our example, what should our attitude toward sinners be? Does your attitude need improvement?

FRIDAY

Jesus' Great Compassion for His Lost Sheep

Matthew 9:18—10:10

Jesus Gives Life to a Dead Girl and Heals a Sick Woman

While Jesus was saying these things, a leader of the synagogue came to him. He bowed down before Jesus and said, "My daughter has just died. But if you come and lay your hand on her, she will live again." So Jesus and his followers stood up and went with the leader.

Then a woman who had been bleeding for twelve years came behind Jesus and touched the edge of his coat. She was thinking, "If I can just touch his clothes, I will be healed."

Jesus turned and saw the woman and said, "Be encouraged, dear woman. You are made well because you believed." And the woman was healed from that moment on.

Jesus continued along with the leader and went into his house. There he saw the funeral musicians and many people crying. Jesus said, "Go away. The girl is not dead, only asleep." But the people laughed at him. After the crowd had been thrown out of the house, Jesus went into the girl's room and took hold of her hand, and she stood up. The news about this spread all around the area.

Jesus Heals More People

When Jesus was leaving there, two blind men followed him. They cried out, "Have mercy on us, Son of David!"

After Jesus went inside, the blind men went with him. He asked the men, "Do you believe that I can make you see again?"

They answered, "Yes, Lord."

Then Jesus touched their eyes and said, "Because you believe I can make you see again, it will happen." Then the men were able to see. But Jesus warned them strongly, saying, "Don't tell anyone about this." But the blind men left and spread the news about Jesus all around that area.

When the two men were leaving, some people brought another man to Jesus. This man could not talk because he had a demon in him. After Jesus forced the demon to leave the man, he was able to speak. The crowd was amazed and said, "We have never seen anything like this in Israel."

But the Pharisees said, "The prince of demons is the one that gives him power to force demons out."

Jesus traveled through all the towns and villages, teaching in their synagogues, preaching the Good News about the kingdom, and healing all kinds of diseases and sicknesses. When he saw the crowds, he felt sorry for them because they were hurting and helpless, like sheep without a shepherd. Jesus said to his followers, "There are many people to harvest but only a few workers to help harvest them. Pray to the Lord, who owns the harvest, that he will send more workers to gather his harvest."

Jesus Sends Out His Apostles

Jesus called his twelve followers together and gave them authority to drive out evil spirits and to heal every kind of disease and sickness. These are the names of the twelve apostles: Simon (also called Peter) and his brother Andrew; James son of Zebedee, and his brother John; Philip and Bartholomew; Thomas and Matthew, the tax collector; James son of Alphaeus, and Thaddaeus; Simon the Zealot and Judas Iscariot, who turned against Jesus.

Jesus sent out these twelve men with the following order: "Don't go to the non-Jewish people or to any town where the Samaritans live. But go to the people of Israel, who are like lost sheep. When you go, preach this: 'The kingdom of heaven is near.' Heal the sick, raise the dead to life again, heal those who have skin diseases, and force demons out of people. I give you these powers freely, so help other people freely. Don't carry any money with you—gold or silver or copper. Don't carry a bag or extra clothes or sandals or a walking stick. Workers should be given what they need."

*T*he LORD is my strength and shield.
I trust him, and he helps me.
I am very happy,
and I praise him with my song.
The Lord is powerful;
he gives victory to his chosen one.
Save your people
and bless those who are your own.
Be their shepherd and carry them
forever.

Psalm 28:7–9

*M*y whole being, praise the LORD;
all my being, praise his holy name.
My whole being, praise the LORD
and do not forget all his kindnesses.
He forgives all my sins
and heals all my diseases.
He saves my life from the grave
and loads me with love and mercy.
He satisfies me with good things
and makes me young again, like the
eagle.

Psalm 103:1–5

*H*e takes care of his people like a
shepherd.
He gathers them like lambs in his
arms
and carries them close to him.
He gently leads the mothers of the
lambs.

Isaiah 40:11

*T*his is what the Lord God says: I, myself, will search for my sheep and take care of them. As a shepherd takes care of his scattered flock when it is found, I will take care of my sheep. I will save them from all the places where they were scattered on a cloudy and dark day. I will bring them out from the nations and gather them from the countries. I will bring them to their own land and pasture them on the mountains of Israel, in the ravines, and in all the places where people live in the land. I will feed them in a good pasture, and they will eat grass on the high mountains of Israel. They will lie down on good ground where they eat grass, and they will eat in rich grassland on the mountains of Israel. I will feed my flock and lead them to rest, says the Lord GOD. I will search for the lost, bring back those that strayed away, put bandages on those that were hurt, and make the weak strong. But I will destroy those sheep that are fat and strong. I will tend the sheep with fairness.'"

Ezekiel 34:11–16

INSIGHTS

*T*he nature of God is to seek and to save sinners. From the opening pages of human history, it was God who sought the fallen couple in the garden. . . . The Almighty was portrayed as a Savior throughout the Old Testament (Psalm 106:21; Isaiah 43:11; Hosea 13:4), so it is appropriate that when Christ entered the world of men as God in human flesh, He was known first of all as a Savior.

Even His name was divinely chosen to be the name of a Savior. An angel told Joseph in a dream, "You shall call His name Jesus, for it is He who will save His people from their sins" (Matthew 1:21). The very heart of all redemptive teaching is that Jesus entered this world on a search-and-rescue mission for sinners. That truth is what characterizes the gospel as good news.

But it is good news only for those who perceive themselves as sinners. The unequivocal teaching of Jesus is that those who will not acknowledge and repent of their sin are beyond the reach of saving grace. All are sinners, but not all are willing to admit their depravity. If they do, He becomes their friend (cf. Matthew 11:19). Those who will not can know Him only as a Judge.

John F. MacArthur

ACTION POINT

*I*n what ways is God's compassion for the lost expressed in these passages of Scripture? How does God want to care for his people? Thank him for the ways he has shown his compassion to you.

WEEKEND:

The Price of Following Jesus

Matthew 10:11–40

NEW TESTAMENT READING

*W*hen you enter a city or town, find some worthy person there and stay in that home until you leave. When you enter that home, say, 'Peace be with you.' If the people there welcome you, let your peace stay there. But if they don't welcome you, take back the peace you wished for them. And if a home or town refuses to welcome you or listen to you, leave that place and shake its dust off your feet. I tell you the truth, on the Judgment Day it will be better for the towns of Sodom and Gomorrah than for the people of that town.

Jesus Warns His Apostles

*L*isten, I am sending you out like sheep among wolves. So be as smart as snakes and as innocent as doves. Be careful of people, because they will arrest you and take you to court and whip you in their synagogues. Because of me you will be taken to stand before governors and kings, and you will tell them and the non-Jewish people about me. When you are arrested, don't worry about what to say or how to say it. At that time you will be given the things to say. It will not really be you speaking but the Spirit of your Father speaking through you.

"Brothers will give their own brothers to be killed, and fathers will give their own children to be killed. Children will fight against their own parents and have them put to death. All people will hate you because you follow me, but those people who keep their faith until the end will be saved. When you are treated badly in one city, run to another city. I tell you the truth, you will not finish going through all the cities of Israel before the Son of Man comes.

"A student is not better than his teacher, and a servant is not better than his master. A student should be satisfied to become like his teacher; a servant should be satisfied to become like his master. If the head of the family is called Beelzebul, then the other members of the family will be called worse names!

Fear God, Not People

*S*o don't be afraid of those people, because everything that is hidden will be shown. Everything that is secret will be made known. I tell you these things in the dark, but I want you to tell them in the light. What you hear whispered in your ear you should shout from the housetops. Don't be afraid of people, who can kill the body but cannot kill the soul. The only one you should fear is the one who can destroy the soul and the body in hell. Two sparrows cost only a penny, but not even one of them can die without your Father's knowing it. God even knows how many hairs are on your head. So don't be afraid. You are worth much more than many sparrows.

Tell People About Your Faith

*A*ll those who stand before others and say they believe in me, I will say before my Father in heaven that they belong to me. But all who stand before others and say they do not believe in me, I will say before my Father in heaven that they do not belong to me.

"Don't think that I came to bring peace to the earth. I did not come to bring peace, but a sword. I have come so that

> 'a son will be against his father,
>   a daughter will be against her mother,
> a daughter-in-law will be against her
>   mother-in-law.
> A person's enemies will be members
>   of his own family.'   *Micah 7:6*

"Those who love their father or mother more than they love me are not worthy to be my followers. Those who love their son or daughter more than they love me are not worthy to be my followers. Whoever is not willing to carry the cross and follow me is not worthy of me. Those who try to hold on to their lives will give up true life. Those who give up their lives for me will hold on to true life. Whoever accepts you also accepts me, and whoever accepts me also accepts the One who sent me. "

24

I am an example to many people,
because you are my strong protection.
I am always praising you;
all day long I honor you.
Do not reject me when I am old;
do not leave me when my strength is
gone.
My enemies make plans against me,
and they meet together to kill me.
They say, "God has left him.
Go after him and take him,
because no one will save him."

God, don't be far off.
My God, hurry to help me.
Let those who accuse me
be ashamed and destroyed.
Let those who are trying to hurt me
be covered with shame and disgrace.
But I will always have hope
and will praise you more and more.
I will tell how you do what is right.
I will tell about your salvation all day
long,
even though it is more than I can tell.
I will come and tell about your powerful
works, Lord GOD.
I will remind people that only you do
what is right.

Psalm 71:7–16

*L*ORD, show me your love,
and save me as you have promised.
I have an answer for people who insult
me,
because I trust what you say.
Never keep me from speaking your
truth,
because I depend on your fair laws.
I will obey your teachings
forever and ever.
So I will live in freedom,
because I want to follow your orders.
I will discuss your rules with kings
and will not be ashamed.

Psalm 119:41–46

I have become a joke;
everyone makes fun of me all day
long.

Every time I speak, I shout.
I am always shouting about violence
and destruction.
I tell the people about the message I
received from the LORD,
but this only brings me insults.
The people make fun of me all day
long.
Sometimes I say to myself,
"I will forget about the LORD.
I will not speak anymore in his name."
But then his message becomes like a
burning fire inside me,
deep within my bones.
I get tired of trying to hold it inside of me,
and finally, I cannot hold it in.

Jeremiah 20:7b–9

INSIGHTS

*I*n *the Sermon on the Mount Jesus said that
those who suffer unjust treatment will have a
"great" reward in heaven (see Matt. 5:10).
The elect who have been abused, abandoned,
stolen from, taken advantage of—all will be
rewarded for their pain. . . .
God knows when we suffer unjustly.
. . . God has not abandoned you to the
whims and wishes of those who are more
powerful. He knows when His children are
overlooked for advancement because of their
religious views. Young lady, He knows when
less talented women are advanced past you
because you refuse to compromise morally. He
sees the abandoned mother who never knows
from month to month if her estranged husband is going to send a check. God is taking
it all in. He has already appointed a pros-
ecuting attorney, a jury, and a judge. And
they are all the same person—the Lord Jesus.
On that court date He will bring about justice
for His elect.*

Charles Stanley

PAUSE   FOR   REFLECTION

*H*ow *intensely does the desire to speak about
Jesus burn within you? What price are you
willing to pay to follow Jesus? What gives you
comfort as you seek to follow him? What is
your reward?*

MONDAY:

God Has Sent His Kingdom; Don't Reject It Foolishly!

Matthew 10:41—11:24

*W*hoever meets a prophet and accepts him will receive the reward of a prophet. And whoever accepts a good person because that person is good will receive the reward of a good person. Those who give one of these little ones a cup of cold water because they are my followers will truly get their reward."

Jesus and John the Baptist

*A*fter Jesus finished telling these things to his twelve followers, he left there and went to the towns in Galilee to teach and preach.

John the Baptist was in prison, but he heard about what Christ was doing. So John sent some of his followers to Jesus. They asked him, "Are you the One who is to come, or should we wait for someone else?"

Jesus answered them, "Go tell John what you hear and see: The blind can see, the crippled can walk, and people with skin diseases are healed. The deaf can hear, the dead are raised to life, and the Good News is preached to the poor. Those who do not stumble in their faith because of me are blessed."

As John's followers were leaving, Jesus began talking to the people about John. Jesus said, "What did you go out into the desert to see? A reed blown by the wind? What did you go out to see? A man dressed in fine clothes? No, those who wear fine clothes live in kings' palaces. So why did you go out? To see a prophet? Yes, and I tell you, John is more than a prophet. This was written about him:

'I will send my messenger ahead of
you,
who will prepare the way for you.'
Malachi 3:1

I tell you the truth, John the Baptist is greater than any other person ever born, but even the least important person in the kingdom of heaven is greater than John. Since the time John the Baptist came until now, the kingdom of heaven has been going forward in strength, and people have been trying to take it by force. All the prophets and the law of Moses told about what would happen until the time John came. And if you will believe what they said, you will believe that John is Elijah, whom they said would come. You people who can hear me, listen!

"What can I say about the people of this time? What are they like? They are like children sitting in the marketplace, who call out to each other,

'We played music for you, but you did
not dance;
we sang a sad song, but you did not
cry.'

John came and did not eat or drink like other people. So people say, 'He has a demon.' The Son of Man came, eating and drinking, and people say, 'Look at him! He eats too much and drinks too much wine, and he is a friend of tax collectors and sinners.' But wisdom is proved to be right by what it does."

Jesus Warns Unbelievers

*T*hen Jesus criticized the cities where he did most of his miracles, because the people did not change their lives and stop sinning. He said, "How terrible for you, Korazin! How terrible for you, Bethsaida! If the same miracles I did in you had happened in Tyre and Sidon, those people would have changed their lives a long time ago. They would have worn rough cloth and put ashes on themselves to show they had changed. But I tell you, on the Judgment Day it will be better for Tyre and Sidon than for you. And you, Capernaum, will you be lifted up to heaven? No, you will be thrown down to the depths. If the miracles I did in you had happened in Sodom, its people would have stopped sinning, and it would still be a city today. But I tell you, on the Judgment Day it will be better for Sodom than for you."

*Y*ou fools, how long will you be
foolish?

26

How long will you make fun of
    wisdom
    and hate knowledge?
If only you had listened when I cor-
    rected you,
    I would have told you what's in my
        heart;
    I would have told you what I am
        thinking.
I called, but you refused to listen;
    I held out my hand, but you paid no
        attention.
You did not follow my advice
    and did not listen when I corrected
        you.
So I will laugh when you are in
    trouble.
    I will make fun when disaster strikes
        you,
when disaster comes over you like a
    storm,
    when trouble strikes you like a
        whirlwind,
    when pain and trouble overwhelm
        you.
"Then you will call to me,
    but I will not answer.
You will look for me,
    but you will not find me.
It is because you rejected knowledge
    and did not choose to respect the
        LORD.
You did not accept my advice,
    and you rejected my correction.
So you will get what you deserve;
    you will get what you planned for
        others.

Proverbs 1:22–31

*C*ome to me and listen;
    listen to me so you may live.
I will make an agreement with you that
    will last forever.
    I will give you the blessings I
        promised to David.

So you should look for the LORD before
    it is too late;
    you should call to him while he is
        near.
The wicked should stop doing wrong,
    and they should stop their evil
        thoughts.

They should return to the LORD so he
    may have mercy on them.
They should come to our God,
    because he will freely forgive
        them.

Isaiah 55:3, 6–7

*T*he LORD All-Powerful says, "I will send my messenger, who will prepare the way for me. Suddenly, the Lord you are looking for will come to his Temple; the messenger of the agreement, whom you want, will come."

Malachi 3:1

INSIGHTS

*G*enerally speaking, God's kingdom is a synonym for God's rule. Those who choose to live in His kingdom (though still very much alive on Planet Earth) choose to live under His authority. . . .
    . . . The kingdom is the invisible realm where God rules as supreme authority. That's helpful news. The bad news is that we, by nature, don't want Him to rule over us; we much prefer to please ourselves. . . .
    . . . To put it bluntly, we don't want anybody other than ourselves ruling over us! Much like those people in a story Jesus once told, "We do not want this man to reign over us!" (Luke 19:14). Not until we experience a spiritual rebirth will we submit to God's rule.

Charles Swindoll

PAUSE FOR REFLECTION

*W*hat is the penalty for rejecting God's wisdom and knowledge? What does God promise to those who listen to him? What change occurs in those who accept God's kingdom? Has that change occurred in you?

27

TUESDAY:

God Wants Faithful Love More than Sacrifices

Matthew 11:25—12:21

Jesus Offers Rest to People

*A*t that time Jesus said, "I praise you, Father, Lord of heaven and earth, because you have hidden these things from the people who are wise and smart. But you have shown them to those who are like little children. Yes, Father, this is what you really wanted.

"My Father has given me all things. No one knows the Son, except the Father. And no one knows the Father, except the Son and those whom the Son chooses to tell.

"Come to me, all of you who are tired and have heavy loads, and I will give you rest. Accept my teachings and learn from me, because I am gentle and humble in spirit, and you will find rest for your lives. The teaching that I ask you to accept is easy; the load I give you to carry is light."

Jesus Is Lord of the Sabbath

*A*t that time Jesus was walking through some fields of grain on a Sabbath day. His followers were hungry, so they began to pick the grain and eat it. When the Pharisees saw this, they said to Jesus, "Look! Your followers are doing what is unlawful to do on the Sabbath day."

Jesus answered, "Have you not read what David did when he and the people with him were hungry? He went into God's house, and he and those with him ate the holy bread, which was lawful only for priests to eat. And have you not read in the law of Moses that on every Sabbath day the priests in the Temple break this law about the Sabbath day? But the priests are not wrong for doing that. I tell you that there is something here that is greater than the Temple. The Scripture says, 'I want kindness more than I want animal sacrifices.' You don't really know what those words mean. If you understood them, you would not judge those who have done nothing wrong.

"So the Son of Man is Lord of the Sabbath day."

Jesus Heals a Man's Hand

*J*esus left there and went into their synagogue, where there was a man with a crippled hand. They were looking for a reason to accuse Jesus, so they asked him, "Is it right to heal on the Sabbath day?"

Jesus answered, "If any of you has a sheep, and it falls into a ditch on the Sabbath day, you will help it out of the ditch. Surely a human being is more important than a sheep. So it is lawful to do good things on the Sabbath day."

Then Jesus said to the man with the crippled hand, "Hold out your hand." The man held out his hand, and it became well again, like the other hand. But the Pharisees left and made plans to kill Jesus.

Jesus Is God's Chosen Servant

*J*esus knew what the Pharisees were doing, so he left that place. Many people followed him, and he healed all who were sick. But Jesus warned the people not to tell who he was. He did these things to bring about what Isaiah the prophet had said:

"Here is my servant whom I have
   chosen.
I love him, and I am pleased with
   him.
I will put my Spirit upon him,
   and he will tell of my justice to all
   people.
He will not argue or cry out;
   no one will hear his voice in the
   streets.
He will not break a crushed blade of
   grass
   or put out even a weak flame
until he makes justice win the victory.
   In him will the non-Jewish people
   find hope." *Isaiah 42:1–4*

*T*he sacrifice God wants is a broken
   spirit.
God, you will not reject a heart that
   is broken and sorry for sin.
      Psalm 51:17

*N*ow, Israel, this is what the LORD your God wants you to do: Respect the LORD your God, and do what he has told you to do. Love him. Serve the LORD your God with your whole being, and obey the LORD's commands and laws that I am giving you today for your own good.

Give yourselves completely to serving him, and do not be stubborn any longer. Respect the LORD your God and serve him. Be loyal to him and make your promises in his name. He is the one you should praise; he is your God, who has done great and wonderful things for you, which you have seen with your own eyes.

Deuteronomy 10:12–13, 16, 20–21

*Y*ou say, "What can I bring with me
    when I come before the LORD,
    when I bow before God on high?
Should I come before him with burnt
    offerings,
    with year-old calves?
Will the LORD be pleased with a thou-
    sand male sheep?
    Will he be pleased with ten thousand
      rivers of oil?
Should I give my first child for the evil I
    have done?
    Should I give my very own child for
      my sin?"
The LORD has told you, human, what is
    good;
    he has told you what he wants from
      you:
to do what is right to other people,
    love being kind to others,
    and live humbly, obeying your God.

Micah 6:6–8

His answer surprised me. He replied, "Not really."

"Not a day has gone by since the beginning of time,
That someone hasn't offered meager nickels and dimes,
Golden altars and crosses, contributions and penance,
Stone monuments and steeples; but why not repentance?

"The money, the statues, the cathedrals you've built,
Do you really think I need your offerings of guilt?
What good is money that's meant only to salve
The hurting conscience that so many of you have?

"Your lips know no prayers. Your eyes, no compassion.
But you will go to church (when church-going's in fashion).

"Just give me a tear—a heart ready to mold.
And I'll give you a mission, a message so bold—
That a fire will be stirred where there was only death,
And your heart will be flamed by my life and my breath."

I stuck my hands in my pockets and kicked at the dirt.
It's tough to be corrected (I guess my feelings were hurt).
But it was worth the struggle to realize the thought.
That the cross isn't for sale and Christ's blood can't be bought.

Max Lucado

INSIGHTS

*L*ord," I said, "I want to be your man, not my own.
So to you I give my money, my car—even my home."
Then, smug and content, I relaxed with a smile
And whispered to God, "I bet it's been a while,
Since anyone has given so much—so freely?"

APPLICATION

*W*hat does God want from his people? Be specific! Think about what it means for God to want those things from you. Pray that you will understand what he wants and that your heart will be open to obey him.

WEDNESDAY:

Our Words Reveal What Is in Our Hearts

Matthew 12:22–42

N E W   T E S T A M E N T   R E A D I N G

Jesus' Power Is from God

*T*hen some people brought to Jesus a man who was blind and could not talk, because he had a demon. Jesus healed the man so that he could talk and see. All the people were amazed and said, "Perhaps this man is the Son of David!"

When the Pharisees heard this, they said, "Jesus uses the power of Beelzebul, the ruler of demons, to force demons out of people."

Jesus knew what the Pharisees were thinking, so he said to them, "Every kingdom that is divided against itself will be destroyed. And any city or family that is divided against itself will not continue. And if Satan forces out himself, then Satan is divided against himself, and his kingdom will not continue. You say that I use the power of Beelzebul to force out demons. If that is true, then what power do your people use to force out demons? So they will be your judges. But if I use the power of God's Spirit to force out demons, then the kingdom of God has come to you.

"If anyone wants to enter a strong person's house and steal his things, he must first tie up the strong person. Then he can steal the things from the house.

"Whoever is not with me is against me. Whoever does not work with me is working against me. So I tell you, people can be forgiven for every sin and everything they say against God. But whoever speaks against the Holy Spirit will not be forgiven. Anyone who speaks against the Son of Man can be forgiven, but anyone who speaks against the Holy Spirit will not be forgiven, now or in the future.

People Know You by Your Words

*I*f you want good fruit, you must make the tree good. If your tree is not good, it will have bad fruit. A tree is known by the kind of fruit it produces. You snakes! You are evil people, so how can you say anything good? The mouth speaks the things that are in the heart. Good people have good things in their hearts, and so they say good things. But evil people have evil in their hearts, so they say evil things. And I tell you that on the Judgment Day people will be responsible for every careless thing they have said. The words you have said will be used to judge you. Some of your words will prove you right, but some of your words will prove you guilty."

The People Ask for a Miracle

*T*hen some of the Pharisees and teachers of the law answered Jesus, saying, "Teacher, we want to see you work a miracle as a sign."

Jesus answered, "Evil and sinful people are the ones who want to see a miracle for a sign. But no sign will be given to them, except the sign of the prophet Jonah. Jonah was in the stomach of the big fish for three days and three nights. In the same way, the Son of Man will be in the grave three days and three nights. On the Judgment Day the people from Nineveh will stand up with you people who live now, and they will show that you are guilty. When Jonah preached to them, they were sorry and changed their lives. And I tell you that someone greater than Jonah is here. On the Judgment Day, the Queen of the South will stand up with you people who live today. She will show that you are guilty, because she came from far away to listen to Solomon's wise teaching. And I tell you that someone greater than Solomon is here.

People Today Are Full of Evil

*W*hen an evil spirit comes out of a person, it travels through dry places, looking for a place to rest, but it doesn't find it. So the spirit says, 'I will go back to the house I left.' When the spirit comes back, it finds the house still empty, swept clean, and made neat. Then the evil spirit goes out and brings seven other spirits even more evil than it is, and they go in and live there. So the person has even more trouble than before. It is the same way with the evil people who live today."

*T*he words of a good person are like
pure silver,
but an evil person's thoughts are
worth very little.
Good people's words will help many
others,
but fools will die because they don't
have wisdom.

Proverbs 10:20–21

A gentle answer will calm a person's
anger,
but an unkind answer will cause
more anger.
Wise people use knowledge when they
speak,
but fools pour out foolishness.
The LORD's eyes see everything;
he watches both evil and good
people.
As a tree gives fruit, healing words give
life;
but dishonest words crush the spirit.
The LORD hates evil thoughts
but is pleased with kind words.

Proverbs 15:1–4, 26

*L*ORD, who may enter your Holy Tent?
Who may live on your holy mountain?
Only those who are innocent
and who do what is right.
Such people speak the truth from their
hearts
and do not tell lies about others.
They do no wrong to their neighbors
and do not gossip.
They do not respect hateful people
but honor those who honor the
LORD.
They keep their promises to their
neighbors,
even when it hurts.
They do not charge interest on money
they lend
and do not take money to hurt
innocent people.
Whoever does all these things will
never be destroyed.

Psalm 15

*M*y God, I want to do what you want.
Your teachings are in my heart."
I will tell about your goodness in the
great meeting of your people.
LORD, you know my lips are not
silent.
I do not hide your goodness in my
heart;
I speak about your loyalty and
salvation.
I do not hide your love and truth
from the people in the great
meeting.

Psalm 40:8–10

INSIGHTS

*T*he tongue is the indicator of the person.
What we talk about all the time is what we
love. The words we use and the words we don't
use define what we are thinking, feeling, and
becoming. . . .

We Christians must learn to undergo rig-
orous self-examination; we must honestly
discern what we are really saying if we are
going to understand who we are. . . .

We must listen closely to the inner reminder of this Holy Spirit. In essence, what
we are doing is sticking out our tongues for
the Great Physician to examine. . . . If some
symptoms indicate mouth disease, we must
confess to him the words that were unpleasing
to him and ask forgiveness. Then we should
take a dose of medicine and read from those
Scriptures that emphasize healthy mouth
habits. We should place the medicinal verses
dealing with word usage under our tongues
nightly, and let them accomplish a cathartic
cleaning as we sleep so that tomorrow we can
begin the day with renewed strength to speak
words of life.

Karen Burton Mains

ACTION   POINT

*A*re you intimidated by the thought of explaining every careless word you have said?
Listen to your words today and write down
what they reveal about your heart. Pray that
your words will prove your heart to be innocent before God.

THURSDAY:
Not Everyone Who Hears Understands
Matthew 12:43—13:17

N E W   T E S T A M E N T   R E A D I N G

Jesus' True Family

*W*hile Jesus was talking to the people, his mother and brothers stood outside, trying to find a way to talk to him. Someone told Jesus, "Your mother and brothers are standing outside, and they want to talk to you."

He answered, "Who is my mother? Who are my brothers?" Then he pointed to his followers and said, "Here are my mother and my brothers. My true brother and sister and mother are those who do what my Father in heaven wants."

A Story About Planting Seed

*T*hat same day Jesus went out of the house and sat by the lake. Large crowds gathered around him, so he got into a boat and sat down, while the people stood on the shore. Then Jesus used stories to teach them many things. He said: "A farmer went out to plant his seed. While he was planting, some seed fell by the road, and the birds came and ate it all up. Some seed fell on rocky ground, where there wasn't much dirt. That seed grew very fast, because the ground was not deep. But when the sun rose, the plants dried up, because they did not have deep roots. Some other seed fell among thorny weeds, which grew and choked the good plants. Some other seed fell on good ground where it grew and produced a crop. Some plants made a hundred times more, some made sixty times more, and some made thirty times more. You people who can hear me, listen."

Why Jesus Used Stories to Teach

*T*he followers came to Jesus and asked, "Why do you use stories to teach the people?"

Jesus answered, "You have been chosen to know the secrets about the kingdom of heaven, but others cannot know these secrets. Those who have understanding will be given more, and they will have all they need. But those who do not have understanding, even what they have will be taken away from them. This is why I use stories to teach the people: They see, but they don't really see. They hear, but they don't really hear or understand. So they show that the things Isaiah said about them are true:

'You will listen and listen, but you will
     not understand.
 You will look and look, but you will
     not learn.
 For the minds of these people have
     become stubborn.
 They do not hear with their ears,
 and they have closed their eyes.
 Otherwise they might really understand
     what they see with their eyes
 and hear with their ears.
 They might really understand in their
     minds
 and come back to me and be healed.'
                              Isaiah 6:9–10

But you are blessed, because you see with your eyes and hear with your ears. I tell you the truth, many prophets and good people wanted to see the things that you now see, but they did not see them. And they wanted to hear the things that you now hear, but they did not hear them."

O L D   T E S T A M E N T   R E A D I N G

*H*ow I love your teachings!
     I think about them all day long.
 Your commands make me wiser than
     my enemies,
     because they are mine forever.
 I am wiser than all my teachers,
     because I think about your rules.
 I have more understanding than the
     older leaders,
     because I follow your orders.
 I have avoided every evil way
     so I could obey your word.
 I haven't walked away from your laws,
     because you yourself are my
     teacher.
 Your promises are sweet to me,
     sweeter than honey in my mouth!
 Your orders give me understanding,
     so I hate lying ways.

Your word is like a lamp for my feet
   and a light for my path.
I will do what I have promised
   and obey your fair laws.

Psalm 119:97–106

*T*o whom can I speak? Whom can I
   warn?
Who will listen to me?
The people of Israel have closed ears,
   so they cannot hear my warnings.
They don't like the word of the LORD;
   they don't want to listen to it!

Jeremiah 6:10

*T*he LORD has sent all his servants the prophets to you over and over again, but you have not listened or paid any attention to them. Those prophets have said, "Stop your evil ways. Stop doing what is wrong so you can stay in the land that the LORD gave to you and your ancestors to live in forever."

"But you people of Judah did not listen to me," says the LORD. "You made me angry by worshiping idols that were the work of your own hands, so I punished you."

Jeremiah 25:4–5, 7

*A*gain the LORD spoke his word to me, saying: "Human, you are living among a people who refuse to obey. They have eyes to see, but they do not see, and they have ears to hear, but they do not hear, because they are a people who refuse to obey."

Ezekiel 12:1–2

*B*ut they refused to pay attention; they were stubborn and did not want to listen anymore. They made their hearts as hard as rock and would not listen to the teachings of the LORD All-Powerful. And they would not hear the words he sent by his Spirit through the earlier prophets. So the LORD All-Powerful became very angry."

Zechariah 7:11–12

INSIGHTS

*O*ur Lord warns that the human heart can be so pounded and beaten down with the traffic of sin that it becomes completely in-sensitive to the gospel. This is the heart that knows no repentance, no sorrow over sin, no guilt, and no concern for the things of God. It allows itself to be trampled by an endless procession of evil thoughts, cherished sins, and ungodly activities. It is careless, callous, indifferent, never broken up or softened by conviction or sorrow for wrongdoing. This is the heart of the fool described in Proverbs. The fool hates knowledge, and resists instruction. The fool despises wisdom and says in his heart there is no God. He will not hear. His mind is closed. And he does not want to be bothered with a gospel invitation.

Many people have hearts like that. You can shower them with seed, but it just lies there. It does not penetrate. And it does not stay very long before Satan comes and takes it away completely. Each time you try to witness to such a person, you must start again at the beginning.

Dry, hard, soil on the edge of the field does not necessarily signify someone who is anti-religious. Some of the hardest individuals in the world remain on the fringes of true religion. But because sin has so hardened their hearts, they are utterly unproductive and unresponsive to God.

John F. MacArthur

A C T I O N   P O I N T

*H*ow are the teachings of Jesus received by those who follow him? By those who reject him? Why is it that some people are unable to understand God's words? Pray for a soft heart that wants to understand all that God teaches.

FRIDAY:

Hide God's Teachings in Your Heart

Matthew 13:18–43

Jesus Explains the Seed Story

So listen to the meaning of that story about the farmer. What is the seed that fell by the road? That seed is like the person who hears the message about the kingdom but does not understand it. The Evil One comes and takes away what was planted in that person's heart. And what is the seed that fell on rocky ground? That seed is like the person who hears the teaching and quickly accepts it with joy. But he does not let the teaching go deep into his life, so he keeps it only a short time. When trouble or persecution comes because of the teaching he accepted, he quickly gives up. And what is the seed that fell among the thorny weeds? That seed is like the person who hears the teaching but lets worries about this life and the temptation of wealth stop that teaching from growing. So the teaching does not produce fruit in that person's life. But what is the seed that fell on the good ground? That seed is like the person who hears the teaching and understands it. That person grows and produces fruit, sometimes a hundred times more, sometimes sixty times more, and sometimes thirty times more."

A Story About Wheat and Weeds

Then Jesus told them another story: "The kingdom of heaven is like a man who planted good seed in his field. That night, when everyone was asleep, his enemy came and planted weeds among the wheat and then left. Later, the wheat sprouted and the heads of grain grew, but the weeds also grew. Then the man's servants came to him and said, 'You planted good seed in your field. Where did the weeds come from?' The man answered, 'An enemy planted weeds.' The servants asked, 'Do you want us to pull up the weeds?' The man answered, 'No, because when you pull up the weeds, you might also pull up the wheat. Let the weeds and the wheat grow together until the harvest time. At harvest time I will tell the workers, "First gather the weeds and tie them together to be burned. Then gather the wheat and bring it to my barn."'"

Stories of Mustard Seed and Yeast

Then Jesus told another story: "The kingdom of heaven is like a mustard seed that a man planted in his field. That seed is the smallest of all seeds, but when it grows, it is one of the largest garden plants. It becomes big enough for the wild birds to come and build nests in its branches."

Then Jesus told another story: "The kingdom of heaven is like yeast that a woman took and hid in a large tub of flour until it made all the dough rise."

Jesus used stories to tell all these things to the people; he always used stories to teach them. This is as the prophet said:

"I will speak using stories;
I will tell things that have been
secret since the world was made."

Psalm 78:2

Jesus Explains About the Weeds

Then Jesus left the crowd and went into the house. His followers came to him and said, "Explain to us the meaning of the story about the weeds in the field."

Jesus answered, "The man who planted the good seed in the field is the Son of Man. The field is the world, and the good seed are all of God's children who belong to the kingdom. The weeds are those people who belong to the Evil One. And the enemy who planted the bad seed is the devil. The harvest time is the end of the world, and the workers who gather are God's angels.

"Just as the weeds are pulled up and burned in the fire, so it will be at the end of the world. The Son of Man will send out his angels, and they will gather out of his kingdom all who cause sin and all who do evil. The angels will throw them into the blazing furnace, where the people will cry and grind their teeth with pain. Then the good people will shine like the sun in the kingdom of their Father. You people who can hear me, listen."

*R*emember my words with your whole being. Write them down and tie them to your hands as a sign; tie them on your foreheads to remind you. Teach them well to your children, talking about them when you sit at home and walk along the road, when you lie down and when you get up. Write them on your doors and gates so that both you and your children will live a long time in the land the LORD promised your ancestors, as long as the skies are above the earth.

Deuteronomy 11:18–21

*M*y child, listen to what I say
and remember what I command you.
Listen carefully to wisdom;
set your mind on understanding.
Cry out for wisdom,
and beg for understanding.
Search for it like silver,
and hunt for it like hidden treasure.
Then you will understand respect for
the LORD,
and you will find that you know God.

Proverbs 2:1–5

*W*ith all my heart I try to obey you.
Don't let me break your commands.
I have taken your words to heart
so I would not sin against you.
LORD, you should be praised.
Teach me your demands.
My lips will tell about
all the laws you have spoken.
I enjoy living by your rules
as people enjoy great riches.
I think about your orders
and study your ways.
I enjoy obeying your demands,
and I will not forget your word.

Get away from me, you who do evil,
so I can keep my God's commands.
Support me as you promised so I can
live.
Don't let me be embarrassed
because of my hopes.
Help me, and I will be saved.
I will always respect your demands.

You reject those who ignore your
demands,
because their lies mislead them.
You throw away the wicked of the
world like trash.
So I will love your rules.
I shake in fear of you;
I respect your laws.

Psalm 119:10–16, 115–120

INSIGHTS

*T*oday, in the twentieth century, Jesus does not speak to us and teach us as He did early in the morning in the Temple [Luke 21:38], but He still speaks to us through His Word, God's Word—the Holy Bible. We have the benefit of hearing the very same teaching that these heard who came at the dawning of the day to the Temple. We can sit at the feet of Jesus today by reading His Word.

H. A. Ironside told of a godly man named Andrew Frazer who had come to southern California to recover from a serious illness. Though this Irishman was quite weak, he opened his worn Bible and began expounding the truths of God's Word in a way that Ironside had never heard before. So moved by Frazer's words was Ironside that his curiosity drove him to ask, "Where did you learn these things? Did you learn them in some college or seminary?" The sickly man said, "My dear young man, I learned these things on my knees on the mud floor of a little sod cottage in the north of Ireland. There with my open Bible before me I used to kneel for hours at a time and ask the Spirit of God to reveal Christ to my soul and to open the Word to my heart. He taught me more on my knees on that mud floor than I ever could have learned in all the seminaries or colleges in the world."

Woodrow Kroll

APPLICATION

*W*hat happens when a person understands and lives by God's teaching? How important is it to you to learn and treasure God's Word? What are you willing to do in order to remember it with your whole heart?

35

WEEKEND:

Jesus Tells His Followers About God's Kingdom

Matthew 13:44—14:12

Stories of a Treasure and a Pearl

*T*he kingdom of heaven is like a treasure hidden in a field. One day a man found the treasure, and then he hid it in the field again. He was so happy that he went and sold everything he owned to buy that field.

"Also, the kingdom of heaven is like a man looking for fine pearls. When he found a very valuable pearl, he went and sold everything he had and bought it.

A Story of a Fishing Net

*A*lso, the kingdom of heaven is like a net that was put into the lake and caught many different kinds of fish. When it was full, the fishermen pulled the net to the shore. They sat down and put all the good fish in baskets and threw away the bad fish. It will be this way at the end of the world. The angels will come and separate the evil people from the good people. The angels will throw the evil people into the blazing furnace, where people will cry and grind their teeth with pain."

Jesus asked his followers, "Do you understand all these things?"

They answered, "Yes, we understand."

Then Jesus said to them, "So every teacher of the law who has been taught about the kingdom of heaven is like the owner of a house. He brings out both new things and old things he has saved."

Jesus Goes to His Hometown

*W*hen Jesus finished teaching with these stories, he left there. He went to his hometown and taught the people in the synagogue, and they were amazed. They said, "Where did this man get this wisdom and this power to do miracles? He is just the son of a carpenter. His mother is Mary, and his brothers are James, Joseph, Simon, and Judas. And all his sisters are here with us. Where then does this man get all these things?" So the people were upset with Jesus.

But Jesus said to them, "A prophet is honored everywhere except in his hometown and in his own home."

So he did not do many miracles there because they had no faith.

How John the Baptist Was Killed

*A*t that time Herod, the ruler of Galilee, heard the reports about Jesus. So he said to his servants, "Jesus is John the Baptist, who has risen from the dead. That is why he can work these miracles."

Sometime before this, Herod had arrested John, tied him up, and put him into prison. Herod did this because of Herodias, who had been the wife of Philip, Herod's brother. John had been telling Herod, "It is not lawful for you to be married to Herodias." Herod wanted to kill John, but he was afraid of the people, because they believed John was a prophet.

On Herod's birthday, the daughter of Herodias danced for Herod and his guests, and she pleased him. So he promised with an oath to give her anything she wanted. Herodias told her daughter what to ask for, so she said to Herod, "Give me the head of John the Baptist here on a platter." Although King Herod was very sad, he had made a promise, and his dinner guests had heard him. So Herod ordered that what she asked for be done. He sent soldiers to the prison to cut off John's head. And they brought it on a platter and gave it to the girl, and she took it to her mother. John's followers came and got his body and buried it. Then they went and told Jesus.

A child has been born to us;
    God has given a son to us.
    He will be responsible for leading
      the people.
His name will be Wonderful Counselor,
      Powerful God,
    Father Who Lives Forever, Prince of
      Peace.
Power and peace will be in his kingdom
    and will continue to grow forever.

He will rule as king on David's throne
and over David's kingdom.
He will make it strong
by ruling with justice and goodness
from now on and forever.
The LORD All-Powerful will do this
because of his strong love for his
people.

Isaiah 9:6–7

*T*ell the nations, "The LORD is king."
The earth is set, and it cannot be
moved.
He will judge the people fairly.
Let the skies rejoice and the earth be
glad;
let the sea and everything in it shout.
Let the fields and everything in them
rejoice.
Then all the trees of the forest will sing
for joy
before the LORD, because he is
coming.
He is coming to judge the world;
he will judge the world with fairness
and the peoples with truth.

Psalm 96:10–13

*L*ORD, everything you have made will
praise you;
those who belong to you will bless
you.
They will tell about the glory of your
kingdom
and will speak about your power.
Then everyone will know the mighty
things you do
and the glory and majesty of your
kingdom.
Your kingdom will go on and on,
and you will rule forever.

Psalm 145:10–13a

*T*here is a day coming that will burn like
a hot furnace, and all the proud and evil
people will be like straw. On that day they
will be completely burned up so that not a
root or branch will be left," says the LORD
All-Powerful. "But for you who honor me,
goodness will shine on you like the sun,
with healing in its rays. You will jump
around, like well-fed calves."

Malachi 4:1–2

*D*uring the Civil War, the army of the Union
and the army of the Confederacy were locked
in a vicious battle to the death just outside
the city of Richmond. As night fell after the
first day of the battle, cheers were heard from
the Confederate lines. When General Grant
asked what was going on behind the enemy's
line, he was told that the wife of General
George Pickett had given birth to a baby boy,
and that his troops were celebrating. . . .

Upon receiving the news, General Grant
ordered bonfires to be lit and a toast to be
given. Cheers and hoorahs rang out all night
long. For a few hours, the shooting stopped
and warring soldiers were drawn together for
a birthday party. The birth of Pickett's son only
temporarily stopped a war. But it stands as
evidence of what a good birthday party can
do. . . .

The good news is that another Son was
born, and there were some who stopped what
they were doing and enjoyed a little bit of
peace for just a little while. There was singing in the sky—at least some shepherds said
there was. And some strange visitors came
looking for a baby whom they nicknamed the
Prince of Peace. Everyone has not gotten the
message, so not everyone knows about the
baby. But the baby started a movement and
we know that someday everyone will come to
His party and call Him the Lord of the feast.

There's a great day coming when the world
will change. The lion will lie down with the
lamb. Swords will be beaten into plowshares.
And people will forget about war. What
started as a birthday party will end with a
wedding feast. We will call it the "Kingdom
of God." We must pray for it, and we must
work for it.

Tony Campolo

P A U S E   F O R   R E F L E C T I O N

*W*hat do you understand about God's kingdom from the three images Jesus presented to
his followers? Is the coming of God's kingdom
exciting enough for you to stop doing your own
thing and celebrate?

MONDAY:

Trust in God to Meet Our Needs

Matthew 14:13–36

More than Five Thousand Fed

*W*hen Jesus heard what had happened to John, he left in a boat and went to a lonely place by himself. But the crowds heard about it and followed him on foot from the towns. When he arrived, he saw a great crowd waiting. He felt sorry for them and healed those who were sick.

When it was evening, his followers came to him and said, "No one lives in this place, and it is already late. Send the people away so they can go to the towns and buy food for themselves."

But Jesus answered, "They don't need to go away. You give them something to eat."

They said to him, "But we have only five loaves of bread and two fish."

Jesus said, "Bring the bread and the fish to me." Then he told the people to sit down on the grass. He took the five loaves and the two fish and, looking to heaven, he thanked God for the food. Jesus divided the bread and gave it to his followers, who gave it to the people. All the people ate and were satisfied. Then the followers filled twelve baskets with the leftover pieces of food. There were about five thousand men there who ate, not counting women and children.

Jesus Walks on the Water

*I*mmediately Jesus told his followers to get into the boat and go ahead of him across the lake. He stayed there to send the people home. After he had sent them away, he went by himself up into the hills to pray. It was late, and Jesus was there alone. By this time, the boat was already far away from land. It was being hit by waves, because the wind was blowing against it.

Between three and six o'clock in the morning, Jesus came to them, walking on the water. When his followers saw him walking on the water, they were afraid. They said, "It's a ghost!" and cried out in fear.

But Jesus quickly spoke to them, "Have courage! It is I. Do not be afraid."

Peter said, "Lord, if it is really you, then command me to come to you on the water."

Jesus said, "Come."

And Peter left the boat and walked on the water to Jesus. But when Peter saw the wind and the waves, he became afraid and began to sink. He shouted, "Lord, save me!"

Immediately Jesus reached out his hand and caught Peter. Jesus said, "Your faith is small. Why did you doubt?"

After they got into the boat, the wind became calm. Then those who were in the boat worshiped Jesus and said, "Truly you are the Son of God!"

When they had crossed the lake, they came to shore at Gennesaret. When the people there recognized Jesus, they told people all around there that Jesus had come, and they brought all their sick to him. They begged Jesus to let them touch just the edge of his coat, and all who touched it were healed.

*P*raise the LORD!

I will thank the LORD with all my heart
　　in the meeting of his good people.
The LORD does great things;
　　those who enjoy them seek them.
What he does is glorious and splendid,
　　and his goodness continues forever.
His miracles are unforgettable.
　　The LORD is kind and merciful.
He gives food to those who fear him.
　　He remembers his agreement
　　forever.

Psalm 111:1–5

I love the LORD,
　　because he listens to my prayers for
　　help.
He paid attention to me,
　　so I will call to him for help as long
　　as I live.
The ropes of death bound me,

and the fear of the grave took hold
of me.
I was troubled and sad.
Then I called out the name of the LORD.
I said, "Please, LORD, save me!"

The LORD is kind and does what is
right;
our God is merciful.
The LORD watches over the foolish;
when I was helpless, he saved me.
I said to myself, "Relax,
because the LORD takes care of you."
LORD, you saved me from death.
You stopped my eyes from crying;
you kept me from being defeated.
So I will walk with the LORD
in the land of the living.

Psalm 116:1–9

*Y*ou, LORD, give true peace
to those who depend on you,
because they trust you.
So, trust the LORD always,
because he is our Rock forever.

Isaiah 26:3–4

*T*he LORD says, "People of Israel, you
are my servants.
People of Jacob, I chose you.
You are from the family of my friend
Abraham.
I took you from places far away on the
earth
and called you from a faraway
country.
I said, 'You are my servants.'
I have chosen you and have not
turned against you.
So don't worry, because I am with you.
Don't be afraid, because I am your
God.
I will make you strong and will help
you;
I will support you with my right
hand that saves you."

Isaiah 41:8–10

*B*ut the LORD says, 'Zerubbabel, be brave.
Also, Joshua son of Jehozadak, the high
priest, be brave. And all you people who live
in the land, be brave,' says the LORD. 'Work,
because I am with you,' says the LORD All-
Powerful. 'I made a promise to you when

you came out of Egypt, and my Spirit is still
with you. So don't be afraid.'"

Haggai 2:4–5

INSIGHTS

*T*oday many fears fill our lives. We fear
poverty, sickness, loneliness, death. We fear
the dangers of the night and the pressures of
the day.

David learned that the only way to be released from fears was to TRUST the Lord.
"What time I am afraid, I will trust in thee."
He changed the focus of his eyes from his
situation to the Lord. Faith replaced fear. He
PUT his trust in the Lord. This was an act of
his will. "In God have I put my trust: I will
not be afraid what man can do unto me" (Ps.
56:11).

Freedom from fear is the result of confidence and trust in God. We may be helpless
against fear, but God is not. When trusting
God, there is nothing to fear.

Faith is more than believing what God can
do. It is trust in the Person of God Himself.
"But without faith it is impossible to please
him: for he that cometh to God must believe
that He IS, and that He is a rewarder of them
that diligently seek Him" (Heb. 11:6). . . .

One day a father discovered his little boy
had climbed an old tree. The limbs were beginning to break under the boy's weight. The
father held up his arms and called, "Jump!
I'll catch you." The little son considered the
offer for a moment. Then, as more limbs began to break, he said, "Shall I let go of everything, Daddy, and trust you?"

What a lesson for us. Our Heavenly Father wants us to let go of everything and trust
Him.

Millie Stamm

PAUSE FOR REFLECTION

*T*hink about the fears and needs in your
life. In what ways have you "let go of everything" and put your trust in God to meet
those needs? Pray or write you own psalm
of trust to God. Praise him for his faithfulness to you.

TUESDAY:
Warnings Against Hypocrisy
Matthew 15:1–31

NEW TESTAMENT READING

Obey God's Law

*T*hen some Pharisees and teachers of the law came to Jesus from Jerusalem. They asked him, "Why don't your followers obey the unwritten laws which have been handed down to us? They don't wash their hands before they eat."

Jesus answered, "And why do you refuse to obey God's command so that you can follow your own teachings? God said, 'Honor your father and your mother,' and 'Anyone who says cruel things to his father or mother must be put to death.' But you say a person can tell his father or mother, 'I have something I could use to help you, but I have given it to God already.' You teach that person not to honor his father or his mother. You rejected what God said for the sake of your own rules. You are hypocrites! Isaiah was right when he said about you:

'These people show honor to me with words, but their hearts are far from me.

Their worship of me is worthless.

The things they teach are nothing
but human rules.'" *Isaiah 29:13*

After Jesus called the crowd to him, he said, "Listen and understand what I am saying. It is not what people put into their mouths that makes them unclean. It is what comes out of their mouths that makes them unclean."

Then his followers came to him and asked, "Do you know that the Pharisees are angry because of what you said?"

Jesus answered, "Every plant that my Father in heaven has not planted himself will be pulled up by the roots. Stay away from the Pharisees; they are blind leaders. And if a blind person leads a blind person, both will fall into a ditch."

Peter said, "Explain the example to us."

Jesus said, "Do you still not understand? Surely you know that all the food that enters the mouth goes into the stomach and then goes out of the body. But what people say with their mouths comes from the way they think; these are the things that make people unclean. Out of the mind come evil thoughts, murder, adultery, sexual sins, stealing, lying, and speaking evil of others. These things make people unclean; eating with unwashed hands does not make them unclean."

Jesus Helps a Non-Jewish Woman

*J*esus left that place and went to the area of Tyre and Sidon. A Canaanite woman from that area came to Jesus and cried out, "Lord, Son of David, have mercy on me! My daughter has a demon, and she is suffering very much."

But Jesus did not answer the woman. So his followers came to Jesus and begged him, "Tell the woman to go away. She is following us and shouting."

Jesus answered, "God sent me only to the lost sheep, the people of Israel."

Then the woman came to Jesus again and bowed before him and said, "Lord, help me!"

Jesus answered, "It is not right to take the children's bread and give it to the dogs."

The woman said, "Yes, Lord, but even the dogs eat the crumbs that fall from their masters' table."

Then Jesus answered, "Woman, you have great faith! I will do what you asked." And at that moment the woman's daughter was healed.

Jesus Heals Many People

*A*fter leaving there, Jesus went along the shore of Lake Galilee. He went up on a hill and sat there.

Great crowds came to Jesus, bringing with them the lame, the blind, the crippled, those who could not speak, and many others. They put them at Jesus' feet, and he healed them. The crowd was amazed when they saw that people who could not speak before were now able to speak. The crippled were made strong. The lame could walk, and the blind could see. And they praised the God of Israel for this.

OLD TESTAMENT READING

*T*he Lord says:
"These people say they love me;

they show honor to me with words,
  but their hearts are far from me.
The honor they show me
  is nothing but human rules.
So I will continue to amaze these
    people
  by doing more and more miracles.
Their wise men will lose their wisdom;
  their wise men will not be able to
    understand."
Isaiah 29:13–14

*T*hose who hate you may try to fool
  you with their words,
  but in their minds they are planning
    evil.
People's words may be kind, but don't
    believe them,
  because their minds are full of evil
    thoughts.
Lies can hide hate,
  but the evil will be plain to everyone."
Proverbs 26:24–26

*S*ome people curse their fathers
  and do not bless their mothers.
Some people think they are pure,
  but they are not really free from evil.
Some people have such a proud look!
  They look down on others."
Proverbs 30:11–13

*A*ll day long I stood ready to accept
  people who turned against me,
but the way they continue to live is not
    good;
  they do anything they want to do.
Right in front of me
  they continue to do things that make
    me angry.
  They offer sacrifices to their gods in
    their gardens,
  and they burn incense on altars of
    brick.
They sit among the graves
  and spend their nights waiting to get
    messages from the dead.
They eat the meat of pigs,
  and their pots are full of soup made
    from meat that is wrong to eat.
But they tell others, 'Stay away, and
    don't come near me.
  I am too holy for you.'

These people are like smoke in my nose.
Like a fire that burns all the time,
  they continue to make me angry.
Isaiah 65:2–5

INSIGHTS

*I*n the ancient Greek plays, the actors were called hypocrites. On the stage they professed to be something they weren't. Unfortunately, there are many people who go through life playacting. They profess to be something they are not. They are hypocrites. They fool no one with this false veneer, this facade, this hypocrisy, except themselves. What they really are is well-known to God and their acquaintances with the result that they are displeasing to both. . . .

. . . Through the years innumerable people have gone to a Christless grave to spend eternity in hell because of the hypocrisy of many who call themselves Christians.

It is said that Thomas K. Beecher could not stand deceit of any kind. When he discovered that the clock in his church ran habitually either too slow or too fast, he reportedly put a placard on the wall above it that read in large letters, "Don't blame my hands—the trouble lies deeper." Don't make the mistake of promising to be a better Christian. The trouble is not on the outside; it is in the inner recesses of a person's being. Only Christ can cure this malady. This He will do if a person in genuine repentance seeks His forgiveness and turns himself over to Him in simple childlike faith.

Harold Fickett

APPLICATION

*W*hy is hypocrisy so displeasing to God? Where does hypocrisy originate? What is the cure for hypocrisy? What hypocrisy in your life needs to be healed by Christ's forgiveness?

WEDNESDAY:

Jesus Offers Real Food

Matthew 15:32—16:20

NEW TESTAMENT READING

More than Four Thousand Fed

Jesus called his followers to him and said, "I feel sorry for these people, because they have already been with me three days, and they have nothing to eat. I don't want to send them away hungry. They might faint while going home."

His followers asked him, "How can we get enough bread to feed all these people? We are far away from any town."

Jesus asked, "How many loaves of bread do you have?"

They answered, "Seven, and a few small fish."

Jesus told the people to sit on the ground. He took the seven loaves of bread and the fish and gave thanks to God. Then he divided the food and gave it to his followers, and they gave it to the people. All the people ate and were satisfied. Then his followers filled seven baskets with the leftover pieces of food. There were about four thousand men there who ate, besides women and children. After sending the people home, Jesus got into the boat and went to the area of Magadan.

The Leaders Ask for a Miracle

The Pharisees and Sadducees came to Jesus, wanting to trick him. So they asked him to show them a miracle from God.

Jesus answered, "At sunset you say we will have good weather, because the sky is red. And in the morning you say that it will be a rainy day, because the sky is dark and red. You see these signs in the sky and know what they mean. In the same way, you see the things that I am doing now, but you don't know their meaning. Evil and sinful people ask for a miracle as a sign, but they will not be given any sign, except the sign of Jonah." Then Jesus left them and went away.

Guard Against Wrong Teachings

Jesus' followers went across the lake, but they had forgotten to bring bread. Jesus said to them, "Be careful! Beware of the yeast of the Pharisees and the Sadducees."

His followers discussed the meaning of this, saying, "He said this because we forgot to bring bread."

Knowing what they were talking about, Jesus asked them, "Why are you talking about not having bread? Your faith is small. Do you still not understand? Remember the five loaves of bread that fed the five thousand? And remember that you filled many baskets with the leftovers? Or the seven loaves of bread that fed the four thousand and the many baskets you filled then also? I was not talking to you about bread. Why don't you understand that? I am telling you to beware of the yeast of the Pharisees and the Sadducees." Then the followers understood that Jesus was not telling them to beware of the yeast used in bread but to beware of the teaching of the Pharisees and the Sadducees.

Peter Says Jesus Is the Christ

When Jesus came to the area of Caesarea Philippi, he asked his followers, "Who do people say the Son of Man is?"

They answered, "Some say you are John the Baptist. Others say you are Elijah, and still others say you are Jeremiah or one of the prophets."

Then Jesus asked them, "And who do you say I am?"

Simon Peter answered, "You are the Christ, the Son of the living God."

Jesus answered, "You are blessed, Simon son of Jonah, because no person taught you that. My Father in heaven showed you who I am. So I tell you, you are Peter. On this rock I will build my church, and the power of death will not be able to defeat it. I will give you the keys of the kingdom of heaven; the things you don't allow on earth will be the things that God does not allow, and the things you allow on earth will be the things that God allows." Then Jesus warned his followers not to tell anyone he was the Christ.

OLD TESTAMENT READING

Moses said, "LORD, here are six hundred thousand people standing around me, and

42

you say, 'I will give them enough meat to eat for a month!' If we killed all the flocks and herds, that would not be enough. If we caught all the fish in the sea, that would not be enough."

But the LORD said to Moses, "Do you think I'm weak? Now you will see if I can do what I say."

The LORD sent a strong wind from the sea, and it blew quail into the area all around the camp. The quail were about three feet deep on the ground, and there were quail a day's walk in any direction. The people went out and gathered quail all that day, that night, and the next day. Everyone gathered at least sixty bushels, and they spread them around the camp.

Numbers 11:21–23, 31–32

God, you are my God.
　I search for you.
I thirst for you
　　like someone in a dry, empty land
　　where there is no water.
I have seen you in the Temple
　　and have seen your strength and
　　　glory.
Because your love is better than life,
　I will praise you.
I will praise you as long as I live.
　I will lift up my hands in prayer to
　　your name.
I will be content as if I had eaten the
　　best foods.
　My lips will sing, and my mouth will
　　praise you.

Psalm 63:1–5

The LORD says, "All you who are thirsty,
　come and drink.
Those of you who do not have money,
　come, buy and eat!
Come buy wine and milk
　without money and without cost.
Why spend your money on something
　　that is not real food?
　Why work for something that
　　doesn't really satisfy you?
Listen closely to me, and you will eat
　　what is good;
　your soul will enjoy the rich food
　　that satisfies.

Isaiah 55:1–2

Our Lord's mission of grace and truth was at its height. His help was sought with the utmost eagerness. Large numbers of sick were cast at his feet in hot haste. The crumb was given to the woman of Canaan, but whole loaves were distributed to the crowds of Jews, because it was befitting that they should have a full chance to appreciate and accept Christ. For a brief moment they glorified the God of Israel, but the spasm of gratitude was transient. "His own" rejected Jesus. They would have his miracles, but would not own his claims. Take care that you do not become content with getting his help; love him for himself.

Do not suppose that these miracles were confined to his earthly life. He is still the great storehouse of divine and healing energy. He is still moved with compassion, and longs to help each weary and sin-sick soul. His thought still is "lest they faint in the way." The wilderness can place no bar on "the saving strength of his right hand."

F. B. Meyer

What does the "real food" that Jesus offers satisfy? How does a person receive that food? Why do you want to be close to Jesus? Do you want his miracles or his claims? Physical food or spiritual food?

43

THURSDAY:

Jesus' Suffering Will Be Followed by His Judgment

Matthew 16:21—17:13

Jesus Says that He Must Die

*F*rom that time on Jesus began telling his followers that he must go to Jerusalem, where the older Jewish leaders, the leading priests, and the teachers of the law would make him suffer many things. He told them he must be killed and then be raised from the dead on the third day.

Peter took Jesus aside and told him not to talk like that. He said, "God save you from those things, Lord! Those things will never happen to you!"

Then Jesus said to Peter, "Go away from me, Satan! You are not helping me! You don't care about the things of God, but only about the things people think are important."

Then Jesus said to his followers, "If people want to follow me, they must give up the things they want. They must be willing even to give up their lives to follow me. Those who want to save their lives will give up true life, and those who give up their lives for me will have true life. It is worth nothing for them to have the whole world if they lose their souls. They could never pay enough to buy back their souls. The Son of Man will come again with his Father's glory and with his angels. At that time, he will reward them for what they have done. I tell you the truth, some people standing here will see the Son of Man coming with his kingdom before they die."

Jesus Talks with Moses and Elijah

*S*ix days later, Jesus took Peter, James, and John, the brother of James, up on a high mountain by themselves. While they watched, Jesus' appearance was changed; his face became bright like the sun, and his clothes became white as light. Then Moses and Elijah appeared to them, talking with Jesus.

Peter said to Jesus, "Lord, it is good that we are here. If you want, I will put up three tents here—one for you, one for Moses, and one for Elijah."

While Peter was talking, a bright cloud covered them. A voice came from the cloud and said, "This is my Son, whom I love, and I am very pleased with him. Listen to him!"

When his followers heard the voice, they were so frightened they fell to the ground. But Jesus went to them and touched them and said, "Stand up. Don't be afraid." When they looked up, they saw Jesus was now alone.

As they were coming down the mountain, Jesus commanded them not to tell anyone about what they had seen until the Son of Man had risen from the dead.

Then his followers asked him, "Why do the teachers of the law say that Elijah must come first?"

Jesus answered, "They are right to say that Elijah is coming and that he will make everything the way it should be. But I tell you that Elijah has already come, and they did not recognize him. They did to him whatever they wanted to do. It will be the same with the Son of Man; those same people will make the Son of Man suffer." Then the followers understood that Jesus was talking about John the Baptist.

*G*od has said this,
    and I have heard it over and over:
    God is strong.
The Lord is loving.
    You reward people for what they
      have done.

Psalm 62:11–12

*W*e all have wandered away like
    sheep;
    each of us has gone his own way.
But the LORD has put on him the
    punishment
    for all the evil we have done.
He was beaten down and punished,
    but he didn't say a word.
He was like a lamb being led to be
    killed.

He was quiet, as a sheep is quiet
while its wool is being cut;
he never opened his mouth.
Men took him away roughly and
unfairly.
He died without children to continue
his family.
He was put to death;
he was punished for the sins of my
people.
He was buried with wicked men,
and he died with the rich.
He had done nothing wrong,
and he had never lied.

But it was the LORD who decided
to crush him and make him suffer.
The LORD made his life a penalty
offering,
but he will still see his descendants and
live a long life.
He will complete the things the
LORD wants him to do.

Isaiah 53:6–10

*B*ut I, the LORD, look into a person's
heart
and test the mind.
So I can decide what each one deserves;
I can give each one the right payment for what he does."

Jeremiah 17:10

*A*t that time Michael, the great prince who
protects your people, will stand up. There
will be a time of much trouble, the worst
time since nations have been on earth, but
your people will be saved. Everyone whose
name is written in God's book will be saved.
Many people who have already died will live
again. Some of them will wake up to have
life forever, but some will wake up to find
shame and disgrace forever. The wise
people will shine like the brightness of the
sky. Those who teach others to live right
will shine like stars forever and ever."

Daniel 12:1–3

INSIGHTS

*W*e are all of us judged every day. We are
judged by the face that looks back at us from
the bathroom mirror. We are judged by the
faces of the people we love and by the faces
and lives of our children and by our dreams.
Each day finds us at the junction of many
roads, and we are judged as much by the
roads we have not taken as by the roads we
have.

The New Testament proclaims that at
some unforeseeable time in the future God
will ring down the final curtain on history,
and there will come a Day on which all our
days and all the judgments upon us and
all our judgments upon each other will
themselves be judged. The judge will be Christ.
In other words, the one who judges us
most finally will be the one who loves us most
fully.

Romantic love is blind to everything except
what is lovable and lovely, but Christ's love
sees us with terrible clarity and sees us whole.
Christ's love so wishes our joy that it is ruthless
against everything in us that diminishes our
joy. The worst sentence Love can pass is that
we behold the suffering which Love has endured for our sake, and that is also our ac-
quittal. The justice and mercy of the judge
are ultimately one.

Frederick Buechner

ACTION POINT

*W*hat was most important to Jesus when he
suffered and died for us? What did he promise would follow? Think about the statement,
"the one who judges us most finally will be
the one who loves us most fully." Pray now
and thank God that our Judge is also our
Savior!

FRIDAY:

Greatness in God's Kingdom Begins with Humility

Matthew 17:14—18:9

NEW TESTAMENT READING

Jesus Heals a Sick Boy

*W*hen Jesus and his followers came back to the crowd, a man came to Jesus and bowed before him. The man said, "Lord, have mercy on my son. He has epilepsy and is suffering very much, because he often falls into the fire or into the water. I brought him to your followers, but they could not cure him."

Jesus answered, "You people have no faith, and your lives are all wrong. How long must I put up with you? How long must I continue to be patient with you? Bring the boy here." Jesus commanded the demon inside the boy. Then the demon came out, and the boy was healed from that time on.

The followers came to Jesus when he was alone and asked, "Why couldn't we force the demon out?"

Jesus answered, "Because your faith is too small. I tell you the truth, if your faith is as big as a mustard seed, you can say to this mountain, 'Move from here to there,' and it will move. All things will be possible for you."

Jesus Talks About His Death

*W*hile Jesus' followers were gathering in Galilee, he said to them, "The Son of Man will be handed over to people, and they will kill him. But on the third day he will be raised from the dead." And the followers were filled with sadness.

Jesus Talks About Paying Taxes

*W*hen Jesus and his followers came to Capernaum, the men who collected the Temple tax came to Peter. They asked, "Does your teacher pay the Temple tax?"

Peter answered, "Yes, Jesus pays the tax."

Peter went into the house, but before he could speak, Jesus said to him, "What do you think? The kings of the earth collect different kinds of taxes. But who pays the taxes—the king's children or others?"

Peter answered, "Other people pay the taxes."

Jesus said to Peter, "Then the children of the king don't have to pay taxes. But we don't want to upset these tax collectors. So go to the lake and fish. After you catch the first fish, open its mouth and you will find a coin. Take that coin and give it to the tax collectors for you and me."

Who Is the Greatest?

*A*t that time the followers came to Jesus and asked, "Who is greatest in the kingdom of heaven?"

Jesus called a little child to him and stood the child before his followers. Then he said, "I tell you the truth, you must change and become like little children. Otherwise, you will never enter the kingdom of heaven. The greatest person in the kingdom of heaven is the one who makes himself humble like this child.

"Whoever accepts a child in my name accepts me. If one of these little children believes in me, and someone causes that child to sin, it would be better for that person to have a large stone tied around the neck and be drowned in the sea. How terrible for the people of the world because of the things that cause them to sin. Such things will happen, but how terrible for the one who causes them to happen! If your hand or your foot causes you to sin, cut it off and throw it away. It is better for you to lose part of your body and live forever than to have two hands and two feet and be thrown into the fire that burns forever. If your eye causes you to sin, take it out and throw it away. It is better for you to have only one eye and live forever than to have two eyes and be thrown into the fire of hell."

OLD TESTAMENT READING

*L*ORD, you are loyal to those who are
    loyal,
  and you are good to those who are
    good.

You are pure to those who are pure,
 but you are against those who are
 bad.
You save the humble,
 but you bring down those who are
 proud.

Psalm 18:25–27

*L*ORD, I will thank you with all my heart;
 I will sing to you before the gods.
I will bow down facing your holy
 Temple,
 and I will thank you for your love
 and loyalty.
You have made your name and your
 word
 greater than anything.
On the day I called to you, you an-
 swered me.
 You made me strong and brave.

LORD, let all the kings of the earth
 praise you
 when they hear the words you
 speak.
They will sing about what the
 LORD has done,
 because the LORD's glory is great.

Though the LORD is supreme,
 he takes care of those who are
 humble,
 but he stays away from the proud.

Psalm 138:1–6

*P*ride will ruin people,
 but those who are humble will be
 honored.

Proverbs 29:23

*A*s Manasseh suffered, he begged the
LORD his God for help and humbled himself
before the God of his ancestors. When
Manasseh prayed, the LORD heard him and
had pity on him. So the LORD let him return
to Jerusalem and to his kingdom. Then Manasseh knew that the LORD is the true God.

2 Chronicles 33:12–13

*E*ven to this day the people of Judah are
still too proud. They have not learned to respect me or to follow my teachings. They
have not obeyed the laws I gave you and
your ancestors.

"So this is what the LORD All-Powerful,
the God of Israel, says: I am determined to
bring disasters on you. I will destroy the
whole family of Judah."

Jeremiah 44:10–11

INSIGHTS

*I was once considering what the reason was
our Lord loved humility in us so much. I
suddenly remembered that He is essentially
the supreme truth and that humility is just
our walking in truth. For it is a very great
truth that we have no good in us; we have
only misery and nothingness. He who does not
understand this walks in lies. But he who
understands this the best is the most pleasing
to the Supreme Truth. May God grant us this
favor, sisters, never to be without the hum-
bling knowledge of ourselves. . . .*

*His Majesty seeks and loves courageous
souls. But they must be humble in all their
ways and have no confidence in themselves. . . .*

*. . . I often used to think of those words
of the Apostle Paul: "All things are possible
with God" (Philippians 4:13). I saw clearly
that I could do nothing of myself. This was of
great help to me to see this. So also was the
saying of Augustine: "Give me, Lord, what
You command, and command what You desire." . . .*

*. . . But it is necessary that we should
understand what this humility is like. For I
believe Satan will try to do great harm. He
hinders those who begin to pray from going
forward by suggesting to them false notions
of humility. He makes them think that it is
pride to have spiritual ambitions, desires to
imitate the saints, and longings to be like
martyrs.*

St. Teresa of Avila

ACTION POINT

*H*ow does God view pride? Why do you think
he places such a high value on humility? In
your own words, describe the attitudes and
actions of true humility, and pray that God
will cause you to want to be humble.

47

WEEKEND:

The Magnitude of God's Forgiveness

Matthew 18:10–35

A Lost Sheep

*B*e careful. Don't think these little children are worth nothing. I tell you that they have angels in heaven who are always with my Father in heaven.

"If a man has a hundred sheep but one of the sheep gets lost, he will leave the other ninety-nine on the hill and go to look for the lost sheep. I tell you the truth, he is happier about that one sheep than about the ninety-nine that were never lost. In the same way, your Father in heaven does not want any of these little children to be lost.

When a Person Sins Against You

*I*f your fellow believer sins against you, go and tell him in private what he did wrong. If he listens to you, you have helped that person to be your brother or sister again. But if he refuses to listen, go to him again and take one or two other people with you. 'Every case may be proved by two or three witnesses.' If he refuses to listen to them, tell the church. If he refuses to listen to the church, then treat him like a person who does not believe in God or like a tax collector.

"I tell you the truth, the things you don't allow on earth will be the things God does not allow. And the things you allow on earth will be the things that God allows.

"Also, I tell you that if two of you on earth agree about something and pray for it, it will be done for you by my Father in heaven. This is true because if two or three people come together in my name, I am there with them."

An Unforgiving Servant

*T*hen Peter came to Jesus and asked, "Lord, when my fellow believer sins against me, how many times must I forgive him? Should I forgive him as many as seven times?"

Jesus answered, "I tell you, you must forgive him more than seven times. You must forgive him even if he does wrong to you seventy-seven times.

"The kingdom of heaven is like a king who decided to collect the money his servants owed him. When the king began to collect his money, a servant who owed him several million dollars was brought to him. But the servant did not have enough money to pay his master, the king. So the master ordered that everything the servant owned should be sold, even the servant's wife and children. Then the money would be used to pay the king what the servant owed.

"But the servant fell on his knees and begged, 'Be patient with me, and I will pay you everything I owe.' The master felt sorry for his servant and told him he did not have to pay it back. Then he let the servant go free.

"Later, that same servant found another servant who owed him a few dollars. The servant grabbed him around the neck and said, 'Pay me the money you owe me!'

"The other servant fell on his knees and begged him, 'Be patient with me, and I will pay you everything I owe.'

"But the first servant refused to be patient. He threw the other servant into prison until he could pay everything he owed. When the other servants saw what had happened, they were very sorry. So they went and told their master all that had happened.

"Then the master called his servant in and said, 'You evil servant! Because you begged me to forget what you owed, I told you that you did not have to pay anything. You should have showed mercy to that other servant, just as I showed mercy to you.' The master was very angry and put the servant in prison to be punished until he could pay everything he owed.

"This king did what my heavenly Father will do to you if you do not forgive your brother or sister from your heart."

---

*B*ut suppose the wicked stop doing all the sins they have done and obey all my rules and do what is fair and right. Then they will surely live; they will not die. Their sins will be forgotten. Because they have done what is right, they will live. I do not really want the wicked to die, says the Lord GOD. I want them to stop their bad ways and live."

Ezekiel 18:21–23

*G*od, be merciful to me
    because you are loving.
Because you are always ready to be
    merciful,
    wipe out all my wrongs.
Wash away all my guilt
    and make me clean again.

I know about my wrongs,
    and I can't forget my sin.
You are the only one I have sinned
    against;
    I have done what you say is wrong.
You are right when you speak
    and fair when you judge.
I was brought into this world in sin.
    In sin my mother gave birth to me.

You want me to be completely truthful,
    so teach me wisdom.
Take away my sin, and I will be clean.
    Wash me, and I will be whiter than
      snow.
Make me hear sounds of joy and
    gladness;
    let the bones you crushed be happy
      again.
Turn your face from my sins
    and wipe out all my guilt.

Create in me a pure heart, God,
    and make my spirit right again.
Do not send me away from you
    or take your Holy Spirit away from
      me.
Give me back the joy of your salvation.
    Keep me strong by giving me a
      willing spirit.
Then I will teach your ways to those
    who do wrong,
    and sinners will turn back to you.

God, save me from the guilt of murder,
    God of my salvation,
    and I will sing about your goodness.
Lord, let me speak
    so I may praise you.

You are not pleased by sacrifices, or I
    would give them.
You don't want burnt offerings.
The sacrifice God wants is a broken
    spirit.
God, you will not reject a heart that
    is broken and sorry for sin.

Psalm 51:1–17

INSIGHTS

*F*orgiving and being forgiven are all of one piece. They cannot be separated. In giving we receive. In accepting those who have injured us we open ourselves to God's acceptance.

It is not a matter of which comes first. There is no sequence of time or priority. The two are one. Anyone who loves God must also love his neighbor. Anyone who hates another does not and cannot love God. Love of God and our neighbor are interlocking and indivisible. We only learn to love as we learn to know God. And we truly learn to know God as we learn to love our brother and sister. It's all of a piece. The life that is open to the love of God is loving to others. The person who truly receives the forgiveness of God is truly forgiving of others. . . .

God's forgiveness gives us the freedom to love and live creatively. The rush of God's strength, which brings forgiveness, gives in turn the ability to forgive, and forgive, and forgive, not just seven times, as the apostle Peter once volunteered, but seventy times seven. . . .

The contrast between our debt to God and the debts others may owe us is immeasurable.

And when God has forgiven us the debt we owe Him, how can we be unforgiving to others who owe us so little in comparison?

David Augsburger

APPLICATION

*A*s you think about the parable of the servants, what debt that God has forgiven you can serve as a model of how you ought to forgive others? In what ways does Ezekiel 18 affect how you think about God?

MONDAY:

Jesus Talks About Marriage and Divorce

Matthew 19:1–26

Jesus Teaches About Divorce

*A*fter Jesus said all these things, he left Galilee and went into the area of Judea on the other side of the Jordan River. Large crowds followed him, and he healed them there.

Some Pharisees came to Jesus and tried to trick him. They asked, "Is it right for a man to divorce his wife for any reason he chooses?"

Jesus answered, "Surely you have read in the Scriptures: When God made the world, 'he made them male and female.' And God said, 'So a man will leave his father and mother and be united with his wife, and the two will become one body.' So there are not two, but one. God has joined the two together, so no one should separate them."

The Pharisees asked, "Why then did Moses give a command for a man to divorce his wife by giving her divorce papers?"

Jesus answered, "Moses allowed you to divorce your wives because you refused to accept God's teaching, but divorce was not allowed in the beginning. I tell you that anyone who divorces his wife and marries another woman is guilty of adultery. The only reason for a man to divorce his wife is if his wife has sexual relations with another man."

The followers said to him, "If that is the only reason a man can divorce his wife, it is better not to marry."

Jesus answered, "Not everyone can accept this teaching, but God has made some able to accept it. There are different reasons why some men cannot marry. Some men were born without the ability to become fathers. Others were made that way later in life by other people. And some men have given up marriage because of the kingdom of heaven. But the person who can marry should accept this teaching about marriage."

Jesus Welcomes Children

*T*hen the people brought their little children to Jesus so he could put his hands on them and pray for them. His followers told them to stop, but Jesus said, "Let the little children come to me. Don't stop them, because the kingdom of heaven belongs to people who are like these children." After Jesus put his hands on the children, he left there.

A Rich Young Man's Question

A man came to Jesus and asked, "Teacher, what good thing must I do to have life forever?"

Jesus answered, "Why do you ask me about what is good? Only God is good. But if you want to have life forever, obey the commands."

The man asked, "Which commands?"

Jesus answered, "'You must not murder anyone; you must not be guilty of adultery; you must not steal; you must not tell lies about your neighbor; honor your father and mother; and love your neighbor as you love yourself.'"

The young man said, "I have obeyed all these things. What else do I need to do?"

Jesus answered, "If you want to be perfect, then go and sell your possessions and give the money to the poor. If you do this, you will have treasure in heaven. Then come and follow me."

But when the young man heard this, he left sorrowfully, because he was rich.

Then Jesus said to his followers, "I tell you the truth, it will be hard for a rich person to enter the kingdom of heaven. Yes, I tell you that it is easier for a camel to go through the eye of a needle than for a rich person to enter the kingdom of God."

When Jesus' followers heard this, they were very surprised and asked, "Then who can be saved?"

Jesus looked at them and said, "This is something people cannot do, but God can do all things."

*T*his is another thing you do. You cover the LORD's altar with your tears. You cry and moan, because he does not accept your offerings and is not pleased with what you bring. You ask, "Why?" It is because the LORD sees how you treated the wife you married when you were young. You broke your promise to her, even though she was your partner and you had an agreement with her. God made husbands and wives to become one body and one spirit for his purpose—so they would have children who are true to God.

So be careful, and do not break your promise to the wife you married when you were young.

The LORD God of Israel says, "I hate divorce. And I hate people who do cruel things as easily as they put on clothes," says the LORD All-Powerful.

So be careful. And do not break your trust.

Malachi 2:13–16

*T*hen the LORD God said, "It is not good for the man to be alone. I will make a helper who is right for him."

From the ground God formed every wild animal and every bird in the sky, and he brought them to the man so the man could name them. Whatever the man called each living thing, that became its name. The man gave names to all the tame animals, to the birds in the sky, and to all the wild animals. But Adam did not find a helper that was right for him. So the LORD God caused the man to sleep very deeply, and while he was asleep, God removed one of the man's ribs. Then God closed up the man's skin at the place where he took the rib. The LORD God used the rib from the man to make a woman, and then he brought the woman to the man.

And the man said,

"Now, this is someone whose bones
        came from my bones,
    whose body came from my body.
I will call her 'woman,'
        because she was taken out of man."

So a man will leave his father and mother and be united with his wife, and the two will become one body.

Genesis 2:18–24

---

*T*he marriage law must conform with the purpose for which marriage was instituted by God. It was instituted to create a new unity of two persons, and no provision was made for the dissolving of that unity. Jesus does not idealize marriage. He does not say that every marriage is made in heaven; he says that marriage itself is made in heaven—that is, instituted by God. To the question, 'Is it lawful for a man to divorce his wife?' his answer, in effect, is 'No; not for any cause.' . . .

. . . It is by God's ordinance that the two become one; men are given no authority to modify that ordinance. . . .

Is it wise to take Jesus's rulings on this or other practical issues and give them legislative force? Perhaps not. The trouble is that, if they are given legislative force, exceptive clauses are bound to be added to cover special cases, and arguments will be prolonged about the various situations which are, or are not, included in the terms of those exceptive clauses. It is better probably, to let his words stand in the uncompromising rigour as the ideal at which his followers ought to aim. Legislation has to make provision for the hardness of men's hearts, but Jesus showed a more excellent way than the way of legislation and supplies the power to change the human heart and make his ideal a practical possibility.

F. F. Bruce

---

*W*hat is God's purpose for marriage (Malachi 2:15)? Did you realize that marriage had such a vital, spiritual purpose? In what ways does knowing God's purpose for marriage affect your view of marriage and divorce?

TUESDAY:
God's View of Fairness
Matthew 19:27—20:19

NEW   TESTAMENT   READING

*P*eter said to Jesus, "Look, we have left everything and followed you. So what will we have?"

Jesus said to them, "I tell you the truth, when the age to come has arrived, the Son of Man will sit on his great throne. All of you who followed me will also sit on twelve thrones, judging the twelve tribes of Israel. And all those who have left houses, brothers, sisters, father, mother, children, or farms to follow me will get much more than they left, and they will have life forever. Many who have the highest place now will have the lowest place in the future. And many who have the lowest place now will have the highest place in the future.

A Story About Workers

*T*he kingdom of heaven is like a person who owned some land. One morning, he went out very early to hire some people to work in his vineyard. The man agreed to pay the workers one coin for working that day. Then he sent them into the vineyard to work. About nine o'clock the man went to the marketplace and saw some other people standing there, doing nothing. So he said to them, 'If you go and work in my vineyard, I will pay you what your work is worth.' So they went to work in the vineyard. The man went out again about twelve o'clock and three o'clock and did the same thing. About five o'clock the man went to the marketplace again and saw others standing there. He asked them, 'Why did you stand here all day doing nothing?' They answered, 'No one gave us a job.' The man said to them, 'Then you can go and work in my vineyard.'

"At the end of the day, the owner of the vineyard said to the boss of all the workers, 'Call the workers and pay them. Start with the last people I hired and end with those I hired first.'

"When the workers who were hired at five o'clock came to get their pay, each received one coin. When the workers who were hired first came to get their pay, they thought they would be paid more than the others. But each one of them also received one coin. When they got their coin, they complained to the man who owned the land. They said, 'Those people were hired last and worked only one hour. But you paid them the same as you paid us who worked hard all day in the hot sun.' But the man who owned the vineyard said to one of those workers, 'Friend, I am being fair to you. You agreed to work for one coin. So take your pay and go. I want to give the man who was hired last the same pay that I gave you. I can do what I want with my own money. Are you jealous because I am good to those people?'

"So those who have the last place now will have the first place in the future, and those who have the first place now will have the last place in the future."

Jesus Talks About His Death

*W*hile Jesus was going to Jerusalem, he took his twelve followers aside privately and said to them, "Look, we are going to Jerusalem. The Son of Man will be turned over to the leading priests and the teachers of the law, and they will say that he must die. They will give the Son of Man to the non-Jewish people to laugh at him and beat him with whips and crucify him. But on the third day, he will be raised to life again."

OLD   TESTAMENT   READING

*T*here is no one holy like the LORD.
    There is no God but you;
    there is no Rock like our God.

"Don't continue bragging,
    don't speak proud words.
The LORD is a God who knows everything,
    and he judges what people do.

"The bows of warriors break,
    but weak people become strong.
Those who once had plenty of food now
    must work for food,
    but people who were hungry are
    hungry no more.

The woman who could not have
    children now has seven,
  but the woman who had many
    children now is sad.

"The LORD sends death,
  and he brings to life.
He sends people to the grave,
  and he raises them to life again.
The LORD makes some people poor,
  and others he makes rich.
He makes some people humble,
  and others he makes great.
The LORD raises the poor up from the
    dust,
  and he lifts the needy from the
    ashes.
He lets the poor sit with princes
  and receive a throne of honor.

"The foundations of the earth belong to
    the LORD,
  and the LORD set the world upon
    them.
He protects those who are loyal to him,
  but evil people will be silenced in
    darkness.
Power is not the key to success.
The LORD destroys his enemies;
  he will thunder in heaven against
    them.
The LORD will judge all the earth.
  He will give power to his king
  and make his appointed king
    strong."

1 Samuel 2:2–10

*B*ut our ancestors were proud and
    stubborn
  and did not obey your commands.
They refused to listen;
  they forgot the miracles you did for
    them.
So they became stubborn and turned
    against you,
  choosing a leader to take them back
    to slavery.
But you are a forgiving God.
  You are kind and full of mercy.
You do not become angry quickly, and
    you have great love.
  So you did not leave them."

Nehemiah 9:16–17

*T*he message of the parable is that the
revolution of God brought by Jesus is a
marvellously generous revolution, offering a
full place and reward even to the late-comer
or outsider. For the rich and the religious such
egalitarian salvation did not always seem
good news, since it meant giving up their
present advantage and special position. . . .
In the parable those who had worked all day
complained of the master's unfair generosity.
But for those in need of employment at the
eleventh hour the master's generosity was
good news indeed. . . .

   . . . The revolution of God is a levelling
revolution; not, however, a negatively levelling revolution bringing everyone down, but
a positively levelling revolution in which
God's amazing generosity welcomes even late-
comers . . . and gives them the full day's
wage. . . .

   . . . To put it simply: entry into the kingdom of God is through God's generosity to
sinners; being in the kingdom of God entails
running the race to obtain the prize (1 Cor
9:24). There is truth in the old saying that
the entry fee to Christianity is completely free,
but the annual subscription is everything
we've got. No one will be in the coming
kingdom of God on the basis of his or her own
achievements, but only on the basis of God's
generosity; but everyone will be called to account on the day of judgement and will be
rewarded according to his or her response to
the Lord's generosity.

David Wenham

*T*hink about God's fairness and mercy. In
what ways are you tempted to be jealous of
his generosity shown to others? Pray for a
greater understanding of his goodness, and
extend his generosity to others.

WEDNESDAY:
Jerusalem Honors Jesus as King
Matthew 20:20—21:11

A Mother Asks Jesus a Favor

Then the wife of Zebedee came to Jesus with her sons. She bowed before him and asked him to do something for her.

Jesus asked, "What do you want?"

She said, "Promise that one of my sons will sit at your right side and the other will sit at your left side in your kingdom."

But Jesus said, "You don't understand what you are asking. Can you drink the cup that I am about to drink?"

The sons answered, "Yes, we can."

Jesus said to them, "You will drink from my cup. But I cannot choose who will sit at my right or my left; those places belong to those for whom my Father has prepared them."

When the other ten followers heard this, they were angry with the two brothers.

Jesus called all the followers together and said, "You know that the rulers of the non-Jewish people love to show their power over the people. And their important leaders love to use all their authority. But it should not be that way among you. Whoever wants to become great among you must serve the rest of you like a servant. Whoever wants to become first among you must serve the rest of you like a slave. In the same way, the Son of Man did not come to be served. He came to serve others and to give his life as a ransom for many people."

Jesus Heals Two Blind Men

When Jesus and his followers were leaving Jericho, a great many people followed him. Two blind men sitting by the road heard that Jesus was going by, so they shouted, "Lord, Son of David, have mercy on us!"

The people warned the blind men to be quiet, but they shouted even more, "Lord, Son of David, have mercy on us!"

Jesus stopped and said to the blind men, "What do you want me to do for you?"

They answered, "Lord, we want to see."

Jesus felt sorry for the blind men and touched their eyes, and at once they could see. Then they followed Jesus.

Jesus Enters Jerusalem as a King

As Jesus and his followers were coming closer to Jerusalem, they stopped at Bethphage at the hill called the Mount of Olives. From there Jesus sent two of his followers and said to them, "Go to the town you can see there. When you enter it, you will quickly find a donkey tied there with its colt. Untie them and bring them to me. If anyone asks you why you are taking the donkeys, say that the Master needs them, and he will send them at once."

This was to bring about what the prophet had said:

"Tell the people of Jerusalem,
'Your king is coming to you.
He is gentle and riding on a donkey,
on the colt of a donkey.'"

Isaiah 62:11; Zechariah 9:9

The followers went and did what Jesus told them to do. They brought the donkey and the colt to Jesus and laid their coats on them, and Jesus sat on them. Many people spread their coats on the road. Others cut branches from the trees and spread them on the road. The people were walking ahead of Jesus and behind him, shouting,

"Praise to the Son of David!
God bless the One who comes in the
name of the Lord! *Psalm 118:26*
Praise to God in heaven!"

When Jesus entered Jerusalem, all the city was filled with excitement. The people asked, "Who is this man?"

The crowd said, "This man is Jesus, the prophet from the town of Nazareth in Galilee."

Come, let's sing for joy to the LORD.
Let's shout praises to the Rock who
saves us.
Let's come to him with thanksgiving.
Let's sing songs to him,

because the LORD is the great God,
the great King over all gods.

Psalm 95:1–3

*T*his is the day that the LORD has made.
Let us rejoice and be glad today!

Please, LORD, save us;
please, LORD, give us success.
God bless the one who comes in the
name of the LORD.
We bless all of you from the Temple
of the LORD.
The LORD is God,
and he has shown kindness to us.
With branches in your hands, join the
feast.
Come to the corners of the altar.

Psalm 118:24–27

*T*he LORD has made a promise,
and by his power he will keep his
promise.
He said, "I will never again give your
grain
as food to your enemies.
I will not let your enemies drink the
new wine
that you have worked to make.
The person who gathers food will eat it,
and he will praise the LORD.
The person who gathers the grapes will
drink the wine
in the courts of my Temple."

Go through, go through the gates!
Make the way ready for the people.
Build up, build up the road!
Move all the stones off the road.
Raise the banner as a sign for the
people.

The Lord is speaking
to all the faraway lands:
"Tell the people of Jerusalem,
'Look, your Savior is coming.
He is bringing your reward to you;
he is bringing his payment with him.'"
His people will be called the Holy People,
the Saved People of the LORD,
and Jerusalem will be called the City
God Wants,
the City God Has Not Rejected.

Isaiah 62:8–12

*Y*ou can almost hear the roar of the crowds as Jesus proceeds slowly into Jerusalem, like a triumphant general returning from a great victory. . . .

From the dusty roads of this earth, where the lips of little children sang his praises, to the very throne of heaven where surely angel anthems rolled, this was Jesus' moment. . . .

Not only on this day of days, but down through the centuries, Jesus has reigned in triumph in the hearts of men and women who have accepted his glorious life and teaching. The Pharisees could hardly have realized how prophetic their words would be: "Look how the whole world has gone after him!"

And why wouldn't we follow Jesus? He leads us in triumph! Just when we think we have had all the trouble we can handle, Jesus reaches down and lifts us gently onto the colt he is riding into Jerusalem. Just when we think nobody cares, he opens our ears and we can hear the crowds shout, "Look who's riding with the King!" And just when we think there is no reward for being righteous, Jesus smiles and quietly reassures us, "My Father will honor the one who serves me."

Not all of our hurt will go away, and our problems won't magically disappear. But through faith we can be a child of the King— a king of triumph!

F. LaGard Smith

*L*ist the ways Jesus has shown himself to be a king of triumph in your life. Spend some time in prayer, celebrating your praise to him. If you would like, write down your praises, or express them in another visible way.

THURSDAY:
God Seeks Sincere Worship
Matthew 21:12–32

NEW TESTAMENT READING

Jesus Goes to the Temple

*J*esus went into the Temple and threw out all the people who were buying and selling there. He turned over the tables of those who were exchanging different kinds of money, and he upset the benches of those who were selling doves. Jesus said to all the people there, "It is written in the Scriptures, 'My Temple will be called a house for prayer.' But you are changing it into a 'hideout for robbers.'"

The blind and crippled people came to Jesus in the Temple, and he healed them. The leading priests and the teachers of the law saw that Jesus was doing wonderful things and that the children were praising him in the Temple, saying, "Praise to the Son of David." All these things made the priests and the teachers of the law very angry.

They asked Jesus, "Do you hear the things these children are saying?"

Jesus answered, "Yes. Haven't you read in the Scriptures, 'You have taught children and babies to sing praises'?"

Then Jesus left and went out of the city to Bethany, where he spent the night.

The Power of Faith

*E*arly the next morning, as Jesus was going back to the city, he became hungry. Seeing a fig tree beside the road, Jesus went to it, but there were no figs on the tree, only leaves. So Jesus said to the tree, "You will never again have fruit." The tree immediately dried up.

When his followers saw this, they were amazed. They asked, "How did the fig tree dry up so quickly?"

Jesus answered, "I tell you the truth, if you have faith and do not doubt, you will be able to do what I did to this tree and even more. You will be able to say to this mountain, 'Go, fall into the sea.' And if you have faith, it will happen. If you believe, you will get anything you ask for in prayer."

Leaders Doubt Jesus' Authority

*J*esus went to the Temple, and while he was teaching there, the leading priests and the older leaders of the people came to him. They said, "What authority do you have to do these things? Who gave you this authority?"

Jesus answered, "I also will ask you a question. If you answer me, then I will tell you what authority I have to do these things. Tell me: When John baptized people, did that come from God or just from other people?"

They argued about Jesus' question, saying, "If we answer, 'John's baptism was from God,' Jesus will say, 'Then why didn't you believe him?' But if we say, 'It was from people,' we are afraid of what the crowd will do because they all believe that John was a prophet."

So they answered Jesus, "We don't know."

Jesus said to them, "Then I won't tell you what authority I have to do these things.

A Story About Two Sons

*T*ell me what you think about this: A man had two sons. He went to the first son and said, 'Son, go and work today in my vineyard.' The son answered, 'I will not go.' But later the son changed his mind and went. Then the father went to the other son and said, 'Son, go and work today in my vineyard.' The son answered, 'Yes, sir, I will go and work,' but he did not go. Which of the two sons obeyed his father?"

The priests and leaders answered, "The first son."

Jesus said to them, "I tell you the truth, the tax collectors and the prostitutes will enter the kingdom of God before you do. John came to show you the right way to live. You did not believe him, but the tax collectors and prostitutes believed him. Even after seeing this, you still refused to change your ways and believe him."

OLD TESTAMENT READING

*L*ORD, I love the Temple where you live, where your glory is.

Psalm 26:8

Sing to the LORD a new song;
  sing to the LORD, all the earth.
Sing to the LORD and praise his name;
  every day tell how he saves us.
Tell the nations of his glory;
  tell all peoples the miracles he does,

because the LORD is great; he should be
    praised at all times.
  He should be honored more than all
    the gods,
because all the gods of the nations are
    only idols,
  but the LORD made the heavens.
The LORD has glory and majesty;
  he has power and beauty in his
    Temple.

Praise the LORD, all nations on earth;
  praise the LORD's glory and power.
Praise the glory of the LORD's name.
  Bring an offering and come into his
    Temple courtyards.
Worship the LORD because he is holy.
  Tremble before him, everyone on
    earth.

Psalm 96:1–9

I will bring these people to my holy
    mountain
  and give them joy in my house of
    prayer.
The offerings and sacrifices
  they place on my altar will please me,
because my Temple will be called
  a house for prayer for people from
    all nations."

Isaiah 56:7

If you do that, do you think you can come before me and stand in this place where I have chosen to be worshiped? Do you think you can say, "We are safe!" When you do all these hateful things? This place where I have chosen to be worshiped is nothing more to you than a hideout for robbers. I have been watching you, says the LORD.

"'You people of Judah, go now to the town of Shiloh, where I first made a place to be worshiped. See what I did to it because of the evil things the people of Israel had done. You people of Judah have done all these evil things too, says the LORD. I spoke to you again and again, but you did not listen

to me. I called you, but you did not answer. So I will destroy the place where I have chosen to be worshiped in Jerusalem."

Jeremiah 7:10–14a

Then he brought me into the inner courtyard of the Temple. There I saw about twenty-five men at the entrance to the Temple of the LORD, between the porch and the altar. With their backs turned to the Temple of the LORD, they faced east and were worshiping the sun in the east.

He said to me, "Do you see, human? Is it unimportant that the people of Judah are doing the hateful things they have done here? They have filled the land with violence and made me continually angry. Look, they are insulting me every way they can. So I will act in anger. I will have no pity, nor will I show mercy. Even if they shout in my ears, I won't listen to them."

Ezekiel 8:16–18

INSIGHTS

In both the Old and New Testaments, God's purpose in revealing himself, in redeeming, and in bringing a people into existence was to create a worshiping community to be a sign of his redeeming work. For example, when God entered into a covenant with the people of Israel, they met him at Mt. Sinai in the first public meeting between God and his people. This meeting with God became the prototype for public worship in Israel. And it was through public worship that God's revelation, redemption, and covenant were remembered and passed down in history. . . .

. . . We go to worship in praise and thank God for what he has done, is doing, and will do.

Robert Webber

PAUSE FOR REFLECTION

In God's eyes, worship is no casual, Sunday-morning time filler! How does your worship experience stand as a continuing reminder of God's redeeming work in your life? How might it be made stronger and more meaningful?

F R I D A Y:

The Kingdom of Heaven Is for All Who Obey

Matthew 21:33—22:14

A Story About God's Son

*L*isten to this story: There was a man who owned a vineyard. He put a wall around it and dug a hole for a winepress and built a tower. Then he leased the land to some farmers and left for a trip. When it was time for the grapes to be picked, he sent his servants to the farmers to get his share of the grapes. But the farmers grabbed the servants, beat one, killed another, and then killed a third servant with stones. So the man sent some other servants to the farmers, even more than he sent the first time. But the farmers did the same thing to the servants that they had done before. So the man decided to send his son to the farmers. He said, 'They will respect my son.' But when the farmers saw the son, they said to each other, 'This son will inherit the vineyard. If we kill him, it will be ours!' Then the farmers grabbed the son, threw him out of the vineyard, and killed him. So what will the owner of the vineyard do to these farmers when he comes?"

The priests and leaders said, "He will surely kill those evil men. Then he will lease the vineyard to some other farmers who will give him his share of the crop at harvest time."

Jesus said to them, "Surely you have read this in the Scriptures:

'The stone that the builders rejected
    became the cornerstone.
The Lord did this,
    and it is wonderful to us.'

Psalm 118:22–23

"So I tell you that the kingdom of God will be taken away from you and given to people who do the things God wants in his kingdom. The person who falls on this stone will be broken, and on whomever that stone falls, that person will be crushed."

When the leading priests and the Pharisees heard these stories, they knew Jesus was talking about them. They wanted to arrest him, but they were afraid of the people, because the people believed that Jesus was a prophet.

A Story About a Wedding Feast

*J*esus again used stories to teach the people. He said, "The kingdom of heaven is like a king who prepared a wedding feast for his son. The king invited some people to the feast. When the feast was ready, the king sent his servants to tell the people, but they refused to come.

"Then the king sent other servants, saying, 'Tell those who have been invited that my feast is ready. I have killed my best bulls and calves for the dinner, and everything is ready. Come to the wedding feast.'

"But the people refused to listen to the servants and left to do other things. One went to work in his field, and another went to his business. Some of the other people grabbed the servants, beat them, and killed them. The king was furious and sent his army to kill the murderers and burn their city.

"After that, the king said to his servants, 'The wedding feast is ready. I invited those people, but they were not worthy to come. So go to the street corners and invite everyone you find to come to my feast.' So the servants went into the streets and gathered all the people they could find, both good and bad. And the wedding hall was filled with guests.

"When the king came in to see the guests, he saw a man who was not dressed for a wedding. The king said, 'Friend, how were you allowed to come in here? You are not dressed for a wedding.' But the man said nothing. So the king told some servants, 'Tie this man's hands and feet. Throw him out into the darkness, where people will cry and grind their teeth with pain.'

"Yes, many people are invited, but only a few are chosen."

*F*oreigners who have joined the LORD
    should not say,
"The LORD will not accept me with
    his people."

The eunuch should not say,
    "Because I cannot have children, the
        LORD will not accept me."
This is what the LORD says:
"The eunuchs should obey the law
        about the Sabbath
    and do what I want
    and keep my agreement.
If they do, I will make their names
        remembered
    within my Temple and its walls.
    It will be better for them than
        children.
I will give them a name that will last
        forever,
    that will never be forgotten.
Foreigners will join the LORD
    to worship him and love him,
    to serve him,
to obey the law about the Sabbath,
    and to keep my agreement."

                                    Isaiah 56:3–6

*A*ll people everywhere,
    follow me and be saved.
    I am God. There is no other God.
I will make a promise by my own
        power,
    and my promise is true;
    what I say will not be changed.
I promise that everyone will bow before
        me
    and will promise to follow me."

                                    Isaiah 45:22–23

*H*uman life is like grass;
    we grow like a flower in the field.
After the wind blows, the flower is
        gone,
    and there is no sign of where it was.
But the LORD's love for those who
        respect him
    continues forever and ever,
    and his goodness continues to their
        grandchildren
and to those who keep his agreement
    and who remember to obey his
        orders.

The LORD has set his throne in heaven,
    and his kingdom rules over every-
        thing.
You who are his angels, praise the
    LORD.

You are the mighty warriors who do
        what he says
    and who obey his voice.
You, his armies, praise the LORD;
    you are his servants who do what he
        wants.
Everything the LORD has made
    should praise him in all the places
        he rules.
My whole being, praise the LORD.

                                    Psalm 103:15–22

INSIGHTS

*W*ho can became a Christian? The answer
in a nutshell is that anyone can. Anyone who
wants to can "take the free gift of the water of
life" (Revelation 22:17). Whosoever will may
come. Everyone has an invitation to the
marriage supper of the Lamb (Matthew
22:9). . . .
    . . . It is certainly true that not all do
make the decision to give their lives over to
God. Some stubbornly insist on going their
own way. "Whoever rejects the Son will not
see life, for God's wrath remains on him"
(John 3:36). Such people will not enjoy the
salvation God has for the world. "Yet to all
who received him, to those who believed in
his name, he gave the right to become children of God" (John 1:12). . . .
    Who can become a Christian? Anyone can,
because God's grace closes nobody out. There
are no limits to his grace except those that
sinners impose upon themselves. Jesus Christ,
our Advocate, has become "the atoning sacrifice for our sins, and not only for ours but
also for the sins of the whole world" (1 John
2:2). Salvation is so broad as to encompass
potentially the entire human race.

                                    Clark H. Pinnock

APPLICATION

*T*o whom is God's kingdom given? For what
reasons do people refuse God's invitation? Are
there ways by which you limit God's grace in
your life? Pray that you will obey and keep
your agreement with God.

WEEKEND:
The Most Important Command
Matthew 22:15–40

NEW TESTAMENT READING

Is It Right to Pay Taxes or Not?

*T*hen the Pharisees left that place and made plans to trap Jesus in saying something wrong. They sent some of their own followers and some people from the group called Herodians. They said, "Teacher, we know that you are an honest man and that you teach the truth about God's way. You are not afraid of what other people think about you, because you pay no attention to who they are. So tell us what you think. Is it right to pay taxes to Caesar or not?"

But knowing that these leaders were trying to trick him, Jesus said, "You hypocrites! Why are you trying to trap me? Show me a coin used for paying the tax." So the men showed him a coin. Then Jesus asked, "Whose image and name are on the coin?"

The men answered, "Caesar's."

Then Jesus said to them, "Give to Caesar the things that are Caesar's, and give to God the things that are God's."

When the men heard what Jesus said, they were amazed and left him and went away.

Some Sadducees Try to Trick Jesus

*T*hat same day some Sadducees came to Jesus and asked him a question. (Sadducees believed that people would not rise from the dead.) They said, "Teacher, Moses said if a married man dies without having children, his brother must marry the widow and have children for him. Once there were seven brothers among us. The first one married and died. Since he had no children, his brother married the widow. Then the second brother also died. The same thing happened to the third brother and all the other brothers. Finally, the woman died. Since all seven men had married her, when people rise from the dead, whose wife will she be?"

Jesus answered, "You don't understand, because you don't know what the Scriptures say, and you don't know about the power of God. When people rise from the dead, they will not marry, nor will they be given to someone to marry. They will be like the angels in heaven. Surely you have read what God said to you about rising from the dead. God said, 'I am the God of Abraham, the God of Isaac, and the God of Jacob.' God is the God of the living, not the dead."

When the people heard this, they were amazed at Jesus' teaching.

The Most Important Command

*W*hen the Pharisees learned that the Sadducees could not argue with Jesus' answers to them, the Pharisees met together. One Pharisee, who was an expert on the law of Moses, asked Jesus this question to test him: "Teacher, which command in the law is the most important?"

Jesus answered, "'Love the Lord your God with all your heart, all your soul, and all your mind.' This is the first and most important command. And the second command is like the first: 'Love your neighbor as you love yourself.' All the law and the writings of the prophets depend on these two commands."

OLD TESTAMENT READING

*L*isten, people of Israel! The LORD our God is the only LORD. Love the LORD your God with all your heart, all your soul, and all your strength. Always remember these commands I give you today. Teach them to your children, and talk about them when you sit at home and walk along the road, when you lie down and when you get up. Write them down and tie them to your hands as a sign. Tie them on your forehead to remind you, and write them on your doors and gates.

Deuteronomy 6:4–9

*S*o know that the LORD your God is God, the faithful God. He will keep his agreement of love for a thousand lifetimes for people who love him and obey his commands. But he will pay back those people who hate him. He will destroy them, and he will not be slow to pay back those who hate him. So be careful to obey the commands, rules, and laws I give you today.

Deuteronomy 7:9–11

*T*hen Joshua called a meeting of all the people from the tribes of Reuben, Gad, and East Manasseh. He said to them, "You have done everything Moses, the LORD's servant, told you to do. You have also obeyed all my commands. But be careful to obey the teachings and laws Moses, the LORD's servant, gave you: to love the LORD your God and obey his commands, to continue to follow him and serve him the very best you can."

Joshua 22:1–2, 5

I love those who love me,
and those who seek me find me.

Proverbs 8:17

*T*his is what the LORD All-Powerful, the God of Israel, says: Offer burnt offerings along with your other sacrifices, and eat the meat yourselves! When I brought your ancestors out of Egypt, I did not speak to them and give them commands only about burnt offerings and sacrifices. I also gave them this command: Obey me, and I will be your God and you will be my people. Do all that I command so that good things will happen to you.'"

Jeremiah 7:21–23

*L*ove the LORD, all you who belong to
him.
The LORD protects those who truly
believe,
but he punishes the proud as much
as they have sinned.

Psalm 31:23

INSIGHTS

I have tried giving myself to other gods—the gods of education and knowledge, success and money, accomplishment and work. I have given good works First Place in my affection. I have tried to get other people to be god for me; I have even let the church assume top priority in my time and energy. I have placed my neck in other worldly nooses and yokes, but only the yoke of Christ grants me freedom.

Surrendering my will to His yoke is a constant process. As I continue to allow the presence of God to permeate the various parts of my life, I am understanding more clearly that anything or anyone, other than God, to whom I turn for meaning, purpose, or strength will ultimately disappoint me or destroy me. God affirmed the first commandment for my benefit; He knew I would never be whole as long as I worshiped anything or anyone besides Himself. I have tried to fill my life with other people, pleasure, work, and acquisition, but these things only partially satisfy.

I am learning that that which is empty cannot fill me, and so I am able more and more to turn aside from dried up, empty wells of fame and fortune, success, power, and achievement to partake of the Living Water. I am learning that the God of Abraham, Joseph, and Isaac is indeed the Source of everything I need and that His intent is always for good.

Jeanie Miley

APPLICATION

*H*ow do we demonstrate that we love God with all our heart, soul, and mind? What are the rewards for loving God or for rejecting him? How are you loving God today? How is he satisfying your soul?

MONDAY:

Judgment Against False Spiritual Leaders

Matthew 22:41—23:22

NEW TESTAMENT READING

Jesus Questions the Pharisees

*W*hile the Pharisees were together, Jesus asked them, "What do you think about the Christ? Whose son is he?"

They answered, "The Christ is the Son of David."

Then Jesus said to them, "Then why did David call him 'Lord'? David, speaking by the power of the Holy Spirit, said,

'The Lord said to my Lord:

Sit by me at my right side,

until I put your enemies under your control.'   *Psalm 110:1*

David calls the Christ 'Lord,' so how can the Christ be his son?"

None of the Pharisees could answer Jesus' question, and after that day no one was brave enough to ask him any more questions.

Jesus Accuses Some Leaders

*T*hen Jesus said to the crowds and to his followers, "The teachers of the law and the Pharisees have the authority to tell you what the law of Moses says. So you should obey and follow whatever they tell you, but their lives are not good examples for you to follow. They tell you to do things, but they themselves don't do them. They make strict rules and try to force people to obey them, but they are unwilling to help those who struggle under the weight of their rules.

"They do good things so that other people will see them. They make the boxes of Scriptures that they wear bigger, and they make their special prayer clothes very long. Those Pharisees and teachers of the law love to have the most important seats at feasts and in the synagogues. They love people to greet them with respect in the marketplaces, and they love to have people call them 'Teacher.'

"But you must not be called 'Teacher,' because you have only one Teacher, and you are all brothers and sisters together. And don't call any person on earth 'Father,' because you have one Father, who is in heaven. And you should not be called 'Master,' because you have only one Master, the Christ. Whoever is your servant is the greatest among you. Whoever makes himself great will be made humble. Whoever makes himself humble will be made great.

"How terrible for you, teachers of the law and Pharisees! You are hypocrites! You close the door for people to enter the kingdom of heaven. You yourselves don't enter, and you stop others who are trying to enter.

"How terrible for you, teachers of the law and Pharisees! You are hypocrites! You travel across land and sea to find one person who will change to your ways. When you find that person, you make him more fit for hell than you are.

"How terrible for you! You guide the people, but you are blind. You say, 'If people swear by the Temple when they make a promise, that means nothing. But if they swear by the gold that is in the Temple, they must keep that promise.' You are blind fools! Which is greater: the gold or the Temple that makes that gold holy? And you say, 'If people swear by the altar when they make a promise, that means nothing. But if they swear by the gift on the altar, they must keep that promise.' You are blind! Which is greater: the gift or the altar that makes the gift holy? The person who swears by the altar is really using the altar and also everything on the altar. And the person who swears by the Temple is really using the Temple and also everything in the Temple. The person who swears by heaven is also using God's throne and the One who sits on that throne."

OLD TESTAMENT READING

*S*o this is what the Lord GOD says: Because you prophets spoke things that are false and saw visions that do not come true, I am against you, says the Lord GOD. I will punish the prophets who see false visions and prophesy lies. They will have no place among my people. Their names will not be written on the list of the people of Israel, and they will not enter the land of Israel. Then you will know that I am the Lord GOD.

"'It is because they lead my people the wrong way by saying, "Peace!" when there is no peace. When the people build a weak wall, the prophets cover it with whitewash to make it look strong. So tell those who cover a weak wall with whitewash that it will fall down. Rain will pour down, hailstones will fall, and a stormy wind will break the wall down. When the wall has fallen, people will ask you, "Where is the whitewash you used on the wall?"

"'So this is what the Lord GOD says: I will break the wall with a stormy wind. In my anger rain will pour down, and hailstones will destroy the wall. I will tear down the wall on which you put whitewash. I will level it to the ground so that people will see the wall's foundation. And when the wall falls, you will be destroyed under it. Then you will know that I am the LORD. So I will carry out my anger on the wall and against those who covered it with whitewash. Then I will tell you, "The wall is gone, and those who covered it with whitewash are gone. The prophets of Israel who prophesy to Jerusalem and who see visions of peace for the city, when there is no peace, will be gone, says the Lord GOD."'"

Ezekiel 13:8–16

A terrible and shocking thing
      has happened in the land of Judah:
The prophets speak lies,
      and the priests take power into their
         own hands,
and my people love it this way.
   But what will you do when the end
      comes?"

Jeremiah 5:30–31

alone a disciple of Christ in the tough, modern world. . . .

. . . Americans used to speak much of their "exceptionalism." Today there is only one place left where America is still exceptional— the strength of religion. In a world in which modernity and secularity seem to go hand in hand, the U.S. is simultaneously the most modern and the most religious of modern countries. Yet with the striking discrepancy between indicators (church attendance, giving, praying) and the social influence—the former up and the latter down—the exception cannot continue for long. There is too little religion and too much religiosity in the church. The church's showdown period is beginning too, when its true integrity and effectiveness will be revealed. . . .

. . . Having visited almost all the countries in the English-speaking world, I would say that I know none where the churches are more full and the sermons more empty than in America. There are magnificent exceptions, of course. But by and large, I am never hungrier and rarely angrier than when I come out of an American evangelical church after what passes for the preaching of the Word of God.

The problem is not just the heresy, though doubtless there is some of that. Nor is it just the degree of entertainment, and there is lots of that. Nor is it even the appalling gaps in the theology, for there is far too much of that. The real problem is that in what is said there is almost no sense of announcement from God; and in what is shown, there is almost no sense of anointing by God.

Jeremiah attacked the false prophets of his day with the damning question, "Which of them has stood in the council of the LORD, seen him and heard his word?" (Jer 23:18). Are we who profess a high view of authority much better in practice? Is such a standard too demanding?

Os Guinness

INSIGHTS

*F*rom the Hallmark-card theology of a thousand churches to the nauseating nonsense of PTL, American evangelicalism is awash in a sloppy, sentimental, superficial theology that wouldn't empower a clockwork mouse, let

PAUSE   FOR   REFLECTION

*S*tudy these readings and list the things that God's teachers are supposed to do. Why will God punish false spiritual leaders? How well do you think today's religious leaders measure up?

TUESDAY:

God Will Punish Those Who Persecute His Messengers

Matthew 23:23—24:8

NEW TESTAMENT READING

*H*ow terrible for you, teachers of the law and Pharisees! You are hypocrites! You give to God one-tenth of everything you earn—even your mint, dill, and cumin. But you don't obey the really important teachings of the law—justice, mercy, and being loyal. These are the things you should do, as well as those other things. You guide the people, but you are blind! You are like a person who picks a fly out of a drink and then swallows a camel!

"How terrible for you, teachers of the law and Pharisees! You are hypocrites! You wash the outside of your cups and dishes, but inside they are full of things you got by cheating others and by pleasing only yourselves. Pharisees, you are blind! First make the inside of the cup clean, and then the outside of the cup can be truly clean.

"How terrible for you, teachers of the law and Pharisees! You are hypocrites! You are like tombs that are painted white. Outside, those tombs look fine, but inside, they are full of the bones of dead people and all kinds of unclean things. It is the same with you. People look at you and think you are good, but on the inside you are full of hypocrisy and evil.

"How terrible for you, teachers of the law and Pharisees! You are hypocrites! You build tombs for the prophets, and you show honor to the graves of those who lived good lives. You say, 'If we had lived during the time of our ancestors, we would not have helped them kill the prophets.' But you give proof that you are children of those who murdered the prophets. And you will complete the sin that your ancestors started.

"You are snakes! A family of poisonous snakes! How are you going to escape God's judgment? So I tell you this: I am sending to you prophets and wise men and teachers. Some of them you will kill and crucify. Some of them you will beat in your synagogues and chase from town to town. So you will be guilty for the death of all the good people who have been killed on earth—from the murder of that good man Abel to the murder of Zechariah son of Berakiah, whom you murdered between the Temple and the altar. I tell you the truth, all of these things will happen to you people who are living now.

Jesus Feels Sorry for Jerusalem

*J*erusalem, Jerusalem! You kill the prophets and stone to death those who are sent to you. Many times I wanted to gather your people as a hen gathers her chicks under her wings, but you did not let me. Now your house will be left completely empty. I tell you, you will not see me again until that time when you will say, 'God bless the One who comes in the name of the Lord.'"

The Temple Will Be Destroyed

*A*s Jesus left the Temple and was walking away, his followers came up to show him the Temple's buildings. Jesus asked, "Do you see all these buildings? I tell you the truth, not one stone will be left on another. Every stone will be thrown down to the ground."

Later, as Jesus was sitting on the Mount of Olives, his followers came to be alone with him. They said, "Tell us, when will these things happen? And what will be the sign that it is time for you to come again and for this age to end?"

Jesus answered, "Be careful that no one fools you. Many will come in my name, saying, 'I am the Christ,' and they will fool many people. You will hear about wars and stories of wars that are coming, but don't be afraid. These things must happen before the end comes. Nations will fight against other nations; kingdoms will fight against other kingdoms. There will be times when there is no food for people to eat, and there will be earthquakes in different places. These things are like the first pains when something new is about to be born.

OLD TESTAMENT READING

I punished your people, but it did not help.

They didn't come back when they
were punished.
With your swords you killed your
prophets
like a hungry lion.

"Even on your clothes you have the
blood
of poor and innocent people,
but they weren't thieves you caught
breaking in.
You do all these things,
but you say, 'I am innocent.
God is not angry with me.'
But I will judge you guilty of lying,
because you say, 'I have not
sinned.'"

Jeremiah 2:30, 34–35

*C*rooked leaders cannot be your
friends.
They use the law to cause suffering.
They join forces against people who do
right
and sentence to death the innocent.
But the LORD is my defender;
my God is the rock of my protection.
God will pay them back for their sins
and will destroy them for their evil.
The LORD our God will destroy them.

Psalm 94:20–23

*P*ashhur son of Immer was a priest and the
highest officer in the Temple of the LORD.
When he heard Jeremiah prophesying in
the Temple courtyard, he had Jeremiah the
prophet beaten. And he locked Jeremiah's
hands and feet between large blocks of
wood at the Upper Gate of Benjamin of the
LORD's Temple. The next day when Pashhur
took Jeremiah out of the blocks of wood,
Jeremiah said to him, "The LORD's name for
you is not Pashhur. Now his name for you
is Terror on Every Side. This is what the
LORD says: 'I will soon make you a terror to
yourself and to all your friends. You will
watch enemies killing your friends with
swords. And I will give all the people of
Judah to the king of Babylon, who will take
them away as captives to Babylon and then
will kill them with swords. I will give all the
wealth of this city to its enemies—its goods,
its valuables, and the treasures of the kings

of Judah. The enemies will carry all those
valuables off to Babylon. And Pashhur, you
and everyone in your house will be taken
captive. You will be forced to go to Babylon,
where you will die and be buried, you and
your friends to whom you have prophesied
lies."

Jeremiah 20:1–6

INSIGHTS

*A young man came to D. L. Moody and
said, "Mr. Moody, I want to be a Christian;
but must I give up the world?" Moody char-
acteristically replied, "Young man, if you live
the out-and-out Christian life, the world will
soon give you up." If we are popular with
the crowd of worldlings, or if we are not
penalised in some way for our attachment
to Christ, we have good cause to inspect our
discipleship. . . .*

*The world varies its ways of persecuting
us. Sometimes it uses the sword, and sometimes the lip of scorn. Most of us can stand
the sword far better than derision or sar-
casm. . . .*

*Let us remember, also, that there is an-
other side to this being penalised for Christian godliness. It is equally true that all who
live ungodly, and persecute God's people, shall
suffer punishment. Old Testament incidents,
as Paul tells us, were recorded for our admonition, as warnings and example to us.
Under the old dispensation God frequently
visited punishment upon persons immediately
after their committing of wrongs, so that the
connection between the sin and the punishment might be clearly seen. In this present
age, the judgment of the ungodly may be de-
ferred; but it is none the less certain, and will
be awful when at last it falls.*

J. Sydlow Baxter

PAUSE FOR REFLECTION

*W*hat are Jesus' accusations against the
teachers and Pharisees? What are his warnings to them? How can we be sure that God
will punish those who persecute his servants?

WEDNESDAY:

The Unmistakable and Terrible Signs of the End Times

Matthew 24:9–35

NEW TESTAMENT READING

*T*hen people will arrest you, hand you over to be hurt, and kill you. They will hate you because you believe in me. At that time, many will lose their faith, and they will turn against each other and hate each other. Many false prophets will come and cause many people to believe lies. There will be more and more evil in the world, so most people will stop showing their love for each other. But those people who keep their faith until the end will be saved. The Good News about God's kingdom will be preached in all the world, to every nation. Then the end will come.

"Daniel the prophet spoke about 'the destroying terror.' You will see this standing in the holy place." (You who read this should understand what it means.) "At that time, the people in Judea should run away to the mountains. If people are on the roofs of their houses, they must not go down to get anything out of their houses. If people are in the fields, they must not go back to get their coats. At that time, how terrible it will be for women who are pregnant or have nursing babies! Pray that it will not be winter or a Sabbath day when these things happen and you have to run away, because at that time there will be much trouble. There will be more trouble than there has ever been since the beginning of the world until now, and nothing as bad will ever happen again. God has decided to make that terrible time short. Otherwise, no one would go on living. But God will make that time short to help the people he has chosen. At that time, someone might say to you, 'Look, there is the Christ!' Or another person might say, 'There he is!' But don't believe them. False Christs and false prophets will come and perform great wonders and miracles. They will try to fool even the

people God has chosen, if that is possible. Now I have warned you about this before it happens.

"If people tell you, 'The Christ is in the desert,' don't go there. If they say, 'The Christ is in the inner room,' don't believe it. When the Son of Man comes, he will be seen by everyone, like lightning flashing from the east to the west. Wherever the dead body is, there the vultures will gather.

"Soon after the trouble of those days,
'the sun will grow dark,
    and the moon will not give its light.
The stars will fall from the sky.
And the powers of the heavens will
        be shaken.' *Isaiah 13:10; 34:4*

"At that time, the sign of the Son of Man will appear in the sky. Then all the peoples of the world will cry. They will see the Son of Man coming on clouds in the sky with great power and glory. He will use a loud trumpet to send his angels all around the earth, and they will gather his chosen people from every part of the world.

"Learn a lesson from the fig tree: When its branches become green and soft and new leaves appear, you know summer is near. In the same way, when you see all these things happening, you will know that the time is near, ready to come. I tell you the truth, all these things will happen while the people of this time are still living. Earth and sky will be destroyed, but the words I have said will never be destroyed."

OLD TESTAMENT READING

*I*n my vision at night I saw in front of me someone who looked like a human being coming on the clouds in the sky. He came near God, who has been alive forever, and he was led to God. He was given authority, glory, and the strength of a king. People of every tribe, nation, and language will serve him. His rule will last forever, and his kingdom will never be destroyed."

Daniel 7:13–14

*T*he day that your watchmen warned
    you about has come.
Now they will be confused.

Don't believe your neighbor
  or trust a friend.
Don't say anything,
  even to your wife.
A son will not honor his father,
  a daughter will turn against her
    mother,
and a daughter-in-law will be against
    her mother-in-law;
  a person's enemies will be members
    of his own family.

Micah 7:4b–6

*L*ook, the LORD's day of judging is
    coming—
  a terrible day, a day of God's anger.
He will destroy the land
  and the sinners who live in it.
The stars will not show their light;
  the skies will be dark.
The sun will grow dark as it rises,
  and the moon will not give its light.

Isaiah 13:9–10

*A*ll you nations, come near and
    listen.
  Pay attention, you peoples!
The earth and all the people in it should
    listen,
  the world and everything in it.
The LORD is angry with all the nations;
  he is angry with their armies.
He will destroy them and kill them all.
Their bodies will be thrown outside.
  The stink will rise from the bodies,
  and the blood will flow down the
    mountains.
The sun, moon, and stars will dissolve,
  and the sky will be rolled up like a
    scroll.
The stars will fall
  like dead leaves from a vine
  or dried-up figs from a fig tree.

Isaiah 34:1–4

INSIGHTS

*T*o a unique degree this generation has witnessed the universal and dramatic fulfillment
of prophecy. Many of the signs Jesus said
would herald His return have developed before our eyes.

There is the evangelistic sign: "This gospel of the kingdom will be preached in the
whole world as a testimony to all nations, and
then the end will come" (Matthew 24:14).

This prophecy has been fulfilled in our
generation to a degree that has never before
been the case. There is now no major nation
in which there is no Christian witness. . . .

There is the religious sign: "That day
will not come until the rebellion occurs
and the man of lawlessness is revealed" (2
Thessalonians 2:3).

Unfortunately, we can see this sign being
fulfilled all around us. As Jesus foretold, the
love of the many is growing cold (Matthew
24:12). . . .

Political signs abound. Could prevailing
world conditions have been more accurately
and comprehensively described than in our
Lord's words in Luke 21:25–26? "There will
be signs. . . . On the earth, nations will be
in anguish and perplexity. . . . Men will
faint from terror, apprehensive of what is
coming on the world."

There is the Jewish sign: "Jerusalem will
be trampled on by the Gentiles until the
times of the Gentiles are fulfilled" (Luke
21:24). . . .

. . . For the first time in 2,500 years,
Jerusalem is not dominated by Gentiles. . . .

Whatever view we hold regarding the details surrounding the second coming of Christ,
history is moving rapidly—not to cataclysm
merely, but to consummation.

J. Oswald Sanders

PAUSE FOR REFLECTION

*W*hy did Jesus warn his followers about
the end times? What event will be perfectly
clear to all people? Despite the horror of these
events, what glorious hope does Jesus promise to his people at the end?

THURSDAY:

Always Be Ready for the Lord's Coming

Matthew 24:36—25:13

NEW TESTAMENT READING

When Will Jesus Come Again?

No one knows when that day or time will be, not the angels in heaven, not even the Son. Only the Father knows. When the Son of Man comes, it will be like what happened during Noah's time. In those days before the flood, people were eating and drinking, marrying and giving their children to be married, until the day Noah entered the boat. They knew nothing about what was happening until the flood came and destroyed them. It will be the same when the Son of Man comes. Two men will be in the field. One will be taken, and the other will be left. Two women will be grinding grain with a mill. One will be taken, and the other will be left.

"So always be ready, because you don't know the day your Lord will come. Remember this: If the owner of the house knew what time of night a thief was coming, the owner would watch and not let the thief break in. So you also must be ready, because the Son of Man will come at a time you don't expect him.

"Who is the wise and loyal servant that the master trusts to give the other servants their food at the right time? When the master comes and finds the servant doing his work, the servant will be blessed. I tell you the truth, the master will choose that servant to take care of everything he owns. But suppose that evil servant thinks to himself, 'My master will not come back soon,' and he begins to beat the other servants and eat and get drunk with others like him? The master will come when that servant is not ready and is not expecting him. Then the master will cut him in pieces and send him away to be with the hypocrites, where people will cry and grind their teeth with pain.

A Story About Ten Bridesmaids

At that time the kingdom of heaven will be like ten bridesmaids who took their lamps and went to wait for the bridegroom. Five of them were foolish and five were wise. The five foolish bridesmaids took their lamps, but they did not take more oil for the lamps to burn. The wise bridesmaids took their lamps and more oil in jars. Because the bridegroom was late, they became sleepy and went to sleep.

"At midnight someone cried out, 'The bridegroom is coming! Come and meet him!' Then all the bridesmaids woke up and got their lamps ready. But the foolish ones said to the wise, 'Give us some of your oil, because our lamps are going out.' The wise bridesmaids answered, 'No, the oil we have might not be enough for all of us. Go to the people who sell oil and buy some for yourselves.'

"So while the five foolish bridesmaids went to buy oil, the bridegroom came. The bridesmaids who were ready went in with the bridegroom to the wedding feast. Then the door was closed and locked.

"Later the others came back and said, 'Sir, sir, open the door to let us in.' But the bridegroom answered, 'I tell you the truth, I don't want to know you.'

"So always be ready, because you don't know the day or the hour the Son of Man will come."

OLD TESTAMENT READING

The LORD All-Powerful says, "I will send my messenger, who will prepare the way for me. Suddenly, the Lord you are looking for will come to his Temple; the messenger of the agreement, whom you want, will come." No one can live through that time; no one can survive when he comes. He will be like a purifying fire and like laundry soap. Like someone who heats and purifies silver, he will purify the Levites and make them pure like gold and silver. Then they will bring offerings to the LORD in the right way. And the LORD will accept the offerings from Judah and Jerusalem, as it was in the past. The LORD All-Powerful says, "Then I will come to you and judge you. I will be quick to testify against those who take part in evil magic, adultery, and lying under oath, those who cheat workers of their pay and who cheat widows and orphans, those who are unfair to foreigners, and those who do not respect me.

"You have said, 'It is useless to serve God. It did no good to obey his laws and to show the LORD All-Powerful that we were sorry for what we did. So we say that proud people are happy. Evil people succeed. They challenge God and get away with it.'"

Then those who honored the LORD spoke with each other, and the LORD listened and heard them. The names of those who honored the LORD and respected him were written in his presence in a book to be remembered.

The LORD All-Powerful says, "They belong to me; on that day they will be my very own. As a parent shows mercy to his child who serves him, I will show mercy to my people. You will again see the difference between good and evil people, between those who serve God and those who don't."

Malachi 3:1–5, 14–18

*G*ather together, gather,
    you unwanted people.
Do it before it's too late,
    before you are blown away like
      chaff,
before the LORD's terrible anger
    reaches you,
    before the day of the LORD's anger
      comes to you.
Come to the LORD, all you who are not
    proud,
    who obey his laws.
Do what is right. Learn to be humble.
    Maybe you will escape
    on the day the LORD shows his
      anger.

Zephaniah 2:1–3

INSIGHTS

*W*e look for the return of the Lord because He said many times that He would come— and because it is one of the most frequently mentioned subjects in the Bible. Christ is with us today through His Holy Spirit, and He will be with Christians and with the church down to the end of the age. When He ascended up into heaven, the disciples were told by two angels standing by that He would return again as they were now seeing Him go (see Acts 1:11).

The climactic event of history is yet in the future. It will be sudden and final—the culmination of the ages. It will take the unbelieving world by surprise, and people will try to hide from His holy presence. At the return of Christ the resurrection of believers will take place. They will be gathered together to be with the Lord forever. We can only speculate about the exact details of His return. The important thing is that He is coming again and that we yet have time to trust in Him as our Savior and Lord. The Bible says all people must face Him at that time—as either Savior or Judge: "When the Son of Man comes in his glory . . . he will sit on his throne in heavenly glory" (Matthew 25:31).

Billy Graham

APPLICATION

*W*hat do you want to be doing when Jesus comes again? Will you be with those who say it is useless to serve God, or will you stand with those who honor the Lord? What are the consequences of each position? Pray that you will remain faithful to God's calling in your life.

FRIDAY:

God Rewards Kindness

Matthew 25:14–40

A Story About Three Servants

*T*he kingdom of heaven is like a man who was going to another place for a visit. Before he left, he called for his servants and told them to take care of his things while he was gone. He gave one servant five bags of gold, another servant two bags of gold, and a third servant one bag of gold, to each one as much as he could handle. Then he left. The servant who got five bags went quickly to invest the money and earned five more bags. In the same way, the servant who had two bags invested them and earned two more. But the servant who got one bag went out and dug a hole in the ground and hid the master's money.

"After a long time the master came home and asked the servants what they did with his money. The servant who was given five bags of gold brought five more bags to the master and said, 'Master, you trusted me to care for five bags of gold, so I used your five bags to earn five more.' The master answered, 'You did well. You are a good and loyal servant. Because you were loyal with small things, I will let you care for much greater things. Come and share my joy with me.'

"Then the servant who had been given two bags of gold came to the master and said, 'Master, you gave me two bags of gold to care for, so I used your two bags to earn two more.' The master answered, 'You did well. You are a good and loyal servant. Because you were loyal with small things, I will let you care for much greater things. Come and share my joy with me.'

"Then the servant who had been given one bag of gold came to the master and said, 'Master, I knew that you were a hard man. You harvest things you did not plant. You gather crops where you did not sow any seed. So I was afraid and went and hid your money in the ground. Here is your bag of gold.' The master answered, 'You are a wicked and lazy servant! You say you knew that I harvest things I did not plant and that I gather crops where I did not sow any seed. So you should have put my gold in the bank. Then, when I came home, I would have received my gold back with interest.'

"So the master told his other servants, 'Take the bag of gold from that servant and give it to the servant who has ten bags of gold. Those who have much will get more, and they will have much more than they need. But those who do not have much will have everything taken away from them.' Then the master said, 'Throw that useless servant outside, into the darkness where people will cry and grind their teeth with pain.'

The King Will Judge All People

*T*he Son of Man will come again in his great glory, with all his angels. He will be King and sit on his great throne. All the nations of the world will be gathered before him, and he will separate them into two groups as a shepherd separates the sheep from the goats. The Son of Man will put the sheep on his right and the goats on his left.

"Then the King will say to the people on his right, 'Come, my Father has given you his blessing. Receive the kingdom God has prepared for you since the world was made. I was hungry, and you gave me food. I was thirsty, and you gave me something to drink. I was alone and away from home, and you invited me into your house. I was without clothes, and you gave me something to wear. I was sick, and you cared for me. I was in prison, and you visited me.'

"Then the good people will answer, 'Lord, when did we see you hungry and give you food, or thirsty and give you something to drink? When did we see you alone and away from home and invite you into our house? When did we see you without clothes and give you something to wear? When did we see you sick or in prison and care for you?'

Then the King will answer, 'I tell you the truth, anything you did for even the least of my people here, you also did for me.'

*H*appy is the person who thinks about
the poor.
When trouble comes, the LORD will
save him.
The LORD will protect him and spare his
life
and will bless him in the land.
He will not let his enemies take him.
The LORD will give him strength when
he is sick,
and he will make him well again.

Psalm 41:1–3

*I*t is good to be merciful and generous.
Those who are fair in their business
will never be defeated.
Good people will always be remembered.
They won't be afraid of bad news;
their hearts are steady because they
trust the LORD.
They are confident and will not be
afraid;
they will look down on their enemies.
They give freely to the poor.
The things they do are right and will
continue forever.
They will be given great honor.

Psalm 112:5–9

*W*hoever mistreats the poor insults
their Maker,
but whoever is kind to the needy
honors God.

Proverbs 14:31

*B*eing kind to the poor is like lending
to the LORD;
he will reward you for what you have
done.

Proverbs 19:17

*S*hare your food with the hungry
and bring poor, homeless people
into your own homes.
When you see someone who has no
clothes, give him yours,
and don't refuse to help your own
relatives.
Then your light will shine like the dawn,

and your wounds will quickly heal.
Your God will walk before you,
and the glory of the LORD will protect
you from behind.
Then you will call out, and the LORD will
answer.
You will cry out, and he will say,
'Here I am.'"

Isaiah 58:7–9a

INSIGHTS

*O*ne *kind word can warm three winter
months," says a Japanese proverb.*
*Kind words indeed warm the human
spirit. Kindness is literally love in action,
showing genuine friendship to others by regarding them as important in God's sight and
worthy of dignity and respect. It involves
treating others with courtesy, lending encouragement, and freely offering yourself or
your resources to help a person in need, no
strings attached. . . .*
*In the book of Proverbs, we read that
kindness is a prime quality of a virtuous
woman: "When she speaks, her words are
wise, and kindness is the rule for everything
she says" (Proverbs 31:26). Men, these vir-
tues are for us, too!*
*Jim has discovered the pleasure of kind-
ness. He makes a special effort to brighten
someone's day with an unexpected kind word
or gesture. . . . At work, he frequently expresses appreciation to others for the jobs they
do. With his neighbors, he is quick to lend a
helping hand or offer encouragement.*
*Imagine the impact Christians could have
on the world if kindness were the rule in all
we do!*

Bill Bright

APPLICATION

*W*hat *in these readings shows that God
considers mistreatment of the poor, homeless,
sick, and downtrodden to be a personal insult? How does that inspire you to be merciful, kind, and generous?*

71

WEEKEND:
Honoring God Is a Beautiful Thing
Matthew 25:41—26:19

*T*hen the King will say to those on his left, 'Go away from me. You will be punished. Go into the fire that burns forever that was prepared for the devil and his angels. I was hungry, and you gave me nothing to eat. I was thirsty, and you gave me nothing to drink. I was alone and away from home, and you did not invite me into your house. I was without clothes, and you gave me nothing to wear. I was sick and in prison, and you did not care for me.'

"Then those people will answer, 'Lord, when did we see you hungry or thirsty or alone and away from home or without clothes or sick or in prison? When did we see these things and not help you?'

"Then the King will answer, 'I tell you the truth, anything you refused to do for even the least of my people here, you refused to do for me.'

"These people will go off to be punished forever, but the good people will go to live forever."

The Plan to Kill Jesus

*A*fter Jesus finished saying all these things, he told his followers, "You know that the day after tomorrow is the day of the Passover Feast. On that day the Son of Man will be given to his enemies to be crucified."

Then the leading priests and the older Jewish leaders had a meeting at the palace of the high priest, named Caiaphas. At the meeting, they planned to set a trap to arrest Jesus and kill him. But they said, "We must not do it during the feast, because the people might cause a riot."

Perfume for Jesus' Burial

*J*esus was in Bethany at the house of Simon, who had a skin disease. While Jesus was there, a woman approached him with an alabaster jar filled with expensive perfume.

She poured this perfume on Jesus' head while he was eating.

His followers were upset when they saw the woman do this. They asked, "Why waste that perfume? It could have been sold for a great deal of money and the money given to the poor."

Knowing what had happened, Jesus said, "Why are you troubling this woman? She did an excellent thing for me. You will always have the poor with you, but you will not always have me. This woman poured perfume on my body to prepare me for burial. I tell you the truth, wherever the Good News is preached in all the world, what this woman has done will be told, and people will remember her."

Judas Becomes an Enemy of Jesus

*T*hen one of the twelve apostles, Judas Iscariot, went to talk to the leading priests. He said, "What will you pay me for giving Jesus to you?" And they gave him thirty silver coins. After that, Judas watched for the best time to turn Jesus in.

Jesus Eats the Passover Meal

*O*n the first day of the Feast of Unleavened Bread, the followers came to Jesus. They said, "Where do you want us to prepare for you to eat the Passover meal?"

Jesus answered, "Go into the city to a certain man and tell him, 'The Teacher says: The chosen time is near. I will have the Passover with my followers at your house.'" The followers did what Jesus told them to do, and they prepared the Passover meal.

*M*anoah said to the angel of the Lord, "We would like you to stay awhile so we can cook a young goat for you."

The angel of the Lord answered, "Even if I stay awhile, I would not eat your food. But if you want to prepare something, offer a burnt offering to the Lord." (Manoah did not understand that the man was really the angel of the Lord.)

Then Manoah asked the angel of the Lord, "What is your name? Then we will honor you when what you have said really happens."

The angel of the LORD said, "Why do you ask my name? It is too amazing for you to understand." So Manoah sacrificed a young goat on a rock and offered some grain as a gift to the LORD. Then an amazing thing happened as Manoah and his wife watched. The flames went up to the sky from the altar. As the fire burned, the angel of the LORD went up to heaven in the flame. When Manoah and his wife saw that, they bowed facedown on the ground. The angel of the LORD did not appear to them again. Then Manoah understood that the man was really the angel of the LORD. Manoah said, "We have seen God, so we will surely die."

But his wife said to him, "If the LORD wanted to kill us, he would not have accepted our burnt offering or grain offering. He would not have shown us all these things or told us all this."

Judges 13:15–23

*M*y father David wanted to build a temple for the LORD, the God of Israel. But the LORD said to my father David, 'It was good that you wanted to build a temple for me. But you are not the one to build it. Your son, who comes from your own body, is the one who will build my temple.'"

1 Kings 8:17–19

*S*o Noah went out with his sons, his wife, and his sons' wives. Every animal, everything that crawls on the earth, and every bird went out of the boat by families.

Then Noah built an altar to the LORD. He took some of all the clean birds and animals, and he burned them on the altar as offerings to God. The LORD was pleased with these sacrifices and said to himself, "I will never again curse the ground because of human beings. Their thoughts are evil even when they are young, but I will never again destroy every living thing on the earth as I did this time."

Genesis 8:18–21

*I*t was said of the soldiers of the first Napoleon that they were content to die in the ditch if only he rode over them to victory. With their last breath they cried, "Long live the Emperor!" It seemed as though they had lost all thought and care of their own interests, so long as glory was given to his name. So should it be of us. Higher than our own comfort, or success, or popularity, should be the one thought of the glory of our God. Let Christ be honored, loved, exalted, at whatever cost to us. . . .

. . . Live to please God, and He will breathe on you His peace. Seek His glory, and He will make your heart His home. Do His will, and thereby good shall come to you.

F. B. Meyer

*R*eview the ways people honored God in these readings (including the Matthew 25 parable). Spend some time honoring God in prayer today. Then, list the ways you want to honor God. Start glorifying him today!

MONDAY:

God Cares for
His Scattered Sheep

Matthew 26:20–46

*I*n the evening Jesus was sitting at the table with his twelve followers. As they were eating, Jesus said, "I tell you the truth, one of you will turn against me."

This made the followers very sad. Each one began to say to Jesus, "Surely, Lord, I am not the one who will turn against you, am I?"

Jesus answered, "The man who has dipped his hand with me into the bowl is the one who will turn against me. The Son of Man will die, just as the Scriptures say. But how terrible it will be for the person who hands the Son of Man over to be killed. It would be better for him if he had never been born."

Then Judas, who would give Jesus to his enemies, said to Jesus, "Teacher, surely I am not the one, am I?"

Jesus answered, "Yes, it is you."

The Lord's Supper

*W*hile they were eating, Jesus took some bread and thanked God for it and broke it. Then he gave it to his followers and said, "Take this bread and eat it; this is my body."

Then Jesus took a cup and thanked God for it and gave it to the followers. He said, "Every one of you drink this. This is my blood which is the new agreement that God makes with his people. This blood is poured out for many to forgive their sins. I tell you this: I will not drink of this fruit of the vine again until that day when I drink it new with you in my Father's kingdom."

After singing a hymn, they went out to the Mount of Olives.

Jesus' Followers Will Leave Him

*J*esus told his followers, "Tonight you will all stumble in your faith on account of me, because it is written in the Scriptures:
'I will kill the shepherd,
and the sheep will scatter.'
Zechariah 13:7

But after I rise from the dead, I will go ahead of you into Galilee."

Peter said, "Everyone else may stumble in their faith because of you, but I will not."

Jesus said, "I tell you the truth, tonight before the rooster crows you will say three times that you don't know me."

But Peter said, "I will never say that I don't know you! I will even die with you!" And all the other followers said the same thing.

Jesus Prays Alone

*T*hen Jesus went with his followers to a place called Gethsemane. He said to them, "Sit here while I go over there and pray." He took Peter and the two sons of Zebedee with him, and he began to be very sad and troubled. He said to them, "My heart is full of sorrow, to the point of death. Stay here and watch with me."

After walking a little farther away from them, Jesus fell to the ground and prayed, "My Father, if it is possible, do not give me this cup of suffering. But do what you want, not what I want." Then Jesus went back to his followers and found them asleep. He said to Peter, "You men could not stay awake with me for one hour? Stay awake and pray for strength against temptation. The spirit wants to do what is right, but the body is weak."

Then Jesus went away a second time and prayed, "My Father, if it is not possible for this painful thing to be taken from me, and if I must do it, I pray that what you want will be done."

Then he went back to his followers, and again he found them asleep, because their eyes were heavy. So Jesus left them and went away and prayed a third time, saying the same thing.

Then Jesus went back to his followers and said, "Are you still sleeping and resting? The time has come for the Son of Man to be handed over to sinful people. Get up, we must go. Look, here comes the man who has turned against me."

*G*od is truly good to Israel,
to those who have pure hearts.

But I had almost stopped believing;
   I had almost lost my faith
because I was jealous of proud people.
   I saw wicked people doing well.

They are not suffering;
   they are healthy and strong.
They don't have troubles like the rest
      of us;
   they don't have problems like other
      people.

Psalm 73:1–5

*K*ill the shepherd,
   and the sheep will scatter,
   and I will punish the little ones."
The LORD says, "Two-thirds of the
      people
   through all the land will die. They
      will be gone,
   and one-third will be left.
The third that is left I will test with fire,
   purifying them like silver,
   testing them like gold.
Then they will call on me,
   and I will answer them.
I will say, 'You are my people,'
   and they will say, 'The LORD is our
      God.'"

Zechariah 13:7b–9

*T*he sheep were scattered, because there
was no shepherd, and they became food for
every wild animal. My flock wandered over
all the mountains and on every high hill.
They were scattered all over the face of the
earth, and no one searched or looked for
them.

   "'This is what the Lord GOD says: I, myself, will search for my sheep and take care
of them. As a shepherd takes care of his
scattered flock when it is found, I will take
care of my sheep. I will save them from all
the places where they were scattered on a
cloudy and dark day. I will bring them out
from the nations and gather them from the
countries. I will bring them to their own land
and pasture them on the mountains of Israel, in the ravines, and in all the places
where people live in the land. I will feed
them in a good pasture, and they will eat
grass on the high mountains of Israel. They
will lie down on good ground where they
eat grass, and they will eat in rich grassland
on the mountains of Israel. I will feed my
flock and lead them to rest, says the Lord
GOD. I will search for the lost, bring back
those that strayed away, put bandages on
those that were hurt, and make the weak
strong. But I will destroy those sheep that
are fat and strong. I will tend the sheep with
fairness.'"

Ezekiel 34:5–6, 11–16

*L*ambs are wont to lag behind, prone to wander, and apt to grow weary, but from all the
danger of these infirmities the Shepherd protects them with His arm of power. He finds
new-born souls, like young lambs, ready to
perish—He nourishes them till life becomes
vigorous; He finds weak minds ready to faint
and die—He consoles them and renews their
strength. All the little ones He gathers, for it
is not the will of our heavenly Father that
one of them should perish. What a quick eye
He must have to see them all! What a tender heart to care for them all! What a far-
reaching and potent arm, to gather them all!
In His lifetime on earth He was a great gath-
erer of the weaker sort, and now that He
dwells in heaven, His loving heart yearns towards the meek and contrite, the timid and
feeble, the fearful and fainting here below.
How gently did He gather me to Himself, to
His truth, to His blood, to His love, to His
church! With what effectual grace did He com-
pel me to Himself! Since my first conversion,
how frequently has He restored me from my
wanderings, and once again folded me within
the circle of His everlasting arm! The best of
all is, that He does it all Himself personally,
not delegating the task of love, but condescending Himself to rescue and preserve His most
unworthy servant.

Charles Spurgeon

APPLICATION

*W*hen have you felt discouraged or abandoned—perhaps ready to lose your faith?
What prompted those feelings? How do these
readings comfort you? Thank God that he
promises to care for you.

TUESDAY:
The Pain of Being Betrayed by Friends
Matthew 26:47–68

NEW   TESTAMENT   READING

Jesus Is Arrested

*W*hile Jesus was still speaking, Judas, one of the twelve apostles, came up. With him were many people carrying swords and clubs who had been sent from the leading priests and the older Jewish leaders of the people. Judas had planned to give them a signal, saying, "The man I kiss is Jesus. Arrest him." At once Judas went to Jesus and said, "Greetings, Teacher!" and kissed him.

Jesus answered, "Friend, do what you came to do."

Then the people came and grabbed Jesus and arrested him. When that happened, one of Jesus' followers reached for his sword and pulled it out. He struck the servant of the high priest and cut off his ear.

Jesus said to the man, "Put your sword back in its place. All who use swords will be killed with swords. Surely you know I could ask my Father, and he would give me more than twelve armies of angels. But it must happen this way to bring about what the Scriptures say."

Then Jesus said to the crowd, "You came to get me with swords and clubs as if I were a criminal. Every day I sat in the Temple teaching, and you did not arrest me there. But all these things have happened so that it will come about as the prophets wrote." Then all of Jesus' followers left him and ran away.

Jesus Before the Leaders

*T*hose people who arrested Jesus led him to the house of Caiaphas, the high priest, where the teachers of the law and the older Jewish leaders were gathered. Peter followed far behind to the courtyard of the high priest's house, and he sat down with the guards to see what would happen to Jesus.

The leading priests and the whole Jewish council tried to find something false against Jesus so they could kill him. Many people came and told lies about him, but the council could find no real reason to kill him. Then two people came and said, "This man said, 'I can destroy the Temple of God and build it again in three days.'"

Then the high priest stood up and said to Jesus, "Aren't you going to answer? Don't you have something to say about their charges against you?" But Jesus said nothing.

Again the high priest said to Jesus, "I command you by the power of the living God: Tell us if you are the Christ, the Son of God."

Jesus answered, "Those are your words. But I tell you, in the future you will see the Son of Man sitting at the right hand of God, the Powerful One, and coming on clouds in the sky."

When the high priest heard this, he tore his clothes and said, "This man has said things that are against God! We don't need any more witnesses; you all heard him say these things against God. What do you think?"

The people answered, "He should die."

Then the people there spat in Jesus' face and beat him with their fists. Others slapped him. They said, "Prove to us that you are a prophet, you Christ! Tell us who hit you!"

OLD   TESTAMENT   READING

*I*t was not an enemy insulting me.
    I could stand that.
It was not someone who hated me.
    I could hide from him.
But it is you, a person like me,
    my companion and good friend.
We had a good friendship
    and walked together to God's Temple.
The one who was my friend attacks his
    friends
    and breaks his promises.
His words are slippery like butter,
    but war is in his heart.
His words are smoother than oil,
    but they cut like knives.

Psalm 55:12–14, 20–21

*T*hen the LORD said to Gideon, "You have too many men to defeat the Midianites. I don't want the Israelites to brag that they saved themselves. So now, announce to the people, 'Anyone who is afraid may leave Mount Gilead and go back home.'" So twenty-two thousand men returned home, but ten thousand remained.

Judges 7:2–3

*G*od has made my brothers my enemies,
　and my friends have become strangers.
My relatives have gone away,
　and my friends have forgotten me.
My guests and my female servants
　　treat me like a stranger;
　they look at me as if I were a foreigner.
I call for my servant, but he does not answer,
　even when I beg him with my own mouth.
My wife can't stand my breath,
　and my own family dislikes me.
Even the little boys hate me
　and talk about me when I leave.
All my close friends hate me;
　even those I love have turned against me."

Job 19:13–19

*B*ut when you are free, remember me. Be kind to me, and tell the king about me so I can get out of this prison. I was taken by force from the land of the Hebrews, and I have done nothing here to deserve being put in prison."

But the officer who served wine did not remember Joseph. He forgot all about him.

Genesis 40:14–15, 23

INSIGHTS

*H*ave you ever been betrayed by a friend? If so, you know the pain of separation which resembles the grief of death. When Judas agreed to betray Jesus, he might as well have hammered the spikes that would later be driven through Jesus' hands.

Have you ever wondered how it was possible for one of the apostles (who had witnessed Jesus' power, teaching, and love) to turn him over to his enemies for any amount of money? This, of course, was not Judas' first act of betrayal. As treasurer for the disciples, Judas had been dipping into the till all along. He was a dishonest and greedy man. Even so, the mind races: How in the world could he have betrayed Jesus? . . .

Perhaps we have a clue when we are told about others who refused to accept Jesus as the Christ: "Even after Jesus had done all these miraculous signs in their presence, they still would not believe in him." Judas was not the only one to betray Jesus. All those who refused to believe on him despite the overwhelming evidence of his deity might as well have picked up their own 30 silver coins when Judas did.

Even today there are those who, despite the evidence, continue to betray Jesus through disbelief. How is it possible? Why do they choose to ignore him? . . .

. . . We can choose Christ, or we can choose the world with its false allure. Yet it is not a choice that we make just once in a lifetime. Each day that Judas robbed Jesus was a day of betrayal. And for those who heard Jesus teach, and watched his miracles, yet refused to believe—for them, every day was a day of betrayal.

Do we believe in Jesus, yet live our lives as if we didn't? If so, we too betray Jesus. Will today be a day of faith or a day of betrayal?

F. LaGard Smith

PAUSE FOR REFLECTION

*W*hen Jesus answered Judas' betrayal with the words, "Friend, do the thing you came to do," Jesus showed that he knew exactly what was in Judas' heart. How do you think his words affected Judas? If Jesus said the same thing today about your plans, how would you be affected?

77

WEDNESDAY:

God Can Speak to Powerful Leaders Through Dreams

Matthew 26:69—27:20

NEW TESTAMENT READING

Peter Says He Doesn't Know Jesus

*A*t that time, as Peter was sitting in the courtyard, a servant girl came to him and said, "You also were with Jesus of Galilee."

But Peter said to all the people there that he was never with Jesus. He said, "I don't know what you are talking about."

When he left the courtyard and was at the gate, another girl saw him. She said to the people there, "This man was with Jesus of Nazareth."

Again, Peter said he was never with him, saying, "I swear I don't know this man Jesus!"

A short time later, some people standing there went to Peter and said, "Surely you are one of those who followed Jesus. The way you talk shows it."

Then Peter began to place a curse on himself and swear, "I don't know the man." At once, a rooster crowed. And Peter remembered what Jesus had told him: "Before the rooster crows, you will say three times that you don't know me." Then Peter went outside and cried painfully.

Jesus Is Taken to Pilate

*E*arly the next morning, all the leading priests and older leaders of the people decided that Jesus should die. They tied him, led him away, and turned him over to Pilate, the governor.

Judas Kills Himself

*J*udas, the one who had given Jesus to his enemies, saw that they had decided to kill Jesus. Then he was very sorry for what he had done. So he took the thirty silver coins back to the priests and the leaders, saying, "I sinned; I handed over to you an innocent man."

The leaders answered, "What is that to us? That's your problem, not ours."

So Judas threw the money into the Temple. Then he went off and hanged himself.

The leading priests picked up the silver coins in the Temple and said, "Our law does not allow us to keep this money with the Temple money, because it has paid for a man's death." So they decided to use the coins to buy Potter's Field as a place to bury strangers who died in Jerusalem. That is why that field is still called the Field of Blood. So what Jeremiah the prophet had said came true: "They took thirty silver coins. That is how little the Israelites thought he was worth. They used those thirty silver coins to buy the potter's field, as the Lord commanded me."

Pilate Questions Jesus

*J*esus stood before Pilate the governor, and Pilate asked him, "Are you the king of the Jews?"

Jesus answered, "Those are your words."

When the leading priests and the older leaders accused Jesus, he said nothing.

So Pilate said to Jesus, "Don't you hear them accusing you of all these things?"

But Jesus said nothing in answer to Pilate, and Pilate was very surprised at this.

Pilate Tries to Free Jesus

*E*very year at the time of Passover the governor would free one prisoner whom the people chose. At that time there was a man in prison, named Barabbas, who was known to be very bad. When the people gathered at Pilate's house, Pilate said, "Whom do you want me to set free: Barabbas or Jesus who is called the Christ?" Pilate knew that the people turned Jesus in to him because they were jealous.

While Pilate was sitting there on the judge's seat, his wife sent this message to him: "Don't do anything to that man, because he is innocent. Today I had a dream about him, and it troubled me very much."

But the leading priests and older leaders convinced the crowd to ask for Barabbas to be freed and for Jesus to be killed.

King Abimelech Responds to God's Warning

*B*ut one night God spoke to Abimelech in a dream and said, "You will die. The woman you took is married."

But Abimelech had not gone near Sarah, so he said, "Lord, would you destroy an innocent nation? Abraham himself told me, 'This woman is my sister,' and she also said, 'He is my brother.' I am innocent. I did not know I was doing anything wrong."

Then God said to Abimelech in the dream, "Yes, I know you did not realize what you were doing. So I did not allow you to sin against me and touch her. Give Abraham his wife back. He is a prophet. He will pray for you, and you will not die. But if you do not give Sarah back, you and all your family will surely die."

So early the next morning, Abimelech called all his officers and told them everything that had happened in the dream. They were very afraid. Then Abimelech called Abraham to him and said, "What have you done to us? What wrong did I do against you? Why did you bring this trouble to my kingdom? You should not have done these things to me. What were you thinking that caused you to do this?"

Then Abraham answered, "I thought no one in this place respected God and that someone would kill me to get Sarah."

Then Abimelech gave Abraham some sheep, cattle, and male and female slaves. He also gave Sarah, Abraham's wife, back to him and said, "Look around you at my land. You may live anywhere you want."

Genesis 20:3–11, 14–15

A Warning to King Nebuchadnezzar

*T*his is the meaning of the dream, O king. The Most High God has commanded these things to happen to my master the king: You will be forced away from people to live among the wild animals. People will feed you grass like an ox, and dew from the sky will make you wet. Seven years will pass, and then you will learn this lesson: The Most High God is ruler over every kingdom on earth, and he gives those kingdoms to anyone he chooses.

"Since the stump of the tree and its roots were left in the ground, your kingdom will be given back to you when you learn that one in heaven rules your kingdom. So, O king, please accept my advice. Stop sinning and do what is right. Stop doing wicked things and be kind to the poor. Then you might continue to be successful."

Daniel 4:24–27

---

*O*n one occasion when I was in prayer, I had a vision in which I saw how all things are seen in God. I cannot explain what I saw, but what I saw remains to this day, deeply imprinted upon my soul. It was a great act of grace in God to give me that vision. It puts me to unspeakable confusion, shame, and horror whenever I recall that magnificent sight, and then think of my sin. I believe that had the Lord been pleased to send me that great revelation of Himself earlier in my life, it would have kept me back from much sin. . . .

. . . To make use of an illustration, it was something like what follows.

Suppose the Godhead to be like a vast globe of light, a globe larger than the whole world, and that all our actions are seen in that all-embracing globe. . . . I saw all my most filthy actions gathered up and reflected back upon me from that world of light. I tell you it was the most pitiful and dreadful thing to see. I did not know where to hide myself, for that shining light, in which there was no darkness at all, held the whole world within it, and all worlds. . . .

. . . Oh that those who commit deeds of darkness could be made to see this! . . . Oh, the madness of committing sin in the immediate presence of a Majesty so great.

St. Teresa of Avila

---

*C*onsider the situation in which Pilate's wife sent him the message about Jesus. Was it normal to interrupt him while he was judging? Why did Pilate ignore her urgent warning? What important messages from God are you ignoring?

THURSDAY:

The Wicked Insult the Righteous

Matthew 27:21–44

NEW TESTAMENT READING

*P*ilate said, "I have Barabbas and Jesus. Which do you want me to set free for you?"

The people answered, "Barabbas."

Pilate asked, "So what should I do with Jesus, the one called the Christ?"

They all answered, "Crucify him!"

Pilate asked, "Why? What wrong has he done?"

But they shouted louder, "Crucify him!"

When Pilate saw that he could do nothing about this and that a riot was starting, he took some water and washed his hands in front of the crowd. Then he said, "I am not guilty of this man's death. You are the ones who are causing it!"

All the people answered, "We and our children will be responsible for his death."

Then he set Barabbas free. But Jesus was beaten with whips and handed over to the soldiers to be crucified.

The governor's soldiers took Jesus into the governor's palace, and they all gathered around him. They took off his clothes and put a red robe on him. Using thorny branches, they made a crown, put it on his head, and put a stick in his right hand. Then the soldiers bowed before Jesus and made fun of him, saying, "Hail, King of the Jews!" They spat on Jesus. Then they took his stick and began to beat him on the head. After they finished, the soldiers took off the robe and put his own clothes on him again. Then they led him away to be crucified.

Jesus Is Crucified

*A*s the soldiers were going out of the city with Jesus, they forced a man from Cyrene, named Simon, to carry the cross for Jesus. They all came to the place called Golgotha, which means the Place of the Skull. The soldiers gave Jesus wine mixed with gall to drink. He tasted the wine but refused to drink it. When the soldiers had crucified him, they threw lots to decide who would get his clothes. The soldiers sat there and continued watching him. They put a sign above Jesus' head with a charge against him. It said: THIS IS JESUS, THE KING OF THE JEWS. Two robbers were crucified beside Jesus, one on the right and the other on the left. People walked by and insulted Jesus and shook their heads, saying, "You said you could destroy the Temple and build it again in three days. So save yourself! Come down from that cross if you are really the Son of God!"

The leading priests, the teachers of the law, and the older Jewish leaders were also making fun of Jesus. They said, "He saved others, but he can't save himself! He says he is the king of Israel! If he is the king, let him come down now from the cross. Then we will believe in him. He trusts in God, so let God save him now, if God really wants him. He himself said, 'I am the Son of God.'" And in the same way, the robbers who were being crucified beside Jesus also insulted him.

OLD TESTAMENT READING

*B*ut I am like a worm instead of a man.
  People make fun of me and hate me.
Those who look at me laugh.
  They stick out their tongues and
    shake their heads.
They say, "Turn to the LORD for help.
  Maybe he will save you.
If he likes you,
  maybe he will rescue you."

Psalm 22:6–8

*A*s a deer thirsts for streams of water,
  so I thirst for you, God.
I thirst for the living God.
  When can I go to meet with him?
Day and night, my tears have been my
    food.
People are always saying,
  "Where is your God?"
When I remember these things,
  I speak with a broken heart.
I used to walk with the crowd
  and lead them to God's Temple
    with songs of praise.

Psalm 42:1–4

*Y*ou made us a joke to our neighbors;
　　those around us laugh and make fun
　　　of us.
You made us a joke to the other
　　nations;
　　people shake their heads.
I am always in disgrace,
　　and I am covered with shame.
My enemy is getting even
　　with insults and curses.

Psalm 44:13–16

*W*ho would have believed what we
　　heard?
　　Who saw the LORD's power in this?
He grew up like a small plant before
　　the LORD,
　　like a root growing in a dry land.
He had no special beauty or form to
　　make us notice him;
　　there was nothing in his appearance
　　　to make us desire him.
He was hated and rejected by people.
　　He had much pain and suffering.
People would not even look at him.
　　He was hated, and we didn't even
　　　notice him.

But he took our suffering on him
　　and felt our pain for us.
We saw his suffering
　　and thought God was punishing
　　　him.
But he was wounded for the wrong we
　　did;
　　he was crushed for the evil we did.
The punishment, which made us well,
　　was given to him,
　　and we are healed because of his
　　　wounds.

Isaiah 53:1–5

I N S I G H T S

*H*ave you ever been persecuted because of
your faith in Christ? If so, how did you respond?

While Francis Xavier was preaching one
day in one of the cities of Japan, a man
walked up to him as if he had something to
say to him privately. As the missionary
leaned closer to hear what he had to say, the
man spat on his face.

Without a word or the least sign of annoy-
ance, Xavier pulled out a handkerchief and
wiped his face. Then he went on with his important message as if nothing had happened.
The scorn of the audience was turned to ad-
miration.

The most learned doctor of the city happened to be present.

"A law which teaches men such virtue,
inspires them with such courage, and gives
them such complete mastery over themselves,"
he said, "could not but be from God."

Supernatural power and enablement by
God's Holy Spirit make that kind of behavior
possible for every believer. Furthermore, that
kind of behavior probably will do more to attract and influence an unbelieving world than
words ever can.

With Christ as our example, love as our
motive, and humility as our covering, let us
depend on God's Holy Spirit for the wisdom
and strength required to respond to mistreatment in a Christlike way. Then, and only
then, are we in a position to reflect honor and
glory to the Lord Jesus Christ.

Bill Bright

A C T I O N　　P O I N T

*D*o these readings indicate that we don't feel
the pain of insults and suffering we bear for
God's sake? Study the model of grace Christ
provides by not lashing out against his tor-
mentors. Pray that God will give you grace
to bear the pain of whatever insults come your
way.

FRIDAY:

The Eternal Impact of Jesus' Death and Resurrection

Matthew 27:45—28:10

NEW TESTAMENT READING

Jesus Dies

*A*t noon the whole country became dark, and the darkness lasted for three hours. About three o'clock Jesus cried out in a loud voice, "Eli, Eli, lama sabachthani?" This means, "My God, my God, why have you rejected me?"

Some of the people standing there who heard this said, "He is calling Elijah."

Quickly one of them ran and got a sponge and filled it with vinegar and tied it to a stick and gave it to Jesus to drink. But the others said, "Don't bother him. We want to see if Elijah will come to save him."

But Jesus cried out again in a loud voice and died.

Then the curtain in the Temple was torn into two pieces, from the top to the bottom. Also, the earth shook and rocks broke apart. The graves opened, and many of God's people who had died were raised from the dead. They came out of the graves after Jesus was raised from the dead and went into the holy city, where they appeared to many people.

When the army officer and the soldiers guarding Jesus saw this earthquake and everything else that happened, they were very frightened and said, "He really was the Son of God!"

Many women who had followed Jesus from Galilee to help him were standing at a distance from the cross, watching. Mary Magdalene, and Mary the mother of James and Joseph, and the mother of James and John were there.

Jesus Is Buried

*T*hat evening a rich man named Joseph, a follower of Jesus from the town of Arimathea, came to Jerusalem. Joseph went to Pilate and asked to have Jesus' body. So Pilate gave orders for the soldiers to give it to Joseph.

Then Joseph took the body and wrapped it in a clean linen cloth. He put Jesus' body in a new tomb that he had cut out of a wall of rock, and he rolled a very large stone to block the entrance of the tomb. Then Joseph went away. Mary Magdalene and the other woman named Mary were sitting near the tomb.

The Tomb of Jesus Is Guarded

*T*he next day, the day after Preparation Day, the leading priests and the Pharisees went to Pilate. They said, "Sir, we remember that while that liar was still alive he said, 'After three days I will rise from the dead.' So give the order for the tomb to be guarded closely till the third day. Otherwise, his followers might come and steal the body and tell people that he has risen from the dead. That lie would be even worse than the first one."

Pilate said, "Take some soldiers and go guard the tomb the best way you know." So they all went to the tomb and made it safe from thieves by sealing the stone in the entrance and putting soldiers there to guard it.

Jesus Rises from the Dead

*T*he day after the Sabbath day was the first day of the week. At dawn on the first day, Mary Magdalene and another woman named Mary went to look at the tomb.

At that time there was a strong earthquake. An angel of the Lord came down from heaven, went to the tomb, and rolled the stone away from the entrance. Then he sat on the stone. He was shining as bright as lightning, and his clothes were white as snow. The soldiers guarding the tomb shook with fear because of the angel, and they became like dead men.

The angel said to the women, "Don't be afraid. I know that you are looking for Jesus, who has been crucified. He is not here. He has risen from the dead as he said he would. Come and see the place where his body was. And go quickly and tell his followers, 'Jesus has risen from the dead. He is going into Galilee ahead of you, and you will see him there.'" Then the angel said, "Now I have told you."

The women left the tomb quickly. They were afraid, but they were also very happy.

They ran to tell Jesus' followers what had happened. Suddenly, Jesus met them and said, "Greetings." The women came up to him, took hold of his feet, and worshiped him. Then Jesus said to them, "Don't be afraid. Go and tell my followers to go on to Galilee, and they will see me there."

O L D   T E S T A M E N T   R E A D I N G

*T*he LORD All-Powerful will prepare a feast
    on this mountain for all people.
It will be a feast with all the best food and wine,
    the finest meat and wine.
On this mountain God will destroy
    the veil that covers all nations,
the veil that stretches over all peoples;
    he will destroy death forever.
The Lord GOD will wipe away every tear
    from every face.
He will take away the shame of his
    people from the earth.
The LORD has spoken.

Isaiah 25:6–8

*W*hy do you mountains with many peaks look with envy
    on the mountain that God chose for his home?
The LORD will live there forever.
God comes with millions of chariots;
    the Lord comes from Mount Sinai to his holy place.
When you went up to the heights,
    you led a parade of captives.
You received gifts from the people,
    even from those who turned against you.
And the LORD God will live there.

Praise the Lord, God our Savior,
    who helps us every day.   *Selah*
Our God is a God who saves us;
    the LORD God saves us from death.

Psalm 68:16–20

I keep the LORD before me always.
    Because he is close by my side
    I will not be hurt.
So I rejoice and am glad.

Even my body has hope,
    because you will not leave me in the grave.
You will not let your holy one rot.
You will teach me how to live a holy life.
Being with you will fill me with joy;
    at your right hand I will find pleasure forever.

Psalm 16:8–11

I N S I G H T S

*T*he power of the resurrection is the power of personal regeneration. Resurrection spells regeneration. The two things must always be kept together: the new world and the new person. Resurrection is not just a passport to heaven, but a power to change us now. It is a present gift, not a wistful longing. Paul says he wants to know Christ and the power of his resurrection. The two are the same. To know Christ today is to come under the influence of the same power that raised Him from the dead. All life is meant to be an Eastertide full of perpetual renewal. Christ's mission is to change us and make us like Himself. What a cruel thing an example is without the power to live it. Christ is the best of all examples, but more than that, He can come within us and give us His own Spirit to fulfill the example. The result is we actually become like Him, we are able to do the things He did, and most of all, we are able to love as He loved. The resurrection is the right angle where all the disillusionment, discouragement, and disappointment with life, people, and ourselves is met with power to change us and give us a new beginning.

Lloyd Ogilvie

P A U S E   F O R   R E F L E C T I O N

*W*hy did the Pharisees fear the possibility of Jesus' resurrection? When he rose again, what did Jesus destroy forever? What difference did his resurrection make in the lives of his followers? How has his resurrection regenerated your life?

WEEKEND:
Tell the Good News!
Matthew 28:11—Mark 1:20

NEW TESTAMENT READING

Soldiers Report to the Leaders

While the women went to tell Jesus' followers, some of the soldiers who had been guarding the tomb went into the city to tell the leading priests everything that had happened. Then the priests met with the older Jewish leaders and made a plan. They paid the soldiers a large amount of money and said to them, "Tell the people that Jesus' followers came during the night and stole the body while you were asleep. If the governor hears about this, we will satisfy him and save you from trouble." So the soldiers kept the money and did as they were told. And that story is still spread among the Jewish people even today.

Jesus Talks to His Followers

The eleven followers went to Galilee to the mountain where Jesus had told them to go. On the mountain they saw Jesus and worshiped him, but some of them did not believe it was really Jesus. Then Jesus came to them and said, "All power in heaven and on earth is given to me. So go and make followers of all people in the world. Baptize them in the name of the Father and the Son and the Holy Spirit. Teach them to obey everything that I have taught you, and I will be with you always, even until the end of this age."

John Prepares for Jesus

This is the beginning of the Good News about Jesus Christ, the Son of God, as the prophet Isaiah wrote:
"I will send my messenger ahead of
  you,
  who will prepare your way."

Malachi 3:1

"This is a voice of one
  who calls out in the desert:
'Prepare the way for the Lord.
  Make the road straight for him.'"

Isaiah 40:3

John was baptizing people in the desert and preaching a baptism of changed hearts and lives for the forgiveness of sins. All the people from Judea and Jerusalem were going out to him. They confessed their sins and were baptized by him in the Jordan River. John wore clothes made from camel's hair, had a leather belt around his waist, and ate locusts and wild honey. This is what John preached to the people: "There is one coming after me who is greater than I; I am not good enough even to kneel down and untie his sandals. I baptize you with water, but he will baptize you with the Holy Spirit."

Jesus Is Baptized

At that time Jesus came from the town of Nazareth in Galilee and was baptized by John in the Jordan River. Immediately, as Jesus was coming up out of the water, he saw heaven open. The Holy Spirit came down on him like a dove, and a voice came from heaven: "You are my Son, whom I love, and I am very pleased with you."

Then the Spirit sent Jesus into the desert. He was in the desert forty days and was tempted by Satan. He was with the wild animals, and the angels came and took care of him.

Jesus Chooses Some Followers

After John was put in prison, Jesus went into Galilee, preaching the Good News from God. He said, "The right time has come. The kingdom of God is near. Change your hearts and lives and believe the Good News!"

When Jesus was walking by Lake Galilee, he saw Simon and his brother Andrew throwing a net into the lake because they were fishermen. Jesus said to them, "Come follow me, and I will make you fish for people." So Simon and Andrew immediately left their nets and followed him.

Going a little farther, Jesus saw two more brothers, James and John, the sons of Zebedee. They were in a boat, mending their nets. Jesus immediately called them, and they left their father in the boat with the hired workers and followed Jesus.

Sing to the LORD, all the earth.
   Every day tell how he saves us.
Tell the nations about his glory;
   tell all peoples the miracles he does.
The LORD is great; he should be praised.
   He should be respected more than
     all the gods.

1 Chronicles 16:23–25

The LORD spoke his word to Jonah again and said, "Get up, go to the great city Nineveh, and preach to it what I tell you to say."

So Jonah obeyed the LORD and got up and went to Nineveh. It was a very large city; just to walk across it took a person three days. After Jonah had entered the city and walked for one day, he preached to the people, saying, "After forty days, Nineveh will be destroyed!"

The people of Nineveh believed God. They announced that they would stop eating for a while, and they put on rough cloth to show their sadness. All the people in the city did this, from the most important to the least important.

When God saw what the people did, that they stopped doing evil, he changed his mind and did not do what he had warned. He did not punish them.

Jonah 3:1–5, 10

The Lord GOD has put his Spirit in me,
   because the LORD has appointed me
     to tell the good news to the poor.
He has sent me to comfort those
     whose hearts are broken,
to tell the captives they are free,
   and to tell the prisoners they are
     released.
He has sent me to announce the time
     when the LORD will show his
     kindness
   and the time when our God will
     punish evil people.
He has sent me to comfort all those
     who are sad
   and to help the sorrowing people of
     Jerusalem.
I will give them a crown to replace their
     ashes,
and the oil of gladness to replace
     their sorrow,
and clothes of praise to replace their
     spirit of sadness.
Then they will be called Trees of
     Goodness,
   trees planted by the LORD to show
     his greatness.

Isaiah 61:1–3

INSIGHTS

For the New Testament Christians, witness was not a sales pitch.

They simply shared, each in his own way, what they had received. Theirs was not a formally prepared, carefully worked-out presentation with a gimmick to manipulate conversation, and a "closer" for an on-the-spot-decision . . . but the spontaneous, irrepressible, effervescent enthusiasm of those who had met the most fascinating Person who ever lived.

The gospel is not theology. It's a Person. Theology doesn't save. Jesus Christ saves. The first-century disciples were totally involved with a Person. They were followers of Jesus. They were learners of Jesus. They were committed to Jesus. They were filled with Jesus.

They had encountered Jesus Christ and it simply could not be concealed. They witnessed not because they had to, but because they could not help it.

Their school of witnessing was the school of the Spirit where they learned continuously. Authentic Christian witness is born of the Spirit.

Madison Avenue, with all its sophisticated know-how, can't improve on the strategy. Nothing is more convincing than the simple, unembellished word of a satisfied customer.

Richard Halverson

ACTION POINT

Is your salvation real enough to comfort the brokenhearted, to set free the captives, to boldly announce the Good News? Pray that God's salvation will be so real to you that you will tell others.

MONDAY:
God Is Compassionate and Brings Healing to Body and Soul
Mark 1:21–45

NEW TESTAMENT READING

Jesus Forces Out an Evil Spirit

*J*esus and his followers went to Capernaum. On the Sabbath day He went to the synagogue and began to teach. The people were amazed at his teaching, because he taught like a person who had authority, not like their teachers of the law. Just then, a man was there in the synagogue who had an evil spirit in him. He shouted, "Jesus of Nazareth! What do you want with us? Did you come to destroy us? I know who you are— God's Holy One!"

Jesus commanded the evil spirit, "Be quiet! Come out of the man!" The evil spirit shook the man violently, gave a loud cry, and then came out of him.

The people were so amazed they asked each other, "What is happening here? This man is teaching something new, and with authority. He even gives commands to evil spirits, and they obey him." And the news about Jesus spread quickly everywhere in the area of Galilee.

Jesus Heals Many People

*A*s soon as Jesus and his followers left the synagogue, they went with James and John to the home of Simon and Andrew. Simon's mother-in-law was sick in bed with a fever, and the people told Jesus about her. So Jesus went to her bed, took her hand, and helped her up. The fever left her, and she began serving them.

That evening, after the sun went down, the people brought to Jesus all who were sick and had demons in them. The whole town gathered at the door. Jesus healed many who had different kinds of sicknesses, and he forced many demons to leave people. But he would not allow the demons to speak, because they knew who he was.

Early the next morning, while it was still dark, Jesus woke and left the house. He went to a lonely place, where he prayed. Simon and his friends went to look for Jesus. When they found him, they said, "Everyone is looking for you!"

Jesus answered, "We should go to other towns around here so I can preach there too. That is the reason I came." So he went everywhere in Galilee, preaching in the synagogues and forcing out demons.

Jesus Heals a Sick Man

A man with a skin disease came to Jesus. He fell to his knees and begged Jesus, "You can heal me if you will."

Jesus felt sorry for the man, so he reached out his hand and touched him and said, "I will. Be healed!" Immediately the disease left the man, and he was healed.

Jesus told the man to go away at once, but he warned him strongly, "Don't tell anyone about this. But go and show yourself to the priest. And offer the gift Moses commanded for people who are made well. This will show the people what I have done." The man left there, but he began to tell everyone that Jesus had healed him, and so he spread the news about Jesus. As a result, Jesus could not enter a town if people saw him. He stayed in places where nobody lived, but people came to him from everywhere.

OLD TESTAMENT READING

*L*ORD, I trust you.
  I have said, "You are my God."
My life is in your hands.
  Save me from my enemies
  and from those who are chasing me.
Show your kindness to me, your
    servant.
  Save me because of your love.
Psalm 31:14–16

*T*he LORD wants to show his mercy to
    you.
  He wants to rise and comfort you.
The LORD is a fair God,
  and everyone who waits for his help
    will be happy.
Isaiah 30:18

*C*ome, let's go back to the LORD.
    He has hurt us, but he will heal us.
    He has wounded us, but he will
       bandage our wounds.
In two days he will put new life in us;
    on the third day he will raise us up
    so that we may live in his presence
    and know him.
Let's try to learn about the LORD;
    He will come to us as surely as the
       dawn comes.
He will come to us like rain,
    like the spring rain that waters the
       ground."

Hosea 6:1–3

*T*he LORD is kind and shows mercy.
    He does not become angry quickly
       but is full of love.
The LORD is good to everyone;
    he is merciful to all he has made.

Psalm 145:8–9

*B*efore Isaiah had left the middle court-yard, the LORD spoke his word to Isaiah: "Go back and tell Hezekiah, the leader of my people: 'This is what the LORD, the God of your ancestor David, says: I have heard your prayer and seen your tears, so I will heal you."

2 Kings 20:4–5a

I have seen what they have done, but I
    will heal them.
    I will guide them and comfort them
       and those who felt sad for them.
    They will all praise me.
I will give peace, real peace, to those far
    and near,
    and I will heal them," says the LORD.

Isaiah 57:18–19

*L*ORD, heal me, and I will truly be
    healed.
Save me, and I will truly be saved.
You are the one I praise.

Jeremiah 17:14

INSIGHTS

*B*ethlehem, Galilee, Gethsemane—He walked there. But today Christ walks the concrete sidewalks of *Times Square, 47th Street, and Broadway. And as He walks, His feet are soiled—not with the sand of the seashore or the reddish dust of the Emmaus Road, but with the soot and filth of the city.*

He walks the "Great White Way," and His face is lit by the gaudy neon signboards of materialism. He walks in the shadows of the dark alleyways, where faces are not lit at all. . . .

He is pushed and shoved through Grand Central Station, elbowed and ignored, yet in the crowd He feels a measure of virtue flow from His being and searches through the faces for an honest seeker passing by. . . .

Christ walks the city and . . . weaves the cloth that transforms rags into a lovely tapestry. . . . He acts the part that tells the story of how that Love invaded humankind, for only story tells the Story. Christ incarnate. Christ the living, walking parable, takes the stage to be the Story. . . .

. . . He is the broken, and He is the healer. He is the hungry, and He is the Bread of Life. He is the homeless, yet it is He who says "Come to Me all you who are overloaded, and I will be your resting place." He is the loser who makes losing the only way to win. He is the omnipotent who calls all who follow to choose powerlessness and teaches us by laying down all power in heaven and in earth. He is the sick, and He is the wholeness.

Gloria Gaither

A C T I O N   P O I N T

*C*an there be any greater healing than that given by the Healer? Can you imagine any greater compassion than that shown in the love of his Son? Meditate on one of these readings and let it become your prayer of praise to God today.

TUESDAY:

Jesus Has the Authority to Forgive

Mark 2:1–22

Jesus Heals a Paralyzed Man

A few days later, when Jesus came back to Capernaum, the news spread that he was at home. Many people gathered together so that there was no room in the house, not even outside the door. And Jesus was teaching them God's message. Four people came, carrying a paralyzed man. Since they could not get to Jesus because of the crowd, they dug a hole in the roof right above where he was speaking. When they got through, they lowered the mat with the paralyzed man on it. When Jesus saw the faith of these people, he said to the paralyzed man, "Young man, your sins are forgiven."

Some of the teachers of the law were sitting there, thinking to themselves, "Why does this man say things like that? He is speaking as if he were God. Only God can forgive sins."

Jesus knew immediately what these teachers of the law were thinking. So he said to them, "Why are you thinking these things? Which is easier: to tell this paralyzed man, 'Your sins are forgiven,' or to tell him, 'Stand up. Take your mat and walk'? But I will prove to you that the Son of Man has authority on earth to forgive sins." So Jesus said to the paralyzed man, "I tell you, stand up, take your mat, and go home." Immediately the paralyzed man stood up, took his mat, and walked out while everyone was watching him.

The people were amazed and praised God. They said, "We have never seen anything like this!"

Jesus went to the lake again. The whole crowd followed him there, and he taught them. While he was walking along, he saw a man named Levi son of Alphaeus, sitting in the tax collector's booth. Jesus said to him, "Follow me," and he stood up and followed Jesus.

Later, as Jesus was having dinner at Levi's house, many tax collectors and "sinners" were eating there with Jesus and his followers. Many people like this followed Jesus. When the teachers of the law who were Pharisees saw Jesus eating with the tax collectors and "sinners," they asked his followers, "Why does he eat with tax collectors and sinners?"

Jesus heard this and said to them, "It is not the healthy people who need a doctor, but the sick. I did not come to invite good people but to invite sinners."

Jesus' Followers Are Criticized

*N*ow the followers of John and the Pharisees often gave up eating for a certain time. Some people came to Jesus and said, "Why do John's followers and the followers of the Pharisees often give up eating, but your followers don't?"

Jesus answered, "The friends of the bridegroom do not give up eating while the bridegroom is still with them. As long as the bridegroom is with them, they cannot give up eating. But the time will come when the bridegroom will be taken from them, and then they will give up eating.

"No one sews a patch of unshrunk cloth over a hole in an old coat. Otherwise, the patch will shrink and pull away—the new patch will pull away from the old coat. Then the hole will be worse. Also, no one ever pours new wine into old leather bags. Otherwise, the new wine will break the bags, and the wine will be ruined along with the bags. But new wine should be put into new leather bags."

*P*eople of Jacob, you have not called to
  me;
    people of Israel, you have become
      tired of me.
You have not brought me your sacri-
    fices of sheep
  nor honored me with your sacrifices.

I did not weigh you down with sacrifices to offer
or make you tired with incense to
burn.
So you did not buy incense for me;
you did not freely bring me fat from
your sacrifices.
Instead you have weighed me down
with your many sins;
you have made me tired of your
many wrongs.

"I, I am the One who forgives all your
sins, for my sake;
I will not remember your sins."

Isaiah 43:22–25

*B*ut it was the Lord who decided
to crush him and make him suffer.
The Lord made his life a penalty
offering,
but he will still see his descendants and
live a long life.
He will complete the things the Lord
wants him to do.
"After his soul suffers many things,
he will see life and be satisfied.
My good servant will make many
people right with God;
he will carry away their sins.
For this reason I will make him a great
man among people,
and he will share in all things with
those who are strong.
He willingly gave his life
and was treated like a criminal.
But he carried away the sins of many
people
and asked forgiveness for those who
sinned."

Isaiah 53:10–12

*T*his is the agreement I will make
with the people of Israel at that
time," says the Lord:
"I will put my teachings in their minds
and write them on their hearts.
I will be their God,
and they will be my people.
People will no longer have to teach
their neighbors and relatives
to know the Lord,

because all people will know me,
from the least to the most important," says the Lord.
"I will forgive them for the wicked
things they did,
and I will not remember their sins
anymore."

Jeremiah 31:33–34

---

*F*orgiveness is one of the first and most glorious blessings we receive from God. It is the
transition from the old to the new life; the sign
and pledge of God's love: with it we receive
the right to all the spiritual gifts which are
prepared for us in Christ. The believer can
never forget, either here or in eternity, that
he is a forgiven sinner. Nothing more in-
flames his love, awakens his joy, or strengthens his courage than the continually renewed
experience of God's forgiving love. Every day,
yes, every thought of God reminds him: I owe
all to pardoning grace.

This forgiving love is one of the greatest
manifestations of the divine nature. In it God
finds His glory and blessedness and wants to
share this with His redeemed people.

Andrew Murray

APPLICATION

*W*hat is the most important characteristic
of the good servant promised Isaiah 53? Is it
then surprising that Jesus forgave sins while
he was on earth? Has your spirit been healed
by Jesus' forgiveness of your sins?

WEDNESDAY:

Jesus Teaches About the Rules of the Sabbath

Mark 2:23—3:27

NEW TESTAMENT READING

Jesus Is Lord of the Sabbath

One Sabbath day, as Jesus was walking through some fields of grain, his followers began to pick some grain to eat. The Pharisees said to Jesus, "Why are your followers doing what is not lawful on the Sabbath day?"

Jesus answered, "Have you never read what David did when he and those with him were hungry and needed food? During the time of Abiathar the high priest, David went into God's house and ate the holy bread, which is lawful only for priests to eat. And David also gave some of the bread to those who were with him."

Then Jesus said to the Pharisees, "The Sabbath day was made to help people; they were not made to be ruled by the Sabbath day. So then, the Son of Man is Lord even of the Sabbath day."

Jesus Heals a Man's Hand

Another time when Jesus went into a synagogue, a man with a crippled hand was there. Some people watched Jesus closely to see if he would heal the man on the Sabbath day so they could accuse him.

Jesus said to the man with the crippled hand, "Stand up here in the middle of everyone."

Then Jesus asked the people, "Which is lawful on the Sabbath day: to do good or to do evil, to save a life or to kill?" But they said nothing to answer him.

Jesus was angry as he looked at the people, and he felt very sad because they were stubborn. Then he said to the man, "Hold out your hand." The man held out his hand and it was healed. Then the Pharisees left and began making plans with the Herodians about a way to kill Jesus.

Many People Follow Jesus

Jesus left with his followers for the lake, and a large crowd from Galilee followed him. Also many people came from Judea, from Jerusalem, from Idumea, from the lands across the Jordan River, and from the area of Tyre and Sidon. When they heard what Jesus was doing, many people came to him. When Jesus saw the crowds, he told his followers to get a boat ready for him to keep people from crowding against him. He had healed many people, so all the sick were pushing toward him to touch him. When evil spirits saw Jesus, they fell down before him and shouted, "You are the Son of God!" But Jesus strongly warned them not to tell who he was.

Jesus Chooses His Apostles

Then Jesus went up on a mountain and called to him the men he wanted, and they came to him. Jesus chose twelve men and called them apostles. He wanted them to be with him, and he wanted to send them out to preach and to have the authority to force demons out of people. These are the twelve men he chose: Simon (Jesus named him Peter), James and John, the sons of Zebedee (Jesus named them Boanerges, which means "Sons of Thunder"), Andrew, Philip, Bartholomew, Matthew, Thomas, James the son of Alphaeus, Thaddaeus, Simon the Zealot, and Judas Iscariot, who later turned against Jesus.

People Say Jesus Has a Devil

Then Jesus went home, but again a crowd gathered. There were so many people that Jesus and his followers could not eat. When his family heard this, they went to get him because they thought he was out of his mind. But the teachers of the law from Jerusalem were saying, "Beelzebul is living inside him! He uses power from the ruler of demons to force demons out of people."

So Jesus called the people together and taught them with stories. He said, "Satan will not force himself out of people. A kingdom that is divided cannot continue, and a family that is divided cannot continue. And if Satan is against himself and fights against his own people, he cannot continue; that is the end of Satan. No one can enter a strong person's house and steal his things unless he first ties up the strong person. Then he can steal things from the house.

David and His Men Eat the Holy Bread

*T*hen at the entrance of the Meeting Tent, Aaron and his sons must eat the meat of the sheep and the bread that is in the basket. They should eat these offerings that were used to remove their sins and to make them holy when they were made priests. But no one else is to eat them, because they are holy things. If any of the meat from that sheep or any of the bread is left the next morning, it must be burned. It must not be eaten, because it is holy."

Exodus 29:32–34

*D*avid went to Nob to see Ahimelech the priest. Ahimelech shook with fear when he saw David, and he asked, "Why are you alone? Why is no one with you?"

David answered him, "The king gave me a special order. He told me, 'No one must know what I am sending you to do or what I told you to do.' I told my men where to meet me. Now, what food do you have with you? Give me five loaves of bread or anything you find."

The priest said to David, "I don't have any plain bread here, but I do have some holy bread. You may eat it if your men have kept themselves from women."

David answered, "No women have been near us for days. My men always keep themselves holy, even when we do ordinary work. And this is especially true when the work is holy."

So the priest gave David the holy bread from the presence of God because there was no other. Each day the holy bread was replaced with hot bread.

1 Samuel 21:1–6

*T*his is what the LORD says:
"Give justice to all people,
    and do what is right,
because my salvation will come to you
        soon.
    Soon everyone will know that I do
        what is right.

The person who obeys the law about
        the Sabbath
    will be blessed,
and the person who does no evil
    will be blessed."

Isaiah 56:1–2

*S*abbath rest means worship with the Christian family. In proper worship we will have a chance to exercise all three aspects that lead to the rest of our private worlds: looking backward, upward, and ahead. Such worship is non-negotiable to the person committed to walking with God. . . .

. . . Sabbath means a deliberate acceptance of personal rest and tranquility within the individual life. Sabbath means a rest that brings peace into the private world. As Christ pressed stillness into a storm, order into a being of a demon-possessed maniac, health into a desperately sick woman, and life into a dead friend, so He seeks to press peace into the harried private world of the man or woman who has been in the marketplace all week. But there is a condition. We must accept this peace as a gift and take the time to receive it.

Gordon MacDonald

*T*hink about Jesus' statement that the Sabbath was meant to help people. In what ways do you think keeping the Sabbath is good for us? How do you think Jesus feels about the way you keep the Sabbath? Are you going to make any changes?

THURSDAY:

Those Who Obey God Belong to Him

Mark 3:28—4:20

NEW TESTAMENT READING

I tell you the truth, all sins that people do and all the things people say against God can be forgiven. But anyone who speaks against the Holy Spirit will never be forgiven; he is guilty of a sin that continues forever."

Jesus said this because the teachers of the law said that he had an evil spirit inside him.

Jesus' True Family

*T*hen Jesus' mother and brothers arrived. Standing outside, they sent someone in to tell him to come out. Many people were sitting around Jesus, and they said to him, "Your mother and brothers are waiting for you outside."

Jesus asked, "Who are my mother and my brothers?" Then he looked at those sitting around him and said, "Here are my mother and my brothers! My true brother and sister and mother are those who do what God wants."

A Story About Planting Seed

*A*gain Jesus began teaching by the lake. A great crowd gathered around him, so he sat down in a boat near the shore. All the people stayed on the shore close to the water. Jesus taught them many things, using stories. He said, "Listen! A farmer went out to plant his seed. While he was planting, some seed fell by the road, and the birds came and ate it up. Some seed fell on rocky ground where there wasn't much dirt. That seed grew very fast, because the ground was not deep. But when the sun rose, the plants dried up because they did not have deep roots. Some other seed fell among thorny weeds, which grew and choked the good plants. So those plants did not produce a crop. Some other seed fell on good ground and began to grow. It got taller and produced a crop. Some plants made thirty times more, some made sixty times more, and some made a hundred times more."

Then Jesus said, "You people who can hear me, listen!"

Jesus Tells Why He Used Stories

*L*ater, when Jesus was alone, the twelve apostles and others around him asked him about the stories.

Jesus said, "You can know the secret about the kingdom of God. But to other people I tell everything by using stories so that:

'They will look and look, but they will
   not learn.
They will listen and listen, but they
   will not understand.
If they did learn and understand,
   they would come back to me and be
   forgiven.'" *Isaiah 6:9–10*

Jesus Explains the Seed Story

*T*hen Jesus said to his followers, "Don't you understand this story? If you don't, how will you understand any story? The farmer is like a person who plants God's message in people. Sometimes the teaching falls on the road. This is like the people who hear the teaching of God, but Satan quickly comes and takes away the teaching that was planted in them. Others are like the seed planted on rocky ground. They hear the teaching and quickly accept it with joy. But since they don't allow the teaching to go deep into their lives, they keep it only a short time. When trouble or persecution comes because of the teaching they accepted, they quickly give up. Others are like the seed planted among the thorny weeds. They hear the teaching, but the worries of this life, the temptation of wealth, and many other evil desires keep the teaching from growing and producing fruit in their lives. Others are like the seed planted in the good ground. They hear the teaching and accept it. Then they grow and produce fruit— sometimes thirty times more, sometimes sixty times more, and sometimes a hundred times more."

*T*hen Moses went up on the mountain to God. The LORD called to him from the mountain and said, "Say this to the family of Jacob, and tell the people of Israel: 'Every one of you has seen what I did to the people of Egypt. You saw how I carried you out of Egypt, as if on eagle's wings. And I brought you here to me. So now if you obey me and keep my agreement, you will be my own possession, chosen from all nations.'"

Exodus 19:3–5

*T*oday the LORD your God commands you to obey all these rules and laws; be careful to obey them with your whole being. Today you have said that the LORD is your God, and you have promised to do what he wants you to do—to keep his rules, commands, and laws. You have said you will obey him. And today the LORD has said that you are his very own people, as he has promised you. But you must obey his commands. He will make you greater than all the other nations he made. He will give you praise, fame, and honor, and you will be a holy people to the LORD your God, as he has said.

Deuteronomy 26:16–19

*Y*ou must completely obey the LORD your God, and you must carefully follow all his commands I am giving you today. Then the LORD your God will make you greater than any other nation on earth. Obey the LORD your God so that all these blessings will come and stay with you:

You will be blessed in the city and blessed in the country.

Your children will be blessed, as well as your crops; your herds will be blessed with calves and your flocks with lambs.

Your basket and your kitchen will be blessed.

You will be blessed when you come in and when you go out.

The LORD will help you defeat the enemies that come to fight you. They will attack you from one direction, but they will run from you in seven directions.

The LORD your God will bless you with full barns, and he will bless everything you do. He will bless the land he is giving you.

The LORD will make you his holy people, as he promised. But you must obey his commands and do what he wants you to do. Then everyone on earth will see that you are the LORD's people, and they will be afraid of you.

Deuteronomy 28:1–10

---

*T*he source of Christ's victory, the secret of His power, and of ours, lies in obedience. . . .

In an obedient heart there is a way prepared for God. There are many Christians who always seek pleasure and satisfaction for themselves. These have not yet learned that only obedient children are happy children. That which in truth brings abiding happiness is nothing else than obedience toward God. For a healthy soul there is only one thing that counts—to be obedient. . . .

Why have so many of God's lambs so little assurance of salvation? Why are their souls not satisfied with the peace of God? God gives us the answer in Isaiah 48:18: "Oh, that thou hadst hearkened to my commandments! Then had thy peace been as a river, and thy righteousness as the waves of the sea." People say, "I lack faith. I have too little faith; therefore I have no assurance of salvation, no peace." But in most instances it is not faith which is lacking, for even with a trembling hand one can receive costly gifts. It is rather obedience which is lacking. There is something in their lives which they will not let go, and which hinders the Holy Spirit from giving them the assurance that they are God's children. . . . No one who is disobedient to God can have confidence in Him. Confidence is a result of obedience.

G. Steinberger

---

*W*hat one thing does God require of those who would be his people? What do those who obey God receive from him? How's your obedience? Is it obvious that you belong to God?

FRIDAY:
Jesus Demonstrates His Power over All
Mark 4:21—5:10

Use What You Have

*T*hen Jesus said to them, "Do you hide a lamp under a bowl or under a bed? No! You put the lamp on a lampstand. Everything that is hidden will be made clear and every secret thing will be made known. You people who can hear me, listen!

"Think carefully about what you hear. The way you give to others is the way God will give to you, but God will give you even more. Those who have understanding will be given more. But those who do not have understanding, even what they have will be taken away from them."

Jesus Uses a Story About Seed

*T*hen Jesus said, "The kingdom of God is like someone who plants seed in the ground. Night and day, whether the person is asleep or awake, the seed still grows, but the person does not know how it grows. By itself the earth produces grain. First the plant grows, then the head, and then all the grain in the head. When the grain is ready, the farmer cuts it, because this is the harvest time."

A Story About Mustard Seed

*T*hen Jesus said, "How can I show you what the kingdom of God is like? What story can I use to explain it? The kingdom of God is like a mustard seed, the smallest seed you plant in the ground. But when planted, this seed grows and becomes the largest of all garden plants. It produces large branches, and the wild birds can make nests in its shade."

Jesus used many stories like these to teach the crowd God's message—as much as they could understand. He always used stories to teach them. But when he and his followers were alone, Jesus explained everything to them.

Jesus Calms a Storm

*T*hat evening, Jesus said to his followers, "Let's go across the lake." Leaving the crowd behind, they took him in the boat just as he was. There were also other boats with them. A very strong wind came up on the lake. The waves came over the sides and into the boat so that it was already full of water. Jesus was at the back of the boat, sleeping with his head on a cushion. His followers woke him and said, "Teacher, don't you care that we are drowning!"

Jesus stood up and commanded the wind and said to the waves, "Quiet! Be still!" Then the wind stopped, and it became completely calm.

Jesus said to his followers, "Why are you afraid? Do you still have no faith?"

The followers were very afraid and asked each other, "Who is this? Even the wind and the waves obey him!"

A Man with Demons Inside Him

*J*esus and his followers went to the other side of the lake to the area of the Gerasene people. When Jesus got out of the boat, instantly a man with an evil spirit came to him from the burial caves. This man lived in the caves, and no one could tie him up, not even with a chain. Many times people had used chains to tie the man's hands and feet, but he always broke them off. No one was strong enough to control him. Day and night he would wander around the burial caves and on the hills, screaming and cutting himself with stones. While Jesus was still far away, the man saw him, ran to him, and fell down before him.

The man shouted in a loud voice, "What do you want with me, Jesus, Son of the Most High God? I command you in God's name not to torture me!" He said this because Jesus was saying to him, "You evil spirit, come out of the man."

Then Jesus asked him, "What is your name?"

He answered, "My name is Legion, because we are many spirits." He begged Jesus again and again not to send them out of that area.

I remember what the LORD did;
  I remember the miracles you did
    long ago.
I think about all the things you did
  and consider your deeds.

God, your ways are holy.
  No god is as great as our God.
You are the God who does miracles;
  you showed people your power.
By your power you have saved your
    people,
  the descendants of Jacob and
    Joseph. *Selah*

God, the waters saw you;
  they saw you and became afraid;
  the deep waters shook with fear.
The clouds poured down their rain.
  The sky thundered.
  Your lightning flashed back and
    forth like arrows.
Your thunder sounded in the whirlwind.
  Lightning lit up the world.
  The earth trembled and shook.
You made a way through the sea
  and paths through the deep waters,
  but your footprints were not seen.
Psalm 77:11–19

*P*raise the LORD, you angels;
  praise the LORD's glory and power.
Praise the LORD for the glory of his
    name;
  worship the LORD because he is holy.

The LORD's voice is heard over the sea.
  The glorious God thunders;
  the LORD thunders over the ocean.
The LORD's voice is powerful;
  the LORD's voice is majestic.
The LORD's voice breaks the trees;
  the LORD breaks the cedars of
    Lebanon.
He makes the land of Lebanon dance
    like a calf
  and Mount Hermon jump like a baby
    bull.
The LORD's voice makes the lightning
    flash.
The LORD's voice shakes the desert;

the LORD shakes the Desert of
  Kadesh.
The LORD's voice shakes the oaks
  and strips the leaves off the trees.
In his Temple everyone says, "Glory to
  God!"

The LORD controls the flood.
  The LORD will be King forever.
Psalm 29:1–10

INSIGHTS

There is a power that destroys. There is also a power that creates. The power that creates gives life and joy and peace. It is freedom and not bondage, life and not death, transformation and not coercion. The power that creates restores relationship and gives the gift of wholeness to all. The power that creates is spiritual power, the power that proceeds from God. . . .

In the crucifixion the power that creates reached its apex. At the cross Satan sought to use all the power at his disposal to destroy Christ, but God turned it into the ultimate act of creative power. The penalty for sin was paid; the justice of God was satisfied. Through the cross of Christ, you and I can receive forgiveness and know the restoring of our relationship to God. Christ died for our sins, and in that death we see the power that creates.

Our response to this supreme act of power is gratitude. It is "love divine, all loves excelling." We can never hope or want to duplicate this act of power. We simply thank God for what he has done.

Richard Foster

ACTION POINT

Think about the many kinds of awesome power God has at his disposal. What has his power done for you? How has he used his power to draw you to himself? Thank him for saving you by his power.

WEEKEND:
The Power of Faith
Mark 5:11–36

N E W   T E S T A M E N T   R E A D I N G

A large herd of pigs was feeding on a hill near there. The demons begged Jesus, "Send us into the pigs; let us go into them." So Jesus allowed them to do this. The evil spirits left the man and went into the pigs. Then the herd of pigs—about two thousand of them—rushed down the hill into the lake and were drowned.

The herdsmen ran away and went to the town and to the countryside, telling everyone about this. So people went out to see what had happened. They came to Jesus and saw the man who used to have the many evil spirits, sitting, clothed, and in his right mind. And they were frightened. The people who saw this told the others what had happened to the man who had the demons living in him, and they told about the pigs. Then the people began to beg Jesus to leave their area.

As Jesus was getting back into the boat, the man who was freed from the demons begged to go with him.

But Jesus would not let him. He said, "Go home to your family and tell them how much the Lord has done for you and how he has had mercy on you." So the man left and began to tell the people in the Ten Towns about what Jesus had done for him. And everyone was amazed.

Jesus Gives Life to a Dead Girl and Heals a Sick Woman

*W*hen Jesus went in the boat back to the other side of the lake, a large crowd gathered around him there. A leader of the synagogue, named Jairus, came there, saw Jesus, and fell at his feet. He begged Jesus, saying again and again, "My daughter is dying. Please come and put your hands on her so she will be healed and will live." So Jesus went with him.

A large crowd followed Jesus and pushed very close around him. Among them was a woman who had been bleeding for twelve years. She had suffered very much from many doctors and had spent all the money she had, but instead of improving, she was getting worse. When the woman heard about Jesus, she came up behind him in the crowd and touched his coat. She thought, "If I can just touch his clothes, I will be healed." Instantly her bleeding stopped, and she felt in her body that she was healed from her disease.

At once Jesus felt power go out from him. So he turned around in the crowd and asked, "Who touched my clothes?"

His followers said, "Look at how many people are pushing against you! And you ask, 'Who touched me?'"

But Jesus continued looking around to see who had touched him. The woman, knowing that she was healed, came and fell at Jesus' feet. Shaking with fear, she told him the whole truth. Jesus said to her, "Dear woman, you are made well because you believed. Go in peace; be healed of your disease."

While Jesus was still speaking, some people came from the house of the synagogue leader. They said, "Your daughter is dead. There is no need to bother the teacher anymore."

But Jesus paid no attention to what they said. He told the synagogue leader, "Don't be afraid; just believe."

O L D   T E S T A M E N T   R E A D I N G

*T*hen Elijah said to the prophets of Baal, "There are many of you, so you go first. Choose a bull and prepare it. Pray to your god, but don't start the fire."

So they took the bull that was given to them and prepared it. They prayed to Baal from morning until noon, shouting "Baal, answer us!" But there was no sound, and no one answered. They danced around the altar they had built.

At noon Elijah began to make fun of them. "Pray louder!" he said. "If Baal really is a god, maybe he is thinking, or busy, or traveling! Maybe he is sleeping so you will have to wake him!" The prophets prayed louder, cutting themselves with swords and spears until their blood flowed, which was the way they worshiped. The afternoon passed, and the prophets continued to act like this until it was time for the evening sacrifice. But no voice was heard; Baal did not answer, and no one paid attention.

Then Elijah said to all the people, "Now come to me." So they gathered around him, and Elijah rebuilt the altar of the LORD, which had been torn down. He took twelve stones, one stone for each of the twelve tribes, the number of Jacob's sons. (The LORD changed Jacob's name to Israel.) Elijah used these stones to rebuild the altar in honor of the LORD. Then he dug a ditch around the altar that was big enough to hold about thirteen quarts of seed. Elijah put the wood on the altar, cut the bull into pieces, and laid the pieces on the wood. Then he said, "Fill four jars with water, and pour it on the meat and on the wood." Then Elijah said, "Do it again," and they did it again. Then he said, "Do it a third time," and they did it the third time. So the water ran off the altar and filled the ditch.

At the time for the evening sacrifice, the prophet Elijah went near the altar. "LORD, you are the God of Abraham, Isaac, and Israel," he prayed. "Prove that you are the God of Israel and that I am your servant. Show these people that you commanded me to do all these things. LORD, answer my prayer so these people will know that you, LORD, are God and that you will change their minds."

Then fire from the LORD came down and burned the sacrifice, the wood, the stones, and the ground around the altar. It also dried up the water in the ditch. When all the people saw this, they fell down to the ground, crying, "The LORD is God! The LORD is God!"

1 Kings 18:25–39

INSIGHTS

The doctrine of the Bible is that Christ saves His people from sin through faith; that Christ's Spirit is received by faith to dwell in the heart. It is faith that works by love. Love is wrought and sustained by faith. By faith, Christians "overcome the world, the flesh, and the devil." It is by faith that they "quench all

the fiery darts of the wicked." It is by faith that they "put on the Lord Jesus Christ, and put off the old man, with his deeds." It is by faith that we "stand," by resolutions we fall. This is the victory that overcometh the world, even our faith.

It is by faith that the flesh is kept under and carnal desires subdued, and by faith that we receive the Spirit of Christ to work in us to will and to do, according to His good pleasure. He sheds abroad His own love in our hearts, and thereby enkindles ours. . . . Nothing but the life and energy of the Spirit of Christ can save us from sin, and trust is the universal condition for the working of His saving energy within us. . . .

. . . When we open the door by implicit trust, He enters in and takes up His abode with us and in us. By shedding abroad His love, He quickens our souls into sympathy with himself, and in this way, and in this way alone, He purifies our hearts through faith.

Charles Finney

PAUSE FOR REFLECTION

What has the Lord done for you? How has he shown himself to you? How has he responded to your faith in him? In what way does his mercy amaze you? With whom does he want you to share your faith?

MONDAY:

The Consequences of Unbelief

Mark 5:37—6:20

N E W   T E S T A M E N T   R E A D I N G

*J*esus let only Peter, James, and John the brother of James go with him. When they came to the house of the synagogue leader, Jesus found many people there making lots of noise and crying loudly. Jesus entered the house and said to them, "Why are you crying and making so much noise? The child is not dead, only asleep." But they laughed at him. So, after throwing them out of the house, Jesus took the child's father and mother and his three followers into the room where the child was. Taking hold of the girl's hand, he said to her, "Talitha, koum!" (This means, "Young girl, I tell you to stand up!") At once the girl stood right up and began walking. (She was twelve years old.) Everyone was completely amazed. Jesus gave them strict orders not to tell people about this. Then he told them to give the girl something to eat.

Jesus Goes to His Hometown

*J*esus left there and went to his hometown, and his followers went with him. On the Sabbath day he taught in the synagogue. Many people heard him and were amazed, saying, "Where did this man get these teachings? What is this wisdom that has been given to him? And where did he get the power to do miracles? He is just the carpenter, the son of Mary and the brother of James, Joseph, Judas, and Simon. And his sisters are here with us." So the people were upset with Jesus.

Jesus said to them, "A prophet is honored everywhere except in his hometown and with his own people and in his own home." So Jesus was not able to work any miracles there except to heal a few sick people by putting his hands on them. He was amazed at how many people had no faith.

Then Jesus went to other villages in that area and taught. He called his twelve followers together and got ready to send them out two by two and gave them authority over evil spirits. This is what Jesus commanded them: "Take nothing for your trip except a walking stick. Take no bread, no bag, and no money in your pockets. Wear sandals, but take only the clothes you are wearing. When you enter a house, stay there until you leave that town. If the people in a certain place refuse to welcome you or listen to you, leave that place. Shake its dust off your feet as a warning to them."

So the followers went out and preached that people should change their hearts and lives. They forced many demons out and put olive oil on many sick people and healed them.

How John the Baptist Was Killed

*K*ing Herod heard about Jesus, because he was now well known. Some people said, "He is John the Baptist, who has risen from the dead. That is why he can work these miracles."

Others said, "He is Elijah."

Other people said, "Jesus is a prophet, like the prophets who lived long ago."

When Herod heard this, he said, "I killed John by cutting off his head. Now he has risen from the dead!"

Herod himself had ordered his soldiers to arrest John and put him in prison in order to please his wife, Herodias. She had been the wife of Philip, Herod's brother, but then Herod had married her. John had been telling Herod, "It is not lawful for you to be married to your brother's wife." So Herodias hated John and wanted to kill him. But she couldn't, because Herod was afraid of John and protected him. He knew John was a good and holy man. Also, though John's preaching always bothered him, he enjoyed listening to John.

O L D   T E S T A M E N T   R E A D I N G

*B*ut you refused to go. You would not obey the command of the LORD your God, but grumbled in your tents, saying, "The LORD hates us. He brought us out of Egypt just to give us to the Amorites, who will destroy us. Where can we go now? The spies we sent have made us afraid, because they said, 'The people there are stronger and taller than we are. The cities are big, with walls up to the sky. And we saw the Anakites there!'"

Then I said to you, "Don't be frightened; don't be afraid of those people. The LORD your God will go ahead of you and fight for you as he did in Egypt; you saw him do it. And in the desert you saw how the LORD your God carried you, like one carries a child. And he has brought you safely all the way to this place."

But you still did not trust the LORD your God, even though he had always gone before you to find places for you to camp. In a fire at night and in a cloud during the day, he showed you which way to go.

When the LORD heard what you said, he was angry and made an oath, saying, "I promised a good land to your ancestors, but none of you evil people will see it. Only Caleb son of Jephunneh will see it. I will give him and his descendants the land he walked on, because he followed the LORD completely."

Then you said to me, "We have sinned against the LORD, but now we will go up and fight, as the LORD our God commanded us." Then all of you put on weapons, thinking it would be easy to go into the mountains.

But the LORD said to me, "Tell the people, 'You must not go up there and fight. I will not be with you, and your enemies will defeat you.'"

So I told you, but you would not listen. You would not obey the LORD's command. You were proud, so you went on up into the mountains, and the Amorites who lived in those mountains came out and fought you. They chased you like bees and defeated you from Edom to Hormah. So you came back and cried before the LORD, but the LORD did not listen to you; he refused to pay attention to you.

Deuteronomy 1:26–36, 41–45

INSIGHTS

*G*od had told the people to enter and possess the land, but they preferred to spy it out just to see if God was really telling the truth! Well, He was—it was a rich land, a beautiful land, and a fruitful land. But there were giants! "We are not able to overcome!" This was the majority report.

The minority report came from Caleb and Joshua, and Moses agreed with them: "We are well able to overcome it!" This is the Old Testament version of Romans 8:31: "If God be for us, who can be against us?" The majority saw the obstacles, and they were bigger than their God. The minority saw God, and the obstacles disappeared!

Unbelief always cries and complains. It plays the same tune: "We are not able!" The nation had the promises of God to lean on and the presence of God to depend on, but they preferred to walk by sight. It cost them forty years in the wilderness, the world's longest funeral march!

Christians do not fight for victory; we fight from victory. Jesus said, "In the world ye shall have tribulation: but be of good cheer; I have overcome the world" (John 16:33). John said, "This is the victory that overcometh the world, even our faith" (1 John 5:4).

Either we are overcomers—or overcome.

Warren Wiersbe

APPLICATION

*L*ist the consequences of unbelief described in these Scripture readings. What are the rewards of faith? What about your life? Are you reaping consequences or rewards? Will you be an overcomer or be overcome?

TUESDAY:
Trust God for His Provision
Mark 6:21–44

*T*hen the perfect time came for Herodias to cause John's death. On Herod's birthday, he gave a dinner party for the most important government leaders, the commanders of his army, and the most important people in Galilee. When the daughter of Herodias came in and danced, she pleased Herod and the people eating with him.

So King Herod said to the girl, "Ask me for anything you want, and I will give it to you." He promised her, "Anything you ask for I will give to you—up to half of my kingdom."

The girl went to her mother and asked, "What should I ask for?"

Her mother answered, "Ask for the head of John the Baptist."

At once the girl went back to the king and said to him, "I want the head of John the Baptist right now on a platter."

Although the king was very sad, he had made a promise, and his dinner guests had heard it. So he did not want to refuse what she asked. Immediately the king sent a soldier to bring John's head. The soldier went and cut off John's head in the prison and brought it back on a platter. He gave it to the girl, and the girl gave it to her mother. When John's followers heard this, they came and got John's body and put it in a tomb.

More than Five Thousand Fed

*T*he apostles gathered around Jesus and told him about all the things they had done and taught. Crowds of people were coming and going so that Jesus and his followers did not even have time to eat. He said to them, "Come away by yourselves, and we will go to a lonely place to get some rest."

So they went in a boat by themselves to a lonely place. But many people saw them leave and recognized them. So from all the towns they ran to the place where Jesus was going, and they got there before him. When he arrived, he saw a great crowd waiting.

He felt sorry for them, because they were like sheep without a shepherd. So he began to teach them many things.

When it was late in the day, his followers came to him and said, "No one lives in this place, and it is already very late. Send the people away so they can go to the countryside and towns around here to buy themselves something to eat."

But Jesus answered, "You give them something to eat."

They said to him, "We would all have to work a month to earn enough money to buy that much bread!"

Jesus asked them, "How many loaves of bread do you have? Go and see."

When they found out, they said, "Five loaves and two fish."

Then Jesus told his followers to have the people sit in groups on the green grass. So they sat in groups of fifty or a hundred. Jesus took the five loaves and two fish and, looking up to heaven, he thanked God for the food. He divided the bread and gave it to his followers for them to give to the people. Then he divided the two fish among them all. All the people ate and were satisfied. The followers filled twelve baskets with the leftover pieces of bread and fish. There were five thousand men who ate.

I praise your greatness, my God the King;
  I will praise you forever and ever.
I will praise you every day;
  I will praise you forever and ever.
The LORD is great and worthy of our praise;
  no one can understand how great he is.

Parents will tell their children what you have done.
  They will retell your mighty acts,
wonderful majesty, and glory.
  And I will think about your miracles.
They will tell about the amazing things you do,
  and I will tell how great you are.
They will remember your great goodness

and will sing about your fairness.
The LORD will keep all his promises;
   he is loyal to all he has made.
The LORD helps those who have been
   defeated
   and takes care of those who are in
   trouble.
All living things look to you for food,
   and you give it to them at the right
   time.
You open your hand,
   and you satisfy all living things.

Everything the LORD does is right.
   He is loyal to all he has made.
Psalm 145:1–7, 13b–17

I will praise God in a song
   and will honor him by giving thanks.
That will please the LORD more than
   offering him cattle,
   more than sacrificing a bull with
   horns and hoofs.
Poor people will see this and be glad.
   Be encouraged, you who worship
   God.
The LORD listens to those in need
   and does not look down on captives.

Heaven and earth should praise him,
   the seas and everything in them.
Psalm 69:30–34

L et them give thanks to the LORD for
   his love
   and for the miracles he does for
   people.
He satisfies the thirsty
   and fills up the hungry.
Psalm 107:8–9

INSIGHTS

It is better to trust in God than to accumulate riches. . . .

Trust in God gives clearness of vision. When we are thinking partly of doing God's work in the world, and partly of lining our own nest, we are in the condition of the man whose eyes do not look in the same direction. . . . We are endeavouring to serve two masters, and our judgment is therefore distorted. Who has not often experienced this? You have tried to ascertain God's will, or to

form a right judgment about your life, but constantly your perception of duty has been obscured by the thought that, if you decided in a certain direction, you would interfere with your interests in another. Your eye has not been single, and you have walked in darkness. When, however, you feel so absorbed in God's interests that you are indifferent to your own, all becomes clear, and you leave Him to care for all results. . . .

Let us not think that God is niggardly and stinting in His gifts. He gives fish as well as bread when He feeds the crowds; colours as well as leaves when He clothes the flowers. You have been adopted into His Family, and may call Him "Abba, Father." Surely this act of grace shows a special love on His part. Would He have taken such care of the spiritual, and have none for the physical? The ungodly may worry about the maintenance; but a child of God may be sure that His needs will be supplied.

F. B. Meyer

APPLICATION

*W*hat *is the difference between Jesus' perspective on feeding the crowd and his disciples' perspective? Do you face similar conflict between feeling a need to provide for yourself and trusting God to provide? Let these psalms be your prayer of trust and thanks for God's provision!*

WEDNESDAY:

God Is Merciful, Even to Those Who Do Not Understand

Mark 6:45—7:13

NEW TESTAMENT READING

Jesus Walks on the Water

*I*mmediately Jesus told his followers to get into the boat and go ahead of him to Bethsaida across the lake. He stayed there to send the people home. After sending them away, he went into the hills to pray.

That night, the boat was in the middle of the lake, and Jesus was alone on the land. He saw his followers struggling hard to row the boat, because the wind was blowing against them. Between three and six o'clock in the morning, Jesus came to them, walking on the water, and he wanted to walk past the boat. But when they saw him walking on the water, they thought he was a ghost and cried out. They all saw him and were afraid. But quickly Jesus spoke to them and said, "Have courage! It is I. Do not be afraid." Then he got into the boat with them, and the wind became calm. The followers were greatly amazed. They did not understand about the miracle of the five loaves, because their minds were closed.

When they had crossed the lake, they came to shore at Gennesaret and tied the boat there. When they got out of the boat, people immediately recognized Jesus. They ran everywhere in that area and began to bring sick people on mats wherever they heard he was. And everywhere he went—into towns, cities, or countryside—the people brought the sick to the market-places. They begged him to let them touch just the edge of his coat, and all who touched it were healed.

Obey God's Law

*W*hen some Pharisees and some teachers of the law came from Jerusalem, they gathered around Jesus. They saw that some of Jesus' followers ate food with hands that were not clean, that is, they hadn't washed them. (The Pharisees and all the Jews never eat before washing their hands in a special way according to their unwritten laws. And when they buy something in the market, they never eat it until they wash themselves in a special way. They also follow many other unwritten laws, such as the washing of cups, pitchers, and pots.)

The Pharisees and the teachers of the law said to Jesus, "Why don't your followers obey the unwritten laws which have been handed down to us? Why do your followers eat their food with hands that are not clean?"

Jesus answered, "Isaiah was right when he spoke about you hypocrites. He wrote,

'These people show honor to me with
    words,
  but their hearts are far from me.
Their worship of me is worthless.
  The things they teach are nothing
    but human rules.'   *Isaiah 29:13*

You have stopped following the commands of God, and you follow only human teachings."

Then Jesus said to them, "You cleverly ignore the commands of God so you can follow your own teachings. Moses said, 'Honor your father and your mother,' and 'Anyone who says cruel things to his father or mother must be put to death.' But you say a person can tell his father or mother, 'I have something I could use to help you, but it is Corban—a gift to God.' You no longer let that person use that money for his father or his mother. By your own rules, which you teach people, you are rejecting what God said. And you do many things like that."

OLD TESTAMENT READING

*T*hey didn't keep their agreement with God
  and refused to live by his teachings.
They forgot what he had done
  and the miracles he had shown them.
He did miracles while their ancestors
    watched,
  in the fields of Zoan in Egypt.
He divided the Red Sea and led them
    through.

He made the water stand up like a
  wall.
He led them with a cloud by day
  and by the light of a fire by night.
He split the rocks in the desert
  and gave them more than enough
    water, as if from the deep ocean.
He brought streams out of the rock
  and caused water to flow down like
    rivers.

But they kept on sinning;
  they did not believe even with the
    miracles.
So he ended their days without meaning
  and their years in terror.
Anytime he killed them, they would
    look to him for help;
  they would come back to God and
    follow him.
They would remember that God was
    their Rock,
  that God Most High had saved
    them.
But their words were false,
  and their tongues lied to him.
Their hearts were not really loyal to
    God;
  they did not keep his agreement.
Still God was merciful.
  He forgave their sins
  and did not destroy them.
Many times he held back his anger
  and did not stir up all his anger.
He remembered that they were only
    human,
  like a wind that blows and does not
    come back.

                    Psalm 78:10–16, 32–39

In Christ, God has broken the cycle of judgment and retaliation. We have received mercy—undeserved and unearned love. In the fifth Beatitude, Jesus invites us to share His character trait of mercy. But inflow and outgo must be matched. Mercy must be given away if we want to live in its flow. . . .

*The test of the greatness Christ offers us is to be merciful to those who do not return it. When we've endured disappointments, injus-*tice, or hurts, we do not become bitter or sour but draw on and express mercy. This is not easy—not until we remember how merciful Christ has been to us. We are called to be a channel of divine mercy flowing through us to others. This is the source of the silent strength of greatness.*

                    Lloyd Ogilvie

Did Jesus condemn his followers for their lack of faith and understanding? What did he do for those who want his healing and miracles, but little else? How was Jesus merciful to the Pharisees and teachers of the law? In what way is God merciful, even to those who don't live by his teachings? Write your own psalm of praise to God for his unending mercy.

THURSDAY:

Evil Comes from Within

Mark 7:14–37

*A*fter Jesus called the crowd to him again, he said, "Every person should listen to me and understand what I am saying. There is nothing people put into their bodies that makes them unclean. People are made unclean by the things that come out of them."

When Jesus left the people and went into the house, his followers asked him about this story. Jesus said, "Do you still not understand? Surely you know that nothing that enters someone from the outside can make that person unclean. It does not go into the mind, but into the stomach. Then it goes out of the body." (When Jesus said this, he meant that no longer was any food unclean for people to eat.)

And Jesus said, "The things that come out of people are the things that make them unclean. All these evil things begin inside people, in the mind: evil thoughts, sexual sins, stealing, murder, adultery, greed, evil actions, lying, doing sinful things, jealousy, speaking evil of others, pride, and foolish living. All these evil things come from inside and make people unclean."

Jesus Helps a Non-Jewish Woman

*J*esus left that place and went to the area around Tyre. When he went into a house, he did not want anyone to know he was there, but he could not stay hidden. A woman whose daughter had an evil spirit in her heard that he was there. So she quickly came to Jesus and fell at his feet. She was Greek, born in Phoenicia, in Syria. She begged Jesus to force the demon out of her daughter.

Jesus told the woman, "It is not right to take the children's bread and give it to the dogs. First let the children eat all they want."

But she answered, "Yes, Lord, but even the dogs under the table can eat the children's crumbs."

Then Jesus said, "Because of your answer, you may go. The demon has left your daughter."

The woman went home and found her daughter lying in bed; the demon was gone.

Jesus Heals a Deaf Man

*T*hen Jesus left the area around Tyre and went through Sidon to Lake Galilee, to the area of the Ten Towns. While he was there, some people brought a man to him who was deaf and could not talk plainly. The people begged Jesus to put his hand on the man to heal him.

Jesus led the man away from the crowd, by himself. He put his fingers in the man's ears and then spit and touched the man's tongue. Looking up to heaven, he sighed and said to the man, "Ephphatha!" (This means, "Be opened.") Instantly the man was able to hear and to use his tongue so that he spoke clearly.

Jesus commanded the people not to tell anyone about what happened. But the more he commanded them, the more they told about it. They were completely amazed and said, "Jesus does everything well. He makes the deaf hear! And those who can't talk he makes able to speak."

*S*ome people are wicked and no good.
They go around telling lies,
winking with their eyes, tapping with
their feet,
and making signs with their fingers.
They make evil plans in their hearts
and are always starting arguments.
So trouble will strike them in an
instant;
suddenly they will be so hurt no one
can help them.

There are six things the LORD hates.
There are seven things he cannot
stand:
a proud look,
a lying tongue,
hands that kill innocent people,
a mind that thinks up evil plans,
feet that are quick to do evil,
a witness who lies,

and someone who starts arguments among families.

Proverbs 6:12–19

*I*t is your evil that has separated
you from your God.
Your sins cause him to turn away from
you,
so he does not hear you.
With your hands you have killed
others,
and with your fingers you have done
wrong.
With your lips you have lied,
and with your tongue you say evil
things.

Isaiah 59:2–3

*P*eople of Jerusalem, clean the evil
from your hearts so that you can
be saved.
Don't continue making evil plans.

Jeremiah 4:14

*M*ore than anything else, a person's
mind is evil
and cannot be healed.
No one truly understands it."

Jeremiah 17:9

*D*on't follow the ways of the wicked;
don't do what evil people do.
Avoid their ways, and don't follow
them.
Stay away from them and keep on
going,
because they cannot sleep until they do
evil.
They cannot rest until they harm
someone.
They feast on wickedness and cruelty
as if they were eating bread and
drinking wine.

Proverbs 4:14–17

*S*in speaks to the wicked in their
hearts.
They have no fear of God.
They think too much of themselves
so they don't see their sin and hate
it.
Their words are wicked lies;
they are no longer wise or good.

At night they make evil plans;
what they do leads to nothing good.
They don't refuse things that are
evil.

Psalm 36:1–4

INSIGHTS

*A friend received a significant honor. I can't
remember struggling with envy and jealousy
before, but on that day, I was swept up into a
whirlwind of envy. I drove back to my office
in a complete state of shock. Where in creation did that come from? It leaked through
the pinholes of my otherwise good character.
A Christian's good character is the character
of Jesus breathed into each of us by the Holy
Spirit. Once we stop allowing the Spirit to
fill us with power, the pinholes leak sin from
our old nature.*

*Accepting our total depravity—our ca-
pacity to sin, that our character is filled with
pinholes—is essential to living a victorious
Christian life. If we presume that when we
become Christian we are now good, we have
missed the point. Jesus Christ shed His blood
to forgive our sin, not to remove our sin. We
have a continuing sinful nature which requires us to guard our heart and mind. We
must post a twenty-four-hour guard at the gate
to our mind.*

Patrick Morley

APPLICATION

*What evil things does Jesus say come from
within a person? Why is it necessary to have
a clean heart? Does your life show any evidence of "heart" trouble? What commitment
will you make to guard those areas of weakness?*

FRIDAY:

Miracles Won't Soften Hard Hearts

Mark 8:1–26

More than Four Thousand Fed

*A*nother time there was a great crowd with Jesus that had nothing to eat. So Jesus called his followers and said, "I feel sorry for these people, because they have already been with me for three days, and they have nothing to eat. If I send them home hungry, they will faint on the way. Some of them live a long way from here."

Jesus' followers answered, "How can we get enough bread to feed all these people? We are far away from any town."

Jesus asked, "How many loaves of bread do you have?"

They answered, "Seven."

Jesus told the people to sit on the ground. Then he took the seven loaves, gave thanks to God, and divided the bread. He gave the pieces to his followers to give to the people, and they did so. The followers also had a few small fish. After Jesus gave thanks for the fish, he told his followers to give them to the people also. All the people ate and were satisfied. Then his followers filled seven baskets with the leftover pieces of food. There were about four thousand people who ate. After they had eaten, Jesus sent them home. Then right away he got into a boat with his followers and went to the area of Dalmanutha.

The Leaders Ask for a Miracle

*T*he Pharisees came to Jesus and began to ask him questions. Hoping to trap him, they asked Jesus for a miracle from God. Jesus sighed deeply and said, "Why do you people ask for a miracle as a sign? I tell you the truth, no sign will be given to you." Then Jesus left the Pharisees and went in the boat to the other side of the lake.

Guard Against Wrong Teachings

*H*is followers had only one loaf of bread with them in the boat; they had forgotten to bring more. Jesus warned them, "Be careful! Beware of the yeast of the Pharisees and the yeast of Herod."

His followers discussed the meaning of this, saying, "He said this because we have no bread."

Knowing what they were talking about, Jesus asked them, "Why are you talking about not having bread? Do you still not see or understand? Are your minds closed? You have eyes, but you don't really see. You have ears, but you don't really listen. Remember when I divided five loaves of bread for the five thousand? How many baskets did you fill with leftover pieces of food?"

They answered, "Twelve."

"And when I divided seven loaves of bread for the four thousand, how many baskets did you fill with leftover pieces of food?"

They answered, "Seven."

Then Jesus said to them, "Don't you understand yet?"

Jesus Heals a Blind Man

*J*esus and his followers came to Bethsaida. There some people brought a blind man to Jesus and begged him to touch the man. So Jesus took the blind man's hand and led him out of the village. Then he spit on the man's eyes and put his hands on the man and asked, "Can you see now?"

The man looked up and said, "Yes, I see people, but they look like trees walking around."

Again Jesus put his hands on the man's eyes. Then the man opened his eyes wide and they were healed, and he was able to see everything clearly. Jesus told him to go home, saying, "Don't go into the town."

*T*hey turned against God so often in the desert
and grieved him there.
Again and again they tested God
and brought pain to the Holy One of Israel.
They did not remember his power
or the time he saved them from the enemy.

They forgot the signs he did in Egypt
and his wonders in the fields of
Zoan.
He turned their rivers to blood
so no one could drink the water.
He sent flies that bit the people.
He sent frogs that destroyed them.
He gave their crops to grasshoppers
and what they worked for to locusts.
He destroyed their vines with hail
and their sycamore trees with sleet.
He killed their animals with hail
and their cattle with lightning.
He showed them his hot anger.
He sent his strong anger against
them,
his destroying angels.
He found a way to show his anger.
He did not keep them from dying
but let them die by a terrible disease.
God killed all the firstborn sons in
Egypt,
the oldest son of each family of
Ham.
But God led his people out like
sheep,
and he guided them like a flock
through the desert.
He led them to safety so they had
nothing to fear,
but their enemies drowned in the
sea.
So God brought them to his holy land,
to the mountain country he took
with his own power.
He forced out the other nations,
and he had his people inherit the
land.
He let the tribes of Israel settle there
in tents.

But they tested God
and turned against God Most High;
they did not keep his rules.
They turned away and were disloyal
just like their ancestors.
They were like a crooked bow that
does not shoot straight.
They made God angry by building
places to worship gods;
they made him jealous with their
idols.

When God heard them, he became
very angry
and rejected the people of Israel
completely.

Psalm 78:40–59

INSIGHTS

*F*or three years, day in and day out, he [Ju-
das] occupied himself with Jesus Christ. He
saw the Lord's miracles, heard His words,
even participated in His ministry. In all that
time, no one ever questioned his faith. He had
the same status as the other disciples. Except
for the Savior Himself, who knew the thoughts
of Judas's heart, no one ever suspected that
this man would betray Christ.

Yet, while the others were growing into
apostles, Judas was quietly becoming a vile,
calculating tool of Satan. Whatever his character seemed to be at the beginning, his faith
was not real (John 13:10–11). He was un-
regenerate, and his heart gradually hardened
so that he became the treacherous man who
sold the Savior for a fistful of coins. . . .

It was not the will of God apart from
Judas's own choice that he should betray
Christ. At every opportunity, Jesus warned
Judas and entreated him to repent and be
saved, but at every point Judas turned away.
Judas had heard the gospel according to
Jesus, yet he refused to turn from his sin and
selfishness. Jesus' words in John 13 represent
His final, loving appeal to this man. In the
end, however, the Savior's merciful entreaty
would condemn Judas in the hardness of his
heart.

John F. MacArthur

PAUSE FOR REFLECTION

*W*ho has witnessed more miracles of God
than the Israelites or those who walked with
Jesus while he was on earth? Do miracles lead
people to salvation? What is more important
than miracles in causing a person to turn
toward God?

WEEKEND:

Learn to Value
What God Values

Mark 8:27—9:13

Peter Says Jesus Is the Christ

Jesus and his followers went to the towns around Caesarea Philippi. While they were traveling, Jesus asked them, "Who do people say I am?"

They answered, "Some say you are John the Baptist. Others say you are Elijah, and others say you are one of the prophets."

Then Jesus asked, "But who do you say I am?"

Peter answered, "You are the Christ."

Jesus warned his followers not to tell anyone who he was.

Then Jesus began to teach them that the Son of Man must suffer many things and that he would be rejected by the older Jewish leaders, the leading priests, and the teachers of the law. He told them that the Son of Man must be killed and then rise from the dead after three days. Jesus told them plainly what would happen. Then Peter took Jesus aside and began to tell him not to talk like that. But Jesus turned and looked at his followers. Then he told Peter not to talk that way. He said, "Go away from me, Satan! You don't care about the things of God, but only about things people think are important."

Then Jesus called the crowd to him, along with his followers. He said, "If people want to follow me, they must give up the things they want. They must be willing even to give up their lives to follow me. Those who want to save their lives will give up true life. But those who give up their lives for me and for the Good News will have true life. It is worth nothing for them to have the whole world if they lose their souls. They could never pay enough to buy back their souls. The people who live now are living in a sinful and evil time. If people are ashamed of me and my teaching, the Son of Man will be ashamed of them when he comes with his Father's glory and with the holy angels."

Then Jesus said to the people, "I tell you the truth, some people standing here will see the kingdom of God come with power before they die."

Jesus Talks with Moses and Elijah

Six days later, Jesus took Peter, James, and John up on a high mountain by themselves. While they watched, Jesus' appearance was changed. His clothes became shining white, whiter than any person could make them. Then Elijah and Moses appeared to them, talking with Jesus.

Peter said to Jesus, "Teacher, it is good that we are here. Let us make three tents— one for you, one for Moses, and one for Elijah." Peter did not know what to say, because he and the others were so frightened.

Then a cloud came and covered them, and a voice came from the cloud, saying, "This is my Son, whom I love. Listen to him!"

Suddenly Peter, James, and John looked around, but they saw only Jesus there alone with them.

As they were coming down the mountain, Jesus commanded them not to tell anyone about what they had seen until the Son of Man had risen from the dead.

So the followers obeyed Jesus, but they discussed what he meant about rising from the dead.

Then they asked Jesus, "Why do the teachers of the law say that Elijah must come first?"

Jesus answered, "They are right to say that Elijah must come first and make everything the way it should be. But why does the Scripture say that the Son of Man will suffer much and that people will treat him as if he were nothing? I tell you that Elijah has already come. And people did to him whatever they wanted to do, just as the Scriptures said it would happen."

Anything I saw and wanted, I got for
  myself;

108

I did not miss any pleasure I desired.
I was pleased with everything I did,
and this pleasure was the reward for
all my hard work.
But then I looked at what I had done,
and I thought about all the hard
work.
Suddenly I realized it was useless, like
chasing the wind.
There is nothing to gain from
anything we do here on earth.

Ecclesiastes 2:10–11

*N*ow, everything has been heard,
so I give my final advice:
Honor God and obey his commands,
because this is all people must do.
God will judge everything,
even what is done in secret,
the good and the evil.

Ecclesiastes 12:13–14

*W*hen they arrived, Samuel saw Eliab, and
he thought, "Surely the LORD has appointed this person standing here before
him."

But the LORD said to Samuel, "Don't look
at how handsome Eliab is or how tall he is,
because I have not chosen him. God does
not see the same way people see. People
look at the outside of a person, but the LORD
looks at the heart."

1 Samuel 16:6–7

*S*amuel spoke to the whole group of Israel,
saying, "If you're turning back to the LORD
with all your hearts, you must remove your
foreign gods and your idols of Ashtoreth.
You must give yourselves fully to the LORD
and serve only him. Then he will save you
from the Philistines."

So the Israelites put away their idols of
Baal and Ashtoreth, and they served only
the LORD.

1 Samuel 7:3–4

*L*ORD, teach me your demands,
and I will keep them until the end.
Help me understand, so I can keep
your teachings,
obeying them with all my heart.
Lead me in the path of your commands,
because that makes me happy.

Make me want to keep your rules
instead of wishing for riches.
Keep me from looking at worthless
things.
Let me live by your word.

Psalm 119:33–37

I N S I G H T S

*I will hear what God the Lord will speak"
(Ps. 85:8). Blessed is the soul which hears
the Lord speaking within, and from His
mouth receives the word of consolation.
Blessed are the ears that catch the pulses of
the divine whisper (Matt. 13:16, 17), and
give no heed to the whisperings of this world.
Blessed indeed are those ears which listen not
after the voice which is sounding without, but
for the truth teaching inwardly. Blessed are
the eyes that are shut to outward things, but
intent on things inward. Blessed are they that
enter far into things within, and endeavor to
prepare themselves more and more, by daily
exercises, for the receiving of heavenly secrets.
Blessed are they who are glad to have time to
spare for God, and who shake off all worldly
hindrances.*

*Consider these things, O my soul, and shut
up the door of your sensual desires, that you
may hear what the Lord your God speaks in
you (Ps. 85:8).*

*Thus says your Beloved, "I am thy salva-
tion," your Peace, and your Life: keep yourself
with Me, and you shall find peace. Let go all
transitory things, and seek the things eternal.
What are all transitory objects but seductive
things? And what can all creatures avail, if
you are forsaken by the Creator?*

*Renounce therefore all things, and labor
to please your Creator, and to be faithful unto
Him, that you may be able to attain unto true
blessedness.*

Thomas à Kempis

A C T I O N   P O I N T

*L*ist and evaluate the things in your life that
seem worth pursuing. Might Jesus criticize
you in the same way he criticized Peter (Mark
8:33–38)? If you want to follow Jesus, what
priorities do you need to rearrange?*

MONDAY:

God Wants to Teach Us His Ways

Mark 9:14–37

Jesus Heals a Sick Boy

*W*hen Jesus, Peter, James, and John came back to the other followers, they saw a great crowd around them and the teachers of the law arguing with them. But as soon as the crowd saw Jesus, the people were surprised and ran to welcome him.

Jesus asked, "What are you arguing about?"

A man answered, "Teacher, I brought my son to you. He has an evil spirit in him that stops him from talking. When the spirit attacks him, it throws him on the ground. Then my son foams at the mouth, grinds his teeth, and becomes very stiff. I asked your followers to force the evil spirit out, but they couldn't."

Jesus answered, "You people have no faith. How long must I stay with you? How long must I put up with you? Bring the boy to me."

So the followers brought him to Jesus. As soon as the evil spirit saw Jesus, it made the boy lose control of himself, and he fell down and rolled on the ground, foaming at the mouth.

Jesus asked the boy's father, "How long has this been happening?"

The father answered, "Since he was very young. The spirit often throws him into a fire or into water to kill him. If you can do anything for him, please have pity on us and help us."

Jesus said to the father, "You said, 'If you can!' All things are possible for the one who believes."

Immediately the father cried out, "I do believe! Help me to believe more!"

When Jesus saw that a crowd was quickly gathering, he ordered the evil spirit, saying, "You spirit that makes people unable to hear or speak, I command you to come out of this boy and never enter him again!"

The evil spirit screamed and caused the boy to fall on the ground again. Then the spirit came out. The boy looked as if he were dead, and many people said, "He is dead!" But Jesus took hold of the boy's hand and helped him to stand up.

When Jesus went into the house, his followers began asking him privately, "Why couldn't we force that evil spirit out?"

Jesus answered, "That kind of spirit can only be forced out by prayer."

Jesus Talks About His Death

*T*hen Jesus and his followers left that place and went through Galilee. He didn't want anyone to know where he was, because he was teaching his followers. He said to them, "The Son of Man will be handed over to people, and they will kill him. After three days, he will rise from the dead." But the followers did not understand what Jesus meant, and they were afraid to ask him.

Who Is the Greatest?

*J*esus and his followers went to Capernaum. When they went into a house there, he asked them, "What were you arguing about on the road?" But the followers did not answer, because their argument on the road was about which one of them was the greatest.

Jesus sat down and called the twelve apostles to him. He said, "Whoever wants to be the most important must be last of all and servant of all."

Then Jesus took a small child and had him stand among them. Taking the child in his arms, he said, "Whoever accepts a child like this in my name accepts me. And whoever accepts me accepts the One who sent me."

*M*oses used to take a tent and set it up a long way outside the camp; he called it the "Meeting Tent." Anyone who wanted to ask the LORD about something would go to the Meeting Tent outside the camp. Whenever Moses went out to the Tent, all the people would rise and stand at the entrances of their tents, watching him until he entered the Meeting Tent. When Moses went into the Tent, the pillar of cloud would always come down and stay at the entrance of the Tent while the LORD spoke with Moses. Whenever the people saw the pillar of cloud at the entrance of the Tent, they stood and worshiped, each person at the entrance of his own tent.

The LORD spoke to Moses face to face as a man speaks with his friend. Then Moses would return to the camp, but Moses' young helper, Joshua son of Nun, did not leave the Tent.

Exodus 33:7–11

*J*ob, pay attention and listen to me;
  be quiet, and I will speak.
If you have anything to say, answer me;
  speak up, because I want to prove
    you right.
But if you have nothing to say, then
    listen to me;
  be quiet, and I will teach you wisdom."
Job 33:31–33

*T*he LORD says, "I will make you wise
    and show you where to go.
I will guide you and watch over you."
Psalm 32:8

*I*n the last days
the mountain on which the Lord's
    Temple stands
  will become the most important of
    all mountains.
It will be raised above the hills,
  and people from other nations will
    come streaming to it.
Many nations will come and say,
  "Come, let us go up to the mountain
    of the LORD,
  to the Temple of the God of Jacob,
so that he can teach us his ways,
  and we can obey his teachings."
His teachings will go out from Jerusa-
    lem,
  the word of the LORD from that city.
Micah 4:1–2

child, and so longs to have his life in step with His will and His love, that He is willing to keep the child's guidance entirely in His own hand. He knows so well that we do not do what is really holy and heavenly, except when He works it in us, that He intends His very demands to become promises of what He will do, in watching over and leading us all day long. We may count on Him to teach us His way and show us His path not only in special trials and hard times, but in every-day life. . . .

. . . So simple and delightful can it be-come to a soul that has practiced waiting on God, to walk all day in the enjoyment of God's light and leading. What is needed to help us find such a life is one thing: the real knowl-edge and faith of God as the only source of wisdom and goodness, as always ready and longing to be to us all that we can possibly need. Yes, this is the one thing we need.

Andrew Murray

ACTION POINT

*W*hat special teaching did Jesus want to give his followers when they were alone? As you read these Old Testament passages, think about how much God wants to teach his people. Thank him for his great outpouring of love. Pray that your heart will listen for his wisdom.

INSIGHTS

*T*he Father in heaven is so interested in His

TUESDAY:
Flee All Evil
Mark 9:38—10:16

Anyone Not Against Us Is for Us

*T*hen John said, "Teacher, we saw someone using your name to force demons out of a person. We told him to stop, because he does not belong to our group."

But Jesus said, "Don't stop him, because anyone who uses my name to do powerful things will not easily say evil things about me. Whoever is not against us is with us. I tell you the truth, whoever gives you a drink of water because you belong to the Christ will truly get his reward.

"If one of these little children believes in me, and someone causes that child to sin, it would be better for that person to have a large stone tied around his neck and be drowned in the sea. If your hand causes you to sin, cut it off. It is better for you to lose part of your body and live forever than to have two hands and go to hell, where the fire never goes out. If your foot causes you to sin, cut it off. It is better for you to lose part of your body and to live forever than to have two feet and be thrown into hell. If your eye causes you to sin, take it out. It is better for you to enter the kingdom of God with only one eye than to have two eyes and be thrown into hell. In hell the worm does not die; the fire is never put out. Every person will be salted with fire.

"Salt is good, but if the salt loses its salty taste, you cannot make it salty again. So, be full of salt, and have peace with each other."

Jesus Teaches About Divorce

*T*hen Jesus left that place and went into the area of Judea and across the Jordan River. Again, crowds came to him, and he taught them as he usually did.

Some Pharisees came to Jesus and tried to trick him. They asked, "Is it right for a man to divorce his wife?"

Jesus answered, "What did Moses command you to do?"

They said, "Moses allowed a man to write out divorce papers and send her away."

Jesus said, "Moses wrote that command for you because you were stubborn. But when God made the world, 'he made them male and female.' 'So a man will leave his father and mother and be united with his wife, and the two will become one body.' So there are not two, but one. God has joined the two together, so no one should separate them."

Later, in the house, his followers asked Jesus again about the question of divorce. He answered, "Anyone who divorces his wife and marries another woman is guilty of adultery against her. And the woman who divorces her husband and marries another man is also guilty of adultery."

Jesus Accepts Children

*S*ome people brought their little children to Jesus so he could touch them, but his followers told them to stop. When Jesus saw this, he was upset and said to them, "Let the little children come to me. Don't stop them, because the kingdom of God belongs to people who are like these children. I tell you the truth, you must accept the kingdom of God as if you were a little child, or you will never enter it." Then Jesus took the children in his arms, put his hands on them, and blessed them.

*N*ow Joseph was well built and handsome. After some time the wife of Joseph's master began to desire Joseph, and one day she said to him, "Have sexual relations with me."

But Joseph refused and said to her, "My master trusts me with everything in his house. He has put me in charge of everything he owns. There is no one in his house greater than I. He has not kept anything from me except you, because you are his wife. How can I do such an evil thing? It is a sin against God."

The woman talked to Joseph every day, but he refused to have sexual relations with her or even spend time with her.

One day Joseph went into the house to do his work as usual and was the only man in the house at that time. His master's wife grabbed his coat and said to him, "Come and have sexual relations with me." But Joseph left his coat in her hand and ran out of the house.

Genesis 39:6b–12

*T*hen they made an agreement to obey the LORD, the God of their ancestors, with their whole being. Anyone who refused to obey the LORD, the God of Israel, was to be killed. It did not matter if that person was important or unimportant, a man or woman. Then Asa and the people made a promise before the LORD, shouting with a loud voice and blowing trumpets and sheep's horns. All the people of Judah were happy about the promise, because they had promised with all their heart. They looked for God and found him. So the LORD gave them peace in all the country.

King Asa also removed Maacah, his grandmother, from being queen mother, because she had made a terrible Asherah idol. Asa cut down that idol, smashed it into pieces, and burned it in the Kidron Valley.

2 Chronicles 15:12–16

*N*ow, my sons, listen to me,
    and don't ignore what I say.
Stay away from such a woman.
    Don't even go near the door of her house,
or you will give your riches to others,
    and the best years of your life will be given to someone cruel.

Proverbs 5:7–9

INSIGHTS

*R*epentance is a definite turn from every thought, word, deed and habit which is known to be wrong. It is not sufficient to feel pangs of remorse or to make some kind of apology to God. Fundamentally, repentance is a matter neither of emotion nor of speech. It is an inward change of mind and attitude towards sin which leads to a change of behaviour.

There can be no compromise here. There may be sins in our lives which we do not think we ever could renounce; but we must be willing to let them go as we cry to God for deliverance from them. If you are in doubt regarding what is right and what is wrong, what must go and what may be retained, do not be too greatly influenced by the customs and conventions of Christians you may know. Go by the clear teaching of the Bible and by the prompting of your conscience, and Christ will gradually lead you further along the path of righteousness. When he puts his finger on anything, give it up. It may be some association or recreation, some literature we read, or some attitude of pride, jealousy or resentment, or an unforgiving spirit.

Jesus told his followers to pluck out their eye and cut off their hand or foot if these caused them to sin. We are not to obey this with dead literalism, of course, and mutilate our bodies. It is a vivid figure of speech for dealing ruthlessly with the avenues along which temptation comes to us.

John Stott

APPLICATION

*H*ow serious a problem does Jesus consider sin to be? Is there anything casual about his attitude? What about your attitude toward sin? Do you vigorously run from it or politely coexist with it? What sin needs to be purged from your life? Is your spirit truly repentant?

WEDNESDAY:

The Righteous Will Be Rewarded in Heaven

Mark 10:17–41

NEW   TESTAMENT   READING

A Rich Young Man's Question

As Jesus started to leave, a man ran to him and fell on his knees before Jesus. The man asked, "Good teacher, what must I do to have life forever?"

Jesus answered, "Why do you call me good? Only God is good. You know the commands: 'You must not murder anyone. You must not be guilty of adultery. You must not steal. You must not tell lies about your neighbor. You must not cheat. Honor your father and mother.'"

The man said, "Teacher, I have obeyed all these things since I was a boy."

Jesus, looking at the man, loved him and said, "There is one more thing you need to do. Go and sell everything you have, and give the money to the poor, and you will have treasure in heaven. Then come and follow me."

He was very sad to hear Jesus say this, and he left sorrowfully, because he was rich.

Then Jesus looked at his followers and said, "How hard it will be for the rich to enter the kingdom of God!"

The followers were amazed at what Jesus said. But he said again, "My children, it is very hard to enter the kingdom of God! It is easier for a camel to go through the eye of a needle than for a rich person to enter the kingdom of God."

The followers were even more surprised and said to each other, "Then who can be saved?"

Jesus looked at them and said, "This is something people cannot do, but God can. God can do all things."

Peter said to Jesus, "Look, we have left everything and followed you."

Jesus said, "I tell you the truth, all those who have left houses, brothers, sisters, mother, father, children, or farms for me and for the Good News will get more than they left. Here in this world they will have a hundred times more homes, brothers, sisters, mothers, children, and fields. And with those things, they will also suffer for their belief. But in the age that is coming they will have life forever. Many who have the highest place now will have the lowest place in the future. And many who have the lowest place now will have the highest place in the future."

Jesus Talks About His Death

As Jesus and the people with him were on the road to Jerusalem, he was leading the way. His followers were amazed, but others in the crowd who followed were afraid. Again Jesus took the twelve apostles aside and began to tell them what was about to happen in Jerusalem. He said, "Look, we are going to Jerusalem. The Son of Man will be turned over to the leading priests and the teachers of the law. They will say that he must die, and they will turn him over to the non-Jewish people, who will laugh at him and spit on him. They will beat him with whips and crucify him. But on the third day, he will rise to life again."

Two Followers Ask Jesus a Favor

Then James and John, sons of Zebedee, came to Jesus and said, "Teacher, we want to ask you to do something for us."

Jesus asked, "What do you want me to do for you?"

They answered, "Let one of us sit at your right side and one of us sit at your left side in your glory in your kingdom."

Jesus said, "You don't understand what you are asking. Can you drink the cup that I must drink? And can you be baptized with the same kind of baptism that I must go through?"

They answered, "Yes, we can."

Jesus said to them, "You will drink the same cup that I will drink, and you will be baptized with the same baptism that I must go through. But I cannot choose who will sit at my right or my left; those places belong to those for whom they have been prepared."

When the other ten followers heard this, they began to be angry with James and John.

*T*hen people will say,
"There really are rewards for doing
   what is right.
There really is a God who judges the
   world."

Psalm 58:11

*Y*ou guide me with your advice,
   and later you will receive me in
      honor.
I have no one in heaven but you;
   I want nothing on earth besides you.
My body and my mind may become
      weak,
   but God is my strength.
He is mine forever.

Psalm 73:24–26

*T*he LORD will always lead you.
   He will satisfy your needs in dry
      lands
   and give strength to your bones.
You will be like a garden that has much
      water,
   like a spring that never runs dry.

"You must obey God's law about the
      Sabbath
   and not do what pleases yourselves
      on that holy day.
You should call the Sabbath a joyful
      day
   and honor it as the LORD's holy day.
You should honor it by not doing
      whatever you please
   nor saying whatever you please on
      that day.
Then you will find joy in the LORD,
   and I will carry you to the high
      places above the earth.
I will let you eat the crops of the land
   your ancestor Jacob had."
The LORD has said these things.

Isaiah 58:11, 13–14

*T*he people the LORD has freed will
      return
   and enter Jerusalem with joy.
   Their happiness will last forever.
They will have joy and gladness,

and all sadness and sorrow will be
   gone far away.

Isaiah 51:11

I N S I G H T S

*B*e not wearied by the labors which you have undertaken for my sake, nor let tribulations cast you down. But let My promise strengthen and comfort you under every circumstance. I am well able to reward you, above all measure and degree.

You shall not long toil here, nor always be oppressed with griefs. Wait a little while, and you shall see a speedy end of your evils. There will come an hour when all labor and tumult shall cease. Poor and brief is all that which passes away with time.

Do in earnest what you do; labor faithfully in My vineyard (Matt. 20:7); I will be your recompense. Write, read, chant, mourn, keep silence, pray, endure crosses manfully. Life everlasting is worth all these battles, and greater than these. Peace shall come in one day which is known unto the Lord, and there shall be "not day, nor night" (Zech. 14:7) (that is, of this present time), but unceasing light, infinite brightness, steadfast peace, and secure rest. Then you shall not say: "Who shall deliver me from the body of this death?" (Rom. 7:24); nor cry: "Woe is me, that I sojourn in Mesech" (Ps. 120:5). For death shall be cast down headlong, and there shall be salvation which can never fail, no more anxiety, blessed joy, companionship sweet and noble. . . .

Lift up your face therefore to Heaven. Behold, I and all My saints with Me, who in this world had great conflict, do now rejoice, now are comforted, now secure, now at rest, and shall remain with Me everlastingly in the kingdom of My Father!

Thomas à Kempis

A P P L I C A T I O N

*W*hat areas of personal commitment to God's kingdom do you find difficult? What is hard for you to leave behind? Pray that you will truly believe—deep inside—that God will reward your faithfulness far above what you can even imagine.

115

THURSDAY:
Being a Servant of God
Mark 10:42—11:14

*J*esus called them together and said, "The non-Jewish people have rulers. You know that those rulers love to show their power over the people, and their important leaders love to use all their authority. But it should not be that way among you. Whoever wants to become great among you must serve the rest of you like a servant. Whoever wants to become the first among you must serve all of you like a slave. In the same way, the Son of Man did not come to be served. He came to serve others and to give his life as a ransom for many people."

Jesus Heals a Blind Man

*T*hen they came to the town of Jericho. As Jesus was leaving there with his followers and a great many people, a blind beggar named Bartimaeus son of Timaeus was sitting by the road. When he heard that Jesus from Nazareth was walking by, he began to shout, "Jesus, Son of David, have mercy on me!"

Many people warned the blind man to be quiet, but he shouted even more, "Son of David, have mercy on me!"

Jesus stopped and said, "Tell the man to come here."

So they called the blind man, saying, "Cheer up! Get to your feet. Jesus is calling you." The blind man jumped up, left his coat there, and went to Jesus.

Jesus asked him, "What do you want me to do for you?"

The blind man answered, "Teacher, I want to see."

Jesus said, "Go, you are healed because you believed." At once the man could see, and he followed Jesus on the road.

Jesus Enters Jerusalem as a King

*A*s Jesus and his followers were coming closer to Jerusalem, they came to the towns of Bethphage and Bethany near the Mount of Olives. From there Jesus sent two of his followers and said to them, "Go to the town you can see there. When you enter it, you will quickly find a colt tied, which no one has ever ridden. Untie it and bring it here to me. If anyone asks you why you are doing this, tell him its Master needs the colt, and he will send it at once."

The followers went into the town, found a colt tied in the street near the door of a house, and untied it. Some people were standing there and asked, "What are you doing? Why are you untying that colt?" The followers answered the way Jesus told them to answer, and the people let them take the colt.

They brought the colt to Jesus and put their coats on it, and Jesus sat on it. Many people spread their coats on the road. Others cut branches in the fields and spread them on the road. The people were walking ahead of Jesus and behind him, shouting,

"Praise God!
God bless the One who comes in the
    name of the Lord!   *Psalm 118:26*
God bless the kingdom of our father
    David!
    That kingdom is coming!
Praise to God in heaven!"

Jesus entered Jerusalem and went into the Temple. After he had looked at everything, since it was already late, he went out to Bethany with the twelve apostles.

The next day as Jesus was leaving Bethany, he became hungry. Seeing a fig tree in leaf from far away, he went to see if it had any figs on it. But he found no figs, only leaves, because it was not the right season for figs. So Jesus said to the tree, "May no one ever eat fruit from you again." And Jesus' followers heard him say this.

Abraham Serves God Above All Else

*T*he LORD said to Abram, "Leave your country, your relatives, and your father's family, and go to the land I will show you."
    Genesis 12:1

*A*fter these things God tested Abraham's faith. God said to him, "Abraham!"

And he answered, "Here I am."

Then God said, "Take your only son, Isaac, the son you love, and go to the land of Moriah. Kill him there and offer him as a whole burnt offering on one of the mountains I will tell you about."

Then Abraham took his knife and was about to kill his son.

But the angel of the LORD called to him from heaven and said, "Abraham! Abraham!"

Abraham answered, "Yes."

The angel said, "Don't kill your son or hurt him in any way. Now I can see that you trust God and that you have not kept your son, your only son, from me."

Genesis 22:1–2, 10–12

God Blesses Abraham

*T*he LORD has greatly blessed my master in everything, and he has become a rich man. The LORD has given him many flocks of sheep, herds of cattle, silver and gold, male and female servants, camels, and horses."

Genesis 24:35

God Remembers Abraham

*S*tay in this land, and I will be with you and bless you. I will give you and your descendants all these lands, and I will keep the oath I made to Abraham your father. I will give you many descendants, as hard to count as the stars in the sky, and I will give them all these lands. Through your descendants all the nations on the earth will be blessed. I will do this because your father Abraham obeyed me. He did what I said and obeyed my commands, my teachings, and my rules."

From there Isaac went to Beersheba. The LORD appeared to him that night and said, "I am the God of your father Abraham. Don't be afraid, because I am with you. I will bless you and give you many descendants because of my servant Abraham." So Isaac built an altar and worshiped the LORD there. He also made a camp there, and his servants dug a well.

Genesis 26:3–5, 23–25

---

*W*e must squarely face the fact that the thought of service, except as a token or temporary activity, is distasteful. To accept a lower place is bad enough, but to choose a lower place—preposterous!

Words like obey, submit, serve, or worse, the expression "know your place," are met with defiance from a people who are obsessed with their "rights." Of course these rights are not wrong, and it is appropriate that there is legislation to protect rights. The problem is that legislation can only protect us from the bad; it cannot produce good in us. And it certainly cannot suggest to us that there might be some value in renouncing our rights for something or someone else. The Cross is the best evidence that there is much more to love than justice, much more to right than rights. A person who has won a public battle for human rights has done a good thing. But a person who has won a personal battle and given up human rights in the interest of human obligation has done a great thing. More often than not, the action will be labeled demeaning or ridiculous. So was the Cross.

Thomas Schmidt

---

*W*ho is our greatest example of being a servant of God? How far was he willing to go in serving others? What did God call his servant Abraham to do? How is God calling you to serve him? Are you willing to be his servant?

FRIDAY:
Pray with Conviction
Mark 11:15—12:12

NEW   TESTAMENT   READING

Jesus Goes to the Temple

*W*hen Jesus returned to Jerusalem, he went into the Temple and began to throw out those who were buying and selling there. He turned over the tables of those who were exchanging different kinds of money, and he upset the benches of those who were selling doves. Jesus refused to allow anyone to carry goods through the Temple courts. Then he taught the people, saying, "It is written in the Scriptures, 'My Temple will be called a house for prayer for people from all nations.' But you are changing God's house into a 'hideout for robbers.'"

The leading priests and the teachers of the law heard all this and began trying to find a way to kill Jesus. They were afraid of him, because all the people were amazed at his teaching. That evening, Jesus and his followers left the city.

The Power of Faith

*T*he next morning as Jesus was passing by with his followers, they saw the fig tree dry and dead, even to the roots. Peter remembered the tree and said to Jesus, "Teacher, look! The fig tree you cursed is dry and dead!"

Jesus answered, "Have faith in God. I tell you the truth, you can say to this mountain, 'Go, fall into the sea.' And if you have no doubts in your mind and believe that what you say will happen, God will do it for you. So I tell you to believe that you have received the things you ask for in prayer, and God will give them to you. When you are praying, if you are angry with someone, forgive him so that your Father in heaven will also forgive your sins."

Leaders Doubt Jesus' Authority

*J*esus and his followers went again to Jerusalem. As Jesus was walking in the Temple, the leading priests, the teachers of the law, and the older leaders came to him. They said to him, "What authority do you have to do these things? Who gave you this authority?"

Jesus answered, "I will ask you one question. If you answer me, I will tell you what authority I have to do these things. Tell me: When John baptized people, was that authority from God or just from other people?"

They argued about Jesus' question, saying, "If we answer, 'John's baptism was from God,' Jesus will say, 'Then why didn't you believe him?' But if we say, 'It was from other people,' the crowd will be against us." (These leaders were afraid of the people, because all the people believed that John was a prophet.)

So they answered Jesus, "We don't know."

Jesus said to them, "Then I won't tell you what authority I have to do these things."

A Story About God's Son

*J*esus began to use stories to teach the people. He said, "A man planted a vineyard. He put a wall around it and dug a hole for a winepress and built a tower. Then he leased the land to some farmers and left for a trip. When it was time for the grapes to be picked, he sent a servant to the farmers to get his share of the grapes. But the farmers grabbed the servant and beat him and sent him away empty-handed. Then the man sent another servant. They hit him on the head and showed no respect for him. So the man sent another servant, whom they killed. The man sent many other servants; the farmers beat some of them and killed others.

"The man had one person left to send, his son whom he loved. He sent him last of all, saying, 'They will respect my son.'

"But the farmers said to each other, 'This son will inherit the vineyard. If we kill him, it will be ours.' So they took the son, killed him, and threw him out of the vineyard.

"So what will the owner of the vineyard do? He will come and kill those farmers and will give the vineyard to other farmers. Surely you have read this Scripture:

'The stone that the builders rejected
    became the cornerstone.

The Lord did this,
and it is wonderful to us.'"

Psalm 118:22–23

The Jewish leaders knew that the story was about them. So they wanted to find a way to arrest Jesus, but they were afraid of the people. So the leaders left him and went away.

OLD TESTAMENT READING

*O*n the day that the LORD gave up the Amorites to the Israelites, Joshua stood before all the people of Israel and said to the LORD:

"Sun, stand still over Gibeon.
Moon, stand still over the Valley of
Aijalon."
So the sun stood still,
and the moon stopped
until the people defeated their
enemies.

These words are written in the Book of Jashar.

The sun stopped in the middle of the sky and waited to go down for a full day. That has never happened at any time before that day or since. That was the day the LORD listened to a human being. Truly the LORD was fighting for Israel!

Joshua 10:12–14

*T*he LORD is close to everyone who
prays to him,
to all who truly pray to him.
He gives those who respect him what
they want.
He listens when they cry, and he
saves them.

Psalm 145:18–19

*W*hen my life had almost gone,
I remembered the LORD.
I prayed to you,
and you heard my prayers in your
Holy Temple.

"People who worship useless idols
give up their loyalty to you.
But I will praise and thank you
while I give sacrifices to you,
and I will keep my promises to you.

Salvation comes from the LORD!"

Jonah 2:7–9

INSIGHTS

*H*ow do you pray a prayer so filled with faith that it can move a mountain? By shifting the focus from the size of your mountain to the sufficiency of the mountain mover, and by stepping forward in obedience. As you walk with God, your faith will grow, your confidence will increase and your prayer will have power.

While the children of Israel are perched on the edge of the Promised Land, twelve spies go out to survey it. Ten come back saying, "You wouldn't believe the size of the cities, the armies, the giants. We'd better look somewhere else." Two come back saying, "The God who is faithful promised he would give us the land, so let's go in his strength." Ten looked at the size of the mountain and fell back; only two looked at the sufficiency of the mountain mover and wanted to move forward. . . .

Probably every human being alive is standing in the shadow of at least one mountain that just will not move: a destructive habit, a character flaw, an impossible marriage or work situation, a financial problem, a physical disability. What is your immovable mountain? Have you stood in its shadow for so long that you've grown accustomed to the darkness? Do you end your prayers by thinking, What's the use?

I challenge you to shift the focus of your prayer. Don't spend a lot of time describing your mountain to the Lord. He knows what it is. Instead, focus your attention on the mountain mover—his glory, power and faithfulness. Then start walking in faith, following his leading, and watch that mountain step aside.

Bill Hybels

ACTION POINT

*H*ow does God want us to ask him for what we need (Mark 11:22–26)? In what remarkable ways has God answered your prayers? Write a psalm about prayer that will help you pray with conviction.

WEEKEND:
The Wicked Persecute the Righteous
Mark 12:13–31

Is It Right To Pay Taxes or Not?

*L*ater, the Jewish leaders sent some Pharisees and Herodians to Jesus to trap him in saying something wrong. They came to him and said, "Teacher, we know that you are an honest man. You are not afraid of what other people think about you, because you pay no attention to who they are. And you teach the truth about God's way. Tell us: Is it right to pay taxes to Caesar or not? Should we pay them, or not?"

But knowing what these men were really trying to do, Jesus said to them, "Why are you trying to trap me? Bring me a coin to look at." They gave Jesus a coin, and he asked, "Whose image and name are on the coin?"

They answered, "Caesar's."

Then Jesus said to them, "Give to Caesar the things that are Caesar's, and give to God the things that are God's." The men were amazed at what Jesus said.

Some Sadducees Try to Trick Jesus

*T*hen some Sadducees came to Jesus and asked him a question. (Sadducees believed that people would not rise from the dead.) They said, "Teacher, Moses wrote that if a man's brother dies, leaving a wife but no children, then that man must marry the widow and have children for his brother. Once there were seven brothers. The first brother married and died, leaving no children. So the second brother married the widow, but he also died and had no children. The same thing happened with the third brother. All seven brothers married her and died, and none of the brothers had any children. Finally the woman died too. Since all seven brothers had married her, when people rise from the dead, whose wife will she be?"

Jesus answered, "Why don't you understand? Don't you know what the Scriptures say, and don't you know about the power of God? When people rise from the dead, they will not marry, nor will they be given to someone to marry. They will be like the angels in heaven. Surely you have read what God said about people rising from the dead. In the book in which Moses wrote about the burning bush, it says that God told Moses, 'I am the God of Abraham, the God of Isaac, and the God of Jacob.' God is the God of the living, not the dead. You Sadducees are wrong!"

The Most Important Command

*O*ne of the teachers of the law came and heard Jesus arguing with the Sadducees. Seeing that Jesus gave good answers to their questions, he asked Jesus, "Which of the commands is most important?"

Jesus answered, "The most important command is this: 'Listen, people of Israel! The Lord our God is the only Lord. Love the Lord your God with all your heart, all your soul, all your mind, and all your strength.' The second command is this: 'Love your neighbor as you love yourself.' There are no commands more important than these."

*T*hose who lead good people to do wrong
 will be ruined by their own evil,
 but the innocent will be rewarded
  with good things.

Proverbs 28:10

*L*ORD, rescue me from evil people;
 protect me from cruel people
who make evil plans,
 who always start fights.
They make their tongues sharp as a
  snake's;
 their words are like snake poison.

Selah

LORD, guard me from the power of
  wicked people;
 protect me from cruel people
who plan to trip me up.
The proud hid a trap for me.
 They spread out a net beside the road;
 they set traps for me. *Selah*

120

I said to the LORD, "You are my God."
  LORD, listen to my prayer for help.
LORD God, my mighty savior,
  you protect me in battle.
LORD, do not give the wicked what they
  want.
  Don't let their plans succeed,
  or they will become proud.   *Selah*
                              Psalm 140:1–8

LORD my God, I trust in you for
    protection.
  Save me and rescue me
  from those who are chasing me.
Otherwise, like a lion they will tear me
    apart.
  They will rip me to pieces, and no
    one can save me.

There are people who think up evil
  and plan trouble and tell lies.
They dig a hole to trap others,
  but they will fall into it themselves.
They will get themselves into trouble;
  the violence they cause will hurt
    only themselves.

I praise the LORD because he does what
  is right.
  I sing praises to the LORD Most
    High.
                              Psalm 7:1–2, 14–17

Hide me from those who plan wicked
    things,
  from that gang who does evil.
They sharpen their tongues like swords
  and shoot bitter words like arrows.
From their hiding places they shoot at
    innocent people;
  they shoot suddenly and are not
    afraid.
They encourage each other to do
    wrong.
  They talk about setting traps,
  thinking no one will see them.
                              Psalm 64:2–5

The reproach we experience is the natural resentment in the hearts of men toward all that is godly and righteous. This is the cross

we are to bear. This is why Christians are often persecuted. . . .

Let us not forget that there is happiness and blessing in persecution. As George MacDonald puts it, we become "hearty through hardship." . . .

Our Lord instructs the persecuted to be happy. "Rejoice," He said, "and be exceeding glad: for great is your reward in heaven: for so persecuted they the prophets which were before you" (Matthew 5:12).

The word joy has all but disappeared from our current Christian vocabulary. One of the reasons is that we have thought that joy and happiness were found in comfort, ease and luxury. James did not say, "Count it all joy when you fall into an easy chair," but he said "Count it all joy when you fall into divers temptations" (James 1:2).

The persecuted are happy because they are being processed for heaven. Persecution is one of the natural consequences of living the Christian life. It is to the Christian what "growing pains" are to the growing child. No pain, no development. No suffering, no glory. No struggle, no victory. No persecution, no reward! Jesus predicted that if they persecuted Him, they would persecute you who follow Him, too.

                              Billy Graham

*H*ave you ever felt that you've unwittingly walked into a trap designed to test your Christian commitment? If so, be glad—you must be an effective witness! Pray that God will give you the strength and wisdom to face such encounters.

MONDAY:

Give Generously, Even Sacrificially, to God

Mark 12:32—13:10

*T*he man answered, "That was a good answer, Teacher. You were right when you said God is the only Lord and there is no other God besides him. One must love God with all his heart, all his mind, and all his strength. And one must love his neighbor as he loves himself. These commands are more important than all the animals and sacrifices we offer to God."

When Jesus saw that the man answered him wisely, Jesus said to him, "You are close to the kingdom of God." And after that, no one was brave enough to ask Jesus any more questions.

As Jesus was teaching in the Temple, he asked, "Why do the teachers of the law say that the Christ is the son of David? David himself, speaking by the Holy Spirit, said:
'The Lord said to my Lord:
Sit by me at my right side,
until I put your enemies under your control.' *Psalm 110:1*
David himself calls the Christ 'Lord,' so how can the Christ be his son?" The large crowd listened to Jesus with pleasure.

Jesus continued teaching and said, "Beware of the teachers of the law. They like to walk around wearing fancy clothes, and they love for people to greet them with respect in the marketplaces. They love to have the most important seats in the synagogues and at feasts. But they cheat widows and steal their houses and then try to make themselves look good by saying long prayers. They will receive a greater punishment."

True Giving

*J*esus sat near the Temple money box and watched the people put in their money. Many rich people gave large sums of money. Then a poor widow came and put in two small copper coins, which were only worth a few cents.

Calling his followers to him, Jesus said, "I tell you the truth, this poor widow gave more than all those rich people. They gave only what they did not need. This woman is very poor, but she gave all she had; she gave all she had to live on."

The Temple Will Be Destroyed

*A*s Jesus was leaving the Temple, one of his followers said to him, "Look, Teacher! How beautiful the buildings are! How big the stones are!"

Jesus said, "Do you see all these great buildings? Not one stone will be left on another. Every stone will be thrown down to the ground."

Later, as Jesus was sitting on the Mount of Olives, opposite the Temple, he was alone with Peter, James, John, and Andrew. They asked Jesus, "Tell us, when will these things happen? And what will be the sign that they are going to happen?"

Jesus began to answer them, "Be careful that no one fools you. Many people will come in my name, saying, 'I am the One,' and they will fool many people. When you hear about wars and stories of wars that are coming, don't be afraid. These things must happen before the end comes. Nations will fight against other nations, and kingdoms against other kingdoms. There will be earthquakes in different places, and there will be times when there is no food for people to eat. These things are like the first pains when something new is about to be born.

"You must be careful. People will arrest you and take you to court and beat you in their synagogues. You will be forced to stand before kings and governors, to tell them about me. This will happen to you because you follow me. But before these things happen, the Good News must be told to all people."

*S*hould a person rob God? But you are robbing me.

"You ask, 'How have we robbed you?'

"You have robbed me in your offerings and the tenth of your crops. So a curse is on you, because the whole nation has robbed me. Bring to the storehouse a full tenth of what you earn so there will be food in my house. Test me in this," says the LORD All-Powerful. "I will open the windows of heaven for you and pour out all the blessings you need. I will stop the insects so they won't eat your crops. The grapes won't fall from your vines before they are ready to pick," says the LORD All-Powerful. "All the nations will call you blessed, because you will have a pleasant country," says the LORD All-Powerful.

Malachi 3:8–12

*H*onor the LORD with your wealth
　　and the firstfruits from all your
　　　　crops.
Then your barns will be full,
　　and your wine barrels will overflow
　　　　with new wine.

Proverbs 3:9–10

*M*oses said to all the Israelites, "This is what the LORD has commanded: From what you have, take an offering for the LORD. Let everyone who is willing bring this offering to the LORD: gold, silver, bronze, blue, purple and red thread, and fine linen, goat hair and male sheepskins that are colored red. They may also bring fine leather, acacia wood, olive oil for the lamps, spices for the special olive oil used for appointing priests and for the sweet-smelling incense, onyx stones, and other jewels to be put on the holy vest and chest covering of the priests."

Exodus 35:4–9

*T*hey received from Moses everything the people of Israel had brought as gifts to build the Holy Tent. The people continued to bring gifts each morning because they wanted to. So all the skilled workers left the work they were doing on the Holy Tent, and they said to Moses, "The people are bringing more than we need to do the work the LORD commanded."

Then Moses sent this command throughout the camp: "No man or woman should make anything else as a gift for the Holy Tent." So the people were kept from giving more, because what they had was already more than enough to do all the work.

Exodus 36:3–7

---

*M*any beloved saints are depriving themselves of wondrous spiritual blessing by not giving as stewards what is entrusted to them. They act as if it were their own, as if all belonged to them, as if already they were in possession of the inheritance incorruptible and undefiled; forgetting that they have nothing whatever which is their own, that they are bought by the precious blood of Christ, and all they possess—their bodily strength, their time, their talents, their business, their professions, their eyes, their hands, their feet, all belong to the Lord Jesus Christ; because He has bought them with his precious blood. . . .

Just as we are constrained by the love of Christ, so God condescends to use us; and as we give, He is pleased to entrust to us more and more. . . .

My advice is this: if the reader has as yet but little knowledge and little grace, let him accordingly begin with a small percentage, yea, though it were ever so small a percentage, only let him be true to God, and put aside for Him habitually as He may be pleased to prosper him. In this way blessing for the soul will be reaped, will be abundantly reaped, and soon will the desire spring up in the heart to increase the proportion of returns to the Lord. This way will more and more lead the heart to such a state to be only a steward for the Lord, and to be willing to stand with all we have and are before the Lord as His stewards.

George Müller

PAUSE　FOR　REFLECTION

*W*hat does God promise to those who give generously to him? To those who do not? Reread the Exodus passages. Can you imagine God's people today giving so much that they would have to be told to stop?

TUESDAY:

Be Strong
During the End Times
Mark 13:11–37

NEW TESTAMENT READING

*W*hen you are arrested and judged, don't worry ahead of time about what you should say. Say whatever is given you to say at that time, because it will not really be you speaking; it will be the Holy Spirit.

"Brothers will give their own brothers to be killed, and fathers will give their own children to be killed. Children will fight against their own parents and cause them to be put to death. All people will hate you because you follow me, but those people who keep their faith until the end will be saved.

"You will see 'the destroying terror' standing where it should not be." (You who read this should understand what it means.) "At that time, the people in Judea should run away to the mountains. If people are on the roofs of their houses, they must not go down or go inside to get anything out of their houses. If people are in the fields, they must not go back to get their coats. At that time, how terrible it will be for women who are pregnant or have nursing babies! Pray that these things will not happen in winter, because those days will be full of trouble. There will be more trouble than there has ever been since the beginning, when God made the world, until now, and nothing as bad will ever happen again. God has decided to make that terrible time short. Otherwise, no one would go on living. But God will make that time short to help the people he has chosen. At that time, someone might say to you, 'Look, there is the Christ!' Or another person might say, 'There he is!' But don't believe them. False Christs and false prophets will come and perform great wonders and miracles. They will try to fool even the people God has chosen, if that is possible. So be careful. I have warned you about all this before it happens.

"During the days after this trouble comes,
 'the sun will grow dark,
  and the moon will not give its light.
 The stars will fall from the sky.
 And the powers of the heavens will
  be shaken.' *Isaiah 13:10; 34:4*

"Then people will see the Son of Man coming in clouds with great power and glory. Then he will send his angels all around the earth to gather his chosen people from every part of the earth and from every part of heaven.

"Learn a lesson from the fig tree: When its branches become green and soft and new leaves appear, you know summer is near. In the same way, when you see these things happening, you will know that the time is near, ready to come. I tell you the truth, all these things will happen while the people of this time are still living. Earth and sky will be destroyed, but the words I have said will never be destroyed.

"No one knows when that day or time will be, not the angels in heaven, not even the Son. Only the Father knows. Be careful! Always be ready, because you don't know when that time will be. It is like a man who goes on a trip. He leaves his house and lets his servants take care of it, giving each one a special job to do. The man tells the servant guarding the door always to be watchful. So always be ready, because you don't know when the owner of the house will come back. It might be in the evening, or at midnight, or in the morning while it is still dark, or when the sun rises. Always be ready. Otherwise he might come back suddenly and find you sleeping. I tell you this, and I say this to everyone: 'Be ready!'"

OLD TESTAMENT READING

*T*hose who are wise will help the others understand what is happening. But they will be killed with swords, or burned, or taken captive, or robbed of their homes and possessions. These things will continue for many days. When the wise ones are suffering, they will get a little help, but many who join the wise ones will not help them in their time of need. Some of the wise ones will be killed. But the hard times must come so they can be made stronger and purer and without faults until the time of the end comes. Then, at the right time, the end will come."

Daniel 11:33–35

I trust in the LORD for protection.
So why do you say to me,
"Fly like a bird to your mountain.
Like hunters, the wicked string their
bows;
they set their arrows on the bow-
strings.
They shoot from dark places
at those who are honest.
When all that is good falls apart,
what can good people do?"

The LORD is in his holy temple;
the LORD sits on his throne in heaven.
He sees what people do;
he keeps his eye on them.
The LORD tests those who do right,
but he hates the wicked and those
who love to hurt others.
He will send hot coals and burning
sulfur on the wicked.
A whirlwind is what they will get.
The LORD does what is right, and he
loves justice,
so honest people will see his face.

Psalm 11

*A*fter the four hundred thirty-four years the appointed leader will be killed; he will have nothing. The people of the leader who is to come will destroy the city and the holy place. The end of the city will come like a flood, and war will continue until the end. God has ordered that place to be completely destroyed. That leader will make firm an agreement with many people for seven years. He will stop the offerings and sacrifices after three and one-half years. A destroyer will do terrible things until the ordered end comes to the destroyed city."

Daniel 9:26–27

INSIGHTS

My hope is built on nothing less
Than Jesus' blood and righteousness;
I dare not trust the sweetest frame,

But wholly lean on Jesus' name.
On Christ, the solid Rock, I stand:
All other ground is sinking sand.

When darkness veils His lovely face,
I rest on His unchanging grace;
In ev'ry high and stormy gale,
My anchor holds within the veil.
On Christ, the solid Rock, I stand:
All other ground is sinking sand.

His oath, His covenant, His blood,
Support me in the whelming flood;
When all around my soul gives way,
He then is all my hope and stay.
On Christ, the solid Rock I stand:
All other ground is sinking sand.

When He shall come with trumpet sound,
O may I then in Him be found:
Dressed in His righteousness alone,
Faultless to stand before the throne.
On Christ, the solid Rock, I stand:
All other ground is sinking sand.

Edward Mote

PAUSE FOR REFLECTION

*W*hat are God's people to be and do during the end times? What is the purpose of their suffering during that time? On what can God's righteous ones depend during that time?

125

WEDNESDAY:

The Passover and the Lord's Supper

Mark 14:1–26

NEW TESTAMENT READING

The Plan to Kill Jesus

*I*t was now only two days before the Passover and the Feast of Unleavened Bread. The leading priests and teachers of the law were trying to find a trick to arrest Jesus and kill him. But they said, "We must not do it during the feast, because the people might cause a riot."

A Woman with Perfume for Jesus

*J*esus was in Bethany at the house of Simon, who had a skin disease. While Jesus was eating there, a woman approached him with an alabaster jar filled with very expensive perfume, made of pure nard. She opened the jar and poured the perfume on Jesus' head.

Some who were there became upset and said to each other, "Why waste that perfume? It was worth a full year's work. It could have been sold and the money given to the poor." And they got very angry with the woman.

Jesus said, "Leave her alone. Why are you troubling her? She did an excellent thing for me. You will always have the poor with you, and you can help them anytime you want. But you will not always have me. This woman did the only thing she could do for me; she poured perfume on my body to prepare me for burial. I tell you the truth, wherever the Good News is preached in all the world, what this woman has done will be told, and people will remember her."

Judas Becomes an Enemy of Jesus

*O*ne of the twelve apostles, Judas Iscariot, went to talk to the leading priests to offer to hand Jesus over to them. These priests were pleased about this and promised to pay Judas money. So he watched for the best time to turn Jesus in.

Jesus Eats the Passover Meal

*I*t was now the first day of the Feast of Unleavened Bread when the Passover lamb was sacrificed. Jesus' followers said to him, "Where do you want us to go and prepare for you to eat the Passover meal?"

Jesus sent two of his followers and said to them, "Go into the city and a man carrying a jar of water will meet you. Follow him. When he goes into a house, tell the owner of the house, 'The Teacher says: Where is my guest room in which I can eat the Passover meal with my followers?' The owner will show you a large room upstairs that is furnished and ready. Prepare the food for us there."

So the followers left and went into the city. Everything happened as Jesus had said, so they prepared the Passover meal.

In the evening, Jesus went to that house with the twelve. While they were all eating, Jesus said, "I tell you the truth, one of you will turn against me—one of you eating with me now."

The followers were very sad to hear this. Each one began to say to Jesus, "I am not the one, am I?"

Jesus answered, "It is one of the twelve— the one who dips his bread into the bowl with me. The Son of Man will die, just as the Scriptures say. But how terrible it will be for the person who hands the Son of Man over to be killed. It would be better for him if he had never been born."

The Lord's Supper

*W*hile they were eating, Jesus took some bread and thanked God for it and broke it. Then he gave it to his followers and said, "Take it; this is my body."

Then Jesus took a cup and thanked God for it and gave it to the followers, and they all drank from the cup.

Then Jesus said, "This is my blood which is the new agreement that God makes with his people. This blood is poured out for many. I tell you the truth, I will not drink of this fruit of the vine again until that day when I drink it new in the kingdom of God."

After singing a hymn, they went out to the Mount of Olives.

*T*he LORD spoke to Moses and Aaron in the land of Egypt: "This month will be the beginning of months, the first month of the year for you. Tell the whole community of Israel that on the tenth day of this month each man must get one lamb for the people in his house. If there are not enough people in his house to eat a whole lamb, he must share it with his closest neighbor, considering the number of people. There must be enough lamb for everyone to eat. The lamb must be a one-year-old male that has nothing wrong with it. This animal can be either a young sheep or a young goat. Take care of the animals until the fourteenth day of the month. On that day all the people of the community of Israel will kill them in the evening before dark. The people must take some of the blood and put it on the sides and tops of the doorframes of the houses where they eat the lambs. On this night they must roast the lamb over a fire. They must eat it with bitter herbs and bread made without yeast. Do not eat the lamb raw or boiled in water. Roast the whole lamb over a fire—with its head, legs, and inner organs. You must not leave any of it until morning, but if any of it is left over until morning, you must burn it with fire.

"This is the way you must eat it: You must be fully dressed as if you were going on a trip. You must have your sandals on and your walking stick in your hand. You must eat it in a hurry; this is the LORD's Passover.

"That night I will go through the land of Egypt and kill all the firstborn animals and people in the land of Egypt. I will also punish all the gods of Egypt. I am the LORD. But the blood will be a sign on the houses where you are. When I see the blood, I will pass over you. Nothing terrible will hurt you when I punish the land of Egypt.

"You are always to remember this day and celebrate it with a feast to the LORD. Your descendants are to honor the LORD with this feast from now on.

"You must keep this command as a law for you and your descendants from now on.

Do this when you go to the land the LORD has promised to give you. When your children ask you, 'Why are we doing these things?' you will say, 'This is the Passover sacrifice to honor the LORD. When we were in Egypt, the LORD passed over the houses of Israel, and when he killed the Egyptians, he saved our homes.'" Then the people bowed down and worshiped the LORD.

Exodus 12:1–14, 24–27

INSIGHTS

*R*ight *down to the present, Jews reenact the Passover-event in celebration of their redemption from Egypt. . . .*

In this service, words are connected with ritual, symbol, and gesture. It is a drama, a reenactment of the flight of Israel from the land of Pharaoh. It is not only a past event, but a present reality. For, although the Exodus happened in the past, its power and meaning reach down into history and change the lives of people now as did the original event. Reenactment of the action still has the power to change lives. . . .

The church has also retained the Old Testament principle that the event being celebrated becomes contemporaneous: Paul referred to the Table as a "participation" in Christ (1 Cor. 10:16). It is important to understand, though, that the death and resurrection of Jesus Christ is not an event which we memorialize. Its power, like that of the Exodus, reaches down through history and becomes a present reality to the people who celebrate it in faith.

Robert Webber

PAUSE FOR REFLECTION

*R*eread *the Old Testament passage and try to feel the drama and significance of the Passover celebration. With this worship experience in mind, what feelings and awareness related to Jesus' celebration of the Lord's Supper (Mark 14:22–26) stir within you?*

127

THURSDAY:
Kneel Before God in Prayer
Mark 14:27–52

NEW TESTAMENT READING

Jesus' Followers Will Leave Him

*T*hen Jesus told the followers, "You will all stumble in your faith, because it is written in the Scriptures:
'I will kill the shepherd,
and the sheep will scatter.'

Zechariah 13:7

But after I rise from the dead, I will go ahead of you into Galilee."

Peter said, "Everyone else may stumble in their faith, but I will not."

Jesus answered, "I tell you the truth, tonight before the rooster crows twice you will say three times you don't know me."

But Peter insisted, "I will never say that I don't know you! I will even die with you!" And all the other followers said the same thing.

Jesus Prays Alone

*J*esus and his followers went to a place called Gethsemane. He said to them, "Sit here while I pray." Jesus took Peter, James, and John with him, and he began to be very sad and troubled. He said to them, "My heart is full of sorrow, to the point of death. Stay here and watch."

After walking a little farther away from them, Jesus fell to the ground and prayed that, if possible, he would not have this time of suffering. He prayed, "Abba, Father! You can do all things. Take away this cup of suffering. But do what you want, not what I want."

Then Jesus went back to his followers and found them asleep. He said to Peter, "Simon, are you sleeping? Couldn't you stay awake with me for one hour? Stay awake and pray for strength against temptation. The spirit wants to do what is right, but the body is weak."

Again Jesus went away and prayed the same thing. Then he went back to his fol-lowers, and again he found them asleep, because their eyes were very heavy. And they did not know what to say to him.

After Jesus prayed a third time, he went back to his followers and said to them, "Are you still sleeping and resting? That's enough. The time has come for the Son of Man to be handed over to sinful people. Get up, we must go. Look, here comes the man who has turned against me."

Jesus Is Arrested

*A*t once, while Jesus was still speaking, Judas, one of the twelve apostles, came up. With him were many people carrying swords and clubs who had been sent from the leading priests, the teachers of the law, and the older Jewish leaders.

Judas had planned a signal for them, saying, "The man I kiss is Jesus. Arrest him and guard him while you lead him away." So Judas went straight to Jesus and said, "Teacher!" and kissed him. Then the people grabbed Jesus and arrested him. One of his followers standing nearby pulled out his sword and struck the servant of the high priest and cut off his ear.

Then Jesus said, "You came to get me with swords and clubs as if I were a criminal. Every day I was with you teaching in the Temple, and you did not arrest me there. But all these things have happened to make the Scriptures come true." Then all of Jesus' followers left him and ran away.

A young man, wearing only a linen cloth, was following Jesus, and the people also grabbed him. But the cloth he was wearing came off, and he ran away naked.

OLD TESTAMENT READING

*S*olomon prayed this prayer to the LORD, kneeling in front of the altar with his arms raised toward heaven. When he finished praying, he got up. Then, in a loud voice, he stood and blessed all the people of Israel, saying: "Praise the LORD! He promised he would give rest to his people Israel, and he has given us rest. The LORD has kept all the good promises he gave through his servant Moses. May the LORD our God be with us as he was with our ancestors. May he never leave us, and may he turn us to himself so we will follow him. Let us obey all the laws and commands he gave our ancestors. May the LORD our God remember this prayer day and night and do what is right for his servant and his people Israel day by day.

1 Kings 8:54–59

*E*ven though Daniel knew that the new law had been written, he went to pray in an upstairs room in his house, which had windows that opened toward Jerusalem. Three times each day Daniel would kneel down to pray and thank God, just as he always had done.

Daniel 6:10

*A*fter these things had been done, the leaders came to me and said, "Ezra, the Israelites, including the priests and Levites, have not kept themselves separate from the people around us. Those neighbors do evil things, as the Canaanites, Hittites, Perizzites, Jebusites, Ammonites, Moabites, Egyptians, and Amorites did. The Israelite men and their sons have married these women. They have mixed the people who belong to God with the people around them. The leaders and officers of Israel have led the rest of the Israelites to do this unfaithful thing."

When I heard this, I angrily tore my robe and coat, pulled hair from my head and beard, and sat down in shock. Everyone who trembled in fear at the word of the God of Israel gathered around me because of the unfaithfulness of the captives who had returned. I sat there in shock until the evening sacrifice.

At the evening sacrifice I got up from where I had shown my shame. My robe and coat were torn, and I fell on my knees with my hands spread out to the LORD my God. I prayed,

"My God, I am too ashamed and embarrassed to lift up my face to you, my God, because our sins are so many. They are higher than our heads. Our guilt even reaches up to the sky."

Ezra 9:1–6

That when I kneel in Your presence
To ask Your forgiveness
I am utterly stripped of facade.
You accept no big-name references
No high-caliber recommendations.
Extenuating circumstances
Crumble to dust
In Your court of appeal . . .
I am forgiven never
Because of inherited tendencies
Or emotional discomfort
Or nagging weakness . . .
I can never plead
Corrupt environment
Or life's strange twistings
Or my own unbelievable stupidity . . .
Ultimately I have one solitary defense.
Only one—
But always one:
Forgive me, God
For Jesus' sake.
Like a song unending
The words keep singing . . .
I am totally forgiven
I am continually cleansed
Just for Jesus' sake.

Ruth Calkin

PAUSE FOR REFLECTION

*W*hat physical posture did these men of God assume when they offered their heartfelt prayers to God? Do you think there is a difference between kneeling, sitting, or standing before God in prayer? How do you pray most earnestly to God?

INSIGHTS

*T*he powerful reality grips me, Lord

FRIDAY:

Accused by the Wicked, the Blameless Stand Innocent Before God

Mark 14:52—15:5

Jesus Before the Leaders

*T*he people who arrested Jesus led him to the house of the high priest, where all the leading priests, the older Jewish leaders, and the teachers of the law were gathered. Peter followed far behind and entered the courtyard of the high priest's house. There he sat with the guards, warming himself by the fire.

The leading priests and the whole Jewish council tried to find something that Jesus had done wrong so they could kill him. But the council could find no proof of anything. Many people came and told false things about him, but all said different things—none of them agreed.

Then some people stood up and lied about Jesus, saying, "We heard this man say, 'I will destroy this Temple that people made. And three days later, I will build another Temple not made by people.'" But even the things these people said did not agree.

Then the high priest stood before them and asked Jesus, "Aren't you going to answer? Don't you have something to say about their charges against you?" But Jesus said nothing; he did not answer.

The high priest asked Jesus another question: "Are you the Christ, the Son of the blessed God?"

Jesus answered, "I am. And in the future you will see the Son of Man sitting at the right hand of God, the Powerful One, and coming on clouds in the sky."

When the high priest heard this, he tore his clothes and said, "We don't need any more witnesses! You all heard him say these things against God. What do you think?"

They all said that Jesus was guilty and should die. Some of the people there began to spit at Jesus. They blindfolded him and beat him with their fists and said, "Prove you are a prophet!" Then the guards led Jesus away and beat him.

Peter Denies Knowing Jesus

*W*hile Peter was in the courtyard, a servant girl of the high priest came there. She saw Peter warming himself at the fire and looked closely at him.

Then she said, "You also were with Jesus, that man from Nazareth."

But Peter said that he was never with Jesus. He said, "I don't know or understand what you are talking about." Then Peter left and went toward the entrance of the courtyard. And the rooster crowed.

The servant girl saw Peter there, and again she said to the people who were standing nearby, "This man is one of those who followed Jesus." Again Peter said that it was not true.

A short time later, some people were standing near Peter saying, "Surely you are one of those who followed Jesus, because you are from Galilee, too."

Then Peter began to place a curse on himself and swear, "I don't know this man you're talking about!"

At once, the rooster crowed the second time. Then Peter remembered what Jesus had told him: "Before the rooster crows twice, you will say three times that you don't know me." Then Peter lost control of himself and began to cry.

Pilate Questions Jesus

*V*ery early in the morning, the leading priests, the older leaders, the teachers of the law, and all the Jewish council decided what to do with Jesus. They tied him, led him away, and turned him over to Pilate, the governor.

Pilate asked Jesus, "Are you the king of the Jews?"

Jesus answered, "Those are your words."

The leading priests accused Jesus of many things. So Pilate asked Jesus another question, "You can see that they are accusing you of many things. Aren't you going to answer?"

But Jesus still said nothing, so Pilate was very surprised.

*T*he LORD is my light and the one who
saves me.
I fear no one.
The LORD protects my life;
I am afraid of no one.
Evil people may try to destroy my
body.
My enemies and those who hate me
attack me,
but they are overwhelmed and de-
feated.
If an army surrounds me,
I will not be afraid.
If war breaks out,
I will trust the LORD.

I ask only one thing from the LORD.
This is what I want:
Let me live in the LORD's house
all my life.
Let me see the Lord's beauty
and look with my own eyes at his
Temple.

Psalm 27:1–4

*L*ORD, defend me because I have lived
an innocent life.
I have trusted the LORD and never
doubted.
LORD, try me and test me;
look closely into my heart and mind.
I see your love,
and I live by your truth.
I do not spend time with liars,
nor do I make friends with those
who hide their sin.
I hate the company of evil people,
and I won't sit with the wicked.
I wash my hands to show I am
innocent,
and I come to your altar, LORD.

Psalm 26:1–6

*O*ne witness is not enough to accuse a person of a crime or sin. A case must be proved
by two or three witnesses.

If a witness lies and accuses a person of
a crime, the two people who are arguing
must stand in the presence of the LORD
before the priests and judges who are on

duty. The judges must check the matter
carefully. The witness who is a liar, lying
about a fellow Israelite, must be punished.
He must be punished in the same way the
other person would have been punished.
You must get rid of the evil among you.

Deuteronomy 19:15–19

INSIGHTS

*H*ere is a secret to the spiritual strength that
willingly suffers wrong: accustom yourself in
everything that happens to recognize the hand
and will of God. Whether it be some great
wrong that is done you, or some little offense
that you meet in daily life, before you consider
the person who did it, first be still and remember, God allows me to come into this
trouble to see if I will glorify Him in it. This
trial, be it great or small, is allowed by God
and is His will concerning me. Let me first
recognize and submit to God's will in it. Then
with the peace of God which this gives, I will
receive wisdom to know how to behave in it.
With my eye turned from man to God, suffering wrong takes on this new dimension.
. . . Jesus saw beyond the temporal injus-
tice and was satisfied to leave the vindica-
tion of His rights and honor in God's hands;
He knew they were safe with Him. Peter
writes, "He committed himself to him that
judgeth righteously" (2:23). It was settled
between the Father and the Son: the Son was
not to care for His own honor, but only for
the Father's. The Father would care for the
Son's honor. Let the believer follow Christ's
example in this; it will give him such rest and
peace. Commit your right and your honor into
God's keeping. Meet every offense that man
commits against you with the firm trust that
God will watch over and care for you.

Andrew Murray

PAUSE   FOR   REFLECTION

*H*ow important is innocence in God's eyes?
Think about the total trust Jesus had in his
Father—a trust that enabled him to stand
innocent before God without having to prove
his innocence to his accusers.

WEEKEND:
Jesus Suffered for Us
Mark 15:6–32

Pilate Tries to Free Jesus

*E*very year at the time of the Passover the governor would free one prisoner whom the people chose. At that time, there was a man named Barabbas in prison who was a rebel and had committed murder during a riot. The crowd came to Pilate and began to ask him to free a prisoner as he always did.

So Pilate asked them, "Do you want me to free the king of the Jews?" Pilate knew that the leading priests had turned Jesus in to him because they were jealous. But the leading priests had persuaded the people to ask Pilate to free Barabbas, not Jesus.

Then Pilate asked the crowd again, "So what should I do with this man you call the king of the Jews?"

They shouted, "Crucify him!"

Pilate asked, "Why? What wrong has he done?"

But they shouted even louder, "Crucify him!"

Pilate wanted to please the crowd, so he freed Barabbas for them. After having Jesus beaten with whips, he handed Jesus over to the soldiers to be crucified.

The soldiers took Jesus into the governor's palace (called the Praetorium) and called all the other soldiers together. They put a purple robe on Jesus and used thorny branches to make a crown for his head. They began to call out to him, "Hail, King of the Jews!" The soldiers beat Jesus on the head many times with a stick. They spit on him and made fun of him by bowing on their knees and worshiping him. After they finished, the soldiers took off the purple robe and put his own clothes on him again. Then they led him out of the palace to be crucified.

Jesus Is Crucified

A man named Simon from Cyrene, the father of Alexander and Rufus, was coming from the fields to the city. The soldiers forced Simon to carry the cross for Jesus. They led Jesus to the place called Golgotha, which means the Place of the Skull. The soldiers tried to give Jesus wine mixed with myrrh to drink, but he refused. The soldiers crucified Jesus and divided his clothes among themselves, throwing lots to decide what each soldier would get.

It was nine o'clock in the morning when they crucified Jesus. There was a sign with this charge against Jesus written on it: THE KING OF THE JEWS. They also put two robbers on crosses beside Jesus, one on the right, and the other on the left. People walked by and insulted Jesus and shook their heads, saying, "You said you could destroy the Temple and build it again in three days. So save yourself! Come down from that cross!"

The leading priests and the teachers of the law were also making fun of Jesus. They said to each other, "He saved other people, but he can't save himself. If he is really the Christ, the king of Israel, let him come down now from the cross. When we see this, we will believe in him." The robbers who were being crucified beside Jesus also insulted him.

---

*E*vil people have surrounded me;
    like dogs they have trapped me.
    They have bitten my arms and legs.
I can count all my bones;
    people look and stare at me.
They divided my clothes among them,
    and they threw lots for my clothing.

But, LORD, don't be far away.
    You are my strength; hurry to help
    me.
Save me from the sword;
    save my life from the dogs.
Rescue me from the lion's mouth;
    save me from the horns of the bulls.

Then I will tell my fellow Israelites
    about you;
I will praise you in the public
    meeting.
Praise the LORD, all you who respect
    him.

All you descendants of Jacob, honor
him;
fear him, all you Israelites.
He does not ignore those in trouble.
He doesn't hide from them
but listens when they call out to him.
LORD, I praise you in the great meeting
of your people;
these worshipers will see me do
what I promised.
Poor people will eat until they are full;
those who look to the LORD will
praise him.
May your hearts live forever!
People everywhere will remember
and will turn to the LORD.
All the families of the nations
will worship him
because the LORD is King,
and he rules the nations.

All the powerful people on earth will eat
and worship.
Everyone will bow down to him,
all who will one day die.
The people in the future will serve him;
they will always be told about the
Lord.
They will tell that he does what is right.
People who are not yet born
will hear what God has done.

Psalm 22:16–31

text. I have often thought I would, but it is so
high that I can never climb to its height, I
have just quoted it and passed on. Who can
fathom the depth of those words: "God so loved
the world"? We can never scale the heights of
His love, or fathom its depths. Paul prayed
that he might know the height, the depth, the
length, and the breadth of the love of God;
but it was past his finding out. . . .*

*Nothing speaks to us of the love of God like
the Cross of Christ. Come with me to Calvary,
and look upon the Son of God as He hangs
there. Can you hear that piercing cry from
His dying lips: "Father, forgive them; for they
know not what they do!" and say that He does
not love you? "Greater love hath no man than
this, that a man lay down his life for his
friends" (John 15:13). But Jesus Christ laid
down His life for His enemies.*

*Another thought is this: He loved us long
before we ever thought of Him. The idea that
He does not love us until we first love Him is
not to be found in Scripture. In 1 John 4:10
it is written: "Herein is love, not that we love
God, but that He loved us, and sent His Son
to be the propitiation for our sins." He loved
us before we ever thought of loving Him. You
loved your children before they knew anything
about your love. And so, long before we ever
thought of God, we were in His thoughts.*

D. L. Moody

INSIGHTS

*T*hink *of the love that God must have had
when He gave His son to die for the world! I
used to think a good deal more of Christ than
I did of the Father. Somehow or other I had
the idea that God was a stern judge; that
Christ came between me and God, and ap-
peased the anger of God. But after I became
a father, and for years had an only son, as I
looked at my boy I thought of the Father giving
His Son to die, and it seemed to me as if it
required more love for the Father to give His
Son than for the Son to die. Oh, the love that
God must have had for the world when He
gave His Son to die for it! "God so loved the
world, that He gave His only begotten Son,
that whosoever believeth in Him should not
perish, but have everlasting life" (John 3:16).
I have never been able to preach from that*

PAUSE FOR REFLECTION

*H*ow *does your image of God's love change
as you read about the way Jesus suffered injury, insult, and degradation in order to save
you? Perhaps now would be a good time for
a thoughtful prayer of thanks for God's love.*

MONDAY:

Jesus Dies, but Rises as He Promised

Mark 15:33—16:8

NEW   TESTAMENT   READING

Jesus Dies

*A*t noon the whole country became dark, and the darkness lasted for three hours. At three o'clock Jesus cried in a loud voice, "Eloi, Eloi, lama sabachthani." This means, "My God, my God, why have you rejected me?"

When some of the people standing there heard this, they said, "Listen! He is calling Elijah."

Someone there ran and got a sponge, filled it with vinegar, tied it to a stick, and gave it to Jesus to drink. He said, "We want to see if Elijah will come to take him down from the cross."

Then Jesus cried in a loud voice and died.

The curtain in the Temple was torn into two pieces, from the top to the bottom. When the army officer who was standing in front of the cross saw what happened when Jesus died, he said, "This man really was the Son of God!"

Some women were standing at a distance from the cross, watching; among them were Mary Magdalene, Salome, and Mary the mother of James and Joseph. (James was her youngest son.) These women had followed Jesus in Galilee and helped him. Many other women were also there who had come with Jesus to Jerusalem.

Jesus Is Buried

*T*his was Preparation Day. (That means the day before the Sabbath day.) That evening, Joseph from Arimathea was brave enough to go to Pilate and ask for Jesus' body. Joseph, an important member of the Jewish council, was one of the people who was waiting for the kingdom of God to come. Pilate was amazed that Jesus would have already died, so he called the army officer who had guarded Jesus and asked him if Jesus had already died. The officer told Pilate that he was dead, so Pilate told

Joseph he could have the body. Joseph bought some linen cloth, took the body down from the cross, and wrapped it in the linen. He put the body in a tomb that was cut out of a wall of rock. Then he rolled a very large stone to block the entrance of the tomb. And Mary Magdalene and Mary the mother of Joseph saw the place where Jesus was laid.

Jesus Rises from the Dead

*T*he day after the Sabbath day, Mary Magdalene, Mary the mother of James, and Salome bought some sweet-smelling spices to put on Jesus' body. Very early on that day, the first day of the week, soon after sunrise, the women were on their way to the tomb. They said to each other, "Who will roll away for us the stone that covers the entrance of the tomb?"

Then the women looked and saw that the stone had already been rolled away, even though it was very large. The women entered the tomb and saw a young man wearing a white robe and sitting on the right side, and they were afraid.

But the man said, "Don't be afraid. You are looking for Jesus from Nazareth, who has been crucified. He has risen from the dead; he is not here. Look, here is the place they laid him. Now go and tell his followers and Peter, 'Jesus is going into Galilee ahead of you, and you will see him there as he told you before.'"

The women were confused and shaking with fear, so they left the tomb and ran away. They did not tell anyone about what happened, because they were afraid.

OLD   TESTAMENT   READING

Jesus Suffers and Dies . . .

*Y*ou see my shame and disgrace.
>You know all my enemies and what
>they have said.
Insults have broken my heart
>and left me weak.
I looked for sympathy, but there was
>none;
>I found no one to comfort me.
They put poison in my food
>and gave me vinegar to drink.

Psalm 69:19–21

But He Will Fulfill His Promise

*M*ake the weak hands strong
   and the weak knees steady.
Say to people who are frightened,
   "Be strong. Don't be afraid.
Look, your God will come,
   and he will punish your enemies.
He will make them pay for the wrongs
      they did,
   but he will save you."

Then the blind people will see again,
   and the deaf will hear.
Crippled people will jump like deer,
   and those who can't talk now will
      shout with joy.
Water will flow in the desert,
   and streams will flow in the dry land.
The burning desert will have pools of
      water,
   and the dry ground will have
      springs.
Where wild dogs once lived,
   grass and water plants will grow.
A road will be there;
   this highway will be called "The
      Road to Being Holy."
Evil people will not be allowed to walk
      on that road;
   only good people will walk on it.
   No fools will go on it.
No lions will be there,
   nor will dangerous animals be on
      that road.
   They will not be found there.
That road will be for the people God
      saves;
   the people the LORD has freed will
      return there.
They will enter Jerusalem with joy,
   and their happiness will last forever.
Their gladness and joy will fill them
      completely,
   and sorrow and sadness will go far
      away.

Isaiah 35:3–10

that His work on the cross for sinners so satisfied divine justice and divine character and
divine righteousness, that I would never see
my sins again. God raised Him from the dead
as a guarantee to me personally that death
has no more authority over the man in Christ.
It has been shorn of its power. . . . At the
cross we see His love, but in resurrection we
see His power.

To grasp the meaning of Jesus' resurrection there at the tomb changed my whole
outlook on life. God made it real to me that
the One who had died on the cross of shame
was no longer on the cross, no longer in the
tomb. We've been joined to a risen Savior.
That is why the apostles gave witness with
such great power in the book of Acts. Paul
stood before Felix, before Festus, before
Agrippa, before the Sanhedrin, before the
philosophers of Athens, and before the corrupt
Corinthians with only one message. He
preached the risen Christ.

But why is the resurrection of Christ one
of the rarest messages you ever hear today?
Even among evangelicals, where is this
wonderful truth? . . .

. . . The cross is a tragedy if there is no
resurrection. Would to God that His people
would continually rejoice that our Savior is
alive forevermore.

John G. Mitchell

ACTION   POINT

*M*editate on the Isaiah 35 reading until
you begin to understand the awesome reality
of Christ's resurrection. Pray now and thank
God that Jesus not only died, but that he lives
today!

INSIGHTS

I will never forget the day that I looked into
the tomb. It changed my whole ministry. It
came to me that my Savior was really alive,

TUESDAY:

Those Who Don't Believe Will Be Judged Guilty

Mark 16:9—Luke 1:13

Some Followers See Jesus

*A*fter Jesus rose from the dead early on the first day of the week, he showed himself first to Mary Magdalene. One time in the past, he had forced seven demons out of her. After Mary saw Jesus, she went and told his followers, who were very sad and were crying. But Mary told them that Jesus was alive. She said that she had seen him, but the followers did not believe her.

Later, Jesus showed himself to two of his followers while they were walking in the country, but he did not look the same as before. These followers went back to the others and told them what had happened, but again, the followers did not believe them.

Jesus Talks to the Apostles

*L*ater Jesus showed himself to the eleven apostles while they were eating, and he criticized them because they had no faith. They were stubborn and refused to believe those who had seen him after he had risen from the dead.

Jesus said to his followers, "Go everywhere in the world, and tell the Good News to everyone. Anyone who believes and is baptized will be saved, but anyone who does not believe will be punished. And those who believe will be able to do these things as proof: They will use my name to force out demons. They will speak in new languages. They will pick up snakes and drink poison without being hurt. They will touch the sick, and the sick will be healed."

After the Lord Jesus said these things to his followers, he was carried up into heaven, and he sat at the right side of God. The followers went everywhere in the world and told the Good News to people, and the Lord helped them. The Lord proved that the Good News they told was true by giving them power to work miracles.

Luke Writes About Jesus' Life

*M*any have tried to report on the things that happened among us. They have written the same things that we learned from others—the people who saw those things from the beginning and served God by telling people his message. Since I myself have studied everything carefully from the beginning, most excellent Theophilus, it seemed good for me to write it out for you. I arranged it in order to help you know that what you have been taught is true.

Zechariah and Elizabeth

*D*uring the time Herod ruled Judea, there was a priest named Zechariah who belonged to Abijah's group. Zechariah's wife, Elizabeth, came from the family of Aaron. Zechariah and Elizabeth truly did what God said was good. They did everything the Lord commanded and were without fault in keeping his law. But they had no children, because Elizabeth could not have a baby, and both of them were very old.

One day Zechariah was serving as a priest before God, because his group was on duty. According to the custom of the priests, he was chosen by lot to go into the Temple of the Lord and burn incense. There were a great many people outside praying at the time the incense was offered. Then an angel of the Lord appeared to Zechariah, standing on the right side of the incense table. When he saw the angel, Zechariah was startled and frightened. But the angel said to him, "Zechariah, don't be afraid. God has heard your prayer. Your wife, Elizabeth, will give birth to a son, and you will name him John."

*T*hat night all the people in the camp began crying loudly. All the Israelites complained against Moses and Aaron, and all the people said to them, "We wish we had died in Egypt or in this desert. Why is the LORD bringing us to this land to be killed with swords? Our wives and children will be taken away. We would be better off going back to Egypt." They said to each other,

"Let's choose a leader and go back to Egypt."

Then Moses and Aaron bowed facedown in front of all the Israelites gathered there. Joshua son of Nun and Caleb son of Jephunneh, who had explored the land, tore their clothes. They said to all of the Israelites, "The land we explored is very good. If the LORD is pleased with us, he will lead us into that land and give us that fertile land. Don't turn against the LORD! Don't be afraid of the people in that land! We will chew them up. They have no protection, but the LORD is with us. So don't be afraid of them."

Then all the people talked about killing them with stones. But the glory of the LORD appeared at the Meeting Tent to all the Israelites. The LORD said to Moses, "How long will these people ignore me? How long will they not believe me in spite of the miracles I have done among them?"

The LORD answered, "I have forgiven them as you asked. But, as surely as I live and as surely as my glory fills the whole earth, I make this promise: All these men saw my glory and the miracles I did in Egypt and in the desert, but they disobeyed me and tested me ten times. So not one of them will see the land I promised to their ancestors. No one who rejected me will see that land. But my servant Caleb thinks differently and follows me completely. So I will bring him into the land he has already seen, and his children will own that land.

Numbers 14:1–11, 20–24

*W*hen the LORD heard them, he was
    very angry.
  His anger was like fire to the people
    of Jacob;
  his anger grew against the people of
    Israel.
They had not believed God
  and had not trusted him to save
    them.

Psalm 78:21–22

INSIGHTS

*Y*ou may ask how people wind up in hell if God is a loving God. People wind up in hell by trampling the love of God instead of treasuring it. They ignore it, spurn it, yawn over it, close their hearts to it, keep saying "someday, someday, someday."

The Bible says there will be a someday. It's a day of reckoning. To those who have spurned His love, God will say in effect, "I loved you every day of your life. I loved you with a perfect love. I extended Myself to you. I made My wisdom available to you. I made My comfort and My strength and My Spirit available to you. I made My offer of salvation to you. But you trampled and spurned My love. You had it your way on earth, so now you can have it your way in eternity."

Are you facing that scenario? Will you continue to trample the love of God? That's the question of the ages, and it is one you yourself must answer.

Bill Hybels

PAUSE FOR REFLECTION

*W*hat is the essential message of the Good News? After Jesus returned to heaven, how did he prove that the Good News was true? Is it really easier to believe God when we see his miracles? What is the fate of all those who—even though they have witnessed miracles—choose to reject God?

WEDNESDAY:

God Sends Special Messengers

Luke 1:14–45

*H*e will bring you joy and gladness, and many people will be happy because of his birth. John will be a great man for the Lord. He will never drink wine or beer, and even from birth, he will be filled with the Holy Spirit. He will help many people of Israel return to the Lord their God. He will go before the Lord in spirit and power like Elijah. He will make peace between parents and their children and will bring those who are not obeying God back to the right way of thinking, to make a people ready for the coming of the Lord."

Zechariah said to the angel, "How can I know that what you say is true? I am an old man, and my wife is old, too."

The angel answered him, "I am Gabriel. I stand before God, who sent me to talk to you and to tell you this good news. Now, listen! You will not be able to speak until the day these things happen, because you did not believe what I told you. But they will really happen."

Outside, the people were still waiting for Zechariah and were surprised that he was staying so long in the Temple. When Zechariah came outside, he could not speak to them, and they knew he had seen a vision in the Temple. He could only make signs to them and remained unable to speak. When his time of service at the Temple was finished, he went home.

Later, Zechariah's wife, Elizabeth, became pregnant and did not go out of her house for five months. Elizabeth said, "Look what the Lord has done for me! My people were ashamed of me, but now the Lord has taken away that shame."

An Angel Appears to Mary

*D*uring Elizabeth's sixth month of pregnancy, God sent the angel Gabriel to Nazareth, a town in Galilee, to a virgin. She was engaged to marry a man named Joseph from the family of David. Her name was Mary. The angel came to her and said, "Greetings! The Lord has blessed you and is with you."

But Mary was very startled by what the angel said and wondered what this greeting might mean.

The angel said to her, "Don't be afraid, Mary; God has shown you his grace. Listen! You will become pregnant and give birth to a son, and you will name him Jesus. He will be great and will be called the Son of the Most High. The Lord God will give him the throne of King David, his ancestor. He will rule over the people of Jacob forever, and his kingdom will never end."

Mary said to the angel, "How will this happen since I am a virgin?"

The angel said to Mary, "The Holy Spirit will come upon you, and the power of the Most High will cover you. For this reason the baby will be holy and will be called the Son of God. Now Elizabeth, your relative, is also pregnant with a son though she is very old. Everyone thought she could not have a baby, but she has been pregnant for six months. God can do anything!"

Mary said, "I am the servant of the Lord. Let this happen to me as you say!" Then the angel went away.

Mary Visits Elizabeth

*M*ary got up and went quickly to a town in the hills of Judea. She came to Zechariah's house and greeted Elizabeth. When Elizabeth heard Mary's greeting, the unborn baby inside her jumped, and Elizabeth was filled with the Holy Spirit. She cried out in a loud voice, "God has blessed you more than any other woman, and he has blessed the baby to which you will give birth. Why has this good thing happened to me, that the mother of my Lord comes to me? When I heard your voice, the baby inside me jumped with joy. You are blessed because you believed that what the Lord said to you would really happen."

*T*here was a man named Manoah from the tribe of Dan, who lived in the city of Zorah.

He had a wife, but she could not have children. The angel of the LORD appeared to Manoah's wife and said, "You have not been able to have children, but you will become pregnant and give birth to a son. Be careful not to drink wine or beer or eat anything that is unclean, because you will become pregnant and have a son. You must never cut his hair, because he will be a Nazirite, given to God from birth. He will begin to save Israel from the power of the Philistines."

Then Manoah's wife went to him and told him what had happened. She said, "A man from God came to me. He looked like an angel from God; his appearance was frightening. I didn't ask him where he was from, and he didn't tell me his name. But he said to me, 'You will become pregnant and will have a son. Don't drink wine or beer or eat anything that is unclean, because the boy will be a Nazirite to God from his birth until the day of his death.'"

Then Manoah prayed to the LORD: "Lord, I beg you to let the man of God come to us again. Let him teach us what we should do for the boy who will be born to us."

God heard Manoah's prayer, and the angel of God came to Manoah's wife again while she was sitting in the field. But her husband Manoah was not with her. So she ran to tell him, "He is here! The man who appeared to me the other day is here!"

Manoah got up and followed his wife. When he came to the man, he said, "Are you the man who spoke to my wife?"

The man said, "I am."

So Manoah asked, "When what you say happens, what kind of life should the boy live? What should he do?"

The angel of the LORD said, "Your wife must be careful to do everything I told her to do. She must not eat anything that grows on a grapevine, or drink any wine or beer, or eat anything that is unclean. She must do everything I have commanded her."

So the woman gave birth to a boy and named him Samson. He grew, and the LORD blessed him.

Judges 13:2–14, 24

*B*ut I will send you Elijah the prophet before that great and terrifying day of the LORD's judging. Elijah will help parents love their children and children love their parents. Otherwise, I will come and put a curse on the land."

Malachi 4:5–6

*R*eports continually flow to my attention from many places around the world telling of visitors of the angelic order appearing, ministering, fellowshiping and disappearing. They warn of God's impending judgment; they spell out the tenderness of His love; they meet a desperate need; then they are gone. Of one thing we can be sure: angels never draw attention to themselves but ascribe glory to God and press His message upon the hearers as a delivering and sustaining word of the highest order.

Demonic activity and Satan worship are on the increase in all parts of the world. The devil is alive and more at work than at any other time. The Bible says that since he realizes his time is short, his activity will increase. Through his demonic influences he does succeed in turning many away from true faith; but we can still say that his evil activities are countered for the people of God by His ministering spirits, the holy ones of the angelic order. They are vigorous in delivering the heirs of salvation from the stratagems of evil men. They cannot fail.

Believers, look up—take courage. The angels are nearer than you think. For after all, God has given "his angels charge of you, to guard you in all your ways. On their hands they will bear you up, lest you dash your foot against a stone" (Psalm 91:11, 12 RSV).

Billy Graham

*W*hen an angel delivers God's message to a person, what response does God expect? In these instances, what are the consequences of believing or doubting God's message? Are you open to receiving his message for you?

139

THURSDAY:

God Is Merciful to His People

Luke 1:46–77

Mary Praises God

*T*hen Mary said,
"My soul praises the Lord;
   my heart rejoices in God my Savior,
because he has shown his concern for
      his humble servant girl.
From now on, all people will say that I
      am blessed,
   because the Powerful One has done
      great things for me.
   His name is holy.
God will show his mercy forever and
      ever
   to those who worship and serve him.
He has done mighty deeds by his
      power.
   He has scattered the people who are
      proud
   and think great things about them-
      selves.
He has brought down rulers from their
      thrones
   and raised up the humble.
He has filled the hungry with good
      things
   and sent the rich away with nothing.
He has helped his servant, the people
      of Israel,
   remembering to show them mercy
as he promised to our ancestors,
   to Abraham and to his children
      forever."
Mary stayed with Elizabeth for about
three months and then returned home.

The Birth of John

*W*hen it was time for Elizabeth to give
birth, she had a boy. Her neighbors and
relatives heard how good the Lord was to
her, and they rejoiced with her.

When the baby was eight days old, they
came to circumcise him. They wanted to
name him Zechariah because this was his
father's name, but his mother said, "No! He
will be named John."

The people said to Elizabeth, "But no one
in your family has this name." Then they
made signs to his father to find out what he
would like to name him.

Zechariah asked for a writing tablet and
wrote, "His name is John," and everyone
was surprised. Immediately Zechariah
could talk again, and he began praising
God. All their neighbors became alarmed,
and in all the mountains of Judea people
continued talking about all these things.
The people who heard about them wondered, saying, "What will this child be?"
because the Lord was with him.

Zechariah Praises God

*T*hen Zechariah, John's father, was filled
with the Holy Spirit and prophesied:
"Let us praise the Lord, the God of
      Israel,
   because he has come to help his
      people and has given them
      freedom.
He has given us a powerful Savior
   from the family of God's servant
      David.
He said that he would do this
   through his holy prophets who lived
      long ago:
He promised he would save us from
      our enemies
   and from the power of all those who
      hate us.
He said he would give mercy to our
      fathers
   and that he would remember his
      holy promise.
God promised Abraham, our father,
   that he would save us from the
      power of our enemies
   so we could serve him without fear,
being holy and good before God as
      long as we live.

"Now you, child, will be called a
      prophet of the Most High God.
You will go before the Lord to
      prepare his way.
You will make his people know that
      they will be saved
   by having their sins forgiven."

140

*T*here is no God like you.
You forgive those who are guilty of
sin;
you don't look at the sins of your people
who are left alive.
You will not stay angry forever,
because you enjoy being kind.
You will have mercy on us again;
you will conquer our sins.
You will throw away all our sins
into the deepest part of the sea.
You will be true to the people of Jacob,
and you will be kind to the people of
Abraham
as you promised to our ancestors long
ago.
Micah 7:18–20

*B*ut I have hope
when I think of this:
The LORD's love never ends;
his mercies never stop.
They are new every morning;
LORD, your loyalty is great.
I say to myself, "The LORD is mine,
so I hope in him."
The LORD is good to those who hope in
him,
to those who seek him.
It is good to wait quietly
for the LORD to save.
Lamentations 3:21–26

*G*o and speak this message toward the
north:
'Come back, unfaithful people of Israel,'
says the LORD.
'I will stop being angry at you,
because I am full of mercy,' says the
LORD.
'I will not be angry with you forever.

"I, the LORD, said,
'How happy I would be to treat you as
my own children
and give you a pleasant land,
a land more beautiful than that of
any other nation.'
I thought you would call me 'My Father'
and not turn away from me.

But like a woman who is unfaithful to
her husband,
family of Israel, you have been
unfaithful to me," says the LORD.

"Come back to me, you unfaithful
children,
and I will forgive you for being
unfaithful."
Jeremiah 3:12, 19–20, 22a

*T*he Israelites were always worshiping the
idols of the peoples around them in spite of
the warning and the pleadings of the prophets. It wasn't until their captivity in Babylon
that they were cured of these dangerous liai-
sons with "other gods." From the days of their
captivity until now—two-and-a-half millen-
nia—the Jews have never again been guilty
of this sin. But in many places in Scripture,
the Holy Spirit takes up the refrain to make
sure the people of God would never slip
back. . . .

God is still dealing mercifully with those
who wander away in rebellion and pride, but
return in humility and faith. We have our
Golden Calves, our substitutes for the living
God. We have things in our lives that seem
more important because they promise more
immediate gratification. We, too, grow discouraged in a wilderness—a treadmill of
monotonous busyness without tangible or
meaningful results. To banish our sense of
emptiness and lostness in this secular world,
we may have looked for satisfaction in lesser
gods, although we would never call them
Golden Calves. Even so, God is patiently
waiting for us to forsake these idols. He may
discipline us, but in His mercy, He will never
forsake us.

William Stoddard

*D*o you sense how greatly Mary, Elizabeth,
and Zechariah felt God's mercy to them and
to all of God's people? Thank God that no
matter how greatly we sin he is merciful and
forgiving to everyone who repents!

FRIDAY:

Praise God for His Salvation!

Luke 1:78—2:27

*W*ith the loving mercy of our God,
a new day from heaven will dawn
upon us.
It will shine on those who live in
darkness,
in the shadow of death.
It will guide us into the path of peace."
And so the child grew up and became strong in spirit. John lived in the desert until the time when he came out to preach to Israel.

The Birth of Jesus

*A*t that time, Augustus Caesar sent an order that all people in the countries under Roman rule must list their names in a register. This was the first registration; it was taken while Quirinius was governor of Syria. And all went to their own towns to be registered.

So Joseph left Nazareth, a town in Galilee, and went to the town of Bethlehem in Judea, known as the town of David. Joseph went there because he was from the family of David. Joseph registered with Mary, to whom he was engaged and who was now pregnant. While they were in Bethlehem, the time came for Mary to have the baby, and she gave birth to her first son. Because there were no rooms left in the inn, she wrapped the baby with pieces of cloth and laid him in a box where animals are fed.

Shepherds Hear About Jesus

*T*hat night, some shepherds were in the fields nearby watching their sheep. Then an angel of the Lord stood before them. The glory of the Lord was shining around them, and they became very frightened. The angel said to them, "Do not be afraid. I am bringing you good news that will be a great joy to all the people. Today your Savior was born in the town of David. He is Christ, the Lord. This is how you will know him: You will find a baby wrapped in pieces of cloth and lying in a feeding box."

Then a very large group of angels from heaven joined the first angel, praising God and saying:
"Give glory to God in heaven,
and on earth let there be peace
among the people who please
God."

When the angels left them and went back to heaven, the shepherds said to each other, "Let's go to Bethlehem. Let's see this thing that has happened which the Lord has told us about."

So the shepherds went quickly and found Mary and Joseph and the baby, who was lying in a feeding box. When they had seen him, they told what the angels had said about this child. Everyone was amazed at what the shepherds said to them. But Mary treasured these things and continued to think about them. Then the shepherds went back to their sheep, praising God and thanking him for everything they had seen and heard. It had been just as the angel had told them.

When the baby was eight days old, he was circumcised and was named Jesus, the name given by the angel before the baby began to grow inside Mary.

Jesus Is Presented in the Temple

*W*hen the time came for Mary and Joseph to do what the law of Moses taught about being made pure, they took Jesus to Jerusalem to present him to the Lord. (It is written in the law of the Lord: "Every firstborn male shall be given to the Lord.") Mary and Joseph also went to offer a sacrifice, as the law of the Lord says: "You must sacrifice two doves or two young pigeons."

Simeon Sees Jesus

*I*n Jerusalem lived a man named Simeon who was a good man and godly. He was waiting for the time when God would take away Israel's sorrow, and the Holy Spirit was in him. Simeon had been told by the Holy Spirit that he would not die before he saw the Christ promised by the Lord.

*P*raise the LORD!
My whole being, praise the LORD.
I will praise the LORD all my life;
    I will sing praises to my God as long
      as I live.

Do not put your trust in princes
    or other people, who cannot save
      you.
When people die, they are buried.
    Then all of their plans come to an
      end.
Happy are those who are helped by the
    God of Jacob.
    Their hope is in the LORD their God.
He made heaven and earth,
    the sea and everything in it.
    He remains loyal forever.
He does what is fair for those who have
    been wronged.
    He gives food to the hungry.
The LORD sets the prisoners free.
    The LORD gives sight to the blind.
The LORD lifts up people who are in
    trouble.
    The LORD loves those who do right.
Psalm 146:1–8

*P*raise the LORD!

It is good to sing praises to our God;
    it is good and pleasant to praise him.
The LORD rebuilds Jerusalem;
    he brings back the captured Israel-
      ites.
He heals the brokenhearted
    and bandages their wounds.
Psalm 147:1–3

*P*raise the LORD,
    because he alone is great.
    He is more wonderful than heaven
      and earth.
God has given his people a king.
    He should be praised by all who
      belong to him,
    he should be praised by the Israel-
      ites, the people closest to his
      heart.

Praise the LORD!
Psalm 148:13–14

*T*he LORD, the LORD gives me strength
    and makes me sing.
    He has saved me."
You will receive your salvation with joy
    as you would draw water from a well.

At that time you will say,
"Praise the LORD and worship him.
    Tell everyone what he has done
    and how great he is.
Sing praise to the LORD, because he has
    done great things.
Isaiah 12:2b–5a

*I*n His holiness and love God could not wink at sin. He could not compromise either His justice or His mercy. Therefore, out of grace He sent His Son. . . . By God's mercy, He came in Christ to pay the full price, and at the cross, exposed His heart. God abhors, condemns, and judges sin, and yet by the power of the cross, He forgives sinners—people like you and me! . . .

. . . We have all gone over the line in breaking the Ten Commandments and Jesus' commandment to love. We've brought hurt, pain and suffering to ourselves and others by what we've done or said or refused to be. We've broken His heart. And even before we asked Him, He forgave us. He reconciled us. He exonerated us. We stutter out our yearning to be free in response to His cross, melted by His love, and healed by His forgiveness.

The same voice that cried, "Father forgive them," from Calvary, says to us with the commanding power of His cross-shaped heart, "The ransom has been paid for all time. And now in this propitious moment in your time it is a pardon for you. You are forgiven. You are free!"

Oh, the wonder of it all, indeed!
Lloyd Ogilvie

Think about all the things Jesus' birth represented to his parents, the shepherds, and Simeon. What does Jesus' coming to earth signify to you? Meditate on the wonder of it all. Thank him for his salvation.

WEEKEND:
Called to Do the Father's Work
Luke 2:28–52

NEW TESTAMENT READING

*T*he Spirit led Simeon to the Temple. When Mary and Joseph brought the baby Jesus to the Temple to do what the law said they must do, Simeon took the baby in his arms and thanked God:

"Now, Lord, you can let me, your servant,
die in peace as you said.
With my own eyes I have seen your salvation,
which you prepared before all people.
It is a light for the non-Jewish people to see
and an honor for your people, the Israelites."

Jesus' father and mother were amazed at what Simeon had said about him. Then Simeon blessed them and said to Mary, "God has chosen this child to cause the fall and rise of many in Israel. He will be a sign from God that many people will not accept so that the thoughts of many will be made known. And the things that will happen will make your heart sad, too."

Anna Sees Jesus

*T*here was a prophetess, Anna, from the family of Phanuel in the tribe of Asher. Anna was very old. She had once been married for seven years. Then her husband died, and she was a widow for eighty-four years. Anna never left the Temple but worshiped God, going without food and praying day and night. Standing there at that time, she thanked God and spoke about Jesus to all who were waiting for God to free Jerusalem.

Joseph and Mary Return Home

*W*hen Joseph and Mary had done everything the law of the Lord commanded, they went home to Nazareth, their own town in Galilee. The little child grew and became strong. He was filled with wisdom, and God's goodness was upon him.

Jesus As a Boy

*E*very year Jesus' parents went to Jerusalem for the Passover Feast. When he was twelve years old, they went to the feast as they always did. After the feast days were over, they started home. The boy Jesus stayed behind in Jerusalem, but his parents did not know it. Thinking that Jesus was with them in the group, they traveled for a whole day. Then they began to look for him among their family and friends. When they did not find him, they went back to Jerusalem to look for him there. After three days they found Jesus sitting in the Temple with the teachers, listening to them and asking them questions. All who heard him were amazed at his understanding and answers. When Jesus' parents saw him, they were astonished. His mother said to him, "Son, why did you do this to us? Your father and I were very worried about you and have been looking for you."

Jesus said to them, "Why were you looking for me? Didn't you know that I must be in my Father's house?" But they did not understand the meaning of what he said.

Jesus went with them to Nazareth and was obedient to them. But his mother kept in her mind all that had happened. Jesus became wiser and grew physically. People liked him, and he pleased God.

OLD TESTAMENT READING

Samuel Is Called to Do God's Work

*W*hen Samuel was old enough to eat, Hannah took him to the house of the LORD at Shiloh, along with a three-year-old bull, one-half bushel of flour, and a leather bag filled with wine. After they had killed the bull for the sacrifice, Hannah brought Samuel to Eli. She said to Eli, "As surely as you live, sir, I am the same woman who stood near you praying to the LORD. I prayed for this child, and the LORD answered my prayer and gave him to me. Now I give him back to the LORD. He will belong to the LORD all his life." And he worshiped the LORD there.

1 Samuel 1:24–28

Then the Lord called Samuel, and Samuel answered, "I am here!" He ran to Eli and said, "I am here. You called me."

But Eli said, "I didn't call you. Go back to bed." So Samuel went back to bed.

The Lord called again, "Samuel!"

Samuel again went to Eli and said, "I am here. You called me."

Again Eli said, "I didn't call you. Go back to bed."

Samuel did not yet know the Lord, and the Lord had not spoken directly to him yet.

The Lord called Samuel for the third time. Samuel got up and went to Eli and said, "I am here. You called me."

Then Eli realized the Lord was calling the boy. So he told Samuel, "Go to bed. If he calls you again, say, 'Speak, Lord. I am your servant and I am listening.'" So Samuel went and lay down in bed.

The Lord came and stood there and called as he had before, "Samuel, Samuel!"

Samuel said, "Speak, Lord. I am your servant and I am listening."

The Lord was with Samuel as he grew up; he did not let any of Samuel's messages fail to come true. Then all Israel, from Dan to Beersheba, knew Samuel was a true prophet of the Lord. And the Lord continued to show himself at Shiloh, and he showed himself to Samuel through his word.

1 Samuel 3:4–10, 19–21

INSIGHTS

Many people have the idea that God only calls preachers and missionaries, and the rest of us can do whatever we want to. But God has a calling for all of His children. . . .

. . . The people that God calls, the people God uses and chooses, His all-stars, are common ordinary people. . . .

. . . I thank God for the wise, noble, and mighty who love the Lord. I thank God for any athlete, movie star, or millionaire who will give his or her life to Christ. But God's work is going to be done primarily not through the superstar preachers, evangelists, or celebrities; God's work is going to be done through His ordinary everyday run-of-the-mill people. . . .

. . . By and large, the kind of people that God is able to use, fall into three categories: the foolish, feeble, and familiar. . . .

. . . God called a timid man with a stutter—a speech impediment—by the name of Moses and made him the greatest leader in the Old Testament. God called David, a little shepherd boy, right out of the pasture and made him the greatest king who ever ruled over Israel. . . . God's ways are above our ways, His thoughts are above our thoughts, and His calling confounds the wise. . . .

. . . Someone has said, "It doesn't take much of a man to be a Christian. It just takes all that there is of him." God takes the weak, feeble, sick, infirm, handicapped, and shames those things which are strong.

When I think of the weak I recall the life of Jonathan Edwards. He was one of the greatest revival preachers America or the world has ever known. . . .

He was an asthmatic. Whenever he would preach he would cough and hack and wheeze during most of the message. He was a very thin, frail man. He had horrible eyesight. . . .

. . . Jonathan Edwards' sermons, despite his disabilities, caused people to come writhing in anguish down the aisles wanting to get right with God. . . .

. . . The people that God uses and chooses, God's all-stars, are not people of ability; they are people of availability who have learned the secret of giving their praise to God. If you use your life for the glory of God, God will use your life for His glory.

James Merritt

ACTION POINT

Jesus knew he was called to do the Father's work. So did Samuel. What about you? Do you long for His clear call? Why not begin today to offer yourself to God and pray that you will be made useful for his glory?

MONDAY:

The Hope of the Coming Christ

Luke 3:1–22

NEW TESTAMENT READING

The Preaching of John

*I*t was the fifteenth year of the rule of Tiberius Caesar. These men were under Caesar: Pontius Pilate, the ruler of Judea; Herod, the ruler of Galilee; Philip, Herod's brother, the ruler of Iturea and Trachonitis; and Lysanias, the ruler of Abilene. Annas and Caiaphas were the high priests. At this time, the word of God came to John son of Zechariah in the desert. He went all over the area around the Jordan River preaching a baptism of changed hearts and lives for the forgiveness of sins. As it is written in the book of Isaiah the prophet:

"This is a voice of one
　who calls out in the desert:
'Prepare the way for the Lord.
　Make the road straight for him.
Every valley should be filled in,
　and every mountain and hill should
　　be made flat.
Roads with turns should be made
　　straight,
　and rough roads should be made
　　smooth.
And all people will know about the
　　salvation of God!'" *Isaiah 40:3–5*

To the crowds of people who came to be baptized by John, he said, "You are all snakes! Who warned you to run away from God's coming punishment? Do the things that show you really have changed your hearts and lives. Don't begin to say to yourselves, 'Abraham is our father.' I tell you that God could make children for Abraham from these rocks. The ax is now ready to cut down the trees, and every tree that does not produce good fruit will be cut down and thrown into the fire."

The people asked John, "Then what should we do?"

John answered, "If you have two shirts, share with the person who does not have one. If you have food, share that also."

Even tax collectors came to John to be baptized. They said to him, "Teacher, what should we do?"

John said to them, "Don't take more taxes from people than you have been ordered to take."

The soldiers asked John, "What about us? What should we do?"

John said to them, "Don't force people to give you money, and don't lie about them. Be satisfied with the pay you get."

Since the people were hoping for the Christ to come, they wondered if John might be the one.

John answered everyone, "I baptize you with water, but there is one coming who is greater than I am. I am not good enough to untie his sandals. He will baptize you with the Holy Spirit and fire. He will come ready to clean the grain, separating the good grain from the chaff. He will put the good part of the grain into his barn, but he will burn the chaff with a fire that cannot be put out." And John continued to preach the Good News, saying many other things to encourage the people.

But John spoke against Herod, the governor, because of his sin with Herodias, the wife of Herod's brother, and because of the many other evil things Herod did. So Herod did something even worse: He put John in prison.

Jesus Is Baptized by John

*W*hen all the people were being baptized by John, Jesus also was baptized. While Jesus was praying, heaven opened and the Holy Spirit came down on him in the form of a dove. Then a voice came from heaven, saying, "You are my Son, whom I love, and I am very pleased with you."

OLD TESTAMENT READING

*Y*our God says,
　"Comfort, comfort my people.
Speak kindly to the people of Jerusalem
　and tell them
that their time of service is finished,
　that they have paid for their sins,
that the LORD has punished Jerusalem
　twice for every sin they did."

146

This is the voice of one who calls out:
"Prepare in the desert
　the way for the Lord.
Make a straight road in the dry lands
　for our God.
Every valley should be raised up,
　and every mountain and hill should
　　be made flat.
The rough ground should be made
　level,
　and the rugged ground should be
　　made smooth.
Then the glory of the Lord will be
　shown,
　and all people together will see it.
The Lord himself said these things."

A voice says, "Cry out!"
　Then I said, "What shall I cry out?"

"Say all people are like the grass,
　and all their glory is like the flowers
　　of the field.
The grass dies and the flowers fall
　when the breath of the Lord blows
　　on them.
　Surely the people are like grass.
The grass dies and the flowers fall,
　but the word of our God will live
　　forever."
Jerusalem, you have good news to tell.
　Go up on a high mountain.
Jerusalem, you have good news to tell.
　Shout out loud the good news.
Shout it out and don't be afraid.
　Say to the towns of Judah,
"Here is your God."
Look, the Lord God is coming with
　power
　to rule all the people.
Look, he will bring reward for his
　people;
　he will have their payment with him.

Isaiah 40:1–10

INSIGHTS

*Is it a waste to focus on the Lord's descent?
Quite the contrary. It's biblical; it's the very
thing Titus 2:13 says we ought to do:*

　*"Looking for the blessed hope and the ap-
pearing of the glory of our great God and
Savior, Christ Jesus."*

*When's the last time you—on your own—
meditated on that fact? If you're like me it's
been too long. People who are more practical
than mystical, who are realistic rather than
idealistic, tend to shove that stuff to times like
funerals or near-death experiences. . . .
Listen, this Bible of ours is full and running
over with promises and encouragements
directly related to the return of our Lord
Christ. . . .*

*Critics have denied it. Cynics have laughed
at it. Scholars have ignored it. Liberal theologians have explained it away (they call that
"rethinking" it) and fanatics have perverted
it. . . . The return of our Savior will continue to be attacked and misused and denied.
But there it stands, solid as a stone, soon to
be fulfilled, ready to offer us hope and encouragement amidst despair and unbelief.*

*"Okay, swell. But what do I do in the
meantime?" I can hear a dozen or more prag-
matists asking that question. First, it might
be best for you to understand what
you don't do. You don't sit around, listening
for some bugle call. You don't keep staring
up into the sky, looking for the rapture
cloud. . . .*

*You do get your act together. You do live
every day (as if it's your last) for His glory.
You do work diligently on your job and in
your home (as if He isn't coming for another
ten years) for His Name's sake. You do shake
salt out every chance you get . . . and do
shine the light . . . and remain balanced,
cheerful, winsome, and stable, anticipating
His return day by day.*

Charles Swindoll

APPLICATION

*Do you feel the excitement of John's listen-
ers? They truly believed Christ was coming
and wanted to know what to do to be ready.
How about you? Do you await Christ's second coming with a yawn, or are you living
each day as he wants you to?*

TUESDAY:

Jesus: The Promised King in David's Line

Luke 3:23–38

The Family History of Jesus

*W*hen Jesus began his ministry, he was about thirty years old. People thought that Jesus was Joseph's son.

Joseph was the son of Heli.
Heli was the son of Matthat.
Matthat was the son of Levi.
Levi was the son of Melki.
Melki was the son of Jannai.
Jannai was the son of Joseph.
Joseph was the son of Mattathias.
Mattathias was the son of Amos.
Amos was the son of Nahum.
Nahum was the son of Esli.
Esli was the son of Naggai.
Naggai was the son of Maath.
Maath was the son of Mattathias.
Mattathias was the son of Semein.
Semein was the son of Josech.
Josech was the son of Joda.
Joda was the son of Joanan.
Joanan was the son of Rhesa.
Rhesa was the son of Zerubbabel.
Zerubbabel was the grandson of
    Shealtiel.
Shealtiel was the son of Neri.
Neri was the son of Melchi.
Melchi was the son of Addi.
Addi was the son of Cosam.
Cosam was the son of Elmadam.
Elmadam was the son of Er.
Er was the son of Joshua.
Joshua was the son of Eliezer.
Eliezer was the son of Jorim.
Jorim was the son of Matthat.
Matthat was the son of Levi.
Levi was the son of Simeon.
Simeon was the son of Judah.
Judah was the son of Joseph.
Joseph was the son of Jonam.
Jonam was the son of Eliakim.
Eliakim was the son of Melea.
Melea was the son of Menna.
Menna was the son of Mattatha.
Mattatha was the son of Nathan.
Nathan was the son of David.
David was the son of Jesse.
Jesse was the son of Obed.
Obed was the son of Boaz.
Boaz was the son of Salmon.
Salmon was the son of Nahshon.
Nahshon was the son of Amminadab.
Amminadab was the son of Admin.
Admin was the son of Arni.
Arni was the son of Hezron.
Hezron was the son of Perez.
Perez was the son of Judah.
Judah was the son of Jacob.
Jacob was the son of Isaac.
Isaac was the son of Abraham.
Abraham was the son of Terah.
Terah was the son of Nahor.
Nahor was the son of Serug.
Serug was the son of Reu.
Reu was the son of Peleg.
Peleg was the son of Eber.
Eber was the son of Shelah.
Shelah was the son of Cainan.
Cainan was the son of Arphaxad.
Arphaxad was the son of Shem.
Shem was the son of Noah.
Noah was the son of Lamech.
Lamech was the son of Methuselah.
Methuselah was the son of Enoch.
Enoch was the son of Jared.
Jared was the son of Mahalalel.
Mahalalel was the son of Kenan.
Kenan was the son of Enosh.
Enosh was the son of Seth.
Seth was the son of Adam.
Adam was the son of God.

A new branch will grow
    from a stump of a tree;
so a new king will come
    from the family of Jesse.
The Spirit of the LORD will rest upon
        that king.
    The Spirit will give him wisdom and
        understanding, guidance and
        power.
    The Spirit will teach him to know
        and respect the LORD.

This king will be glad to obey the LORD.
He will not judge by the way things look
    or decide by what he hears.
But he will judge the poor honestly;
    he will be fair in his decisions for the
    poor people of the land.
At his command evil people will be
    punished,
    and by his words the wicked will be
    put to death.
Goodness and fairness will give him
    strength,
    like a belt around his waist.

Isaiah 11:1–5

*T*he LORD says, "The time is coming
when I will do the good thing I promised to the people of Israel and Judah.
In those days and at that time,
    I will make a good branch sprout
        from David's family.
    He will do what is fair and right in
        the land.
At that time Judah will be saved,
    and the people of Jerusalem will live
        in safety.
The branch will be named:
    The LORD Does What Is Right."
This is what the LORD says: "Someone
from David's family will always sit on the
throne of the family of Israel."

Jeremiah 33:14–17

I will pour out on David's family and the
people in Jerusalem a spirit of kindness and
mercy. They will look at me, the one they
have stabbed, and they will cry like someone crying over the death of an only child.
They will be as sad as someone who has lost
a firstborn son.

Zechariah 12:10

of Israel is transferred from Benjamin to
Judah (1 Sam. 16). David, a man after God's
own heart, is chosen and anointed king (1
Sam. 16:13; 2 Sam. 2:4; 5:2). And with such
a change, there commences the desperate and
determined attack of Satan upon "the seed
royal," that is, the house of Judah, from which
the Messiah must spring. . . .

Saul, the God-forsaken, Satan-possessed
monarch (1 Sam. 16:14), tried his utmost
to destroy the Lord's anointed one, and thus
David is obliged to flee as a fugitive, hiding
in caves and holes from his father-in-
law. . . .

In the union of Jehoram and Athaliah, the
daughter of Ahab, king of Israel, Satan continues his assault upon the house of
Judah. . . .

At this critical moment, God's word appears to be at stake. Those of the royal seed
are becoming fewer and fewer. In fact, the
light was almost quenched, for Athaliah
"arose and destroyed all the seed royal of the
house of Judah" (2 Chron. 22:10). What followed? "But Jehoshabeath [another blessed,
divine "but" the devil hates], the daughter of
the king, took Joash the son of Ahaziah, and
stole him . . . [and] hid him from Athaliah,
so that she slew him not" (2 Chron. 22:11,
12). . . .

How much depended upon the preservation of Joash! If he dies, then Judah's
light and hope will be completely extin-
guished. . . . Carefully he is hid and cared
for while Athaliah reigns on in blissful ignorance until the day dawns when Joash is presented and crowned as king over Judah and
Athaliah is slain (2 Kings 11:4–16;
2 Chron. 23:11, 15). Thus God, in a marvelous way, defeated the evil tactics of the
devil, thereby fulfilling the promise of giving
a light forever (2 Chron. 21:7).

Herbert Lockyer

INSIGHTS

*I*n coming to the kingdom-phase of Satan's
antagonism, we believe that he was aware of
Jacob's prophetic utterance in Genesis 49:10,
that "the sceptre shall not depart from Judah,
nor a lawgiver from between his feet, until
Shiloh come; and unto him shall the gathering of the people be." . . .

With the abandonment of Saul, the throne

PAUSE   FOR   REFLECTION

*A*lthough family history may not be very
important you, a king must be able to prove
his royal heritage. What do these prophetic
and genealogical verses tell you about the
nature of Jesus' kingship?

WEDNESDAY:

Jesus Claims to Be the One of Whom Isaiah Spoke

Luke 4:1–30

NEW TESTAMENT READING

Jesus Is Tempted by the Devil

Jesus, filled with the Holy Spirit, returned from the Jordan River. The Spirit led Jesus into the desert where the devil tempted Jesus for forty days. Jesus ate nothing during that time, and when those days were ended, he was very hungry.

The devil said to Jesus, "If you are the Son of God, tell this rock to become bread."

Jesus answered, "It is written in the Scriptures: 'A person does not live by eating only bread.'"

Then the devil took Jesus and showed him all the kingdoms of the world in an instant. The devil said to Jesus, "I will give you all these kingdoms and all their power and glory. It has all been given to me, and I can give it to anyone I wish. If you worship me, then it will all be yours."

Jesus answered, "It is written in the Scriptures: 'You must worship the Lord your God and serve only him.'"

Then the devil led Jesus to Jerusalem and put him on a high place of the Temple. He said to Jesus, "If you are the Son of God, jump down. It is written in the Scriptures:
'He has put his angels in charge of you
to watch over you.' *Psalm 91:11*
It is also written:
'They will catch you in their hands
so that you will not hit your foot on a rock.'" *Psalm 91:12*

Jesus answered, "But it also says in the Scriptures: 'Do not test the Lord your God.'"

After the devil had tempted Jesus in every way, he left him to wait until a better time.

Jesus Teaches the People

Jesus returned to Galilee in the power of the Holy Spirit, and stories about him spread all through the area. He began to teach in their synagogues, and everyone praised him.

Jesus traveled to Nazareth, where he had grown up. On the Sabbath day he went to the synagogue, as he always did, and stood up to read. The book of Isaiah the prophet was given to him. He opened the book and found the place where this is written:
"The Lord has put his Spirit in me,
because he appointed me to tell the
Good News to the poor.
He has sent me to tell the captives they
are free
and to tell the blind that they can see
again. *Isaiah 61:1*
God sent me to free those who have
been treated unfairly *Isaiah 58:6*
and to announce the time when the
Lord will show his kindness." *Isaiah 61:2*

Jesus closed the book, gave it back to the assistant, and sat down. Everyone in the synagogue was watching Jesus closely. He began to say to them, "While you heard these words just now, they were coming true!"

All the people spoke well of Jesus and were amazed at the words of grace he spoke. They asked, "Isn't this Joseph's son?"

Jesus said to them, "I know that you will tell me the old saying: 'Doctor, heal yourself.' You want to say, 'We heard about the things you did in Capernaum. Do those things here in your own town!'" Then Jesus said, "I tell you the truth, a prophet is not accepted in his hometown. But I tell you the truth, there were many widows in Israel during the time of Elijah. It did not rain in Israel for three and one-half years, and there was no food anywhere in the whole country. But Elijah was sent to none of those widows, only to a widow in Zarephath, a town in Sidon. And there were many with skin diseases living in Israel during the time of the prophet Elisha. But none of them were healed, only Naaman, who was from the country of Syria."

When all the people in the synagogue heard these things, they became very angry. They got up, forced Jesus out of town, and took him to the edge of the cliff on which the town was built. They planned to throw him off the edge, but Jesus walked through the crowd and went on his way.

*T*he Lord GOD has put his Spirit in me,
because the LORD has appointed me
to tell the good news to the poor.
He has sent me to comfort those
whose hearts are broken,
to tell the captives they are free,
and to tell the prisoners they are
released.
He has sent me to announce the time
when the LORD will show his
kindness
and the time when our God will
punish evil people.
He has sent me to comfort all those
who are sad
and to help the sorrowing people of
Jerusalem.
I will give them a crown to replace their
ashes,
and the oil of gladness to replace
their sorrow,
and clothes of praise to replace their
spirit of sadness.
Then they will be called Trees of
Goodness,
trees planted by the LORD to show
his greatness.

Isaiah 61:1–3

I will tell you the kind of special day I
want:
Free the people you have put in prison
unfairly
and undo their chains.
Free those to whom you are unfair
and stop their hard labor.
Share your food with the hungry
and bring poor, homeless people
into your own homes.
When you see someone who has no
clothes, give him yours,
and don't refuse to help your own
relatives.
Then your light will shine like the dawn,
and your wounds will quickly heal.
Your God will walk before you,
and the glory of the LORD will protect
you from behind.
Then you will call out, and the LORD will
answer.

You will cry out, and he will say,
'Here I am.'"

Isaiah 58:6–9

I N S I G H T S

Jesus' words in the synagogue at Nazareth, spoken near the beginning of his public ministry, throb with hope for the poor. . . . Jesus informed his audience that this Scripture was now fulfilled in himself. The mission of the Incarnate One was to free the oppressed. . . .

Jesus' actual ministry corresponded precisely to the words of Luke 4. He spent most of his time not among the rich and powerful in Jerusalem, but among the poor in the cultural and economic backwater of Galilee. He healed the sick and blind. He fed the hungry. And he warned his followers in the strongest possible words that those who do not feed the hungry, clothe the naked, and visit the prisoners will experience eternal damnation (Matt. 25:31–46).

At the supreme moment of history when God took on human flesh, the God of Israel was still liberating the poor and oppressed and summoning his people to do the same.

Ronald Sider

PAUSE FOR REFLECTION

*W*hy *do you think Jesus so clearly proclaimed who he was in the synagogue at Nazareth? How was his message received? Why do you think he identified himself with these particular portions of Isaiah?*

THURSDAY:

Obedience Leads to Blessing and Faith

Luke 4:31—5:11

NEW TESTAMENT READING

Jesus Forces Out an Evil Spirit

Jesus went to Capernaum, a city in Galilee, and on the Sabbath day, he taught the people. They were amazed at his teaching, because he spoke with authority. In the synagogue a man who had within him an evil spirit shouted in a loud voice, "Jesus of Nazareth! What do you want with us? Did you come to destroy us? I know who you are—God's Holy One!"

Jesus commanded the evil spirit, "Be quiet! Come out of the man!" The evil spirit threw the man down to the ground before all the people and then left the man without hurting him.

The people were amazed and said to each other, "What does this mean? With authority and power he commands evil spirits, and they come out." And so the news about Jesus spread to every place in the whole area.

Jesus Heals Many People

Jesus left the synagogue and went to the home of Simon. Simon's mother-in-law was sick with a high fever, and they asked Jesus to help her. He came to her side and commanded the fever to leave. It left her, and immediately she got up and began serving them.

When the sun went down, the people brought those who were sick to Jesus. Putting his hands on each sick person, he healed every one of them. Demons came out of many people, shouting, "You are the Son of God." But Jesus commanded the demons and would not allow them to speak, because they knew Jesus was the Christ.

At daybreak, Jesus went to a lonely place, but the people looked for him. When they found him, they tried to keep him from leaving. But Jesus said to them, "I must preach about God's kingdom to other towns, too. This is why I was sent."

Then he kept on preaching in the synagogues of Judea.

Jesus' First Followers

One day while Jesus was standing beside Lake Galilee, many people were pressing all around him to hear the word of God. Jesus saw two boats at the shore of the lake. The fishermen had left them and were washing their nets. Jesus got into one of the boats, the one that belonged to Simon, and asked him to push off a little from the land. Then Jesus sat down and continued to teach the people from the boat.

When Jesus had finished speaking, he said to Simon, "Take the boat into deep water, and put your nets in the water to catch some fish."

Simon answered, "Master, we worked hard all night trying to catch fish, and we caught nothing. But you say to put the nets in the water, so I will." When the fishermen did as Jesus told them, they caught so many fish that the nets began to break. They called to their partners in the other boat to come and help them. They came and filled both boats so full that they were almost sinking.

When Simon Peter saw what had happened, he bowed down before Jesus and said, "Go away from me, Lord. I am a sinful man!" He and the other fishermen were amazed at the many fish they caught, as were James and John, the sons of Zebedee, Simon's partners.

Jesus said to Simon, "Don't be afraid. From now on you will fish for people." When the men brought their boats to the shore, they left everything and followed Jesus.

OLD TESTAMENT READING

Naaman was commander of the army of the king of Aram. He was honored by his master, and he had much respect because the LORD used him to give victory to Aram. He was a mighty and brave man, but he had a skin disease.

Naaman went to the king and told him what the girl from Israel had said. The king of Aram said, "Go ahead, and I will send a letter to the king of Israel." So Naaman left and took with him about seven hundred fifty pounds of silver, as well as one hundred fifty pounds of gold and ten changes of clothes. He brought the letter to the king of Israel, which read, "I am sending my servant Naaman to you so you can heal him of his skin disease."

When the king of Israel read the letter, he tore his clothes to show how upset he was. He said, "I'm not God! I can't kill and make alive again! Why does this man send someone with a skin disease for me to heal? You can see that the king of Aram is trying to start trouble with me."

When Elisha, the man of God, heard that the king of Israel had torn his clothes, he sent the king this message: "Why have you torn your clothes? Let Naaman come to me. Then he will know there is a prophet in Israel." So Naaman went with his horses and chariots to Elisha's house and stood outside the door.

Elisha sent Naaman a messenger who said, "Go and wash in the Jordan River seven times. Then your skin will be healed, and you will be clean."

Naaman became angry and left. He said, "I thought Elisha would surely come out and stand before me and call on the name of the LORD his God. I thought he would wave his hand over the place and heal the disease. The Abana and the Pharpar, the rivers of Damascus, are better than all the waters of Israel. Why can't I wash in them and become clean?" So Naaman went away very angry.

Naaman's servants came near and said to him, "My father, if the prophet had told you to do some great thing, wouldn't you have done it? Doesn't it make more sense just to do it? After all, he only told you, 'Wash, and you will be clean.'" So Naaman went down and dipped in the Jordan seven times, just as Elisha had said. Then his skin became new again, like the skin of a child. And he was clean.

Naaman and all his group returned to Elisha. He stood before Elisha and said, "Look, I now know there is no God in all the earth except in Israel. Now please accept a gift from me."

2 Kings 5:1, 4–15

T rust and obey, for there's no other way
To be happy in Jesus, but to trust and obey."

All too often we glibly sing the words of this familiar Christian hymn without giving them much thought. These important words convey exactly what the Bible teaches. The secret of spiritual happiness and blessing is simply trusting and obeying the Lord. . . . The divine method for happiness and blessing is full trust in God and complete obedience to His Word. Lack of faith and partial obedience not only result in unhappiness and loss of blessing; they bring serious consequences in the life of the believer.

The Bible contains many passages that teach the trust-and-obey-for-happiness principle (see Psalm 119, for instance). In addition, many character studies from the Scriptures illustrate this same truth. Jacob is one such example. Jacob was a believer who had to learn over and over again throughout his life that halfway trust and obedience do not bring happiness and blessing. . . .

. . . God had stated in no uncertain terms His promises to Jacob, and yet Jacob had the audacity to hold back with an "if" type of faith and obedience. But let's not mock Jacob's faith and obedience before we examine our own. Can we say without reservation that we simply trust and obey, or must we confess that we selfishly bargain with God? . . .

. . . God does not expect us to question or change or compromise His commands; He expects us to simply trust Him and obey Him. That's the way to find spiritual blessing and happiness.

David Reid

D id Naaman and Simon expect God to work the way he did? Could they bargain with God or change his requirements for obedience? Do you think anything less than total obedience will accomplish God's work and blessing in your life?

FRIDAY:
Jesus Often Slipped Away to Be Alone and Pray
Luke 5:12–35

Jesus Heals a Sick Man

*W*hen Jesus was in one of the towns, there was a man covered with a skin disease. When he saw Jesus, he bowed before him and begged him, "Lord, you can heal me if you will."

Jesus reached out his hand and touched the man and said, "I will. Be healed!" Immediately the disease disappeared. Then Jesus said, "Don't tell anyone about this, but go and show yourself to the priest and offer a gift for your healing, as Moses commanded. This will show the people what I have done."

But the news about Jesus spread even more. Many people came to hear Jesus and to be healed of their sicknesses, but Jesus often slipped away to be alone so he could pray.

Jesus Heals a Paralyzed Man

*O*ne day as Jesus was teaching the people, the Pharisees and teachers of the law from every town in Galilee and Judea and from Jerusalem were there. The Lord was giving Jesus the power to heal people. Just then, some men were carrying on a mat a man who was paralyzed. They tried to bring him in and put him down before Jesus. But because there were so many people there, they could not find a way in. So they went up on the roof and lowered the man on his mat through the ceiling into the middle of the crowd right before Jesus. Seeing their faith, Jesus said, "Friend, your sins are forgiven."

The Jewish teachers of the law and the Pharisees thought to themselves, "Who is this man who is speaking as if he were God? Only God can forgive sins."

But Jesus knew what they were thinking and said, "Why are you thinking these things? Which is easier: to say, 'Your sins are forgiven,' or to say, 'Stand up and walk'? But I will prove to you that the Son of Man has authority on earth to forgive sins." So Jesus said to the paralyzed man, "I tell you, stand up, take your mat, and go home."

At once the man stood up before them, picked up his mat, and went home, praising God. All the people were fully amazed and began to praise God. They were filled with much respect and said, "Today we have seen amazing things!"

Levi Follows Jesus

*A*fter this, Jesus went out and saw a tax collector named Levi sitting in the tax collector's booth. Jesus said to him, "Follow me!" So Levi got up, left everything, and followed him.

Then Levi gave a big dinner for Jesus at his house. Many tax collectors and other people were eating there, too. But the Pharisees and the men who taught the law for the Pharisees began to complain to Jesus' followers, "Why do you eat and drink with tax collectors and sinners?"

Jesus answered them, "It is not the healthy people who need a doctor, but the sick. I have not come to invite good people but sinners to change their hearts and lives."

Jesus Answers a Question

*T*hey said to Jesus, "John's followers often give up eating for a certain time and pray, just as the Pharisees do. But your followers eat and drink all the time."

Jesus said to them, "You cannot make the friends of the bridegroom give up eating while he is still with them. But the time will come when the bridegroom will be taken away from them, and then they will give up eating."

*L*ORD, every morning you hear my
   voice.
Every morning, I tell you what I
   need,
and I wait for your answer.

You are not a God who is pleased with
   the wicked;

you do not live with those who do evil.
Those people who make fun of you cannot stand before you.
You hate all those who do evil.
You destroy liars;
the LORD hates those who kill and trick others.

Because of your great love,
I can come into your Temple.
Because I fear and respect you,
I can worship in your holy Temple.
LORD, since I have many enemies,
show me the right thing to do.
Show me clearly how you want me to live.

My enemies' mouths do not tell the truth;
in their hearts they want to destroy others.
Their throats are like open graves;
they use their tongues for telling lies.
God, declare them guilty!
Let them fall into their own traps.
Send them away because their sins are many;
they have turned against you.

But let everyone who trusts you be happy;
let them sing glad songs forever.
Protect those who love you
and who are happy because of you.
LORD, you bless those who do what is right;
you protect them like a soldier's shield.

Psalm 5:3–12

*L*ORD, I call to you with all my heart.
Answer me, and I will keep your demands.
I call to you.
Save me so I can obey your rules.
I wake up early in the morning and cry out.
I hope in your word.
I stay awake all night
so I can think about your promises.
Listen to me because of your love;
LORD, give me life by your laws.

Those who love evil are near,
but they are far from your teachings.
But, LORD, you are also near,
and all your commands are true.

Psalm 119:145–151

*J*esus needed solitude simply because he was human—the only fully human person who has ever lived. He sought solitude. . . .

He went apart to cure his loneliness. He needed the silence of eternity as a thirsting man in the desert needs water. And he essentially needed the silence of eternity which was interpreted by love. For he who was love incarnate had his own needs to love and be loved. His deepest need, and likewise ours, could be met only by God. Ultimately no human being, no matter how close or dear, can fully satisfy our need for love. Those who imagine they can end up devouring one another.

Jesus longed for time apart to bask and sunbathe in his Father's love, to soak in it and repose in it. No matter how drained he felt, it seems that this deep, silent communion refreshed him more than a good night's sleep. . . .

. . . Human love and friendship indeed enrich our lives and partly meet this need—but not entirely, for at the core of our being [is] . . . a lovelonging for God which will only be met by converting our loneliness into deep solitude, by fleeing the sweets and cordials that may give temporary satisfaction, and finding the real thing in him.

Margaret Magdalen

PAUSE FOR REFLECTION

*I*t seems as if the psalmist thrived on his time with God, doesn't it? What is in your heart and on your lips when you slip away from life's demands to bask in the nearness of God's love? Isn't it about time you again slipped away to be refreshed by solitude with God?

WEEKEND:

God Cares for Those
Who Trust Him,
But Will Judge the Wicked

Luke 5:36—6:23

*J*esus told them this story: "No one takes cloth off a new coat to cover a hole in an old coat. Otherwise, he ruins the new coat, and the cloth from the new coat will not be the same as the old cloth. Also, no one ever pours new wine into old leather bags. Otherwise, the new wine will break the bags, the wine will spill out, and the leather bags will be ruined. New wine must be put into new leather bags. No one after drinking old wine wants new wine, because he says, 'The old wine is better.'"

Jesus Is Lord over the Sabbath

*O*ne Sabbath day Jesus was walking through some fields of grain. His followers picked the heads of grain, rubbed them in their hands, and ate them. Some Pharisees said, "Why do you do what is not lawful on the Sabbath day?"

Jesus answered, "Have you not read what David did when he and those with him were hungry? He went into God's house and took and ate the holy bread, which is lawful only for priests to eat. And he gave some to the people who were with him." Then Jesus said to the Pharisees, "The Son of Man is Lord of the Sabbath day."

Jesus Heals a Man's Hand

*O*n another Sabbath day Jesus went into the synagogue and was teaching, and a man with a crippled right hand was there. The teachers of the law and the Pharisees were watching closely to see if Jesus would heal on the Sabbath day so they could accuse him. But he knew what they were thinking, and he said to the man with the crippled hand, "Stand up here in the middle of everyone." The man got up and stood there. Then Jesus said to them, "I ask you, which is lawful on the Sabbath day: to do good or to do evil, to save a life or to destroy it?"

Jesus looked around at all of them and said to the man, "Hold out your hand." The man held out his hand, and it was healed.

But the Pharisees and the teachers of the law were very angry and discussed with each other what they could do to Jesus.

Jesus Chooses His Apostles

*A*t that time Jesus went off to a mountain to pray, and he spent the night praying to God. The next morning, Jesus called his followers to him and chose twelve of them, whom he named apostles: Simon (Jesus named him Peter), his brother Andrew, James, John, Philip, Bartholomew, Matthew, Thomas, James son of Alphaeus, Simon (called the Zealot), Judas son of James, and Judas Iscariot, who later turned Jesus over to his enemies.

Jesus Teaches and Heals

*J*esus and the apostles came down from the mountain, and he stood on level ground. A large group of his followers was there, as well as many people from all around Judea, Jerusalem, and the seacoast cities of Tyre and Sidon. They all came to hear Jesus teach and to be healed of their sicknesses, and he healed those who were troubled by evil spirits. All the people were trying to touch Jesus, because power was coming from him and healing them all.

Jesus looked at his followers and said,
"You people who are poor are happy,
   because the kingdom of God
      belongs to you.
You people who are now hungry are happy,
   because you will be satisfied.
You people who are now crying are happy,
   because you will laugh with joy.
"People will hate you, shut you out, insult you, and say you are evil because you follow the Son of Man. But when they do, you will be happy. Be full of joy at that time, because you have a great reward waiting for you in heaven. Their ancestors did the same things to the prophets."

*W*ait and trust the LORD.
   Don't be upset when others get rich

or when someone else's plans
  succeed.
Don't get angry.
  Don't be upset; it only leads to
    trouble.
Evil people will be sent away,
  but those who trust the LORD will
    inherit the land.
In a little while the wicked will be no
    more.
  You may look for them, but they will
    be gone.
People who are not proud will inherit
    the land
  and will enjoy complete peace.

The wicked make evil plans against
    good people.
  They grind their teeth at them in
    anger.
But the Lord laughs at the wicked,
  because he sees that their day is
    coming.

Psalm 37:7–13

I call to you, God,
  and you answer me.
Listen to me now,
  and hear what I say.
Your love is wonderful.
  By your power you save those who
    trust you
  from their enemies.
Protect me as you would protect your
    own eye.
  Hide me under the shadow of your
    wings.
Keep me from the wicked who attack me,
  from my enemies who surround me.

LORD, rise up, face the enemy, and
    throw them down.
  Save me from the wicked with your
    sword.
LORD, save me by your power
  from those whose reward is in this
    life.
They have plenty of food.
  They have many sons
  and leave much money to their
    children.

Because I have lived right, I will see
    your face.

When I wake up, I will see your
  likeness and be satisfied.

Psalm 17:6–9, 13–15

---

*T*he representations of the Bible with regard
to the final doom of the wicked are exceed-
ingly striking. Spiritual truths are revealed
by natural objects: e.g., the gates and walls of
the New Jerusalem, to present the splendours
and glories of the heavenly state. A spiritual
telescope is put into our hands; we are per-
mitted to point it towards the glorious city
"whose builder and Maker is God"; we may
survey its inner sanctuary, where the wor-
shipping hosts praise God without ceasing. We
see their flowing robes of white—the palms of
victory in their hands—the beaming joy of
their faces—the manifestations of ineffable
bliss in their souls. . . .

Then we have the other side. The veil is
lifted, and you come to the very verge of hell
to see what is there. Whereas on the one hand
all was glorious, on the other all is fearful,
and full of horrors.

There is a bottomless pit. A deathless soul
is cast therein; it sinks and sinks and sinks,
going down that awful pit which knows no
bottom, weeping and wailing as it descends,
and you hear its groans as they echo and re-
echo from the sides of that dread cavern of
woe!

Charles Finney

PAUSE FOR REFLECTION

*S*tudy the contrasting images of reward and
suffering on earth and in heaven for both
the wicked and God's people. What do these
images reveal to you about God's love and
compassion? Thank God that he sees all and
cares for those who love him.

M O N D A Y:

Do Good to All—Show Mercy, as God Shows Mercy

Luke 6:24–45

*B*ut how terrible it will be for you who
are rich,
  because you have had your easy life.
How terrible it will be for you who are
full now,
  because you will be hungry.
How terrible it will be for you who are
laughing now,
  because you will be sad and cry.
"How terrible when everyone says only
good things about you, because their ancestors said the same things about the false
prophets.

Love Your Enemies

*B*ut I say to you who are listening, love your
enemies. Do good to those who hate you,
bless those who curse you, pray for those
who are cruel to you. If anyone slaps you on
one cheek, offer him the other cheek, too. If
someone takes your coat, do not stop him
from taking your shirt. Give to everyone who
asks you, and when someone takes something that is yours, don't ask for it back. Do
to others what you would want them to do
to you. If you love only the people who love
you, what praise should you get? Even sinners love the people who love them. If you
do good only to those who do good to you,
what praise should you get? Even sinners do
that! If you lend things to people, always
hoping to get something back, what praise
should you get? Even sinners lend to other
sinners so that they can get back the same
amount! But love your enemies, do good to
them, and lend to them without hoping to
get anything back. Then you will have a great
reward, and you will be children of the Most
High God, because he is kind even to people
who are ungrateful and full of sin. Show
mercy, just as your Father shows mercy.

Look at Yourselves

*D*on't judge other people, and you will not

be judged. Don't accuse others of being
guilty, and you will not be accused of being
guilty. Forgive, and you will be forgiven.
Give, and you will receive. You will be given
much. Pressed down, shaken together, and
running over, it will spill into your lap. The
way you give to others is the way God will
give to you."

Jesus told them this story: "Can a blind
person lead another blind person? No! Both
of them will fall into a ditch. A student is not
better than the teacher, but the student who
has been fully trained will be like the teacher.

"Why do you notice the little piece of
dust in your friend's eye, but you don't notice the big piece of wood in your own eye?
How can you say to your friend, 'Friend, let
me take that little piece of dust out of your
eye' when you cannot see that big piece of
wood in your own eye! You hypocrite! First,
take the wood out of your own eye. Then
you will see clearly to take the dust out of
your friend's eye.

Two Kinds of Fruit

A good tree does not produce bad fruit,
nor does a bad tree produce good fruit.
Each tree is known by its own fruit. People
don't gather figs from thornbushes, and
they don't get grapes from bushes. Good
people bring good things out of the good
they stored in their hearts. But evil people
bring evil things out of the evil they stored
in their hearts. People speak the things that
are in their hearts."

*D*avid used these words to stop his men;
he did not let them attack Saul. Then Saul
left the cave and went his way.

When David came out of the cave, he
shouted to Saul, "My master and king!" Saul
looked back, and David bowed facedown on
the ground. He said to Saul, "Why do you
listen when people say, 'David wants to
harm you'? You have seen something with
your own eyes today. The LORD put you in
my power in the cave. They said I should
kill you, but I was merciful. I said, 'I won't
harm my master, because he is the LORD's
appointed king.' My father, look at this
piece of your robe in my hand! I cut off the

corner of your robe, but I didn't kill you. Now understand and know I am not planning any evil against you. I did nothing wrong to you, but you are hunting me to kill me. May the LORD judge between us, and may he punish you for the wrong you have done to me! But I am not against you. There is an old saying: 'Evil things come from evil people.' But I am not against you."

When David finished saying these words, Saul asked, "Is that your voice, David my son?" And he cried loudly. He said, "You are a better man than I am. You have been good to me, but I have done wrong to you. You told me what good things you did. The LORD handed me over to you, but you did not kill me. If a person finds his enemy, he doesn't just send him on his way, does he? May the LORD reward you because you were good to me today. I know you will surely be king, and you will rule the kingdom of Israel. Now swear to me by the LORD that you will not kill my descendants and that you won't wipe out my name from my father's family."

So David made the promise to Saul. Then Saul went back home, and David and his men went up to their hideout.

1 Samuel 24:7–13, 16–22

*B*ut this made Jonah very unhappy, and he became angry. He prayed to the LORD, "When I was still in my own country this is what I said would happen, and that is why I quickly ran away to Tarshish. I knew that you are a God who is kind and shows mercy. You don't become angry quickly, and you have great love. I knew you would choose not to cause harm."

Jonah 4:1–2

*B*ut Lord, you are a God who shows mercy and is kind.
You don't become angry quickly.
You have great love and faithfulness.

Psalm 86:15

INSIGHTS

*M*ercy is concern for people in need. It is ministry to the miserable. Offering help for those who hurt . . .

Those special servants of God who extend mercy to the miserable often do so with much encouragement because they identify with the sorrowing—they "get inside their skin." Rather than watching from a distance or keeping the needy safely at arm's length, they get in touch, involved, and offer assistance that alleviates some of the pain.

A large group of the collegians in our church in Fullerton, California, pile into our bus one weekend a month and travel together—not to a mountain resort or the beach for fun-n-games, but to a garbage dump in Tijuana, Mexico, where hundreds of poverty-stricken Mexican families live. Our young adults, under the encouraging leadership of Kenneth Kemp (one of our pastoral staff team members), bring apples and other foodstuff plus money they have collected to share with those in that miserable existence. . . .

What are they doing? They are showing mercy . . . a ministry to others that is born out of the womb of identification. . . .

True servants are merciful. They care. They get involved. They get dirty, if necessary. They offer more than pious words.

And what do they get in return? What does Christ promise? ". . . they shall receive mercy." Those who remain detached, distant, and disinterested in others will receive like treatment. But God promises that those who reach out and demonstrate mercy will, in turn, receive it. . . .

That is exactly what Jesus, our Savior, did for us when He came to earth. By becoming human. He got right inside our skin, literally. That made it possible for Him to see life through our eyes, feel the sting of our pain, and identify with the anguish of human need. He understands.

Charles Swindoll

ACTION POINT

*W*ho is our model for mercy? Are any of his instructions in mercy difficult for you to practice? Pray that God will continue to reveal his mercy to you and enable you to be merciful—to those who suffer as well as to those who hate you.

TUESDAY:

Build Your Life on a Solid Foundation

Luke 6:46—7:23

Two Kinds of People

*W*hy do you call me, 'Lord, Lord,' but do not do what I say? I will show you what everyone is like who comes to me and hears my words and obeys. That person is like a man building a house who dug deep and laid the foundation on rock. When the floods came, the water tried to wash the house away, but it could not shake it, because the house was built well. But the one who hears my words and does not obey is like a man who built his house on the ground without a foundation. When the floods came, the house quickly fell and was completely destroyed."

Jesus Heals a Soldier's Servant

*W*hen Jesus finished saying all these things to the people, he went to Capernaum. There was an army officer who had a servant who was very important to him. The servant was so sick he was nearly dead. When the officer heard about Jesus, he sent some older Jewish leaders to him to ask Jesus to come and heal his servant. The men went to Jesus and begged him, saying, "This officer is worthy of your help. He loves our people, and he built us a synagogue."

So Jesus went with the men. He was getting near the officer's house when the officer sent friends to say, "Lord, don't trouble yourself, because I am not worthy to have you come into my house. That is why I did not come to you myself. But you only need to command it, and my servant will be healed. I, too, am a man under the authority of others, and I have soldiers under my command. I tell one soldier, 'Go,' and he goes. I tell another soldier, 'Come,' and he comes. I say to my servant, 'Do this,' and my servant does it."

When Jesus heard this, he was amazed. Turning to the crowd that was following him, he said, "I tell you, this is the greatest faith I have found anywhere, even in Israel."

Those who had been sent to Jesus went back to the house where they found the servant in good health.

Jesus Brings a Man Back to Life

*S*oon afterwards Jesus went to a town called Nain, and his followers and a large crowd traveled with him. When he came near the town gate, he saw a funeral. A mother, who was a widow, had lost her only son. A large crowd from the town was with the mother while her son was being carried out. When the Lord saw her, he felt very sorry for her and said, "Don't cry." He went up and touched the coffin, and the people who were carrying it stopped. Jesus said, "Young man, I tell you, get up!" And the son sat up and began to talk. Then Jesus gave him back to his mother.

All the people were amazed and began praising God, saying, "A great prophet has come to us! God has come to help his people."

This news about Jesus spread through all Judea and into all the places around there.

John Asks a Question

*J*ohn's followers told him about all these things. He called for two of his followers and sent them to the Lord to ask, "Are you the One who is to come, or should we wait for someone else?"

When the men came to Jesus, they said, "John the Baptist sent us to you with this question: 'Are you the One who is to come, or should we wait for someone else?'"

At that time, Jesus healed many people of their sicknesses, diseases, and evil spirits, and he gave sight to many blind people. Then Jesus answered John's followers, "Go tell John what you saw and heard here. The blind can see, the crippled can walk, and people with skin diseases are healed. The deaf can hear, the dead are raised to life, and the Good News is preached to the poor. Those who do not stumble in their faith because of me are blessed!"

I love you, LORD. You are my strength.

The LORD is my rock, my protection,
　　my Savior.
　　My God is my rock.
　　I can run to him for safety.
　　He is my shield and my saving
　　　　strength, my defender.
I will call to the LORD, who is worthy of
　　　praise,
　　and I will be saved from my enemies.

The ropes of death came around me;
　　the deadly rivers overwhelmed me.
The ropes of death wrapped around me.
　　The traps of death were before me.
In my trouble I called to the LORD.
　　I cried out to my God for help.
From his temple he heard my voice;
　　my call for help reached his ears.

The LORD reached down from above
　　　and took me;
　　he pulled me from the deep water.
He saved me from my powerful enemies,
　　from those who hated me, because
　　　they were too strong for me.
They attacked me at my time of trouble,
　　but the LORD supported me.
He took me to a safe place.
　　Because he delights in me, he saved
　　　me.

The LORD spared me because I did what
　　was right.
　　Because I have not done evil, he has
　　　rewarded me.
I have followed the ways of the LORD;
　　I have not done evil by turning away
　　　from my God.
I remember all his laws
　　and have not broken his rules.
I am innocent before him;
　　I have kept myself from doing evil.
The LORD rewarded me because I did
　　what was right,
　　because I did what the LORD said was
　　　right.

The LORD lives!
　　May my Rock be praised.
　　Praise the God who saves me!
　　　　　Psalm 18:1–6, 16–24, 46

*S*uppose it were possible for a man never to
have seen any season but summer. Then
suppose that this man was called upon to
advise in the erection of a building. You can
imagine his procedure; everything is to be
light, because he never heard a high wind.
Waterpipes may be exposed, for he never felt
the severity of frost. The most flimsy roof will
be sufficient, for he knows nothing of the great
rains of winter and spring.

Tell such a man that the winds will become stormy, that the rivers will be chilled
into ice, that his windows will be blinded with
snow, and that floods will beat upon his roof.
If he is a wise man, he will say, "I must not
build for one season, but for all seasons. I must
not build for fine days, but for days that will
be tempestuous. I must, as far as possible,
prepare for the most inclement and trying
weather." That is simple common sense.

Why be less sensible in building a character than in building a house? We build our
bricks for severity as well as for sunshine, so
why build our character with less care? If in
summer we think about the frost, why not in
prosperity have some thought for adversity?
If in July we prepare for December, why not
in the flattering hour of exultation think of
the judgment that is at once infallible and
irresistible?

As he would be infinitely foolish who would
build his house without thinking of the natural forces that will try its strength, so is he
cursed with insanity who builds his character
without thinking of the fire with which God
will try every man's work.

Joseph Parker

*O*n what are you building your life? Will
your house stand firm against any storm?
Write your own psalm that reminds you both
of God's steadfast protection and your need
to follow his ways.

WEDNESDAY:
Be Sorry for Your Sin
Luke 7:24–50

NEW TESTAMENT READING

*W*hen John's followers left, Jesus began talking to the people about John: "What did you go out into the desert to see? A reed blown by the wind? What did you go out to see? A man dressed in fine clothes? No, people who have fine clothes and much wealth live in kings' palaces. But what did you go out to see? A prophet? Yes, and I tell you, John is more than a prophet. This was written about him:

'I will send my messenger ahead of you,
who will prepare the way for you.'

Malachi 3:1

I tell you, John is greater than any other person ever born, but even the least important person in the kingdom of God is greater than John."

(When the people, including the tax collectors, heard this, they all agreed that God's teaching was good, because they had been baptized by John. But the Pharisees and experts on the law refused to accept God's plan for themselves; they did not let John baptize them.)

Then Jesus said, "What shall I say about the people of this time? What are they like? They are like children sitting in the marketplace, calling to one another and saying,

'We played music for you, but you did not dance;
we sang a sad song, but you did not cry.'

John the Baptist came and did not eat bread or drink wine, and you say, 'He has a demon in him.' The Son of Man came eating and drinking, and you say, 'Look at him! He eats too much and drinks too much wine, and he is a friend of tax collectors and sinners!' But wisdom is proved to be right by what it does."

A Woman Washes Jesus' Feet

*O*ne of the Pharisees asked Jesus to eat with him, so Jesus went into the Pharisee's house and sat at the table. A sinful woman in the town learned that Jesus was eating at the Pharisee's house. So she brought an alabaster jar of perfume and stood behind Jesus at his feet, crying. She began to wash his feet with her tears, and she dried them with her hair, kissing them many times and rubbing them with the perfume. When the Pharisee who asked Jesus to come to his house saw this, he thought to himself, "If Jesus were a prophet, he would know that the woman touching him is a sinner!"

Jesus said to the Pharisee, "Simon, I have something to say to you."

Simon said, "Teacher, tell me."

Jesus said, "Two people owed money to the same banker. One owed five hundred coins and the other owed fifty. They had no money to pay what they owed, but the banker told both of them they did not have to pay him. Which person will love the banker more?"

Simon, the Pharisee, answered, "I think it would be the one who owed him the most money."

Jesus said to Simon, "You are right." Then Jesus turned toward the woman and said to Simon, "Do you see this woman? When I came into your house, you gave me no water for my feet, but she washed my feet with her tears and dried them with her hair. You gave me no kiss of greeting, but she has been kissing my feet since I came in. You did not put oil on my head, but she poured perfume on my feet. I tell you that her many sins are forgiven, so she showed great love. But the person who is forgiven only a little will love only a little."

Then Jesus said to her, "Your sins are forgiven."

The people sitting at the table began to say among themselves, "Who is this who even forgives sins?"

Jesus said to the woman, "Because you believed, you are saved from your sins. Go in peace."

OLD TESTAMENT READING

*T*here is more hope for a foolish person than for those who think they are wise.

Proverbs 26:12

*H*ow terrible it will be for people who
   call good things bad
   and bad things good,
who think darkness is light
   and light is darkness,
who think sour is sweet
   and sweet is sour.

How terrible it will be for people who
   think they are wise
   and believe they are clever.

How terrible it will be for people who
   are famous for drinking wine
   and are champions at mixing drinks.
They take money to set the guilty free
   and don't allow good people to be
   judged fairly.
They will be destroyed
   just as fire burns straw or dry grass.
They will be destroyed
   like a plant whose roots rot
   and whose flower dies and blows
   away like dust.
They have refused to obey the teachings of the LORD All-Powerful
   and have hated the message from
   the Holy God of Israel.
                    Isaiah 5:20–24

*Y*ou say, 'My teachings are right,
   and I am clean in God's sight.'
I wish God would speak
   and open his lips against you
and tell you the secrets of wisdom,
   because wisdom has two sides.
Know this: God has even forgotten
   some of your sin.

"You must give your whole heart to him
   and hold out your hands to him for
   help.
Put away the sin that is in your hand;
   let no evil remain in your tent.
Then you can lift up your face without
   shame,
   and you can stand strong without fear.
You will forget your trouble
   and remember it only as water gone by.
Your life will be as bright as the noon-
   day sun,
   and darkness will seem like morning."
                    Job 11:4–6, 13–17

*B*efore I can become wise, I must first realize that I am foolish. Before I can receive
power, I must first confess that I am powerless. I must lament my sins before I can rejoice in a Savior. Mourning, in God's sequence,
always comes before exultation. Blessed are
those who mourn their unworthiness, their
helplessness, and their inadequacy.

Isaiah, the mighty prophet of God, knew
by experience that one must bow the knee in
mourning before one can lift the voice in ju-
bilation. When his sin appeared ugly and
venomous in the bright light of God's holiness,
he said: "Woe is me! for I am undone; because
I am a man of unclean lips: for mine eyes
have seen the King, the LORD of hosts" (Isaiah
6:5).

We cannot be satisfied with our goodness
after beholding the holiness of God. But our
mourning over our unworthiness and sinful-
ness should be of short duration, for God has
said: "I, even I, am he that blotteth out thy
transgressions for mine own sake, and will
not remember thy sins" (Isaiah 43:25).

Isaiah had to experience the mourning
inadequacy before he could realize the joy of
forgiveness. . . .

In God's economy, a person must go down
into the valley of grief before he or she can
scale the heights of spiritual glory. One must
become tired and weary of living without
Christ before he or she can seek and find His
fellowship. One must come to the end of "self"
before one can really begin to live.

Billy Graham

*A*re you, like the Pharisees, ever tempted to
brush your sins off as being of little consequence? Pray that you will truly mourn the
burden of your sin and love God deeply because of his great forgiveness.

THURSDAY:

Jesus Understands the Hearts of Spiritually Closed People

Luke 8:1–21

The Group with Jesus

*A*fter this, while Jesus was traveling through some cities and small towns, he preached and told the Good News about God's kingdom. The twelve apostles were with him, and also some women who had been healed of sicknesses and evil spirits: Mary, called Magdalene, from whom seven demons had gone out; Joanna, the wife of Chuza (the manager of Herod's house); Susanna; and many others. These women used their own money to help Jesus and his apostles.

A Story About Planting Seed

*W*hen a great crowd was gathered, and people were coming to Jesus from every town, he told them this story:

"A farmer went out to plant his seed. While he was planting, some seed fell by the road. People walked on the seed, and the birds ate it up. Some seed fell on rock, and when it began to grow, it died because it had no water. Some seed fell among thorny weeds, but the weeds grew up with it and choked the good plants. And some seed fell on good ground and grew and made a hundred times more."

As Jesus finished the story, he called out, "You people who can hear me, listen!"

Jesus' followers asked him what this story meant.

Jesus said, "You have been chosen to know the secrets about the kingdom of God. But I use stories to speak to other people so that:

'They will look, but they may not see.
They will listen, but they may not
understand.'   *Isaiah 6:9*

"This is what the story means: The seed is God's message. The seed that fell beside the road is like the people who hear God's teaching, but the devil comes and takes it away from them so they cannot believe it and be saved. The seed that fell on rock is like those who hear God's teaching and accept it gladly, but they don't allow the teaching to go deep into their lives. They believe for a while, but when trouble comes, they give up. The seed that fell among the thorny weeds is like those who hear God's teaching, but they let the worries, riches, and pleasures of this life keep them from growing and producing good fruit. And the seed that fell on the good ground is like those who hear God's teaching with good, honest hearts and obey it and patiently produce good fruit.

Use What You Have

*N*o one after lighting a lamp covers it with a bowl or hides it under a bed. Instead, the person puts it on a lampstand so those who come in will see the light. Everything that is hidden will become clear, and every secret thing will be made known. So be careful how you listen. Those who have understanding will be given more. But those who do not have understanding, even what they think they have will be taken away from them."

Jesus' True Family

*J*esus' mother and brothers came to see him, but there was such a crowd they could not get to him. Someone said to Jesus, "Your mother and your brothers are standing outside, wanting to see you."

Jesus answered them, "My mother and my brothers are those who listen to God's teaching and obey it!"

*M*y people, listen to my teaching;
     listen to what I say.
I will speak using stories;
     I will tell secret things from long
     ago.
We have heard them and known them
     by what our ancestors have told us.
We will not keep them from our
     children;
     we will tell those who come later
     about the praises of the LORD.

We will tell about his power
and the miracles he has done.

Psalm 78:1–4

*T*his is what the LORD All-Powerful says:
"Gather the few people of Israel who
are left alive,
as you would gather the last grapes
on a grapevine.
Check each vine again,
like someone who gathers grapes."

To whom can I speak? Whom can I
warn?
Who will listen to me?
The people of Israel have closed ears,
so they cannot hear my warnings.
They don't like the word of the LORD;
they don't want to listen to it!

Jeremiah 6:9–10

*T*hen the Lord said, "Go and tell this
to the people:
'You will listen and listen, but you will
not understand.
You will look and look, but you will
not learn.'
Make the minds of these people dumb.
Shut their ears. Cover their eyes.
Otherwise, they might really understand
what they see with their eyes
and hear with their ears.
They might really understand in their
minds
and come back to me and be
healed."

Isaiah 6:9–10

*H*eaven and earth, listen,
because the LORD is speaking:
"I raised my children and helped them
grow up,
but they have turned against me.
An ox knows its master,
and a donkey knows where its
owner feeds it.
but the people of Israel do not know me;
my people do not understand."

Isaiah 1:2–3

INSIGHTS

*N*ot all of Christ's parables are explained.

In fact, most are not. But this one is. . . .

The first type of soil represents the hard heart, of which there are many today as well as in Christ's time. . . . What is it that makes the human heart hard? There can be only one answer: sin. Sin hardens the heart, and the heart that is hardened sins even more.

. . . . That type of person is described in the first chapter of Romans. He or she begins by suppressing the truth about God that may be known from nature (vv. 18–20), plunges inevitably into spiritual ignorance and moral degradation (vv. 21–31), and eventually comes not only to practice the sins of the heathen but to approve them as well (v. 32). Here we see both halves of the circle; sin leads to a rejection of God and God's truth, and the rejection of God's truth leads to even greater sin. What is it that leads such a person to reject the truth of God in the first place? According to Paul, it is a determined opposition to the nature of God Himself, which the apostle describes as human "godlessness and wickedness" (Rom. 1:18).

Virtually all of God's attributes—whether sovereignty, holiness, omniscience, immutability, or even the divine love—are offensive to the natural man, if properly understood. So rather than repent of sin and turn for mercy to a God who is altogether sovereign, holy, knowing, and unchangeable, men and women suppress what knowledge they have and refuse to seek out that additional knowledge that could be the salvation of their souls. . . .

. . . When Jesus came preaching the kingdom of God, He came preaching God's right to rule over the minds and hearts of all people. But that is precisely what the people involved did not want. . . .

So it is also today. That is probably the greatest reason for the rejection of the gospel of God's grace in Jesus Christ.

James Boice

APPLICATION

*W*hy do you think Jesus twice warns his hearers to listen to his teaching carefully? What message do you think Jesus wants you to hear? What difference do his words make in your heart and life?

F R I D A Y:

God Meets Us in Our Suffering

Luke 8:22–48

Jesus Calms a Storm

*O*ne day Jesus and his followers got into a boat, and he said to them, "Let's go across the lake." And so they started across. While they were sailing, Jesus fell asleep. A very strong wind blew up on the lake, causing the boat to fill with water, and they were in danger.

The followers went to Jesus and woke him, saying, "Master! Master! We will drown!"

Jesus got up and gave a command to the wind and the waves. They stopped, and it became calm. Jesus said to his followers, "Where is your faith?"

The followers were afraid and amazed and said to each other, "Who is this that commands even the wind and the water, and they obey him?"

A Man with Demons Inside Him

*J*esus and his followers sailed across the lake from Galilee to the area of the Gerasene people. When Jesus got out on the land, a man from the town who had demons inside him came to Jesus. For a long time he had worn no clothes and had lived in the burial caves, not in a house. When he saw Jesus, he cried out and fell down before him. He said with a loud voice, "What do you want with me, Jesus, Son of the Most High God? I beg you, don't torture me!" He said this because Jesus was commanding the evil spirit to come out of the man. Many times it had taken hold of him. Though he had been kept under guard and chained hand and foot, he had broken his chains and had been forced by the demon out into a lonely place.

Jesus asked him, "What is your name?"

He answered, "Legion," because many demons were in him. The demons begged Jesus not to send them into eternal darkness. A large herd of pigs was feeding on a hill, and the demons begged Jesus to allow them to go into the pigs. So Jesus allowed them to do this. When the demons came out of the man, they went into the pigs, and the herd ran down the hill into the lake and was drowned.

When the herdsmen saw what had happened, they ran away and told about this in the town and the countryside. And people went to see what had happened. When they came to Jesus, they found the man sitting at Jesus' feet, clothed and in his right mind, because the demons were gone. But the people were frightened. The people who saw this happen told the others how Jesus had made the man well. All the people of the Gerasene country asked Jesus to leave, because they were all very afraid. So Jesus got into the boat and went back to Galilee.

The man whom Jesus had healed begged to go with him, but Jesus sent him away, saying, "Go back home and tell people how much God has done for you." So the man went all over town telling how much Jesus had done for him.

Jesus Gives Life to a Dead Girl and Heals a Sick Woman

*W*hen Jesus got back to Galilee, a crowd welcomed him, because everyone was waiting for him. A man named Jairus, a leader of the synagogue, came to Jesus and fell at his feet, begging him to come to his house. Jairus' only daughter, about twelve years old, was dying.

While Jesus was on his way to Jairus' house, the people were crowding all around him. A woman was in the crowd who had been bleeding for twelve years, but no one was able to heal her. She came up behind Jesus and touched the edge of his coat, and instantly her bleeding stopped. Then Jesus said, "Who touched me?"

When all the people said they had not touched him, Peter said, "Master, the people are all around you and are pushing against you."

But Jesus said, "Someone did touch me, because I felt power go out from me." When the woman saw she could not hide, she came forward, shaking, and fell down before Jesus. While all the people listened, she told why she had touched him and how she had been instantly healed. Jesus said to her, "Dear woman, you are made well because you believed. Go in peace."

*B*ut the LORD looks after those who
 fear him,
  those who put their hope in his love.
He saves them from death
  and spares their lives in times of
   hunger.
So our hope is in the LORD.
  He is our help, our shield to protect
   us.
We rejoice in him,
  because we trust his holy name.
LORD, show your love to us
  as we put our hope in you.

          Psalm 33:18–22

*T*he LORD said, "I have seen the troubles my people have suffered in Egypt, and I have heard their cries when the Egyptian slave masters hurt them. I am concerned about their pain, and I have come down to save them from the Egyptians. I will bring them out of that land and lead them to a good land with lots of room—a fertile land. It is the land of the Canaanites, Hittites, Amorites, Perizzites, Hivites, and Jebusites. I have heard the cries of the people of Israel, and I have seen the way the Egyptians have made life hard for them. So now I am sending you to the king of Egypt. Go! Bring my people, the Israelites, out of Egypt!"

          Exodus 3:7–10

*T*he LORD defends those who suffer;
  he defends them in times of trouble.
Those who know the LORD trust him,
  because he will not leave those who
   come to him.
Sing praises to the LORD who is king on
  Mount Zion.
Tell the nations what he has done.

          Psalm 9:9–11

*T*he LORD hears good people when
  they cry out to him,
  and he saves them from all their
   troubles.

The LORD is close to the brokenhearted,
  and he saves those whose spirits
   have been crushed.

People who do what is right may have
  many problems,
  but the LORD will solve them all.
He will protect their very bones;
  not one of them will be broken.

          Psalm 34:17–20

*T*he image Jesus left with the world, the cross, . . . is proof that God cares about our suffering and pain. He died of it. . . .

 . . . Jesus, who had said He could call down angels at any moment and rescue Himself from the horror, chose not to— because of us. For God so loved us, that He sent His only Son to die for us.

And thus the cross, an eternal stumbling block to some, became the cornerstone of our faith. . . .

By taking it on Himself, Jesus in a sense dignified pain. Of all the kinds of lives He could have lived, He chose a suffering one. . . . Even though Jesus died, His death became the great victory of history, pulling man and God together. God made a supreme good out of that awful day.

Jesus' followers are not insulated from the tragedies of this world, just as He was not. God has never promised that tornados will skip our houses on the way to our pagan neighbors'. Microbes do not flee from Christian bodies. Rather, Peter could say to suffering Christians, "This suffering is all part of the work God has given you. Christ, who suffered for you, is your example. Follow in his steps" (1 Peter 2:21 LB).

         Philip Yancey

*T*hese verses show Jesus surrounded by suffering. How did he respond? How much does he care about your suffering? Thank him that he not only relieves our suffering, but took our greatest suffering upon himself on the cross.

WEEKEND:
God Is in Control
Luke 8:49—9:17

*W*hile Jesus was still speaking, someone came from the house of the synagogue leader and said to him, "Your daughter is dead. Don't bother the teacher anymore."

When Jesus heard this, he said to Jairus, "Don't be afraid. Just believe, and your daughter will be well."

When Jesus went to the house, he let only Peter, John, James, and the girl's father and mother go inside with him. All the people were crying and feeling sad because the girl was dead, but Jesus said, "Stop crying. She is not dead, only asleep."

The people laughed at Jesus because they knew the girl was dead. But Jesus took hold of her hand and called to her, "My child, stand up!" Her spirit came back into her, and she stood up at once. Then Jesus ordered that she be given something to eat. The girl's parents were amazed, but Jesus told them not to tell anyone what had happened.

Jesus Sends Out the Apostles

*J*esus called the twelve apostles together and gave them power and authority over all demons and the ability to heal sicknesses. He sent the apostles out to tell about God's kingdom and to heal the sick. He said to them, "Take nothing for your trip, neither a walking stick, bag, bread, money, or extra clothes. When you enter a house, stay there until it is time to leave. If people do not welcome you, shake the dust off of your feet as you leave the town, as a warning to them."

So the apostles went out and traveled through all the towns, preaching the Good News and healing people everywhere.

Herod Is Confused About Jesus

*H*erod, the governor, heard about all the things that were happening and was confused, because some people said, "John the Baptist has risen from the dead." Others said, "Elijah has come to us." And still others said, "One of the prophets who lived long ago has risen from the dead." Herod said, "I cut off John's head, so who is this man I hear such things about?" And Herod kept trying to see Jesus.

More than Five Thousand Fed

*W*hen the apostles returned, they told Jesus everything they had done. Then Jesus took them with him to a town called Bethsaida where they could be alone together. But the people learned where Jesus went and followed him. He welcomed them and talked with them about God's kingdom and healed those who needed to be healed.

Late in the afternoon, the twelve apostles came to Jesus and said, "Send the people away. They need to go to the towns and countryside around here and find places to sleep and something to eat, because no one lives in this place."

But Jesus said to them, "You give them something to eat."

They said, "We have only five loaves of bread and two fish, unless we go buy food for all these people." (There were about five thousand men there.)

Jesus said to his followers, "Tell the people to sit in groups of about fifty people."

So the followers did this, and all the people sat down. Then Jesus took the five loaves of bread and two fish, and looking up to heaven, he thanked God for the food. Then he divided the food and gave it to the followers to give to the people. They all ate and were satisfied, and what was left over was gathered up, filling twelve baskets.

A man from Baal Shalishah came to Elisha, bringing him twenty loaves of barley bread from the first harvest. He also brought fresh grain in his sack. Elisha said, "Give it to the people to eat."

Elisha's servant asked, "How can I feed a hundred people with so little?"

"Give the bread to the people to eat," Elisha said. "This is what the LORD says: 'They will eat and will have food left over.'"

After he gave it to them, the people ate and had food left over, as the LORD had said.

2 Kings 4:42–44

*L*ord, you have been our home
 since the beginning.
Before the mountains were born
 and before you created the earth and
  the world,
you are God.
 You have always been, and you will
  always be.

You turn people back into dust.
 You say, "Go back into dust, human
  beings."
To you, a thousand years
 is like the passing of a day,
 or like a few hours in the night.
While people sleep, you take their lives.
 They are like grass that grows up in
  the morning.
In the morning they are fresh and new,
 but by evening they dry up and die.

Psalm 90:1–6

*N*ow you will see that I am the one
  God!
 There is no god but me.
I send life and death;
 I can hurt, and I can heal.
 No one can escape from me."

Deuteronomy 32:39

*B*ut ask the animals, and they will
  teach you,
 or ask the birds of the air, and they
  will tell you.
Speak to the earth, and it will teach
  you,
 or let the fish of the sea tell you.
Every one of these knows
 that the hand of the LORD has done
  this.
The life of every creature
 and the breath of all people are in
  God's hand."

Job 12:7–10

*N*o two days were ever exactly the same on my bit of beach. Part of its great appeal lay in the ever-changing appearance of its shoreline.

The subtle play of sunlight and shadow on the cliff faces altered their contours. Some mornings the rugged rocks seemed softened by the muted shades of the rising sun. They glowed warm, golden, wrapped in sunshine and serenity.

Other days the same rock buttresses stood gray and forbidding in the fog and mist that swirled in off the sea. The shoreline looked almost black, dark with dampness, soaked with sea spray.

Always, always, always the ocean is at work on the land. Summer and winter, spring and autumn the changing tides rise and ebb, shaping the character of the coast. Their force is utterly relentless—their power immeasurable—their titanic thrust untamed.

Great mysteries surround the majestic, awesome action of the tides. With incredible precision they move billions of tons of water from surface to surface upon the sea. They are the reflection of gigantic energy within the cosmos that knows no rest, that never slumbers, that never sleeps.

In the same overshadowing way, our Father watches over His children, quietly overseeing the events of their lives that they might accomplish His purposes for Him.

W. Phillip Keller

*W*hat do these readings show that God controls? Is there anything more for him to control? What experience in your life or image from nature reminds you that God is in control? Think of it often, and praise God for his great sovereignty!

M O N D A Y:

God Is a Patient Teacher

Luke 9:18–43a

Jesus Is the Christ

*O*ne time when Jesus was praying alone, his followers were with him, and he asked them, "Who do the people say I am?"

They answered, "Some say you are John the Baptist. Others say you are Elijah. And others say you are one of the prophets from long ago who has come back to life."

Then Jesus asked, "But who do you say I am?"

Peter answered, "You are the Christ from God."

Jesus warned them not to tell anyone, saying, "The Son of Man must suffer many things. He will be rejected by the older Jewish leaders, the leading priests, and the teachers of the law. He will be killed and after three days will be raised from the dead."

Jesus said to all of them, "If people want to follow me, they must give up the things they want. They must be willing to give up their lives daily to follow me. Those who want to save their lives will give up true life. But those who give up their lives for me will have true life. It is worth nothing for them to have the whole world if they themselves are destroyed or lost. If people are ashamed of me and my teaching, then the Son of Man will be ashamed of them when he comes in his glory and with the glory of the Father and the holy angels. I tell you the truth, some people standing here will see the kingdom of God before they die."

Jesus Talks with Moses and Elijah

*A*bout eight days after Jesus said these things, he took Peter, John, and James and went up on a mountain to pray. While Jesus was praying, the appearance of his face changed, and his clothes became shining white. Then two men, Moses and Elijah, were talking with Jesus. They appeared in heavenly glory, talking about his departure which he would soon bring about in Jerusalem. Peter and the others were very sleepy, but when they awoke fully, they saw the glory of Jesus and the two men standing with him. When Moses and Elijah were about to leave, Peter said to Jesus, "Master, it is good that we are here. Let us make three tents—one for you, one for Moses, and one for Elijah." (Peter did not know what he was talking about.)

While he was saying these things, a cloud came and covered them, and they became afraid as the cloud covered them. A voice came from the cloud, saying, "This is my Son, whom I have chosen. Listen to him!"

When the voice finished speaking, only Jesus was there. Peter, John, and James said nothing and told no one at that time what they had seen.

Jesus Heals a Sick Boy

*T*he next day, when they came down from the mountain, a large crowd met Jesus. A man in the crowd shouted to him, "Teacher, please come and look at my son, because he is my only child. An evil spirit seizes my son, and suddenly he screams. It causes him to lose control of himself and foam at the mouth. The evil spirit keeps on hurting him and almost never leaves him. I begged your followers to force the evil spirit out, but they could not do it."

Jesus answered, "You people have no faith, and your lives are all wrong. How long must I stay with you and put up with you? Bring your son here."

While the boy was coming, the demon threw him on the ground and made him lose control of himself. But Jesus gave a strong command to the evil spirit and healed the boy and gave him back to his father. All the people were amazed at the great power of God.

God Patiently Teaches
the Children of Israel

*Y*ou have great mercy,
   so you did not leave them in the
   desert.

The pillar of cloud guided them by day,
and the pillar of fire led them at night,
lighting the way they were to go.
You gave your good Spirit to teach them.
You gave them manna to eat
and water when they were thirsty.
You took care of them for forty years in
the desert;
they needed nothing.
Their clothes did not wear out,
and their feet did not swell.

"But they were disobedient and turned
against you
and ignored your teachings.
Your prophets warned them to come
back to you,
but they killed those prophets
and spoke against you.
So you handed them over to their
enemies,
and their enemies treated them badly.
But in this time of trouble our ancestors cried out to you,
and you heard from heaven.
You had great mercy
and gave them saviors who saved
them from the power of their
enemies.
But as soon as they had rest,
they again did what was evil.
So you left them to their enemies
who ruled over them.
When they cried out to you again,
you heard from heaven.
Because of your mercy, you saved
them again and again.
You warned them to return to your
teachings,
but they were proud and did not
obey your commands.
If someone obeys your laws, he will
live,
but they sinned against your laws.
They were stubborn, unwilling, and
disobedient.
You were patient with them for many
years
and warned them by your Spirit
through the prophets,
but they did not pay attention.
So you handed them over to other
countries.

But because your mercy is great, you
did not kill them all or leave them.
You are a kind and merciful God."
Nehemiah 9:19–21, 26–31

In Judaism it was the custom for the pupil to select the rabbi of his choice and attach himself to him for instruction. Thus Paul sat "at the feet of Gamaliel" (Acts 22:3, KJV). But here it was Jesus and not the disciples who took the initiative. "When day came, He called His disciples to Him; and chose twelve of them" (Luke 6:13). . . . He called them personally and bound them to Him with bonds of affection that stood the test of time. Thus He chose to invest His life and channel it into that little group of men. . . .

. . . They were not theologians or politi-cal leaders—just ordinary men who became extraordinary under the molding hand of the Master Potter. That makes His selection of them the more wonderful. . . .

Their imperfections were painfully appar-ent, but those did not debar them from His fellowship and friendship. If God required perfection before He admitted us into the circle of His fellowship, who would qualify? Quirks of temperament did not disqualify them, or Peter with his volatile nature would not have been counted in. Nor would James and John with their selfish ambition and callous racism. Thomas's disbelief would have placed him outside the circle. But Jesus wel-comed them all into the circle of His love and intimacy.

J. Oswald Sanders

PAUSE FOR REFLECTION

Chronicle your own spiritual journey in a way similar to Nehemiah's account of God's dealings with the children of Israel. In what ways has God stood beside you as a patient, wise, and ever-merciful teacher? Thank him for claiming you as his own.

TUESDAY:

God Seeks Those Who Follow Him Faithfully

Luke 9:43b—10:7

NEW TESTAMENT READING

Jesus Talks About His Death

*W*hile everyone was wondering about all that Jesus did, he said to his followers, "Don't forget what I tell you now: The Son of Man will be handed over to people." But the followers did not understand what this meant; the meaning was hidden from them so they could not understand. But they were afraid to ask Jesus about it.

Who Is the Greatest?

*J*esus' followers began to have an argument about which one of them was the greatest. Jesus knew what they were thinking, so he took a little child and stood the child beside him. Then Jesus said, "Whoever accepts this little child in my name accepts me. And whoever accepts me accepts the One who sent me, because whoever is least among you all is really the greatest."

Anyone Not Against Us Is for Us

*J*ohn answered, "Master, we saw someone using your name to force demons out of people. We told him to stop, because he does not belong to our group."

But Jesus said to him, "Don't stop him, because whoever is not against you is for you."

A Town Rejects Jesus

*W*hen the time was coming near for Jesus to depart, he was determined to go to Jerusalem. He sent some men ahead of him, who went into a town in Samaria to make everything ready for him. But the people there would not welcome him, because he was set on going to Jerusalem. When James and John, followers of Jesus, saw this, they said, "Lord, do you want us to call fire down from heaven and destroy those people?"

But Jesus turned and scolded them. Then they went to another town.

Following Jesus

*A*s they were going along the road, someone said to Jesus, "I will follow you any place you go."

Jesus said to them, "The foxes have holes to live in, and the birds have nests, but the Son of Man has no place to rest his head."

Jesus said to another man, "Follow me!"

But he said, "Lord, first let me go and bury my father."

But Jesus said to him, "Let the people who are dead bury their own dead. You must go and tell about the kingdom of God."

Another man said, "I will follow you, Lord, but first let me go and say good-bye to my family."

Jesus said, "Anyone who begins to plow a field but keeps looking back is of no use in the kingdom of God."

Jesus Sends Out the Seventy-Two

*A*fter this, the Lord chose seventy-two others and sent them out in pairs ahead of him into every town and place where he planned to go. He said to them, "There are a great many people to harvest, but there are only a few workers. So pray to God, who owns the harvest, that he will send more workers to help gather his harvest. Go now, but listen! I am sending you out like sheep among wolves. Don't carry a purse, a bag, or sandals, and don't waste time talking with people on the road. Before you go into a house, say, 'Peace be with this house.' If peaceful people live there, your blessing of peace will stay with them, but if not, then your blessing will come back to you. Stay in the peaceful house, eating and drinking what the people there give you. A worker should be given his pay. Don't move from house to house."

OLD TESTAMENT READING

I have followed the ways of the LORD;
    I have not done evil by turning from
      my God.
I remember all his laws
    and have not broken his rules.
I am innocent before him;
    I have kept myself from doing evil.

The LORD rewarded me because I did
what was right,
because I did what the LORD said
was right.

"LORD, you are loyal to those who are
loyal,
and you are good to those who are
good.
You are pure to those who are pure,
but you are against those who are
evil.
You save the humble,
but you bring down those who are
proud.
LORD, you give light to my lamp.
The LORD brightens the darkness
around me.
With your help I can attack an army.
With God's help I can jump over a
wall."

2 Samuel 22:22–30

*H*ezekiah did what the LORD said was
right, just as his ancestor David had done.
Hezekiah trusted in the LORD, the God of
Israel. There was no one like him among all
the kings of Judah, either before him or after him. Hezekiah was loyal to the LORD and
did not stop following him; he obeyed the
commands the LORD had given Moses. And
the LORD was with Hezekiah, so he had success in everything he did. He turned against
the king of Assyria and stopped serving
him. Hezekiah defeated the Philistines all
the way to Gaza and its borders, including the
watchtowers and the strong, walled cities.

2 Kings 18:3, 5–8

*A*t that time Hanani the seer came to Asa
king of Judah and said to him, "You depended
on the king of Aram to help you and not on
the LORD your God. So the king of Aram's
army escaped from you. The Cushites and
Libyans had a large and powerful army and
many chariots and horsemen. But you depended on the LORD to help you, so he
handed them over to you. The LORD searches
all the earth for people who have given
themselves completely to him. He wants to
make them strong. Asa, you did a foolish
thing, so from now on you will have wars."

2 Chronicles 16:7–9

*W*hen you begin to pray, your life can take
on all kinds of perils and problems that you
never had before. Think about it. As far as
we know, Abraham was living a comfortable,
trouble-free life until he began to pray. It was
through prayer that he heard God's message
to leave home, move out, hit the road for an
unknown destination, and start a journey of
indeterminate length. His life became ex-
ceedingly difficult and dangerous. . . .

Prayer was the launching pad for Moses
as well. He was quietly tending sheep in the
Midian hills, leading a settled life with his
wife and sons and his father-in-law. Things
changed when he started to pray. It started
dramatically enough at a burning bush,
where he heard God speak to him and entrust
him with an impossible task—that of leading
the Israelites out of Egypt. From one perspective, that was the last really comfortable
day of Moses' life. . . .

Peter, James, John, and Andrew were
comfortable, middle-class businessmen, settled
and respected in their community, until their
dialog with Jesus began. As they responded to
his invitation to, "Follow me," all of that
ended. They embarked on three years of intense ministry and then carried out the commission to "go and make disciples of all nations" (Matt. 28:19) in the face of unimag-
inable adversity and persecution. . . .

That is the peril of prayer. . . . As we
begin to talk to God and hear him speak to
us, life may never be the same.

Bruce Larson

*W*hen Jesus walked on earth, he literally
called his disciples to follow him. How does
he call people when he isn't living on earth?
Is God calling you, through your prayers, to
break out into new territory, to follow him
more faithfully?

WEDNESDAY:
God Gives His Wisdom and Power to His Servants
Luke 10:8–29

*I*f you go into a town and the people welcome you, eat what they give you. Heal the sick who live there, and tell them, 'The kingdom of God is near you.' But if you go into a town, and the people don't welcome you, then go into the streets and say, 'Even the dirt from your town that sticks to our feet we wipe off against you. But remember that the kingdom of God is near.' I tell you, on the Judgment Day it will be better for the people of Sodom than for the people of that town.

Jesus Warns Unbelievers

*H*ow terrible for you, Korazin! How terrible for you, Bethsaida! If the miracles I did in you had happened in Tyre and Sidon, those people would have changed their lives long ago. They would have worn rough cloth and put ashes on themselves to show they had changed. But on the Judgment Day it will be better for Tyre and Sidon than for you. And you, Capernaum, will you be lifted up to heaven? No! You will be thrown down to the depths!

"Whoever listens to you listens to me, and whoever refuses to accept you refuses to accept me. And whoever refuses to accept me refuses to accept the One who sent me."

Satan Falls

*W*hen the seventy-two came back, they were very happy and said, "Lord, even the demons obeyed us when we used your name!"

Jesus said, "I saw Satan fall like lightning from heaven. Listen, I have given you power to walk on snakes and scorpions, power that is greater than the enemy has. So nothing will hurt you. But you should not be happy because the spirits obey you but because your names are written in heaven."

Jesus Prays to the Father

*T*hen Jesus rejoiced in the Holy Spirit and said, "I praise you, Father, Lord of heaven and earth, because you have hidden these things from the people who are wise and smart. But you have shown them to those who are like little children. Yes, Father, this is what you really wanted.

"My Father has given me all things. No one knows who the Son is, except the Father. And no one knows who the Father is, except the Son and those whom the Son chooses to tell."

Then Jesus turned to his followers and said privately, "You are blessed to see what you now see. I tell you, many prophets and kings wanted to see what you now see, but they did not, and they wanted to hear what you now hear, but they did not."

The Good Samaritan

*T*hen an expert on the law stood up to test Jesus, saying, "Teacher, what must I do to get life forever?"

Jesus said, "What is written in the law? What do you read there?"

The man answered, "Love the Lord your God with all your heart, all your soul, all your strength, and all your mind." Also, "Love your neighbor as you love yourself."

Jesus said to him, "Your answer is right. Do this and you will live."

But the man, wanting to show the importance of his question, said to Jesus, "And who is my neighbor?"

Others Who Showed God's Spirit

*T*hen the king's mother, who had heard the voices of the king and his royal guests, came into the banquet room. She said, "O king, live forever! Don't be afraid or let your face be white with fear! There is a man in your kingdom who has the spirit of the holy gods. In the days of your father, this man showed understanding, knowledge, and wisdom like the gods. Your father, King Nebuchadnezzar, put this man in charge of all the wise men, fortune-tellers, magicians, and wizards. The man I am talking about is named Daniel, whom the king named Belteshazzar. He was very smart and had knowledge and understanding. He could explain dreams and secrets and could answer very hard problems. Call for Daniel. He will tell you what the writing on the wall means."

So they brought Daniel to the king, and the king asked, "Is your name Daniel? Are you one of the captives my father the king brought from Judah? I have heard that the spirit of the gods is in you, and that you are very smart and have knowledge and extraordinary understanding."

Daniel 5:10–14

When the people of Israel heard about King Solomon's decision, they respected him very much. They saw he had wisdom from God to make the right decisions.

1 Kings 3:28

God gave Solomon great wisdom so he could understand many things. His wisdom was as hard to measure as the grains of sand on the seashore. His wisdom was greater than any wisdom of the East, or any wisdom in Egypt. He was wiser than anyone on earth. He was even wiser than Ethan the Ezrahite, as well as Heman, Calcol, and Darda—the three sons of Mahol. King Solomon became famous in all the surrounding countries. During his life he spoke three thousand wise sayings and also wrote one thousand five songs. He taught about many kinds of plants—everything from the great cedar trees of Lebanon to the weeds that grow out of the walls. He also taught about animals, birds, crawling things, and fish. People from all nations came to listen to King Solomon's wisdom. The kings of all nations sent them to him, because they had heard of Solomon's wisdom.

1 Kings 4:29–34

INSIGHTS

Too many Christians do not believe Christ's promise that He would endue the Church with spiritual power; they doubt that His promise is to every believer. Consequently, they have no faith to lay hold of Christ's power. If His promise does not belong to all, how can they know to whom it does belong? Of course, with this limited understanding they cannot lay hold of the promise by faith.

Another lack in Christians is persistence in waiting upon God for that which He has promised to us in the Scriptures. People give up before they have prevailed, and hence, the enduement of spiritual power is not received.

Of great concern also is the extent to which the Church has practically lost sight of the necessity of the enduement of spiritual power. Much is said about our dependence upon the Holy Spirit by almost everybody, but how little is this dependence realized. Christians and even ministers go to work without any spiritual power. I mourn to be obliged to say that the ranks of the ministry seem to be filling up with those who do not possess spiritual power. May the Lord have mercy upon us! Will this last remark be thought uncharitable? If so, let the current state of the Church and her success in evangelism be heard on this subject. Surely, something is wrong.

Charles Finney

APPLICATION

What is the source of the believer's wisdom and power? What is the believer's true reason for happiness? Take a look at your life. In what do you find happiness? Is spiritual power evident in your life? Pray that God's spirit will be alive in you.

175

THURSDAY:
It Is Good to Show Kindness to Others
Luke 10:30—11:13

N E W   T E S T A M E N T   R E A D I N G

*J*esus answered, "As a man was going down from Jerusalem to Jericho, some robbers attacked him. They tore off his clothes, beat him, and left him lying there, almost dead. It happened that a Jewish priest was going down that road. When he saw the man, he walked by on the other side. Next, a Levite came there, and after he went over and looked at the man, he walked by on the other side of the road. Then a Samaritan traveling down the road came to where the hurt man was. When he saw the man, he felt very sorry for him. The Samaritan went to him, poured olive oil and wine on his wounds, and bandaged them. Then he put the hurt man on his own donkey and took him to an inn where he cared for him. The next day, the Samaritan brought out two coins, gave them to the innkeeper, and said, 'Take care of this man. If you spend more money on him, I will pay it back to you when I come again.'"

Then Jesus said, "Which one of these three men do you think was a neighbor to the man who was attacked by the robbers?"

The expert on the law answered, "The one who showed him mercy."

Jesus said to him, "Then go and do what he did."

Mary and Martha

*W*hile Jesus and his followers were traveling, Jesus went into a town. A woman named Martha let Jesus stay at her house. Martha had a sister named Mary, who was sitting at Jesus' feet and listening to him teach. But Martha was busy with all the work to be done. She went in and said, "Lord, don't you care that my sister has left me alone to do all the work? Tell her to help me."

But the Lord answered her, "Martha, Martha, you are worried and upset about many things. Only one thing is important. Mary has chosen the better thing, and it will never be taken away from her."

Jesus Teaches About Prayer

*O*ne time Jesus was praying in a certain place. When he finished, one of his followers said to him, "Lord, teach us to pray as John taught his followers."

Jesus said to them, "When you pray, say:
'Father, may your name always be kept holy.
May your kingdom come.
Give us the food we need for each day.
Forgive us for our sins,
   because we forgive everyone who
      has done wrong to us.
And do not cause us to be tempted.'"

Continue to Ask

*T*hen Jesus said to them, "Suppose one of you went to your friend's house at midnight and said to him, 'Friend, loan me three loaves of bread. A friend of mine has come into town to visit me, but I have nothing for him to eat.' Your friend inside the house answers, 'Don't bother me! The door is already locked, and my children and I are in bed. I cannot get up and give you anything.' I tell you, if friendship is not enough to make him get up to give you the bread, your boldness will make him get up and give you whatever you need. So I tell you, ask, and God will give to you. Search, and you will find. Knock, and the door will open for you. Yes, everyone who asks will receive. The one who searches will find. And everyone who knocks will have the door opened. If your children ask for a fish, which of you would give them a snake instead? Or, if your children ask for an egg, would you give them a scorpion? Even though you are bad, you know how to give good things to your children. How much more your heavenly Father will give the Holy Spirit to those who ask him!"

O L D   T E S T A M E N T   R E A D I N G

*M*y child, do not forget my teaching,
   but keep my commands in mind.
Then you will live a long time,

and your life will be successful.

Don't ever forget kindness and truth.
 Wear them like a necklace.
 Write them on your heart as if on a
  tablet.
Then you will be respected
 and will please both God and people.

Whenever you are able,
 do good to people who need help.
If you have what your neighbor asks for,
 don't say, "Come back later.
 I will give it to you tomorrow."

Proverbs 3:1–4, 27–28

*P*raise the LORD!

Happy are those who respect the LORD,
 who want what he commands.
A light shines in the dark for honest
  people,
 for those who are merciful and kind
  and good.
It is good to be merciful and generous.

Psalm 112:1, 4–5a

*T*here was a priest in Midian who had seven daughters. His daughters went to that well to get water to fill the water troughs for their father's flock. Some shepherds came and chased the girls away, but Moses defended the girls and watered their flock.

When they went back to their father Reuel, he asked them, "Why have you come home early today?"

The girls answered, "The shepherds chased us away, but an Egyptian defended us. He got water for us and watered our flock."

He asked his daughters, "Where is this man? Why did you leave him? Invite him to eat with us."

Exodus 2:16–20

*B*ut the LORD was with Joseph and showed him kindness and caused the prison warden to like Joseph. The prison warden chose Joseph to take care of all the prisoners, and he was responsible for whatever was done in the prison. The warden paid no attention to anything that was in Joseph's care because the LORD was with

Joseph and made him successful in everything he did.

Genesis 39:21–23

INSIGHTS

*K*indness is a sincere desire for the happiness of others; goodness is the activity calculated to advance that happiness. . . .

. . . The New Testament has much to say about the kindness of God. The first mention is in Luke 6: Jesus says that God "is kind to the ungrateful and wicked." Next we find that God's kindness leads sinners toward repentance (Romans 2:4). In Ephesians 2:7, in the context of our utter lostness and sin, Paul speaks of the incomparable riches of God's grace, expressed in his kindness to us in Christ Jesus. . . .

What lesson can we draw from these accounts of the kindness of God? He is kind to all men—the ungrateful, the wicked, the utterly lost and hopeless, the rebellious—without distinction. . . .

Our natural inclination is to show kindness only to those for whom we have some natural affinity—family, friends, likable neighbors. But God shows kindness to those who are most despicable—the ungrateful and wicked. Have you ever tried to be kind to someone who was ungrateful? Unless God's grace was working in your heart in a significant way, your reaction to his ingratitude may well have been, "I'll never do anything for him again!" But God doesn't turn his back on the ungrateful. . . .

We need to develop a kind disposition, to be sensitive to others and truly desire their happiness. But sensitivity alone is not enough: the grace of goodness impels us to take action to meet those needs.

Jerry Bridges

ACTION POINT

*T*hink about contemporary parallels to the story of the good Samaritan that show what it means for you to do good to anyone who needs help even when it is inconvenient or unpleasant. Diligently pray that you will seek ways to express God's kindness.

177

FRIDAY:

Focus Your Eyes on the Things of God

Luke 11:14–36

NEW TESTAMENT READING

Jesus' Power Is from God

*O*ne time Jesus was sending out a demon that could not talk. When the demon came out, the man who had been unable to speak, then spoke. The people were amazed. But some of them said, "Jesus uses the power of Beelzebul, the ruler of demons, to force demons out of people."

Other people, wanting to test Jesus, asked him to give them a sign from heaven. But knowing their thoughts, he said to them, "Every kingdom that is divided against itself will be destroyed. And a family that is divided against itself will not continue. So if Satan is divided against himself, his kingdom will not continue. You say that I use the power of Beelzebul to force out demons. But if I use the power of Beelzebul to force out demons, what power do your people use to force demons out? So they will be your judges. But if I use the power of God to force out demons, then the kingdom of God has come to you.

"When a strong person with many weapons guards his own house, his possessions are safe. But when someone stronger comes and defeats him, the stronger one will take away the weapons the first man trusted and will give away the possessions.

"Anyone who is not with me is against me, and anyone who does not work with me is working against me.

The Empty Person

*W*hen an evil spirit comes out of a person, it travels through dry places, looking for a place to rest. But when it finds no place, it says, 'I will go back to the house I left.' And when it comes back, it finds that house swept clean and made neat. Then the evil spirit goes out and brings seven other spirits more evil than it is, and they go in and live there. So the person has even more trouble than before."

People Who Are Truly Happy

*A*s Jesus was saying these things, a woman in the crowd called out to Jesus, "Happy is the mother who gave birth to you and nursed you."

But Jesus said, "No, happy are those who hear the teaching of God and obey it."

The People Want a Miracle

*A*s the crowd grew larger, Jesus said, "The people who live today are evil. They want to see a miracle for a sign, but no sign will be given them, except the sign of Jonah. As Jonah was a sign for those people who lived in Nineveh, the Son of Man will be a sign for the people of this time. On the Judgment Day the Queen of the South will stand up with the people who live now. She will show they are guilty, because she came from far away to listen to Solomon's wise teaching. And I tell you that someone greater than Solomon is here. On the Judgment Day the people of Nineveh will stand up with the people who live now, and they will show that you are guilty. When Jonah preached to them, they were sorry and changed their lives. And I tell you that someone greater than Jonah is here.

Be a Light for the World

*N*o one lights a lamp and puts it in a secret place or under a bowl, but on a lampstand so the people who come in can see. Your eye is a light for the body. When your eyes are good, your whole body will be full of light. But when your eyes are evil, your whole body will be full of darkness. So be careful not to let the light in you become darkness. If your whole body is full of light, and none of it is dark, then you will shine bright, as when a lamp shines on you."

OLD TESTAMENT READING

*T*he way of the good person is like the
    light of dawn,
        growing brighter and brighter until
        full daylight.
But the wicked walk around in the dark;

they can't even see what makes
    them stumble.

My child, pay attention to my words;
    listen closely to what I say.
Don't ever forget my words;
    keep them always in mind.
They are the key to life for those who
    find them;
    they bring health to the whole body.
Be careful what you think,
    because your thoughts run your life.
Don't use your mouth to tell lies;
    don't ever say things that are not
    true.
Keep your eyes focused on what is right,
    and look straight ahead to what is
    good.
Be careful what you do,
    and always do what is right.
Don't turn off the road of goodness;
    keep away from evil paths.

Proverbs 4:18–27

*T*he LORD said to Moses, "Speak to the Israelites and tell them this: 'Tie several
pieces of thread together and attach them
to the corners of your clothes. Put a blue
thread in each one of these tassels. Wear
them from now on. You will have these tassels to look at to remind you of all the LORD's
commands. Then you will obey them and
not be disloyal by following what your bodies and eyes want. Then you will remember to obey all my commands, and you will
be God's holy people. I am the LORD your
God, who brought you out of Egypt to be
your God. I am the LORD your God.'"

Numbers 15:37–41

*D*o good to me, your servant, so I can
    live,
    so I can obey your word.
Open my eyes to see
    the miracles in your teachings.
I am a stranger on earth.
    Do not hide your commands from
    me.

Psalm 119:17–19

*L*ORD, you give light to my lamp.
    My God brightens the darkness
    around me.

Psalm 18:28

INSIGHTS

*T*he nature of the Christian life is Christ's
life taking hold upon all the inner life of a
man, changing, dominating, pulsating. It is
seen therefore, and I do not think we can be
too careful in emphasizing this, that Christian life is neither human imitation of Christ,
nor correct intellectual positions concerning
Christ. Neither is it a cult, or a system of
thought. I may attempt to imitate Christ sincerely through long years, and yet never be a
Christian. I may hold absolutely correct intellectual views concerning Christ as a person,
and His power, and yet never be a Christian.
It is possible for me to admire Him, and attempt with all the power of my life to imitate
Him, and yet never realize Him. It is quite
possible for a person to believe most sincerely
in His Deity, and in the fact of His atoning
work, and moreover, in the necessity for regeneration, and yet never be submitted to His
Lordship, never to have personal share in the
work of His atonement, never to be born
again.

Nothing short of the coming into life of the
individual of Christ Himself constitutes a
Christian. If Jesus Christ is external to your
life there will be times when the world will
not see Him and hear Him, and will not know
you belong to Him. But if Christ be in you,
living, reigning there absolutely, and you are
obeying Him, there never will be a moment
when the truth will not be evident. You cannot
hide Christ if once He comes within. If the
light is there, it simply must shine.

G. Campbell Morgan

APPLICATION

*W*hat happens when a person focuses his or
her eyes on the good things of God? Is your
body filled with the light of Christ? What
practical reminder (like the tassels on the
Israelites' clothes) will help you keep your eyes
focused on God?

WEEKEND:
Trust God; Don't Fear People
Luke 11:37—12:7

Jesus Accuses the Pharisees

After Jesus had finished speaking, a Pharisee asked Jesus to eat with him. So Jesus went in and sat at the table. But the Pharisee was surprised when he saw that Jesus did not wash his hands before the meal. The Lord said to him, "You Pharisees clean the outside of the cup and the dish, but inside you are full of greed and evil. You foolish people! The same one who made what is outside also made what is inside. So give what is in your dishes to the poor, and then you will be fully clean. How terrible for you Pharisees! You give God one-tenth of even your mint, your rue, and every other plant in your garden. But you fail to be fair to others and to love God. These are the things you should do while continuing to do those other things. How terrible for you Pharisees, because you love to have the most important seats in the synagogues, and you love to be greeted with respect in the marketplaces. How terrible for you, because you are like hidden graves, which people walk on without knowing."

Jesus Talks to Experts on the Law

One of the experts on the law said to Jesus, "Teacher, when you say these things, you are insulting us, too."

Jesus answered, "How terrible for you, you experts on the law! You make strict rules that are very hard for people to obey, but you yourselves don't even try to follow those rules. How terrible for you, because you build tombs for the prophets whom your ancestors killed! And now you show that you approve of what your ancestors did. They killed the prophets, and you build tombs for them! This is why in his wisdom God said, 'I will send prophets and apostles to them. They will kill some, and they will treat others cruelly.' So you who live now will be punished for the deaths of all the prophets who were killed since the beginning of the world—from the killing of Abel to the killing of Zechariah, who died between the altar and the Temple. Yes, I tell you that you who are alive now will be punished for them all.

"How terrible for you, you experts on the law. You have taken away the key to learning about God. You yourselves would not learn, and you stopped others from learning, too."

When Jesus left, the teachers of the law and the Pharisees began to give him trouble, asking him questions about many things, trying to catch him saying something wrong.

Don't Be Like the Pharisees

So many thousands of people had gathered that they were stepping on each other. Jesus spoke first to his followers, saying, "Beware of the yeast of the Pharisees, because they are hypocrites. Everything that is hidden will be shown, and everything that is secret will be made known. What you have said in the dark will be heard in the light, and what you have whispered in an inner room will be shouted from the housetops.

"I tell you, my friends, don't be afraid of people who can kill the body but after that can do nothing more to hurt you. I will show you the one to fear. Fear the one who has the power to kill you and also to throw you into hell. Yes, this is the one you should fear.

"Five sparrows are sold for only two pennies, and God does not forget any of them. But God even knows how many hairs you have on your head. Don't be afraid. You are worth much more than many sparrows."

You people who know what is right
 should listen to me;
 you people who follow my teachings
 should hear what I say.
Don't be afraid of the evil things people
 say,
 and don't be upset by their insults.
Moths will eat those people as if they
 were clothes,
 and worms will eat them as if they
 were wool.

But my goodness will continue forever,
and my salvation will continue from
now on."

The LORD says, "I am the one who
comforts you.
So why should you be afraid of
people, who die?
Why should you fear people who die
like the grass?
Have you forgotten the LORD who made
you,
who stretched out the skies
and made the earth?
Why are you always afraid
of those angry people who trouble
you
and who want to destroy?
But where are those angry people now?
People in prison will soon be set free;
they will not die in prison,
and they will have enough food.
I am the LORD your God,
who stirs the sea and makes the
waves roar.
My name is the LORD All-Powerful.
I will give you the words I want you to
say.
I will cover you with my hands and
protect you.
I made the heavens and the earth,
and I say to Jerusalem, 'You are my
people.'"

Isaiah 51:7–8, 12–16

*B*eing afraid of people can get you
into trouble,
but if you trust the LORD, you will be
safe.

Proverbs 29:25

*W*hen I am afraid,
I will trust you.
I praise God for his word.
I trust God, so I am not afraid.
What can human beings do to me?

Psalm 56:3–4

*M*any of us have lost the fear of the Lord.
We have forgotten our deep awe for the
character of God, His holiness, His eternality,
His sovereignty over all the affairs of men.
We let Him get smaller. We let our impression of ourselves get bigger. We see ourselves
as larger in intellect and capabilities, as more
technologically advanced and more scientific.
As we prosper, we don't need God as we once
did.

What is the fear of the Lord? And how can
we get it into our lives? The fear of the Lord
is to love what God loves and to hate what
God hates. The fear of the Lord is both positive
and negative. . . .

The positive is to love what God loves—
wisdom. God loves wisdom. The fear of the
Lord is to love wisdom. "My son, if you accept my words and store up my commands
within you, turning your ear to wisdom and
applying your heart to understanding . . . then you will understand the fear
of the Lord and find the knowledge of God.
For the Lord gives wisdom." (Proverbs 2:1–
2, 5–6). . . .

The negative is to hate what God hates—
evil. God hates evil. "To fear the Lord is to
hate evil." (Proverbs 8:13). "Through the fear
of the Lord a man avoids evil" (Proverbs
16:6). "To shun evil is understanding" (Job
28:28). The person who would understand
the fear of the Lord will hate what God hates.
God hates evil, so he will hate evil. . . .

The person gripped by godly fear cannot
tolerate evil because God does not tolerate
evil. He hates evil with the intensity that God
hates evil, or at least he tries to. He is a re-
former, not a recluse. His hatred of evil
sanctions him no occasion to tolerate.

Patrick Morley

*W*hat kind of fear of God did Jesus tell the
Pharisees and teachers of the law they should
have? In your own words, describe the two
kinds of fear that those who trust the Lord
should have.

MONDAY:

Where Is Your Treasure?

Luke 12:8–34

NEW TESTAMENT READING

Don't Be Ashamed of Jesus

I tell you, all those who stand before others and say they believe in me, I, the Son of Man, will say before the angels of God that they belong to me. But all who stand before others and say they do not believe in me, I will say before the angels of God that they do not belong to me.

"Anyone who speaks against the Son of Man can be forgiven, but anyone who speaks against the Holy Spirit will not be forgiven.

"When you are brought into the synagogues before the leaders and other powerful people, don't worry about how to defend yourself or what to say. At that time the Holy Spirit will teach you what you must say."

Jesus Warns Against Selfishness

*S*omeone in the crowd said to Jesus, "Teacher, tell my brother to divide with me the property our father left us."

But Jesus said to him, "Who said I should judge or decide between you?" Then Jesus said to them, "Be careful and guard against all kinds of greed. Life is not measured by how much one owns."

Then Jesus told this story: "There was a rich man who had some land, which grew a good crop. He thought to himself, 'What will I do? I have no place to keep all my crops.' Then he said, 'This is what I will do: I will tear down my barns and build bigger ones, and there I will store all my grain and other goods. Then I can say to myself, "I have enough good things stored to last for many years. Rest, eat, drink, and enjoy life!"'

"But God said to him, 'Foolish man! Tonight your life will be taken from you. So who will get those things you have prepared for yourself?'

"This is how it will be for those who store up things for themselves and are not rich toward God."

Don't Worry

*J*esus said to his followers, "So I tell you, don't worry about the food you need to live, or about the clothes you need for your body. Life is more than food, and the body is more than clothes. Look at the birds. They don't plant or harvest, they don't have storerooms or barns, but God feeds them. And you are worth much more than birds. You cannot add any time to your life by worrying about it. If you cannot do even the little things, then why worry about the big things? Consider how the lilies grow; they don't work or make clothes for themselves. But I tell you that even Solomon with his riches was not dressed as beautifully as one of these flowers. God clothes the grass in the field, which is alive today but tomorrow is thrown into the fire. So how much more will God clothe you? Don't have so little faith! Don't always think about what you will eat or what you will drink, and don't keep worrying. All the people in the world are trying to get these things, and your Father knows you need them. But seek God's kingdom, and all the other things you need will be given to you.

Don't Trust in Money

*D*on't fear, little flock, because your Father wants to give you the kingdom. Sell your possessions and give to the poor. Get for yourselves purses that will not wear out, the treasure in heaven that never runs out, where thieves can't steal and moths can't destroy. Your heart will be where your treasure is."

OLD TESTAMENT READING

I ask two things from you, LORD.
    Don't refuse me before I die.
Keep me from lying and being dishonest.
    And don't make me either rich or
        poor;
        just give me enough food for each
        day.
If I have too much, I might reject you
    and say, 'I don't know the LORD.'
If I am poor, I might steal
    and disgrace the name of my God."

Proverbs 30:7–9

*D*on't wear yourself out trying to get
   rich;
   be wise enough to control yourself.
Wealth can vanish in the wink of an
      eye.
   It can seem to grow wings
   and fly away like an eagle.

Proverbs 23:4–5

*W*hoever loves money
   will never have enough money;
Whoever loves wealth
   will not be satisfied with it.
   This is also useless.
The more wealth people have,
   the more friends they have to help
      spend it.
So what do people really gain?
   They gain nothing except to look at
      their riches.

Ecclesiastes 5:10–11

*E*vil people never lack an appetite,
   and nothing escapes their selfish-
      ness.
But nothing will be left for them to eat;
   their riches will not continue.
When they still have plenty, trouble will
      catch up to them,
   and great misery will come down on
      them.
When the wicked fill their stomachs,
   God will send his burning anger
      against them,
   and blows of punishment will fall on
      them like rain."

Job 20:20–23

I have not put my trust in gold
   or said to pure gold, 'You are my
      security.'
I have not celebrated my great wealth
   or the riches my hands had gained.
I have not thought about worshiping
      the sun in its brightness
   nor admired the moon moving in
      glory
so that my heart was pulled away from
      God.
   My hand has never offered the sun
      and moon a kiss of worship.
If I had, these also would have been
      sins to be punished,

because I would have been unfaith-
      ful to God."

Job 31:24–28

INSIGHTS

*C*onstantly the Bible deals decisively with
the inner spirit of slavery that an idolatrous
attachment to wealth brings. "If riches increase, set not your heart on them," counsels
the psalmist (Ps. 62:10). . . .
   . . . Jesus . . . saw the grip that wealth
can have on a person. He knew that "where
your treasure is, there will your heart be also,"
which is precisely why he commanded his
followers: "Do not lay up for yourselves treasures on earth" (Matt. 6:21, 19). He is not
saying that the heart should or should not be
where the treasure is. He is stating the plain
fact that wherever you find the treasure, you
will find the heart.
   He exhorted the rich young ruler not just
to have an inner attitude of detachment from
his possessions, but literally to get rid of his
possessions if he wanted the kingdom of God
(Matt. 19:16–22). He counseled people who
came seeking God, "Sell your possessions, and
give alms; provide yourselves with purses that
do not grow old, with a treasure in the heavens that does not fail . . ." (Luke 12:33). He
told the parable of the rich farmer whose life
centered in hoarding—we would call him
prudent; Jesus called him a fool (Luke 12:16–
21). He states that if we really want the
kingdom of God we must, like a merchant in
search of fine pearls, be willing to sell everything we have to get it (Matt. 13:45, 46). He
calls all who would follow him to a joyful life
of carefree unconcern for possessions: "Give
to every one who begs from you; and of him
who takes away your goods do not ask them
again" (Luke 6:30).

Richard Foster

PAUSE   FOR   REFLECTION

*W*hat things does God say are important in
life? What causes people to be greedy? What
necessities are we to trust God to provide?
Why is it important for those who follow Christ
to guard against greed?

TUESDAY:
Live a Godly Life While You Wait for Christ's Return
Luke 12:35–56

NEW TESTAMENT READING

Always Be Ready

*B*e dressed, ready for service, and have your lamps shining. Be like servants who are waiting for their master to come home from a wedding party. When he comes and knocks, the servants immediately open the door for him. They will be blessed when their master comes home, because he sees that they were watching for him. I tell you the truth, the master will dress himself to serve and tell the servants to sit at the table, and he will serve them. Those servants will be happy when he comes in and finds them still waiting, even if it is midnight or later.

"Remember this: If the owner of the house knew what time a thief was coming, he would not allow the thief to enter his house. So you also must be ready, because the Son of Man will come at a time when you don't expect him!"

Who Is the Trusted Servant?

*P*eter said, "Lord, did you tell this story to us or to all people?"

The Lord said, "Who is the wise and trusted servant that the master trusts to give the other servants their food at the right time? When the master comes and finds the servant doing his work, the servant will be blessed. I tell you the truth, the master will choose that servant to take care of everything he owns. But suppose the servant thinks to himself, 'My master will not come back soon,' and he begins to beat the other servants, men and women, and to eat and drink and get drunk. The master will come when that servant is not ready and is not expecting him. Then the master will cut him in pieces and send him away to be with the others who don't obey.

"The servant who knows what his master wants but is not ready, or who does not do what the master wants, will be beaten with many blows! But the servant who does not know what his master wants and does things that should be punished will be beaten with few blows. From everyone who has been given much, much will be demanded. And from the one trusted with much, much more will be expected.

Jesus Causes Division

I came to set fire to the world, and I wish it were already burning! I have a baptism to suffer through, and I feel very troubled until it is over. Do you think I came to give peace to the earth? No, I tell you, I came to divide it. From now on, a family with five people will be divided, three against two, and two against three. They will be divided: father against son and son against father, mother against daughter and daughter against mother, mother-in-law against daughter-in-law and daughter-in-law against mother-in-law."

Understanding the Times

*T*hen Jesus said to the people, "When you see clouds coming up in the west, you say, 'It's going to rain,' and it happens. When you feel the wind begin to blow from the south, you say, 'It will be a hot day,' and it happens. Hypocrites! You know how to understand the appearance of the earth and sky. Why don't you understand what is happening now?"

OLD TESTAMENT READING

*T*he earth belongs to the LORD, and
everything in it—
the world and all its people.
He built it on the waters
and set it on the rivers.

Who may go up on the mountain of the LORD?
Who may stand in his holy Temple?
Only those with clean hands and pure hearts,
who have not worshiped idols,
who have not made promises in the name of a false god.
They will receive a blessing from the LORD;

the God who saves them will declare
them right.
They try to follow God;
they look to the God of Jacob for
help. *Selah*

Psalm 24:1–6

*T*he path of life is level for those who
are right with God;
LORD, you make the way of life
smooth for those people.
But, LORD, we are waiting
for your way of justice.
Our souls want to remember
you and your name.
My soul wants to be with you at night,
and my spirit wants to be with you at
the dawn of every day.
When your way of justice comes to the
land,
people of the world will learn the
right way of living.
Evil people will not learn to do good
even if you show them kindness.
They will continue doing evil, even if
they live in a good world;
they never see the LORD's greatness.
LORD, you are ready to punish those
people,
but they do not see that.
Show them your strong love for your
people.
Then those who are evil will be
ashamed.
Burn them in the fire
you have prepared for your enemies.
LORD, all our success is because of what
you have done,
so give us peace.

Isaiah 26:7–12

INSIGHTS

*T*he last message the risen Christ gave his
people was the promise of his soon return.
Couple this with Paul's admonition to the
Thessalonian Christians and you get a good
rule for life: Live both expectantly and patiently, and you will be fulfilling the Lord's
will until he returns.

What are some of the blessings awaiting
the believer when Jesus Christ comes back?

*First of all, the faithful ones can confi-
dently expect to be rewarded for their faithfulness. . . .*

*There is also a clear-cut promise of reward
to the obedient Christian. . . .*

*But in addition to waiting expectantly, we
are also admonished to wait patiently, to
"occupy 'til he comes." And while we are
waiting, we are to be yielded to the "love of
God" operative in our lives. If the love of God
flows through us, we will find ourselves sharing that love with those around us, for God is
love, and that love is bigger than its container,
the Christian, so it must overflow. Those
around us long for love, for our world is full
of hate, Satan's legacy since the Garden of
Eden episode. Let us as Christians share God's
love as we await the return of his Son from
heaven.*

Al Bryant

PAUSE FOR REFLECTION

*W*hat warnings does Jesus give to servants
who are not ready for his return? What does
he promise to those who are ready? What
must your life be like in order to obey Jesus'
words, "Be ready! Be dressed for service and
have your lamps shining"?

WEDNESDAY:
Produce Good Fruit or Be Destroyed
Luke 12:57—13:21

NEW TESTAMENT READING

Settle Your Problems

*W*hy can't you decide for yourselves what is right? If your enemy is taking you to court, try hard to settle it on the way. If you don't, your enemy might take you to the judge, and the judge might turn you over to the officer, and the officer might throw you into jail. I tell you, you will not get out of there until you have paid everything you owe."

Change Your Hearts

*A*t that time some people were there who told Jesus that Pilate had killed some people from Galilee while they were worshiping. He mixed their blood with the blood of the animals they were sacrificing to God. Jesus answered, "Do you think this happened to them because they were more sinful than all others from Galilee? No, I tell you. But unless you change your hearts and lives, you will be destroyed as they were! What about those eighteen people who died when the tower of Siloam fell on them? Do you think they were more sinful than all the others who live in Jerusalem? No, I tell you. But unless you change your hearts and lives, you will all be destroyed too!"

The Useless Tree

*J*esus told this story: "A man had a fig tree planted in his vineyard. He came looking for some fruit on the tree, but he found none. So the man said to his gardener, 'I have been looking for fruit on this tree for three years, but I never find any. Cut it down. Why should it waste the ground?' But the servant answered, 'Master, let the tree have one more year to produce fruit. Let me dig up the dirt around it and put on some fertilizer. If the tree produces fruit next year, good. But if not, you can cut it down.'"

Jesus Heals on the Sabbath

*J*esus was teaching in one of the synagogues on the Sabbath day. A woman was there who, for eighteen years, had an evil spirit in her that made her crippled. Her back was always bent; she could not stand up straight. When Jesus saw her, he called her over and said, "Woman, you are free from your sickness." Jesus put his hands on her, and immediately she was able to stand up straight and began praising God.

The synagogue leader was angry because Jesus healed on the Sabbath day. He said to the people, "There are six days when one has to work. So come to be healed on one of those days, and not on the Sabbath day."

The Lord answered, "You hypocrites! Doesn't each of you untie your work animals and lead them to drink water every day—even on the Sabbath day? This woman that I healed, a daughter of Abraham, has been held by Satan for eighteen years. Surely it is not wrong for her to be freed from her sickness on a Sabbath day!" When Jesus said this, all of those who were criticizing him were ashamed, but the entire crowd rejoiced at all the wonderful things Jesus was doing.

Stories of Mustard Seed and Yeast

*T*hen Jesus said, "What is God's kingdom like? What can I compare it with? It is like a mustard seed that a man plants in his garden. The seed grows and becomes a tree, and the wild birds build nests in its branches."

Jesus said again, "What can I compare God's kingdom with? It is like yeast that a woman took and hid in a large tub of flour until it made all the dough rise."

OLD TESTAMENT READING

*N*ow I will sing for my friend a song
    about his vineyard.
My friend had a vineyard
    on a hill with very rich soil.
He dug and cleared the field of stones
    and planted the best grapevines
      there.
He built a tower in the middle of it
    and cut out a winepress as well.

He hoped good grapes would grow
there,
but only bad ones grew.

My friend says, "You people living in
Jerusalem,
and you people of Judah,
judge between me and my vineyard.
What more could I have done for my
vineyard
than I have already done?
Although I expected good grapes to
grow,
why were there only bad ones?
Now I will tell you
what I will do to my vineyard:
I will remove the hedge,
and it will be burned.
I will break down the stone wall,
and it will be walked on.
I will ruin my field.
It will not be trimmed or hoed,
and weeds and thorns will grow there.
I will command the clouds
not to rain on it."

The vineyard belonging to the LORD All-
Powerful
is the nation of Israel;
the garden that he loves
is the people of Judah.
He looked for justice, but there was
only killing.
He hoped for right living, but there
were only cries of pain.

So the common people and the great
people will be brought down;
those who are proud will be
humbled.
The LORD All-Powerful will receive
glory by judging fairly;
the holy God will show himself holy
by doing what is right.

Isaiah 5:1–7, 15–16

We all know what fruit is. The produce of the branch, by which men are refreshed and nourished. The fruit is not for the branch, but for those who come to carry it away. As soon as the fruit is ripe, the branch gives it off, to commence afresh its work of beneficence, and

anew prepare its fruit for another season. A fruit-bearing tree lives not for itself, but wholly for those to whom its fruit brings refreshment and life. And so the branch exists only and entirely for the sake of the fruit. To make glad the heart of the husbandman is its object, its safety, and its glory.

Beautiful image of the believer, abiding in Christ! He not only grows in strength, the union with the vine becoming ever surer and firmer, he also bears fruit, yea, much fruit. He has the power to offer that to others of which they can eat and live. Amid all who surround him he becomes like a tree of life, of which they can taste and be refreshed. He is in his circle a centre of life and of blessing, and that simply because he abides in Christ, and receives from Him the Spirit and the life of which he can impart to others. Learn thus, if you would bless others, to abide in Christ, and that if you do abide, you shall surely bless.

Andrew Murray

What result did Christ's healing work have on the people? Does he expect anything less from those who follow him? What does he do to nurture his people so they will bear good fruit? What does he promise if they don't ? Are you bearing the fruit Christ has prepared you to bear?

THURSDAY:
Pride Leads to Dishonor
Luke 13:22—14:14

The Narrow Door

*J*esus was teaching in every town and village as he traveled toward Jerusalem. Someone said to Jesus, "Lord, will only a few people be saved?"

Jesus said, "Try hard to enter through the narrow door, because many people will try to enter there, but they will not be able. When the owner of the house gets up and closes the door, you can stand outside and knock on the door and say, 'Sir, open the door for us.' But he will answer, 'I don't know you or where you come from.' Then you will say, 'We ate and drank with you, and you taught in the streets of our town.' But he will say to you, 'I don't know you or where you come from. Go away from me, all you who do evil!' You will cry and grind your teeth with pain when you see Abraham, Isaac, Jacob, and all the prophets in God's kingdom, but you yourselves thrown outside. People will come from the east, west, north, and south and will sit down at the table in the kingdom of God. There are those who have the lowest place in life now who will have the highest place in the future. And there are those who have the highest place now who will have the lowest place in the future."

Jesus Will Die in Jerusalem

*A*t that time some Pharisees came to Jesus and said, "Go away from here! Herod wants to kill you!"

Jesus said to them, "Go tell that fox Herod, 'Today and tomorrow I am forcing demons out and healing people. Then, on the third day, I will reach my goal.' Yet I must be on my way today and tomorrow and the next day. Surely it cannot be right for a prophet to be killed anywhere except in Jerusalem.

"Jerusalem, Jerusalem! You kill the prophets and stone to death those who are sent to you. Many times I wanted to gather your people as a hen gathers her chicks under her wings, but you would not let me. Now your house is left completely empty. I tell you, you will not see me until that time when you will say, 'God bless the One who comes in the name of the Lord.'"

Healing on the Sabbath

*O*n a Sabbath day, when Jesus went to eat at the home of a leading Pharisee, the people were watching Jesus very closely. And in front of him was a man with dropsy. Jesus said to the Pharisees and experts on the law, "Is it right or wrong to heal on the Sabbath day?" But they would not answer his question. So Jesus took the man, healed him, and sent him away. Jesus said to the Pharisees and teachers of the law, "If your child or ox falls into a well on the Sabbath day, will you not pull him out quickly?" And they could not answer him.

Don't Make Yourself Important

*W*hen Jesus noticed that some of the guests were choosing the best places to sit, he told this story: "When someone invites you to a wedding feast, don't take the most important seat, because someone more important than you may have been invited. The host, who invited both of you, will come to you and say, 'Give this person your seat.' Then you will be embarrassed and will have to move to the last place. So when you are invited, go sit in a seat that is not important. When the host comes to you, he may say, 'Friend, move up here to a more important place.' Then all the other guests will respect you. All who make themselves great will be made humble, but those who make themselves humble will be made great."

You Will Be Rewarded

*T*hen Jesus said to the man who had invited him, "When you give a lunch or a dinner, don't invite only your friends, your family, your other relatives, and your rich neighbors. At another time they will invite you to eat with them, and you will be repaid. Instead, when you give a feast, invite the poor, the crippled, the lame, and the blind. Then you will be blessed, because they have nothing and cannot pay you back. But you will be repaid when the good people rise from the dead."

*T*he LORD All-Powerful has a certain
    day planned
  when he will punish the proud and
    those who brag,
  and they will no longer be important.
He will bring down the tall cedar trees
    from Lebanon
  and the great oak trees of Bashan,
all the tall mountains
  and the high hills,
every tall tower
  and every high, strong wall,
all the trading ships
  and the beautiful ships.
At that time proud people will be made
    humble,
  and they will bow low with shame.
At that time only the LORD will be praised.

Isaiah 2:12–17

*R*espect for the LORD will teach you
    wisdom.
  If you want to be honored, you must
    be humble.

Proverbs 15:33

*P*roud people will be ruined,
  but the humble will be honored.

Proverbs 18:12

*T*he LORD laughs at those who laugh
    at him,
  but he gives grace to those who are
    not proud.

Proverbs 3:34

*T*hen Jerusalem will not be ashamed
  of the wrongs done against me,
because I will remove from this city
  those who like to brag;
there will never be any more proud
    people
  on my holy mountain in Jerusalem.
But I will leave in the city
  the humble and those who are not
    proud,
  and they will trust in the LORD.
Those who are left alive in Israel won't
    do wrong
  or tell lies;

they won't trick people with their
    words.
They will eat and lie down
  with no one to make them afraid."

Zephaniah 3:11–13

INSIGHTS

*G*od does not denigrate pride in its positive
sense. The Bible has a hundred ways to illustrate the quiet feeling of competence that lies
behind one's ability to do what he knows he
has to do and can do. The apostle Paul's
ministry was grounded on the assurance that
Christ would help him finish what he had
started. If that is what is meant by pride, we
should certainly cultivate it and thank God
for it. . . .

*Pride in the dictionary sense of conceited
and overbearing behavior . . . brings out
the worst in antisocial relationships. Such
pride is not the answer to the human problem;
it is the human problem. . . . All of the
major transgressions to inflict woe upon the
human race—fear, greed, avarice, cruelty,
lust, unbelief—can be traced to runaway
pride. . . .*

*As to whether or not our pride is sin, the
answer ultimately rests with each of us. The
Christian knows the condition of his own
heart. He measures it by the Word of God. Is
he at peace? Is his conscience clear? Is he
filled with the Spirit? . . . Then his personal
life should reflect the modest, open, worship-
ful, loving stance of a humble creature of God
who has been in the presence of his Creator.*

Sherwood Wirt

PAUSE FOR REFLECTION

*W*hy do you think Jesus spoke out against
the seemingly mild form of pride he saw at
the Pharisee's dinner? Why does God so detest
pride? Why is humility necessary in the lives
of those who belong to God? How does God
honor humility?

189

FRIDAY:
Count the Cost of Serving Christ
Luke 14:15—15:10

A Story About a Big Banquet

One of those at the table with Jesus heard these things and said to him, "Happy are the people who will share in the meal in God's kingdom."

Jesus said to him, "A man gave a big banquet and invited many people. When it was time to eat, the man sent his servant to tell the guests, 'Come. Everything is ready.'

"But all the guests made excuses. The first one said, 'I have just bought a field, and I must go look at it. Please excuse me.' Another said, 'I have just bought five pairs of oxen; I must go and try them. Please excuse me.' A third person said, 'I just got married; I can't come.' So the servant returned and told his master what had happened. Then the master became angry and said, 'Go at once into the streets and alleys of the town, and bring in the poor, the crippled, the blind, and the lame.' Later the servant said to him, 'Master, I did what you commanded, but we still have room.' The master said to the servant, 'Go out to the roads and country lanes, and urge the people there to come so my house will be full. I tell you, none of those whom I invited first will eat with me.'"

The Cost of Being Jesus' Follower

Large crowds were traveling with Jesus, and he turned and said to them, "If anyone comes to me but loves his father, mother, wife, children, brothers, or sisters—or even life—more than me, he cannot be my follower. Whoever is not willing to carry the cross and follow me cannot be my follower. If you want to build a tower, you first sit down and decide how much it will cost, to see if you have enough money to finish the job. If you don't, you might lay the foundation, but you would not be able to finish. Then all who would see it would make fun of you, saying, 'This person began to build but was not able to finish.'

"If a king is going to fight another king, first he will sit down and plan. He will decide if he and his ten thousand soldiers can defeat the other king who has twenty thousand soldiers. If he can't, then while the other king is still far away, he will send some people to speak to him and ask for peace. In the same way, you must give up everything you have to be my follower.

Don't Lose Your Influence

Salt is good, but if it loses its salty taste, you cannot make it salty again. It is no good for the soil or for manure; it is thrown away.

"You people who can hear me, listen."

A Lost Sheep, a Lost Coin

The tax collectors and sinners all came to listen to Jesus. But the Pharisees and the teachers of the law began to complain: "Look, this man welcomes sinners and even eats with them."

Then Jesus told them this story: "Suppose one of you has a hundred sheep but loses one of them. Then he will leave the other ninety-nine sheep in the open field and go out and look for the lost sheep until he finds it. And when he finds it, he happily puts it on his shoulders and goes home. He calls to his friends and neighbors and says, 'Be happy with me because I found my lost sheep.' In the same way, I tell you there is more joy in heaven over one sinner who changes his heart and life, than over ninety-nine good people who don't need to change.

"Suppose a woman has ten silver coins, but loses one. She will light a lamp, sweep the house, and look carefully for the coin until she finds it. And when she finds it, she will call her friends and neighbors and say, 'Be happy with me because I have found the coin that I lost.' In the same way, there is joy in the presence of the angels of God when one sinner changes his heart and life."

Then some Babylonians came up to the king and began speaking against the men of Judah. They said to King Nebuchadnezzar, "O king, live forever! O king, you gave a command that everyone who heard the horns, lyres, zithers, harps, pipes, and all the other musical instruments would have to bow down and worship the gold statue. Anyone who wouldn't do this was to be thrown into a blazing furnace. O king, there are some men of Judah whom you made officers in the area of Babylon that did not pay attention to your order. Their names are Shadrach, Meshach, and Abednego. They do not serve your gods and do not worship the gold statue you have set up."

Shadrach, Meshach, and Abednego answered the king, saying, "Nebuchadnezzar, we do not need to defend ourselves to you. If you throw us into the blazing furnace, the God we serve is able to save us from the furnace. He will save us from your power, O king. But even if God does not save us, we want you, O king, to know this: We will not serve your gods or worship the gold statue you have set up."

Then Nebuchadnezzar was furious with Shadrach, Meshach, and Abednego, and he changed his mind. He ordered the furnace to be heated seven times hotter than usual. Then he commanded some of the strongest soldiers in his army to tie up Shadrach, Meshach, and Abednego and throw them into the blazing furnace.

Then Nebuchadnezzar went to the opening of the blazing furnace and shouted, "Shadrach, Meshach, and Abednego, come out! Servants of the Most High God, come here!"

So Shadrach, Meshach, and Abednego came out of the fire. When they came out, the governors, assistant governors, captains of the soldiers, and royal advisers crowded around them and saw that the fire had not harmed their bodies. Their hair was not burned, their robes were not burned, and they didn't even smell like smoke!

Then Nebuchadnezzar said, "Praise the God of Shadrach, Meshach, and Abednego. Their God has sent his angel and saved his servants from the fire! These three men trusted their God and refused to obey my command. They were willing to die rather than serve or worship any god other than their own."

Daniel 3:8–12, 16–20, 26–28

INSIGHTS

When Christ said time after time that one must "deny himself and take up his cross and follow me" He was indicating that it is not easy to be His true follower. The apostle Paul warned, "Everyone who wants to live a godly life in Christ Jesus will be persecuted" (2 Timothy 3:12). He offers no cheap grace, no easy life. As someone has said, "Salvation is free but not cheap. . . ."

The Christian faith brings its own "blood, sweat and tears" to those who would follow Jesus Christ. Christ calls us to discipleship. When we come to Him, He takes away one set of burdens—the burden of sin, the burden of guilt, the burden of separation from God, the burden of hopelessness. But He also calls upon us to "Take my yoke upon you and learn from me" (Matthew 11:29). It is not a yoke that is too heavy for us to bear, for Christ bears it with us: "For my yoke is easy and my burden is light" (Matthew 11:30). Nevertheless, Christ calls us to follow Him, regardless of the cost, and He has never promised that our path will always be smooth. . . .

But in the midst of the suffering, trials and temptations, He will provide His peace, joy and fellowship. . . . In the midst of every situation of life He can give an inner calm and strength that you could never imagine apart from Him.

Billy Graham

APPLICATION

What price were Shadrach, Meshach, and Abednego willing to pay to serve God? What might it cost you to serve Christ, given your family or social setting? Are you willing to pay that price?

WEEKEND:

God Welcomes All Who Come to Him

Luke 15:11—16:8

The Son Who Left Home

*T*hen Jesus said, "A man had two sons. The younger son said to his father, 'Give me my share of the property.' So the father divided the property between his two sons. Then the younger son gathered up all that was his and traveled far away to another country. There he wasted his money in foolish living. After he had spent everything, a time came when there was no food anywhere in the country, and the son was poor and hungry. So he got a job with one of the citizens there who sent the son into the fields to feed pigs. The son was so hungry that he wanted to eat the pods the pigs were eating, but no one gave him anything. When he realized what he was doing, he thought, 'All of my father's servants have plenty of food. But I am here, almost dying with hunger. I will leave and return to my father and say to him, "Father, I have sinned against God and have done wrong to you. I am no longer worthy to be called your son, but let me be like one of your servants."' So the son left and went to his father.

"While the son was still a long way off, his father saw him and felt sorry for his son. So the father ran to him and hugged and kissed him. The son said, 'Father, I have sinned against God and have done wrong to you. I am no longer worthy to be called your son.' But the father said to his servants, 'Hurry! Bring the best clothes and put them on him. Also, put a ring on his finger and sandals on his feet. And get our fat calf and kill it so we can have a feast and celebrate. My son was dead, but now he is alive again! He was lost, but now he is found!' So they began to celebrate.

"The older son was in the field, and as he came closer to the house, he heard the sound of music and dancing. So he called to one of the servants and asked what all this meant. The servant said, 'Your brother has come back, and your father killed the fat calf, because your brother came home safely.' The older son was angry and would not go in to the feast. So his father went out and begged him to come in. But the older son said to his father, 'I have served you like a slave for many years and have always obeyed your commands. But you never gave me even a young goat to have at a feast with my friends. But your other son, who wasted all your money on prostitutes, comes home, and you kill the fat calf for him!' The father said to him, 'Son, you are always with me, and all that I have is yours. We had to celebrate and be happy because your brother was dead, but now he is alive. He was lost, but now he is found.'"

True Wealth

*J*esus also said to his followers, "Once there was a rich man who had a manager to take care of his business. This manager was accused of cheating him. So he called the manager in and said to him, 'What is this I hear about you? Give me a report of what you have done with my money, because you can't be my manager any longer.' The manager thought to himself, 'What will I do since my master is taking my job away from me? I am not strong enough to dig ditches, and I am ashamed to beg. I know what I'll do so that when I lose my job people will welcome me into their homes.'

"So the manager called in everyone who owed the master any money. He asked the first one, 'How much do you owe?' He answered, 'Eight hundred gallons of olive oil.' The manager said to him, 'Take your bill, sit down quickly, and write four hundred gallons.' Then the manager asked another one, 'How much do you owe?' He answered, 'One thousand bushels of wheat.' Then the manager said to him, 'Take your bill and write eight hundred bushels.' So, the master praised the dishonest manager for being smart. Yes, worldly people are smarter with their own kind than spiritual people are."

So you, human, say to Israel: 'You have said: Surely our law-breaking and sins are hurting us. They will kill us. What can we do so we will live?' Say to them: 'The Lord GOD says: As surely as I live, I do not want any who are wicked to die. I want them to stop doing evil and live. Stop! Stop your wicked ways! You don't want to die, do you, people of Israel?'

"Human, say to your people: 'The goodness of those who do right will not save them when they sin. The evil of wicked people will not cause them to be punished if they stop doing it. If good people sin, they will not be able to live by the good they did earlier.' If I tell good people, 'You will surely live,' they might think they have done enough good and then do evil. Then none of the good things they did will be remembered. They will die because of the evil they have done. Or, if I say to the wicked people, 'You will surely die,' they may stop sinning and do what is right and honest. For example, they may return what somebody gave them as a promise to repay a loan, or pay back what they stole. If they live by the rules that give life and do not sin, then they will surely live, and they will not die."

Ezekiel 33:10–15

If you hide your sins, you will not
    succeed.
If you confess and reject them, you
    will receive mercy.

Proverbs 28:13

There may come a time when I will speak about a nation or a kingdom that I will pull up by its roots or will pull down to destroy it. But if the people of that nation stop doing the evil they have done, I will change my mind and not carry out my plans to bring disaster to them.

Jeremiah 18:7–8

INSIGHTS

Acknowledging guilt and accountability before God; standing before Him, as it were, offering no excuses and sorrowfully admitting that one has done wrong. It's a very difficult moment, perhaps the hardest of the human condition. The Bible uses the word repentance to describe this action.

Repentance is a rather dramatic word. It refers to the act of traveling in one direction and then suddenly changing to go the opposite way. Both John the Baptizer and Jesus used repentance as the centerpoint of their teaching because they were talking to a generation of people whose personal worlds were terribly broken. Yet the people would not face up to the changes necessary to make their worlds come back together again. Stubborn people do not repent very easily, and those people were stubborn.

Repentance is activated, first, in the act of confession: the candid acknowledgment before God, and perhaps to others, that one has sinned and is in need of forgiveness. Both by example and by teaching, the Scriptures place a high priority on confessing, for in so doing, one actually reveals the secrets of the heart. And until the heart is voluntarily opened up, the process of rebuilding a broken world cannot begin. . . .

. . . Restoration looks to the damage done in a broken-world experience and asks how it can be repaired. Broken relationships must be examined and, if possible, glued back together again. Forgiveness must be requested and granted, and that requires people to come together and offer mercy and grace to one another. These are not simple or easy things to give . . .

But restoration is one of the unique acts of the Christian community. In the final analysis, it cannot be demanded or even earned by the broken-world person; it must be freely given as God once freely gave grace to whoever wished to receive it.

Gordon MacDonald

PAUSE FOR REFLECTION

W*hat does God want every person to do? What does he promise to those who confess and reject their sins? Is repentance a one-time or ongoing action? How freely do you extend mercy to restore repentant sinners?*

MONDAY:
God Knows Our Hearts
Luke 16:9—17:4

I tell you, make friends for yourselves using worldly riches so that when those riches are gone, you will be welcomed in those homes that continue forever. Whoever can be trusted with a little can also be trusted with a lot, and whoever is dishonest with a little is dishonest with a lot. If you cannot be trusted with worldly riches, then who will trust you with true riches? And if you cannot be trusted with things that belong to someone else, who will give you things of your own?

"No servant can serve two masters. The servant will hate one master and love the other, or will follow one master and refuse to follow the other. You cannot serve both God and worldly riches."

God's Law Cannot Be Changed

*T*he Pharisees, who loved money, were listening to all these things and made fun of Jesus. He said to them, "You make yourselves look good in front of people, but God knows what is really in your hearts. What is important to people is hateful in God's sight.

"The law of Moses and the writings of the prophets were preached until John came. Since then the Good News about the kingdom of God is being told, and everyone tries to enter it by force. It would be easier for heaven and earth to pass away than for the smallest part of a letter in the law to be changed.

Divorce and Remarriage

*I*f a man divorces his wife and marries another woman, he is guilty of adultery, and the man who marries a divorced woman is also guilty of adultery."

The Rich Man and Lazarus

*J*esus said, "There was a rich man who always dressed in the finest clothes and lived in luxury every day. And a very poor man named Lazarus, whose body was covered with sores, was laid at the rich man's gate. He wanted to eat only the small pieces of food that fell from the rich man's table. And the dogs would come and lick his sores. Later, Lazarus died, and the angels carried him to the arms of Abraham. The rich man died, too, and was buried. In the place of the dead, he was in much pain. The rich man saw Abraham far away with Lazarus at his side. He called, 'Father Abraham, have mercy on me! Send Lazarus to dip his finger in water and cool my tongue, because I am suffering in this fire!' But Abraham said, 'Child, remember when you were alive you had the good things in life, but bad things happened to Lazarus. Now he is comforted here, and you are suffering. Besides, there is a big pit between you and us, so no one can cross over to you, and no one can leave there and come here.' The rich man said, 'Father, then please send Lazarus to my father's house. I have five brothers, and Lazarus could warn them so that they will not come to this place of pain.' But Abraham said, 'They have the law of Moses and the writings of the prophets; let them learn from them.' The rich man said, 'No, father Abraham! If someone goes to them from the dead, they would believe and change their hearts and lives.' But Abraham said to him, 'If they will not listen to Moses and the prophets, they will not listen to someone who comes back from the dead.'"

Sin and Forgiveness

*J*esus said to his followers, "Things that cause people to sin will happen, but how terrible for the person who causes them to happen! It would be better for you to be thrown into the sea with a large stone around your neck than to cause one of these little ones to sin. So be careful!

"If another follower sins, warn him, and if he is sorry and stops sinning, forgive him. If he sins against you seven times in one day and says that he is sorry each time, forgive him."

*L*ORD, you have examined me
and know all about me.

You know when I sit down and when I
get up.
You know my thoughts before I
think them.
You know where I go and where I lie
down.
You know thoroughly everything I
do.
LORD, even before I say a word,
you already know it.
You are all around me—in front and in
back—
and have put your hand on me.
Your knowledge is amazing to me;
it is more than I can understand.

Where can I go to get away from your
Spirit?
Where can I run from you?
If I go up to the heavens, you are there.
If I lie down in the grave, you are
there.
If I rise with the sun in the east
and settle in the west beyond the
sea,
even there you would guide me.
With your right hand you would
hold me.

I could say, "The darkness will hide me.
Let the light around me turn into
night."
But even the darkness is not dark to
you.
The night is as light as the day;
darkness and light are the same to
you.

You made my whole being;
you formed me in my mother's body.
I praise you because you made me in
an amazing and wonderful way.
What you have done is wonderful.
I know this very well.
You saw my bones being formed
as I took shape in my mother's body.
When I was put together there,
you saw my body as it was formed.
All the days planned for me
were written in your book
before I was one day old.

God, examine me and know my heart;
test me and know my nervous
thoughts.

See if there is any bad thing in me.
Lead me on the road to everlasting
life.

Psalm 139:1–16, 23–24

*Making good judgments in this world is
sometimes a hit-and-miss proposition. Often
we fail. In baseball, a hitter is constantly trying to guess what the pitcher will throw next.
In football, a defensive coach tries to predict
where the offense will run next. Basketball
coaches continually try to outmaneuver each
other. Sometimes they are right, and sometimes they are wrong. We fail because we
seldom have all the facts. We have no idea
what the other person is thinking. We're
looking for a fast ball, and the pitcher throws
a curve ball, or we're looking for a pass and
they run! . . . We don't know all the facts,
we don't know the future, and sometimes we
don't even react properly when we do know!
But with God, life is not a guessing game.
His judgments are sure, because He knows
all the facts. God knows everything about us.
He knows our thoughts before we think them
(Psalm 139:1–6). No one can escape His
sight (Psalm 139:7–12). He even judges the
thoughts and intentions of our hearts (Hebrews 4:12–13). God's judgment is always
perfect, because He knows all the facts. Those
who think they are getting away with something may escape our notice, but they will
never escape the notice of God. The eyes of
the Lord are in every place, watching the evil
and the good (Proverbs 15:3). Take comfort,
righteous ones, for goodness will be vindicated
and evil will be punished!*

Elliot Johnson/Al Schierbaum

ACTION POINT

*What feelings do you have when you real-
ize that God knows what is in your heart and
that he knows it even better than you do? Pray
that God's knowledge of you will lead you
closer to him. Take comfort that he not only
knows you, but loves you! Praise him for his
amazing knowledge!*

TUESDAY:

When God's Judgment Comes, There Will Be No Turning Back

Luke 17:5–38

N E W   T E S T A M E N T   R E A D I N G

How Big Is Your Faith?

*T*he apostles said to the Lord, "Give us more faith!"

The Lord said, "If your faith were the size of a mustard seed, you could say to this mulberry tree, 'Dig yourself up and plant yourself in the sea,' and it would obey you.

Be Good Servants

*S*uppose one of you has a servant who has been plowing the ground or caring for the sheep. When the servant comes in from working in the field, would you say, 'Come in and sit down to eat'? No, you would say to him, 'Prepare something for me to eat. Then get yourself ready and serve me. After I finish eating and drinking, you can eat.' The servant does not get any special thanks for doing what his master commanded. It is the same with you. When you have done everything you are told to do, you should say, 'We are unworthy servants; we have only done the work we should do.'"

Be Thankful

*W*hile Jesus was on his way to Jerusalem, he was going through the area between Samaria and Galilee. As he came into a small town, ten men who had a skin disease met him there. They did not come close to Jesus but called to him, "Jesus! Master! Have mercy on us!"

When Jesus saw the men, he said, "Go and show yourselves to the priests."

As the ten men were going, they were healed. When one of them saw that he was healed, he went back to Jesus, praising God in a loud voice. Then he bowed down at Jesus' feet and thanked him. (And this man was a Samaritan.) Jesus said, "Weren't ten men healed? Where are the other nine? Is this Samaritan the only one who came back to thank God?" Then Jesus said to him, "Stand up and go on your way. You were healed because you believed."

God's Kingdom Is Within You

*S*ome of the Pharisees asked Jesus, "When will the kingdom of God come?"

Jesus answered, "God's kingdom is coming, but not in a way that you will be able to see with your eyes. People will not say, 'Look, here it is!' or, 'There it is!' because God's kingdom is within you."

Then Jesus said to his followers, "The time will come when you will want very much to see one of the days of the Son of Man. But you will not see it. People will say to you, 'Look, there he is!' or, 'Look, here he is!' Stay where you are; don't go away and search.

When Jesus Comes Again

*W*hen the Son of Man comes again, he will shine like lightning, which flashes across the sky and lights it up from one side to the other. But first he must suffer many things and be rejected by the people of this time. When the Son of Man comes again, it will be as it was when Noah lived. People were eating, drinking, marrying, and giving their children to be married until the day Noah entered the boat. Then the flood came and killed them all. It will be the same as during the time of Lot. People were eating, drinking, buying, selling, planting, and building. But the day Lot left Sodom, fire and sulfur rained down from the sky and killed them all. This is how it will be when the Son of Man comes again.

"On that day, a person who is on the roof and whose belongings are in the house should not go inside to get them. A person who is in the field should not go back home. Remember Lot's wife. Those who try to keep their lives will lose them. But those who give up their lives will save them. I tell you, on that night two people will be sleeping in one bed; one will be taken and the other will be left. There will be two women grinding grain together; one will be taken, and the other will be left."

The followers asked Jesus, "Where will this be, Lord?"

Jesus answered, "Where there is a dead body, there the vultures will gather."

OLD TESTAMENT READING

*T*hen the LORD said, "I have heard many complaints against the people of Sodom and Gomorrah. They are very evil. I will go down and see if they are as bad as I have heard. If not, I will know."

Genesis 18:20–21

*T*he two angels came to Sodom in the evening as Lot was sitting near the city gate. When he saw them, he got up and went to them and bowed facedown on the ground. Lot said, "Sirs, please come to my house and spend the night. There you can wash your feet, and then tomorrow you may continue your journey."

The angels answered, "No, we will spend the night in the city's public square."

But Lot begged them to come, so they agreed and went to his house. Then Lot prepared a meal for them. He baked bread without yeast, and they ate it.

The two men said to Lot, "Do you have any other relatives in this city? Do you have any sons-in-law, sons, daughters, or any other relatives? If you do, tell them to leave now, because we are about to destroy this city. The LORD has heard of all the evil that is here, so he has sent us to destroy it."

So Lot went out and said to his future sons-in-law who were pledged to marry his daughters, "Hurry and leave this city! The LORD is about to destroy it!" But they thought Lot was joking.

At dawn the next morning, the angels begged Lot to hurry. They said, "Go! Take your wife and your two daughters with you so you will not be destroyed when the city is punished."

But Lot delayed. So the two men took the hands of Lot, his wife, and his two daughters and led them safely out of the city. So the LORD was merciful to Lot and his family. After they brought them out of the city, one of the men said, "Run for your lives! Don't look back or stop anywhere in the valley. Run to the mountains, or you will be destroyed."

The LORD sent a rain of burning sulfur down from the sky on Sodom and Gomorrah and destroyed those cities. He also destroyed the whole Jordan Valley, everyone living in the cities, and even all the plants.

Genesis 19:1–3, 12–17, 24–25

INSIGHTS

*I*n John's vision . . . you will get a feeling for the absolute horror of this final judgment for those who do not believe. Picture it. Carefully the Lamb opens the sixth seal (Revelation 6:12–17). Suddenly, chaos grips the universe. An earthquake shakes the entire world, no Richter scale could measure its fury. There is a complete eclipse of the sun. In fact, reports John, "the sun turned black . . . the whole moon turned blood red, and the stars in the sky fell to earth, as late figs drop from a fig tree when shaken by a strong wind" (Revelation 6:12, 13).

The world is trembling with terror. The great cities collapse. John sees kings, princes, generals; the rich, the mighty, slave and free— every human being left on the earth running to escape the horror of God's final judgment. They flee to mountain caves. They cower behind rocks and boulders. But there is no escape. Desperately they cry out, "Hide us from the face of him who sits on the throne and from the wrath of the Lamb! For the great day of their wrath has come, and who can stand?" (Revelation 6:16, 17).

There will be a day of reckoning when God closes His books on time and judges every creature, living and dead.

Billy Graham

APPLICATION

*W*hen God decides it's time for judgment, is there any room for doubt about what he is doing? Will there by any doubt about his coming judgment? How does Jesus' warning about his coming judgment affect your everyday life?

WEDNESDAY:

Trust in God, Not in Pride or Riches

Luke 18:1–25

NEW TESTAMENT READING

God Will Answer His People

*T*hen Jesus used this story to teach his followers that they should always pray and never lose hope. "In a certain town there was a judge who did not respect God or care about people. In that same town there was a widow who kept coming to this judge, saying, 'Give me my rights against my enemy.' For a while the judge refused to help her. But afterwards, he thought to himself, 'Even though I don't respect God or care about people, I will see that she gets her rights. Otherwise she will continue to bother me until I am worn out.'"

The Lord said, "Listen to what the unfair judge said. God will always give what is right to his people who cry to him night and day, and he will not be slow to answer them. I tell you, God will help his people quickly. But when the Son of Man comes again, will he find those on earth who believe in him?"

Being Right with God

*J*esus told this story to some people who thought they were very good and looked down on everyone else: "A Pharisee and a tax collector both went to the Temple to pray. The Pharisee stood alone and prayed, 'God, I thank you that I am not like other people who steal, cheat, or take part in adultery, or even like this tax collector. I give up eating twice a week, and I give one-tenth of everything I get!'

"The tax collector, standing at a distance, would not even look up to heaven. But he beat on his chest because he was so sad. He said, 'God, have mercy on me, a sinner.' I tell you, when this man went home, he was right with God, but the Pharisee was not. All who make themselves great will be made humble, but all who make themselves humble will be made great."

Who Will Enter God's Kingdom?

*S*ome people brought even their babies to Jesus so he could touch them. When the followers saw this, they told them to stop. But Jesus called for the children, saying, "Let the little children come to me. Don't stop them, because the kingdom of God belongs to people who are like these children. I tell you the truth, you must accept the kingdom of God as if you were a child, or you will never enter it."

A Rich Man's Question

A certain leader asked Jesus, "Good Teacher, what must I do to have life forever?"

Jesus said to him, "Why do you call me good? Only God is good. You know the commands: 'You must not be guilty of adultery. You must not murder anyone. You must not steal. You must not tell lies about your neighbor. Honor your father and mother.'"

But the leader said, "I have obeyed all these commands since I was a boy."

When Jesus heard this, he said to him, "There is still one more thing you need to do. Sell everything you have and give it to the poor, and you will have treasure in heaven. Then come and follow me." But when the man heard this, he became very sad, because he was very rich.

Jesus looked at him and said, "It is very hard for rich people to enter the kingdom of God. It is easier for a camel to go through the eye of a needle than for a rich person to enter the kingdom of God."

OLD TESTAMENT READING

*B*e careful! Don't be led away from
        God by riches;
    don't let much money turn you away.
Neither your wealth nor all your great
        strength
    will keep you out of trouble."

Job 36:18–19

*T*his is what the LORD says:
"The wise must not brag about their
    wisdom.

The strong must not brag about
their strength.
The rich must not brag about their
money.
But if someone wants to brag, let him
brag
that he understands and knows me.
Let him brag that I am the LORD,
and that I am kind and fair,
and that I do things that are right on
earth.
This kind of bragging pleases me," says
the LORD.

Jeremiah 9:23–24

*L*isten to this, all you nations;
listen, all you who live on earth.
Listen, both great and small,
rich and poor together.
What I say is wise,
and my heart speaks with understanding.
I will pay attention to a wise saying;
I will explain my riddle on the harp.

Why should I be afraid of bad days?
Why should I fear when evil men
surround me?
They trust in their money
and brag about their riches.
No one can buy back the life of an-
other.
No one can pay God for his own life,
because the price of a life is high.
No payment is ever enough.
Do people live forever?
Don't they all face death?

See, even wise people die.
Fools and stupid people also die
and leave their wealth to others.
Their graves will always be their
homes.
They will live there from now on,
even though they named places after
themselves.
Even rich people do not live forever;
like the animals, people die.

This is what will happen to those who
trust in themselves
and to their followers who believe
them. *Selah*

Psalm 49:1–13

*T*o receive what we have as a gift from God is the first inner attitude of simplicity. We work but we know that it is not our work that gives us what we have. We live by grace even when it comes to "daily bread." We are dependent upon God for the simplest elements of life: air, water, sun. What we have is not the result of our labor, but of the gracious care of God. When we are tempted to think that what we own is the result of our personal efforts, it takes only a little drought or a small accident to show us once again how utterly dependent we are for everything.

To know that it is God's business, and not ours, to care for what we have is the second inner attitude of simplicity. God is able to protect what we possess. We can trust him. . . . Obviously, these matters are not restricted to possessions but include such things as our reputation and our employment. Simplicity means the freedom to trust God for these (and all) things.

To have our goods available to others marks the third inner attitude of simplicity. If our goods are not available to the community when it is clearly right and good, then they are stolen goods. . . . We cling to our possessions rather than sharing them because we are anxious about tomorrow. But if we truly believe that God is who Jesus says he is, then we do not need to be afraid. When we come to see God as the almighty Creator and our loving Father, we can share because we know that he will care for us. . . .

When we are seeking first the kingdom of God, these three attitudes will characterize our lives. Taken together they define what Jesus means by "do not be anxious." They comprise the inner reality of Christian simplicity.

Richard Foster

APPLICATION

*W*hat great risk do we face when our hearts are focused on our abilities, goodness, strength, or riches? Can we truly achieve anything for ourselves? What is the next step for you to take in trusting God?

THURSDAY:

When God Changes Our Hearts, Our Actions Change, Too

Luke 18:26—19:10

Who Can Be Saved?

*W*hen the people heard this, they asked, "Then who can be saved?"

Jesus answered, "God can do things that are not possible for people to do."

Peter said, "Look, we have left everything and followed you."

Jesus said, "I tell you the truth, all those who have left houses, wives, brothers, parents, or children for the kingdom of God will get much more in this life. And in the age that is coming, they will have life forever."

Jesus Will Rise from the Dead

*T*hen Jesus took the twelve apostles aside and said to them, "We are going to Jerusalem. Everything the prophets wrote about the Son of Man will happen. He will be turned over to those who are not Jews. They will laugh at him, insult him, spit on him, beat him with whips, and kill him. But on the third day, he will rise to life again." The apostles did not understand this; the meaning was hidden from them, and they did not realize what was said.

Jesus Heals a Blind Man

*A*s Jesus came near the city of Jericho, a blind man was sitting beside the road, begging. When he heard the people coming down the road, he asked, "What is happening?"

They told him, "Jesus, from Nazareth, is going by."

The blind man cried out, "Jesus, Son of David, have mercy on me!"

The people leading the group warned the blind man to be quiet. But the blind man shouted even more, "Son of David, have mercy on me!"

Jesus stopped and ordered the blind man to be brought to him. When he came near,

Jesus asked him, "What do you want me to do for you?"

He said, "Lord, I want to see."

Jesus said to him, "Then see. You are healed because you believed."

At once the man was able to see, and he followed Jesus, thanking God. All the people who saw this praised God.

Zacchaeus Meets Jesus

*J*esus was going through the city of Jericho. A man was there named Zacchaeus, who was a very important tax collector, and he was wealthy. He wanted to see who Jesus was, but he was not able because he was too short to see above the crowd. He ran ahead to a place where Jesus would come, and he climbed a sycamore tree so he could see him. When Jesus came to that place, he looked up and said to him, "Zacchaeus, hurry and come down! I must stay at your house today."

Zacchaeus came down quickly and welcomed him gladly. All the people saw this and began to complain, "Jesus is staying with a sinner!"

But Zacchaeus stood and said to the Lord, "I will give half of my possessions to the poor. And if I have cheated anyone, I will pay back four times more."

Jesus said to him, "Salvation has come to this house today, because this man also belongs to the family of Abraham. The Son of Man came to find lost people and save them."

*T*he LORD spoke his word to Jonah again and said, "Get up, go to the great city Nineveh, and preach to it what I tell you to say."

So Jonah obeyed the LORD and got up and went to Nineveh. It was a very large city; just to walk across it took a person three days. After Jonah had entered the city and walked for one day, he preached to the people, saying, "After forty days, Nineveh will be destroyed!"

The people of Nineveh believed God. They announced that they would stop eating for a while, and they put on rough cloth to show their sadness. All the people in the city did this, from the most important to the least important.

When the king of Nineveh heard this news, he got up from his throne, took off his robe, and covered himself with rough cloth and sat in ashes to show how upset he was.

He sent this announcement through Nineveh:

By command of the king and his important men: No person or animal, herd or flock, will be allowed to taste anything. Do not let them eat food or drink water. But every person and animal should be covered with rough cloth, and people should cry loudly to God. Everyone must turn away from evil living and stop doing harm all the time. Who knows? Maybe God will change his mind. Maybe he will stop being angry, and then we will not die.

When God saw what the people did, that they stopped doing evil, he changed his mind and did not do what he had warned. He did not punish them.

Jonah 3:1–10

*W*hen the Passover celebration was finished, all the Israelites in Jerusalem went out to the towns of Judah. There they smashed the stone pillars used to worship gods. They cut down the Asherah idols and destroyed the altars and places for worshiping gods in all of Judah, Benjamin, Ephraim, and Manasseh. After they had destroyed all of them, the Israelites returned to their own towns and homes.

2 Chronicles 31:1

*T*rue repentance occurs when we begin to see sin from God's point of view—when we see the way our sin has broken his heart. Perhaps the idea that God's heart can be broken by our sin is new to you. In Genesis 6:5–6 we are told, "Then the LORD saw that the wickedness of man was great on the earth, and that every intent of the thoughts of his heart was only evil continually. And the LORD was

sorry that he had made man on the earth, and he was grieved in his heart" (NASB). God was so disappointed with what he saw that there was a grief or sorrow in his heart.

Jesus also was brokenhearted as he wept over Jerusalem. "O Jerusalem, Jerusalem, you who kill the prophets and stone those sent to you, how often I have longed to gather your children together, as a hen gathers her chicks under her wings, but you were not willing!" (Lk 13:34). God's heart aches over our sin. It alienates us from him and from our fellow believers.

If we want to have victory over sin and turn our lives wholeheartedly over to God, then we must see our sin from God's perspective. No sermon on hell can ever change a person's heart like seeing the grief sin has brought to the heart of the One who created us. We must ask God to show us what our sin does to him. As we do this and begin to understand his great love for us, despite how much we have hurt and grieved his heart, turning away from that sin is the natural thing to do. This is the test of our sincerity and of the level of our desperation to be right with God.

Floyd McClung

*D*o you think the people mentioned in these passages recognized that their sin grieved God? Why? What is the evidence that God changed their hearts? How about you? What in your life grieves God? Will you turn away from it—today?

F R I D A Y:
God Will Reward the Righteous and Punish Those Who Don't Serve Him
Luke 19:11–40

A Story About Three Servants

As the people were listening to this, Jesus told them a story because he was near Jerusalem and they thought God's kingdom would appear immediately. He said: "A very important man went to a country far away to be made a king and then to return home. So he called ten of his servants and gave a coin to each servant. He said, 'Do business with this money until I get back.' But the people in the kingdom hated the man. So they sent a group to follow him and say, 'We don't want this man to be our king.'

"But the man became king. When he returned home, he said, 'Call those servants who have my money so I can know how much they earned with it.'

"The first servant came and said, 'Sir, I earned ten coins with the one you gave me.' The king said to the servant, 'Excellent! You are a good servant. Since I can trust you with small things, I will let you rule over ten of my cities.'

"The second servant said, 'Sir, I earned five coins with your one.' The king said to this servant, 'You can rule over five cities.'

"Then another servant came in and said to the king, 'Sir, here is your coin which I wrapped in a piece of cloth and hid. I was afraid of you, because you are a hard man. You even take money that you didn't earn and gather food that you didn't plant.' Then the king said to the servant, 'I will condemn you by your own words, you evil servant. You knew that I am a hard man, taking money that I didn't earn and gathering food that I didn't plant. Why then didn't you put my money in the bank? Then when I came back, my money would have earned some interest.'

"The king said to the men who were standing by, 'Take the coin away from this servant and give it to the servant who earned ten coins.' They said, 'But sir, that servant already has ten coins.' The king said, 'Those who have will be given more, but those who do not have anything will have everything taken away from them. Now where are my enemies who didn't want me to be king? Bring them here and kill them before me.'"

Jesus Enters Jerusalem as a King

After Jesus said this, he went on toward Jerusalem. As Jesus came near Bethphage and Bethany, towns near the hill called the Mount of Olives, he sent out two of his followers. He said, "Go to the town you can see there. When you enter it, you will find a colt tied there, which no one has ever ridden. Untie it and bring it here to me. If anyone asks you why you are untying it, say that the Master needs it."

The two followers went into town and found the colt just as Jesus had told them. As they were untying it, its owners came out and asked the followers, "Why are you untying our colt?"

The followers answered, "The Master needs it." So they brought it to Jesus, threw their coats on the colt's back, and put Jesus on it. As Jesus rode toward Jerusalem, others spread their coats on the road before him.

As he was coming close to Jerusalem, on the way down the Mount of Olives, the whole crowd of followers began joyfully shouting praise to God for all the miracles they had seen. They said,

"God bless the king who comes in the
name of the Lord!   *Psalm 118:26*
There is peace in heaven and glory to
God!"

Some of the Pharisees in the crowd said to Jesus, "Teacher, tell your followers not to say these things."

But Jesus answered, "I tell you, if my followers didn't say these things, then the stones would cry out."

People will be rewarded for what they say,

and they will also be rewarded for
what they do.

Proverbs 12:14

*I*f you say, "We don't know anything
about this,"
God, who knows what's in your
mind, will notice.
He is watching you, and he will know.
He will reward each person for what
he has done.

Proverbs 24:12

*T*ell those who do what is right that
things will go well for them,
because they will receive a reward
for what they do.
But how terrible it will be for the
wicked!
They will be punished for all the
wrong they have done.

Isaiah 3:10–11

*S*top doing evil and do good,
so you will live forever.
The LORD loves justice
and will not leave those who worship
him.
He will always protect them,
but the children of the wicked will
die.
Good people will inherit the land
and will live in it forever.

Psalm 37:27–29

*T*he LORD will pay back his enemies
for what they have done.
He will show his anger to those who
were against him;
he will punish the people in faraway
places as they deserve.

Isaiah 59:18

*G*reat and powerful God, your name is the
LORD All-Powerful. You plan and do great
things. You see everything that people do,
and you reward people for the way they live
and for what they do. You did miracles and
wonderful things in the land of Egypt. You
have continued doing them in Israel and
among the other nations even until today.
So you have become well known. You
brought your people, the Israelites, out of
Egypt using signs and miracles and your
great power and strength. You brought
great terror on everyone. You gave them
this land that you promised to their ancestors long ago, a fertile land. They came into
this land and took it for their own, but they
did not obey you or follow your teachings.
They did not do everything you commanded. So you made all these terrible
things happen to them.

Jeremiah 32:18b–23

INSIGHTS

*H*ow does free forgiveness and justification
by faith square with judgment according to
works? The answer seems to be as follows.
First, the gift of justification certainly shields
believers from being condemned and banished
from God's presence as sinners. This appears
from the vision of judgment in Revelation
20:11–15, where alongside 'the books' re-
cording each man's work 'the book of life' is
opened, and those whose names are written
there are not 'cast into the lake of fire' as the
rest of men are. But, second, the gift of justification does not at all shield believers from
being assessed as Christians, and from for-
feiting good which others will enjoy if it turns
out that as Christians they have been slack,
mischievous and destructive. This appears
from Paul's warning to the Corinthians to be
careful what life-style they build on Christ, the
one foundation. 'If any man builds upon this
foundation . . . If any man's work abide
. . . he shall receive a reward. If any man's
work shall be burned, he shall suffer loss: but
he himself shall be saved; yet so as by fire' (1
Corinthians 3:12–15). 'Reward' and 'loss'
signify an enriched or impoverished relationship with God, though in what ways it is
beyond our present power to know.

J. I. Packer

APPLICATION

*F*or what does God punish or reward people?
What do you think God expects his servants
to do while they wait for his return? What
kind of servant do you want to be for your
Lord? How can you be a better one?

WEEKEND:

God Judges His People

Luke 19:41—20:19

N E W T E S T A M E N T R E A D I N G

Jesus Cries for Jerusalem

*A*s Jesus came near Jerusalem, he saw the city and cried for it, saying, "I wish you knew today what would bring you peace. But now it is hidden from you. The time is coming when your enemies will build a wall around you and will hold you in on all sides. They will destroy you and all your people, and not one stone will be left on another. All this will happen because you did not recognize the time when God came to save you."

Jesus Goes to the Temple

*J*esus went into the Temple and began to throw out the people who were selling things there. He said, "It is written in the Scriptures, 'My Temple will be a house for prayer.' But you have changed it into a 'hideout for robbers'!"

Jesus taught in the Temple every day. The leading priests, the experts on the law, and some of the leaders of the people wanted to kill Jesus. But they did not know how they could do it, because all the people were listening closely to him.

Jewish Leaders Question Jesus

*O*ne day Jesus was in the Temple, teaching the people and telling them the Good News. The leading priests, teachers of the law, and older Jewish leaders came up to talk with him, saying, "Tell us what authority you have to do these things? Who gave you this authority?"

Jesus answered, "I will also ask you a question. Tell me: When John baptized people, was that authority from God or just from other people?"

They argued about this, saying, "If we answer, 'John's baptism was from God,' Jesus will say, 'Then why did you not believe him?' But if we say, 'It was from other people,' all the people will stone us to death, because they believe John was a prophet."

So they answered that they didn't know where it came from.

Jesus said to them, "Then I won't tell you what authority I have to do these things."

A Story About God's Son

*T*hen Jesus told the people this story: "A man planted a vineyard and leased it to some farmers. Then he went away for a long time. When it was time for the grapes to be picked, he sent a servant to the farmers to get some of the grapes. But they beat the servant and sent him away empty-handed. Then he sent another servant. They beat this servant also, and showed no respect for him, and sent him away empty-handed. So the man sent a third servant. The farmers wounded him and threw him out. The owner of the vineyard said, 'What will I do now? I will send my son whom I love. Maybe they will respect him.' But when the farmers saw the son, they said to each other, 'This son will inherit the vineyard. If we kill him, it will be ours.' So the farmers threw the son out of the vineyard and killed him.

"What will the owner of this vineyard do to them? He will come and kill those farmers and will give the vineyard to other farmers."

When the people heard this story, they said, "Let this never happen!"

But Jesus looked at them and said, "Then what does this verse mean:
'The stone that the builders rejected
became the cornerstone'?

Psalm 118:22

Everyone who falls on that stone will be broken, and the person on whom it falls, that person will be crushed!"

The teachers of the law and the leading priests wanted to arrest Jesus at once, because they knew the story was about them. But they were afraid of what the people would do.

O L D T E S T A M E N T R E A D I N G

*J*erusalem is left alone
like an empty shelter in a vineyard,
like a hut left in a field of melons,
like a city surrounded by enemies.

The Lord All-Powerful
    allowed a few of our people to live.
Otherwise we would have been
    completely destroyed
like the cities of Sodom and
    Gomorrah.

Jerusalem, your rulers are like those of
    Sodom,
    and your people are like those of
    Gomorrah.
Hear the word of the Lord;
    listen to the teaching of our God!
The Lord says,
    "I do not want all these sacrifices.
I have had enough of your burnt
    sacrifices
    of male sheep and fat from fine
    animals.
I am not pleased
    by the blood of bulls, lambs, and
    goats.
You come to meet with me,
    but who asked you to do
    all this running in and out of my
    Temple's rooms?
Don't continue bringing me worthless
    sacrifices!
    I hate the incense you burn.
I can't stand your New Moons, Sab-
    baths, and other feast days;
    I can't stand the evil you do in your
    holy meetings.
I hate your New Moon feasts
    and your other yearly feasts.
They have become a heavy weight on me,
    and I am tired of carrying it.
When you raise your arms to me in
    prayer,
    I will refuse to look at you.
Even if you say many prayers,
    I will not listen to you,
because your hands are full of blood.
Wash yourselves and make yourselves
    clean.
    Stop doing the evil things I see you do.
Stop doing wrong.
    Learn to do good.
Seek justice.
    Punish those who hurt others.
Help the orphans.
    Stand up for the rights of widows."
Isaiah 1:8–17

APPLICATION

Jerusalem is identified in Scripture as God's holy city. For what reasons did Jesus weep over it? In a broader sense, what does this scene reveal about how Jesus views sin? Does Jesus weep or rejoice over the condition of your heart?

MONDAY:

Jesus Warns Against False Religious Leaders

Luke 20:20–47

Is It Right to Pay Taxes or Not?

So they watched Jesus and sent some spies who acted as if they were sincere. They wanted to trap Jesus in saying something wrong so they could hand him over to the authority and power of the governor. So the spies asked Jesus, "Teacher, we know that what you say and teach is true. You pay no attention to who people are, and you always teach the truth about God's way. Tell us, is it right for us to pay taxes to Caesar or not?"

But Jesus, knowing they were trying to trick him, said, "Show me a coin. Whose image and name are on it?"

They said, "Caesar's."

Jesus said to them, "Then give to Caesar the things that are Caesar's, and give to God the things that are God's."

So they were not able to trap Jesus in anything he said in the presence of the people. And being amazed at his answer, they became silent.

Some Sadducees Try to Trick Jesus

Some Sadducees, who believed people would not rise from the dead, came to Jesus. They asked, "Teacher, Moses wrote that if a man's brother dies and leaves a wife but no children, then that man must marry the widow and have children for his brother. Once there were seven brothers. The first brother married and died, but had no children. Then the second brother married the widow, and he died. And the third brother married the widow, and he died. The same thing happened with all seven brothers; they died and had no children. Finally, the woman died also. Since all seven brothers had married her, whose wife will she be when people rise from the dead?"

Jesus said to them, "On earth, people marry and are given to someone to marry. But those who will be worthy to be raised from the dead and live again will not marry, nor will they be given to someone to marry. In that life they are like angels and cannot die. They are children of God, because they have been raised from the dead. Even Moses clearly showed that the dead are raised to life. When he wrote about the burning bush, he said that the Lord is 'the God of Abraham, the God of Isaac, and the God of Jacob.' God is the God of the living, not the dead, because all people are alive to him."

Some of the teachers of the law said, "Teacher, your answer was good." No one was brave enough to ask him another question.

Is the Christ the Son of David?

Then Jesus said, "Why do people say that the Christ is the Son of David? In the book of Psalms, David himself says:

'The Lord said to my Lord:
　Sit by me at my right side,
　until I put your enemies under your
　　control.'   *Psalm 110:1*

David calls the Christ 'Lord,' so how can the Christ be his son?"

Jesus Accuses Some Leaders

While all the people were listening, Jesus said to his followers, "Beware of the teachers of the law. They like to walk around wearing fancy clothes, and they love for people to greet them with respect in the marketplaces. They love to have the most important seats in the synagogues and at feasts. But they cheat widows and steal their houses and then try to make themselves look good by saying long prayers. They will receive a greater punishment."

How terrible it will be for people who
　plan wickedness,
　who lie on their beds and make evil
　　plans.
When the morning light comes, they
　do what they planned,
　because they have the power to do
　　so.

They want fields, so they take them;
  they want houses, so they take them
    away.
They cheat people to get their houses;
  they rob them even of their prop-
    erty.

That is why the LORD says:
"Look, I am planning trouble against
    such people,
  and you won't be able to save
    yourselves.
You will no longer walk proudly,
  because it will be a terrible time.
                                    Micah 2:1–3

*T*he LORD spoke his word to me, saying:
"Human, prophesy against the leaders of
Israel, who are like shepherds. Prophesy
and say to them: 'This is what the Lord GOD
says: How terrible it will be for the shepherds of Israel who feed only themselves!
Why don't the shepherds feed the flock?
You eat the milk curds, and you clothe
yourselves with the wool. You kill the fat
sheep, but you do not feed the flock. You
have not made the weak strong. You have
not healed the sick or put bandages on
those that were hurt. You have not brought
back those who strayed away or searched
for the lost. But you have ruled the sheep
with cruel force.

"'So, you shepherds, hear the word of the
LORD. This is what the Lord GOD says: As
surely as I live, my flock has been caught
and eaten by all the wild animals, because
the flock has no shepherd. The shepherds
did not search for my flock. No, they fed
themselves instead of my flock. So, you
shepherds, hear the word of the LORD. This
is what the Lord GOD says: I am against the
shepherds. I will blame them for what has
happened to my sheep and will not let them
tend the flock anymore. Then the shepherds will stop feeding themselves, and I
will take my flock from their mouths so they
will no longer be their food."
                              Ezekiel 34:1–4, 7–10

I appeal to you, my brothers, who are already
in the ministry; I appeal to your churches; I
appeal to the onlookers, and inquire: How
many forms of sin are allowed to exist in you
and in your churches without anything like
that pointed rebuke which the nature of the
case demands? My brothers, do not many of
you satisfy yourselves simply with preaching
against sin, while you are afraid to so much
as name the different forms of sin that exist
among those to whom you are preaching? Do
you not preach against sin in the abstract,
with very little or no descending to par-
ticulars? . . . Or are the consciences of some
of you so seared as to render you almost blind
to anything like the details of the sins that
exist around you?

Not long ago a discerning man said that
his minister preaches against sin, but he does
not tell what sin is. He preaches against sin
in general, but never against any particular
sin. He denounces it in the aggregate, but
never meddles with it in detail as it exists
among his people. . . .

Do you see the importance of praying
continually for a quick and tender and powerful conscience? Do you see the importance
of great watchfulness lest we should abuse and
seduce our conscience by indulgence in sin?
Do you see the great importance of faithful
dealings with the consciences all around you,
so as to keep your own and their consciences
fully awake and as quick and sensitive as the
apple of the eye? . . .

It is impossible for me to understand how
some could really be in love with the law of
God, earnestly and honestly engaged in sup-
porting it in all the length and breadth of its
claims, and yet indulge in so many forms of
violating it with so little compunction or
misgiving. Is there not, my beloved brethren,
some delusion in this?

                                    Charles Finney

*W*hat are the leaders of God's people responsible to do? What does God promise to
spiritual leaders who plan wickedness? Pray
that God will open your eyes and protect you
from the blinding influence of false spiritual
leaders.

TUESDAY:
God Gives His People Words to Say
Luke 21:1–28

True Giving

*A*s Jesus looked up, he saw some rich people putting their gifts into the Temple money box. Then he saw a poor widow putting two small copper coins into the box. He said, "I tell you the truth, this poor widow gave more than all those rich people. They gave only what they did not need. This woman is very poor, but she gave all she had to live on."

The Temple Will Be Destroyed

*S*ome people were talking about the Temple and how it was decorated with beautiful stones and gifts offered to God.

But Jesus said, "As for these things you are looking at, the time will come when not one stone will be left on another. Every stone will be thrown down."

They asked Jesus, "Teacher, when will these things happen? What will be the sign that they are about to take place?"

Jesus said, "Be careful so you are not fooled. Many people will come in my name, saying, 'I am the One' and, 'The time has come!' But don't follow them. When you hear about wars and riots, don't be afraid, because these things must happen first, but the end will come later."

Then he said to them, "Nations will fight against other nations, and kingdoms against other kingdoms. In various places there will be great earthquakes, sicknesses, and a lack of food. Fearful events and great signs will come from heaven.

"But before all these things happen, people will arrest you and treat you cruelly. They will judge you in their synagogues and put you in jail and force you to stand before kings and governors, because you follow me. But this will give you an opportunity to tell about me. Make up your minds not to worry ahead of time about what you will say.

I will give you the wisdom to say things that none of your enemies will be able to stand against or prove wrong. Even your parents, brothers, relatives, and friends will turn against you, and they will kill some of you. All people will hate you because you follow me. But none of these things can really harm you. By continuing to have faith you will save your lives.

Jerusalem Will Be Destroyed

*W*hen you see armies all around Jerusalem, you will know it will soon be destroyed. At that time, the people in Judea should run away to the mountains. The people in Jerusalem must get out, and those who are near the city should not go in. These are the days of punishment to bring about all that is written in the Scriptures. How terrible it will be for women who are pregnant or have nursing babies! Great trouble will come upon this land, and God will be angry with these people. They will be killed by the sword and taken as prisoners to all nations. Jerusalem will be crushed by non-Jewish people until their time is over.

Don't Fear

*T*here will be signs in the sun, moon, and stars. On earth, nations will be afraid and confused because of the roar and fury of the sea. People will be so afraid they will faint, wondering what is happening to the world, because the powers of the heavens will be shaken. Then people will see the Son of Man coming in a cloud with power and great glory. When these things begin to happen, look up and hold your heads high, because the time when God will free you is near!"

*B*ut Moses said to the LORD, "Please, Lord, I have never been a skilled speaker. Even now, after talking to you, I cannot speak well. I speak slowly and can't find the best words."

Then the LORD said to him, "Who made a person's mouth? And who makes someone deaf or not able to speak? Or who gives a person sight or blindness? It is I, the LORD.

Now go! I will help you speak, and I will teach you what to say."

But Moses said, "Please, Lord, send someone else."

The LORD became angry with Moses and said, "Your brother Aaron, from the family of Levi, is a skilled speaker. He is already coming to meet you, and he will be happy when he sees you. You will speak to Aaron and tell him what to say. I will help both of you to speak and will teach you what to do. Aaron will speak to the people for you. You will tell him what God says, and he will speak for you."

Exodus 4:10–16

The LORD told Balaam what he should say. Then the LORD said, "Go back to Balak and give him this message."

So Balaam went back to Balak. Balak and all the leaders of Moab were still standing beside his burnt offering when Balaam gave them this message:

"Balak brought me here from Aram;
   the king of Moab brought me from
      the eastern mountains.
Balak said, 'Come, put a curse on the
   people of Jacob for me.
Come, call down evil on the people
   of Israel.'
But God has not cursed them,
   so I cannot curse them.
The LORD has not called down evil on
   them,
   so I cannot call down evil on them.
I see them from the top of the mountains;
   I see them from the hills.
I see a people who live alone,
   who think they are different from
      other nations.
No one can number the many people of
   Jacob,
   and no one can count a fourth of
      Israel.
Let me die like good men,
   and let me end up like them!"

Balak said to Balaam, "What have you done to me? I brought you here to curse my enemies, but you have only blessed them!"

But Balaam answered, "I must say what the LORD tells me to say."

Numbers 23:5–12

What in the world will I say?"

At some time in life we're all confronted with this challenge. . . .

In today's passage Jesus is talking about our concern over what to say when we are faced with giving testimony about Him in a setting which is hostile to the Christian faith. He assures us that the Holy Spirit will give us the thoughts, the words, and the courage which we so often lack. . . . There may be times when you are concerned about sharing your faith in Christ with someone or when you are challenged in your faith by other people. Rely upon the fact that God is the source of your thoughts and words at those times. Dr. Lloyd Ogilvie says:

> *Our only task is to open our minds in calm expectation of wisdom beyond our own capacity. We were never meant to be adequate on our own. It is when we think we are adequate that we get into trouble. A Christian is not one who works for the Lord but one in whom and through whom the Lord works. We are not to speak for God but to yield our tongues to express the thoughts the Lord has implanted.*

What can we draw from these words? Listen to the Lord before you speak and, after you have heard Him, speak with confidence and concern.

H. Norman Wright

What did God promise to do for both Moses and Aaron? Have you ever been (or are you) worried about what to say? Pray for a willing spirit that God can use, then trust him to give his message through you!

WEDNESDAY:

Focus Your Eyes on God; Be Ready for His Coming

Luke 21:29—22:20

Jesus' Words Will Live Forever

*T*hen Jesus told this story: "Look at the fig tree and all the other trees. When their leaves appear, you know that summer is near. In the same way, when you see these things happening, you will know that God's kingdom is near.

"I tell you the truth, all these things will happen while the people of this time are still living. Earth and sky will be destroyed, but the words I have spoken will never be destroyed.

Be Ready All the Time

*B*e careful not to spend your time feasting, drinking, or worrying about worldly things. If you do, that day might come on you suddenly, like a trap on all people on earth. So be ready all the time. Pray that you will be strong enough to escape all these things that will happen and that you will be able to stand before the Son of Man."

During the day, Jesus taught the people in the Temple, and at night he went out of the city and stayed on the Mount of Olives. Every morning all the people got up early to go to the Temple to listen to him.

Judas Becomes an Enemy of Jesus

*I*t was almost time for the Feast of Unleavened Bread, called the Passover Feast. The leading priests and teachers of the law were trying to find a way to kill Jesus, because they were afraid of the people.

Satan entered Judas Iscariot, one of Jesus' twelve apostles. Judas went to the leading priests and some of the soldiers who guarded the Temple and talked to them about a way to hand Jesus over to them. They were pleased and agreed to give Judas money. He agreed and watched for the best time to hand Jesus over to them when he was away from the crowd.

Jesus Eats the Passover Meal

*T*he Day of Unleavened Bread came when the Passover lambs had to be sacrificed. Jesus said to Peter and John, "Go and prepare the Passover meal for us to eat."

They asked, "Where do you want us to prepare it?" Jesus said to them, "After you go into the city, a man carrying a jar of water will meet you. Follow him into the house that he enters, and tell the owner of the house, 'The Teacher says: Where is the guest room in which I may eat the Passover meal with my followers?' Then he will show you a large, furnished room upstairs. Prepare the Passover meal there."

So Peter and John left and found everything as Jesus had said. And they prepared the Passover meal.

The Lord's Supper

*W*hen the time came, Jesus and the apostles were sitting at the table. He said to them, "I wanted very much to eat this Passover meal with you before I suffer. I will not eat another Passover meal until it is given its true meaning in the kingdom of God."

Then Jesus took a cup, gave thanks, and said, "Take this cup and share it among yourselves. I will not drink again from the fruit of the vine until God's kingdom comes."

Then Jesus took some bread, gave thanks, broke it, and gave it to the apostles, saying, "This is my body, which I am giving for you. Do this to remember me." In the same way, after supper, Jesus took the cup and said, "This cup is the new agreement that God makes with his people. This new agreement begins with my blood which is poured out for you."

*H*appy are those who live pure lives,
  who follow the LORD's teachings.
Happy are those who keep his rules,
  who try to obey him with their whole
    heart.
They don't do what is wrong;
  they follow his ways.
LORD, you gave your orders

to be obeyed completely.
I wish I were more loyal
  in obeying your demands.
Then I would not be ashamed
  when I study your commands.
When I learned that your laws are fair,
  I praised you with an honest heart.
I will obey your demands,
  so please don't ever leave me.

Psalm 119:1–8

*M*y child, listen and accept what I say.
  Then you will have a long life.
I am guiding you in the way of wisdom,
  and I am leading you on the right
    path.
Nothing will hold you back;
  you will not be overwhelmed.
Always remember what you have been
    taught,
  and don't let go of it.
Keep all that you have learned;
  it is the most important thing in life.
Don't follow the ways of the wicked;
  don't do what evil people do.
Avoid their ways, and don't follow
    them.
  Stay away from them and keep on
    going.

Proverbs 4:10–15

*L*isten, my child, and be wise.
  Keep your mind on what is right.
Don't drink too much wine
  or eat too much food.

Proverbs 23:19–20

*L*ORD, you are my share in life;
  I have promised to obey your words.
I prayed to you with all my heart.
  Have mercy on me as you have
    promised.
I thought about my life,
  and I decided to follow your rules.
I hurried and did not wait
  to obey your commands.

Psalm 119:57–60

INSIGHTS

*T*he coming of God's Son is the real hope of
the believers. . . . The early Christians

*constantly looked forward to it. The Church
in its first love waited for its Lord. How
often too Jesus Himself and His apostles admonished us to wait for His coming and to
hasten to meet Him! The return of the Lord
is not a theme with which certain specialists
occupy themselves, but it is the great theme
of Scripture and it must also become ours.
We are all deeply aware of the fact that our
congregations need a spiritual renewal.
"How can this take place?" I asked a missionary. "When the hope of the Lord's return
becomes living in our congregations," he
answered. . . .*

*Think of a congregation of three hundred
in which there were thirty who really were
waiting for the Lord. What holiness and what
light these could give to a congregation! John
says, "Everyone that hath this hope set on him
purifieth himself even as he is pure." He that
does not have this hope, does not cleanse
himself. Those who are really waiting need
not be exhorted to cleanse themselves; they do
it without outward prompting. They do not
need to be urged to press forward, to deny
themselves, to humble themselves; they just
naturally strive to be like the Lamb. . . . As
long as we do not have this Hope, we are
really without hope; and the state of such
persons is known to us all. . . .*

*Hitherto many of us have been like the
brother who once said: "For many years I
have known that I was converted, but I did
not know for what purpose. I have long known
that I was sealed with the Holy Spirit, but not
to what end. But I understood it when I Thess.
1:9–10 and Eph. 4:30 became clear to me:
we are converted to serve the true and living
God, and to wait for His Son from Heaven."*

G. Steinberger

ACTION POINT

*W*hy is it important to be ready for Jesus'
return? What must we do to be ready? What
causes believers to be unprepared for his
coming? Will you pray daily to be strong and
ready for that day?

211

THURSDAY:
Jesus Sought the Will of the Father

Luke 22:21–53

N E W   T E S T A M E N T   R E A D I N G

Who Will Turn Against Jesus?

But one of you will turn against me, and his hand is with mine on the table. What God has planned for the Son of Man will happen, but how terrible it will be for that one who turns against the Son of Man."

Then the apostles asked each other which one of them would do that.

Be Like a Servant

The apostles also began to argue about which one of them was the most important. But Jesus said to them, "The kings of the non-Jewish people rule over them, and those who have authority over others like to be called 'friends of the people.' But you must not be like that. Instead, the greatest among you should be like the youngest, and the leader should be like the servant. Who is more important: the one sitting at the table or the one serving? You think the one at the table is more important, but I am like a servant among you.

"You have stayed with me through my struggles. Just as my Father has given me a kingdom, I also give you a kingdom so you may eat and drink at my table in my kingdom. And you will sit on thrones, judging the twelve tribes of Israel.

Don't Lose Your Faith!

Simon, Simon, Satan has asked to test all of you as a farmer sifts his wheat. I have prayed that you will not lose your faith! Help your brothers be stronger when you come back to me."

But Peter said to Jesus, "Lord, I am ready to go with you to prison and even to die with you!"

But Jesus said, "Peter, before the rooster crows this day, you will say three times that you don't know me."

Be Ready for Trouble

Then Jesus said to the apostles, "When I sent you out without a purse, a bag, or sandals, did you need anything?"

They said, "No."

He said to them, "But now if you have a purse or a bag, carry that with you. If you don't have a sword, sell your coat and buy one. The Scripture says, 'He was treated like a criminal,' and I tell you this scripture must have its full meaning. It was written about me, and it is happening now."

His followers said, "Look, Lord, here are two swords."

He said to them, "That is enough."

Jesus Prays Alone

Jesus left the city and went to the Mount of Olives, as he often did, and his followers went with him. When he reached the place, he said to them, "Pray for strength against temptation."

Then Jesus went about a stone's throw away from them. He kneeled down and prayed, "Father, if you are willing, take away this cup of suffering. But do what you want, not what I want." Then an angel from heaven appeared to him to strengthen him. Being full of pain, Jesus prayed even harder. His sweat was like drops of blood falling to the ground. When he finished praying, he went to his followers and found them asleep because of their sadness. Jesus said to them, "Why are you sleeping? Get up and pray for strength against temptation."

Jesus Is Arrested

While Jesus was speaking, a crowd came up, and Judas, one of the twelve apostles, was leading them. He came close to Jesus so he could kiss him.

But Jesus said to him, "Judas, are you using the kiss to give the Son of Man to his enemies?"

When those who were standing around him saw what was happening, they said, "Lord, should we strike them with our swords?" And one of them struck the servant of the high priest and cut off his right ear.

Jesus said, "Stop! No more of this." Then he touched the servant's ear and healed him.

Those who came to arrest Jesus were the leading priests, the soldiers who guarded the Temple, and the older Jewish leaders. Jesus said to them, "You came out here with swords and clubs as though I am a criminal. I was with you every day in the Temple, and you didn't arrest me there. But this is your time—the time when darkness rules."

OLD TESTAMENT READING

David Prays for God's Will

LORD, listen to me and answer me.
   I am poor and helpless.
Protect me, because I worship you.
   My God, save me, your servant who
      trusts in you.
Lord, have mercy on me,
   because I have called to you all day.
Give happiness to me, your servant,
   because I give my life to you, Lord.
Lord, you are kind and forgiving
   and have great love for those who
      call to you.
LORD, hear my prayer,
   and listen when I ask for mercy.
I call to you in times of trouble,
   because you will answer me.

Lord, there is no god like you
   and no works like yours.
Lord, all the nations you have made
   will come and worship you.
   They will honor you.
You are great and you do miracles.
   Only you are God.

LORD, teach me what you want me to do,
   and I will live by your truth.

Psalm 86:1–11a

I lift my hands to you in prayer.
   As a dry land needs rain, I thirst for
      you.   *Selah*

LORD, answer me quickly,
   because I am getting weak.
Don't turn away from me,
   or I will be like those who are dead.
Tell me in the morning about your love,
   because I trust you.
Show me what I should do,
   because my prayers go up to you.

LORD, save me from my enemies;
   I hide in you.
Teach me to do what you want,
   because you are my God.
Let your good Spirit
   lead me on level ground.

Psalm 143:6–10

INSIGHTS

I seek at the beginning to get my heart in such a state that it has no will of its own in regard to a given matter. Nine tenths of the trouble with people generally is just here. Nine tenths of the difficulties are overcome when our hearts are ready to do the Lord's will, whatever it may be. When one is truly in this state, it is usually but a little way to the knowledge of what His will is.

Having done this, I do not leave the result to feeling or simple impression. If so, I make myself liable to great delusions.

I seek the will of the Spirit of God through, or in connection with, the Word of God. The Spirit and the Word must be combined. If I look to the Spirit alone without the Word, I lay myself open to great delusions also. If the Holy Spirit guides us at all, He will do it according to the Scriptures and never contrary to them.

Next I take into account providential circumstances. These often plainly indicate God's will in connection with His Word and Spirit.

I ask God in prayer to reveal His will to me aright.

Thus through prayer to God, the study of the Word, and reflection, I come to a deliberate judgment according to the best of my ability and knowledge; and if my mind is thus at peace, and continues so after two or three more petitions, I proceed accordingly. In trivial matters, and in transactions involving most important issues, I have found this method always effective.

George Müller

PAUSE FOR REFLECTION

What did Jesus do to know God's will? When Jesus struggled to know God's will, what did he do? What do you do to discover God's will?

FRIDAY:
Deceit Leads to Great Pain
Luke 22:54—23:12

NEW TESTAMENT READING

Peter Says He Doesn't Know Jesus

They arrested Jesus, and led him away, and brought him into the house of the high priest. Peter followed far behind them. After the soldiers started a fire in the middle of the courtyard and sat together, Peter sat with them. A servant girl saw Peter sitting there in the firelight, and looking closely at him, she said, "This man was also with him."

But Peter said this was not true; he said, "Woman, I don't know him."

A short time later, another person saw Peter and said, "You are also one of them."

But Peter said, "Man, I am not!"

About an hour later, another man insisted, "Certainly this man was with him, because he is from Galilee, too."

But Peter said, "Man, I don't know what you are talking about!"

At once, while Peter was still speaking, a rooster crowed. Then the Lord turned and looked straight at Peter. And Peter remembered what the Lord had said: "Before the rooster crows this day, you will say three times that you don't know me." Then Peter went outside and cried painfully.

The People Make Fun of Jesus

The men who were guarding Jesus began making fun of him and beating him.

They blindfolded him and said, "Prove that you are a prophet, and tell us who hit you." They said many cruel things to Jesus.

Jesus Before the Leaders

When day came, the council of the older leaders of the people, both the leading priests and the teachers of the law, came together and led Jesus to their highest court. They said, "If you are the Christ, tell us."

Jesus said to them, "If I tell you, you will not believe me. And if I ask you, you will not answer. But from now on, the Son of Man will sit at the right hand of the powerful God."

They all said, "Then are you the Son of God?"

Jesus said to them, "You say that I am."

They said, "Why do we need witnesses now? We ourselves heard him say this."

Pilate Questions Jesus

Then the whole group stood up and led Jesus to Pilate. They began to accuse Jesus, saying, "We caught this man telling things that mislead our people. He says that we should not pay taxes to Caesar, and he calls himself the Christ, a king."

Pilate asked Jesus, "Are you the king of the Jews?"

Jesus answered, "Those are your words."

Pilate said to the leading priests and the people, "I find nothing against this man."

They were insisting, saying, "But Jesus makes trouble with the people, teaching all around Judea. He began in Galilee, and now he is here."

Pilate Sends Jesus to Herod

Pilate heard this and asked if Jesus was from Galilee. Since Jesus was under Herod's authority, Pilate sent Jesus to Herod, who was in Jerusalem at that time. When Herod saw Jesus, he was very glad, because he had heard about Jesus and had wanted to meet him for a long time. He was hoping to see Jesus work a miracle. Herod asked Jesus many questions, but Jesus said nothing. The leading priests and teachers of the law were standing there, strongly accusing Jesus. After Herod and his soldiers had made fun of Jesus, they dressed him in a kingly robe and sent him back to Pilate. In the past, Pilate and Herod had always been enemies, but on that day they became friends.

OLD TESTAMENT READING

Isaac said, "I am old and don't know when I might die. So take your bow and arrows and go hunting in the field for an animal for me to eat. When you prepare the tasty food that I love, bring it to me, and I will eat. Then

I will bless you before I die." So Esau went out in the field to hunt.

Rebekah was listening as Isaac said this to his son Esau. She said to her son Jacob, "Listen, I heard your father saying to your brother Esau, 'Kill an animal and prepare some tasty food for me to eat. Then I will bless you in the presence of the LORD before I die.' So obey me, my son, and do what I tell you. Go out to our goats and bring me two of the best young ones. I will prepare them just the way your father likes them. Then you will take the food to your father, and he will bless you before he dies."

Isaac finished blessing Jacob. Then, just as Jacob left his father Isaac, Esau came in from hunting. He also prepared some tasty food and brought it to his father. He said, "Father, rise and eat the food that your son killed for you and then bless me."

Isaac asked, "Who are you?"

He answered, "I am your son—your firstborn son—Esau."

Then Isaac trembled greatly and said, "Then who was it that hunted the animals and brought me food before you came? I ate it, and I blessed him, and it is too late now to take back my blessing."

When Esau heard the words of his father, he let out a loud and bitter cry. He said to his father, "Bless me—me, too, my father!"

But Isaac said, "Your brother came and tricked me. He has taken your blessing."

Esau said, "Jacob is the right name for him. He has tricked me these two times. He took away my share of everything you own, and now he has taken away my blessing." Then Esau asked, "Haven't you saved a blessing for me?"

Isaac answered, "I gave Jacob the power to be master over you, and all his brothers will be his servants. And I kept him strong with grain and wine. There is nothing left to give you, my son."

After that Esau hated Jacob because of the blessing from Isaac. He thought to himself, "My father will soon die, and I will be sad for him. Then I will kill Jacob."

Genesis 27:2–10, 30–37, 41

INSIGHTS

*F*or the Old Testament Jew, truth was a sacred matter. Truth involved a proper understanding of reality, but it also involved much more than that. For the Jew truth also had a personal dimension, an emotional dimension, and an ethical dimension.

Truth is personal—it is a special part of any close human relationship. Trust is a by-product of truth, and personal relationships are built upon trust. I trust people who demonstrate that they are truthful. I do not trust people who show themselves to be habitual liars. A person who is trustworthy is a person who is truthful. . . .

Broken truth hurts. Satan, "the father of lies," loves to attack and distort truth. The Scripture says that Satan was a liar from the beginning. It is painful for anybody to invest his heart in a lie. A broken truth often means a broken heart.

This is the problem with lies. We do invest our hearts in the promises people make and the stories they tell us. When the promises are not kept and the stories prove to be false, we are hurt. We are disillusioned. We sometimes grow bitter. Trust is a fragile commodity and is as precious as it is delicate. Deep levels of trust take years to develop. Yet, such trust can be smashed to pieces in seconds.

R. C. Sproul

PAUSE FOR REFLECTION

*H*ow did deceit in Isaac's family change the family relationships? When Peter lied about knowing Jesus, how did he feel? How did his relationship with Jesus change? Thank Jesus that his trust never fails!

WEEKEND:
God Always Welcomes Repentant Sinners
Luke 23:13–43

Jesus Must Die

*P*ilate called the people together with the leading priests and the Jewish leaders. He said to them, "You brought this man to me, saying he makes trouble among the people. But I have questioned him before you all, and I have not found him guilty of what you say. Also, Herod found nothing wrong with him; he sent him back to us. Look, he has done nothing for which he should die. So, after I punish him, I will let him go free."

But the people shouted together, "Take this man away! Let Barabbas go free!" (Barabbas was a man who was in prison for his part in a riot in the city and for murder.)

Pilate wanted to let Jesus go free and told this to the crowd. But they shouted again, "Crucify him! Crucify him!"

A third time Pilate said to them, "Why? What wrong has he done? I can find no reason to kill him. So I will have him punished and set him free."

But they continued to shout, demanding that Jesus be crucified. Their yelling became so loud that Pilate decided to give them what they wanted. He set free the man who was in jail for rioting and murder, and he handed Jesus over to them to do with him as they wished.

Jesus Is Crucified

*A*s they led Jesus away, Simon, a man from Cyrene, was coming in from the fields. They forced him to carry Jesus' cross and to walk behind him.

A large crowd of people was following Jesus, including some women who were sad and crying for him. But Jesus turned and said to them, "Women of Jerusalem, don't cry for me. Cry for yourselves and for your children. The time is coming when people will say, 'Happy are the women who cannot have children and who have no babies to nurse.' Then people will say to the mountains, 'Fall on us!' And they will say to the hills, 'Cover us!' If they act like this now when life is good, what will happen when bad times come?"

There were also two criminals led out with Jesus to be put to death. When they came to a place called the Skull, the soldiers crucified Jesus and the criminals—one on his right and the other on his left. Jesus said, "Father, forgive them, because they don't know what they are doing."

The soldiers threw lots to decide who would get his clothes. The people stood there watching. And the leaders made fun of Jesus, saying, "He saved others. Let him save himself if he is God's Chosen One, the Christ."

The soldiers also made fun of him, coming to Jesus and offering him some vinegar. They said, "If you are the king of the Jews, save yourself!" At the top of the cross these words were written: THIS IS THE KING OF THE JEWS.

One of the criminals on a cross began to shout insults at Jesus: "Aren't you the Christ? Then save yourself and us."

But the other criminal stopped him and said, "You should fear God! You are getting the same punishment he is. We are punished justly, getting what we deserve for what we did. But this man has done nothing wrong." Then he said, "Jesus, remember me when you come into your kingdom."

Jesus said to him, "I tell you the truth, today you will be with me in paradise."

*N*ow write this on a sign for the
people,
write this on a scroll,
so that for the days to come
this will be a witness forever.
These people are like children who lie
and refuse to obey;
they refuse to listen to the LORD's
teachings.
They tell the seers,
"Don't see any more visions!"
They say to the prophets,
"Don't tell us the truth!

Say things that will make us feel good;
  see only good things for us.
Stop blocking our path.
  Get out of our way.
Stop telling us
  about God, the Holy One of Israel."

So this is what the Holy One of Israel
says:
  "You people have refused to accept this
    message
  and have depended on cruelty and
    lies to help you.
You are guilty of these things.
  So you will be like a high wall with
    cracks in it
  that falls suddenly and breaks into
    small pieces.
You will be like a clay jar that breaks,
  smashed into many pieces.
Those pieces will be too small
  to take coals from the fire
  or to get water from a well."

This is what the Lord God, the Holy One
of Israel, says:
  "If you come back to me and trust me,
    you will be saved.
  If you will be calm and trust me, you
    will be strong."
  But you don't want to do that.
The Lord wants to show his mercy to
  you.
He wants to rise and comfort you.
The Lord is a fair God,
  and everyone who waits for his help
    will be happy.

Isaiah 30:8–15, 18

Get a scroll. Write on it all the words I
have spoken to you about Israel and Judah
and all the nations. Write everything from
when I first spoke to you, when Josiah was
king, until now. Maybe the family of Judah
will hear what disasters I am planning to
bring on them and will stop doing wicked
things. Then I would forgive them for the
sins and the evil things they have done."

Jeremiah 36:2–3

INSIGHTS

*The prisoners in the Montinlupa Prison who
gathered for a large assembly were astonished*
*to see a woman in her seventies make her way
up the steps of the platform to address them.
What would an old woman have to say to
them? . . .*

*. . . She told how she and her family had
hidden Jews from the Nazis during World
War II and how German police, because of a
tip from two of her fellow citizens, had
pounded on their door one frigid February day
in 1944 with warrants for their arrest. The
speaker was Corrie ten Boom. . . .*

*After the war was over, the two Dutchmen
who had betrayed her family were taken into
custody and put on trial. . . . "My sister
Nollie," Corrie told her audience, "heard of
the trial of these two men who told the Gestapo
about us, and she wrote a letter to both of
them. . . She told them that we had forgiven
them and that we could do this because of
Jesus, who is in our hearts."*

*Both men responded. One wrote: "I have
received Jesus as my Savior. When you can
give such ability to forgive to people like
Corrie ten Boom and her sister, then there is
hope for me. I brought my sins to Him." The
other letter gave an opposite viewpoint: "I
know what I have done to your family, that I
have caused the death of several of you who
have saved Jews, and above that I have helped
to kill many hundreds of Jewish people. The
only thing I regret is that I have not been able
to kill more of your kind." Corrie went on to
challenge the prisoners that every one of
them—even as those criminals who had been
on the cross—could accept or reject Christ and
his forgiveness.*

Ruth Tucker

APPLICATION

*How much evil will God forgive? What does
he require to receive forgiveness? Are you
willing to turn away from a life of sin and
trust God for your salvation?*

MONDAY:

The Resurrected Christ Saves His People

Luke 23:44—24:12

NEW TESTAMENT READING

Jesus Dies

*I*t was about noon, and the whole land became dark until three o'clock in the afternoon, because the sun did not shine. The curtain in the Temple was torn in two. Jesus cried out in a loud voice, "Father, I give you my life." After Jesus said this, he died.

When the army officer there saw what happened, he praised God, saying, "Surely this was a good man!"

When all the people who had gathered there to watch saw what happened, they returned home, beating their chests because they were so sad. But those who were close friends of Jesus, including the women who had followed him from Galilee, stood at a distance and watched.

Joseph Takes Jesus' Body

*T*here was a good and religious man named Joseph who was a member of the Jewish council. But he had not agreed to the other leaders' plans and actions against Jesus. He was from the Jewish town of Arimathea and was waiting for the kingdom of God to come. Joseph went to Pilate to ask for the body of Jesus. He took the body down from the cross, wrapped it in cloth, and put it in a tomb that was cut out of a wall of rock. This tomb had never been used before. This was late on Preparation Day, and when the sun went down, the Sabbath day would begin.

The women who had come from Galilee with Jesus followed Joseph and saw the tomb and how Jesus' body was laid. Then the women left to prepare spices and perfumes.

On the Sabbath day they rested, as the law of Moses commanded.

Jesus Rises from the Dead

*V*ery early on the first day of the week, at dawn, the women came to the tomb, bringing the spices they had prepared. They found the stone rolled away from the entrance of the tomb, but when they went in, they did not find the body of the Lord Jesus. While they were wondering about this, two men in shining clothes suddenly stood beside them. The women were very afraid and bowed their heads to the ground. The men said to them, "Why are you looking for a living person in this place for the dead? He is not here; he has risen from the dead. Do you remember what he told you in Galilee? He said the Son of Man must be handed over to sinful people, be crucified, and rise from the dead on the third day." Then the women remembered what Jesus had said.

The women left the tomb and told all these things to the eleven apostles and the other followers. It was Mary Magdalene, Joanna, Mary the mother of James, and some other women who told the apostles everything that had happened at the tomb. But they did not believe the women, because it sounded like nonsense. But Peter got up and ran to the tomb. Bending down and looking in, he saw only the cloth that Jesus' body had been wrapped in. Peter went away to his home, wondering about what had happened.

OLD TESTAMENT READING

*H*ere is my servant, the one I support.
    He is the one I chose, and I am
      pleased with him.
I have put my Spirit upon him,
    and he will bring justice to all
      nations.
He will not cry out or yell
    or speak loudly in the streets.
He will not break a crushed blade of
      grass
    or put out even a weak flame.
He will truly bring justice;
    he will not lose hope or give up
until he brings justice to the world.
    And people far away will trust his
      teachings."

God, the LORD, said these things.
He created the skies and stretched
    them out.

He spread out the earth and everything on it.
He gives life to all people on earth,
to everyone who walks on the earth.
The LORD says, "I, the LORD, called you
to do right,
and I will hold your hand
and protect you.
You will be the sign of my agreement with the people,
a light to shine for all people.
You will help the blind to see.
You will free those who are in prison,
and you will lead those who live in
darkness out of their prison.

"I am the LORD. That is my name.
I will not give my glory to another;
I will not let idols take the praise that
should be mine.
The things I said would happen have
happened,
and now I tell you about new things.
Before those things happen,
I tell you about them."

Isaiah 42:1–9

I am the LORD your God,
who holds your right hand,
and I tell you, 'Don't be afraid.
I will help you.'
You few people of Israel who are left,
do not be afraid even though you are
weak as a worm.
I myself will help you," says the LORD.
"The one who saves you is the Holy
One of Israel."

Isaiah 41:13–14

*N*ever underestimate the power of a seed.
God didn't. When his kingdom was rav-
aged and his people had forgotten his name,
he planted his seed. When the soil of the human heart had grown crusty, he planted his
seed. When religion had become a ritual and
the temple a trading post, he planted his seed.
Want to see a miracle? Watch him as he
places the seed of his own self in the fertile
womb of a Jewish girl.
Up it grew, "like a tender green shoot,
sprouting from a root in dry and sterile

ground." The seed spent a lifetime pushing
back the stones that tried to keep it under-
ground. The seed made a ministry out of
shoving away the rocks that cluttered his
father's soil.
The stones of legalism that burdened backs.
The stones of oppression that broke bones.
The stones of prejudice that fenced out the
needy.
But it was the final stone that proved to
be the supreme test of the seed. The stone of
death—rolled by humans and sealed by Satan
in front of the tomb. For a moment it appeared the seed would be stuck in the earth.
For a moment, it looked like this rock was
too big to be budged.
But then, somewhere in the heart of the
earth, the seed of God stirred, shoved, and
sprouted. The ground trembled, and the rock
of the tomb tumbled. And the flower of Easter
blossomed.
Never underestimate the power of a seed.

Max Lucado

*W*hat warnings did Jesus' followers have
that he would die and rise again? How well
did they handle the reality of his resurrection?
When you ponder Christ's awesome salvation,
do you, like Peter, take time alone to take it
all in?

TUESDAY:

Jesus Sends His Witnesses to All Nations

Luke 24:13–53

NEW TESTAMENT READING

Jesus on the Road to Emmaus

*T*hat same day two of Jesus' followers were going to a town named Emmaus, about seven miles from Jerusalem. They were talking about everything that had happened. While they were talking and discussing, Jesus himself came near and began walking with them, but they were kept from recognizing him. Then he said, "What are these things you are talking about while you walk?"

The two followers stopped, looking very sad. The one named Cleopas answered, "Are you the only visitor in Jerusalem who does not know what just happened there?"

Jesus said to them, "What are you talking about?"

They said, "About Jesus of Nazareth. He was a prophet who said and did many powerful things before God and all the people. Our leaders and the leading priests handed him over to be sentenced to death, and they crucified him.

"But we were hoping that he would free Israel. Besides this, it is now the third day since this happened. And today some women among us amazed us. Early this morning they went to the tomb, but they did not find his body there. They came and told us that they had seen a vision of angels who said that Jesus was alive! So some of our group went to the tomb, too. They found it just as the women said, but they did not see Jesus."

Then Jesus said to them, "You are foolish and slow to believe everything the prophets said. They said that the Christ must suffer these things before he enters his glory." Then starting with what Moses and all the prophets had said about him, Jesus began to explain everything that had been written about himself in the Scriptures.

They came near the town of Emmaus, and Jesus acted as if he were going farther.

But they begged him, "Stay with us, because it is late; it is almost night." So he went in to stay with them.

When Jesus was at the table with them, he took some bread, gave thanks, divided it, and gave it to them. And then, they were allowed to recognize Jesus. But when they saw who he was, he disappeared. They said to each other, "It felt like a fire burning in us when Jesus talked to us on the road and explained the Scriptures to us."

So the two followers got up at once and went back to Jerusalem. There they found the eleven apostles and others gathered. They were saying, "The Lord really has risen from the dead! He showed himself to Simon."

Then the two followers told what had happened on the road and how they recognized Jesus when he divided the bread.

Jesus Appears to His Followers

*W*hile the two followers were telling this, Jesus himself stood right in the middle of them and said, "Peace be with you."

They were fearful and terrified and thought they were seeing a ghost. But Jesus said, "Why are you troubled? Why do you doubt what you see? Look at my hands and my feet. It is I myself! Touch me and see, because a ghost does not have a living body as you see I have."

After Jesus said this, he showed them his hands and feet. While they still could not believe it because they were amazed and happy, Jesus said to them, "Do you have any food here?" They gave him a piece of broiled fish. While the followers watched, Jesus took the fish and ate it.

He said to them, "Remember when I was with you before? I said that everything written about me must happen—everything in the law of Moses, the books of the prophets, and the Psalms."

Then Jesus opened their minds so they could understand the Scriptures. He said to them, "It is written that the Christ would suffer and rise from the dead on the third day and that a change of hearts and lives and forgiveness of sins would be preached in his name to all nations, starting at Jerusalem. You are witnesses of these things. I will send you what my Father has promised, but you must stay in Jerusalem until you have received that power from heaven."

Jesus Goes Back to Heaven

*J*esus led his followers as far as Bethany, and he raised his hands and blessed them. While he was blessing them, he was separated from them and carried into heaven. They worshiped him and returned to Jerusalem very happy. They stayed in the Temple all the time, praising God.

OLD TESTAMENT READING

*H*ow beautiful is the person
　who comes over the mountains to
　　bring good news,
who announces peace
　and brings good news,
　who announces salvation
and says to Jerusalem,
　"Your God is King."
Listen! Your guards are shouting.
　They are all shouting for joy!
They all will see with their own eyes
　when the LORD returns to Jerusalem.
Jerusalem, your buildings are de-
　stroyed now,
　but shout and rejoice together,
because the LORD has comforted his
　people.
He has saved Jerusalem.
The LORD will show his holy power
　to all the nations.
Then everyone on earth
　will see the salvation of our God.
　　　　　　　　　　　Isaiah 52:7–10

*H*ear, heavens, and I will speak.
　Listen, earth, to what I say.
My teaching will drop like rain;
　my words will fall like dew.
They will be like showers on the grass;
　they will pour down like rain on
　　young plants.
I will announce the name of the LORD.
　Praise God because he is great!
He is like a rock; what he does is perfect,
　and he is always fair.
He is a faithful God who does no wrong,
　who is right and fair.
　　　　　　　　　　Deuteronomy 32:1–4

*J*erusalem, you have good news to tell.
　Go up on a high mountain.
Jerusalem, you have good news to tell.
　Shout out loud the good news.
Shout it out and don't be afraid.
　Say to the towns of Judah,
　"Here is your God."
Look, the Lord GOD is coming with
　power
　to rule all the people.
Look, he will bring reward for his
　people;
　he will have their payment with him.
He takes care of his people like a
　shepherd.
He gathers them like lambs in his
　arms
　and carries them close to him.
　　　　　　　　　　Isaiah 40:9–11a

*S*ing praises to the LORD who is king
　on Mount Zion.
Tell the nations what he has done.
　　　　　　　　　　Psalm 9:11

INSIGHTS

*E*veryone has the great responsibility to win as many people as possible to Christ. This is the great privilege and the great duty of all disciples of Christ. . . .

I fear I must say that the great mass of people professing to be believers seem never to have been impressed with this truth. The work of saving souls is something they feel they can leave to ministers.

Many believers suppose it belongs only to those who are called to preach the gospel as a life work. They fail to realize that all are called to preach the gospel, that the whole life of every believer is to be a proclamation of the glad tidings.

Charles Finney

ACTION POINT

*W*rite, in your own words, the essential message of salvation that Jesus wants his followers to proclaim. To whom does he want you to deliver that message? Will you?

WEDNESDAY:

Christ: The True Light of the World

John 1:1–28

Christ Comes to the World

*I*n the beginning there was the Word. The Word was with God, and the Word was God. He was with God in the beginning. All things were made by him, and nothing was made without him. In him there was life, and that life was the light of all people. The Light shines in the darkness, and the darkness has not overpowered it.

There was a man named John who was sent by God. He came to tell people the truth about the Light so that through him all people could hear about the Light and believe. John was not the Light, but he came to tell people the truth about the Light. The true Light that gives light to all was coming into the world!

The Word was in the world, and the world was made by him, but the world did not know him. He came to the world that was his own, but his own people did not accept him. But to all who did accept him and believe in him he gave the right to become children of God. They did not become his children in any human way—by any human parents or human desire. They were born of God.

The Word became a human and lived among us. We saw his glory—the glory that belongs to the only Son of the Father —and he was full of grace and truth. John tells the truth about him and cries out, saying, "This is the One I told you about: 'The One who comes after me is greater than I am, because he was living before me.'"

Because he was full of grace and truth, from him we all received one gift after another. The law was given through Moses, but grace and truth came through Jesus Christ. No one has ever seen God. But God the only Son is very close to the Father, and he has shown us what God is like.

John Tells People About Jesus

*H*ere is the truth John told when the Jews in Jerusalem sent priests and Levites to ask him, "Who are you?"

John spoke freely and did not refuse to answer. He said, "I am not the Christ."

So they asked him, "Then who are you? Are you Elijah?"

He answered, "No, I am not."

"Are you the Prophet?" they asked.

He answered, "No."

Then they said, "Who are you? Give us an answer to tell those who sent us. What do you say about yourself?"

John told them in the words of the prophet Isaiah:

"I am the voice of one
    calling out in the desert:
'Make the road straight for the Lord.'"

Isaiah 40:3

Some Pharisees who had been sent asked John: "If you are not the Christ or Elijah or the Prophet, why do you baptize people?"

John answered, "I baptize with water, but there is one here with you that you don't know about. He is the One who comes after me. I am not good enough to untie the strings of his sandals."

This all happened at Bethany on the other side of the Jordan River, where John was baptizing people.

*T*he stone that the builders rejected
    became the cornerstone.
The LORD did this,
    and it is wonderful to us.
This is the day that the LORD has made.
    Let us rejoice and be glad today!

Please, LORD, save us;
    please, LORD, give us success.
God bless the one who comes in the
        name of the LORD.
    We bless all of you from the Temple
        of the LORD.
The LORD is God,
    and he has shown kindness to us.
With branches in your hands, join the
        feast.

Come to the corners of the altar.

You are my God, and I will thank you;
you are my God, and I will praise
your greatness.

Thank the LORD because he is good.
His love continues forever.

Psalm 118:22–29

*B*efore those people lived in darkness,
but now they have seen a great light.
They lived in a dark land,
but a light has shined on them.
A child has been born to us;
God has given a son to us.
He will be responsible for leading
the people.
His name will be Wonderful Counselor,
Powerful God,
Father Who Lives Forever, Prince of
Peace.

Isaiah 9:2, 6

*T*he LORD made me in the body of my
mother
to be his servant,
to lead the people of Jacob back to him
so that Israel might be gathered to
him.
The LORD will honor me,
and I will get my strength from my
God.
Now he told me,
"You are an important servant to me
to bring back the tribes of Jacob,
to bring back the people of Israel
who are left alive.
But, more importantly, I will make you
a light for all nations
to show people all over the world the
way to be saved."

Isaiah 49:5–6

INSIGHTS

*T*hanks to the great mercy and marvel of the
Incarnation, the cosmic scene is resolved into
a human drama. God reaches down to relate
himself to man, and man reaches up to relate
himself to God. Time looks into eternity and
eternity into time, making now always and
always now. Everything is transformed by this

*sublime drama of the Incarnation, God's
special parable for fallen man in a fallen
world. The way opens before us that was
charted in the birth, ministry, death, and
resurrection of Jesus Christ, a way that suc-
cessive generations of believers have striven
to follow. They have derived therefrom
the moral, spiritual, and intellectual creativity out of which has come everything truly
great in our art, our literature, our music. . . .*

*. . . Whatever may happen, however
seemingly inimical to it may be the world's
going and those who preside over the world's
affairs, the truth of the Incarnation remains
intact and inviolate. . . .*

*. . . Christ shows what life really is, and
what our true destiny is. We escape from the
cave. We emerge from the darkness and instead of shadows we have all around us the
glory of God's creation. Instead of darkness
we have light; instead of despair, hope; instead of time and the clocks ticking inexorably
on, eternity, which never began and never
ends and yet is sublimely now. . . . By
identifying ourselves with Christ, by absorbing
ourselves in his teaching, by living out the
drama of his life with him, including especially the passion, that powerhouse of love and
creativity—by living with, by, and in him, we
can be reborn to become new men and women
in a new world.*

Malcolm Muggeridge

PAUSE   FOR   REFLECTION

*I*n *what ways would you say Christ's coming to earth enlightened the world? What did
Christ's coming reveal? What difference does
being reborn of God—becoming one of his
children—make in your life?*

223

THURSDAY:

Jesus Comes as the Lamb of God

John 1:29–51

*T*he next day John saw Jesus coming toward him. John said, "Look, the Lamb of God, who takes away the sin of the world! This is the One I was talking about when I said, 'A man will come after me, but he is greater than I am, because he was living before me.' Even I did not know who he was, although I came baptizing with water so that the people of Israel would know who he is."

Then John said, "I saw the Spirit come down from heaven in the form of a dove and rest on him. Until then I did not know who the Christ was. But the God who sent me to baptize with water told me, 'You will see the Spirit come down and rest on a man; he is the One who will baptize with the Holy Spirit.' I have seen this happen, and I tell you the truth: This man is the Son of God."

The First Followers of Jesus

*T*he next day John was there again with two of his followers. When he saw Jesus walking by, he said, "Look, the Lamb of God!"

The two followers heard John say this, so they followed Jesus. When Jesus turned and saw them following him, he asked, "What are you looking for?"

They said, "Rabbi, where are you staying?" ("Rabbi" means "Teacher.")

He answered, "Come and see." So the two men went with Jesus and saw where he was staying and stayed there with him that day. It was about four o'clock in the afternoon.

One of the two men who followed Jesus after they heard John speak about him was Andrew, Simon Peter's brother. The first thing Andrew did was to find his brother Simon and say to him, "We have found the Messiah." ("Messiah" means "Christ.")

Then Andrew took Simon to Jesus. Jesus looked at him and said, "You are Simon son of John. You will be called Cephas." ("Cephas" means "Peter.")

The next day Jesus decided to go to Galilee. He found Philip and said to him, "Follow me." Philip was from the town of Bethsaida, where Andrew and Peter lived. Philip found Nathanael and told him, "We have found the man that Moses wrote about in the law, and the prophets also wrote about him. He is Jesus, the son of Joseph, from Nazareth."

But Nathanael said to Philip, "Can anything good come from Nazareth?"

Philip answered, "Come and see."

As Jesus saw Nathanael coming toward him, he said, "Here is truly an Israelite. There is nothing false in him."

Nathanael asked, "How do you know me?"

Jesus answered, "I saw you when you were under the fig tree, before Philip told you about me."

Then Nathanael said to Jesus, "Teacher, you are the Son of God; you are the King of Israel."

Jesus said to Nathanael, "Do you believe simply because I told you I saw you under the fig tree? You will see greater things than that." And Jesus said to them, "I tell you the truth, you will all see heaven open and 'angels of God going up and coming down' on the Son of Man."

---

*B*ut he took our suffering on him
and felt our pain for us.
We saw his suffering
and thought God was punishing him.
But he was wounded for the wrong we did;
he was crushed for the evil we did.
The punishment, which made us well, was given to him,
and we are healed because of his wounds.
We all have wandered away like sheep;
each of us has gone his own way.
But the LORD has put on him the punishment
for all the evil we have done.

224

He was beaten down and punished,
  but he didn't say a word.
He was like a lamb being led to be
    killed.
  He was quiet, as a sheep is quiet
      while its wool is being cut;
  he never opened his mouth.
Men took him away roughly and
    unfairly.
  He died without children to continue
    his family.
He was put to death;
  he was punished for the sins of my
    people.
He was buried with wicked men,
  and he died with the rich.
He had done nothing wrong,
  and he had never lied.

But it was the LORD who decided
  to crush him and make him suffer.
  The LORD made his life a penalty
    offering,
but he will still see his descendants and
    live a long life.
  He will complete the things the LORD
    wants him to do.
"After his soul suffers many things,
  he will see life and be satisfied.
My good servant will make many
      people right with God;
  he will carry away their sins.
For this reason I will make him a great
    man among people,
  and he will share in all things with
    those who are strong.
He willingly gave his life
  and was treated like a criminal.
But he carried away the sins of many
    people
  and asked forgiveness for those who
    sinned."

Isaiah 53:4–12

It was never meant
to burst from the body
so fiercely, to pour
unchannelled from
the five wounds
and the unbandaged brow,
drowning the dark wood,

staining the stones
and the gravel below,
clotting in the air
dark with God's absence.

It was created for
a closed system—
the unbroken
rhythms of human blood
binding the body
of God, circulating
hot, brilliant,
saline, without
interruption
between heart, lungs
and all cells.

But because he
was once emptied
I am each day refilled;
my spirit-arteries
pulse with the vital red
of love; poured out,
it is his life
that now pumps through
my own heart's core.
He bled, and died, and I
have been transfused.

Luci Shaw

PAUSE FOR REFLECTION

What an awesome thing to be saved by the
Lamb of God! How well do you know the
Lamb of God? As certainly as John, Andrew,
and Philip did? Or are you a bit skeptical, as
Nathanael was? Reread the Isaiah passage
and pray for a renewed knowledge of the
Lamb of God—in your mind and in your
heart.

FRIDAY:

Jesus Shows His Love for God's Temple and His Hatred of Sin

John 2:1–25

The Wedding at Cana

*T*wo days later there was a wedding in the town of Cana in Galilee. Jesus' mother was there, and Jesus and his followers were also invited to the wedding. When all the wine was gone, Jesus' mother said to him, "They have no more wine."

Jesus answered, "Dear woman, why come to me? My time has not yet come."

His mother said to the servants, "Do whatever he tells you to do."

In that place there were six stone water jars that the Jews used in their washing ceremony. Each jar held about twenty or thirty gallons.

Jesus said to the servants, "Fill the jars with water." So they filled the jars to the top.

Then he said to them, "Now take some out and give it to the master of the feast."

So they took the water to the master. When he tasted it, the water had become wine. He did not know where the wine came from, but the servants who had brought the water knew. The master of the wedding called the bridegroom and said to him, "People always serve the best wine first. Later, after the guests have been drinking awhile, they serve the cheaper wine. But you have saved the best wine till now."

So in Cana of Galilee Jesus did his first miracle. There he showed his glory, and his followers believed in him.

Jesus in the Temple

*A*fter this, Jesus went to the town of Capernaum with his mother, brothers, and followers. They stayed there for just a few days. When it was almost time for the Jewish Passover Feast, Jesus went to Jerusalem. In the Temple he found people selling cattle, sheep, and doves. He saw others sitting at tables, exchanging different kinds of money. Jesus made a whip out of cords and forced all of them, both the sheep and cattle, to leave the Temple. He turned over the tables and scattered the money of those who were exchanging it. Then he said to those who were selling pigeons, "Take these things out of here! Don't make my Father's house a place for buying and selling!"

When this happened, the followers remembered what was written in the Scriptures: "My strong love for your Temple completely controls me."

The Jews said to Jesus, "Show us a miracle to prove you have the right to do these things."

Jesus answered them, "Destroy this temple, and I will build it again in three days."

The Jews answered, "It took forty-six years to build this Temple! Do you really believe you can build it again in three days?"

(But the temple Jesus meant was his own body. After Jesus was raised from the dead, his followers remembered that Jesus had said this. Then they believed the Scripture and the words Jesus had said.)

When Jesus was in Jerusalem for the Passover Feast, many people believed in him because they saw the miracles he did. But Jesus did not trust himself to them because he knew them all. He did not need anyone to tell him about people, because he knew what was in people's minds.

David's Psalms About Love for God and His Temple

*L*ORD, defend me because I have lived
>an innocent life.
I have trusted the LORD and never
>doubted.
LORD, try me and test me;
>look closely into my heart and mind.
I see your love,
>and I live by your truth.
I do not spend time with liars,
>nor do I make friends with those
>who hide their sin.
I hate the company of evil people,

and I won't sit with the wicked.
I wash my hands to show I am innocent,
and I come to your altar, LORD.
I raise my voice in praise
and tell of all the miracles you have
done.
LORD, I love the Temple where you
live,
where your glory is.
Do not kill me with those sinners
or take my life with those murderers.
Evil is in their hands,
and they do wrong for money.
But I have lived an innocent life,
so save me and have mercy on me.
I stand in a safe place.
LORD, I praise you in the great
meeting.

Psalm 26:1–12

*L*ord GOD All-Powerful,
do not let those who hope in you be
ashamed because of me.
God of Israel,
do not let your worshipers be
disgraced because of me.
For you, I carry this shame,
and my face is covered with disgrace.
I am like a stranger to my closest
relatives
and a foreigner to my mother's
children.
My strong love for your Temple
completely controls me.
When people insult you, it hurts
me.

Psalm 69:6–9

I will look for trustworthy people
so I can live with them in the land.
Only those who live innocent lives
will be my servants.
No one who is dishonest will live in my
house;
no liars will stay around me.
Every morning I will destroy the
wicked in the land.
I will rid the LORD's city of people
who do evil.

Psalm 101:6–8

*I*n Cana Jesus manifested His power as the Creator. Now He came to manifest His authority as the Messiah, the Son of God. Not only did He drive the sheep and oxen out of the temple, but He whipped the merchants out of the place. These Jews knew that He was right. The law and their consciences were witnesses against them. Christ was filled with righteous indignation in His zeal for His Father's house.

Christ cleansed the temple by crying, "Make not my Father's house an house of merchandise." Mark that He calls the temple "My Father's house." Christ was claiming a unique relationship with the Living God. . . .

When Christ drove the merchandisers out of the temple, they experienced something of the terror of the Lord. In the future men will cry to the mountains and rocks to hide them "from the face of him that sitteth on the throne, and from the wrath of the Lamb: For the great day of his wrath is come; and who shall be able to stand?" (Revelation 6:16–17).

Sometimes we forget that He is a righteous God and that every one of us must one day stand in His presence and give an account to Him. "It is a fearful thing to fall into the hands of the living God" (Hebrews 10:31). . . .

. . . Christ cleansed the temple when men sinned and made it unclean. Similarly, the Lord has a right to cleanse us when we sin. It is much better for us to willingly confess our sins so that He may forgive and cleanse us. And He is willing and ready to do just that. How wonderful it is to know that the blood of Jesus Christ, God's Son, cleanseth us from all sin (1 John 1:7).

John G. Mitchell

*W*hat does the Jews' demand that Jesus prove he had the right to cleanse God's temple reveal? In what ways do you demand that Jesus prove his right to purge the sin from your heart (which is also his temple)? Ask for his forgiveness.

WEEKEND:

God's Love Caused Him to Send Salvation Through His Son

John 3:1–30

Nicodemus Comes to Jesus

There was a man named Nicodemus who was one of the Pharisees and an important Jewish leader. One night Nicodemus came to Jesus and said, "Teacher, we know you are a teacher sent from God, because no one can do the miracles you do unless God is with him."

Jesus answered, "I tell you the truth, unless one is born again, he cannot be in God's kingdom."

Nicodemus said, "But if a person is already old, how can he be born again? He cannot enter his mother's body again. So how can a person be born a second time?"

But Jesus answered, "I tell you the truth, unless one is born from water and the Spirit, he cannot enter God's kingdom. Human life comes from human parents, but spiritual life comes from the Spirit. Don't be surprised when I tell you, 'You must all be born again.' The wind blows where it wants to and you hear the sound of it, but you don't know where the wind comes from or where it is going. It is the same with every person who is born from the Spirit."

Nicodemus asked, "How can this happen?"

Jesus said, "You are an important teacher in Israel, and you don't understand these things? I tell you the truth, we talk about what we know, and we tell about what we have seen, but you don't accept what we tell you. I have told you about things here on earth, and you do not believe me. So you will not believe me if I tell you about things of heaven. The only one who has ever gone up to heaven is the One who came down from heaven—the Son of Man.

"Just as Moses lifted up the snake in the desert, the Son of Man must also be lifted up. So that everyone who believes can have eternal life in him.

"God loved the world so much that he gave his one and only Son so that whoever believes in him may not be lost, but have eternal life. God did not send his Son into the world to judge the world guilty, but to save the world through him. People who believe in God's Son are not judged guilty. Those who do not believe have already been judged guilty, because they have not believed in God's one and only Son. They are judged by this fact: The Light has come into the world, but they did not want light. They wanted darkness, because they were doing evil things. All who do evil hate the light and will not come to the light, because it will show all the evil things they do. But those who follow the true way come to the light, and it shows that the things they do were done through God."

Jesus and John the Baptist

After this, Jesus and his followers went into the area of Judea, where he stayed with his followers and baptized people. John was also baptizing in Aenon, near Salim, because there was plenty of water there. People were going there to be baptized. (This was before John was put into prison.)

Some of John's followers had an argument with a Jew about religious washing. So they came to John and said, "Teacher, remember the man who was with you on the other side of the Jordan River, the one you spoke about so much? He is baptizing, and everyone is going to him."

John answered, "A man can get only what God gives him. You yourselves heard me say, 'I am not the Christ, but I am the one sent to prepare the way for him.' The bride belongs only to the bridegroom. But the friend who helps the bridegroom stands by and listens to him. He is thrilled that he gets to hear the bridegroom's voice. In the same way, I am really happy. He must become greater, and I must become less important."

We have done many wrong things
   against our God;
   our sins show we are wrong.

We know we have turned against
    God;
  we know the evil things we have
    done:
sinning and rejecting the LORD,
  turning away from our God,
planning to hurt others and to disobey
    God,
  planning and speaking lies.
So we have driven away justice,
  and we have kept away from what is
    right.
Truth is not spoken in the streets;
  what is honest is not allowed to
    enter the city.
Truth cannot be found anywhere,
  and people who refuse to do evil are
    attacked.

The LORD looked and could not find any
    justice,
  and he was displeased.
He could not find anyone to help the
    people,
  and he was surprised that there was
    no one to help.
So he used his own power to save the
    people;
  his own goodness gave him
    strength.
He covered himself with goodness like
    armor.
  He put the helmet of salvation on his
    head.
He put on the clothes of punishment
  and wrapped himself in the coat of
    his strong love.

Isaiah 59:12–17

*N*ow he told me,
"You are an important servant to me
  to bring back the tribes of Jacob,
  to bring back the people of Israel
    who are left alive.
But, more importantly, I will make you
    a light for all nations
  to show people all over the world the
    way to be saved."

The LORD who saves you
  is the Holy One of Israel.
He speaks to the one who is hated by
    the people,
  to the servant of rulers.

This is what he says: "Kings will see
    you and stand to honor you;
  great leaders will bow down before
    you,
because the LORD can be trusted.
  He is the Holy One of Israel, who
    has chosen you."

Isaiah 49:6–7

*G*od loves us, not only as a host of human
beings who are living on the earth at this time,
but as individuals whom He knows by name.
He has a personal interest in each one. He
has a perfect plan for every detail in the life
of each individual. He is not willing that any
should perish, but wants all mankind to be
saved and come to the knowledge of the truth
(1 Timothy 2:4).

The greatest and most profound expression
of God's love for us is in the death of Christ
on the cross. Men rejected the Lord Jesus
Christ as God's Son, falsely accused Him,
condemned Him to death, beat Him, crowned
Him with thorns, spit on Him, made sport of
Him, crucified Him with thieves, and ridi-
culed Him. While they were doing this, He
forgave them and paid the penalty of their sin
by dying for them.

This speaks most powerfully of the extent
of God's unchanging, everlasting love. There
is no greater expression of love than for a man
to lay down his life for his friends.

Lucille Sollenberger

*W*hat motivated God to use his own power,
to send his own son, to save us? Why do some
reject God's salvation? Reread Isaiah 59:12–
17 and as you do, ask God for his forgiveness
of your wrongs and praise him for offering
himself to save you.

MONDAY:
Jesus Gives Living Water
John 3:31—4:26

The One Who Comes from Heaven

The One who comes from above is greater than all. The one who is from the earth belongs to the earth and talks about things on the earth. But the One who comes from heaven is greater than all. He tells what he has seen and heard, but no one accepts what he says. Whoever accepts what he says has proven that God is true. The One whom God sent speaks the words of God, because God gives him the Spirit fully. The Father loves the Son and has given him power over everything. Those who believe in the Son have eternal life, but those who do not obey the Son will never have life. God's anger stays on them."

Jesus and a Samaritan Woman

The Pharisees heard that Jesus was making and baptizing more followers than John, although Jesus himself did not baptize people, but his followers did. Jesus knew that the Pharisees had heard about him, so he left Judea and went back to Galilee. But on the way he had to go through the country of Samaria.

In Samaria Jesus came to the town called Sychar, which is near the field Jacob gave to his son Joseph. Jacob's well was there. Jesus was tired from his long trip, so he sat down beside the well. It was about twelve o'clock noon. When a Samaritan woman came to the well to get some water, Jesus said to her, "Please give me a drink." (This happened while Jesus' followers were in town buying some food.)

The woman said, "I am surprised that you ask me for a drink, since you are a Jewish man and I am a Samaritan woman." (Jewish people are not friends with Samaritans.)

Jesus said, "If you only knew the free gift of God and who it is that is asking you for water, you would have asked him, and he would have given you living water."

The woman said, "Sir, where will you get this living water? The well is very deep, and you have nothing to get water with. Are you greater than Jacob, our father, who gave us this well and drank from it himself along with his sons and flocks?"

Jesus answered, "Everyone who drinks this water will be thirsty again, but whoever drinks the water I give will never be thirsty. The water I give will become a spring of water gushing up inside that person, giving eternal life."

The woman said to him, "Sir, give me this water so I will never be thirsty again and will not have to come back here to get more water."

Jesus told her, "Go get your husband and come back here."

The woman answered, "I have no husband."

Jesus said to her, "You are right to say you have no husband. Really you have had five husbands, and the man you live with now is not your husband. You told the truth."

The woman said, "Sir, I can see that you are a prophet. Our ancestors worshiped on this mountain, but you Jews say that Jerusalem is the place where people must worship."

Jesus said, "Believe me, woman. The time is coming when neither in Jerusalem nor on this mountain will you actually worship the Father. You Samaritans worship something you don't understand. We understand what we worship, because salvation comes from the Jews. The time is coming when the true worshipers will worship the Father in spirit and truth, and that time is here already. You see, the Father too is actively seeking such people to worship him. God is spirit, and those who worship him must worship in spirit and truth."

The woman said, "I know that the Messiah is coming." (Messiah is the One called Christ.) "When the Messiah comes, he will explain everything to us."

Then Jesus said, "I am he—I, the one talking to you."

At that time you will say:
"I praise you, LORD!

You were angry with me,
but you are not angry with me now!
    You have comforted me.
God is the one who saves me;
    I will trust him and not be afraid.
The LORD, the LORD gives me strength
        and makes me sing.
    He has saved me."
You will receive your salvation with joy
    as you would draw water from a well.

At that time you will say,
"Praise the LORD and worship him.
    Tell everyone what he has done
    and how great he is.
Sing praise to the LORD, because he has
        done great things.
    Let all the world know what he has
        done.
Shout and sing for joy, you people of
        Jerusalem,
    because the Holy One of Israel does
        great things before your eyes."

Isaiah 12:1–6

Skies, be shocked at the things that
        have happened
    and shake with great fear!" says the
        LORD.
"My people have done two evils:
They have turned away from me,
    the spring of living water.
And they have dug their own wells,
    which are broken wells that cannot
        hold water.
It did not help to go to Egypt
    and drink from the Shihor River.
It did not help to go to Assyria
    and drink from the Euphrates River.
Your evil will bring punishment to you,
    and the wrong you have done will
        teach you a lesson.
Think about it and understand
that it is a terrible evil to turn away from
        the LORD your God.
    It is wrong not to fear me,"
says the Lord GOD All-Powerful.

Jeremiah 2:12–13, 18–19

LORD, hope of Israel,
    those who leave you will be shamed.
People who quit following the LORD will
    be like a name written in the dust,

because they have left the LORD, the
    spring of living water.

Jeremiah 17:13

INSIGHTS

The flow of life surging and pulsing through me to refresh this weary old world must be from God Himself. It must be the continuous outpouring of His Presence by His Spirit which touches and transforms all around me. Any person naive enough, arrogant enough, stupid enough to believe that it is his or her own charm, charisma, or capabilities that change and enliven others, lives in utter self-delusion.

One of the terrible tragedies of human behavior is for people to turn to other human beings in an effort to find sustenance for their spirits. They are always deluded, ever disappointed. Our spirits can only find life in the Living Spirit of the Living Lord. Our eternal quest for life-giving water can only be quenched by the eternal life of God Himself coming to us through the hidden springs of His own person who indwells those who are open channels for His life.

W. Phillip Keller

PAUSE FOR REFLECTION

What do those who drink of Jesus' living water receive? How does one receive living water? What happens to everyone who rejects God's living water? What is the source of your sustenance?

TUESDAY:
When People Believe, God Does Great Things
John 4:27–54

*J*ust then his followers came back from town and were surprised to see him talking with a woman. But none of them asked, "What do you want?" or "Why are you talking with her?"

Then the woman left her water jar and went back to town. She said to the people, "Come and see a man who told me everything I ever did. Do you think he might be the Christ?" So the people left the town and went to see Jesus.

Meanwhile, his followers were begging him, "Teacher, eat something."

But Jesus answered, "I have food to eat that you know nothing about."

So the followers asked themselves, "Did somebody already bring him food?"

Jesus said, "My food is to do what the One who sent me wants me to do and to finish his work. You have a saying, 'Four more months till harvest.' But I tell you, open your eyes and look at the fields ready for harvest now. Already, the one who harvests is being paid and is gathering crops for eternal life. So the one who plants and the one who harvests celebrate at the same time. Here the saying is true, 'One person plants, and another harvests.' I sent you to harvest a crop that you did not work on. Others did the work, and you get to finish up their work."

Many of the Samaritans in that town believed in Jesus because of what the woman said: "He told me everything I ever did." When the Samaritans came to Jesus, they begged him to stay with them, so he stayed there two more days. And many more believed because of the things he said.

They said to the woman, "First we believed in Jesus because of your speech, but now we believe because we heard him ourselves. We know that this man really is the Savior of the world."

Jesus Heals an Officer's Son

*T*wo days later, Jesus left and went to Galilee. (Jesus had said before that a prophet is not respected in his own country.) When Jesus arrived in Galilee, the people there welcomed him. They had seen all the things he did at the Passover Feast in Jerusalem, because they had been there, too.

Jesus went again to visit Cana in Galilee where he had changed the water into wine. One of the king's important officers lived in the city of Capernaum, and his son was sick. When he heard that Jesus had come from Judea to Galilee, he went to Jesus and begged him to come to Capernaum and heal his son, because his son was almost dead. Jesus said to him, "You people must see signs and miracles before you will believe in me."

The officer said, "Sir, come before my child dies."

Jesus answered, "Go. Your son will live."

The man believed what Jesus told him and went home. On the way the man's servants came and met him and told him, "Your son is alive."

The man asked, "What time did my son begin to get well?"

They answered, "Yesterday at one o'clock the fever left him."

The father knew that one o'clock was the exact time that Jesus had said, "Your son will live." So the man and all the people who lived in his house believed in Jesus.

That was the second miracle Jesus did after coming from Judea to Galilee.

*O*ur God, punish those people. We have no power against this large army that is attacking us. We don't know what to do, so we look to you for help."

All the men of Judah stood before the LORD with their babies, wives, and children. Then the Spirit of the LORD entered Jahaziel. (Jahaziel was Zechariah's son. Zechariah was Benaiah's son. Benaiah was Jeiel's son, and Jeiel was Mattaniah's son.) Jahaziel, a Levite and a descendant of Asaph, stood up in the meeting. He said, "Listen to me, King

Jehoshaphat and all you people living in Judah and Jerusalem. The LORD says this to you: 'Don't be afraid or discouraged because of this large army. The battle is not your battle, it is God's. Tomorrow go down there and fight those people. They will come up through the Pass of Ziz. You will find them at the end of the ravine that leads to the Desert of Jeruel. You won't need to fight in this battle. Just stand strong in your places, and you will see the LORD save you. Judah and Jerusalem, don't be afraid or discouraged, because the LORD is with you. So go out against those people tomorrow.'"

Jehoshaphat's army went out into the Desert of Tekoa early in the morning. As they were starting out, Jehoshaphat stood and said, "Listen to me, people of Judah and Jerusalem. Have faith in the LORD your God, and you will stand strong. Have faith in his prophets, and you will succeed." Jehoshaphat listened to the people's advice. Then he chose men to be singers to the LORD, to praise him because he is holy and wonderful. As they marched in front of the army, they said,

"Thank the LORD,
    because his love continues forever."

As they began to sing and praise God, the LORD set ambushes for the people of Ammon, Moab, and Edom who had come to attack Judah. And they were defeated. The Ammonites and Moabites attacked the Edomites, destroying them completely. After they had killed the Edomites, they killed each other.

When the men from Judah came to a place where they could see the desert, they looked at the enemy's large army. But they only saw dead bodies lying on the ground; no one had escaped.

2 Chronicles 20:12–17, 20–24

INSIGHTS

*G*od gives us faith as we walk with him.

An Old Testament story illustrates this principle well. As Joshua 3 opens, the Israelites are camped on the bank of the Jordan River. . . . They are in sight of the Promised Land, Canaan, but they have an enormous problem: a river is right in their path,

and there's no convenient way around it. To make matters worse, it is flood season, and any usual fording places are impassable. The waters are deep and turbulent and menacing.

God could easily make the river subside right before their eyes. He could throw a wide bridge across it. But he doesn't. Instead, he gives Joshua some strange orders that he passes on . . .

. . . Joshua commands the priests to pick up the ark and go stand in the river. . . .

In spite of the problems, the priests had faith enough to obey, and this is what happened: "As soon as the priests who carried the ark reached the Jordan and their feet touched the water's edge, the water from upstream stopped flowing. . . . The priests who carried the ark of the covenant of the LORD stood firm on dry ground in the middle of the Jordan, while all Israel passed by until the whole nation had completed the crossing on dry ground" (Josh 3:15–17).

God didn't give the priests absolute proof or even overwhelming evidence that the waters would part. He did nothing until they put their feet in the water, taking the first step of commitment and obedience. Only then did he stop the flow of the river. In the same way, mountain-moving faith will be given to us as we step out and follow the Lord's direction.

    Bill Hybels

PAUSE   FOR   REFLECTION

*W*hoever heard of an army singing its way into battle? A flooding river that stopped instantly? An adulterous woman bringing others to Christ? For what do you believe God? Pray that he will strengthen your belief!

WEDNESDAY:

God Gives Eternal Life to Those Who Believe

John 5:1–29

Jesus Heals a Man at a Pool

Later Jesus went to Jerusalem for a special Jewish feast. In Jerusalem there is a pool with five covered porches, which is called Bethzatha in the Jewish language. This pool is near the Sheep Gate. Many sick people were lying on the porches beside the pool. Some were blind, some were crippled, and some were paralyzed. A man was lying there who had been sick for thirty-eight years. When Jesus saw the man and knew that he had been sick for such a long time, Jesus asked him, "Do you want to be well?"

The sick man answered, "Sir, there is no one to help me get into the pool when the water starts moving. While I am coming to the water, someone else always gets in before me."

Then Jesus said, "Stand up. Pick up your mat and walk." And immediately the man was well; he picked up his mat and began to walk.

The day this happened was a Sabbath day. So the Jews said to the man who had been healed, "Today is the Sabbath. It is against our law for you to carry your mat on the Sabbath day."

But he answered, "The man who made me well told me, 'Pick up your mat and walk.'"

Then they asked him, "Who is the man who told you to pick up your mat and walk?"

But the man who had been healed did not know who it was, because there were many people in that place, and Jesus had left.

Later, Jesus found the man at the Temple and said to him, "See, you are well now. Stop sinning so that something worse does not happen to you."

Then the man left and told the Jews that Jesus was the one who had made him well. Because Jesus was doing this on the Sabbath day, the Jews began to persecute him. But Jesus said to them, "My Father never stops working, and so I keep working, too."

This made the Jews try still harder to kill him. They said, "First Jesus was breaking the law about the Sabbath day. Now he says that God is his own Father, making himself equal with God!"

Jesus Has God's Authority

But Jesus said, "I tell you the truth, the Son can do nothing alone. The Son does only what he sees the Father doing, because the Son does whatever the Father does. The Father loves the Son and shows the Son all the things he himself does. But the Father will show the Son even greater things than this so that you can all be amazed. Just as the Father raises the dead and gives them life, so also the Son gives life to those he wants to. In fact, the Father judges no one, but he has given the Son power to do all the judging so that all people will honor the Son as much as they honor the Father. Anyone who does not honor the Son does not honor the Father who sent him.

"I tell you the truth, whoever hears what I say and believes in the One who sent me has eternal life. That person will not be judged guilty but has already left death and entered life. I tell you the truth, the time is coming and is already here when the dead will hear the voice of the Son of God, and those who hear will have life. Life comes from the Father himself, and he has allowed the Son to have life in himself as well. And the Father has given the Son the power to judge, because he is the Son of Man. Don't be surprised at this: A time is coming when all who are dead and in their graves will hear his voice. Then they will come out of their graves. Those who did good will rise and have life forever, but those who did evil will rise to be judged guilty."

Sin speaks to the wicked in their
    hearts.
They have no fear of God.
They think too much of themselves

234

so they don't see their sin and hate
it.
Their words are wicked lies;
they are no longer wise or good.
At night they make evil plans;
what they do leads to nothing good.
They don't refuse things that are evil.

LORD, your love reaches to the heavens,
your loyalty to the skies.
Your goodness is as high as the
mountains.
Your justice is as deep as the great
ocean.
LORD, you protect both people and
animals.
God, your love is so precious!
You protect people in the shadow of
your wings.
They eat the rich food in your house,
and you let them drink from your
river of pleasure.
You are the giver of life.
Your light lets us enjoy life.

Psalm 36:1–9

*E*vil will kill the wicked;
those who hate good people will be
judged guilty.
But the LORD saves his servants' lives;
no one who trusts him will be judged
guilty.

Psalm 34:21–22

*T*he LORD is my light and the one who
saves me.
I fear no one.
The LORD protects my life;
I am afraid of no one.

Psalm 27:1

*P*rotect me, God,
because I trust in you.
I said to the LORD, "You are my Lord.
Every good thing I have comes from
you."

So I rejoice and am glad.
Even my body has hope,
because you will not leave me in the
grave.
You will not let your holy one rot.
You will teach me how to live a holy
life.

Being with you will fill me with joy;
at your right hand I will find pleasure forever.

Psalm 16:1–2, 9–11

INSIGHTS

*T*he New Testament teaching is not that
everyone has eternal life, but that those who
come to God through Jesus Christ are given
eternal life as a gift. Many passages contain
this teaching; it is not found in only one or
two texts. The new birth, being "born of the
Spirit," is to have the life of God given to us.
Not all are born of the Spirit. The Scripture
rejects the idea that everybody has a spark of
deity within. In fact, the Bible says that man,
in his natural condition, is "dead to God" and
that rebirth, an action of the Holy Spirit, is
required to plant the life of God.

That "the gift of God is eternal life" doesn't
mean that our lives just go on and on and
on. It means that we share in the divine nature of God, which is itself eternal. It is His
life, then, that is lived in our bodies. That's
what's meant by eternal life. We don't begin
eternal life when we die; we begin it while
we still live. Eternity begins with belief in
Christ. . . .

. . . Eternal life comes to those who believe in the Son of Man, who has been lifted
up on the cross—that act of obedience to the
Father, His death, that brought salvation to
all who believe in Him. It belongs to those
who will share in the resurrection victory of
Jesus Christ over death.

Terry Fullam

APPLICATION

*I*n the Old Testament, God is clearly recognized as the source and giver of life. What
claims does Jesus make regarding his ability
to give eternal life? Have you accepted Jesus'
daring offer of eternal life?

THURSDAY:

People Choose Whether or Not to Believe in Christ

John 5:30—6:15

Jesus Is God's Son

I can do nothing alone. I judge only the way I am told, so my judgment is fair. I don't try to please myself, but I try to please the One who sent me.

"If only I tell people about myself, what I say is not true. But there is another who tells about me, and I know that the things he says about me are true.

"You have sent people to John, and he has told you the truth. It is not that I accept such human telling; I tell you this so you can be saved. John was like a burning and shining lamp, and you were happy to enjoy his light for a while.

"But I have a proof about myself that is greater than that of John. The things I do, which are the things my Father gave me to do, prove that the Father sent me. And the Father himself who sent me has given proof about me. You have never heard his voice or seen what he looks like. His teaching does not live in you, because you don't believe in the One the Father sent. You carefully study the Scriptures because you think they give you eternal life. They do in fact tell about me, but you refuse to come to me to have that life.

"I don't need praise from people. But I know you—I know that you don't have God's love in you. I have come from my Father and speak for him, but you don't accept me. But when another person comes, speaking only for himself, you will accept him. You try to get praise from each other, but you do not try to get the praise that comes from the only God. So how can you believe? Don't think that I will stand before the Father and say you are wrong. The one who says you are wrong is Moses, the one you hoped would save you. If you really believed Moses, you would believe me, because Moses wrote about me. But if you

don't believe what Moses wrote, how can you believe what I say?"

More than Five Thousand Fed

*A*fter this, Jesus went across Lake Galilee (or, Lake Tiberias). Many people followed him because they saw the miracles he did to heal the sick. Jesus went up on a hill and sat down there with his followers. It was almost the time for the Jewish Passover Feast.

When Jesus looked up and saw a large crowd coming toward him, he said to Philip, "Where can we buy enough bread for all these people to eat?" (Jesus asked Philip this question to test him, because Jesus already knew what he planned to do.)

Philip answered, "We would all have to work a month to buy enough bread for each person to have only a little piece."

Another one of his followers, Andrew, Simon Peter's brother, said, "Here is a boy with five loaves of barley bread and two little fish, but that is not enough for so many people."

Jesus said, "Tell the people to sit down." This was a very grassy place, and about five thousand men sat down there. Then Jesus took the loaves of bread, thanked God for them, and gave them to the people who were sitting there. He did the same with the fish, giving as much as the people wanted.

When they had all had enough to eat, Jesus said to his followers, "Gather the leftover pieces of fish and bread so that nothing is wasted." So they gathered up the pieces and filled twelve baskets with the pieces left from the five barley loaves.

When the people saw this miracle that Jesus did, they said, "He must truly be the Prophet who is coming into the world."

Jesus knew that the people planned to come and take him by force and make him their king, so he left and went into the hills alone.

*T*he LORD your God will give you a prophet like me, who is one of your own people. Listen to him. This is what you asked the LORD your God to do when you were gathered at Mount Sinai. You said,

"Don't make us listen to the voice of the LORD our God again, and don't make us look at this terrible fire anymore, or we will die."

So the LORD said to me, "What they have said is good. So I will give them a prophet like you, who is one of their own people. I will tell him what to say, and he will tell them everything I command. This prophet will speak for me; anyone who does not listen when he speaks will answer to me. But if a prophet says something I did not tell him to say as though he were speaking for me, or if a prophet speaks in the name of other gods, that prophet must be killed."

You might be thinking, "How can we know if a message is not from the LORD?" If what a prophet says in the name of the LORD does not happen, it is not the LORD's message. That prophet was speaking his own ideas. Don't be afraid of him.

Deuteronomy 18:15–22

*T*he LORD God said to the snake,
"Because you did this,
    a curse will be put on you.
You will be cursed as no other
        animal, tame or wild, will ever be.
You will crawl on your stomach,
    and you will eat dust all the days of
        your life.
I will make you and the woman
    enemies to each other.
Your descendants and her descendants
    will be enemies.
One of her descendants will crush your
        head,
    and you will bite his heel."

Genesis 3:14–15

*J*udah, your brothers will praise you.
You will grab your enemies by the
        neck,
    and your brothers will bow down to
        you.
Judah is like a young lion.
You have returned from killing, my
        son.
Like a lion, he stretches out and lies
        down to rest,
    and no one is brave enough to wake
        him.
Kings will come from Judah's family;

someone from Judah will always be
        on the throne.
Judah will rule until Shiloh comes,
    and the nations will obey him."

Genesis 49:8–10

INSIGHTS

*W*hat *God did makes sense. It makes sense that Jesus would be our sacrifice because a sacrifice was needed to justify man's presence before God. It makes sense that God would use the Old Law to tutor Israel on their need for grace. It makes sense that Jesus would be our High Priest. What God did makes sense. It can be taught, charted, and put in books on systematic theology.*

However, why God did it is absolutely absurd. When one leaves the method and examines the motive, the carefully stacked blocks of logic begin to tumble. That type of love isn't logical; it can't be neatly outlined in a sermon or explained in a term paper. . . .

Even after generations of people had spit in his face, he still loved them. After a nation of chosen ones had stripped him naked and ripped his incarnated flesh, he still died for them. And even today, after billions have chosen to prostitute themselves before pimps of power, fame, and wealth, he still waits for them.

It is inexplicable. It doesn't have a drop of logic nor a thread of rationality. . . .

Bloodstained royalty. A God with tears. A creator with a heart. God became earth's mockery to save his children.

How absurd to think that such nobility would go to such poverty to share such a treasure with such thankless souls.

But he did.

In fact, the only thing more absurd than the gift is our stubborn unwillingness to receive it.

Max Lucado

APPLICATION

*W*hat *evidence from his life and from the Scriptures proves that Jesus was who he said he was? Why didn't most Jews believe Jesus? Do you believe and trust him?*

FRIDAY:

Believe in the God of Miracles

John 6:16–40

Jesus Walks on the Water

*T*hat evening Jesus' followers went down to Lake Galilee. It was dark now, and Jesus had not yet come to them. The followers got into a boat and started across the lake to Capernaum. By now a strong wind was blowing, and the waves on the lake were getting bigger. When they had rowed the boat about three or four miles, they saw Jesus walking on the water, coming toward the boat. The followers were afraid, but Jesus said to them, "It is I. Do not be afraid." Then they were glad to take him into the boat. At once the boat came to land at the place where they wanted to go.

The People Seek Jesus

*T*he next day the people who had stayed on the other side of the lake knew that Jesus had not gone in the boat with his followers but that they had left without him. And they knew that only one boat had been there. But then some boats came from Tiberias and landed near the place where the people had eaten the bread after the Lord had given thanks. When the people saw that Jesus and his followers were not there now, they got into boats and went to Capernaum to find Jesus.

Jesus, the Bread of Life

*W*hen the people found Jesus on the other side of the lake, they asked him, "Teacher, when did you come here?"

Jesus answered, "I tell you the truth, you aren't looking for me because you saw me do miracles. You are looking for me because you ate the bread and were satisfied. Don't work for the food that spoils. Work for the food that stays good always and gives eternal life. The Son of Man will give you this food, because on him God the Father has put his power."

The people asked Jesus, "What are the things God wants us to do?"

Jesus answered, "The work God wants you to do is this: Believe the One he sent."

So the people asked, "What miracle will you do? If we see a miracle, we will believe you. What will you do? Our fathers ate the manna in the desert. This is written in the Scriptures: 'He gave them bread from heaven to eat.'"

Jesus said, "I tell you the truth, it was not Moses who gave you bread from heaven; it is my Father who is giving you the true bread from heaven. God's bread is the One who comes down from heaven and gives life to the world."

The people said, "Sir, give us this bread always."

Then Jesus said, "I am the bread that gives life. Whoever comes to me will never be hungry, and whoever believes in me will never be thirsty. But as I told you before, you have seen me and still don't believe. The Father gives me my people. Every one of them will come to me, and I will always accept them. I came down from heaven to do what God wants me to do, not what I want to do. Here is what the One who sent me wants me to do: I must not lose even one whom God gave me, but I must raise them all on the last day. Those who see the Son and believe in him have eternal life, and I will raise them on the last day. This is what my Father wants."

*E*verything on earth, shout with joy to
   God!
Sing about his glory!
   Make his praise glorious!
Say to God, "Your works are amazing!
   Because your power is great,
   your enemies fall before you.
All the earth worships you
   and sings praises to you.
   They sing praises to your name."

Selah

Come and see what God has done,
   the amazing things he has done for
     people.
He turned the sea into dry land.

The people crossed the river on foot.
So let us rejoice because of what he
did.
He rules forever with his power.
He keeps his eye on the nations,
so people should not turn against
him. *Selah*

Psalm 66:1–7

*W*hen the Israelites went out of
Egypt,
the people of Jacob left that foreign
country.
Then Judah became God's holy place;
Israel became the land he ruled.

The Red Sea looked and ran away;
the Jordan River turned back.
The mountains danced like sheep
and the hills like little lambs.
Sea, why did you run away?
Jordan, why did you turn back?
Mountains, why did you dance like
sheep?
Hills, why did you dance like little
lambs?

Earth, shake with fear before the Lord,
before the God of Jacob.
He turned a rock into a pool of water,
a hard rock into a spring of water.

Psalm 114:1–8

*G*ive thanks to the LORD and pray to
him.
Tell the nations what he has done.
Sing to him; sing praises to him.
Tell about all his miracles.
Be glad that you are his;
let those who seek the LORD be
happy.
Depend on the LORD and his strength;
always go to him for help.
Remember the miracles he has done,
his wonders, and his decisions.

1 Chronicles 16:8–12

INSIGHTS

*M*om, I need new shoes," Nicky announced
as he burst through the door after school.
"Miss Bell says it's dangerous to run in gym
with my toe sticking out."

I looked down at my son's blue tennies.
Hadn't I just bought them last month? But
the protruding toe, a slit along the side, and
tattered laces told me he'd had them longer.
"You're right, Nicky. It's time for some new
tennies, but you'll have to wait until our next
paycheck. . . ."

"But, Mother," Nicky protested, "I can't
wear these shoes for gym anymore. Miss Bell
said!"

I launched into an elaborate discourse on
budgeting principles. "So you see, Nicky," I
concluded, "that's how Mommy and Daddy
spend money. Tennis shoes are not in the
budget this time; next time they will be."

"Then I'll pray about my shoes," Nicky
announced. "I'll tell God I need the money by
tomorrow." . . .

. . . When he left for school the next
morning, new tennis shoes were still uppermost on his mind. "Can we buy my shoes tonight? You'll get the money today, because I
prayed about it."

"We'll see, Nicky," I replied as I kissed him
good-bye. There wasn't time to explain just
then.

But the need to explain didn't come;
Nicky's answer came instead. "This is long
overdue . . . sorry for the oversight," said the
note I received in the mail that afternoon. The
enclosed check, payment for an article I'd
written long ago and forgotten, was more
than enough to pay for Nicky's new shoes.

After school, Nicky's blue eyes danced. "See,
Mom I told you it would come. Now can we
buy my shoes?"

Today Nicky wears new blue-and-gold
tennis shoes—poignant reminders of a child's
simple trust and of my need to continually
relearn what faith is all about.

Ruth Senter

ACTION POINT

*W*hat is your psalm of praise to the God of
miracles? What wonders has he done for you?
Praise him with joy! Believe him and seek
after the food that gives eternal life.

WEEKEND:

When Difficulties Come, Some Want to Reject God's Ways

John 6:41–71

*T*he Jews began to complain about Jesus because he said, "I am the bread that comes down from heaven." They said, "This is Jesus, the son of Joseph. We know his father and mother. How can he say, 'I came down from heaven'?"

But Jesus answered, "Stop complaining to each other. The Father is the One who sent me. No one can come to me unless the Father draws him to me, and I will raise that person up on the last day. It is written in the prophets, 'They will all be taught by God.' Everyone who listens to the Father and learns from him comes to me. No one has seen the Father except the One who is from God; only he has seen the Father. I tell you the truth, whoever believes has eternal life. I am the bread that gives life. Your ancestors ate the manna in the desert, but still they died. Here is the bread that comes down from heaven. Anyone who eats this bread will never die. I am the living bread that came down from heaven. Anyone who eats this bread will live forever. This bread is my flesh, which I will give up so that the world may have life."

Then the Jews began to argue among themselves, saying, "How can this man give us his flesh to eat?"

Jesus said, "I tell you the truth, you must eat the flesh of the Son of Man and drink his blood. Otherwise, you won't have real life in you. Those who eat my flesh and drink my blood have eternal life, and I will raise them up on the last day. My flesh is true food, and my blood is true drink. Those who eat my flesh and drink my blood live in me, and I live in them. The living Father sent me, and I live because of the Father. So whoever eats me will live because of me. I am not like the bread your ancestors ate. They ate that bread and still died. I am the bread that came down from heaven, and whoever eats this bread will live forever." Jesus said all these things while he was teaching in the synagogue in Capernaum.

The Words of Eternal Life

*W*hen the followers of Jesus heard this, many of them said, "This teaching is hard. Who can accept it?"

Knowing that his followers were complaining about this, Jesus said, "Does this teaching bother you? Then will it also bother you to see the Son of Man going back to the place where he came from? It is the Spirit that gives life. The flesh doesn't give life. The words I told you are spirit, and they give life. But some of you don't believe." (Jesus knew from the beginning who did not believe and who would turn against him.) Jesus said, "That is the reason I said, 'If the Father does not bring a person to me, that one cannot come.'"

After Jesus said this, many of his followers left him and stopped following him.

Jesus asked the twelve followers, "Do you want to leave, too?"

Simon Peter answered him, "Lord, where would we go? You have the words that give eternal life. We believe and know that you are the Holy One from God."

Then Jesus answered, "I chose all twelve of you, but one of you is a devil."

Jesus was talking about Judas, the son of Simon Iscariot. Judas was one of the twelve, but later he was going to turn against Jesus.

*W*hen the king sent the people out of Egypt, God did not lead them on the road through the Philistine country, though that was the shortest way. God said, "If they have to fight, they might change their minds and go back to Egypt." So God led them through the desert toward the Red Sea.

Exodus 13:17–18a

*M*oses sent them to explore Canaan and said, "Go through southern Canaan and then into the mountains. See what the land looks like. Are the people who live there strong or weak? Are there a few or many? What kind of land do they live in? Is it good or bad? What about the towns they live in—are they open like camps, or do they have walls? What about the soil? Is it fertile or poor? Are there trees there? Try to bring back some of the fruit from that land." (It was the season for the first grapes.)

So they went up and explored the land, from the Desert of Zin all the way to Rehob by Lebo Hamath.

They came back to Moses and Aaron and all the Israelites at Kadesh, in the Desert of Paran. The men reported to them and showed everybody the fruit from the land. They told Moses, "We went to the land where you sent us, and it is a fertile land! Here is some of its fruit. But the people who live there are strong. Their cities are walled and very large. We even saw some Anakites there. The Amalekites live in the southern area; the Hittites, Jebusites, and Amorites live in the mountains; and the Canaanites live near the sea and along the Jordan River."

Then Caleb told the people near Moses to be quiet, and he said, "We should certainly go up and take the land for ourselves. We can certainly do it."

But the men who had gone with him said, "We can't attack those people; they are stronger than we are." And those men gave the Israelites a bad report about the land they explored, saying, "The land that we explored is too large to conquer. All the people we saw are very tall. We saw the Nephilim people there. (The Anakites come from the Nephilim people.) We felt like grasshoppers, and we looked like grasshoppers to them."

Numbers 13:17–21, 26–33

*T*hat night all the people in the camp began crying loudly. All the Israelites complained against Moses and Aaron, and all the people said to them, "We wish we had died in Egypt or in this desert. Why is the LORD bringing us to this land to be killed with swords? Our wives and children will be taken away. We would be better off going back to Egypt." They said to each other, "Let's choose a leader and go back to Egypt."

Numbers 14:1–4

INSIGHTS

*A*s God's children, through having accepted Christ's work for us, accusations are definitely always off limits. As we stand before the Creator of the universe, the all-wise, perfectly holy, mighty God, who made us in His image, who upholds the universe, who understands all things, who has shown His compassion in providing a way for us to come to Him through the Messiah, the Lamb . . . how dare we shake our fist in His face? How dare we question God and say, "Why did you do this to me?". . .

. . . We can be angry at a person when we are caught in the awful results of cause-and-effect history following the Fall, or following attacks of Satan, or following human choices of one kind or another—but that person is never God. We may not understand our tragic situation. We may not feel we can face life after a terrible shock. We may not feel that we know how to cope in the midst of a war, or avalanche, or earthquake, or famine. But it is always off limits to blame God. We are not to run away from God, shaking our fist at Him and screaming. We are to run to Him when we are shaking with grief or trembling with fear.

He is our refuge and strength; a very present help in trouble. Our help is to come from Him as we run into the shelter of His arms, away from the noise of the battle, or the storm. He has promised us comfort, and we need to climb on His lap as a weeping, hurt child, not to kick at Him.

Edith Schaeffer

PAUSE FOR REFLECTION

*W*hat difficulties or lack of understanding in life have tempted you to turn away from God? Did you reject or run toward God? What gives you confidence that Jesus is the "Holy One from God," the one on whom you can believe and run to for shelter?

MONDAY:
The World Hates Those Who Expose Evil
John 7:1–31

Jesus' Brothers Don't Believe

*A*fter this, Jesus traveled around Galilee. He did not want to travel in Judea, because the Jews there wanted to kill him. It was time for the Jewish Feast of Shelters. So Jesus' brothers said to him, "You should leave here and go to Judea so your followers there can see the miracles you do. Anyone who wants to be well known does not hide what he does. If you are doing these things, show yourself to the world." (Even Jesus' brothers did not believe in him.)

Jesus said to his brothers, "The right time for me has not yet come, but any time is right for you. The world cannot hate you, but it hates me, because I tell it the evil things it does. So you go to the feast. I will not go yet to this feast, because the right time for me has not yet come." After saying this, Jesus stayed in Galilee.

But after Jesus' brothers had gone to the feast, Jesus went also. But he did not let people see him. At the feast the Jews were looking for him and saying, "Where is that man?"

Within the large crowd there, many people were whispering to each other about Jesus. Some said, "He is a good man."

Others said, "No, he fools the people." But no one was brave enough to talk about Jesus openly, because they were afraid of the Jews.

Jesus Teaches at the Feast

*W*hen the feast was about half over, Jesus went to the Temple and began to teach. The Jews were amazed and said, "This man has never studied in school. How did he learn so much?"

Jesus answered, "The things I teach are not my own, but they come from him who sent me. If people choose to do what God wants, they will know that my teaching comes from God and not from me. Those who teach their own ideas are trying to get honor for themselves. But those who try to bring honor to the one who sent him speak the truth, and there is nothing false in them. Moses gave you the law, but none of you obeys that law. Why are you trying to kill me?"

The people answered, "A demon has come into you. We are not trying to kill you."

Jesus said to them, "I did one miracle, and you are all amazed. Moses gave you the law about circumcision. (But really Moses did not give you circumcision; it came from our ancestors.) And yet you circumcise a baby on a Sabbath day. If a baby can be circumcised on a Sabbath day to obey the law of Moses, why are you angry at me for healing a person's whole body on the Sabbath day? Stop judging by the way things look, but judge by what is really right."

Is Jesus the Christ?

*T*hen some of the people who lived in Jerusalem said, "This is the man they are trying to kill. But he is teaching where everyone can see and hear him, and no one is trying to stop him. Maybe the leaders have decided he really is the Christ. But we know where this man is from. And when the real Christ comes, no one will know where he comes from."

Jesus, teaching in the Temple, cried out, "Yes, you know me, and you know where I am from. But I have not come by my own authority. I was sent by the One who is true, whom you don't know. But I know him, because I am from him, and he sent me."

When Jesus said this, the people tried to take him. But no one was able to touch him, because it was not yet the right time. But many of the people believed in Jesus. They said, "When the Christ comes, will he do more miracles than this man has done?"

---

*T*hese are the people I am pleased with:
> those who are not proud or stubborn
> and who fear my word.

242

But those people who kill bulls as a
    sacrifice to me
  are like those who kill people.
Those who kill sheep as a sacrifice
  are like those who break the necks
    of dogs.
Those who give me grain offerings
  are like those who offer me the
    blood of pigs.
Those who burn incense
  are like those who worship idols.
These people choose their own ways,
    not mine,
  and they love the terrible things they
    do.
So I will choose their punishments,
  and I will punish them with what
    they fear most.
This is because I called to them, but
    they did not listen.
  I spoke to them, but they did not
    hear me.
They did things I said were evil;
  they chose to do things I did not
    like."

You people who obey the words of the
    LORD,
  listen to what he says:
"Your brothers hated you
  and turned against you because you
    followed me.
Your brothers said, 'Let the LORD be
    honored
  so we may see you rejoice,'
  but they will be punished."

Isaiah 66:2b–5

*B*ut Jehoshaphat asked, "Isn't there a prophet of the LORD here? Let's ask him what we should do."

Then King Ahab said to Jehoshaphat, "There is one other prophet. We could ask the LORD through him, but I hate him. He never prophesies anything good about me, but something bad. He is Micaiah son of Imlah."

1 Kings 22:7–8a

A few years ago one of the leading golfers on the professional tour was invited to play in a foursome with Gerald Ford, then president of the United States, Jack Nicklaus, and Billy Graham. . . .

After the round of golf was finished, one of the other pros came up to the golfer and asked, "Hey, what was it like playing with the President and with Billy Graham?"

The pro unleashed a torrent of cursing, and in a disgusted manner said, "I don't need Billy Graham stuffing religion down my throat." With that he turned on his heel and stormed off, heading for the practice tee. . . .

Astonishing. Billy Graham had said not a word about God, Jesus, or religion, yet the pro had stormed away after the game accusing Billy of trying to ram religion down his throat. How can we explain this? It's really not difficult. Billy Graham didn't have to say a word; he didn't have to give a single sideward glance to make the pro feel uncomfortable. Billy Graham is so identified with religion, so associated with the things of God, that his very presence is enough to smother the wicked man who flees when no man pursues. Luther was right, the pagan does tremble at the rustling of a leaf. He feels the hound of heaven breathing down his neck. He feels crowded by holiness even if it is only made present by an imperfect, partially sanctified human vessel. . . .

. . . Holiness provokes hatred. The greater the holiness the greater the human hostility toward it. It seems insane. No man was ever more loving than Jesus Christ. Yet even His love provoked men to anger. His love was a perfect love, a transcendent and holy love, but His very love brought trauma to people. This kind of love is so majestic we can't stand it.

R. C. Sproul

F or what reasons did the leaders of the Jews hate Jesus? Was their hatred for righteousness anything new (see Old Testament readings)? Is your life holy enough to incur the wrath of the unrighteous?

TUESDAY:
Everyone Has Sinned
John 7:32—8:11

The Leaders Try to Arrest Jesus

The Pharisees heard the crowd whispering these things about Jesus. So the leading priests and the Pharisees sent some Temple guards to arrest him. Jesus said, "I will be with you a little while longer. Then I will go back to the One who sent me. You will look for me, but you will not find me. And you cannot come where I am."

The Jews said to each other, "Where will this man go so we cannot find him? Will he go to the Greek cities where our people live and teach the Greek people there? What did he mean when he said, 'You will look for me, but you will not find me,' and 'You cannot come where I am'?"

Jesus Talks About the Spirit

On the last and most important day of the feast Jesus stood up and said in a loud voice, "Let anyone who is thirsty come to me and drink. If anyone believes in me, rivers of living water will flow out from that person's heart, as the Scripture says." Jesus was talking about the Holy Spirit. The Spirit had not yet been given, because Jesus had not yet been raised to glory. But later, those who believed in Jesus would receive the Spirit.

The People Argue About Jesus

When the people heard Jesus' words, some of them said, "This man really is the Prophet."

Others said, "He is the Christ."

Still others said, "The Christ will not come from Galilee. The Scripture says that the Christ will come from David's family and from Bethlehem, the town where David lived." So the people did not agree with each other about Jesus. Some of them wanted to arrest him, but no one was able to touch him.

Some Leaders Won't Believe

The Temple guards went back to the leading priests and the Pharisees, who asked, "Why didn't you bring Jesus?"

The guards answered, "The words he says are greater than the words of any other person who has ever spoken!"

The Pharisees answered, "So Jesus has fooled you also! Have any of the leaders or the Pharisees believed in him? No! But these people, who know nothing about the law, are under God's curse."

Nicodemus, who had gone to see Jesus before, was in that group. He said, "Our law does not judge a man without hearing him and knowing what he has done."

They answered, "Are you from Galilee, too? Study the Scriptures, and you will learn that no prophet comes from Galilee."

And everyone left and went home.

The Woman Caught in Adultery

Jesus went to the Mount of Olives. But early in the morning he went back to the Temple, and all the people came to him, and he sat and taught them. The teachers of the law and the Pharisees brought a woman who had been caught in adultery. They forced her to stand before the people. They said to Jesus, "Teacher, this woman was caught having sexual relations with a man who is not her husband. The law of Moses commands that we stone to death every woman who does this. What do you say we should do?" They were asking this to trick Jesus so that they could have some charge against him.

But Jesus bent over and started writing on the ground with his finger. When they continued to ask Jesus their question, he raised up and said, "Anyone here who has never sinned can throw the first stone at her." Then Jesus bent over again and wrote on the ground.

Those who heard Jesus began to leave one by one, first the older men and then the others. Jesus was left there alone with the woman standing before him. Jesus raised up again and asked her, "Woman, where are they? Has no one judged you guilty?"

She answered, "No one, sir."

Then Jesus said, "I also don't judge you guilty. You may go now, but don't sin anymore."

*N*o one can say, "I am innocent;
I have never done anything wrong."
Proverbs 20:9

*F*ools say to themselves,
"There is no God."
Fools are evil and do terrible things;
there is no one who does anything good.

The LORD looked down from heaven on all people
to see if anyone understood,
if anyone was looking to God for help.
But all have turned away.
Together, everyone has become evil.
There is no one who does anything good,
not even one.
Psalm 14:1–3

*S*urely there is not a good person on earth
who always does good and never sins.
Ecclesiastes 7:20

*B*ut you were angry because we sinned.
For a long time we disobeyed,
so how can we be saved?
All of us are dirty with sin.
All the right things we have done are like filthy pieces of cloth.
All of us are like dead leaves,
and our sins, like the wind, have carried us away.
No one worships you
or even asks you to help us.
That is because you have turned away from us
and have let our sins destroy us.
Isaiah 64:5b–7

*H*ow can anyone be pure?
How can someone born to a woman be good?
God places no trust in his holy ones,
and even the heavens are not pure in his eyes.
How much less pure is one who is terrible and rotten
and drinks up evil as if it were water!
Job 15:14–16

We were born wrong with God. The same sin that Adam introduced has polluted the entire human race. No one is immune to the sin disease. And no human accomplishment can erase the internal stain that separates us from God. Because Adam sinned, all have sinned. This leads to one conclusion: We all need help. We need forgiveness. We need a Savior.

So . . . how do we get out of this mess? Read the next two verses slowly and carefully.

So then as through one transgression there resulted condemnation to all men, even so through one act of righteousness there resulted justification of life to all men. For as through the one man's disobedience the many were made sinners, even so through the obedience of the One the many will be made righteous. (Rom. 5:18–19)

Wonderful! Marvelous reassurance!
"You're telling me, Chuck, that by simply believing in Jesus Christ I can have eternal life with God, my sins forgiven, a destiny secure in heaven, all of this and much more without my working for that?" Yes, that is precisely what Scripture teaches. I remind you, it is called grace. It's what the Protestant Reformation was all about. Salvation is offered by divine grace, not by human works.
Charles Swindoll

*L*ist the ways these Scripture readings show *that every person has sinned. What did Jesus say to the woman caught in adultery? Is it different than what he says to you? How have you responded?*

WEDNESDAY:
Jesus' Relationship with His Father
John 8:12–41

NEW TESTAMENT READING

Jesus Is the Light of the World

*L*ater, Jesus talked to the people again, saying, "I am the light of the world. The person who follows me will never live in darkness but will have the light that gives life."

The Pharisees said to Jesus, "When you talk about yourself, you are the only one to say these things are true. We cannot accept what you say."

Jesus answered, "Yes, I am saying these things about myself, but they are true. I know where I came from and where I am going. But you don't know where I came from or where I am going. You judge by human standards. I am not judging anyone. But when I do judge, my judging is true, because I am not alone. The Father who sent me is with me. Your own law says that when two witnesses say the same thing, you must accept what they say. I am one of the witnesses who speaks about myself, and the Father who sent me is the other witness."

They asked, "Where is your father?"

Jesus answered, "You don't know me or my Father. If you knew me, you would know my Father, too." Jesus said these things while he was teaching in the Temple, near where the money is kept. But no one arrested him, because the right time for him had not yet come.

The People Misunderstand Jesus

*A*gain, Jesus said to the people, "I will leave you, and you will look for me, but you will die in your sins. You cannot come where I am going."

So the Jews asked, "Will Jesus kill himself? Is that why he said, 'You cannot come where I am going'?"

Jesus said, "You people are from here below, but I am from above. You belong to this world, but I don't belong to this world.

So I told you that you would die in your sins. Yes, you will die in your sins if you don't believe that I am he."

They asked, "Then who are you?"

Jesus answered, "I am what I have told you from the beginning. I have many things to say and decide about you. But I tell people only the things I have heard from the One who sent me, and he speaks the truth."

The people did not understand that he was talking to them about the Father. So Jesus said to them, "When you lift up the Son of Man, you will know that I am he. You will know that these things I do are not by my own authority but that I say only what the Father has taught me. The One who sent me is with me. I always do what is pleasing to him, so he has not left me alone." While Jesus was saying these things, many people believed in him.

Freedom from Sin

*S*o Jesus said to the Jews who believed in him, "If you continue to obey my teaching, you are truly my followers. Then you will know the truth, and the truth will make you free."

They answered, "We are Abraham's children, and we have never been anyone's slaves. So why do you say we will be free?"

Jesus answered, "I tell you the truth, everyone who lives in sin is a slave to sin. A slave does not stay with a family forever, but a son belongs to the family forever. So if the Son makes you free, you will be truly free. I know you are Abraham's children, but you want to kill me because you don't accept my teaching. I am telling you what my Father has shown me, but you do what your father has told you."

They answered, "Our father is Abraham."

Jesus said, "If you were really Abraham's children, you would do the things Abraham did. I am a man who has told you the truth which I heard from God, but you are trying to kill me. Abraham did nothing like that. So you are doing the things your own father did."

But they said, "We are not like children who never knew who their father was. God is our Father; he is the only Father we have."

*T*he kings of the earth prepare to fight,
and their leaders make plans
together
against the LORD
and his appointed one.
They say, "Let's break the chains that
hold us back
and throw off the ropes that tie us
down."

But the one who sits in heaven laughs;
the Lord makes fun of them.
Then the LORD warns them
and frightens them with his anger.
He says, "I have appointed my own
king
to rule in Jerusalem on my holy
mountain, Zion."

Now I will tell you what the LORD has
declared:
He said to me, "You are my son.
Today I have become your father.
If you ask me, I will give you the
nations;
all the people on earth will be yours.
You will rule over them with an iron
rod.
You will break them into pieces like
pottery."

So, kings, be wise;
rulers, learn this lesson.
Obey the LORD with great fear.
Be happy, but tremble.
Show that you are loyal to his son,
or you will be destroyed by his
anger,
because he can quickly become angry.
But happy are those who trust him
for protection.

Psalm 2:2–12

*T*he LORD said to my Lord,
"Sit by me at my right side
until I put your enemies under your
control."
The LORD will enlarge your kingdom
beyond Jerusalem,
and you will rule over your enemies.
Your people will join you on your day of
battle.

You have been dressed in holiness
from birth;
you have the freshness of a child.

Psalm 110:1–3

I N S I G H T S

*T*hink first of the origin of that life of Christ
in the Father. They were ONE—one in life and
one in love. In this His abiding in the Father
had its root. Though dwelling here on earth,
He knew that He was one with the Father;
that the Father's life was in Him, and His
love on Him. . . .

. . . The Son is not afraid of losing aught
by giving up all to the Father, for He knows
that the Father loves Him, and can have no
interest apart from that of the beloved Son.
He knows that as complete as is the dependence on His part is the communication on
the part of the Father of all He possesses.
Hence when He had said, "The Son can do
nothing of Himself, except he see the Father
do it," He adds at once, "Whatsoever things
the Father doeth, them also doeth the Son
likewise: for the Father loveth the Son, and
showeth Him all things that Himself
doeth. . . ."

Think of the glory of this life of Christ in
the Father's love. Because He gave Himself
wholly to the Father's will and glory, the Father crowned him with glory and honour. He
acknowledged Him as His only representa-
tive; He made him partaker of His power and
authority; He exalted him to share His throne
as God. . . .

. . . Christ was the revelation of the Father on earth. He could not be this if there
were not the most perfect unity, the most
complete communication of all the Father
had to the Son. He could be it because the
Father loved Him, and He abode in that love.

Andrew Murray

P A U S E   F O R   R E F L E C T I O N

*H*ow many different ways in this passage did
Jesus tell the people he was the Son of God?
How does God say the people of earth are to
treat his son? What convinced you that Jesus
is God's son?

THURSDAY:

What Does It Mean to Honor God?

John 8:42—9:12

NEW TESTAMENT READING

*J*esus said to them, "If God were really your Father, you would love me, because I came from God and now I am here. I did not come by my own authority; God sent me. You don't understand what I say, because you cannot accept my teaching. You belong to your father the devil, and you want to do what he wants. He was a murderer from the beginning and was against the truth, because there is no truth in him. When he tells a lie, he shows what he is really like, because he is a liar and the father of lies. But because I speak the truth, you don't believe me. Can any of you prove that I am guilty of sin? If I am telling the truth, why don't you believe me? The person who belongs to God accepts what God says. But you don't accept what God says, because you don't belong to God."

Jesus Is Greater than Abraham

*T*he Jews answered, "We say you are a Samaritan and have a demon in you. Are we not right?"

Jesus answered, "I have no demon in me. I give honor to my Father, but you dishonor me. I am not trying to get honor for myself. There is One who wants this honor for me, and he is the judge. I tell you the truth, whoever obeys my teaching will never die."

The Jews said to Jesus, "Now we know that you have a demon in you! Even Abraham and the prophets died. But you say, 'Whoever obeys my teaching will never die.' Do you think you are greater than our father Abraham, who died? And the prophets died, too. Who do you think you are?"

Jesus answered, "If I give honor to myself, that honor is worth nothing. The One who gives me honor is my Father, and you say he is your God. You don't really know him, but I know him. If I said I did not know him, I would be a liar like you. But I

do know him, and I obey what he says. Your father Abraham was very happy that he would see my day. He saw that day and was glad."

The Jews said to him, "You have never seen Abraham! You are not even fifty years old."

Jesus answered, "I tell you the truth, before Abraham was even born, I am!" When Jesus said this, the people picked up stones to throw at him. But Jesus hid himself, and then he left the Temple.

Jesus Heals a Man Born Blind

*A*s Jesus was walking along, he saw a man who had been born blind. His followers asked him, "Teacher, whose sin caused this man to be born blind—his own sin or his parents' sin?"

Jesus answered, "It is not this man's sin or his parents' sin that made him be blind. This man was born blind so that God's power could be shown in him. While it is daytime, we must continue doing the work of the One who sent me. Night is coming, when no one can work. While I am in the world, I am the light of the world."

After Jesus said this, he spit on the ground and made some mud with it and put the mud on the man's eyes. Then he told the man, "Go and wash in the Pool of Siloam." (Siloam means Sent.) So the man went, washed, and came back seeing.

The neighbors and some people who had earlier seen this man begging said, "Isn't this the same man who used to sit and beg?"

Some said, "He is the one," but others said, "No, he only looks like him."

The man himself said, "I am the man."

They asked, "How did you get your sight?"

He answered, "The man named Jesus made some mud and put it on my eyes. Then he told me to go to Siloam and wash. So I went and washed, and then I could see."

They asked him, "Where is this man?"

"I don't know," he answered.

OLD TESTAMENT READING

*W*hile the people of Israel were still camped at Acacia, the men began sinning sexually with Moabite women. The women invited them to their sacrifices to their gods, and the Israelites ate food there and worshiped these gods. So the Israelites began to worship Baal of Peor, and the LORD was very angry with them.

The LORD said to Moses, "Get all the leaders of the people and kill them in open daylight in the presence of the LORD. Then the LORD will not be angry with the people of Israel."

So Moses said to Israel's judges, "Each of you must put to death your people who have become worshipers of Baal of Peor."

Moses and the Israelites were gathered at the entrance to the Meeting Tent, crying there. Then an Israelite man brought a Midianite woman to his brothers in plain sight of Moses and all the people. Phinehas son of Eleazar, the son of Aaron, the priest, saw this, so he left the meeting and got his spear. He followed the Israelite into his tent and drove his spear through both the Israelite man and the Midianite woman. Then the terrible sickness among the Israelites stopped.

This sickness had killed twenty-four thousand people.

The LORD said to Moses, "Phinehas son of Eleazar, the son of Aaron, the priest, has saved the Israelites from my anger. He hates sin as much as I do. Since he tried to save my honor among them, I will not kill them. So tell Phinehas that I am making my peace agreement with him. He and his descendants will always be priests, because he had great concern for the honor of his God. He removed the sins of the Israelites so they would belong to God."

Numbers 25:1–13

*P*riests, this command is for you. Listen to me. Pay attention to what I say. Honor my name," says the LORD All-Powerful. "If you don't, I will send a curse on you and on your blessings. I have already cursed them, because you don't pay attention to what I say.

"My agreement for priests was with the tribe of Levi. I promised them life and peace so they would honor me. And they did honor me and fear me. They taught the true teachings and spoke no lies. With peace and honesty they did what I said they should do, and they kept many people from sinning."

Malachi 2:1–2, 5–6

*J*esus glorified God by giving himself for the work of His redeeming love. God's glory is His holiness, and God's holiness is His redeeming love—love that triumphs over sin by conquering the sin and rescuing the sinner. Jesus not only told of the Father being the righteous One, whose condemnation must rest on sin, and the loving One, who saves everyone who turns from his sin, but He gave himself to be a sacrifice to that righteousness, a servant to that love, even unto death. It was not only in acts of obedience or words of confession that He glorified God, but in giving himself to magnify the holiness of God, to vindicate at once His law and His love by His atonement. He gave himself, His whole life and being, to show how the Father loved, how the Father must condemn the sin, and yet would save the sinner. He counted nothing too great a sacrifice. He lived and died only that the glory of the Father, the glory of His holiness, of His redeeming love, might break through the dark veil of sin and flesh, and shine into the hearts of the children. . . .

If we want to know the way, let us again study Jesus. He obeyed the Father. Let simple obedience mark our whole life. Let humble, childlike waiting for direction, a Christlike dependence on the Father's showing us His way, be our daily attitude. Let everything be done to the Lord, according to His will, for His glory, in direct relationship to himself. Let God's glory shine out in the holiness of our life.

Andrew Murray

*W*hat brings honor to God? How did Jesus honor God? How did Phinehas honor God? How did the Levites honor God? How do you think God wants you to honor him? Are you willing to honor him with a holy life?

FRIDAY:

Jesus Opens the Eyes of Those Who Believe

John 9:13–41

Pharisees Question the Healing

Then the people took to the Pharisees the man who had been blind. The day Jesus had made mud and healed his eyes was a Sabbath day. So now the Pharisees asked the man, "How did you get your sight?"

He answered, "He put mud on my eyes, I washed, and now I see."

So some of the Pharisees were saying, "This man does not keep the Sabbath day, so he is not from God."

But others said, "A man who is a sinner can't do miracles like these." So they could not agree with each other.

They asked the man again, "What do you say about him since it was your eyes he opened?"

The man answered, "He is a prophet."

The Jews did not believe that he had been blind and could now see again. So they sent for the man's parents and asked them, "Is this your son who you say was born blind? Then how does he now see?"

His parents answered, "We know that this is our son and that he was born blind. But we don't know how he can now see. We don't know who opened his eyes. Ask him. He is old enough to speak for himself." His parents said this because they were afraid of the Jews, who had already decided that anyone who said Jesus was the Christ would be put out of the synagogue. That is why his parents said, "He is old enough. Ask him."

So for the second time, they called the man who had been blind. They said, "You should give God the glory by telling the truth. We know that this man is a sinner."

He answered, "I don't know if he is a sinner. One thing I do know: I was blind, and now I see."

They asked, "What did he do to you? How did he make you see again?"

He answered, "I already told you, and you didn't listen. Why do you want to hear it again? Do you want to become his followers, too?"

Then they insulted him and said, "You are his follower, but we are followers of Moses. We know that God spoke to Moses, but we don't even know where this man comes from."

The man answered, "This is a very strange thing. You don't know where he comes from, and yet he opened my eyes. We all know that God does not listen to sinners, but he listens to anyone who worships and obeys him. Nobody has ever heard of anyone giving sight to a man born blind. If this man were not from God, he could do nothing."

They answered, "You were born full of sin! Are you trying to teach us?" And they threw him out.

Spiritual Blindness

When Jesus heard that they had thrown him out, Jesus found him and said, "Do you believe in the Son of Man?"

He asked, "Who is the Son of Man, sir, so that I can believe in him?"

Jesus said to him, "You have seen him. The Son of Man is the one talking with you."

He said, "Lord, I believe!" Then the man worshiped Jesus.

Jesus said, "I came into this world so that the world could be judged. I came so that the blind would see and so that those who see will become blind."

Some of the Pharisees who were nearby heard Jesus say this and asked, "Are you saying we are blind, too?"

Jesus said, "If you were blind, you would not be guilty of sin. But since you keep saying you see, your guilt remains."

Do good to me, your servant, so I can
live,
  so I can obey your word.
Open my eyes to see
  the miracles in your teachings.
I am a stranger on earth.
  Do not hide your commands from me.

I wear myself out with desire
for your laws all the time.
You scold proud people;
those who ignore your commands
are cursed.
Don't let me be insulted and hated
because I keep your rules.
Even if princes speak against me,
I, your servant, will think about your
demands.
Your rules give me pleasure;
they give me good advice.

Psalm 119:17–24

*H*appy are those who are helped by
the God of Jacob.
Their hope is in the Lord their God.
He made heaven and earth,
the sea and everything in it.
He remains loyal forever.
He does what is fair for those who have
been wronged.
He gives food to the hungry.
The Lord sets the prisoners free.
The Lord gives sight to the blind.
The Lord lifts up people who are in
trouble.
The Lord loves those who do right.
The Lord protects the foreigners.
He defends the orphans and widows,
but he blocks the way of the wicked.

The Lord will be King forever.
Jerusalem, your God is everlasting.

Praise the Lord!

Psalm 146:5–10

*Y*ou who are deaf, hear me.
You who are blind, look and see.
No one is more blind than my servant
Israel
or more deaf than the messenger I
send.
No one is more blind than the person I
own
or more blind than the servant of the
Lord.
Israel, you have seen much, but you
have not obeyed.
You hear, but you refuse to listen."
The Lord made his teachings wonderful,
because he is good.

Isaiah 42:18–21

*T*he Lord loves to do things differently. At
least four times He opened blind eyes, and He
does it a different way each time, depending
on the personality and the circumstances.

*The Lord deals with each of us, not en
masse, but as individuals. Each of us is a
special object of the grace and care and
faithfulness of God. If you were the only one
on the face of the earth, He would still take
care of you. This is demonstrated here. He
made clay and put it on the man's eyes. And
this calls for two things from the man: faith
and obedience. The moment he obeyed, he had
deliverance. Deliverance comes from obedience.*

*. . . To follow Him means not to walk in
darkness. Here is a man who has never seen
the light of day, or seen a tree or a flower, or
seen his mother. He has never seen anything.
He has always lived in the dark. How glad I
am the Savior is the light of the world and
can come into any darkened heart that wants
to know God. The moment your heart is open
to Him, the light shines in.*

John G. Mitchell

APPLICATION

*W*hat words of faith and wisdom did the
blind man speak to the Jewish leaders? Why
do you think Jesus looked for him after he was
thrown out of the temple? Pray that you will
see how much Jesus wants you to believe and
trust him.

WEEKEND:
Jesus Is Our Caring Shepherd
John 10:1–33

The Shepherd and His Sheep

*J*esus said, "I tell you the truth, the person who does not enter the sheepfold by the door, but climbs in some other way, is a thief and a robber. The one who enters by the door is the shepherd of the sheep. The one who guards the door opens it for him. And the sheep listen to the voice of the shepherd. He calls his own sheep by name and leads them out. When he brings all his sheep out, he goes ahead of them, and they follow him because they know his voice. But they will never follow a stranger. They will run away from him because they don't know his voice." Jesus told the people this story, but they did not understand what it meant.

Jesus Is the Good Shepherd

*S*o Jesus said again, "I tell you the truth, I am the door for the sheep. All the people who came before me were thieves and robbers. The sheep did not listen to them. I am the door, and the person who enters through me will be saved and will be able to come in and go out and find pasture. A thief comes to steal and kill and destroy, but I came to give life—life in all its fullness.

"I am the good shepherd. The good shepherd gives his life for the sheep. The worker who is paid to keep the sheep is different from the shepherd who owns them. When the worker sees a wolf coming, he runs away and leaves the sheep alone. Then the wolf attacks the sheep and scatters them. The man runs away because he is only a paid worker and does not really care about the sheep.

"I am the good shepherd. I know my sheep, as the Father knows me. And my sheep know me, as I know the Father. I give my life for the sheep. I have other sheep that are not in this flock, and I must bring them also. They will listen to my voice, and there will be one flock and one shepherd. The Father loves me because I give my life so that I can take it back again. No one takes it away from me; I give my own life freely. I have the right to give my life, and I have the right to take it back. This is what my Father commanded me to do."

Again the Jews did not agree with each other because of these words of Jesus. Many of them said, "A demon has come into him and made him crazy. Why listen to him?"

But others said, "A man who is crazy with a demon does not say things like this. Can a demon open the eyes of the blind?"

Jesus Is Rejected

*T*he time came for the Feast of Dedication at Jerusalem. It was winter, and Jesus was walking in the Temple in Solomon's Porch. The Jews gathered around him and said, "How long will you make us wonder about you? If you are the Christ, tell us plainly."

Jesus answered, "I told you already, but you did not believe. The miracles I do in my Father's name show who I am. But you don't believe, because you are not my sheep. My sheep listen to my voice; I know them, and they follow me. I give them eternal life, and they will never die, and no one can steal them out of my hand. My Father gave my sheep to me. He is greater than all, and no person can steal my sheep out of my Father's hand. The Father and I are one."

Again the Jews picked up stones to kill Jesus. But he said to them, "I have done many good works from the Father. Which of these good works are you killing me for?"

The Jews answered, "We are not killing you because of any good work you did, but because you speak against God. You are only a human, but you say you are the same as God!"

*T*he LORD is my shepherd;
I have everything I need.
He lets me rest in green pastures.
He leads me to calm water.
He gives me new strength.

He leads me on paths that are right
   for the good of his name.
Even if I walk through a very dark
    valley,
   I will not be afraid,
because you are with me.
   Your rod and your walking stick
    comfort me.

You prepare a meal for me
   in front of my enemies.
You pour oil on my head;
   you fill my cup to overflowing.
Surely your goodness and love will be
    with me
   all my life,
and I will live in the house of the LORD
   forever.

                   Psalm 23:1–6

Shout to the LORD, all the earth.
   Serve the LORD with joy;
   come before him with singing.
Know that the LORD is God.
   He made us, and we belong to him;
   we are his people, the sheep he
    tends.
Come into his city with songs of
   thanksgiving
   and into his courtyards with songs of
    praise.
   Thank him and praise his name.
The LORD is good. His love is forever,
   and his loyalty goes on and on.

                  Psalm 100:1–5

He takes care of his people like a
   shepherd.
   He gathers them like lambs in his
    arms
   and carries them close to him.
He gently leads the mothers of the
   lambs.

                Isaiah 40:11

Nations, listen to the message from
   the LORD.
   Tell this message in the faraway
    lands by the sea:
'The one who scattered the people of
   Israel will bring them back,
   and he will watch over his people
    like a shepherd.'"

              Jeremiah 31:10

INSIGHTS

Do you need guidance as to your path? Look unto Jesus; it is always possible to discern His form, though partially veiled in mist; and when it is lost, be sure to stand still until He comes back to find and re-establish the blessed connection. . . . Do not get anxious or flurried. Put the government of your life upon His shoulder, and leave Him to execute His plan.

Sometimes He guides us to the rest of the green pastures, and the quiet of the still waters. In other words, we are left through happy months and years to fulfil the ordinary commonplaces of life, content to fill a little space, and receiving great increments of spiritual force for future service. At other times, we are guided from the lowland pastures up into the hills. The way is sunny, above us the precipitous cliffs, beneath the dark turbid stream; but this is well; we would not always be lying the pastures or walking softly by the waters. It is good to climb the heights with their far view and bracing air.

In the late afternoon the Shepherd may lead his flock back into the valleys, through the dark woods, where the branches meet overhead and the wild beast lurks in ambush, but we know that in one hand He has the rod or club, with which to belabour anything that may attack; and in the other the crook to drag us out of the hole. He would not lead us into the dark valley which He had not explored, and whose perils He was not prepared to overcome. Darkness, sorrow, or death do not prove that we have missed His guidance, or have taken the wrong path, but rather that He accounts us able to bear the trial by faith in Himself.

                F. B. Meyer

PAUSE FOR REFLECTION

What does Jesus promise to give his sheep who follow him? Study the qualities of the good shepherd that Jesus describes and think about the ways Jesus has been your shepherd. Praise him for his goodness!

M O N D A Y:
Trust in God to Protect and Care for You
John 10:34—11:27

*J*esus answered, "It is written in your law that God said, 'I said, you are gods.' This Scripture called those people gods who received God's message, and Scripture is always true. So why do you say that I speak against God because I said, 'I am God's Son'? I am the one God chose and sent into the world. If I don't do what my Father does, then don't believe me. But if I do what my Father does, even though you don't believe in me, believe what I do. Then you will know and understand that the Father is in me and I am in the Father."

They tried to take Jesus again, but he escaped from them.

Then he went back across the Jordan River to the place where John had first baptized. Jesus stayed there, and many people came to him and said, "John never did a miracle, but everything John said about this man is true." And in that place many believed in Jesus.

The Death of Lazarus

A man named Lazarus was sick. He lived in the town of Bethany, where Mary and her sister Martha lived. Mary was the woman who later put perfume on the Lord and wiped his feet with her hair. Mary's brother was Lazarus, the man who was now sick. So Mary and Martha sent someone to tell Jesus, "Lord, the one you love is sick."

When Jesus heard this, he said, "This sickness will not end in death. It is for the glory of God, to bring glory to the Son of God." Jesus loved Martha and her sister and Lazarus. But when he heard that Lazarus was sick, he stayed where he was for two more days. Then Jesus said to his followers, "Let's go back to Judea."

The followers said, "But Teacher, the Jews there tried to stone you to death only a short time ago. Now you want to go back there?"

Jesus answered, "Are there not twelve hours in the day? If anyone walks in the daylight, he will not stumble, because he can see by this world's light. But if anyone walks at night, he stumbles because there is no light to help him see."

After Jesus said this, he added, "Our friend Lazarus has fallen asleep, but I am going there to wake him."

The followers said, "But Lord, if he is only asleep, he will be all right."

Jesus meant that Lazarus was dead, but his followers thought he meant Lazarus was really sleeping. So then Jesus said plainly, "Lazarus is dead. And I am glad for your sakes I was not there so that you may believe. But let's go to him now."

Then Thomas (the one called Didymus) said to the other followers, "Let us also go so that we can die with him."

Jesus in Bethany

*W*hen Jesus arrived, he learned that Lazarus had already been dead and in the tomb for four days. Bethany was about two miles from Jerusalem. Many of the Jews had come there to comfort Martha and Mary about their brother.

When Martha heard that Jesus was coming, she went out to meet him, but Mary stayed home. Martha said to Jesus, "Lord, if you had been here, my brother would not have died. But I know that even now God will give you anything you ask."

Jesus said, "Your brother will rise and live again."

Martha answered, "I know that he will rise and live again in the resurrection on the last day."

Jesus said to her, "I am the resurrection and the life. Those who believe in me will have life even if they die. And everyone who lives and believes in me will never die. Martha, do you believe this?"

Martha answered, "Yes, Lord. I believe that you are the Christ, the Son of God, the One coming to the world."

I waited patiently for the LORD.
He turned to me and heard my cry.

He lifted me out of the pit of destruction,
    out of the sticky mud.
He stood me on a rock
    and made my feet steady.
He put a new song in my mouth,
    a song of praise to our God.
Many people will see this and worship
    him.
    Then they will trust the LORD.

Happy is the person
    who trusts the LORD,
who doesn't turn to those who are proud
    or to those who worship gods.
LORD my God, you have done many
    miracles.
    Your plans for us are many.
If I tried to tell them all,
    there would be too many to count.

Psalm 40:1–5

*T*he LORD says, "Whoever loves me, I
    will save.
I will protect those who know me.
They will call to me, and I will answer
    them.
I will be with them in trouble;
I will rescue them and honor them.
I will give them a long, full life,
    and they will see how I can save."

Psalm 91:14–16

*L*ORD, you are my God.
    I honor you and praise you,
because you have done amazing things.
    You have always done what you said
        you would do;
    you have done what you planned
        long ago.

He will destroy death forever.
    The Lord GOD will wipe away every
        tear from every face.
He will take away the shame of his people
    from the earth.
The LORD has spoken.
At that time people will say,
    "Our God is doing this!
We have waited for him, and he has
        come to save us.
    This is the LORD. We waited for him,
so we will rejoice and be happy when
        he saves us."

Isaiah 25:1, 8–9

A *pair of scientists and botanists were exploring in the Alps for some special kinds of flowers. One day they spied through their field glass a flower of rare beauty. But it was in a ravine with perpendicular cliffs on both sides. Someone must be lowered over the cliff to get it.*

A native boy was watching. They said to him, "We will give you five pounds if you will let us lower you into the valley to get the flower." The boy looked into the valley and said, "Just a moment. I'll be back." He soon returned with a man. "I'll go over the cliff," he said, "and get the flower for you if this man holds the rope. He's my dad." Have we learned to trust the Lord as this little boy did his father?

Sometimes we find ourselves putting our confidence in man and what we think he can do for us. But man can let us down. Man can disappoint us. Not so the Lord. Needs may be pressing in but we can look up, trusting an all-wise, all-loving God to do all for our good and His glory.

We can trust the rope of our circumstances to Him. Man may become weary and let the rope drop; or he may be distracted or become impatient. But God never wearies of holding the rope. We can confidently leave it in His strong hand.

Millie Stamm

*H*ow long had Lazarus been dead before Jesus reached out and saved him? Doesn't that stretch your ability to trust in his protection? Can you, like the psalmist, confidently praise God for his protection?

255

TUESDAY:
God Honors Our Faith
John 11:28–57

Jesus Cries

After Martha said this, she went back and talked to her sister Mary alone. Martha said, "The Teacher is here and he is asking for you." When Mary heard this, she got up quickly and went to Jesus. Jesus had not yet come into the town but was still at the place where Martha had met him. The Jews were with Mary in the house, comforting her. When they saw her stand and leave quickly, they followed her, thinking she was going to the tomb to cry there. But Mary went to the place where Jesus was. When she saw him, she fell at his feet and said, "Lord, if you had been here, my brother would not have died."

When Jesus saw Mary crying and the Jews who came with her also crying, he was upset and was deeply troubled. He asked, "Where did you bury him?"

"Come and see, Lord," they said.

Jesus cried.

So the Jews said, "See how much he loved him."

But some of them said, "If Jesus opened the eyes of the blind man, why couldn't he keep Lazarus from dying?"

Jesus Raises Lazarus

Again feeling very upset, Jesus came to the tomb. It was a cave with a large stone covering the entrance. Jesus said, "Move the stone away."

Martha, the sister of the dead man, said, "But, Lord, it has been four days since he died. There will be a bad smell."

Then Jesus said to her, "Didn't I tell you that if you believed you would see the glory of God?"

So they moved the stone away from the entrance. Then Jesus looked up and said, "Father, I thank you that you heard me. I know that you always hear me, but I said these things because of the people here around me. I want them to believe that you sent me." After Jesus said this, he cried out in a loud voice, "Lazarus, come out!" The dead man came out, his hands and feet wrapped with pieces of cloth, and a cloth around his face.

Jesus said to them, "Take the cloth off of him and let him go."

The Plan to Kill Jesus

Many of the Jews, who had come to visit Mary and saw what Jesus did, believed in him. But some of them went to the Pharisees and told them what Jesus had done. Then the leading priests and Pharisees called a meeting of the Jewish council. They asked, "What should we do? This man is doing many miracles. If we let him continue doing these things, everyone will believe in him. Then the Romans will come and take away our Temple and our nation."

One of the men there was Caiaphas, the high priest that year. He said, "You people know nothing! You don't realize that it is better for one man to die for the people than for the whole nation to be destroyed."

Caiaphas did not think of this himself. As high priest that year, he was really prophesying that Jesus would die for the Jewish nation and for God's scattered children to bring them all together and make them one. That day they started planning to kill Jesus. So Jesus no longer traveled openly among the Jews. He left there and went to a place near the desert, to a town called Ephraim and stayed there with his followers.

It was almost time for the Jewish Passover Feast. Many from the country went up to Jerusalem before the Passover to do the special things to make themselves pure. The people looked for Jesus and stood in the Temple asking each other, "Is he coming to the Feast? What do you think?" But the leading priests and the Pharisees had given orders that if anyone knew where Jesus was, he must tell them. Then they could arrest him.

The woman answered, "As surely as the LORD your God lives, I have no bread. I have only a handful of flour in a jar and only a little olive oil in a jug. I came here to gather some wood so I could go home and cook our last meal. My son and I will eat it and then die from hunger."

"Don't worry," Elijah said to her. "Go home and cook your food as you have said. But first make a small loaf of bread from the flour you have, and bring it to me. Then cook something for yourself and your son. The LORD, the God of Israel, says, 'That jar of flour will never be empty, and the jug will always have oil in it, until the day the LORD sends rain to the land.'"

So the woman went home and did what Elijah told her to do. And the woman and her son and Elijah had enough food every day. The jar of flour and the jug of oil were never empty, just as the LORD, through Elijah, had promised.

Elijah Brings a Boy Back to Life

Some time later the son of the woman who owned the house became sick. He grew worse and worse and finally stopped breathing. The woman said to Elijah, "Man of God, what have you done to me? Did you come here to remind me of my sin and to kill my son?"

Elijah said to her, "Give me your son." Elijah took the boy from her, carried him upstairs, and laid him on the bed in the room where he was staying. Then he prayed to the LORD: "LORD my God, this widow is letting me stay in her house. Why have you done this terrible thing to her and caused her son to die?" Then Elijah lay on top of the boy three times. He prayed to the LORD, "Lord my God, let this boy live again!"

The LORD answered Elijah's prayer; the boy began breathing again and was alive. Elijah carried the boy downstairs and gave him to his mother and said, "See! Your son is alive!"

"Now I know you really are a man from God," the woman said to Elijah. "I know that the LORD truly speaks through you!"

1 Kings 17:12–24

INSIGHTS

*F*aith is man's response to God's initiative. . . .

To realize that faith is your response to something God does or says, will take pressure off you and enable you to adopt a more constructive attitude to it. Do not look inside yourself and ask, "How much faith do I have?" Look to God and ask, "What is he saying to me? What would he have me do?" When Jesus praised the great faith of different men and women in the Gospels, he was not praising a mystical inner state. He was usually commenting on a concrete action by which someone responded to him. . . .

Once you understand this you will also begin to see why the amount of faith you have is a less crucial issue than you might have thought. The saying of Jesus about the grain of mustard seed begins to make sense. . . .

How much faith did Martha need to get Lazarus back from the dead? Precious little (Jn. 11:38–40). If we are to go by mystical inner states, every evidence points to Martha having no faith at all. No, what she needed (and what she had) was enough faith to give orders for the tombstone to be moved, in spite of the doubts she felt. And Lazarus was raised from the dead. . . .

Faith then is your decision to respond to God's Word. The decision may either manifest itself in some outward action or else in what we might call an "interior action"—like the committing of your eternal destiny into the hands of Christ. In time the decision grows into an attitude, an attitude of always being ready to respond positively to God's Word.

John White

PAUSE FOR REFLECTION

*W*hen Jesus came to them, did Mary and Martha believe he had come to raise Lazarus from the dead? What faith did they have in Jesus? Is your faith in Jesus enough for him to accomplish his purposes?

257

WEDNESDAY:

Evil People Have Always Conspired Against the Righteous and Innocent

John 12:1–26

Jesus with Friends in Bethany

Six days before the Passover Feast, Jesus went to Bethany, where Lazarus lived. (Lazarus is the man Jesus raised from the dead.) There they had a dinner for Jesus. Martha served the food, and Lazarus was one of the people eating with Jesus. Mary brought in a pint of very expensive perfume made from pure nard. She poured the perfume on Jesus' feet, and then she wiped his feet with her hair. And the sweet smell from the perfume filled the whole house.

Judas Iscariot, one of Jesus' followers who would later turn against him, was there. Judas said, "This perfume was worth three hundred coins. Why wasn't it sold and the money given to the poor?" But Judas did not really care about the poor; he said this because he was a thief. He was the one who kept the money box, and he often stole from it.

Jesus answered, "Leave her alone. It was right for her to save this perfume for today, the day for me to be prepared for burial. You will always have the poor with you, but you will not always have me."

The Plot Against Lazarus

A large crowd of Jews heard that Jesus was in Bethany. So they went there to see not only Jesus but Lazarus, whom Jesus raised from the dead. So the leading priests made plans to kill Lazarus, too. Because of Lazarus many of the Jews were leaving them and believing in Jesus.

Jesus Enters Jerusalem

The next day a great crowd who had come to Jerusalem for the Passover Feast heard that Jesus was coming there. So they took branches of palm trees and went out to meet Jesus, shouting,

"Praise God!
God bless the One who comes in the
  name of the Lord!
God bless the King of Israel!"

Psalm 118:25–26

Jesus found a colt and sat on it. This was as the Scripture says,

"Don't be afraid, people of Jerusalem!
Your king is coming,
  sitting on the colt of a donkey."

Zechariah 9:9

The followers of Jesus did not understand this at first. But after Jesus was raised to glory, they remembered that this had been written about him and that they had done these things to him.

People Tell About Jesus

There had been many people with Jesus when he raised Lazarus from the dead and told him to come out of the tomb. Now they were telling others about what Jesus did. Many people went out to meet Jesus, because they had heard about this miracle. So the Pharisees said to each other, "You can see that nothing is going right for us. Look! The whole world is following him."

Jesus Talks About His Death

There were some Greek people, too, who came to Jerusalem to worship at the Passover Feast. They went to Philip, who was from Bethsaida in Galilee, and said, "Sir, we would like to see Jesus." Philip told Andrew, and then Andrew and Philip told Jesus.

Jesus said to them, "The time has come for the Son of Man to receive his glory. I tell you the truth, a grain of wheat must fall to the ground and die to make many seeds. But if it never dies, it remains only a single seed. Those who love their lives will lose them, but those who hate their lives in this world will keep true life forever. Whoever serves me must follow me. Then my servant will be with me everywhere I am. My Father will honor anyone who serves me."

Lord, why are you so far away?
  Why do you hide when there is
    trouble?

Proudly the wicked chase down those
who suffer.
Let them be caught in their own
traps.
They brag about the things they want.
They bless the greedy but hate the
LORD.
The wicked people are too proud.
They do not look for God;
there is no room for God in their
thoughts.
They always succeed.
They are far from keeping your laws;
they make fun of their enemies.
They say to themselves, "Nothing bad
will ever happen to me;
I will never be ruined."
Their mouths are full of curses, lies,
and threats;
they use their tongues for sin and
evil.
They hide near the villages.
They look for innocent people to kill;
they watch in secret for the helpless.
They wait in hiding like a lion.
They wait to catch poor people;
they catch the poor in nets.
The poor are thrown down and
crushed;
they are defeated because the others
are stronger.
The wicked think, "God has forgotten
us.
He doesn't see what is happening."

LORD, rise up and punish the wicked.
Don't forget those who need help.
Why do wicked people hate God?
They say to themselves, "God won't
punish us."
LORD, surely you see these cruel and
evil things;
look at them and do something.
People in trouble look to you for help.
You are the one who helps the
orphans.
Break the power of wicked people.
Punish them for the evil they have
done.

The LORD is King forever and ever.
Destroy from your land those
nations that do not worship you.

Psalm 10:1–16

*Charles Haddon Spurgeon remains one of
the most colorful and gifted preachers in the
history of the church. . . . The new Taber-
nacle was filled to overflowing every Lord's
Day as people came miles by horse and buggy
to hear the gifted man handle the Word of
God. They were challenged, encouraged, exhorted, fed, and built up in the Christian
faith. He was truly a phenomenon. As a result, he became the object of great criticism
by the press, by other pastors, by influential
people in London, and by petty parishio-
ners. . . .*

*I am told that his wife, seeing the results
of those verbal blows on her husband, decided
to assist him in getting back on his feet and
regaining his powerful stature in the pulpit.
She found in her Bible Matthew 5:10–12—
and she printed in beautiful old English the
words of this passage on a large sheet of paper.
Then she tacked that sheet to the ceiling of
their bedroom, directly above Charles' side of
the bed! . . .*

*Blessed are those who have been perse-
cuted for the sake of righteousness, for
theirs is the kingdom of heaven.*

*Blessed are you when men revile you,
and persecute you, and say all kinds of
evil against you falsely, on account of
Me.*

*Rejoice, and be glad, for your reward
in heaven is great, for so they persecuted
the prophets who were before you. . . .*

*. . . Servants, that statement will help us
call a halt to the next pity party we are
tempted to throw for ourselves. We are not
alone. It has been going on for centuries.*

Charles Swindoll

*Why did the religious leaders of the day hate
Jesus and Lazarus? From whom does persecution come in your life? What portion of
Scripture encourages and comforts you during such times?*

THURSDAY:
Some Who See God's Work Still Do Not Believe
John 12:27—13:5

NEW TESTAMENT READING

*N*ow I am very troubled. Should I say, 'Father, save me from this time'? No, I came to this time so I could suffer. Father, bring glory to your name!"

Then a voice came from heaven, "I have brought glory to it, and I will do it again."

The crowd standing there, who heard the voice, said it was thunder.

But others said, "An angel has spoken to him."

Jesus said, "That voice was for your sake, not mine. Now is the time for the world to be judged; now the ruler of this world will be thrown down. If I am lifted up from the earth, I will draw all people toward me." Jesus said this to show how he would die.

The crowd said, "We have heard from the law that the Christ will live forever. So why do you say, 'The Son of Man must be lifted up'? Who is this 'Son of Man'?"

Then Jesus said, "The light will be with you for a little longer, so walk while you have the light. Then the darkness will not catch you. If you walk in the darkness, you will not know where you are going. Believe in the light while you still have it so that you will become children of light." When Jesus had said this, he left and hid himself from them.

Some Won't Believe in Jesus

*T*hough Jesus had done many miracles in front of the people, they still did not believe in him. This was to bring about what Isaiah the prophet had said:

"Lord, who believed what we told
    them?
Who saw the Lord's power in this?"

Isaiah 53:1

This is why the people could not believe: Isaiah also had said,

"He has blinded their eyes,
    and he has closed their minds.

Otherwise they would see with their
    eyes
and understand in their minds
and come back to me and be healed."

Isaiah 6:10

Isaiah said this because he saw Jesus' glory and spoke about him.

But many believed in Jesus, even many of the leaders. But because of the Pharisees, they did not say they believed in him for fear they would be put out of the synagogue. They loved praise from people more than praise from God.

Then Jesus cried out, "Whoever believes in me is really believing in the One who sent me. Whoever sees me sees the One who sent me. I have come as light into the world so that whoever believes in me would not stay in darkness.

"Anyone who hears my words and does not obey them, I do not judge, because I did not come to judge the world, but to save the world. There is a judge for those who refuse to believe in me and do not accept my words. The word I have taught will be their judge on the last day. The things I taught were not from myself. The Father who sent me told me what to say and what to teach. And I know that eternal life comes from what the Father commands. So whatever I say is what the Father told me to say."

Jesus Washes His Followers' Feet

*I*t was almost time for the Jewish Passover Feast. Jesus knew that it was time for him to leave this world and go back to the Father. He had always loved those who were his own in the world, and he loved them all the way to the end.

Jesus and his followers were at the evening meal. The devil had already persuaded Judas Iscariot, the son of Simon, to turn against Jesus. Jesus knew that the Father had given him power over everything and that he had come from God and was going back to God. So during the meal Jesus stood up and took off his outer clothing. Taking a towel, he wrapped it around his waist. Then he poured water into a bowl and began to wash the followers' feet, drying them with the towel that was wrapped around him.

*O*ne day Moses was taking care of Jethro's flock. (Jethro was the priest of Midian and also Moses' father-in-law.) When Moses led the flock to the west side of the desert, he came to Sinai, the mountain of God. There the angel of the LORD appeared to him in flames of fire coming out of a bush. Moses saw that the bush was on fire, but it was not burning up. So he said, "I will go closer to this strange thing. How can a bush continue burning without burning up?"

When the LORD saw Moses was coming to look at the bush, God called to him from the bush, "Moses, Moses!"

And Moses said, "Here I am."

Then God said, "Do not come any closer. Take off your sandals, because you are standing on holy ground. I am the God of your ancestors—the God of Abraham, the God of Isaac, and the God of Jacob." Moses covered his face because he was afraid to look at God.

Exodus 3:1–6

*T*hen the LORD told Moses, "Raise your hand toward the sky, and darkness will cover the land of Egypt. It will be so dark you will be able to feel it." Moses raised his hand toward the sky, and total darkness was everywhere in Egypt for three days. No one could see anyone else, and no one could go anywhere for three days. But the Israelites had light where they lived.

Exodus 10:21–23

*M*oses heard every family crying as they stood in the entrances of their tents. Then the LORD became very angry, and Moses got upset. He asked the LORD, "Why have you brought me, your servant, this trouble? What have I done wrong that you made me responsible for all these people? I am not the father of all these people, and I didn't give birth to them. So why do you make me carry them to the land you promised to our ancestors? Must I carry them in my arms as a nurse carries a baby? Where can I get meat for all these people? They keep crying to me, 'We want meat!' I can't take care of all these people alone. It is too much for

me. If you are going to continue doing this to me, then kill me now. If you care about me, put me to death, and then I won't have any more troubles.

"Tell the people this: 'Make yourselves holy for tomorrow, and you will eat meat. You cried to the LORD, "We want meat! We were better off in Egypt!" So now the LORD will give you meat to eat.'"

Moses said, "LORD, here are six hundred thousand people standing around me, and you say, 'I will give them enough meat to eat for a month!' If we killed all the flocks and herds, that would not be enough. If we caught all the fish in the sea, that would not be enough."

But the LORD said to Moses, "Do you think I'm weak? Now you will see if I can do what I say."

Numbers 11:10–15, 18, 21–23

INSIGHTS

*T*he late Dr. Heugh, of Glasgow, a short time before he breathed his last, said, "There is nothing I feel more than the criminality of not trusting Christ without doubt—without doubt. Oh, to think what Christ is, what he did, and whom he did it for, and then not to believe him, not to trust him! There is no wickedness like the wickedness of unbelief!"

Charles Spurgeon

PAUSE FOR REFLECTION

*D*oes it surprise you that Moses, even after all the miracles he had seen (and been a part of), still struggled with unbelief? Why is it important for us to believe Jesus? In what ways do you find it difficult to trust and believe Jesus? What "miracles" have you seen that ought to strengthen your belief?

FRIDAY:

Jesus Gives a New Commandment to His People

John 13:6–35

*J*esus came to Simon Peter, who said to him, "Lord, are you going to wash my feet?"

Jesus answered, "You don't understand now what I am doing, but you will understand later."

Peter said, "No, you will never wash my feet."

Jesus answered, "If I don't wash your feet, you are not one of my people."

Simon Peter answered, "Lord, then wash not only my feet, but wash my hands and my head, too!"

Jesus said, "After a person has had a bath, his whole body is clean. He needs only to wash his feet. And you men are clean, but not all of you." Jesus knew who would turn against him, and that is why he said, "Not all of you are clean."

When he had finished washing their feet, he put on his clothes and sat down again. He asked, "Do you understand what I have just done for you? You call me 'Teacher' and 'Lord,' and you are right, because that is what I am. If I, your Lord and Teacher, have washed your feet, you also should wash each other's feet. I did this as an example so that you should do as I have done for you. I tell you the truth, a servant is not greater than his master. A messenger is not greater than the one who sent him. If you know these things, you will be happy if you do them.

"I am not talking about all of you. I know those I have chosen. But this is to bring about what the Scripture said: 'The man who ate at my table has turned against me.' I am telling you this now before it happens so that when it happens, you will believe that I am he. I tell you the truth, whoever accepts anyone I send also accepts me. And whoever accepts me also accepts the One who sent me."

Jesus Talks About His Death

*A*fter Jesus said this, he was very troubled.

He said openly, "I tell you the truth, one of you will turn against me."

The followers all looked at each other, because they did not know whom Jesus was talking about. One of the followers sitting next to Jesus was the follower Jesus loved. Simon Peter motioned to him to ask Jesus whom he was talking about.

That follower leaned closer to Jesus and asked, "Lord, who is it?"

Jesus answered, "I will dip this bread into the dish. The man I give it to is the man who will turn against me." So Jesus took a piece of bread, dipped it, and gave it to Judas Iscariot, the son of Simon. As soon as Judas took the bread, Satan entered him. Jesus said to him, "The thing that you will do—do it quickly." No one at the table understood why Jesus said this to Judas. Since he was the one who kept the money box, some of the followers thought Jesus was telling him to buy what was needed for the feast or to give something to the poor.

Judas took the bread Jesus gave him and immediately went out. It was night.

When Judas was gone, Jesus said, "Now the Son of Man receives his glory, and God receives glory through him. If God receives glory through him, then God will give glory to the Son through himself. And God will give him glory quickly."

Jesus said, "My children, I will be with you only a little longer. You will look for me, and what I told the Jews, I tell you now: Where I am going you cannot come.

"I give you a new command: Love each other. You must love each other as I have loved you. All people will know that you are my followers if you love each other."

God Gives His People His Commandments at Sinai

*T*hen Moses went up on the mountain to God. The LORD called to him from the mountain and said, "Say this to the family of Jacob, and tell the people of Israel: 'Every one of you has seen what I did to the people of Egypt. You saw how I carried you out of Egypt, as if on eagle's wings. And I brought you here to me. So now if you obey me and keep my agreement, you will be my own possession, chosen from all nations. Even though the whole earth is mine, you will be my kingdom of priests and a holy nation.' You must tell the Israelites these words."

Exodus 19:3–6

*T*hen God spoke all these words:

"I am the LORD your God, who brought you out of the land of Egypt where you were slaves.

"You must not have any other gods except me.

"You must not make for yourselves an idol that looks like anything in the sky above or on the earth below or in the water below the land. You must not worship or serve any idol, because I, the LORD your God, am a jealous God. If you hate me, I will punish your children, and even your grandchildren and great-grandchildren. But I show kindness to thousands who love me and obey my commands.

"You must not use the name of the LORD your God thoughtlessly; the LORD will punish anyone who misuses his name.

"Remember to keep the Sabbath holy. Work and get everything done during six days each week, but the seventh day is a day of rest to honor the LORD your God. On that day no one may do any work: not you, your son or daughter, your male or female slaves, your animals, or the foreigners living in your cities. The reason is that in six days the LORD made everything—the sky, the earth, the sea, and everything in them. On the seventh day he rested. So the LORD blessed the Sabbath day and made it holy.

"Honor your father and your mother so that you will live a long time in the land that the LORD your God is going to give you.

"You must not murder anyone.

"You must not be guilty of adultery.

"You must not steal.

"You must not tell lies about your neighbor.

"You must not want to take your neighbor's house. You must not want his wife or his male or female slaves, or his ox or his donkey, or anything that belongs to your neighbor."

Exodus 20:1–17

INSIGHTS

*W*ith the resurrection of the Lord Jesus and the day of Pentecost came a breath of heavenly love. Those who received Jesus, the incarnation of love, into their lives and who chose to obey His command began to love one another. The pagan world looked on in amazement and said of the believers, "How they love one another!"

Within a few years following this command to love one another, the gospel had spread like a prairie fire throughout the known world. The miracle of God's love, His supernatural agape, had captivated multitudes throughout the decadent, wicked Roman Empire.

Tragically, today one seldom hears "How they love one another!" about Christians. Instead there is far too much suspicion, jealousy, criticism and conflict between Christians, churches and denominations. The unbelieving world often laughs at our publicized conflicts.

But those individuals who do demonstrate this supernatural love are usually warmly received by nonbelievers as well as believers. The churches that obey our Lord's command to "love one another" usually are filled to overflowing and are making a great impact for good and for the glory of God. They represent a highly desirable alternative to secular society.

How does one love supernaturally? By faith. God's Word commands us to love (John 13:34, 35). God's Word promises that He will enable us to do what He commands us to do (1 John 5:14, 15).

Bill Bright

APPLICATION

*A*s Jesus prepared to leave his disciples, what one command did he give them? Why do you think this command differs from those given at Mount Sinai? How can you more fully follow this command in your life today?

WEEKEND:

Our Obedience Demonstrates Our Love for God

John 13:36—14:26

Peter Will Say He Doesn't Know Jesus

Simon Peter asked Jesus, "Lord, where are you going?"

Jesus answered, "Where I am going you cannot follow now, but you will follow later."

Peter asked, "Lord, why can't I follow you now? I am ready to die for you!"

Jesus answered, "Are you ready to die for me? I tell you the truth, before the rooster crows, you will say three times that you don't know me."

Jesus Comforts His Followers

Jesus said, "Don't let your hearts be troubled. Trust in God, and trust in me. There are many rooms in my Father's house; I would not tell you this if it were not true. I am going there to prepare a place for you. After I go and prepare a place for you, I will come back and take you to be with me so that you may be where I am. You know the way to the place where I am going."

Thomas said to Jesus, "Lord, we don't know where you are going. So how can we know the way?"

Jesus answered, "I am the way, and the truth, and the life. The only way to the Father is through me. If you really knew me, you would know my Father, too. But now you do know him, and you have seen him."

Philip said to him, "Lord, show us the Father. That is all we need."

Jesus answered, "I have been with you a long time now. Do you still not know me, Philip? Whoever has seen me has seen the Father. So why do you say, 'Show us the Father'? Don't you believe that I am in the Father and the Father is in me? The words I say to you don't come from me, but the Father lives in me and does his own work. Believe me when I say that I am in the Father and the Father is in me. Or believe be-

cause of the miracles I have done. I tell you the truth, whoever believes in me will do the same things that I do. Those who believe will do even greater things than these, because I am going to the Father. And if you ask for anything in my name, I will do it for you so that the Father's glory will be shown through the Son. If you ask me for anything in my name, I will do it.

The Promise of the Holy Spirit

If you love me, you will obey my commands. I will ask the Father, and he will give you another Helper to be with you forever—the Spirit of truth. The world cannot accept him, because it does not see him or know him. But you know him, because he lives with you and he will be in you.

"I will not leave you all alone like orphans; I will come back to you. In a little while the world will not see me anymore, but you will see me. Because I live, you will live, too. On that day you will know that I am in my Father, and that you are in me and I am in you. Those who know my commands and obey them are the ones who love me, and my Father will love those who love me. I will love them and will show myself to them."

Then Judas (not Judas Iscariot) said, "But, Lord, why do you plan to show yourself to us and not to the rest of the world?"

Jesus answered, "If people love me, they will obey my teaching. My Father will love them, and we will come to them and make our home with them. Those who do not love me do not obey my teaching. This teaching that you hear is not really mine; it is from my Father, who sent me.

"I have told you all these things while I am with you. But the Helper will teach you everything and will cause you to remember all that I told you. This Helper is the Holy Spirit whom the Father will send in my name."

Love the LORD your God and always obey his orders, rules, laws, and commands. Remember today it was not your children who saw and felt the correction of the LORD your

God. They did not see his majesty, his power, his strength, or his signs and the things he did in Egypt to the king and his whole country. They did not see what he did to the Egyptian army, its horses and chariots, when he drowned them in the Red Sea as they were chasing you. The LORD ruined them forever. They did not see what he did for you in the desert until you arrived here. They did not see what he did to Dathan and Abiram, the sons of Eliab the Reubenite, when the ground opened up and swallowed them, their families, their tents, and everyone who stood with them in Israel. It was you who saw all these great things the LORD has done.

So obey all the commands I am giving you today so that you will be strong and can go in and take the land you are going to take as your own. Then you will live a long time in the land that the LORD promised to give to your ancestors and their descendants, a fertile land. The land you are going to take is not like Egypt, where you were. There you had to plant your seed and water it, like a vegetable garden, by using your feet. But the land that you will soon cross the Jordan River to take is a land of hills and valleys, a land that drinks rain from heaven. It is a land the LORD your God cares for. His eyes are on it continually, and he watches it from the beginning of the year to the end.

If you carefully obey the commands I am giving you today and love the LORD your God and serve him with your whole being, then he will send rain on your land at the right time, in the fall and spring, and you will be able to gather your grain, new wine, and oil. He will put grass in the fields for your cattle, and you will have plenty to eat.

If you are careful to obey every command I am giving you to follow, and love the LORD your God, and do what he has told you to do, and are loyal to him, then the LORD will force all those nations out of the land ahead of you, and you will take the land from nations that are bigger and stronger than you.

See, today I am letting you choose a blessing or a curse. You will be blessed if you obey the commands of the LORD your God that I am giving you today. But you will be cursed if you disobey the commands of the LORD your God. So do not disobey the commands I am giving you today, and do not worship other gods you do not know.

Deuteronomy 11:1–15, 22–23, 26–28

The Master has revealed Himself to you, and is calling for your complete surrender, and you shrink and hesitate. A measure of surrender you are willing to make, and think indeed it is fit and proper that you should. But an utter abandonment, without any reserves, seems to you too much to be asked for. You are afraid of it. It involves too much, you think, and is too great a risk. . . .

. . . Your Lord says, "He that hath my commandments, and keepeth them, he it is that loveth me; and he that loveth me shall be loved of my Father, and I will love him, and will manifest myself to him. . . ."

He loves you with more than the love of friendship. . . . He has given you all, and He asks for all in return. The slightest reserve will grieve Him to the heart. He spared not Himself, and how can you spare yourself? . . .

Oh, be generous in your self-surrender! Meet His measureless devotion for you with a measureless devotion to Him. . . . Whatever there is of you, let Him have it all. Give up forever everything that is separate from Him. . . .

. . . The obligations of love will be to you its sweetest privileges; and the right you have acquired to lavish the uttermost wealth of abandonment of all that you have upon your Lord will seem to lift you into a region of unspeakable glory. The perfect happiness of perfect obedience will dawn upon your soul, and you will begin to know something of what Jesus meant when He said, "I delight to do thy will, O my God."

Hannah Whitall Smith

PAUSE FOR REFLECTION

Why do you obey God? Out of obligation? Because it is the "right" thing to do? God wants us to obey him simply because we love him! Pray for such a love-filled heart that obedience will be a delight!

MONDAY:
Serving God Brings Joy
John 14:27—15:27

I leave you peace; my peace I give you. I do not give it to you as the world does. So don't let your hearts be troubled or afraid. You heard me say to you, 'I am going, but I am coming back to you.' If you loved me, you should be happy that I am going back to the Father, because he is greater than I am. I have told you this now, before it happens, so that when it happens, you will believe. I will not talk with you much longer, because the ruler of this world is coming. He has no power over me, but the world must know that I love the Father, so I do exactly what the Father told me to do.

"Come now, let us go.

Jesus Is Like a Vine

I am the true vine; my Father is the gardener. He cuts off every branch of mine that does not produce fruit. And he trims and cleans every branch that produces fruit so that it will produce even more fruit. You are already clean because of the words I have spoken to you. Remain in me, and I will remain in you. A branch cannot produce fruit alone but must remain in the vine. In the same way, you cannot produce fruit alone but must remain in me.

"I am the vine, and you are the branches. If any remain in me and I remain in them, they produce much fruit. But without me they can do nothing. If any do not remain in me, they are like a branch that is thrown away and then dies. People pick up dead branches, throw them into the fire, and burn them. If you remain in me and follow my teachings, you can ask anything you want, and it will be given to you. You should produce much fruit and show that you are my followers, which brings glory to my Father. I loved you as the Father loved me. Now remain in my love. I have obeyed my Father's commands, and I remain in his love. In the same way, if you obey my commands, you will remain in my love. I have

told you these things so that you can have the same joy I have and so that your joy will be the fullest possible joy.

"This is my command: Love each other as I have loved you. The greatest love a person can show is to die for his friends. You are my friends if you do what I command you. I no longer call you servants, because a servant does not know what his master is doing. But I call you friends, because I have made known to you everything I heard from my Father. You did not choose me; I chose you. And I gave you this work: to go and produce fruit, fruit that will last. Then the Father will give you anything you ask for in my name. This is my command: Love each other.

Jesus Warns His Followers

*I*f the world hates you, remember that it hated me first. If you belonged to the world, it would love you as it loves its own. But I have chosen you out of the world, so you don't belong to it. That is why the world hates you. Remember what I told you: A servant is not greater than his master. If people did wrong to me, they will do wrong to you, too. And if they obeyed my teaching, they will obey yours, too. They will do all this to you on account of me, because they do not know the One who sent me. If I had not come and spoken to them, they would not be guilty of sin, but now they have no excuse for their sin. Whoever hates me also hates my Father. I did works among them that no one else has ever done. If I had not done these works, they would not be guilty of sin. But now they have seen what I have done, and yet they have hated both me and my Father. But this happened so that what is written in their law would be true: 'They hated me for no reason.'

"I will send you the Helper from the Father; he is the Spirit of truth who comes from the Father. When he comes, he will tell about me, and you also must tell people about me, because you have been with me from the beginning."

*C*reate in me a pure heart, God,
  and make my spirit right again.

Do not send me away from you
  or take your Holy Spirit away from
  me.
Give me back the joy of your salvation.
  Keep me strong by giving me a
  willing spirit.
Then I will teach your ways to those
  who do wrong,
  and sinners will turn back to you.

Psalm 51:10–13

Sing to the LORD, you who do what is
  right;
  honest people should praise him.
Praise the LORD on the harp;
  make music for him on a ten-
  stringed lyre.
Sing a new song to him;
  play well and joyfully.

God's word is true,
  and everything he does is right.
He loves what is right and fair;
  the LORD's love fills the earth.

Happy is the nation whose God is the
  LORD,
  the people he chose for his very own.
The LORD looks down from heaven
  and sees every person.
From his throne he watches
  all who live on earth.
He made their hearts
  and understands everything they
  do.
No king is saved by his great army.
  No warrior escapes by his great
  strength.
Horses can't bring victory;
  they can't save by their strength.
But the LORD looks after those who fear
  him,
  those who put their hope in his love.
He saves them from death
  and spares their lives in times of
  hunger.
So our hope is in the LORD.
  He is our help, our shield to protect
  us.
We rejoice in him,
  because we trust his holy name.
LORD, show your love to us
  as we put our hope in you.

Psalm 33:1–5, 12–22

May my friends sing and shout for joy.
  May they always say, "Praise the
  greatness of the LORD,
  who loves to see his servants do
  well."
I will tell of your goodness
  and will praise you every day.

Psalm 35:27–28

INSIGHTS

If anyone asks the question, "How can I be a happy Christian?" our Lord's answer is very simple: . . . "You cannot have My joy without My life. Abide in Me, and let Me abide in you, and My joy will be in you." . . .

. . . There is no joy like love. There is no joy but love. Christ had just spoken of the Father's love and His own abiding in it, and of His having loved us with that same love. His joy is nothing but the joy of love, of being loved and of loving. It was the joy of receiving His Father's love and abiding in it, and then the joy of passing on that love and pouring it out on sinners. It is this joy He wants us to share: the joy of being loved of the Father and of Him; the joy of in our turn loving and living for those around us. . . .

. . . How sad that we should so need to be reminded that as God alone is the fountain of all joy, "God our exceeding joy," the only way to be perfectly happy is to have as much of God, as much of His will and fellowship, as possible! Religion is meant to be in everyday life a thing of unspeakable joy. And why do so many complain that it is not so? Because they do not believe that there is no joy like the joy of abiding in Christ and in His love, and being branches through whom He can pour out His love on a dying world.

Andrew Murray

PAUSE FOR REFLECTION

In what ways do you think the peace that Jesus promises (John 14:27) differs from the world's peace? What does Jesus say about the relationship between love, joy, and obedience to God?

TUESDAY:
God Cares for Those Who Serve Him
John 16:1–28

N E W   T E S T A M E N T   R E A D I N G

I have told you these things to keep you from giving up. People will put you out of their synagogues. Yes, the time is coming when those who kill you will think they are offering service to God. They will do this because they have not known the Father and they have not known me. I have told you these things now so that when the time comes you will remember that I warned you.

The Work of the Holy Spirit

I did not tell you these things at the beginning, because I was with you then. Now I am going back to the One who sent me. But none of you asks me, 'Where are you going?' Your hearts are filled with sadness because I have told you these things. But I tell you the truth, it is better for you that I go away. When I go away, I will send the Helper to you. If I do not go away, the Helper will not come. When the Helper comes, he will prove to the people of the world the truth about sin, about being right with God, and about judgment. He will prove to them that sin is not believing in me. He will prove to them that being right with God comes from my going to the Father and not being seen anymore. And the Helper will prove to them that judgment happened when the ruler of this world was judged.

"I have many more things to say to you, but they are too much for you now. But when the Spirit of truth comes, he will lead you into all truth. He will not speak his own words, but he will speak only what he hears, and he will tell you what is to come. The Spirit of truth will bring glory to me, because he will take what I have to say and tell it to you. All that the Father has is mine. That is why I said that the Spirit will take what I have to say and tell it to you.

Sadness Will Become Happiness

*A*fter a little while you will not see me, and then after a little while you will see me again."

Some of the followers said to each other, "What does Jesus mean when he says, 'After a little while you will not see me, and then after a little while you will see me again'? And what does he mean when he says, 'Because I am going to the Father'?" They also asked, "What does he mean by 'a little while'? We don't understand what he is saying."

Jesus saw that the followers wanted to ask him about this, so he said to them, "Are you asking each other what I meant when I said, 'After a little while you will not see me, and then after a little while you will see me again'? I tell you the truth, you will cry and be sad, but the world will be happy. You will be sad, but your sadness will become joy. When a woman gives birth to a baby, she has pain, because her time has come. But when her baby is born, she forgets the pain, because she is so happy that a child has been born into the world. It is the same with you. Now you are sad, but I will see you again and you will be happy, and no one will take away your joy. In that day you will not ask me for anything. I tell you the truth, my Father will give you anything you ask for in my name. Until now you have not asked for anything in my name. Ask and you will receive, so that your joy will be the fullest possible joy.

Victory over the World

I have told you these things, using stories that hide the meaning. But the time will come when I will not use stories like that to tell you things; I will speak to you in plain words about the Father. In that day you will ask the Father for things in my name. I mean, I will not need to ask the Father for you. The Father himself loves you. He loves you because you loved me and believed that I came from God. I came from the Father into the world. Now I am leaving the world and going back to the Father."

O L D   T E S T A M E N T   R E A D I N G

*P*eople of Jacob, why do you complain?

268

People of Israel, why do you say,
"The LORD does not see what happens
    to me;
he does not care if I am treated
    fairly"?
Surely you know.
Surely you have heard.
The LORD is the God who lives forever,
    who created all the world.
He does not become tired or need to
    rest.
    No one can understand how great
    his wisdom is.
He gives strength to those who are tired
    and more power to those who are
    weak.
Even children become tired and need
    to rest,
    and young people trip and fall.
But the people who trust the LORD will
    become strong again.
They will rise up as an eagle in the sky;
    they will run and not need rest;
    they will walk and not become tired.
Isaiah 40:27–31

LORD, teach me your ways,
    and guide me to do what is right
    because I have enemies.
Do not hand me over to my enemies,
    because they tell lies about me
    and say they will hurt me.

I truly believe
    I will live to see the LORD's goodness.
Wait for the LORD's help.
    Be strong and brave,
    and wait for the LORD's help.
Psalm 27:11–14

Trust the LORD and do good.
    Live in the land and feed on truth.
Enjoy serving the LORD,
    and he will give you what you want.
Depend on the LORD;
    trust him, and he will take care of
    you.
Then your goodness will shine like the
    sun,
    and your fairness like the noonday
    sun.
Psalm 37:3–6

The LORD does not listen to the
    wicked,
but he hears the prayers of those
    who do right.
Proverbs 15:29

INSIGHTS

*You walk your daughter down the aisle.
"When did she grow up?"*

*You wake up in an emergency room to the
beeping of a machine and find wires suction-
cupped to your chest.*

*Be the event pleasant or painful, the re-
sult is the same. Reality breaks through the
papier-mâché mask and screams at you like
a Marine drill sergeant. "You are getting old!
You are going to die! You can't be someone
you are not!". . .*

*Jesus does his best work at such moments.
Just when the truth about life sinks in, his
truth starts to surface. He takes us by the hand
and dares us not to sweep the facts under the
rug but to confront them with him at our side.*

*Aging? A necessary process to pass on to a
better world.*

Death? Merely a brief passage, a tunnel.

*Self? Designed and created for a purpose,
purchased by God himself.*

There, was that so bad?

*Funerals, divorces, illnesses, and stays in
the hospital—you can't lie about life at such
times. Maybe that's why he's always present
at such moments.*

*The next time you find yourself alone in a
dark alley facing the undeniables of life, don't
cover them with a blanket, or ignore them
with a nervous grin. Don't turn up the TV
and pretend they aren't there. Instead, stand
still, whisper his name, and listen. He is
nearer than you think.*

Max Lucado

PAUSE   FOR   REFLECTION

*Who did Jesus promise to send to his follow-
ers? What would he do for them? Why does
God love Jesus' followers? What does God do
for those he loves? How is he comforting and
caring for you today?*

WEDNESDAY:

God Protects Those Who Follow Him

John 16:29—17:20

NEW TESTAMENT READING

*T*hen the followers of Jesus said, "You are speaking clearly to us now and are not using stories that are hard to understand. We can see now that you know all things. You can answer a person's question even before it is asked. This makes us believe you came from God."

Jesus answered, "So now you believe? Listen to me; a time is coming when you will be scattered, each to his own home. That time is now here. You will leave me alone, but I am never really alone, because the Father is with me.

"I told you these things so that you can have peace in me. In this world you will have trouble, but be brave! I have defeated the world."

Jesus Prays for His Followers

*A*fter Jesus said these things, he looked toward heaven and prayed, "Father, the time has come. Give glory to your Son so that the Son can give glory to you. You gave the Son power over all people so that the Son could give eternal life to all those you gave him. And this is eternal life: that people know you, the only true God, and that they know Jesus Christ, the One you sent. Having finished the work you gave me to do, I brought you glory on earth. And now, Father, give me glory with you; give me the glory I had with you before the world was made.

"I showed what you are like to those you gave me from the world. They belonged to you, and you gave them to me, and they have obeyed your teaching. Now they know that everything you gave me comes from you. I gave them the teachings you gave me, and they accepted them. They knew that I truly came from you, and they believed that you sent me. I am praying for them. I am not praying for people in the world but for those you gave me, because they are yours. All I have is yours, and all you have is mine. And my glory is shown through them. I am coming to you; I will not stay in the world any longer. But they are still in the world. Holy Father, keep them safe by the power of your name, the name you gave me, so that they will be one, just as you and I are one. While I was with them, I kept them safe by the power of your name, the name you gave me. I protected them, and only one of them, the one worthy of destruction, was lost so that the Scripture would come true.

"I am coming to you now. But I pray these things while I am still in the world so that these followers can have all of my joy in them. I have given them your teaching. And the world has hated them, because they don't belong to the world, just as I don't belong to the world. I am not asking you to take them out of the world but to keep them safe from the Evil One. They don't belong to the world, just as I don't belong to the world. Make them ready for your service through your truth; your teaching is truth. I have sent them into the world, just as you sent me into the world. For their sake, I am making myself ready to serve so that they can be ready for their service of the truth.

"I pray for these followers, but I am also praying for all those who will believe in me because of their teaching."

OLD TESTAMENT READING

*T*hose who go to God Most High for
    safety
  will be protected by the Almighty.
I will say to the LORD, "You are my
    place of safety and protection.
  You are my God and I trust you."

God will save you from hidden traps
  and from deadly diseases.
He will cover you with his feathers,
  and under his wings you can hide.
  His truth will be your shield and
    protection.
You will not fear any danger by night
  or an arrow during the day.
You will not be afraid of diseases that
    come in the dark
  or sickness that strikes at noon.

At your side one thousand people may
die,
　or even ten thousand right beside
　　you,
but you will not be hurt.
You will only watch
　and see the wicked punished.

The LORD is your protection;
　you have made God Most High your
　　place of safety.
Nothing bad will happen to you;
　no disaster will come to your home.
He has put his angels in charge of you
　to watch over you wherever you go.
They will catch you in their hands
　so that you will not hit your foot on a
　　rock.
You will walk on lions and cobras;
　you will step on strong lions and
　　snakes.

The LORD says, "Whoever loves me, I
　will save.
I will protect those who know me.
They will call to me, and I will answer
　them.
I will be with them in trouble;
I will rescue them and honor them.
I will give them a long, full life,
　and they will see how I can save."

Psalm 91:1–16

*I*srael, you are blessed!
　No one else is like you,
　because you are a people saved by
　　the LORD.
He is your shield and helper,
　your glorious sword.
Your enemies will be afraid of you,
　and you will walk all over their holy
　　places."

Deuteronomy 33:29

INSIGHTS

*S*omeone has said that Psalm 91 is an ex-
*panded commentary on the great cry of the
apostle Paul: "If God is for us, who can be
against us?" (Rom. 8:31). What is the message of the Psalm? . . .
　. . . God promises us shelter, covering,
and comprehensive protection based on His*

*very nature. Those who claim the promise
and dwell in the shelter of the Most High
will rest in the shadow of the Almighty. God
offers us security, says the psalmist, by providing secret shelter. . . .
　. . . If we make the choice to dwell in His
secret place, as the psalmist puts it, then God's
response will be to treat us as His guests. . . .
Almighty God is saying, in effect, "When you
dwell in My most secret place, I promise to
be your divine host with the sacred responsibility of covering and caring for you." When
we deposit our trust in Him, then He guarantees He will give us His sheltering protection against all that harms us—until our duty
is done and our race is finished in His service.
　We will still go through trials. That is part
of life. But . . . if we are "dwelling" in communion with God, if we are accepting the
shelter only He can give, then we will be safe
until our work for the Lord is over, until our
time on this earth is done. . . .
　Our security does not rest in our weak,
feeble, timid, fragile, finite humanity—not for
a moment. Our security is in clinging to a
God who takes care of those who take the
conscious step of faith to believe.*

Joel Gregory

PAUSE　FOR　REFLECTION

*W*hy did Jesus pray for protection for all of
*his followers? What kind of protection did
Jesus want for his followers? What assurances
does Psalm 91 give to you? As you read Jesus'
prayer, do you feel his personal love and care
for you? Thank him.*

THURSDAY:
The Unity of All Believers
John 17:21—18:18

N E W   T E S T A M E N T   R E A D I N G

*F*ather, I pray that they can be one. As you are in me and I am in you, I pray that they can also be one in us. Then the world will believe that you sent me. I have given these people the glory that you gave me so that they can be one, just as you and I are one. I will be in them and you will be in me so that they will be completely one. Then the world will know that you sent me and that you loved them just as much as you loved me.

"Father, I want these people that you gave me to be with me where I am. I want them to see my glory, which you gave me because you loved me before the world was made. Father, you are the One who is good. The world does not know you, but I know you, and these people know you sent me. I showed them what you are like, and I will show them again. Then they will have the same love that you have for me, and I will live in them."

Jesus Is Arrested

*W*hen Jesus finished praying, he went with his followers across the Kidron Valley. On the other side there was a garden, and Jesus and his followers went into it.

Judas knew where this place was, because Jesus met there often with his followers. Judas was the one who turned against Jesus. So Judas came there with a group of soldiers and some guards from the leading priests and the Pharisees. They were carrying torches, lanterns, and weapons.

Knowing everything that would happen to him, Jesus went out and asked, "Who is it you are looking for?"

They answered, "Jesus from Nazareth."

"I am he," Jesus said. (Judas, the one who turned against Jesus, was standing there with them.) When Jesus said, "I am he," they moved back and fell to the ground.

Jesus asked them again, "Who is it you are looking for?"

They said, "Jesus of Nazareth."

"I told you that I am he," Jesus said. "So if you are looking for me, let the others go." This happened so that the words Jesus said before would come true: "I have not lost any of the ones you gave me."

Simon Peter, who had a sword, pulled it out and struck the servant of the high priest, cutting off his right ear. (The servant's name was Malchus.) Jesus said to Peter, "Put your sword back. Shouldn't I drink the cup the Father gave me?"

Jesus Is Brought Before Annas

*T*hen the soldiers with their commander and the Jewish guards arrested Jesus. They tied him and led him first to Annas, the father-in-law of Caiaphas, the high priest that year. Caiaphas was the one who told the Jews that it would be better if one man died for all the people.

Peter Says He Doesn't Know Jesus

*S*imon Peter and another one of Jesus' followers went along after Jesus. This follower knew the high priest, so he went with Jesus into the high priest's courtyard. But Peter waited outside near the door. The follower who knew the high priest came back outside, spoke to the girl at the door, and brought Peter inside. The girl at the door said to Peter, "Aren't you also one of that man's followers?"

Peter answered, "No, I am not!"

It was cold, so the servants and guards had built a fire and were standing around it, warming themselves. Peter also was standing with them, warming himself.

O L D   T E S T A M E N T   R E A D I N G

*I*t is good and pleasant
　　when God's people live together in
　　　peace!
It is like perfumed oil poured on the
　　· priest's head
　　and running down his beard.
It ran down Aaron's beard
　　and on to the collar of his robes.
It is like the dew of Mount Hermon
　　falling on the hills of Jerusalem.

There the LORD gives his blessing
  of life forever.

Psalm 133:1–3

I will put a mark on some of the people, and I will send some of these saved people to the nations: to Tarshish, Libya, Lud (the land of archers), Tubal, Greece, and all the faraway lands. These people have never heard about what I have done nor seen my glory. So the saved people will tell the nations about my glory. And they will bring all your fellow Israelites from all nations to my holy mountain in Jerusalem. Your fellow Israelites will come on horses, donkeys, and camels and in chariots and wagons. They will be like the grain offerings that the people bring in clean containers to the Temple," says the LORD. "And I will choose even some of these people to be priests and Levites," says the LORD.

"I will make new heavens and the new earth, which will last forever," says the LORD. "In the same way, your names and your children will always be with me. All people will come to worship me every Sabbath and every New Moon," says the LORD.

Isaiah 66:19–23

*S*o Abram, his wife, and Lot left Egypt, taking everything they owned, and traveled to southern Canaan. Abram was very rich in cattle, silver, and gold.

He left southern Canaan and went back to Bethel where he had camped before, between Bethel and Ai, and where he had built an altar. So he worshiped the LORD there.

During this time Lot was traveling with Abram, and Lot also had flocks, herds, and tents. Abram and Lot had so many animals that the land could not support both of them together, so Abram's herdsmen and Lot's herdsmen began to argue. The Canaanites and the Perizzites were living in the land at this time.

Abram said to Lot, "There should be no arguing between you and me, or between your herdsmen and mine, because we are brothers. We should separate. The whole land is there in front of you. If you go to the left, I will go to the right. If you go to the right, I will go to the left."

Genesis 13:1–9

INSIGHTS

Our God is a God of unity. It is against His nature to work in the midst of division. That is why in His high priestly prayer (John 17) Jesus repeatedly prayed that "they may be one, just as We are one." Jesus knew that Satan would try to destroy the church through disunity. Thus, He earnestly prayed that the church would be a unified body through which God could accomplish His work.

God's insistence on unity is why so much of the New Testament gives instruction for maintaining the unity of the church. For example, 1 Corinthians 14:40 instructs the church to do all things properly and in order. Ephesians 4:3 exhorts believers to be "diligent to preserve the unity of the Spirit in the bond of peace." . . .

Satan recognizes the power of God's people. He knows that we are the only ones in the world who can keep him from messing up God's plan. So he is desperate to stop us. That is why the church is always under attack from Satan. He wants to get choir folks fighting each other. He wants to get church leaders fighting each other. He wants to get members fighting each other. He wants husbands and wives to be fighting each other. If he succeeds, God's people become ineffective.

As God's people, we must overcome disunity before we can fight any other battles. When we see disunity, we should not join Satan's side and keep it going. We should stop, recognize the source, and act under God's authority to restore our unity so He can continue His work through us.

Anthony Evans

ACTION POINT

Why does Jesus want his followers to be one? In what ways does disunity limit God's work through your life? Prayerfully read Psalm 133 and begin working for the unity that is such a precious blessing to God.

F R I D A Y:

God Is Truth

John 18:19—19:3

The High Priest Questions Jesus

The high priest asked Jesus questions about his followers and his teaching. Jesus answered, "I have spoken openly to everyone. I have always taught in synagogues and in the Temple, where all the Jews come together. I never said anything in secret. So why do you question me? Ask the people who heard my teaching. They know what I said."

When Jesus said this, one of the guards standing there hit him. The guard said, "Is that the way you answer the high priest?"

Jesus answered him, "If I said something wrong, then show what it was. But if what I said is true, why do you hit me?"

Then Annas sent Jesus, who was still tied, to Caiaphas the high priest.

Peter Again Denies He Knows Jesus

As Simon Peter was standing and warming himself, they said to him, "Aren't you one of that man's followers?"

Peter said it was not true; he said, "No, I am not."

One of the servants of the high priest was there. This servant was a relative of the man whose ear Peter had cut off. The servant said, "Didn't I see you with him in the garden?"

Again Peter said it wasn't true. At once a rooster crowed.

Jesus Is Brought Before Pilate

Early in the morning they led Jesus from Caiaphas's house to the Roman governor's palace. They would not go inside the palace, because they did not want to make themselves unclean; they wanted to eat the Passover meal. So Pilate went outside to them and asked, "What charges do you bring against this man?"

They answered, "If he were not a criminal, we wouldn't have brought him to you."

Pilate said to them, "Take him yourselves and judge him by your own law."

"But we are not allowed to put anyone to death," the Jews answered. (This happened so that what Jesus said about how he would die would come true.)

Then Pilate went back inside the palace and called Jesus to him and asked, "Are you the king of the Jews?"

Jesus said, "Is that your own question, or did others tell you about me?"

Pilate answered, "I am not Jewish. It was your own people and their leading priests who handed you over to me. What have you done wrong?"

Jesus answered, "My kingdom does not belong to this world. If it belonged to this world, my servants would fight so that I would not be given over to the Jews. But my kingdom is from another place."

Pilate said, "So you are a king!"

Jesus answered, "You are the one saying I am a king. This is why I was born and came into the world: to tell people the truth. And everyone who belongs to the truth listens to me."

Pilate said, "What is truth?" After he said this, he went out to the Jews again and said to them, "I find nothing against this man. But it is your custom that I free one prisoner to you at Passover time. Do you want me to free the 'king of the Jews'?"

They shouted back, "No, not him! Let Barabbas go free!" (Barabbas was a robber.)

Then Pilate ordered that Jesus be taken away and whipped. The soldiers made a crown from some thorny branches and put it on Jesus' head and put a purple robe around him. Then they came to him many times and said, "Hail, King of the Jews!" and hit him in the face.

All you nations, praise the LORD.
  All you people, praise him
because the LORD loves us very much,
  and his truth is everlasting.

Praise the LORD!

Psalm 117:1–2

LORD, you do what is right,
  and your laws are fair.

The rules you commanded are right
and completely trustworthy.
I am so upset I am worn out,
because my enemies have forgotten
your words.
Your promises are proven,
so I, your servant, love them.
I am unimportant and hated,
but I have not forgotten your orders.
Your goodness continues forever,
and your teachings are true.

Psalm 119:137–142

God's word is true,
and everything he does is right.
He loves what is right and fair;
the LORD's love fills the earth.

Psalm 33:4–5

LORD, I trust in you;
let me never be disgraced.
Save me because you do what is right.
I give you my life.
Save me, LORD, God of truth.

Psalm 31:1, 5

The LORD created the heavens.
He is the God who formed the earth
and made it.
He did not want it to be empty,
but he wanted life on the earth.
This is what the LORD says:
"I am the LORD. There is no other
God.
I did not speak in secret
or hide my words in some dark
place.
I did not tell the family of Jacob
to look for me in empty places.
I am the LORD, and I speak the truth;
I say what is right.

"Tell these people to come to me.
Let them talk about these things
together.
Who told you long ago that this would
happen?
Who told about it long ago?
I, the LORD, said these things.
There is no other God besides me.
I am the only good God. I am the Savior.
There is no other God."

Isaiah 45:18–19, 21

What is truth? I have often wondered how Pilate asked this question. What was his tone of voice? What kind of expression did he have on his face? Was the question raised in jest? Was it cynical? Was Pilate pensive for a moment? We don't really know. If Pilate was momentarily concerned for truth, his mood soon gave way to a spirit of expediency. If he cared about knowing the truth, he certainly didn't care much about doing the truth. . . .

To declare that Jesus was without fault and then minutes later to turn Him over to a barbarous mob was to slaughter the truth. Pilate judged the Truth. He sentenced the Truth. He scourged the Truth. He mocked the Truth. He crucified the Truth.

The irony is that at the very moment he asked his question "What is truth?" he was staring at the pure incarnation of Truth. The One who is the Truth had just said to him, "Everyone who is of the truth hears My voice."

Pilate missed that voice. The words bounced off his ears. He was not "of the truth."

R. C. Sproul

How ironic that Pilate was so close to the God of truth, yet failed to understand truth. What claims to truth does God make? Does he make his truth available to people? How? Pray that you will draw close to God and trust his truth.

WEEKEND:

All Power on Earth Is Given by God

John 19:4–27

N E W   T E S T A M E N T   R E A D I N G

*A*gain Pilate came out and said to them, "Look, I am bringing Jesus out to you. I want you to know that I find nothing against him." So Jesus came out, wearing the crown of thorns and the purple robe. Pilate said to them, "Here is the man!"

When the leading priests and the guards saw Jesus, they shouted, "Crucify him! Crucify him!"

But Pilate answered, "Crucify him yourselves, because I find nothing against him."

The Jews answered, "We have a law that says he should die, because he said he is the Son of God."

When Pilate heard this, he was even more afraid. He went back inside the palace and asked Jesus, "Where do you come from?" But Jesus did not answer him. Pilate said, "You refuse to speak to me? Don't you know I have power to set you free and power to have you crucified?"

Jesus answered, "The only power you have over me is the power given to you by God. The man who turned me in to you is guilty of a greater sin."

After this, Pilate tried to let Jesus go. But the Jews cried out, "Anyone who makes himself king is against Caesar. If you let this man go, you are no friend of Caesar."

When Pilate heard what they were saying, he brought Jesus out and sat down on the judge's seat at the place called The Stone Pavement. (In the Jewish language the name is Gabbatha.) It was about noon on Preparation Day of Passover week. Pilate said to the Jews, "Here is your king!"

They shouted, "Take him away! Take him away! Crucify him!"

Pilate asked them, "Do you want me to crucify your king?"

The leading priests answered, "The only king we have is Caesar."

So Pilate handed Jesus over to them to be crucified.

Jesus Is Crucified

*T*he soldiers took charge of Jesus. Carrying his own cross, Jesus went out to a place called The Place of the Skull, which in the Jewish language is called Golgotha. There they crucified Jesus. They also crucified two other men, one on each side, with Jesus in the middle. Pilate wrote a sign and put it on the cross. It read: JESUS OF NAZARETH, THE KING OF THE JEWS. The sign was written in the Jewish language, in Latin, and in Greek. Many of the Jews read the sign, because the place where Jesus was crucified was near the city. The leading Jewish priests said to Pilate, "Don't write, 'The King of the Jews.' But write, 'This man said, "I am the King of the Jews."'"

Pilate answered, "What I have written, I have written."

After the soldiers crucified Jesus, they took his clothes and divided them into four parts, with each soldier getting one part. They also took his long shirt, which was all one piece of cloth, woven from top to bottom. So the soldiers said to each other, "We should not tear this into parts. Let's throw lots to see who will get it." This happened so that this Scripture would come true:

"They divided my clothes among them,
    and they threw lots for my clothing."

Psalm 22:18

So the soldiers did this.

Standing near his cross were Jesus' mother, his mother's sister, Mary the wife of Clopas, and Mary Magdalene. When Jesus saw his mother and the follower he loved standing nearby, he said to his mother, "Dear woman, here is your son." Then he said to the follower, "Here is your mother." From that time on, the follower took her to live in his home.

O L D   T E S T A M E N T   R E A D I N G

*T*he people of Judah and Jerusalem met in front of the new courtyard in the Temple of the LORD. Then Jehoshaphat stood up, and he said, "LORD, God of our ancestors, you are the God in heaven. You rule over all the kingdoms of the nations. You have power and strength, so no one can stand against you.

2 Chronicles 20:5–6

*H*ezekiah put army commanders over the people and met with them at the open place near the city gate. Hezekiah encouraged them, saying, "Be strong and brave. Don't be afraid or worried because of the king of Assyria or his large army. There is a greater power with us than with him. He only has men, but we have the LORD our God to help us and to fight our battles." The people were encouraged by the words of Hezekiah king of Judah.

2 Chronicles 32:6–8

*T*ell them to give this message to their masters: 'The LORD All-Powerful, the God of Israel, says: "Tell your masters: I made the earth, its people, and all its animals with my great power and strength. I can give the earth to anyone I want. Now I have given all these lands to Nebuchadnezzar king of Babylon, my servant. I will make even the wild animals obey him. All nations will serve Nebuchadnezzar and his son and grandson. Then the time will come for Babylon to be defeated, and many nations and great kings will make Babylon their servant."'"

Jeremiah 27:4–7

*A*ll these things happened to King Nebuchadnezzar. Twelve months later as he was walking on the roof of his palace in Babylon, he said, "I have built this great Babylon as my royal home. I built it by my power to show my glory and my majesty."

The words were still in his mouth when a voice from heaven said, "King Nebuchadnezzar, these things will happen to you: Your royal power has been taken away from you. You will be forced away from people. You will live with the wild animals and will be fed grass like an ox. Seven years will pass before you learn this lesson: The Most High God rules over every kingdom on earth and gives those kingdoms to anyone he chooses."

Immediately the words came true.

Nebuchadnezzar was forced to go away from people, and he began eating grass like an ox. He became wet from dew. His hair grew long like the feathers of an eagle, and his nails grew like the claws of a bird.

Daniel 4:28–33

INSIGHTS

*O*ur sovereign Lord . . . exerts control over His entire universe from beginning to end! His sovereignty means that He either causes or He allows all things to happen that do happen. He is absolutely independent, subject to no one, and influenced by no one. Despite the suffering, violence, and filth of this world, God remains in control—whether or not we acknowledge him. Before time began, God was in control. He has ruled over all creation ever since He created heaven and earth. . . .

The Israelites must have wondered whether God was in control, as they spent four hundred years of bondage in Egypt. Driven day after day by cruel taskmasters, they surely asked, "If there is a God, where is He?" . . . They probably reasoned that either there is no God, or that God did not have the power to stop the madness. But what happened? The sovereign God who controls every circumstance led Israel out of Egypt with mighty demonstrations of His power! Israel never forgot His deliverance. The entire world was shaken! Nations trembled at the prospect of confronting God's people.

Elliot Johnson/Al Schierbaum

PAUSE FOR REFLECTION

*W*ho holds the only real power there is? Why does God give power to certain people for a time? What happens to those who think their power is their own? Submit your heart to his power today!

MONDAY:
Rejoice! Jesus Has Risen
John 19:28—20:9

NEW TESTAMENT READING

Jesus Dies

*A*fter this, Jesus knew that everything had been done. So that the Scripture would come true, he said, "I am thirsty." There was a jar full of vinegar there, so the soldiers soaked a sponge in it, put the sponge on a branch of a hyssop plant, and lifted it to Jesus' mouth. When Jesus tasted the vinegar, he said, "It is finished." Then he bowed his head and died.

This day was Preparation Day, and the next day was a special Sabbath day. Since the Jews did not want the bodies to stay on the cross on the Sabbath day, they asked Pilate to order that the legs of the men be broken and the bodies be taken away. So the soldiers came and broke the legs of the first man on the cross beside Jesus. Then they broke the legs of the man on the other cross beside Jesus. But when the soldiers came to Jesus and saw that he was already dead, they did not break his legs. But one of the soldiers stuck his spear into Jesus' side, and at once blood and water came out. (The one who saw this happen is the one who told us this, and whatever he says is true. And he knows that he tells the truth, and he tells it so that you might believe.) These things happened to make the Scripture come true: "Not one of his bones will be broken." And another Scripture says, "They will look at the one they stabbed."

Jesus Is Buried

*L*ater, Joseph from Arimathea asked Pilate if he could take the body of Jesus. (Joseph was a secret follower of Jesus, because he was afraid of the Jews.) Pilate gave his permission, so Joseph came and took Jesus' body away. Nicodemus, who earlier had come to Jesus at night, went with Joseph. He brought about seventy-five pounds of myrrh and aloes. These two men took Jesus' body and wrapped it with the spices in pieces of linen cloth, which is how the Jewish people bury the dead. In the place where Jesus was crucified, there was a garden. In the garden was a new tomb that had never been used before. The men laid Jesus in that tomb because it was nearby, and the Jews were preparing to start their Sabbath day.

Jesus' Tomb Is Empty

*E*arly on the first day of the week, Mary Magdalene went to the tomb while it was still dark. When she saw that the large stone had been moved away from the tomb, she ran to Simon Peter and the follower whom Jesus loved. Mary said, "They have taken the Lord out of the tomb, and we don't know where they have put him."

So Peter and the other follower started for the tomb. They were both running, but the other follower ran faster than Peter and reached the tomb first. He bent down and looked in and saw the strips of linen cloth lying there, but he did not go in. Then following him, Simon Peter arrived and went into the tomb and saw the strips of linen lying there. He also saw the cloth that had been around Jesus' head, which was folded up and laid in a different place from the strips of linen. Then the other follower, who had reached the tomb first, also went in. He saw and believed. (They did not yet understand from the Scriptures that Jesus must rise from the dead.)

OLD TESTAMENT READING

*C*lap your hands, all you people.
  Shout to God with joy.
The LORD Most High is wonderful.
  He is the great King over all the earth!
He defeated nations for us
  and put them under our control.
He chose the land we would inherit.
  We are the children of Jacob, whom he loved. *Selah*
God has risen with a shout of joy;
  the LORD has risen as the trumpets sounded.

Sing praises to God. Sing praises.
  Sing praises to our King. Sing praises.

God is King of all the earth,
  so sing a song of praise to him.
God is King over the nations.
  God sits on his holy throne.
The leaders of the nations meet
  with the people of the God of
    Abraham,
because the leaders of the earth belong
    to God.
  He is supreme.

Psalm 47:1–9

*B*ut it was the Lord who decided
  to crush him and make him suffer.
  The Lord made his life a penalty
    offering,
but he will still see his descendants and
    live a long life.
  He will complete the things the Lord
    wants him to do.
"After his soul suffers many things,
  he will see life and be satisfied.
My good servant will make many
    people right with God;
  he will carry away their sins.
For this reason I will make him a great
    man among people,
  and he will share in all things with
    those who are strong.
He willingly gave his life
  and was treated like a criminal.
But he carried away the sins of many
    people
  and asked forgiveness for those who
    sinned."

Isaiah 53:10–12

I know that my Defender lives,
  and in the end he will stand upon the
    earth.
Even after my skin has been destroyed,
  in my flesh I will see God.
I will see him myself;
  I will see him with my very own
    eyes.
  How my heart wants that to happen!

Job 19:25–27

INSIGHTS

*C*hrist is risen:
  The world below lies desolate.

Christ is risen:
  The spirits of evil are fallen.
Christ is risen:
  The angels of God are rejoicing.
Christ is risen:
  The tombs of the dead are empty.
Christ is risen indeed from the dead,
  The first of the sleepers.
Glory and power are his forever and ever.
  Amen.

Hippolytus of Rome

ACTION POINT

*W*hen Mary revealed the stunning news that Jesus was no longer in the tomb, the disciples took off running to see it for themselves! Does the realization that Jesus is truly alive set your heart racing? Ask God to renew your excitement and joy in Jesus' resurrection.

TUESDAY:
Thomas Wasn't Alone in His Unbelief
John 20:10—21:3

NEW TESTAMENT READING

Jesus Appears to Mary Magdalene

Then the followers went back home. But Mary stood outside the tomb, crying. As she was crying, she bent down and looked inside the tomb. She saw two angels dressed in white, sitting where Jesus' body had been, one at the head and one at the feet.

They asked her, "Woman, why are you crying?"

She answered, "They have taken away my Lord, and I don't know where they have put him." When Mary said this, she turned around and saw Jesus standing there, but she did not know it was Jesus.

Jesus asked her, "Woman, why are you crying? Whom are you looking for?"

Thinking he was the gardener, she said to him, "Did you take him away, sir? Tell me where you put him, and I will get him."

Jesus said to her, "Mary."

Mary turned toward Jesus and said in the Jewish language, "Rabboni." (This means Teacher.)

Jesus said to her, "Don't hold on to me, because I have not yet gone up to the Father. But go to my brothers and tell them, 'I am going back to my Father and your Father, to my God and your God.'"

Mary Magdalene went and said to the followers, "I saw the Lord!" And she told them what Jesus had said to her.

Jesus Appears to His Followers

When it was evening on the first day of the week, the followers were together. The doors were locked, because they were afraid of the Jews. Then Jesus came and stood right in the middle of them and said, "Peace be with you." After he said this, he showed them his hands and his side. The followers were thrilled when they saw the Lord.

Then Jesus said again, "Peace be with you. As the Father sent me, I now send you." After he said this, he breathed on them and said, "Receive the Holy Spirit. If you forgive anyone his sins, they are forgiven. If you don't forgive them, they are not forgiven."

Jesus Appears to Thomas

Thomas (called Didymus), who was one of the twelve, was not with them when Jesus came. The other followers kept telling Thomas, "We saw the Lord."

But Thomas said, "I will not believe it until I see the nail marks in his hands and put my finger where the nails were and put my hand into his side."

A week later the followers were in the house again, and Thomas was with them. The doors were locked, but Jesus came in and stood right in the middle of them. He said, "Peace be with you." Then he said to Thomas, "Put your finger here, and look at my hands. Put your hand here in my side. Stop being an unbeliever and believe."

Thomas said to him, "My Lord and my God!"

Then Jesus told him, "You believe because you see me. Those who believe without seeing me will be truly happy."

Why John Wrote This Book

Jesus did many other miracles in the presence of his followers that are not written in this book. But these are written so that you may believe that Jesus is the Christ, the Son of God. Then, by believing, you may have life through his name.

Jesus Appears to Seven Followers

Later, Jesus showed himself to his followers again—this time at Lake Galilee. This is how he showed himself: Some of the followers were together: Simon Peter, Thomas (called Didymus), Nathanael from Cana in Galilee, the two sons of Zebedee, and two other followers. Simon Peter said, "I am going out to fish."

The others said, "We will go with you." So they went out and got into the boat. They fished that night but caught nothing.

*T*he angel of the LORD appeared to Gideon and said, "The LORD is with you, mighty warrior!"

Then Gideon said, "Sir, if the LORD is with us, why are we having so much trouble? Where are the miracles our ancestors told us he did when the LORD brought them out of Egypt? But now he has left us and has handed us over to the Midianites."

The LORD turned to Gideon and said, "Go with your strength and save Israel from the Midianites. I am the one who is sending you."

But Gideon answered, "Lord, how can I save Israel? My family group is the weakest in Manasseh, and I am the least important member of my family."

The LORD answered him, "I will be with you. It will seem as if the Midianites you are fighting are only one man."

Then Gideon said to the LORD, "If you are pleased with me, give me proof that it is really you talking with me. Please wait here until I come back to you. Let me bring my offering and set it in front of you."

And the LORD said, "I will wait until you return."

So Gideon went in and cooked a young goat, and with twenty quarts of flour, made bread without yeast. Then he put the meat into a basket and the broth into a pot. He brought them out and gave them to the angel under the oak tree.

The angel of God said to Gideon, "Put the meat and the bread without yeast on that rock over there. Then pour the broth on them." And Gideon did as he was told. The angel of the LORD touched the meat and the bread with the end of the stick that was in his hand. Then fire jumped up from the rock and completely burned up the meat and the bread! And the angel of the LORD disappeared! Then Gideon understood he had been talking to the angel of the LORD. So Gideon cried out, "Lord GOD! I have seen the angel of the LORD face to face!"

Then Gideon said to God, "You said you would help me save Israel. I will put some wool on the threshing floor. If there is dew only on the wool but all of the ground is dry,

then I will know that you will use me to save Israel, as you said." And that is just what happened. When Gideon got up early the next morning and squeezed the wool, he got a full bowl of water from it.

Then Gideon said to God, "Don't be angry with me if I ask just one more thing. Please let me make one more test. Let only the wool be dry while the ground around it gets wet with dew." That night God did that very thing. Just the wool was dry, but the ground around it was wet with dew.

Judges 6:12–22, 36–40

---

*G*ive your whole being to God without holding back and without doubting. He will prove himself to you, and work in you that which is pleasing in His sight through Jesus Christ. Keep His ways as you know them in the Word. Keep His ways, as nature teaches them, in always doing what appears right. Keep His ways as providence points them out. Keep His ways as the Holy Spirit suggests. Do not think of waiting on God while you say you are not willing to walk in His path. However weak you feel, only be willing, and he who has worked to will, will work to do by His power. . . .

. . . So come with every temptation you feel in yourself, every memory of unwillingness, unwatchfulness, unfaithfulness, and all that causes your unceasing self-condemnation. Put your powerlessness in God's almighty power, and find in waiting on God your deliverance.

Andrew Murray

---

*H*ow does God treat those who doubt? What did he do for Gideon, for Mary, for Thomas? What was their response? Do you struggle with unbelief? Ask God to prove himself to you; his answer will overwhelm you!

WEDNESDAY:

God's People Need a Shepherd

John 21:4–25

*E*arly the next morning Jesus stood on the shore, but the followers did not know it was Jesus. Then he said to them, "Friends, did you catch any fish?"

They answered, "No."

He said, "Throw your net on the right side of the boat, and you will find some." So they did, and they caught so many fish they could not pull the net back into the boat.

The follower whom Jesus loved said to Peter, "It is the Lord!" When Peter heard him say this, he wrapped his coat around himself. (Peter had taken his clothes off.) Then he jumped into the water. The other followers went to shore in the boat, dragging the net full of fish. They were not very far from shore, only about a hundred yards. When the followers stepped out of the boat and onto the shore, they saw a fire of hot coals. There were fish on the fire, and there was bread.

Then Jesus said, "Bring some of the fish you just caught."

Simon Peter went into the boat and pulled the net to the shore. It was full of big fish, one hundred fifty-three in all, but even though there were so many, the net did not tear. Jesus said to them, "Come and eat." None of the followers dared ask him, "Who are you?" because they knew it was the Lord. Jesus came and took the bread and gave it to them, along with the fish.

This was now the third time Jesus showed himself to his followers after he was raised from the dead.

Jesus Talks to Peter

*W*hen they finished eating, Jesus said to Simon Peter, "Simon son of John do you love me more than these?"

He answered, "Yes, Lord, you know that I love you."

Jesus said, "Feed my lambs."

Again Jesus said, "Simon son of John do you love me?"

He answered, "Yes, Lord, you know that I love you."

Jesus said, "Take care of my sheep."

A third time he said, "Simon son of John do you love me?"

Peter was hurt because Jesus asked him the third time, "Do you love me?" Peter said, "Lord, you know everything; you know that I love you!"

He said to him, "Feed my sheep. I tell you the truth, when you were younger, you tied your own belt and went where you wanted. But when you are old, you will put out your hands and someone else will tie you and take you where you don't want to go." (Jesus said this to show how Peter would die to give glory to God.) Then Jesus said to Peter, "Follow me!"

Peter turned and saw that the follower Jesus loved was walking behind them. (This was the follower who had leaned against Jesus at the supper and had said, "Lord, who will turn against you?") When Peter saw him behind them, he asked Jesus, "Lord, what about him?"

Jesus answered, "If I want him to live until I come back, that is not your business. You follow me."

So a story spread among the followers that this one would not die. But Jesus did not say he would not die. He only said, "If I want him to live until I come back, that is not your business."

That follower is the one who is telling these things and who has now written them down. We know that what he says is true.

There are many other things Jesus did. If every one of them were written down, I suppose the whole world would not be big enough for all the books that would be written.

*M*oses said to the LORD, "The LORD is the God of the spirits of all people. May he choose a leader for these people, who will go in and out before them. He must lead them out like sheep and bring them in; the

LORD's people must not be like sheep without a shepherd."

Numbers 27:15–17

*T*hen all the tribes of Israel came to David at Hebron and said to him, "Look, we are your own family. Even when Saul was king, you were the one who led Israel in battle. The LORD said to you, 'You will be a shepherd for my people Israel. You will be their leader.'"

2 Samuel 5:1–2

*H*e chose David to be his servant
and took him from the sheep pens.
He brought him from tending the
sheep
so he could lead the flock, the
people of Jacob,
his own people, the people of Israel.
And David led them with an innocent
heart
and guided them with skillful hands.

Psalm 78:70–72

*T*he LORD spoke his word to me, saying: "Human, prophesy against the leaders of Israel, who are like shepherds. Prophesy and say to them: 'This is what the Lord GOD says: How terrible it will be for the shepherds of Israel who feed only themselves! Why don't the shepherds feed the flock? You eat the milk curds, and you clothe yourselves with the wool. You kill the fat sheep, but you do not feed the flock. You have not made the weak strong. You have not healed the sick or put bandages on those that were hurt. You have not brought back those who strayed away or searched for the lost. But you have ruled the sheep with cruel force. The sheep were scattered, because there was no shepherd, and they became food for every wild animal. My flock wandered over all the mountains and on every high hill. They were scattered all over the face of the earth, and no one searched or looked for them.

" 'This is what the Lord GOD says: I, myself, will search for my sheep and take care of them.

" 'Then they will know that I, the LORD their God, am with them. The nation of Is-

rael will know that they are my people, says the Lord GOD. You, my human sheep, are the sheep I care for, and I am your God, says the Lord GOD.' "

Ezekiel 34:1–6, 11, 30–31

INSIGHTS

*T*he shepherd is at the very center of the life of the sheep. He provides for their every need, satisfying them completely.

Sheep will not lie down if they have cause to be fearful. They are easily frightened. However, as soon as the shepherd appears and moves in the midst of the restless flock, they become quiet.

. . . Our Good Shepherd appears, saying, "Fear THOU not; for I am with thee" (Isa. 41:10). His presence in the midst of our need removes fear and gives rest.

Sheep will not lie down if they are hungry. The shepherd searches for the best pasture land available for his sheep. Our Good Shepherd knows we need to be well nourished for inner satisfaction. He provides nourishment for us from the green pastures of His Word. Nourished by it, we can lie down in quiet contentment.

Occasionally He has to MAKE us lie down. It may take illness, loneliness, heartache, or sorrow to accomplish this.

Not only does the shepherd lead his sheep in the green meadows of nourishment and rest, but beside the still waters. We are refreshed at the waters of quietness. . . .

Our Good Shepherd loves to see His sheep contented and relaxed, refreshed and satisfied with Him.

Millie Stamm

PAUSE FOR REFLECTION

*W*hy is it important that God's people be led by a shepherd? How will a good shepherd lead the Lord's sheep? What relationship do you see between loving Jesus and caring for his sheep?

THURSDAY:
Tell All the Nations that Jesus Will Return!
Acts 1:1–26

Luke Writes Another Book

To Theophilus.

The first book I wrote was about everything Jesus began to do and teach until the day he was taken up into heaven. Before this, with the help of the Holy Spirit, Jesus told the apostles he had chosen what they should do. After his death, he showed himself to them and proved in many ways that he was alive. The apostles saw Jesus during the forty days after he was raised from the dead, and he spoke to them about the kingdom of God. Once when he was eating with them, he told them not to leave Jerusalem. He said, "Wait here to receive the promise from the Father which I told you about. John baptized people with water, but in a few days you will be baptized with the Holy Spirit."

Jesus Is Taken Up Into Heaven

When the apostles were all together, they asked Jesus, "Lord, are you now going to give the kingdom back to Israel?"

Jesus said to them, "The Father is the only One who has the authority to decide dates and times. These things are not for you to know. But when the Holy Spirit comes to you, you will receive power. You will be my witnesses—in Jerusalem, in all of Judea, in Samaria, and in every part of the world."

After he said this, as they were watching, he was lifted up, and a cloud hid him from their sight. As he was going, they were looking into the sky. Suddenly, two men wearing white clothes stood beside them. They said, "Men of Galilee, why are you standing here looking into the sky? Jesus, whom you saw taken up from you into heaven, will come back in the same way you saw him go."

A New Apostle Is Chosen

Then they went back to Jerusalem from the Mount of Olives. (This mountain is about half a mile from Jerusalem.) When they entered the city, they went to the upstairs room where they were staying. Peter, John, James, Andrew, Philip, Thomas, Bartholomew, Matthew, James son of Alphaeus, Simon (known as the Zealot), and Judas son of James were there. They all continued praying together with some women, including Mary the mother of Jesus, and Jesus' brothers.

During this time there was a meeting of the believers (about one hundred twenty of them). Peter stood up and said, "Brothers and sisters, in the Scriptures the Holy Spirit said through David something that must happen involving Judas. He was one of our own group and served together with us. He led those who arrested Jesus." (Judas bought a field with the money he got for his evil act. But he fell to his death, his body burst open, and all his intestines poured out. Everyone in Jerusalem learned about this so they named this place Akeldama. In their language Akeldama means "Field of Blood.") "In the Book of Psalms," Peter said, "this is written:

'May his place be empty;
    leave no one to live in it.'   *Psalm 69:25*
And it is also written:
'Let another man replace him as
    leader.'   *Psalm 109:8*

"So now a man must become a witness with us of Jesus' being raised from the dead. He must be one of the men who were part of our group during all the time the Lord Jesus was among us—from the time John was baptizing people until the day Jesus was taken up from us to heaven."

They put the names of two men before the group. One was Joseph Barsabbas, who was also called Justus. The other was Matthias. The apostles prayed, "Lord, you know the thoughts of everyone. Show us which one of these two you have chosen to do this work. Show us who should be an apostle in place of Judas, who turned away and went where he belongs." Then they used lots to choose between them, and the lots showed that Matthias was the one. So he became an apostle with the other eleven.

*S*ing to the LORD a new song,
  because he has done miracles.
By his right hand and holy arm
  he has won the victory.
The LORD has made known his power to
    save;
  he has shown the other nations his
    victory for his people.
He has remembered his love
  and his loyalty to the people of
    Israel.
All the ends of the earth have seen
  God's power to save.

Shout with joy to the LORD, all the
    earth;
  burst into songs and make music.
Make music to the LORD with harps,
  with harps and the sound of singing.
Blow the trumpets and the sheep's
    horns;
  shout for joy to the LORD the King.

Let the sea and everything in it shout;
  let the world and everyone in it sing.
Let the rivers clap their hands;
  let the mountains sing together for
    joy.
Let them sing before the LORD,
  because he is coming to judge the
    world.
He will judge the world fairly;
  he will judge the peoples with
    fairness.

Psalm 98:1–9

*H*ear this, all you nations;
  listen, earth and all you who live on
    it.
The Lord GOD will be a witness against
    you,
  the Lord from his Holy Temple.

Micah 1:2

*T*ell the nations, "The LORD is king."
  The earth is set, and it cannot be
    moved.

He will judge the people fairly.
Let the skies rejoice and the earth be
    glad;
  let the sea and everything in it shout.
Let the fields and everything in them
    rejoice.
Then all the trees of the forest will sing
    for joy
  before the LORD, because he is
    coming.
He is coming to judge the world;
he will judge the world with fairness
  and the peoples with truth.

Psalm 96:10–13

*A*ll true Christians believe that Jesus Christ is coming again. They may differ in their views of when certain promised events will occur, but they all agree that He is returning as He promised. Furthermore, all Christians agree that this faith in future glory ought to motivate the church. . . .

Because we do not know the day or the hour of our Lord's return, we must constantly be ready. The believer who starts to neglect the "blessed hope" (Titus 2:13) will gradually develop a cold heart, a worldly attitude, and an unfaithful life (Luke 12:35–48). . . .

Not only should this expectant attitude make a difference in our conduct, but it should also make a difference in our witness. . . .

Since this is the day of salvation, we must be diligent to do all we can to win the lost. . . . We must understand what the Bible teaches about God's program for this present age, and we must be motivated by a love for the lost (2 Cor. 5:14) and a desire to be pleasing to Him when He returns.

Warren Wiersbe

*W*hat were Jesus' last words to his apostles? After he went up into heaven, what did God's messengers promise them? Praise God that his people still take his message into every part of the world!

FRIDAY:
God's Spirit Fills His People
Acts 2:1–28

The Coming of the Holy Spirit

*W*hen the day of Pentecost came, they were all together in one place. Suddenly a noise like a strong, blowing wind came from heaven and filled the whole house where they were sitting. They saw something like flames of fire that were separated and stood over each person there. They were all filled with the Holy Spirit, and they began to speak different languages by the power the Holy Spirit was giving them.

There were some religious Jews staying in Jerusalem who were from every country in the world. When they heard this noise, a crowd came together. They were all surprised, because each one heard them speaking in his own language. They were completely amazed at this. They said, "Look! Aren't all these people that we hear speaking from Galilee? Then how is it possible that we each hear them in our own languages? We are from different places: Parthia, Media, Elam, Mesopotamia, Judea, Cappadocia, Pontus, Asia, Phrygia, Pamphylia, Egypt, the areas of Libya near Cyrene, Rome (both Jews and those who had become Jews), Crete, and Arabia. But we hear them telling in our own languages about the great things God has done!" They were all amazed and confused, asking each other, "What does this mean?"

But others were making fun of them, saying, "They have had too much wine."

Peter Speaks to the People

*B*ut Peter stood up with the eleven apostles, and in a loud voice he spoke to the crowd: "My fellow Jews, and all of you who are in Jerusalem, listen to me. Pay attention to what I have to say. These people are not drunk, as you think; it is only nine o'clock in the morning! But Joel the prophet wrote about what is happening here today:

'God says: In the last days
   I will pour out my Spirit on all kinds
     of people.
Your sons and daughters will prophesy.
   Your young men will see visions,
   and your old men will dream
     dreams.
At that time I will pour out my Spirit
   also on my male slaves and female
     slaves,
   and they will prophesy.
I will show miracles
   in the sky and on the earth:
   blood, fire, and thick smoke.
The sun will become dark,
   the moon red as blood,
   before the overwhelming and
     glorious day of the Lord will
     come.
Then anyone who calls on the Lord
   will be saved.'   *Joel 2:28–32*

"People of Israel, listen to these words: Jesus from Nazareth was a very special man. God clearly showed this to you by the miracles, wonders, and signs he did through Jesus. You all know this, because it happened right here among you. Jesus was given to you, and with the help of those who don't know the law, you put him to death by nailing him to a cross. But this was God's plan which he had made long ago; he knew all this would happen. God raised Jesus from the dead and set him free from the pain of death, because death could not hold him. For David said this about him:

'I keep the Lord before me always.
   Because he is close by my side,
   I will not be hurt.
So I am glad, and I rejoice.
   Even my body has hope,
because you will not leave me in the
     grave.
   You will not let your Holy One rot.
You will teach me how to live a holy
     life.
   Being with you will fill me with joy.'
     Psalm 16:8–11

*T*he LORD says, "People of Jacob, you are my servants. Listen to me!

People of Israel, I chose you."
This is what the LORD says, who made
you,
who formed you in your mother's
body,
who will help you:
"People of Jacob, my servants, don't be
afraid.
Israel, I chose you.
I will pour out water for the thirsty land
and make streams flow on dry land.
I will pour out my Spirit into your
children
and my blessing on your descendants.
Your children will grow like a tree in
the grass,
like poplar trees growing beside
streams of water.
One person will say, 'I belong to the
LORD,'
and another will use the name Jacob.
Another will sign his name 'I am the
LORD's,'
and another will use the name
Israel."

The LORD, the king of Israel,
is the LORD All-Powerful, who saves
Israel.
This is what he says: "I am the begin-
ning and the end.
I am the only God.
Who is a god like me?
That god should come and prove it.
Let him tell and explain all that has
happened since I set up my
ancient people.
He should also tell what will happen
in the future.
Don't be afraid! Don't worry!
I have always told you what will
happen.
You are my witnesses.
There is no other God but me.
I know of no other Rock; I am the
only One."

Isaiah 44:1–8

---

*O*ne day while I was sailing, the wind went
down and the sea became calm and flat.

*There was nothing to do but sit in irons and
wait for the wind. "Irons" is a sailing term
for a windless time of drifting. While waiting
for the wind, I drifted past another sailboat
that was floating aimlessly. The people on
board the craft waved and made a flat of the
hand gesture of complaint about the lack of
wind. One man stood by the sails and blew
on them.*

*I thought about that for a long time after-
ward. How like many Christians and far too
many churches. Human breath blowing on
the sails—no wonder we make so little
progress!*

*The Spirit of God in Hebrew is ruach,
meaning "breath" and "wind." At Pentecost
the power of the Holy Spirit was like a mighty
wind. The Spirit filled the disciples and got
them moving again. What we need is a
mighty wind—a fresh, bracing wind of a new
Pentecost. . . .*

*. . . So stop blowing your own breath into
the sails of your life or your church. Ask for a
fresh wind to fill the sails. Without the Holy
Spirit, we'll drift in irons and be lost at
sea. . . .*

Lloyd Ogilvie

*Almighty God, Father of our Lord Jesus
Christ,
grant, we pray, that we might be
grounded and settled in your truth by
the coming of your Holy Spirit into our
hearts.
What we do not know,
reveal to us;
What is lacking within us,
make complete;
That which we do know,
confirm in us;
And keep us blameless in your service,
through Jesus Christ our Lord.*

Clement of Rome

---

*W*hat did God's Spirit enable the believers
to do? For what purpose? Has your life been
renewed by God's Spirit? Pray that God's
Spirit will fill you, direct you, and enable you
to complete God's work in your life!

WEEKEND:
Change Your Hearts, and God Will Forgive
Acts 2:29—3:10

*B*rothers and sisters, I can tell you truly that David, our ancestor, died and was buried. His grave is still here with us today. He was a prophet and knew God had promised him that he would make a person from David's family a king just as he was. Knowing this before it happened, David talked about the Christ rising from the dead. He said:

'He was not left in the grave.
His body did not rot.'

So Jesus is the One whom God raised from the dead. And we are all witnesses to this. Jesus was lifted up to heaven and is now at God's right side. The Father has given the Holy Spirit to Jesus as he promised. So Jesus has poured out that Spirit, and this is what you now see and hear. David was not the one who was lifted up to heaven, but he said:

'The Lord said to my Lord,
"Sit by me at my right side,
until I put your enemies under your
control."' *Psalm 110:1*

"So, all the people of Israel should know this truly: God has made Jesus—the man you nailed to the cross—both Lord and Christ."

When the people heard this, they felt guilty and asked Peter and the other apostles, "What shall we do?"

Peter said to them, "Change your hearts and lives and be baptized, each one of you, in the name of Jesus Christ for the forgiveness of your sins. And you will receive the gift of the Holy Spirit. This promise is for you, for your children, and for all who are far away. It is for everyone the Lord our God calls to himself."

Peter warned them with many other words. He begged them, "Save yourselves from the evil of today's people!" Then those people who accepted what Peter said were baptized. About three thousand people were added to the number of believers that day. They spent their time learning the apostles'

teaching, sharing, breaking bread, and praying together.

The Believers Share

*T*he apostles were doing many miracles and signs, and everyone felt great respect for God. All the believers were together and shared everything. They would sell their land and the things they owned and then divide the money and give it to anyone who needed it. The believers met together in the Temple every day. They ate together in their homes, happy to share their food with joyful hearts. They praised God and were liked by all the people. Every day the Lord added those who were being saved to the group of believers.

Peter Heals a Crippled Man

*O*ne day Peter and John went to the Temple at three o'clock, the time set each day for the afternoon prayer service. There, at the Temple gate called Beautiful Gate, was a man who had been crippled all his life. Every day he was carried to this gate to beg for money from the people going into the Temple. The man saw Peter and John going into the Temple and asked them for money. Peter and John looked straight at him and said, "Look at us!" The man looked at them, thinking they were going to give him some money. But Peter said, "I don't have any silver or gold, but I do have something else I can give you. By the power of Jesus Christ from Nazareth, stand up and walk!" Then Peter took the man's right hand and lifted him up. Immediately the man's feet and ankles became strong. He jumped up, stood on his feet, and began to walk. He went into the Temple with them, walking and jumping and praising God. All the people recognized him as the crippled man who always sat by the Beautiful Gate begging for money. Now they saw this same man walking and praising God, and they were amazed. They wondered how this could happen.

*L*ORD, I am in great trouble,
so I call out to you.

288

Lord, hear my voice;
  listen to my prayer for help.
LORD, if you punished people for all
    their sins,
  no one would be left, Lord.
But you forgive us,
  so you are respected.

I wait for the LORD to help me,
  and I trust his word.
I wait for the Lord to help me
  more than night watchmen wait for
    the dawn,
  more than night watchmen wait for
    the dawn.

People of Israel, put your hope in the
    LORD
  because he is loving
  and able to save.
He will save Israel
  from all their sins.

Psalm 130:1–8

Come, let's go back to the LORD.
  He has hurt us, but he will heal us.
  He has wounded us, but he will
    bandage our wounds.
In two days he will put new life in us;
  on the third day he will raise us up
  so that we may live in his presence
    and know him.
Let's try to learn about the LORD;
  He will come to us as surely as the
    dawn comes.
He will come to us like rain,
  like the spring rain that waters the
    ground."

The LORD says, "Israel, what should I
    do with you?
  Judah, what should I do with you?
Your faithfulness is like a morning mist,
  like the dew that goes away early in
    the day.
I have warned you by my prophets
  that I will kill you and destroy you.
  My justice comes out like bright
    light.
I want faithful love
  more than I want animal sacrifices.
I want people to know me
  more than I want burnt offerings.

Hosea 6:1–6

INSIGHTS

Are you running on empty because of sin in your life that you think is well hidden? God sees and knows all about it. He wants you to face it, name it, confess it, turn from it, and, where you can, put things right. Self-flagellation will not make any lasting difference. Listen to David: "You do not delight in sacrifice, or I would bring it; you do not take pleasure in burnt offerings. The sacrifices of God are a broken spirit; a broken and contrite heart, O God, you will not despise" (Ps. 51:16–17).

God looks for brokenness of spirit—for a contrite, humble heart that, quickened by the Holy Spirit, teaches us to regard our sin as He does. We learn to pray, in the words of the old hymn:

> *Throw light into the darkened cells,*
> *Where passion reigns within;*
> *Quicken my conscience till it feels*
> *The loathsomeness of sin.*

And when we have seen our sin for what it is and rejected it, God will help us to have the right spirit in our hearts. Then we will be able to add:

> *Thus prostrate I shall learn of Thee,*
> *What now I feebly prove,*
> *That God alone in Christ can be*
> *Unutterable love.*

Jill Briscoe

ACTION POINT

How did Peter's audience respond when they learned the truth about Christ? What did he tell them to do? Do your sins make you sick at heart? Then there is hope for you! Peter's message applies to you as well. Do what he says!

MONDAY:

Jesus Is the Only Way to Salvation

Acts 3:11—4:12

NEW TESTAMENT READING

Peter Speaks to the People

*W*hile the man was holding on to Peter and John, all the people were amazed and ran to them at Solomon's Porch. When Peter saw this, he said to them, "People of Israel, why are you surprised? You are looking at us as if it were our own power or goodness that made this man walk. The God of Abraham, Isaac, and Jacob, the God of our ancestors, gave glory to Jesus, his servant. But you handed him over to be killed. Pilate decided to let him go free, but you told Pilate you did not want Jesus. You did not want the One who is holy and good but asked Pilate to give you a murderer instead. And so you killed the One who gives life, but God raised him from the dead. We are witnesses to this. It was faith in Jesus that made this crippled man well. You can see this man, and you know him. He was made completely well because of trust in Jesus, and you all saw it happen!

"Brothers and sisters, I know you did those things to Jesus because neither you nor your leaders understood what you were doing. God said through the prophets that his Christ would suffer and die. And now God has made these things come true in this way. So you must change your hearts and lives! Come back to God, and he will forgive your sins. Then the Lord will send the time of rest. And he will send Jesus, the One he chose to be the Christ. But Jesus must stay in heaven until the time comes when all things will be made right again. God told about this time long ago when he spoke through his holy prophets. Moses said, 'The Lord your God will give you a prophet like me, who is one of your own people. You must listen to everything he tells you. Anyone who does not listen to that prophet will die, cut off from God's people.' Samuel, and all the other prophets who spoke for God after Samuel, told about this time now. You are descendants of the prophets. You have received the agreement God made with your ancestors. He said to your father Abraham, 'Through your descendants all the nations on the earth will be blessed.' God has raised up his servant Jesus and sent him to you first to bless you by turning each of you away from doing evil."

Peter and John at the Council

*W*hile Peter and John were speaking to the people, Jewish priests, the captain of the soldiers that guarded the Temple, and Sadducees came up to them. They were upset because the two apostles were teaching the people and were preaching that people will rise from the dead through the power of Jesus. The Jewish leaders grabbed Peter and John and put them in jail. Since it was already night, they kept them in jail until the next day. But many of those who had heard Peter and John preach believed the things they said. There were now about five thousand in the group of believers.

The next day the Jewish rulers, the older Jewish leaders, and the teachers of the law met in Jerusalem. Annas the high priest, Caiaphas, John, and Alexander were there, as well as everyone from the high priest's family. They made Peter and John stand before them and then asked them, "By what power or authority did you do this?"

Then Peter, filled with the Holy Spirit, said to them, "Rulers of the people and you older leaders, are you questioning us about a good thing that was done to a crippled man? Are you asking us who made him well? We want all of you and all the Jewish people to know that this man was made well by the power of Jesus Christ from Nazareth. You crucified him, but God raised him from the dead. This man was crippled, but he is now well and able to stand here before you because of the power of Jesus. Jesus is

'the stone that you builders rejected,
which has become the cornerstone.'

Psalm 118:22

Jesus is the only One who can save people. His name is the only power in the world that has been given to save people. We must be saved through him."

Shouts of joy and victory
    come from the tents of those who do
      right:
    "The LORD has done powerful
      things."
The power of the LORD has won the
    victory;
    with his power the LORD has done
      mighty things.

I will not die, but live,
    and I will tell what the LORD has done.
The LORD has taught me a hard lesson,
    but he did not let me die.

Open for me the Temple gates.
    Then I will come in and thank the
      LORD.
This is the LORD's gate;
    only those who are good may enter
      through it.
LORD, I thank you for answering me.
    You have saved me.

The stone that the builders rejected
    became the cornerstone.
The LORD did this,
    and it is wonderful to us.
This is the day that the LORD has made.
    Let us rejoice and be glad today!
Psalm 118:15–24

So listen to the LORD's message, you
    who brag,
    you leaders in Jerusalem.
You say, "We have made an agreement
    with death;
    we have a contract with death.
When terrible punishment passes by,
    it won't hurt us.
Our lies will keep us safe,
    and our tricks will hide us."

Because of these things, this is what the
Lord GOD says:
    "I will put a stone in the ground in
      Jerusalem,
    a tested stone.
Everything will be built on this impor-
    tant and precious rock.
    Anyone who trusts in it will never be
      disappointed.

I will use justice as a measuring line
    and goodness as the standard.
The lies you hide behind will be
    destroyed as if by hail.
    They will be washed away as if in a
      flood.
Your agreement with death will be
    erased;
    your contract with death will not
      help you.
When terrible punishment comes,
    you will be crushed by it."
Isaiah 28:14–18

INSIGHTS

*I am the way and the truth and the life. No
one comes to the Father except through me"
(John 14:6). . . .*

*   . . . Jesus did not merely show the way to
God; He said, "I am the way." He did not
claim merely to know the truth; He said, "I
am the truth." He did not merely point to the
abundant life; He said, "I am the life."
Therefore, within Christianity if there is no
Christ, there is no way to God, no truth about
God, and no vitality.*

*   How could Jesus make such claims? If He
was only a man, His claims are preposterous.
But if He is who He said He is, and if He did
what He said He would do, His claims make
sense. Jesus claimed to be God and to have
come to earth to die for our own sin. We
deserve to die for our own sin, but Jesus died
in our place. He who was sinless accepted the
guilt of our sin and died for us. No one else
could do it, but He could and did. Thus, He
literally became the door by which sinful men
and women can approach the Father.*

James Boice

APPLICATION

*Who is the rock on whom God's salvation is
built? What is the way of salvation? Why does
no other way of salvation exist? Have you
followed God's way of salvation?*

TUESDAY:
Christ's Witnesses Have Nothing to Fear
Acts 4:13–37

NEW TESTAMENT READING

*T*he Jewish leaders saw that Peter and John were not afraid to speak, and they understood that these men had no special training or education. So they were amazed. Then they realized that Peter and John had been with Jesus. Because they saw the healed man standing there beside the two apostles, they could say nothing against them. After the Jewish leaders ordered them to leave the meeting, they began to talk to each other. They said, "What shall we do with these men? Everyone in Jerusalem knows they have done a great miracle, and we cannot say it is not true. But to keep it from spreading among the people, we must warn them not to talk to people anymore using that name."

So they called Peter and John in again and told them not to speak or to teach at all in the name of Jesus. But Peter and John answered them, "You decide what God would want. Should we obey you or God? We cannot keep quiet. We must speak about what we have seen and heard." The Jewish leaders warned the apostles again and let them go free. They could not find a way to punish them, because all the people were praising God for what had been done. The man who received the miracle of healing was more than forty years old.

The Believers Pray

*A*fter Peter and John left the meeting of Jewish leaders, they went to their own group and told them everything the leading priests and the older Jewish leaders had said to them. When the believers heard this, they prayed to God together, "Lord, you are the One who made the sky, the earth, the sea, and everything in them. By the Holy Spirit, through our father David your servant, you said:

'Why are the nations so angry?
    Why are the people making useless
        plans?
The kings of the earth prepare to fight,
    and their leaders make plans
        together
against the Lord
    and his Christ.'   *Psalm 2:1–2*

These things really happened when Herod, Pontius Pilate, those who are not Jews, and the Jewish people all came together against Jesus here in Jerusalem. Jesus is your holy servant, the One you made to be the Christ. These people made your plan happen because of your power and your will. And now, Lord, listen to their threats. Lord, help us, your servants, to speak your word without fear. Help us to be brave by showing us your power to heal. Give proofs and make miracles happen by the power of Jesus, your holy servant."

After they had prayed, the place where they were meeting was shaken. They were all filled with the Holy Spirit, and they spoke God's word without fear.

The Believers Share

*T*he group of believers were united in their hearts and spirit. All those in the group acted as though their private property belonged to everyone in the group. In fact, they shared everything. With great power the apostles were telling people that the Lord Jesus was truly raised from the dead. And God blessed all the believers very much. No one in the group needed anything. From time to time those who owned fields or houses sold them, brought the money, and gave it to the apostles. Then the money was given to anyone who needed it.

One of the believers was named Joseph, a Levite born in Cyprus. The apostles called him Barnabas (which means "one who encourages"). Joseph owned a field, sold it, brought the money, and gave it to the apostles.

OLD TESTAMENT READING

*N*ow this is what the Lord says.
    He created you, people of Jacob;
    he formed you, people of Israel.

He says, "Don't be afraid, because I
　　have saved you.
　I have called you by name, and you
　　are mine.
When you pass through the waters, I
　　will be with you.
　When you cross rivers, you will not
　　drown.
When you walk through fire, you will
　　not be burned,
　nor will the flames hurt you.
This is because I, the LORD, am your
　　God,
　the Holy One of Israel, your Savior.
I gave Egypt to pay for you,
　and I gave Cush and Seba to make
　　you mine.
Because you are precious to me,
　because I give you honor and love
　　you,
I will give other people in your place;
　I will give other nations to save your
　　life.
Don't be afraid, because I am with you.
　I will bring your children from the
　　east
　and gather you from the west.
I will tell the north: Give my people to
　　me.
　I will tell the south: Don't keep my
　　people in prison.
Bring my sons from far away
　and my daughters from faraway
　　places.
Bring to me all the people who are mine,
　whom I made for my glory,
　whom I formed and made."

Judah Is God's Witness

Bring out the people who have eyes but
　　don't see
　and those who have ears but don't
　　hear.
The LORD says, "You are my witnesses
　　and the servant I chose.
I chose you so you would know and
　　believe me,
　so you would understand that I am
　　the true God.
There was no God before me,
　and there will be no God after me.
I myself am the LORD;
　I am the only Savior.

I myself have spoken to you, saved you,
　　and told you these things.
　It was not some foreign god among
　　you.
You are my witnesses, and I am God,"
　says the LORD.
　"I have always been God.
No one can save people from my
　　power;
　when I do something, no one can
　　change it."

Isaiah 43:1–8, 10–13

I N S I G H T S

If we are Christians, we have all been delivered to be deliverers! The Word of God commands us to tell people they are in bondage to sin and that God would love to set them free from that taskmaster. . . .

Sometimes this is disappointing work. The people we go to may not want us to deliver them. Moses knew that particular scenario (Exod. 2:13–14). Or it can even be dangerous work. We may not be in danger of losing our life . . . but we may be in danger of losing our popularity, our friends, or in some extreme cases, even our job. Yes, a delivering work can be a disappointing work and even a dangerous work. But it is above all, a directed work, and that's what helps. To have a sense of God's direction when we are disappointed or in danger is a huge boost to our morale. The inner thrill that God has invited us to cooperate with Him takes the worry out of the work. People work is His work, and He will show us what to do, and even how to do it.

Jill Briscoe

P A U S E　　F O R　　R E F L E C T I O N

Notice how, in both of these readings, the recitation of one's spiritual heritage served as encouragement to be God's fearless witness. How does your spiritual heritage encourage you to bravely proclaim God's truth?

WEDNESDAY:

Give to God What Is His

Acts 5:1–26

Ananias and Sapphira Die

*B*ut a man named Ananias and his wife Sapphira sold some land. He kept back part of the money for himself; his wife knew about this and agreed to it. But he brought the rest of the money and gave it to the apostles. Peter said, "Ananias, why did you let Satan rule your thoughts to lie to the Holy Spirit and to keep for yourself part of the money you received for the land? Before you sold the land, it belonged to you. And even after you sold it, you could have used the money any way you wanted. Why did you think of doing this? You lied to God, not to us!" When Ananias heard this, he fell down and died. Some young men came in, wrapped up his body, carried it out, and buried it. And everyone who heard about this was filled with fear.

About three hours later his wife came in, but she did not know what had happened. Peter said to her, "Tell me, was the money you got for your field this much?"

Sapphira answered, "Yes, that was the price."

Peter said to her, "Why did you and your husband agree to test the Spirit of the Lord? Look! The men who buried your husband are at the door, and they will carry you out." At that moment Sapphira fell down by his feet and died. When the young men came in and saw that she was dead, they carried her out and buried her beside her husband. The whole church and all the others who heard about these things were filled with fear.

The Apostles Heal Many

*T*he apostles did many signs and miracles among the people. And they would all meet together on Solomon's Porch. None of the others dared to join them, but all the people respected them. More and more men and women believed in the Lord and were added to the group of believers. The people placed their sick on beds and mats in the streets, hoping that when Peter passed by at least his shadow might fall on them. Crowds came from all the towns around Jerusalem, bringing their sick and those who were bothered by evil spirits, and all of them were healed.

Leaders Try to Stop the Apostles

*T*he high priest and all his friends (a group called the Sadducees) became very jealous. They took the apostles and put them in jail. But during the night, an angel of the Lord opened the doors of the jail and led the apostles outside. The angel said, "Go stand in the Temple and tell the people everything about this new life." When the apostles heard this, they obeyed and went into the Temple early in the morning and continued teaching.

When the high priest and his friends arrived, they called a meeting of the Jewish leaders and all the important older Jewish men. They sent some men to the jail to bring the apostles to them. But, upon arriving, the officers could not find the apostles. So they went back and reported to the Jewish leaders. They said, "The jail was closed and locked, and the guards were standing at the doors. But when we opened the doors, the jail was empty!" Hearing this, the captain of the Temple guards and the leading priests were confused and wondered what was happening.

Then someone came and told them, "Listen! The men you put in jail are standing in the Temple teaching the people." Then the captain and his men went out and brought the apostles back. But the soldiers did not use force, because they were afraid the people would stone them to death.

*I*f you make a promise to give something to the LORD your God, do not be slow to pay it, because the LORD your God demands it from you. Do not be guilty of sin. But if you do not make the promise, you will not be guilty. You must do whatever you say you will do, because you chose to make the promise to the LORD your God.

Deuteronomy 23:21–23

*T*hink before you speak,
　　and be careful about what you say to
　　　　God.
God is in heaven,
　　and you are on the earth,
　　so say only a few words to God.
The saying is true: Bad dreams come
　　　　from too much worrying,
　　and too many words come from
　　　　foolish people.

If you make a promise to God, don't be slow to keep it. God is not happy with fools, so give God what you promised. It is better not to promise anything than to promise something and not do it. Don't let your words cause you to sin, and don't say to the priest at the Temple, "I didn't mean what I promised." If you do, God will become angry with your words and will destroy everything you have worked for. Many useless promises are like so many dreams; they mean nothing. You should respect God.

Ecclesiastes 5:2–7

Achan Keeps What Belongs to God

*D*on't take any of the things that are to be destroyed as an offering to the LORD. If you take them and bring them into our camp, you yourselves will be destroyed, and you will bring trouble to all of Israel. All the silver and gold and things made from bronze and iron belong to the LORD and must be saved for him."

Joshua 6:18–19

*A*chan answered, "It is true! I have sinned against the LORD, the God of Israel. This is what I did: Among the things I saw a beautiful coat from Babylonia and about five pounds of silver and more than one and one-fourth pounds of gold. I wanted these things very much for myself, so I took them. You will find them buried in the ground under my tent, with the silver underneath."

Then Joshua and all the people led Achan son of Zerah to the Valley of Trouble. They also took the silver, the coat, the gold, Achan's sons, daughters, cattle, donkeys,

sheep, tent, and everything he owned. Joshua said, "I don't know why you caused so much trouble for us, but now the LORD will bring trouble to you." Then all the people threw stones at Achan and his family until they died. Then the people burned them.

Joshua 7:20–21, 24–25

INSIGHTS

*W*hen I have made it, I'll have time for . . ." How was that again?

"I want to make a lot of money for God. I must make money now so I can give money later." What was that again?

A farmer was explaining to a minister, "Well, if I'd get enough, I'd give half to the Lord."

"If you had two thousand acres of oil wells," asked the preacher, "would you give revenues from one thousand acres to the Lord?"

"Why, sure," the farmer gloated. "Anyone could live off a thousand acres of oil."

"If you had two hogs, would you give one to the Lord?" queried the minister.

At that, the farmer complained, "That's not fair. You know I have two pigs!"

We don't suddenly, someday, have an abundance of time and money to give. We begin with the little pieces. We are in training now, learning bit by bit to manage money, power, time, relationships and temptation. Then maybe someday we will find ourselves competent to manage life on a grander scale.

Lynn Anderson

PAUSE　FOR　REFLECTION

*W*hat was Ananias' and Sapphira's sin against God? Achan's sin? Are you waiting to acquire enough to satisfy yourself before you give to God? What do you have now that you give to him?

THURSDAY:

God's Will Can't Be Thwarted

Acts 5:27—6:7

NEW TESTAMENT READING

*T*he soldiers brought the apostles to the meeting and made them stand before the Jewish leaders. The high priest questioned them, saying, "We gave you strict orders not to continue teaching in that name. But look, you have filled Jerusalem with your teaching and are trying to make us responsible for this man's death."

Peter and the other apostles answered, "We must obey God, not human authority! You killed Jesus by hanging him on a cross. But God, the God of our ancestors, raised Jesus up from the dead! Jesus is the One whom God raised to be on his right side, as Leader and Savior. Through him, all Jewish people could change their hearts and lives and have their sins forgiven. We saw all these things happen. The Holy Spirit, whom God has given to all who obey him, also proves these things are true."

When the Jewish leaders heard this, they became angry and wanted to kill them. But a Pharisee named Gamaliel stood up in the meeting. He was a teacher of the law, and all the people respected him. He ordered the apostles to leave the meeting for a little while. Then he said, "People of Israel, be careful what you are planning to do to these men. Remember when Theudas appeared? He said he was a great man, and about four hundred men joined him. But he was killed, and all his followers were scattered; they were able to do nothing. Later, a man named Judas came from Galilee at the time of the registration. He also led a group of followers and was killed, and all his followers were scattered. And so now I tell you: Stay away from these men, and leave them alone. If their plan comes from human authority, it will fail. But if it is from God, you will not be able to stop them. You might even be fighting against God himself!"

The Jewish leaders agreed with what Gamaliel said. They called the apostles in, beat them, and told them not to speak in the name of Jesus again. Then they let them go free. The apostles left the meeting full of joy because they were given the honor of suffering disgrace for Jesus. Every day in the Temple and in people's homes they continued teaching the people and telling the Good News—that Jesus is the Christ.

Seven Leaders Are Chosen

*T*he number of followers was growing. But during this same time, the Greek-speaking followers had an argument with the other Jewish followers. The Greek-speaking widows were not getting their share of the food that was given out every day. The twelve apostles called the whole group of followers together and said, "It is not right for us to stop our work of teaching God's word in order to serve tables. So, brothers and sisters, choose seven of your own men who are good, full of the Spirit and full of wisdom. We will put them in charge of this work. Then we can continue to pray and to teach the word of God."

The whole group liked the idea, so they chose these seven men: Stephen (a man with great faith and full of the Holy Spirit), Philip, Procorus, Nicanor, Timon, Parmenas, and Nicolas (a man from Antioch who had become a Jew). Then they put these men before the apostles, who prayed and laid their hands on them.

The word of God was continuing to spread. The group of followers in Jerusalem increased, and a great number of the Jewish priests believed and obeyed.

OLD TESTAMENT READING

*R*emember this, and do not forget it!
　　Think about these things, you who
　　　turn against God.
Remember what happened long ago.
　　Remember that I am God, and there
　　　is no other God.
　　I am God, and there is no one like
　　　me.
From the beginning I told you what
　　would happen in the end.

A long time ago I told you things
that have not yet happened.
When I plan something, it happens.
What I want to do, I will do.
I am calling a man from the east to
carry out my plan;
he will come like a hawk from a
country far away.
I will make what I have said come true;
I will do what I have planned.
Listen to me, you stubborn people,
who are far from what is right.
I will soon do the things that are right.
I will bring salvation soon.
I will save Jerusalem
and bring glory to Israel."

Isaiah 46:8–13

I know that everything God does will continue forever. People cannot add anything to what God has done, and they cannot take anything away from it. God does it this way to make people respect him.

What happens now has happened in
the past,
and what will happen in the future
has happened before.
God makes the same things happen
again and again.

Ecclesiastes 3:14–15

*I*f the LORD doesn't build the house,
the builders are working for nothing.
If the LORD doesn't guard the city,
the guards are watching for nothing.

Psalm 127:1

*B*ut he is the only God.
Who can come against him?
He does anything he wants.
He will do to me what he said he would
do,
and he has many plans like this.
That is why I am frightened of him;
when I think of this, I am afraid of him.
God has made me afraid;
the Almighty terrifies me."

Job 23:13–16

toward "an expected end." . . . God is working with a motive. All things are working together for one object: the good of those who love God. We see only the beginning; God sees the end from the beginning. He knows every letter of the Book of Providence; He sees not only what He is doing, but what will come of what He is doing.

As to our present pain and grief, God sees not these things exclusively, but He sees the future joy and usefulness which will come of them. He regards not only the tearing up of the soil with the plow, but the clothing of that soil with the golden harvest. He sees the after consequences of affliction, and He accounts those painful incidents to be blessed which lead up to so much of happiness. Let us comfort ourselves with this. . . .

You have never seen the Great Artist's masterpiece; you have seen the rough marble, you have marked the chippings that fall on the ground; you have felt the edge of His chisel, you know the weight of His hammer, and you are full of the memory of these things; but oh, could you see that glorious image as it will be when He has put the finishing stroke to it, you would then understand the chisel, and the hammer, and the Worker better than you now do!

Charles Spurgeon

APPLICATION

*D*id Gamaliel speak to the Jews with true wisdom? What do you learn about God's sovereign will in these readings? Pray to remember that God is working toward "an expected end" and to understand that what happens in your life is part of his work.

INSIGHTS

*T*he Lord's thoughts are all working

FRIDAY:
Tell the Nations What God Has Done
Acts 6:8—7:16

Stephen Is Accused

Stephen was richly blessed by God who gave him the power to do great miracles and signs among the people. But some Jewish people were against him. They belonged to the synagogue of Free Men (as it was called), which included Jewish people from Cyrene, Alexandria, Cilicia, and Asia. They all came and argued with Stephen.

But the Spirit was helping him to speak with wisdom, and his words were so strong that they could not argue with him. So they secretly urged some men to say, "We heard Stephen speak against Moses and against God."

This upset the people, the older Jewish leaders, and the teachers of the law. They came and grabbed Stephen and brought him to a meeting of the Jewish leaders. They brought in some people to tell lies about Stephen, saying, "This man is always speaking against this holy place and the law of Moses. We heard him say that Jesus from Nazareth will destroy this place and that Jesus will change the customs Moses gave us." All the people in the meeting were watching Stephen closely and saw that his face looked like the face of an angel.

Stephen's Speech

The high priest said to Stephen, "Are these things true?"

Stephen answered, "Brothers and fathers, listen to me. Our glorious God appeared to Abraham, our ancestor, in Mesopotamia before he lived in Haran. God said to Abraham, 'Leave your country and your relatives, and go to the land I will show you.' So Abraham left the country of Chaldea and went to live in Haran. After Abraham's father died, God sent him to this place where you now live. God did not give Abraham any of this land, not even a foot of it. But God promised that he would give this land to him and his descendants, even before Abraham had a child. This is what God said to him: 'Your descendants will be strangers in a land they don't own. The people there will make them slaves and will mistreat them for four hundred years. But I will punish the nation where they are slaves. Then your descendants will leave that land and will worship me in this place.' God made an agreement with Abraham, the sign of which was circumcision. And so when Abraham had his son Isaac, Abraham circumcised him when he was eight days old. Isaac also circumcised his son Jacob, and Jacob did the same for his sons, the twelve ancestors of our people.

"Jacob's sons became jealous of Joseph and sold him to be a slave in Egypt. But God was with him and saved him from all his troubles. The king of Egypt liked Joseph and respected him because of the wisdom God gave him. The king made him governor of Egypt and put him in charge of all the people in his palace.

"Then all the land of Egypt and Canaan became so dry that nothing would grow, and the people suffered very much. Jacob's sons, our ancestors, could not find anything to eat. But when Jacob heard there was grain in Egypt, he sent his sons there. This was their first trip to Egypt. When they went there a second time, Joseph told his brothers who he was, and the king learned about Joseph's family. Then Joseph sent messengers to invite Jacob, his father, to come to Egypt along with all his relatives (seventy-five persons altogether). So Jacob went down to Egypt, where he and his sons died. Later their bodies were moved to Shechem and put in a grave there. (It was the same grave Abraham had bought for a sum of money from the sons of Hamor in Shechem.)"

Give thanks to the LORD and pray to
  him.
Tell the nations what he has done.
Sing to him; sing praises to him.
Tell about all his miracles.

Be glad that you are his;
let those who seek the LORD be
happy.
Depend on the LORD and his strength;
always go to him for help.
Remember the miracles he has done;
remember his wonders and his
decisions.
You are descendants of his servant
Abraham,
the children of Jacob, his chosen
people.
He is the LORD our God.
His laws are for all the world.

He will keep his agreement forever;
he will keep his promises always.
He will keep the agreement he made
with Abraham
and the promise he made to Isaac.
He made it a law for the people of Jacob;
he made it an agreement with Israel
to last forever.
The LORD said, "I will give you the land
of Canaan,
and it will belong to you."

Then God's people were few in number.
They were strangers in the land.
They went from one nation to another,
from one kingdom to another.
But the LORD did not let anyone hurt
them;
he warned kings not to harm them.
He said, "Don't touch my chosen
people,
and don't harm my prophets."

God ordered a time of hunger in the
land,
and he destroyed all the food.
Then he sent a man ahead of them—
Joseph, who was sold as a slave.
They put chains around his feet
and an iron ring around his neck.
Then the time he had spoken of came,
and the LORD's words proved that
Joseph was right.
The king of Egypt sent for Joseph and
freed him;
the ruler of the people set him free.
He made him the master of his house;
Joseph was in charge of his riches.
He could order the princes as he
wished.

He taught the older men to be wise.
Then his father Israel came to Egypt;
Jacob lived in Egypt.

Psalm 105:1–23

What appears to be foolish in the eyes of society is often that which is most effective in
the work of the kingdom. The ignorant, the
uneducated, the despised of the world are
sometimes God's choicest servants. So it was
with Sophie "the scrubwoman" Lichtenfels,
"whose sermons rose not from an exalted po-
dium or pulpit but from callused hands and
knees and with the rhythm of a lowly washtub
and scrub brush." . . .

. . . Her testimony was simple.

"God called me to scrub and preach. I was
born a preacher, but since I was poor I had
to work. My work is good and I can be trusted,
so they want me. But if they have me, they
must hear me preach. No preach, no work. I
scrub as unto the Lord and I preach to all in
the house. When I am out of work I tell my
father. He is the best employment office. You
don't have to pay or wait. . . .

"Sometimes we pray so foolish. For 12
years I prayed the Lord make me a foreign
missionary. One day I prayed like that and
my Father said, 'Stop Sophie. Where were you
born?' 'In Germany,' I replied. 'And where
are you now?' 'In America.' 'Well, aren't you
already a foreign missionary?' Then He said
to me, 'Who lives on the floor above you?' 'A
family of Swedes.' 'And above them?' 'Some
Swiss.' . . .

"'Yes, and in back are Italians, and a block
away Chinese. You have never spoken to them
about My Son. Do you think I'll send you a
thousand miles away when you've got foreigners, even heathen all around you?'"

Ruth Tucker

---

*S*tephen was a powerful witness for God
among Jews from many nations. What message did both Stephen and the psalmist have
to share? What message has God given you
to share to the "nations" around you?

WEEKEND:

God Is Faithful to His People

Acts 7:17–42a

*T*he promise God made to Abraham was soon to come true, and the number of people in Egypt grew large. Then a new king, who did not know who Joseph was, began to rule Egypt. This king tricked our people and was cruel to our ancestors, forcing them to leave their babies outside to die. At this time Moses was born, and he was very beautiful. For three months Moses was cared for in his father's house. When they put Moses outside, the king's daughter adopted him and raised him as if he were her own son. The Egyptians taught Moses everything they knew, and he was a powerful man in what he said and did.

"When Moses was about forty years old, he thought it would be good to visit his own people, the people of Israel. Moses saw an Egyptian mistreating an Israelite, so he defended the Israelite and punished the Egyptian by killing him. Moses thought his own people would understand that God was using him to save them, but they did not. The next day when Moses saw two men of Israel fighting, he tried to make peace between them. He said, 'Men, you are brothers. Why are you hurting each other?' The man who was hurting the other pushed Moses away and said, 'Who made you our ruler and judge? Are you going to kill me as you killed the Egyptian yesterday?' When Moses heard him say this, he left Egypt and went to live in the land of Midian where he was a stranger. While Moses lived in Midian, he had two sons.

"Forty years later an angel appeared to Moses in the flames of a burning bush as he was in the desert near Mount Sinai. When Moses saw this, he was amazed and went near to look closer. Moses heard the Lord's voice say, 'I am the God of your ancestors, the God of Abraham, Isaac, and Jacob.' Moses began to shake with fear and was afraid to look. The Lord said to him, 'Take off your sandals, because you are standing on holy ground. I have seen the troubles my people have suffered in Egypt. I have heard their cries and have come down to save them. And now, Moses, I am sending you back to Egypt.'

"This Moses was the same man the two men of Israel rejected, saying, 'Who made you a ruler and judge?' Moses is the same man God sent to be a ruler and savior, with the help of the angel that Moses saw in the burning bush. So Moses led the people out of Egypt. He worked miracles and signs in Egypt, at the Red Sea, and then in the desert for forty years. This is the same Moses that said to the people of Israel, 'God will give you a prophet like me, who is one of your own people.' This is the Moses who was with the gathering of the Israelites in the desert. He was with the angel that spoke to him at Mount Sinai, and he was with our ancestors. He received commands from God that give life, and he gave those commands to us.

"But our ancestors did not want to obey Moses. They rejected him and wanted to go back to Egypt. They said to Aaron, 'Make us gods who will lead us. Moses led us out of Egypt, but we don't know what has happened to him.' So the people made an idol that looked like a calf. Then they brought sacrifices to it and were proud of what they had made with their own hands. But God turned against them and did not try to stop them from worshiping the sun, moon, and stars."

*T*he LORD made his people grow in
number,
    and he made them stronger than
their enemies.
He caused the Egyptians to hate his
people
    and to make plans against his
servants.
Then he sent his servant Moses,
    and Aaron, whom he had chosen.
They did many signs among the
Egyptians
    and worked wonders in Egypt.

The LORD sent darkness and made the
land dark,
but the Egyptians turned against
what he said.
So he changed their water into blood
and made their fish die.
Then their country was filled with frogs,
even in the bedrooms of their rulers.
The LORD spoke and flies came,
and gnats were everywhere in the
country.
He made hail fall like rain
and sent lightning through their land.
He struck down their grapevines and
fig trees,
and he destroyed every tree in the
country.
He spoke and grasshoppers came;
the locusts were too many to count.
They ate all the plants in the land
and everything the earth produced.
The LORD also killed all the firstborn
sons in the land,
the oldest son of each family.

Then he brought his people out,
and they carried with them silver
and gold.
Not one of his people stumbled.
The Egyptians were glad when they
left,
because the Egyptians were afraid of
them.
The LORD covered them with a cloud
and lit up the night with fire.
When they asked, he brought them
quail
and filled them with bread from
heaven.
God split the rock, and water flowed out;
it ran like a river through the desert.
He remembered his holy promise
to his servant Abraham.

So God brought his people out with joy,
his chosen ones with singing.
He gave them lands of other nations,
so they received what others had
worked for.
This was so they would keep his orders
and obey his teachings.

Praise the LORD!

Psalm 105:24–45

---

*Great is Thy faithfulness, O God my
Father,
There is no shadow of turning with Thee;
Thou changest not, Thy compassions they
fail not;
As Thou hast been Thou forever wilt be.*

*Summer and winter, and spring-time and
harvest,
Sun, moon and stars in their courses above
Join with all nature in manifold witness
To Thy great faithfulness, mercy and love.*

*Pardon for sin and a peace that endureth,
Thy own dear presence to cheer and to
guide;
Strength for today and bright hope for
tomorrow,
Blessings all mine, with ten thousand
beside!*

*Great is Thy faithfulness! Great is Thy
faithfulness!
Morning by morning new mercies I see;
All I have needed Thy hand hath provided.
Great is Thy faithfulness, Lord, unto me!*
Thomas O. Chisholm

ACTION POINT

*From what trials did God, in his faithful-
ness, deliver the people of Israel? List as many
as you can. When you doubt his faithfulness in your life, reread your list and
believe that God is and always will be faithful!*

MONDAY:

Some Refuse to Hear God's Messengers

Acts 7:42b—8:1

*T*his is what is written in the book of the prophets: God says,

'People of Israel, you did not bring me
 sacrifices and offerings
 while you traveled in the desert for
 forty years.
You have carried with you
 the tent to worship Molech
 and the idols of the star god Rephan
 that you made to worship.
So I will send you away beyond
 Babylon.'   *Amos 5:25–27*

"The Holy Tent where God spoke to our ancestors was with them in the desert. God told Moses how to make this Tent, and he made it like the plan God showed him. Later, Joshua led our ancestors to capture the lands of the other nations. Our people went in, and God forced the other people out. When our people went into this new land, they took with them this same Tent they had received from their ancestors. They kept it until the time of David, who pleased God and asked God to let him build a house for him, the God of Jacob. But Solomon was the one who built the Temple.

"But the Most High does not live in houses that people build with their hands. As the prophet says:

'Heaven is my throne,
 and the earth is my footstool.
So do you think you can build a house
 for me? says the Lord.
 Do I need a place to rest?
Remember, my hand made all these
 things!'"   *Isaiah 66:1–2*

Stephen continued speaking: "You stubborn people! You have not given your hearts to God, nor will you listen to him! You are always against what the Holy Spirit is trying to tell you, just as your ancestors were. Your ancestors tried to hurt every prophet who ever lived. Those prophets said long ago that the One who is good would come, but your ancestors killed them. And now you have turned against and killed the One who is good. You received the law of Moses, which God gave you through his angels, but you haven't obeyed it."

Stephen Is Killed

*W*hen the leaders heard this, they became furious. They were so mad they were grinding their teeth at Stephen. But Stephen was full of the Holy Spirit. He looked up to heaven and saw the glory of God and Jesus standing at God's right side. He said, "Look! I see heaven open and the Son of Man standing at God's right side."

Then they shouted loudly and covered their ears and all ran at Stephen. They took him out of the city and began to throw stones at him to kill him. And those who told lies against Stephen left their coats with a young man named Saul. While they were throwing stones, Stephen prayed, "Lord Jesus, receive my spirit." He fell on his knees and cried in a loud voice, "Lord, do not hold this sin against them." After Stephen said this, he died.

Saul agreed that the killing of Stephen was good.

Troubles for the Believers

*O*n that day the church of Jerusalem began to be persecuted, and all the believers, except the apostles, were scattered throughout Judea and Samaria.

*T*he king and these leaders stopped worshiping in the Temple of the Lord, the God of their ancestors. Instead, they began to worship the Asherah idols and other idols. Because they did wrong, God was angry with the people of Judah and Jerusalem. Even though the Lord sent prophets to the people to turn them back to him and even though the prophets warned them, they refused to listen.

Then the Spirit of God entered Zechariah son of Jehoiada the priest. Zechariah stood before the people and said, "This is what God says: 'Why do you disobey the Lord's

302

commands? You will not be successful. Because you have left the Lord, he has also left you.'"

But the king and his officers made plans against Zechariah. At the king's command they threw stones at him in the courtyard of the Temple of the Lord until he died. King Joash did not remember Jehoiada's kindness to him, so Joash killed Zechariah, Jehoiada's son. Before Zechariah died, he said, "May the Lord see what you are doing and punish you."

2 Chronicles 24:18–22

Zedekiah did what the Lord his God said was wrong. The prophet Jeremiah spoke messages from the Lord, but Zedekiah did not obey. Zedekiah turned against King Nebuchadnezzar, who had forced him to swear in God's name to be loyal to him. But Zedekiah became stubborn and refused to obey the Lord, the God of Israel. Also, all the leaders of the priests and the people of Judah became more wicked, following the evil example of the other nations. The Lord had made the Temple in Jerusalem holy, but the leaders made it unholy.

The Lord, the God of their ancestors, sent prophets again and again to warn his people, because he had pity on them and on his Temple. But they made fun of God's prophets and hated God's messages. They refused to listen to the prophets until, finally, the Lord became so angry with his people that he could not be stopped. So God brought the king of Babylon to attack them. The king killed the young men even when they were in the Temple. He had no mercy on the young men or women, the old men or those who were sick. God handed all of them over to Nebuchadnezzar.

2 Chronicles 36:12–17

INSIGHTS

In his remarkable and eloquent sermon, Stephen revealed his accurate grasp of Jewish history and its relevance to the new faith he had embraced. He turned the tables on his attackers and charged them with being the guilty ones. He refuted their charges in a closely reasoned, eloquent speech that reviewed their history from the time of Abraham onward. From it he demonstrated that the presence of the eternal God cannot be localized and confined to an earthly temple, be it ever so magnificent.

He cited God's presence with Joseph even when he was in Egypt. He reminded them that as a nation they had persistently rejected and resisted the messengers of God. They had envied and mistreated Joseph, whom God had sent as their preserver. They had rebelled against Moses and rejected his message. They had stoned the prophets and abused the functions of the Temple. They boasted of the angelic mediation of the Law, yet they failed to keep it. . . .

When Stephen delivered his final, blistering denunciation, he did it with his eyes open. He knew what the inevitable reaction of those bigoted men would be when he told them that they were stiff-necked, uncircumcised in heart, and murderers and betrayers of the Righteous One (Acts 7:51–52).

J. Oswald Sanders

PAUSE FOR REFLECTION

Was Stephen's martyrdom a unique event in Jewish history? Why did the religious leaders kill him? Why did they kill those who had preceded him? Is your heart in any way hardened to God's message today?

TUESDAY:

There Is No Room for Jealousy in God's Kingdom

Acts 8:2–25

*A*nd some religious people buried Stephen and cried loudly for him. Saul was also trying to destroy the church, going from house to house, dragging out men and women and putting them in jail. And wherever they were scattered, they told people the Good News.

Philip Preaches in Samaria

*P*hilip went to the city of Samaria and preached about the Christ. When the people there heard Philip and saw the miracles he was doing, they all listened carefully to what he said. Many of these people had evil spirits in them, but Philip made the evil spirits leave. The spirits made a loud noise when they came out. Philip also healed many weak and crippled people there. So the people in that city were very happy.

But there was a man named Simon in that city. Before Philip came there, Simon had practiced magic and amazed all the people of Samaria. He bragged and called himself a great man. All the people—the least important and the most important—paid attention to Simon, saying, "This man has the power of God, called 'the Great Power'!" Simon had amazed them with his magic so long that the people became his followers. But when Philip told them the Good News about the kingdom of God and the power of Jesus Christ, men and women believed Philip and were baptized. Simon himself believed, and after he was baptized, he stayed very close to Philip. When he saw the miracles and the powerful things Philip did, Simon was amazed.

When the apostles who were still in Jerusalem heard that the people of Samaria had accepted the word of God, they sent Peter and John to them. When Peter and John arrived, they prayed that the Samaritan believers might receive the Holy Spirit.

These people had been baptized in the name of the Lord Jesus, but the Holy Spirit had not yet come upon any of them. Then, when the two apostles began laying their hands on the people, they received the Holy Spirit.

Simon saw that the Spirit was given to people when the apostles laid their hands on them. So he offered the apostles money, saying, "Give me also this power so that anyone on whom I lay my hands will receive the Holy Spirit."

Peter said to him, "You and your money should both be destroyed, because you thought you could buy God's gift with money. You cannot share with us in this work since your heart is not right before God. Change your heart! Turn away from this evil thing you have done, and pray to the Lord. Maybe he will forgive you for thinking this. I see that you are full of bitter jealousy and ruled by sin."

Simon answered, "Both of you pray for me to the Lord so the things you have said will not happen to me."

After Peter and John told the people what they had seen Jesus do and after they had spoken the message of the Lord, they went back to Jerusalem. On the way, they went through many Samaritan towns and preached the Good News to the people.

*K*orah, Dathan, Abiram, and On turned against Moses. (Korah was the son of Izhar, the son of Kohath, the son of Levi; Dathan and Abiram were brothers, the sons of Eliab; and On was the son of Peleth; Dathan, Abiram, and On were from the tribe of Reuben.) These men gathered two hundred fifty other Israelite men, well-known leaders chosen by the community, and challenged Moses. They came as a group to speak to Moses and Aaron and said, "You have gone too far. All the people are holy, every one of them, and the LORD is among them. So why do you put yourselves above all the people of the LORD?"

Moses also said to Korah, "Listen, you Levites. The God of Israel has separated you from the rest of the Israelites. He brought you near to himself to do the work in the LORD's Holy Tent and to stand before all the Israelites and serve them. Isn't that enough? He has brought you and all your fellow Levites near to himself, yet now you want to be priests. You and your followers have joined together against the LORD. Your complaint is not against Aaron."

Then Moses said, "Now you will know that the LORD has sent me to do all these things; it was not my idea. If these men die a normal death—the way men usually die—then the LORD did not really send me. But if the LORD does something new, you will know they have insulted the LORD. The ground will open and swallow them. They will be buried alive and will go to the place of the dead, and everything that belongs to them will go with them."

When Moses finished saying these things, the ground under the men split open. The earth opened and swallowed them and all their families. All Korah's men and everything they owned went down. They were buried alive, going to the place of the dead, and everything they owned went with them. Then the earth covered them. They died and were gone from the community. The people of Israel around them heard their screams and ran away, saying, "The earth will swallow us, too!"

Then a fire came down from the LORD and destroyed the two hundred fifty men who had presented the incense.

Numbers 16:1–3, 8–11, 28–35

*T*he people in the camp were jealous of Moses
 and of Aaron, the holy priest of the
  LORD.
Then the ground opened up and
  swallowed Dathan
 and closed over Abiram's group.
A fire burned among their followers,
 and flames burned up the wicked.

Psalm 106:16–18

*D*elight yourself in the spiritual victories
 of others:

*Delight in all triumphs
 in Christ Jesus.
Rejoice when another's success is greater
 than yours:
 Be glad when another receives
 what you need.
Remain at peace when another receives
 the attention
 you think you deserve.
You must not strive:
You must war against
 all jealousy and contention.*

*Say today:
 I will not be jealous.
 I will not contend.
 I will not strive.
 I will rejoice at another's victories.
 I will delight in the success of others.
 I will not think others less worthy
  or less important than I.
 I will not see my work as more impor-
  tant than someone else's.
 I will pray for those who are my com-
  petitors.
 I will rejoice in my relationship with
  the Lord.*

And so it will be.

Marie Chapian

*B*efore reading Numbers 16, did you know that God considers jealousy of his chosen servants to be an insult to him, not an insult to his servants? God takes the bitter sin of jealousy quite seriously, doesn't he? For what sins of jealousy do you need to ask God's forgiveness?

WEDNESDAY:
God's Word Brings Joy to Those Who Understand It
Acts 8:26—9:9

Philip Teaches an Ethiopian

*A*n angel of the Lord said to Philip, "Get ready and go south to the road that leads down to Gaza from Jerusalem—the desert road." So Philip got ready and went. On the road he saw a man from Ethiopia, a eunuch. He was an important officer in the service of Candace, the queen of the Ethiopians; he was responsible for taking care of all her money. He had gone to Jerusalem to worship. Now, as he was on his way home, he was sitting in his chariot reading from the Book of Isaiah, the prophet. The Spirit said to Philip, "Go to that chariot and stay near it."

So when Philip ran toward the chariot, he heard the man reading from Isaiah the prophet. Philip asked, "Do you understand what you are reading?"

He answered, "How can I understand unless someone explains it to me?" Then he invited Philip to climb in and sit with him. The portion of Scripture he was reading was this:

"He was like a sheep being led to be
killed.
He was quiet, as a lamb is quiet
while its wool is being cut;
he never opened his mouth.
He was shamed and was treated
unfairly.
He died without children to continue
his family.
His life on earth has ended."

Isaiah 53:7–8

The officer said to Philip, "Please tell me, who is the prophet talking about—himself or someone else?" Philip began to speak, and starting with this same Scripture, he told the man the Good News about Jesus.

While they were traveling down the road, they came to some water. The officer said, "Look, here is water. What is stopping me from being baptized?" Then the officer commanded the chariot to stop. Both Philip and the officer went down into the water, and Philip baptized him. When they came up out of the water, the Spirit of the Lord took Philip away; the officer never saw him again. And the officer continued on his way home, full of joy. But Philip appeared in a city called Azotus and preached the Good News in all the towns on the way from Azotus to Caesarea.

Saul Is Converted

*I*n Jerusalem Saul was still threatening the followers of the Lord by saying he would kill them. So he went to the high priest and asked him to write letters to the synagogues in the city of Damascus. Then if Saul found any followers of Christ's Way, men or women, he would arrest them and bring them back to Jerusalem.

So Saul headed toward Damascus. As he came near the city, a bright light from heaven suddenly flashed around him. Saul fell to the ground and heard a voice saying to him, "Saul, Saul! Why are you persecuting me?"

Saul said, "Who are you, Lord?"

The voice answered, "I am Jesus, whom you are persecuting. Get up now and go into the city. Someone there will tell you what you must do."

The people traveling with Saul stood there but said nothing. They heard the voice, but they saw no one. Saul got up from the ground and opened his eyes, but he could not see. So those with Saul took his hand and led him into Damascus. For three days Saul could not see and did not eat or drink.

*A*ll the people of Israel gathered together in the square by the Water Gate. They asked Ezra the teacher to bring out the Book of the Teachings of Moses, which the LORD had given to Israel.

So on the first day of the seventh month, Ezra the priest brought out the Teachings for the crowd. Men, women, and all who could listen and understand had gathered.

At the square by the Water Gate Ezra read the Teachings out loud from early morning until noon to the men, women, and everyone who could listen and understand. All the people listened carefully to the Book of the Teachings.

Ezra the teacher stood on a high wooden platform that had been built just for this time. On his right were Mattithiah, Shema, Anaiah, Uriah, Hilkiah, and Maaseiah. And on his left were Pedaiah, Mishael, Malkijah, Hashum, Hashbaddanah, Zechariah, and Meshullam.

Ezra opened the book in full view of everyone, because he was above them. As he opened it, all the people stood up. Ezra praised the LORD, the great God, and all the people held up their hands and said, "Amen! Amen!" Then they bowed down and worshiped the LORD with their faces to the ground.

These Levites explained the Teachings to the people as they stood there: Jeshua, Bani, Sherebiah, Jamin, Akkub, Shabbethai, Hodiah, Maaseiah, Kelita, Azariah, Jozabad, Hanan, and Pelaiah. They read from the Book of the Teachings of God and explained what it meant so the people understood what was being read.

Then Nehemiah the governor, Ezra the priest and teacher, and the Levites who were teaching said to all the people, "This is a holy day to the LORD your God. Don't be sad or cry." All the people had been crying as they listened to the words of the Teachings.

Nehemiah said, "Go and enjoy good food and sweet drinks. Send some to people who have none, because today is a holy day to the Lord. Don't be sad, because the joy of the LORD will make you strong."

The Levites helped calm the people, saying, "Be quiet, because this is a holy day. Don't be sad."

Then all the people went away to eat and drink, to send some of their food to others, and to celebrate with great joy. They finally understood what they had been taught.

Nehemiah 8:1–12

*L*ORD, teach me your demands,
and I will keep them until the end.

Help me understand, so I can keep
your teachings,
obeying them with all my heart.
Lead me in the path of your commands,
because that makes me happy.

I am as happy over your promises
as if I found a great treasure.
I hate and despise lies,
but I love your teachings.
Seven times a day I praise you
for your fair laws.
Those who love your teachings will find
true peace,
and nothing will defeat them.
I am waiting for you to save me, LORD.
I will obey your commands.
I obey your rules,
and I love them very much.

Psalm 119:33–35, 162–67

INSIGHTS

*T*he Word of God is a constant and continuing source of joy for the Christian. I don't think I've ever met a joyless Christian who was regularly employed in searching the Scriptures. The result of such searching is to see beyond the words the One who inspired them. Of all the habits the Christian can cultivate, this is one of the most blessed and profitable. Some books are exhausting and exhaustible. The Bible is the only Book that rewards the student with increasing insight as he allows the Word of God to flow through and cleanse him. Indeed, it is the only Book that can cleanse and purify the life of its reader. Other books can inform, but only the Scripture can transform, infill, and inspire.

Al Bryant

ACTION POINT

*W*hy were the Israelites saddened when they first heard the Lord's teachings? What enabled them to be joyous? What brought great joy to the Ethiopian officer? Who has helped you understand God's Word? Thank God for that person and pray that you will experience the joy of living by God's Word.

THURSDAY:
"Here I Am, Lord"
Acts 9:10–35

NEW TESTAMENT READING

*T*here was a follower of Jesus in Damascus named Ananias. The Lord spoke to Ananias in a vision, "Ananias!"

Ananias answered, "Here I am, Lord."

The Lord said to him, "Get up and go to Straight Street. Find the house of Judas, and ask for a man named Saul from the city of Tarsus. He is there now, praying. Saul has seen a vision in which a man named Ananias comes to him and lays his hands on him. Then he is able to see again."

But Ananias answered, "Lord, many people have told me about this man and the terrible things he did to your holy people in Jerusalem. Now he has come here to Damascus, and the leading priests have given him the power to arrest everyone who worships you."

But the Lord said to Ananias, "Go! I have chosen Saul for an important work. He must tell about me to those who are not Jews, to kings, and to the people of Israel. I will show him how much he must suffer for my name."

So Ananias went to the house of Judas. He laid his hands on Saul and said, "Brother Saul, the Lord Jesus sent me. He is the one you saw on the road on your way here. He sent me so that you can see again and be filled with the Holy Spirit." Immediately, something that looked like fish scales fell from Saul's eyes, and he was able to see again! Then Saul got up and was baptized. After he ate some food, his strength returned.

Saul Preaches in Damascus

*S*aul stayed with the followers of Jesus in Damascus for a few days. Soon he began to preach about Jesus in the synagogues, saying, "Jesus is the Son of God."

All the people who heard him were amazed. They said, "This is the man who was in Jerusalem trying to destroy those who trust in this name! He came here to arrest the followers of Jesus and take them back to the leading priests."

But Saul grew more powerful. His proofs that Jesus is the Christ were so strong that the Jewish people in Damascus could not argue with him.

After many days, some Jewish people made plans to kill Saul. They were watching the city gates day and night, but Saul learned about their plan. One night some followers of Saul helped him leave the city by lowering him in a basket through an opening in the city wall.

Saul Preaches in Jerusalem

*W*hen Saul went to Jerusalem, he tried to join the group of followers, but they were all afraid of him. They did not believe he was really a follower. But Barnabas accepted Saul and took him to the apostles. Barnabas explained to them that Saul had seen the Lord on the road and the Lord had spoken to Saul. Then he told them how boldly Saul had preached in the name of Jesus in Damascus.

And so Saul stayed with the followers, going everywhere in Jerusalem, preaching boldly in the name of the Lord. He would often talk and argue with the Jewish people who spoke Greek, but they were trying to kill him. When the followers learned about this, they took Saul to Caesarea and from there sent him to Tarsus.

The church everywhere in Judea, Galilee, and Samaria had a time of peace and became stronger. Respecting the Lord by the way they lived, and being encouraged by the Holy Spirit, the group of believers continued to grow.

Peter Heals Aeneas

*A*s Peter was traveling through all the area, he visited God's people who lived in Lydda. There he met a man named Aeneas, who was paralyzed and had not been able to leave his bed for the past eight years. Peter said to him, "Aeneas, Jesus Christ heals you. Stand up and make your bed." Aeneas stood up immediately. All the people living in Lydda and on the Plain of Sharon saw him and turned to the Lord.

*T*he Lᴏʀᴅ said to Samuel, "How long will you continue to feel sorry for Saul? I have rejected him as king of Israel. Fill your container with olive oil and go. I am sending you to Jesse who lives in Bethlehem, because I have chosen one of his sons to be king."

But Samuel said, "If I go, Saul will hear the news and will try to kill me."

The Lᴏʀᴅ said, "Take a young calf with you. Say, 'I have come to offer a sacrifice to the Lᴏʀᴅ.' Invite Jesse to the sacrifice. Then I will tell you what to do. You must appoint the one I show you."

Samuel did what the Lᴏʀᴅ told him to do. When he arrived at Bethlehem, the older leaders of Bethlehem shook with fear. They met him and asked, "Are you coming in peace?"

Samuel answered, "Yes, I come in peace. I have come to make a sacrifice to the Lᴏʀᴅ. Set yourselves apart to the Lᴏʀᴅ and come to the sacrifice with me." Then he set Jesse and his sons apart to the Lᴏʀᴅ, and he invited them to come to the sacrifice.

When they arrived, Samuel saw Eliab, and he thought, "Surely the Lᴏʀᴅ has appointed this person standing here before him."

But the Lᴏʀᴅ said to Samuel, "Don't look at how handsome Eliab is or how tall he is, because I have not chosen him. God does not see the same way people see. People look at the outside of a person, but the Lᴏʀᴅ looks at the heart."

Then Jesse called Abinadab and told him to pass by Samuel. But Samuel said, "The Lᴏʀᴅ has not chosen this man either." Then Jesse had Shammah pass by. But Samuel said, "No, the Lᴏʀᴅ has not chosen this one." Jesse had seven of his sons pass by Samuel. But Samuel said to him, "The Lᴏʀᴅ has not chosen any of these."

Then he asked Jesse, "Are these all the sons you have?"

Jesse answered, "I still have the youngest son. He is out taking care of the sheep."

Samuel said, "Send for him. We will not sit down to eat until he arrives."

So Jesse sent and had his youngest son brought in. He was a fine boy, tanned, and handsome.

The Lᴏʀᴅ said to Samuel, "Go, appoint him, because he is the one."

So Samuel took the container of olive oil and poured it on Jesse's youngest son to appoint him in front of his brothers. From that day on, the Lᴏʀᴅ's Spirit worked in David. Samuel then went back to Ramah.

1 Samuel 16:1–13

---

*B*lessed and happy are they who have a sweet faith in Jesus, intertwined with deep affection for Him, for this is a restful confidence. These lovers of Jesus are charmed with His character and delighted with His mission; they are carried away by the loving-kindness that He has manifested, and therefore they cannot help trusting Him because they so much admire, revere, and love Him. . . .

. . . We love Him and He loves us, and therefore we put ourselves into His hands, accept whatever He prescribes, and do whatever He bids. We feel that nothing can be wrongly ordered while He is the Director of our affairs, for He loves us too well to let us perish or suffer a single needless pang.

Faith is the root of obedience, and this may be clearly seen in the affairs of life. When a captain trusts a pilot to steer his vessel into port, he manages the vessel according to his direction. When a traveler trusts a guide to conduct him over a difficult pass, he follows the track which his guide points out. When a patient believes in a physician, he carefully follows his prescriptions and directions. Faith which refuses to obey the commands of the Saviour is a mere pretence and will never save the soul.

Charles Spurgeon

---

*W*hat kind of faith is needed to earnestly say the words, "Here I am, Lord"? Is your faith sufficient to do anything your Savior may ask? What objections to complete obedience must you overcome?

FRIDAY:
God Hears and Answers Our Prayers
Acts 9:36—10:23a

Peter Heals Tabitha

*I*n the city of Joppa there was a follower named Tabitha (whose Greek name was Dorcas). She was always doing good deeds and kind acts. While Peter was in Lydda, Tabitha became sick and died. Her body was washed and put in a room upstairs. Since Lydda is near Joppa and the followers in Joppa heard that Peter was in Lydda, they sent two messengers to Peter. They begged him, "Hurry, please come to us!" So Peter got ready and went with them. When he arrived, they took him to the upstairs room where all the widows stood around Peter, crying. They showed him the shirts and coats Tabitha had made when she was still alive. Peter sent everyone out of the room and kneeled and prayed. Then he turned to the body and said, "Tabitha, stand up." She opened her eyes, and when she saw Peter, she sat up. He gave her his hand and helped her up. Then he called the saints and the widows into the room and showed them that Tabitha was alive. People everywhere in Joppa learned about this, and many believed in the Lord. Peter stayed in Joppa for many days with a man named Simon who was a tanner.

Peter Teaches Cornelius

*A*t Caesarea there was a man named Cornelius, an officer in the Italian group of the Roman army. Cornelius was a religious man. He and all the other people who lived in his house worshiped the true God. He gave much of his money to the poor and prayed to God often. One afternoon about three o'clock, Cornelius clearly saw a vision. An angel of God came to him and said, "Cornelius!"

Cornelius stared at the angel. He became afraid and said, "What do you want, Lord?"

The angel said, "God has heard your prayers. He has seen that you give to the poor, and he remembers you. Send some men now to Joppa to bring back a man named Simon who is also called Peter. He is staying with a man, also named Simon, who is a tanner and has a house beside the sea." When the angel who spoke to Cornelius left, Cornelius called two of his servants and a soldier, a religious man who worked for him. Cornelius explained everything to them and sent them to Joppa.

About noon the next day as they came near Joppa, Peter was going up to the roof to pray. He was hungry and wanted to eat, but while the food was being prepared, he had a vision. He saw heaven opened and something coming down that looked like a big sheet being lowered to earth by its four corners. In it were all kinds of animals, reptiles, and birds. Then a voice said to Peter, "Get up, Peter; kill and eat."

But Peter said, "No, Lord! I have never eaten food that is unholy or unclean."

But the voice said to him again, "God has made these things clean so don't call them 'unholy'!" This happened three times, and at once the sheet was taken back to heaven.

While Peter was wondering what this vision meant, the men Cornelius sent had found Simon's house and were standing at the gate. They asked, "Is Simon Peter staying here?"

While Peter was still thinking about the vision, the Spirit said to him, "Listen, three men are looking for you. Get up and go downstairs. Go with them without doubting, because I have sent them to you."

So Peter went down to the men and said, "I am the one you are looking for. Why did you come here?"

They said, "A holy angel spoke to Cornelius, an army officer and a good man; he worships God. All the Jewish people respect him. The angel told Cornelius to ask you to come to his house so that he can hear what you have to say." So Peter asked the men to come in and spend the night.

*L*ORD, I give myself to you;
my God, I trust you.

Do not let me be disgraced;
    do not let my enemies laugh at me.
No one who trusts you will be dis-
    graced,
    but those who sin without excuse
    will be disgraced.

LORD, tell me your ways.
    Show me how to live.
Guide me in your truth,
    and teach me, my God, my Savior.
    I trust you all day long.
LORD, remember your mercy and love
    that you have shown since long ago.
Do not remember the sins
    and wrong things I did when I was
    young.
But remember to love me always
    because you are good, LORD.

The LORD is good and right;
    he points sinners to the right way.
He shows those who are humble how
    to do right,
    and he teaches them his ways.
All the LORD's ways are loving and true
    for those who follow the demands of
    his agreement.
For the sake of your name, LORD,
    forgive my many sins.
Are there those who respect the LORD?
    He will point them to the best way.
They will enjoy a good life,
    and their children will inherit the
    land.

Psalm 25:1–13

*B*ut please listen to my prayer and my request, because I am your servant. LORD my
God, hear this prayer your servant prays to
you today. Night and day please watch over
this Temple where you have said, 'I will be
worshiped there.' Hear the prayer I pray
facing this Temple. Hear my prayers and
the prayers of your people Israel when we
pray facing this place. Hear from your home
in heaven, and when you hear, forgive us.

1 Kings 8:28–30

*S*olomon finished building the Temple of
the LORD and his royal palace and everything
he wanted to build. Then the LORD appeared
to him again just as he had done before, in
Gibeon. The LORD said to him: "I have heard

your prayer and what you have asked me
to do. You built this Temple, and I have
made it a holy place. I will be worshiped
there forever and will watch over it and
protect it always."

1 Kings 9:1–3

INSIGHTS

*T*he Lord God of the universe, the Creator
and Sustainer of all things, . . . not only
commands us to pray, but also invites us to
make our requests known. Jesus says that we
have not because we ask not. James tells us
that the effectual, fervent prayer of a righteous
man accomplishes much. Time and again the
Bible says that prayer is an effective tool. It is
useful; it works. . . .

Prayer, like everything else in the Christian life, is for God's glory and for our benefit,
in that order. Everything that God does, everything that God allows and ordains, is in
the supreme sense for His glory. It is also true
that while God seeks His own glory supremely,
man benefits when God is glorified. We pray
to glorify God, but also to receive the benefits
of prayer from His hand. . . .

One of the great themes of the Reformation was the idea that all of our life is to be
lived under the authority of God, to the glory
of God, in the presence of God. . . . Prayer
is discourse with the personal God Himself.
There, in the act and dynamic of praying, I
bring my whole life under His gaze. Yes, He
knows what is in my mind, but I still have
the privilege of articulating to Him what is
there. He says, "Come. Speak to Me. Make
your requests known to Me." And so, we come
in order to know Him and to be known by
Him.

R. C. Sproul

ACTION POINT

*D*o you feel that your prayers are really
in touch with God—powerful enough to
raise the dead? No? Then take these Scriptures to heart. Pray as if God is the ultimate
reality in your life. Then listen. His response
will come!

WEEKEND:

God Forgives All Who Come to Him

Acts 10:23b–48

*T*he next day Peter got ready and went with them, and some of the followers from Joppa joined him. On the following day they came to Caesarea. Cornelius was waiting for them and had called together his relatives and close friends. When Peter entered, Cornelius met him, fell at his feet, and worshiped him. But Peter helped him up, saying, "Stand up. I too am only a human." As he talked with Cornelius, Peter went inside where he saw many people gathered. He said, "You people understand that it is against our Jewish law for Jewish people to associate with or visit anyone who is not Jewish. But God has shown me that I should not call any person 'unholy' or 'unclean.' That is why I did not argue when I was asked to come here. Now, please tell me why you sent for me."

Cornelius said, "Four days ago, I was praying in my house at this same time—three o'clock in the afternoon. Suddenly, there was a man standing before me wearing shining clothes. He said, 'Cornelius, God has heard your prayer and has seen that you give to the poor and remembers you. So send some men to Joppa and ask Simon Peter to come. Peter is staying in the house of a man, also named Simon, who is a tanner and has a house beside the sea.' So I sent for you immediately, and it was very good of you to come. Now we are all here before God to hear everything the Lord has commanded you to tell us."

Peter began to speak: "I really understand now that to God every person is the same. In every country God accepts anyone who worships him and does what is right. You know the message that God has sent to the people of Israel is the Good News that peace has come through Jesus Christ. Jesus is the Lord of all people! You know what has happened all over Judea, beginning in Galilee after John preached to the people about baptism. You know about Jesus from Nazareth, that God gave him the Holy Spirit and power. You know how Jesus went everywhere doing good and healing those who were ruled by the devil, because God was with him. We saw what Jesus did in Judea and in Jerusalem, but the Jews in Jerusalem killed him by hanging him on a cross. Yet, on the third day, God raised Jesus to life and caused him to be seen, not by all the people, but only by the witnesses God had already chosen. And we are those witnesses who ate and drank with him after he was raised from the dead. He told us to preach to the people and to tell them that he is the one whom God chose to be the judge of the living and the dead. All the prophets say it is true that all who believe in Jesus will be forgiven of their sins through Jesus' name."

While Peter was still saying this, the Holy Spirit came down on all those who were listening. The Jewish believers who came with Peter were amazed that the gift of the Holy Spirit had been given even to those who were not Jews. These Jewish believers heard them speaking in different languages and praising God. Then Peter said, "Can anyone keep these people from being baptized with water? They have received the Holy Spirit just as we did!" So Peter ordered that they be baptized in the name of Jesus Christ. Then they asked Peter to stay with them for a few days.

*T*he LORD says,
  "Come, let us talk about these things.
Though your sins are like scarlet,
  they can be as white as snow.
Though your sins are deep red,
  they can be white like wool.
If you become willing and obey me,
  you will eat good crops from the land.
But if you refuse to obey and if you turn
  against me,
  you will be destroyed by your
  enemies' swords."
The LORD himself said these things.
Isaiah 1:18–20

God, you will be praised in Jerusalem.
We will keep our promises to you.
You hear our prayers.
All people will come to you.
Our guilt overwhelms us,
but you forgive our sins.
Happy are the people you choose
and invite to stay in your court.
We are filled with good things in your
house,
your holy Temple.

You give the year a good harvest,
and you load the wagons with many
crops.
The desert is covered with grass
and the hills with happiness.
The pastures are full of flocks,
and the valleys are covered with
grain.
Everything shouts and sings for joy.

Psalm 65:1–4, 11–13

The wicked should stop doing wrong,
and they should stop their evil
thoughts.
They should return to the LORD so he
may have mercy on them.
They should come to our God,
because he will freely forgive
them.

Isaiah 55:7

The LORD passed in front of Moses and said, "I am the LORD. The LORD is a God who shows mercy, who is kind, who doesn't become angry quickly, who has great love and faithfulness and is kind to thousands of people. The LORD forgives people for evil, for sin, and for turning against him, but he does not forget to punish guilty people. He will punish not only the guilty people, but also their children, their grandchildren, their great-grandchildren, and their great-great-grandchildren."

Exodus 34:6–7

INSIGHTS

At the heart of God is the desire to give and to forgive. Because of this, he set into motion the entire redemptive process that culminated in the cross and was confirmed in the resurrection. The usual notion of what Jesus did on the cross runs something like this: people were so bad and so mean and God was so angry with them that he could not forgive them unless somebody big enough took the rap for the whole lot of them.

Nothing could be further from the truth. Love, not anger, brought Jesus to the cross. Golgotha came as a result of God's great desire to forgive, not his reluctance. Jesus knew that by his vicarious suffering he could actually absorb all the evil of humanity and so heal it, forgive it, redeem it. . . .

Having accomplished this greatest of all his works, Jesus then took refreshment. "It is finished," he announced. That is, this great work of redemption was completed. He could feel the last dregs of the misery of humankind flow through him and into the care of the Father. The last twinges of evil, hostility, anger, and fear drained out of him, and he was able to turn again into the light of God's presence. . . .

This redemptive process is a great mystery hidden in the heart of God. But I know that it is true. I know this not only because the Bible says it is true, but because I have seen its effects in the lives of many people, including myself. It is the ground upon which we can know that confession and forgiveness are realities that transform us. Without the cross the Discipline of confession would be only psychologically therapeutic. But it is so much more. It involves an objective change in our relationship with God and a subjective change in us. It is a means of healing and transforming the inner spirit.

Richard Foster

PAUSE FOR REFLECTION

Peter was one of Jesus' closest disciples, yet we see here that he discovers a new, wonderful, and unexpected truth about God's forgiveness. What is it? Thank God for his awesome gift of salvation to you!

MONDAY:

God's People Are to Care for One Another

Acts 11:1–30

NEW TESTAMENT READING

Peter Returns to Jerusalem

*T*he apostles and the believers in Judea heard that some who were not Jewish had accepted God's teaching too. But when Peter came to Jerusalem, some Jewish believers argued with him. They said, "You went into the homes of people who are not circumcised and ate with them!"

So Peter explained the whole story to them. He said, "I was in the city of Joppa, and while I was praying, I had a vision. I saw something that looked like a big sheet being lowered from heaven by its four corners. It came very close to me. I looked inside it and saw animals, wild beasts, reptiles, and birds. I heard a voice say to me, 'Get up, Peter. Kill and eat.' But I said, 'No, Lord! I have never eaten anything that is unholy or unclean.' But the voice from heaven spoke again, 'God has made these things clean, so don't call them unholy.' This happened three times. Then the whole thing was taken back to heaven. Right then three men who were sent to me from Caesarea came to the house where I was staying. The Spirit told me to go with them without doubting. These six believers here also went with me, and we entered the house of Cornelius. He told us about the angel he saw standing in his house. The angel said to him, 'Send some men to Joppa and invite Simon Peter to come. By the words he will say to you, you and all your family will be saved.' When I began my speech, the Holy Spirit came on them just as he came on us at the beginning. Then I remembered the words of the Lord. He said, 'John baptized with water, but you will be baptized with the Holy Spirit.' Since God gave them the same gift he gave us who believed in the Lord Jesus Christ, how could I stop the work of God?"

When the Jewish believers heard this, they stopped arguing. They praised God and said, "So God is allowing even those who are not Jewish to turn to him and live."

The Good News Comes to Antioch

*M*any of the believers were scattered when they were persecuted after Stephen was killed. Some of them went as far as Phoenicia, Cyprus, and Antioch telling the message to others, but only to Jews. Some of these believers were people from Cyprus and Cyrene. When they came to Antioch, they spoke also to Greeks, telling them the Good News about the Lord Jesus. The Lord was helping the believers, and a large group of people believed and turned to the Lord.

The church in Jerusalem heard about all of this, so they sent Barnabas to Antioch. Barnabas was a good man, full of the Holy Spirit and full of faith. When he reached Antioch and saw how God had blessed the people, he was glad. He encouraged all the believers in Antioch always to obey the Lord with all their hearts, and many people became followers of the Lord.

Then Barnabas went to the city of Tarsus to look for Saul, and when he found Saul, he brought him to Antioch. For a whole year Saul and Barnabas met with the church and taught many people there. In Antioch the followers were called Christians for the first time.

About that time some prophets came from Jerusalem to Antioch. One of them, named Agabus, stood up and spoke with the help of the Holy Spirit. He said, "A very hard time is coming to the whole world. There will be no food to eat." (This happened when Claudius ruled.) The believers all decided to help the followers who lived in Judea, as much as each one could. They gathered the money and gave it to Barnabas and Saul, who brought it to the elders in Judea.

OLD TESTAMENT READING

*A*nyone who heard me spoke well of me,
  and those who saw me praised me,
because I saved the poor who called out
  and the orphan who had no one to
  help.
The dying person blessed me,
  and I made the widow's heart sing.

I put on right living as if it were clothing;
I wore fairness like a robe and a
turban.
I was eyes for the blind
and feet for the lame.
I was like a father to needy people,
and I took the side of strangers who
were in trouble.

Job 29:11–16

*G*enerous people will be blessed,
because they share their food with
the poor.

Proverbs 22:9

*B*ut there should be no poor people among you, because the LORD your God will richly bless you in the land he is giving you as your own. He will bless you if you obey the LORD your God completely, but you must be careful to obey all the commands I am giving you today. The LORD your God will bless you as he promised, and you will lend to other nations, but you will not need to borrow from them. You will rule over many nations, but none will rule over you.

If there are poor among you, in one of the towns of the land the LORD your God is giving you, do not be selfish or greedy toward them. But give freely to them, and freely lend them whatever they need. Beware of evil thoughts. Don't think, "The seventh year is near, the year to cancel what people owe." You might be mean to the needy and not give them anything. Then they will complain to the LORD about you, and he will find you guilty of sin. Give freely to the poor person, and do not wish that you didn't have to give. The LORD your God will bless your work and everything you touch. There will always be poor people in the land, so I command you to give freely to your neighbors and to the poor and needy in your land.

Deuteronomy 15:4–11

INSIGHTS

*S*omeone has said, "We have no permission from Jesus to be selective in our compassion." It is our natural tendency, however, to choose whom we will reach out to. Perhaps this was the problem of the priest and the Levite in the parable of the good Samaritan. In any event, we know it is often our problem. Jesus mingled with all men, the rich and the poor, the socially acceptable and the backward and undesirable. This willingness to enter into others' lives is costly. A contemporary poet, Michael Quoist, pinpoints our problem:

Lord, why did you tell me to love all men as my brothers?
I have tried, but I come back to you frightened.
Lord, I was so peaceful at home, so comfortably settled.
It was well-furnished, and I felt so cozy.
I was alone—I was at peace.
Sheltered from the wind and the rain, kept clean.

Our God wants to dislodge us from our comfortable, smug existence, to move us to mingle with our needy brothers, to stir us to touch those we might otherwise shun. Another poet, whose name is lost in history, expresses the challenge well: "Love has a hem to her garment that trails in the very dust; it can reach the stains of the streets and lanes, and because it can, it must." This is clearly the brand of compassion Jesus exemplified, and it is the kind of loving outreach he calls us to in our modern world. Answering his call is often a struggle for us. We may pay lip service to such compassion, but the performance is often costly, and we're inclined to back away. . . .

True compassion is an expression of the life of our Lord Jesus Christ. It is always ready to give, and always willing to sacrifice.

William Fletcher

ACTION POINT

*W*hen has God shaken up your view of how you are to live for him or to care for others? Does your view of Christian compassion need some adjustment? Pray for a heart that will gladly give and sacrifice for Jesus' sake.

TUESDAY:

God Intervenes to Save His People

Acts 12:1–25

NEW TESTAMENT READING

Herod Agrippa Hurts the Church

*D*uring that same time King Herod began to mistreat some who belonged to the church. He ordered James, the brother of John, to be killed by the sword. Herod saw that the Jewish people liked this, so he decided to arrest Peter, too. (This happened during the time of the Feast of Unleavened Bread.)

After Herod arrested Peter, he put him in jail and handed him over to be guarded by sixteen soldiers. Herod planned to bring Peter before the people for trial after the Passover Feast. So Peter was kept in jail, but the church prayed earnestly to God for him.

Peter Leaves the Jail

*T*he night before Herod was to bring him to trial, Peter was sleeping between two soldiers, bound with two chains. Other soldiers were guarding the door of the jail. Suddenly, an angel of the Lord stood there, and a light shined in the cell. The angel struck Peter on the side and woke him up. "Hurry! Get up!" the angel said. And the chains fell off Peter's hands. Then the angel told him, "Get dressed and put on your sandals." And Peter did. Then the angel said, "Put on your coat and follow me." So Peter followed him out, but he did not know if what the angel was doing was real; he thought he might be seeing a vision. They went past the first and second guards and came to the iron gate that separated them from the city. The gate opened by itself for them, and they went through it. When they had walked down one street, the angel suddenly left him.

Then Peter realized what had happened. He thought, "Now I know that the Lord really sent his angel to me. He rescued me from Herod and from all the things the Jewish people thought would happen."

When he considered this, he went to the home of Mary, the mother of John Mark.

Many people were gathered there, praying. Peter knocked on the outside door, and a servant girl named Rhoda came to answer it. When she recognized Peter's voice, she was so happy she forgot to open the door. Instead, she ran inside and told the group, "Peter is at the door!"

They said to her, "You are crazy!" But she kept on saying it was true, so they said, "It must be Peter's angel."

Peter continued to knock, and when they opened the door, they saw him and were amazed. Peter made a sign with his hand to tell them to be quiet. He explained how the Lord led him out of the jail, and he said, "Tell James and the other believers what happened." Then he left to go to another place.

The next day the soldiers were very upset and wondered what had happened to Peter. Herod looked everywhere for him but could not find him. So he questioned the guards and ordered that they be killed.

The Death of Herod Agrippa

*L*ater Herod moved from Judea and went to the city of Caesarea, where he stayed. Herod was very angry with the people of Tyre and Sidon, but the people of those cities all came in a group to him. After convincing Blastus, the king's personal servant, to be on their side, they asked Herod for peace, because their country got its food from his country.

On a chosen day Herod put on his royal robes, sat on his throne, and made a speech to the people. They shouted, "This is the voice of a god, not a human!" Because Herod did not give the glory to God, an angel of the Lord immediately caused him to become sick, and he was eaten by worms and died.

God's message continued to spread and reach people.

After Barnabas and Saul finished their task in Jerusalem, they returned to Antioch, taking John Mark with them.

OLD TESTAMENT READING

*W*hen the Israelites saw the king and his army coming after them, they were very frightened and cried to the LORD for help.

Then the LORD said to Moses, "Why are you crying out to me? Command the Israelites to start moving. Raise your walking stick and hold it over the sea so that the sea will split and the people can cross it on dry land. I will make the Egyptians stubborn so they will chase the Israelites, but I will be honored when I defeat the king and all of his chariot drivers and chariots. When I defeat the king, his chariot drivers, and chariots, the Egyptians will know that I am the LORD."

Now the angel of God that usually traveled in front of Israel's army moved behind them. Also, the pillar of cloud moved from in front of the people and stood behind them. So the cloud came between the Egyptians and the Israelites. This made it dark for the Egyptians but gave light to the Israelites. So the cloud kept the two armies apart all night.

Then Moses held his hand over the sea. All that night the LORD drove back the sea with a strong east wind, making the sea become dry ground. The water was split, and the Israelites went through the sea on dry land, with a wall of water on their right and on their left.

Then all the king's horses, chariots, and chariot drivers followed them into the sea. When morning came, the LORD looked down from the pillar of cloud and fire at the Egyptian army and made them panic. He kept the wheels of the chariots from turning, making it hard to drive the chariots. The Egyptians shouted, "Let's get away from the Israelites! The LORD is fighting for them and against Egypt."

Then the LORD told Moses, "Hold your hand over the sea so that the water will come back over the Egyptians, their chariots, and chariot drivers." So Moses raised his hand over the sea, and at dawn the sea returned to its place. The Egyptians tried to run from it, but the LORD swept them away into the sea. The water returned, covering the chariots, chariot drivers, and all the king's army that had followed the Israelites into the sea. Not one of them survived.

But the Israelites crossed the sea on dry land, with a wall of water on their right and on their left. So that day the LORD saved the Israelites from the Egyptians, and the Israelites saw the Egyptians lying dead on the seashore. When the Israelites saw the great power the LORD had used against the Egyptians, they feared the LORD, and they trusted him and his servant Moses.

Exodus 14:10, 15–31

Interestingly, the Book of Daniel opens with a story of the Babylonian invasion of Judah. In the invasion the Babylonians were totally successful and a number of the children of Israel were deported into captivity, including Daniel and his three friends. . . . These young men understood that they were not in Babylon by chance. God had put them there. . . .

God knew what kind of persecution His children were facing and what He would have to do to deliver them out of it. . . . The fiery furnace, the intensity of the heat, and the anger of Nebuchadnezzar were all human efforts to thwart the will of God. But He overcame them all! At the moment of His children's greatest need, He sent His Son to deliver them from the fire. In so doing, God gives us a beautiful picture of His working in our lives. He does not always choose to keep us from the fire, but often brings about our deliverance while we are in the fire itself.

If God could deliver these young men from a fiery furnace, it should seem evident He can deliver us from whatever trouble we find ourselves in. . . .

. . . He may use these difficulties to teach us great lessons and to bring us to a point of repentance, but ultimately, He can also use these difficulties to produce a wonderful result that only He could bring to pass.

Richard Lee

PAUSE FOR REFLECTION

God never ceases to amaze his people, does he? How did God's miraculous deliverance in each of these instances build up the faith of those involved? What result does his intervention bring about in your life?

WEDNESDAY:

God's Miracles May Cause Us to Believe

Acts 13:1–25

Barnabas and Saul Are Chosen

*I*n the church at Antioch there were these prophets and teachers: Barnabas, Simeon (also called Niger), Lucius (from the city of Cyrene), Manaen (who had grown up with Herod, the ruler), and Saul. They were all worshiping the Lord and giving up eating for a certain time. During this time the Holy Spirit said to them, "Set apart for me Barnabas and Saul to do a special work for which I have chosen them."

So after they gave up eating and prayed, they laid their hands on Barnabas and Saul and sent them out.

Barnabas and Saul in Cyprus

*B*arnabas and Saul, sent out by the Holy Spirit, went to the city of Seleucia. From there they sailed to the island of Cyprus. When they came to Salamis, they preached the Good News of God in the Jewish synagogues. John Mark was with them to help.

They went across the whole island to Paphos where they met a Jewish magician named Bar-Jesus. He was a false prophet who always stayed close to Sergius Paulus, the governor and a smart man. He asked Barnabas and Saul to come to him, because he wanted to hear the message of God. But Elymas, the magician, was against them. (Elymas is the name for Bar-Jesus in the Greek language.) He tried to stop the governor from believing in Jesus. But Saul, who was also called Paul, was filled with the Holy Spirit. He looked straight at Elymas and said, "You son of the devil! You are an enemy of everything that is right! You are full of evil tricks and lies, always trying to change the Lord's truths into lies. Now the Lord will touch you, and you will be blind. For a time you will not be able to see anything—not even the light from the sun."

Then everything became dark for Elymas, and he walked around, trying to find someone to lead him by the hand. When the governor saw this, he believed because he was amazed at the teaching about the Lord.

Paul and Barnabas Leave Cyprus

*P*aul and those with him sailed from Paphos and came to Perga, in Pamphylia. There John Mark left them to return to Jerusalem. They continued their trip from Perga and went to Antioch, a city in Pisidia. On the Sabbath day they went into the synagogue and sat down. After the law of Moses and the writings of the prophets were read, the leaders of the synagogue sent a message to Paul and Barnabas: "Brothers, if you have any message that will encourage the people, please speak."

Paul stood up, raised his hand, and said, "You Israelites and you who worship God, please listen! The God of the Israelites chose our ancestors. He made the people great during the time they lived in Egypt, and he brought them out of that country with great power. And he was patient with them for forty years in the desert. God destroyed seven nations in the land of Canaan and gave the land to his people. All this happened in about four hundred fifty years.

"After this, God gave them judges until the time of Samuel the prophet. Then the people asked for a king, so God gave them Saul son of Kish. Saul was from the tribe of Benjamin and was king for forty years. After God took him away, God made David their king. God said about him: 'I have found in David son of Jesse the kind of man I want. He will do all I want him to do.' So God has brought Jesus, one of David's descendants, to Israel to be its Savior, as he promised. Before Jesus came, John preached to all the people of Israel about a baptism of changed hearts and lives. When he was finishing his work, he said, 'Who do you think I am? I am not the Christ. He is coming later, and I am not worthy to untie his sandals.'"

*O*ur ancestors in Egypt
did not learn from your miracles.

318

They did not remember all your
kindnesses,
so they turned against you at the
Red Sea.
But the LORD saved them for his own
sake,
to show his great power.
He commanded the Red Sea, and it
dried up.
He led them through the deep sea as
if it were a desert.
He saved them from those who hated
them.
He saved them from their enemies,
and the water covered their foes.
Not one of them escaped.
Then the people believed what the
LORD said,
and they sang praises to him.

Psalm 106:7–12

*M*oses told Aaron everything the LORD
had said to him when he sent him to Egypt.
He also told him about the miracles which
the LORD had commanded him to do.

Moses and Aaron gathered all the older
leaders of the Israelites, and Aaron told
them everything that the LORD had told
Moses. Then Moses did the miracles for all
the people to see, and the Israelites believed. When they heard that the LORD was
concerned about them and had seen their
troubles, they bowed down and worshiped
him.

Exodus 4:28–31

*S*o Naaman went down and dipped in
the Jordan seven times, just as Elisha
had said. Then his skin became new
again, like the skin of a child. And he was
clean.

Naaman and all his group returned to
Elisha. He stood before Elisha and said,
"Look, I now know there is no God in all
the earth except in Israel. Now please accept a gift from me."

But Elisha said, "As surely as the LORD
lives whom I serve, I won't accept anything."
Naaman urged him to take the gift, but he
refused.

Then Naaman said, "If you won't take the
gift, then please give me some soil—as
much as two of my mules can carry. From

now on I'll not offer any burnt offering or
sacrifice to any other gods but the LORD.

2 Kings 5:14–17

INSIGHTS

*G*od, who made the visible heaven and
earth, does not disdain to work visible
miracles in heaven or earth, that He may
thereby awaken the soul which is immersed
in things visible to worship Himself, the Invisible. . . .

*He restored to the blind those eyes which
death was sure some time to close; He raised
Lazarus from the dead, who was to die again.
And whatever He did for the health of bodies,
He did it not to the end that they should exist
for evermore; whereas at the last He will give
eternal health even to the body itself. But because those things which were not seen were
not believed, by means of those temporal
things which were seen He built up faith in
those things which were not seen. Let no one
therefore say that our Lord Jesus Christ doeth
not those things now, and on this account
prefer the former to the present ages of the
Church. . . . The Lord did those things to
invite us to the faith.*

St. Augustine

PAUSE FOR REFLECTION

*I*n each of these Scripture readings, what did
the miracles reveal about God? What was the
result? In what way has God revealed himself
to you? How have you responded?

THURSDAY:
Those Who Believe Are Happy
Acts 13:26–52

NEW TESTAMENT READING

*B*rothers, sons of the family of Abraham, and those of you who are not Jews who worship God, listen! The news about this salvation has been sent to us. Those who live in Jerusalem and their leaders did not realize that Jesus was the Savior. They did not understand the words that the prophets wrote, which are read every Sabbath day. But they made them come true when they said Jesus was guilty. They could not find any real reason for Jesus to be put to death, but they asked Pilate to have him killed. When they had done to him all that the Scriptures had said, they took him down from the cross and laid him in a tomb. But God raised him up from the dead! After this, for many days, those who had gone with Jesus from Galilee to Jerusalem saw him. They are now his witnesses to the people. We tell you the Good News about the promise God made to our ancestors. God has made this promise come true for us, his children, by raising Jesus from the dead. We read about this also in Psalm 2:

'You are my Son.
Today I have become your Father.'

Psalm 2:7

God raised Jesus from the dead, and he will never go back to the grave and become dust. So God said:

'I will give you the holy and sure
blessings
that I promised to David.'

Isaiah 55:3

But in another place God says:

'You will not let your Holy One rot.'

Psalm 16:10

David did God's will during his lifetime. Then he died and was buried beside his ancestors, and his body did rot in the grave. But the One God raised from the dead did not rot in the grave. Brothers, understand what we are telling you: You can have forgiveness of your sins through Jesus. The law of Moses could not free you from your sins. But through Jesus everyone who believes is free from all sins. Be careful! Don't let what the prophets said happen to you:

'Listen, you people who doubt!
You can wonder, and then die.
I will do something in your lifetime
that you won't believe even when
you are told about it!'

Habakkuk 1:5

While Paul and Barnabas were leaving the synagogue, the people asked them to tell them more about these things on the next Sabbath. When the meeting was over, many Jews and those who had changed to the Jewish religion and who worshiped God followed Paul and Barnabas from that place. Paul and Barnabas were persuading them to continue trusting in God's grace.

On the next Sabbath day, almost everyone in the city came to hear the word of the Lord. Seeing the crowd, the Jewish people became very jealous and said insulting things and argued against what Paul said. But Paul and Barnabas spoke very boldly, saying, "We must speak the message of God to you first. But you refuse to listen. You are judging yourselves not worthy of having eternal life! So we will now go to the people of other nations. This is what the Lord told us to do, saying:

'I have made you a light for the nations;
you will show people all over the
world the way to be saved.'

Isaiah 49:6

When those who were not Jewish heard Paul say this, they were happy and gave honor to the message of the Lord. And the people who were chosen to have life forever believed the message.

So the message of the Lord was spreading through the whole country. But the Jewish people stirred up some of the important religious women and the leaders of the city. They started trouble against Paul and Barnabas and forced them out of their area. So Paul and Barnabas shook the dust off their feet and went to Iconium. But the followers were filled with joy and the Holy Spirit.

*I*t is good to praise you, Lord,
    to sing praises to God Most High.
It is good to tell of your love in the
    morning
    and of your loyalty at night.
It is good to praise you with the ten-
    stringed lyre
    and with the soft-sounding harp.

Lord, you have made me happy by
    what you have done;
    I will sing for joy about what your
    hands have done.
Lord, you have done such great things!
    How deep are your thoughts!
Stupid people don't know these things,
    and fools don't understand.
Wicked people grow like the grass.
    Evil people seem to do well,
    but they will be destroyed forever.
But, Lord, you will be honored forever.
Psalm 92:1–8

*S*ing praises to the Lord, you who
    belong to him;
    praise his holy name.
His anger lasts only a moment,
    but his kindness lasts for a lifetime.
Crying may last for a night,
    but joy comes in the morning.

You changed my sorrow into dancing.
    You took away my clothes of sad-
    ness,
    and clothed me in happiness.
I will sing to you and not be silent.
    Lord, my God, I will praise you
    forever.
Psalm 30:4–5, 11–12

*Y*our words came to me, and I listened
    carefully to them.
    Your words made me very happy,
because I am called by your name,
    Lord God All–Powerful.
Jeremiah 15:16

*T*he Lord makes me very happy;
    all that I am rejoices in my God.
He has covered me with clothes of
    salvation

and wrapped me with a coat of
    goodness,
like a bridegroom dressed for his
    wedding,
like a bride dressed in jewels.
Isaiah 61:10

INSIGHTS

I'm convinced that enjoyment is the ultimate stage of knowledge. When we set out to learn the basic truths of an intellectual discipline, we are confounded by all we don't know. Little by little, we become more secure in ideas and theories. Then one day, we suddenly realize that we have captured the subject and know how to use our knowledge. . . .

. . . Enjoyment of our faith grows in the same way. In the beginning, God seems distant and aloof. Biblical and theological terms are like a foreign language. Our prayers are strained and shallow. . . . And then, with the touch of the Father's hand, we discover how much He loves us and wants us to know Him personally. Secondary theories about Him are replaced by an intimate relationship with Him. None of our awe and adoration is lost as we begin to enjoy Him. . . .

Enjoying God is really a vital expression of glorifying Him. The glory of God is the manifestation and revelation of all that He is as Creator, Sustainer, Redeemer, and Lord of all. We glorify Him when we worship Him for His lovingkindness, goodness, and mercifulness. Our worship becomes intimate when we joyfully experience God's nature and attributes. From that joy springs our desire to glorify Him by serving Him. Our faithful obedience becomes an enjoyable response.

Lloyd Ogilvie

PAUSE FOR REFLECTION

*H*ow did the people respond when Paul and Barnabas spoke God's Word in Antioch? In what ways does the Lord make you happy? How has your happiness grown as you have come to know him better?*

FRIDAY:
Seek God's Guidance When Making Decisions
Acts 14:1–28

Paul and Barnabas in Iconium

*I*n Iconium, Paul and Barnabas went as usual to the Jewish synagogue. They spoke so well that a great many Jews and Greeks believed. But some of the Jews who did not believe excited the non-Jewish people and turned them against the believers. Paul and Barnabas stayed in Iconium a long time and spoke bravely for the Lord. He showed that their message about his grace was true by giving them the power to work miracles and signs. But the city was divided. Some of the people agreed with the Jews, and others believed the apostles.

Some who were not Jews, some Jews, and some of their rulers wanted to mistreat Paul and Barnabas and to stone them to death. When Paul and Barnabas learned about this, they ran away to Lystra and Derbe, cities in Lycaonia, and to the areas around those cities. They announced the Good News there, too.

Paul in Lystra and Derbe

*I*n Lystra there sat a man who had been born crippled; he had never walked. As this man was listening to Paul speak, Paul looked straight at him and saw that he believed God could heal him. So he cried out, "Stand up on your feet!" The man jumped up and began walking around. When the crowds saw what Paul did, they shouted in the Lycaonian language, "The gods have become like humans and have come down to us!" Then the people began to call Barnabas "Zeus" and Paul "Hermes," because he was the main speaker. The priest in the temple of Zeus, which was near the city, brought some bulls and flowers to the city gates. He and the people wanted to offer a sacrifice to Paul and Barnabas. But when the apostles, Barnabas and Paul, heard about it, they tore their clothes. They ran in among the people, shouting, "Friends, why are you doing these things? We are only human beings like you. We are bringing you the Good News and are telling you to turn away from these worthless things and turn to the living God. He is the One who made the sky, the earth, the sea, and everything in them. In the past, God let all the nations do what they wanted. Yet he proved he is real by showing kindness, by giving you rain from heaven and crops at the right times, by giving you food and filling your hearts with joy." Even with these words, they were barely able to keep the crowd from offering sacrifices to them.

Then some Jewish people came from Antioch and Iconium and persuaded the people to turn against Paul. So they threw stones at him and dragged him out of town, thinking they had killed him. But the followers gathered around him, and he got up and went back into the town. The next day he and Barnabas left and went to the city of Derbe.

The Return to Antioch in Syria

*P*aul and Barnabas told the Good News in Derbe, and many became followers. Paul and Barnabas returned to Lystra, Iconium, and Antioch, making the followers of Jesus stronger and helping them stay in the faith. They said, "We must suffer many things to enter God's kingdom." They chose elders for each church, by praying and giving up eating for a certain time. These elders had trusted the Lord, so Paul and Barnabas put them in the Lord's care.

Then they went through Pisidia and came to Pamphylia. When they had preached the message in Perga, they went down to Attalia. And from there they sailed away to Antioch where the believers had put them into God's care and had sent them out to do this work. Now they had finished.

When they arrived in Antioch, Paul and Barnabas gathered the church together. They told the church all about what God had done with them and how God had made it possible for those who were not Jewish to believe. And they stayed there a long time with the followers.

*W*hen the Philistines heard that David had been made king of all Israel, they went to look for him. But David heard about it and went out to fight them. The Philistines had attacked and robbed the people in the Valley of Rephaim. David asked God, "Should I go and attack the Philistines? Will you hand them over to me?"

The LORD answered him, "Go, I will hand them over to you."

So David and his men went up to the town of Baal Perazim and defeated the Philistines. David said, "Like a flood of water, God has broken through my enemies by using me." So that place was named Baal Perazim. The Philistines had left their idols there, so David ordered his men to burn them.

Soon the Philistines attacked the people in the valley again. David prayed to God again, and God answered him, saying, "Don't attack the Philistines from the front. Instead, go around them and attack them in front of the balsam trees. When you hear the sound of marching in the tops of the balsam trees, then attack. I, God, will have gone out before you to defeat the Philistine army." David did as God commanded, and he and his men defeated the Philistine army all the way from Gibeon to Gezer.

So David became famous in all the countries, and the LORD made all nations afraid of him.

1 Chronicles 14:8–17

*T*rust the LORD with all your heart,
and don't depend on your own
understanding.
Remember the LORD in all you do,
and he will give you success.

Don't depend on your own wisdom.
Respect the LORD and refuse to do
wrong.

Proverbs 3:5–7

*A*hab king of Israel asked Jehoshaphat king of Judah, "Will you go with me to attack Ramoth in Gilead?"

Jehoshaphat answered, "I will go with you, and my soldiers are yours. We will join you in the battle." Jehoshaphat also said to Ahab, "But first we should ask if this is the LORD's will."

So King Ahab called four hundred prophets together and asked them, "Should we go to war against Ramoth in Gilead or not?"

They answered, "Go, because God will hand them over to you."

But Jehoshaphat asked, "Isn't there a prophet of the LORD here? Let's ask him what we should do."

2 Chronicles 18:3–6

I N S I G H T S

*W*hen I was in my late teens I had life all figured out . . . . Now I realize how uncertain this world is, how limited my own experience is, how deceptive the evil one is, how easily I can be duped. I desperately need a guide though the maze of options every day. Don't you?

I need a guide who knows me, who understands me and has my best interests in mind. The best guide would understand my personality, my temperament, my gifts and abilities, my likes and dislikes. Wouldn't it be something to have a guide who takes all that into consideration as He charts a path for your life?

Such a guide exists, friend. God reaches out to you and says, in effect, "Take My hand. You matter to Me. I am trustworthy. I know you. I understand you. I know what will fulfill you. I created you." . . .

. . . He wants to guide your life. Will you let Him? Will you read and heed the Word? Will you be yielded and listen to and trust the leadings of the Holy Spirit? Will you submit your plans to others for their input? When you do, you'll find that life can truly be an adventure.

Bill Hybels

A P P L I C A T I O N

*W*hy do you think Paul and Barnabas especially sought God's guidance in choosing elders for the churches? For what decisions do you seek God's guidance? Should you be seeking his wisdom more?

WEEKEND:

God Accepts Anyone Who Comes to Him

Acts 15:1–21

The Meeting at Jerusalem

*T*hen some people came to Antioch from Judea and began teaching the non-Jewish believers: "You cannot be saved if you are not circumcised as Moses taught us." Paul and Barnabas were against this teaching and argued with them about it. So the church decided to send Paul, Barnabas, and some others to Jerusalem where they could talk more about this with the apostles and elders.

The church helped them leave on the trip, and they went through the countries of Phoenicia and Samaria, telling all about how those who were not Jewish had turned to God. This made all the believers very happy. When they arrived in Jerusalem, they were welcomed by the apostles, the elders, and the church. Paul, Barnabas, and the others told about everything God had done with them. But some of the believers who belonged to the Pharisee group came forward and said, "The non-Jewish believers must be circumcised. They must be told to obey the law of Moses."

The apostles and the elders gathered to consider this problem. After a long debate, Peter stood up and said to them, "Brothers, you know that in the early days God chose me from among you to preach the Good News to those who are not Jewish. They heard the Good News from me, and they believed. God, who knows the thoughts of everyone, accepted them. He showed this to us by giving them the Holy Spirit, just as he did to us. To God, those people are not different from us. When they believed, he made their hearts pure. So now why are you testing God by putting a heavy load around the necks of the non-Jewish believers? It is a load that neither we nor our ancestors were able to carry. But we believe that we and they too will be saved by the grace of the Lord Jesus."

Then the whole group became quiet. They listened to Paul and Barnabas tell about all the miracles and signs that God did through them among the non-Jewish people. After they finished speaking, James said, "Brothers, listen to me. Simon has told us how God showed his love for the non-Jewish people. For the first time he is accepting from among them a people to be his own. The words of the prophets agree with this too:

'After these things I will return.
  The kingdom of David is like a fallen tent.
But I will rebuild its ruins,
  and I will set it up.
Then those people who are left alive
  may ask the Lord for help,
  and the other nations that belong to me,
says the Lord,
  who will make it happen.
And these things have been known
  for a long time.'   *Amos 9:11–12*

"So I think we should not bother the non-Jewish people who are turning to God. Instead, we should write a letter to them telling them these things: Stay away from food that has been offered to idols (which makes it unclean), any kind of sexual sin, eating animals that have been strangled, and blood. They should do these things, because for a long time in every city the law of Moses has been taught. And it is still read in the synagogue every Sabbath day."

*G*od, have mercy on us and bless us
  and show us your kindness   *Selah*
so the world will learn your ways,
  and all nations will learn that you can save.
God, the people should praise you;
  all people should praise you.
The nations should be glad and sing
  because you judge people fairly.
  You guide all the nations on earth.
      Selah
God, the people should praise you;
  all people should praise you.
      Psalm 67:1–5

*P*eople everywhere will remember
  and will turn to the Lord.
All the families of the nations
  will worship him
because the Lord is King,
  and he rules the nations.

Psalm 22:27–28

*A*ll people everywhere,
  follow me and be saved.
I am God. There is no other God.

Isaiah 45:22

*T*his is what the Lord said to me: "Here is what I will do to all my wicked neighbors who take the land I gave my people Israel. I will pull them up and throw them out of their land. And I will pull up the people of Judah from among them. But after I pull them up, I will feel sorry for them again. I will bring each person back to his own property and to his own land. I want them to learn their lessons well. In the past they taught my people to swear by Baal's name. But if they will now learn to swear by my name, saying 'As surely as the Lord lives . . .' I will allow them to rebuild among my people. But if a nation will not listen to my message, I will pull it up completely and destroy it," says the Lord.

Jeremiah 12:14–17

*F*oreigners will join the Lord
  to worship him and love him,
  to serve him,
to obey the law about the Sabbath,
  and to keep my agreement.
I will bring these people to my holy
    mountain
  and give them joy in my house of
    prayer.
The offerings and sacrifices
  they place on my altar will please me,
because my Temple will be called
  a house for prayer for people from
    all nations."
The Lord God says—
  he who gathers the Israelites that
    were forced to leave their country:
"I will bring together other people
  to join those who are already
    gathered."

Isaiah 56:6–8

INSIGHTS

*T*he Law came and in bold letters etched by the finger of God it read, "This is holiness! Honor My Name by keeping My Law!" But the fact is, nobody could keep it, which explains the statement in Romans 5:20 that says "sin increased." The Law arouses sin but never arrests it. So how can the tailspin stop? What hope is there? The answer is found in the same verse: ". . . but where sin increased, grace abounded all the more." . . .

Let me amplify the scriptural statement even more. Where sin overflowed, grace flooded in. Where sin measurably increased, grace immeasurably increased. Where sin was finite, grace was infinite. Where sin was colossal, grace was supercolossal. Where sin abounds, grace superabounds. The sin identified by the Law in no way stopped the flow of the grace of God. Jesus' death on the cross was the sufficient payment for sin, putting grace into action that was not simply adequate but abundant. . . .

. . . God, in grace, offers you the free gift of forgiveness. All you can do is take it. Once you take it, you will be given the power to give up, to put on, to take off, to quit, to start—whatever. But don't confuse the issue of salvation. It is yours strictly on the basis of God's free gift. In spite of all the stuff you may hear to the contrary, the emphasis is not on what we do for God; instead, it is on what God has done for us.

Charles Swindoll

PAUSE FOR REFLECTION

*T*o whom was the law of Moses given? Why? What evidence in the Old and New Testaments reveals that God offers salvation through Jesus Christ to all people—Jew and non-Jew?

325

MONDAY:
The Value of Encouragement
Acts 15:22—16:10

Letter to Non-Jewish Believers

The apostles, the elders, and the whole church decided to send some of their men with Paul and Barnabas to Antioch. They chose Judas Barsabbas and Silas, who were respected by the believers. They sent the following letter with them:

From the apostles and elders, your brothers.

To all the non-Jewish believers in Antioch, Syria, and Cilicia:

Greetings!

We have heard that some of our group have come to you and said things that trouble and upset you. But we did not tell them to do this. We have all agreed to choose some messengers and send them to you with our dear friends Barnabas and Paul—people who have given their lives to serve our Lord Jesus Christ. So we are sending Judas and Silas, who will tell you the same things. It has pleased the Holy Spirit that you should not have a heavy load to carry, and we agree. You need to do only these things: Stay away from any food that has been offered to idols, eating any animals that have been strangled, and blood, and any kind of sexual sin. If you stay away from these things, you will do well.

Good-bye.

So they left Jerusalem and went to Antioch where they gathered the church and gave them the letter. When they read it, they were very happy because of the encouraging message. Judas and Silas, who were also prophets, said many things to encourage the believers and make them stronger. After some time Judas and Silas were sent off in peace by the believers, and they went back to those who had sent them.

But Paul and Barnabas stayed in Antioch and, along with many others, preached the Good News and taught the people the message of the Lord.

Paul and Barnabas Separate

After some time, Paul said to Barnabas, "We should go back to all those towns where we preached the message of the Lord. Let's visit the believers and see how they are doing."

Barnabas wanted to take John Mark with them, but he had left them at Pamphylia; he did not continue with them in the work. So Paul did not think it was a good idea to take him. Paul and Barnabas had such a serious argument about this that they separated and went different ways. Barnabas took Mark and sailed to Cyprus, but Paul chose Silas and left. The believers in Antioch put Paul into the Lord's care, and he went through Syria and Cilicia, giving strength to the churches.

Timothy Goes with Paul

Paul came to Derbe and Lystra, where a follower named Timothy lived. Timothy's mother was Jewish and a believer, but his father was a Greek.

The believers in Lystra and Iconium respected Timothy and said good things about him. Paul wanted Timothy to travel with him, but all the Jews living in that area knew that Timothy's father was Greek. So Paul circumcised Timothy to please the Jews. Paul and those with him traveled from town to town and gave the decisions made by the apostles and elders in Jerusalem for the people to obey. So the churches became stronger in the faith and grew larger every day.

Paul Is Called Out of Asia

Paul and those with him went through the areas of Phrygia and Galatia since the Holy Spirit did not let them preach the Good News in the country of Asia. When they came near the country of Mysia, they tried to go into Bithynia, but the Spirit of Jesus did not let them. So they passed by Mysia and went to Troas. That night Paul saw in a vision a man from Macedonia. The man stood and begged, "Come over to Macedonia and help us." After Paul had seen the vision, we immediately prepared to leave for Macedonia, understanding that God had called us to tell the Good News to those people.

*T*he right word spoken at the right
time
   is as beautiful as gold apples in a
silver bowl.

Proverbs 25:11

*T*hen Boaz said to Ruth, "Listen, my daughter. Don't go to gather grain for yourself in another field. Don't even leave this field at all, but continue following closely behind my women workers. Watch to see into which fields they go to cut grain and follow them. I have warned the young men not to bother you. When you are thirsty, you may go and drink from the water jugs that the young men have filled."

Then Ruth bowed low with her face to the ground and said to him, "I am not an Israelite. Why have you been so kind to notice me?"

Boaz answered her, "I know about all the help you have given your mother-in-law after your husband died. You left your father and mother and your own country to come to a nation where you did not know anyone. May the LORD reward you for all you have done. May your wages be paid in full by the LORD, the God of Israel, under whose wings you have come for shelter."

Then Ruth said, "I hope I can continue to please you, sir. You have said kind and encouraging words to me, your servant, though I am not one of your servants."

Ruth 2:8–13

*N*ow Job had three friends: Eliphaz the Temanite, Bildad the Shuhite, and Zophar the Naamathite. When these friends heard about Job's troubles, they agreed to meet and visit him. They wanted to show their concern and to comfort him.

Job 2:11

*J*oab went into the king's house and said, "Today you have shamed all your men. They saved your life and the lives of your sons, daughters, wives, and slave women. You have shamed them because you love those who hate you, and you hate those who love you. Today you have made it clear that your commanders and men mean nothing to you. What if Absalom had lived and all of us were dead? I can see you would be pleased. Now go out and encourage your servants. I swear by the LORD that if you don't go out, no man will be left with you by tonight! That will be worse than all the troubles you have had from your youth until today."

So the king went to the city gate. When the news spread that the king was at the gate, everyone came to see him.

2 Samuel 19:5–8b

I N S I G H T S

I was rushing around trying to get dinner ready for my husband and houseguests. . . .

. . . Just as I began last-minute preparations, the doorbell rang. I ran to answer it. A friend had stopped by to drop off a folder of information for my husband.

"How are you, Doris?"

I began to tell her that I was a little tired and frazzled around the edges, when I noticed she wasn't listening. Before I could finish my response, she said, "That's good. It's nice to see you." And with that she left.

I walked slowly back to my kitchen, feeling lonely and deflated. My friend had let me down when I could have used just a word of encouragement, maybe even a quick prayer.

Mechanically, I began to set the table. Why didn't she hear me? Doesn't she care how I am? I just needed a little of her time.

And then I heard the words: Doris, you've done this to people, too. Let this be a lesson to you. Listen to those I send across your path. Give them at least five minutes, even if you are in a hurry. Stop and pray with them.

Doris Greig

A P P L I C A T I O N

*O*ur *Proverbs reading summarizes the beauty of encouragement well, doesn't it? What has been your most encouraging experience? What kind of encouragement is offered in each of these examples? How do they help you know how to encourage others?*

TUESDAY:
"Come Stay in My House"
Acts 16:11–34

NEW TESTAMENT READING

Lydia Becomes a Christian

*W*e left Troas and sailed straight to the island of Samothrace. The next day we sailed to Neapolis. Then we went by land to Philippi, a Roman colony and the leading city in that part of Macedonia. We stayed there for several days.

On the Sabbath day we went outside the city gate to the river where we thought we would find a special place for prayer. Some women had gathered there, so we sat down and talked with them. One of the listeners was a woman named Lydia from the city of Thyatira whose job was selling purple cloth. She worshiped God, and he opened her mind to pay attention to what Paul was saying. She and all the people in her house were baptized. Then she invited us to her home, saying, "If you think I am truly a believer in the Lord, then come stay in my house." And she persuaded us to stay with her.

Paul and Silas in Jail

*O*nce, while we were going to the place for prayer, a servant girl met us. She had a special spirit in her, and she earned a lot of money for her owners by telling fortunes. This girl followed Paul and us, shouting, "These men are servants of the Most High God. They are telling you how you can be saved."

She kept this up for many days. This bothered Paul, so he turned and said to the spirit, "By the power of Jesus Christ, I command you to come out of her!" Immediately, the spirit came out.

When the owners of the servant girl saw this, they knew that now they could not use her to make money. So they grabbed Paul and Silas and dragged them before the city rulers in the marketplace. They brought Paul and Silas to the Roman rulers and said, "These men are Jews and are making trouble in our city. They are teaching things that are not right for us as Romans to do."

The crowd joined the attack against them. The Roman officers tore the clothes of Paul and Silas and had them beaten with rods. Then Paul and Silas were thrown into jail, and the jailer was ordered to guard them carefully. When he heard this order, he put them far inside the jail and pinned their feet down between large blocks of wood.

About midnight Paul and Silas were praying and singing songs to God as the other prisoners listened. Suddenly, there was a strong earthquake that shook the foundation of the jail. Then all the doors of the jail broke open, and all the prisoners were freed from their chains. The jailer woke up and saw that the jail doors were open. Thinking that the prisoners had already escaped, he got his sword and was about to kill himself. But Paul shouted, "Don't hurt yourself! We are all here."

The jailer told someone to bring a light. Then he ran inside and, shaking with fear, fell down before Paul and Silas. He brought them outside and said, "Men, what must I do to be saved?"

They said to him, "Believe in the Lord Jesus and you will be saved—you and all the people in your house." So Paul and Silas told the message of the Lord to the jailer and all the people in his house. At that hour of the night the jailer took Paul and Silas and washed their wounds. Then he and all his people were baptized immediately. After this the jailer took Paul and Silas home and gave them food. He and his family were very happy because they now believed in God.

OLD TESTAMENT READING

*L*ater, the LORD again appeared to Abraham near the great trees of Mamre. Abraham was sitting at the entrance of his tent during the hottest part of the day. He looked up and saw three men standing near him. When Abraham saw them, he ran from his tent to meet them. He bowed facedown on the ground before them and said, "Sir, if you think well of me, please stay awhile with me, your servant. I will bring some water so all of you can wash your feet.

You may rest under the tree, and I will get some bread for you so you can regain your strength. Then you may continue your journey."

The three men said, "That is fine. Do as you said."

Abraham hurried to the tent where Sarah was and said to her, "Hurry, prepare twenty quarts of fine flour, and make it into loaves of bread." Then Abraham ran to his herd and took one of his best calves. He gave it to a servant, who hurried to kill it and to prepare it for food. Abraham gave the three men the calf that had been cooked and milk curds and milk. While they ate, he stood under the tree near them.

Genesis 18:1–8

*O*ne day Elisha went to Shunem, where an important woman lived. She begged Elisha to stay and eat. So every time Elisha passed by, he stopped there to eat. The woman said to her husband, "I know that this is a holy man of God who passes by our house all the time. Let's make a small room on the roof and put a bed in the room for him. We can put a table, a chair, and a lampstand there. Then when he comes by, he can stay there."

2 Kings 4:8–10

*F*inally, in the evening an old man came in from his work in the fields. His home was in the mountains of Ephraim, but now he was living in Gibeah. (The people of Gibeah were from the tribe of Benjamin.) He saw the traveler in the public square and asked, "Where are you going? Where did you come from?"

The Levite answered, "We are traveling from Bethlehem in Judah to my home in the mountains of Ephraim. I have been to Bethlehem in Judah, but now I am going to the Holy Tent of the LORD. No one has invited me to stay in his house. We already have straw and food for our donkeys and bread and wine for me, the young woman, and my servant. We don't need anything."

The old man said, "You are welcome to stay at my house. Let me give you anything you need, but don't spend the night in the public square." So the old man took the Levite into his house, and he fed their donkeys. They washed their feet and had something to eat and drink.

Judges 19:16–21

THERE IS ROOM

*Y*ou know how it happened, Lord:
She said, "May I live with you
Just a little while?
I have no place to go.
I'm lonely
And afraid."
I hastily glanced at the small room.
I thought of other rooms
Smaller and extremely crowded.
I said, "You see my small house.
There is really no room.
But I have room in my heart
For caring
For praying
I'll make phone calls—
There must be a family somewhere . . ."
That was this morning, Lord.
All day long
I prayed
I called
I waited . . .
Then You accomplished
What I cannot explain.
Through the hours
You pushed back the walls—
Until suddenly, tonight
There is room for her in my house
As well as in my heart
You are indeed a Master Builder!

Ruth Calkin

*W*hat do you find particularly interesting about these examples of hospitality? What do you think it means to express Christian hospitality to people today? Pray about how God wants you to use your home to serve him.

WEDNESDAY:

It's Important to Know God's Powerful Word

Acts 16:35—17:15

*T*he next morning, the Roman officers sent the police to tell the jailer, "Let these men go free."

The jailer said to Paul, "The officers have sent an order to let you go free. You can leave now. Go in peace."

But Paul said to the police, "They beat us in public without a trial, even though we are Roman citizens. And they threw us in jail. Now they want to make us go away quietly. No! Let them come themselves and bring us out."

The police told the Roman officers what Paul said. When the officers heard that Paul and Silas were Roman citizens, they were afraid. So they came and told Paul and Silas they were sorry and took them out of jail and asked them to leave the city. So when they came out of the jail, they went to Lydia's house where they saw some of the believers and encouraged them. Then they left.

Paul and Silas in Thessalonica

*P*aul and Silas traveled through Amphipolis and Apollonia and came to Thessalonica where there was a Jewish synagogue. Paul went into the synagogue as he always did, and on each Sabbath day for three weeks, he talked with the Jews about the Scriptures. He explained and proved that the Christ must die and then rise from the dead. He said, "This Jesus I am telling you about is the Christ." Some of the Jews were convinced and joined Paul and Silas, along with many of the Greeks who worshiped God and many of the important women.

But the Jews became jealous. So they got some evil men from the marketplace, formed a mob, and started a riot. They ran to Jason's house, looking for Paul and Silas, wanting to bring them out to the people. But when they did not find them, they dragged Jason and some other believers to the leaders of the city. The people were yelling, "These people have made trouble everywhere in the world, and now they have come here too! Jason is keeping them in his house. All of them do things against the laws of Caesar, saying there is another king, called Jesus."

When the people and the leaders of the city heard these things, they became very upset. They made Jason and the others put up a sum of money. Then they let the believers go free.

Paul and Silas Go to Berea

*T*hat same night the believers sent Paul and Silas to Berea where they went to the Jewish synagogue. These Jews were more willing to listen than the Jews in Thessalonica. The Bereans were eager to hear what Paul and Silas said and studied the Scriptures every day to find out if these things were true. So, many of them believed, as well as many important Greek women and men. But the Jews in Thessalonica learned that Paul was preaching the word of God in Berea, too. So they came there, upsetting the people and making trouble. The believers quickly sent Paul away to the coast, but Silas and Timothy stayed in Berea. The people leading Paul went with him to Athens. Then they carried a message from Paul back to Silas and Timothy for them to come to him as soon as they could.

---

*R*ain and snow fall from the sky
    and don't return without watering
        the ground.
They cause the plants to sprout and
        grow,
    making seeds for the farmer
    and bread for the people.
The same thing is true of the words I
        speak.
    They will not return to me empty.
They make the things happen that I
        want to happen,
    and they succeed in doing what I
        send them to do.

Isaiah 55:10–11

*A*fter Moses finished writing all the words of the teachings in a book, he gave a command to the Levites, who carried the Ark of the Agreement with the LORD. He said, "Take this Book of the Teachings and put it beside the Ark of the Agreement with the LORD your God. It must stay there as a witness against you. I know how stubborn and disobedient you are. You have disobeyed the LORD while I am alive and with you, and you will disobey even more after I die! Gather all the older leaders of your tribes and all your officers to me so that I may say these things for them to hear, and so that I may ask heaven and earth to testify against them. I know that after I die you will become completely evil. You will turn away from the commands I have given you.

Deuteronomy 31:24–29b

*T*he teachings of the LORD are perfect;
   they give new strength.
The rules of the LORD can be trusted;
   they make plain people wise.
The orders of the LORD are right;
   they make people happy.
The commands of the LORD are pure;
   they light up the way.
Respect for the LORD is good;
   it will last forever.
The judgments of the LORD are true;
   they are completely right.
They are worth more than gold,
   even the purest gold.
They are sweeter than honey,
   even the finest honey.
By them your servant is warned.
   Keeping them brings great
     reward.

Psalm 19:7–11

*Y*our word is like a lamp for my feet
   and a light for my path.
I will do what I have promised
   and obey your fair laws.
I have suffered for a long time.
   LORD, give me life by your word.
LORD, accept my willing praise
   and teach me your laws.

Psalm 119:105–108

I never pretend to make but one book my study. I read them occasionally, but have little time or inclination to read other books much while I have so much to learn of my Bible. I find it like a deep mine, the more I work it, the richer it grows. We must read that more than any or all other books. We must pause and pray over it, verse after verse, and compare part with part, dwell on it, digest it, and get it into our minds, till we feel that the Spirit of God has filled us with the spirit of holiness.

Will you do it? Will you lay your hearts open to God, and not give him rest, till he has filled you with divine knowledge? Will you search the scriptures? I have often been asked by young converts, and young men preparing for the ministry, what they should read. Read the Bible. I would give the same answer five hundred times. Over and above all other things, study the Bible.

Charles Finney

*W*hat was unusual about the Jews in Berea? Is it, then, surprising that many of them believed? What does God say about his word in Isaiah? How much do you treasure and seek after God's Word? Will you begin today to search after it more diligently?

THURSDAY:
Paul Tells Others About the True God
Acts 17:16—18:4

NEW TESTAMENT READING

Paul Preaches in Athens

While Paul was waiting for Silas and Timothy in Athens, he was troubled because he saw that the city was full of idols. In the synagogue, he talked with the Jews and the Greeks who worshiped God. He also talked every day with people in the marketplace.

Some of the Epicurean and Stoic philosophers argued with him, saying, "This man doesn't know what he is talking about. What is he trying to say?" Others said, "He seems to be telling us about some other gods," because Paul was telling them about Jesus and his rising from the dead. They got Paul and took him to a meeting of the Areopagus, where they said, "Please explain to us this new idea you have been teaching. The things you are saying are new to us, and we want to know what this teaching means." (All the people of Athens and those from other countries who lived there always used their time to talk about the newest ideas.)

Then Paul stood before the meeting of the Areopagus and said, "People of Athens, I can see you are very religious in all things. As I was going through your city, I saw the objects you worship. I found an altar that had these words written on it: TO A GOD WHO IS NOT KNOWN. You worship a god that you don't know, and this is the God I am telling you about! The God who made the whole world and everything in it is the Lord of the land and the sky. He does not live in temples built by human hands. This God is the One who gives life, breath, and everything else to people. He does not need any help from them; he has everything he needs. God began by making one person, and from him came all the different people who live everywhere in the world. God decided exactly when and where they must live. God wanted them to look for him and perhaps search all around for him and find him, though he is not far from any of us: 'We live in him. We walk in him. We are in him.' Some of your own poets have said: 'For we are his children.' Since we are God's children, you must not think that God is like something that people imagine or make from gold, silver, or rock. In the past, people did not understand God, and he ignored this. But now, God tells all people in the world to change their hearts and lives. God has set a day that he will judge all the world with fairness, by the man he chose long ago. And God has proved this to everyone by raising that man from the dead!"

When the people heard about Jesus being raised from the dead, some of them laughed. But others said, "We will hear more about this from you later." So Paul went away from them. But some of the people believed Paul and joined him. Among those who believed was Dionysius, a member of the Areopagus, a woman named Damaris, and some others.

Paul in Corinth

Later Paul left Athens and went to Corinth. Here he met a Jew named Aquila who had been born in the country of Pontus. But Aquila and his wife, Priscilla, had recently moved to Corinth from Italy, because Claudius commanded that all Jews must leave Rome. Paul went to visit Aquila and Priscilla. Because they were tentmakers, just as he was, he stayed with them and worked with them. Every Sabbath day he talked with the Jews and Greeks in the synagogue, trying to persuade them to believe in Jesus.

OLD TESTAMENT READING

This is the story of the creation of the sky and the earth. When the LORD God first made the earth and the sky, there were still no plants on the earth. Nothing was growing in the fields because the LORD God had not yet made it rain on the land. And there was no person to care for the ground, but a mist would rise up from the earth and water all the ground.

Then the LORD God took dust from the ground and formed a man from it. He breathed the breath of life into the man's nose, and the man became a living person.

Genesis 2:4–7

*T*hen the LORD answered Job from the storm. He said:

"Where were you when I made the
　　earth's foundation?
　Tell me, if you understand.
Who marked off how big it should be?
　Surely you know!
　Who stretched a ruler across it?
What were the earth's foundations set
　on,
　or who put its cornerstone in place
while the morning stars sang together
　and all the angels shouted with joy?

"Have you ever gone into the store-
　　house of the snow
　or seen the storehouses for hail,
which I save for times of trouble,
　for days of war and battle?
Where is the place from which light
　comes?
　Where is the place from which the
　　east winds blow over the earth?
Who cuts a waterway for the heavy
　　rains
　and sets a path for the thunder-
　　storm?

"Who put wisdom inside the mind
　or understanding in the heart?"

Job 38:1, 4–7, 22–25, 36

*W*ould you say that I am unfair?
　Would you blame me to make
　　yourself look right?
Are you as strong as God?
　Can your voice thunder like his?
If so, then decorate yourself with glory
　and beauty;
　dress in honor and greatness as if
　　they were clothing.
Let your great anger punish;
　look at the proud and bring them
　　down.
Look at the proud and make them
　　humble.
　Crush the wicked wherever they are.

Bury them all in the dirt together;
　cover their faces in the grave.
If you can do that, then I myself will
　praise you,
　because you are strong enough to
　　save yourself."

Job 40:8–14

INSIGHTS

I WILL WORSHIP

*G*od, you are with me
　and you can help me;
You were with me when I was taken,
　and you are with me now.
You strengthen me.

The God I serve is everywhere—
　in heaven and earth and the sea,
but he is above them all,
　for all live in him:
All were created by him,
　and by him only do they remain.

I will worship only the true God;
　you will I carry in my heart;
No one on earth shall be able to
　separate me from you.

Quirinus of Siscia

MY COMFORT

*J*esus Christ is my comfort.
It is you who created us all.
There is only you, one God,
　Father, Son, and Holy Spirit,
　to whom homage and praise are due.

Januarius of Cordova

PAUSE FOR REFLECTION

*I*n order to help them understand the Good News, what did Paul tell the philosophers and important people of Athens about the true God? What knowledge of God helps you to understand, trust, and worship him?

FRIDAY:

"Don't Be Afraid . . .
I Am with You"

Acts 18:5–28

Silas and Timothy came from Macedonia and joined Paul in Corinth. After this, Paul spent all his time telling people the Good News, showing the Jews that Jesus is the Christ. But they would not accept Paul's teaching and said some evil things. So he shook off the dust from his clothes and said to them, "If you are not saved, it will be your own fault! I have done all I can do! After this, I will go only to those who are not Jewish." Paul left the synagogue and moved into the home of Titius Justus, next to the synagogue. This man worshiped God. Crispus was the leader of that synagogue, and he and all the people living in his house believed in the Lord. Many others in Corinth also listened to Paul and believed and were baptized.

During the night, the Lord told Paul in a vision: "Don't be afraid. Continue talking to people and don't be quiet. I am with you, and no one will hurt you because many of my people are in this city." Paul stayed there for a year and a half, teaching God's word to the people.

Paul Is Brought Before Gallio

When Gallio was the governor of the country of Southern Greece, some of the Jews came together against Paul and took him to the court. They said, "This man is teaching people to worship God in a way that is against our law."

Paul was about to say something, but Gallio spoke to the Jews, saying, "I would listen to you Jews if you were complaining about a crime or some wrong. But the things you are saying are only questions about words and names—arguments about your own law. So you must solve this problem yourselves. I don't want to be a judge of these things." And Gallio made them leave the court.

Then they all grabbed Sosthenes, the leader of the synagogue, and beat him there before the court. But this did not bother Gallio.

Paul Returns to Antioch

Paul stayed with the believers for many more days. Then he left and sailed for Syria, with Priscilla and Aquila. At Cenchrea Paul cut off his hair, because he had made a promise to God. Then they went to Ephesus, where Paul left Priscilla and Aquila. While Paul was there, he went into the synagogue and talked with the Jews. When they asked him to stay with them longer, he refused. But as he left, he said, "I will come back to you again if God wants me to." And so he sailed away from Ephesus.

When Paul landed at Caesarea, he went and gave greetings to the church in Jerusalem. After that, Paul went to Antioch. He stayed there for a while and then left and went through the regions of Galatia and Phrygia. He traveled from town to town in these regions, giving strength to all the followers.

Apollos in Ephesus and Corinth

A Jew named Apollos came to Ephesus. He was born in the city of Alexandria and was a good speaker who knew the Scriptures well. He had been taught about the way of the Lord and was always very excited when he spoke and taught the truth about Jesus. But the only baptism Apollos knew about was the baptism that John taught. Apollos began to speak very boldly in the synagogue, and when Priscilla and Aquila heard him, they took him to their home and helped him better understand the way of God. Now Apollos wanted to go to the country of Southern Greece. So the believers helped him and wrote a letter to the followers there, asking them to accept him. These followers had believed in Jesus because of God's grace, and when Apollos arrived, he helped them very much. He argued very strongly with the Jews before all the people, clearly proving with the Scriptures that Jesus is the Christ.

The LORD guards you.
The LORD is the shade that protects
you from the sun.

The sun cannot hurt you during the
day,
  and the moon cannot hurt you at
  night.
The LORD will protect you from all
dangers;
  he will guard your life.
The LORD will guard you as you come
and go,
  both now and forever.

Psalm 121:5–8

*G*od is our protection and our
strength.
  He always helps in times of trouble.
So we will not be afraid even if the
earth shakes,
  or the mountains fall into the sea,
even if the oceans roar and foam,
  or the mountains shake at the raging
  sea.   *Selah*

The LORD All-Powerful is with us;
  the God of Jacob is our defender.

Selah

Psalm 46:1–3, 7

*S*o don't worry, because I am with you.
  Don't be afraid, because I am your
  God.
I will make you strong and will help
you;
  I will support you with my right
  hand that saves you.

"All those people who are angry with
you
  will be ashamed and disgraced.
Those who are against you
  will disappear and be lost.
You will look for your enemies,
  but you will not find them.
Those who fought against you
  will vanish completely.
I am the LORD your God,
  who holds your right hand,
and I tell you, 'Don't be afraid.
  I will help you.'"

Isaiah 41:10–13

*Y*ou might say to yourselves, "Because
these nations are stronger than we are, we
can't force them out." But don't be afraid of
them. Remember what the LORD your God

did to all of Egypt and its king. You saw for
yourselves the troubles, signs, and miracles
he did, how the LORD's great power and
strength brought you out of Egypt. The
LORD your God will do the same thing to all
the nations you now fear. The LORD your
God will also send terror among them so
that even those who are alive and hiding
from you will die. Don't be afraid of them,
because the LORD your God is with you; he
is a great God and people are afraid of him.

Deuteronomy 7:17–21

I am with you and will protect you everywhere you go and will bring you back to this
land. I will not leave you until I have done
what I have promised you."

Genesis 28:15

INSIGHTS

*H*ow *tenderly God soothes our fears! How
sweetly He says, . . . "Fear thou not; for I
am with thee: be not dismayed; for I am thy
God: . . . I will uphold thee with the right
hand of my righteousness" (Isaiah 41:10).
And yet again, still with tender thoughtful-
ness, "I the Lord thy God will hold thy right
hand, saying unto thee, Fear not; I will help
thee" (Isaiah 41:13). He does not say it only
once, but He keeps holding our right hand and
repeating such promises.*

*The blessed Lord condensed it all into one
single message of eternal comfort spoken to
the disciples on the Sea of Galilee, It is I; be
not afraid. He is the antidote to fear; He is
the remedy for trouble; He is the substance
and the sum of deliverance. We should,
therefore, rise above fear. Let us keep our eyes
fastened upon Him; let us abide continually
in Him; let us be content with Him.*

Let us cling closely to Him.

A. B. Simpson

ACTION POINT

*W*hat *encouragement from the Lord have
you received in times of fear? Which of the
Old Testament readings assures you that God
is with you? Pray that you will always cling
to God and feel the blessing of his presence!*

WEEKEND:

True Repentance Involves Abandoning Sinful Practices

Acts 19:1–22

NEW TESTAMENT READING

Paul in Ephesus

*W*hile Apollos was in Corinth, Paul was visiting some places on the way to Ephesus. There he found some followers and asked them, "Did you receive the Holy Spirit when you believed?"

They said, "We have never even heard of a Holy Spirit."

So he asked, "What kind of baptism did you have?"

They said, "It was the baptism that John taught."

Paul said, "John's baptism was a baptism of changed hearts and lives. He told people to believe in the one who would come after him, and that one is Jesus."

When they heard this, they were baptized in the name of the Lord Jesus. Then Paul laid his hands on them, and the Holy Spirit came upon them. They began speaking different languages and prophesying. There were about twelve people in this group.

Paul went into the synagogue and spoke out boldly for three months. He talked with the Jews and persuaded them to accept the things he said about the kingdom of God. But some of the Jews became stubborn. They refused to believe and said evil things about the Way of Jesus before all the people. So Paul left them, and taking the followers with him, he went to the school of a man named Tyrannus. There Paul talked with people every day for two years. Because of his work, every Jew and Greek in the country of Asia heard the word of the Lord.

The Sons of Sceva

*G*od used Paul to do some very special miracles. Some people took handkerchiefs and clothes that Paul had used and put them on the sick. When they did this, the sick were healed and evil spirits left them.

But some Jews also were traveling around and making evil spirits go out of people. They tried to use the name of the Lord Jesus to force the evil spirits out. They would say, "By the same Jesus that Paul talks about, I order you to come out!" Seven sons of Sceva, a leading Jewish priest, were doing this.

But one time an evil spirit said to them, "I know Jesus, and I know about Paul, but who are you?"

Then the man who had the evil spirit jumped on them. Because he was so much stronger than all of them, they ran away from the house naked and hurt. All the people in Ephesus—Jews and Greeks—learned about this and were filled with fear and gave great honor to the Lord Jesus. Many of the believers began to confess openly and tell all the evil things they had done. Some of them who had used magic brought their magic books and burned them before everyone. Those books worth about fifty thousand silver coins.

So in a powerful way the word of the Lord kept spreading and growing.

After these things, Paul decided to go to Jerusalem, planning to go through the countries of Macedonia and Southern Greece and then on to Jerusalem. He said, "After I have been to Jerusalem, I must also visit Rome." Paul sent Timothy and Erastus, two of his helpers, ahead to Macedonia, but he himself stayed in Asia for a while.

OLD TESTAMENT READING

*T*hen Jehoiada made an agreement between the LORD and the king and the people that they would be the LORD's special people. He also made an agreement between the king and the people. All the people of the land went to the temple of Baal and tore it down, smashing the altars and idols. They also killed Mattan, the priest of Baal, in front of the altars.

Then Jehoiada the priest placed guards at the Temple of the LORD.

2 Kings 11:17–18

*T*he king must not have many wives, or his heart will be led away from God. He must not have too much silver and gold.

When he becomes king, he should write a copy of the teachings on a scroll for himself, a copy taken from the priests and Levites. He should keep it with him all the time and read from it every day of his life. Then he will learn to respect the LORD his God, and he will obey all the teachings and commands.

Deuteronomy 17:17–19

*J*osiah was eight years old when he became king, and he ruled thirty-one years in Jerusalem. He did what the LORD said was right. He lived as his ancestor David had lived, and he did not stop doing what was right.

In his eighth year as king while he was still young, Josiah began to obey the God of his ancestor David. In his twelfth year as king, Josiah began to remove from Judah and Jerusalem the gods, the places for worshiping gods, the Asherah idols, and the wooden and metal idols. The people tore down the altars for the Baal gods as Josiah directed. Then Josiah cut down the incense altars that were above them. He broke up the Asherah idols and the wooden and metal idols and beat them into powder. Then he sprinkled the powder on the graves of the people who had offered sacrifices to these gods. He burned the bones of their priests on their own altars. So Josiah removed idol worship from Judah and Jerusalem, and from the towns in the areas of Manasseh, Ephraim, and Simeon all the way to Naphtali, and in the ruins near these towns. Josiah broke down the altars and Asherah idols and beat the idols into powder. He cut down all the incense altars in all of Israel. Then he went back to Jerusalem.

2 Chronicles 34:1–7

INSIGHTS

*W*hen I was a boy, each Saturday my father would make a list of chores for me to do before I could go and play. When he came home in the evening, he would take the list and—walking with me beside him—check how each job had been done. Sometimes he would point out a hidden, unswept corner that I had missed or find a small, untrimmed area of the yard that I had overlooked. When he did so, I would take a brush or clippers right then and finish the job properly. And you can be sure that, the next week, I would remember to carefully check those places I'd missed.

In checking on my work, my father was not being unkind or critical of what I'd done. He was helping me learn to do a job right the first time. And when I did, he would always encourage me and say, "That's good work, son."

That's how we should be with the Lord. We need to learn to be quick to take care of everything we see on the Father's "list" in his Word and then be open and ready for him to point out the things we have overlooked or neglected. We must offer daily confession, both for known sins that blot a day's activities and for sins we overlooked.

When we do these things, we know that through the blood of Christ we have instant and complete forgiveness: "If we confess our sins to him, he can be depended on to forgive us and to cleanse us from every wrong" (1 John 1:9).

"Hidden corners" do slip by unnoticed, and there are many believers caught up in sinful habits that at first they don't even recognize as sin. We might find, as we open to the Lord, that he begins to confront and adjust a pattern of our relationships, an aspect of our daily activities or entertainment, or some continued practice from childhood. We need to bring all aspects of our lives, regardless of what the world says is right or acceptable, under the searching eyes of the Lord.

Jack Hayford

APPLICATION

*W*hat happens when God's people turn away from sin and truly seek to obey him? These readings show that God's people must continually put away their hidden sins and follow God more diligently. What sins in your life need to be put away?

MONDAY:

God Can Defeat Those Who Stir Up Trouble for His People

Acts 19:23—20:6

Trouble in Ephesus

*A*nd during that time, there was some serious trouble in Ephesus about the way of Jesus. A man named Demetrius, who worked with silver, made little silver models that looked like the temple of the goddess Artemis. Those who did this work made much money. Demetrius had a meeting with them and some others who did the same kind of work. He told them, "Men, you know that we make a lot of money from our business. But look at what this man Paul is doing. He has convinced and turned away many people in Ephesus and in almost all of Asia! He says the gods made by human hands are not real. There is a danger that our business will lose its good name, but there is also another danger: People will begin to think that the temple of the great goddess Artemis is not important. Her greatness will be destroyed, and Artemis is the goddess that everyone in Asia and the whole world worships."

When the others heard this, they became very angry and shouted, "Artemis, the goddess of Ephesus, is great!" The whole city became confused. The people grabbed Gaius and Aristarchus, who were from Macedonia and were traveling with Paul, and ran to the theater. Paul wanted to go in and talk to the crowd, but the followers did not let him. Also, some leaders of Asia who were friends of Paul sent him a message, begging him not to go into the theater. Some people were shouting one thing, and some were shouting another. The meeting was completely confused; most of them did not know why they had come together. The Jews put a man named Alexander in front of the people, and some of them told him what to do. Alexander waved his hand so he could explain things to the people. But when they saw that Alexander was a Jew, they all shouted the same thing for two hours: "Great is Artemis of Ephesus!"

Then the city clerk made the crowd be quiet. He said, "People of Ephesus, everyone knows that Ephesus is the city that keeps the temple of the great goddess Artemis and her holy stone that fell from heaven. Since no one can say this is not true, you should be quiet. Stop and think before you do anything. You brought these men here, but they have not said anything evil against our goddess or stolen anything from her temple. If Demetrius and those who work with him have a charge against anyone they should go to the courts and judges where they can argue with each other. If there is something else you want to talk about, it can be decided at the regular town meeting of the people. I say this because some people might see this trouble today and say that we are rioting. We could not explain this, because there is no real reason for this meeting." After the city clerk said these things, he told the people to go home.

Paul in Macedonia and Greece

*W*hen the trouble stopped, Paul sent for the followers to come to him. After he encouraged them and then told them good-bye, he left and went to the country of Macedonia. He said many things to strengthen the followers in the different places on his way through Macedonia. Then he went to Greece, where he stayed for three months. He was ready to sail for Syria, but some Jews were planning something against him. So Paul decided to go back through Macedonia to Syria. The men who went with him were Sopater son of Pyrrhus, from the city of Berea; Aristarchus and Secundus, from the city of Thessalonica; Gaius, from Derbe; Timothy; and Tychicus and Trophimus, two men from the country of Asia. These men went on ahead and waited for us at Troas. We sailed from Philippi after the Feast of Unleavened Bread. Five days later we met them in Troas, where we stayed for seven days.

*W*hat if the LORD had not been on our
side?
(Let Israel repeat this.)
What if the LORD had not been on our
side
when we were attacked?
When they were angry with us,
they would have swallowed us alive.
They would have been like a flood
drowning us;
they would have poured over us like
a river.
They would have swept us away like
a mighty stream.
Praise the LORD,
who did not let them chew us up.
We escaped like a bird
from the hunter's trap.
The trap broke,
and we escaped.
Our help comes from the LORD,
who made heaven and earth.

Psalm 124:1–8

A greedy person causes trouble,
but the one who trusts the LORD will
succeed.

Proverbs 28:25

*B*ut Sanballat, Tobiah, the Arabs, the Ammonites, and the people from Ashdod were
very angry when they heard that the repairs
to Jerusalem's walls were continuing and
that the holes in the wall were being closed.
So they all made plans to come to Jerusalem and fight and stir up trouble. But we
prayed to our God and appointed guards to
watch for them day and night.

So I put people behind the lowest places
along the wall—the open places—and I put
families together with their swords, spears,
and bows. Then I looked around and stood
up and said to the important men, the leaders, and the rest of the people: "Don't be
afraid of them. Remember the Lord, who
is great and powerful. Fight for your brothers, your sons and daughters, your wives,
and your homes."

Then our enemies heard that we knew
about their plans and that God had ruined
their plans. So we all went back to the wall,
each to his own work.

Nehemiah 4:7–9, 13–15

A mighty fortress is our God,
A bulwark never failing;
Our helper He amid the flood
Of mortal ills prevailing.
For still our ancient foe
Doth seek to work us woe—
His craft and pow'r are great,
And, armed with cruel hate,
On earth is not his equal.

Did we in our own strength confide,
Our striving would be losing,
Were not the right man on our side,
The man of God's own choosing.
Dost ask who that may be?
Christ Jesus, it is He—
Lord Sabaoth His name,
From age to age the same,
And He must win the battle.

And tho this world, with devils filled,
Should threaten to undo us,
We will not fear, for God hath willed
His truth to triumph thru us.
The prince of darkness grim,
We tremble not for him—
His rage we can endure,
For lo, his doom is sure:
One little word shall fell him.

That word above all earthly pow'rs,
No thanks to them, abideth;
The Spirit and the gifts are ours
Thru Him who with us sideth.
Let goods and kindred go,
This mortal life also—
The body they may kill;
God's truth abideth still:
His kingdom is forever.

Martin Luther

---

*W*hat motivated Demetrius to start the
trouble in Ephesus? For what other reasons
do people cause trouble for God's people?
What comfort and strength do you find in
Psalm 124 and Luther's famous hymn?

TUESDAY:

Serving God Is Most Important . . . Even If We Risk Our Lives

Acts 20:7–38

NEW TESTAMENT READING

Paul's Last Visit to Troas

On the first day of the week, we all met together to break bread, and Paul spoke to the group. Because he was planning to leave the next day, he kept on talking until midnight. We were all together in a room upstairs, and there were many lamps in the room. A young man named Eutychus was sitting in the window. As Paul continued talking, Eutychus was falling into a deep sleep. Finally, he went sound asleep and fell to the ground from the third floor. When they picked him up, he was dead. Paul went down to Eutychus, knelt down, and put his arms around him. He said, "Don't worry. He is alive now." Then Paul went upstairs again, broke bread, and ate. He spoke to them a long time, until it was early morning, and then he left. They took the young man home alive and were greatly comforted.

The Trip from Troas to Miletus

We went on ahead of Paul and sailed for the city of Assos, where he wanted to join us on the ship. Paul planned it this way because he wanted to go to Assos by land. When he met us there, we took him aboard and went to Mitylene. We sailed from Mitylene and the next day came to a place near Chios. The following day we sailed to Samos, and the next day we reached Miletus. Paul had already decided not to stop at Ephesus, because he did not want to stay too long in the country of Asia. He was hurrying to be in Jerusalem on the day of Pentecost, if that were possible.

The Elders from Ephesus

Now from Miletus Paul sent to Ephesus and called for the elders of the church. When they came to him, he said, "You know about my life from the first day I came to Asia. You know the way I lived all the time I was with you. The Jews made plans against me, which troubled me very much. But you know I always served the Lord unselfishly, and I often cried. You know I preached to you and did not hold back anything that would help you. You know that I taught you in public and in your homes. I warned both Jews and Greeks to change their lives and turn to God and believe in our Lord Jesus. But now I must obey the Holy Spirit and go to Jerusalem. I don't know what will happen to me there. I know only that in every city the Holy Spirit tells me that troubles and even jail wait for me. I don't care about my own life. The most important thing is that I complete my mission, the work that the Lord Jesus gave me—to tell people the Good News about God's grace.

"And now, I know that none of you among whom I was preaching the kingdom of God will ever see me again. So today I tell you that if any of you should be lost, I am not responsible, because I have told you everything God wants you to know. Be careful for yourselves and for all the people the Holy Spirit has given to you to care for. You must be like shepherds to the church of God, which he bought with the death of his own son. I know that after I leave, some people will come like wild wolves and try to destroy the flock. Also, some from your own group will rise up and twist the truth and will lead away followers after them. So be careful! Always remember that for three years, day and night, I never stopped warning each of you, and I often cried over you.

"Now I am putting you in the care of God and the message about his grace. It is able to give you strength, and it will give you the blessings God has for all his holy people. When I was with you, I never wanted anyone's money or fine clothes. You know I always worked to take care of my own needs and the needs of those who were with me. I showed you in all things that you should work as I did and help the weak. I taught you to remember the words Jesus said: 'It is more blessed to give than to receive.'"

When Paul had said this, he knelt down with all of them and prayed. And they all cried because Paul had said they would never see him again. They put their arms around him and kissed him. Then they went with him to the ship.

*T*hen Elijah said, "Capture the prophets of Baal! Don't let any of them run away!" The people captured all the prophets. Then Elijah led them down to the Kishon Valley, where he killed them.

1 Kings 18:40

*K*ing Ahab told Jezebel everything Elijah had done and how Elijah had killed all the prophets with a sword. So Jezebel sent a messenger to Elijah, saying, "May the gods punish me terribly if by this time tomorrow I don't kill you just as you killed those prophets."

When Elijah heard this, he was afraid and ran for his life, taking his servant with him. When they came to Beersheba in Judah, Elijah left his servant there. Then Elijah walked for a whole day into the desert. He sat down under a bush and asked to die. "I have had enough, LORD," he prayed. "Let me die. I am no better than my ancestors." Then he lay down under the tree and slept.

Suddenly an angel came to him and touched him. "Get up and eat," the angel said. Elijah saw near his head a loaf baked over coals and a jar of water, so he ate and drank. Then he went back to sleep.

Later the LORD's angel came to him a second time. The angel touched him and said, "Get up and eat. If you don't, the journey will be too hard for you." So Elijah got up and ate and drank. The food made him strong enough to walk for forty days and nights to Mount Sinai, the mountain of God. There Elijah went into a cave and stayed all night.

Then the LORD spoke his word to him: "Elijah! Why are you here?"

He answered, "LORD God All-Powerful, I have always served you as well as I could. But the people of Israel have broken their agreement with you, destroyed your altars, and killed your prophets with swords. I am the only prophet left, and now they are trying to kill me, too."

The LORD said to him, "Go back on the road that leads to the desert around Damascus. Enter that city, and pour olive oil on Hazael to make him king over Aram. Then pour oil on Jehu son of Nimshi to make him king over Israel. Next, pour oil on Elisha son of Shaphat from Abel Meholah to make him a prophet in your place."

So Elijah left that place and found Elisha.

1 Kings 19:1–10, 15–16, 19a

*D*avid Brainerd, early missionary to the Indians of the United States, was so consumed with a passion for the glory of Christ in the salvation of souls that he claimed: "I cared not how or where I lived, or what hardships I endured, so that I could but gain souls for Christ."

Paul was a passionately ambitious man, even before his conversion. . . .

. . . Whereas his old ambition had been to efface the name of Jesus and exterminate His church, now he had a passion to exalt the name of Jesus and establish and edify His church. His new ambition found its center in the glory of Christ and the advancement of His kingdom. . . .

Our Lord was gripped by a master ambition that integrated the whole of His life. It can be summarized in a single sentence: "I have come to do your will, O God" (Hebrews 10:7). When at life's end He offered His wonderful high-priestly prayer, He was able to report the complete achievement of this ambition: "I have brought you glory on earth by completing the work you gave me to do" (John 17:4).

J. Oswald Sanders

*W*hat was Paul's most important goal in life? What personal hardship did that commitment cost him? What sustains a person who makes such a commitment? Is serving God most important for you?

WEDNESDAY:

God Requires Uncompromising Faithfulness

Acts 21:1–25

NEW TESTAMENT READING

Paul Goes to Jerusalem

*A*fter we all said good-bye to them, we sailed straight to the island of Cos. The next day we reached Rhodes, and from there we went to Patara. There we found a ship going to Phoenicia, so we went aboard and sailed away. We sailed near the island of Cyprus, seeing it to the north, but we sailed on to Syria. We stopped at Tyre because the ship needed to unload its cargo there. We found some followers in Tyre and stayed with them for seven days. Through the Holy Spirit they warned Paul not to go to Jerusalem. When we finished our visit, we left and continued our trip. All the followers, even the women and children, came outside the city with us. After we all knelt on the beach and prayed, we said good-bye and got on the ship, and the followers went back home.

We continued our trip from Tyre and arrived at Ptolemais, where we greeted the believers and stayed with them for a day. The next day we left Ptolemais and went to the city of Caesarea. There we went into the home of Philip the preacher, one of the seven helpers, and stayed with him. He had four unmarried daughters who had the gift of prophesying. After we had been there for some time, a prophet named Agabus arrived from Judea. He came to us and borrowed Paul's belt and used it to tie his own hands and feet. He said, "The Holy Spirit says, 'This is how the Jews in Jerusalem will tie up the man who wears this belt. Then they will give him to those who are not Jews.'"

When we all heard this, we and the people there begged Paul not to go to Jerusalem. But he said, "Why are you crying and making me so sad? I am not only ready to be tied up in Jerusalem, I am ready to die for the Lord Jesus!"

We could not persuade him to stay away from Jerusalem. So we stopped begging him and said, "We pray that what the Lord wants will be done."

After this, we got ready and started on our way to Jerusalem. Some of the followers from Caesarea went with us and took us to the home of Mnason, where we would stay. He was from Cyprus and was one of the first followers.

Paul Visits James

*I*n Jerusalem the believers were glad to see us. The next day Paul went with us to visit James, and all the elders were there. Paul greeted them and told them everything God had done among the non-Jewish people through him. When they heard this, they praised God. Then they said to Paul, "Brother, you can see that many thousands of Jews have become believers. And they think it is very important to obey the law of Moses. They have heard about your teaching, that you tell the Jews who live among those who are not Jews to leave the law of Moses. They have heard that you tell them not to circumcise their children and not to obey Jewish customs. What should we do? They will learn that you have come. So we will tell you what to do: Four of our men have made a promise to God. Take these men with you and share in their cleansing ceremony. Pay their expenses so they can shave their heads. Then it will prove to everyone that what they have heard about you is not true and that you follow the law of Moses in your own life. We have already sent a letter to the non-Jewish believers. The letter said: 'Do not eat food that has been offered to idols, or blood, or animals that have been strangled. Do not take part in sexual sin.'"

OLD TESTAMENT READING

*T*he people saw that a long time had passed and Moses had not come down from the mountain. So they gathered around Aaron and said, "Moses led us out of Egypt, but we don't know what has happened to him. Make us gods who will lead us."

Aaron said to the people, "Take off the gold earrings that your wives, sons, and daughters are wearing, and bring them to

me." So all the people took their gold earrings and brought them to Aaron. He took
the gold from the people and formed it
with a tool and made a statue of a calf. Then
the people said, "Israel, these are your
gods who brought you out of the land of
Egypt!"

Then the LORD said to Moses, "Go down
from this mountain, because your people,
the people you brought out of the land of
Egypt, have ruined themselves. They have
quickly turned away from the things I
commanded them to do. They have made
for themselves a calf covered with gold,
and they have worshiped it and offered
sacrifices to it. They have said, 'Israel, these
are your gods who brought you out of
Egypt.'"

So Moses stood at the entrance to the
camp and said, "Let anyone who wants to
follow the LORD come to me." And all the
people from the family of Levi gathered
around Moses.

Then Moses said to them, "The LORD,
the God of Israel, says this: 'Every man
must put on his sword and go through the
camp from one end to the other. Each man
must kill his brother, his friend, and his
neighbor.'" The people from the family of
Levi obeyed Moses, and that day about
three thousand of the Israelites died. Then
Moses said, "Today you have been given for
service to the LORD. You were willing to kill
your own sons and brothers, and God has
blessed you for this."

The next day Moses told the people,
"You have done a terrible sin. But now I will
go up to the LORD. Maybe I can do something so your sins will be removed." So
Moses went back to the LORD and said,
"How terribly these people have sinned!
They have made for themselves gods from
gold. Now, please forgive them of this sin.
If you will not, then erase my name from
the book in which you have written the
names of your people."

But the LORD told Moses, "I will erase
from my book the names of the people who
sin against me. So now, go. Lead the people
where I have told you, and my angel will
lead you. When the time comes to punish,
I will punish them for their sin."

So the LORD caused terrible things to
happen to the people because of what they
did with the calf Aaron had made.

Exodus 32:1–4, 7–8, 26–35

INSIGHTS

*S*ometimes King Saul was among the
*prophets, easily turned into a prophet, and
then afterwards among the witches; sometimes in one place and then another, and
insincere in everything. How many such we
have in every Christian assembly; men who
are very easily molded. They have affection-
ate dispositions, very likely a tender conscience; but then the conscience is so remark-
ably tender, that when touched it seems to
give, and you are afraid to probe deeper; it
heals as soon as it is wounded. You may press
then whichever way you wish, they are so
elastic you can always win your purpose, but
then they are not fixed in character and soon
return to be what they were before.*

*Pray God to send a few men with "grit" in
them; men, who when they know a thing to
be right, will not turn away, or turn aside, or
stop; men who will persevere all the more
because there are difficulties to meet or foes
to encounter; who stand all the more true to
their Master because they are opposed; who,
the more they are thrust into the fire, the
hotter they become; who, just like the bow,
the further the string is drawn the more powerfully it sends forth its arrows, and so the
more they are trodden upon, the more mighty
will they become in the cause of truth against
error.*

Charles Spurgeon

PAUSE   FOR   REFLECTION

*L*ook at the examples of faithful service to
*God in these Scripture readings. Are you so
convinced of the reality of God in your life
that you would risk your life to serve him?*

THURSDAY:
Proclaim God's Truth Boldly
Acts 21:26—22:5

NEW   TESTAMENT   READING

*T*he next day Paul took the four men and shared in the cleansing ceremony with them. Then he went to the Temple and announced the time when the days of the cleansing ceremony would be finished. On the last day an offering would be given for each of the men.

When the seven days were almost over, some Jews from Asia saw Paul at the Temple. They caused all the people to be upset and grabbed Paul. They shouted, "People of Israel, help us! This is the man who goes everywhere teaching against the law of Moses, against our people, and against this Temple. Now he has brought some Greeks into the Temple and has made this holy place unclean!" (The Jews said this because they had seen Trophimus, a man from Ephesus, with Paul in Jerusalem. The Jews thought that Paul had brought him into the Temple.)

All the people in Jerusalem became upset. Together they ran, took Paul, and dragged him out of the Temple. The Temple doors were closed immediately. While they were trying to kill Paul, the commander of the Roman army in Jerusalem learned that there was trouble in the whole city. Immediately he took some officers and soldiers and ran to the place where the crowd was gathered. When the people saw them, they stopped beating Paul. The commander went to Paul and arrested him. He told his soldiers to tie Paul with two chains. Then he asked who he was and what he had done wrong. Some in the crowd were yelling one thing, and some were yelling another. Because of all this confusion and shouting, the commander could not learn what had happened. So he ordered the soldiers to take Paul to the army building. When Paul came to the steps, the soldiers had to carry him because the people were ready to hurt him. The whole mob was following them, shouting, "Kill him!"

As the soldiers were about to take Paul into the army building, he spoke to the commander, "May I say something to you?"

The commander said, "Do you speak Greek? I thought you were the Egyptian who started some trouble against the government not long ago and led four thousand killers out to the desert."

Paul said, "No, I am a Jew from Tarsus in the country of Cilicia. I am a citizen of that important city. Please, let me speak to the people."

The commander gave permission, so Paul stood on the steps and waved his hand to quiet the people. When there was silence, he spoke to them in the Jewish language.

Paul Speaks to the People

*P*aul said, "Friends, fellow Jews, listen to my defense to you." When the Jews heard him speaking the Jewish language, they became very quiet. Paul said, "I am a Jew, born in Tarsus in the country of Cilicia, but I grew up in this city. I was a student of Gamaliel, who carefully taught me everything about the law of our ancestors. I was very serious about serving God, just as are all of you here today. I persecuted the people who followed the Way of Jesus, and some of them were even killed. I arrested men and women and put them in jail. The high priest and the whole council of older Jewish leaders can tell you this is true. They gave me letters to the Jewish brothers in Damascus. So I was going there to arrest these people and bring them back to Jerusalem to be punished."

OLD   TESTAMENT   READING

*H*e said to me, "Human, stand up on your feet so I may speak with you." While he spoke to me, the Spirit entered me and put me on my feet. Then I heard the LORD speaking to me.

He said, "Human, I am sending you to the people of Israel. That nation has turned against me and broken away from me. They and their ancestors have sinned against me until this very day. I am sending you to people who are stubborn and who do not obey. You will say to them, 'This is what the

Lord God says.' They may listen, or they may not, since they are a people who have turned against me. But they will know that a prophet has been among them. You, human, don't be afraid of the people or their words. Even though they may be like thorny branches and stickers all around you, and though you may feel like you live with poisonous insects, don't be afraid. Don't be afraid of their words or their looks, because they are a people who turn against me. But speak my words to them. They may listen, or they may not, because they turn against me."

Ezekiel 2:1–7

*T*hen he said to me, "Human, go to the people of Israel, and speak my words to them. You are not being sent to people whose speech you can't understand, whose language is difficult. You are being sent to Israel. You are not being sent to many nations whose speech you can't understand, whose language is difficult, whose words you cannot understand. If I had sent you to them, they would have listened to you. But the people of Israel will not be willing to listen to you, because they are not willing to listen to me. Yes, all the people of Israel are stubborn and will not obey. See, I now make you as stubborn and as hard as they are. I am making you as hard as a diamond, harder than stone. Don't be afraid of them or be frightened by them, though they are a people who turn against me."

Also, he said to me, "Human, believe all the words I will speak to you, and listen carefully to them. Then go to the captives, your own people, and say to them, 'The Lord God says this.' Tell them this whether they listen or not."

Ezekiel 3:4–11

INSIGHTS

*J*ohan is young, tall, blond, and Dutch. I got to know him through my cousin, who attended the same Bible school in England. Gifted and handsome, Johan could have carved out a comfortable youth ministry in his native Netherlands—or most anywhere in the world, for that matter.

Comfort, however, isn't one of Johan's major goals. He chose to take the gospel of Christ to the bedouins and nomads near Israel's desolate Sinai desert. A forgotten people in one of the most desolate corners of the world.

Johan works by an oasis near the sea, attracting travelers and bedouins by offering hot meals, clothing, and first aid. . . .

From the bedouins, Johan learned it is considered worse than murder if you know of a water source and yet neglect to tell your fellow man.

Few of us will ever live in a wilderness like the one where young Johan has pitched his tent. Not many among us will ever proclaim salvation to desert nomads. But all around us, no matter where we reside or work, there are thirsty men and women. The neighbor down the street, the man at the service station, the boy who carries our groceries, the secretary who types and files, or even the distant aunt who occasionally comes by for visits.

If these people don't know Christ, they're going to die of thirst. . . .

Do you know the Source of living water? If you do, please don't withhold a drink from somebody who is thirsty.

It's not just a matter of hospitality. It's a matter of life and death.

Joni Eareckson Tada

APPLICATION

*W*hat difficulties did Paul and Ezekiel face in proclaiming God's message? Why did they speak God's Word, even at great personal risk? To whom is God leading you to share Christ? Will you take the risk?

F R I D A Y:

God Has Plans for Those He Has Chosen

Acts 22:6–29

NEW TESTAMENT READING

*A*bout noon when I came near Damascus, a bright light from heaven suddenly flashed all around me. I fell to the ground and heard a voice saying, 'Saul, Saul, why are you persecuting me?' I asked, 'Who are you, Lord?' The voice said, 'I am Jesus from Nazareth whom you are persecuting.' Those who were with me did not hear the voice, but they saw the light. I said, 'What shall I do, Lord?' The Lord answered, 'Get up and go to Damascus. There you will be told about all the things I have planned for you to do.' I could not see, because the bright light had made me blind. So my companions led me into Damascus.

"There a man named Ananias came to me. He was a religious man; he obeyed the law of Moses, and all the Jews who lived there respected him. He stood by me and said, 'Brother Saul, see again!' Immediately I was able to see him. He said, 'The God of our ancestors chose you long ago to know his plan, to see the Righteous One, and to hear words from him. You will be his witness to all people, telling them about what you have seen and heard. Now, why wait any longer? Get up, be baptized, and wash your sins away, trusting in him to save you.'

"Later, when I returned to Jerusalem, I was praying in the Temple, and I saw a vision. I saw the Lord saying to me, 'Hurry! Leave Jerusalem now! The people here will not accept the truth about me.' But I said, 'Lord, they know that in every synagogue I put the believers in jail and beat them. They also know I was there when Stephen, your witness, was killed. I stood there agreeing and holding the coats of those who were killing him!' But the Lord said to me, 'Leave now. I will send you far away to the non-Jewish people.'"

The crowd listened to Paul until he said this. Then they began shouting, "Kill him! Get him out of the world! He should not be allowed to live!" They shouted, threw off their coats, and threw dust into the air.

Then the commander ordered the soldiers to take Paul into the army building and beat him. He wanted to make Paul tell why the people were shouting against him like this. But as the soldiers were tying him up, preparing to beat him, Paul said to an officer nearby, "Do you have the right to beat a Roman citizen who has not been proven guilty?"

When the officer heard this, he went to the commander and reported it. The officer said, "Do you know what you are doing? This man is a Roman citizen."

The commander came to Paul and said, "Tell me, are you really a Roman citizen?"

He answered, "Yes."

The commander said, "I paid a lot of money to become a Roman citizen."

But Paul said, "I was born a citizen."

The men who were preparing to question Paul moved away from him immediately. The commander was frightened because he had already tied Paul, and Paul was a Roman citizen.

OLD TESTAMENT READING

*T*he sky was made at the Lord's
    command.
  By the breath from his mouth, he
    made all the stars.
He gathered the water of the sea into a
    heap.
  He made the great ocean stay in its
    place.
All the earth should worship the Lord;
    the whole world should fear him.
He spoke, and it happened.
  He commanded, and it appeared.
The Lord upsets the plans of nations;
    he ruins all their plans.
But the Lord's plans will stand forever;
    his ideas will last from now on.
Happy is the nation whose God is the
    Lord,
  the people he chose for his very
    own.

Psalm 33:6–12

*P*eople may make plans in their minds,
    but the LORD decides what they will
    do.

Proverbs 16:9

I say this because I know what I am planning for you," says the LORD. "I have good
plans for you, not plans to hurt you. I will
give you hope and a good future. Then you
will call my name. You will come to me and
pray to me, and I will listen to you. You will
search for me. And when you search for me
with all your heart, you will find me!"

Jeremiah 29:11–13

*Y*ou saw that the walls of Jerusalem
    had many cracks that needed
        repairing.
    You stored up water in the lower
        pool.
    You counted the houses of Jerusalem,
        and you tore down houses to repair
        the walls with their stones.
    You made a pool between the two walls
        to save water from the old pool,
    but you did not trust the God who
            made these things;
        you did not respect the One who
            planned them long ago.

Isaiah 22:9–11

*L*ORD, you are my God.
    I honor you and praise you,
    because you have done amazing
        things.
    You have always done what you said
        you would do;
    you have done what you planned
        long ago.

Isaiah 25:1

INSIGHTS

*G*od is at work in all the kaleidoscoping
family transitions: not only in the high points
but in the endings, beginnings, detours, dead
ends, and in-between times. His powerful tools
are not just the promotions and graduations
but the failures and firings and losses and
sicknesses and shocks and periods of boredom.
In them all He's silently, busily, unceasingly
encouraging, punishing, shaping. . . .

*. . . And during all His working—all
God's silent activity in the disappointments,
surprises, delights, irritations—transforma-
tions are taking place. . . .*

*Do you feel as if nothing is happen-
ing . . . ?*

*I guess so does a lobster, encased in that
ridiculous armor. As he grows it even gets
crowded inside. But he sheds it fourteen times
during his first year of life. Each shedding
takes ten days, and each time in the period
between shells—when he's naked, exposed,
vulnerable—he grows about seven percent.*

*You feel stifled, unfulfilled? You don't know
when you'll break out into change?*

Wait for God.

Wait on God.

Wait with God.

*Life is not fixed. Let it happen; don't rush
it. "It is God who works in you to will and to
act according to his good purpose. Do everything without complaining or arguing" (Phil.
2:13, 14). Keep your eyes fixed on Him, live
in obedience as you see it, and then just be
there.*

Anne Ortlund

APPLICATION

*I*magine yourself as Paul. How would
you have taken the news that God had very
different plans than what you had chosen?
Pray that you will trust God's plans and obey
them as they are revealed to you.

WEEKEND:

Be Brave; God Stands by His Own

Acts 22:30—23:22

Paul Speaks to Jewish Leaders

The next day the commander decided to learn why the Jews were accusing Paul. So he ordered the leading priests and the Jewish council to meet. The commander took Paul's chains off. Then he brought Paul out and stood him before their meeting.

Paul looked at the Jewish council and said, "Brothers, I have lived my life without guilt feelings before God up to this day." Ananias, the high priest, heard this and told the men who were standing near Paul to hit him on the mouth. Paul said to Ananias, "God will hit you, too! You are like a wall that has been painted white. You sit there and judge me, using the law of Moses, but you are telling them to hit me, and that is against the law."

The men standing near Paul said to him, "You cannot insult God's high priest like that!"

Paul said, "Brothers, I did not know this man was the high priest. It is written in the Scriptures, 'You must not curse a leader of your people.'"

Some of the men in the meeting were Sadducees, and others were Pharisees. Knowing this, Paul shouted to them, "My brothers, I am a Pharisee, and my father was a Pharisee. I am on trial here because I believe that people will rise from the dead."

When Paul said this, there was an argument between the Pharisees and the Sadducees, and the group was divided. (The Sadducees do not believe in angels or spirits or that people will rise from the dead. But the Pharisees believe in them all.) So there was a great uproar. Some of the teachers of the law, who were Pharisees, stood up and argued, "We find nothing wrong with this man. Maybe an angel or a spirit did speak to him."

The argument was beginning to turn into such a fight that the commander was afraid the Jews would tear Paul to pieces. So he told the soldiers to go down and take Paul away and put him in the army building.

The next night the Lord came and stood by Paul. He said, "Be brave! You have told people in Jerusalem about me. You must do the same in Rome."

In the morning some of the Jews made a plan to kill Paul, and they took an oath not to eat or drink anything until they had killed him. There were more than forty Jews who made this plan. They went to the leading priests and the older Jewish leaders and said, "We have taken an oath not to eat or drink until we have killed Paul. So this is what we want you to do: Send a message to the commander to bring Paul out to you as though you want to ask him more questions. We will be waiting to kill him while he is on the way here."

But Paul's nephew heard about this plan and went to the army building and told Paul. Then Paul called one of the officers and said, "Take this young man to the commander. He has a message for him."

So the officer brought Paul's nephew to the commander and said, "The prisoner, Paul, asked me to bring this young man to you. He wants to tell you something."

The commander took the young man's hand and led him to a place where they could be alone. He asked, "What do you want to tell me?"

The young man said, "The Jews have decided to ask you to bring Paul down to their council meeting tomorrow. They want you to think they are going to ask him more questions. But don't believe them! More than forty men are hiding and waiting to kill Paul. They have all taken an oath not to eat or drink until they have killed him. Now they are waiting for you to agree."

The commander sent the young man away, ordering him, "Don't tell anyone that you have told me about their plan."

God, we thank you;
we thank you because you are near.

348

We tell about the miracles you do.

You say, "I set the time for trial,
and I will judge fairly.
The earth with all its people may shake,
but I am the one who holds it steady.

Selah

I say to those who are proud, 'Don't
brag,'
and to the wicked, 'Don't show your
power.
Don't try to use your power against
heaven.
Don't be stubborn.'"

No one from the east or the west
or the desert can judge you.
God is the judge;
he judges one person as guilty and
another as innocent.
The Lord holds a cup of anger in his
hand;
it is full of wine mixed with spices.
He pours it out even to the last drop,
and the wicked drink it all.

I will tell about this forever;
I will sing praise to the God of Jacob.
He will take all power away from the
wicked,
but the power of good people will
grow.

Psalm 75:1–10

Lord, surely your enemies,
surely your enemies will be destroyed,
and all who do evil will be scattered.
But you have made me as strong as an
ox.
You have poured fine oils on me.
When I looked, I saw my enemies;
I heard the cries of those who are
against me.

But good people will grow like palm
trees;
they will be tall like the cedars of
Lebanon.
Like trees planted in the Temple of the
Lord,
they will grow strong in the courtyards of our God.
When they are old, they will still
produce fruit;

they will be healthy and fresh.
They will say that the Lord is good.
He is my Rock, and there is no
wrong in him.

Psalm 92:9–15

*Now on whom dost thou trust?" (2 Kings
18:20). Such was the challenge which the
blatant Assyrian field-marshal, Rab-shakeh,
flung at the beleagured king Hezekiah, more
than two-and-a-half millenniums ago. Little
did he guess that before many more sunrises
185,000 of his proud army would be corpses,
cut down by an invisible scythe of the Almighty! Hezekiah did not reply to Rab-shakeh,
but despite the hopeless-looking circumstances
his heart was fixed, trusting in Jehovah
(18:5). This was his secret of victory.*

*Even so today, the first mark of the true
Christian is reliance on Jehovah-Jesus. We
rely on Him exclusively as the vicarious
Sinbearer through whom we have the salvation of our souls.*

*But we are to rely on Him continually as
our victorious Champion through whom we
have victory in our daily life. . . . So long
as we rely on Him we have victory. Temper,
fear, lust, pride, envy, grudging, moodiness,
impatience, despondency, worry; over all such
we gain victory as we really rely on Jesus.*

*Again, we are to rely on Him as our vigi-
lant Provider, who "supplies all our need"
(Phil. 4:19; Ps. 34:22). He does not always
employ ravens to feed His Elijahs, but by one
means or another He sustains them if they
really rely on Him.*

J. Sydlow Baxter

*In what ways has the Lord stood next to you
and encouraged you to be brave for his sake?
For what in your life do you need confidence
that he is standing with you? Pray for his
protection. Trust him. He will supply the
victory!*

MONDAY:

God Wants His People to Do What Is Right

Acts 23:23—24:16

Paul Is Sent to Caesarea

*T*hen the commander called two officers and said, "I need some men to go to Caesarea. Get two hundred soldiers, seventy horsemen, and two hundred men with spears ready to leave at nine o'clock tonight. Get some horses for Paul to ride so he can be taken to Governor Felix safely." And he wrote a letter that said:

From Claudius Lysias.

To the Most Excellent Governor Felix: Greetings.

The Jews had taken this man and planned to kill him. But I learned that he is a Roman citizen, so I went with my soldiers and saved him. I wanted to know why they were accusing him, so I brought him before their council meeting. I learned that the Jews said Paul did some things that were wrong by their own laws, but no charge was worthy of jail or death. When I was told that some of the Jews were planning to kill Paul, I sent him to you at once. I also told those Jews to tell you what they have against him.

So the soldiers did what they were told and took Paul and brought him to the city of Antipatris that night. The next day the horsemen went with Paul to Caesarea, but the other soldiers went back to the army building in Jerusalem. When the horsemen came to Caesarea and gave the letter to the governor, they turned Paul over to him. The governor read the letter and asked Paul, "What area are you from?" When he learned that Paul was from Cilicia, he said, "I will hear your case when those who are against you come here, too." Then the governor gave orders for Paul to be kept under guard in Herod's palace.

Paul Is Accused

*F*ive days later Ananias, the high priest, went to the city of Caesarea with some of the older Jewish leaders and a lawyer named Tertullus. They had come to make charges against Paul before the governor. Paul was called into the meeting, and Tertullus began to accuse him, saying, "Most Excellent Felix! Our people enjoy much peace because of you, and many wrong things in our country are being made right through your wise help. We accept these things always and in every place, and we are thankful for them. But not wanting to take any more of your time, I beg you to be kind and listen to our few words. We have found this man to be a troublemaker, stirring up the Jews everywhere in the world. He is a leader of the Nazarene group. Also, he was trying to make the Temple unclean, but we stopped him. By asking him questions yourself, you can decide if all these things are true." The other Jews agreed and said that all of this was true.

When the governor made a sign for Paul to speak, Paul said, "Governor Felix, I know you have been a judge over this nation for a long time. So I am happy to defend myself before you. You can learn for yourself that I went to worship in Jerusalem only twelve days ago. Those who are accusing me did not find me arguing with anyone in the Temple or stirring up the people in the synagogues or in the city. They cannot prove the things they are saying against me now. But I will tell you this: I worship the God of our ancestors as a follower of the Way of Jesus. The Jews say that the Way of Jesus is not the right way. But I believe everything that is taught in the law of Moses and that is written in the books of the Prophets. I have the same hope in God that they have—the hope that all people, good and bad, will surely be raised from the dead. This is why I always try to do what I believe is right before God and people."

*T*his is what King Hezekiah did in Judah. He did what was good and right and obedient before the LORD his God. Hezekiah tried to obey God in his service of the Temple of God, and he tried to obey God's teachings and commands. He gave himself fully to his work for God. So he had success.

2 Chronicles 31:20–21

*H*ezekiah trusted in the LORD, the God of Israel. There was no one like him among all the kings of Judah, either before him or after him. Hezekiah was loyal to the LORD and did not stop following him; he obeyed the commands the LORD had given Moses.

2 Kings 18:5–6

*A*braham's children will certainly become a great and powerful nation, and all nations on the earth will be blessed through him. I have chosen him so he would command his children and his descendants to live the way the LORD wants them to, to live right and be fair. Then I, the LORD, will give Abraham what I promised him."

Genesis 18:18–19

*T*he LORD was with Jehoshaphat, because he lived as his ancestor David had lived when he first became king. Jehoshaphat did not ask for help from the Baal idols, but from the God of his father. He obeyed God's commands and did not live as the people of Israel lived. The LORD made Jehoshaphat a strong king over Judah. All the people of Judah brought gifts to Jehoshaphat, so he had much wealth and honor. He wanted very much to obey the LORD. He also removed the places for worshiping gods and the Asherah idols from Judah.

2 Chronicles 17:3–6

*S*amuel answered, "Don't be afraid. It's true that you did wrong, but don't turn away from the LORD. Serve the LORD with all your heart. Idols are of no use, so don't worship them. They can't help you or save you. They are useless! For his own sake, the LORD won't leave his people. Instead, he was pleased to make you his own people. I will surely not stop praying for you, because that would be sinning against the LORD. I will teach you what is good and right. You must honor the LORD and truly serve him with all your heart. Remember the wonderful things he did for you!"

1 Samuel 12:20–24

*Y*our father was satisfied to have food and drink.
He did what was right and fair,
so everything went well for him.
He helped those who were poor and needy,
so everything went well for him.
That is what it means to know God,"
says the LORD.

Jeremiah 22:15b–16

INSIGHTS

*F*aithfully pleasing God" is an activity, not just a nice set of beliefs. It must be a way of life.

. . . Twenty years ago, people were asking the question: Does God exist? Today that question has changed to: What difference does He make? The answer for too many people is: Not much. Even for many people who have an enormous amount of Bible knowledge, God makes little difference in how they actually live their lives.

. . . If Christ doesn't make any difference in my ethics and values at my job; if He doesn't affect my speech and attitudes toward co-workers; . . . if He makes absolutely no difference in the way I live and work, then pray tell, what difference does He make?! What's the point of playing a religious game that is all talk and no action?

I take the matter of obedience as an action quite seriously. I challenge you to do the same. Whenever you're exposed to Scripture, ask yourself: How can I apply this to my life? What practical thing can I do to embed this truth in my attitude, character, and behavior? Where does it need to make a difference? That's a commitment to life-change.

Doug Sherman/William Hendricks

ACTION POINT

*W*hy did Paul try to do what was right before God and men? What does God say it means to know him (Jeremiah 22:16)? Pray that you, like King Hezekiah, will give yourself fully to obeying God's commands!

TUESDAY:

The Unrighteous Fear God's Judgment

Acts 24:17—25:12

*A*fter being away from Jerusalem for several years, I went back to bring money to my people and to offer sacrifices. I was doing this when they found me in the Temple. I had finished the cleansing ceremony and had not made any trouble; no people were gathering around me. But there were some Jews from the country of Asia who should be here, standing before you. If I have really done anything wrong, they are the ones who should accuse me. Or ask these Jews here if they found any wrong in me when I stood before the Jewish council in Jerusalem. But I did shout one thing when I stood before them: 'You are judging me today because I believe that people will rise from the dead!'"

Felix already understood much about the Way of Jesus. He stopped the trial and said, "When commander Lysias comes here, I will decide your case." Felix told the officer to keep Paul guarded but to give him some freedom and to let his friends bring what he needed.

Paul Speaks to Felix and His Wife

*A*fter some days Felix came with his wife, Drusilla, who was Jewish, and asked for Paul to be brought to him. He listened to Paul talk about believing in Christ Jesus. But Felix became afraid when Paul spoke about living right, self-control, and the time when God will judge the world. He said, "Go away now. When I have more time, I will call for you." At the same time Felix hoped that Paul would give him some money, so he often sent for Paul and talked with him.

But after two years, Felix was replaced by Porcius Festus as governor. But Felix had left Paul in prison to please the Jews.

Paul Asks to See Caesar

*T*hree days after Festus became governor, he went from Caesarea to Jerusalem. There the leading priests and the important Jewish leaders made charges against Paul before Festus. They asked Festus to do them a favor. They wanted him to send Paul back to Jerusalem, because they had a plan to kill him on the way. But Festus answered that Paul would be kept in Caesarea and that he himself was returning there soon. He said, "Some of your leaders should go with me. They can accuse the man there in Caesarea, if he has really done something wrong."

Festus stayed in Jerusalem another eight or ten days and then went back to Caesarea. The next day he told the soldiers to bring Paul before him. Festus was seated on the judge's seat when Paul came into the room. The Jewish people who had come from Jerusalem stood around him, making serious charges against him, which they could not prove. This is what Paul said to defend himself: "I have done nothing wrong against the Jewish law, against the Temple, or against Caesar."

But Festus wanted to please the Jews. So he asked Paul, "Do you want to go to Jerusalem for me to judge you there on these charges?"

Paul said, "I am standing at Caesar's judgment seat now, where I should be judged. I have done nothing wrong to the Jews; you know this is true. If I have done something wrong and the law says I must die, I do not ask to be saved from death. But if these charges are not true, then no one can give me to them. I want Caesar to hear my case!"

Festus talked about this with his advisors. Then he said, "You have asked to see Caesar, so you will go to Caesar!"

---

*T*hen, it was as if their eyes were opened. They realized they were naked, so they sewed fig leaves together and made something to cover themselves.

Then they heard the LORD God walking in the garden during the cool part of the day, and the man and his wife hid from the LORD God among the trees in the garden. But the LORD God called to the man and said, "Where are you?"

The man answered, "I heard you walking in the garden, and I was afraid because I was naked, so I hid."

Genesis 3:7–10

*T*he LORD is a jealous God who punishes;
    the LORD punishes and is filled with
    anger.
The LORD punishes those who are
    against him,
    and he stays angry with his enemies.
The mountains shake in front of him,
    and the hills melt.
The earth trembles when he comes;
    the world and all who live in it shake
    with fear.
No one can stay alive when he is angry;
    no one can survive his strong anger.
His anger is poured out like fire;
    the rocks are smashed by him.

Nahum 1:2, 5–6

*T*he people lose their courage, and
    their knees knock.
Stomachs ache, and everyone's face
    grows pale.

Nahum 2:10b–c

*T*hen the LORD spoke his word to me, saying: "Human, look toward Jerusalem and speak against the holy place. Prophesy against the land of Israel. Say to Israel: 'This is what the LORD says: I am against you. I will pull my sword out of its holder, and I will cut off from you both the wicked and those who do right. Because I am going to cut off the wicked and those who do right, my sword will come out from its holder and attack all people from south to north. Then all people will know that I, the LORD, have pulled my sword out from its holder. My sword will not go back in again.'

"So, human, groan with breaking heart and great sadness. Groan in front of the people. When they ask you, 'Why are you groaning?' you will say, 'Because of what I have heard is going to happen. When it happens, every heart will melt with fear, and all hands will become weak. Everyone will be afraid; all knees will become weak as water. Look, it is coming, and it will happen, says the Lord GOD.'"

Ezekiel 21:1–7

If our fathers emphasized God's "awful purity" at the expense of His love, we have emphasized His love at the expense of His "awful purity." We delight in these days to say, "Gentle, gentle, gentle, is the God and Father." We have almost forgotten that cherubim and seraphim, with veiled faces, continually cry, "Holy, holy, holy is the Lord of Hosts."

In our absorption in the thought of God as Father, we have almost lost sight of the fact that He is the Holy Sovereign, ruling the world in righteousness. The result has been that to a large extent we have lost the sense of religious awe, of reverence, and of godly fear. . . .

We have only to realize that God is the Holy Sovereign, and the awe is bound to come back. . . .

To believe that an Almighty God is on the throne, working out His own holy and perfect and acceptable righteousness—is there not enough in that to fill the hearts of sinful men with "godly fear"? Is there not enough in that to make us "tremble"?

The Puritan's religion was a serious religion. He was afraid of God—afraid of Him in a worthy sense. He conceived of God as with him and about him always, and he was afraid of sinning against His holiness.

And is there not enough in the mere realization of the fact that a Holy God sits upon the throne, a God who is actively and unceasingly asserting His holiness—is there not enough in that one fact to make us, who are so prone to sin, serious and fearful?

John Jones

*H*ow do you respond to God's insistence on purity and his declarations of coming judgment? Pray that God will convince you of his holiness and your need for him!

WEDNESDAY:

The Testimony of a Blameless Life

Acts 25:13—26:8

NEW TESTAMENT READING

Paul Before King Agrippa

A few days later King Agrippa and Bernice came to Caesarea to visit Festus. They stayed there for some time, and Festus told the king about Paul's case. Festus said, "There is a man that Felix left in prison. When I went to Jerusalem, the leading priests and the older Jewish leaders there made charges against him, asking me to sentence him to death. But I answered, 'When a man is accused of a crime, Romans do not hand him over until he has been allowed to face his accusers and defend himself against their charges.' So when these Jews came here to Caesarea for the trial, I did not waste time. The next day I sat on the judge's seat and commanded that the man be brought in. The Jews stood up and accused him, but not of any serious crime as I thought they would. The things they said were about their own religion and about a man named Jesus who died. But Paul said that he is still alive. Not knowing how to find out about these questions, I asked Paul, 'Do you want to go to Jerusalem and be judged there?' But he asked to be kept in Caesarea. He wants a decision from the emperor. So I ordered that he be held until I could send him to Caesar."

Agrippa said to Festus, "I would also like to hear this man myself."

Festus said, "Tomorrow you will hear him."

The next day Agrippa and Bernice appeared with great show, acting like very important people. They went into the judgment room with the army leaders and the important men of Caesarea. Then Festus ordered the soldiers to bring Paul in. Festus said, "King Agrippa and all who are gathered here with us, you see this man. All the Jewish people, here and in Jerusalem, have complained to me about him, shouting that he should not live any longer. When I judged him, I found no reason to order his death. But since he asked to be judged by Caesar, I decided to send him. But I have nothing definite to write the emperor about him. So I have brought him before all of you—especially you, King Agrippa. I hope you can question him and give me something to write. I think it is foolish to send a prisoner to Caesar without telling what charges are against him."

Paul Defends Himself

A grippa said to Paul, "You may now speak to defend yourself."

Then Paul raised his hand and began to speak. He said, "King Agrippa, I am very happy to stand before you and will answer all the charges the Jewish people make against me. You know so much about all the Jewish customs and the things the Jews argue about, so please listen to me patiently.

"All the Jewish people know about my whole life, how I lived from the beginning in my own country and later in Jerusalem. They have known me for a long time. If they want to, they can tell you that I was a good Pharisee. And the Pharisees obey the laws of the Jewish religion more carefully than any other group. Now I am on trial because I hope for the promise that God made to our ancestors. This is the promise that the twelve tribes of our people hope to receive as they serve God day and night. My king, the Jews have accused me because I hope for this same promise! Why do any of you people think it is impossible for God to raise people from the dead?"

OLD TESTAMENT READING

T he LORD spared me because I did
    what was right.
  Because I have not done evil, he has
    rewarded me.
I have followed the ways of the LORD;
  I have not done evil by turning from
    my God.
I remember all his laws
  and have not broken his rules.
I am innocent before him;
  I have kept myself from doing evil.

The Lord rewarded me because I did
   what was right,
   because I did what the Lord said was
   right.
                              2 Samuel 22:21–25

*T*he power of the wicked will be
   broken,
   but the Lord supports those who do
   right.
The Lord watches over the lives of the
   innocent,
   and their reward will last forever.
They will not be ashamed when trouble
   comes.

A good person speaks with wisdom,
   and he says what is fair.
The teachings of his God are in his
   heart,
   so he does not fail to keep them.
The wicked watch for good people
   so that they may kill them.
But the Lord will not take away his
   protection
   or let good people be judged guilty.

The Lord saves good people;
   he is their strength in times of trouble.
The Lord helps them and saves them;
   he saves them from the wicked,
   because they trust in him for
   protection.
                      Psalm 37:17–19a, 30–33, 39–40

A man named Job lived in the land of Uz.
He was an honest and innocent man; he
honored God and stayed away from evil.
                              Job 1:1

*T*hen the Lord said to Satan, "Have you
noticed my servant Job? No one else on
earth is like him. He is an honest and innocent man, honoring God and staying away
from evil. You caused me to ruin him for
no good reason, but he continues to be
without blame."
                              Job 2:3

*W*e must show nonbelievers what it looks
like to be at peace with ourselves, and to truly
*love other people. The best means of creating
an interest in Christ and the Christian way
of life is to so thoroughly live and enjoy it that
others will want to know how they, too, can
have it.*

   *. . . Most Americans believe that you
cannot tell a born-again Christian from nonbelievers because there is no difference in the
way they live. The only distinction, people say,
is that Christians are more religious, more
fanatical or more closed-minded. There is no
widespread sense that the religious experience
of Christians has changed the fabric of our
thinking or the nature of our life-styles (other
than requiring regular participation in
church activities).*

   *To convince a hardened and cynical world
that we are not just different, but better off
for those differences, we must allow them to
see how our struggles in life have been altered
for the better as a result of our relationship
with Christ.*

                              George Barna

*H*ow might Paul's testimony to King
*Agrippa have been different if he hadn't been
so careful to live in a way that honored God?
Is living in a way that pleases God most important to you? Pray that your life will make
a positive difference in the world around you!*

THURSDAY:
Called to Be God's Witnesses
Acts 26:9–32

I, too, thought I ought to do many things against Jesus from Nazareth. And that is what I did in Jerusalem. The leading priests gave me the power to put many of God's people in jail, and when they were being killed, I agreed it was a good thing. In every synagogue, I often punished them and tried to make them speak against Jesus. I was so angry against them I even went to other cities to find them and punish them.

"One time the leading priests gave me permission and the power to go to Damascus. On the way there, at noon, I saw a light from heaven. It was brighter than the sun and flashed all around me and those who were traveling with me. We all fell to the ground. Then I heard a voice speaking to me in the Jewish language, saying, 'Saul, Saul, why are you persecuting me? You are only hurting yourself by fighting me.' I said, 'Who are you, Lord?' The Lord said, 'I am Jesus, the one you are persecuting. Stand up! I have chosen you to be my servant and my witness—you will tell people the things that you have seen and the things that I will show you. This is why I have come to you today. I will keep you safe from your own people and also from those who are not Jewish. I am sending you to them to open their eyes so that they may turn away from darkness to the light, away from the power of Satan and to God. Then their sins can be forgiven, and they can have a place with those people who have been made holy by believing in me.'

"King Agrippa, after I had this vision from heaven, I obeyed it. I began telling people that they should change their hearts and lives and turn to God and do things to show they really had changed. I told this first to those in Damascus, then in Jerusalem, and in every part of Judea, and also to those who are not Jewish. This is why the Jews took me and were trying to kill me in the Temple. But God has helped me, and so I stand here today, telling all people, small and great, what I have seen. But I am saying only what Moses and the prophets said would happen—that the Christ would die, and as the first to rise from the dead, he would bring light to the Jewish and non-Jewish people."

Paul Tries to Persuade Agrippa

*W*hile Paul was saying these things to defend himself, Festus said loudly, "Paul, you are out of your mind! Too much study has driven you crazy!"

Paul said, "Most excellent Festus, I am not crazy. My words are true and sensible. King Agrippa knows about these things, and I can speak freely to him. I know he has heard about all of these things, because they did not happen off in a corner. King Agrippa, do you believe what the prophets wrote? I know you believe."

King Agrippa said to Paul, "Do you think you can persuade me to become a Christian in such a short time?"

Paul said, "Whether it is a short or a long time, I pray to God that not only you but every person listening to me today would be saved and be like me—except for these chains I have."

Then King Agrippa, Governor Festus, Bernice, and all the people sitting with them stood up and left the room. Talking to each other, they said, "There is no reason why this man should die or be put in jail." And Agrippa said to Festus, "We could let this man go free, but he has asked Caesar to hear his case."

God Chose the Nation of Israel to Be His Witness

*A*re there any gods like you, LORD?
There are no gods like you.
You are wonderfully holy,
amazingly powerful,
a worker of miracles.
You reached out with your right hand,
and the earth swallowed our enemies.
You keep your loving promise
and lead the people you have saved.

With your strength you will guide them
to your holy place.
"The other nations will hear this and
tremble with fear."

Exodus 15:11–14a

*L*ook, I have taught you the laws and rules the LORD my God commanded me. Now you can obey the laws in the land you are entering, in the land you will take. Obey these laws carefully, in order to show the other nations that you have wisdom and understanding. When they hear about these laws, they will say, "This great nation of Israel is wise and understanding." No other nation is as great as we are. Their gods do not come near them, but the LORD our God comes near when we pray to him. And no other nation has such good teachings and commands as those I am giving to you today.

Deuteronomy 4:5–8

*T*hen King David went in and sat in front of the LORD. David said, "Lord GOD, who am I? What is my family? Why did you bring me to this point? But even this is not enough for you, Lord GOD. You have also made promises about my future family. This is not normal, Lord GOD.

"What more can I say to you, Lord GOD, since you know me, your servant, so well! You have done this great thing because you said you would and because you wanted to, and you have let me know about it. This is why you are great, Lord GOD! There is no one like you. There is no God except you. We have heard all this ourselves! There is no nation like your people Israel. They are the only people on earth that God chose to be his own. You made your name well known. You did great and wonderful miracles for them. You went ahead of them and forced other nations and their gods out of the land. You freed your people from slavery in Egypt. You made the people of Israel your very own people forever, and, LORD, you are their God."

2 Samuel 7:18–24

INSIGHTS

*T*he best instrument for evangelism is the ordinary church member bearing witness to a vital faith. It always has been; it always will be. . . .

There is a high probability that if you are a Christian, it is because a member of the church invited you and then some of the people of the church loved you into making a decision for Christ. Generally, people are led into a personal relationship with Christ because there have been church members who cared enough to talk to them and love them into the Kingdom. . . .

. . . Our lifestyle as Christians should be a testimony to the validity of our message, but if we had to be spiritually perfect in order to witness for Christ, no one would qualify. . . . According to Paul, we must share the gospel while we are still in the process of changing into truly Christianized people. He wanted us to know that if we wait until we are the kind of people we ought to be before witnessing, we will never get the evangelistic job done. As imperfect people who are heirs to the grace of God, we are called to invite people to join us as we strive together to become more and more like Christ.

Tony Campolo

APPLICATION

*H*ave you ever felt unworthy to be God's witness? Have you felt, like David, that what God was doing in your life wasn't normal? Despite your feelings, how is God making his name known through you? Pray to be a diligent and faithful witness!

F R I D A Y:

We Can Trust God to Keep His Promises

Acts 27:1–26

Paul Sails for Rome

*I*t was decided that we would sail for Italy. An officer named Julius, who served in the emperor's army, guarded Paul and some other prisoners. We got on a ship that was from the city of Adramyttium and was about to sail to different ports in the country of Asia. Aristarchus, a man from the city of Thessalonica in Macedonia, went with us. The next day we came to Sidon. Julius was very good to Paul and gave him freedom to go visit his friends, who took care of his needs. We left Sidon and sailed close to the island of Cyprus, because the wind was blowing against us. We went across the sea by Cilicia and Pamphylia and landed at the city of Myra, in Lycia. There the officer found a ship from Alexandria that was going to Italy, so he put us on it.

We sailed slowly for many days. We had a hard time reaching Cnidus because the wind was blowing against us, and we could not go any farther. So we sailed by the south side of the island of Crete near Salmone. Sailing past it was hard. Then we came to a place called Fair Havens, near the city of Lasea.

We had lost much time, and it was now dangerous to sail, because it was already after the Day of Cleansing. So Paul warned them, "Men, I can see there will be a lot of trouble on this trip. The ship, the cargo, and even our lives may be lost." But the captain and the owner of the ship did not agree with Paul, and the officer believed what the captain and owner of the ship said. Since that harbor was not a good place for the ship to stay for the winter, most of the men decided that the ship should leave. They hoped we could go to Phoenix and stay there for the winter. Phoenix, a city on the island of Crete, had a harbor which faced southwest and northwest.

The Storm

*W*hen a good wind began to blow from the south, the men on the ship thought, "This is the wind we wanted, and now we have it." So they pulled up the anchor, and we sailed very close to the island of Crete. But then a very strong wind named the "northeaster" came from the island. The ship was caught in it and could not sail against it. So we stopped trying and let the wind carry us. When we went below a small island named Cauda, we were barely able to bring in the lifeboat. After the men took the lifeboat in, they tied ropes around the ship to hold it together. The men were afraid that the ship would hit the sandbanks of Syrtis, so they lowered the sail and let the wind carry the ship. The next day the storm was blowing us so hard that the men threw out some of the cargo. A day later with their own hands they threw out the ship's equipment. When we could not see the sun or the stars for many days, and the storm was very bad, we lost all hope of being saved.

After the men had gone without food for a long time, Paul stood up before them and said, "Men, you should have listened to me. You should not have sailed from Crete. Then you would not have all this trouble and loss. But now I tell you to cheer up because none of you will die. Only the ship will be lost. Last night an angel came to me from the God I belong to and worship. The angel said, 'Paul, do not be afraid. You must stand before Caesar. And God has promised you that he will save the lives of everyone sailing with you.' So men, have courage. I trust in God that everything will happen as his angel told me. But we will crash on an island."

*G*od is not a human being, and he will
    not lie.
  He is not a human, and he does not
    change his mind.
What he says he will do, he does.
  What he promises, he makes come
    true.

Numbers 23:19

*A*fter Moses, the servant of the LORD, died, the LORD spoke to Joshua son of Nun, Moses' assistant. The LORD said, "My servant Moses is dead. Now you and all these people go across the Jordan River into the land I am giving to the Israelites. I promised Moses I would give you this land, so I will give you every place you go in the land. All the land from the desert in the south to Lebanon in the north will be yours. All the land from the great river, the Euphrates, in the east, to the Mediterranean Sea in the west will be yours, too, including the land of the Hittites. No one will be able to defeat you all your life. Just as I was with Moses, so I will be with you. I will not leave you or forget you.

"Joshua, be strong and brave! You must lead these people so they can take the land that I promised their fathers I would give them. Be strong and brave. Be sure to obey all the teachings my servant Moses gave you. If you follow them exactly, you will be successful in everything you do. Always remember what is written in the Book of the Teachings. Study it day and night to be sure to obey everything that is written there. If you do this, you will be wise and successful in everything. Remember that I commanded you to be strong and brave. Don't be afraid, because the LORD your God will be with you everywhere you go."

Joshua 1:1–9

*T*hen Solomon stood facing the LORD's altar, and all the Israelites were standing behind him. He spread out his hands toward the sky and said:

"LORD, God of Israel, there is no god like you in heaven above or on earth below. You keep your agreement of love with your servants who truly follow you. You have kept the promise you made to your servant David, my father. You spoke it with your own mouth and finished it with your hands today.

"Praise the LORD! He promised he would give rest to his people Israel, and he has given us rest. The LORD has kept all the good promises he gave through his servant Moses."

1 Kings 8:22–24, 56

*T*he story of Jericho's conquest is a fine example of the completed promises of God. . . .

. . . On the seventh circuit of the seventh day the people shouted and the walls of Jericho fell down flat. The army of Israel entered the city unhindered and utterly destroyed all that was in the city, with one notable exception—the household of Rahab. Because they obeyed the Lord explicitly, the people saw two great promises of the Lord performed on the same day. The city of Jericho, the strongest outpost of the Canaanite defenses, had been utterly destroyed as God had promised. Likewise Rahab and her household had been spared destruction, as God had promised.

But there is one final promise of God that can be seen in the conquest of Jericho. . . . To show that God means business when He makes a promise, Joshua imprecated a solemn curse on anyone who would rebuild the now-destroyed Jericho. This curse was literally fulfilled in the fate of Heil, the Bethelite, who rebuilt Jericho in the reign of Ahab (about 925 B.C.). Heil's firstborn son, Abiram, died as he was laying the foundation for the rebuilding of Jericho. Also his youngest son, Segub, died while he was setting up the gates of the city (1 Kings 16:34). What God promises, God performs.

Whether the promise is for salvation, as in the case of Rahab, or for destruction, as in the case of Heil, the promises of God must never be taken lightly. Whatever God promises, God performs. You can count on it.

Woodrow Kroll

PAUSE FOR REFLECTION

*H*ow did Paul and Joshua respond to God's promises? How well do you face great challenges with only the hope offered by a yet-to-be-fulfilled promise? Pray that you will trust God to keep his word!

WEEKEND:
God Saves His Own for His Purposes
Acts 27:27—28:11a

*O*n the fourteenth night we were still being carried around in the Adriatic Sea. About midnight the sailors thought we were close to land, so they lowered a rope with a weight on the end of it into the water. They found that the water was one hundred twenty feet deep. They went a little farther and lowered the rope again. It was ninety feet deep. The sailors were afraid that we would hit the rocks, so they threw four anchors into the water and prayed for daylight to come. Some of the sailors wanted to leave the ship, and they lowered the lifeboat, pretending they were throwing more anchors from the front of the ship. But Paul told the officer and the other soldiers, "If these men do not stay in the ship, your lives cannot be saved." So the soldiers cut the ropes and let the lifeboat fall into the water.

Just before dawn Paul began persuading all the people to eat something. He said, "For the past fourteen days you have been waiting and watching and not eating. Now I beg you to eat something. You need it to stay alive. None of you will lose even one hair off your heads." After he said this, Paul took some bread and thanked God for it before all of them. He broke off a piece and began eating. They all felt better and started eating, too. There were two hundred seventy-six people on the ship. When they had eaten all they wanted, they began making the ship lighter by throwing the grain into the sea.

The Ship Is Destroyed

*W*hen daylight came, the sailors saw land. They did not know what land it was, but they saw a bay with a beach and wanted to sail the ship to the beach if they could. So they cut the ropes to the anchors and left the anchors in the sea. At the same time, they untied the ropes that were holding the rudders. Then they raised the front sail into the wind and sailed toward the beach. But the ship hit a sandbank. The front of the ship stuck there and could not move, but the back of the ship began to break up from the big waves.

The soldiers decided to kill the prisoners so none of them could swim away and escape. But Julius, the officer, wanted to let Paul live and did not allow the soldiers to kill the prisoners. Instead he ordered everyone who could swim to jump into the water first and swim to land. The rest were to follow using wooden boards or pieces of the ship. And this is how all the people made it safely to land.

Paul on the Island of Malta

*W*hen we were safe on land, we learned that the island was called Malta. The people who lived there were very good to us. Because it was raining and very cold, they made a fire and welcomed all of us. Paul gathered a pile of sticks and was putting them on the fire when a poisonous snake came out because of the heat and bit him on the hand. The people living on the island saw the snake hanging from Paul's hand and said to each other, "This man must be a murderer! He did not die in the sea, but Justice does not want him to live." But Paul shook the snake off into the fire and was not hurt. The people thought that Paul would swell up or fall down dead. They waited and watched him for a long time, but nothing bad happened to him. So they changed their minds and said, "He is a god!"

There were some fields around there owned by Publius, an important man on the island. He welcomed us into his home and was very good to us for three days. Publius' father was sick with a fever and dysentery. Paul went to him, prayed, and put his hands on the man and healed him. After this, all the other sick people on the island came to Paul, and he healed them, too. The people on the island gave us many honors. When we were ready to leave, three months later, they gave us the things we needed.

*T*hank the LORD because he is good. His love continues forever.

That is what those whom the LORD has
saved should say.

Others went out to sea in ships
and did business on the great oceans.
They saw what the LORD could do,
the miracles he did in the deep
oceans.
He spoke, and a storm came up,
which blew up high waves.
The ships were tossed as high as the
sky and fell low to the depths.
The storm was so bad that they lost
their courage.
They stumbled and fell like people who
were drunk.
They did not know what to do.
In their misery they cried out to the
LORD,
and he saved them from their
troubles.
He stilled the storm
and calmed the waves.
They were happy that it was quiet,
and God guided them to the port
they wanted.
Let them give thanks to the LORD for
his love
and for the miracles he does for
people.
Let them praise his greatness in the
meeting of the people;
let them praise him in the meeting of
the older leaders.

Psalm 107:1–2a, 23–32

*B*ut the LORD sent a great wind on the sea,
which made the sea so stormy that the ship
was in danger of breaking apart. The sailors
were afraid, and each man cried to his own
god. They began throwing the cargo from
the ship into the sea to make the ship
lighter.

Jonah said to them, "Pick me up, and
throw me into the sea, and then it will calm
down. I know it is my fault that this great
storm has come on you."

So they picked up Jonah and threw him
into the sea, and the sea became calm. Then
they began to fear the LORD very much; they
offered a sacrifice to the LORD and made
promises to him.

Jonah 1:4–5a, 12, 15–16

*J*ob did not understand the trials that came
to him, but he passed the test because he could
say, "'Though He slay me, I will hope in Him
. . .'" (Job 13:15). Mary and Martha did not
understand why Jesus waited until after
Lazarus died before He came to them (John
11:21). The disciples did not understand why
Jesus took them through Samaria, or why He
waited at the well rather than go with them
to buy food (John 4:8). Peter did not understand why Jesus let the soldiers arrest Him
(John 18:10–11). Today, we understand the
reason for these things because we can see the
end result.

Job was tested because Satan said Job loved
and served God only because of the protection
and blessing God gave him. Job stood the test
and Satan was defeated (Job 42:10–17).

After Jesus had raised Lazarus from the
dead, Mary and Martha understood how the
sickness and death of their brother had
brought glory to God (John 11:43–45).

By the time they left Samaria, the disciples
realized why they had to go through Samaria.
A whole city, which otherwise would have
been closed to them, heard the gospel and believed in Christ, all because Jesus talked to a
woman while he waited at the well (John
4:39–41).

When difficulties come, we can know they
have a purpose. We need not be confused. If
we are in right relationship with God, we may
not understand at the time, but we can know
He will make all that happens to us work out
for our good and His glory.

Lucille Sollenberger

*N*otice how God used each of these adven-
tures at sea to bring glory to himself. Pray for
faithful confidence in God's perfect plan, even
when you face the most difficult and confusing
situations.

MONDAY:

God's People Welcome All Who Visit Them

Acts 28:11b–31

N E W   T E S T A M E N T   R E A D I N G

Paul Goes to Rome

*W*e got on a ship from Alexandria that had stayed on the island during the winter. On the front of the ship was the sign of the twin gods. We stopped at Syracuse for three days. From there we sailed to Rhegium. The next day a wind began to blow from the south, and a day later we came to Puteoli. We found some believers there who asked us to stay with them for a week. Finally, we came to Rome. The believers in Rome heard that we were there and came out as far as the Market of Appius and the Three Inns to meet us. When Paul saw them, he was encouraged and thanked God.

Paul in Rome

*W*hen we arrived at Rome, Paul was allowed to live alone, with the soldier who guarded him.

Three days later Paul sent for the Jewish leaders there. When they came together, he said, "Brothers, I have done nothing against our people or the customs of our ancestors. But I was arrested in Jerusalem and given to the Romans. After they asked me many questions, they could find no reason why I should be killed. They wanted to let me go free, but the Jewish people there argued against that. So I had to ask to come to Rome to have my trial before Caesar. But I have no charge to bring against my own people. That is why I wanted to see you and talk with you. I am bound with this chain because I believe in the hope of Israel."

They answered Paul, "We have received no letters from Judea about you. None of our Jewish brothers who have come from there brought news or told us anything bad about you. But we want to hear your ideas, because we know that people everywhere are speaking against this religious group."

Paul and the Jewish people chose a day for a meeting and on that day many more of the Jews met with Paul at the place he was staying. He spoke to them all day long. Using the law of Moses and the prophets' writings, he explained the kingdom of God, and he tried to persuade them to believe these things about Jesus. Some believed what Paul said, but others did not. So they argued and began leaving after Paul said one more thing to them: "The Holy Spirit spoke the truth to your ancestors through Isaiah the prophet, saying,

'Go to this people and say:
You will listen and listen, but you will not understand.
You will look and look, but you will not learn,
because these people have become stubborn.
They don't hear with their ears,
and they have closed their eyes.
Otherwise, they might really understand
what they see with their eyes
and hear with their ears.
They might really understand in their minds
and come back to me and be healed.'

Isaiah 6:9–10

"I want you to know that God has also sent his salvation to those who are not Jewish, and they will listen!"

Paul stayed two full years in his own rented house and welcomed all people who came to visit him. He boldly preached about the kingdom of God and taught about the Lord Jesus Christ, and no one tried to stop him.

O L D   T E S T A M E N T   R E A D I N G

*T*he servant ran to her and said, "Please give me a little water from your jar."

Rebekah said, "Drink, sir." She quickly lowered the jar from her shoulder and gave him a drink. After he finished drinking, Rebekah said, "I will also pour some water for your camels." So she quickly poured all the water from her jar into the drinking trough for the camels. Then she kept running to the well until she had given all the camels enough to drink.

The servant quietly watched her. He wanted to be sure the LORD had made his trip successful. After the camels had finished drinking, he gave Rebekah a gold ring weighing one-fifth of an ounce and two gold arm bracelets weighing about four ounces each. He asked, "Who is your father? Is there a place in his house for me and my men to spend the night?"

Rebekah answered, "My father is Bethuel, the son of Milcah and Nahor." Then she said, "And, yes, we have straw for your camels and a place for you to spend the night."

The servant bowed and worshiped the LORD and said, "Blessed is the LORD, the God of my master Abraham. The LORD has been kind and truthful to him and has led me to my master's relatives."

Then Rebekah ran and told her mother's family about all these things. She had a brother named Laban, who ran out to Abraham's servant, who was still at the spring. Laban had heard what she had said and had seen the ring and the bracelets on his sister's arms. So he ran out to the well, and there was the man standing by the camels at the spring. Laban said, "Sir, you are welcome to come in; you don't have to stand outside. I have prepared the house for you and also a place for your camels."

So Abraham's servant went into the house. After Laban unloaded the camels and gave them straw and food, he gave water to Abraham's servant so he and the men with him could wash their feet. Then Laban gave the servant food.

Genesis 24:17–33a

INSIGHTS

*R*ecently I finally got around to inviting a couple from our home church over for Sunday lunch. Sandy and Mike are young college graduates with promising careers and an adorable new baby. They are busy people and had not yet gotten involved in our church. I was ashamed to discover that although they'd been members of our church for nearly three years, ours was the first personal invitation they had received from anyone in our congregation. . . .

. . . In addition to providing examples of hospitality, Scripture gives us specific instructions to practice this kind of loving care for others. In his letters to Timothy and Titus, Paul listed it as a necessary qualification of an elder of the church. He combined encouragement and hospitality as important Christian traits in Titus 1:8–9. . . .

Paul's instructions in Romans 12:9–13 emphasize that this ministry of love in action belongs not just to elders, but should be a trademark of all believers. . . .

Webster defines hospitality as "the reception and entertainment of guests or strangers with liberality and kindness." . . . Liberality means giving generously; kindness means treating gently and considerately. Doesn't this definition of hospitality create a picture of a loving, encouraging atmosphere? . . .

The emphasis in our practice of hospitality should be on how we give of ourselves to minister to others—not on how we perform to entertain others. The Bible commands us to carry out this ministry; it does not set up requirements for housing or meals. We do not need a large, beautifully decorated, immaculately tidy house in order to invite others into our home. "Breaking bread" with others does not require serving filet mignon or lobster tails. The issue is not spending money, but spending our time—not giving things, but giving ourselves. . . .

. . . Focus on people, not preparations. In the Lord's hands, a few loaves and fishes go a long way.

Rachael Crabb

PAUSE FOR REFLECTION

*D*o you think Paul, a prisoner, offered his guests luxurious accommodations? Do you think Rebekah and her family expected anything in return for the hospitality they offered? What do you think are the biblical standards for hospitality?

TUESDAY:

All of Creation Tells Us About God

Romans 1:1–27

NEW TESTAMENT READING

*F*rom Paul, a servant of Christ Jesus. God called me to be an apostle and chose me to tell the Good News.

God promised this Good News long ago through his prophets, as it is written in the Holy Scriptures. The Good News is about God's Son, Jesus Christ our Lord. As a man, he was born from the family of David. But through the Spirit of holiness he was appointed to be God's Son with great power by rising from the dead. Through Christ, God gave me the special work of an apostle, which was to lead people of all nations to believe and obey. I do this work for him. And you who are in Rome are also called to belong to Jesus Christ.

To all of you in Rome whom God loves and has called to be his holy people:

Grace and peace to you from God our Father and the Lord Jesus Christ.

A Prayer of Thanks

*F*irst I want to say that I thank my God through Jesus Christ for all of you, because people everywhere in the world are talking about your faith. God, whom I serve with my whole heart by telling the Good News about his Son, knows that I always mention you every time I pray. I pray that I will be allowed to come to you, and this will happen if God wants it. I want very much to see you, to give you some spiritual gift to make you strong. I mean that I want us to help each other with the faith we have. Your faith will help me, and my faith will help you. Brothers and sisters, I want you to know that I planned many times to come to you, but this has not been possible. I wanted to come so that I could help you grow spiritually as I have helped the other non-Jewish people.

I have a duty to all people—Greeks and those who are not Greeks, the wise and the foolish. That is why I want so much to preach the Good News to you in Rome.

I am proud of the Good News, because it is the power God uses to save everyone who believes—to save the Jews first, and also to save those who are not Jews. The Good News shows how God makes people right with himself—that it begins and ends with faith. As the Scripture says, "But those who are right with God will live by trusting in him."

All People Have Done Wrong

*G*od's anger is shown from heaven against all the evil and wrong things people do. By their own evil lives they hide the truth. God shows his anger because some knowledge of him has been made clear to them. Yes, God has shown himself to them. There are things about him that people cannot see—his eternal power and all the things that make him God. But since the beginning of the world those things have been easy to understand by what God has made. So people have no excuse for the bad things they do. They knew God, but they did not give glory to God or thank him. Their thinking became useless. Their foolish minds were filled with darkness. They said they were wise, but they became fools. They traded the glory of God who lives forever for the worship of idols made to look like earthly people, birds, animals, and snakes.

Because they did these things, God left them and let them go their sinful way, wanting only to do evil. As a result, they became full of sexual sin, using their bodies wrongly with each other. They traded the truth of God for a lie. They worshiped and served what had been created instead of the God who created those things, who should be praised forever. Amen.

Because people did those things, God left them and let them do the shameful things they wanted to do. Women stopped having natural sex and started having sex with other women. In the same way, men stopped having natural sex and began wanting each other. Men did shameful things with other men, and in their bodies they received the punishment for those wrongs.

*T*he heavens tell the glory of God,
    and the skies announce what his
        hands have made.
Day after day they tell the story;
    night after night they tell it again.
They have no speech or words;
    they have no voice to be heard.
But their message goes out through all
        the world;
    their words go everywhere on earth.
                    Psalm 19:1–4b

*L*ORD, your word is everlasting;
    it continues forever in heaven.
Your loyalty will go on and on;
    you made the earth, and it still
        stands.
All things continue to this day because
    of your laws,
    because all things serve you.
                    Psalm 119:89–91

*T*he LORD is king. Let the earth rejoice;
    faraway lands should be glad.
Thick, dark clouds surround him.
    His kingdom is built on what is right
        and fair.
A fire goes before him
    and burns up his enemies all around.
His lightning lights up the world;
    when the people see it, they tremble.
The mountains melt like wax before the
    LORD,
    before the Lord of all the earth.
The heavens tell about his goodness,
    and all the people see his glory.
                    Psalm 97:1–6

*T*he God of gods, the LORD, speaks.
    He calls the earth from the rising to
        the setting sun.
God shines from Jerusalem,
    whose beauty is perfect.
Our God comes, and he will not be
        silent.
    A fire burns in front of him,
    and a powerful storm surrounds
        him.
He calls to the sky above and to the
    earth

that he might judge his people.
He says, "Gather around, you who
        worship me,
    who have made an agreement with
        me, using a sacrifice."
God is the judge,
    and even the skies say he is right.
                    Selah
                    Psalm 50:1–6

INSIGHTS

*T*his is my Father's world,
And to my listening ears
All nature sings, and round me rings
The music of the spheres.
This is my Father's world:
I rest me in the thought
Of rocks and trees, of skies and seas—
His hand the wonders wrought.

This is my Father's world,
The birds their carols raise,
The morning light, the lily white,
Declare their Makers praise.
This is my Father's world:
He shines in all that's fair;
In the rustling grass I hear Him pass,
He speaks to me everywhere.

This is my Father's world,
O let me ne'er forget
That though the wrong seems oft so strong,
God is the Ruler yet.
This is my Father's world:
The battle is not done;
Jesus who died shall be satisfied,
And earth and heav'n be one.

                    Maltbie Babcock

PAUSE FOR REFLECTION

*A*ccording to Paul, what excuses do people
have of not knowing God? What testifies to
God's glory and goodness? Describe the ways
in which God's creation has influenced your
beliefs about God.

WEDNESDAY:

People Do What They Want, but God Holds Them Accountable

Romans 1:28—2:16

NEW TESTAMENT READING

*P*eople did not think it was important to have a true knowledge of God. So God left them and allowed them to have their own worthless thinking and to do things they should not do. They are filled with every kind of sin, evil, selfishness, and hatred. They are full of jealousy, murder, fighting, lying, and thinking the worst about each other. They gossip and say evil things about each other. They hate God. They are rude and conceited and brag about themselves. They invent ways of doing evil. They do not obey their parents. They are foolish, they do not keep their promises, and they show no kindness or mercy to others. They know God's law says that those who live like this should die. But they themselves not only continue to do these evil things, they applaud others who do them.

You People Also Are Sinful

*I*f you think you can judge others, you are wrong. When you judge them, you are really judging yourself guilty, because you do the same things they do. God judges those who do wrong things, and we know that his judging is right. You judge those who do wrong, but you do wrong yourselves. Do you think you will be able to escape the judgment of God? He has been very kind and patient, waiting for you to change, but you think nothing of his kindness. Perhaps you do not understand that God is kind to you so you will change your hearts and lives. But you are stubborn and refuse to change, so you are making your own punishment even greater on the day he shows his anger. On that day everyone will see God's right judgments. God will reward or punish every person for what that person has done. Some people, by always continuing to do good, live for God's glory, for honor, and for life that has no end. God will give them life forever. But other people are selfish. They refuse to follow truth and, instead, follow evil. God will give them his punishment and anger. He will give trouble and suffering to everyone who does evil—to the Jews first and also to those who are not Jews. But he will give glory, honor, and peace to everyone who does good—to the Jews first and also to those who are not Jews. For God judges all people in the same way.

People who do not have the law and who are sinners will be lost, although they do not have the law. And, in the same way, those who have the law and are sinners will be judged by the law. Hearing the law does not make people right with God. It is those who obey the law who will be right with him. (Those who are not Jews do not have the law, but when they freely do what the law commands, they are the law for themselves. This is true even though they do not have the law. They show that in their hearts they know what is right and wrong, just as the law commands. And they show this by their consciences. Sometimes their thoughts tell them they did wrong, and sometimes their thoughts tell them they did right.) All these things will happen on the day when God, through Christ Jesus, will judge people's secret thoughts. The Good News that I preach says this.

OLD TESTAMENT READING

*T*he LORD is a God who punishes.
　　God, show your greatness and
　　　　punish!
Rise up, Judge of the earth,
　　and give the proud what they
　　　　deserve.
How long will the wicked be happy?
　　How long, LORD?

They are full of proud words;
　　those who do evil brag about what
　　　　they have done.
LORD, they crush your people
　　and make your children suffer.
They kill widows and foreigners
　　and murder orphans.

They say, "The LORD doesn't see;
   the God of Jacob doesn't notice."

You stupid ones among the people, pay
      attention.
   You fools, when will you under-
      stand?
Can't the creator of ears hear?
   Can't the maker of eyes see?
Won't the one who corrects nations
      punish you?
   Doesn't the teacher of people know
      everything?
The LORD knows what people think.
   He knows their thoughts are just a
      puff of wind.

LORD, those you correct are happy;
   you teach them from your law.
You give them rest from times of
      trouble
   until a pit is dug for the wicked.
The LORD won't leave his people
   nor give up his children.
Judgment will again be fair,
   and all who are honest will follow it.
                              Psalm 94:1–15

*T*he LORD sees everything you do,
   and he watches where you go.
An evil man will be caught in his
      wicked ways;
   the ropes of his sins will tie him up.
He will die because he does not control
      himself,
   and he will be held captive by his
      foolishness.
                              Proverbs 5:21–23

*T*he LORD hates what evil people do,
   but he loves those who do what is
      right.

The person who quits doing what is
      right will be punished,
   and the one who hates to be cor-
      rected will die.

The LORD knows what is happening in
      the world of the dead,
   so he surely knows the thoughts of
      the living.
                              Proverbs 15:9–11

*T*he Bible's proclamation of God's work as Judge is part of its witness to His character. It confirms what is said elsewhere of His moral perfection, His righteousness and justice, His wisdom, omniscience, and omnipotence. It shows us also that the heart of the justice which expresses God's nature is retribution, the rendering to men what they have deserved; for this is the essence of the judge's task. To reward good with good, and evil with evil, is natural to God. So, when the New Testament speaks of the final judgment, it always represents it in terms of retribution. God will judge all men, it says, 'according to their works' (Matthew 16:27; Revelation 20:12f.). Paul amplifies. 'God . . . will render to every man according to his deeds: to them who by patient continuance in well doing seek for glory and honour and immortality, eternal life; but unto them that are contentious, and do not obey the truth, but obey unrighteousness, indignation and wrath, tribulation and anguish, upon every soul of man that doeth evil . . . but glory, honour, and peace, to every man that worketh good . . . for there is no respect of persons throughout: Christians, as well as non-Christians, will receive 'according to their works'. . . .*

Thus retribution appears as a natural and predetermined expression of the divine character. God has resolved to be every man's Judge, rewarding every man according to his works. Retribution is the inescapable moral law of creation; God will see that each man sooner or later receives what he deserves—if not here, then hereafter.

                                          J. I. Packer

PAUSE   FOR   REFLECTION

*W*hat do people do when God gives them freedom to do as they please? What does God, in his kindness, wait for people to do? What will God, the Judge of the earth, do when people refuse to change their hearts and live in obedience to him?

THURSDAY:

God Wants Us to Change Our Hearts and Lives

Romans 2:17—3:18

NEW TESTAMENT READING

The Jews and the Law

*W*hat about you? You call yourself a Jew. You trust in the law of Moses and brag that you are close to God. You know what he wants you to do and what is important, because you have learned the law.

You think you are a guide for the blind and a light for those who are in darkness. You think you can show foolish people what is right and teach those who know nothing. You have the law; so you think you know everything and have all truth. You teach others, so why don't you teach yourself? You tell others not to steal, but you steal. You say that others must not take part in adultery, but you are guilty of that sin. You hate idols, but you steal from temples. You brag about having God's law, but you bring shame to God by breaking his law, just as the Scriptures say: "Those who are not Jews speak against God's name because of you."

If you follow the law, your circumcision has meaning. But if you break the law, it is as if you were never circumcised. People who are not Jews are not circumcised, but if they do what the law says, it is as if they were circumcised. You Jews have the written law and circumcision, but you break the law. So those who are not circumcised in their bodies, but still obey the law, will show that you are guilty. They can do this because a person is not a true Jew if he is only a Jew in his physical body; true circumcision is not only on the outside of the body. A person is a Jew only if he is a Jew inside; true circumcision is done in the heart by the Spirit, not by the written law. Such a person gets praise from God rather than from people.

So, do Jews have anything that other people do not have? Is there anything special about being circumcised? Yes, of course, there is in every way. The most im-portant thing is this: God trusted the Jews with his teachings. If some Jews were not faithful to him, will that stop God from doing what he promised? No! God will continue to be true even when every person is false. As the Scriptures say:

"So you will be shown to be right when
    you speak,
and you will win your case."

Psalm 51:4

When we do wrong, that shows more clearly that God is right. So can we say that God is wrong to punish us? (I am talking as people might talk.) No! If God could not punish us, he could not judge the world.

A person might say, "When I lie, it really gives him glory, because my lie shows God's truth. So why am I judged a sinner?" It would be the same to say, "We should do evil so that good will come." Some people find fault with us and say we teach this, but they are wrong and deserve the punishment they will receive.

All People Are Guilty

*S*o are we Jews better than others? No! We have already said that Jews and those who are not Jews are all guilty of sin. As the Scriptures say:

"There is no one who always does what
    is right,
    not even one.
There is no one who understands.
There is no one who looks to God
    for help.
All have turned away.
    Together, everyone has become
    useless.
There is no one who does anything good;
    there is not even one."   *Psalm 14:1–3*
"Their throats are like open graves;
    they use their tongues for telling
    lies."   *Psalm 5:9*
"Their words are like snake poison."

Psalm 140:3

"Their mouths are full of cursing and
    hate."   *Psalm 10:7*
"They are always ready to kill people.
Everywhere they go they cause ruin
    and misery.
They don't know how to live in peace."

Isaiah 59:7–8

They have no fear of God."   *Psalm 36:1*

*T*he LORD says, "The time is coming when I will punish all those who are circumcised only in the flesh: the people of Egypt, Judah, Edom, Ammon, Moab, and the desert people who cut their hair short. The men in all those countries are not circumcised. And the whole family of Israel does not give itself to serving me."

Jeremiah 9:25–26

*G*ive yourselves to the service of the
    LORD,
   and decide to obey him,
   people of Judah and people of
      Jerusalem.
If you don't, my anger will spread
      among you like a fire,
   and no one will be able to put it out,
because of the evil you have done."

Jeremiah 4:4

*T*his is what the LORD All-Powerful, the God of Israel, says: Change your lives and do what is right! Then I will let you live in this place. You must change your lives and do what is right. Be fair to each other. You must not be hard on strangers, orphans, and widows. Don't kill innocent people in this place! Don't follow other gods, or they will ruin your lives.

Jeremiah 7:3, 5–6

*B*ut I am filled with power,
   with the Spirit of the LORD,
   and with justice and strength,
to tell the people of Jacob how they
      have turned against God,
   and the people of Israel how they
      have sinned.
Leaders of Jacob and rulers of Israel,
      listen to me,
you who hate fairness
   and twist what is right.
You build Jerusalem by murdering
      people;
   you build it with evil.
Its judges take money
   to decide who wins in court.
Its priests only teach for pay,
   and its prophets only look into the
      future when they get paid.

But they lean on the LORD and say,
   "The LORD is here with us,
   so nothing bad will happen to us."
Because of you,
   Jerusalem will be plowed like a field.
The city will become a pile of rocks,
   and the hill on which the Temple
      stands will be covered with bushes.

Micah 3:8–12

*E*verywhere Jesus went He proclaimed the twofold message of repentance and faith in God (Mark 1:15). The faith He proclaimed was not mere mental assent, but the kind of faith that produces change in people's lives. There is no such thing as biblical faith that does not produce obedience. . . .

It is important to note that the Bible identifies both a true and a false repentance. Second Corinthians 7:10 says, "Godly grief produces a repentance that leads to salvation and brings no regret, but worldly grief produces death." Godly grief is true repentance, and true repentance is more than contrition. A person may be sorrowful over his sins yet unrepentant because he is sorrowing for the wrong reasons. Instead of sorrowing because his sins have hurt and disappointed God, he may just feel bad because his sins have been personally painful, stressful, or costly, or because his sins have been found out. If there is no change in character, there has been no true repentance. . . .

The results of false repentance are seen everywhere in the church. Hearts are unbroken. Sin is covered up. . . . And many professing Christians do not walk in the light with God and one another. The fruit of true repentance is a change of mind, heart, and behavior.

Floyd McClung

*W*hat value does God place on outward signs of obedience to his law? What does circumcision represent? How does God want those who are called "his people" to live?

FRIDAY:

Faith in God Is Our Salvation

Romans 3:19—4:12

*W*e know that the law's commands are for those who have the law. This stops all excuses and brings the whole world under God's judgment, because no one can be made right with God by following the law. The law only shows us our sin.

How God Makes People Right

*B*ut God has a way to make people right with him without the law, and he has now shown us that way which the law and the prophets told us about. God makes people right with himself through their faith in Jesus Christ. This is true for all who believe in Christ, because all people are the same: All have sinned and are not good enough for God's glory, and all need to be made right with God by his grace, which is a free gift. They need to be made free from sin through Jesus Christ. God gave him as a way to forgive sin through faith in the blood of Jesus' death. This showed that God always does what is right and fair, as in the past when he was patient and did not punish people for their sins. And God gave Jesus to show today that he does what is right. God did this so he could judge rightly and so he could make right any person who has faith in Jesus.

So do we have a reason to brag about ourselves? No! And why not? It is the way of faith that stops all bragging, not the way of trying to obey the law. A person is made right with God through faith, not through obeying the law. Is God only the God of the Jews? Is he not also the God of those who are not Jews? Of course he is, because there is only one God. He will make Jews right with him by their faith, and he will also make those who are not Jews right with him through their faith. So do we destroy the law by following the way of faith? No! Faith causes us to be what the law truly wants.

The Example of Abraham

*S*o what can we say that Abraham, the father of our people, learned about faith? If Abraham was made right by the things he did, he had a reason to brag. But this is not God's view, because the Scripture says, "Abraham believed God, and God accepted Abraham's faith, and that faith made him right with God."

When people work, their pay is not given as a gift, but as something earned. But people cannot do any work that will make them right with God. So they must trust in him, who makes even evil people right in his sight. Then God accepts their faith, and that makes them right with him. David said the same thing. He said that people are truly blessed when God, without paying attention to good deeds, makes people right with himself.

"Happy are they
   whose sins are forgiven,
   whose wrongs are pardoned.
Happy is the person
   whom the Lord does not consider
      guilty."   *Psalm 32:1–2*

Is this blessing only for those who are circumcised or also for those who are not circumcised? We have already said that God accepted Abraham's faith and that faith made him right with God. So how did this happen? Did God accept Abraham before or after he was circumcised? It was before his circumcision. Abraham was circumcised to show that he was right with God through faith before he was circumcised. So Abraham is the father of all those who believe but are not circumcised; he is the father of all believers who are accepted as being right with God. And Abraham is also the father of those who have been circumcised and who live following the faith that our father Abraham had before he was circumcised.

*A*fter these things happened, the LORD spoke his word to Abram in a vision:

"Abram, don't be afraid. I will defend you, and I will give you a great reward."

But Abram said, "Lord GOD, what can you give me? I have no son, so my slave Eliezer from Damascus will get everything I own after I die." Abram said, "Look, you have given me no son, so a slave born in my house will inherit everything I have."

Then the LORD spoke his word to Abram: "He will not be the one to inherit what you have. You will have a son of your own who will inherit what you have."

Then God led Abram outside and said, "Look at the sky. There are so many stars you cannot count them. Your descendants also will be too many to count."

Abram believed the LORD. And the LORD accepted Abram's faith, and that faith made him right with God.

Genesis 15:1–6

Now I know the LORD helps his
    appointed king.
He answers him from his holy heaven
    and saves him with his strong right
      hand.
Some trust in chariots, others in
      horses,
    but we trust the LORD our God.
They are overwhelmed and defeated,
    but we march forward and win.

Psalm 20:6–8

Wicked people have many troubles,
    but the LORD's love surrounds those
      who trust him.
Good people, rejoice and be happy in
      the LORD.
Sing all you whose hearts are right.

Psalm 32:10–11

Sing praises to the LORD;
    praise our God with harps.
He fills the sky with clouds
    and sends rain to the earth
    and makes grass grow on the hills.
He gives food to cattle
    and to the little birds that call.

He does not enjoy the strength of a
      horse
    or the strength of a man.

The LORD is pleased with those who
    respect him,
  with those who trust his love.

Psalm 147:7–11

INSIGHTS

Faith is believing that Christ is what He is said to be and that He will do what He has promised to do, and then to expect this of Him. The Scriptures speak of Jesus Christ as being God in human flesh, as being perfect in His character, as being made a sin offering on our behalf, as bearing our sins in His own body on the tree. . . . The sacred records further tell us that He "rose again" (1 Co 15:4) from the dead, that He "ever liveth to make intercession for us" (Heb 7:25), that He has gone up into glory and has taken possession of heaven on the behalf of His people, and that he will shortly come again "to judge the . . . world with righteousness, and the peoples with equity" (Ps 98:9, ASV). . . .

. . . Jesus is what He is said to be. Jesus will do what He says He will do. Therefore, we must each trust Him, saying, "He will be to me what He says He is, and He will do to me what He has promised to do. I leave myself in the hands of Him who is appointed to save, that he may save me. I rest upon His promise that He will do even as He has said." This is saving faith, and he that has it has everlasting life. Whatever his dangers and difficulties, whatever his darkness and depression, whatever his infirmities and sins, he that believes thus on Christ Jesus is not condemned, and shall never come into condemnation.

Charles Spurgeon

PAUSE FOR REFLECTION

How are people made right with God? Who can be made right with God? How did God enable us to be made right with him? How does God bless those who trust him? Have you received that blessing?

WEEKEND:
God Has Great Love for Us
Romans 4:13—5:11

God Keeps His Promise

*A*braham and his descendants received the promise that they would get the whole world. He did not receive that promise through the law, but through being right with God by his faith. If people could receive what God promised by following the law, then faith is worthless. And God's promise to Abraham is worthless, because the law can only bring God's anger. But if there is no law, there is nothing to disobey.

So people receive God's promise by having faith. This happens so the promise can be a free gift. Then all of Abraham's children can have that promise. It is not only for those who live under the law of Moses but for anyone who lives with faith like that of Abraham, who is the father of us all. As it is written in the Scriptures: "I am making you a father of many nations." This is true before God, the God Abraham believed, the God who gives life to the dead and who creates something out of nothing.

There was no hope that Abraham would have children. But Abraham believed God and continued hoping, and so he became the father of many nations. As God told him, "Your descendants also will be too many to count." Abraham was almost a hundred years old, much past the age for having children, and Sarah could not have children. Abraham thought about all this, but his faith in God did not become weak. He never doubted that God would keep his promise, and he never stopped believing. He grew stronger in his faith and gave praise to God. Abraham felt sure that God was able to do what he had promised. So, "God accepted Abraham's faith, and that faith made him right with God." Those words ("God accepted Abraham's faith") were written not only for Abraham but also for us. God will accept us also because we believe in the One who raised Jesus our Lord from the dead. Jesus was given to die for our sins, and he was raised from the dead to make us right with God.

Right with God

*S*ince we have been made right with God by our faith, we have peace with God. This happened through our Lord Jesus Christ, who has brought us into that blessing of God's grace that we now enjoy. And we are happy because of the hope we have of sharing God's glory. We also have joy with our troubles, because we know that these troubles produce patience. And patience produces character, and character produces hope. And this hope will never disappoint us, because God has poured out his love to fill our hearts. He gave us his love through the Holy Spirit, whom God has given to us.

When we were unable to help ourselves, at the moment of our need, Christ died for us, although we were living against God. Very few people will die to save the life of someone else. Although perhaps for a good person someone might possibly die. But God shows his great love for us in this way: Christ died for us while we were still sinners.

So through Christ we will surely be saved from God's anger, because we have been made right with God by the blood of Christ's death. While we were God's enemies, he made friends with us through the death of his Son. Surely, now that we are his friends, he will save us through his Son's life. And not only that, but now we are also very happy in God through our Lord Jesus Christ. Through him we are now God's friends again.

He Saves Us Because of His Love

I find rest in God;
  only he gives me hope.
He is my rock and my salvation.
  He is my defender;
  I will not be defeated.
My honor and salvation come from God.
  He is my mighty rock and my
  protection.

Psalm 62:5–7

*B*ut I pray to you, L<small>ORD</small>, for favor.
God, because of your great love,
    answer me.
You are truly able to save.

Psalm 69:13

I will tell about the L<small>ORD</small>'s kindness
    and praise him for everything he has
        done.
I will praise the L<small>ORD</small> for the many good
        things he has given us
    and for his goodness to the people of
        Israel.
He has shown great mercy to us
    and has been very kind to us.
He said, "These are my people;
    my children will not lie to me."
So he saved them.
When they suffered, he suffered also.
    He sent his own angel to save them.
Because of his love and kindness, he
        saved them.
    Since long ago he has picked them
        up and carried them.

Isaiah 63:7–9

He Purifies Us for His Glory

I have made you pure, but not by fire,
    as silver is made pure.
    I have purified you by giving you
        troubles.
I do this for myself, for my own sake.
    I will not let people speak evil
        against me,
    and I will not let some god take my
        glory."

Isaiah 48:10–11

He Builds Our Character
Through Troubles

*W*hat can I say?
    The Lord told me what would
        happen and then made it happen.
I have had these troubles in my soul,
    so now I will be humble all my life.
Lord, because of you, people live.
    Because of you, my spirit also lives;
you made me well and let me live.
It was for my own good
    that I had such troubles.

Because you love me very much,
    you did not let me die
but threw my sins
    far away.

Isaiah 38:15–17

I N S I G H T S

*M*ay God through His Holy Spirit teach
you to cherish the unfathomable mystery of
His love. Jesus said, "None is good save one,
even God." The glory of God in heaven is that
everything He wills and does is good. . . .

The God who wills only good is a God of
love. He does not seek His own. He does not
live for himself. He pours out His love upon
all living creatures. . . .

Love "seeketh not her own." Love finds
happiness in giving to others. Love sacrifices
wholly for others. Therefore, God offered
himself to us in the person of His Son. And
the Son offered himself upon the cross to bring
love to us and to win our hearts. The everlasting love with which the Father loves the
Son is the same love with which the Son loves
us. This same love of the Father, Jesus Christ
has poured into our hearts through the Holy
Spirit. God desires that our whole life be
permeated with this love's vital power. . . .

. . . Love is the power of the Godhead: in
the Father, Son, and Holy Spirit. All who are
members of the body of Christ possess the love
of God, and this love streams forth from them
to take the whole world within its compass.

Andrew Murray

A C T I O N   P O I N T

*H*ow has God shown his love for the world?
When we place our faith in his love, what are
the results? Write your own psalm of thanksgiving, praising God for his gift of love.

MONDAY:

Christ Frees Us from the Power of Sin

Romans 5:12—6:14

NEW TESTAMENT READING

Adam and Christ Compared

Sin came into the world because of what one man did, and with sin came death. This is why everyone must die—because everyone sinned. Sin was in the world before the law of Moses, but sin is not counted against us as breaking a command when there is no law. But from the time of Adam to the time of Moses, everyone had to die, even those who had not sinned by breaking a command, as Adam had.

Adam was like the One who was coming in the future. But God's free gift is not like Adam's sin. Many people died because of the sin of that one man. But the grace from God was much greater; many people received God's gift of life by the grace of the one man, Jesus Christ. After Adam sinned once, he was judged guilty. But the gift of God is different. God's free gift came after many sins, and it makes people right with God. One man sinned, and so death ruled all people because of that one man. But now those people who accept God's full grace and the great gift of being made right with him will surely have true life and rule through the one man, Jesus Christ.

So as one sin of Adam brought the punishment of death to all people, one good act that Christ did makes all people right with God. And that brings true life for all. One man disobeyed God, and many became sinners. In the same way, one man obeyed God, and many will be made right. The law came to make sin worse. But when sin grew worse, God's grace increased. Sin once used death to rule us, but God gave people more of his grace so that grace could rule by making people right with him. And this brings life forever through Jesus Christ our Lord.

Dead to Sin but Alive in Christ

So do you think we should continue sinning so that God will give us even more grace? No! We died to our old sinful lives, so how can we continue living with sin? Did you forget that all of us became part of Christ when we were baptized? We shared his death in our baptism. When we were baptized, we were buried with Christ and shared his death. So, just as Christ was raised from the dead by the wonderful power of the Father, we also can live a new life.

Christ died, and we have been joined with him by dying too. So we will also be joined with him by rising from the dead as he did. We know that our old life died with Christ on the cross so that our sinful selves would have no power over us and we would not be slaves to sin. Anyone who has died is made free from sin's control.

If we died with Christ, we know we will also live with him. Christ was raised from the dead, and we know that he cannot die again. Death has no power over him now. Yes, when Christ died, he died to defeat the power of sin one time—enough for all time. He now has a new life, and his new life is with God. In the same way, you should see yourselves as being dead to the power of sin and alive with God through Christ Jesus.

So, do not let sin control your life here on earth so that you do what your sinful self wants to do. Do not offer the parts of your body to serve sin, as things to be used in doing evil. Instead, offer yourselves to God as people who have died and now live. Offer the parts of your body to God to be used in doing good. Sin will not be your master, because you are not under law but under God's grace.

OLD TESTAMENT READING

Without God's Salvation, We Are Slaves to Sin

How terrible! Israel is a nation of sin,
    a people loaded down with guilt,
a group of children doing evil,
    children who are full of evil.
They have left the LORD;
    they hate God, the Holy One of Israel,

and have turned away from him as if
he were a stranger.
Wash yourselves and make yourselves
clean.
Stop doing the evil things I see you
do.
Stop doing wrong.

Isaiah 1:4, 16

I, the LORD, said,
'How happy I would be to treat you as
my own children
and give you a pleasant land,
a land more beautiful than that of
any other nation.'
I thought you would call me 'My
Father'
and not turn away from me.
But like a woman who is unfaithful to
her husband,
family of Israel, you have been
unfaithful to me," says the LORD.

You can hear crying on the bare
hilltops.
It is the people of Israel crying and
praying for mercy.
They have become very evil
and have forgotten the LORD their
God.

"Come back to me, you unfaithful
children,
and I will forgive you for being
unfaithful."

"Yes, we will come to you,
because you are the LORD our God.
It was foolish to worship idols on the hills
and on the mountains.
Surely the salvation of Israel
comes from the LORD our God."

Jeremiah 3:19–23

*S*o, say this to the people of Judah and
those who live in Jerusalem: 'This is what
the LORD says: I am preparing disaster for
you and making plans against you. So stop
doing evil. Change your ways and do what
is right.' But the people of Judah will answer, 'It won't do any good to try! We will
continue to do what we want. Each of us will
do what his stubborn, evil heart wants!'"

Jeremiah 18:11–12

*If we would know what Christ wants to be
to us, we must first of all know Him as our
Saviour from sin. When the angel came down
from heaven to proclaim that He was to be
born into the world, you remember he gave
His name, "He shall be called Jesus, for he
shall save his people from their sins." HAVE WE
BEEN DELIVERED FROM SIN? He did not come to
save us in our sins, but from our sins. . . .*

*Let us look at Him as He hangs upon the
Cross, and see how He has put away sin. He
was manifested that He might take away our
sins. . . .*

*But Christ is not only a Saviour. I might
save a man from drowning and rescue him
from an untimely grave; but I might probably
not be able to do any more for him. Christ is
something more than a Saviour. When the
children of Israel were placed behind the
blood, that blood was their salvation; but they
would still have heard the crack of the slave-
driver's whip, if they had not been delivered
from the Egyptian yoke of bondage: then it
was that God delivered them from the hand
of the King of Egypt. I have little sympathy
with the idea that God comes down to save
us, and then leaves us in prison, the slaves of
our besetting sins. No; He has come to deliver
us, and to give us victory over our evil tempers, our passions, and our lusts. Are you a
professed Christian, but one who is a slave to
some besetting sin? If you want to get victory
over that temper or that lust, go on to know
Christ more intimately. He brings deliverance
for the past, the present, and the future.*

D. L. Moody

*In your own words, describe what the bur-
den of sin does to people. How have you been
enslaved to sin? Does your life give evidence
that you are no longer a slave to sin? What
can you do so that God will truly be your
master?*

TUESDAY:
God's People Belong to Him
Romans 6:15—7:13

Be Slaves of Righteousness

So what should we do? Should we sin because we are under grace and not under law? No! Surely you know that when you give yourselves like slaves to obey someone, then you are really slaves of that person. The person you obey is your master. You can follow sin, which brings spiritual death, or you can obey God, which makes you right with him. In the past you were slaves to sin—sin controlled you. But thank God, you fully obeyed the things that you were taught. You were made free from sin, and now you are slaves to goodness. I use this example because this is hard for you to understand. In the past you offered the parts of your body to be slaves to sin and evil; you lived only for evil. In the same way now you must give yourselves to be slaves of goodness. Then you will live only for God.

In the past you were slaves to sin, and goodness did not control you. You did evil things, and now you are ashamed of them. Those things only bring death. But now you are free from sin and have become slaves of God. This brings you a life that is only for God, and this gives you life forever. When people sin, they earn what sin pays—death. But God gives us a free gift—life forever in Christ Jesus our Lord.

An Example from Marriage

Brothers and sisters, all of you understand the law of Moses. So surely you know that the law rules over people only while they are alive. For example, a woman must stay married to her husband as long as he is alive. But if her husband dies, she is free from the law of marriage. But if she marries another man while her husband is still alive, the law says she is guilty of adultery. But if her husband dies, she is free from the law of marriage. Then if she marries another man, she is not guilty of adultery.

In the same way, my brothers and sisters, your old selves died, and you became free from the law through the body of Christ. This happened so that you might belong to someone else—the One who was raised from the dead—and so that we might be used in service to God. In the past, we were ruled by our sinful selves. The law made us want to do sinful things that controlled our bodies, so the things we did were bringing us death. In the past, the law held us like prisoners, but our old selves died, and we were made free from the law. So now we serve God in a new way with the Spirit, and not in the old way with written rules.

Our Fight Against Sin

You might think I am saying that sin and the law are the same thing. That is not true. But the law was the only way I could learn what sin meant. I would never have known what it means to want to take something belonging to someone else if the law had not said, "You must not want to take your neighbor's things." And sin found a way to use that command and cause me to want all kinds of things I should not want. But without the law, sin has no power. I was alive before I knew the law. But when the law's command came to me, then sin began to live, and I died. The command was meant to bring life, but for me it brought death. Sin found a way to fool me by using the command to make me die.

So the law is holy, and the command is holy and right and good. Does this mean that something that is good brought death to me? No! Sin used something that is good to bring death to me. This happened so that I could see what sin is really like; the command was used to show that sin is very evil.

Come, let's worship him and bow
    down.
    Let's kneel before the LORD who
        made us,
because he is our God

and we are the people he takes care of
and the sheep that he tends.

Psalm 95:6–7a

You are holy people who belong to the
LORD your God. He has chosen you from all
the people on earth to be his very own.

The LORD did not care for you and choose
you because there were many of you—you
are the smallest nation of all. But the LORD
chose you because he loved you, and he
kept his promise to your ancestors. So he
brought you out of Egypt by his great power
and freed you from the land of slavery, from
the power of the king of Egypt.

Deuteronomy 7:6–8

This is what the LORD All-Powerful says: "I
will save my people from countries in the
east and west. I will bring them back, and
they will live in Jerusalem. They will be my
people, and I will be their good and loyal
God."

Zechariah 8:7–8

Now, Israel, this is what the LORD your
God wants you to do: Respect the LORD your
God, and do what he has told you to do.
Love him. Serve the LORD your God with
your whole being.

Respect the LORD your God and serve
him. Be loyal to him and make your promises in his name. He is the one you should
praise; he is your God, who has done great
and wonderful things for you, which you
have seen with your own eyes.

Deuteronomy 10:12, 20–21

These are the words that the LORD spoke
to Jeremiah: "Listen to the words of this
agreement and tell them to the people of
Judah and those living in Jerusalem.
Tell them this is what the LORD, the God of
Israel, says: 'Cursed is the person who
does not obey the words of this agreement
that I made with your ancestors when I
brought them out of Egypt. Egypt was
like a furnace for melting iron!' I told
them, 'Obey me and do everything I command you. Then you will be my people,
and I will be your God."

Jeremiah 11:1–4

This is because the people of Israel are
servants to me. They are my servants,
whom I brought out of Egypt. I am the LORD
your God.

Leviticus 25:55

INSIGHTS

We are chosen to be holy. This is what the
word "saint" means. In Greek, the word is
hagios, meaning holy, set apart, and belonging to God. It does not mean the spiritual
elitism of a "Holy Joe" or the aloof smugness
of a "Perfect Pat." Rather, it indicates ownership. God says to us, "You belong to Me!"

When Paul addressed the saints, he was
not writing to church leaders or to spiritually advanced people. Rather, Paul wrote to
all of God's people who stood equally with him
as those chosen, called, and cherished.

We, then, can also enjoy our status as loved
and forgiven people.

This is a lofty thought, but what does it
mean practically? Nothing less than that all
we are and have belongs to God. This means
our minds, emotions, will and bodies belong
to God. We expand God's reign in our lives
to include the people, the possessions, and the
plans of our lives. And we don't stop here. Our
list grows to include the memories that shape
our present and the values that etch our future. In addition, we must be sure to include
our work world where we spend most of our
days. We must also remember that our money
is holy, too.

Choosing to be chosen means accepting
Christ's lordship over our total lives. This requires our committed surrender to Him.

Lloyd Ogilvie

APPLICATION

Describe as fully as you can what it means
to be a slave to sin. Describe what it means
to belong to God. What difference does belonging to God make in a person's life? In
your life? Have you surrendered to him as
your Lord?

WEDNESDAY:

We Must Choose Either to Follow Sin or Serve God

Romans 7:14—8:17

The War Within Us

*W*e know that the law is spiritual, but I am not spiritual since sin rules me as if I were its slave. I do not understand the things I do. I do not do what I want to do, and I do the things I hate. And if I do not want to do the hated things I do, that means I agree that the law is good. But I am not really the one who is doing these hated things; it is sin living in me that does them. Yes, I know that nothing good lives in me—I mean nothing good lives in the part of me that is earthly and sinful. I want to do the things that are good, but I do not do them. I do not do the good things I want to do, but I do the bad things I do not want to do. So if I do things I do not want to do, then I am not the one doing them. It is sin living in me that does those things.

So I have learned this rule: When I want to do good, evil is there with me. In my mind, I am happy with God's law. But I see another law working in my body, which makes war against the law that my mind accepts. That other law working in my body is the law of sin, and it makes me its prisoner. What a miserable man I am! Who will save me from this body that brings me death? I thank God for saving me through Jesus Christ our Lord!

So in my mind I am a slave to God's law, but in my sinful self I am a slave to the law of sin.

Be Ruled by the Spirit

*S*o now, those who are in Christ Jesus are not judged guilty. Through Christ Jesus the law of the Spirit that brings life made me free from the law that brings sin and death. The law was without power, because the law was made weak by our sinful selves. But God did what the law could not do. He sent his own Son to earth with the same

human life that others use for sin. By sending his Son to be an offering to pay for sin, God used a human life to destroy sin. He did this so that we could be the kind of people the law correctly wants us to be. Now we do not live following our sinful selves, but we live following the Spirit.

Those who live following their sinful selves think only about things that their sinful selves want. But those who live following the Spirit are thinking about the things the Spirit wants them to do. If people's thinking is controlled by the sinful self, there is death. But if their thinking is controlled by the Spirit, there is life and peace. When people's thinking is controlled by the sinful self, they are against God, because they refuse to obey God's law and really are not even able to obey God's law. Those people who are ruled by their sinful selves cannot please God.

But you are not ruled by your sinful selves. You are ruled by the Spirit, if that Spirit of God really lives in you. But the person who does not have the Spirit of Christ does not belong to Christ. Your body will always be dead because of sin. But if Christ is in you, then the Spirit gives you life, because Christ made you right with God. God raised Jesus from the dead, and if God's Spirit is living in you, he will also give life to your bodies that die. God is the One who raised Christ from the dead, and he will give life through his Spirit that lives in you.

So, my brothers and sisters, we must not be ruled by our sinful selves or live the way our sinful selves want. If you use your lives to do the wrong things your sinful selves want, you will die spiritually. But if you use the Spirit's help to stop doing the wrong things you do with your body, you will have true life.

The true children of God are those who let God's Spirit lead them. The Spirit we received does not make us slaves again to fear; it makes us children of God. With that Spirit we cry out, "Father." And the Spirit himself joins with our spirits to say we are God's children. If we are God's children, we will receive blessings from God together with Christ. But we must suffer as Christ suffered so that we will have glory as Christ has glory.

*J*oshua gathered all the tribes of Israel together at Shechem. He called the older leaders, heads of families, judges, and officers of Israel to stand before God.

Then Joshua said to the people, "Now respect the LORD and serve him fully and sincerely. Throw away the gods that your ancestors worshiped on the other side of the Euphrates River and in Egypt. Serve the LORD. But if you don't want to serve the LORD, you must choose for yourselves today whom you will serve. You may serve the gods that your ancestors worshiped when they lived on the other side of the Euphrates River, or you may serve the gods of the Amorites who lived in this land. As for me and my family, we will serve the LORD."

Then the people answered, "We will never stop following the LORD to serve other gods! It was the LORD our God who brought our ancestors out of Egypt. We were slaves in that land, but the LORD did great things for us there. He brought us out and protected us while we traveled through other lands. Then he forced out all the people living in these lands, even the Amorites. So we will serve the LORD, because he is our God."

Then Joshua said, "You are not be able to serve the LORD because he is a holy God and a jealous God. If you turn against him and sin, he will not forgive you. If you leave the LORD and serve other gods, he will send you great trouble. The LORD may have been good to you, but if you turn against him, he will destroy you."

But the people said to Joshua, "No! We will serve the LORD."

Then Joshua said, "You are your own witnesses that you have chosen to serve the Lord."

The people said, "Yes, we are."

Then Joshua said, "Now throw away the gods that you have. Love the LORD, the God of Israel, with all your heart."

Then the people said to Joshua, "We will serve the LORD our God, and we will obey him."

On that day at Shechem Joshua made an agreement for the people. He made rules and laws for them to follow. Joshua wrote these things in the Book of the Teachings of God. Then he took a large stone and set it up under the oak tree near the LORD's Holy Tent.

Joshua said to all the people, "See this stone! It will remind you of what we did today. It was here the LORD spoke to us today. It will remind you of what happened so you will not turn against your God."

Joshua 24:1, 14–27

INSIGHTS

*T*he Bible does not leave us floundering as to what is right and what is wrong in the basic areas of life. We do have an absolute base for choosing. The choices are not so vague that we need to be frightened that we are choosing the wrong thing. . . .

. . . Through Joshua God challenged the Israelites to choose among "the gods . . . on the other side of the River, or the gods of the Amorites," or the Lord. Elijah presented the choice on Mount Carmel, and made the difference very vivid. Choice continues to be important time after time for each of us, but there are crisis moments in each of our lives when we are tempted to make a tremendously wrong choice. . . .

What are your choices? Whom are your choices for? Not just for yourself. Choose now whom you will serve, and that choice is going to affect the next generation, and the next generation, and the next. Choice never affects one single person alone. It goes on and on and the effect goes out into geography and history. You are a part of history and your choices become a part of history.

Edith Schaeffer

ACTION POINT

*I*n what ways are you aware of your life struggle between choosing God or the way of sin? Pray that you will see clearly the choices you must make and that you will unfailingly obey God's way of life.

THURSDAY:

Nothing Can Separate Us from God's Love

Romans 8:18–39

Our Future Glory

The sufferings we have now are nothing compared to the great glory that will be shown to us. Everything God made is waiting with excitement for God to show his children's glory completely. Everything God made was changed to become useless, not by its own wish but because God wanted it and because all along there was this hope: that everything God made would be set free from ruin to have the freedom and glory that belong to God's children.

We know that everything God made has been waiting until now in pain, like a woman ready to give birth. Not only the world, but we also have been waiting with pain inside us. We have the Spirit as the first part of God's promise. So we are waiting for God to finish making us his own children, which means our bodies will be made free. We were saved, and we have this hope. If we see what we are waiting for, that is not really hope. People do not hope for something they already have. But we are hoping for something we do not have yet, and we are waiting for it patiently.

Also, the Spirit helps us with our weakness. We do not know how to pray as we should. But the Spirit himself speaks to God for us, even begs God for us with deep feelings that words cannot explain. God can see what is in people's hearts. And he knows what is in the mind of the Spirit, because the Spirit speaks to God for his people in the way God wants.

We know that in everything God works for the good of those who love him. They are the people he called, because that was his plan. God knew them before he made the world, and he decided that they would be like his Son so that Jesus would be the firstborn of many brothers. God planned for them to be like his Son; and those he planned to be like his Son, he also called; and those he called, he also made right with him; and those he made right, he also glorified.

God's Love in Christ Jesus

So what should we say about this? If God is with us, no one can defeat us. He did not spare his own Son but gave him for us all. So with Jesus, God will surely give us all things. Who can accuse the people God has chosen? No one, because God is the One who makes them right. Who can say God's people are guilty? No one, because Christ Jesus died, but he was also raised from the dead, and now he is on God's right side, begging God for us. Can anything separate us from the love Christ has for us? Can troubles or problems or sufferings or hunger or nakedness or danger or violent death? As it is written in the Scriptures:

"For you we are in danger of death all
    the time.
People think we are worth no more
    than sheep to be killed."

Psalm 44:22

But in all these things we have full victory through God who showed his love for us. Yes, I am sure that neither death, nor life, nor angels, nor ruling spirits, nothing now, nothing in the future, no powers, nothing above us, nothing below us, nor anything else in the whole world will ever be able to separate us from the love of God that is in Christ Jesus our Lord.

We have done many wrong things
    against our God;
    our sins show we are wrong.
We know we have turned against God;
    we know the evil things we have
      done:
sinning and rejecting the LORD,
    turning away from our God,
planning to hurt others and to disobey
    God,
    planning and speaking lies.
So we have driven away justice,
    and we have kept away from what is
      right.

Truth is not spoken in the streets;
  what is honest is not allowed to
    enter the city.
Truth cannot be found anywhere,
  and people who refuse to do evil are
    attacked.

The LORD looked and could not find any
    justice,
  and he was displeased.
He could not find anyone to help the
    people,
  and he was surprised that there was
    no one to help.
So he used his own power to save the
    people;
  his own goodness gave him
    strength.
He covered himself with goodness like
    armor.
  He put the helmet of salvation on his
    head.
He put on the clothes of punishment
  and wrapped himself in the coat of
    his strong love.

The LORD says, "This is my agreement
with these people: My Spirit and my words
that I give you will never leave you or your
children or your grandchildren, now and
forever."

Isaiah 59:12–17, 21

Give thanks to the LORD because he is
    good.
  His love continues forever.
Give thanks to the God of gods.
  His love continues forever.
Give thanks to the Lord of lords.
  His love continues forever.
He remembered us when we were in
    trouble.
  His love continues forever.
He freed us from our enemies.
  His love continues forever.
He gives food to every living creature.
  His love continues forever.

Psalm 136:1–3, 23–25

INSIGHTS

*In the very nature of things we soon discover
in life that in order to be loved either in a*
*physical or filial dimension we must show
ourselves lovable. Somehow we have to demonstrate to others that we are worth loving.
We have to prove that we are worthy of their
love. And, sad to say, in most cases, the moment we fail to do this we discover that we
are being cut of. . . .*

*Now, amazing as it may sound, and in-
credible as it may seem, there is none of this
in the love of God. The simple truth is that
His love for me does not in any way depend
on my worthiness of it. In other words, I do
not have to merit His love. I do not, so to
speak, have to earn His love.*

*Scripture repeats this theme again and
again. For example, in that most poignant
of all the stories told by Jesus, the account of
the prodigal son, we see clearly portrayed for
us what the love of God is like. . . .*

*No doubt the dear old man had died
a thousand deaths after his son's departure. . . .*

*Yet his attitude of devotion, affection, and
utter selflessness never altered. It mattered not
what happened to himself as long as his son
could be restored and redeemed and remade.
His care and concern for this one's welfare
never abated.*

This is the love of God.

Phillip Keller

ACTION POINT

*List the things (as many as you want) that,
powerful and dreadful as they may be, cannot separate us from the love of God. Thank
God that his love for you is greater than every
one of those things!*

F R I D A Y:
Is God Unfair?
Romans 9:1–29

God and the Jewish People

I am in Christ, and I am telling you the truth; I do not lie. My conscience is ruled by the Holy Spirit, and it tells me I am not lying. I have great sorrow and always feel much sadness. I wish I could help my Jewish brothers and sisters, my people. I would even wish that I were cursed and cut off from Christ if that would help them.

They are the people of Israel, God's chosen children. They have seen the glory of God, and they have the agreements that God made between himself and his people. God gave them the law of Moses and the right way of worship and his promises. They are the descendants of our great ancestors, and they are the earthly family into which Christ was born, who is God over all. Praise him forever! Amen.

It is not that God failed to keep his promise to them. But only some of the people of Israel are truly God's people, and only some of Abraham's descendants are true children of Abraham. But God said to Abraham: "The descendants I promised you will be from Isaac." This means that not all of Abraham's descendants are God's true children. Abraham's true children are those who become God's children because of the promise God made to Abraham. God's promise to Abraham was this: "At the right time I will return, and Sarah will have a son." And that is not all. Rebekah's sons had the same father, our father Isaac. But before the two boys were born, God told Rebekah, "The older will serve the younger." This was before the boys had done anything good or bad. God said this so that the one chosen would be chosen because of God's own plan. He was chosen because he was the one God wanted to call, not because of anything he did. As the Scripture says, "I loved Jacob, but I hated Esau."

So what should we say about this? Is God unfair? In no way. God said to Moses, "I will show kindness to anyone to whom I want to show kindness, and I will show mercy to anyone to whom I want to show mercy." So God will choose the one to whom he decides to show mercy; his choice does not depend on what people want or try to do. The Scripture says to the king of Egypt: "I made you king for this reason: to show my power in you so that my name will be talked about in all the earth." So God shows mercy where he wants to show mercy, and he makes stubborn the people he wants to make stubborn.

So one of you will ask me: "Then why does God blame us for our sins? Who can fight his will?" You are only human, and human beings have no right to question God. An object should not ask the person who made it, "Why did you make me like this?" The potter can make anything he wants to make. He can use the same clay to make one thing for special use and another thing for daily use.

It is the same way with God. He wanted to show his anger and to let people see his power. But he patiently stayed with those people he was angry with—people who were made ready to be destroyed. He waited with patience so that he could make known his rich glory to the people who receive his mercy. He has prepared these people to have his glory, and we are those people whom God called. He called us not from the Jews only but also from those who are not Jews. As the Scripture says in Hosea:
"I will say, 'You are my people'
    to those I had called 'not my people.'
And I will show my love
    to those people I did not love."

Hosea 2:1, 23

"They were called,
    'You are not my people,'
but later they will be called
    'children of the living God.'"

Hosea 1:10

And Isaiah cries out about Israel:
"The people of Israel are many,
    like the grains of sand by the sea.
But only a few of them will be saved,
    because the Lord will quickly and
        completely punish the people on
        the earth." *Isaiah 10:22–23*

It is as Isaiah said:
"The Lord All-Powerful
allowed a few of our descendants to
live.
Otherwise we would have been completely destroyed
like the cities of Sodom and
Gomorrah."   *Isaiah 1:9*

*T*he Lord said to Job:
"Will the person who argues with the
Almighty correct him?
Let the person who accuses God
answer him."

Then Job answered the Lord:
"I am not worthy; I cannot answer you
anything,
so I will put my hand over my
mouth.
I spoke one time, but I will not answer
again;
I even spoke two times, but I will say
nothing more."

Then the Lord spoke to Job from the
storm:
"Be strong, like a man!
I will ask you questions,
and you must answer me.
Would you say that I am unfair?
Would you blame me to make
yourself look right?"

Then Job answered the Lord:
"I know that you can do all things
and that no plan of yours can be
ruined.
You asked, 'Who is this that made my
purpose unclear by saying things
that are not true?'
Surely I spoke of things I did not
understand;
I talked of things too wonderful for
me to know."
                    Job 40:1–8; 42:1–3

I alone am the Lord.
I made the light and the darkness.
I bring peace, and I cause troubles.
I, the Lord, do all these things.

"How terrible it will be for those who
argue with the God who made
them.
They are like a piece of broken
pottery among many pieces.
The clay does not ask the potter,
'What are you doing?'
The thing that is made doesn't say to its
maker,
'You have no hands.'"
                    Isaiah 45:6b–7, 9

*C*hild, don't try to understand Me. Just love
Me. Just let Me love you. You don't have to
understand Me to open yourself to My love.
  You're right—I do ride the wild winds into
town sometimes. I do appear in forms you
have never seen, sound notes you have never
heard. This makes you wonder if I get My
signals crossed, if I take you south in order to
get you north. I seem to have plopped you
down, reasonable creature that you are, into
an unreasonable world. You do not understand all this because I am God and you are
you.
  May I remind you how different we really
are? You are human; I am divine. You are
finite; I am infinite. You need love; I delight
in love but do not need it. You need to be
understood; I am above the need to be understood. You cannot understand; I understand
perfectly. You are of time; I am of eternity.
You are of reason; I am above reason. You
are blown by the wind; I blow the wind.
                    Ruth Senter

*W*hat did Job learn when he questioned
God? Are you comfortable with the fact that
God is the potter and you are the clay? Pray
for the humility to accept God's love for you
in the way that he gives it.

WEEKEND:

Salvation Comes to Those Who Believe

Romans 9:30—10:21

So what does all this mean? Those who are not Jews were not trying to make themselves right with God, but they were made right with God because of their faith. The people of Israel tried to follow a law to make themselves right with God. But they did not succeed, because they tried to make themselves right by the things they did instead of trusting in God to make them right. They stumbled over the stone that causes people to stumble. As it is written in the Scripture:

"I will put in Jerusalem a stone that
    causes people to stumble,
a rock that makes them fall.
Anyone who trusts in him will never be
    disappointed." *Isaiah 8:14; 28:16*

Brothers and sisters, the thing I want most is for all the Jews to be saved. That is my prayer to God. I can say this about them: They really try to follow God, but they do not know the right way. Because they did not know the way that God makes people right with him, they tried to make themselves right in their own way. So they did not accept God's way of making people right. Christ ended the law so that everyone who believes in him may be right with God.

Moses writes about being made right by following the law. He says, "A person who obeys these things will live because of them." But this is what the Scripture says about being made right through faith: "Don't say to yourself, 'Who will go up into heaven?'" (That means, "Who will go up to heaven and bring Christ down to earth?") "And do not say, 'Who will go down into the world below?'" (That means, "Who will go down and bring Christ up from the dead?") This is what the Scripture says: "The word is near you; it is in your mouth and in your heart." That is the teaching of faith that we are telling. If you use your mouth to say,

"Jesus is Lord," and if you believe in your heart that God raised Jesus from the dead, you will be saved. We believe with our hearts, and so we are made right with God. And we use our mouths to say that we believe, and so we are saved. As the Scripture says, "Anyone who trusts in him will never be disappointed." That Scripture says "anyone" because there is no difference between those who are Jews and those who are not. The same Lord is the Lord of all and gives many blessings to all who trust in him, as the Scripture says, "Anyone who calls on the Lord will be saved."

But before people can ask the Lord for help, they must believe in him; and before they can believe in him, they must hear about him; and for them to hear about the Lord, someone must tell them; and before someone can go and tell them, that person must be sent. It is written, "How beautiful is the person who comes to bring good news."

But not all the Jews accepted the good news. Isaiah said, "Lord, who believed what we told them?" So faith comes from hearing the Good News, and people hear the Good News when someone tells them about Christ.

But I ask: Didn't people hear the Good News? Yes, they heard—as the Scripture says:

"Their message went out through all
    the world;
their words go everywhere on
    earth." *Psalm 19:4*

Again I ask: Didn't the people of Israel understand? Yes, they did understand. First, Moses says:

"I will use those who are not a nation to
    make you jealous.
I will use a nation that does not
    understand to make you angry."
    Deuteronomy 32:21

Then Isaiah is bold enough to say:

"I was found by those who were not
    asking me for help.
I made myself known to people who
    were not looking for me."
    Isaiah 65:1

But about Israel God says,

"All day long I stood ready to accept
    people who disobey and are stubborn."
    Isaiah 65:2

Those Who Obey the Law Will Live

The LORD said to Moses, "Tell the people of Israel: 'I am the LORD your God. In the past you lived in Egypt, but you must not do what was done in that country. And you must not do as they do in the land of Canaan, where I am bringing you. Do not follow their customs. You must obey my rules and follow them. I am the LORD your God. Obey my laws and rules; a person who obeys them will live because of them. I am the LORD."

Leviticus 18:1–5

Salvation Is Not Far Away

This command I give you today is not too hard for you; it is not beyond what you can do. It is not up in heaven. You do not have to ask, "Who will go up to heaven and get it for us so we can obey it and keep it?" It is not on the other side of the sea. You do not have to ask, "Who will go across the sea and get it? Who will tell it to us so we can keep it?" No, the word is very near you. It is in your mouth and in your heart so you may obey it.

Deuteronomy 30:11–14

The Good News Has Been Told Throughout the Earth

The heavens tell the glory of God,
 and the skies announce what his
  hands have made.
Day after day they tell the story;
 night after night they tell it again.
They have no speech or words;
 they have no voice to be heard.
But their message goes out through all
  the world;
 their words go everywhere on earth.

Psalm 19:1–4a

Salvation Is for Everyone Who Calls on the Lord

Your sons and daughters will prophesy,
 your old men will dream dreams,
 and your young men will see visions.
At that time I will pour out my Spirit
 also on male slaves and female
  slaves.

I will show miracles
 in the sky and on the earth:
  blood, fire, and thick smoke.
The sun will become dark,
 the moon red as blood,
  before the overwhelming and
   terrible day of the LORD comes.
Then anyone who calls on the LORD
  will be saved,
because on Mount Zion and in Jerusalem
 there will be people who will be
  saved,
just as the LORD has said.
Those left alive after the day of punishment
 are the people whom the LORD
  called.

Joel 2:28b–32

INSIGHTS

It's not through wisdom that people come to the knowledge of God and their absolute equality before Him. It's not through endless arguments of fine points of theology that they will find a humble heart. The doorway into the kingdom is so low down that one must bend in humility to get through. I've never known a single person who has been convinced of the kingdom of God through head knowledge—a person just can't think his or her way into the kingdom of God. Nor can anyone come into the kingdom of God based on a religious experience. It is knowledge of and faith in Christ that enables the equality of life in the kingdom to be real. "For Jews request a sign, and Greeks seek after wisdom; but we preach Christ crucified, to the Jews a stumbling block and to the Greeks foolishness, but to those who are called, both Jews and Greeks, Christ the power of God and the wisdom of God" (1 Cor 1:22–25).

Terry Fullam

PAUSE FOR REFLECTION

Can a person successfully follow God in his or her own way (Romans 10:1–4)? What is the way of salvation? To whom does God offer it?

MONDAY:

God's Mercy and Kindness Are Great

Romans 11:1–21

NEW TESTAMENT READING

God Shows Mercy to All People

So I ask: Did God throw out his people? No! I myself am an Israelite from the family of Abraham, from the tribe of Benjamin. God chose the Israelites to be his people before they were born, and he has not thrown his people out. Surely you know what the Scripture says about Elijah, how he prayed to God against the people of Israel. "Lord," he said, "they have killed your prophets, and they have destroyed your altars. I am the only prophet left, and now they are trying to kill me, too." But what answer did God give Elijah? He said, "But I have left seven thousand people in Israel who have never bowed down before Baal." It is the same now. There are a few people that God has chosen by his grace. And if he chose them by grace, it is not for the things they have done. If they could be made God's people by what they did, God's gift of grace would not really be a gift.

So this is what has happened: Although the Israelites tried to be right with God, they did not succeed, but the ones God chose did become right with him. The others were made stubborn and refused to listen to God. As it is written in the Scriptures:

"God gave the people a dull mind so
    they could not understand."

Isaiah 29:10

"He closed their eyes so they could not
    see
    and their ears so they could not hear.
This continues until today."

Deuteronomy 29:4

And David says:
"Let their own feasts trap them and
    cause their ruin;
    let their feasts cause them to
        stumble and be paid back.
Let their eyes be closed so they cannot
    see

and their backs be forever weak
    from troubles." *Psalm 69:22–23*

So I ask: When the Jews fell, did that fall destroy them? No! But their mistake brought salvation to those who are not Jews, in order to make the Jews jealous. The Jews' mistake brought rich blessings for the world, and the Jews' loss brought rich blessings for the non-Jewish people. So surely the world will receive much richer blessings when enough Jews become the kind of people God wants.

Now I am speaking to you who are not Jews. I am an apostle to those who are not Jews, and since I have that work, I will make the most of it. I hope I can make my own people jealous and, in that way, help some of them to be saved. When God turned away from the Jews, he became friends with other people in the world. So when God accepts the Jews, surely that will bring them life after death.

If the first piece of bread is offered to God, then the whole loaf is made holy. If the roots of a tree are holy, then the tree's branches are holy too.

It is as if some of the branches from an olive tree have been broken off. You non-Jewish people are like the branch of a wild olive tree that has been joined to that first tree. You now share the strength and life of the first tree, the Jews. So do not brag about those branches that were broken off. If you brag, remember that you do not support the root, but the root supports you. You will say, "Branches were broken off so that I could be joined to their tree." That is true. But those branches were broken off because they did not believe, and you continue to be part of the tree only because you believe. Do not be proud, but be afraid. If God did not let the natural branches of that tree stay, then he will not let you stay if you don't believe.

OLD TESTAMENT READING

*B*ut suppose the wicked stop doing all the sins they have done and obey all my rules and do what is fair and right. Then they will surely live; they will not die. Their sins will be forgotten. Because they have done what is right, they will live. I do not really want

the wicked to die, says the Lord GOD. I want
them to stop their bad ways and live."

Ezekiel 18:21–23

*L*ORD, show us your love,
and save us.

I will listen to God the LORD.
He has ordered peace for those who
worship him.
Don't let them go back to foolishness.
God will soon save those who respect
him,
and his glory will be seen in our land.
Love and truth belong to God's people;
goodness and peace will be theirs.
On earth people will be loyal to God,
and God's goodness will shine down
from heaven.
The LORD will give his goodness,
and the land will give its crops.
Goodness will go before God
and prepare the way for him.

Psalm 85:7–13

*L*ord, there is no god like you
and no works like yours.
Lord, all the nations you have made
will come and worship you.
They will honor you.
You are great and you do miracles.
Only you are God.

Psalm 86:8–10

*A*ll people everywhere,
follow me and be saved.
I am God. There is no other God.
I will make a promise by my own
power,
and my promise is true;
what I say will not be changed.
I promise that everyone will bow before
me
and will promise to follow me.
People will say about me, 'Goodness
and power
come only from the LORD.'"
Everyone who has been angry with him
will come to him and be ashamed.

Isaiah 45:22–24

*T*he LORD will show his holy power
to all the nations.

Then everyone on earth
will see the salvation of our God.

Isaiah 52:10

INSIGHTS

*K*indness is invariably associated with
mercy. It is impossible to be kind without being merciful. Likewise to be merciful is to be
kind. It implies that there is a deep and
genuine concern for another. This concern is
one of compassion and mercy. . . .

Throughout the Scriptures the great theme
of God's unrelenting kindness throbs like a
powerful heartbeat. . . .

The kindness of God has drawn me to Him
with bonds of love stronger than steel. The
mercy of my Lord has endeared me to Him
with enormous gratitude and thanksgiving. . . .

It is the kindness of God, expressed in
Christ and revealed to us by His Spirit that
supplies my salvation. His kindness makes
provision for my pardon from sins and selfishness at the cost of His own laid down life.
It is His kindness that forgives my faults and
accepts me into His family as His dearly
beloved child. His kindness enables me to
stand acquitted of my wrongdoing, justified
freely in His presence. God's kindness removes
my guilt and I am at one with Him and others in peace. It is the kindness of God that
enables Him to share Himself with me in the
inner sanctuary of my spirit, soul, and body.
His kindness enables me to be re-made,
refashioned, re-formed gently into His likeness. His kindness gives enormous meaning
and dignity to this life and endless delight in
the life yet to come.

It is the constant, enduring, unchanging
kindness of God that gives me every reason
to rejoice and revel in life . . . all of
life . . . this one and the next.

W. Phillip Keller

PAUSE FOR REFLECTION

*I*s there anyone to whom God doesn't want
to offer his forgiveness? In what ways has God
shown his forgiveness and mercy to the Jews?
To non-Jews? Describe how God's unfailing
kindness has touched your heart.

TUESDAY:

God Wants Our Lives to Be a Sacrifice of Obedience

Romans 11:22—12:8

NEW TESTAMENT READING

So you see that God is kind and also very strict. He punishes those who stop following him. But God is kind to you, if you continue following in his kindness. If you do not, you will be cut off from the tree. And if the Jews will believe in God again, he will accept them back. God is able to put them back where they were. It is not natural for a wild branch to be part of a good tree. And you who are not Jews are like a branch cut from a wild olive tree and joined to a good olive tree. But since those Jews are like a branch that grew from the good tree, surely they can be joined to their own tree again.

I want you to understand this secret, brothers and sisters, so you will understand that you do not know everything: Part of Israel has been made stubborn, but that will change when many who are not Jews have come to God. And that is how all Israel will be saved. It is written in the Scriptures:

"The Savior will come from Jerusalem;
   he will take away all evil from the
      family of Jacob.
And I will make this agreement with
      those people
   when I take away their sins."

Isaiah 59:20–21; 27:9

The Jews refuse to accept the Good News, so they are God's enemies. This has happened to help you who are not Jews. But the Jews are still God's chosen people, and he loves them very much because of the promises he made to their ancestors. God never changes his mind about the people he calls and the things he gives them. At one time you refused to obey God. But now you have received mercy, because those people refused to obey. And now the Jews refuse to obey, because God showed mercy to you. But this happened so that they also can receive mercy from him. God has given all people over to their stubborn ways so that he can show mercy to all.

Praise to God

Yes, God's riches are very great, and his wisdom and knowledge have no end! No one can explain the things God decides or understand his ways. As the Scripture says,

"Who has known the mind of the Lord,
   or who has been able to give him
      advice?"   *Isaiah 40:13*
"No one has ever given God anything
   that he must pay back."   *Job 41:11*

Yes, God made all things, and everything continues through him and for him. To him be the glory forever! Amen.

Give Your Lives to God

So brothers and sisters, since God has shown us great mercy, I beg you to offer your lives as a living sacrifice to him. Your offering must be only for God and pleasing to him, which is the spiritual way for you to worship. Do not change yourselves to be like the people of this world, but be changed within by a new way of thinking. Then you will be able to decide what God wants for you; you will know what is good and pleasing to him and what is perfect. Because God has given me a special gift, I have something to say to everyone among you. Do not think you are better than you are. You must decide what you really are by the amount of faith God has given you. Each one of us has a body with many parts, and these parts all have different uses. In the same way, we are many, but in Christ we are all one body. Each one is a part of that body, and each part belongs to all the other parts. We all have different gifts, each of which came because of the grace God gave us. The person who has the gift of prophecy should use that gift in agreement with the faith. Anyone who has the gift of serving should serve. Anyone who has the gift of teaching should teach. Whoever has the gift of encouraging others should encourage. Whoever has the gift of giving to others should give freely. Anyone who has the gift of being a leader should try hard when he leads. Whoever has the gift of showing mercy to others should do so with joy.

*Y*ou know that the LORD has chosen for
himself those who are loyal to
him.
The LORD listens when I pray to him.
When you are angry, do not sin.
Think about these things quietly
as you go to bed.   *Selah*
Do what is right as a sacrifice to the
LORD
and trust the LORD.

Psalm 4:3–5

*W*hen Samuel came to Saul, Saul said,
"May the LORD bless you! I have obeyed the
LORD's commands."

But Samuel said, "Then why do I hear
cattle mooing and sheep bleating?"

Saul answered, "The soldiers took them
from the Amalekites. They saved the best
sheep and cattle to offer as sacrifices to the
LORD your God, but we destroyed all the
other animals."

Samuel said to Saul, "Stop! Let me tell
you what the LORD said to me last night."

Saul answered, "Tell me."

Samuel said, "Once you didn't think much
of yourself, but now you have become the
leader of the tribes of Israel. The LORD appointed you to be king over Israel. And he
sent you on a mission. He said, 'Go and
destroy those evil people, the Amalekites.
Make war on them until all of them are
dead.' Why didn't you obey the LORD? Why
did you take the best things? Why did you
do what the LORD said was wrong?"

Saul said, "But I did obey the LORD. I did
what the LORD told me to do. I destroyed all
the Amalekites, and I brought back Agag
their king. The soldiers took the best sheep
and cattle to sacrifice to the LORD your God
at Gilgal."

But Samuel answered,
"What pleases the LORD more:
burnt offerings and sacrifices
or obedience to his voice?
It is better to obey than to sacrifice.
It is better to listen to God than to
offer the fat of sheep.
Disobedience is as bad as the sin of
sorcery.
Pride is as bad as the sin of worship-
ing idols.
You have rejected the LORD's com-
mand.
Now he rejects you as king."

1 Samuel 15:13–23

---

*M*en *would understand; they do not care
to obey. They try to understand where it is
impossible they could understand except by
obeying. They would search into the work of
the Lord instead of doing their part in it—
thus making it impossible for the Lord to go
on with his work, and for themselves to become capable of seeing and understanding
what he does. Instead of immediately obeying the Lord of life, the one condition upon
which he can help them, and in itself the beginning of their deliverance, they set themselves to question their unenlightened intel-
lects as to his plans for their deliverance—
and not merely how he means to carry it out,
but whether he is able to carry it out. They
would bind their Samson until they have
scanned his limbs and muscles. They delay
in setting their foot on the stair that alone
can lead them to the house of wisdom until
they shall have determined the material and
mode of its construction.*

*For the sake of knowing, they postpone that
which alone can enable them to know, and
substitute for the true understanding that lies
beyond, a false persuasion that they already
understand. They will not accept, that is, act
upon, their highest privilege, that of obeying
the Son of God.*

*It is on them that do his will that the day
dawns. To them the Daystar rises in their
hearts. Obedience is the soul of knowledge.*

George MacDonald

---

*I*n *what ways is your life an offering to God?
In what ways are you tempted to fall short of
full obedience? Pray that your deepest desire
will be to give yourself fully as a living sacrifice to God.*

WEDNESDAY:
Owe Nothing but Love
Romans 12:9—13:14

NEW TESTAMENT READING

*Y*our love must be real. Hate what is evil, and hold on to what is good. Love each other like brothers and sisters. Give each other more honor than you want for yourselves. Do not be lazy but work hard, serving the Lord with all your heart. Be joyful because you have hope. Be patient when trouble comes, and pray at all times. Share with God's people who need help. Bring strangers in need into your homes.

Wish good for those who harm you; wish them well and do not curse them. Be happy with those who are happy, and be sad with those who are sad. Live in peace with each other. Do not be proud, but make friends with those who seem unimportant. Do not think how smart you are.

If someone does wrong to you, do not pay him back by doing wrong to him. Try to do what everyone thinks is right. Do your best to live in peace with everyone. My friends, do not try to punish others when they wrong you, but wait for God to punish them with his anger. It is written: "I will punish those who do wrong; I will repay them," says the Lord. But you should do this:

"If your enemy is hungry, feed him;
    if he is thirsty, give him a drink.
Doing this will be like pouring burning
    coals on his head."

Proverbs 25:21–22

Do not let evil defeat you, but defeat evil by doing good.

Christians Should Obey the Law

*A*ll of you must yield to the government rulers. No one rules unless God has given him the power to rule, and no one rules now without that power from God. So those who are against the government are really against what God has commanded. And they will bring punishment on themselves. Those who do right do not have to fear the rulers; only those who do wrong fear them.

Do you want to be unafraid of the rulers? Then do what is right, and they will praise you. The ruler is God's servant to help you. But if you do wrong, then be afraid. He has the power to punish; he is God's servant to punish those who do wrong. So you must yield to the government, not only because you might be punished, but because you know it is right.

This is also why you pay taxes. Rulers are working for God and give their time to their work. Pay everyone, then, what you owe. If you owe any kind of tax, pay it. Show respect and honor to them all.

Loving Others

*D*o not owe people anything, except always owe love to each other, because the person who loves others has obeyed all the law. The law says, "You must not be guilty of adultery. You must not murder anyone. You must not steal. You must not want to take your neighbor's things." All these commands and all others are really only one rule: "Love your neighbor as you love yourself." Love never hurts a neighbor, so loving is obeying all the law.

Do this because we live in an important time. It is now time for you to wake up from your sleep, because our salvation is nearer now than when we first believed. The "night" is almost finished, and the "day" is almost here. So we should stop doing things that belong to darkness and take up the weapons used for fighting in the light. Let us live in a right way, like people who belong to the day. We should not have wild parties or get drunk. There should be no sexual sins of any kind, no fighting or jealousy. But clothe yourselves with the Lord Jesus Christ and forget about satisfying your sinful self.

OLD TESTAMENT READING

*T*he wicked borrow and don't pay back,
    but those who do right give freely to
    others.
Good people always lend freely to others,
    and their children are a blessing.

Psalm 37:21, 26

*T*he rich rule over the poor,
and borrowers are servants to
lenders.

Proverbs 22:7

*M*y child, be careful about giving a
guarantee for somebody else's
loan,
about promising to pay what someone
else owes.
You might get trapped by what you say;
you might be caught by your own
words.
My child, if you have done this and are
under your neighbor's control,
here is how to get free.
Don't be proud. Go to your neighbor
and beg to be free from your promise.
Don't go to sleep .
or even rest your eyes,
but free yourself like a deer running
from a hunter,
like a bird flying away from a trapper.

Proverbs 6:1–5

A light shines in the dark for honest
people,
for those who are merciful and kind
and good.
It is good to be merciful and generous.
Those who are fair in their business
will never be defeated.
Good people will always be remembered.
They won't be afraid of bad news;
their hearts are steady because they
trust the LORD.
They are confident and will not be afraid;
they will look down on their enemies.
They give freely to the poor.
The things they do are right and will
continue forever.
They will be given great honor.

Psalm 112:4–9

*G*ive freely to the poor person, and do not
wish that you didn't have to give. The LORD
your God will bless your work and everything you touch. There will always be poor
people in the land, so I command you to give
freely to your neighbors and to the poor and
needy in your land.

Deuteronomy 15:10–11

INSIGHTS

*T*he context of this passage does . . . set up
a principle that says, "If I owe anyone anything, I am not free to give love to that person." Anyone who has borrowed money from
another person, and especially another
Christian, realizes the wall that immediately
goes up from being in a debtor/lender relationship. Debtors and lenders are not really
free to love one another. This verse suggests
principles for both sides. Lending to another
Christian needs to be considered very, very
seriously before it is done. On the other side,
before you borrow from anyone for anything,
consider the ramifications of being in bondage
to that person. Are you, in fact, free to love
that person? . . .

. . . The reality is that whenever you have
borrowed from anyone, you are a servant to
that person. . . .

. . . "Why is so much written about debt
in God's Word?" I believe there are three
reasons. First of all, debt is extremely deceptive. As we said earlier, getting into debt is
easy—getting out is next to impossible. Second, debt creates bondage, and if that bondage
is to the world system, we are no longer free
to be the witnesses in this world that God has
called us to be. Third, debt is almost blas-
phemous when we use it and deny God an
opportunity to work. . . .

. . . Being in debt is never the real problem; it is only symptomatic of the real problem, which is usually greed, self-indulgence,
impatience, fear, poor self-image, lack of self-
discipline, and perhaps others. So, if you find
yourself in debt, your first question is not,
"How do I get out of debt?" Ask first of all,
"Why am I in this situation?" and answer that
question. Then getting out of debt will become
much easier.

Ron Blue

PAUSE FOR REFLECTION

*W*hat is Jesus' greatest commandment? Examine the relationships between love, debt,
ministry, and giving in your life. How do your
lifestyle choices hinder your obedience to
Christ's commandment to love one another?

THURSDAY:

Live in a Way that Pleases God; He Will Judge Our Actions

Romans 14:1—15:3

NEW TESTAMENT READING

Do Not Criticize Other People

*A*ccept into your group someone who is weak in faith, and do not argue about opinions. One person believes it is right to eat all kinds of food. But another, who is weak, believes it is right to eat only vegetables. The one who knows that it is right to eat any kind of food must not reject the one who eats only vegetables. And the person who eats only vegetables must not think that the one who eats all foods is wrong, because God has accepted that person. You cannot judge another person's servant. The master decides if the servant is doing well or not. And the Lord's servant will do well because the Lord helps him do well.

Some think that one day is more important than another, and others think that every day is the same. Let all be sure in their own mind. Those who think one day is more important than other days are doing that for the Lord. And those who eat all kinds of food are doing that for the Lord, and they give thanks to God. Others who refuse to eat some foods do that for the Lord, and they give thanks to God. We do not live or die for ourselves. If we live, we are living for the Lord, and if we die, we are dying for the Lord. So living or dying, we belong to the Lord.

The reason Christ died and rose from the dead to live again was so he would be Lord over both the dead and the living. So why do you judge your brothers or sisters in Christ? And why do you think you are better than they are? We will all stand before God to be judged, because it is written in the Scriptures:

"'As surely as I live,' says the Lord,
'Everyone will bow before me;
everyone will say that I am God.'"

Isaiah 45:23

So each of us will have to answer to God.

Do Not Cause Others to Sin

*F*or that reason we should stop judging each other. We must make up our minds not to do anything that will make another Christian sin. I am in the Lord Jesus, and I know that there is no food that is wrong to eat. But if a person believes something is wrong, that thing is wrong for him. If you hurt your brother's or sister's faith because of something you eat, you are not really following the way of love. Do not destroy someone's faith by eating food he thinks is wrong, because Christ died for him. Do not allow what you think is good to become what others say is evil. In the kingdom of God, eating and drinking are not important. The important things are living right with God, peace, and joy in the Holy Spirit. Anyone who serves Christ by living this way is pleasing God and will be accepted by other people.

So let us try to do what makes peace and helps one another. Do not let the eating of food destroy the work of God. All foods are all right to eat, but it is wrong to eat food that causes someone else to sin. It is better not to eat meat or drink wine or do anything that will cause your brother or sister to sin.

Your beliefs about these things should be kept secret between you and God. People are happy if they can do what they think is right without feeling guilty. But those who eat something without being sure it is right are wrong because they did not believe it was right. Anything that is done without believing it is right is a sin.

We who are strong in faith should help the weak with their weaknesses, and not please only ourselves. Let each of us please our neighbors for their good, to help them be stronger in faith. Even Christ did not live to please himself. It was as the Scriptures said: "When people insult you, it hurts me."

OLD TESTAMENT READING

*P*eople will be rewarded for what they say,
and they will also be rewarded for what they do.

Proverbs 12:14

392

Now, everything has been heard,
  so I give my final advice:
Honor God and obey his commands,
  because this is all people must do.
God will judge everything,
  even what is done in secret,
the good and the evil.

Ecclesiastes 12:13–14

Bring to me all the people who are mine,
  whom I made for my glory,
  whom I formed and made."

Isaiah 43:7

We Live to Honor God's Name

Human, when the nation of Israel was living in their own land, they made it unclean by their ways and the things they did. Their ways were like a woman's uncleanness in her time of monthly bleeding. So I poured out my anger against them, because they murdered in the land and because they made the land unclean with their idols. I scattered them among the nations, and they were spread through the countries. I punished them for how they lived and what they did. They dishonored my holy name in the nations where they went. The nations said about them: 'These are the people of the LORD, but they had to leave the land which he gave them.' But I had concern for my holy name, which the nation of Israel had dishonored among the nations where they went.

"So say to the people of Israel, 'This is what the Lord God says: Israel, I am going to act, but not for your sake. I will do something to help my holy name, which you have dishonored among the nations where you went. I will prove the holiness of my great name, which has been dishonored among the nations. You have dishonored it among these nations, but the nations will know that I am the LORD when I prove myself holy before their eyes, says the Lord GOD.

"Also, I will teach you to respect me completely, and I will put a new way of thinking inside you. I will take out the stubborn hearts of stone from your bodies, and I will give you obedient hearts of flesh. I will put my Spirit inside you and help you live by my rules and carefully obey my laws."

Ezekiel 36:17–23, 26–27

W*hen we please God, we have peace. We're not trying to juggle a dozen different things in order to please everyone around us. Instead, we have a single purpose—to please God.*

When we try to please ourselves or others, however, things get out of balance. Far too many of us have become overly involved in various causes and have lost our perspective. Our priorities no longer are established by God, but by all the voices—many of which are sincere and good—clamoring around us. We have forgotten that our purpose is to please God.

But as spiritually renewed Christians who aim to please God, we can walk with security and confidence. We no longer view life and its problems with the short-sighted limitations of a merely human perspective. Instead, we view life with the long-term assurance that comes only from God's eternal perspective.

Luis Palau

PAUSE FOR REFLECTION

F*or whom do believers live and die? How does that affect our lifestyle? What is our guideline for living in a way that pleases God? Who exemplifies such a lifestyle? How are we to treat those whose faith is weak? Why?*

F R I D A Y:

God Is the Source of Our Hope and Joy

Romans 15:4–29

NEW TESTAMENT READING

*E*verything that was written in the past was written to teach us. The Scriptures give us patience and encouragement so that we can have hope. Patience and encouragement come from God. And I pray that God will help you all agree with each other the way Christ Jesus wants. Then you will all be joined together, and you will give glory to God the Father of our Lord Jesus Christ. Christ accepted you, so you should accept each other, which will bring glory to God. I tell you that Christ became a servant of the Jews to show that God's promises to the Jewish ancestors are true. And he also did this so that those who are not Jews could give glory to God for the mercy he gives to them. It is written in the Scriptures:

"So I will praise you among the non-
Jewish people.
I will sing praises to your name."
Psalm 18:49

The Scripture also says,

"Be happy, you who are not Jews,
together with his people."
Deuteronomy 32:43

Again the Scripture says,

"All you who are not Jews, praise the Lord.
All you people, sing praises to him."
Psalm 117:1

And Isaiah says,

"A new king will come from the family
of Jesse.
He will come to rule over the non-
Jewish people,
and they will have hope because of
him." *Isaiah 11:10*

I pray that the God who gives hope will fill you with much joy and peace while you trust in him. Then your hope will overflow by the power of the Holy Spirit.

Paul Talks About His Work

*M*y brothers and sisters, I am sure that you are full of goodness. I know that you have all the knowledge you need and that you are able to teach each other. But I have written to you very openly about some things I wanted you to remember. I did this because God gave me this special gift: to be a minister of Christ Jesus to those who are not Jews. I served God by teaching his Good News, so that the non-Jewish people could be an offering that God would accept—an offering made holy by the Holy Spirit.

So I am proud of what I have done for God in Christ Jesus. I will not talk about anything except what Christ has done through me in leading those who are not Jews to obey God. They have obeyed God because of what I have said and done, because of the power of miracles and the great things they saw, and because of the power of the Holy Spirit. I preached the Good News from Jerusalem all the way around to Illyricum, and so I have finished that part of my work. I always want to preach the Good News in places where people have never heard of Christ, because I do not want to build on the work someone else has already started. But it is written in the Scriptures:

"Those who were not told about him
will see,
and those who have not heard about
him will understand." *Isaiah 52:15*

Paul's Plan to Visit Rome

*T*his is the reason I was stopped many times from coming to you. Now I have finished my work here. Since for many years I have wanted to come to you, I hope to visit you on my way to Spain. After I enjoy being with you for a while, I hope you can help me on my trip. Now I am going to Jerusalem to help God's people. The believers in Macedonia and Southern Greece were happy to give their money to help the poor among God's people at Jerusalem. They were happy to do this, and really they owe it to them. These who are not Jews have shared in the Jews' spiritual blessings, so they should use their material possessions to help the Jews. After I am sure the poor in Jerusalem get the money that has been given for them, I will leave for Spain and stop and visit you. I know that when I come to you I will bring Christ's full blessing.

OLD TESTAMENT READING

*B*ut the Lord looks after those who
fear him,
those who put their hope in his love.
He saves them from death
and spares their lives in times of
hunger.
So our hope is in the Lord.
He is our help, our shield to protect
us.
We rejoice in him,
because we trust his holy name.
Lord, show your love to us
as we put our hope in you.

Psalm 33:18–22

*R*emember your promise to me, your
servant;
it gives me hope.
When I suffer, this comforts me:
Your promise gives me life.

Psalm 119:49–50

*T*he Lord gives strength to his people;
the Lord blesses his people with
peace.

Psalm 29:11

*B*ut I have hope
when I think of this:

The Lord's love never ends;
his mercies never stop.
They are new every morning;
Lord, your loyalty is great.
I say to myself, "The Lord is mine,
so I hope in him."

The Lord is good to those who hope in
him,
to those who seek him.

Lamentations 3:21–25

*L*ight shines on those who do right;
joy belongs to those who are
honest.
Rejoice in the Lord, you who do right.
Praise his holy name.

Psalm 97:11–12

*B*ut let everyone who trusts you be
happy;
let them sing glad songs forever.
Protect those who love you
and who are happy because of you.

Psalm 5:11

INSIGHTS

*A*s Jesus was entering into the last days of
his life on earth, he prayed for his disciples
and for all disciples to come. His petitions
were for union with the Father, joy, protection, and usefulness. The sequence of those
petitions is significant (John 17:11–17).

Friendship with Christ is the first priority
and is basic for the qualities that follow. Out
of that intimate, love relationship, joy is a
logical consequence. Jesus knew, as he prayed
for his disciples, that if they did indeed come
into fellowship with him and exhibit the kind
of full-fledged joy that he gives, there would
be opposition from the world, and so he prayed
not that his disciples would be protected from
the world or taken out of it into a kind of insulated, holy huddle, but that they would be
protected from anything that would destroy
that union and joy. Then, out of that dynamic
partnership, usefulness would naturally flow.

Many of us, brought up in the work ethic
of our churches, have tried to get the union
by our works. We have tried to exhibit joy we
didn't have or have hoped to earn joy by
working hard. While joy comes through giving myself away, I become burned out unless
that joy and my service flow from friendship
with Christ. . . .

. . . The more I know Him, the more I
experience that deep inner well of joy that is
not dependent on external circumstances.
This joy is present even in the midst of suffering and sorrow; it is a motivating power even
in discouragement and dismay.

Jeanie Miley

ACTION POINT

*W*ho does God fill with hope and joy? Why
is God worthy of our trust and hope? What
has God done that comforts you and brings
you hope, even when life is difficult? Thank
him. Rejoice in his unfailing love!

WEEKEND:

Watch Out for False Prophets

Romans 15:30—16:27

*B*rothers and sisters, I beg you to help me in my work by praying to God for me. Do this because of our Lord Jesus and the love that the Holy Spirit gives us. Pray that I will be saved from the non-believers in Judea and that this help I bring to Jerusalem will please God's people there. Then, if God wants me to, I will come to you with joy, and together you and I will have a time of rest. The God who gives peace be with you all. Amen.

Greetings to the Christians

I recommend to you our sister Phoebe, who is a helper in the church in Cenchrea. I ask you to accept her in the Lord in the way God's people should. Help her with anything she needs, because she has helped me and many other people also.

Give my greetings to Priscilla and Aquila, who work together with me in Christ Jesus and who risked their own lives to save my life. I am thankful to them, and all the non-Jewish churches are thankful as well. Also, greet for me the church that meets at their house.

Greetings to my dear friend Epenetus, who was the first person in the country of Asia to follow Christ. Greetings to Mary, who worked very hard for you. Greetings to Andronicus and Junia, my relatives, who were in prison with me. They are very important apostles. They were believers in Christ before I was. Greetings to Ampliatus, my dear friend in the Lord. Greetings to Urbanus, a worker together with me for Christ. And greetings to my dear friend Stachys. Greetings to Apelles, who was tested and proved that he truly loves Christ. Greetings to all those who are in the family of Aristobulus. Greetings to Herodion, my fellow citizen. Greetings to all those in the family of Narcissus who belong to the Lord. Greetings to Tryphena and Tryphosa, women who work very hard for the Lord. Greetings to my dear friend Persis, who also has worked very hard for the Lord. Greetings to Rufus, who is a special person in the Lord, and to his mother, who has been like a mother to me also. Greetings to Asyncritus, Phlegon, Hermes, Patrobas, Hermas, and all the brothers who are with them. Greetings to Philologus and Julia, Nereus and his sister, and Olympas, and to all God's people with them. Greet each other with a holy kiss. All of Christ's churches send greetings to you.

Brothers and sisters, I ask you to look out for those who cause people to be against each other and who upset other people's faith. They are against the true teaching you learned, so stay away from them. Such people are not serving our Lord Christ but are only doing what pleases themselves. They use fancy talk and fine words to fool the minds of those who do not know about evil. All the believers have heard that you obey, so I am very happy because of you. But I want you to be wise in what is good and innocent in what is evil.

The God who brings peace will soon defeat Satan and give you power over him.

The grace of our Lord Jesus be with you.

Timothy, a worker together with me, sends greetings, as well as Lucius, Jason, and Sosipater, my relatives.

I am Tertius, and I am writing this letter from Paul. I send greetings to you in the Lord.

Gaius is letting me and the whole church here use his home. He also sends greetings to you, as do Erastus, the city treasurer, and our brother Quartus.

Glory to God who can make you strong in faith by the Good News that I tell people and by the message about Jesus Christ. The message about Christ is the secret that was hidden for long ages past but is now made known. It has been made clear through the writings of the prophets. And by the command of the eternal God it is made known to all nations that they might believe and obey.

To the only wise God be glory forever through Jesus Christ! Amen.

*P*rophets or those who tell the future with dreams might come to you and say they will show you a miracle or a sign. The miracle or sign might even happen, and then they might say, "Let's serve other gods" (gods you have not known) "and let's worship them." But you must not listen to those prophets or dreamers. The LORD your God is testing you, to find out if you love him with your whole being. Serve only the LORD your God. Respect him, keep his commands, and obey him. Serve him and be loyal to him. The prophets or dreamers must be killed, because they said you should turn against the LORD your God, who brought you out of Egypt and saved you from the land where you were slaves. They tried to turn you from doing what the LORD your God commanded you to do. You must get rid of the evil among you.

Someone might try to lead you to serve other gods—it might be your brother, your son or daughter, the wife you love, or a close friend. The person might say, "Let's go and worship other gods." (These are gods that neither you nor your ancestors have known, gods of the people who live around you, either nearby or far away, from one end of the land to the other.) Do not give in to such people. Do not listen or feel sorry for them, and do not let them go free or protect them. You must put them to death. You must be the first one to start to kill them, and then everyone else must join in. You must throw stones at them until they die, because they tried to turn you away from the LORD your God, who brought you out of the land of Egypt, where you were slaves.

Deuteronomy 13:1–10

*T*hen the prophet Jeremiah said to the prophet Hananiah, "Listen, Hananiah! The LORD did not send you, and you have made the people of Judah trust in lies. So this is what the LORD says: 'Soon I will remove you from the earth. You will die this year, because you taught the people to turn against the LORD.'"

Jeremiah 28:15–16

*T*his is what the Lord GOD says: How terrible it will be for the foolish prophets who follow their own ideas and have not seen a vision from me! You said, "This is the message of the LORD," but that is a false vision. Your prophecies are lies, because I have not spoken.

Ezekiel 13:3, 7

INSIGHTS

*F*or the last sixty or so years professors and teachers in centers of theological training have had Satan's special attention, and so successful has he been that modernism has thoroughly penetrated the church. His ministers—yes, the devil's ministers, for he has many in the ministry!—are masquerading as ministers of truth and righteousness.

. . . Modern heresies and criticism are pitted against the infallible Word, the infallible Christ, the fact of sin, the redemptive works of the cross, the witness of the Holy Spirit. Knowing how completely the deity and death of Christ destroyed his works, Satan, through religious teachers, has been attacking the virgin birth, the sinlessness, the efficacious death, and the resurrection of our blessed Lord. . . .

By modernism, Satan has succeeded in robbing the church of her power in the world. With a humanized Christ, a mutilated Bible, and a glorified self, modernism is bankrupt. Nothing can damn evangelism like modernism, and Satan knows that—hence his untiring efforts to create an ever-increasing army of false teachers. . . . Let us pray for spiritual perception, whereby we can detect, and that immediately, the subtle error in a good deal we hear from some of the pulpits of our land.

Herbert Lockyer

APPLICATION

*H*ow seriously does God want his people to view the problem of false teachers? How can we guard against their deception?

MONDAY:
God's Wisdom Defies the Wisdom of People
1 Corinthians 1:1–25

NEW TESTAMENT READING

*F*rom Paul. God called me to be an apostle of Christ Jesus because that is what God wanted. Also from Sosthenes, our brother in Christ.

To the church of God in Corinth, to you who have been made holy in Christ Jesus. You were called to be God's holy people with all people everywhere who pray in the name of the Lord Jesus Christ—their Lord and ours:

Grace and peace to you from God our Father and the Lord Jesus Christ.

Paul Gives Thanks to God

I always thank my God for you because of the grace God has given you in Christ Jesus. I thank God because in Christ you have been made rich in every way, in all your speaking and in all your knowledge. Just as our witness about Christ has been guaranteed to you, so you have every gift from God while you wait for our Lord Jesus Christ to come again. Jesus will keep you strong until the end so that there will be no wrong in you on the day our Lord Jesus Christ comes again. God, who has called you to share everything with his Son, Jesus Christ our Lord, is faithful.

Problems in the Church

I beg you, brothers and sisters, by the name of our Lord Jesus Christ that all of you agree with each other and not be split into groups. I beg that you be completely joined together by having the same kind of thinking and the same purpose. My brothers and sisters, some people from Chloe's family have told me quite plainly that there are quarrels among you. This is what I mean: One of you says, "I follow Paul"; another says, "I follow Apollos"; another says, "I follow Peter"; and another says, "I follow Christ." Christ has been divided up into different groups! Did Paul die on the cross for you? No! Were you baptized in the name of Paul? No! I thank God I did not baptize any of you except Crispus and Gaius so that now no one can say you were baptized in my name. (I also baptized the family of Stephanas, but I do not remember that I baptized anyone else.) Christ did not send me to baptize people but to preach the Good News. And he sent me to preach the Good News without using words of human wisdom so that the cross of Christ would not lose its power.

Christ Is God's Power and Wisdom

*T*he teaching about the cross is foolishness to those who are being lost, but to us who are being saved it is the power of God. It is written in the Scriptures:

"I will cause the wise men to lose their
    wisdom;
I will make the wise men unable to
    understand."   *Isaiah 29:14*

Where is the wise person? Where is the educated person? Where is the skilled talker of this world? God has made the wisdom of the world foolish. In the wisdom of God the world did not know God through its own wisdom. So God chose to use the message that sounds foolish to save those who believe. The Jews ask for miracles, and the Greeks want wisdom. But we preach a crucified Christ. This is a big problem to the Jews, and it is foolishness to those who are not Jews. But Christ is the power of God and the wisdom of God to those people God has called—Jews and Greeks. Even the foolishness of God is wiser than human wisdom, and the weakness of God is stronger than human strength.

OLD TESTAMENT READING

*O*lder people are wise,
    and long life brings understanding.

"But only God has wisdom and power,
    good advice and understanding.

"He is strong and victorious;
    both the one who fools others and the
        one who is fooled belong to him.
God leads the wise away as captives
    and turns judges into fools.

He takes off chains that kings put on
    and puts a garment on their bodies.
He leads priests away naked
    and destroys the powerful.
He makes trusted people be silent
    and takes away the wisdom of older
        leaders.
He brings disgrace on important people
    and takes away the weapons of the
        strong.
He uncovers the deep things of dark-
    ness
    and brings dark shadows into the
        light.
He makes nations great and then
    destroys them;
    he makes nations large and then
        scatters them.
He takes understanding away from the
    leaders of the earth
    and makes them wander through a
        pathless desert.
They feel around in darkness with no
    light;
    he makes them stumble like drunks."

Job 12:12–13, 16–25

*T*hese are the wise words of Solomon
son of David, king of Israel.

They make the uneducated smarter
    and give knowledge and sense to the
        young.
Wise people can also listen and learn;
    even smart people can find good
        advice in these words.

Knowledge begins with respect for the
    LORD,
    but fools hate wisdom and self-
        control.

Proverbs 1:1, 4–5, 7

I, the LORD, made everything,
    stretching out the skies by myself
    and spreading out the earth all
        alone.
I show that the lying prophets' signs
    are false;
    I make fools of those who do
        magic.
I confuse even wise men;
    they think they know much, but I
        make them look foolish.

I make the messages of my servants
    come true;
    I make the advice of my messengers
        come true."

Isaiah 44:24b–26a

INSIGHTS

*T*he Jews sought after wonders, but the
Greeks sought after wisdom. The Greeks were
known for their great philosophers and their
knowledge. They had come to the point where
they literally deified wisdom. They were worshiping at the shrine of science and knowledge. Does that sound familiar today in the
twentieth century?

We have people today who say, "If you can't
put it into the test tube or in a mathematical
equation, we will not believe it." But you can't
put the Cross in a crucible, and you can't put
faith in a formula. The great philosopher,
Pascal, said, "The heart has its reasons that
reason knows nothing of." . . .

. . . God is too wise to let man come to
know Him by his own wisdom. Man cannot
solve his problems because he will not recognize their source, which is sin. Furthermore,
he will not recognize the solution, which is
salvation. God is so wise that He is not going
to let man come to Him by his own wisdom.

As a matter of fact, we are told in 1
Corinthians 3:19 that "the wisdom of this
world is foolishness with God." Think about
it, a world full of wisdom is just a thimble
full of foolishness to God. The Prophet
Jeremiah said, "The wise men are ashamed.
They are dismayed and taken. Behold they
have rejected the Word of the Lord; so what
wisdom do they have?" (Jer. 8:9). . . .

. . . If a person is going to come to God,
he or she will have to come as a little child
(Matt. 18:3).

James Merritt

PAUSE FOR REFLECTION

*W*hy do you think Paul says, "If I used
worldly wisdom to tell the Good News, the
cross of Christ would lose its power"? Do you
agree? Why? Why do you think that God, the
source of all wisdom, turns the world's wisdom
into foolishness?

TUESDAY:

God Is the Source of Wisdom

1 Corinthians 1:26—2:16

NEW TESTAMENT READING

*B*rothers and sisters, look at what you were when God called you. Not many of you were wise in the way the world judges wisdom. Not many of you had great influence. Not many of you came from important families. But God chose the foolish things of the world to shame the wise, and he chose the weak things of the world to shame the strong. He chose what the world thinks is unimportant and what the world looks down on and thinks is nothing in order to destroy what the world thinks is important. God did this so that no one can brag in his presence. Because of God you are in Christ Jesus, who has become for us wisdom from God. In Christ we are put right with God, and have been made holy, and have been set free from sin. So, as the Scripture says, "If someone wants to brag, he should brag only about the Lord."

The Message of Christ's Death

*D*ear brothers and sisters, when I came to you, I did not come preaching God's secret with fancy words or a show of human wisdom. I decided that while I was with you I would forget about everything except Jesus Christ and his death on the cross. So when I came to you, I was weak and fearful and trembling. My teaching and preaching were not with words of human wisdom that persuade people but with proof of the power that the Spirit gives. This was so that your faith would be in God's power and not in human wisdom.

God's Wisdom

*H*owever, I speak a wisdom to those who are mature. But this wisdom is not from this world or from the rulers of this world, who are losing their power. I speak God's secret wisdom, which he has kept hidden. Before the world began, God planned this wisdom for our glory. None of the rulers of this world understood it. If they had, they would not have crucified the Lord of glory. But as it is written in the Scriptures:

"No one has ever seen this,
and no one has ever heard about it.
No one has ever imagined
what God has prepared for those
who love him." *Isaiah 64:4*

But God has shown us these things through the Spirit.

The Spirit searches out all things, even the deep secrets of God. Who knows the thoughts that another person has? Only a person's spirit that lives within him knows his thoughts. It is the same with God. No one knows the thoughts of God except the Spirit of God. Now we did not receive the spirit of the world, but we received the Spirit that is from God so that we can know all that God has given us. And we speak about these things, not with words taught us by human wisdom but with words taught us by the Spirit. And so we explain spiritual truths to spiritual people. A person who does not have the Spirit does not accept the truths that come from the Spirit of God. That person thinks they are foolish and cannot understand them, because they can only be judged to be true by the Spirit. The spiritual person is able to judge all things, but no one can judge him. The Scripture says:

"Who has known the mind of the Lord?
Who has been able to teach him?"
Isaiah 40:13

But we have the mind of Christ.

OLD TESTAMENT READING

*P*eople do not understand the value of
wisdom;
it cannot be found among those who
are alive.
The deep ocean says, 'It's not in me';
the sea says, 'It's not in me.'
Wisdom cannot be bought with gold,
and its cost cannot be weighed in
silver.
Wisdom cannot be bought with fine gold
or with valuable onyx or sapphire
gems.

Gold and crystal are not as valuable as
wisdom,
and you cannot buy it with jewels of
gold.
Coral and jasper are not worth talking
about,
and the price of wisdom is much
greater than rubies.
The topaz from Cush cannot compare
to wisdom;
it cannot be bought with the purest
gold.

"So from where does wisdom come,
and where does understanding live?
It is hidden from the eyes of every
living thing,
even from the birds of the air.
The places of destruction and death
say,
'We have heard reports about it.'
Only God understands the way to
wisdom,
and he alone knows where it lives,
because he looks to the farthest parts
of the earth
and sees everything under the sky.
When God gave power to the wind
and measured the water,
when he made rules for the rain
and set a path for a thunderstorm to
follow,
then he looked at wisdom and decided
its worth;
he set wisdom up and tested it.
Then he said to humans,
'The fear of the Lord is wisdom;
to stay away from evil is understanding.'"

Job 28:13–28

*L*isten carefully to wisdom;
set your mind on understanding.
Search for it like silver,
and hunt for it like hidden treasure.
Then you will understand respect for
the LORD,
and you will find that you know God.
Only the LORD gives wisdom;
he gives knowledge and understanding.

Proverbs 2:2, 4–6

WEDNESDAY:

Christ Is the Cornerstone of Our Faith, so Our Works Must Stand His Test

1 Corinthians 3:1—4:5

Following People Is Wrong

*B*rothers and sisters, in the past I could not talk to you as I talk to spiritual people. I had to talk to you as I would to people without the Spirit—babies in Christ. The teaching I gave you was like milk, not solid food, because you were not able to take solid food. And even now you are not ready. You are still not spiritual, because there is jealousy and quarreling among you, and this shows that you are not spiritual. You are acting like people of the world. One of you says, "I belong to Paul," and another says, "I belong to Apollos." When you say things like this, you are acting like people of the world.

Is Apollos important? No! Is Paul important? No! We are only servants of God who helped you believe. Each one of us did the work God gave us to do. I planted the seed, and Apollos watered it. But God is the One who made it grow. So the one who plants is not important, and the one who waters is not important. Only God, who makes things grow, is important. The one who plants and the one who waters have the same purpose, and each will be rewarded for his own work. We are God's workers, working together; you are like God's farm, God's house.

Using the gift God gave me, I laid the foundation of that house like an expert builder. Others are building on that foundation, but all people should be careful how they build on it. The foundation that has already been laid is Jesus Christ, and no one can lay down any other foundation. But if people build on that foundation, using gold, silver, jewels, wood, grass, or straw, their work will be clearly seen, because the Day of Judgment will make it visible. That Day will appear with fire, and the fire will test everyone's work to show what sort of work it was. If the building that has been put on the foundation still stands, the builder will get a reward. But if the building is burned up, the builder will suffer loss. The builder will be saved, but it will be as one who escaped from a fire.

Don't you know that you are God's temple and that God's Spirit lives in you? If anyone destroys God's temple, God will destroy that person, because God's temple is holy and you are that temple.

Do not fool yourselves. If you think you are wise in this world, you should become a fool so that you can become truly wise, because the wisdom of this world is foolishness with God. It is written in the Scriptures, "He catches those who are wise in their own clever traps." It is also written in the Scriptures, "The Lord knows what wise people think. He knows their thoughts are just a puff of wind." So you should not brag about human leaders. All things belong to you: Paul, Apollos, and Peter; the world, life, death, the present, and the future—all these belong to you. And you belong to Christ, and Christ belongs to God.

Apostles Are Servants of Christ

*P*eople should think of us as servants of Christ, the ones God has trusted with his secrets. Now in this way those who are trusted with something valuable must show they are worthy of that trust. As for myself, I do not care if I am judged by you or by any human court. I do not even judge myself. I know of no wrong I have done, but this does not make me right before the Lord. The Lord is the One who judges me. So do not judge before the right time; wait until the Lord comes. He will bring to light things that are now hidden in darkness, and will make known the secret purposes of people's hearts. Then God will praise each one of them.

*T*he LORD says, "Two-thirds of the people
  through all the land will die. They will be gone,
  and one-third will be left.
The third that is left I will test with fire,
  purifying them like silver,
  testing them like gold.

Then they will call on me,
    and I will answer them.
I will say, 'You are my people,'
    and they will say, 'The LORD is our
        God.'"

Zechariah 13:8–9

So this is what the LORD All-Powerful
says:
"I will test the people of Judah as a
        person tests metal in a fire.
    I have no other choice,
    because my people have sinned."

Jeremiah 9:7

Idols tell lies;
    fortune-tellers see false visions
and tell about false dreams.
    The comfort they give is worth
        nothing.
So the people are like lost sheep.
    They are abused, because there is
        no shepherd.

The LORD says, "I am angry at my
        shepherds,
    and I will punish the leaders.
I, the LORD All-Powerful, care
    for my flock, the people of Judah.
    I will make them like my proud war
        horses.
From Judah will come the cornerstone,
    and the tent peg,
    the battle bow,
    and every ruler.
Together they will be like soldiers
    marching to battle through muddy
        streets.
The LORD is with them,
    so they will fight and defeat the
        horsemen.

"I will strengthen the people of Judah
    and save the people of Joseph.
I will bring them back,
    because I care about them.
It will be as though
    I had never left them,
because I am the LORD their God,
    and I will answer them."

Zechariah 10:2–6

The stone that the builders rejected
    became the cornerstone.

Psalm 118:22

*What does it mean to build your house on
the rock or to dig deeply and lay a foundation? . . . It is a matter of building on
Jesus Himself. . . . To practice His words
means . . . to believe that He is who He says
He is and to turn from sin to faith in Him as
the way of salvation. . . .*

*Isaiah writes, "This is what the Sovereign
LORD says: 'See I lay a stone in Zion, a tested
stone, a precious cornerstone for a sure
foundation'" (Isa. 28:16). Paul declares,
"You are . . . built on the foundation of the
apostles and prophets, with Christ Jesus himself as the chief cornerstone" (Eph 2:19–
20). . . . That is the true sense of Christ's
teaching: "If you want a life that will last for
eternity, build on Me." We sing:*

> *My hope is built on nothing less
> Than Jesus' blood and righteousness;
> I dare not trust the sweetest frame,
> But wholly lean on Jesus' name.*

> *On Christ, the solid rock, I stand;
> All other ground is sinking sand. . . .*

*. . . A life built on Jesus and His teach-
ings will stand—it will stand in the trials
and testings of this life, and it will stand in
eternity. . . .*

*. . . Jesus says that although rains will
fall, floods will rise, and winds will blow, the
life that is constructed on Him will survive
the blast and last forever.*

James Boice

*Who will test our works? Why? On what
foundation are you building your life's work?
Is your work worthy of the foundation; will it
stand the test? Pray that your works will be
proven worthy.*

THURSDAY:

God Will Not Tolerate Sin Among His People

1 Corinthians 4:6—5:8

NEW TESTAMENT READING

*B*rothers and sisters, I have used Apollos and myself as examples so you could learn through us the meaning of the saying, "Follow only what is written in the Scriptures." Then you will not be more proud of one person than another. Who says you are better than others? What do you have that was not given to you? And if it was given to you, why do you brag as if you did not receive it as a gift?

You think you already have everything you need. You think you are rich. You think you have become kings without us. I wish you really were kings so we could be kings together with you. But it seems to me that God has put us apostles in last place, like those sentenced to die. We are like a show for the whole world to see—angels and people. We are fools for Christ's sake, but you are very wise in Christ. We are weak, but you are strong. You receive honor, but we are shamed. Even to this very hour we do not have enough to eat or drink or to wear. We are often beaten, and we have no homes in which to live. We work hard with our own hands for our food. When people curse us, we bless them. When they hurt us, we put up with it. When they tell evil lies about us, we speak nice words about them. Even today, we are treated as though we were the garbage of the world—the filth of the earth.

I am not trying to make you feel ashamed. I am writing this to give you a warning as my own dear children. For though you may have ten thousand teachers in Christ, you do not have many fathers. Through the Good News I became your father in Christ Jesus, so I beg you, please follow my example. That is why I am sending to you Timothy, my son in the Lord. I love Timothy, and he is faithful. He will help you remember my way of life in Christ Jesus, just as I teach it in all the churches everywhere.

Some of you have become proud, thinking that I will not come to you again. But I will come to you very soon if the Lord wishes. Then I will know what the proud ones do, not what they say, because the kingdom of God is present not in talk but in power. Which do you want: that I come to you with punishment or with love and gentleness?

Wickedness in the Church

*I*t is actually being said that there is sexual sin among you. And it is a kind that does not happen even among people who do not know God. A man there has his father's wife. And you are proud! You should have been filled with sadness so that the man who did this should be put out of your group. I am not there with you in person, but I am with you in spirit. And I have already judged the man who did that sin as if I were really there. When you meet together in the name of our Lord Jesus, and I meet with you in spirit with the power of our Lord Jesus, then hand this man over to Satan. So his sinful self will be destroyed, and his spirit will be saved on the day of the Lord.

Your bragging is not good. You know the saying, "Just a little yeast makes the whole batch of dough rise." Take out all the old yeast so that you will be a new batch of dough without yeast, which you really are. For Christ, our Passover lamb, has been sacrificed. So let us celebrate this feast, but not with the bread that has the old yeast—the yeast of sin and wickedness. Let us celebrate this feast with the bread that has no yeast—the bread of goodness and truth.

OLD TESTAMENT READING

A man or woman in one of the towns the LORD gave you might be found doing something evil and breaking the Agreement. That person may have served other gods and bowed down to them or to the sun or moon or stars of the sky, which I have commanded should not be done. If someone has told you about it, you must look into the matter carefully. If it is true that such a hateful thing has happened in Israel, take the man or woman who has done the evil thing to the city gates and throw stones at that person until he dies. There must be two or three witnesses that it is true before the person is put to death; if there is only one witness, the person should not be put to death. The witnesses must be the first to throw stones at the person, and then everyone else will follow. You must get rid of the evil among you.

The person who does not show respect for the judge or priest who is there serving the LORD your God must be put to death. You must get rid of that evil from Israel. Then everyone will hear about this and will be afraid, and they will not show disrespect anymore.

Deuteronomy 17:2–7, 12–13

So the Lord GOD All-Powerful,
   the Mighty One of Israel, says:
"You, my enemies, will not cause me
      any more trouble.
   I will pay you back for what you did.
I will turn against you
   and clean away all your wrongs as if
      with soap;
   I will take all the worthless things
      out of you.
I will bring back judges as you had long
      ago;
   your counselors will be like those
      you had in the beginning.
Then you will be called the City That Is
      Right with God,
   the Loyal City."

By doing what is fair,
   Jerusalem will be free again.
By doing what is right,
   her people who come back to the
      LORD will have freedom.
But sinners and those who turn against
      him will be destroyed;
   those who have left the LORD will
      die.

Isaiah 1:24–28

Evil is like a small fire.
   First, it burns weeds and thorns.
Next, it burns the larger bushes in the
      forest,

and they all go up in a column of
   smoke.

Isaiah 9:18

INSIGHTS

C*an a Christian get away with sin? Some people seem to think so. However, a closer look points to another answer. God is always opposed to sin. He is never deceived and cannot be outwitted. He may allow sin to continue for a time, but there will be a day of accountability.*

Nothing leads to evil quite as much as the idea that this world is all there is. Those who commit violent crimes and who harm the innocent have usually first convinced themselves that there will never be a day of judgment. Even the motorist speeding down the highway has convinced himself he will not receive a speeding ticket.

However, Jesus says that people who believe they will never be found out are wrong: "There is nothing covered up that will not be revealed, and hidden that will not be known" (Luke 12:2). . . .

. . . God totally opposes sin. Take a favorable attitude toward sin and God must take an unfavorable attitude toward you. No Christian can entertain sin and get away with it.

The Royal Canadian Mounted Police have taken as their motto, "We always get our man." The implication is that no matter where a wanted man runs, he will be found. Sin is the same way. No matter how hard we try, we cannot hide our sins. Regardless of how much good we do, it will not cover our disobedience.

God will not allow sin in the lives of His children to go unchecked.

George Sweeting/Donald Sweeting

APPLICATION

W*hy does God tell his people to punish the sinners among them? What was Paul's response to sin in the Corinthian church? What is your response to sin? How might your response be more pleasing to God?*

F R I D A Y:

Honor God with Your Body;
Keep Yourself from Sexual Sin

1 Corinthians 5:9—6:20

I wrote you in my earlier letter not to associate with those who sin sexually. But I did not mean you should not associate with those of this world who sin sexually, or with the greedy, or robbers, or those who worship idols. To get away from them you would have to leave this world. I am writing to tell you that you must not associate with those who call themselves believers in Christ but who sin sexually, or are greedy, or worship idols, or abuse others with words, or get drunk, or cheat people. Do not even eat with people like that.

It is not my business to judge those who are not part of the church. God will judge them. But you must judge the people who are part of the church. The Scripture says, "You must get rid of the evil person among you."

Judging Problems Among Christians

*W*hen you have something against another Christian, how can you bring yourself to go before judges who are not right with God? Why do you not let God's people decide who is right? Surely you know that God's people will judge the world. So if you are to judge the world, are you not able to judge small cases as well? You know that in the future we will judge angels, so surely we can judge the ordinary things of this life. If you have ordinary cases that must be judged, are you going to appoint people as judges who mean nothing to the church? I say this to shame you. Surely there is someone among you wise enough to judge a complaint between believers. But now one believer goes to court against another believer—and you do this in front of unbelievers!

The fact that you have lawsuits against each other shows that you are already defeated. Why not let yourselves be wronged? Why not let yourselves be cheated? But you yourselves do wrong and cheat, and you do this to other believers!

Surely you know that the people who do wrong will not inherit God's kingdom. Do not be fooled. Those who sin sexually, worship idols, take part in adultery, those who are male prostitutes, or men who have sexual relations with other men, those who steal, are greedy, get drunk, lie about others, or rob—these people will not inherit God's kingdom. In the past, some of you were like that, but you were washed clean. You were made holy, and you were made right with God in the name of the Lord Jesus Christ and in the Spirit of our God.

Use Your Bodies for God's Glory

I am allowed to do all things," but all things are not good for me to do. "I am allowed to do all things," but I will not let anything make me its slave. "Food is for the stomach, and the stomach for food," but God will destroy them both. The body is not for sexual sin but for the Lord, and the Lord is for the body. By his power God has raised the Lord from the dead and will also raise us from the dead. Surely you know that your bodies are parts of Christ himself. So I must never take the parts of Christ and join them to a prostitute! It is written in the Scriptures, "The two will become one body." So you should know that anyone who joins with a prostitute becomes one body with the prostitute. But the one who joins with the Lord is one spirit with the Lord.

So run away from sexual sin. Every other sin people do is outside their bodies, but those who sin sexually sin against their own bodies. You should know that your body is a temple for the Holy Spirit who is in you. You have received the Holy Spirit from God. So you do not belong to yourselves, because you were bought by God for a price. So honor God with your bodies.

*W*hile the people of Israel were still camped at Acacia, the men began sinning sexually with Moabite women. The women invited them to their sacrifices to their gods, and the Israelites ate food there and worshiped these gods. So the Israelites began to worship Baal of Peor, and the LORD was very angry with them.

Moses and the Israelites were gathered at the entrance to the Meeting Tent, crying there. Then an Israelite man brought a Midianite woman to his brothers in plain sight of Moses and all the people. Phinehas son of Eleazar, the son of Aaron, the priest, saw this, so he left the meeting and got his spear. He followed the Israelite into his tent and drove his spear through both the Israelite man and the Midianite woman. Then the terrible sickness among the Israelites stopped.

This sickness had killed twenty-four thousand people.

The LORD said to Moses, "Phinehas son of Eleazar, the son of Aaron, the priest, has saved the Israelites from my anger. He hates sin as much as I do. Since he tried to save my honor among them, I will not kill them. So tell Phinehas that I am making my peace agreement with him. He and his descendants will always be priests, because he had great concern for the honor of his God. He removed the sins of the Israelites so they would belong to God."

Numbers 25:1–3, 6–13

*I*f I have desired another woman
    or have waited at my neighbor's
        door for his wife,
then let my wife grind another man's
        grain,
    and let other men have sexual
        relations with her.
That would be shameful,
    a sin to be punished.
It is like a fire that burns and destroys;
    all I have done would be plowed up."

Job 31:9–12

A prostitute will treat you like a loaf of
        bread,
    and a woman who takes part in
        adultery may cost you your life.
You cannot carry hot coals against your
        chest
    without burning your clothes,
and you cannot walk on hot coals
    without burning your feet.

The same is true if you have sexual relations with another man's wife. Anyone who does so will be punished.

Proverbs 6:26–29

*I*t's often said that people "fall" into immorality. The expression is as revealing as it is faulty and dangerous. The very term fall betrays a victim mentality. It sounds as if we were walking down a street and someone tripped us or kicked our feet out from under us. It implies that moral collapse comes out of nowhere, that there is little or nothing we could have done to prevent what happened.

We do not fall into immorality. We walk into it. Indeed, sometimes we run headlong into it. We must realize from the beginning that immorality is a choice. It is not something that happens to people. . . .

Sexual sin never comes out of the clear blue sky. It is often the result of a long process in which a mind susceptible to sin is granted unguarded exposure to immoral input.

"Sow a thought, reap an action. Sow an action, reap a habit. Sow a habit, reap a character. Sow a character, reap a destiny." Our thoughts are the fabric with which we weave our character and destiny. We must actively fight off thoughts of impurity. But the key to doing this is not simply saying "I will not lust, I will not lust"—that often has the same effect as saying, "I will not think of purple elephants." We must cultivate our hearts and minds with what is godly and pure. These better thoughts will displace others (Phil 4:8).

Randy Alcorn

P A U S E F O R R E F L E C T I O N

*W*hat does Paul say about judging the lifestyles of other Christians? What sins, in addition to sexual sins, does Paul take a hard line against? Why are we to run away from sin? What are the penalties for continuing in sin?

WEEKEND:

*Marriage Is a Gift from God
Not to Be Taken Lightly*

1 Corinthians 7:1–24

About Marriage

*N*ow I will discuss the things you wrote me about. It is good for a man not to have sexual relations with a woman. But because sexual sin is a danger, each man should have his own wife, and each woman should have her own husband. The husband should give his wife all that he owes her as his wife. And the wife should give her husband all that she owes him as her husband. The wife does not have full rights over her own body; her husband shares them. And the husband does not have full rights over his own body; his wife shares them. Do not refuse to give your bodies to each other, unless you both agree to stay away from sexual relations for a time so you can give your time to prayer. Then come together again so Satan cannot tempt you because of a lack of self-control. I say this to give you permission to stay away from sexual relations for a time. It is not a command to do so. I wish that everyone were like me, but each person has his own gift from God. One has one gift, another has another gift.

Now for those who are not married and for the widows I say this: It is good for them to stay unmarried as I am. But if they cannot control themselves, they should marry. It is better to marry than to burn with sexual desire.

Now I give this command for the married people. (The command is not from me; it is from the Lord.) A wife should not leave her husband. But if she does leave, she must not marry again, or she should make up with her husband. Also the husband should not divorce his wife.

For all the others I say this (I am saying this, not the Lord): If a Christian man has a wife who is not a believer, and she is happy to live with him, he must not divorce her. And if a Christian woman has a husband who is not a believer, and he is happy to live with her, she must not divorce him. The husband who is not a believer is made holy through his believing wife. And the wife who is not a believer is made holy through her believing husband. If this were not true, your children would not be clean, but now your children are holy.

But if those who are not believers decide to leave, let them leave. When this happens, the Christian man or woman is free. But God called us to live in peace. Wife, you don't know; maybe you will save your husband. And husband, you don't know; maybe you will save your wife.

Live as God Called You

*B*ut in any case each one of you should continue to live the way God has given you to live—the way you were when God called you. This is a rule I make in all the churches. If a man was already circumcised when he was called, he should not undo his circumcision. If a man was without circumcision when he was called, he should not be circumcised. It is not important if a man is circumcised or not. The important thing is obeying God's commands. Each one of you should stay the way you were when God called you. If you were a slave when God called you, do not let that bother you. But if you can be free, then make good use of your freedom. Those who were slaves when the Lord called them are free persons who belong to the Lord. In the same way, those who were free when they were called are now Christ's slaves. You all were bought at a great price, so do not become slaves of people. Brothers and sisters, each of you should stay as you were when you were called, and stay there with God.

*A*nd the man said,
"Now, this is someone whose bones
came from my bones,
whose body came from my body.
I will call her 'woman,'
because she was taken out of man."
So a man will leave his father and mother

and be united with his wife, and the two will become one body.

Genesis 2:23–24

When a man finds a wife, he finds something good.
It shows that the LORD is pleased with him.

Proverbs 18:22

This is another thing you do. You cover the LORD's altar with your tears. You cry and moan, because he does not accept your offerings and is not pleased with what you bring. You ask, "Why?" It is because the LORD sees how you treated the wife you married when you were young. You broke your promise to her, even though she was your partner and you had an agreement with her. God made husbands and wives to become one body and one spirit for his purpose—so they would have children who are true to God.

So be careful, and do not break your promise to the wife you married when you were young.

The LORD God of Israel says, "I hate divorce. And I hate people who do cruel things as easily as they put on clothes," says the LORD All-Powerful.

Malachi 2:13–16a

Abraham was now very old, and the LORD had blessed him in every way. Abraham said to his oldest servant, who was in charge of everything he owned, "Put your hand under my leg. Make a promise to me before the LORD, the God of heaven and earth. Don't get a wife for my son from the Canaanite girls who live around here. Instead, go back to my country, to the land of my relatives, and get a wife for my son Isaac."

The servant said to him, "What if this woman does not want to return with me to this land? Then, should I take your son with me back to your homeland?"

Abraham said to him, "No! Don't take my son back there. The LORD, the God of heaven, brought me from the home of my father and the land of my relatives. And he promised me, 'I will give this land to your descendants.' The LORD will send his angel before you to help you get a wife for my son

there. If the girl won't come back with you, you will be free from this promise. But you must not take my son back there."

Genesis 24:1–8

INSIGHTS

If Paul is writing anything, he is writing this, "When you marry, you marry for life." He has permanence in mind.
- The wife should not leave her husband (v. 10).
- The husband should not leave his wife (v. 11).
- Let him not send her away (v. 12).
- Let her not send him away (v. 13).

To write it once would be sufficient. Twice would be extremely and unmistakably clear. Three times would be more than enough. But four times? The man means business!

Years ago Cynthia and I took the ugly word divorce out of our dialogues. We agreed we would not even store it in the arsenal of our argument vocabulary. No matter how heated our disagreements may be, we'd not threaten each other with that term. It does something to a marriage when you can count on your partner to stick around and hammer out your differences with each other instead of walking away from them.

What does it take to stick it out . . . to be permanently committed to each other? I repeat, it takes grace! It takes an enormous amount of grace to negotiate through the mine field of disagreements. It takes grace to forgive and go on. Grace to hang tough even though the same mistake is made over and over or the same sin committed again and again. A marriage well-oiled by grace is durable, longlasting—protected against the wear and tear of friction.

Charles Swindoll

APPLICATION

What do you learn about the seriousness of marriage from these Scripture readings? What adjustments need to be made in your thinking toward marriage? Will you make them?

MONDAY:

To Marry or Not to Marry?

1 Corinthians 7:25—8:8

Questions About Getting Married

*N*ow I write about people who are not married. I have no command from the Lord about this; I give my opinion. But I can be trusted, because the Lord has shown me mercy. The present time is a time of trouble, so I think it is good for you to stay the way you are. If you have a wife, do not try to become free from her. If you are not married, do not try to find a wife. But if you decide to marry, you have not sinned. And if a girl who has never married decides to marry, she has not sinned. But those who marry will have trouble in this life, and I want you to be free from trouble.

Brothers and sisters, this is what I mean: We do not have much time left. So starting now, those who have wives should live as if they had no wives. Those who are crying should live as if they were not crying. Those who are happy should live as if they were not happy. Those who buy things should live as if they own nothing. Those who use the things of the world should live as if they were not using them, because this world in its present form will soon be gone.

I want you to be free from worry. A man who is not married is busy with the Lord's work, trying to please the Lord. But a man who is married is busy with things of the world, trying to please his wife. He must think about two things—pleasing his wife and pleasing the Lord. A woman who is not married or a girl who has never married is busy with the Lord's work. She wants to be holy in body and spirit. But a married woman is busy with things of the world, as to how she can please her husband. I am saying this to help you, not to limit you. But I want you to live in the right way, to give yourselves fully to the Lord without concern for other things.

If a man thinks he is not doing the right thing with the girl he is engaged to, if she is almost past the best age to marry and he feels he should marry her, he should do what he wants. They should get married. It is no sin. But if a man is sure in his mind that there is no need for marriage, and has his own desires under control, and has decided not to marry the one to whom he is engaged, he is doing the right thing. So the man who marries his girl does right, but the man who does not marry will do better.

A woman must stay with her husband as long as he lives. But if her husband dies, she is free to marry any man she wants, but she must marry in the Lord. The woman is happier if she does not marry again. This is my opinion, but I believe I also have God's Spirit.

About Food Offered to Idols

*N*ow I will write about meat that is sacrificed to idols. We know that "we all have knowledge." Knowledge puffs you up with pride, but love builds up. If you think you know something, you do not yet know anything as you should. But if any person loves God, that person is known by God.

So this is what I say about eating meat sacrificed to idols: We know that an idol is really nothing in the world, and we know there is only one God. Even though there are things called gods, in heaven or on earth (and there are many "gods" and "lords"), for us there is only one God—our Father. All things came from him, and we live for him. And there is only one Lord—Jesus Christ. All things were made through him, and we also were made through him.

But not all people know this. Some people are still so used to idols that when they eat meat, they still think of it as being sacrificed to an idol. Because their conscience is weak, when they eat it, they feel guilty. But food will not bring us closer to God. Refusing to eat does not make us less pleasing to God, and eating does not make us better in God's sight.

God Calls Jeremiah for Special Service, Not Marriage

*T*he LORD spoke his word to me, saying: "Before I made you in your mother's womb, I chose you.

Before you were born, I set you
apart for a special work.
I appointed you as a prophet to the
nations."

Then I said, "But Lord GOD, I don't know
how to speak. I am only a boy."

But the LORD said to me, "Don't say, 'I am
only a boy.' You must go everywhere that I
send you, and you must say everything I
tell you to say. Don't be afraid of anyone,
because I am with you to protect you," says
the LORD.

Then the LORD reached out with his hand
and touched my mouth. He said to me, "See,
I am putting my words in your mouth. Today I have put you in charge of nations and
kingdoms. You will pull up and tear down,
destroy and overthrow, build up and plant."

Jeremiah 1:4–10

*T*hen the LORD spoke his word to me: "You
must not get married or have sons or
daughters in this place."

Jeremiah 16:1–2

*I*t is hard to find a good wife,
because she is worth more than
rubies.
Give her the reward she has earned;
she should be praised in public for
what she has done.

Proverbs 31:10, 31

*W*hen you enter the land the LORD your
God is giving you, taking it as your own and
living in it, you will say, "Let's appoint a king
over us like the nations all around us." Be
sure to appoint over you the king the LORD
your God chooses. He must be one of your
own people. Do not appoint as your king a
foreigner who is not a fellow Israelite. The
king must not have many wives, or his heart
will be led away from God. He must not
have too much silver and gold.

Deuteronomy 17:14–15, 17

*T*he LORD had told the Israelites, "You
must not marry people of other nations. If
you do, they will cause you to follow their
gods." But Solomon fell in love with these
women. He had seven hundred wives who
were from royal families and three hundred
slave women who gave birth to his children.
His wives caused him to turn away from
God. As Solomon grew old, his wives
caused him to follow other gods. He did not
follow the LORD completely as his father
David had done. Solomon worshiped Ashtoreth, the goddess of the people of Sidon,
and Molech, the hated god of the Ammonites. So Solomon did what the LORD said
was wrong and did not follow the LORD
completely as his father David had done.

1 Kings 11:2–6

I N S I G H T S

*S*ome have a special call of God to a single
life, as both Jesus and Paul taught. This was
a genuine contribution. . . .

Jesus declared that there were those who
were single "for the sake of the kingdom of
heaven" (Matt. 19:12). And Paul builds on
this foundation by suggesting that the unmarried can focus their energies toward the
work of God in a way that the married simply cannot (1 Cor. 7:32–35).

Some have railed at Paul for urging people
to seriously consider the single life, but the
truth is that his words are filled with practical
wisdom. He was not against marriage—in
fact his great contribution to Christian sexual
theology is the way he compares the sexual
union in marriage to the union of Christ and
his Church. But Paul did insist that we count
the cost. You see, no one should enter the
covenant of marriage without realizing the
immense time and energy required to make
that relationship work.

Richard Foster

A P P L I C A T I O N

*W*hat does a person's marital status have
to do with his or her spiritual service? What
is more important than whether a person is
married or single? Pray that you will be true
to God's calling for you.

TUESDAY:

Don't Do Anything to Cause Someone to Sin

1 Corinthians 8:9—9:18

*B*ut be careful that your freedom does not cause those who are weak in faith to fall into sin. You have "knowledge," so you eat in an idol's temple. But someone who is weak in faith might see you eating there and be encouraged to eat meat sacrificed to idols while thinking it is wrong to do so. This weak believer for whom Christ died is ruined because of your "knowledge." When you sin against your brothers and sisters in Christ like this and cause them to do what they feel is wrong, you are also sinning against Christ. So if the food I eat causes them to fall into sin, I will never eat meat again so that I will not cause any of them to sin.

Paul Is like the Other Apostles

I am a free man. I am an apostle. I have seen Jesus our Lord. You people are all an example of my work in the Lord. If others do not accept me as an apostle, surely you do, because you are proof that I am an apostle in the Lord.

This is the answer I give people who want to judge me: Do we not have the right to eat and drink? Do we not have the right to bring a believing wife with us when we travel as do the other apostles and the Lord's brothers and Peter? Are Barnabas and I the only ones who must work to earn our living? No soldier ever serves in the army and pays his own salary. No one ever plants a vineyard without eating some of the grapes. No person takes care of a flock without drinking some of the milk.

I do not say this by human authority; God's law also says the same thing. It is written in the law of Moses: "When an ox is working in the grain, do not cover its mouth to keep it from eating." When God said this, was he thinking only about oxen? No. He was really talking about us. Yes, that Scripture was written for us, because it goes on to say: "The one who plows and the one who works in the grain should hope to get some of the grain for their work." Since we planted spiritual seed among you, is it too much if we should harvest from you some things for this life? If others have the right to get something from you, surely we have this right, too. But we do not use it. No, we put up with everything ourselves so that we will not keep anyone from believing the Good News of Christ. Surely you know that those who work at the Temple get their food from the Temple, and those who serve at the altar get part of what is offered at the altar. In the same way, the Lord has commanded that those who tell the Good News should get their living from this work.

But I have not used any of these rights. And I am not writing this now to get anything from you. I would rather die than to have my reason for bragging taken away. Telling the Good News does not give me any reason for bragging. Telling the Good News is my duty—something I must do. And how terrible it will be for me if I do not tell the Good News. If I preach because it is my own choice, I have a reward. But if I preach and it is not my choice to do so, I am only doing the duty that was given to me. So what reward do I get? This is my reward: that when I tell the Good News I can offer it freely. I do not use my full rights in my work of preaching the Good News.

I made some of your children to be prophets
  and some of your young people to be Nazirites.
People of Israel, isn't this true?" says the LORD.
"But you made the Nazirites drink wine
  and told the prophets not to prophesy.
Now I will make you get stuck,
  as a wagon loaded with grain gets stuck.
No one will escape, not even the fastest runner.

Strong people will not be strong
enough;
warriors will not be able to save
themselves.
Soldiers with bows and arrows will not
stand and fight,
and even fast runners will not get
away;
soldiers on horses will not escape
alive.
At that time even the bravest warriors
will run away without their armor,"
says the LORD.

Amos 2:11–16

*T*he LORD said to Moses, "Tell the Israelites: 'If men or women want to promise to
belong to the LORD in a special way, they will
be called Nazirites. During this time, they
must not drink wine or beer, or vinegar
made from wine or beer. They must not
even drink grape juice or eat grapes or rai-
sins. While they are Nazirites, they must
not eat anything that comes from the
grapevine, even the seeds or the skin.

"'During the time they have promised
to belong to the LORD, they must not cut
their hair. They must be holy until this special time is over. They must let their hair
grow long. During their special time of belonging to the LORD, Nazirites must not go
near a dead body. Even if their own father,
mother, brother, or sister dies, they must
not touch them, or they will become unclean. They must still keep their promise
to belong to God in a special way. While
they are Nazirites, they belong to the LORD
in a special way.'"

Numbers 6:1–8

A priest should teach what he knows, and
people should learn the teachings from him,
because he is the messenger of the LORD
All-Powerful. But you priests have stopped
obeying me. With your teachings you have
caused many people to do wrong. You have
broken the agreement with the tribe of
Levi!" says the LORD All-Powerful. "You have
not been careful to do what I say, but instead
you take sides in court cases. So I have
caused you to be hated and disgraced in
front of everybody."

Malachi 2:7–9

*F*ew would question the assertion that we
should renounce the wrong things in our lives.
It is self-evident that such things mar our
lives, spoil our enjoyment of life, and limit
our usefulness to God and man. But not everyone is equally convinced that in the interest of the gospel the disciple of Christ may need
to renounce some things that are perfectly
right and legitimate. . . .

*Four times in 1 Corinthians 9 Paul as-
serts his rights in the gospel. Three times he
claims that he has refrained from exercising
these rights in the higher interests of spreading
the gospel. He affirms that he is ready to forgo
any right he may have, and forsake any
privilege, out of love for Christ and in the
interests of the progress of the gospel. . . .*

*Oswald Chambers had some trenchant
words to say in this connection: "If we are
willing to give up only wrong things for Jesus,
never let us talk about being in love with Him.
Anyone will give up wrong things if he knows
how, but are we prepared to give up the best
we have for Jesus Christ? The only right a
Christian has is the right to give up his rights.
If we are to be the best for God, there must be
victory in the realm of legitimate desire as
well as in the realm of unlawful indulgence." . . .*

*. . . The disciple must choose his priori-
ties very carefully, even in things that are right
in themselves. If we are aiming at the heights
of Christian experience, there will always
come the challenge to voluntary renunciation
of some rights.*

J. Oswald Sanders

*D*efine Christian freedom in your own
words. What is the objective of Christian
freedom? What legitimate freedoms did Paul
sacrifice for the sake of the Gospel? How much
freedom will you sacrifice for the cause of
Christ?

WEDNESDAY:

Stand Firm Against Temptation

1 Corinthians 9:19—10:22

NEW TESTAMENT READING

I am free and belong to no one. But I make myself a slave to all people to win as many as I can. To the Jews I became like a Jew to win the Jews. I myself am not ruled by the law. But to those who are ruled by the law I became like a person who is ruled by the law. I did this to win those who are ruled by the law. To those who are without the law I became like a person who is without the law. I did this to win those people who are without the law. (But really, I am not without God's law—I am ruled by Christ's law.) To those who are weak, I became weak so I could win the weak. I have become all things to all people so I could save some of them in any way possible. I do all this because of the Good News and so I can share in its blessings.

You know that in a race all the runners run, but only one gets the prize. So run to win! All those who compete in the games use self-control so they can win a crown. That crown is an earthly thing that lasts only a short time, but our crown will never be destroyed. So I do not run without a goal. I fight like a boxer who is hitting something—not just the air. I treat my body hard and make it my slave so that I myself will not be disqualified after I have preached to others.

Warnings from Israel's Past

*B*rothers and sisters, I want you to know what happened to our ancestors who followed Moses. They were all under the cloud and all went through the sea. They were all baptized as followers of Moses in the cloud and in the sea. They all ate the same spiritual food, and all drank the same spiritual drink. They drank from that spiritual rock that followed them, and that rock was Christ. But God was not pleased with most of them, so they died in the desert.

And these things happened as examples for us, to stop us from wanting evil things as those people did. Do not worship idols, as some of them did. Just as it is written in the Scriptures: "They sat down to eat and drink, and then they got up and sinned sexually." We must not take part in sexual sins, as some of them did. In one day twenty-three thousand of them died because of their sins. We must not test Christ as some of them did; they were killed by snakes. Do not complain as some of them did; they were killed by the angel that destroys.

The things that happened to those people are examples. They were written down to teach us, because we live in a time when all these things of the past have reached their goal. If you think you are strong, you should be careful not to fall. The only temptation that has come to you is that which everyone has. But you can trust God, who will not permit you to be tempted more than you can stand. But when you are tempted, he will also give you a way to escape so that you will be able to stand it.

So, my dear friends, run away from the worship of idols. I am speaking to you as to intelligent people; judge for yourselves what I say. We give thanks for the cup of blessing, which is a sharing in the blood of Christ. And the bread that we break is a sharing in the body of Christ. Because there is one loaf of bread, we who are many are one body, because we all share that one loaf.

Think about the Israelites: Do not those who eat the sacrifices share in the altar? I do not mean that the food sacrificed to an idol is important. I do not mean that an idol is anything at all. But I say that what is sacrificed to idols is offered to demons, not to God. And I do not want you to share anything with demons. You cannot drink the cup of the Lord and the cup of demons also. You cannot share in the Lord's table and the table of demons. Are we trying to make the Lord jealous? We are not stronger than he is, are we?

OLD TESTAMENT READING

Eve Is Enticed by Satan

*N*ow the snake was the most clever of all the wild animals the LORD God had made.

414

One day the snake said to the woman, "Did God really say that you must not eat fruit from any tree in the garden?"

The woman answered the snake, "We may eat fruit from the trees in the garden. But God told us, 'You must not eat fruit from the tree that is in the middle of the garden. You must not even touch it, or you will die.'"

But the snake said to the woman, "You will not die. God knows that if you eat the fruit from that tree, you will learn about good and evil and you will be like God!"

The woman saw that the tree was beautiful, that its fruit was good to eat, and that it would make her wise. So she took some of its fruit and ate it. She also gave some of the fruit to her husband, and he ate it.

Genesis 3:1–6

Joseph Runs from Temptation

One day Joseph went into the house to do his work as usual and was the only man in the house at that time. His master's wife grabbed his coat and said to him, "Come and have sexual relations with me." But Joseph left his coat in her hand and ran out of the house.

Genesis 39:11–12

Job Refuses to Sin

Then the LORD said to Satan, "Have you noticed my servant Job? No one else on earth is like him. He is an honest and innocent man, honoring God and staying away from evil. You caused me to ruin him for no good reason, but he continues to be without blame."

"One skin for another!" Satan answered. "A man will give all he has to save his own life. But reach out your hand and destroy his flesh and bones, and he will curse you to your face."

The LORD said to Satan, "All right, then. Job is in your power, but you may not take his life."

So Satan left the LORD's presence. He put painful sores on Job's body, from the top of his head to the soles of his feet. Job took a piece of broken pottery to scrape himself, and he sat in ashes in misery.

Job's wife said to him, "Why are you trying to stay innocent? Curse God and die!"

Job answered, "You are talking like a foolish woman. Should we take only good things from God and not trouble?" In spite of all this Job did not sin in what he said.

Job 2:3–10

I have often heard my husband tell our teenagers, "Temptation is not only an opportunity to do the wrong thing, but an opportunity to do the right!" Although we usually consider temptation in negative terms, God allows us to be tempted in order to provide us with a chance to be obedient. If we are to learn to say no, and we are certainly supposed to say no sometimes to some things, then circumstances become life's workshop to that end. Saying no when you want to say yes strengthens you, produces endurance, and builds character—Christian character.

Jill Briscoe

What did Paul mean when he said he made his body a slave? Why did he do that? What things does the example of the Israelites in the desert warn us against? How seriously did Paul take that warning? How seriously do you take it?

415

THURSDAY:

Everything We Do Should Honor God

1 Corinthians 10:23—11:22

NEW TESTAMENT READING

How to Use Christian Freedom

*W*e are allowed to do all things," but all things are not good for us to do. "We are allowed to do all things," but not all things help others grow stronger. Do not look out only for yourselves. Look out for the good of others also.

Eat any meat that is sold in the meat market. Do not ask questions to see if it is meat you think is wrong to eat. You may eat it, "because the earth belongs to the Lord, and everything in it."

Those who are not believers may invite you to eat with them. If you want to go, eat anything that is put before you. Do not ask questions to see if you think it might be wrong to eat. But if anyone says to you, "That food was offered to idols," do not eat it. Do not eat it because of that person who told you and because eating it might be thought to be wrong. I don't mean you think it is wrong, but the other person might. But why, you ask, should my freedom be judged by someone else's conscience? If I eat the meal with thankfulness, why am I criticized because of something for which I thank God?

The answer is, if you eat or drink, or if you do anything, do it all for the glory of God. Never do anything that might hurt others—Jews, Greeks, or God's church— just as I, also, try to please everybody in every way. I am not trying to do what is good for me but what is good for most people so they can be saved.

Follow my example, as I follow the example of Christ.

Being Under Authority

I praise you because you remember me in everything, and you follow closely the teachings just as I gave them to you. But I want you to understand this: The head of every man is Christ, the head of a woman is the man, and the head of Christ is God. Every man who prays or prophesies with his head covered brings shame to his head. But every woman who prays or prophesies with her head uncovered brings shame to her head. She is the same as a woman who has her head shaved. If a woman does not cover her head, she should have her hair cut off. But since it is shameful for a woman to cut off her hair or to shave her head, she should cover her head. But a man should not cover his head, because he is the likeness and glory of God. But woman is man's glory. Man did not come from woman, but woman came from man. And man was not made for woman, but woman was made for man. So that is why a woman should have a symbol of authority on her head, because of the angels.

But in the Lord women are not independent of men, and men are not independent of women. This is true because woman came from man, but also man is born from woman. But everything comes from God. Decide this for yourselves: Is it right for a woman to pray to God with her head uncovered? Even nature itself teaches you that wearing long hair is shameful for a man. But long hair is a woman's glory. Long hair is given to her as a covering. Some people may still want to argue about this, but I would add that neither we nor the churches of God have any other practice.

The Lord's Supper

*I*n the things I tell you now I do not praise you, because when you come together you do more harm than good. First, I hear that when you meet together as a church you are divided, and I believe some of this. (It is necessary to have differences among you so that it may be clear which of you really have God's approval.) When you come together, you are not really eating the Lord's Supper. This is because when you eat, each person eats without waiting for the others. Some people do not get enough to eat, while others have too much to drink. You can eat and drink in your own homes! You seem to think God's church is not important, and you embarrass those who are poor. What should I tell you? Should I praise you? I do not praise you for doing this.

416

Eli's Sons Refuse to Honor God

Now Eli's sons were evil men; they did not care about the LORD.

The LORD saw that the sin of the servants was very great because they did not show respect for the offerings made to the LORD.

Now Eli was very old. He heard about everything his sons were doing to all the Israelites and how his sons had sexual relations with the women who served at the entrance to the Meeting Tent. Eli said to his sons, "Why do you do these evil things that the people tell me about? No, my sons. The LORD's people are spreading a bad report about you. If you sin against someone, God can help you. But if you sin against the LORD himself, no one can help you!" But Eli's sons would not listen to him, because the LORD had decided to put them to death.

A man of God came to Eli and said, "This is what the LORD says: 'I clearly showed myself to the family of your ancestor Aaron when they were slaves to the king of Egypt. I chose them from all the tribes of Israel to be my priests. I wanted them to go up to my altar, to burn incense, and to wear the holy vest. I also let the family of your ancestor have part of all the offerings sacrificed by the Israelites. So why don't you respect the sacrifices and gifts? You honor your sons more than me. You grow fat on the best parts of the meat the Israelites bring to me.'

"So the LORD, the God of Israel, says: 'I promised that your family and your ancestor's family would serve me always.' But now the LORD says: 'This must stop! I will honor those who honor me, but I will dishonor those who ignore me. The time is coming when I will destroy the descendants of both you and your ancestors. No man will grow old in your family. You will see trouble in my house. No matter what good things happen to Israel, there will never be an old man in your family. I will not totally cut off your family from my altar. But your eyes will cry and your heart be sad, because all your descendants will die.'"

1 Samuel 2:12, 17, 22–25, 27–33

*E*verything created was through Christ and His power, and furthermore, it was created for His honor. That includes everyday things today. You have a good job? It's to be enjoyed for Him. You have a nice salary? It's to be enjoyed and invested for Him. You have good health? It is for Him. You have a family? The family members are for Him. You're planning a move? It's to be for Him. You're thinking about a career change? It needs to be for Him. That is true because He's the ruler of our kingdom. He is Lord. And that's not simply the title of a chorus Christians sing; it's a statement of faith. He has the right to take charge of our decisions so that He might be honored through them. Every day I live I must address that. Again, it is a matter of priorities. . . .

. . . If Christ is going to have top priority, it must be according to the standard of His righteousness. There has to be credibility in what we do or it doesn't fall into the category of seeking His kingdom and His righteousness, does it? Why am I coming on so strong? Because He is to have first place in everything. Those who are really committed to excellence give Him top priority.

Charles Swindoll

*T*hink about Jesus' commandment to love God and to love one another. Notice how Paul's instructions fulfill his command. In what practical ways can you obey Christ's commandments and honor God in your daily life?

FRIDAY:
The Holy Spirit Gives Gifts
1 Corinthians 11:23—12:13

NEW TESTAMENT READING

*T*he teaching I gave you is the same teaching I received from the Lord: On the night when the Lord Jesus was handed over to be killed, he took bread and gave thanks for it. Then he broke the bread and said, "This is my body; it is for you. Do this to remember me." In the same way, after they ate, Jesus took the cup. He said, "This cup is the new agreement that is sealed with the blood of my death. When you drink this, do it to remember me." Every time you eat this bread and drink this cup you are telling others about the Lord's death until he comes.

So a person who eats the bread or drinks the cup of the Lord in a way that is not worthy of it will be guilty of sinning against the body and the blood of the Lord. Look into your own hearts before you eat the bread and drink the cup, because all who eat the bread and drink the cup without recognizing the body eat and drink judgment against themselves. That is why many in your group are sick and weak, and many have died. But if we judged ourselves in the right way, God would not judge us. But when the Lord judges us, he punishes us so that we will not be destroyed along with the world.

So my brothers and sisters, when you come together to eat, wait for each other. Anyone who is too hungry should eat at home so that in meeting together you will not bring God's judgment on yourselves. I will tell you what to do about the other things when I come.

Gifts from the Holy Spirit

*N*ow, brothers and sisters, I want you to understand about spiritual gifts. You know the way you lived before you were believers. You let yourselves be influenced and led away to worship idols—things that could not speak. So I want you to understand that no one who is speaking with the help of God's Spirit says, "Jesus be cursed." And no one can say, "Jesus is Lord," without the help of the Holy Spirit.

There are different kinds of gifts, but they are all from the same Spirit. There are different ways to serve but the same Lord to serve. And there are different ways that God works through people but the same God. God works in all of us in everything we do. Something from the Spirit can be seen in each person, for the common good. The Spirit gives one person the ability to speak with wisdom, and the same Spirit gives another the ability to speak with knowledge. The same Spirit gives faith to one person. And, to another, that one Spirit gives gifts of healing. The Spirit gives to another person the power to do miracles, to another the ability to prophesy. And he gives to another the ability to know the difference between good and evil spirits. The Spirit gives one person the ability to speak in different kinds of languages and to another the ability to interpret those languages. One Spirit, the same Spirit, does all these things, and the Spirit decides what to give each person.

The Body of Christ Works Together

A person's body is only one thing, but it has many parts. Though there are many parts to a body, all those parts make only one body. Christ is like that also. Some of us are Jews, and some are Greeks. Some of us are slaves, and some are free. But we were all baptized into one body through one Spirit. And we were all made to share in the one Spirit.

OLD TESTAMENT READING

Gift of Wisdom and Understanding

A new branch will grow
    from a stump of a tree;
so a new king will come
    from the family of Jesse.
The Spirit of the LORD will rest upon
    that king.

Isaiah 11:1–2a

Gift of Speaking with knowledge

*J*oshua son of Nun was then filled with wisdom, because Moses had put his hands on him. So the Israelites listened to Joshua, and they did what the LORD had commanded Moses.

Deuteronomy 34:9

*T*hese are the last words of David.

This is the message of David son of Jesse.
The man made great by the Most
High God speaks.
He is the appointed king of the God of
Jacob;
he is the sweet singer of Israel:

"The LORD's Spirit spoke through me,
and his word was on my tongue."

2 Samuel 23:1–2

Gift of Miracles

*T*here has never been another prophet in Israel like Moses. The LORD knew Moses face to face and sent him to do signs and miracles in Egypt—to the king, to all his officers, and to the whole land of Egypt. Moses had great power, and he did great and wonderful things for all the Israelites to see.

Deuteronomy 34:10–12

Gift of Prophecy

*S*o Moses went out to the people and told them what the LORD had said. He gathered seventy of the older leaders together and had them stand around the Tent. Then the LORD came down in the cloud and spoke to Moses. The LORD took some of the Spirit Moses had, and he gave it to the seventy leaders. With the Spirit in them, they prophesied, but just that one time.

Numbers 11:24–25

Gift of Creativity

*T*hen the LORD said to Moses, "See, I have chosen Bezalel son of Uri from the tribe of Judah. (Uri was the son of Hur.) I have filled Bezalel with the Spirit of God and have given him the skill, ability, and knowledge to do all kinds of work. He is able to design pieces to be made from gold, silver, and bronze, to cut jewels and put them in metal, to carve wood, and to do all kinds of work. I have also chosen Oholiab son of Ahisamach from the tribe of Dan to work with Bezalel. I have given skills to all the craftsmen, and they will be able to make all these

things I have commanded you: the Meeting Tent, the Ark of the Agreement, the lid that covers the Ark, and everything in the Tent."

Exodus 31:1–7

INSIGHTS

*I*t may take another Christian to pinpoint for us a particular talent we have. For instance, in the course of speaking at a meeting, I started, "I'm a one-talent person." . . . The meeting was scarcely over when a young woman dashed up to me and said, "That's not true what you said tonight. . . . I know about your writing and other things you do, but the best part is that you're good at sitting by the fire and being a friend."

It's evident, then, that we can be using a talent even when we do not recognize that we possess it. . . .

Perhaps we wish we could have had some choice as to which gift or ability would be ours. Maybe we would gladly trade ours off for something that has more appeal for us. But our all-wise God has apportioned His gifts as He wills, and one day He will require from each of us an accounting of our use of those gifts. . . .

If you and I really want to be used by our Lord, it will pay us to ferret out what our particular ability is, then get busy putting it to use.

Jeanette Lockerbie

PAUSE FOR REFLECTION

*H*ow are the gifts that the Spirit gives to different individuals intended to work together (1 Cor. 12:1–13)? What do the Scriptures reveal to you about the purpose of spiritual gifts?

WEEKEND:
The Great Gift of Love
1 Corinthians 12:14—13:13

*T*he human body has many parts. The foot might say, "Because I am not a hand, I am not part of the body." But saying this would not stop the foot from being a part of the body. The ear might say, "Because I am not an eye, I am not part of the body." But saying this would not stop the ear from being a part of the body. If the whole body were an eye, it would not be able to hear. If the whole body were an ear, it would not be able to smell. If each part of the body were the same part, there would be no body. But truly God put all the parts, each one of them, in the body as he wanted them. So then there are many parts, but only one body.

The eye cannot say to the hand, "I don't need you!" And the head cannot say to the foot, "I don't need you!" No! Those parts of the body that seem to be the weaker are really necessary. And the parts of the body we think are less are the parts to which we give the most honor. We give special respect to the parts we want to hide. The more respectable parts of our body need no special care. But God put the body together and gave more honor to the parts that need it so our body would not be divided. God wanted the different parts to care the same for each other. If one part of the body suffers, all the other parts suffer with it. Or if one part of our body is honored, all the other parts share its honor.

Together you are the body of Christ, and each one of you is a part of that body. In the church God has given a place first to apostles, second to prophets, and third to teachers. Then God has given a place to those who do miracles, those who have gifts of healing, those who can help others, those who are able to govern, and those who can speak in different languages. Not all are apostles. Not all are prophets. Not all are teachers. Not all do miracles. Not all have gifts of healing. Not all speak in different languages. Not all interpret those languages. But you should truly want to have the greater gifts.

Love Is the Greatest Gift

*A*nd now I will show you the best way of all.

I may speak in different languages of people or even angels. But if I do not have love, I am only a noisy bell or a crashing cymbal. I may have the gift of prophecy. I may understand all the secret things of God and have all knowledge, and I may have faith so great I can move mountains. But even with all these things, if I do not have love, then I am nothing. I may give away everything I have, and I may even give my body as an offering to be burned. But I gain nothing if I do not have love.

Love is patient and kind. Love is not jealous, it does not brag, and it is not proud. Love is not rude, is not selfish, and does not get upset with others. Love does not count up wrongs that have been done. Love is not happy with evil but is happy with the truth. Love patiently accepts all things. It always trusts, always hopes, and always remains strong.

Love never ends. There are gifts of prophecy, but they will be ended. There are gifts of speaking in different languages, but those gifts will stop. There is the gift of knowledge, but it will come to an end. The reason is that our knowledge and our ability to prophesy are not perfect. But when perfection comes, the things that are not perfect will end. When I was a child, I talked like a child, I thought like a child, I reasoned like a child. When I became a man, I stopped those childish ways. It is the same with us. Now we see a dim reflection, as if we were looking into a mirror, but then we shall see clearly. Now I know only a part, but then I will know fully, as God has known me. So these three things continue forever: faith, hope, and love. And the greatest of these is love.

Boaz Shows Love to Ruth

*A*t mealtime Boaz told Ruth, "Come here. Eat some of our bread and dip it in our sauce."

So Ruth sat down beside the workers. Boaz handed her some roasted grain, and she ate until she was full; she even had some food left over. When Ruth rose and went back to work, Boaz commanded his workers, "Let her gather even around the piles of cut grain. Don't tell her to go away. In fact, drop some full heads of grain for her from what you have in your hands, and let her gather them. Don't tell her to stop."

So Ruth gathered grain in the field until evening. Then she separated the grain from the chaff, and there was about one-half bushel of barley. Ruth carried the grain into town, and her mother-in-law saw how much she had gathered. Ruth also took out the food that was left over from lunch and gave it Naomi.

Naomi asked her, "Where did you gather all this grain today? Where did you work? Blessed be whoever noticed you!"

Ruth told her mother-in-law whose field she had worked in. She said, "The man I worked with today is named Boaz."

Naomi told her daughter-in-law, "The LORD bless him! He continues to be kind to us—both the living and the dead!"

Ruth 2:14–20b

Jonathan Shows Love to David

So David said, "Look, tomorrow is the New Moon festival. I am supposed to eat with the king, but let me hide in the field until the third evening. If your father notices I am gone, tell him, 'David begged me to let him go to his hometown of Bethlehem. Every year at this time his family group offers a sacrifice.' If your father says, 'Fine,' I am safe. But if he becomes angry, you will know that he wants to hurt me. Jonathan, be loyal to me, your servant. You have made an agreement with me before the LORD. If I am guilty, you may kill me yourself! Why hand me over to your father?"

Jonathan answered, "No, never! If I learn that my father plans to hurt you, I will warn you!"

1 Samuel 20:5–9

INSIGHTS

Jesus never wrote a book, yet the nature of his love was indelibly impressed upon the minds of his followers. They could never forget their three years experience with the Master. He was the Model. His very life clearly defined love for them.

- *Jesus was concerned about their families, homes, and health.*
- *Jesus was willing to take time for people in need even though he was engaged in a busy ministry.*
- *Jesus provided faithful support in the spiritual battle by intercessory prayer.*
- *Jesus extended complete forgiveness, even when it seemed undeserved.*
- *Jesus humbly served his followers, exemplified in his washing their feet.*
- *Jesus ultimately gave himself in his death on Calvary's cross.*

In all of these acts of compassion, Jesus modeled a practical brand of love. His was a love that ministered to his disciples' pressing needs. Calvary, of course, tied it all together: The cross dealt finally with their sins and opened the way for them to experience all the blessings of God. . . .

So it is with us. If we are to love our brothers and sisters as Jesus commanded, we must learn to express a practical love for the whole person. It must be the kind of love our Master has shown to us.

William Fletcher

APPLICATION

What examples of Christian love that you have experienced stand out in your mind? What did those experiences teach you about love? What example of Jesus' love do you want to put into practice in your life?

MONDAY:

Desire Spiritual Gifts that Strengthen the Church

1 Corinthians 14:1–25

Desire Spiritual Gifts

*Y*ou should seek after love, and you should truly want to have the spiritual gifts, especially the gift of prophecy. I will explain why. Those who have the gift of speaking in different languages are not speaking to people; they are speaking to God. No one understands them; they are speaking secret things through the Spirit. But those who prophesy are speaking to people to give them strength, encouragement, and comfort. The ones who speak in different languages are helping only themselves, but those who prophesy are helping the whole church. I wish all of you had the gift of speaking in different kinds of languages, but more, I wish you would prophesy. Those who prophesy are greater than those who can only speak in different languages—unless someone is there who can explain what is said so that the whole church can be helped.

Brothers and sisters, will it help you if I come to you speaking in different languages? No! It will help you only if I bring you a new truth or some new knowledge, or prophecy, or teaching. It is the same as with lifeless things that make sounds—like a flute or a harp. If they do not make clear musical notes, you will not know what is being played. And in a war, if the trumpet does not give a clear sound, who will prepare for battle? It is the same with you. Unless you speak clearly with your tongue, no one can understand what you are saying. You will be talking into the air! It may be true that there are all kinds of sounds in the world, and none is without meaning. But unless I understand the meaning of what someone says to me, I will be a foreigner to him, and he will be a foreigner to me. It is the same with you. Since you want spiritual gifts very much, seek most of all to have the gifts that help the church grow stronger.

The one who has the gift of speaking in a different language should pray for the gift to interpret what is spoken. If I pray in a different language, my spirit is praying, but my mind does nothing. So what should I do? I will pray with my spirit, but I will also pray with my mind. I will sing with my spirit, but I will also sing with my mind. If you praise God with your spirit, those persons there without understanding cannot say amen to your prayer of thanks, because they do not know what you are saying. You may be thanking God in a good way, but the other person is not helped.

I thank God that I speak in different kinds of languages more than all of you. But in the church meetings I would rather speak five words I understand in order to teach others than thousands of words in a different language.

Brothers and sisters, do not think like children. In evil things be like babies, but in your thinking you should be like adults. It is written in the Scriptures:

> "With people who use strange words
> and foreign languages
> I will speak to these people.
> But even then they will not listen to
> me,"   *Isaiah 28:11–12*

says the Lord.

So the gift of speaking in different kinds of languages is a proof for those who do not believe, not for those who do believe. And prophecy is for people who believe, not for those who do not believe. Suppose the whole church meets together and everyone speaks in different languages. If some people come in who do not understand or do not believe, they will say you are crazy. But suppose everyone is prophesying and some people come in who do not believe or do not understand. If everyone is prophesying, their sin will be shown to them, and they will be judged by all that they hear. The secret things in their hearts will be made known. So they will bow down and worship God saying, "Truly, God is with you."

*T*he LORD commanded a man of God from Judah to go to Bethel. When he arrived,

Jeroboam was standing by the altar to offer a sacrifice. The LORD had commanded the man of God to speak against the altar. The man said, "Altar, altar, the LORD says to you: 'David's family will have a son named Josiah. The priests for the places of worship now make their sacrifices on you, but Josiah will sacrifice those priests on you. Human bones will be burned on you.'" That same day the man of God gave proof that these things would happen. "This is the LORD's sign that this will happen," he said. "This altar will break apart, and the ashes on it will fall to the ground."

1 Kings 13:1–3

*K*ing Josiah ruined the places where gods were worshiped east of Jerusalem, south of the Mount of Olives. Solomon king of Israel had built these places. One was for Ashtoreth, the hated goddess of the Sidonians. One was for Chemosh, the hated god of Moab. And one was for Molech, the hated god of the Ammonites. Josiah smashed to pieces the stone pillars they worshiped, and he cut down the Asherah idols. Then he covered the places with human bones.

Josiah also broke down the altar at Bethel—the place of worship made by Jeroboam son of Nebat, who had led Israel to sin. Josiah burned that place, broke the stones of the altar into pieces, then beat them into dust. He also burned the Asherah idol. When he turned around, he saw the graves on the mountain. He had the bones taken from the graves, and he burned them on the altar to ruin it. This happened as the LORD had said it would through the man of God.

2 Kings 23:13–16

*T*hen Joshua made this oath:
"Anyone who tries to rebuild this city of Jericho
  will be cursed by the LORD.
The one who lays the foundation of this city
  will lose his oldest son,
and the one who sets up the gates
  will lose his youngest son."

So the LORD was with Joshua, and Joshua became famous through all the land.

Joshua 6:26–27

*D*uring the time of Ahab, Hiel from Bethel rebuilt the city of Jericho. It cost Hiel the life of Abiram, his oldest son, to begin work on the city, and it cost the life of Segub, his youngest son, to build the city gates. This happened just as the LORD, speaking through Joshua son of Nun, said it would happen.

1 Kings 16:34

INSIGHTS

*T*he gifts of the Spirit . . . come to us from the Holy Spirit. He chooses who gets which gifts, and He dispenses them at His good pleasure. While we are held accountable for the use of any gifts He gives us, we have no responsibility for gifts we have not been given. Nor are we to covet what someone else has or be envious of that person. We may wish to have certain gifts and even ask for them, but if it is not the will of the Holy Spirit, we will not get what we ask for. And if we are dissatisfied because the Holy Spirit does not give us the gifts we want, we sin. . . .

Paul says that the purpose of these spiritual gifts is, "for the equipping of the saints for the work of service, to the building up of the body of Christ" (Eph. 4:12). In other words, God has given each of us a task to do, and supernatural gifts to equip us for it. . . .

In 1 Corinthians 12:7, the apostle Paul says the gifts are given "for the common good" so we are not to use them selfishly. Instead, we are to use them to help each other. . . .

God has also designed the gifts to help "unite" the body of Christ. . . .

Thus the gifts of the Spirit should never divide the body of Christ; they should unify it.

Billy Graham

APPLICATION

*W*hat is the purpose of spiritual gifts? What is the difference between prophesying and speaking in tongues? Why do you desire spiritual gifts? Pray that you will use your gift to God's glory.

TUESDAY:

The Essentials of Christian Faith

1 Corinthians 14:26—15:11

Meetings Should Help the Church

So, brothers and sisters, what should you do? When you meet together, one person has a song, and another has a teaching. Another has a new truth from God. Another speaks in a different language, and another person interprets that language. The purpose of all these things should be to help the church grow strong. When you meet together, if anyone speaks in a different language, it should be only two, or not more than three, who speak. They should speak one after the other, and someone else should interpret. But if there is no interpreter, then those who speak in a different language should be quiet in the church meeting. They should speak only to themselves and to God.

Only two or three prophets should speak, and the others should judge what they say. If a message from God comes to another person who is sitting, the first speaker should stop. You can all prophesy one after the other. In this way all the people can be taught and encouraged. The spirits of prophets are under the control of the prophets themselves. God is not a God of confusion but a God of peace.

As is true in all the churches of God's people, women should keep quiet in the church meetings. They are not allowed to speak, but they must yield to this rule as the law says. If they want to learn something, they should ask their own husbands at home. It is shameful for a woman to speak in the church meeting. Did God's teaching come from you? Or are you the only ones to whom it has come?

Those who think they are prophets or spiritual persons should understand that what I am writing to you is the Lord's command. Those who ignore this will be ignored by God.

So my brothers and sisters, you should truly want to prophesy. But do not stop people from using the gift of speaking in different kinds of languages. But let everything be done in a right and orderly way.

The Good News About Christ

Now, brothers and sisters, I want you to remember the Good News I brought to you. You received this Good News and continue strong in it. And you are being saved by it if you continue believing what I told you. If you do not, then you believed for nothing.

I passed on to you what I received, of which this was most important: that Christ died for our sins, as the Scriptures say; that he was buried and was raised to life on the third day as the Scriptures say; and that he was seen by Peter and then by the twelve apostles. After that, Jesus was seen by more than five hundred of the believers at the same time. Most of them are still living today, but some have died. Then he was seen by James and later by all the apostles. Last of all he was seen by me—as by a person not born at the normal time. All the other apostles are greater than I am. I am not even good enough to be called an apostle, because I persecuted the church of God. But God's grace has made me what I am, and his grace to me was not wasted. I worked harder than all the other apostles. (But it was not I really; it was God's grace that was with me.) So if I preached to you or the other apostles preached to you, we all preach the same thing, and this is what you believed.

Christ Died for Our Sins

But he took our suffering on him
  and felt our pain for us.
We saw his suffering
  and thought God was punishing him.
But he was wounded for the wrong we
    did;
  he was crushed for the evil we did.
The punishment, which made us well,
    was given to him,
  and we are healed because of his
    wounds.

We all have wandered away like sheep;
  each of us has gone his own way.
But the LORD has put on him the
    punishment
  for all the evil we have done.

He was beaten down and punished,
  but he didn't say a word.
He was like a lamb being led to be killed.
  He was quiet, as a sheep is quiet
    while its wool is being cut;
  he never opened his mouth.
Men took him away roughly and
    unfairly.
  He died without children to continue
    his family.
He was put to death;
  he was punished for the sins of my
    people.
He was buried with wicked men,
  and he died with the rich.
He had done nothing wrong,
  and he had never lied.

But it was the LORD who decided
  to crush him and make him suffer.
The LORD made his life a penalty
    offering,
but he will still see his descendants and
    live a long life.
  He will complete the things the LORD
    wants him to do.

Isaiah 53:4–10

Christ Rose Again

*G*od has risen with a shout of joy;
  the LORD has risen as the trumpets
    sounded.
Sing praises to God. Sing praises.
  Sing praises to our King. Sing
    praises.
God is King of all the earth,
  so sing a song of praise to him.
God is King over the nations.
  God sits on his holy throne.

Psalm 47:5–8

*I*n the guise of a man, Jesus the Christ, was
born, lived, grew up, worked, was crucified,
and rose from the grave among us, He ascended back to His splendor among us.

*In all of this, though subject to the strains
and stresses of our human society, he never
sinned. His was a perfect performance. His
was a life without a single stain. His was the
"perfect doing" and "perfect dying" required
to redeem all men for all time from all their
wrongs and sins and stains. . . .*

*It was in my stead He did all this: He paid
the penalty for all my wrongs. He bled and
suffered and died for me. He took my sins to
set me free. It was to satisfy His own righteousness that He became my substitute. He
did this to impute to me His own wondrous
righteousness.*

*This is a titanic transaction of eternal di-
mensions. God, very God, in Christ takes my
sins and gives me His goodness . . . His own
righteousness.*

*Nothing else can satisfy my searching
spirit. I look away from myself to see the
splendor of His supreme self-sacrifice for my
salvation. I see that He has made me whole.
He has enfolded and filled me with His righteousness. He has accepted me as His own
son. He is my living Lord and Savior. He is
my Father!*

*My spirit leaps for joy, where before it was
sunk with sin and despair. His Spirit bears
witness with my spirit that I am now His son.
In overwhelming appreciation and gratitude,
I look up and my spirit cries, "Abba Father!"*

W. Phillip Keller

*W*hat are the essential elements of the
Christian faith? How fully was the Good News
foretold in the Old Testament? Why must we
continue believing the Good News? Pray that
your faith will continue strong!

425

WEDNESDAY:

God's People Will Be Raised to Life Again

1 Corinthians 15:12–44a

NEW TESTAMENT READING

We Will Be Raised from the Dead

*N*ow since we preached that Christ was raised from the dead, why do some of you say that people will not be raised from the dead? If no one is ever raised from the dead, then Christ has not been raised. And if Christ has not been raised, then our preaching is worth nothing, and your faith is worth nothing. And also, we are guilty of lying about God, because we testified of him that he raised Christ from the dead. But if people are not raised from the dead, then God never raised Christ. If the dead are not raised, Christ has not been raised either. And if Christ has not been raised, then your faith has nothing to it; you are still guilty of your sins. And those in Christ who have already died are lost. If our hope in Christ is for this life only, we should be pitied more than anyone else in the world.

But Christ has truly been raised from the dead—the first one and proof that those who sleep in death will also be raised. Death has come because of what one man did, but the rising from death also comes because of one man. In Adam all of us die. In the same way, in Christ all of us will be made alive again. But everyone will be raised to life in the right order. Christ was first to be raised. When Christ comes again, those who belong to him will be raised to life, and then the end will come. At that time Christ will destroy all rulers, authorities, and powers, and he will hand over the kingdom to God the Father. Christ must rule until he puts all enemies under his control. The last enemy to be destroyed will be death. The Scripture says that God put all things under his control. When it says "all things" are under him, it is clear this does not include God himself. God is the One who put everything under his control. After everything has been put under the Son, then he will put himself under God, who had put all things under him. Then God will be the complete ruler over everything.

If the dead are never raised, what will people do who are being baptized for the dead? If the dead are not raised at all, why are people being baptized for them?

And what about us? Why do we put ourselves in danger every hour? I die every day. That is true, brothers and sisters, just as it is true that I brag about you in Christ Jesus our Lord. If I fought wild animals in Ephesus only with human hopes, I have gained nothing. If the dead are not raised, "Let us eat and drink, because tomorrow we will die."

Do not be fooled: "Bad friends will ruin good habits." Come back to your right way of thinking and stop sinning. Some of you do not know God—I say this to shame you.

What Kind of Body Will We Have?

*B*ut someone may ask, "How are the dead raised? What kind of body will they have?" Foolish person! When you sow a seed, it must die in the ground before it can live and grow. And when you sow it, it does not have the same "body" it will have later. What you sow is only a bare seed, maybe wheat or something else. But God gives it a body that he has planned for it, and God gives each kind of seed its own body. All things made of flesh are not the same: People have one kind of flesh, animals have another, birds have another, and fish have another. Also there are heavenly bodies and earthly bodies. But the beauty of the heavenly bodies is one kind, and the beauty of the earthly bodies is another. The sun has one kind of beauty, the moon has another beauty, and the stars have another. And each star is different in its beauty.

It is the same with the dead who are raised to life. The body that is "planted" will ruin and decay, but it is raised to a life that cannot be destroyed. When the body is "planted," it is without honor, but it is raised in glory. When the body is "planted," it is weak, but when it is raised, it is powerful. The body that is "planted" is a physical body. When it is raised, it is a spiritual body.

426

*T*he LORD All-Powerful will prepare a
feast
on this mountain for all people.
It will be a feast with all the best food
and wine,
the finest meat and wine.
On this mountain God will destroy
the veil that covers all nations,
the veil that stretches over all peoples;
he will destroy death forever.

Isaiah 25:6–8a

*A*t that time Michael, the great prince who protects your people, will stand up. There will be a time of much trouble, the worst time since nations have been on earth, but your people will be saved. Everyone whose name is written in God's book will be saved. Many people who have already died will live again. Some of them will wake up to have life forever, but some will wake up to find shame and disgrace forever. The wise people will shine like the brightness of the sky. Those who teach others to live right will shine like stars forever and ever."

Daniel 12:1–3

*T*his is what will happen those who
trust in themselves
and to their followers who believe
them.   *Selah*
Like sheep, they must die,
and death will be their shepherd.
Honest people will rule over them in
the morning,
and their bodies will rot in a grave
far from home.
But God will save my life
and will take me from the grave.   *Selah*

Psalm 49:13–15

*T*hen he said to me, "Human, these bones are like all the people of Israel. They say, 'Our bones are dried up, and our hope has gone. We are destroyed.' So, prophesy and say to them, 'This is what the Lord GOD says: My people, I will open your graves and cause you to come up out of your graves. Then I will bring you into the land of Israel. My people, you will know that I am the LORD when I open your graves and cause you to come up from them. And I will put my Spirit inside you, and you will come to life. Then I will put you in your own land. And you will know that I, the LORD, have spoken and done it, says the LORD.'"

Ezekiel 37:11–14

*O*ften *when we are racked with pain and unable to think or worship, we feel that this indeed is "the body of our humiliation," and when we are tempted by the passions which rise from the flesh we do not think the word vile at all too vigorous a translation. Our bodies humble us; and that is about the best thing they do for us. Oh, that we were duly lowly, because our bodies ally us with animals and even link us with the dust!*

But our Savior, the Lord Jesus, shall change all this. We shall be fashioned like His own body of glory. This will take place in all who believe in Jesus. By faith their souls have been transformed, and their bodies will undergo such a renewal as shall fit them for their regenerated spirits. How soon this grand transformation will happen we cannot tell; but the thought of it should help us to bear the trials of today and all the woes of the flesh. In a little while we shall be as Jesus now is. No more aching brows, no more swollen limbs, no more dim eyes, no more fainting hearts. The old man shall be no more a bundle of infirmities, nor the sick man a mass of agony. "Like unto his glorious body [Phil 3:21]." What an expression! Even our flesh shall rest in hope of such a resurrection!

Charles Spurgeon

*W*hat *is the significance and what are the results of Christ's resurrection? What will all those who rise up in Christ be given? What about the resurrection gives you the greatest hope?*

THURSDAY:

Be Prepared for Opposition as You Serve God

1 Corinthians 15:44b—16:24

*T*here is a physical body, and there is also a spiritual body. It is written in the Scriptures: "The first man, Adam, became a living person." But the last Adam became a spirit that gives life. The spiritual did not come first, but the physical and then the spiritual. The first man came from the dust of the earth. The second man came from heaven. People who belong to the earth are like the first man of earth. But those people who belong to heaven are like the man of heaven. Just as we were made like the man of earth, so we will also be made like the man of heaven.

I tell you this, brothers and sisters: Flesh and blood cannot have a part in the kingdom of God. Something that will ruin cannot have a part in something that never ruins. But look! I tell you this secret: We will not all sleep in death, but we will all be changed. It will take only a second—as quickly as an eye blinks—when the last trumpet sounds. The trumpet will sound, and those who have died will be raised to live forever, and we will all be changed. This body that can be destroyed must clothe itself with something that can never be destroyed. And this body that dies must clothe itself with something that can never die. So this body that can be destroyed will clothe itself with that which can never be destroyed, and this body that dies will clothe itself with that which can never die. When this happens, this Scripture will be made true:

"Death is destroyed forever in victory."

Isaiah 25:8

"Death, where is your victory?
  Death, where is your pain?"

Hosea 13:14

Death's power to hurt is sin, and the power of sin is the law. But we thank God! He gives us the victory through our Lord Jesus Christ.

So my dear brothers and sisters, stand strong. Do not let anything change you. Always give yourselves fully to the work of the Lord, because you know that your work in the Lord is never wasted.

The Gift for Other Believers

*N*ow I will write about the collection of money for God's people. Do the same thing I told the Galatian churches to do: On the first day of every week, each one of you should put aside money as you have been blessed. Save it up so you will not have to collect money after I come. When I arrive, I will send whomever you approve to take your gift to Jerusalem. I will send them with letters of introduction, and if it seems good for me to go also, they will go along with me.

Paul's Plans

I plan to go through Macedonia, so I will come to you after I go through there. Perhaps I will stay with you for a time or even all winter. Then you can help me on my trip, wherever I go. I do not want to see you now just in passing. I hope to stay a longer time with you if the Lord allows it. But I will stay at Ephesus until Pentecost, because a good opportunity for a great and growing work has been given to me now. And there are many people working against me.

If Timothy comes to you, see to it that he has nothing to fear with you, because he is working for the Lord just as I am. So none of you should treat Timothy as unimportant, but help him on his trip in peace so that he can come back to me. I am expecting him to come with the brothers.

Now about our brother Apollos: I strongly encouraged him to visit you with the other brothers. He did not at all want to come now; he will come when he has the opportunity.

Paul Ends His Letter

*B*e alert. Continue strong in the faith. Have courage, and be strong. Do everything in love.

You know that the family of Stephanas were the first believers in Southern Greece and that they have given themselves to the service of God's people. I ask you, brothers and sisters, to follow the leading of people like these and anyone else who works and serves with them.

I am happy that Stephanas, Fortunatus, and Achaicus have come. You are not here, but they have filled your place. They have refreshed my spirit and yours. You should recognize the value of people like these.

The churches in the country of Asia send greetings to you. Aquila and Priscilla greet you in the Lord, as does the church that meets in their house. All the brothers and sisters here send greetings. Give each other a holy kiss when you meet.

I, Paul, am writing this greeting with my own hand.

If anyone does not love the Lord, let him be separated from God—lost forever!

Come, O Lord!

The grace of the Lord Jesus be with you. My love be with all of you in Christ Jesus.

OLD TESTAMENT READING

*W*hen the enemies of the people of Judah and Benjamin heard that the returned captives were building a Temple for the LORD, the God of Israel, they came to Zerubbabel and the leaders of the families. The enemies said, "Let us help you build, because we are like you and want to worship your God. We have been offering sacrifices to him since the time of Esarhaddon king of Assyria, who brought us here."

But Zerubbabel, Jeshua, and the leaders of Israel answered, "You will not help us build a Temple to our God. We will build it ourselves for the LORD, the God of Israel, as King Cyrus, the king of Persia, commanded us to do."

Then the people around them tried to discourage the people of Judah by making them afraid to build. Their enemies hired others to delay the building plans during the time Cyrus was king of Persia. And it continued to the time Darius was king of Persia.

Ezra 4:1–5

*T*hen the people said, "Come, let's make plans against Jeremiah. Surely the teaching of the law by the priest will not be lost. We will still have the advice from the wise men and the words of the prophets. So let's ruin him by telling lies about him. We won't pay attention to anything he says."

Jeremiah 18:18

*L*ORD, battle with those who battle with me.
Fight against those who fight against me.
For no reason they spread out their net to trap me;
for no reason they dug a pit for me.
So let ruin strike them suddenly.
Let them be caught in their own nets;
let them fall into the pit and die.

Psalm 35:1, 7–8

INSIGHTS

*F*or many years as a struggling young Christian I was led to believe that if I was just good enough, and kind enough, and loving enough, the whole of the world would be bound to hug me to its heart. Unfortunately and unhappily one learns in time that simply is not so. It is one of the sobering shocks that comes to us as mature Christians.

If God, very God, who was all perfection, suffered such abuse at the hands of His adversaries when He was here among us as the Man Christ Jesus, how can we expect less? . . .

Any man, any woman, who will determine to live righteously for Christ's sake will suffer persecution (2 Tim. 3:12). And in passing it must be said here that the attacks made upon him may not always necessarily come just from the unrighteous. . . .

If in truth persecution does come to me because of my righteous character and commendable, Christlike conduct, it is proof positive that I am indeed God's person.

W. Phillip Keller

APPLICATION

*W*hy did Paul plan to stay in Ephesus? What was taking place that he was so excited about? Do you gain or lose enthusiasm for the Lord's work when you face opposition?

FRIDAY:

When Troubles Come, Trust in the God Who Comforts Us

2 Corinthians 1:1–17

Paul Answers His Accusers

*F*rom Paul, an apostle of Christ Jesus. I am an apostle because that is what God wanted. Also from Timothy our brother in Christ.

To the church of God in Corinth, and to all of God's people everywhere in Southern Greece:

Grace and peace to you from God our Father and the Lord Jesus Christ.

Paul Gives Thanks to God

*P*raise be to the God and Father of our Lord Jesus Christ. God is the Father who is full of mercy and all comfort. He comforts us every time we have trouble, so when others have trouble, we can comfort them with the same comfort God gives us. We share in the many sufferings of Christ. In the same way, much comfort comes to us through Christ. If we have troubles, it is for your comfort and salvation, and if we have comfort, you also have comfort. This helps you to accept patiently the same sufferings we have. Our hope for you is strong, knowing that you share in our sufferings and also in the comfort we receive.

Brothers and sisters, we want you to know about the trouble we suffered in Asia. We had great burdens there that were beyond our own strength. We even gave up hope of living. Truly, in our own hearts we believed we would die. But this happened so we would not trust in ourselves but in God, who raises people from the dead. God saved us from these great dangers of death, and he will continue to save us. We have put our hope in him, and he will save us again. And you can help us with your prayers. Then many people will give thanks for us—that God blessed us because of their many prayers.

The Change in Paul's Plans

*T*his is what we are proud of, and I can say it with a clear conscience: In everything we have done in the world, and especially with you, we have had an honest and sincere heart from God. We did this by God's grace, not by the kind of wisdom the world has. We write to you only what you can read and understand. And I hope that as you have understood some things about us, you may come to know everything about us. Then you can be proud of us, as we will be proud of you on the day our Lord Jesus Christ comes again.

I was so sure of all this that I made plans to visit you first so you could be blessed twice. I planned to visit you on my way to Macedonia and again on my way back. I wanted to get help from you for my trip to Judea. Do you think that I made these plans without really meaning it? Or maybe you think I make plans as the world does, so that I say yes, yes and at the same time no, no.

*G*od, be merciful to me because
    people are chasing me;
    the battle has pressed me all day
      long.
My enemies have chased me all
    day;
    there are many proud people
      fighting me.
When I am afraid,
    I will trust you.
I praise God for his word.
    I trust God, so I am not afraid.
    What can human beings do to me?
        Psalm 56:1–4

*L*ord, your love fills the earth.
    Teach me your demands.

You have done good things for your
    servant,
    as you have promised, Lord.
Teach me wisdom and knowledge
    because I trust your commands.
Before I suffered, I did wrong,
    but now I obey your word.

You are good, and you do what is good.
　　Teach me your demands.
Proud people have made up lies about
　　me,
　　but I will follow your orders with all
　　my heart.
Those people have no feelings,
　　but I love your teachings.
It was good for me to suffer
　　so I would learn your demands.
Your teachings are worth more to me
　　than thousands of pieces of gold and
　　silver.
You made me and formed me with your
　　hands.
　　Give me understanding so I can
　　learn your commands.
Let those who respect you rejoice when
　　they see me,
　　because I put my hope in your word.
LORD, I know that your laws are right
　　and that it was right for you to
　　punish me.
Comfort me with your love,
　　as you promised me, your servant.
Have mercy on me so that I may live.
　　I love your teachings.
Make proud people ashamed because
　　they lied about me.
　　But I will think about your orders.
Let those who respect you return to me,
　　those who know your rules.
Let me obey your demands perfectly
　　so I will not be ashamed.

Psalm 119:64–80

INSIGHTS

It has been well said that "earthly cares are a heavenly discipline." But they are even something better than discipline,—they are God's chariots, sent to take the soul to its high places of triumph. . . .

Everything that comes to us becomes a chariot the moment we treat it as such; and on the other hand, even the smallest trials may be a Juggernaut car to crush us into misery or despair if we so consider them. It lies with each of us to choose which they shall be. . . .

Look upon your chastenings then, no matter how grievous they may be for the

present, as God's chariots sent to carry your souls into the "high places" of spiritual achievement and uplifting, and you will find that they are, after all, "paved with love."

The Bible tells us that when God went forth for the salvation of His people, then He "did ride upon His horses and chariots of salvation." And it is the same now. Everything becomes a "chariot of salvation" when God rides upon it. He maketh even the "clouds his chariot," we are told, and "rideth on the wings of the wind." Therefore the clouds and storms that darken our skies and seem to shut out the shining of the sun of righteousness are really only God's chariots, into which we may mount with Him, and "ride prosperously" over all the darkness.

Hannah Whitall Smith

ACTION POINT

How well acquainted are you with the God Paul describes in 2 Corinthians 1:3? The next time you are ready to give up hope, why not trust the God of comfort to turn your troubles into triumphs of his making?

WEEKEND:

The Healing Power of Forgiveness

2 Corinthians 1:18—3:3

*B*ut if you can believe God, you can believe that what we tell you is never both yes and no. The Son of God, Jesus Christ, that Silas and Timothy and I preached to you, was not yes and no. In Christ it has always been yes. The yes to all of God's promises is in Christ, and through Christ we say yes to the glory of God. Remember, God is the One who makes you and us strong in Christ. God made us his chosen people. He put his mark on us to show that we are his, and he put his Spirit in our hearts to be a guarantee for all he has promised.

I tell you this, and I ask God to be my witness that this is true: The reason I did not come back to Corinth was to keep you from being punished or hurt. We are not trying to control your faith. You are strong in faith. But we are workers with you for your own joy.

So I decided that my next visit to you would not be another one to make you sad. If I make you sad, who will make me glad? Only you can make me glad—particularly the person whom I made sad. I wrote you a letter for this reason: that when I came to you I would not be made sad by the people who should make me happy. I felt sure of all of you, that you would share my joy. When I wrote to you before, I was very troubled and unhappy in my heart, and I wrote with many tears. I did not write to make you sad, but to let you know how much I love you.

Forgive the Sinner

*S*omeone there among you has caused sadness, not to me, but to all of you. I mean he caused sadness to all in some way. (I do not want to make it sound worse than it really is.) The punishment that most of you gave him is enough for him. But now you should forgive him and comfort him to keep him from having too much sadness and giving up completely. So I beg you to show that you love him. I wrote you to test you and to see if you obey in everything. If you forgive someone, I also forgive him. And what I have forgiven—if I had anything to forgive—I forgave it for you, as if Christ were with me. I did this so that Satan would not win anything from us, because we know very well what Satan's plans are.

Paul's Concern in Troas

*W*hen I came to Troas to preach the Good News of Christ, the Lord gave me a good opportunity there. But I had no peace, because I did not find my brother Titus. So I said good-bye to them at Troas and went to Macedonia.

Victory Through Christ

*B*ut thanks be to God, who always leads us in victory through Christ. God uses us to spread his knowledge everywhere like a sweet-smelling perfume. Our offering to God is this: We are the sweet smell of Christ among those who are being saved and among those who are being lost. To those who are lost, we are the smell of death that brings death, but to those who are being saved, we are the smell of life that brings life. So who is able to do this work? We do not sell the word of God for a profit as many other people do. But in Christ we speak the truth before God, as messengers of God.

Servants of the New Agreement

*A*re we starting to brag about ourselves again? Do we need letters of introduction to you or from you, like some other people? You yourselves are our letter, written on our hearts, known and read by everyone. You show that you are a letter from Christ sent through us. This letter is not written with ink but with the Spirit of the living God. It is not written on stone tablets but on human hearts.

*A*fter Jacob died, Joseph's brothers said, "What if Joseph is still angry with us? We did many wrong things to him. What if he plans to pay us back?" So they sent a message to Joseph that said, "Your father gave this command before he died. He said to us, 'You have done wrong and have sinned and done evil to Joseph. Tell Joseph to forgive you, his brothers.' So now, Joseph, we beg you to forgive our wrong. We are the servants of the God of your father." When Joseph received the message, he cried.

And his brothers went to him and bowed low before him and said, "We are your slaves."

Then Joseph said to them, "Don't be afraid. Can I do what only God can do? You meant to hurt me, but God turned your evil into good to save the lives of many people, which is being done. So don't be afraid. I will take care of you and your children." So Joseph comforted his brothers and spoke kind words to them.

Genesis 50:15–21

*H*appy is the person
　whose sins are forgiven,
　whose wrongs are pardoned.
Happy is the person
　whom the LORD does not consider
　　guilty
　and in whom there is nothing false.

When I kept things to myself,
　I felt weak deep inside me.
　I moaned all day long.
Day and night you punished me.
　My strength was gone as in the
　　summer heat.　　　　　　*Selah*
Then I confessed my sins to you
　and didn't hide my guilt.
I said, "I will confess my sins to the
　LORD,"
and you forgave my guilt.　　*Selah*

For this reason, all who obey you
　should pray to you while they still
　　can.

Psalm 32:1–6a

*T*he messengers returned to Jacob and said, "We went to your brother Esau. He is coming to meet you and has four hundred men with him."

Then Jacob was very afraid and worried. He divided the people who were with him and all the flocks, herds, and camels into two camps. Jacob thought, "Esau might come and destroy one camp, but the other camp can run away and be saved."

Then Jacob said, "God of my father Abraham! God of my father Isaac! LORD, you told me to return to my country and my family. You said that you would treat me well. I am not worthy of the kindness and continual goodness you have shown me. The first time I traveled across the Jordan River, I had only my walking stick, but now I own enough to have two camps."

Genesis 32:6–10

INSIGHTS

*F*orgiveness of sins is a great all-embracing gift of God. In His mercy, God sets the sinner free and receives him back into His love and favor. When we are forgiven, we have confidence toward God in prayer. We can be thankful every day of our lives because we are free and nothing stands between us and God. With the door open to communion with Him, God desires that we spend time with Him in His Word each day as people whose sins are forgiven. We need to live in the light of His countenance daily.

And God desires that this assurance affect our relationship with others. Those who are forgiven are free to forgive others. If it is difficult to forgive, we should consider how freely God has forgiven us of every offense toward Him. . . .

Remember these words daily: "As I need God's forgiveness each day, so let me be ready each day to forgive my brother." God grant you grace to do it!

Andrew Murray

APPLICATION

*W*hat healing has God's forgiveness accomplished in your life? What are the consequences when God's people don't forgive one another? Who do you need to forgive? Pray that you will always follow God's merciful example in forgiving others.

MONDAY:

God's Spirit Brings Glory and Understanding to Those Who Believe

2 Corinthians 3:4—4:15

N E W   T E S T A M E N T   R E A D I N G

*W*e can say this, because through Christ we feel certain before God. We are not saying that we can do this work ourselves. It is God who makes us able to do all that we do. He made us able to be servants of a new agreement from himself to his people. This new agreement is not a written law, but it is of the Spirit. The written law brings death, but the Spirit gives life.

The law that brought death was written in words on stone. It came with God's glory, which made Moses' face so bright that the Israelites could not continue to look at it. But that glory later disappeared. So surely the new way that brings the Spirit has even more glory. If the law that judged people guilty of sin had glory, surely the new way that makes people right with God has much greater glory. That old law had glory, but it really loses its glory when it is compared to the much greater glory of this new way. If that law which disappeared came with glory, then this new way which continues forever has much greater glory.

We have this hope, so we are very bold. We are not like Moses, who put a covering over his face so the Israelites would not see it. The glory was disappearing, and Moses did not want them to see it end. But their minds were closed, and even today that same covering hides the meaning when they read the old agreement. That covering is taken away only through Christ. Even today, when they read the law of Moses, there is a covering over their minds. But when a person changes and follows the Lord, that covering is taken away. The Lord is the Spirit, and where the Spirit of the Lord is, there is freedom. Our faces, then, are not covered. We all show the Lord's glory, and we are being changed to be like him. This change in us brings ever greater glory, which comes from the Lord, who is the Spirit.

Preaching the Good News

*G*od, with his mercy, gave us this work to do, so we don't give up. But we have turned away from secret and shameful ways. We use no trickery, and we do not change the teaching of God. We teach the truth plainly, showing everyone who we are. Then they can know in their hearts what kind of people we are in God's sight. If the Good News that we preach is hidden, it is hidden only to those who are lost. The devil who rules this world has blinded the minds of those who do not believe. They cannot see the light of the Good News—the Good News about the glory of Christ, who is exactly like God. We do not preach about ourselves, but we preach that Jesus Christ is Lord and that we are your servants for Jesus. God once said, "Let the light shine out of the darkness!" This is the same God who made his light shine in our hearts by letting us know the glory of God that is in the face of Christ.

Spiritual Treasure in Clay Jars

*W*e have this treasure from God, but we are like clay jars that hold the treasure. This shows that the great power is from God, not from us. We have troubles all around us, but we are not defeated. We do not know what to do, but we do not give up the hope of living. We are persecuted, but God does not leave us. We are hurt sometimes, but we are not destroyed. We carry the death of Jesus in our own bodies so that the life of Jesus can also be seen in our bodies. We are alive, but for Jesus we are always in danger of death so that the life of Jesus can be seen in our bodies that die. So death is working in us, but life is working in you.

It is written in the Scriptures, "I believed, so I spoke." Our faith is like this, too. We believe, and so we speak. God raised the Lord Jesus from the dead, and we know that God will also raise us with Jesus. God will bring us together with you, and we will stand before him. All these things are for you. And so the grace of God that is being given to more and more people will bring increasing thanks to God for his glory.

*H*ow terrible it will be for people who
    rise early in the morning
to look for strong drink,
    who stay awake late at night,
    becoming drunk with wine.
At their parties they have lyres, harps,
    tambourines, flutes, and wine.
They don't see what the LORD has done
    or notice the work of his hands.

Isaiah 5:11–12

*T*he way of the good person is like the
    light of dawn,
    growing brighter and brighter until
    full daylight.
But the wicked walk around in the
    dark;
    they can't even see what makes
    them stumble.

Proverbs 4:18–19

*A*nnounce this message to the family
    of Jacob,
    and tell it to the nation of Judah:
Hear this message, you foolish people
    who have no sense.
    They have eyes, but they don't really
    see.
    They have ears, but they don't really
    listen.
Surely you are afraid of me," says the
    LORD.
    "You should shake with fear in my
    presence.
I am the one who made the beaches to
    be a border for the sea,
    a border the water can never go
    past.
The waves may pound the beach, but
    they can't win over it.
    They may roar, but they cannot go
    beyond it.
But the people of Judah are stubborn
    and have turned against me.
    They have turned aside and gone
    away from me.
They do not say to themselves,
'We should fear the LORD our God,
    who gives us autumn and spring rains
    in their seasons,

who makes sure we have the harvest
    at the right time.'"

Jeremiah 5:20–24

*T*hose who fight against the light
    do not know God's ways
    or stay in his paths.

"God may let these evil people feel safe,
    but he is watching their ways.
For a little while they are important,
    and then they die;
    they are laid low and buried like
    everyone else;
    they are cut off like the heads of
    grain."

Job 24:13, 23–24

*G*lory, I've learned, is what God is all about.
His essential being. Whenever you talk about
His character or attributes—like holiness,
love, compassion, justice, truth, or mercy—
that's God's glory. . . .

    So how is it that you and I can glorify God?
It happens every time we reveal His attributes
in the course of our daily lives. Everytime you
share the good news of Christ with another.
Everytime you reflect patience in the middle
of an upsetting or perplexing problem. Every
time you smile from the heart or offer an encouraging word. Whenever those around you
see God's character displayed in your attitudes
and responses, you are displaying His glory.

    . . . God's glory isn't reserved for a temple
of stone or some heavenly vista. It can shine
out clearly while you're changing a flat on
the freeway . . . or counseling an angry co-
worker . . . or lying in a hospital bed . . .
or balancing two crying babies in the church
nursery.

Joni Eareckson Tada

*H*ow is God's glory shown through believers
different from that shown by Moses? How has
God's Spirit opened up your mind? How is
God's glory shining in your life?

TUESDAY:

The Righteous Will Receive Eternal Glory

2 Corinthians 4:16—6:2

Living by Faith

So we do not give up. Our physical body is becoming older and weaker, but our spirit inside us is made new every day. We have small troubles for a while now, but they are helping us gain an eternal glory that is much greater than the troubles. We set our eyes not on what we see but on what we cannot see. What we see will last only a short time, but what we cannot see will last forever.

We know that our body—the tent we live in here on earth—will be destroyed. But when that happens, God will have a house for us. It will not be a house made by human hands; instead, it will be a home in heaven that will last forever. But now we groan in this tent. We want God to give us our heavenly home, because it will clothe us so we will not be naked. While we live in this body, we have burdens, and we groan. We do not want to be naked, but we want to be clothed with our heavenly home. Then this body that dies will be fully covered with life. This is what God made us for, and he has given us the Spirit to be a guarantee for this new life.

So we always have courage. We know that while we live in this body, we are away from the Lord. We live by what we believe, not by what we can see. So I say that we have courage. We really want to be away from this body and be at home with the Lord. Our only goal is to please God whether we live here or there, because we must all stand before Christ to be judged. Each of us will receive what we should get—good or bad—for the things we did in the earthly body.

Becoming Friends with God

Since we know what it means to fear the Lord, we try to help people accept the truth about us. God knows what we really are, and I hope that in your hearts you know, too. We are not trying to prove ourselves to you again, but we are telling you about ourselves so you will be proud of us. Then you will have an answer for those who are proud about things that can be seen rather than what is in the heart. If we are out of our minds, it is for God. If we have our right minds, it is for you. The love of Christ controls us, because we know that One died for all, so all have died. Christ died for all so that those who live would not continue to live for themselves. He died for them and was raised from the dead so that they would live for him.

From this time on we do not think of anyone as the world does. In the past we thought of Christ as the world thinks, but we no longer think of him in that way. If anyone belongs to Christ, there is a new creation. The old things have gone; everything is made new! All this is from God. Through Christ, God made peace between us and himself, and God gave us the work of telling everyone about the peace we can have with him. God was in Christ, making peace between the world and himself. In Christ, God did not hold the world guilty of its sins. And he gave us this message of peace. So we have been sent to speak for Christ. It is as if God is calling to you through us. We speak for Christ when we beg you to be at peace with God. Christ had no sin, but God made him become sin so that in Christ we could become right with God.

We are workers together with God, so we beg you: Do not let the grace that you received from God be for nothing. God says,

"At the right time I heard your prayers.
On the day of salvation I helped
you."   *Isaiah 49:8*

I tell you that the "right time" is now, and the "day of salvation" is now.

Who may go up on the mountain of
the LORD?
Who may stand in his holy Temple?
Only those with clean hands and pure
hearts,
who have not worshiped idols,

who have not made promises in the
name of a false god.
They will receive a blessing from the
LORD;
the God who saves them will declare
them right.
They try to follow God;
they look to the God of Jacob for
help. *Selah*
Gates, open all the way.
Open wide, aged doors
so the glorious King will come in.
Who is this glorious King?
The LORD, strong and mighty.
The LORD, the powerful warrior.
Gates, open all the way.
Open wide, aged doors
so the glorious King will come in.
Who is this glorious King?
The LORD All-Powerful—
he is the glorious King. *Selah*

Psalm 24:3–10

*T*he desert and dry land will become
happy;
the desert will be glad and will
produce flowers.
Like a flower, it will have many
blooms.
It will show its happiness, as if it
were shouting with joy.
It will be beautiful like the forest of
Lebanon,
as beautiful as the hill of Carmel and
the Plain of Sharon.
Everyone will see the glory of the LORD
and the splendor of our God.

Isaiah 35:1–2

*J*erusalem, get up and shine, because
your light has come,
and the glory of the LORD shines on
you.

You will name your walls Salvation
and your gates Praise.
The sun will no longer be your light
during the day
nor will the brightness from the
moon be your light,
because the LORD will be your light
forever,
and your God will be your glory.

Your sun will never set again,
and your moon will never be dark,
because the LORD will be your light
forever,
and your time of sadness will end.

Isaiah 60:1, 18b–20

INSIGHTS

*M*an's place in creation was very remarkable. The Psalmist says, "For thou hast made
him a little lower than the angels, and hast
crowned him with glory and honor. Thou
madest him to have dominion over the works
of thy hands; thou hast put all things under
his feet: all sheep and oxen, yea, and the beasts
of the field; the fowl of the air, and the fish of
the sea, and whatsoever passeth through the
paths of the seas." . . .

What a man will become we can scarcely
tell when he is remade in the image of God,
and made like unto our divine Lord who is
"the firstborn among many brethren." Our
bodies are to be developed into something
infinitely brighter and better than the bodies
of men here below: and as for the soul, we
cannot guess to what an elevation it shall be
raised in Christ Jesus. There is room for
the largest expectation here, as we conjecture
what will be the full accomplishment of
the vast intent of eternal love, an intent
which has involved the sacrifice of the only-
begotten Son of God. That can be no mean
design which has been carried on at the expense of the best that heaven itself possessed.

Charles Spurgeon

ACTION POINT

*S*top now and focus your eyes on what you
cannot yet see. Imagine yourself standing in
God's temple with clean hands and a pure
heart. Imagine God as your glory and light
forever. Praise him for his eternal glory that
is to come!

WEDNESDAY:

The Importance of Living a Pure Life

2 Corinthians 6:3—7:7

NEW TESTAMENT READING

*W*e do not want anyone to find fault with our work, so nothing we do will be a problem for anyone. But in every way we show we are servants of God: in accepting many hard things, in troubles, in difficulties, and in great problems. We are beaten and thrown into prison. We meet those who become upset with us and start riots. We work hard, and sometimes we get no sleep or food. We show we are servants of God by our pure lives, our understanding, patience, and kindness, by the Holy Spirit, by true love, by speaking the truth, and by God's power. We use our right living to defend ourselves against everything. Some people honor us, but others blame us. Some people say evil things about us, but others say good things. Some people say we are liars, but we speak the truth. We are not known, but we are well known. We seem to be dying, but we continue to live. We are punished, but we are not killed. We have much sadness, but we are always rejoicing. We are poor, but we are making many people rich in faith. We have nothing, but really we have everything.

We have spoken freely to you in Corinth and have opened our hearts to you. Our feelings of love for you have not stopped, but you have stopped your feelings of love for us. I speak to you as if you were my children. Do to us as we have done—open your hearts to us.

Warning About Non-Christians

*Y*ou are not the same as those who do not believe. So do not join yourselves to them. Good and bad do not belong together. Light and darkness cannot share together. How can Christ and Belial, the devil, have any agreement? What can a believer have together with a nonbeliever? The temple of God cannot have any agreement with idols,

and we are the temple of the living God. As God said: "I will live with them and walk with them. And I will be their God, and they will be my people."

"Leave those people,
and be separate, says the Lord.
Touch nothing that is unclean,
and I will accept you."   *Isaiah 52:11;*
                                    Ezekiel 20:34, 41

"I will be your father,
and you will be my sons and
daughters,
says the Lord Almighty."

2 Samuel 7:14; 7:8

Dear friends, we have these promises from God, so we should make ourselves pure—free from anything that makes body or soul unclean. We should try to become holy in the way we live, because we respect God.

Paul's Joy

*O*pen your hearts to us. We have not done wrong to anyone, we have not ruined the faith of anyone, and we have not cheated anyone. I do not say this to blame you. I told you before that we love you so much we would live or die with you. I feel very sure of you and am very proud of you. You give me much comfort, and in all of our troubles I have great joy.

When we came into Macedonia, we had no rest. We found trouble all around us. We had fighting on the outside and fear on the inside. But God, who comforts those who are troubled, comforted us when Titus came. We were comforted, not only by his coming but also by the comfort you gave him. Titus told us about your wish to see me and that you are very sorry for what you did. He also told me about your great care for me, and when I heard this, I was much happier.

OLD TESTAMENT READING

*H*appy are those who live pure lives,
who follow the LORD's teachings.
Happy are those who keep his rules,
who try to obey him with their whole
heart.
They don't do what is wrong;
they follow his ways.

How can a young person live a pure life?
By obeying your word.
With all my heart I try to obey you.
Don't let me break your commands.
I have taken your words to heart
so I would not sin against you.

Psalm 119:1–3, 9–11

I have followed the ways of the LORD;
I have not done evil by turning away
from my God.
I remember all his laws
and have not broken his rules.
I am innocent before him;
I have kept myself from doing evil.
The LORD rewarded me because I did
what was right,
because I did what the LORD said
was right.

LORD, you are loyal to those who are
loyal,
and you are good to those who are
good.
You are pure to those who are pure,
but you are against those who are bad.

Psalm 18:21–26

*T*he LORD your God will bring you into the
land that you are entering and that you will
have as your own. As you go in, he will force
out these nations: the Hittites, Girgashites,
Amorites, Canaanites, Perizzites, Hivites,
and Jebusites—seven nations that are
stronger than you. The LORD your God will
hand these nations over to you, and when
you defeat them, you must destroy them
completely. Do not make a peace treaty
with them or show them any mercy. Do not
marry any of them, or let your daughters
marry their sons, or let your sons marry
their daughters. If you do, those people will
turn your children away from me, to begin serving other gods. Then the LORD will
be very angry with you, and he will quickly
destroy you.

Deuteronomy 7:1–4

*D*on't follow the ways of the wicked;
don't do what evil people do.
Avoid their ways, and don't follow them.
Stay away from them and keep on
going.

Proverbs 4:14–15

*S*omeone has said, "a belief is what you hold;
a conviction is what holds you." A conviction
is not truly a conviction unless it includes a
commitment to live by what we claim to believe. A commitment is not a vow but a
resolution—a determined purpose to live by
God's word as he applies it to our lives. First,
we need a commitment to holiness as a total
way of life. We must decide that holiness is so
important to God that it deserves priority attention in our lives. We must commit ourselves to obeying God in all of his commands.
We cannot pick and choose according to our
own values. A little bit of fudging on one's
income tax return is sin just as much as outright theft; an unforgiving spirit toward
someone else is sin just as much as murder. I
am not suggesting that all sin is equally offensive to God; I am saying that all sin is offensive to God. The measure of sin is not just
in its effect upon our neighbor, but in its affront to the majesty and holiness of a sovereign God.

Sin is serious to God, and it becomes serious business to us when we reflect upon the
fact that every sin, regardless of how seemingly insignificant it appears to us, is an expression of contempt toward the sovereign
authority of God. . . .

The psalmist recognized the seriousness of
any and all sin when he said, "You have laid
down precepts that are to be fully obeyed"
(Psalm 119:4). He recognized that partial
obedience—for example, refraining from
outright theft of our neighbor's property while
allowing our heart to covet it—is actually
disobedience. God's precepts are to be fully
obeyed.

Jerry Bridges

*L*ist the lifestyle traits that are to characterize those who serve God. Why is purity so
important to God? Why must God's people
seek purity? What is the way to live a pure
life? Is your desire for purity a belief or a
conviction?

THURSDAY:

Godly Sorrow Leads Us to Repentance

2 Corinthians 7:8—8:15

NEW TESTAMENT READING

*E*ven if my letter made you sad, I am not sorry I wrote it. At first I was sorry, because it made you sad, but you were sad only for a short time. Now I am happy, not because you were made sad, but because your sorrow made you change your lives. You became sad in the way God wanted you to, so you were not hurt by us in any way. The kind of sorrow God wants makes people change their hearts and lives. This leads to salvation, and you cannot be sorry for that. But the kind of sorrow the world has brings death. See what this sorrow—the sorrow God wanted you to have—has done to you: It has made you very serious. It made you want to prove you were not wrong. It made you angry and afraid. It made you want to see me. It made you care. It made you want the right thing to be done. You proved you were innocent in the problem. I wrote that letter, not because of the one who did the wrong or because of the person who was hurt. I wrote the letter so you could see, before God, the great care you have for us. That is why we were comforted.

Not only were we very comforted, we were even happier to see that Titus was so happy. All of you made him feel much better. I bragged to Titus about you, and you showed that I was right. Everything we said to you was true, and you have proved that what we bragged about to Titus is true. And his love for you is stronger when he remembers that you were all ready to obey. You welcomed him with respect and fear. I am very happy that I can trust you fully.

Christian Giving

*A*nd now, brothers and sisters, we want you to know about the grace God gave the churches in Macedonia. They have been tested by great troubles, and they are very poor. But they gave much because of their great joy. I can tell you that they gave as much as they were able and even more than they could afford. No one told them to do it. But they begged and pleaded with us to let them share in this service for God's people. And they gave in a way we did not expect: They first gave themselves to the Lord and to us. This is what God wants. So we asked Titus to help you finish this special work of grace since he is the one who started it. You are rich in everything—in faith, in speaking, in knowledge, in truly wanting to help, and in the love you learned from us. In the same way, be strong also in the grace of giving.

I am not commanding you to give. But I want to see if your love is true by comparing you with others that really want to help. You know the grace of our Lord Jesus Christ. You know that Christ was rich, but for you he became poor so that by his becoming poor you might become rich.

This is what I think you should do: Last year you were the first to want to give, and you were the first who gave. So now finish the work you started. Then your "doing" will be equal to your "wanting to do." Give from what you have. If you want to give, your gift will be accepted. It will be judged by what you have, not by what you do not have. We do not want you to have troubles while other people are at ease, but we want everything to be equal. At this time you have plenty. What you have can help others who are in need. Then later, when they have plenty, they can help you when you are in need, and all will be equal. As it is written in the Scriptures, "The person who gathered more did not have too much, nor did the person who gathered less have too little."

OLD TESTAMENT READING

*A*s Ezra was praying and confessing and crying and throwing himself down in front of the Temple, a large group of Israelite men, women, and children gathered around him who were also crying loudly. Then

Shecaniah son of Jehiel the Elamite said to Ezra, "We have been unfaithful to our God by marrying women from the peoples around us. But even so, there is still hope for Israel. Now let us make an agreement before our God. We will send away all these women and their children as you and those who respect the commands of our God advise. Let it be done to obey God's Teachings. Get up, Ezra. You are in charge, and we will support you. Have courage and do it."

So Ezra got up and made the priests, Levites, and all the people of Israel promise to do what was suggested; and they promised.

So within three days all the people of Judah and Benjamin gathered in Jerusalem. It was the twentieth day of the ninth month. All the people were sitting in the open place in front of the Temple and were upset because of the meeting and because it was raining.

Ezra the priest stood up and said to them, "You have been unfaithful and have married non-Jewish women. You have made Israel more guilty. Now, confess it to the LORD, the God of your ancestors. Do his will and separate yourselves from the people living around you and from your non-Jewish wives."

Then the whole group answered Ezra with a loud voice, "Ezra, you're right! We must do what you say. But there are many people here, and it's the rainy season. We can't stand outside, and this problem can't be solved in a day or two, because we have sinned badly. Let our officers make a decision for the whole group. Then let everyone in our towns who has married a non-Jewish woman meet with the older leaders and judges of each town at a planned time, until the hot anger of our God turns away from us." Only Jonathan son of Asahel, Jahzeiah son of Tikvah, Meshullam, and Shabbethai the Levite were against the plan.

So the returned captives did what was suggested. Ezra the priest chose men who were leaders of the family groups and named one from each family division. On the first day of the tenth month they sat down to study each case. By the first day of the first month, they had finished with all the men who had married non-Jewish women.

Ezra 10:1–5, 9–17

Repentance is simply and precisely a change of mind. The original term denotes, a thinking again—a turning of the mind—as when one finds himself going wrong and turns about to pursue the opposite course. The term, when applied to evangelical repentance, means not merely a turning of the mind, but a change of the entire purposes of action, change in the entire attitude of the will. . . .

Conviction of sin as a wrong committed against God is implied in repentance. Without this there can be no rational repentance.

The sinner must become truly honest with God. He must honestly admit the truths affirmed by his reason and pressed on his soul by his conscience. Especially must he recognize God's rights: that he himself is God's property and belongs truly to God. . . .

Repentance implies a universal reformation of life, a reformation extending to all forms of sin. Penitent men turn from all sin as sin, because they regard it as sin, and therefore can have no sympathy with it. All known sin therefore they at once abandon. . . .

When I speak of abandoning sin, I do not imply that the penitent man never for even a moment relapses into it; but I imply that he sets himself against it in real honest earnestness.

Charles Finney

What is the difference between godly sorrow and the world's sorrow? What feelings and actions does godly sorrow bring about? Pray that you will always respond appropriately to godly sorrow!

441

F R I D A Y:

God Encourages Us to Share Liberally with Others

2 Corinthians 8:16—9:15

Titus and His Companions Help

I thank God because he gave Titus the same love for you that I have. Titus accepted what we asked him to do. He wanted very much to go to you, and this was his own idea. We are sending with him the brother who is praised by all the churches because of his service in preaching the Good News. Also, this brother was chosen by the churches to go with us when we deliver this gift of money. We are doing this service to bring glory to the Lord and to show that we really want to help.

We are being careful so that no one will criticize us for the way we are handling this large gift. We are trying hard to do what the Lord accepts as right and also what people think is right.

Also, we are sending with them our brother, who is always ready to help. He has proved this to us in many ways, and he wants to help even more now, because he has much faith in you.

Now about Titus—he is my partner who is working with me to help you. And about the other brothers—they are sent from the churches, and they bring glory to Christ. So show these men the proof of your love and the reason we are proud of you. Then all the churches can see it.

Help for Fellow Christians

I really do not need to write you about this help for God's people. I know you want to help. I have been bragging about this to the people in Macedonia, telling them that you in Southern Greece have been ready to give since last year. And your desire to give has made most of them ready to give also. But I am sending the brothers to you so that our bragging about you in this will not be empty words. I want you to be ready, as I said you would be. If any of the people from Macedonia come with me and find that you are not ready, we will be ashamed that we were so sure of you. (And you will be ashamed, too!) So I thought I should ask these brothers to go to you before we do. They will finish getting in order the generous gift you promised so it will be ready when we come. And it will be a generous gift—not one that you did not want to give.

Remember this: The person who plants a little will have a small harvest, but the person who plants a lot will have a big harvest. Each one should give as you have decided in your heart to give. You should not be sad when you give, and you should not give because you feel forced to give. God loves the person who gives happily. And God can give you more blessings than you need. Then you will always have plenty of everything—enough to give to every good work. It is written in the Scriptures:

"He gives freely to the poor.
The things he does are right and will
continue forever." *Psalm 112:9*

God is the One who gives seed to the farmer and bread for food. He will give you all the seed you need and make it grow so there will be a great harvest from your goodness. He will make you rich in every way so that you can always give freely. And your giving through us will cause many to give thanks to God. This service you do not only helps the needs of God's people, it also brings many more thanks to God. It is a proof of your faith. Many people will praise God because you obey the Good News of Christ—the gospel you say you believe—and because you freely share with them and with all others. And when they pray, they will wish they could be with you because of the great grace that God has given you. Thanks be to God for his gift that is too wonderful for words.

*B*e sure to save one-tenth of all your crops each year. Take it to the place the LORD your God will choose where he is to be worshiped. There, where you will be together with the LORD, eat the tenth of your grain, new wine, and oil, and eat the animals born first to your herds and flocks. Do this so that you will learn to respect the LORD your God always. But if the place the LORD will choose to be worshiped is too far away and he has blessed you so much you cannot carry a tenth, exchange your one-tenth for silver. Then take the silver with you to the place the LORD your God shall choose. Use the silver to buy anything you wish—cattle, sheep, wine, beer, or anything you wish. Then you and your family will eat and celebrate there before the LORD your God. Do not forget the Levites in your town, because they have no land of their own among you.

At the end of every third year, everyone should bring one-tenth of that year's crop and store it in your towns. This is for the Levites so they may eat and be full. (They have no land of their own among you.) It is also for strangers, orphans, and widows who live in your towns so that all of them may eat and be full. Then the LORD your God will bless you and all the work you do.

Deuteronomy 14:22–29

*W*hoever gives to the poor will have
    everything he needs,
  but the one who ignores the poor
    will receive many curses.

Proverbs 28:27

*L*azy people's desire for sleep will kill
    them,
  because they refuse to work.
All day long they wish for more,
  but good people give without
    holding back.

Proverbs 21:25–26

*I*t is good to be merciful and generous.
    Those who are fair in their business
will never be defeated.
  Good people will always be remem-
    bered.
They won't be afraid of bad news;
  their hearts are steady because they
    trust the LORD.
They are confident and will not be
    afraid;
  they will look down on their enemies.
They give freely to the poor.

The things they do are right and will
  continue forever.
They will be given great honor.

Psalm 112:5–9

INSIGHTS

*W*e all know how subtle the materialistic temptations are and how convincing the rationalizations. Only by God's grace and with great effort can we escape the shower of luxuries which has almost suffocated our Christian compassion. All of us face this problem. Some years ago I spent about fifty dollars on an extra suit. That's not much of course. Besides, I persuaded myself, it was a wise investment (thanks to the 75 percent discount). But that money would have fed a starving child in India for about a year. In all honesty we have to ask ourselves: Dare we care at all about current fashions if that means reducing our ability to help hungry neighbors? Dare we care more about obtaining a secure economic future for our family than for living an uncompromisingly Christian lifestyle? . . .

. . . We have been brainwashed to believe that bigger houses, more prosperous businesses, more luxurious gadgets, are worthy goals in life. As a result, we are caught in an absurd, materialistic spiral. The more we make, the more we think we need in order to live decently and respectably. Somehow we have to break this cycle because it makes us sin against our needy brothers and sisters and, therefore, against our Lord. And it also destroys us. Sharing with others is the way to real joy.

Ronald Sider

APPLICATION

*L*ist what God promises those who give generously. What do you think it means to be made "rich in every way so that you can always give freely"? Is your giving such that it brings praise to God from others?

WEEKEND:

*Our Spiritual Weapons
Are Empowered by God*

2 Corinthians 10:1—11:4

Paul Defends His Ministry

I, Paul, am begging you with the gentleness and the kindness of Christ. Some people say that I am easy on you when I am with you and bold when I am away. They think we live in a worldly way, and I plan to be very bold with them when I come. I beg you that when I come I will not need to use that same boldness with you. We do live in the world, but we do not fight in the same way the world fights. We fight with weapons that are different from those the world uses. Our weapons have power from God that can destroy the enemy's strong places. We destroy people's arguments and every proud thing that raises itself against the knowledge of God. We capture every thought and make it give up and obey Christ. We are ready to punish anyone there who does not obey, but first we want you to obey fully.

You must look at the facts before you. If you feel sure that you belong to Christ, you must remember that we belong to Christ just as you do. It is true that we brag freely about the authority the Lord gave us. But this authority is to build you up, not to tear you down. So I will not be ashamed. I do not want you to think I am trying to scare you with my letters. Some people say, "Paul's letters are powerful and sound important, but when he is with us, he is weak. And his speaking is nothing." They should know this: We are not there with you now, so we say these things in letters. But when we are there with you, we will show the same authority that we show in our letters.

We do not dare to compare ourselves with those who think they are very important. They use themselves to measure themselves, and they judge themselves by what they themselves are. This shows that they know nothing. But we will not brag about things outside the work that was given us to do. We will limit our bragging to the work that God gave us, and this includes our work with you. We are not bragging too much, as we would be if we had not already come to you. But we have come to you with the Good News of Christ. We limit our bragging to the work that is ours, not what others have done. We hope that as your faith continues to grow, you will help our work to grow much larger. We want to tell the Good News in the areas beyond your city. We do not want to brag about work that has already been done in another person's area. But, "If someone wants to brag, he should brag only about the Lord." It is not those who say they are good who are accepted but those who the Lord thinks are good.

Paul and the False Apostles

I wish you would be patient with me even when I am a little foolish, but you are already doing that. I am jealous over you with a jealousy that comes from God. I promised to give you to Christ, as your only husband. I want to give you as his pure bride. But I am afraid that your minds will be led away from your true and pure following of Christ just as Eve was tricked by the snake with his evil ways. You are very patient with anyone who comes to you and preaches a different Jesus from the one we preached. You are very willing to accept a spirit or gospel that is different from the Spirit and Good News you received from us.

The Power of Scripture

I have heard the prophets who prophesy lies in my name. They say, 'I have had a dream! I have had a dream!' How long will this continue in the minds of these lying prophets? They prophesy from their own wishful thinking. They are trying to make the people of Judah forget me by telling each other these dreams. In the same way, their ancestors forgot me and worshiped Baal. Is straw the same thing as wheat?" says the LORD. "If a prophet wants to tell about his dreams, let him! But let the person who hears my message speak it truthfully! Isn't my message like a fire?" says the LORD. "Isn't it like a hammer that smashes a rock?"

Jeremiah 23:25–29

The Power of Salvation

*T*he LORD is my rock, my protection, my Savior.
My God is my rock.
   I can run to him for safety.
He is my shield and my saving strength,
   my defender and my place of safety.
   The LORD saves me from those who want to harm me.
I will call to the LORD, who is worthy of praise,
   and I will be saved from my enemies."

2 Samuel 22:2b–4

The Power of Faith

*J*ehoshaphat's army went out into the Desert of Tekoa early in the morning. As they were starting out, Jehoshaphat stood and said, "Listen to me, people of Judah and Jerusalem. Have faith in the LORD your God, and you will stand strong. Have faith in his prophets, and you will succeed." Jehoshaphat listened to the people's advice. Then he chose men to be singers to the LORD, to praise him because he is holy and wonderful. As they marched in front of the army, they said,
   "Thank the LORD,
      because his love continues forever."
As they began to sing and praise God, the LORD set ambushes for the people of Ammon, Moab, and Edom who had come to attack Judah. And they were defeated.

2 Chronicles 20:20–22

The Power of Prayer

*B*ut I will call to God for help,
   and the LORD will save me.
Morning, noon, and night I am troubled and upset,
   but he will listen to me.
Many are against me,
   but he keeps me safe in battle.
God who lives forever

will hear me and punish them.   *Selah*
But they will not change;
   they do not fear God.

Psalm 55:16–19

INSIGHTS

*W*e have no enemies but the enemies of God. Our fights are not against men but against spiritual wickednesses. We war with the devil and the blasphemy and error and despair which he brings into the field of battle. We fight with all the armies of sin—impurity, drunkenness, oppression, infidelity, and ungodliness. With these we contend earnestly, but not with sword or spear; the weapons of our warfare are not carnal.

Jehovah, our God, abhors everything which is evil, and, therefore, He goeth with us to fight for us in this crusade. He will save us, and He will give us grace to war a good warfare and win the victory. We may depend upon it that if we are on God's side God is on our side. With such an august ally the conflict is never in the least degree doubtful. It is not that truth is mighty and must prevail but that might lies with the Father who is almighty, with Jesus who has all power in heaven and in earth, and with the Holy Spirit who worketh His will among men.

Soldiers of Christ, gird on your armor. Strike home in the name of the God of holiness, and by faith grasp His salvation. Let not this day pass without striking a blow for Jesus and holiness.

Charles Spurgeon

ACTION POINT

*A*gainst what enemy does the believer fight? What weapons are in your spiritual arsenal? Are your weapons ready for battle and armed with the power of God? Pray that you will faithfully obey God and diligently fight against the enemy.

MONDAY:

God Brings Good out of Our Suffering

2 Corinthians 11:5–33

I do not think that those "great apostles" are any better than I am. I may not be a trained speaker, but I do have knowledge. We have shown this to you clearly in every way.

I preached God's Good News to you without pay. I made myself unimportant to make you important. Do you think that was wrong? I accepted pay from other churches, taking their money so I could serve you. If I needed something when I was with you, I did not trouble any of you. The brothers who came from Macedonia gave me all that I needed. I did not allow myself to depend on you in any way, and I will never depend on you. No one in Southern Greece will stop me from bragging about that. I say this with the truth of Christ in me. And why do I not depend on you? Do you think it is because I do not love you? God knows that I love you.

And I will continue doing what I am doing now, because I want to stop those people from having a reason to brag. They would like to say that the work they brag about is the same as ours. Such men are not true apostles but are workers who lie. They change themselves to look like apostles of Christ. This does not surprise us. Even Satan changes himself to look like an angel of light. So it does not surprise us if Satan's servants also make themselves look like servants who work for what is right. But in the end they will be punished for what they do.

Paul Tells About His Sufferings

I tell you again: No one should think I am a fool. But if you think so, accept me as you would accept a fool. Then I can brag a little, too. When I brag because I feel sure of myself, I am not talking as the Lord would talk but as a fool. Many people are bragging about their lives in the world. So I will brag too. You are wise, so you will gladly be patient with fools! You are even patient with those who order you around, or use you, or trick you, or think they are better than you, or hit you in the face. It is shameful to me to say this, but we were too "weak" to do those things to you!

But if anyone else is brave enough to brag, then I also will be brave and brag. (I am talking as a fool.) Are they Hebrews? So am I. Are they Israelites? So am I. Are they from Abraham's family? So am I. Are they serving Christ? I am serving him more. (I am crazy to talk like this.) I have worked much harder than they. I have been in prison more often. I have been hurt more in beatings. I have been near death many times. Five times the Jews have given me their punishment of thirty-nine lashes with a whip. Three different times I was beaten with rods. One time I was almost stoned to death. Three times I was in ships that wrecked, and one of those times I spent a night and a day in the sea. I have gone on many travels and have been in danger from rivers, thieves, my own people, the Jews, and those who are not Jews. I have been in danger in cities, in places where no one lives, and on the sea. And I have been in danger with false Christians. I have done hard and tiring work, and many times I did not sleep. I have been hungry and thirsty, and many times I have been without food. I have been cold and without clothes. Besides all this, there is on me every day the load of my concern for all the churches. I feel weak every time someone is weak, and I feel upset every time someone is led into sin.

If I must brag, I will brag about the things that show I am weak. God knows I am not lying. He is the God and Father of the Lord Jesus Christ, and he is to be praised forever. When I was in Damascus, the governor under King Aretas wanted to arrest me, so he put guards around the city. But my friends lowered me in a basket through a hole in the city wall. So I escaped from the governor.

*S*o the Egyptians made life hard for the Israelites. They put slave masters over them, who forced the Israelites to build the cities Pithom and Rameses as supply centers for the king. But the harder the Egyptians forced the Israelites to work, the more the Israelites grew in number and spread out. So the Egyptians became very afraid of them and demanded even more of them. They made their lives bitter. They forced the Israelites to work hard to make bricks and mortar and to do all kinds of work in the fields. The Egyptians were not merciful to them in all their painful work.

So the king commanded all his people, "Every time a boy is born to the Hebrews, you must throw him into the Nile River, but let all the girl babies live."

Exodus 1:11–14, 22

*N*ow a man from the family of Levi married a woman who was also from the family of Levi. She became pregnant and gave birth to a son. When she saw how wonderful the baby was, she hid him for three months. But after three months she was not able to hide the baby any longer, so she got a basket and covered it with tar so that it would float. She put the baby in the basket. Then she put the basket among the tall stalks of grass at the edge of the Nile River.

Then the daughter of the king of Egypt came to the river to take a bath, and her servant girls were walking beside the river. When she saw the basket in the tall grass, she sent her slave girl to get it.

Then the baby's sister asked the king's daughter, "Would you like me to go and find a Hebrew woman to nurse the baby for you?"

The king's daughter said, "Go!" So the girl went and got the baby's own mother.

The king's daughter said to the woman, "Take this baby and nurse him for me, and I will pay you." So the woman took her baby and nursed him. When the child grew older, the woman took him to the king's daughter, and she adopted the baby as her own son. The king's daughter named him Moses, because she had pulled him out of the water.

Exodus 2:1–3, 5, 7–10

*O*ur God who is sovereign does not have "chance" to contend with. He has told us that He is able to take whatever has taken place and to work together all things for the good of those who are His children. We grow in our understanding through difficulties, as God opens to us that which we could not have understood with any other background or in any other set of circumstances. However, that does not eliminate the fact that we simply do not know what flow of factors brought about the accident, the illness, the fire, the earthquakes, the storm, and the combination of events in the middle of it all. Our assurance as children of the Living God is that He is able to bring beauty from ashes and to give the "oil of joy" for the spirit of mourning (see Isaiah 61:3). And, in addition, He refines, purifies, proves, and causes to grow in us something very precious and lasting in our attitudes toward Him and in our actions to other human beings. As we turn to Him in our affliction and ask for help, He does not allow our affliction to be "wasted." As He removed the hedge protecting Job (or any one of us whom Satan accuses of not loving God, but rather the possessions or health or other things which God has given us), he is also able to give us the grace to come through the onslaught that follows. However, there is much more than just "coming through," still hanging on to our trust and love of God. There is a "coming through," with a shinier, more gleaming sheen on our surface. We have the possibility during the hard time to have skimmed off more of the specks and scum which are hindering the more beautiful reality of love, joy, peace, long-suffering, and meekness.

Edith Schaeffer

*F*or Paul, preaching the Good News was "good" enough to willingly bear great suffering, wasn't it? Pray for total confidence that God is bringing about good through the suffering in your life, too.

TUESDAY:

God's Power Is Made Perfect in Weakness

2 Corinthians 12:1—13:4

A Special Blessing in Paul's Life

I must continue to brag. It will do no good, but I will talk now about visions and revelations from the Lord. I know a man in Christ who was taken up to the third heaven fourteen years ago. I do not know whether the man was in his body or out of his body, but God knows. And I know that this man was taken up to paradise. I don't know if he was in his body or away from his body, but God knows. He heard things he is not able to explain, things that no human is allowed to tell. I will brag about a man like that, but I will not brag about myself, except about my weaknesses. But if I wanted to brag about myself, I would not be a fool, because I would be telling the truth. But I will not brag about myself. I do not want people to think more of me than what they see me do or hear me say.

So that I would not become too proud of the wonderful things that were shown to me, a painful physical problem was given to me. This problem was a messenger from Satan, sent to beat me and keep me from being too proud. I begged the Lord three times to take this problem away from me. But he said to me, "My grace is enough for you. When you are weak, my power is made perfect in you." So I am very happy to brag about my weaknesses. Then Christ's power can live in me. For this reason I am happy when I have weaknesses, insults, hard times, sufferings, and all kinds of troubles for Christ. Because when I am weak, then I am truly strong.

Paul's Love for the Christians

I have been talking like a fool, but you made me do it. You are the ones who should say good things about me. I am worth nothing, but those "great apostles" are not worth any more than I am! When I was with

you, I patiently did the things that prove I am an apostle—signs, wonders, and miracles. So you received everything that the other churches have received. Only one thing was different: I was not a burden to you. Forgive me for this!

I am now ready to visit you the third time, and I will not be a burden to you. I want nothing from you, except you. Children should not have to save up to give to their parents. Parents should save to give to their children. So I am happy to give everything I have for you, even myself. If I love you more, will you love me less?

It is clear I was not a burden to you, but you think I was tricky and lied to catch you. Did I cheat you by using any of the messengers I sent to you? No, you know I did not. I asked Titus to go to you, and I sent our brother with him. Titus did not cheat you, did he? No, you know that Titus and I did the same thing and with the same spirit.

Do you think we have been defending ourselves to you all this time? We have been speaking in Christ and before God. You are our dear friends, and everything we do is to make you stronger. I am afraid that when I come, you will not be what I want you to be, and I will not be what you want me to be. I am afraid that among you there may be arguing, jealousy, anger, selfish fighting, evil talk, gossip, pride, and confusion. I am afraid that when I come to you again, my God will make me ashamed before you. I may be saddened by many of those who have sinned because they have not changed their hearts or turned from their sexual sins and the shameful things they have done.

Final Warnings and Greetings

I will come to you for the third time. "Every case must be proved by two or three witnesses." When I was with you the second time, I gave a warning to those who had sinned. Now I am away from you, and I give a warning to all the others. When I come to you again, I will not be easy with them. You want proof that Christ is speaking through me. My proof is that he is not weak among you, but he is powerful. It is true that he was weak when he was killed on the cross, but he lives now by God's power. It is true that we are weak in Christ, but for you we will be alive in Christ by God's power.

So the king prepared his war chariot and took his army with him. He took six hundred of his best chariots, together with all the other chariots of Egypt, each with an officer in it. The LORD made the king of Egypt stubborn, so he chased the Israelites, who were leaving victoriously. The Egyptians—with all the king's horses, chariot drivers, and army—chased the Israelites. They caught up with them while they were camped by the Red Sea, near Pi Hahiroth and Baal Zephon.

When the Israelites saw the king and his army coming after them, they were very frightened and cried to the LORD for help. They said to Moses, "What have you done to us? Why did you bring us out of Egypt to die in the desert? There were plenty of graves for us in Egypt. We told you in Egypt, 'Let us alone; we will stay and serve the Egyptians.' Now we will die in the desert."

But Moses answered, "Don't be afraid! Stand still and you will see the LORD save you today. You will never see these Egyptians again after today. You only need to remain calm; the LORD will fight for you."

Exodus 14:6–14

On the third day, when David and his men arrived at Ziklag, he found that the Amalekites had raided southern Judah and Ziklag, attacking Ziklag and burning it. They captured the women and everyone, young and old, but they had not killed anyone. They had only taken them away.

When David and his men came to Ziklag, they found the town had been burned and their wives, sons, and daughters had been taken as prisoners. Then David and his army cried loudly until they were too weak to cry anymore. David's two wives had also been taken—Ahinoam of Jezreel and Abigail the widow of Nabal from Carmel. The men in the army were threatening to kill David with stones, which greatly upset David. Each man was sad and angry because his sons and daughters had been

captured, but David found strength in the LORD his God. David said to Abiathar the priest, "Bring me the holy vest."

Then David asked the LORD, "Should I chase the people who took our families? Will I catch them?"

The LORD answered, "Chase them. You will catch them, and you will succeed in saving your families."

David fought them from sunset until the evening of the next day. None of them escaped, except four hundred young men who rode off on their camels.

1 Samuel 30:1–8, 17

Upon examining the life of the apostle Paul, one hardly gets the impression that he was a weak man. On the contrary, he debated against Christ's apostles over the question of gentile salvation, and he won! He spent his life preaching in the most hostile of circumstances. He planted churches throughout the major cities of Asia Minor and in the port cities along the Aegean Sea. Paul trained the first pastors and elders of these early congregations. And to top it all off, he wrote half of the New Testament!

I don't know what you think, but that certainly doesn't sound like a weak man to me. . . . He was a mover and a shaker.

So how do we reconcile Paul's claim to weakness with his amazing accomplishments? Simple, the answer is in the phrase, "when I am weak, then I am strong." A paraphrase of his comment would go something like this: "When I, Paul, in and of my own strength, am weak, then I, Paul, relying of the power of Christ in me, become strong, capable of whatever the Lord requires of me, full of energy and zeal to accomplish His will."

Charles Stanley

Why does Paul say that God allowed him to become weak? How did Paul respond to his weakness? What did David and Moses do in their time of weakness? What do the examples of these men of faith teach you?

WEDNESDAY:
God Has Plans for His Own
2 Corinthians 13:5—Galatians 1:21

*L*ook closely at yourselves. Test yourselves to see if you are living in the faith. You know that Jesus Christ is in you—unless you fail the test. But I hope you will see that we ourselves have not failed the test. We pray to God that you will not do anything wrong. It is not important to see that we have passed the test, but it is important that you do what is right, even if it seems we have failed. We cannot do anything against the truth, but only for the truth. We are happy to be weak, if you are strong, and we pray that you will become complete. I am writing this while I am away from you so that when I come I will not have to be harsh in my use of authority. The Lord gave me this authority to build you up, not to tear you down.

Now, brothers and sisters, I say goodbye. Try to be complete. Do what I have asked you to do. Agree with each other, and live in peace. Then the God of love and peace will be with you.

Greet each other with a holy kiss. All of God's holy people send greetings to you.

The grace of the Lord Jesus Christ, the love of God, and the fellowship of the Holy Spirit be with you all.

Christians Are Saved by Grace

*F*rom Paul, an apostle. I was not chosen to be an apostle by human beings, nor was I sent from human beings. I was made an apostle through Jesus Christ and God the Father who raised Jesus from the dead. This letter is also from all those of God's family who are with me.

To the churches in Galatia:

Grace and peace to you from God our Father and the Lord Jesus Christ. Jesus gave himself for our sins to free us from this evil world we live in, as God the Father planned. The glory belongs to God forever and ever. Amen.

The Only Good News

*G*od, by his grace through Christ, called you to become his people. So I am amazed that you are turning away so quickly and believing something different than the Good News. Really, there is no other Good News. But some people are confusing you; they want to change the Good News of Christ. We preached to you the Good News. So if we ourselves, or even an angel from heaven, should preach to you something different, we should be judged guilty! I said this before, and now I say it again: You have already accepted the Good News. If anyone is preaching something different to you, he should be judged guilty!

Do you think I am trying to make people accept me? No, God is the One I am trying to please. Am I trying to please people? If I still wanted to please people, I would not be a servant of Christ.

Paul's Authority Is from God

*B*rothers and sisters, I want you to know that the Good News I preached to you was not made up by human beings. I did not get it from humans, nor did anyone teach it to me, but Jesus Christ showed it to me.

You have heard about my past life in the Jewish religion. I attacked the church of God and tried to destroy it. I was becoming a leader in the Jewish religion, doing better than most other Jews of my age. I tried harder than anyone else to follow the teachings handed down by our ancestors.

But God had special plans for me and set me apart for his work even before I was born. He called me through his grace and showed his son to me so that I might tell the Good News about him to those who are not Jewish. When God called me, I did not get advice or help from any person. I did not go to Jerusalem to see those who were apostles before I was. But, without waiting, I went away to Arabia and later went back to Damascus.

After three years I went to Jerusalem to meet Peter and stayed with him for fifteen days. I met no other apostles, except James, the brother of the Lord. God knows that these things I write are not lies. Later, I went to the areas of Syria and Cilicia.

*N*ow, tell my servant David: 'This is what the LORD All-Powerful says: I took you from the pasture and from tending the sheep and made you king of my people Israel. I have been with you everywhere you have gone. I have defeated your enemies for you. I will make you as famous as any of the great people on the earth. I will choose a place for my people Israel, and I will plant them so they can live in their own homes. They will not be bothered anymore. Wicked people will no longer hurt them as they have in the past when I chose judges for my people Israel. I will defeat all your enemies.

"'I tell you that the LORD will make your descendants kings of Israel after you. When you die and join your ancestors, I will make one of your sons the new king, and I will set up his kingdom.'"

1 Chronicles 17:7–11

*S*aul and the servant went up to the town. Just as they entered it, they saw Samuel coming toward them on his way up to the place of worship.

The day before Saul came, the LORD had told Samuel: "About this time tomorrow I will send you a man from the land of Benjamin. Appoint him to lead my people Israel. He will save my people from the Philistines. I have seen the suffering of my people, and I have listened to their cry."

When Samuel first saw Saul, the LORD said to Samuel, "This is the man I told you about. He will organize my people."

1 Samuel 9:14–17

*Y*ou made my whole being;
    you formed me in my mother's
        body.
I praise you because you made me in
        an amazing and wonderful way.
    What you have done is wonderful.
    I know this very well.
You saw my bones being formed
    as I took shape in my mother's body.
When I was put together there,
    you saw my body as it was formed.
All the days planned for me

were written in your book
before I was one day old.

Psalm 139:13–16

*I*t is better we should not know our future. If we did, we should often spoil God's plan for our life. If we could see into tomorrow and know the troubles it will bring, we might be tempted to seek some way of avoiding them, while really they are God's way to new honor and blessing. God's thoughts for us are always thoughts of love, good, promotion; but sometimes the path to the hilltop lies through dark valleys or up rough paths. Yet to miss the hard bit of road is to fail of gaining the lofty height. It is better, therefore, to walk, not knowing, with God, than it would be to see the way and choose for ourselves. God's way for us is always better than our own.

J. R. Miller

*D*avid, Samuel, Saul, and Paul all knew that they were called by God to fulfill his plans. Is there any reason to believe that God has planned your life to a lesser degree? Are you willing to test yourself to see if you are following his plan for you? Pray that you will be faithful to his plan and calling for your life.

THURSDAY:

"Remember to Help the Poor"

Galatians 1:22—2:21

NEW TESTAMENT READING

*I*n Judea the churches in Christ had never met me. They had only heard it said, "This man who was attacking us is now preaching the same faith that he once tried to destroy." And these believers praised God because of me.

Other Apostles Accepted Paul

*A*fter fourteen years I went to Jerusalem again, this time with Barnabas. I also took Titus with me. I went because God showed me I should go. I met with the believers there, and in private I told their leaders the Good News that I preach to the non-Jewish people. I did not want my past work and the work I am now doing to be wasted. Titus was with me, but he was not forced to be circumcised, even though he was a Greek. We talked about this problem because some false believers had come into our group secretly. They came in like spies to overturn the freedom we have in Christ Jesus. They wanted to make us slaves. But we did not give in to those false believers for a minute. We wanted the truth of the Good News to continue for you.

Those leaders who seemed to be important did not change the Good News that I preach. (It doesn't matter to me if they were "important" or not. To God everyone is the same.) But these leaders saw that I had been given the work of telling the Good News to those who are not Jewish, just as Peter had the work of telling the Jews. God gave Peter the power to work as an apostle for the Jewish people. But he also gave me the power to work as an apostle for those who are not Jews. James, Peter, and John, who seemed to be the leaders, understood that God had given me this special grace, so they accepted Barnabas and me. They agreed that they would go to the Jewish people and that we should go to those who are not Jewish. The only thing they asked us was to remember to help the poor—something I really wanted to do.

Paul Shows that Peter Was Wrong

*W*hen Peter came to Antioch, I challenged him to his face, because he was wrong. Peter ate with the non-Jewish people until some Jewish people sent from James came to Antioch. When they arrived, Peter stopped eating with those who weren't Jewish, and he separated himself from them. He was afraid of the Jews. So Peter was a hypocrite, as were the other Jewish believers who joined with him. Even Barnabas was influenced by what these Jewish believers did. When I saw they were not following the truth of the Good News, I spoke to Peter in front of them all. I said, "Peter, you are a Jew, but you are not living like a Jew. You are living like those who are not Jewish. So why do you now try to force those who are not Jewish to live like Jews?"

We were not born as non-Jewish "sinners," but as Jews. Yet we know that a person is made right with God not by following the law, but by trusting in Jesus Christ. So we, too, have put our faith in Christ Jesus, that we might be made right with God because we trusted in Christ. It is not because we followed the law, because no one can be made right with God by following the law.

We Jews came to Christ, trying to be made right with God, and it became clear that we are sinners, too. Does this mean that Christ encourages sin? No! But I would really be wrong to begin teaching again those things that I gave up. It was the law that put me to death, and I died to the law so that I can now live for God. I was put to death on the cross with Christ, and I do not live anymore—it is Christ who lives in me. I still live in my body, but I live by faith in the Son of God who loved me and gave himself to save me. By saying these things I am not going against God's grace. Just the opposite, if the law could make us right with God, then Christ's death would be useless.

OLD TESTAMENT READING

*W*hoever ignores the poor when they cry for help

will also cry for help and not be
answered.

Proverbs 21:13

*T*hen Nehemiah the governor, Ezra the
priest and teacher, and the Levites who
were teaching said to all the people, "This
is a holy day to the LORD your God. Don't
be sad or cry." All the people had been crying as they listened to the words of the
Teachings.

Nehemiah said, "Go and enjoy good food
and sweet drinks. Send some to people who
have none, because today is a holy day to
the Lord. Don't be sad, because the joy of
the LORD will make you strong."

Nehemiah 8:9–10

*N*o one is like the LORD our God,
    who rules from heaven,
who bends down to look
    at the skies and the earth.
The LORD lifts the poor from the dirt
    and takes the helpless from the
        ashes.
He seats them with princes,
    the princes of his people.

Psalm 113:5–8

*G*od, give the king your good judgment
    and the king's son your goodness.
Help him judge your people fairly
    and decide what is right for the poor.
Let there be peace on the mountains
    and goodness on the hills for the
        people.
Help him be fair to the poor
    and save the needy
    and punish those who hurt them.

Psalm 72:1–4

*I*f anyone from your country becomes too
poor to support himself, help him to live
among you as you would a stranger or foreigner. Do not charge him any interest on
money you loan to him, but respect your
God; let the poor live among you. Don't lend
him money for interest, and don't try to
make a profit from the food he buys. I am
the LORD your God, who brought you out of
the land of Egypt to give the land of Canaan
to you and to become your God.' "

Leviticus 25:35–38

*W*hoever mistreats the poor insults
    their Maker,
but whoever is kind to the needy
    honors God.

Proverbs 14:31

INSIGHTS

*T*he Bible specifically commands believers to
imitate God's special concern for the poor and
oppressed. In the Old Testament, Yahweh
frequently reminded the Israelites of their
former oppression in Egypt when he commanded them to care for the poor. . . .

When Paul took up the collection for the
poor in Jerusalem, he pointedly reminded the
Corinthians that the Lord Jesus became poor
so that they might become rich (2 Cor. 8:9).
When the author of 1 John called on Christians to share with the needy, he first mentioned the example of Christ: "By this we know
love, that he laid down his life for us; and we
ought to lay down our lives for the brethren"
(1 John 3:16). Then, in the very next verse,
he urged Christians to give generously to the
needy. It is the amazing self-sacrifice of Christ
which Christians are to imitate as they relate
to the poor and oppressed.

. . . God's Word commands believers to
care for the poor. In fact the Bible underlines
the command by teaching that when God's
people care for the poor, they imitate God
himself. But that is not all. God's Word
teaches that those who neglect the poor and
oppressed are really not God's people at all—
no matter how frequent their religious rituals
or how orthodox their creeds and confessions.

Ronald Sider

ACTION POINT

*W*hat do these passages reveal to you about
God's attitude toward the poor? Deep in your
heart, do you really want to help the poor?
What more can you do to show God's compassion for the poor? Will you do it?

F R I D A Y:

God Will Bless Those Who Believe

Galatians 3:1–20

Blessing Comes Through Faith

*Y*ou people in Galatia were told very clearly about the death of Jesus Christ on the cross. But you were foolish; you let someone trick you. Tell me this one thing: How did you receive the Holy Spirit? Did you receive the Spirit by following the law? No, you received the Spirit because you heard the Good News and believed it. You began your life in Christ by the Spirit. Now are you trying to make it complete by your own power? That is foolish. Were all your experiences wasted? I hope not! Does God give you the Spirit and work miracles among you because you follow the law? No, he does these things because you heard the Good News and believed it.

The Scriptures say the same thing about Abraham: "Abraham believed God, and God accepted Abraham's faith, and that faith made him right with God." So you should know that the true children of Abraham are those who have faith. The Scriptures, telling what would happen in the future, said that God would make the non-Jewish people right through their faith. This Good News was told to Abraham beforehand, as the Scripture says: "All nations will be blessed through you." So all who believe as Abraham believed are blessed just as Abraham was. But those who depend on following the law to make them right are under a curse, because the Scriptures say, "Anyone will be cursed who does not always obey what is written in the Book of the Law." Now it is clear that no one can be made right with God by the law, because the Scriptures say, "Those who are right with God will live by trusting in him." The law is not based on faith. It says, "A person who obeys these things will live because of them." Christ took away the curse the law put on us. He changed places with us and put himself under that curse. It is written in the Scriptures, "Anyone whose body is displayed on a tree is cursed." Christ did this so that God's blessing promised to Abraham might come through Jesus Christ to those who are not Jews. Jesus died so that by our believing we could receive the Spirit that God promised.

The Law and the Promise

*B*rothers and sisters, let us think in human terms: Even an agreement made between two persons is firm. After that agreement is accepted by both people, no one can stop it or add anything to it. God made promises both to Abraham and to his descendant. God did not say, "and to your descendants." That would mean many people. But God said, "and to your descendant." That means only one person; that person is Christ. This is what I mean: God had an agreement with Abraham and promised to keep it. The law, which came four hundred thirty years later, cannot change that agreement and so destroy God's promise to Abraham. If the law could give us Abraham's blessing, then the promise would not be necessary. But that is not possible, because God freely gave his blessings to Abraham through the promise he had made.

So what was the law for? It was given to show that the wrong things people do are against God's will. And it continued until the special descendant, who had been promised, came. The law was given through angels who used Moses for a mediator to give the law to people. But a mediator is not needed when there is only one side, and God is only one.

*T*he angel of the LORD called to Abraham from heaven a second time and said, "The LORD says, 'Because you did not keep back your son, your only son, from me, I make you this promise by my own name: I will surely bless you and give you many descendants. They will be as many as the stars in the sky and the sand on the seashore, and they will capture the cities of their enemies.

Through your descendants all the nations on the earth will be blessed, because you obeyed me.' "

Genesis 22:15–18

Since it was almost time for David to die, he gave his son Solomon his last commands. David said, "My time to die is near. Be a good and strong leader. Obey the LORD your God. Follow him by obeying his demands, his commands, his laws, and his rules that are written in the teachings of Moses. If you do these things, you will be successful in all you do and wherever you go. And if you obey the LORD, he will keep the promise he made to me. He said: 'If your descendants live as I tell them and have complete faith in me, a man from your family will always be king over the people of Israel.' "

1 Kings 2:1–4

The ways of God are without fault.
The LORD's words are pure.
He is a shield to those who trust him.
Who is God? Only the LORD.
Who is the Rock? Only our God.
God is my protection.
He makes my way free from fault.
He makes me like a deer that does not
stumble;
he helps me stand on the steep
mountains.
He trains my hands for battle
so my arms can bend a bronze bow.
You protect me with your saving shield.
You support me with your right hand.
You have stooped to make me great.
You give me a better way to live,
so I live as you want me to.

Psalm 18:30–36

The LORD is my shepherd;
I have everything I need.
He lets me rest in green pastures.
He leads me to calm water.
He gives me new strength.
He leads me on paths that are right
for the good of his name.
Surely your goodness and love will be
with me all my life,
and I will live in the house of the LORD
forever.

Psalm 23:1–3, 6

*When upon life's billows you are tempest
tossed,*
*When you are discouraged, thinking all is
lost,*
*Count your many blessings, name them one
by one,*
*And it will surprise you what the Lord hath
done.*

Are you ever burdened with a load of care?
*Does the cross seem heavy you are called to
bear?*
*Count your many blessings, ev'ry doubt will
fly,*
And you will be singing as the days go by.

*When you look at others with their lands
and gold,*
*Think that Christ has promised you His
wealth untold;*
*Count your many blessings, money cannot
buy*
*Your reward in heaven, nor your home on
high.*

*So, amid the conflict, whether great or
small,*
Do not be discouraged, God is over all;
*Count your many blessings, angels will
attend,*
*Help and comfort give you to your journey's
end.*

*Count your blessings, name them one by
one;*
*Count your blessings, see what God hath
done;*
*Count your blessings, name them one by
one;*
*Count your many blessings, see what God
hath done.*

Johnson Oatman, Jr.

*What are the differences between obeying the
law and believing the Good News? What was
the purpose of the law? What is promised to
all who believe? Name the blessings God has
bestowed on you!*

WEEKEND:
We Are God's Children

Galatians 3:21—4:20

The Purpose of the Law of Moses

Does this mean that the law is against God's promises? Never! That would be true only if the law could make us right. But God did not give a law that can bring life. Instead, the Scriptures showed that the whole world is bound by sin. This was so the promise would be given through faith to people who believe in Jesus Christ.

Before this faith came, we were all held prisoners by the law. We had no freedom until God showed us the way of faith that was coming. In other words, the law was our guardian leading us to Christ so that we could be made right with God through faith. Now the way of faith has come, and we no longer live under a guardian.

You were all baptized into Christ, and so you were all clothed with Christ. This means that you are all children of God through faith in Christ Jesus. In Christ, there is no difference between Jew and Greek, slave and free person, male and female. You are all the same in Christ Jesus. You belong to Christ, so you are Abraham's descendants. You will inherit all of God's blessings because of the promise God made to Abraham.

I want to tell you this: While those who will inherit their fathers' property are still children, they are no different from slaves. It does not matter that the children own everything. While they are children, they must obey those who are chosen to care for them. But when the children reach the age set by their fathers, they are free. It is the same for us. We were once like children, slaves to the useless rules of this world. But when the right time came, God sent his Son who was born of a woman and lived under the law. God did this so he could buy freedom for those who were under the law and so we could become his children.

Since you are God's children, God sent the Spirit of his Son into your hearts, and the Spirit cries out, "Father." So now you are not a slave; you are God's child, and God will give you the blessing he promised, because you are his child.

Paul's Love for the Christians

In the past you did not know God. You were slaves to gods that were not real. But now you know the true God. Really, it is God who knows you. So why do you turn back to those weak and useless rules you followed before? Do you want to be slaves to those things again? You still follow teachings about special days, months, seasons, and years. I am afraid for you, that my work for you has been wasted.

Brothers and sisters, I became like you, so I beg you to become like me. You were very good to me before. You remember that it was because of an illness that I came to you the first time, preaching the Good News. Though my sickness was a trouble for you, you did not hate me or make me leave. But you welcomed me as an angel from God, as if I were Jesus Christ himself! You were very happy then, but where is that joy now? I am ready to testify that you would have taken out your eyes and given them to me if that were possible. Now am I your enemy because I tell you the truth?

Those people are working hard to persuade you, but this is not good for you. They want to persuade you to turn against us and follow only them. It is good for people to show interest in you, but only if their purpose is good. This is always true, not just when I am with you. My little children, again I feel the pain of childbirth for you until you truly become like Christ. I wish I could be with you now and could change the way I am talking to you, because I do not know what to think about you.

But LORD, you are our father.
   We are like clay, and you are the
      potter;
   your hands made us all.
LORD, don't continue to be angry with
      us;

don't remember our sins forever.
Please, look at us,
because we are your people.

Isaiah 64:8–9

I will announce the name of the LORD.
Praise God because he is great!
They have done evil against him.
To their shame they are no longer
his children;
they are an evil and lying people.
This is not the way to repay the LORD,
you foolish and unwise people.
He is your Father and Maker,
who made you and formed you.

Remember the old days.
Think of the years already passed.
Ask your father and he will tell you;
ask your older leaders and they will
inform you.
God Most High gave the nations their
lands,
dividing up the human race.
He set up borders for the people
and even numbered the Israelites.
The LORD took his people as his share,
the people of Jacob as his very
own.

He found them in a desert,
a windy, empty land.
He surrounded them and brought them
up,
guarding them as those he loved
very much.

Deuteronomy 32:3, 5–10

B ut the number of the Israelites will become like the grains of sand of the sea,
which no one can measure or count. They
were called, 'You are not my people,' but
later they will be called 'children of the living God.' The people of Judah and Israel will
join together again and will choose one
leader for themselves. They will come up
from the land, because the day of Jezreel
will be truly great."

Hosea 1:10–11

Y ou are holy people, who belong to the
LORD your God. He has chosen you from
all the people on earth to be his very own.

Deuteronomy 14:2

INSIGHTS

A doption, by its very nature, is an act of
free kindness to the persons adopted. If you
become a father by adopting a child, you do
so because you choose to, not because you are
bound to. Similarly, God adopts because he
chooses to. He has no duty to do so. He need
not have done anything about our sins save
punish us as we deserved. But he loved us;
he redeemed us, forgave us . . . gave himself to us as our Father.

Nor does his grace stop short with that
initial act, any more than the love of human
parents who adopt stops short with the completing of the legal process that makes the
child theirs. The establishing of the child's
status as a member of the family is only a beginning. The real task remains: to establish
a filial relationship between your adopted
child and yourself to win the child's love by
loving it. You seek to excite affection by showing affection. And so it is with God.
Throughout our life in this world, and to all
eternity beyond, he will constantly be showing us in one way or another more and more
of his love, and thereby increasing our love
to him continually.

J. I. Packer

ACTION POINT

T hink carefully about the implications
of being made a child of God. How does one
live as a child of a living, holy God? Pray
that you will live like a child of God, not like
a child of the world.

MONDAY:
Christ Gives Us Freedom
Galatians 4:21—5:15

The Example of Hagar and Sarah

Some of you still want to be under the law. Tell me, do you know what the law says? The Scriptures say that Abraham had two sons. The mother of one son was a slave woman, and the mother of the other son was a free woman. Abraham's son from the slave woman was born in the normal human way. But the son from the free woman was born because of the promise God made to Abraham.

This story teaches something else: The two women are like the two agreements between God and his people. One agreement is the law that God made on Mount Sinai, and the people who are under this agreement are like slaves. The mother named Hagar is like that agreement. She is like Mount Sinai in Arabia and is a picture of the earthly Jewish city of Jerusalem. This city and its people, the Jews, are slaves to the law. But the heavenly Jerusalem, which is above, is like the free woman. She is our mother. It is written in the Scriptures:

"Be happy, Jerusalem.
    You are like a woman who never
        gave birth to children.
Start singing and shout for joy.
    You never felt the pain of giving birth,
but you will have more children
    than the woman who has a hus-
        band."   *Isaiah 54:1*

My brothers and sisters, you are God's children because of his promise, as Isaac was then. The son who was born in the normal way treated the other son badly. It is the same today. But what does the Scripture say? "Throw out the slave woman and her son. The son of the slave woman should not inherit anything. The son of the free woman should receive it all." So, my brothers and sisters, we are not children of the slave woman, but of the free woman.

Keep Your Freedom

We have freedom now, because Christ made us free. So stand strong. Do not change and go back into the slavery of the law. Listen, I Paul tell you that if you go back to the law by being circumcised, Christ does you no good. Again, I warn every man: If you allow yourselves to be circumcised, you must follow all the law. If you try to be made right with God through the law, your life with Christ is over—you have left God's grace. But we have the true hope that comes from being made right with God, and by the Spirit we wait eagerly for this hope. When we are in Christ Jesus, it is not important if we are circumcised or not. The important thing is faith—the kind of faith that works through love.

You were running a good race. Who stopped you from following the true way? This change did not come from the One who chose you. Be careful! "Just a little yeast makes the whole batch of dough rise." But I trust in the Lord that you will not believe those different ideas. Whoever is confusing you with such ideas will be punished.

My brothers and sisters, I do not teach that a man must be circumcised. If I teach circumcision, why am I still being attacked? If I still taught circumcision, my preaching about the cross would not be a problem. I wish the people who are bothering you would castrate themselves!

My brothers and sisters, God called you to be free, but do not use your freedom as an excuse to do what pleases your sinful self. Serve each other with love. The whole law is made complete in this one command: "Love your neighbor as you love yourself." If you go on hurting each other and tearing each other apart, be careful, or you will completely destroy each other.

After these things happened, the LORD spoke his word to Abram in a vision: "Abram, don't be afraid. I will defend you, and I will give you a great reward."

But Abram said, "Lord GOD, what can you give me? I have no son, so my slave

Eliezer from Damascus will get everything I own after I die." Abram said, "Look, you have given me no son, so a slave born in my house will inherit everything I have."

Then the LORD spoke his word to Abram: "He will not be the one to inherit what you have. You will have a son of your own who will inherit what you have."

Genesis 15:1–4

Sarai, Abram's wife, had no children, but she had a slave girl from Egypt named Hagar. Sarai said to Abram, "Look, the LORD has not allowed me to have children, so have sexual relations with my slave girl. If she has a child, maybe I can have my own family through her."

Abram did what Sarai said. It was after he had lived ten years in Canaan that Sarai gave Hagar to her husband Abram. (Hagar was her slave girl from Egypt.)

Abram had sexual relations with Hagar, and she became pregnant.

Genesis 16:1–4a

Abraham was one hundred years old when his son Isaac was born. And Sarah said, "God has made me laugh. Everyone who hears about this will laugh with me. No one thought that I would be able to have Abraham's child, but even though Abraham is old I have given him a son."

Isaac grew, and when he became old enough to eat food, Abraham gave a great feast. But Sarah saw Ishmael making fun of Isaac. (Ishmael was the son of Abraham by Hagar, Sarah's Egyptian slave.) So Sarah said to Abraham, "Throw out this slave woman and her son. Her son should not inherit anything; my son Isaac should receive it all."

This troubled Abraham very much because Ishmael was also his son. But God said to Abraham, "Don't be troubled about the boy and the slave woman. Do whatever Sarah tells you. The descendants I promised you will be from Isaac. I will also make the descendants of Ishmael into a great nation because he is your son, too."

Early the next morning Abraham took some food and a leather bag full of water. He gave them to Hagar and sent her away. Carrying these things and her son, Hagar went and wandered in the desert of Beersheba.

Genesis 21:5–14

INSIGHTS

Freedom is the privilege of those who are willing to obey. It is a privilege which carries many responsibilities. It is not an automatic right. . . .

Jesus said, ". . . You shall know the truth, and the truth shall make you free" (John 8:32). Truth makes us free because it gives understanding. Understanding helps us accept the necessary conditions, restrictions, and discipline which must prevail if there is to be true freedom. To obey the truth of God's Word makes us free from the slavery of evil habits, desires which harm us, and behavior which dishonors the Lord. Liberty is not the result of human achievement. It is the result of obedience to God. Disobedience means loss of freedom.

If freedom is to be real and lasting, it must be controlled by love. Freedom to do as one pleases, without regard for others or for the circumstances, is destructive. Christian liberty is freedom to love and to serve. It is abused when it is made an excuse for loveless behavior or inconsiderate action.

Real freedom is found in serving God. With our minds centered on Christ and what He would have us do, the self-centered desires and degrading habits of life are crowded out. Life is complete and happy when we surrender ourselves to God, whose yoke is easy and burden is light (Matthew 11:30).

Lucille Sollenberger

PAUSE FOR REFLECTION

What are the differences between the children of the slave woman and the free woman? Who gives true freedom? What privileges does freedom in Christ provide? Do you fully enjoy those privileges?

TUESDAY:
We Harvest What We Plant
Galatians 5:16—6:18

The Spirit and Human Nature

So I tell you: Live by following the Spirit. Then you will not do what your sinful selves want. Our sinful selves want what is against the Spirit, and the Spirit wants what is against our sinful selves. The two are against each other, so you cannot do just what you please. But if the Spirit is leading you, you are not under the law.

The wrong things the sinful self does are clear: being sexually unfaithful, not being pure, taking part in sexual sins, worshiping gods, doing witchcraft, hating, making trouble, being jealous, being angry, being selfish, making people angry with each other, causing divisions among people, feeling envy, being drunk, having wild and wasteful parties, and doing other things like these. I warn you now as I warned you before: Those who do these things will not inherit God's kingdom. But the Spirit produces the fruit of love, joy, peace, patience, kindness, goodness, faithfulness, gentleness, self-control. There is no law that says these things are wrong. Those who belong to Christ Jesus have crucified their own sinful selves. They have given up their old selfish feelings and the evil things they wanted to do. We get our new life from the Spirit, so we should follow the Spirit. We must not be proud or make trouble with each other or be jealous of each other.

Help Each Other

Brothers and sisters, if someone in your group does something wrong, you who are spiritual should go to that person and gently help make him right again. But be careful, because you might be tempted to sin, too. By helping each other with your troubles, you truly obey the law of Christ. If anyone thinks he is important when he really is not, he is only fooling himself. Each person should judge his own actions and not compare himself with others. Then he can be proud for what he himself has done. Each person must be responsible for himself.

Anyone who is learning the teaching of God should share all the good things he has with his teacher.

Life Is like Planting a Field

Do not be fooled: You cannot cheat God. People harvest only what they plant. If they plant to satisfy their sinful selves, their sinful selves will bring them ruin. But if they plant to please the Spirit, they will receive eternal life from the Spirit. We must not become tired of doing good. We will receive our harvest of eternal life at the right time if we do not give up. When we have the opportunity to help anyone, we should do it. But we should give special attention to those who are in the family of believers.

Paul Ends His Letter

See what large letters I use to write this myself. Some people are trying to force you to be circumcised so the Jews will accept them. They are afraid they will be attacked if they follow only the cross of Christ. Those who are circumcised do not obey the law themselves, but they want you to be circumcised so they can brag about what they forced you to do. I hope I will never brag about things like that. The cross of our Lord Jesus Christ is my only reason for bragging. Through the cross of Jesus my world was crucified, and I died to the world. It is not important if a man is circumcised or uncircumcised. The important thing is being the new people God has made. Peace and mercy to those who follow this rule—and to all of God's people.

So do not give me any more trouble. I have scars on my body that show I belong to Christ Jesus.

My brothers and sisters, the grace of our Lord Jesus Christ be with your spirit. Amen.

Joy

If people please God, God will give them wisdom, knowledge, and joy. But sinners will get only the work of gathering and storing wealth that they will have to give to the ones who please God. So all their work is useless, like chasing the wind.

Ecclesiastes 2:26

Kindness

*D*on't ever forget kindness and truth.
Wear them like a necklace.
Write them on your heart as if on a
tablet.
Then you will be respected
and will please both God and people.

Proverbs 3:3–4

Witchcraft

*S*aul died because he was not faithful to the LORD and did not obey the LORD. He even went to a medium and asked her for advice.

1 Chronicles 10:13

Patience

*W*ait and trust the LORD.
Don't be upset when others get rich
or when someone else's plans
succeed.
Don't get angry.
Don't be upset; it only leads to
trouble.
Evil people will be sent away,
but those who trust the LORD will
inherit the land.

Psalm 37:7–9

Peace

*T*hose who plan evil are full of lies,
but those who plan peace are happy.

No harm comes to a good person,
but an evil person's life is full of
trouble.

Proverbs 12:20–21

Drunkenness

*W*ho has trouble? Who has pain?
Who fights? Who complains?
Who has unnecessary bruises?
Who has bloodshot eyes?
It is people who drink too much wine,
who try out all different kinds of
strong drinks.
Don't stare at the wine when it is red,
when it sparkles in the cup,

when it goes down smoothly.
Later it bites like a snake
with poison in its fangs.

Proverbs 23:29–32

---

*O*ur dividends in heaven are determined by what we invest in on earth. We can invest in eternal sureties, or we can invest in wind. . . .

. . . According to the law of the harvest you reap what you sow. If you sow wheat, you reap wheat; if you sow weeds, you reap weeds; if you sow wind, you reap wind. The law of the harvest operates in the spiritual and moral realms as well as the physical. "Do not be deceived, God is not mocked; for whatever a man sows, this he will also reap" (Galatians 6:7). . . . We should guard against sowing too much time, energy, and money on clothes and recreation and parties and other means of self-indulgence. We will reap nothing in terms of our eternal well-being from these seeds. No wonder growing Christians are exhorted to "guard yourselves from idols" (1 John 5:21). Idols are not just the wood and stone types that Israel turned to, but anything that steals our hearts and minds away from total commitment to the Lord. . . .

. . . If we invest our lives in the nothingness of what this world has to offer, we not only reap a harvest of nothing but we destroy our lives as well. Many Christians have lives that are disordered, chaotic, and shattered because of their investment in the wind of this world. . . .

. . . We must have a steady diet of the solid food of the Word of God now if we are going to avoid the stunted growth, starvation, and emptiness that are associated with feeding on wind.

David Reid

ACTION POINT

*E*xamine your life and list what you have sown. Does what you have sown please the Spirit (Gal. 5:16–25)? What do you need to sow on earth in order to receive the heavenly dividends you desire?

WEDNESDAY:

The Importance of Praying for One Another

Ephesians 1:1—2:3

NEW TESTAMENT READING

*F*rom Paul, an apostle of Christ Jesus. I am an apostle because that is what God wanted.

To God's holy people living in Ephesus, believers in Christ Jesus:

Grace and peace to you from God our Father and the Lord Jesus Christ.

Spiritual Blessings in Christ

*P*raise be to the God and Father of our Lord Jesus Christ. In Christ, God has given us every spiritual blessing in the heavenly world. That is, in Christ, he chose us before the world was made so that we would be his holy people—people without blame before him. Because of his love, God had already decided to make us his own children through Jesus Christ. That was what he wanted and what pleased him, and it brings praise to God because of his wonderful grace. God gave that grace to us freely, in Christ, the One he loves. In Christ we are set free by the blood of his death, and so we have forgiveness of sins. How rich is God's grace, which he has given to us so fully and freely. God, with full wisdom and understanding, let us know his secret purpose. This was what God wanted, and he planned to do it through Christ. His goal was to carry out his plan, when the right time came, that all things in heaven and on earth would be joined together in Christ as the head.

In Christ we were chosen to be God's people, because from the very beginning God had decided this in keeping with his plan. And he is the One who makes everything agree with what he decides and wants. We are the first people who hoped in Christ, and we were chosen so that we would bring praise to God's glory. So it is with you. When you heard the true teaching—the Good News about your salvation—you believed in Christ. And in Christ, God put his special mark of ownership on you by giving you the Holy Spirit that he had promised. That Holy Spirit is the guarantee that we will receive what God promised for his people until God gives full freedom to those who are his—to bring praise to God's glory.

Paul's Prayer

*T*hat is why since I heard about your faith in the Lord Jesus and your love for all God's people, I have not stopped giving thanks to God for you. I always remember you in my prayers, asking the God of our Lord Jesus Christ, the glorious Father, to give you a spirit of wisdom and revelation so that you will know him better. I pray also that you will have greater understanding in your heart so you will know the hope to which he has called us and that you will know how rich and glorious are the blessings God has promised his holy people. And you will know that God's power is very great for us who believe. That power is the same as the great strength God used to raise Christ from the dead and put him at his right side in the heavenly world. God has put Christ over all rulers, authorities, powers, and kings, not only in this world but also in the next. God put everything under his power and made him the head over everything for the church, which is Christ's body. The church is filled with Christ, and Christ fills everything in every way.

We Now Have Life

*I*n the past you were spiritually dead because of your sins and the things you did against God. Yes, in the past you lived the way the world lives, following the ruler of the evil powers that are above the earth. That same spirit is now working in those who refuse to obey God. In the past all of us lived like them, trying to please our sinful selves and doing all the things our bodies and minds wanted. We should have suffered God's anger because of the way we were. We were the same as all other people.

OLD TESTAMENT READING

*A*rioch, the commander of the king's guards, was going to kill the wise men of Babylon. But Daniel spoke to him with wisdom and skill, saying, "Why did the king order such a terrible punishment?" Then Arioch explained everything to Daniel. So Daniel went to King Nebuchadnezzar and asked for an appointment so that he could tell the king what his dream meant.

Then Daniel went to his house and explained the whole story to his friends Hananiah, Mishael, and Azariah. Daniel asked his friends to pray that the God of heaven would show them mercy and help them understand this secret so he and his friends would not be killed with the other wise men of Babylon.

Daniel 2:14–18

*A*fter the LORD had said these things to Job, he said to Eliphaz the Temanite, "I am angry with you and your two friends, because you have not said what is right about me, as my servant Job did. Now take seven bulls and seven male sheep, and go to my servant Job, and offer a burnt offering for yourselves. My servant Job will pray for you, and I will listen to his prayer. Then I will not punish you for being foolish. You have not said what is right about me, as my servant Job did." So Eliphaz the Temanite, Bildad the Shuhite, and Zophar that Naamathite did as the LORD said, and the LORD listened to Job's prayer.

Job 42:7–9

*T*hen I again bowed facedown on the ground before the LORD for forty days and forty nights; I did not eat bread or drink water. You had sinned by doing what the LORD said was evil, and you made him angry. I was afraid of the LORD's anger and rage, because he was angry enough with you to destroy you, but the LORD listened to me again. And the LORD was angry enough with Aaron to destroy him, but then I prayed for Aaron, too.

Deuteronomy 9:18–20

INSIGHTS

*C*ompassion lies at the heart of intercession. . . .

When we promise to pray for someone, how often do we truly enter into the reality of what that means? The story of the paralytic borne by four friends to Jesus for healing is a powerful illustration of intercessory love. We 'carry' those for whom we pray (we even speak sometimes of having 'a burden' in prayer). We bring them to the Lord that he may meet them in their need, touch their lives, restore their health and bring them the joy of his wholeness. Self is out of the picture, for we have become that other person experiencing his pain with him, suffering his fears for him, consumed with the same longings.

"Blessed are the merciful," said Jesus (Matt 5:7). Part of the meaning of being merciful is to get inside the skin of someone else, to feel as he feels, think as he thinks, see as he sees, to understand life the way he understands it. That, of course, is at the heart of the incarnation. It is precisely what Jesus did when he 'got inside the skin' of a human being and experienced life as we do.

This kind of intercession is contemplative rather than petitionary. It is gathered up in compassion and empathy more often than words—though words are sometimes helpful to us in focusing on a particular person or need. We can bear people to the Lord, as the friends of the paralytic did, and leave them with him. We do not need to inform him of all the facts or suggest how he should act. We are not able to pray, but the Holy Spirit can pray through and in us. We cannot heal, but God can heal through us.

Margaret Magdalen

PAUSE FOR REFLECTION

*D*o you feel the passion with which Paul, Daniel and his friends, Moses, and Job prayed? These prayers go far deeper than cursory "Lord bless" and "Lord forgive" prayers, don't they? Could your prayers perhaps flow from deeper in your heart?

THURSDAY:

God Gives Mercy and Grace to His People

Ephesians 2:4—3:6

NEW TESTAMENT READING

*B*ut God's mercy is great, and he loved us very much. Though we were spiritually dead because of the things we did against God, he gave us new life with Christ. You have been saved by God's grace. And he raised us up with Christ and gave us a seat with him in the heavens. He did this for those in Christ Jesus so that for all future time he could show the very great riches of his grace by being kind to us in Christ Jesus. I mean that you have been saved by grace through believing. You did not save yourselves; it was a gift from God. It was not the result of your own efforts, so you cannot brag about it. God has made us what we are. In Christ Jesus, God made us to do good works, which God planned in advance for us to live our lives doing.

One in Christ

*Y*ou were not born Jewish. You are the people the Jews call "uncircumcised." Those who call you "uncircumcised" call themselves "circumcised." (Their circumcision is only something they themselves do on their bodies.) Remember that in the past you were without Christ. You were not citizens of Israel, and you had no part in the agreements with the promise that God made to his people. You had no hope, and you did not know God. But now in Christ Jesus, you who were far away from God are brought near through the blood of Christ's death. Christ himself is our peace. He made both Jewish people and those who are not Jews one people. They were separated as if there were a wall between them, but Christ broke down that wall of hate by giving his own body. The Jewish law had many commands and rules, but Christ ended that law. His purpose was to make the two groups of people become one new people in him and in this way make peace. It was also Christ's purpose to end the hatred between the two groups, to make them into one body, and to bring them back to God. Christ did all this with his death on the cross. Christ came and preached peace to you who were far away from God, and to those who were near to God. Yes, it is through Christ we all have the right to come to the Father in one Spirit.

Now you who are not Jewish are not foreigners or strangers any longer, but are citizens together with God's holy people. You belong to God's family. You are like a building that was built on the foundation of the apostles and prophets. Christ Jesus himself is the most important stone in that building, and that whole building is joined together in Christ. He makes it grow and become a holy temple in the Lord. And in Christ you, too, are being built together with the Jews into a place where God lives through the Spirit.

Paul's Work in Telling the Good News

*S*o I, Paul, am a prisoner of Christ Jesus for you who are not Jews. Surely you have heard that God gave me this work through his grace to help you. He let me know his secret by showing it to me. I have already written a little about this. If you read what I wrote then, you can see that I truly understand the secret about the Christ. People who lived in other times were not told that secret. But now, through the Spirit, God has shown that secret to his holy apostles and prophets. This is that secret: that through the Good News those who are not Jews will share with the Jews in God's blessing. They belong to the same body, and they share together in the promise that God made in Christ Jesus.

OLD TESTAMENT READING

I will not accuse forever,
  nor will I always be angry,
because then human life would grow
    weak.
  Human beings, whom I created,
    would die.

I was angry because they were dishonest in order to make money.
I punished them and turned away
 from them in anger,
but they continued to do evil.
I have seen what they have done, but I
 will heal them.
I will guide them and comfort them
 and those who felt sad for them.
They will all praise me.
I will give peace, real peace, to those far
 and near,
 and I will heal them," says the LORD.
Isaiah 57:16–19

*T*here is no God like you.
 You forgive those who are guilty of
  sin;
you don't look at the sins of your
  people
 who are left alive.
You will not stay angry forever,
 because you enjoy being kind.
You will have mercy on us again;
 you will conquer our sins.
You will throw away all our sins
 into the deepest part of the sea.
Micah 7:18–19

*N*ow, our God, hear the prayers of your
servant. Listen to my prayer for help, and
for your sake do good things for your holy
place that is in ruins. My God, pay attention
and hear me. Open your eyes and see all
the terrible things that have happened to us.
See how our lives have been ruined and
what has happened to the city that is called
by your name. We do not ask these things
because we are good; instead, we ask because of your mercy."
Daniel 9:17–18

*L*ord, my God, I will praise you with
 all my heart,
 and I will honor your name forever.
You have great love for me.
 You have saved me from death.

But Lord, you are a God who shows
 mercy and is kind.
 You don't become angry quickly.
You have great love and faithfulness.
Psalm 86:12–13, 15

*In my own life I am acutely aware that I
am a roughhewn man. Because of my rather
tough, rough upbringing in a frontier environment, I simply do not possess the polish of
the "man about the town." There are characteristics in my makeup which may seem harsh
and unyielding. But, despite this, my life has
been deeply touched by the mercy of those who
took the time to try and understand me—who
cared enough to forgive so many faults and
who in mercy made me their friend.*

*Often these were people to whom I had
shown no special kindness. Their bestowal of
mercy on me was something totally unexpected and undeserved. Because of this, it has
been a double delight. More than that, it has
been an enormous inspiration that lifted and
challenged me to respond in a measure beyond my wildest dreams.*

*Mercy does just that to people. It excites
and stimulates their hope. It reassures them
that life can be beautiful. It convinces them
that there is good reason to carry on and push
for better things if others care that much.*

*This all implies that if someone has ex-
tended mercy to me, surely I, in turn, can and
must extend mercy to others.*

*But, to really find the true source of inner
inspiration for this sort of conduct, the Christian simply must look beyond his fellow man.
He must look away to the mercy of God our
Father. Nothing else in all the world will so
humble us. Nothing else will so move our
stony spirits to extend mercy. Nothing else will
so powerfully induce us to do the proper thing
in extending genuine mercy to our contemporaries.*

W. Phillip Keller

PAUSE FOR REFLECTION

*What has God's mercy, as described in
Ephesians, accomplished for all people? How
has God's mercy touched your life? What has
been the result of his merciful touch? How will
you thank him?*

FRIDAY:
Christ's Love Is Greater than Anyone Can Fathom
Ephesians 3:7—4:16

NEW TESTAMENT READING

*B*y God's special gift of grace given to me through his power, I became a servant to tell that Good News. I am the least important of all God's people, but God gave me this gift—to tell those who are not Jews the Good News about the riches of Christ, which are too great to understand fully. And God gave me the work of telling all people about the plan for his secret, which has been hidden in him since the beginning of time. He is the One who created everything. His purpose was that through the church all the rulers and powers in the heavenly world will now know God's wisdom, which has so many forms. This agrees with the purpose God had since the beginning of time, and he carried out his plan through Christ Jesus our Lord. In Christ we can come before God with freedom and without fear. We can do this through faith in Christ. So I ask you not to become discouraged because of the sufferings I am having for you. My sufferings are for your glory.

The Love of Christ

*S*o I bow in prayer before the Father from whom every family in heaven and on earth gets its true name. I ask the Father in his great glory to give you the power to be strong inwardly through his Spirit. I pray that Christ will live in your hearts by faith and that your life will be strong in love and be built on love. And I pray that you and all God's holy people will have the power to understand the greatness of Christ's love—how wide and how long and how high and how deep that love is. Christ's love is greater than anyone can ever know, but I pray that you will be able to know that love. Then you can be filled with the fullness of God.

With God's power working in us, God can do much, much more than anything we can ask or imagine. To him be glory in the church and in Christ Jesus for all time, forever and ever. Amen.

The Unity of the Body

I am in prison because I belong to the Lord. God chose you to be his people, so I urge you now to live the life to which God called you. Always be humble, gentle, and patient, accepting each other in love. You are joined together with peace through the Spirit, so make every effort to continue together in this way. There is one body and one Spirit, and God called you to have one hope. There is one Lord, one faith, and one baptism. There is one God and Father of everything. He rules everything and is everywhere and is in everything.

Christ gave each one of us the special gift of grace, showing how generous he is. That is why it says in the Scriptures,

"When he went up to the heights,
  he led a parade of captives,
  and he gave gifts to people."

Psalm 68:18

When it says, "He went up," what does it mean? It means that he first came down to the earth. So Jesus came down, and he is the same One who went up above all the sky. Christ did that to fill everything with his presence. And Christ gave gifts to people—he made some to be apostles, some to be prophets, some to go and tell the Good News, and some to have the work of caring for and teaching God's people. Christ gave those gifts to prepare God's holy people for the work of serving, to make the body of Christ stronger. This work must continue until we are all joined together in the same faith and in the same knowledge of the Son of God. We must become like a mature person, growing until we become like Christ and have his perfection.

Then we will no longer be babies. We will not be tossed about like a ship that the waves carry one way and then another. We will not be influenced by every new teaching we hear from people who are trying to fool us. They make plans and try any kind of trick to fool people into following the wrong path. No! Speaking the truth with love, we will grow up in every way into

Christ, who is the head. The whole body depends on Christ, and all the parts of the body are joined and held together. Each part does its own work to make the whole body grow and be strong with love.

OLD   TESTAMENT   READING

*P*raise the LORD, all nations on earth.
　　Praise the LORD's glory and power;
　　praise the glory of the LORD's name.
Bring an offering and come to him.
　　Worship the LORD because he is
　　　holy.
Thank the LORD because he is good.
　　His love continues forever.

1 Chronicles 16:28, 29, 34

*D*avid left Zadok the priest and the other priests who served with him in front of the Tent of the LORD at the place of worship in Gibeon. Every morning and evening they offered burnt offerings on the altar of burnt offerings, following the rules written in the Teachings of the LORD, which he had given Israel. With them were Heman and Jeduthun and other Levites. They were chosen by name to sing praises to the LORD because his love continues forever.

1 Chronicles 16:39–41

*G*ive thanks to the LORD because he is
　　good.
　　His love continues forever.
Only he can do great miracles.
　　His love continues forever.
With his wisdom he made the skies.
　　His love continues forever.
He spread out the earth on the seas.
　　His love continues forever.
He made the sun and the moon.
　　His love continues forever.
He made the sun to rule the day.
　　His love continues forever.
He made the moon and stars to rule the
　　night.
　　His love continues forever.
Give thanks to the God of heaven.
　　His love continues forever.

Psalm 136:1, 4–9, 26

I N S I G H T S

*T*he love of Christ in its sweetness, its fulness, its greatness, its faithfulness, passeth all human comprehension. Where shall language be found which shall describe His matchless, His unparalleled love towards the children of men? It is so vast and boundless that, as the swallow but skimmeth the water, and diveth not into its depths, so all descriptive words but touch the surface, while depths immeasurable lie beneath. . . . Before we can have any right idea of the love of Jesus, we must understand His previous glory in its height of majesty, and His incarnation upon the earth in all its depths of shame. But who can tell us the majesty of Christ? When He was enthroned in the highest heavens He was very God of very God; by Him were the heavens made, and all the hosts thereof. His own almighty arm upheld the spheres; the praises of cherubim and seraphim perpetually surrounded Him; the full chorus of the hallelujahs of the universe unceasingly flowed to the foot of his throne: He reigned supreme above all His creatures, God over all, blessed for ever. Who can tell His height of glory then? And who, on the other hand, can tell how low He descended? To be a man was something, to be a man of sorrows was far more; to bleed, and die, and suffer, these were much for Him who was the Son of God; but to suffer such unparalleled agony—to endure a death of shame and desertion by His Father, this is a depth of condescending love which the most inspired mind must utterly fail to fathom. Herein is love! and truly it is love that "passeth knowledge." O let this love fill our hearts with adoring gratitude, and lead us to practical manifestations of its power.

Charles Spurgeon

A C T I O N   P O I N T

*D*escribe in the best way you can, how wide, long, high, and deep Christ's love is. Pray that you will know the fullness of God's love in your life. Offer your own praise to God for his love.

467

WEEKEND:

Guard Against Greed

Ephesians 4:17—5:14

NEW TESTAMENT READING

The Way You Should Live

*I*n the Lord's name, I tell you this. Do not continue living like those who do not believe. Their thoughts are worth nothing. They do not understand, and they know nothing, because they refuse to listen. So they cannot have the life that God gives. They have lost all feeling of shame, and they use their lives for doing evil. They continually want to do all kinds of evil. But what you learned in Christ was not like this. I know that you heard about him, and you are in him, so you were taught the truth that is in Jesus. You were taught to leave your old self—to stop living the evil way you lived before. That old self becomes worse, because people are fooled by the evil things they want to do. But you were taught to be made new in your hearts, to become a new person. That new person is made to be like God—made to be truly good and holy.

So you must stop telling lies. Tell each other the truth, because we all belong to each other in the same body. When you are angry, do not sin, and be sure to stop being angry before the end of the day. Do not give the devil a way to defeat you. Those who are stealing must stop stealing and start working. They should earn an honest living for themselves. Then they will have something to share with those who are poor.

When you talk, do not say harmful things, but say what people need—words that will help others become stronger. Then what you say will do good to those who listen to you. And do not make the Holy Spirit sad. The Spirit is God's proof that you belong to him. God gave you the Spirit to show that God will make you free when the final day comes. Do not be bitter or angry or mad. Never shout angrily or say things to hurt others. Never do anything evil. Be kind and loving to each other, and forgive each other just as God forgave you in Christ.

Living in the Light

*Y*ou are God's children whom he loves, so try to be like him. Live a life of love just as Christ loved us and gave himself for us as a sweet-smelling offering and sacrifice to God.

But there must be no sexual sin among you, or any kind of evil or greed. Those things are not right for God's holy people. Also, there must be no evil talk among you, and you must not speak foolishly or tell evil jokes. These things are not right for you. Instead, you should be giving thanks to God. You can be sure of this: No one will have a place in the kingdom of Christ and of God who sins sexually, or does evil things, or is greedy. Anyone who is greedy is serving a false god.

Do not let anyone fool you by telling you things that are not true, because these things will bring God's anger on those who do not obey him. So have nothing to do with them. In the past you were full of darkness, but now you are full of light in the Lord. So live like children who belong to the light. Light brings every kind of goodness, right living, and truth. Try to learn what pleases the Lord. Have nothing to do with the things done in darkness, which are not worth anything. But show that they are wrong. It is shameful even to talk about what those people do in secret. But the light makes all things easy to see, and everything that is made easy to see can become light. This is why it is said:

"Wake up, sleeper!
    Rise from death,
    and Christ will shine on you."

OLD TESTAMENT READING

*M*y child, if sinners try to lead you
        into sin,
    do not follow them.
My child, do not go along with them;
    do not do what they do.
They are eager to do evil
    and are quick to kill.

It is useless to spread out a net
    right where the birds can see it.
But sinners will fall into their own traps;
    they will only catch themselves!
All greedy people end up this way;
    greed kills selfish people.

Proverbs 1:10, 15–19

*E*veryone, from the least important to
    the greatest,
    is greedy for money.
Even the prophets and priests
    all tell lies.
They tried to heal my people's serious
    injuries
    as if they were small wounds.
They said, "It's all right, it's all right."
    But really, it is not all right.
They should be ashamed of the terrible
    way they act,
    but they are not ashamed at all.
They don't even know how to blush
    about their sins.
So they will fall, along with everyone else.
    They will be thrown to the ground
    when I punish them, says the LORD.

Jeremiah 8:10b–12

A truthful person will have many
    blessings,
    but those eager to get rich will be
    punished.

Proverbs 28:20

*G*reed has two daughters
    named 'Give' and 'Give.'
There are three things that are never
    satisfied,
    really four that never say, 'I've had
    enough!':
the cemetery, the childless mother,
    the land that never gets enough rain,
    and fire that never says, 'I've had
    enough!' "

Proverbs 30:15–16

*S*omeone has well said, "Our pocketbooks
have more to do with heaven and hell than
our hymnbooks." Jesus told the story of the rich
man who had everything, and a beggar who

had nothing. The rich man, blinded by his
abundance, neither saw his need for righteousness nor prepared himself for eternity.
Lazarus, who had received only bad things,
"crumbs from the rich man's table," had prepared well for his future. And their roles in
the future life were completely reversed! (Luke
16:19–31) . . .

Cyprian, the third-century bishop of
Carthage, wrote an amazingly up-to-date de-
scription of the affluent:

Their property held them in
chains . . . which shackled their
courage and choked their faith and
hampered their judgment and throttled
their souls. . . . If they stored up their
treasure in heaven, they would not now
have an enemy and a thief within their
household. . . . They think of themselves as owners, whereas it is they
rather who are owned: enslaved as they
are to their own property, they are not
the masters of their money but its slaves.

How we need to hear the voice of the New
Testament as it calls us to a life of responsible stewardship of our resources.

Art Beals

*W*hy is greed such a hindrance to spiritual
growth? What other lifestyle choices are wrong
for God's holy people? Why? What does your
handling of possessions reveal about your
heart?

MONDAY:

Mutual Love in Marriage

Ephesians 5:15—6:4

NEW TESTAMENT READING

So be very careful how you live. Do not live like those who are not wise, but live wisely. Use every chance you have for doing good, because these are evil times. So do not be foolish but learn what the Lord wants you to do. Do not be drunk with wine, which will ruin you, but be filled with the Spirit. Speak to each other with psalms, hymns, and spiritual songs, singing and making music in your hearts to the Lord. Always give thanks to God the Father for everything, in the name of our Lord Jesus Christ.

Wives and Husbands

Yield to obey each other because you respect Christ.

Wives, yield to your husbands, as you do to the Lord, because the husband is the head of the wife, as Christ is the head of the church. And he is the Savior of the body, which is the church. As the church yields to Christ, so you wives should yield to your husbands in everything.

Husbands, love your wives as Christ loved the church and gave himself for it to make it belong to God. Christ used the word to make the church clean by washing it with water. He died so that he could give the church to himself like a bride in all her beauty. He died so that the church could be pure and without fault, with no evil or sin or any other wrong thing in it. In the same way, husbands should love their wives as they love their own bodies. The man who loves his wife loves himself. No one ever hates his own body, but feeds and takes care of it. And that is what Christ does for the church, because we are parts of his body. The Scripture says, "So a man will leave his father and mother and be united with his wife, and the two will become one body." That secret is very important—I am talking about Christ and the church. But each one of you must love his wife as he loves himself, and a wife must respect her husband.

Children and Parents

Children, obey your parents as the Lord wants, because this is the right thing to do. The command says, "Honor your father and mother." This is the first command that has a promise with it—"Then everything will be well with you, and you will have a long life on the earth."

Fathers, do not make your children angry, but raise them with the training and teaching of the Lord.

OLD TESTAMENT READING

Be happy with the wife you married
  when you were young.
She gives you joy as your fountain
  gives you water.
She is as lovely and graceful as a deer.
  Let her love always make you happy;
  let her love always hold you captive.
My son, don't be held captive by a
  woman who takes part in adultery.
Don't hug another man's wife.

Proverbs 5:18–20

My lover is mine, and I am his.
  He feeds among the lilies
until the day dawns
  and the shadows disappear.
Turn, my lover.
  Be like a gazelle or a young deer
  on the mountain valleys.

Song of Solomon 2:16–17

He said, "I am Abraham's servant. The LORD has greatly blessed my master in everything, and he has become a rich man. The LORD has given him many flocks of sheep, herds of cattle, silver and gold, male and female servants, camels, and horses. Sarah, my master's wife, gave birth to a son when she was old, and my master has given everything he owns to that son. My master had me make a promise to him and said, 'Don't get a wife for my son from the Canaanite girls who live around here. Instead, you must go to my father's people and to my family. There you must get a wife for my son.' I said to my master, 'What if the woman will not come back with me?' But he said, 'I serve the LORD, who will send his angel with you and will help you. You will get a wife for my son from my family and my father's people.'"

Laban and Bethuel answered, "This is clearly from the LORD, and we cannot change what must happen. Rebekah is yours. Take her and go. Let her marry your master's son as the LORD has commanded."

At this time Isaac had left Beer Lahai Roi and was living in southern Canaan. One evening when he went out to the field to think, he looked up and saw camels coming. Rebekah also looked and saw Isaac. Then she jumped down from the camel and asked the servant, "Who is that man walking in the field to meet us?"

The servant answered, "That is my master." So Rebekah covered her face with her veil.

The servant told Isaac everything that had happened. Then Isaac brought Rebekah into the tent of Sarah, his mother, and she became his wife. Isaac loved her very much, and so he was comforted after his mother's death.

Genesis 24:34–40, 50–51, 62–66

INSIGHTS

If you could enter a time machine and emerge back in the first century when Paul's letters hit the culture of the day, you would be in for some real excitement. His instruction to husbands in Ephesians 5:25–27 must have caused a riot! They went contrary to the way men treated women at that time. Paul's writing called the husband to a ministry of loving servanthood to his wife in a culture which treated women as little better than household furnishings!

A husband is to love his wife with the same sacrificial self-abandonment that Christ adopted toward each of us. When a man considers hardship in marriage, he needs to look at the life of Jesus. Jesus said, "The Son of Man came not to be served, but to serve" (Matthew 20:28). Jesus is presented in Scripture as both Head and Servant. He is the "head over everything for the church" *(Ephesians 1:22) who took "the very nature of a servant (Philippians 2:7). And Jesus instructed us, "The greatest among you will be your servant" (Matthew 23:11).*

As believers, we are all called to servanthood as an expression of our new life in Christ. However, when it comes to marriage, modeling this attribute of God's Son is a calling extended to husbands. A husband expresses love to his wife by regarding her as a completely equal partner in everything that concerns their life together. He asserts his headship to see that this equal partnership works. Loving headship affirms and defers; it encourages and stimulates. Loving headship delights to delegate without demanding.

H. Norman Wright

PAUSE FOR REFLECTION

How do Paul's instructions about marriage fit in with the broader scope of instructions on Christian living that he offers in this passage (Ephesians 5:15–21)? What do his instructions reveal about God's desired intent for marriage?

TUESDAY:

We Are Involved in a Spiritual Battle!

Ephesians 6:5–24

Slaves and Masters

Slaves, obey your masters here on earth with fear and respect and from a sincere heart, just as you obey Christ. You must do this not only while they are watching you, to please them. With all your heart you must do what God wants as people who are obeying Christ. Do your work with enthusiasm. Work as if you were serving the Lord, not as if you were serving only men and women. Remember that the Lord will give a reward to everyone, slave or free, for doing good.

Masters, in the same way, be good to your slaves. Do not threaten them. Remember that the One who is your Master and their Master is in heaven, and he treats everyone alike.

Wear the Full Armor of God

Finally, be strong in the Lord and in his great power. Put on the full armor of God so that you can fight against the devil's evil tricks. Our fight is not against people on earth but against the rulers and authorities and the powers of this world's darkness, against the spiritual powers of evil in the heavenly world. That is why you need to put on God's full armor. Then on the day of evil you will be able to stand strong. And when you have finished the whole fight, you will still be standing. So stand strong, with the belt of truth tied around your waist and the protection of right living on your chest. On your feet wear the Good News of peace to help you stand strong. And also use the shield of faith with which you can stop all the burning arrows of the Evil One. Accept God's salvation as your helmet, and take the sword of the Spirit, which is the word of God. Pray in the Spirit at all times with all kinds of prayers, asking for everything you need. To do this you must always be ready

and never give up. Always pray for all God's people.

Also pray for me that when I speak, God will give me words so that I can tell the secret of the Good News without fear. I have been sent to preach this Good News, and I am doing that now, here in prison. Pray that when I preach the Good News I will speak without fear, as I should.

Final Greetings

I am sending to you Tychicus, our brother whom we love and a faithful servant of the Lord's work. He will tell you everything that is happening with me. Then you will know how I am and what I am doing. I am sending him to you for this reason—so that you will know how we are, and he can encourage you.

Peace and love with faith to you from God the Father and the Lord Jesus Christ. Grace to all of you who love our Lord Jesus Christ with love that never ends.

One day the angels came to show themselves before the LORD, and Satan was with them. The LORD said to Satan, "Where have you come from?"

Satan answered the LORD, "I have been wandering around the earth, going back and forth in it."

Then the LORD said to Satan, "Have you noticed my servant Job? No one else on earth is like him. He is an honest and innocent man, honoring God and staying away from evil."

But Satan answered the LORD, "Job honors God for a good reason. You have put a wall around him, his family, and everything he owns. You have blessed the things he has done. His flocks and herds are so large they almost cover the land.

Job 1:6–10

On the twenty-fourth day of the first month, I was standing beside the great Tigris River. While standing there, I looked up and saw a man dressed in linen clothes with a belt of fine gold wrapped around his waist. His body was like shiny yellow quartz.

His face was bright like lightning, and his eyes were like fire. His arms and legs were shiny like polished bronze, and his voice sounded like the roar of a crowd.

I, Daniel, was the only person who saw the vision. The men with me did not see it, because they were so frightened that they ran away and hid.

Then the man said to me, "Daniel, do not be afraid. Some time ago you decided to get understanding and to humble yourself before your God. Since that time God has listened to you, and I have come because of your prayers. But the prince of Persia has been fighting against me for twenty-one days. Then Michael, one of the most important angels, came to help me, because I had been left there with the king of Persia."

Daniel 10:4–7, 12–13

You must destroy all the people the LORD your God hands over to you. Do not feel sorry for them, and do not worship their gods, or they will trap you.

Deuteronomy 7:16

The people did not destroy the other
    nations
  as the LORD had told them to do.
Instead, they mixed with the other
    nations
  and learned their customs.
They worshiped other nations' idols
  and were trapped by them.
They even killed their sons and
    daughters
  as sacrifices to demons.

Psalm 106:34–37

INSIGHTS

*A*wareness that we are involved in a cosmic battle which is supernatural, personal, and futile if fought with natural weapons is the beginning of conquering wisdom. We must be convinced of these things if we are to succeed. We must go beyond evangelical lip service to a deep-souled conviction which bursts our simplistic religious shackles.

Paul is specific about the nature of our evil opponents: "our struggle is . . . against the rulers, against the authorities, against the powers of this dark world and against the spiritual forces of evil in the heavenly realms" (v. 12). . . .

The immediate implication is that Satan is terribly powerful. To be sure he does not possess anything near the power of God, but in God's inscrutable arrangement he temporarily dominates and drives the world, which on the whole is separated from God's grace. . . .

. . . If we are filled with the Spirit (5:18), Satan's forces cannot subdue us. But those of us who neglect our resources, and especially those who give the enemies room in our lives, place ourselves in harm's way. . . .

. . . We cannot fight Satan ourselves. All our own doing will be in vain. Nevertheless there is something we can do, and that is to avail ourselves of the Lord's strength. . . . We are to acknowledge our weakness and invite his power. We must imitate Gideon's going from 32,000 warriors to 10,000 to 300 armed only with trumpets and lanterns (Judges 7). This divestment of natural strength enabled the putting on of God's power—and a mighty victory!

R. Kent Hughes

APPLICATION

*W*hat does Scripture say you need in order to fight spiritual battles? Identify the spiritual battlefields in your life. List the battles you most frequently fail to recognize as spiritual. How can you better avail yourself of God's resources to fight those battles?

WEDNESDAY:

Be Humble and
Give Honor to Others

Philippians 1:1—2:4

Serve Others with Joy

*F*rom Paul and Timothy, servants of Christ Jesus.

To all of God's holy people in Christ Jesus who live in Philippi, including your elders and deacons:

Grace and peace to you from God our Father and the Lord Jesus Christ.

Paul's Prayer

I thank my God every time I remember you, always praying with joy for all of you. I thank God for the help you gave me while I preached the Good News—help you gave from the first day you believed until now. God began doing a good work in you, and I am sure he will continue it until it is finished when Jesus Christ comes again.

And I know that I am right to think like this about all of you, because I have you in my heart. All of you share in God's grace with me while I am in prison and while I am defending and proving the truth of the Good News. God knows that I want to see you very much, because I love all of you with the love of Christ Jesus.

This is my prayer for you: that your love will grow more and more; that you will have knowledge and understanding with your love; that you will see the difference between good and bad and will choose the good; that you will be pure and without wrong for the coming of Christ; that you will do many good things with the help of Christ to bring glory and praise to God.

Paul's Troubles Help the Work

I want you brothers and sisters to know that what has happened to me has helped to spread the Good News. All the palace guards and everyone else knows that I am in prison because I am a believer in Christ. Because I am in prison, most of the believ-ers have become more bold in Christ and are not afraid to speak the word of God.

It is true that some preach about Christ because they are jealous and ambitious, but others preach about Christ because they want to help. They preach because they have love, and they know that God gave me the work of defending the Good News. But the others preach about Christ for selfish and wrong reasons, wanting to make trouble for me in prison.

But it doesn't matter. The important thing is that in every way, whether for right or wrong reasons, they are preaching about Christ. So I am happy, and I will continue to be happy. Because you are praying for me and the Spirit of Jesus Christ is helping me, I know this trouble will bring my freedom. I expect and hope that I will not fail Christ in anything but that I will have the courage now, as always, to show the greatness of Christ in my life here on earth, whether I live or die. To me the only important thing about living is Christ, and dying would be profit for me. If I continue living in my body, I will be able to work for the Lord. I do not know what to choose—living or dying. It is hard to choose between the two. I want to leave this life and be with Christ, which is much better, but you need me here in my body. Since I am sure of this, I know I will stay with you to help you grow and have joy in your faith. You will be very happy in Christ Jesus when I am with you again.

Only one thing concerns me: Be sure that you live in a way that brings honor to the Good News of Christ. Then whether I come and visit you or am away from you, I will hear that you are standing strong with one purpose, that you work together as one for the faith of the Good News, and that you are not afraid of those who are against you. All of this is proof that your enemies will be destroyed but that you will be saved by God. God gave you the honor not only of believing in Christ but also of suffering for him, both of which bring glory to Christ. When I was with you, you saw the struggles I had, and you hear about the struggles I am having now. You yourselves are having the same kind of struggles.

Does your life in Christ give you strength? Does his love comfort you? Do we share together in the spirit? Do you have mercy and kindness? If so, make me very happy by having the same thoughts, sharing the same love, and having one mind and purpose. When you do things, do not let selfishness or pride be your guide. Instead, be humble and give more honor to others than to yourselves. Do not be interested only in your own life, but be interested in the lives of others.

*R*especting the LORD and not being proud will bring you wealth, honor, and life.

Proverbs 22:4

*D*on't praise yourself. Let someone else do it.
Let the praise come from a stranger and not from your own mouth.

Proverbs 27:2

*S*aul said to David, "Here is my older daughter Merab. I will let you marry her. All I ask is that you remain brave and fight the LORD's battles." Saul thought, "I won't have to kill David. The Philistines will do that."

But David answered Saul, saying, "Who am I? My family is not important enough for me to become the king's son-in-law." So, when the time came for Saul's daughter Merab to marry David, Saul gave her instead to Adriel of Meholah.

1 Samuel 18:17–19

*T*he LORD has told you, human, what is good;
he has told you what he wants from you:
to do what is right to other people,
love being kind to others,
and live humbly, obeying your God.

Micah 6:8

*H*e says, "I live in a high and holy place,
but I also live with people who are sad and humble.

I give new life to those who are humble and to those whose hearts are broken.

Isaiah 57:15b

INSIGHTS

Humility inclines us to distrust ourselves and depend only upon God. The proud person has a high opinion of his own wisdom or strength or righteousness and is inordinately self-confident. The humble rely upon God and delight to cast themselves wholly on Him as their refuge, righteousness, and strength.

The humble person will renounce all the glory of the good he has or does and give it all to God. If there is anything good in him or any good done by him, he is not disposed to glorify himself or boast about it before God. . . . The disposition of the humble person is to wholly submit himself to God. His heart is not opposed to a full and absolute subjection to the divine will, but is inclined to it. He is content to be subject to the commands and laws of God, for he sees it is right and good that the creature be subject to His Creator. He wants to give God the honor that belongs to Him, and that is to reign over him and subject him to certain laws and commands that are designed for his own best interests.

Humility tends to prevent an inordinate aspiring to wealth or position—in short, ambitious behavior among people. A humble person is content with such a situation among others as God is pleased to allot to him and is not greedy for honor. Nor does he try to appear uppermost and exalted above his neighbors.

Jonathan Edwards

PAUSE FOR REFLECTION

Why is God opposed to the proud? Why is humility necessary for Christian living? What does God promise to those who are humble? In what ways is humility part of obeying Christ's commandment to love one another?

THURSDAY:

Do Everything Without Complaining or Arguing

Philippians 2:5–30

Be Unselfish like Christ

*I*n your lives you must think and act like Christ Jesus.

Christ himself was like God in everything.

But he did not think that being equal with God was something to be used for his own benefit.

But he gave up his place with God and made himself nothing.

He was born to be a man
and became like a servant.

And when he was living as a man,
he humbled himself and was fully obedient to God,

even when that caused his death—
death on a cross.

So God raised him to the highest place.

God made his name greater than every other name

so that every knee will bow to the name of Jesus—

everyone in heaven, on earth, and under the earth.

And everyone will confess that Jesus Christ is Lord

and bring glory to God the Father.

Be the People God Wants You to Be

*M*y dear friends, you have always obeyed God when I was with you. It is even more important that you obey now while I am away from you. Keep on working to complete your salvation with fear and trembling, because God is working in you to help you want to do and be able to do what pleases him.

Do everything without complaining or arguing. Then you will be innocent and without any wrong. You will be God's children without fault. But you are living with crooked and mean people all around you, among whom you shine like stars in the dark world. You offer the teaching that gives life. So when Christ comes again, I can be happy because my work was not wasted. I ran the race and won.

Your faith makes you offer your lives as a sacrifice in serving God. If I have to offer my own blood with your sacrifice, I will be happy and full of joy with all of you. You also should be happy and full of joy with me.

Timothy and Epaphroditus

I hope in the Lord Jesus to send Timothy to you soon. I will be happy to learn how you are. I have no one else like Timothy, who truly cares for you. Other people are interested only in their own lives, not in the work of Jesus Christ. You know the kind of person Timothy is. You know he has served with me in telling the Good News, as a son serves his father. I plan to send him to you quickly when I know what will happen to me. I am sure that the Lord will help me to come to you soon.

Epaphroditus, my brother in Christ, works and serves with me in the army of Christ. When I needed help, you sent him to me. I think now that I must send him back to you, because he wants very much to see all of you. He is worried because you heard that he was sick. Yes, he was sick, and nearly died, but God had mercy on him and me too so that I would not have more sadness. I want very much to send him to you so that when you see him you can be happy, and I can stop worrying about you. Welcome him in the Lord with much joy. Give honor to people like him, because he almost died for the work of Christ. He risked his life to give me the help you could not give in your service to me.

*Y*ou must do these things
to enjoy life and have many happy days.

You must not say evil things,
and you must not tell lies.

Stop doing evil and do good.

Look for peace and work for it.

Psalm 34:12–14

*F*oolish people are always fighting,
   but avoiding quarrels will bring you
   honor.

Proverbs 20:3

*J*oseph also sent his father ten donkeys
loaded with the best things from Egypt and
ten female donkeys loaded with grain,
bread, and other food for his father on his
trip back. Then Joseph told his brothers to
go. As they were leaving, he said to them,
"Don't quarrel on the way home."

Genesis 45:23–24

*S*tarting a quarrel is like a leak in a dam,
   so stop it before a fight breaks out.

Whoever loves to argue loves to sin.
   Whoever brags a lot is asking for
   trouble.

Proverbs 17:14, 19

*B*ut the people continued to sin
      against him;
   in the desert they turned against
      God Most High.
They decided to test God
   by asking for the food they wanted.
Then they spoke against God,
   saying, "Can God prepare food in the
      desert?
When he hit the rock, water poured out
   and rivers flowed down.
But can he give us bread also?
   Will he provide his people with
      meat?"
When the Lord heard them, he was
      very angry.
   His anger was like fire to the people
      of Jacob;
   his anger grew against the people of
      Israel.

Psalm 78:17–21

*J*ust as charcoal and wood keep a fire
      going,
   a quarrelsome person keeps an
      argument going.

Proverbs 26:21

*P*leasant words are like a honeycomb,
   making people happy and healthy.

Proverbs 16:24

*P*eople without good sense find fault
      with their neighbors,
   but those with understanding keep
      quiet.

Proverbs 11:12

INSIGHTS

*W*hether we admit it or not, unbelief and
disobedience are the underlying reasons for
a complaining spirit.

God's Word is clear: "Do everything without complaining or arguing." This is a command, not an option. He doesn't qualify the
statement and excuse us if things suddenly go
wrong and it's not our fault. He says everything—and I take that to be all-inclusive. He
is talking about every single circumstance
whether desirable or not. When I complain, I
am in essence saying, "I really don't believe
God has arranged these circumstances or that
He could change them if He desired." If I did
believe it, I wouldn't need to complain. I'd
know my only safety is in the center of His
will no matter what happens.

The same God who told me not to complain also said, "In everything give thanks,
for this is the will of God in Christ Jesus concerning you." How is it possible to give thanks
and complain at the same time?

Is it hypocritical to say I'm thankful for my
problems when I don't feel thankful? Not really, because God assures us that ". . . all
things work together for good. . . ." Even
when it looks disastrous, I can be certain that
these self-same predicaments will be miracu-
lously transformed under the skilled knife of
the divine surgeon. He might do a little hurt-
ful cutting on me through the process, but it
will only be for my good.

Madalene Harris

PAUSE FOR REFLECTION

*D*id you realize that arguing and complaining are sins against God? Reread these
Scripture passages and list the results of
resisting the temptation to complain or
argue—in your own life and in the lives of
those around you.

F R I D A Y:

*Pursue God and
His Salvation*

Philippians 3:1–21

The Importance of Christ

*M*y brothers and sisters, be full of joy in the Lord. It is no trouble for me to write the same things to you again, and it will help you to be more ready. Watch out for those who do evil, who are like dogs, who demand to cut the body. We are the ones who are truly circumcised. We worship God through his Spirit, and our pride is in Christ Jesus. We do not put trust in ourselves or anything we can do, although I might be able to put trust in myself. If anyone thinks he has a reason to trust in himself, he should know that I have greater reason for trusting in myself. I was circumcised eight days after my birth. I am from the people of Israel and the tribe of Benjamin. I am a Hebrew, and my parents were Hebrews. I had a strict view of the law, which is why I became a Pharisee. I was so enthusiastic I tried to hurt the church. No one could find fault with the way I obeyed the law of Moses. Those things were important to me, but now I think they are worth nothing because of Christ. Not only those things, but I think that all things are worth nothing compared with the greatness of knowing Christ Jesus my Lord. Because of him, I have lost all those things, and now I know they are worthless trash. This allows me to have Christ and to belong to him. Now I am right with God, not because I followed the law, but because I believed in Christ. God uses my faith to make me right with him. I want to know Christ and the power that raised him from the dead. I want to share in his sufferings and become like him in his death. Then I have hope that I myself will be raised from the dead.

Continuing Toward Our Goal

I do not mean that I am already as God wants me to be. I have not yet reached that goal, but I continue trying to reach it and to make it mine. Christ wants me to do that, which is the reason he made me his. Brothers and sisters, I know that I have not yet reached that goal, but there is one thing I always do. Forgetting the past and straining toward what is ahead, I keep trying to reach the goal and get the prize for which God called me through Christ to the life above.

All of us who are spiritually mature should think this way, too. And if there are things you do not agree with, God will make them clear to you. But we should continue following the truth we already have.

Brothers and sisters, all of you should try to follow my example and to copy those who live the way we showed you. Many people live like enemies of the cross of Christ. I have often told you about them, and it makes me cry to tell you about them now. In the end, they will be destroyed. They do whatever their bodies want, they are proud of their shameful acts, and they think only about earthly things. But our homeland is in heaven, and we are waiting for our Savior, the Lord Jesus Christ, to come from heaven. By his power to rule all things, he will change our simple bodies and make them like his own glorious body.

*A*s a deer thirsts for streams of water,
   so I thirst for you, God.
I thirst for the living God.
   When can I go to meet with him?
Psalm 42:1–2

I am waiting for you to save me, LORD.
   I will obey your commands.
I obey your rules,
   and I love them very much.
I obey your orders and rules,
   because you know everything I do.

Hear my cry to you, LORD.
   Let your word help me understand.
Listen to my prayer;
   save me as you promised.
Let me speak your praise,
   because you have taught me your
     demands.

Let me sing about your promises,
    because all your commands are fair.
Give me your helping hand,
    because I have chosen your com-
      mands.

Psalm 119:166–173

God, you are my God.
    I search for you.
I thirst for you
    like someone in a dry, empty land
    where there is no water.
I have seen you in the Temple
    and have seen your strength and
      glory.
Because your love is better than life,
    I will praise you.
I will praise you as long as I live.
    I will lift up my hands in prayer to
      your name.
I will be content as if I had eaten the
      best foods.
    My lips will sing, and my mouth will
      praise you.

I remember you while I'm lying in bed;
    I think about you through the night.
You are my help.
    Because of your protection, I sing.
I stay close to you;
    you support me with your right
      hand.

Psalm 63:1–8

You guide me with your advice,
    and later you will receive me in
      honor.
I have no one in heaven but you;
    I want nothing on earth besides you.
My body and my mind may become
      weak,
    but God is my strength.
    He is mine forever.

Psalm 73:24–26

INSIGHTS

*Recently, I saw a young New Zealand cy-
clist win a grueling race in which he broke
the national record. In a subsequent interview
by the TV sports commentator, he was asked
the question, "And what do you aim at for
the future?" With not a moment's hesitation*

*the reply came back: "I aim to be one of the
best cyclists in the world."*

*In order to realize his ambition, he was
prepared to pay any price in training—grueling discipline, forfeiture of social life, self-
denial in many areas—and all for a piece of
gold, or even bronze. Why is it that so few
disciples have a similar, fixed ambition to
excel for Christ? Are we "taking time and
trouble to keep spiritually fit," or have we
grown soft and flabby? . . .*

*. . . Winning a race makes great de-
mands on the stamina and perseverance of
the athlete.*

*Once the race has begun, the athlete can-
not afford to look back. He must press on to
the tape without distraction. His eyes must
be fixed on the umpire's stand at the end of
the track if he is to win the prize. . . .*

*So must the disciple run his race with
eyes steadfastly fixed on his encouraging
Lord, who is at once Judge, Umpire, and
Awarder. He is not to look back either wist-
fully or hopelessly but to resolutely forget
what is behind—failures and disappointments as well as successes and victories. He
must strain forward to the tape with eyes
fixed on his welcoming Lord. It was He who
initiated our faith, and it is He who will
strengthen us to complete the course.*

J. Oswald Sanders

PAUSE   FOR   REFLECTION

*In what way does Paul say spiritual matu-
rity changes a person's thinking? How diligently are you pursuing God's calling? May
the psalmist's words be your prayer and praise
to the Lord!*

WEEKEND:

Don't Worry About Anything; Ask God for What You Need

Philippians 4:1–23

What the Christians Are to Do

*M*y dear brothers and sisters, I love you and want to see you. You bring me joy and make me proud of you, so stand strong in the Lord as I have told you.

I ask Euodia and Syntyche to agree in the Lord. And I ask you, my faithful friend, to help these women. They served with me in telling the Good News, together with Clement and others who worked with me, whose names are written in the book of life.

Be full of joy in the Lord always. I will say again, be full of joy.

Let everyone see that you are gentle and kind. The Lord is coming soon. Do not worry about anything, but pray and ask God for everything you need, always giving thanks. And God's peace, which is so great we cannot understand it, will keep your hearts and minds in Christ Jesus.

Brothers and sisters, think about the things that are good and worthy of praise. Think about the things that are true and honorable and right and pure and beautiful and respected. Do what you learned and received from me, what I told you, and what you saw me do. And the God who gives peace will be with you.

Paul Thanks the Christians

I am very happy in the Lord that you have shown your care for me again. You continued to care about me, but there was no way for you to show it. I am not telling you this because I need anything. I have learned to be satisfied with the things I have and with everything that happens. I know how to live when I am poor, and I know how to live when I have plenty. I have learned the secret of being happy at any time in everything that happens, when I have enough to eat and when I go hungry, when I have more than I need and when I do not have

enough. I can do all things through Christ, because he gives me strength.

But it was good that you helped me when I needed it. You Philippians remember when I first preached the Good News there. When I left Macedonia, you were the only church that gave me help. Several times you sent me things I needed when I was in Thessalonica. Really, it is not that I want to receive gifts from you, but I want you to have the good that comes from giving. And now I have everything, and more. I have all I need, because Epaphroditus brought your gift to me. It is like a sweet-smelling sacrifice offered to God, who accepts that sacrifice and is pleased with it. My God will use his wonderful riches in Christ Jesus to give you everything you need. Glory to our God and Father forever and ever! Amen.

Greet each of God's people in Christ. Those who are with me send greetings to you. All of God's people greet you, particularly those from the palace of Caesar.

The grace of the Lord Jesus Christ be with you all.

*G*ive your worries to the LORD,
and he will take care of you.
He will never let good people down.
Psalm 55:22

*G*ive thanks to the LORD and pray to
him.
Tell the nations what he has done.
Sing to him; sing praises to him.
Tell about all his miracles.
Be glad that you are his;
let those who seek the LORD be
happy.
Depend on the LORD and his strength;
always go to him for help.
Psalm 105:1–4

*T*rust the LORD and do good.
Live in the land and feed on truth.
Enjoy serving the LORD,
and he will give you what you want.
Depend on the LORD;
trust him, and he will take care of you.
Psalm 37:3–5

People who love the LORD hate evil.
The LORD watches over those who
follow him
and frees them from the power of
the wicked.
Light shines on those who do right;
joy belongs to those who are honest.
Rejoice in the LORD, you who do right.
Praise his holy name.

Psalm 97:10–12

*L*et God rise up and scatter his
enemies;
let those who hate him run away
from him.
Blow them away as smoke
is driven away by the wind.
As wax melts before a fire,
let the wicked be destroyed before
God.
But those who do right should be glad
and should rejoice before God;
they should be happy and glad.
Praise the Lord, God our Savior,
who helps us every day.   *Selah*
Our God is a God who saves us;
the LORD God saves us from death.

Psalm 68:1–3, 19–20

*P*eople may make plans in their minds,
but only the LORD can make them
come true.

You may believe you are doing right,
but the LORD will judge your reasons.

Depend on the LORD in whatever you do,
and your plans will succeed.

The LORD makes everything go as he
pleases.
He has even prepared a day of
disaster for evil people.

The LORD hates those who are proud.
They will surely be punished.

Love and truth bring forgiveness of sin.
By respecting the LORD you will
avoid evil.
When people live so that they please
the LORD,
even their enemies will make peace
with them.

It is better to be poor and right

than to be wealthy and dishonest.

Proverbs 16:1–8

INSIGHTS

*D*uring the Great Depression the bank in
which my father was an officer was forced to
close. . . .

I was convinced my father would be out of
work. I knew I had to get a job as a boy of
twelve to help support the family. A nearby
corner grocer hired me after school and Sat-
urdays for a dollar a week to sweep the floors
and deliver groceries.

When I told my father, he replied, "I appreciate your concern and desire to help, son,
but I am trusting the Lord to meet our needs.
We belong to Him and He will take care of
His own."

God honored my father's faith. He never
went a day without employment through the
entire Depression.

With similar confidence Paul wrote to the
Philippian Christians, "My God will meet all
your needs" (4:19). This was the encouragement those believers needed because they were
far from affluent (2 Cor. 8:1–5). Out of their
meager resources they had sent an offering to
Paul in Rome (Phil. 4:14–18). Paul assured
them that God would reimburse them.

Two important details about this promise
must be observed. First, God will meet "all
your needs," not your desires. Jesus said,
"Your Father knows what you need" (Matt.
6:8), and His understanding of our needs
may be different from ours.

Second, God will meet our needs "accord-
ing to His glorious riches in Christ Jesus."
God's supply is not "out of" but "according to
His glorious riches." God is "able to do im-
measurably more than we ask or imagine"
(Eph. 3:20). . . .

Whatever your needs are right now, trust
God to meet them and look for His supply.

John Witmer

ACTION POINT

*W*hat does God's peace enable us to do? List
the things on which God wants you to focus
your thoughts. Will you ask God for what you
need and trust him to care for you?

MONDAY:

Christ's Preeminence in All of History

Colossians 1:1–23

*F*rom Paul, an apostle of Christ Jesus. I am an apostle because that is what God wanted. Also from Timothy, our brother.

To the holy and faithful brothers and sisters in Christ that live in Colosse:

Grace and peace to you from God our Father.

In our prayers for you we always thank God, the Father of our Lord Jesus Christ, because we have heard about the faith you have in Christ Jesus and the love you have for all of God's people. You have this faith and love because of your hope, and what you hope for is kept safe for you in heaven. You learned about this hope when you heard the message about the truth, the Good News that was told to you. Everywhere in the world that Good News is bringing blessings and is growing. This has happened with you, too, since you heard the Good News and understood the truth about the grace of God. You learned about God's grace from Epaphras, whom we love. He works together with us and is a faithful servant of Christ for us. He also told us about the love you have from the Holy Spirit.

Because of this, since the day we heard about you, we have continued praying for you, asking God that you will know fully what he wants. We pray that you will also have great wisdom and understanding in spiritual things so that you will live the kind of life that honors and pleases the Lord in every way. You will produce fruit in every good work and grow in the knowledge of God. God will strengthen you with his own great power so that you will not give up when troubles come, but you will be patient. And you will joyfully give thanks to the Father who has made you able to have a share in all that he has prepared for his people in the kingdom of light. God has freed us from the power of darkness, and he brought us into the kingdom of his dear Son. The Son paid for our sins, and in him we have forgiveness.

The Importance of Christ

*N*o one can see God, but Jesus Christ is exactly like him. He ranks higher than everything that has been made. Through his power all things were made—things in heaven and on earth, things seen and unseen, all powers, authorities, lords, and rulers. All things were made through Christ and for Christ. He was there before anything was made, and all things continue because of him. He is the head of the body, which is the church. Everything comes from him. He is the first one who was raised from the dead. So in all things Jesus has first place. God was pleased for all of himself to live in Christ. And through Christ, God has brought all things back to himself again—things on earth and things in heaven. God made peace through the blood of Christ's death on the cross.

At one time you were separated from God. You were his enemies in your minds, and the evil things you did were against God. But now God has made you his friends again. He did this through Christ's death in the body so that he might bring you into God's presence as people who are holy, with no wrong, and with nothing of which God can judge you guilty. This will happen if you continue strong and sure in your faith. You must not be moved away from the hope brought to you by the Good News that you heard. That same Good News has been told to everyone in the world, and I, Paul, help in preaching that Good News.

*B*ut, Lord, you rule forever,
> and your fame goes on and on.
Nations will fear the name of the Lord,
> and all the kings on earth will honor
> you.
The Lord will rebuild Jerusalem;
> there his glory will be seen.
He will answer the prayers of the needy;
> he will not reject their prayers.
Write these things for the future

so that people who are not yet born
will praise the LORD.
The LORD looked down from his holy
place above;
from heaven he looked down at the
earth.
He heard the moans of the prisoners,
and he freed those sentenced to die.
The name of the LORD will be heard in
Jerusalem;
his praise will be heard there.
People will come together,
and kingdoms will serve the LORD.
In the beginning you made the earth,
and your hands made the skies.
They will be destroyed, but you will
remain.
They will all wear out like clothes.
And, like clothes, you will change
them
and throw them away.
But you never change,
and your life will never end.

Psalm 102:12, 15–22, 25–27

*W*ho caused the one to come from
the east?
Who gives him victories everywhere
he goes?
The one who brought him gives
nations over to him
and defeats kings.
He uses his sword, and kings become
like dust.
He uses his bow, and they are blown
away like chaff.
He chases them and is never hurt,
going places he has never been
before.
Who caused this to happen?
Who has controlled history since the
beginning?
I, the LORD, am the one. I was here at
the beginning,
and I will be here when all things are
finished."

Isaiah 41:2–4

*H*e is the one who makes the mountains
and creates the wind
and makes his thoughts known to
people.
He changes the dawn into darkness

and walks over the mountains of the
earth.
His name is the LORD God All-
Powerful.

Amos 4:13

INSIGHTS

*R*ight *through the Old Testament the conviction runs that God is managing all human history for the good of his people and that the climax will be the setting up of the kingdom of God under the Messiah, God's anointed King. In the New Testament, Jesus of Nazareth is shown to be that Messiah or Christ. But his role is not only a kingly one, but prophetic and priestly too. Jesus as prophet preached in God's name; as priest, he offered himself in sacrifice for the sins of the people; as king, having risen triumphantly from the dead, he now reigns at God's right hand. "All authority in heaven and on earth has been given to me," he told his disciples (Matt. 28:18). So the early Christians came to see Jesus of Nazareth as the Christ of God, their Teacher, Savior, and living Lord.*

. . . As Christians we know that Christ is reigning until all things are put under his feet and that we are living in the last days—the period between his first coming, to bring salvation and set up his kingdom, and his second coming, to complete the work of his kingdom in royal triumph and final judgment.

There is increasing chaos and confusion as human history moves to its close, but as Christians we can find stability and hope in Jesus who is the sovereign Lord of history. The Father has promised the Son, "Thy throne, O God, is forever and ever" (Heb. 1:8), and the promise will never fail.

J. I. Packer

ACTION POINT

*H*ow *does Christ's management of heaven and earth affect your view of history? Your hope for the future? Spend time in prayer, praising God for his incomparable greatness and his awesome love for you.*

483

TUESDAY:
Be Strong in Your Faith so No One Turns You Away from God

Colossians 1:24—2:15

Paul's Work for the Church

I am happy in my sufferings for you. There are things that Christ must still suffer through his body, the church. I am accepting, in my body, my part of these things that must be suffered. I became a servant of the church because God gave me a special work to do that helps you, and that work is to tell fully the message of God. This message is the secret that was hidden from everyone since the beginning of time, but now it is made known to God's holy people. God decided to let his people know this rich and glorious secret which he has for all people. This secret is Christ himself, who is in you. He is our only hope for glory. So we continue to preach Christ to each person, using all wisdom to warn and to teach everyone, in order to bring each one into God's presence as a mature person in Christ. To do this, I work and struggle, using Christ's great strength that works so powerfully in me.

I want you to know how hard I work for you, those in Laodicea, and others who have never seen me. I want them to be strengthened and joined together with love so that they may be rich in their understanding. This leads to their knowing fully God's secret, that is, Christ himself. In him all the treasures of wisdom and knowledge are safely kept.

I say this so that no one can fool you by arguments that seem good, but are false. Though I am absent from you in my body, my heart is with you, and I am happy to see your good lives and your strong faith in Christ.

Continue to Live in Christ

*A*s you received Christ Jesus the Lord, so continue to live in him. Keep your roots deep in him and have your lives built on him. Be strong in the faith, just as you were taught, and always be thankful.

Be sure that no one leads you away with false and empty teaching that is only human, which comes from the ruling spirits of this world, and not from Christ. All of God lives in Christ fully (even when Christ was on earth), and you have a full and true life in Christ, who is ruler over all rulers and powers.

Also in Christ you had a different kind of circumcision, a circumcision not done by hands. It was through Christ's circumcision, that is, his death, that you were made free from the power of your sinful self. When you were baptized, you were buried with Christ, and you were raised up with him through your faith in God's power that was shown when he raised Christ from the dead. When you were spiritually dead because of your sins and because you were not free from the power of your sinful self, God made you alive with Christ, and he forgave all our sins. He canceled the debt, which listed all the rules we failed to follow. He took away that record with its rules and nailed it to the cross. God stripped the spiritual rulers and powers of their authority. With the cross, he won the victory and showed the world that they were powerless.

I waited patiently for the LORD.
  He turned to me and heard my cry.
He lifted me out of the pit of destruction,
  out of the sticky mud.
He stood me on a rock
  and made my feet steady.
He put a new song in my mouth,
  a song of praise to our God.
Many people will see this and worship him.
  Then they will trust the LORD.

Happy is the person
  who trusts the LORD,
who doesn't turn to those who are proud
  or to those who worship false gods.
Psalm 40:1–4

Who among you fears the LORD
  and obeys his servant?
That person may walk in the dark
  and have no light.
Then let him trust in the LORD
  and depend on his God.
But instead, some of you want to light
    your own fires
  and make your own light.
So, go, walk in the light of your fires,
    and trust your own light to guide
    you.
But this is what you will receive from
    me:
  You will lie down in a place of pain.

Isaiah 50:10–11

*A*lways remember what you have
    been taught,
  and don't let go of it.
Keep all that you have learned;
  it is the most important thing in life.
Don't follow the ways of the wicked;
  don't do what evil people do.
Avoid their ways, and don't follow
    them.
  Stay away from them and keep on
    going.

Proverbs 4:13–15

Jehosaphat Encourages Faith

*J*ehoshaphat's army went out into the Desert of Tekoa early in the morning. As they were starting out, Jehoshaphat stood and said, "Listen to me, people of Judah and Jerusalem. Have faith in the LORD your God, and you will stand strong. Have faith in his prophets, and you will succeed." Jehoshaphat listened to the people's advice. Then he chose men to be singers to the LORD, to praise him because he is holy and wonderful. As they marched in front of the army, they said,

"Thank the LORD,
  because his love continues forever."

2 Chronicles 20:20–21

INSIGHTS

*I*t is a grand thing to have a faith which cannot be shaken. I saw one day a number of beech trees which had formed a wood: they had all fallen to the ground through a storm. The fact was they leaned upon one another to a great extent, and the thickness of the wood prevented each tree from getting a firm hold of the soil. They kept each other up and also constrained each other to grow up tall and thin, to the neglect of root growth. When the tempest forced down the first few trees the others readily followed one after the other. Close to that same spot I saw another tree in the open, bravely defying the blast, in solitary strength. The hurricane had beaten upon it but it had endured all its force unsheltered. That lone, brave tree seemed to be better rooted than before the storm.

I thought, "Is it not so with professors?" They often hold together, and help each other to grow up, but if they have not firm personal roothold, when a storm arises they fall in rows. A minister dies, or certain leaders are taken away, and over go the members by departure from the faith and from holiness. I would have you be self-contained, growing each man into Christ for himself, rooted and grounded in love and faith and every holy grace. Then when the worst storm that ever blew on mortal man shall come, it will be said of your faith, "It could not shake it."

Charles Spurgeon

PAUSE FOR REFLECTION

*W*hy must believers know and understand God's truth? How deep and strong are your roots in the faith? Can you clearly separate the ideas of humans from the teachings of God? Are his teachings safe within your heart?

WEDNESDAY:

Put Away All Evil and Focus on the Holy Things of God

Colossians 2:16—3:17

Don't Follow People's Rules

So do not let anyone make rules for you about eating and drinking or about a religious feast, a New Moon Festival, or a Sabbath day. These things were like a shadow of what was to come. But what is true and real has come and is found in Christ. Do not let anyone disqualify you by making you humiliate yourself and worship angels. Such people enter into visions, which fill them with foolish pride because of their human way of thinking. They do not hold tightly to Christ, the head. It is from him that all the parts of the body are cared for and held together. So it grows in the way God wants it to grow.

Since you died with Christ and were made free from the ruling spirits of the world, why do you act as if you still belong to this world by following rules like these: "Don't eat this," "Don't taste that," "Don't even touch that thing"? These rules refer to earthly things that are gone as soon as they are used. They are only man-made commands and teachings. They seem to be wise, but they are only part of a man-made religion. They make people pretend not to be proud and make them punish their bodies, but they do not really control the evil desires of the sinful self.

Your New Life in Christ

Since you were raised from the dead with Christ, aim at what is in heaven, where Christ is sitting at the right hand of God. Think only about the things in heaven, not the things on earth. Your old sinful self has died, and your new life is kept with Christ in God. Christ is our life, and when he comes again, you will share in his glory.

So put all evil things out of your life: sexual sinning, doing evil, letting evil thoughts control you, wanting things that are evil, and greed. This is really serving a false god. These things make God angry. In your past, evil life you also did these things.

But now also put these things out of your life: anger, bad temper, doing or saying things to hurt others, and using evil words when you talk. Do not lie to each other. You have left your old sinful life and the things you did before. You have begun to live the new life, in which you are being made new and are becoming like the One who made you. This new life brings you the true knowledge of God. In the new life there is no difference between Greeks and Jews, those who are circumcised and those who are not circumcised, or people who are foreigners, or Scythians. There is no difference between slaves and free people. But Christ is in all believers, and Christ is all that is important.

God has chosen you and made you his holy people. He loves you. So always do these things: Show mercy to others, be kind, humble, gentle, and patient. Get along with each other, and forgive each other. If someone does wrong to you, forgive that person because the Lord forgave you. Do all these things; but most important, love each other. Love is what holds you all together in perfect unity. Let the peace that Christ gives control your thinking, because you were all called together in one body to have peace. Always be thankful. Let the teaching of Christ live in you richly. Use all wisdom to teach and instruct each other by singing psalms, hymns, and spiritual songs with thankfulness in your hearts to God. Everything you do or say should be done to obey Jesus your Lord. And in all you do, give thanks to God the Father through Jesus.

Children, come and listen to me.
  I will teach you to worship the LORD.
You must do these things
    to enjoy life and have many happy days.
You must not say evil things,
    and you must not tell lies.

486

Stop doing evil and do good.
Look for peace and work for it.

Psalm 34:11–14

*T*he LORD said to Moses, "Tell all the people of Israel: 'I am the LORD your God. You must be holy because I am holy.

"'You must respect your mother and father, and you must keep my Sabbaths. I am the LORD your God.

"'Do not worship idols or make statues or gods for yourselves. I am the LORD your God.

"'You must not steal. You must not cheat people, and you must not lie to each other. You must not make a false promise by my name, or you will show that you don't respect your God. I am the LORD.

"'You must not cheat your neighbor or rob him. You must not keep a hired worker's salary all night until morning. You must not curse a deaf person or put something in front of a blind person to make him fall. But you must respect your God. I am the LORD.

"'Be fair in your judging. You must not show special favor to poor people or great people, but be fair when you judge your neighbor. You must not spread false stories against other people, and you must not do anything that would put your neighbor's life in danger. I am the LORD.

"'You must not hate your fellow citizen in your heart. If your neighbor does something wrong, tell him about it, or you will be partly to blame. Forget about the wrong things people do to you, and do not try to get even. Love your neighbor as you love yourself. I am the LORD.

"'Remember all my laws and rules, and obey them. I am the LORD.'"

Leviticus 19:1–4, 11–18, 37

*B*e my holy people. Be holy because I am the LORD your God. Remember and obey my laws. I am the LORD, and I have made you holy.

"'So you must be holy to me because I, the LORD, am holy, and I have set you apart from other people to be my own.'"

Leviticus 20:7–8, 26

*T*he New Testament leaves no doubt that holiness is our responsibility. If we are to pursue holiness, we must take some decisive action. . . .

The action we are to take is to put to death the misdeeds of the body (Romans 8:13). Paul uses the same expression in another book: "Put to death, therefore, whatever belongs to your earthly nature" (Colossians 3:5). . . . To put to death the misdeeds of the body, then, is to destroy the strength and vitality of sin as it tries to reign in our bodies.

It must be clear to us that mortification, though it is something we do, cannot be carried out in our own strength. . . . Mortification must be done by the strength and under the direction of the Holy Spirit. . . .

. . . "How do we destroy the strength and vitality of sin?" If we are to work at this difficult task, we must first have conviction. We must be persuaded that a holy life of God's will for every Christian is important. . . .

Not only must we develop conviction for living a holy life in general, but we must also develop convictions in specific areas of obedience.

These convictions are developed through exposure to the Word of God. . . .

. . . Obedience is the pathway to holiness, but it is only as we have His commands that we can obey them. God's Word must be so strongly fixed in our minds that it becomes the dominant influence in our thoughts, our attitudes, and our actions.

Jerry Bridges

PAUSE   FOR   REFLECTION

*W*hat is the one and only reason that God's people are to be holy? What does a person need to know to be holy? What must a person do to be holy? How does a person have the strength to be holy? What do you need to focus on as you pursue holiness?

THURSDAY:
Honor Your Parents
Colossians 3:18—4:18

Your New Life with Other People

Wives, yield to the authority of your husbands, because this is the right thing to do in the Lord.

Husbands, love your wives and be gentle with them.

Children, obey your parents in all things, because this pleases the Lord.

Fathers, do not nag your children. If you are too hard to please, they may want to stop trying.

Slaves, obey your masters in all things. Do not obey just when they are watching you, to gain their favor, but serve them honestly, because you respect the Lord. In all the work you are doing, work the best you can. Work as if you were doing it for the Lord, not for people. Remember that you will receive your reward from the Lord, which he promised to his people. You are serving the Lord Christ. But remember that anyone who does wrong will be punished for that wrong, and the Lord treats everyone the same.

Masters, give what is good and fair to your slaves. Remember that you have a Master in heaven.

What the Christians Are to Do

Continue praying, keeping alert, and always thanking God. Also pray for us that God will give us an opportunity to tell people his message. Pray that we can preach the secret that God has made known about Christ. This is why I am in prison. Pray that I can speak in a way that will make it clear, as I should.

Be wise in the way you act with people who are not believers, making the most of every opportunity. When you talk, you should always be kind and pleasant so you will be able to answer everyone in the way you should.

The People with Paul

Tychicus is my dear brother in Christ and a faithful minister and servant with me in the Lord. He will tell you all the things that are happening to me. This is why I am sending him: so you may know how we are and he may encourage you. I send him with Onesimus, a faithful and dear brother in Christ, and one of your group. They will tell you all that has happened here.

Aristarchus, a prisoner with me, and Mark, the cousin of Barnabas, greet you. (I have already told you what to do about Mark. If he comes, welcome him.) Jesus, who is called Justus, also greets you. These are the only Jewish believers who work with me for the kingdom of God, and they have been a comfort to me.

Epaphras, a servant of Jesus Christ, from your group, also greets you. He always prays for you that you will grow to be spiritually mature and have everything God wants for you. I know he has worked hard for you and the people in Laodicea and in Hierapolis. Demas and our dear friend Luke, the doctor, greet you.

Greet the brothers in Laodicea. And greet Nympha and the church that meets in her house. After this letter is read to you, be sure it is also read to the church in Laodicea. And you read the letter that I wrote to Laodicea. Tell Archippus, "Be sure to finish the work the Lord gave you."

I, Paul, greet you and write this with my own hand. Remember me in prison. Grace be with you.

My son, keep your father's commands,
    and don't forget your mother's
      teaching.
Keep their words in mind forever
    as though you had them tied around
      your neck.
They will guide you when you walk.
    They will guard you when you sleep.
    They will speak to you when you are
      awake.
These commands are like a lamp;
    this teaching is like a light.

And the correction that comes from
them
will help you have life.
Proverbs 6:20–23

A foolish son makes his father sad
and causes his mother great sorrow.
Proverbs 17:25

*L*isten to your father, who gave you
life,
and do not forget your mother when
she is old.
Learn the truth and never reject it.
Get wisdom, self-control, and
understanding.
The father of a good child is very
happy;
parents who have wise children are
glad because of them.
Make your father and mother happy;
give your mother a reason to be glad.
Proverbs 23:22–25

*A*nyone who curses his father or mother
must be put to death. He has cursed his
father or mother, so he has brought his
own death on himself.'"
Leviticus 20:9

*H*onor your father and your mother as
the LORD your God has commanded you.
Then you will live a long time, and
things will go well for you in the land
that the LORD your God is going to give
you."
Deuteronomy 5:16

*I*f someone has a son who is stubborn, who
turns against his father and mother and
doesn't obey them or listen when they
correct him, his parents must take him to
the older leaders at the city gate. They will
say to the leaders, "Our son is stubborn
and turns against us. He will not obey
us. He eats too much, and he is always
drunk." Then all the men in his town must
throw stones at him until he dies. Get rid
of the evil among you, because then all
the people of Israel will hear about this and
be afraid.
Deuteronomy 21:18–21

*M*uch is being said and written these days
about the care of the elderly. But what is being done in practical ways to relieve them of
their ongoing fears for their future? Such fears
as:

- *financial problems in a day of rising
  costs and a fixed income*
- *fears of sickness with no one to take care
  of them, in a day when families can be
  so scattered as to be unavailable to one
  another . . .*

*Each of us, whatever our age, needs to re-
mind himself that we are of great worth in
the sight of God, that He has plans for each
one. Speaking of the righteous, the psalmist
writes, "They shall still bring forth fruit in old
age" (Psalm 92:14).*

*Ironically, some countries to which we
send missionaries with the gospel message can
teach us much about honoring our fathers
and our mothers. For example, a woman
whom I met on one of my teaching trips to
Asian countries confided to me, "My sister,
who is much wealthier than I, felt that she
should have the pleasure of taking care of our
aged mother. But, as the youngest daughter,
it is my privilege." . . .*

*. . . God knows our heart and our inten-
tions. Where we treat the elderly around us
with love and care, it will be counted as our
obeying the fifth commandment.*

And obedience is its own reward.

*The Lord Jesus Himself set the pattern.
From the cross, in the midst of His own agony,
He remembered His mother and committed
her to the care of "the disciple . . . whom he
loved" (John 19:26–27).*

Jeanette Lockerbie

PAUSE   FOR   REFLECTION

*I*t is good to honor one's parents by caring
for them, but Scripture reveals a broader
perspective on what it means to honor one's
parents. How does this reading expand your
picture of honoring one's parents? How do you
measure up?

F R I D A Y:

God Loves His Chosen People, Who May Endure Suffering

1 Thessalonians 1:1—2:16

*F*rom Paul, Silas, and Timothy.

To the church in Thessalonica, the church in God the Father and the Lord Jesus Christ:

Grace and peace to you.

The Faith of the Thessalonians

*W*e always thank God for all of you and mention you when we pray. We continually recall before God our Father the things you have done because of your faith and the work you have done because of your love. And we thank him that you continue to be strong because of your hope in our Lord Jesus Christ.

Brothers and sisters, God loves you, and we know he has chosen you, because the Good News we brought to you came not only with words, but with power, with the Holy Spirit, and with sure knowledge that it is true. Also you know how we lived when we were with you in order to help you. And you became like us and like the Lord. You suffered much, but still you accepted the teaching with the joy that comes from the Holy Spirit. So you became an example to all the believers in Macedonia and Southern Greece. And the Lord's teaching spread from you not only into Macedonia and Southern Greece, but now your faith in God has become known everywhere. So we do not need to say anything about it. People everywhere are telling about the way you accepted us when we were there with you. They tell how you stopped worshiping idols and began serving the living and true God. And you wait for God's Son, whom God raised from the dead, to come from heaven. He is Jesus, who saves us from God's angry judgment that is sure to come.

Paul's Work in Thessalonica

*B*rothers and sisters, you know our visit to you was not a failure. Before we came to you, we suffered in Philippi. People there insulted us, as you know, and many people were against us. But our God helped us to be brave and to tell you his Good News. Our appeal does not come from lies or wrong reasons, nor were we trying to trick you. But we speak the Good News because God tested us and trusted us to do it. When we speak, we are not trying to please people, but God, who tests our hearts. You know that we never tried to influence you by saying nice things about you. We were not trying to get your money; we had no selfishness to hide from you. God knows that this is true. We were not looking for human praise, from you or anyone else, even though as apostles of Christ we could have used our authority over you.

But we were very gentle with you, like a mother caring for her little children. Because we loved you, we were happy to share not only God's Good News with you, but even our own lives. You had become so dear to us! Brothers and sisters, I know you remember our hard work and difficulties. We worked night and day so we would not burden any of you while we preached God's Good News to you.

When we were with you, we lived in a holy and honest way, without fault. You know this is true, and so does God. You know that we treated each of you as a father treats his own children. We encouraged you, we urged you, and we insisted that you live good lives for God, who calls you to his glorious kingdom.

Also, we always thank God because when you heard his message from us, you accepted it as the word of God, not the words of humans. And it really is God's message which works in you who believe. Brothers and sisters, your experiences have been like those of God's churches in Christ that are in Judea. You suffered from the people of your own country, as they suffered from the Jews, who killed both the Lord Jesus and the prophets and forced us to leave that country. They do not please God and are against all people. They try to stop us from teaching those who are not Jews so they may be saved. By doing this, they are increasing their sins to the limit. The anger of God has come to them at last.

*Y*ou are holy people who belong to the LORD your God. He has chosen you from all the people on earth to be his very own.

The LORD did not care for you and choose you because there were many of you—you are the smallest nation of all. But the LORD chose you because he loved you, and he kept his promise to your ancestors.

Deuteronomy 7:6–8a

*H*appy is the person
　who trusts the LORD,
who doesn't turn to those who are proud
　or to those who worship false gods.
LORD my God, you have done many
　miracles.
　Your plans for us are many.
If I tried to tell them all,
　there would be too many to count.

You do not want sacrifices and offerings.
　But you have made a hole in my ear
　to show that my body and life are
　yours.
You do not ask for burnt offerings
　and sacrifices to take away sins.
Then I said, "Look, I have come.
　It is written about me in the book.
My God, I want to do what you want.
　Your teachings are in my heart."

I will tell about your goodness in the
　great meeting of your people.
LORD, you know my lips are not
　silent.
I do not hide your goodness in my heart;
　I speak about your loyalty and
　salvation.
I do not hide your love and truth
　from the people in the great meeting.

Please, LORD, save me.
　Hurry, LORD, to help me.
People are trying to kill me.
　Shame them and disgrace them.
People want to hurt me.

Let them run away in disgrace.
People are making fun of me.
　Let them be shamed into silence.
But let those who follow you
　be happy and glad.
They love you for saving them.
　May they always say, "Praise the
　LORD!"

Psalm 40:4–10, 13–16

*I*f there be one place where our Lord Jesus most fully becomes the joy and comfort of His people, it is where He plunged deepest into the depths of woe. Come hither, gracious souls, and behold the Man in the garden of Gethsemane; behold His heart so brimming with love that He cannot hold it in—so full of sorrow that it must find a vent. Behold the Man as they drive the nails into His hands and feet. . . .

Most of us know what it is to be overwhelmed in heart. Disappointments and heartbreaks will do this when billow after billow rolls over us, and we are like a broken shell hurled to and fro by the surf. Blessed be God, at such seasons we are not without an all-sufficient solace; our Savior is the harbor of weather-beaten sails, the hospice of forlorn pilgrims. Higher than we are is our God, His mercy higher than our sins, His love higher than our thoughts. A rock He is since He changes not, and a high rock, because the tempests which overwhelm us roll far beneath at His feet. O Lord, our God, by Your Holy Spirit, teach us your way of faith, lead us unto Your rest.

Charles Spurgeon

*H*ow do you think Paul's words encouraged the Thessalonians? When has someone encouraged you with the assurance of God's love? Who can you encourage today?

WEEKEND:
God Requires Holy Living
1 Thessalonians 2:17—4:12

NEW TESTAMENT READING

Paul Wants to Visit Them Again

*B*rothers and sisters, though we were separated from you for a short time, our thoughts were still with you. We wanted very much to see you and tried hard to do so. We wanted to come to you. I, Paul, tried to come more than once, but Satan stopped us. You are our hope, our joy, and the crown we will take pride in when our Lord Jesus Christ comes. Truly you are our glory and our joy.

When we could not wait any longer, we decided it was best to stay in Athens alone and send Timothy to you. Timothy, our brother, works with us for God and helps us tell people the Good News about Christ. We sent him to strengthen and encourage you in your faith so none of you would be upset by these troubles. You yourselves know that we must face these troubles. Even when we were with you, we told you we all would have to suffer, and you know it has happened. Because of this, when I could wait no longer, I sent Timothy to you so I could learn about your faith. I was afraid the devil had tempted you, and then our hard work would have been wasted.

But Timothy now has come back to us from you and has brought us good news about your faith and love. He told us that you always remember us in a good way and that you want to see us just as much as we want to see you. So, brothers and sisters, while we have much trouble and suffering, we are encouraged about you because of your faith. Our life is really full if you stand strong in the Lord. We have so much joy before our God because of you. We cannot thank him enough for all the joy we feel. Night and day we continue praying with all our heart that we can see you again and give you all the things you need to make your faith strong.

Now may our God and Father himself and our Lord Jesus prepare the way for us to come to you. May the Lord make your love grow more and multiply for each other and for all people so that you will love others as we love you. May your hearts be made strong so that you will be holy and without fault before our God and Father when our Lord Jesus comes with all his holy ones.

A Life that Pleases God

*B*rothers and sisters, we taught you how to live in a way that will please God, and you are living that way. Now we ask and encourage you in the Lord Jesus to live that way even more. You know what we told you to do by the authority of the Lord Jesus. God wants you to be holy and to stay away from sexual sins. He wants each of you to learn to control your own body in a way that is holy and honorable. Don't use your body for sexual sin like the people who do not know God. Also, do not wrong or cheat another Christian in this way. The Lord will punish people who do those things as we have already told you and warned you. God called us to be holy and does not want us to live in sin. So the person who refuses to obey this teaching is disobeying God, not simply a human teaching. And God is the One who gives us his Holy Spirit.

We do not need to write you about having love for your Christian family, because God has already taught you to love each other. And truly you do love the Christians in all of Macedonia. Brothers and sisters, now we encourage you to love them even more.

Do all you can to live a peaceful life. Take care of your own business, and do your own work as we have already told you. If you do, then people who are not believers will respect you, and you will not have to depend on others for what you need.

OLD TESTAMENT READING

*R*emember my commands and obey them; I am the LORD. Show respect for my holy name. You Israelites must remember that I am holy; I am the LORD, who has made you holy. I brought you out of Egypt to be your God. I am the LORD."

Leviticus 22:31–33

I am the LORD your God. Keep yourselves holy for me because I am holy. Don't make yourselves unclean with any of these crawling animals. I am the LORD who brought you out of Egypt to be your God; you must be holy because I am holy.'"

Leviticus 11:44–45

*T*his is what the LORD says:
"For the many crimes of Israel,
    I will punish them.
For silver, they sell people who have
        done nothing wrong;
    they sell the poor to buy a pair of
        sandals.
They walk on poor people as if they
        were dirt,
    and they refuse to be fair to those
        who are suffering.
Fathers and sons have sexual relations
        with the same woman,
    and so they ruin my holy name.

Amos 2:6–7

*P*raise the LORD our God,
    and worship at the Temple, his
        footstool.
    He is holy.

Moses and Aaron were among his
        priests,
    and Samuel was among his
        worshipers.
They called to the LORD,
    and he answered them.
He spoke to them from the pillar of
        cloud.
    They kept the rules and laws he
        gave them.

LORD our God, you answered them.
    You showed them that you are a
        forgiving God,
    but you punished them for their
        wrongs.
Praise the LORD our God,
    and worship at his holy mountain,
    because the LORD our God is holy.

Psalm 99:5–9

tion of our faith in Christ. If we have no desire to be holy, we should seriously question the genuineness of our faith in the Lord Jesus.*

Christ not only died to save us from the punishment for our sins, but also from slavery to sin in this worldly culture. To continue to live in sin as a Christian is contradictory to the most basic meaning of Christianity. Christ died to save us from our sins, not to let us remain in our sins (Matthew 1:21; 1 John 1:6, 7). What kind of person would want to follow Christ and not desire to live a holy life? . . .

Holiness, then, is not an option for the believer. Paul wrote to Titus, "For the grace of God has appeared for the salvation of all men, training us to renounce irreligion and worldly passions, and to live sober, upright, and godly lives in this world" (Titus 2:11, 12). Though holiness is not a condition for salvation, it is the natural consequence of salvation. We do not become holy in order to be saved, but because we are saved. We do not do good works to get to heaven, but because heaven has already come into our hearts.

To trust Christ for salvation is to trust him for holiness. If there is no desire for holiness within, then it is doubtful that the Holy Spirit has come to dwell within. The Holy Spirit does not save us without giving us the desire to live a holy life.

Floyd McClung

APPLICATION

*W*hat instruction does Paul give to those who please God? How does Scripture define holy living? If you are to live in a way that pleases God more and more, what is your next step? What is required of you to live a more holy life?*

INSIGHTS

*O*ur daily expression of holiness is a reflec-

MONDAY:

The Hope of Christ's Second Coming

1 Thessalonians 4:13—5:28

The Lord's Coming

*B*rothers and sisters, we want you to know about those Christians who have died so you will not be sad, as others who have no hope. We believe that Jesus died and that he rose again. So, because of him, God will raise with Jesus those who have died. What we tell you now is the Lord's own message. We who are living when the Lord comes again will not go before those who have already died. The Lord himself will come down from heaven with a loud command, with the voice of the archangel, and with the trumpet call of God. And those who have died believing in Christ will rise first. After that, we who are still alive will be gathered up with them in the clouds to meet the Lord in the air. And we will be with the Lord forever. So encourage each other with these words.

Be Ready for the Lord's Coming

*N*ow, brothers and sisters, we do not need to write you about times and dates. You know very well that the day the Lord comes again will be a surprise, like a thief that comes in the night. While people are saying, "We have peace and we are safe," they will be destroyed quickly. It is like pains that come quickly to a woman having a baby. Those people will not escape. But you, brothers and sisters, are not living in darkness, and so that day will not surprise you like a thief. You are all people who belong to the light and to the day. We do not belong to the night or to darkness. So we should not be like other people who are sleeping, but we should be alert and have self-control. Those who sleep, sleep at night. Those who get drunk, get drunk at night. But we belong to the day, so we should control ourselves. We should wear faith and love to protect us, and the hope of salvation

should be our helmet. God did not choose us to suffer his anger but to have salvation through our Lord Jesus Christ. Jesus died for us so that we can live together with him, whether we are alive or dead when he comes. So encourage each other and give each other strength, just as you are doing now.

Final Instructions and Greetings

*N*ow, brothers and sisters, we ask you to appreciate those who work hard among you, who lead you in the Lord and teach you. Respect them with a very special love because of the work they do.

Live in peace with each other. We ask you, brothers and sisters, to warn those who do not work. Encourage the people who are afraid. Help those who are weak. Be patient with everyone. Be sure that no one pays back wrong for wrong, but always try to do what is good for each other and for all people.

Always be joyful. Pray continually, and give thanks whatever happens. That is what God wants for you in Christ Jesus.

Do not hold back the work of the Holy Spirit. Do not treat prophecy as if it were unimportant. But test everything. Keep what is good, and stay away from everything that is evil.

Now may God himself, the God of peace, make you pure, belonging only to him. May your whole self—spirit, soul, and body—be kept safe and without fault when our Lord Jesus Christ comes. You can trust the One who calls you to do that for you.

Brothers and sisters, pray for us.

Give each other a holy kiss when you meet. I tell you by the authority of the Lord to read this letter to all the believers.

The grace of our Lord Jesus Christ be with you.

I know that my Defender lives,
    and in the end he will stand upon the
      earth.
Even after my skin has been destroyed,
    in my flesh I will see God.
I will see him myself;

I will see him with my very own
eyes.
How my heart wants that to happen!
Job 19:25–27

*T*he Lord has made known his power
to save;
he has shown the other nations his
victory for his people.
He has remembered his love
and his loyalty to the people of
Israel.
All the ends of the earth have seen
God's power to save.

Shout with joy to the Lord, all the
earth;
burst into songs and make music.
Make music to the Lord with harps,
with harps and the sound of singing.
Blow the trumpets and the sheep's
horns;
shout for joy to the Lord the King.

Let the sea and everything in it shout;
let the world and everyone in it sing.
Let the rivers clap their hands;
let the mountains sing together for
joy.
Let them sing before the Lord,
because he is coming to judge the
world.
He will judge the world fairly;
he will judge the peoples with
fairness.
Psalm 98:2–9

*Y*our people have died, but they will
live again;
their bodies will rise from death.
You who lie in the ground,
wake up and be happy!
The dew covering you is like the dew of
a new day;
the ground will give birth to the dead.
Isaiah 26:19

*A*t that time Michael, the great prince who
protects your people, will stand up. There
will be a time of much trouble, the worst
time since nations have been on earth, but
your people will be saved. Everyone whose
name is written in God's book will be saved.
Many people who have already died will live

again. Some of them will wake up to have
life forever, but some will wake up to find
shame and disgrace forever. The wise
people will shine like the brightness of the
sky. Those who teach others to live right
will shine like stars forever and ever."
Daniel 12:1–3

INSIGHTS

*W*hat would you say about a person who had
made a hundred promises to you and kept
ninety-nine of them? You probably would
think that he was honest enough to fulfill the
last promise as well, wouldn't you?

*Jesus Christ has fulfilled every promise He
ever made, except one. He has not yet returned. Will He?*

*In both the Old and New Testaments there
are references to the return of the
Lord. . . . Ezekiel tells of a Jerusalem which
is to be restored, a temple which is to be rebuilt, and a land which is to be reclaimed
and blessed with prosperity at the Lord's return. Zephaniah gives us the new song that
He will teach to Israel and describes the
overthrow of the false Christ.*

*In the New Testament, Matthew likens
Christ to a bridegroom coming to receive His
bride. Mark sees Him as a householder going
on a long journey and entrusting certain tasks
to his servants until his return. To Luke, Jesus
is a nobleman going to a far country to
transact business and leaving his possessions
with his servants that they may trade with
them until he comes.*

*John quotes Christ as saying, "I go to pre-
pare a place for you. I will come again to receive you unto myself." The entire book of
Revelation tells of the glorious return of
Christ. And we can say with the apostle John,
who wrote that book, "Amen, even so, come,
Lord Jesus."*

Billy Graham

PAUSE FOR REFLECTION

*W*hat about Christ's second coming gives you
hope? What difference does Paul say the hope
of Christ's second coming should make in the
believer's life? What difference does that hope
make in your life?

TUESDAY:

God's Righteous Judgment Will Destroy Those Who Refuse to Believe

2 Thessalonians 1:1—2:12

NEW TESTAMENT READING

*F*rom Paul, Silas, and Timothy.

To the church in Thessalonica in God our Father and the Lord Jesus Christ:

Grace and peace to you from God the Father and the Lord Jesus Christ.

Paul Talks About God's Judgment

*W*e must always thank God for you, brothers and sisters. This is only right, because your faith is growing more and more, and the love that every one of you has for each other is increasing. So we brag about you to the other churches of God. We tell them about the way you continue to be strong and have faith even though you are being treated badly and are suffering many troubles.

This is proof that God is right in his judgment. He wants you to be counted worthy of his kingdom for which you are suffering. God will do what is right. He will give trouble to those who trouble you. And he will give rest to you who are troubled and to us also when the Lord Jesus appears with burning fire from heaven with his powerful angels. Then he will punish those who do not know God and who do not obey the Good News about our Lord Jesus Christ. Those people will be punished with a destruction that continues forever. They will be kept away from the Lord and from his great power. This will happen on the day when the Lord Jesus comes to receive glory because of his holy people. And all the people who have believed will be amazed at Jesus. You will be in that group, because you believed what we told you.

That is why we always pray for you, asking our God to help you live the kind of life he called you to live. We pray that with his power God will help you do the good things you want and perform the works that come from your faith. We pray all this so that the name of our Lord Jesus Christ will have glory in you, and you will have glory in him. That glory comes from the grace of our God and the Lord Jesus Christ.

Evil Things Will Happen

*B*rothers and sisters, we have something to say about the coming of our Lord Jesus Christ and the time when we will meet together with him. Do not become easily upset in your thinking or afraid if you hear that the day of the Lord has already come. Someone may say this in a prophecy or in a message or in a letter as if it came from us. Do not let anyone fool you in any way. That day of the Lord will not come until the turning away from God happens and the Man of Evil, who is on his way to hell, appears. He will be against and put himself above anything called God or anything that people worship. And that Man of Evil will even go into God's Temple and sit there and say that he is God.

I told you when I was with you that all this would happen. Do you not remember? And now you know what is stopping that Man of Evil so he will appear at the right time. The secret power of evil is already working in the world, but there is one who is stopping that power. And he will continue to stop it until he is taken out of the way. Then that Man of Evil will appear, and the Lord Jesus will kill him with the breath that comes from his mouth and will destroy him with the glory of his coming. The Man of Evil will come by the power of Satan. He will have great power, and he will do many different false miracles, signs, and wonders. He will use every kind of evil to trick those who are lost. They will die, because they refused to love the truth. (If they loved the truth, they would be saved.) For this reason God sends them something powerful that leads them away from the truth so they will believe a lie. So all those will be judged guilty who did not believe the truth, but enjoyed doing evil.

OLD TESTAMENT READING

*B*y doing what is fair,
   Jerusalem will be free again.
By doing what is right,

her people who come back to the
    Lord will have freedom.
But sinners and those who turn against
    him will be destroyed;
    those who have left the Lord will die.

"You will be ashamed,
    because you have worshiped gods
    under the oak trees.
You will be disgraced,
    because you have worshiped idols in
    your gardens.
You will be like an oak whose leaves
    are dying
    or like a garden without water.
Powerful people will be like small, dry
    pieces of wood,
    and their works will be like sparks.
They will burn together,
    and no one will be able to put out
    that fire."

Isaiah 1:27–31

I called, but you refused to listen;
    I held out my hand, but you paid no
    attention.
You did not follow my advice
    and did not listen when I corrected you.
So I will laugh when you are in trouble.
    I will make fun when disaster strikes
    you,
when disaster comes over you like a
    storm,
    when trouble strikes you like a
    whirlwind,
    when pain and trouble overwhelm
    you.

"Then you will call to me,
    but I will not answer.
You will look for me,
    but you will not find me.
It is because you rejected knowledge
    and did not choose to respect the
    Lord.
You did not accept my advice,
    and you rejected my correction.
So you will get what you deserve;
    you will get what you planned for
    others.
Fools will die because they refuse to
    listen;
    they will be destroyed because they
    do not care.

But those who listen to me will live in
    safety
    and be at peace, without fear of
    injury."

Proverbs 1:24–33

INSIGHTS

*D*eath *is the "wages of sin." It is just what sin deserves. Labour earns wages, and creates a rightful claim to such remuneration. So men are conceived as earning wages when they sin. They become entitled to their pay. God deems Himself holden to give them their well-deserved wages. . . .*

We are informed that in the final consummation of earthly scenes, "the judgment shall sit and the books shall be opened." We shall be there, and what is more, there to close up our account with our Lord and receive our allotment. Which will you have on that final settlement day? The wages of sin? . . .

. . . O, sinner, think of hell, and of yourself thrust into it. It pours forth its volumes of smoke and flame forever, never ceasing, never exhausted. Upon that spectacle the universe can look and read—"The wages of sin is death! O, sin not, since such is the doom of the unpardoned sinner!" Think what a demonstration this is in the government of God! What an exhibition of His holy justice, of His inflexible purpose to sustain the interests of holiness and happiness in all His vast dominions! . . .

Sinner, you may now escape this fearful doom. This is the reason why God has revealed hell in His faithful Word.

Charles Finney

PAUSE FOR REFLECTION

*W*hen *will God punish those who don't know him? How can one escape God's punishment? How will God treat those who believe? What will happen before Jesus comes again? How are believers to live until he comes?*

WEDNESDAY:

Called to Work for God's Service

2 Thessalonians 2:13—3:18

You Are Chosen for Salvation

*B*rothers and sisters, whom the Lord loves, God chose you from the beginning to be saved. So we must always thank God for you. You are saved by the Spirit that makes you holy and by your faith in the truth. God used the Good News that we preached to call you to be saved so you can share in the glory of our Lord Jesus Christ. So, brothers and sisters, stand strong and continue to believe the teachings we gave you in our speaking and in our letter.

May our Lord Jesus Christ himself and God our Father encourage you and strengthen you in every good thing you do and say. God loved us, and through his grace he gave us a good hope and encouragement that continues forever.

Pray for Us

*A*nd now, brothers and sisters, pray for us that the Lord's teaching will continue to spread quickly and that people will give honor to that teaching, just as happened with you. And pray that we will be protected from stubborn and evil people, because not all people believe.

But the Lord is faithful and will give you strength and will protect you from the Evil One. The Lord makes us feel sure that you are doing and will continue to do the things we told you. May the Lord lead your hearts into God's love and Christ's patience.

The Duty to Work

*B*rothers and sisters, by the authority of our Lord Jesus Christ we command you to stay away from any believer who refuses to work and does not follow the teaching we gave you. You yourselves know that you should live as we live. We were not lazy when we were with you. And when we ate another person's food, we always paid for it. We worked very hard night and day so we would not be an expense to any of you. We had the right to ask you to help us, but we worked to take care of ourselves so we would be an example for you to follow. When we were with you, we gave you this rule: "Anyone who refuses to work should not eat."

We hear that some people in your group refuse to work. They do nothing but busy themselves in other people's lives. We command those people and beg them in the Lord Jesus Christ to work quietly and earn their own food. But you, brothers and sisters, never become tired of doing good.

If some people do not obey what we tell you in this letter, then take note of them. Have nothing to do with them so they will feel ashamed. But do not treat them as enemies. Warn them as fellow believers.

Final Words

*N*ow may the Lord of peace give you peace at all times and in every way. The Lord be with all of you.

I, Paul, end this letter now in my own handwriting. All my letters have this to show they are from me. This is the way I write.

The grace of our Lord Jesus Christ be with you all.

*I*t is hard to find a good wife,
> because she is worth more than
> rubies.
Her husband trusts her completely.
> With her, he has everything he
> needs.
She does him good and not harm
> for as long as she lives.
She looks for wool and flax
> and likes to work with her hands.
She is like a trader's ship,
> bringing food from far away.
She gets up while it is still dark
> and prepares food for her family
> and feeds her servant girls.
She inspects a field and buys it.
> With money she earned, she plants a
> vineyard.

She does her work with energy,
and her arms are strong.
She knows that what she makes is
good.
Her lamp burns late into the night.
She makes thread with her hands
and weaves her own cloth.
She welcomes the poor
and helps the needy.
She does not worry about her family
when it snows,
because they all have fine clothes to
keep them warm.
She makes coverings for herself;
her clothes are made of linen and
other expensive material.
Her husband is known at the city
meetings,
where he makes decisions as one of
the leaders of the land.
She makes linen clothes and sells
them
and provides belts to the merchants.
She is strong and is respected by the
people.
She looks forward to the future with
joy.
She speaks wise words
and teaches others to be kind.
She watches over her family
and never wastes her time.
Her children speak well of her.
Her husband also praises her,
saying, "There are many fine women,
but you are better than all of them."
Charm can fool you, and beauty can
trick you,
but a woman who respects the LORD
should be praised.
Give her the reward she has earned;
she should be praised in public for
what she has done.

Proverbs 31:10–31

*I*f people please God, God will give them
wisdom, knowledge, and joy. But sinners will get only the work of gathering
and storing wealth that they will have to
give to the ones who please God. So all
their work is useless, like chasing the
wind.

Ecclesiastes 2:26

*T*he common drudgery of daily life can be a
Divine Calling. We often speak of a young
man as "being called to the Ministry"; but it
is as fitting to speak of a carpenter being
called to the bench, the blacksmith to the forge,
and the shoemaker to his last. "Brethren,"
said the Apostle, "let every man wherein he
is called, therein abide with God."

Remember that your life has been appointed by God's wise providence. God as
much sent Joseph to the drudgery and discipline of the prison as to the glory and responsibility of the palace. Nothing happens to us
which is not included in His plan for us; and
the incidents which seem most tiresome are
often contrived to give us opportunities to become nobler, stronger characters.

We are called to be faithful in performing
our assigned duties. Not brilliance, not success, not notoriety which attracts the world's
notice, but the regular, quiet, and careful
performance of trivial and common duties;
faithfulness in that which is least is as great
an attainment in God's sight as in the greatest. . . .

Take up your work, then, you who seem to
be the nobodies, the drudges, the maid-of-all-
work, the clerk, or shop assistant. Do it with
a brave heart, looking up to Him who for
many years toiled at the carpenter's bench.
Amid the many scenes and actions of life, set
the Lord always before your face. Do all as in
His presence, and to win His smile; and be
sure to cultivate a spirit of love to God and
man. Look out for opportunities of cheering
your fellow-workers. Do not murmur or
grumble, but let your heart rise from your toil
to God your Maker, Saviour, and Friend. So
the lowliest service will glisten, as grass-blades
do when sun and dewdrops garnish them.

F. B. Meyer

*S*tudy these readings and describe what it
means to be a diligent and faithful worker
for God's service today. How well do you
measure up? What changes will you make to
bring greater honor to God?

THURSDAY:

God Is Patient and Merciful to Sinners

1 Timothy 1:1–20

*F*rom Paul, an apostle of Christ Jesus, by the command of God our Savior and Christ Jesus our hope.

To Timothy, a true child to me because you believe:

Grace, mercy, and peace from God the Father and Christ Jesus our Lord.

Warning Against False Teaching

I asked you to stay longer in Ephesus when I went into Macedonia so you could command some people there to stop teaching false things. Tell them not to spend their time on stories that are not true and on long lists of names in family histories. These things only bring arguments; they do not help God's work, which is done in faith. The purpose of this command is for people to have love, a love that comes from a pure heart and a good conscience and a true faith. Some people have missed these things and turned to useless talk. They want to be teachers of the law, but they do not understand either what they are talking about or what they are sure about.

But we know that the law is good if someone uses it lawfully. We also know that the law is not made for good people but for those who are against the law and for those who refuse to follow it. It is for people who are against God and are sinful, who are not holy and have no religion, who kill their fathers and mothers, who murder, who take part in sexual sins, who have sexual relations with people of the same sex, who sell slaves, who tell lies, who speak falsely, and who do anything against the true teaching of God. That teaching is part of the Good News of the blessed God that he gave me to tell.

Thanks for God's Mercy

I thank Christ Jesus our Lord, who gave me strength, because he trusted me and gave me this work of serving him. In the past I spoke against Christ and persecuted him and did all kinds of things to hurt him. But God showed me mercy, because I did not know what I was doing. I did not believe. But the grace of our Lord was fully given to me, and with that grace came the faith and love that are in Christ Jesus.

What I say is true, and you should fully accept it: Christ Jesus came into the world to save sinners, of whom I am the worst. But I was given mercy so that in me, the worst of all sinners, Christ Jesus could show that he has patience without limit. His patience with me made me an example for those who would believe in him and have life forever. To the King that rules forever, who will never die, who cannot be seen, the only God, be honor and glory forever and ever. Amen.

Timothy, my child, I am giving you a command that agrees with the prophecies that were given about you in the past. I tell you this so you can follow them and fight the good fight. Continue to have faith and do what you know is right. Some people have rejected this, and their faith has been shipwrecked. Hymenaeus and Alexander have done that, and I have given them to Satan so they will learn not to speak against God.

*B*ut then I will bring health and healing to the people there. I will heal them and let them enjoy great peace and safety. I will bring Judah and Israel back from captivity and make them strong countries as in the past. They sinned against me, but I will wash away that sin. They did evil and turned away from me, but I will forgive them. Then 'Jerusalem' will be to me a name that brings joy! And people from all nations of the earth will praise it when they hear about the good things I am doing there. They will be surprised and shocked at all the good things and the peace I will bring to Jerusalem.'

There will be sounds of joy and gladness and the happy sounds of brides and bridegrooms. There will be the sounds of people bringing to the Temple of the LORD their offerings of thanks to the LORD. They will say,

'Praise the LORD All-Powerful,
    because the LORD is good!
    His love continues forever!'
They will say this because I will again do good things for Judah, as I did in the beginning," says the LORD.

Jeremiah 33:6–9, 11

*T*he wicked should stop doing wrong,
    and they should stop their evil
        thoughts.
They should return to the LORD so he
    may have mercy on them.
    They should come to our God,
        because he will freely forgive
        them.

Isaiah 55:7

*T*he LORD says,
    "Come, let us talk about these
        things.
Though your sins are like scarlet,
    they can be as white as snow.
Though your sins are deep red,
    they can be white like wool."

Isaiah 1:18

*T*he LORD shows mercy and is kind.
    He does not become angry quickly,
        and he has great love.
He will not always accuse us,
    and he will not be angry forever.
He has not punished us as our sins
        should be punished;
    he has not repaid us for the evil we
        have done.
As high as the sky is above the
        earth,
    so great is his love for those who
        respect him.
He has taken our sins away from us
    as far as the east is from west.
The LORD has mercy on those who
        respect him,
    as a father has mercy on his
        children.
He knows how we were made;
    he remembers that we are dust.

Psalm 103:8–14

*I*n amateur baseball, there is a rule known as the "mercy rule." This rule terminates a game after a certain number of innings (usually seven) when one team is ahead by a certain number of runs (usually ten). The "mercy rule" has relieved the misery of many inferior teams or of a team that just had a bad day.

Mercy is an attribute of God for which we should be especially thankful. How wonderful that He has not given us what we really deserve! We all have our "bad days." So many times we've "blown it" with God. But He is merciful! His patience is astounding! It's hard to fathom God's mercy as He looks down upon this wicked world. How many chances He has given us! How many times we have failed to obey! . . .

. . . It is God's mercy that gives us hope for a continued relationship with Him.

Because of his mercy, we are still here! We should be so grateful that God is merciful toward His children. Our God promises to complete what He began in us (Philippians 1:6), and by His mercy He shows compassion toward us in our weaknesses. Psalms 103:14 says, "For He knows how we are formed, He remembers that we are dust." God sees us in our lowly estate and extends His mercy. Our hearts should praise the God of mercy. . . .

. . . It's only by His mercy that we are not destroyed totally and completely. Therefore, we . . . should be imitators of God and show mercy to those God brings our way.

Elliot Johnson/Al Schierbaum

*R*eview the evidence in these readings that God is not begrudgingly merciful, but abundantly merciful! The next time someone accuses God of being harsh or unforgiving, tell about the evidence you have found of God's awesome, unfailing mercy.

FRIDAY:

There Is Only One God, and He Alone Saves Us

1 Timothy 2:1—3:13

Some Rules for Men and Women

*F*irst, I tell you to pray for all people, asking God for what they need and being thankful to him. Pray for rulers and for all who have authority so that we can have quiet and peaceful lives full of worship and respect for God. This is good, and it pleases God our Savior, who wants all people to be saved and to know the truth. There is one God and one way human beings can reach God. That way is through Christ Jesus, who is himself human. He gave himself as a payment to free all people. He is proof that came at the right time. That is why I was chosen to tell the Good News and to be an apostle. (I am telling the truth; I am not lying.) I was chosen to teach those who are not Jews to believe and to know the truth.

So, I want the men everywhere to pray, lifting up their hands in a holy manner, without anger and arguments.

Also, women should wear proper clothes that show respect and self-control, not using braided hair or gold or pearls or expensive clothes. Instead, they should do good deeds, which is right for women who say they worship God.

Let a woman learn by listening quietly and being ready to cooperate in everything. But I do not allow a woman to teach or to have authority over a man, but to listen quietly, because Adam was formed first and then Eve. And Adam was not tricked, but the woman was tricked and became a sinner. But she will be saved through having children if they continue in faith, love, and holiness, with self-control.

Elders in the Church

*W*hat I say is true: Anyone wanting to become an elder desires a good work. An elder must not give people a reason to criticize him, and he must have only one wife.

He must be self-controlled, wise, respected by others, ready to welcome guests, and able to teach. He must not drink too much wine or like to fight, but rather be gentle and peaceable, not loving money. He must be a good family leader, having children who cooperate with full respect. (If someone does not know how to lead the family, how can that person take care of God's church?) But an elder must not be a new believer, or he might be too proud of himself and be judged guilty just as the devil was. An elder must also have the respect of people who are not in the church so he will not be criticized by others and caught in the devil's trap.

Deacons in the Church

*I*n the same way, deacons must be respected by others, not saying things they do not mean. They must not drink too much wine or try to get rich by cheating others. With a clear conscience they must follow the secret of the faith that God made known to us. Test them first. Then let them serve as deacons if you find nothing wrong in them. In the same way, women must be respected by others. They must not speak evil of others. They must be self-controlled and trustworthy in everything. Deacons must have only one wife and be good leaders of their children and their own families. Those who serve well as deacons are making an honorable place for themselves, and they will be very bold in their faith in Christ Jesus.

*T*he LORD says, "You are my witnesses
and the servant I chose.
I chose you so you would know and
believe me,
so you would understand that I am
the true God.
There was no God before me,
and there will be no God after me.
I myself am the LORD;
I am the only Savior.
I myself have spoken to you, saved you,
and told you these things.
It was not some foreign god among
you.

502

You are my witnesses, and I am God,"
    says the LORD.
"I have always been God.
No one can save people from my
        power;
    when I do something, no one can
        change it."

Isaiah 43:10–13

Don't be afraid! Don't worry!
    I have always told you what will
        happen.
You are my witnesses.
    There is no other God but me.
    I know of no other Rock; I am the
        only One."

Isaiah 44:8

No other god has ever taken for himself one nation out of another. But the LORD your God did this for you in Egypt, right before your own eyes. He did it with tests, signs, miracles, war, and great sights, by his great power and strength.

He showed you things so you would know that the LORD is God, and there is no other God besides him. He spoke to you from heaven to teach you. He showed you his great fire on earth, and you heard him speak from the fire. Because the LORD loved your ancestors, he chose you, their descendants, and he brought you out of Egypt himself by his great strength. He forced nations out of their land ahead of you, nations that were bigger and stronger than you were. The LORD did this so he could bring you into their land and give it to you as your own, and this land is yours today.

Know and believe today that the LORD is God. He is God in heaven above and on the earth below. There is no other god! Obey his laws and commands that I am giving you today so that things will go well for you and your children. Then you will live a long time in the land that the LORD your God is giving to you forever.

Deuteronomy 4:34–40

M*en have always stumbled over the simplicity of salvation. That is why there are so* many cults. Each one has a unique slant on the doctrine of salvation, each corrupting the simplicity of the gospel revealed in God's Word (cf. 2 Corinthians 11:3) by espousing salvation by human works. . . .

From start to finish, God's Word disproves them all, and in a wonderfully consistent way. Its message, woven through sixty-six books, written over a span of fifteen hundred years by more than forty different authors, is marvelously unified and congruous. The message is simply that God graciously saves repentant sinners who come to Him in faith. There is no secret here, no mystery, no obscurity, no complexity. . . .

. . . God has come down from heaven and spoken to us by His Son (Hebrews 1:1– 2). We can never gain the right to climb to heaven and find the answers for ourselves. . . .

. . . Jesus is the only source of salvation. Those who do not believe in His name are condemned, excluded from eternal life. No matter how sincere, how religious, how immersed in good works, everyone must be born again. There is no promise of life—only a guarantee of condemnation—for those who will not . . . turn from sin in obedient faith to the One who was lifted up so that they would not have to perish.

John F. MacArthur, Jr.

W*hat truth does God want all people to know? What evidence does Scripture give that God is the only true God? What is the one way of salvation? Do you personally know that way?*

WEEKEND:

Your Life Should Be a Godly Example

1 Timothy 3:14—4:16

The Secret of Our Life

*A*lthough I hope I can come to you soon, I am writing these things to you now. Then, even if I am delayed, you will know how to live in the family of God. That family is the church of the living God, the support and foundation of the truth. Without doubt, the secret of our life of worship is great:

He was shown to us in a human body,
 proved right in spirit,
and seen by angels.
 He was preached to those who are
  not Jews,
believed in by the world,
 and taken up in glory.

A Warning About False Teachers

*N*ow the Holy Spirit clearly says that in the later times some people will stop believing the faith. They will follow spirits that lie and teachings of demons. Such teachings come from the false words of liars whose consciences are destroyed as if by a hot iron. They forbid people to marry and tell them not to eat certain foods which God created to be eaten with thanks by people who believe and know the truth. Everything God made is good, and nothing should be refused if it is accepted with thanks, because it is made holy by what God has said and by prayer.

Be a Good Servant of Christ

*B*y telling these things to the brothers and sisters, you will be a good servant of Christ Jesus. You will be made strong by the words of the faith and the good teaching which you have been following. But do not follow foolish stories that disagree with God's truth, but train yourself to serve God. Training your body helps you in some ways, but serving God helps you in every way by bringing you blessings in this life and in the future life, too. What I say is true, and you should fully accept it. This is why we work and struggle: We hope in the living God who is the Savior of all people, especially of those who believe.

Command and teach these things. Do not let anyone treat you as if you are unimportant because you are young. Instead, be an example to the believers with your words, your actions, your love, your faith, and your pure life. Until I come, continue to read the Scriptures to the people, strengthen them, and teach them. Use the gift you have, which was given to you through prophecy when the group of elders laid their hands on you. Continue to do those things; give your life to doing them so your progress may be seen by everyone. Be careful in your life and in your teaching. If you continue to live and teach rightly, you will save both yourself and those who listen to you.

*J*osiah was eight years old when he became king, and he ruled thirty-one years in Jerusalem. His mother's name was Jedidah daughter of Adaiah, who was from Bozkath. Josiah did what the LORD said was right. He lived as his ancestor David had lived, and he did not stop doing what was right.

2 Kings 22:1–2

*T*hen the king gathered all the older leaders of Judah and Jerusalem together. He went up to the Temple of the LORD, and all the people from Judah and Jerusalem went with him. The priests, prophets, and all the people—from the least important to the most important—went with him. He read to them all the words of the Book of the Agreement that was found in the Temple of the LORD. The king stood by the pillar and made an agreement in the presence of the LORD to follow the LORD and obey his commands, rules, and laws with his whole being, and to obey the words of the agreement written in this book. Then all the people promised to obey the agreement.

Josiah destroyed the mediums, fortune-tellers, house gods, and idols. He also destroyed all the hated gods seen in the land of Judah and Jerusalem. This was to obey the words of the teachings written in the book Hilkiah the priest had found in the Temple of the LORD.

There was no king like Josiah before or after him. He obeyed the LORD with all his heart, soul, and strength, following all the Teachings of Moses.

2 Kings 23:1–3, 24–25

*D*arius thought it would be a good idea to choose one hundred twenty governors who would rule his kingdom. He chose three men as supervisors over those governors, and Daniel was one of the supervisors. The supervisors were to ensure that the governors did not try to cheat the king. Daniel showed that he could do the work better than the other supervisors and governors, so the king planned to put Daniel in charge of the whole kingdom. Because of this, the other supervisors and governors tried to find reasons to accuse Daniel about his work in the government. But they could not find anything wrong with him or any reason to accuse him, because he was trustworthy and not lazy or dishonest. Finally these men said, "We will never find any reason to accuse Daniel unless it is about the law of his God."

Daniel 6:1–5

INSIGHTS

I frequently hear that the call to be holy and the call to demonstrate love to sinners are mutually exclusive. (As if love is the antithesis to holiness!) Jesus welcomed and loved sinners; he did not drive them away by too much affectation of righteousness. He showed genuine compassion for people, but he was also direct and uncompromising in denouncing sin. Jesus had compassion, but there was also toughness in this love. He won them without sacrificing the purity of his life.

The paradox of agape love is that we accept our neighbor unconditionally and with open arms and at the same time desire moral purity for their lives. If Jesus is our Lord, our compassion will be shaped by his moral absolutes. Christ both was merciful and made

judgments. Some things, he said, were immoral and destructive, but he never ceased to love. Indeed, it was his love that prompted his judgment. The enemy of our age is our desire to be tolerant and open-minded. . . .

I know a Christian woman who has cared deeply for a non-Christian woman who has had every variety of sexual experience. One day the non-Christian woman said to the Christian, "It's funny, my non-Christian friends accept me. They say it doesn't matter what I do. I'm free. But it's only with you that I feel loved, that I know I could always come to you. But it's also only when I'm with you that I feel shame and remorse for what I'm doing."

That is holiness. It never abandons; it identifies deeply with individual people. But it also brings the reality of God's presence, the purity of his holiness.

Rebecca Pippert

PAUSE FOR REFLECTION

*L*ist the areas of life in which the believer ought to be an example. What happens when people have a godly example before them? To whom are you an example of godly living? Do you know what impact your example is having?

505

MONDAY:

The Importance of Accountability Among God's People

1 Timothy 5:1–25

Rules for Living with Others

Do not speak angrily to an older man, but plead with him as if he were your father. Treat younger men like brothers, older women like mothers, and younger women like sisters. Always treat them in a pure way.

Take care of widows who are truly widows. But if a widow has children or grandchildren, let them first learn to do their duty to their own family and to repay their parents or grandparents. That pleases God. The true widow, who is all alone, puts her hope in God and continues to pray night and day for God's help. But the widow who uses her life to please herself is really dead while she is alive. Tell the believers to do these things so that no one can criticize them. Whoever does not care for his own relatives, especially his own family members, has turned against the faith and is worse than someone who does not believe in God.

To be on the list of widows, a woman must be at least sixty years old. She must have been faithful to her husband. She must be known for her good works—works such as raising her children, welcoming strangers, washing the feet of God's people, helping those in trouble, and giving her life to do all kinds of good deeds.

But do not put younger widows on that list. After they give themselves to Christ, they are pulled away from him by their physical needs, and then they want to marry again. They will be judged for not doing what they first promised to do. Besides that, they learn to waste their time, going from house to house. And they not only waste their time but also begin to gossip and busy themselves with other people's lives, saying things they should not say. So I want the younger widows to marry, have children, and manage their homes. Then no enemy will have any reason to criticize them. But some have already turned away to follow Satan.

If any woman who is a believer has widows in her family, she should care for them herself. The church should not have to care for them. Then it will be able to take care of those who are truly widows.

The elders who lead the church well should receive double honor, especially those who work hard by speaking and teaching, because the Scripture says: "When an ox is working in the grain, do not cover its mouth to keep it from eating," and "A worker should be given his pay."

Do not listen to someone who accuses an elder, without two or three witnesses. Tell those who continue sinning that they are wrong. Do this in front of the whole church so that the others will have a warning.

Before God and Christ Jesus and the chosen angels, I command you to do these things without showing favor of any kind to anyone.

Think carefully before you lay your hands on anyone, and don't share in the sins of others. Keep yourself pure.

Stop drinking only water, but drink a little wine to help your stomach and your frequent sicknesses.

The sins of some people are easy to see even before they are judged, but the sins of others are seen only later. So also good deeds are easy to see, but even those that are not easily seen cannot stay hidden.

Then Nathan said to David, "You are the man! This is what the LORD, the God of Israel, says: 'I appointed you king of Israel and saved you from Saul. I gave you his kingdom and his wives. And I made you king of Israel and Judah. And if that had not been enough, I would have given you even more. So why did you ignore the LORD's command? Why did you do what he says is wrong? You killed Uriah the Hittite with the sword of the Ammonites and took his wife to be your wife!' "

Then David said to Nathan, "I have sinned against the LORD."

Nathan answered, "The LORD has taken away your sin. You will not die. But what you did caused the LORD's enemies to lose all respect for him. For this reason the son who was born to you will die."

2 Samuel 12:7–9, 13–14

*B*e fair in your judging. You must not show special favor to poor people or great people, but be fair when you judge your neighbor. You must not spread false stories against other people, and you must not do anything that would put your neighbor's life in danger. I am the LORD.

"'You must not hate your fellow citizen in your heart. If your neighbor does something wrong, tell him about it, or you will be partly to blame.'"

Leviticus 19:15–17

*W*hoever accepts correction is on the way to life,
but whoever ignores correction will lead others away from life.

If you talk a lot, you are sure to sin;
if you are wise, you will keep quiet.

The words of a good person are like pure silver,
but an evil person's thoughts are worth very little.
Good people's words will help many others,
but fools will die because they don't have wisdom.

Proverbs 10:17, 19–21

*I*f you listen to correction to improve your life,
you will live among the wise.

Those who refuse correction hate themselves,
but those who accept correction gain understanding.

Respect for the LORD will teach you wisdom.
If you want to be honored, you must be humble.

Proverbs 15:31–33

*T*oo often I have seen marriages go down the drain, relationships deteriorate to the point of destruction, people with glaring personal limitations go unchecked—all because Christians who know precisely what is wrong will not love sufficiently to tackle the problem.

"I was afraid I would hurt their future," is one lame excuse. But that is exactly what happens.

My mind recalls the words of our Lord to Peter when he veered off course; it seems a harsh slash to the disciple who had a short time before confessed him as Lord. "Out of my sight, Satan! You are a stumbling block to me; you do not have in mind the things of God, but the things of men." (Matthew 16:23) These words came from the lips of the One who loves with everlasting love.

A former pastor told me about his experience of sinking into an illicit sexual relationship. He said he felt like an exhausted swimmer battling alone in the pounding surf, unable to escape the strong undertow, about to go down for the last time. On shore he could see all the people of his church. Some were shaking their heads in weeping and despair; others were shouting and shaking their fists in anger and frustration. There were words of encouragement and gestures of good will. There they were, all lined up, watching and waiting for something to happen. Only one man stepped forward and risked everything to plunge into the water and help the victim to safety.

Howard and Jeanne Hendricks

PAUSE FOR REFLECTION

*I*n what ways does Paul urge Christians to hold one another accountable? What are the results of a proper response to correction? Who holds you accountable to live in obedience to God?

TUESDAY:

A Godly Attitude Toward Riches

1 Timothy 6:1–21

*A*ll who are slaves under a yoke should show full respect to their masters so no one will speak against God's name and our teaching. The slaves whose masters are believers should not show their masters any less respect because they are believers. They should serve their masters even better, because they are helping believers they love.

You must teach and preach these things.

False Teaching and True Riches

*A*nyone who has a different teaching does not agree with the true teaching of our Lord Jesus Christ and the teaching that shows the true way to serve God. This person is full of pride and understands nothing, but is sick with a love for arguing and fighting about words. This brings jealousy, fighting, speaking against others, evil mistrust, and constant quarrels from those who have evil minds and have lost the truth. They think that serving God is a way to get rich.

Serving God does make us very rich, if we are satisfied with what we have. We brought nothing into the world, so we can take nothing out. But, if we have food and clothes, we will be satisfied with that. Those who want to become rich bring temptation to themselves and are caught in a trap. They want many foolish and harmful things that ruin and destroy people. The love of money causes all kinds of evil. Some people have left the faith, because they wanted to get more money, but they have caused themselves much sorrow.

Some Things to Remember

*B*ut you, man of God, run away from all those things. Instead, live in the right way, serve God, have faith, love, patience, and gentleness. Fight the good fight of faith, grabbing hold of the life that continues forever. You were called to have that life when you confessed the good confession before many witnesses. In the sight of God, who gives life to everything, and of Christ Jesus, I give you a command. Christ Jesus made the good confession when he stood before Pontius Pilate. Do what you were commanded to do without wrong or blame until our Lord Jesus Christ comes again. God will make that happen at the right time. He is the blessed and only Ruler, the King of all kings and the Lord of all lords. He is the only One who never dies. He lives in light so bright no one can go near it. No one has ever seen God, or can see him. May honor and power belong to God forever. Amen.

Command those who are rich with things of this world not to be proud. Tell them to hope in God, not in their uncertain riches. God richly gives us everything to enjoy. Tell the rich people to do good, to be rich in doing good deeds, to be generous and ready to share. By doing that, they will be saving a treasure for themselves as a strong foundation for the future. Then they will be able to have the life that is true life.

Timothy, guard what God has trusted to you. Stay away from foolish, useless talk and from the arguments of what is falsely called "knowledge." By saying they have that "knowledge," some have missed the true faith.

Grace be with you.

*B*e careful not to forget the LORD your God so that you fail to obey his commands, laws, and rules that I am giving to you today. When you eat all you want and build nice houses and live in them, when your herds and flocks grow large and your silver and gold increase, when you have more of everything, then your heart will become proud. You will forget the LORD your God, who brought you out of the land of Egypt, where you were slaves.

You might say to yourself, "I am rich because of my own power and strength," but remember the LORD your God! It is he who gives you the power to become rich, keeping the agreement he promised to your ancestors, as it is today.

Deuteronomy 8:11–14, 17–18

Whoever loves money
will never have enough money;
Whoever loves wealth
will not be satisfied with it.
This is also useless.
The more wealth people have,
the more friends they have to help spend it.
So what do people really gain?
They gain nothing except to look at their riches.
Those who work hard sleep in peace;
it is not important if they eat little or much.
But rich people worry about their wealth and cannot sleep.

I have seen real misery here on earth:
Money saved is a curse to its owners.
They lose it all in a bad deal
and have nothing to give to their children.
People come into this world with nothing,
and when they die they leave with nothing.
In spite of all their hard work,
they leave just as they came.
This, too, is real misery:
They leave just as they came.
So what do they gain from chasing the wind?
All they get are days full of sadness and sorrow,
and they end up sick, defeated, and angry.

God gives some people the ability to enjoy the wealth and property he gives them, as well as the ability to accept their state in life and enjoy their work. They do not worry about how short life is, because God keeps them busy with what they love to do.

Ecclesiastes 5:10–17, 19–20

INSIGHTS

*T*here will be this difference between the rich that loves his riches and the poor that hates his poverty. When they die, the heart of the one will still be crowded with things and their pleasures, while the heart of the other will be relieved of their lack. The one has had his good things; the other, his sorrowful things.

But the rich man, on the other hand, who held his things lightly and who did not let them nestle in his heart, who was a channel and not a cistern, who was ever and always forsaking his money—this rich man starts in the new world side by side with the man who accepted, not hated, his poverty. Each will say, "I am free."

George MacDonald

God often allows people to accumulate property so they may have an opportunity to extend the cause of truth and righteousness in the earth. . . . Professing Christians acknowledge themselves to be but stewards for God, that everything they possess is His; consequently, their possessions are at His disposal. Now, is it a fact that these people act in harmony with what they profess? Well, God often tries them to see if they are hypocrites or not.

Charles Finney

PAUSE FOR REFLECTION

*W*hat traps await those who accumulate riches? Who is the source of wealth? Write down what it means for you to have a godly attitude toward riches. In what ways do riches tempt you? How well are you handling what God has given to you?

WEDNESDAY:

Disciple One Another in the Teachings of God

2 Timothy 1:1—2:13

*F*rom Paul, an apostle of Christ Jesus by the will of God. God sent me to tell about the promise of life that is in Christ Jesus.

To Timothy, a dear child to me:

Grace, mercy, and peace to you from God the Father and Christ Jesus our Lord.

Encouragement for Timothy

I thank God as I always mention you in my prayers, day and night. I serve him, doing what I know is right as my ancestors did. Remembering that you cried for me, I want very much to see you so I can be filled with joy. I remember your true faith. That faith first lived in your grandmother Lois and in your mother Eunice, and I know you now have that same faith. This is why I remind you to keep using the gift God gave you when I laid my hands on you. Now let it grow, as a small flame grows into a fire. God did not give us a spirit that makes us afraid but a spirit of power and love and self-control.

So do not be ashamed to tell people about our Lord Jesus, and do not be ashamed of me, in prison for the Lord. But suffer with me for the Good News. God, who gives us the strength to do that, saved us and made us his holy people. That was not because of anything we did ourselves but because of God's purpose and grace. That grace was given to us through Christ Jesus before time began, but it is now shown to us by the coming of our Savior Christ Jesus. He destroyed death, and through the Good News he showed us the way to have life that cannot be destroyed. I was chosen to tell that Good News and to be an apostle and a teacher. I am suffering now because I tell the Good News, but I am not ashamed, because I know Jesus, the One in whom I have believed. And I am sure he is able to protect what he has trusted me with until that day. Follow the pattern of true teachings that you heard from me in faith and love, which are in Christ Jesus. Protect the truth that you were given; protect it with the help of the Holy Spirit who lives in us.

You know that everyone in the country of Asia has left me, even Phygelus and Hermogenes. May the Lord show mercy to the family of Onesiphorus, who has often helped me and was not ashamed that I was in prison. When he came to Rome, he looked eagerly for me until he found me. May the Lord allow him to find mercy from the Lord on that day. You know how many ways he helped me in Ephesus.

A Loyal Soldier of Christ Jesus

*Y*ou then, Timothy, my child, be strong in the grace we have in Christ Jesus. You should teach people whom you can trust the things you and many others have heard me say. Then they will be able to teach others. Share in the troubles we have like a good soldier of Christ Jesus. A soldier wants to please the enlisting officer, so no one serving in the army wastes time with everyday matters. Also an athlete who takes part in a contest must obey all the rules in order to win. The farmer who works hard should be the first person to get some of the food that was grown. Think about what I am saying, because the Lord will give you the ability to understand everything.

Remember Jesus Christ, who was raised from the dead, who is from the family of David. This is the Good News I preach, and I am suffering because of it to the point of being bound with chains like a criminal. But God's teaching is not in chains. So I patiently accept all these troubles so that those whom God has chosen can have the salvation that is in Christ Jesus. With that salvation comes glory that never ends.

This teaching is true:

> If we died with him, we will also live with him.
> If we accept suffering, we will also rule with him.
> If we refuse to accept him, he will refuse to accept us.
> If we are not faithful, he will still be faithful,
> because he cannot be false to himself.

*B*ut be careful! Watch out and don't forget the things you have seen. Don't forget them as long as you live, but teach them to your children and grandchildren. Remember the day you stood before the LORD your God at Mount Sinai. He said to me, "Bring the people together so I can tell them what I have to say. Then they will respect me as long as they live in the land, and they will teach these things to their children."

Deuteronomy 4:9–10

*R*emember my words with your whole being. Write them down and tie them to your hands as a sign; tie them on your foreheads to remind you. Teach them well to your children, talking about them when you sit at home and walk along the road, when you lie down and when you get up. Write them on your doors and gates so that both you and your children will live a long time in the land the LORD promised your ancestors, as long as the skies are above the earth.

Deuteronomy 11:18–21

*S*o Moses wrote down these teachings and gave them to the priests and all the older leaders of Israel. (The priests are the sons of Levi, who carry the Ark of the Agreement with the LORD.) Then Moses commanded them: "Read these teachings for all Israel to hear at the end of every seven years, which is the year to cancel what people owe. Do it during the Feast of Shelters, when all the Israelites will come to appear before the LORD your God and stand at the place he will choose. Gather all the people: the men, women, children, and foreigners living in your towns so that they can listen and learn to respect the LORD your God and carefully obey everything in this law. Since their children do not know this law, they must hear it. They must learn to respect the LORD your God for as long as they live in the land you are crossing the Jordan River to take for your own."

Deuteronomy 31:9–13

*T*his Ezra came to Jerusalem from Babylon. He was a teacher and knew well the Teachings of Moses that had been given by the LORD, the God of Israel.

Ezra had worked hard to know and obey the Teachings of the LORD and to teach his rules and commands to the Israelites.

Ezra 7:6, 10

INSIGHTS

*T*he discipling ministry lacks the glamour and excitement of the platform or large meeting type of ministry. But we can hardly overemphasize the importance of investing the right kind of person, one of vision and discipline, totally committed to Jesus Christ, willing to pay any price to have the will of God fulfilled in his life. . . .

. . . The Great Commission given to us in Matthew 28:19–20 says, "Go therefore, and teach [make disciples of] all nations." It takes a disciple-maker to make disciples. Historically, the Church has believed that the Great Commission was not given to a select few people, but to all believers. If this is true, then all believers can be disciple-makers. . . .

. . . If you are not a disciple-maker, then I would suggest that you do the same thing that Timothy did with Paul, or that Peter, James, and John did with the Lord Jesus. Make yourself available to a disciple-maker who can help you to become a disciple-maker. Latch on to them. Learn from them the "how to" involved in developing those qualities needed to spiritually reproduce yourself in the lives of others.

Walter Henrichsen

PAUSE FOR REFLECTION

*I*s disciple-making a new phenomenon? What principles of discipleship did Moses outline for the Israelites? In what ways do those principles apply today? What does Paul and Timothy's relationship teach you about discipleship?

THURSDAY:

Those Who Follow God Must Flee Evil

2 Timothy 2:14—3:11

A Worker Pleasing to God

*C*ontinue teaching these things, warning people in God's presence not to argue about words. It does not help anyone, and it ruins those who listen. Make every effort to give yourself to God as the kind of person he will accept. Be a worker who is not ashamed and who uses the true teaching in the right way. Stay away from foolish, useless talk, because that will lead people further away from God. Their evil teaching will spread like a sickness inside the body. Hymenaeus and Philetus are like that. They have left the true teaching, saying that the rising from the dead has already taken place, and so they are destroying the faith of some people. But God's strong foundation continues to stand. These words are written on the seal: "The Lord knows those who belong to him," and "Everyone who wants to belong to the Lord must stop doing wrong."

In a large house there are not only things made of gold and silver, but also things made of wood and clay. Some things are used for special purposes, and others are made for ordinary jobs. All who make themselves clean from evil will be used for special purposes. They will be made holy, useful to the Master, ready to do any good work.

But run away from the evil young people like to do. Try hard to live right and to have faith, love, and peace, together with those who trust in the Lord from pure hearts. Stay away from foolish and stupid arguments, because you know they grow into quarrels. And a servant of the Lord must not quarrel but must be kind to everyone, a good teacher, and patient. The Lord's servant must gently teach those who disagree. Then maybe God will let them change their minds so they can accept the truth. And they may wake up and escape from the trap of the devil, who catches them to do what he wants.

The Last Days

*R*emember this! In the last days there will be many troubles, because people will love themselves, love money, brag, and be proud. They will say evil things against others and will not obey their parents or be thankful or be the kind of people God wants. They will not love others, will refuse to forgive, will gossip, and will not control themselves. They will be cruel, will hate what is good, will turn against their friends, and will do foolish things without thinking. They will be conceited, will love pleasure instead of God, and will act as if they serve God but will not have his power. Stay away from those people. Some of them go into homes and get control of silly women who are full of sin and are led by many evil desires. These women are always learning new teachings, but they are never able to understand the truth fully. Just as Jannes and Jambres were against Moses, these people are against the truth. Their thinking has been ruined, and they have failed in trying to follow the faith. But they will not be successful in what they do, because as with Jannes and Jambres, everyone will see that they are foolish.

Obey the Teachings

*B*ut you have followed what I teach, the way I live, my goal, faith, patience, and love. You know I never give up. You know how I have been hurt and have suffered, as in Antioch, Iconium, and Lystra. I have suffered, but the Lord saved me from all those troubles.

*D*on't follow the ways of the wicked;
    don't do what evil people do.
Avoid their ways, and don't follow them.
    Stay away from them and keep on
      going,
because they cannot sleep until they do
      evil.
    They cannot rest until they harm
      someone.

They feast on wickedness and cruelty
  as if they were eating bread and
    drinking wine.

My child, pay attention to my words;
  listen closely to what I say.
Don't ever forget my words;
  keep them always in mind.
They are the key to life for those who
    find them;
  they bring health to the whole body.
Be careful what you think,
  because your thoughts run your life.
Don't use your mouth to tell lies;
  don't ever say things that are not
    true.
Keep your eyes focused on what is
    right,
  and look straight ahead to what is
    good.
Be careful what you do,
  and always do what is right.
Don't turn off the road of goodness;
  keep away from evil paths.

Proverbs 4:14–17, 20–27

*Y*ou are not a God who is pleased with
    the wicked;
  you do not live with those who do
    evil.
Those people who make fun of you
    cannot stand before you.
  You hate all those who do evil.

Psalm 5:4–5

I will sing of your love and fairness;
  LORD, I will sing praises to you.
I will be careful to live an innocent life.
  When will you come to me?

I will live an innocent life in my house.
  I will not look at anything wicked.
I hate those who turn against you;
  they will not be found near me.
Let those who want to do wrong stay
    away from me;
  I will have nothing to do with evil.
If anyone secretly says things against
    his neighbor,
  I will stop him.
I will not allow people
  to be proud and look down on
    others.

Psalm 101:1–5

*T*he practice of godliness involves the pursuit of holiness because God has said, "Be holy, because I am holy" (1 Peter 1:16). Paul tells us that we have been called to a holy life; we have been redeemed for that purpose. Any Christian who is not earnestly pursuing holiness in every aspect of his life is flying in the face of God's purpose in saving him.

What is holiness? The best practical definition that I have heard is simply "without sin." . . .

John said he wrote his first letter so that his readers would not sin (1 John 2:1). Most Christians seem content not to sin very much, but John's goal was that we not sin at all. Every sin, no matter how small it may seem to us, is an affront to God's authority, a disregard for his law, a spurning of his love. Because of this, sin cannot be tolerated in any form, to any degree. . . .

. . . When Paul was instructing the Ephesian Christians about the importance of holiness he said, "So I tell you this, and insist on it in the Lord, that you must no longer live as the Gentiles do" (4:17). He insisted on holiness, and he did so with the Lord's authority. Holiness is not an option but a must for every Christian. . . .

. . . If we want to train ourselves to be godly, it must be holiness in every area of our lives.

Jerry Bridges

PAUSE FOR REFLECTION

*W*hat must everyone who believes in God stop doing—and start doing? How important is this teaching for Christians today? In what ways do you share the psalmist's delight in innocence and pure living expressed in Psalm 101?

513

FRIDAY:

God Gave Us Scripture to Teach Us How to Live

2 Timothy 3:12—4:22

*E*veryone who wants to live as God desires, in Christ Jesus, will be hurt. But people who are evil and cheat others will go from bad to worse. They will fool others, but they will also be fooling themselves.

But you should continue following the teachings you learned. You know they are true, because you trust those who taught you. Since you were a child you have known the Holy Scriptures which are able to make you wise. And that wisdom leads to salvation through faith in Christ Jesus. All Scripture is given by God and is useful for teaching, for showing people what is wrong in their lives, for correcting faults, and for teaching how to live right. Using the Scriptures, the person who serves God will be capable, having all that is needed to do every good work.

I give you a command in the presence of God and Christ Jesus, the One who will judge the living and the dead, and by his coming and his kingdom: Preach the Good News. Be ready at all times, and tell people what they need to do. Tell them when they are wrong. Encourage them with great patience and careful teaching, because the time will come when people will not listen to the true teaching but will find many more teachers who please them by saying the things they want to hear. They will stop listening to the truth and will begin to follow false stories. But you should control yourself at all times, accept troubles, do the work of telling the Good News, and complete all the duties of a servant of God.

My life is being given as an offering to God, and the time has come for me to leave this life. I have fought the good fight, I have finished the race, I have kept the faith. Now, a crown is being held for me—a crown for being right with God. The Lord, the judge who judges rightly, will give the crown to me on that day—not only to me but to all those who have waited with love for him to come again.

Personal Words

*D*o your best to come to me as soon as you can, because Demas, who loved this world, left me and went to Thessalonica. Crescens went to Galatia, and Titus went to Dalmatia. Luke is the only one still with me. Get Mark and bring him with you when you come, because he can help me in my work here. I sent Tychicus to Ephesus. When I was in Troas, I left my coat there with Carpus. So when you come, bring it to me, along with my books, particularly the ones written on parchment.

Alexander the metalworker did many harmful things against me. The Lord will punish him for what he did. You also should be careful that he does not hurt you, because he fought strongly against our teaching.

The first time I defended myself, no one helped me; everyone left me. May they be forgiven. But the Lord stayed with me and gave me strength so I could fully tell the Good News to all those who are not Jews. So I was saved from the lion's mouth. The Lord will save me when anyone tries to hurt me, and he will bring me safely to his heavenly kingdom. Glory forever and ever be the Lord's. Amen.

Final Greetings

*G*reet Priscilla and Aquila and the family of Onesiphorus. Erastus stayed in Corinth, and I left Trophimus sick in Miletus. Try as hard as you can to come to me before winter.

Eubulus sends greetings to you. Also Pudens, Linus, Claudia, and all the brothers and sisters in Christ greet you.

The Lord be with your spirit. Grace be with you.

*A*ll the people of Israel gathered together in the square by the Water Gate. They asked Ezra the teacher to bring out the

Book of the Teachings of Moses, which the LORD had given to Israel.

So on the first day of the seventh month, Ezra the priest brought out the Teachings for the crowd. Men, women, and all who could listen and understand had gathered. At the square by the Water Gate Ezra read the Teachings out loud from early morning until noon to the men, women, and everyone who could listen and understand. All the people listened carefully to the Book of the Teachings.

They read from the Book of the Teachings of God and explained what it meant so the people understood what was being read.

This is what they found written in the Teachings: The LORD commanded through Moses that the people of Israel were to live in shelters during the feast of the seventh month. The people were supposed to preach this message and spread it through all their towns and in Jerusalem: "Go out into the mountains, and bring back branches from olive and wild olive trees, myrtle trees, palms, and shade trees. Make shelters with them, as it is written."

So the people went out and got tree branches. They built shelters on their roofs, in their courtyards, in the courtyards of the Temple, in the square by the Water Gate, and in the square next to the Gate of Ephraim. The whole group that had come back from captivity built shelters and lived in them. The Israelites had not done this since the time of Joshua son of Nun. And they were very happy.

Ezra read to them every day from the Book of the Teachings, from the first day to the last. The people of Israel celebrated the feast for seven days, and then on the eighth day the people gathered as the law said.

Nehemiah 8:1–3, 8, 14–18

*T*he LORD used every prophet and seer to warn Israel and Judah. He said, "Stop your evil ways and obey my commands and laws. Follow all the teachings that I commanded your ancestors, the teachings that I gave you through my servants the prophets."

But the people would not listen. They were stubborn, just as their ancestors had been who did not believe in the LORD their God. They rejected the LORD's laws and the agreement he had made with their ancestors. And they refused to listen to his warnings. They worshiped useless idols and became useless themselves. They did what the nations around them did, which the LORD had warned them not to do.

2 Kings 17:13–15

INSIGHTS

*T*here are few joys like the joy of sudden discovery. Instantly, there is forgotten the pain and expense of the search, the inconveniences, the hours, the sacrifices. Bathed in the ecstasy of discovery, time stands still. . . .

Solomon talks about the greatest discovery of all. . . .

"My son, if you will receive my sayings,
And treasure my commandments within you,
Make your ear attentive to wisdom,
Incline your heart to understanding;
For if you cry for discernment,
Lift your voice for understanding;
If you seek her as silver,
And search for her as for hidden treasures;
Then you will discern the fear of the LORD,
And discover the knowledge of God."
(Proverbs 2:1–5)

Talk about a discovery! Hidden in the Scriptures are priceless verbal vaults. Silent. Hard to find. Easy to miss if you're in a hurry. But they are there, awaiting discovery. God's Word, like a deep, deep mine, stands ready to yield its treasures.

Charles Swindoll

PAUSE FOR REFLECTION

*W*hat are the results of learning and obeying God's Word? What are the results of rejecting it? Have you discovered the rich treasures of God's Word for yourself?

WEEKEND:

God's Teachers Must Be Blameless and Trustworthy

Titus 1:1—2:8

*F*rom Paul, a servant of God and an apostle of Jesus Christ. I was sent to help the faith of God's chosen people and to help them know the truth that shows people how to serve God. That faith and that knowledge come from the hope for life forever, which God promised to us before time began. And God cannot lie. At the right time God let the world know about that life through preaching. He trusted me with that work, and I preached by the command of God our Savior.

To Titus, my true child in the faith we share:

Grace and peace from God the Father and Christ Jesus our Savior.

Titus' Work in Crete

I left you in Crete so you could finish doing the things that still needed to be done and so you could appoint elders in every town, as I directed you. An elder must not be guilty of doing wrong, must have only one wife, and must have believing children. They must not be known as children who are wild and do not cooperate. As God's manager, an elder must not be guilty of doing wrong, being selfish, or becoming angry quickly. He must not drink too much wine, like to fight, or try to get rich by cheating others. An elder must be ready to welcome guests, love what is good, be wise, live right, and be holy and self-controlled. By holding on to the trustworthy word just as we teach it, an elder can help people by using true teaching, and he can show those who are against the true teaching that they are wrong.

There are many people who refuse to cooperate, who talk about worthless things and lead others into the wrong way—mainly those who say all who are not Jews must be circumcised. These people must be stopped, because they are upsetting whole families by teaching things they should not teach, which they do to get rich by cheating people. Even one of their own prophets said, "Cretans are always liars, evil animals, and lazy people who do nothing but eat." The words that prophet said are true. So firmly tell those people they are wrong so they may become strong in the faith, not accepting Jewish false stories and the commands of people who reject the truth. To those who are pure, all things are pure, but to those who are full of sin and do not believe, nothing is pure. Both their minds and their consciences have been ruined. They say they know God, but their actions show they do not accept him. They are hateful people, they refuse to obey, and they are useless for doing anything good.

Following the True Teaching

But you must tell everyone what to do to follow the true teaching. Teach older men to be self-controlled, serious, wise, strong in faith, in love, and in patience.

In the same way, teach older women to be holy in their behavior, not speaking against others or enslaved to too much wine, but teaching what is good. Then they can teach the young women to love their husbands, to love their children, to be wise and pure, to be good workers at home, to be kind, and to yield to their husbands. Then no one will be able to criticize the teaching God gave us.

In the same way, encourage young men to be wise. In every way be an example of doing good deeds. When you teach, do it with honesty and seriousness. Speak the truth so that you cannot be criticized. Then those who are against you will be ashamed because there is nothing bad to say about us.

*T*he Lord GOD gave me the ability to teach
 so that I know what to say to make
  the weak strong.
Every morning he wakes me.
 He teaches me to listen like a
  student.

The Lord GOD helps me learn,
and I have not turned against him
nor stopped following him.
I offered my back to those who beat
me.
I offered my cheeks to those who
pulled my beard.
I won't hide my face from them
when they make fun of me and spit
at me.
The Lord GOD helps me,
so I will not be ashamed.
I will be determined,
and I know I will not be disgraced.

Isaiah 50:4–7

God Calls His Priests to Holiness

*T*hey must be holy to their God and show respect for God's name, because they present the offerings made by fire to the LORD, which is the food of their God. So they must be holy.

"'Treat him as holy, because he offers up the food of your God. Think of him as holy; I am the LORD who makes you holy, and I am holy.'"

Leviticus 21:6, 8

*I*f the priests keep all the rules I have given, they will not become guilty; if they are careful, they will not die. I am the LORD who has made them holy.'"

Leviticus 22:9

A Warning Against Dishonorable Teachers

*M*y agreement for priests was with the tribe of Levi. I promised them life and peace so they would honor me. And they did honor me and fear me. They taught the true teachings and spoke no lies. With peace and honesty they did what I said they should do, and they kept many people from sinning.

"A priest should teach what he knows, and people should learn the teachings from him, because he is the messenger of the LORD All-Powerful. But you priests have stopped obeying me. With your teachings you have caused many people to do wrong. You have broken the agreement with the tribe of Levi!" says the LORD All-Powerful.

"You have not been careful to do what I say, but instead you take sides in court cases. So I have caused you to be hated and disgraced in front of everybody."

Malachi 2:5–9

MONDAY:

Our Lives Are a Testimony to God

Titus 2:9—3:15

Slaves should yield to their own masters at all times, trying to please them and not arguing with them. They should not steal from them but should show their masters they can be fully trusted so that in everything they do they will make the teaching of God our Savior attractive.

That is the way we should live, because God's grace that can save everyone has come. It teaches us not to live against God nor to do the evil things the world wants to do. Instead, that grace teaches us to live now in a wise and right way and in a way that shows we serve God. We should live like that while we wait for our great hope and the coming of the glory of our great God and Savior Jesus Christ. He gave himself for us so he might pay the price to free us from all evil and to make us pure people who belong only to him—people who are always wanting to do good deeds.

Say these things and encourage the people and tell them what is wrong in their lives, with all authority. Do not let anyone treat you as if you were unimportant.

The Right Way to Live

Remind the believers to yield to the authority of rulers and government leaders, to obey them, to be ready to do good, to speak no evil about anyone, to live in peace, and to be gentle and polite to all people.

In the past we also were foolish. We did not obey, we were wrong, and we were slaves to many things our bodies wanted and enjoyed. We spent our lives doing evil and being jealous. People hated us, and we hated each other. But when the kindness and love of God our Savior was shown, he saved us because of his mercy. It was not because of good deeds we did to be right with him. He saved us through the washing that made us new people through the

Holy Spirit. God poured out richly upon us that Holy Spirit through Jesus Christ our Savior. Being made right with God by his grace, we could have the hope of receiving the life that never ends.

This teaching is true, and I want you to be sure the people understand these things. Then those who believe in God will be careful to use their lives for doing good. These things are good and will help everyone.

But stay away from those who have foolish arguments and talk about useless family histories and argue and quarrel about the law. Those things are worth nothing and will not help anyone. After a first and second warning, avoid someone who causes arguments. You can know that such people are evil and sinful; their own sins prove them wrong.

Some Things to Remember

When I send Artemas or Tychicus to you, make every effort to come to me at Nicopolis, because I have decided to stay there this winter. Do all you can to help Zenas the lawyer and Apollos on their journey so that they have everything they need. Our people must learn to use their lives for doing good deeds to provide what is necessary so that their lives will not be useless.

All who are with me greet you. Greet those who love us in the faith.

Grace be with you all.

Then those men went as a group and found Daniel praying and asking God for help. So they went to the king and talked to him about the law he had made. They said, "Didn't you sign a law that says no one may pray to any god or human except you, O king? Doesn't it say that anyone who disobeys during the next thirty days will be thrown into the lions' den?"

The king answered, "Yes, that is the law, and the laws of the Medes and Persians cannot be canceled."

Then they said to the king, "Daniel, one of the captives from Judah, is not paying attention to you, O king, or to the law you signed. Daniel still prays to his God three times every day." The king became very upset when he heard this. He wanted to save Daniel, and he worked hard until sunset trying to think of a way to save him.

Then those men went as a group to the king. They said, "Remember, O king, the law of the Medes and Persians says that no law or command given by the king can be changed."

So King Darius gave the order, and Daniel was brought in and thrown into the lions' den. The king said to Daniel, "May the God you serve all the time save you!"

The next morning King Darius got up at dawn and hurried to the lions' den. As he came near the den, he was worried. He called out to Daniel, "Daniel, servant of the living God! Has your God that you always worship been able to save you from the lions?"

Daniel answered, "O king, live forever! My God sent his angel to close the lions' mouths. They have not hurt me, because my God knows I am innocent. I never did anything wrong to you, O king."

King Darius was very happy and told his servants to lift Daniel out of the lions' den. So they lifted him out and did not find any injury on him, because Daniel had trusted in his God.

Then King Darius wrote a letter to all people and all nations, to those who spoke every language in the world:

I wish you great peace and wealth.

I am making a new law for people in every part of my kingdom. All of you must fear and respect the God of Daniel.

Daniel's God is the living God;
    he lives forever.
His kingdom will never be destroyed,
    and his rule will never end.
God rescues and saves people
    and does mighty miracles
    in heaven and on earth.
He is the one who saved Daniel
    from the power of the lions.
Daniel 6:11–16, 19–23, 25–27

If you are a publisher or a pastor, a ditch-digger or a pilot, a fisherman or a fruit grower, a garage mechanic or a furniture maker, a writer or a homemaker, an office worker or a congressman . . . there are unique things involved in your moment-by-moment work since you are a child of the Creator of the universe. . . .

You are to do well, whatever you are doing, to the glory of God (see 1 Peter 4:11). Just as flowers that grow on the Alpine peaks, beauty in the cracks of rocks with perhaps no one ever passing that way, are not growing in vain because God sees them, so it is true of the human being. A person may live alone, walk alone, and feel that no one is recognizing that he or she is being patient in the tribulation of loneliness . . . but God does know, and is aware of the whisper, "I love you, God. Please accept my praise as I walk alone today." This is true of people in prisons, in concentration camps, in hospital beds, or in wheelchairs. . . . "Work" to the glory of God can be done in every part of life . . . which is what makes it all so fair. No one gets a bigger opportunity than another. And no one is "out of work"!

Edith Schaeffer

PAUSE   FOR   REFLECTION

What kind of people are we without Jesus? What kind of people does his death make us? How are believers supposed to use their lives? Who do you know who truly lives like a servant of the living God?

TUESDAY:

All People Are Valuable in God's Eyes

Philemon 1–25

NEW TESTAMENT READING

A Slave Becomes a Christian

*F*rom Paul, a prisoner of Christ Jesus, and from Timothy, our brother.

To Philemon, our dear friend and worker with us; to Apphia, our sister; to Archippus, a worker with us; and to the church that meets in your home:

Grace and peace to you from God our Father and the Lord Jesus Christ.

Philemon's Love and Faith

I always thank my God when I mention you in my prayers, because I hear about the love you have for all God's holy people and the faith you have in the Lord Jesus. I pray that the faith you share may make you understand every blessing we have in Christ. I have great joy and comfort, my brother, because the love you have shown to God's people has refreshed them.

Accept Onesimus as a Brother

*S*o, in Christ, I could be bold and order you to do what is right. But because I love you, I am pleading with you instead. I, Paul, an old man now and also a prisoner for Christ Jesus, am pleading with you for my child Onesimus, who became my child while I was in prison. In the past he was useless to you, but now he has become useful for both you and me.

I am sending him back to you, and with him I am sending my own heart. I wanted to keep him with me so that in your place he might help me while I am in prison for the Good News. But I did not want to do anything without asking you first so that any good you do for me will be because you want to do it, not because I forced you. Maybe Onesimus was separated from you for a short time so you could have him back forever—no longer as a slave, but better than a slave, as a loved brother. I love him very much, but you will love him even more, both as a person and as a believer in the Lord.

So if you consider me your partner, welcome Onesimus as you would welcome me. If he has done anything wrong to you or if he owes you anything, charge that to me. I, Paul, am writing this with my own hand. I will pay it back, and I will say nothing about what you owe me for your own life. So, my brother, I ask that you do this for me in the Lord: Refresh my heart in Christ. I write this letter, knowing that you will do what I ask you and even more.

One more thing—prepare a room for me in which to stay, because I hope God will answer your prayers and I will be able to come to you.

Final Greetings

*E*paphras, a prisoner with me for Christ Jesus, sends greetings to you. And also Mark, Aristarchus, Demas, and Luke, workers together with me, send greetings.

The grace of our Lord Jesus Christ be with your spirit.

OLD TESTAMENT READING

A Slave Becomes a Loved Brother

*J*oseph's brothers saw him coming from far away. Before he reached them, they made a plan to kill him. They said to each other, "Here comes that dreamer. Let's kill him and throw his body into one of the wells. We can tell our father that a wild animal killed him. Then we will see what will become of his dreams."

Then Judah said to his brothers, "What will we gain if we kill our brother and hide his death? Let's sell him to these Ishmaelites. Then we will not be guilty of killing our own brother. After all, he is our brother, our own flesh and blood." And the other brothers agreed. So when the Midianite traders came by, the brothers took Joseph out of the well and sold him to the Ishmaelites for eight ounces of silver. And the Ishmaelites took him to Egypt.

Genesis 37:18–20, 26–28

So the king said to Joseph, "God has shown you all this. There is no one as wise and understanding as you are, so I will put you in charge of my palace. All the people will obey your orders, and only I will be greater than you."

Then the king took off from his own finger his ring with the royal seal on it, and he put it on Joseph's finger. He gave Joseph fine linen clothes to wear, and he put a gold chain around Joseph's neck. The king had Joseph ride in the second royal chariot, and people walked ahead of his chariot calling, "Bow down!" By doing these things, the king put Joseph in charge of all of Egypt.

Genesis 41:39–40, 42–43

So Joseph said to them, "Come close to me." When the brothers came close to him, he said to them, "I am your brother Joseph, whom you sold as a slave to go to Egypt. Now don't be worried or angry with yourselves because you sold me here. God sent me here ahead of you to save people's lives.

"So leave quickly and go to my father. Tell him, 'Your son Joseph says: God has made me master over all Egypt. Come down to me quickly. Live in the land of Goshen where you will be near me. Your children, your grandchildren, your flocks and herds, and all that you have will also be near me. I will care for you during the next five years of hunger so that you and your family and all that you have will not starve.'

"Now you can see for yourselves, and so can my brother Benjamin, that the one speaking to you is really Joseph." Then Joseph hugged his brother Benjamin and cried, and Benjamin cried also. And Joseph kissed all his brothers and cried as he hugged them. After this, his brothers talked with him.

Genesis 45:4–5, 9–12, 14–15

INSIGHTS

Are you still running around trying to milk acceptance and self-esteem out of the world like lost people when you've already got both? Are you still employing the same old methods, such as trying to perform up to your flesh's standards to generate and maintain self-esteem moment by moment? You are of infinite worth. You are accepted. Not by people, perhaps, but of God! If you're rejected by certain people, welcome to the club. So was Jesus. But He didn't go around with His head down. Why? Because He knew it's not a feeling that matters; it's what you know. He knew He was accepted.

Do you know that? . . . You are not to strive to get love; we don't live that way. We live from a posture of knowing that we are loved.

. . . You can accept yourself now as the new person you truly are in Him, just as the Father accepts you—perfectly.

Bill Gillham

PAUSE FOR REFLECTION

In biblical times, who had less value than a slave? In what ways did God affirm the value of Joseph and Onesimus? How was each one received? Who do you need to accept as a beloved brother or sister before God?

WEDNESDAY:

God Has Given Us a Great Salvation

Hebrews 1:1—2:4

God Spoke Through His Son

*I*n the past God spoke to our ancestors through the prophets many times and in many different ways. But now in these last days God has spoken to us through his Son. God has chosen his Son to own all things, and through him he made the world. The Son reflects the glory of God and shows exactly what God is like. He holds everything together with his powerful word. When the Son made people clean from their sins, he sat down at the right side of God, the Great One in heaven. The Son became much greater than the angels, and God gave him a name that is much greater than theirs.

This is because God never said to any of the angels,

"You are my Son.
Today I have become your Father."
Psalm 2:7

Nor did God say of any angel,

"I will be his Father,
and he will be my Son." *2 Samuel 7:14*

And when God brings his firstborn Son into the world, he says,

"Let all God's angels worship him."
Psalm 97:7

This is what God said about the angels:

"God makes his angels become like winds.
He makes his servants become like flames of fire." *Psalm 104:4*

But God said this about his Son:

"God, your throne will last forever and ever.
You will rule your kingdom with fairness.
You love right and hate evil,
so God has chosen you from among your friends;
he has set you apart with much joy."
Psalm 45:6–7

God also says,

"Lord, in the beginning you made the earth,
and your hands made the skies.
They will be destroyed, but you will remain.
They will all wear out like clothes.
You will fold them like a coat.
And, like clothes, you will change them.
But you never change,
and your life will never end."
Psalm 102:25–27

And God never said this to an angel:

"Sit by me at my right side
until I put your enemies under your control." *Psalm 110:1*

All the angels are spirits who serve God and are sent to help those who will receive salvation.

Our Salvation Is Great

*S*o we must be more careful to follow what we were taught. Then we will not stray away from the truth. The teaching God spoke through angels was shown to be true, and anyone who did not follow it or obey it received the punishment that was earned. So surely we also will be punished if we ignore this great salvation. The Lord himself first told about this salvation, and it was proven true to us by those who heard him. God also proved it by using wonders, great signs, many kinds of miracles, and by giving people gifts through the Holy Spirit, just as he wanted.

I will sing to the LORD,
because he is worthy of great honor.
He has thrown the horse and its rider into the sea.
The LORD gives me strength and makes me sing;
he has saved me.
He is my God,
and I will praise him.
He is the God of my fathers,
and I will honor him.
The LORD is a warrior;
the LORD is his name.

Your right hand, LORD,
  is amazingly strong.
LORD, your right hand
  broke the enemy to pieces.
In your great victory
  you destroyed those who were
     against you.
Your anger destroyed them,
  like fire burning straw."
Exodus 15:1b–3, 6–7

*L*ORD, teach me what you want me to
  do,
  and I will live by your truth.
Teach me to respect you completely.
Lord, my God, I will praise you with all
  my heart,
  and I will honor your name forever.
You have great love for me.
  You have saved me from death.
Psalm 86:11–13

*G*od and Savior of Israel,
  you are a God that people cannot
    see.
All the people who make idols will be
    put to great shame;
  they will go off together in disgrace.
But Israel will be saved by the LORD,
  and that salvation will continue
    forever.
  Never again will Israel be put to
    shame.
Isaiah 45:15–17

*L*ORD, I have heard the news about
  you;
  I am amazed at what you have done.

God is coming from Teman;
  the Holy One comes from Mount
    Paran.   *Selah*
His glory covers the skies,
  and his praise fills the earth.
He is like a bright light.
  Rays of light shine from his hand,
  and there he hides his power.

In anger you marched on the earth;
  in anger you punished the nations.
You came out to save your people,
  to save your chosen one.
You crushed the leader of the wicked
  ones

and took everything he had, from
  head to toe.   *Selah*

But I will still be glad in the LORD;
  I will rejoice in God my Savior.
Habakkuk 3:2a, 3–4, 12–13, 18

INSIGHTS

*O*ur salvation is good reason to rejoice.
Hannah rejoiced because of salvation in a
song that Mary echoed when Jesus was born
and salvation had come. The magi rejoiced
when they saw the star that led them to the
infant Jesus and salvation (Matthew 2:10).
The Ethiopian eunuch rejoiced in the dis-
covery of salvation through Philip's ministry
of the Word (Acts 8:39). Christians rejoice
in hope and even in suffering since they have
peace with God (Romans 5:2–3).

Rejoicing and salvation belong together.
The coming of Jesus into this world can never
be a matter of academic aloofness or objective
study. Because it is real and because it means
so much it goes right to the heart to make it
leap with joy. It is the emotion felt when a
woman finds a lost coin or a shepherd finds
a lost sheep or a waiting Father sees his lost
son on the horizon (read Luke 15). It is not
like a student poring over a book in the li-
brary. It is more like a student with a thou-
sand others, rejoicing over a touchdown on
the field. It is like oil drillers watching their
first wild fountain of black gold after days of
hard and fruitless labor. It is a soldier seeing
a light in the window or a returning prisoner
finding yellow ribbons tied all over the tree.
In prayer let us remember all the joy we have
drawn from the wells of salvation. It should
make quite a list.

William Stoddard

ACTION POINT

*I*f you risk living as if salvation were unim-
portant, take notice! What makes salvation
great? Who revealed it? Who has proven it?
Throughout the ages, God's people have re-
joiced and celebrated his salvation. Go ahead,
be amazed, and join them in praising God
for his salvation!

THURSDAY:

Jesus, Our Savior, Makes His People Holy

Hebrews 2:5—3:6

Christ Became like Humans

God did not choose angels to be the rulers of the new world that was coming, which is what we have been talking about. It is written in the Scriptures,

"Why are people important to you?
Why do you take care of human
beings?
You made them a little lower than the
angels
and crowned them with glory and
honor.
You put all things under their
control." *Psalm 8:4-6*

When God put everything under their control, there was nothing left that they did not rule. Still, we do not yet see them ruling over everything. But we see Jesus, who for a short time was made lower than the angels. And now he is wearing a crown of glory and honor because he suffered and died. And by God's grace, he died for everyone.

God is the One who made all things, and all things are for his glory. He wanted to have many children share his glory, so he made the One who leads people to salvation perfect through suffering.

Jesus, who makes people holy, and those who are made holy are from the same family. So he is not ashamed to call them his brothers and sisters. He says,

"Then, I will tell my fellow Israelites
about you;
I will praise you in the public
meeting." *Psalm 22:22*

He also says,

"I will trust in God." *Isaiah 8:17*

And he also says,

"I am here, and with me are the
children God has given me." *Isaiah 8:18*

Since these children are people with physical bodies, Jesus himself became like them. He did this so that, by dying, he could destroy the one who has the power of death—the devil—and free those who were like slaves all their lives because of their fear of death. Clearly, it is not angels that Jesus helps, but the people who are from Abraham. For this reason Jesus had to be made like his brothers in every way so he could be their merciful and faithful high priest in service to God. Then Jesus could bring forgiveness for their sins. And now he can help those who are tempted, because he himself suffered and was tempted.

Jesus Is Greater than Moses

So all of you holy brothers and sisters, who were called by God, think about Jesus, who was sent to us and is the high priest of our faith. Jesus was faithful to God as Moses was in God's family. Jesus has more honor than Moses, just as the builder of a house has more honor than the house itself. Every house is built by someone, but the builder of everything is God himself. Moses was faithful in God's family as a servant, and he told what God would say in the future. But Christ is faithful as a Son over God's house. And we are God's house if we keep on being very sure about our great hope.

I will make them one nation in the land, on the mountains of Israel. One king will rule all of them. They will never again be two nations; they will not be divided into two kingdoms anymore. They will not continue to make themselves unclean by their idols, their statues of gods which I hate, or by their sins. I will save them from all the ways they sin and turn against me, and I will make them clean. Then they will be my people, and I will be their God.

" 'My servant David will be their king, and they will all have one shepherd. They will live by my rules and obey my laws. They will live on the land I gave to my servant Jacob, the land in which your ancestors lived. They will all live on the land forever: they, their children, and their grandchildren. David my servant will be their king forever. I will make an agreement of peace with them, an agreement that continues forever. I will put them in their land and make them grow in number. Then I will put my Temple among them forever. The place where I live will be with them. I will be their God, and they will be my people. When my Temple is among them forever, the nations will know that I, the LORD, make Israel holy.' "

Ezekiel 37:22–28

When the Israelites give their holy offerings to the LORD, the priest must not treat these holy things as though they were not holy. The priests must not allow those who are not priests to eat the holy offerings. If they do, they cause the ones who eat the holy offerings to become guilty, and they will have to pay for it. I am the LORD, who makes them holy.' "

Leviticus 22:15–16

A Warning Against Israel

Now this is what the LORD says.
He created you, people of Jacob;
he formed you, people of Israel.
He says, "Don't be afraid, because I
    have saved you.
I have called you by name, and you
    are mine.

"I, I am the One who forgives all your
    sins, for my sake;
I will not remember your sins.
But you should remind me.
    Let's meet and decide what is right.
    Tell what you have done and show
    you are right.
Your first father sinned,
    and your leaders have turned against
    me.
So I will make your holy rulers unholy.
    I will bring destruction on the people
    of Jacob,
    and I will let Israel be insulted."

Isaiah 43:1, 25–28

Christ in us can manifest His holiness if we will yield our flesh to Him. This is not a human operation; it is a spiritual one. Jesus installs His holiness in us by grace. Not a once-for-all-time transaction, this is a daily, moment-by-moment striving to live more by the Spirit and less by the flesh.

Though becoming more holy is God's work in us, it is not a passive enterprise. Our part is active, to strive and strain toward the high calling we have received. God's part is to forgive our failings based on the merit of Christ's atoning death.

His will is that we become holy. . . . This kind of holiness is not the result of our own best effort. . . .

The forgiveness of Christ makes us holy; He washed away our sin. In reality, God in us—the Holy Spirit—makes us holy. There is no possibility of holiness apart from His grace. He calls us, He justifies us, He sanctifies us (makes us holy), and He will glorify us—all by His grace.

Our part is to surrender in faith; God's part is to implant the sanctifying Holy Spirit in us. "So I say, live by the Spirit, and you will not gratify the desires of the sinful nature" (Galatians 5:16). Because of His everlasting love, we know Him, and He is faithful to mold us into the character of His Son Jesus Christ—to make us holy.

Patrick Morley

ACTION POINT

Meditate on what Jesus did to make his people holy. How significant is it that Jesus considers his holy people to be his family— his brothers? How do these truths inspire you to yield to his holiness?

FRIDAY:

God Demands Obedience and Punishes Unbelief

Hebrews 3:7—4:13

We Must Continue to Follow God

So it is as the Holy Spirit says:
"Today listen to what he says.
Do not be stubborn as in the past
    when you turned against God,
when you tested God in the desert.
There your ancestors tried me and
        tested me
    and saw the things I did for forty
        years.
I was angry with them.
    I said, 'They are not loyal to me
    and have not understood my ways.'
I was angry and made a promise,
    'They will never enter my rest.'"

Psalm 95:7–11

So brothers and sisters, be careful that none of you has an evil, unbelieving heart that will turn you away from the living God. But encourage each other every day while it is "today." Help each other so none of you will become hardened because sin has tricked you. We all share in Christ if we keep till the end the sure faith we had in the beginning. This is what the Scripture says:

"Today listen to what he says.
Do not be stubborn as in the past
    when you turned against God."

Psalm 95:7–8

Who heard God's voice and was against him? It was all those people Moses led out of Egypt. And with whom was God angry for forty years? He was angry with those who sinned, who died in the desert. And to whom was God talking when he promised that they would never enter his rest? He was talking to those who did not obey him. So we see they were not allowed to enter and have God's rest, because they did not believe.

Now, since God has left us the promise that we may enter his rest, let us be very careful so none of you will fail to enter. The Good News was preached to us just as it was to them. But the teaching they heard did not help them, because they heard it but did not accept it with faith. We who have believed are able to enter and have God's rest. As God has said,

"I was angry and made a promise,
'They will never enter my rest.'"

Psalm 95:11

But God's work was finished from the time he made the world. In the Scriptures he talked about the seventh day of the week: "And on the seventh day God rested from all his works." And again in the Scripture God said, "They will never enter my rest."

It is still true that some people will enter God's rest, but those who first heard the way to be saved did not enter, because they did not obey. So God planned another day, called "today." He spoke about that day through David a long time later in the same Scripture used before:

"Today listen to what he says.
Do not be stubborn." *Psalm 95:7–8*

We know that Joshua did not lead the people into that rest, because God spoke later about another day. This shows that the rest for God's people is still coming. Anyone who enters God's rest will rest from his work as God did. Let us try as hard as we can to enter God's rest so that no one will fail by following the example of those who refused to obey.

God's word is alive and working and is sharper than a double-edged sword. It cuts all the way into us, where the soul and the spirit are joined, to the center of our joints and bones. And it judges the thoughts and feelings in our hearts. Nothing in all the world can be hidden from God. Everything is clear and lies open before him, and to him we must explain the way we have lived.

All the Israelites complained against Moses and Aaron, and all the people said to them, "We wish we had died in Egypt or in this desert. Why is the LORD bringing us to this land to be killed with swords? Our wives and children will be taken away.

We would be better off going back to Egypt."

Joshua son of Nun and Caleb son of Jephunneh, who had explored the land, tore their clothes. They said to all of the Israelites, "The land we explored is very good. If the LORD is pleased with us, he will lead us into that land and give us that fertile land. Don't turn against the LORD! Don't be afraid of the people in that land! We will chew them up. They have no protection, but the LORD is with us. So don't be afraid of them."

The LORD answered, "I have forgiven them as you asked. But, as surely as I live and as surely as my glory fills the whole earth, I make this promise: All these men saw my glory and the miracles I did in Egypt and in the desert, but they disobeyed me and tested me ten times. So not one of them will see the land I promised to their ancestors. No one who rejected me will see that land.

Numbers 14:2–3, 6–9, 20–23

*D*uring Darius' first year as king, I, Daniel, was reading the Scriptures. I saw that the LORD told Jeremiah that Jerusalem would be empty ruins for seventy years.

Then I turned to the Lord God and prayed and asked him for help. I did not eat any food. To show my sadness, I put on rough cloth and sat in ashes. I prayed to the LORD my God and told him about all of our sins. I said, "Lord, you are a great God who causes fear and wonder. You keep your agreement of love with all who love you and obey your commands.

"But we have sinned and done wrong. We have been wicked and turned against you, your commands, and your laws. We did not listen to your servants, the prophets, who spoke for you to our kings, our leaders, our ancestors, and all the people of the land.

"But, Lord our God, you show us mercy and forgive us even though we have turned against you. We have not obeyed the LORD our God or the teachings he gave us through his servants, the prophets. All the people of Israel have disobeyed your teachings and have turned away, refusing to obey you. So you brought on us the curses and promises of punishment written in the Teachings of Moses, the servant of God, because we sinned against you."

Daniel 9:2–6, 9–11

I N S I G H T S

*H*ow do we find God and grow in him? Jesus was adamant at this point. He said we must do what he says. We must put into practical obedience the knowledge that we have. He continually asked people to drop their nets, to sell all they had and to follow him.

We might say that Jesus had a theology of obedience. And the object of this obedience was a living person, not a historical norm, not a code of laws, but himself. He called people to be accountable to God whether they were believers or skeptics who were searching. For example, he told his disciples, "What is the point of calling me, 'Lord, Lord,' without doing what I tell you to do?" (Lk. 6:46 Phillips). . . .

Jesus knew that obedience to his and his Father's words yielded faith. . . . If I had to sum up one's response to the gospel message, I would say as William Pannell has said, "It's paint—or get off the ladder." Jesus approached people exactly like that. He told them to pick up their brush and paint something.

Do you want to discover who Jesus is and deal honestly with your doubts? Jesus' style is not to suggest that you go and ponder the virgin birth for three months but to begin doing what he says.

Rebecca Pippert

A P P L I C A T I O N

*W*hat does an unbelieving heart lead us to do? What is the relationship between obedience and belief? When our life is over, what will God ask us to explain? Are you ready to answer him?

WEEKEND:
Jesus Is Our High Priest
Hebrews 4:14—6:8

Since we have a great high priest, Jesus the Son of God, who has gone into heaven, let us hold on to the faith we have. For our high priest is able to understand our weaknesses. When he lived on earth, he was tempted in every way that we are, but he did not sin. Let us, then, feel very sure that we can come before God's throne where there is grace. There we can receive mercy and grace to help us when we need it.

Every high priest is chosen from among other people. He is given the work of going before God for them to offer gifts and sacrifices for sins. Since he himself is weak, he is able to be gentle with those who do not understand and who are doing wrong things. Because he is weak, the high priest must offer sacrifices for his own sins and also for the sins of the people.

To be a high priest is an honor, but no one chooses himself for this work. He must be called by God as Aaron was. So also Christ did not choose himself to have the honor of being a high priest, but God chose him. God said to him,

"You are my Son.

Today I have become your Father."

Psalm 2:7

And in another Scripture God says,

"You are a priest forever,

a priest like Melchizedek." *Psalm 110:4*

While Jesus lived on earth, he prayed to God and asked God for help. He prayed with loud cries and tears to the One who could save him from death, and his prayer was heard because he trusted God. Even though Jesus was the Son of God, he learned obedience by what he suffered. And because his obedience was perfect, he was able to give eternal salvation to all who obey him. In this way God made Jesus a high priest, a priest like Melchizedek.

Warning Against Falling Away

We have much to say about this, but it is hard to explain because you are so slow to understand. By now you should be teachers, but you need someone to teach you again the first lessons of God's message. You still need the teaching that is like milk. You are not ready for solid food. Anyone who lives on milk is still a baby and knows nothing about right teaching. But solid food is for those who are grown up. They have practiced in order to know the difference between good and evil.

So let us go on to grown-up teaching. Let us not go back over the beginning lessons we learned about Christ. We should not again start teaching about faith in God and about turning away from those acts that lead to death. We should not return to the teaching about baptisms, about laying on of hands, about the raising of the dead and eternal judgment. And we will go on to grown-up teaching if God allows.

Some people cannot be brought back again to a changed life. They were once in God's light, and enjoyed heaven's gift, and shared in the Holy Spirit. They found out how good God's word is, and they received the powers of his new world. But they fell away from Christ. It is impossible to bring them back to a changed life again, because they are nailing the Son of God to a cross again and are shaming him in front of others.

Some people are like land that gets plenty of rain. The land produces a good crop for those who work it, and it receives God's blessings. Other people are like land that grows thorns and weeds and is worthless. It is in danger of being cursed by God and will be destroyed by fire.

Who is Melchizedek?

Melchizedek king of Salem brought out bread and wine. He was a priest for God Most High and blessed Abram, saying,

"Abram, may you be blessed by God Most High,

the God who made heaven and earth.

And we praise God Most High,
   who has helped you to defeat your
      enemies."
Then Abram gave Melchizedek a tenth of
everything he had brought back from the
battle.

Genesis 14:18–20

God Chooses Priests for
His Holy Work

*T*ell your brother Aaron to come to you,
along with his sons Nadab, Abihu, Eleazar,
and Ithamar. Separate them from the other
Israelites to serve me as priests. Make holy
clothes for your brother Aaron to give him
honor and beauty. Tell all the skilled craftsmen to whom I have given wisdom to make
special clothes for Aaron—clothes to show
that he belongs to me so that he may serve
me as a priest."

Exodus 28:1–3

*S*o I will make the Meeting Tent and the
altar holy; I will also make Aaron and his
sons holy so they may serve me as priests.
I will live with the people of Israel and be
their God. And they will know that I am the
LORD their God who led them out of Egypt
so that I could live with them. I am the LORD
their God."

Exodus 29:44–46

A Special Role for the High Priest

*T*he high priest, who was chosen from
among his brothers, had the special olive
oil poured on his head. He was also appointed to wear the priestly clothes. So he
must not show his sadness by letting his
hair go uncombed or tearing his clothes. He
must not go into a house where there is a
dead body. He must not make himself unclean, even if it is for his own father or
mother. The high priest must not go out of
the Holy Place, because if he does and becomes unclean, he will make God's Holy
Place unclean. The special oil used in appointing priests was poured on his head to
separate him from the rest of the people. I
am the LORD.
   " 'The high priest must marry a woman
who is a virgin. He must not marry a widow,

a divorced woman, or a prostitute. He must
marry a virgin from his own people so the
people will respect his children as his own.
I am the LORD. I have set the high priest
apart for his special job.' "

Leviticus 21:10–15

INSIGHTS

*A*t one time in history a "NO ACCESS" sign
was posted at the gates of Paradise. Even in
the Old Testament temple there was no access
to the throne of God by the ordinary person.
Even for the High Priest his access was "limited" to once a year under very guarded circumstances. A thick veil separated the Holy
of Holies from the rest of the temple. It was
off-limits. Restricted. No admission was per-
mitted to the rank-and-file believer.
   The moment Jesus was slain, the instant
the Just One died for the unjust, the veil in
the temple was torn. The presence of God became accessible to us. For the Christian the
"NO ACCESS" sign was removed from the
gates of Paradise. We may now trespass freely
on holy ground. We have access to His grace,
but even more, we have access to Him. Justified men need no longer say to the Holy,
"Depart from me, for I am a sinful man."
Now we can be comfortable in the presence
of a holy God. We can take our questions to
Him. He is not too remote to hear our cries.
We come as those covered by the righteousness
of Christ. I repeat: We can be comfortable in
the presence of God. To be sure we still come
in awe, in a spirit of reverence and adoration,
but the tremendous news is that we can . . .
approach the throne of grace with confidence.

R. C. Sproul

PAUSE   FOR   REFLECTION

*F*rom the Old Testament reading, do you
begin to sense the vital role of God's priests?
In what ways does your understanding of
Christ's role as high priest (explained in Hebrews) help you realize how much he has done
to save us?

529

MONDAY:

God's Word Is True: He Keeps His Promises

Hebrews 6:9—7:10

*D*ear friends, we are saying this to you, but we really expect better things from you that will lead to your salvation. God is fair; he will not forget the work you did and the love you showed for him by helping his people. And he will remember that you are still helping them. We want each of you to go on with the same hard work all your lives so you will surely get what you hope for. We do not want you to become lazy. Be like those who through faith and patience will receive what God has promised.

God made a promise to Abraham. And as there is no one greater than God, he used himself when he swore to Abraham, saying, "I will surely bless you and give you many descendants." Abraham waited patiently for this to happen, and he received what God promised.

People always use the name of someone greater than themselves when they swear. The oath proves that what they say is true, and this ends all arguing. God wanted to prove that his promise was true to those who would get what he promised. And he wanted them to understand clearly that his purposes never change, so he made an oath. These two things cannot change: God cannot lie when he makes a promise, and he cannot lie when he makes an oath. These things encourage us who came to God for safety. They give us strength to hold on to the hope we have been given. We have this hope as an anchor for the soul, sure and strong. It enters behind the curtain in the Most Holy Place in heaven, where Jesus has gone ahead of us and for us. He has become the high priest forever, a priest like Melchizedek.

The Priest Melchizedek

*M*elchizedek was the king of Salem and a priest for God Most High. He met Abraham when Abraham was coming back after defeating the kings. When they met, Melchizedek blessed Abraham, and Abraham gave him a tenth of everything he had brought back from the battle. First, Melchizedek's name means "king of goodness," and he is king of Salem, which means "king of peace." No one knows who Melchizedek's father or mother was, where he came from, when he was born, or when he died. Melchizedek is like the Son of God; he continues being a priest forever.

You can see how great Melchizedek was. Abraham, the great father, gave him a tenth of everything that he won in battle. Now the law says that those in the tribe of Levi who become priests must collect a tenth from the people—their own people—even though the priests and the people are from the family of Abraham. Melchizedek was not from the tribe of Levi, but he collected a tenth from Abraham. And he blessed Abraham, the man who had God's promises. Now everyone knows that the more important person blesses the less important person. Priests receive a tenth, even though they are only men who live and then die. But Melchizedek, who received a tenth from Abraham, continues living, as the Scripture says. We might even say that Levi, who receives a tenth, also paid it when Abraham paid Melchizedek a tenth. Levi was not yet born, but he was in the body of his ancestor when Melchizedek met Abraham.

I have found my servant David;
    I appointed him by pouring holy oil
        on him.
He will say to me, 'You are my father,
    my God, the Rock, my Savior.'
I will make him my firstborn son,
    the greatest king on earth.
My love will watch over him forever,
    and my agreement with him will
        never end.
I will make his family continue,
    and his kingdom will last as long as
        the skies.

"If his descendants reject my teachings

and do not follow my laws,
if they ignore my demands
    and disobey my commands,
then I will punish their sins with a rod
    and their wrongs with a whip.
But I will not hold back my love from
    David,
    nor will I stop being loyal.
I will not break my agreement
    nor change what I have said.
I have promised by my holiness,
    I will not lie to David.
His family will go on forever.
    His kingdom will last before me like
    the sun.
It will continue forever, like the moon,
    like a dependable witness in the
    sky."   *Selah*

                        Psalm 89:20, 26–37

*R*emember that your people have been given their land between the Jordan River and the Mediterranean Sea in the west, the land I promised to give you. The LORD your God will force out the people living there. The LORD will push them out ahead of you. And you will own the land, as he has promised you.

"Be strong. You must be careful to obey everything commanded in the Book of the Teachings of Moses. Do exactly as it says.

"It's almost time for me to die. You know and fully believe that the LORD has done great things for you. You know that he has not failed to keep any of his promises. Every good promise that the LORD your God made has come true, and in the same way, his other promises will come true. He promised that evil will come to you and that he will destroy you from this good land that he gave you. This will happen if you don't keep your agreement with the LORD your God. If you go and serve other gods and worship them, the LORD will become very angry with you. Then none of you will be left in this good land he has given you."

                        Joshua 23:4–6, 14–16

INSIGHTS

*T*he Bible is filled with the promises of God. We need to claim each one by faith and activate its truth in our lives. Some folks like to say, "If God said it, I believe it, and that settles it!" The fact of the matter is, if God said it, that settles it, whether we believe it or not.

Someone will question, "How can I be sure God really said this?" or, "How can I be sure this is what it means?" I realize we must interpret each promise in its proper context. But I also believe that we need to take those promises which apply to us and activate them by faith.

In Hebrews 4:3, we read an amazing truth. It says there that God's works were "finished from the foundation of the world." In other words, God had already provided the answer to your every need before the world was ever formed. With His divine foreknowledge He looked down the corridor of time to come, saw your coming problem and provided just exactly what you would need. . . .

. . . Think on the majesty and magnitude of God. Focus on the promises He has given you in His Word. Turn your attention to fulfilling His purpose for your life. Live in the confidence that He is in control. Now you can relax, for there is nothing to worry about. God cares and He keeps His promises to help.

                        Richard Lee

APPLICATION

*W*hat about God's character encourages us to trust in his promises? Of what did Joshua remind the Israelites before he died? Why is it important to remember that God keeps his promises? Will you remember to live by his promises?

TUESDAY:

Jesus Is the High Priest of God's New Agreement

Hebrews 7:11—8:6

NEW TESTAMENT READING

*T*he people were given the law based on a system of priests from the tribe of Levi, but they could not be made perfect through that system. So there was a need for another priest to come, a priest like Melchizedek, not Aaron. And when a different kind of priest comes, the law must be changed, too. We are saying these things about Christ, who belonged to a different tribe. No one from that tribe ever served as a priest at the altar. It is clear that our Lord came from the tribe of Judah, and Moses said nothing about priests belonging to that tribe.

Jesus Is like Melchizedek

*A*nd this becomes even more clear when we see that another priest comes who is like Melchizedek. He was not made a priest by human rules and laws but through the power of his life, which continues forever. It is said about him,

"You are a priest forever,
a priest like Melchizedek." *Psalm 110:4*

The old rule is now set aside, because it was weak and useless. The law of Moses could not make anything perfect. But now a better hope has been given to us, and with this hope we can come near to God. It is important that God did this with an oath. Others became priests without an oath, but Christ became a priest with God's oath. God said:

"The Lord has made a promise
and will not change his mind.
'You are a priest forever.'" *Psalm 110:4*

This means that Jesus is the guarantee of a better agreement from God to his people.

When one of the other priests died, he could not continue being a priest. So there were many priests. But because Jesus lives forever, he will never stop serving as priest. So he is able always to save those who come to God through him because he always lives, asking God to help them.

Jesus is the kind of high priest we need. He is holy, sinless, pure, not influenced by sinners, and he is raised above the heavens. He is not like the other priests who had to offer sacrifices every day, first for their own sins, and then for the sins of the people. Christ offered his sacrifice only once and for all time when he offered himself. The law chooses high priests who are people with weaknesses, but the word of God's oath came later than the law. It made God's Son to be the high priest, and that Son has been made perfect forever.

Jesus Is Our High Priest

*H*ere is the point of what we are saying: We have a high priest who sits on the right side of God's throne in heaven. Our high priest serves in the Most Holy Place, the true place of worship that was made by God, not by humans.

Every high priest has the work of offering gifts and sacrifices to God. So our high priest must also offer something to God. If our high priest were now living on earth, he would not be a priest, because there are already priests here who follow the law by offering gifts to God. The work they do as priests is only a copy and a shadow of what is in heaven. This is why God warned Moses when he was ready to build the Holy Tent: "Be very careful to make everything by the plan I showed you on the mountain." But the priestly work that has been given to Jesus is much greater than the work that was given to the other priests. In the same way, the new agreement that Jesus brought from God to his people is much greater than the old one. And the new agreement is based on promises of better things.

OLD TESTAMENT READING

*T*he LORD said to my Lord,
"Sit by me at my right side
until I put your enemies under your
control."
The LORD will enlarge your kingdom
beyond Jerusalem,
and you will rule over your enemies.
Your people will join you on your day of
battle.

You have been dressed in holiness
from birth;
you have the freshness of a child.

The LORD has made a promise
and will not change his mind.
He said, "You are a priest forever,
a priest like Melchizedek."

Psalm 110:1–4

*L*ook, the time is coming," says the LORD,
"when I will make a new agreement
with the people of Israel
and the people of Judah.
It will not be like the agreement
I made with their ancestors
when I took them by the hand
to bring them out of Egypt.
I was a husband to them,
but they broke that agreement," says
the LORD.
"This is the agreement I will make
with the people of Israel at that
time," says the LORD:
"I will put my teachings in their minds
and write them on their hearts.
I will be their God,
and they will be my people."

Jeremiah 31:31–33

*T*his is what the Lord GOD says: I will do to
you what you have done. You hated and
broke the agreement you promised to keep.
But I will remember my agreement I made
with you when you were young, and I will
make an agreement that will continue forever with you. Then you will remember
what you have done and feel ashamed when
you receive your sisters—both your older
and your younger sisters. I will give them
to you like daughters, but not because they
share in my agreement with you. I will set
up my agreement with you, and you will
know that I am the LORD. You will remember what you did and feel ashamed. You will
not open your mouth again because of your
shame, when I forgive you for all the things
you have done, says the Lord GOD.' "

Ezekiel 16:59–63

INSIGHTS

*W*e need a priest such as Jesus is, to repre-

sent us in heaven. Although we are so completely absolved from guilt, and so fully "accepted in the beloved", yet in ourselves, while
down here, we are still erring, sinning, feeble,
needy creatures, exposed to trials and temptations, liable to stumble, and encompassed
by infirmities. How we need the high priestly
mediation of our dear heavenly Advocate,
whose presence yonder keeps us in all the
benefits of the New Covenant, maintains our
standing in grace, and releases to us the
paraclete ministries of the Holy Spirit. It has
been well said, "We could not stand for a
moment down here, if He were not living for
us up there."
Thank God, "we have such an high priest"!

J. Sydlow Baxter

ACTION POINT

*I*dentify the unique aspects of Christ's priest-
hood and describe why his unique role as high
priest is significant. Pray now and thank God
that he has sent a high priest—like no other—
to offer the only perfect sacrifice for your sins.

WEDNESDAY:

Jesus Takes Away Our Sins Forever

Hebrews 8:7—9:12

*I*f there had been nothing wrong with the first agreement, there would have been no need for a second agreement. But God found something wrong with his people. He says:

"Look, the time is coming, says the Lord,
> when I will make a new agreement
with the people of Israel
> and the people of Judah.
It will not be like the agreement
> I made with their ancestors
when I took them by the hand
> to bring them out of Egypt.
But they broke that agreement,
> and I turned away from them, says the Lord.
This is the agreement I will make
> with the people of Israel at that time, says the Lord.
I will put my teachings in their minds
> and write them on their hearts.
I will be their God,
> and they will be my people.
People will no longer have to teach
> their neighbors and relatives
to know the Lord,
because all people will know me,
> from the least to the most important.
I will forgive them for the wicked
> things they did,
and I will not remember their sins
> anymore." *Jeremiah 31:31–34*

God called this a new agreement, so he has made the first agreement old. And anything that is old and worn out is ready to disappear.

The Old Agreement

*T*he first agreement had rules for worship and a man-made place for worship. The Holy Tent was set up for this. The first area in the Tent was called the Holy Place. In it were the lamp and the table with the bread that was made holy for God. Behind the second curtain was a room called the Most Holy Place. In it was a golden altar for burning incense and the Ark covered with gold that held the old agreement. Inside this Ark was a golden jar of manna, Aaron's rod that once grew leaves, and the stone tablets of the old agreement. Above the Ark were the creatures that showed God's glory, whose wings reached over the lid. But we cannot tell everything about these things now.

When everything in the Tent was made ready in this way, the priests went into the first room every day to worship. But only the high priest could go into the second room, and he did that only once a year. He could never enter the inner room without taking blood with him, which he offered to God for himself and for sins the people did without knowing they did them. The Holy Spirit uses this to show that the way into the Most Holy Place was not open while the system of the old Holy Tent was still being used. This is an example for the present time. It shows that the gifts and sacrifices offered cannot make the conscience of the worshiper perfect. These gifts and sacrifices were only about food and drink and special washings. They were rules for the body, to be followed until the time of God's new way.

The New Agreement

*B*ut when Christ came as the high priest of the good things we now have, he entered the greater and more perfect tent. It is not made by humans and does not belong to this world. Christ entered the Most Holy Place only once—and for all time. He did not take with him the blood of goats and calves. His sacrifice was his own blood, and by it he set us free from sin forever.

*T*he LORD shows mercy and is kind.
> He does not become angry quickly,
> and he has great love.
He will not always accuse us,
> and he will not be angry forever.

He has not punished us as our sins
  should be punished;
    he has not repaid us for the evil we
    have done.
As high as the sky is above the earth,
  so great is his love for those who
    respect him.
He has taken our sins away from us
  as far as the east is from west.

Psalm 103:8–12

*E*verything he does is good and fair;
  all his orders can be trusted.
They will continue forever.
  They were made true and right.
He sets his people free.
  He made his agreement everlasting.
  He is holy and wonderful.

Psalm 111:7–9

*L*ook at the new thing I am going to do.
  It is already happening. Don't you
    see it?
I will make a road in the desert
  and rivers in the dry land.

"People of Jacob, you have not called to
    me;
  people of Israel, you have become
    tired of me.
You have not brought me your sacri-
    fices of sheep
  nor honored me with your sacrifices.
I did not weigh you down with sacri-
    fices to offer
  or make you tired with incense to
    burn.
So you did not buy incense for me;
  you did not freely bring me fat from
    your sacrifices.
Instead you have weighed me down
    with your many sins;
  you have made me tired of your
    many wrongs.

"I, I am the One who forgives all your
    sins, for my sake;
  I will not remember your sins."

Isaiah 43:19, 22–25

*B*ut it was the Lord who decided
  to crush him and make him suffer.
The Lord made his life a penalty
    offering,

but he will still see his descendants and
  live a long life.
He will complete the things the Lord
  wants him to do.
"After his soul suffers many things,
  he will see life and be satisfied.
My good servant will make many
  people right with God;
  he will carry away their sins."

Isaiah 53:10–11

*I*f we confess our sins, he is faithful and just
and will forgive us our sins and purify us from
all unrighteousness" (1 John 1:9). This verse
tells us what to do when we've sinned—we
must confess that we have sinned and need
forgiveness.

Then if we confess, God promises to forgive. He takes care of that sin once and for
all. He restores our relationship with
him. . . .

. . . At the center of forgiveness is always
the cross of Christ. Without his body on the
cross, forgiveness would not even be available.
Forgiveness is costly, and we need to see it
from that perspective. There is no forgiveness
without tears, without a price to be paid,
without the sacrifice of Christ.

Because of Christ's sacrifice, sin need not
defeat us. . . .

Though we cannot eliminate the temptation to sin, we are not left without redemptive resources. God is on our side, Jesus is
advocating for us, and the Holy Spirit is
making us aware of our weaknesses as our
Teacher and Guide.

David McKenna

PAUSE FOR REFLECTION

*D*escribe the many differences between the
old and new agreements. What difference does
it make that Jesus is now our high priest? Pray
and thank God that the blood of Jesus takes
away our sins forever.

THURSDAY:

Christ's Blood: The Perfect Sacrifice

Hebrews 9:13—10:10

*T*he blood of goats and bulls and the ashes of a cow are sprinkled on the people who are unclean, and this makes their bodies clean again. How much more is done by the blood of Christ. He offered himself through the eternal Spirit as a perfect sacrifice to God. His blood will make our consciences pure from useless acts so we may serve the living God.

For this reason Christ brings a new agreement from God to his people. Those who are called by God can now receive the blessings he has promised, blessings that will last forever. They can have those things because Christ died so that the people who lived under the first agreement could be set free from sin.

When there is a will, it must be proven that the one who wrote that will is dead. A will means nothing while the person is alive; it can be used only after the person dies. This is why even the first agreement could not begin without blood to show death. First, Moses told all the people every command in the law. Next he took the blood of calves and mixed it with water. Then he used red wool and a branch of the hyssop plant to sprinkle it on the book of the law and on all the people. He said, "This is the blood that begins the Agreement that God commanded you to obey." In the same way, Moses sprinkled the blood on the Holy Tent and over all the things used in worship. The law says that almost everything must be made clean by blood, and sins cannot be forgiven without blood to show death.

Christ's Death Takes Away Sins

*S*o the copies of the real things in heaven had to be made clean by animal sacrifices. But the real things in heaven need much better sacrifices. Christ did not go into the Most Holy Place made by humans, which is only a copy of the real one. He went into heaven itself and is there now before God to help us. The high priest enters the Most Holy Place once every year with blood that is not his own. But Christ did not offer himself many times. Then he would have had to suffer many times since the world was made. But Christ came only once and for all time at just the right time to take away all sin by sacrificing himself. Just as everyone must die once and be judged, so Christ was offered as a sacrifice one time to take away the sins of many people. And he will come a second time, not to offer himself for sin, but to bring salvation to those who are waiting for him.

The law is only an unclear picture of the good things coming in the future; it is not the real thing. The people under the law offer the same sacrifices every year, but these sacrifices can never make perfect those who come near to worship God. If the law could make them perfect, the sacrifices would have already stopped. The worshipers would be made clean, and they would no longer have a sense of sin. But these sacrifices remind them of their sins every year, because it is impossible for the blood of bulls and goats to take away sins.

So when Christ came into the world, he said:

"You do not want sacrifices and offerings,
　　but you have prepared a body for
　　　me.
You do not ask for burnt offerings
　　and offerings to take away sins.
Then I said, 'Look, I have come.
　　It is written about me in the book.
God, I have come to do what you
　　want.'"　　　　　　　*Psalm 40:6–8*

In this Scripture he first said, "You do not want sacrifices and offerings. You do not ask for burnt offerings and offerings to take away sins." (These are all sacrifices that the law commands.) Then he said, "Look, I have come to do what you want." God ends the first system of sacrifices so he can set up the new system. And because of this, we are made holy through the sacrifice Christ made in his body once and for all time.

The Sacrifices of the Law
Can't Make People Perfect

*M*oses told the people all the LORD's words and laws for living. Then all of the people answered out loud together, "We will do all the things the LORD has said." So Moses wrote down all the words of the LORD. And he got up early the next morning and built an altar near the bottom of the mountain. He set up twelve stones, one stone for each of the twelve tribes of Israel. Then Moses sent young Israelite men to offer whole burnt offerings and to sacrifice young bulls as fellowship offerings to the LORD. Moses put half of the blood of these animals in bowls, and he sprinkled the other half of the blood on the altar. Then he took the Book of the Agreement and read it so the people could hear him. And they said, "We will do everything that the LORD has said; we will obey."

Then Moses took the blood from the bowls and sprinkled it on the people, saying, "This is the blood that begins the Agreement, the Agreement which the LORD has made with you about all these words."

Exodus 24:3–8

*T*hen Aaron will offer the bull as a sin offering for himself, to remove the sins from him and his family so they will belong to the LORD; he will kill the bull for the sin offering for himself.

"Then Aaron must kill the goat of the sin offering for the people and bring its blood into the room behind the curtain. He must do with the goat's blood as he did with the bull's blood, sprinkling it on the lid and in front of the lid. Because the people of Israel have been unclean, Aaron will perform the acts to make the Most Holy Place ready for service to the LORD. Then it will be clean from the sins and crimes of the Israelites. He must also do this for the Meeting Tent, because it stays in the middle of unclean people. When Aaron makes the Most Holy Place ready for service to the LORD, no one is allowed in the Meeting Tent until he comes out. So Aaron will perform the acts to remove sins from himself, his family, and all the people of Israel, so they will belong to the LORD.

"That law for removing the sins of the Israelites so they will belong to the LORD will continue forever. You will do these things once a year."

So they did the things the LORD had commanded Moses.

Leviticus 16:11, 15–17, 34

*W*hen we sin, our only option is repentance. Without repentance there is no forgiveness. We must come before God in contrition. David put it this way:

"For thou has no delight in sacrifice. . . . The sacrifice acceptable to God is a broken spirit; a broken and contrite heart, O God, thou wilt not despise" [Psalm 51:16, 17].

Here David's profound thoughts reveal his understanding of what many Old Testament persons failed to grasp—that the offering of sacrifices in the temple did not gain merit for the sinner. Sacrifices pointed beyond themselves to the perfect Sacrifice. The perfect atonement was offered by the perfect Lamb without blemish. The blood of bulls and goats does not take away sin. The blood of Jesus does. To avail ourselves of the atonement of Christ, to gain that covering, requires that we come before God in brokenness and contrition. The true sacrifices of God are a broken spirit and a contrite heart.

R. C. Sproul

APPLICATION

*W*hat does the sacrifice of Christ's blood accomplish that no other sacrifice can do? What kind of sacrifice does God want from his people? What has Christ's sacrifice done for you personally?

FRIDAY:

The Lord Will Judge His People

Hebrews 10:11–39

*E*very day the priests stand and do their religious service, often offering the same sacrifices. Those sacrifices can never take away sins. But after Christ offered one sacrifice for sins, forever, he sat down at the right side of God. And now Christ waits there for his enemies to be put under his power. With one sacrifice he made perfect forever those who are being made holy.

The Holy Spirit also tells us about this. First he says:

"This is the agreement I will make
  with them at that time, says the
  Lord.
I will put my teachings in their hearts
  and write them on their minds."

Jeremiah 31:33

Then he says:

"Their sins and the evil things they
  do—
  I will not remember anymore."

Jeremiah 31:34

Now when these have been forgiven, there is no more need for a sacrifice for sins.

Continue to Trust God

*S*o, brothers and sisters, we are completely free to enter the Most Holy Place without fear because of the blood of Jesus' death. We can enter through a new and living way that Jesus opened for us. It leads through the curtain—Christ's body. And since we have a great priest over God's house, let us come near to God with a sincere heart and a sure faith, because we have been made free from a guilty conscience, and our bodies have been washed with pure water. Let us hold firmly to the hope that we have confessed, because we can trust God to do what he promised.

Let us think about each other and help each other to show love and do good deeds.

You should not stay away from the church meetings, as some are doing, but you should meet together and encourage each other. Do this even more as you see the day coming.

If we decide to go on sinning after we have learned the truth, there is no longer any sacrifice for sins. There is nothing but fear in waiting for the judgment and the terrible fire that will destroy all those who live against God. Anyone who refused to obey the law of Moses was found guilty from the proof given by two or three witnesses. He was put to death without mercy. So what do you think should be done to those who do not respect the Son of God, who look at the blood of the agreement that made them holy as no different from others' blood, who insult the Spirit of God's grace? Surely they should have a much worse punishment. We know that God said, "I will punish those who do wrong; I will repay them." And he also said, "The Lord will judge his people." It is a terrible thing to fall into the hands of the living God.

Remember those days in the past when you first learned the truth. You had a hard struggle with many sufferings, but you continued strong. Sometimes you were hurt and attacked before crowds of people, and sometimes you shared with those who were being treated that way. You helped the prisoners. You even had joy when all that you owned was taken from you, because you knew you had something better and more lasting.

So do not lose the courage you had in the past, which has a great reward. You must hold on, so you can do what God wants and receive what he has promised. For in a very short time,

"The One who is coming will come
  and will not be delayed.
The person who is right with me
  will live by trusting in me.
But if he turns back with fear,
  I will not be pleased with him."

Habakkuk 2:3–4

But we are not those who turn back and are lost. We are people who have faith and are saved.

*J*erusalem, rejoice.
> All you people who love Jerusalem,
>> be happy.
> Those of you who felt sad for Jerusalem
>> should now feel happy with her."

When you see these things, you will be
>> happy,
> and you will grow like the grass.
The LORD's servants will see his power,
> but his enemies will see his anger.
Look, the LORD is coming with fire
> and his armies with clouds of dust.
He will punish those people with his
> anger;
> he will punish them with flames of
>> fire.
The LORD will judge the people with fire,
> and he will destroy many people
>> with his sword;
> he will kill many people.

Isaiah 66:10, 14–16

*T*his is what the LORD says to the nation
of Israel:
"Come to me and live.
> But do not look in Bethel
or go to Gilgal,
> and do not go down to Beersheba.
The people of Gilgal will be taken away
>> as captives,
> and Bethel will become nothing."
Come to the LORD and live,
> or he will move like fire against the
>> descendants of Joseph.
The fire will burn Bethel,
> and there will be no one to put it out.
You turn justice upside down,
> and you throw on the ground what is
>> right.

I know your many crimes,
> your terrible sins.
You hurt people who do right,
> you take money to do wrong,
> and you keep the poor from getting
>> justice in court.

Try to do good, not evil,
> so that you will live,
and the LORD God All-Powerful will be
> with you

just as you say he is.
Hate evil and love good;
> be fair in the courts.
Maybe the LORD God All-Powerful will
> be kind
> to the people of Joseph who are left
> alive.

Amos 5:4–7, 12, 14–15

INSIGHTS

*W*ithout a physical order in the universe,
there could be no science.

*Much of the genius of our space program
involves achieving the most precise knowledge
and conformity to this order. Failure means
disaster.*

*Tens of thousands of man-hours, the most
sophisticated technology, and the latest advances in space science are involved. . . .
But all of it is helpless without an orderly
universe to count on, and conform to.*

*God, who ordained physical order, also
ordained moral and spiritual order.*

Conformity guarantees fulfillment. Disobedience spells destruction. . . .

*One can reject God's moral absolutes. But
that does not get rid of them. The law of sin
and death is just as inviolable as the law of
gravity. Morality isn't arbitrary. It's part of
the natural law of the universe. God's law
stands whether we like it or not.*

*We ignore this fact to our doom. Violating
God's physical law is destructive, but violating
His moral law is infinitely more serious—for
it has eternal consequences.*

*Every malfunction of the social order in
America derives from our transgression of
God's moral law. If we refuse to turn to God
for mercy and grace, we condemn ourselves
to His inexorable justice and judgment.*

Richard Halverson

APPLICATION

*W*hat will happen to everyone who lives
*against God? What is promised to those who
continue living by faith? Pray for the courage
to live as God wants his people to live.*

539

WEEKEND:
Faith Pleases God
Hebrews 11:1–22

N E W   T E S T A M E N T   R E A D I N G

What Is Faith?

*F*aith means being sure of the things we hope for and knowing that something is real even if we do not see it. Faith is the reason we remember great people who lived in the past.

It is by faith we understand that the whole world was made by God's command so what we see was made by something that cannot be seen.

It was by faith that Abel offered God a better sacrifice than Cain did. God said he was pleased with the gifts Abel offered and called Abel a good man because of his faith. Abel died, but through his faith he is still speaking.

It was by faith that Enoch was taken to heaven so he would not die. He could not be found, because God had taken him away. Before he was taken, the Scripture says that he was a man who truly pleased God. Without faith no one can please God. Anyone who comes to God must believe that he is real and that he rewards those who truly want to find him.

It was by faith that Noah heard God's warnings about things he could not yet see. He obeyed God and built a large boat to save his family. By his faith, Noah showed that the world was wrong, and he became one of those who are made right with God through faith.

It was by faith Abraham obeyed God's call to go to another place God promised to give him. He left his own country, not knowing where he was to go. It was by faith that he lived like a foreigner in the country God promised to give him. He lived in tents with Isaac and Jacob, who had received that same promise from God. Abraham was waiting for the city that has real foundations—the city planned and built by God.

He was too old to have children, and Sarah could not have children. It was by faith that Abraham was made able to be-come a father, because he trusted God to do what he had promised. This man was so old he was almost dead, but from him came as many descendants as there are stars in the sky. Like the sand on the seashore, they could not be counted.

All these great people died in faith. They did not get the things that God promised his people, but they saw them coming far in the future and were glad. They said they were like visitors and strangers on earth. When people say such things, they show they are looking for a country that will be their own. If they had been thinking about the country they had left, they could have gone back. But they were waiting for a bet-ter country—a heavenly country. So God is not ashamed to be called their God, because he has prepared a city for them.

It was by faith that Abraham, when God tested him, offered his son Isaac as a sacri-fice. God made the promises to Abraham, but Abraham was ready to offer his own son as a sacrifice. God had said, "The descen-dants I promised you will be from Isaac." Abraham believed that God could raise the dead, and really, it was as if Abraham got Isaac back from death.

It was by faith that Isaac blessed the fu-ture of Jacob and Esau. It was by faith that Jacob, as he was dying, blessed each one of Joseph's sons. Then he worshiped as he leaned on the top of his walking stick.

It was by faith that Joseph, while he was dying, spoke about the Israelites leaving Egypt and gave instructions about what to do with his body.

O L D   T E S T A M E N T   R E A D I N G

*T*his is the family history of Noah. Noah was a good man, the most innocent man of his time, and he walked with God.

People on earth did what God said was evil, and violence was everywhere. When God saw that everyone on the earth did only evil, he said to Noah, "Because people have made the earth full of violence, I will destroy all of them from the earth. Build a boat of cypress wood for yourself. Make rooms in it and cover it inside and outside with tar. This is how big I want you to build the boat:

four hundred fifty feet long, seventy-five feet wide, and forty-five feet high. Make an opening around the top of the boat that is eighteen inches high from the edge of the roof down. Put a door in the side of the boat. Make an upper, middle, and lower deck in it. I will bring a flood of water on the earth to destroy all living things that live under the sky, including everything that has the breath of life. Everything on the earth will die. But I will make an agreement with you—you, your sons, your wife, and your sons' wives will all go into the boat. Also, you must bring into the boat two of every living thing, male and female. Keep them alive with you. Two of every kind of bird, animal, and crawling thing will come to you to be kept alive. Also gather some of every kind of food and store it on the boat as food for you and the animals."

Noah did everything that God commanded him.

Genesis 6:9, 11–22

*N*oah was six hundred years old when the flood came. He and his wife and his sons and their wives went into the boat to escape the waters of the flood. The clean animals, the unclean animals, the birds, and everything that crawls on the ground came to Noah. They went into the boat in groups of two, male and female, just as God had commanded Noah. Seven days later the flood started.

The rain fell on the earth for forty days and forty nights.

Genesis 7:6–10, 12

*W*hen Noah was six hundred and one years old, in the first day of the first month of that year, the water was dried up from the land.

Then God said to Noah, "You and your wife, your sons, and their wives should go out of the boat."

Then Noah built an altar to the LORD. He took some of all the clean birds and animals, and he burned them on the altar as offerings to God. The LORD was pleased with these sacrifices and said to himself, "I will never again curse the ground because of human beings. Their thoughts are evil even when they are young, but I will never again de-

stroy every living thing on the earth as I did this time."

Genesis 8:13a, 15–16, 20–21

*T*hen God blessed Noah and his sons and said to them, "Have many children; grow in number and fill the earth. Every animal on earth, every bird in the sky, every animal that crawls on the ground, and every fish in the sea will respect and fear you. I have given them to you.

"I make this agreement with you: I will never again destroy all living things by a flood. A flood will never again destroy the earth."

Genesis 9:1–2, 11

INSIGHTS

*F*aith is my deliberate and positive response to the good in another to the extent that I will act on his behalf in a personal, powerful way. . . .

. . . It means that I am willing to share my life along with all its capacities (time, strength, attention, talents, means, energy, affection, acceptance) with another. It means that I actively, energetically give of my best to another outside of and apart from myself.

To speak of faith in any other way than this is to indulge in mere "believism." It is to play around with pious platitudes that pack no punch at all. This sort of superficial spirituality is actually the great bane of Christianity. Literally hundreds of thousands of people claim they trust in God; they claim to have faith in Christ; they claim to be believers, yet their lives and personal conduct are a denial and travesty of true faith. . . .

. . . When our Lord lived amongst us He was continually looking for this dynamic trust and response to Himself. Whenever He found even the tiniest fragment of faith being exercised in Him He was delighted.

W. Phillip Keller

ACTION POINT

*I*s faith for things in the past, present, or future? In what ways is faith a catalyst in your life? Pray that your faith will be a delight to God.

M O N D A Y:

God Corrects Those He Loves

Hebrews 11:23—12:6

*I*t was by faith that Moses' parents hid him for three months after he was born. They saw that Moses was a beautiful baby, and they were not afraid to disobey the king's order.

It was by faith that Moses, when he grew up, refused to be called the son of the king of Egypt's daughter. He chose to suffer with God's people instead of enjoying sin for a short time. He thought it was better to suffer for the Christ than to have all the treasures of Egypt, because he was looking for God's reward. It was by faith that Moses left Egypt and was not afraid of the king's anger. Moses continued strong as if he could see the God that no one can see. It was by faith that Moses prepared the Passover and spread the blood on the doors so the one who brings death would not kill the firstborn sons of Israel.

It was by faith that the people crossed the Red Sea as if it were dry land. But when the Egyptians tried it, they were drowned.

It was by faith that the walls of Jericho fell after the people had marched around them for seven days.

It was by faith that Rahab, the prostitute, welcomed the spies and was not killed with those who refused to obey God.

Do I need to give more examples? I do not have time to tell you about Gideon, Barak, Samson, Jephthah, David, Samuel, and the prophets. Through their faith they defeated kingdoms. They did what was right, received God's promises, and shut the mouths of lions. They stopped great fires and were saved from being killed with swords. They were weak, and yet were made strong. They were powerful in battle and defeated other armies. Women received their dead relatives raised back to life. Others were tortured and refused to accept their freedom so they could be raised from the dead to a better life.

Some were laughed at and beaten. Others were put in chains and thrown into prison. They were stoned to death, they were cut in half, and they were killed with swords. Some wore the skins of sheep and goats. They were poor, abused, and treated badly. The world was not good enough for them! They wandered in deserts and mountains, living in caves and holes in the earth.

All these people are known for their faith, but none of them received what God had promised. God planned to give us something better so that they would be made perfect, but only together with us.

Follow Jesus' Example

*W*e have around us many people whose lives tell us what faith means. So let us run the race that is before us and never give up. We should remove from our lives anything that would get in the way and the sin that so easily holds us back. Let us look only to Jesus, the One who began our faith and who makes it perfect. He suffered death on the cross. But he accepted the shame as if it were nothing because of the joy that God put before him. And now he is sitting at the right side of God's throne. Think about Jesus' example. He held on while wicked people were doing evil things to him. So do not get tired and stop trying.

God Is like a Father

*Y*ou are struggling against sin, but your struggles have not yet caused you to be killed. You have forgotten the encouraging words that call you his children:

> "My child, don't think the Lord's
> discipline is worth nothing,
> and don't stop trying when he
> corrects you.
> The Lord disciplines those he loves,
> and he punishes everyone he
> accepts as his child." *Proverbs 3:11–12*

*T*he one whom God corrects is happy,
> so do not hate being corrected by
> the Almighty.
God hurts, but he also bandages up;
> he injures, but his hands also heal.

He will save you from six troubles;
   even seven troubles will not harm you.
God will buy you back from death in
      times of hunger,
   and in battle he will save you from
      the sword.
You will be protected from the tongue
      that strikes like a whip,
   and you will not be afraid when
      destruction comes."

Job 5:17–21

*Y*ou have done good things for your
      servant,
   as you have promised, LORD.
Teach me wisdom and knowledge
   because I trust your commands.
Before I suffered, I did wrong,
   but now I obey your word.
You are good, and you do what is
      good.
   Teach me your demands.
Proud people have made up lies about
      me,
   but I will follow your orders with all
      my heart.
Those people have no feelings,
   but I love your teachings.
It was good for me to suffer
   so I would learn your demands.
Your teachings are worth more to me
   than thousands of pieces of gold and
      silver.

Psalm 119:65–72

*M*y child, do not reject the LORD's
      discipline,
   and don't get angry when he cor-
      rects you.
The LORD corrects those he loves,
   just as parents correct the child they
      delight in.

Proverbs 3:11–12

*T*he Lord will not reject
   his people forever.
Although he brings sorrow,
   he also has mercy and great love.
He does not like to punish people
   or make them sad.

No one should complain
   when he is punished for his sins.

Let us examine and see what we have
   done
and then return to the LORD.

Lamentations 3:31–33, 39–40

INSIGHTS

*M*ost of us don't want to be broken in the storms of life. We much prefer to protect our personalities from the stresses and strains of our days. We would rather, much rather, be tough and rugged and self-assured than con-trite before Christ, repentant in soul before His Spirit. . . .

Many of us would like to avoid the mills of God. We are tempted to ask Him to deliver us from the upsetting, tumbling tides of time that knock off our rough corners and shape us to His design. We plead for release from the discipline of difficulties, the rub of routine responsibilities, the polish that comes from long perseverance.

We are a restless generation. We of the West want and insist on instant results. We demand a quick fix. We look for shortcuts and immediate results. We are quite sure we can be a rough slab of stone today and a polished gemstone tomorrow.

But God's ways and our ways are not the same. His patience is persistent. His work is meticulous. His years know no end. His per-ception of time is that one day is as a thou-sand years and a thousand years as but a single day.

The shattering of rock, the smoothing of stone, the polishing of a jewel in the sea re-quires eons of time. Can I then expect the breaking of my hard heart, the smoothing of my spirit, the shaping of my character as it is conformed to His own to be any less time-consuming?

W. Phillip Keller

APPLICATION

*W*hat is the relationship between having faith and receiving God's correction? In what way does correction help us remove sin from our lives? Pray that you will feel God's great love as he corrects you!

TUESDAY:

*Accept God's Correction
so You Will Learn
the Right Way to Live*

Hebrews 12:7–29

NEW TESTAMENT READING

So hold on through your sufferings, because they are like a father's discipline. God is treating you as children. All children are disciplined by their fathers. If you are never disciplined (and every child must be disciplined), you are not true children. We have all had fathers here on earth who disciplined us, and we respected them. So it is even more important that we accept discipline from the Father of our spirits so we will have life. Our fathers on earth disciplined us for a short time in the way they thought was best. But God disciplines us to help us, so we can become holy as he is. We do not enjoy being disciplined. It is painful, but later, after we have learned from it, we have peace, because we start living in the right way.

Be Careful How You Live

You have become weak, so make yourselves strong again. Live in the right way so that you will be saved and your weakness will not cause you to be lost.

Try to live in peace with all people, and try to live free from sin. Anyone whose life is not holy will never see the Lord. Be careful that no one fails to receive God's grace and begins to cause trouble among you. A person like that can ruin many of you. Be careful that no one takes part in sexual sin or is like Esau and never thinks about God. As the oldest son, Esau would have received everything from his father, but he sold all that for a single meal. You remember that after Esau did this, he wanted to get his father's blessing, but his father refused. Esau could find no way to change what he had done, even though he wanted the blessing so much that he cried.

You have not come to a mountain that can be touched and that is burning with fire. You have not come to darkness, sadness, and storms. You have not come to the noise of a trumpet or to the sound of a voice like the one the people of Israel heard and begged not to hear another word. They did not want to hear the command: "If anything, even an animal, touches the mountain, it must be put to death with stones." What they saw was so terrible that Moses said, "I am shaking with fear."

But you have come to Mount Zion, to the city of the living God, the heavenly Jerusalem. You have come to thousands of angels gathered together with joy. You have come to the meeting of God's firstborn children whose names are written in heaven. You have come to God, the judge of all people, and to the spirits of good people who have been made perfect. You have come to Jesus, the One who brought the new agreement from God to his people, and you have come to the sprinkled blood that has a better message than the blood of Abel.

So be careful and do not refuse to listen when God speaks. Others refused to listen to him when he warned them on earth, and they did not escape. So it will be worse for us if we refuse to listen to God who warns us from heaven. When he spoke before, his voice shook the earth, but now he has promised, "Once again I will shake not only the earth but also the heavens." The words "once again" clearly show us that everything that was made—things that can be shaken—will be destroyed. Only the things that cannot be shaken will remain.

So let us be thankful, because we have a kingdom that cannot be shaken. We should worship God in a way that pleases him with respect and fear, because our God is like a fire that burns things up.

OLD TESTAMENT READING

The LORD was angry with Israel again, and he caused David to turn against the Israelites. He said, "Go, count the people of Israel and Judah."

So King David said to Joab, the commander of the army, "Go through all the tribes of Israel, from Dan to Beersheba, and count the people. Then I will know how many there are."

But Joab said to the king, "May the LORD your God give you a hundred times more people, and may my master the king live to see this happen. Why do you want to do this?"

But the king commanded Joab and the commanders of the army, so they left the king to count the Israelites.

After nine months and twenty days, they had gone through all the land. Then they came back to Jerusalem.

Joab gave the list of the people to the king. There were eight hundred thousand men in Israel who could use the sword and five hundred thousand men in Judah.

David felt ashamed after he had counted the people. He said to the LORD, "I have sinned greatly by what I have done. LORD, I beg you to forgive me, your servant, because I have been very foolish."

When David got up in the morning, the LORD spoke his word to Gad, who was a prophet and David's seer. The LORD told Gad, "Go and tell David, 'This is what the LORD says: I offer you three choices. Choose one of them and I will do it to you.'"

So Gad went to David and said to him, "Should three years of hunger come to you and your land? Or should your enemies chase you for three months? Or should there be three days of disease in your land? Think about it. Then decide which of these things I should tell the LORD who sent me."

David said to Gad, "I am in great trouble. Let the LORD punish us, because the LORD is very merciful. Don't let my punishment come from human beings!"

So the LORD sent a terrible disease on Israel. It began in the morning and continued until the chosen time to stop. From Dan to Beersheba seventy thousand people died.

When David saw the angel that killed the people, he said to the LORD, "I am the one who sinned and did wrong. These people only followed me like sheep. They did nothing wrong. Please punish me and my family."

That day Gad came to David and said, "Go and build an altar to the LORD on the threshing floor of Araunah the Jebusite." So David did what Gad told him to do, just as the LORD commanded.

He built an altar to the LORD there and offered whole burnt offerings and fellowship offerings. Then the LORD answered his prayer for the country, and the disease in Israel stopped.

2 Samuel 24:1–4, 8–15, 17–19, 25

INSIGHTS

Just as a caring parent will lovingly discipline and train his child, so God lovingly disciplines us. We live in a world of mystery and unexplained enigmas, so it is not surprising that the element of mystery should invade this realm too. Indeed, our Lord indicated that it would be so. "What I do you do not realize now; but you shall understand hereafter" (John 13:7). If we are to experience serenity in this turbulent world, we will need to take firmer grasp of God's sovereignty and trust His love even when we cannot discern His purpose. We must remember that the hand molding the clay is nail-pierced, and that our God's sovereignty will never clash with His paternity. "But now, O LORD, Thou art our Father, we are the clay, and Thou our potter" (Isa. 64:8). If we are to enjoy a deepening intimacy with God, we must react to His providential dealings in a spiritual way, even though they may be inscrutable. These dealings may take various forms, but all are planned in love, and with a view to cultivating a deeper intimacy with God.

J. Oswald Sanders

PAUSE FOR REFLECTION

Why does God punish his people? What did God's punishment accomplish in David's life (2 Samuel 24)? Do you think David realized how seriously he had sinned before God punished him? What causes you to recognize the seriousness of your sin?

WEDNESDAY:
Live in a Way that Pleases God
Hebrews 13:1–25

NEW TESTAMENT READING

*K*eep on loving each other as brothers and sisters. Remember to welcome strangers, because some who have done this have welcomed angels without knowing it. Remember those who are in prison as if you were in prison with them. Remember those who are suffering as if you were suffering with them.

Marriage should be honored by everyone, and husband and wife should keep their marriage pure. God will judge as guilty those who take part in sexual sins. Keep your lives free from the love of money, and be satisfied with what you have. God has said,

"I will never leave you;
I will never forget you." *Deuteronomy 31:6*
So we can be sure when we say,
"I will not be afraid, because the Lord is my helper.
People can't do anything to me."
Psalm 118:6
Remember your leaders who taught God's message to you. Remember how they lived and died, and copy their faith. Jesus Christ is the same yesterday, today, and forever.

Do not let all kinds of strange teachings lead you into the wrong way. Your hearts should be strengthened by God's grace, not by obeying rules about foods, which do not help those who obey them.

We have a sacrifice, but the priests who serve in the Holy Tent cannot eat from it. The high priest carries the blood of animals into the Most Holy Place where he offers this blood for sins. But the bodies of the animals are burned outside the camp. So Jesus also suffered outside the city to make his people holy with his own blood. So let us go to Jesus outside the camp, holding on as he did when we are abused. Here on earth we do not have a city that lasts forever, but we are looking for the city that we will have in the future. So through Jesus let us always offer to God our sacrifice of praise, coming from lips that speak his name. Do not forget to do good to others, and share with them, because such sacrifices please God.

Obey your leaders and act under their authority. They are watching over you, because they are responsible for your souls. Obey them so that they will do this work with joy, not sadness. It will not help you to make their work hard.

Pray for us. We are sure that we have a clear conscience, because we always want to do the right thing. I especially beg you to pray so that God will send me back to you soon.

I pray that the God of peace will give you every good thing you need so you can do what he wants. God raised from the dead our Lord Jesus, the Great Shepherd of the sheep, because of the blood of his death. His blood began the eternal agreement that God made with his people. I pray that God will do in us what pleases him, through Jesus Christ, and to him be glory forever and ever. Amen.

My brothers and sisters, I beg you to listen patiently to this message I have written to encourage you, because it is not very long. I want you to know that our brother Timothy has been let out of prison. If he arrives soon, we will both come to see you.

Greet all your leaders and all of God's people. Those from Italy send greetings to you.

Grace be with you all.

OLD TESTAMENT READING

Moses Tells the Israelites How God Wants Them to Live

*N*ow, Israel, this is what the LORD your God wants you to do: Respect the LORD your God, and do what he has told you to do. Love him. Serve the LORD your God with your whole being, and obey the LORD's commands and laws that I am giving you today for your own good.

The LORD owns the world and everything in it—the heavens, even the highest heavens, are his. But the LORD cared for and loved your ancestors, and he chose you, their descendants, over all the other nations, just as it is today. Give yourselves completely to serving him, and do not be stubborn any longer. The LORD your God is God of all gods and Lord of all lords. He is the great God, who is strong and wonderful. He does not take sides, and he will not be talked into doing evil. He helps orphans and widows, and he loves foreigners and gives them food and clothes. You also must love foreigners, because you were foreigners in Egypt. Respect the LORD your God and serve him. Be loyal to him and make your promises in his name. He is the one you should praise; he is your God, who has done great and wonderful things for you, which you have seen with your own eyes.

Deuteronomy 10:12–21

An Exemplary Life

*I*f I have been dishonest
or lied to others,
then let God weigh me on honest
scales.
Then he will know I have done
nothing wrong.

"If I have desired another woman
or have waited at my neighbor's
door for his wife,
then let my wife grind another man's
grain,
and let other men have sexual
relations with her.
That would be shameful,
a sin to be punished.

"I have never refused the appeals of the
poor
or let widows give up hope while
looking for help.
Since I was young, I have been like a
father to the orphans.
From my birth I guided the widows.
I have not let anyone die for lack of
clothes
or let a needy person go without a
coat.

"I have not put my trust in gold
or said to pure gold, 'You are my
security.'

"No stranger ever had to spend the
night in the street,
because I always let travelers stay in
my home."
Job 31:5–6, 9–11, 16, 18–19, 24, 32

INSIGHTS

In recent decades the phrase "easy believism" has surfaced. Unfortunately, it describes a large number of contemporary Christians who have received Christ as Savior but do not, in practice, regard Him as Lord. They seem to have received Him in order to reach heaven someday or to get help for their problems, but they have never fully committed to trust, obey, honor and serve Him as a way of life.

Our Lord never intended that we be His casual acquaintances. He wants us to be His disciples, fully dedicated to following Him and lifting up His holy name to the world. . . . Our Lord is repulsed by mediocre commitment. . . .

. . . When we acknowledge Christ as our Lord, we affirm that He is our Master for life and that we are dedicated to serving and glorifying Him. In all things, large and small, our deepest desire is to do what our Lord would want us to do. We ask for His guidance—not for our gain, but for His glory. We discipline ourselves in studying and obeying His written Word. We proclaim His love to the world around us. We try to think, speak and act in a way that will attract others to Him.

The misguided person who thinks all this is too difficult or irrelevant misses the point. The Christian life is far more than a fire escape from hell; it is the life of submission and obedience which result in joy and victory.

Bill Bright

ACTION POINT

Describe the kind of life God has called his people to live (in both Old and New Testaments). Pray that living such a life will be of utmost importance to you. Make that commitment today!

THURSDAY:

God Gives Wisdom to Those Who Ask for It

James 1:1–27

NEW TESTAMENT READING

*F*rom James, a servant of God and of the Lord Jesus Christ.

To all of God's people who are scattered everywhere in the world:

Greetings.

Faith and Wisdom

*M*y brothers and sisters, when you have many kinds of troubles, you should be full of joy, because you know that these troubles test your faith, and this will give you patience. Let your patience show itself perfectly in what you do. Then you will be perfect and complete and will have everything you need. But if any of you needs wisdom, you should ask God for it. He is generous and enjoys giving to all people, so he will give you wisdom. But when you ask God, you must believe and not doubt. Anyone who doubts is like a wave in the sea, blown up and down by the wind. Such doubters are thinking two different things at the same time, and they cannot decide about anything they do. They should not think they will receive anything from the Lord.

True Riches

*B*elievers who are poor should be proud, because God has made them spiritually rich. Those who are rich should be proud, because God has shown them that they are spiritually poor. The rich will die like a wild flower in the grass. The sun rises with burning heat and dries up the plants. The flower falls off, and its beauty is gone. In the same way the rich will die while they are still taking care of business.

Temptation Is Not from God

*W*hen people are tempted and still continue strong, they should be happy. After they have proved their faith, God will reward them with life forever. God promised this to all those who love him. When people are tempted, they should not say, "God is tempting me." Evil cannot tempt God, and God himself does not tempt anyone. But people are tempted when their own evil desire leads them away and traps them. This desire leads to sin, and then the sin grows and brings death.

My dear brothers and sisters, do not be fooled about this. Every good action and every perfect gift is from God. These good gifts come down from the Creator of the sun, moon, and stars, who does not change like their shifting shadows. God decided to give us life through the word of truth so we might be the most important of all the things he made.

Listening and Obeying

*M*y dear brothers and sisters, always be willing to listen and slow to speak. Do not become angry easily, because anger will not help you live the right kind of life God wants. So put out of your life every evil thing and every kind of wrong. Then in gentleness accept God's teaching that is planted in your hearts, which can save you.

Do what God's teaching says; when you only listen and do nothing, you are fooling yourselves. Those who hear God's teaching and do nothing are like people who look at themselves in a mirror. They see their faces and then go away and quickly forget what they looked like. But the truly happy people are those who carefully study God's perfect law that makes people free, and they continue to study it. They do not forget what they heard, but they obey what God's teaching says. Those who do this will be made happy.

The True Way to Worship God

*P*eople who think they are religious but say things they should not say are just fooling themselves. Their "religion" is worth nothing. Religion that God accepts as pure and without fault is this: caring for orphans or widows who need help, and keeping yourself free from the world's evil influence.

OLD TESTAMENT READING

*K*ing Solomon went to Gibeon to offer a sacrifice, because it was the most important place of worship. He offered a thousand burnt offerings on that altar. While he was at Gibeon, the LORD appeared to him in a dream during the night. God said, "Ask for whatever you want me to give you."

Solomon answered, "You were very kind to your servant, my father David. He obeyed you, and he was honest and lived right. You showed great kindness to him when you allowed his son to be king after him. LORD my God, now you have made me, your servant, king in my father's place. But I am like a little child; I don't know how to do what must be done. I, your servant, am here among your chosen people, and there are too many of them to count. I ask that you give me an obedient heart so I can rule the people in the right way and will know the difference between right and wrong. Otherwise, it is impossible to rule this great people of yours."

The Lord was pleased that Solomon had asked this. So God said to him, "You did not ask for a long life, or riches for yourself, or the death of your enemies. Since you asked for wisdom to make the right decisions, I will do what you asked. I will give you wisdom and understanding that is greater than anyone has had in the past or will have in the future. I will also give you what you did not ask for: riches and honor. During your life no other king will be as great as you. If you follow me and obey my laws and commands, as your father David did, I will also give you a long life."

1 Kings 3:4–14

*D*aniel asked his friends to pray that the God of heaven would show them mercy and help them understand this secret so he and his friends would not be killed with the other wise men of Babylon.

During the night God explained the secret to Daniel in a vision. Then Daniel praised the God of heaven. Daniel said:
"Praise God forever and ever,
    because he has wisdom and power.
He makes known secrets that are deep
    and hidden;
he knows what is hidden in darkness,
    and light is all around him.
I thank you and praise you, God of my
    ancestors,

because you have given me wisdom
    and power.
You told me what we asked of you;
    you told us about the king's dream."

Daniel 2:18–20, 22–23

---

*I*t has been said that the wisest man in the world is the man who knows he doesn't know.

In the midst of trials how often we say, "If only I knew what to do"; or we may say, "I don't know which way to turn or what to do."

God has promised to give us His wisdom. "If any of you is deficient in wisdom, let him ask of the giving God [Who gives] to every one liberally and ungrudgingly, without reproaching or faultfinding, and it will be given him" (Amplified). . . .

Not only are we to ask God for wisdom but we are to ask in faith. "Only it must be in faith that he asks, with no wavering—no hesitating, no doubting" (vs. 6, Amplified). No wavering—no hesitating—no doubting. Someone has said, "Doubt is a nonconductor of grace."

We are not to be double-minded, wanting partly our way and partly God's way. We are not to vacillate back and forth uncertain of our decision. "[For being as he is] a man of two minds—hesitating, dubious, irresolute—[he is] unstable and unreliable and uncertain about everything (he thinks, feels, decides)" (vs. 8, Amplified).

As we ask of God and ask in faith, God has promised to give liberally. We are to ask for wisdom to face serenely the trials of today, unwaveringly trusting in Him. We are to ask for wisdom to meet each trial of life and to face it triumphantly.

Millie Stamm

PAUSE FOR REFLECTION

*F*or what reasons did Solomon and Daniel ask for God's wisdom? Did God's answer meet or exceed their expectations? For what in your life do you need God's wisdom? Have you asked him for it?

F R I D A Y:

Love Your Neighbor as Yourself

James 2:2–26

Love All People

My dear brothers and sisters, as believers in our glorious Lord Jesus Christ, never think some people are more important than others. Suppose someone comes into your church meeting wearing nice clothes and a gold ring. At the same time a poor person comes in wearing old, dirty clothes. You show special attention to the one wearing nice clothes and say, "Please, sit here in this good seat." But you say to the poor person, "Stand over there," or, "Sit on the floor by my feet." What are you doing? You are making some people more important than others, and with evil thoughts you are deciding that one person is better.

Listen, my dear brothers and sisters! God chose the poor in the world to be rich with faith and to receive the kingdom God promised to those who love him. But you show no respect to the poor. The rich are always trying to control your lives. They are the ones who take you to court. And they are the ones who speak against Jesus, who owns you.

This royal law is found in the Scriptures: "Love your neighbor as you love yourself." If you obey this law, you are doing right. But if you treat one person as being more important than another, you are sinning. You are guilty of breaking God's law. A person who follows all of God's law but fails to obey even one command is guilty of breaking all the commands in that law. The same God who said, "You must not be guilty of adultery," also said, "You must not murder anyone." So if you do not take part in adultery but you murder someone, you are guilty of breaking all of God's law. In everything you say and do, remember that you will be judged by the law that makes people free. So you must show mercy to others, or God will not show mercy to you when he judges you. But the person who shows mercy can stand without fear at the judgment.

Faith and Good Works

My brothers and sisters, if people say they have faith, but do nothing, their faith is worth nothing. Can faith like that save them? A brother or sister in Christ might need clothes or food. If you say to that person, "God be with you! I hope you stay warm and get plenty to eat," but you do not give what that person needs, your words are worth nothing. In the same way, faith that is alone—that does nothing—is dead.

Someone might say, "You have faith, but I have deeds." Show me your faith without doing anything, and I will show you my faith by what I do. You believe there is one God. Good! But the demons believe that, too, and they tremble with fear.

You foolish person! Must you be shown that faith that does nothing is worth nothing? Abraham, our ancestor, was made right with God by what he did when he offered his son Isaac on the altar. So you see that Abraham's faith and the things he did worked together. His faith was made perfect by what he did. This shows the full meaning of the Scripture that says: "Abraham believed God, and God accepted Abraham's faith, and that faith made him right with God." And Abraham was called God's friend. So you see that people are made right with God by what they do, not by faith only.

Another example is Rahab, a prostitute, who was made right with God by something she did. She welcomed the spies into her home and helped them escape by a different road.

Just as a person's body that does not have a spirit is dead, so faith that does nothing is dead!

The LORD says, "On that day
I will surely destroy the wise people from Edom,
and those with understanding from the mountains of Edom.

You did violence to your relatives, the
Israelites,
    so you will be covered with shame
      and destroyed forever.
You stood aside without helping
    while strangers carried Israel's
      treasures away.
When foreigners entered Israel's city
    gate
    and threw lots to decide what part of
      Jerusalem they would take,
    you were like one of them.

"Edom, do not laugh at your brother
    Israel in his time of trouble
or be happy about the people of Judah
    when they are destroyed.
    Do not brag when cruel things are
      done to them.
Do not enter the city gate of my people
    in their time of trouble,
or laugh at their problems
    in their time of trouble.
Do not take their treasures
    in their time of trouble.
Do not stand at the crossroads
    to destroy those who are trying to
      escape.
Do not capture those who escape alive
    and turn them over to their enemy
    in their time of trouble.

"The LORD's day of judging is coming
    soon
    to all the nations.
The same evil things you did to other
    people
    will happen to you;
    they will come back upon your own
      head."

Obadiah 8, 10–15

*B*e fair in your judging. You must not show
special favor to poor people or great people,
but be fair when you judge your neighbor.
You must not spread false stories against
other people, and you must not do anything
that would put your neighbor's life in danger. I am the LORD.' "

Leviticus 19:15–16

*D*oing what is right and fair
    is more important to the LORD than
      sacrifices.

Proverbs 21:3

*M*y life has been deeply touched by the mercy
of those who took the time to try and understand me—who cared enough to forgive so
many of my faults and who in mercy made
me their friend.

Often these were people to whom I had
shown no special kindness. Their bestowal of
mercy on me was something totally unexpected and undeserved. Because of this, it has
been a double delight. More than that, it has
been an enormous inspiration that lifted and
challenged me to respond in a measure beyond my wildest dreams. . . .

. . . To really find the true source of inner inspiration for this sort of conduct, the
Christian simply must look beyond his fellow
man. He must look away to the mercy of God
our Father. Nothing else in all the world will
so humble us. Nothing else will so move our
stony spirits to extend mercy. Nothing else will
so powerfully induce us to do the proper thing
in extending genuine mercy to our contemporaries. . . .

Christ calls us to be merciful. He calls us
to be forgiving and compassionate. This does
not mean we wink at wrong and sweep sin
under the carpet. Rather it demands that we
care enough to bring others to the God of all
mercy. And it is He who will cleanse, re-cre-
ate, and renew them in His loving-kindness
and tender mercy. Bless His dear name!

W. Phillip Keller

ACTION POINT

*I*n what situations does James plead for believers to show mercy? What lack of mercy
does God condemn in Obadiah 8–15? In
what ways does your normal human behavior lack God's mercy? How will you seek to
demonstrate his mercy?

WEEKEND:
Train Your Tongue for God's Service
James 3:1—4:10

NEW TESTAMENT READING

Controlling the Things We Say

*M*y brothers and sisters, not many of you should become teachers, because you know that we who teach will be judged more strictly. We all make many mistakes. If people never said anything wrong, they would be perfect and able to control their entire selves, too. When we put bits into the mouths of horses to make them obey us, we can control their whole bodies. Also a ship is very big, and it is pushed by strong winds. But a very small rudder controls that big ship, making it go wherever the pilot wants. It is the same with the tongue. It is a small part of the body, but it brags about great things.

A big forest fire can be started with only a little flame. And the tongue is like a fire. It is a whole world of evil among the parts of our bodies. The tongue spreads its evil through the whole body. The tongue is set on fire by hell, and it starts a fire that influences all of life. People can tame every kind of wild animal, bird, reptile, and fish, and they have tamed them, but no one can tame the tongue. It is wild and evil and full of deadly poison. We use our tongues to praise our Lord and Father, but then we curse people, whom God made like himself. Praises and curses come from the same mouth! My brothers and sisters, this should not happen. Do good and bad water flow from the same spring? My brothers and sisters, can a fig tree make olives, or can a grapevine make figs? No! And a well full of salty water cannot give good water.

True Wisdom

*A*re there those among you who are truly wise and understanding? Then they should show it by living right and doing good things with a gentleness that comes from wisdom. But if you are selfish and have bitter jealousy in your hearts, do not brag. Your bragging is a lie that hides the truth. That kind of "wisdom" does not come from God but from the world. It is not spiritual; it is from the devil. Where jealousy and selfishness are, there will be confusion and every kind of evil. But the wisdom that comes from God is first of all pure, then peaceful, gentle, and easy to please. This wisdom is always ready to help those who are troubled and to do good for others. It is always fair and honest. People who work for peace in a peaceful way plant a good crop of right-living.

Give Yourselves to God

*D*o you know where your fights and arguments come from? They come from the selfish desires that war within you. You want things, but you do not have them. So you are ready to kill and are jealous of other people, but you still cannot get what you want. So you argue and fight. You do not get what you want, because you do not ask God. Or when you ask, you do not receive because the reason you ask is wrong. You want things so you can use them for your own pleasures.

So, you are not loyal to God! You should know that loving the world is the same as hating God. Anyone who wants to be a friend of the world becomes God's enemy. Do you think the Scripture means nothing that says, "The Spirit that God made to live in us wants us for himself alone." But God gives us even more grace, as the Scripture says,

"God is against the proud,
but he gives grace to the humble."

Proverbs 3:34

So give yourselves completely to God. Stand against the devil, and the devil will run from you. Come near to God, and God will come near to you. You sinners, clean sin out of your lives. You who are trying to follow God and the world at the same time, make your thinking pure. Be sad, cry, and weep! Change your laughter into crying and your joy into sadness. Don't be too proud in the Lord's presence, and he will make you great.

*L*ORD, I call to you. Come quickly.
 Listen to me when I call to you.
Let my prayer be like incense placed
  before you,
 and my praise like the evening
  sacrifice.

LORD, help me control my tongue;
 help me be careful about what I
  say.
Take away my desire to do evil
 or to join others in doing wrong.
Don't let me eat tasty food
 with those who do evil.

Psalm 141:1–4

*T*he words of a good person give life,
 like a fountain of water,
but the words of the wicked contain
 nothing but violence.

A good person says wise things,
 but a liar's tongue will be stopped.
Good people know the right thing to say,
 but evil people only tell lies.

Proverbs 10:11, 31–32

*C*areless words stab like a sword,
 but wise words bring healing.
Truth will continue forever,
 but lies are only for a moment.

Proverbs 12:18–19

*T*hose who are careful about what
  they say protect their lives,
 but whoever speaks without thinking will be ruined.

Proverbs 13:3

*T*he words of the wise bring them
  praise,
 but the words of a fool will destroy
  them.
A fool begins by saying foolish things
 and ends by saying crazy and wicked
  things.
A fool talks too much.
 No one knows the future,
 and no one can tell what will happen
  after death.

Ecclesiastes 10:12–14

*P*eople will be rewarded for what they
  say;
 they will be rewarded by how they
  speak.
What you say can mean life or death.
 Those who speak with care will be
  rewarded.

Proverbs 18:20–21

INSIGHTS

*N*o man can tame the tongue, but the Word
of God encourages us to recognize that the
Holy Spirit can transform and tie the
tongue. . . .
 . . . The tongue is the temperature gauge
on the heart's engine. If the engine overheats,
then the temperature gauge warns us of engine trouble. If the tongue gets out of control,
it is a sure sign that we need to check our
heart. . . . We need to constantly fill the
heart with good things from God's Word in
order to tie our tongues.
 One must also concede to the Spirit's control to tie the tongue successfully. It always
interested me that when James describes the
tongue as a horse's bit that controls the horse
or a ship's rudder that directs the ship, he,
perhaps purposefully, fails to mention that a
horse's bit must, in reality, be controlled by
the rider and the ship's rudder must be controlled by the helmsman. I daily remind myself
that the Lord, through the Holy Spirit, must
be the rider or the helmsman controlling my
tongue. Who is your helmsman?
 If you have difficulty yielding control to the
Lord, ask Him for the desire to give Him
control. . . . When you have the willingness
to concede control of your tongue, you'll soon
discover you also have the strength to do it as
well.

Vicki Lake

PAUSE FOR REFLECTION

*W*hat does your tongue reveal about your
heart? Think about your experiences with the
good and evil things people have said, and
write your own proverb about the tongue.

M O N D A Y:

God Answers the Prayers of His People

James 4:11—5:20

NEW TESTAMENT READING

You Are Not the Judge

*B*rothers and sisters, do not tell evil lies about each other. If you speak against your fellow believers or judge them, you are judging and speaking against the law they follow. And when you are judging the law, you are no longer a follower of the law. You have become a judge. God is the only Law-maker and Judge. He is the only One who can save and destroy. So it is not right for you to judge your neighbor.

Let God Plan Your Life

*S*ome of you say, "Today or tomorrow we will go to some city. We will stay there a year, do business, and make money." But you do not know what will happen tomorrow! Your life is like a mist. You can see it for a short time, but then it goes away. So you should say, "If the Lord wants, we will live and do this or that." But now you are proud and you brag. All of this bragging is wrong. Anyone who knows the right thing to do, but does not do it, is sinning.

A Warning to the Rich

*Y*ou rich people, listen! Cry and be very sad because of the troubles that are coming to you. Your riches have rotted, and your clothes have been eaten by moths. Your gold and silver have rusted, and that rust will be a proof that you were wrong. It will eat your bodies like fire. You saved your treasure for the last days. The pay you did not give the workers who mowed your fields cries out against you, and the cries of the workers have been heard by the Lord All-Powerful. Your life on earth was full of rich living and pleasing yourselves with every-thing you wanted. You made yourselves fat, like an animal ready to be killed. You have judged guilty and then murdered innocent people, who were not against you.

Be Patient

*B*rothers and sisters, be patient until the Lord comes again. A farmer patiently waits for his valuable crop to grow from the earth and for it to receive the autumn and spring rains. You, too, must be patient. Do not give up hope, because the Lord is com-ing soon. Brothers and sisters, do not complain against each other or you will be judged guilty. And the Judge is ready to come! Brothers and sisters, follow the ex-ample of the prophets who spoke for the Lord. They suffered many hard things, but they were patient. We say they are happy because they did not give up. You have heard about Job's patience, and you know the Lord's purpose for him in the end. You know the Lord is full of mercy and is kind.

Be Careful What You Say

*M*y brothers and sisters, above all, do not use an oath when you make a promise. Don't use the name of heaven, earth, or anything else to prove what you say. When you mean yes, say only yes, and when you mean no, say only no so you will not be judged guilty.

The Power of Prayer

*A*nyone who is having troubles should pray. Anyone who is happy should sing praises. Anyone who is sick should call the church's elders. They should pray for and pour oil on the person in the name of the Lord. And the prayer that is said with faith will make the sick person well; the Lord will heal that person. And if the person has sinned, the sins will be forgiven. Confess your sins to each other and pray for each other so God can heal you. When a believ-ing person prays, great things happen. Elijah was a human being just like us. He prayed that it would not rain, and it did not rain on the land for three and a half years! Then Elijah prayed again, and the rain came down from the sky, and the land produced crops again.

Saving a Soul

*M*y brothers and sisters, if one of you wanders away from the truth, and someone helps that person come back, remember this: Anyone who brings a sinner back from the wrong way will save that sinner's soul from death and will cause many sins to be forgiven.

Hezekiah Begs God for His Life

*A*t that time Hezekiah became so sick he almost died. The prophet Isaiah son of Amoz went to see him and told him, "This is what the LORD says: Make arrangements because you are not going to live, but die."

Hezekiah turned toward the wall and prayed to the LORD, "LORD, please remember that I have always obeyed you. I have given myself completely to you and have done what you said was right." Then Hezekiah cried loudly.

Before Isaiah had left the middle courtyard, the LORD spoke his word to Isaiah: "Go back and tell Hezekiah, the leader of my people: 'This is what the LORD, the God of your ancestor David, says: I have heard your prayer and seen your tears, so I will heal you. Three days from now you will go up to the Temple of the LORD. I will add fifteen years to your life. I will save you and this city from the king of Assyria; I will protect the city for my sake and for the sake of my servant David.'"

2 Kings 20:1–6

Esther Asks the Jews to Fast on Her Behalf

*A*nd Mordecai told him to order Esther to go into the king's presence to beg for mercy and to plead with him for her people.

Hathach went back and reported to Esther everything Mordecai had said. Then Esther told Hathach to tell Mordecai, "All the royal officers and people of the royal states know that no man or woman may go to the king in the inner courtyard without being called. There is only one law about this: Anyone who enters must be put to death unless the king holds out his gold scepter. Then that person may live. And I have not been called to go to the king for thirty days."

Esther's message was given to Mordecai. Then Mordecai told them to say to Esther: "Just because you live in the king's palace, don't think that out of all the Jewish people you alone will escape. If you keep quiet at this time, someone else will help and save the Jewish people, but you and your father's family will all die. And who knows, you may have been chosen queen for just such a time as this."

Then Esther sent this answer to Mordecai: "Go and get all the Jewish people in Susa together. For my sake, give up eating; do not eat or drink for three days, night and day. I and my servant girls will also give up eating. Then I will go to the king, even though it is against the law, and if I die, I die."

Esther 4:8c–16

*G*od honors prayer. . . . He longs to demonstrate His power in the tremendous trials that jar us like thunder, and in the pinprick troubles that annoy us. Giant needs are never too great for His power; dwarf-sized ones are never too small for His love. . . .

God can answer prayer because He is the supreme ruler of all. . . . He governs both world events and our individual lives, ready at our request to act, to intervene, to overrule for our good, His glory, and the progress of the gospel. He has decreed that prayer is the way to secure His aid and move His mighty hand. Therefore even in sickness, failure, rejection, or financial distress, we can pray and experience His peace which transcends human understanding. Through prayer we can open a window to let God's love shine into our lives; we can open our hands to receive His riches; we can open our hearts to let His presence fill and empower us. Through it we can also allow Him to provide answers to prayer that are important to Him and to us.

Warren and Ruth Meyers

*W*hat great powers does James attribute to prayer? Do you believe God answers prayer—enough to risk your life on the power of prayer as Esther did?

TUESDAY:
God Will Purify Our Faith
1 Peter 1:1–21

*F*rom Peter, an apostle of Jesus Christ.

To God's chosen people who are away from their homes and are scattered all around the countries of Pontus, Galatia, Cappadocia, Asia, and Bithynia. God planned long ago to choose you by making you his holy people, which is the Spirit's work. God wanted you to obey him and to be made clean by the blood of the death of Jesus Christ.

Grace and peace be yours more and more.

We Have a Living Hope

*P*raise be to the God and Father of our Lord Jesus Christ. In God's great mercy he has caused us to be born again into a living hope, because Jesus Christ rose from the dead. Now we hope for the blessings God has for his children. These blessings, which cannot be destroyed or be spoiled or lose their beauty, are kept in heaven for you. God's power protects you through your faith until salvation is shown to you at the end of time. This makes you very happy, even though now for a short time different kinds of troubles may make you sad. These troubles come to prove that your faith is pure. This purity of faith is worth more than gold, which can be proved to be pure by fire but will ruin. But the purity of your faith will bring you praise and glory and honor when Jesus Christ is shown to you. You have not seen Christ, but still you love him. You cannot see him now, but you believe in him. So you are filled with a joy that cannot be explained, a joy full of glory. And you are receiving the goal of your faith—the salvation of your souls.

The prophets searched carefully and tried to learn about this salvation. They prophesied about the grace that was coming to you. The Spirit of Christ was in the prophets, telling in advance about the sufferings of Christ and about the glory that would follow those sufferings. The prophets tried to learn about what the Spirit was showing them, when those things would happen, and what the world would be like at that time. It was shown them that their service was not for themselves but for you, when they told about the truths you have now heard. Those who preached the Good News to you told you those things with the help of the Holy Spirit who was sent from heaven—things into which angels desire to look.

A Call to Holy Living

*S*o prepare your minds for service and have self-control. All your hope should be for the gift of grace that will be yours when Jesus Christ is shown to you. Now that you are obedient children of God do not live as you did in the past. You did not understand, so you did the evil things you wanted. But be holy in all you do, just as God, the One who called you, is holy. It is written in the Scriptures: "You must be holy, because I am holy."

You pray to God and call him Father, and he judges each person's work equally. So while you are here on earth, you should live with respect for God. You know that in the past you were living in a worthless way, a way passed down from the people who lived before you. But you were saved from that useless life. You were bought, not with something that ruins like gold or silver, but with the precious blood of Christ, who was like a pure and perfect lamb. Christ was chosen before the world was made, but he was shown to the world in these last times for your sake. Through Christ you believe in God, who raised Christ from the dead and gave him glory. So your faith and your hope are in God.

*T*he LORD says, "Family of Jacob, listen
    to me.
  You are called Israel,
    and you come from the family of
      Judah.
  You swear by the LORD's name
    and praise the God of Israel,

but you are not honest or sincere.
You call yourselves people of the holy
  city,
  and you depend on the God of Israel,
  who is named the LORD All-Powerful.

"But you have not heard me; you have
  not understood.
  Even long ago you did not listen to
  me.
I knew you would surely turn against
  me;
  you have fought against me since
  you were born.
I have made you pure, but not by fire,
  as silver is made pure.
  I have purified you by giving you
  troubles."

Isaiah 48:1–2, 8, 10

*B*ut God knows the way that I take,
  and when he has tested me, I will
    come out like gold.
My feet have closely followed his steps;
  I have stayed in his way;
  I did not turn aside.
I have never left the commands he has
    spoken;
  I have treasured his words more
    than my own.

Job 23:10–12

*R*emember how the LORD your God has
led you in the desert for these forty years,
taking away your pride and testing you, because he wanted to know what was in your
heart. He wanted to know if you would obey
his commands. He took away your pride
when he let you get hungry, and then he
fed you with manna, which neither you nor
your ancestors had ever seen. This was to
teach you that a person does not live only
by eating bread, but by everything the LORD
says. Know in your heart that the LORD your
God corrects you as a parent corrects a
child.

Deuteronomy 8:2–3, 5

*T*he third that is left I will test with fire,
  purifying them like silver,
  testing them like gold.
Then they will call on me,
  and I will answer them.

I will say, 'You are my people,'
  and they will say, 'The LORD is our
  God.'"

Zechariah 13:9

---

*W*hat is trouble but that very influence that
brings you nearer to the heart of God than
prayers or hymns? I think sorrows usually
bring us closer to God than joys do. But sorrows, to be of use, must be borne, as Christ's
were, victoriously, carrying with them inti-
mations and sacred prophecies to the heart
of hope. This is not only so we will not be
overcome by them, but also so we will be
strengthened and ennobled and enlarged by
them. . . .

  . . . By fire, by anvil-strokes, by the hammer that breaks the flinty rock, you are made
what you are. You were gold in the rock, and
God played miner, and blasted you out of the
rock. Then He played stamper, and crushed
you. Then He played smelter, and melted you.

  Now you are gold, free from the rock by
the grace of God's severity to you. As you look
back upon those experiences of 5, 10, or 20
years ago and see what they have done for
you, and what you are now, you say, "I would
not exchange what I learned from these things
for all the world.". . .

  When God comes to you wrapped and
wreathed in clouds, and in storms, why should
we not recognize Him, and say, "I know you,
God; and I will not flee you; though you slay
me, I will trust thee"? If a man could see God
in his troubles and take sorrow to be the . . .
sweet discipline of a bitter medicine that
brings health, though the taste is not agree-
able—if one could so look upon his God, how
sorrows would make him strong!

Henry Beecher

APPLICATION

*W*hat is the value of a pure faith? What are
its rewards? How does our faith become pure?
How is God purifying your faith today? Welcome his testing!

WEDNESDAY:

The Lives of God's People Bring Glory to Him

1 Peter 1:22—2:17

NEW TESTAMENT READING

*N*ow that you have made your souls pure by obeying the truth, you can have true love for your Christian brothers and sisters. So love each other deeply with all your heart. You have been born again, and this new life did not come from something that dies, but from something that cannot die. You were born again through God's living message that continues forever. The Scripture says,

"All people are like the grass,
and all their glory is like the flowers of the field.
The grass dies and the flowers fall,
but the word of the Lord will live forever." *Isaiah 40:6–8*

And this is the word that was preached to you.

Jesus Is the Living Stone

*S*o then, rid yourselves of all evil, all lying, hypocrisy, jealousy, and evil speech. As newborn babies want milk, you should want the pure and simple teaching. By it you can grow up and be saved, because you have already examined and seen how good the Lord is.

Come to the Lord Jesus, the "stone" that lives. The people of the world did not want this stone, but he was the stone God chose, and he was precious. You also are like living stones, so let yourselves be used to build a spiritual temple—to be holy priests who offer spiritual sacrifices to God. He will accept those sacrifices through Jesus Christ. The Scripture says:

"I will put a stone in the ground in Jerusalem.
Everything will be built on this important and precious rock.
Anyone who trusts in him will never be disappointed." *Isaiah 28:16*

This stone is worth much to you who believe.

But to the people who do not believe,
"the stone that the builders rejected has become the cornerstone." *Psalm 118:22*

Also, he is
"a stone that causes people to stumble, a rock that makes them fall." *Isaiah 8:14*

They stumble because they do not obey what God says, which is what God planned to happen to them.

But you are a chosen people, royal priests, a holy nation, a people for God's own possession. You were chosen to tell about the wonderful acts of God, who called you out of darkness into his wonderful light. At one time you were not a people, but now you are God's people. In the past you had never received mercy, but now you have received God's mercy.

Live for God

*D*ear friends, you are like foreigners and strangers in this world. I beg you to avoid the evil things your bodies want to do that fight against your soul. People who do not believe are living all around you and might say that you are doing wrong. Live such good lives that they will see the good things you do and will give glory to God on the day when Christ comes again.

Yield to Every Human Authority

*F*or the Lord's sake, yield to the people who have authority in this world: the king, who is the highest authority, and the leaders who are sent by him to punish those who do wrong and to praise those who do right. It is God's desire that by doing good you should stop foolish people from saying stupid things about you. Live as free people, but do not use your freedom as an excuse to do evil. Live as servants of God. Show respect for all people: Love the brothers and sisters of God's family, respect God, honor the king.

OLD TESTAMENT READING

*S*hadrach, Meshach, and Abednego answered the king, saying, "Nebuchadnezzar, we do not need to defend ourselves to you. If you throw us into the blazing furnace,

558

the God we serve is able to save us from the furnace. He will save us from your power, O king. But even if God does not save us, we want you, O king, to know this: We will not serve your gods or worship the gold statue you have set up."

Then Nebuchadnezzar was furious with Shadrach, Meshach, and Abednego, and he changed his mind. He ordered the furnace to be heated seven times hotter than usual. Then he commanded some of the strongest soldiers in his army to tie up Shadrach, Meshach, and Abednego and throw them into the blazing furnace.

Then Nebuchadnezzar went to the opening of the blazing furnace and shouted, "Shadrach, Meshach, and Abednego, come out! Servants of the Most High God, come here!"

So Shadrach, Meshach, and Abednego came out of the fire. When they came out, the governors, assistant governors, captains of the soldiers, and royal advisers crowded around them and saw that the fire had not harmed their bodies. Their hair was not burned, their robes were not burned, and they didn't even smell like smoke!

Then Nebuchadnezzar said, "Praise the God of Shadrach, Meshach, and Abednego. Their God has sent his angel and saved his servants from the fire! These three men trusted their God and refused to obey my command. They were willing to die rather than serve or worship any god other than their own. So I now give this command: Anyone from any nation or language who says anything against the God of Shadrach, Meshach, and Abednego will be torn apart and have his house turned into a pile of stones. No other god can save his people like this."

Daniel 3:16–20, 26–29

*T*his is why you are great, Lord GOD! There is no one like you. There is no God except you. We have heard all this ourselves! There is no nation like your people Israel. They are the only people on earth that God chose to be his own. You made your name well known. You did great and wonderful miracles for them. You went ahead of them and forced other nations and their gods out of the land. You freed your people from slavery in Egypt. You made the people of Israel your very own people forever, and, LORD, you are their God."

2 Samuel 7:22–24

INSIGHTS

*G*od considers himself honored by the high attainments of His children and dishonored by their low attainments. He is honored in the fact that their graces so shine forth that it shall be seen by all around that they have partaken largely of His Spirit.

Exalted piety is honorable to God. Manifestations of great grace and spirituality of mind honor God. He is greatly honored by the fruits of righteousness His people bring forth. Christ himself says, "Herein is my Father glorified that ye bring forth much fruit." Ministers should be greatly fruitful. They should bring forth the fruits of the Spirit in their tempers, in their lives, in the strength of their faith and labors of love. Can you doubt that God has great interest in these things? Indeed His great desire, that you should bring forth fruit to His glory, is shown in the fact that He says, "open thy mouth wide, and I will fill it."

Charles Finney

PAUSE FOR REFLECTION

*W*hat do you think it means to be made "pure by obeying the truth"? What purpose is served when believers live good lives? What have you learned from the lives of those who honor God in such a way? Are you willing to get rid of everything in your life that doesn't bring honor to the King?

THURSDAY:
Live in Peace!
1 Peter 2:18—3:12

NEW TESTAMENT READING

Follow Christ's Example

Slaves, yield to the authority of your masters with all respect, not only those who are good and kind, but also those who are dishonest. A person might have to suffer even when it is unfair, but if he thinks of God and stands the pain, God is pleased. If you are beaten for doing wrong, there is no reason to praise you for being patient in your punishment. But if you suffer for doing good, and you are patient, then God is pleased. This is what you were called to do, because Christ suffered for you and gave you an example to follow. So you should do as he did.

"He had never sinned,
and he had never lied." *Isaiah 53:9*

People insulted Christ, but he did not insult them in return. Christ suffered, but he did not threaten. He let God, the One who judges rightly, take care of him. Christ carried our sins in his body on the cross so we would stop living for sin and start living for what is right. And you are healed because of his wounds. You were like sheep that wandered away, but now you have come back to the Shepherd and Protector of your souls.

Wives and Husbands

In the same way, you wives should yield to your husbands. Then, if some husbands do not obey God's teaching, they will be persuaded to believe without anyone's saying a word to them. They will be persuaded by the way their wives live. Your husbands will see the pure lives you live with your respect for God. It is not fancy hair, gold jewelry, or fine clothes that should make you beautiful. No, your beauty should come from within you—the beauty of a gentle and quiet spirit that will never be destroyed and is very precious to God. In this same way the holy women who lived long ago and followed God made themselves beautiful, yielding to their own husbands. Sarah obeyed Abraham, her husband, and called him her master. And you women are true children of Sarah if you always do what is right and are not afraid.

In the same way, you husbands should live with your wives in an understanding way, since they are weaker than you. But show them respect, because God gives them the same blessing he gives you—the grace that gives true life. Do this so that nothing will stop your prayers.

Suffering for Doing Right

Finally, all of you should be in agreement, understanding each other, loving each other as family, being kind and humble. Do not do wrong to repay a wrong, and do not insult to repay an insult. But repay with a blessing, because you yourselves were called to do this so that you might receive a blessing. The Scripture says,

"A person must do these things
to enjoy life and have many happy
days.
He must not say evil things,
and he must not tell lies.
He must stop doing evil and do good.
He must look for peace and work for it.
The Lord sees the good people
and listens to their prayers.
But the Lord is against
those who do evil." *Psalm 34:12–16*

OLD TESTAMENT READING

Abimelech came from Gerar to see Isaac. He brought with him Ahuzzath, who advised him, and Phicol, the commander of his army. Isaac asked them, "Why have you come to see me? You were my enemy and forced me to leave your country."

They answered, "Now we know that the Lord is with you. Let us swear an oath to each other. Let us make an agreement with you that since we did not hurt you, you will not hurt us. We were good to you and sent you away in peace. Now the Lord has blessed you."

So Isaac prepared food for them, and they all ate and drank. Early the next morning the men swore an oath to each other.

Then Isaac sent them away, and they left in peace.

Genesis 26:26–31

When David came out of the cave, he shouted to Saul, "My master and king!" Saul looked back, and David bowed face-down on the ground. He said to Saul, "Why do you listen when people say, 'David wants to harm you'? You have seen something with your own eyes today. The LORD put you in my power in the cave. They said I should kill you, but I was merciful. I said, 'I won't harm my master, because he is the LORD's appointed king.' My father, look at this piece of your robe in my hand! I cut off the corner of your robe, but I didn't kill you. Now understand and know I am not planning any evil against you. I did nothing wrong to you, but you are hunting me to kill me. May the LORD judge between us, and may he punish you for the wrong you have done to me! But I am not against you."

1 Samuel 24:8–12

Judah and Israel, your names have been used as curses in other nations. But I will save you, and you will become a blessing. So don't be afraid; work hard.

"These are the things you should do: Tell each other the truth. In the courts judge with truth and complete fairness. Do not make plans to hurt your neighbors, and don't love false promises. I hate all these things," says the LORD.

The LORD All-Powerful spoke his word to me again. This is what the LORD All-Powerful says: "The special days when you give up eating in the fourth, fifth, seventh, and tenth months will become good, joyful, happy feasts in Judah. But you must love truth and peace."

Zechariah 8:13, 16–19

INSIGHTS

If the life is opened to receive the divine presence of the risen Christ, He comes in, speaking peace—just as He came again and again to His distraught disciples after His resurrection, saying, "Peace be unto you!"

He comes into our lives there to shed abroad a new love, His own life, that expresses itself in peace. When He enters my experience; when He penetrates my personality; when He becomes Sovereign in my spirit, I in turn become a person of peace. It is then that I begin to know what it means to be at peace with God, at peace with others, at peace with myself.

Increasingly as He is given control of my life the entire complexion of my character, conduct, and conversation alters. I discover that He can change me dramatically. Peace, good will, good cheer, and serenity replace animosity, bitterness, hostility, belligerence, jealousy, bad temper, quarreling, and rivalry. . . .

. . . The peace of God, which is self-sacrificing and self-foregoing, produces healing. It comes to bind up the wounds; to pour in the oil of consolation; to bring repose and quietness; to still the troubled soul; to speak peace to stormy spirits. This peace comes only from Christ. It is one of the genuine, indisputable marks of God's presence in a person's life.

W. Phillip Keller

ACTION POINT

Who set the standard for living in peace? What does living in peace look like? How full of Christ's peace is your life? Pray that God will give you a fuller love and more intimate understanding of his peace and that it will touch every area of your life.

FRIDAY:

Always Be Ready to Explain the Hope of Your Salvation

1 Peter 3:13—4:11

*I*f you are trying hard to do good, no one can really hurt you. But even if you suffer for doing right, you are blessed.

"Don't be afraid of what they fear;
do not dread those things."

Isaiah 8:12-13

But respect Christ as the holy Lord in your hearts. Always be ready to answer everyone who asks you to explain about the hope you have, but answer in a gentle way and with respect. Keep a clear conscience so that those who speak evil of your good life in Christ will be made ashamed. It is better to suffer for doing good than for doing wrong if that is what God wants. Christ himself suffered for sins once. He was not guilty, but he suffered for those who are guilty to bring you to God. His body was killed, but he was made alive in the spirit. And in the spirit he went and preached to the spirits in prison who refused to obey God long ago in the time of Noah. God was waiting patiently for them while Noah was building the boat. Only a few people—eight in all—were saved by water. And that water is like baptism that now saves you—not the washing of dirt from the body, but the promise made to God from a good conscience. And this is because Jesus Christ was raised from the dead. Now Jesus has gone into heaven and is at God's right side ruling over angels, authorities, and powers.

Change Your Lives

*S*ince Christ suffered while he was in his body, strengthen yourselves with the same way of thinking Christ had. The person who has suffered in the body is finished with sin. Strengthen yourselves so that you will live here on earth doing what God wants, not the evil things people want. In the past you wasted too much time doing what nonbelievers enjoy. You were guilty of sexual sins, evil desires, drunkenness, wild and drunken parties, and hateful idol worship. Nonbelievers think it is strange that you do not do the many wild and wasteful things they do, so they insult you. But they will have to explain this to God, who is ready to judge the living and the dead. For this reason the Good News was preached to those who are now dead. Even though they were judged like all people, the Good News was preached to them so they could live in the spirit as God lives.

Use God's Gifts Wisely

*T*he time is near when all things will end. So think clearly and control yourselves so you will be able to pray. Most importantly, love each other deeply, because love will cause many sins to be forgiven. Open your homes to each other, without complaining. Each of you has received a gift to use to serve others. Be good servants of God's various gifts of grace.

Anyone who speaks should speak words from God. Anyone who serves should serve with the strength God gives so that in everything God will be praised through Jesus Christ. Power and glory belong to him forever and ever. Amen.

*H*ow great is your goodness
that you have stored up for those
who fear you,
that you have given to those who trust
you.
You do this for all to see.
You protect them by your presence
from what people plan against them.
You shelter them from evil words.

Love the LORD, all you who belong to
him.
The LORD protects those who truly
believe,
but he punishes the proud as much
as they have sinned.
All you who put your hope in the LORD
be strong and brave.

Psalm 31:19-20, 23-24

I find rest in God;
only he gives me hope.
He is my rock and my salvation.
He is my defender;
I will not be defeated.
My honor and salvation come from God.
He is my mighty rock and my
protection.

People, trust God all the time.
Tell him all your problems,
because God is our protection.   *Selah*
Psalm 62:5–8

L ORD, you are my hope.
LORD, I have trusted you since I was
young.

God, don't be far off.
My God, hurry to help me.
Let those who accuse me
be ashamed and destroyed.
Let those who are trying to hurt me
be covered with shame and disgrace.
But I will always have hope
and will praise you more and more.
I will tell how you do what is right.
I will tell about your salvation all day
long,
even though it is more than I can tell.
I will come and tell about your powerful
works, Lord GOD.
I will remind people that only you do
what is right.
Psalm 71:5, 12–16

B ut I have hope
when I think of this:

The LORD's love never ends;
his mercies never stop.
They are new every morning;
LORD, your loyalty is great.
I say to myself, "The LORD is mine,
so I hope in him."

The LORD is good to those who hope in
him,
to those who seek him.
Lamentations 3:21–25

Because the basis of all hope is knowing who God is. There is no hope without a God who controls the universe and promises to bring us to heaven.

Hope designates a future—that is what we hope in. Time, our period on this earth, can be seen in various ways, but only one way offers hope. Some see time as cyclical: history repeats itself and will continue to repeat itself only to get worse (and finally burn itself up). Others see time in the modern secular view that immortality exists as each generation gives birth to the next, which then gives birth to the next. But Christians see time in a straight line—God began time, has a specific purpose for each person within his divine plan, and he will bring it to an end when he returns as he promised.

Hope is not in most of the things our fellow humans hope in. It cannot be found in possessions, in our own strength or supposed "immortality," in people's love, in the past. Neither can it be found in human achievement, in who we are or what we have done, or in this life itself.

So where is hope? Our hope lies in our Christian growth here on earth—that we are doing what God wants for us in our particular place in time. We hope in the new heaven and new earth God has promised for us (Hebrews 13:14). We hope in Christ's second coming, in eternal life, and in resurrection (1 John 3:2, 3). We hope in the fact that this world is not all there is (Revelation 21:2, 3). And the great thing about our hope is that it is based on fact. It will happen because our hope is based on God, not on us.

YFC Editors

ACTION POINT

D escribe the hope of your salvation. Be specific. How might your hope affect the heart of a nonbeliever? What should be your purpose in everything you do? Ask God to fulfill his purpose through you.

INSIGHTS

C hristians have a corner on hope. Why?

WEEKEND:

Give All Your Worries to God; He Cares for You

1 Peter 4:12—5:14

Suffering as a Christian

*M*y friends, do not be surprised at the terrible trouble which now comes to test you. Do not think that something strange is happening to you. But be happy that you are sharing in Christ's sufferings so that you will be happy and full of joy when Christ comes again in glory. When people insult you because you follow Christ, you are blessed, because the glorious Spirit, the Spirit of God, is with you. Do not suffer for murder, theft, or any other crime, nor because you trouble other people. But if you suffer because you are a Christian, do not be ashamed. Praise God because you wear that name. It is time for judgment to begin with God's family. And if that judging begins with us, what will happen to those people who do not obey the Good News of God?

"If it is very hard for a good person to
    be saved,
  the wicked person and the sinner
    will surely be lost!"

So those who suffer as God wants should trust their souls to the faithful Creator as they continue to do what is right.

The Flock of God

*N*ow I have something to say to the elders in your group. I also am an elder. I have seen Christ's sufferings, and I will share in the glory that will be shown to us. I beg you to shepherd God's flock, for whom you are responsible. Watch over them because you want to, not because you are forced. That is how God wants it. Do it because you are happy to serve, not because you want money. Do not be like a ruler over people you are responsible for, but be good examples to them. Then when Christ, the Chief Shepherd, comes, you will get a glorious crown that will never lose its beauty.

In the same way, younger people should be willing to be under older people. And all of you should be very humble with each other.
  "God is against the proud,
    but he gives grace to the humble."

Proverbs 3:34

Be humble under God's powerful hand so he will lift you up when the right time comes. Give all your worries to him, because he cares about you.

Control yourselves and be careful! The devil, your enemy, goes around like a roaring lion looking for someone to eat. Refuse to give in to him, by standing strong in your faith. You know that your Christian family all over the world is having the same kinds of suffering.

And after you suffer for a short time, God, who gives all grace, will make everything right. He will make you strong and support you and keep you from falling. He called you to share in his glory in Christ, a glory that will continue forever. All power is his forever and ever. Amen.

Final Greetings

I wrote this short letter with the help of Silas, who I know is a faithful brother in Christ. I wrote to encourage you and to tell you that this is the true grace of God. Stand strong in that grace.

The church in Babylon, who was chosen like you, sends you greetings. Mark, my son in Christ, also greets you. Give each other a kiss of Christian love when you meet.

Peace to all of you who are in Christ.

*T*hen the LORD spoke his word to Elijah: "Leave this place and go east and hide near Kerith Ravine east of the Jordan River. You may drink from the stream, and I have commanded ravens to bring you food there."

The birds brought Elijah bread and meat every morning and evening, and he drank water from the stream.

After a while the stream dried up because there was no rain. Then the LORD spoke his word to Elijah, "Go to Zarephath in Sidon and live there. I have commanded a widow there to take care of you."

So Elijah went to Zarephath. When he reached the town gate, he saw a widow gathering wood for a fire. Elijah asked her, "Would you bring me a little water in a cup so I may have a drink." As she was going to get his water, Elijah said, "Please bring me a piece of bread, too."

The woman answered, "As surely as the LORD your God lives, I have no bread. I have only a handful of flour in a jar and only a little olive oil in a jug. I came here to gather some wood so I could go home and cook our last meal. My son and I will eat it and then die from hunger."

"Don't worry," Elijah said to her. "Go home and cook your food as you have said. But first make a small loaf of bread from the flour you have, and bring it to me. Then cook something for yourself and your son. The LORD, the God of Israel, says, 'That jar of flour will never be empty, and the jug will always have oil in it, until the day the LORD sends rain to the land.'"

So the woman went home and did what Elijah told her to do. And the woman and her son and Elijah had enough food every day. The jar of flour and the jug of oil were never empty, just as the LORD, through Elijah, had promised.

1 Kings 17:2–4, 6–16

The LORD is good to everyone;
　he is merciful to all he has made.

The LORD will keep all his promises;
　he is loyal to all he has made.
The LORD helps those who have been
　　defeated
　　and takes care of those who are in
　　　trouble.
You open your hand,
　and you satisfy all living things.

The LORD is close to everyone who
　　prays to him,
　to all who truly pray to him.
He gives those who respect him what
　　they want.
　He listens when they cry, and he
　　saves them.

Psalm 145:9, 13b–14, 16, 18–19

One winter I worked as secretary and receptionist at a mortuary. . . .

My husband had just been affected by a large company layoff, so I had needed to work. One particularly dark and dreary day I sat all by myself in the large office of the mortuary. While I typed a letter, my thoughts drifted to the house payment and utility bills. I soon felt overwhelmed. Tears came as I thought about the fact that we also needed groceries. Furthermore, Christmas was coming.

Suddenly, my thoughts were interrupted by a noise at the window. I walked over to see what it was. Through my tears, I saw that a sparrow had flown into the window and, stunned by the blow, had fallen to the ground.

This little incident reminded me of what God has to say in His Word about the birds of the air. He's aware of and provides for all of their needs. How much more is He aware of His children in need.

I felt so encouraged as I recalled sermons on this topic. I could almost hear the gospel singer: "His Eye Is On the Sparrow." I hummed the song the rest of the day. My faith increased, as I learned to trust God for my every need.

Then one morning a friend stood at the front door. "The Lord laid it on my heart to give you this money," he said. He didn't know it, but it was our house payment. Later, several checks came in the mail from a loving friend, signed, "Love, Jesus." One week we were invited out to dinner every night. And the children ended up having a delightful Christmas.

Barbara Hyatt

What worry did Peter's readers face? For what reasons does he tell them not to worry? What reassurance of God's loving care do the Old Testament readings provide? Will you trust in his care?

MONDAY:

Add Knowledge to Your Faith

2 Peter 1:1–21

*F*rom Simon Peter, a servant and apostle of Jesus Christ.

To you who have received a faith as valuable as ours, because our God and Savior Jesus Christ does what is right.

Grace and peace be given to you more and more, because you truly know God and Jesus our Lord.

God Has Given Us Blessings

*J*esus has the power of God, by which he has given us everything we need to live and to serve God. We have these things because we know him. Jesus called us by his glory and goodness. Through these he gave us the very great and precious promises. With these gifts you can share in being like God, and the world will not ruin you with its evil desires.

Because you have these blessings, do your best to add these things to your lives: to your faith, add goodness; and to your goodness, add knowledge; and to your knowledge, add self-control; and to your self-control, add patience; and to your patience, add service for God; and to your service for God, add kindness for your brothers and sisters in Christ; and to this kindness, add love. If all these things are in you and are growing, they will help you to be useful and productive in your knowledge of our Lord Jesus Christ. But anyone who does not have these things cannot see clearly. He is blind and has forgotten that he was made clean from his past sins.

My brothers and sisters, try hard to be certain that you really are called and chosen by God. If you do all these things, you will never fall. And you will be given a very great welcome into the eternal kingdom of our Lord and Savior Jesus Christ.

You know these things, and you are very strong in the truth, but I will always help you remember them. I think it is right for me to help you remember as long as I am in this body. I know I must soon leave this body, as our Lord Jesus Christ has shown me. I will try my best so that you may be able to remember these things even after I am gone.

We Saw Christ's Glory

*W*hen we told you about the powerful coming of our Lord Jesus Christ, we were not telling just smart stories that someone invented. But we saw the greatness of Jesus with our own eyes. Jesus heard the voice of God, the Greatest Glory, when he received honor and glory from God the Father. The voice said, "This is my Son, whom I love, and I am very pleased with him." We heard that voice from heaven while we were with Jesus on the holy mountain.

This makes us more sure about the message the prophets gave. It is good for you to follow closely what they said as you would follow a light shining in a dark place, until the day begins and the morning star rises in your hearts. Most of all, you must understand this: No prophecy in the Scriptures ever comes from the prophet's own interpretation. No prophecy ever came from what a person wanted to say, but people led by the Holy Spirit spoke words from God.

*T*hat night God appeared to Solomon and said to him, "Ask for whatever you want me to give you."

Solomon answered, "You have been very kind to my father David, and you have made me king in his place. Now, LORD God, may your promise to my father David come true. You have made me king of a people who are as many as the dust of the earth. Now give me wisdom and knowledge so I can lead these people in the right way, because no one can rule them without your help."

God said to Solomon, "You have not asked for wealth or riches or honor, or for the death of your enemies, or for a long life. But since you have asked for wisdom and knowledge to lead my people, over whom I have made you king, I will give you wisdom and knowledge."

2 Chronicles 1:7–12a

Cry out for wisdom,
 and beg for understanding.
Search for it like silver,
 and hunt for it like hidden treasure.
Then you will understand respect for
  the LORD,
 and you will find that you know God.
Only the LORD gives wisdom;
 he gives knowledge and understanding.

Proverbs 2:3–6

These are the wise words of Solomon son of David, king of Israel.

They teach wisdom and self-control;
 they will help you understand wise
  words.
They will teach you how to be wise and
  self-controlled
 and will teach you to do what is
  honest and fair and right.
They make the uneducated smarter
 and give knowledge and sense to the
  young.
Wise people can also listen and learn;
 even smart people can find good
  advice in these words.

Knowledge begins with respect for the
  LORD,
 but fools hate wisdom and self-
  control.

Proverbs 1:1–5, 7

People with good sense know what I
  say is true;
 and those with knowledge know my
  words are right.
Choose my teachings instead of silver,
 and knowledge rather than the finest
  gold.

Proverbs 8:9–10

I N S I G H T S

W*e are to make every effort to increase our faith, knowledge, self-control, steadfastness and brotherly affection. Each of us is expected to be spiritually self-sustaining. We cannot* rely on pastors or Christian leaders to keep our faith propped up.

Some Christians live from Sunday to Sunday. They start their week ready for action, but by Saturday are drained of their enthusiasm and can barely drag themselves to church the next day for another boost. Paul talks of digesting the milk of the Word (1 Cor 3:2). Babies need someone to feed them milk, and in the same way, new Christians need someone to help them understand biblical truth. Yet, we have all seen retarded adults who are incapable of feeding themselves. Behavior that is natural and cute in an infant is saddening to watch in these adults. Sadly, there are Christians who have not made "every effort to supplement their faith," and they too are retarded in their spiritual development.

Prayer and Bible study are important in supplementing our faith. God reveals himself to us in the Bible, and through prayer we have direct access to him with our problems and questions. . . .

. . . Once Bible study is a regular part of our lives, we will begin to reap the rewards of a more stable and mature relationship with the Lord. We will also have the personal confidence to go to the Bible and find our own answers to life's questions.

God does not want us to be spiritually retarded and unable to sustain the new life he has given us. He wants us to reach a place of maturity where we can spiritually feed ourselves and be able to stand firm in the face of any adversity.

Floyd McClung

P A U S E   F O R   R E F L E C T I O N

W*hat things does Peter say to add to your faith? What is the purpose and the result of doing these things? Consider your own life, and write down what you think will be accomplished if you add each of these things to your faith. Be specific (the Old Testament readings have some ideas)!*

TUESDAY:

*God Condemns False Teachers
Who Lead People into Evil*

2 Peter 2:1–22

NEW TESTAMENT READING

False Teachers

There used to be false prophets among God's people, just as you will have some false teachers in your group. They will secretly teach things that are wrong— teachings that will cause people to be lost. They will even refuse to accept the Master, Jesus, who bought their freedom. So they will bring quick ruin on themselves. Many will follow their evil ways and say evil things about the way of truth. Those false teachers only want your money, so they will use you by telling you lies. Their judgment spoken against them long ago is still coming, and their ruin is certain.

When angels sinned, God did not let them go free without punishment. He sent them to hell and put them in caves of darkness where they are being held for judgment. And God punished the world long ago when he brought a flood to the world that was full of people who were against him. But God saved Noah, who preached about being right with God, and seven other people with him. And God also destroyed the evil cities of Sodom and Gomorrah by burning them until they were ashes. He made those cities an example of what will happen to those who are against God. But he saved Lot from those cities. Lot, a good man, was troubled because of the filthy lives of evil people. (Lot was a good man, but because he lived with evil people every day, his good heart was hurt by the evil things he saw and heard.) So the Lord knows how to save those who serve him when troubles come. He will hold evil people and punish them, while waiting for the Judgment Day. That punishment is especially for those who live by doing the evil things their sinful selves want and who hate authority.

These false teachers are bold and do anything they want. They are not afraid to speak against the angels. But even the angels, who are much stronger and more powerful than false teachers, do not accuse them with insults before the Lord. But these people speak against things they do not understand. They are like animals that act without thinking, animals born to be caught and killed. And, like animals, these false teachers will be destroyed. They have caused many people to suffer, so they themselves will suffer. That is their pay for what they have done. They take pleasure in openly doing evil, so they are like dirty spots and stains among you. They delight in trickery while eating meals with you. Every time they look at a woman they want her, and their desire for sin is never satisfied. They lead weak people into the trap of sin, and they have taught their hearts to be greedy. God will punish them! These false teachers left the right road and lost their way, following the way Balaam went. Balaam was the son of Beor, who loved being paid for doing wrong. But a donkey, which cannot talk, told Balaam he was sinning. It spoke with a man's voice and stopped the prophet's crazy thinking.

Those false teachers are like springs without water and clouds blown by a storm. A place in the blackest darkness has been kept for them. They brag with words that mean nothing. By their evil desires they lead people into the trap of sin—people who are just beginning to escape from others who live in error. They promise them freedom, but they themselves are not free. They are slaves of things that will be destroyed. For people are slaves of anything that controls them. They were made free from the evil in the world by knowing our Lord and Savior Jesus Christ. But if they return to evil things and those things control them, then it is worse for them than it was before. Yes, it would be better for them to have never known the right way than to know it and to turn away from the holy teaching that was given to them. What they did is like this true saying: "A dog goes back to what it has thrown up," and, "After a pig is washed, it goes back and rolls in the mud."

*A*ll you animals of the field,
    all you animals of the forest, come to
       eat.
The leaders who are to guard the
       people are blind;
    they don't know what they are
       doing.
All of them are like quiet dogs
    that don't know how to bark.
They lie down and dream
    and love to sleep.
They are like hungry dogs
    that are never satisfied.
They are like shepherds
    who don't know what they are doing.
They all have gone their own way;
    all they want to do is satisfy them-
       selves.
They say, "Come, let's drink some wine;
    let's drink all the beer we want.
And tomorrow we will do this again,
    or, maybe we will have an even
       better time."

Isaiah 56:9–12

*M*y people will be destroyed,
    because they have no knowledge.
You have refused to learn,
    so I will refuse to let you be priests
       to me.
You have forgotten the teachings of
       your God,
    so I will forget your children.
The more priests there are,
    the more they sin against me.
I will take away their honor
    and give them shame.
Since the priests live off the sin offer-
       ings of the people,
    they want the people to sin more and
       more.
The priests are as wrong as the people,
    and I will punish them both for what
       they have done.
    I will repay them for the wrong they
       have done.

"They will eat
    but not have enough;
they will have sexual relations with the
       prostitutes,

but they will not have children,
because they have left the LORD."

Hosea 4:6–10

INSIGHTS

*D*eception is on the rise within the Christian church and we ignore it to our peril.

    Sometimes it is difficult—even for a Christian—to recognize the deceivers. Jesus spoke of false prophets who "perform great signs and miracles to deceive even the elect." . . .

    Satan does not want to build a church and call it "The First Church of Satan." He is far too clever for that. He invades the Sunday school, the youth department, the Christian education program, the pulpit and the seminary classroom.

    The apostle Paul warned that many will follow false teachers, not knowing that in feeding upon what these people say they are taking the devil's poison into their own lives. Thousands of uninstructed Christians are being deceived today. False teachers use high-sounding words that seem like the height of logic, scholarship and culture. They are intellectually clever and crafty in their sophistry. They are adept at beguiling thoughtless, untaught men and women. . . .

    The best advice against deception that I can give is to urge you to spend your time looking at the real Christ. Then, when a counterfeit appears, you'll have less trouble spotting him.

Billy Graham

ACTION POINT

*L*ist the lifestyle patterns that serve as clues that a false teacher is at work. How can a person guard against the practiced deception of false teachers? How do you plan to learn God's truth?

WEDNESDAY:
Be Strong in Your Faith
2 Peter 3:1–18

Jesus Will Come Again

*M*y friends, this is the second letter I have written you to help your honest minds remember. I want you to think about the words the holy prophets spoke in the past, and remember the command our Lord and Savior gave us through your apostles. It is most important for you to understand what will happen in the last days. People will laugh at you. They will live doing the evil things they want to do. They will say, "Jesus promised to come again. Where is he? Our fathers have died, but the world continues the way it has been since it was made." But they do not want to remember what happened long ago. By the word of God heaven was made, and the earth was made from water and with water. Then the world was flooded and destroyed with water. And that same word of God is keeping heaven and earth that we now have to be destroyed by fire. They are being kept for the Judgment Day and the destruction of all who are against God.

But do not forget this one thing, dear friends: To the Lord one day is as a thousand years, and a thousand years is as one day. The Lord is not slow in doing what he promised—the way some people understand slowness. But God is being patient with you. He does not want anyone to be lost, but he wants all people to change their hearts and lives.

But the day of the Lord will come like a thief. The skies will disappear with a loud noise. Everything in them will be destroyed by fire, and the earth and everything in it will be burned up. In that way everything will be destroyed. So what kind of people should you be? You should live holy lives and serve God, as you wait for and look forward to the coming of the day of God. When that day comes, the skies will be destroyed with fire, and everything in them will melt with heat. But God made a promise to us, and we are waiting for a new heaven and a new earth where goodness lives.

Dear friends, since you are waiting for this to happen, do your best to be without sin and without fault. Try to be at peace with God. Remember that we are saved because our Lord is patient. Our dear brother Paul told you the same thing when he wrote to you with the wisdom that God gave him. He writes about this in all his letters. Some things in Paul's letters are hard to understand, and people who are ignorant and weak in faith explain these things falsely. They also falsely explain the other Scriptures, but they are destroying themselves by doing this.

Dear friends, since you already know about this, be careful. Do not let those evil people lead you away by the wrong they do. Be careful so you will not fall from your strong faith. But grow in the grace and knowledge of our Lord and Savior Jesus Christ. Glory be to him now and forever! Amen.

*Y*ou sit as the Holy One.
   The praises of Israel are your
      throne.
Our ancestors trusted you;
   they trusted, and you saved them.
They called to you for help
   and were rescued.
They trusted you
   and were not disappointed.

But I am like a worm instead of a man.
   People make fun of me and hate me.
Those who look at me laugh.
   They stick out their tongues and
      shake their heads.
They say, "Turn to the Lord for help.
   Maybe he will save you.
If he likes you,
   maybe he will rescue you."

Psalm 22:3–8

*H*ow terrible it will be for those people!
   They pull their guilt and sins behind
      them
   as people pull wagons with ropes.

They say, "Let God hurry;
    let him do his work soon
    so we may see it.
Let the plan of the Holy One of Israel
        happen soon
    so that we will know what it is."
                                        Isaiah 5:18–19

*L*ORD, heal me, and I will truly be
        healed.
    Save me, and I will truly be saved.
    You are the one I praise.
The people of Judah keep asking me,
    "Where is the word from the LORD?
    Let's see that message come true!"

LORD, I didn't run away from being the
        shepherd you wanted.
    I didn't want the terrible day to
        come.
You know everything I have said;
    you see all that is happening.
Don't be a terror to me.
    I run to you for safety in times of
        trouble.
Make those who are hurting me be
        ashamed,
    but don't bring shame to me.
Let them be terrified,
    but keep me from terror.
Bring the day of disaster on my en-
        emies.
    Destroy them, and destroy them
        again.
                                        Jeremiah 17:14–18

---

*T*hey laughed at me and made fun of me because I wouldn't participate in what they were
doing."

"I lost the promotion at work because I
refused to take my clients to that sleazy night-
club."

"I lost several 'friends' because I didn't go
along with their gossiping when we got together."

Modern day persecution because of our
faith? Perhaps. It hurts to be misunderstood
and not accepted. Believers in China and
other parts of the world still face intense persecution. They lose their homes, some end up
in prison, and many are killed because of
their faith.

Most of us have never really felt the piercing sting of persecution. It could happen to
us as it does in other countries like China. It
could happen in ways hard to imagine if our
democratic society were overturned. You
never know. But whatever type of persecution
you experience, do you know how Jesus wants
you to respond? It's quite simple. Rejoice and
be glad. That's all. Be glad. Don't retaliate.
Don't sulk. Don't complain. Don't just grin
and bear it. Rejoice and actually "leap for joy"
(Luke 6:23).

. . . Expect opposition to your Christian
stance. That's normal. If you are persecuted
because of your stance for Jesus Christ, it
means you are really committed to Him and
your commitment is evident to others. You are
having an impact in the world around you.
Isn't it strange that living for Him brings
discomfort? But why not? Living for Christ
means confronting a world that is living
contrary to the way God intended. Your
Christian life bothers them. It's convicting. So
they will react to you. But I guess Jesus understands that pretty well, doesn't He? Look
at what it cost Him.

                                        H. Norman Wright

A P P L I C A T I O N

*W*hat perspective does Peter offer to help his
readers bear persecution? Will God hurry to
fulfill his plan for anyone? In what ways does
focusing on God—his eternal timelessness
and omnipotent power—help you face the
challenges of unbelievers?

THURSDAY:

Live in the Light!

1 John 1:1—2:14

*W*e write you now about what has always existed, which we have heard, we have seen with our own eyes, we have looked at, and we have touched with our hands. We write to you about the Word that gives life. He who gives life was shown to us. We saw him and can give proof about it. And now we announce to you that he has life that continues forever. He was with God the Father and was shown to us. We announce to you what we have seen and heard, because we want you also to have fellowship with us. Our fellowship is with God the Father and with his Son, Jesus Christ. We write this to you so you can be full of joy with us.

God Forgives Our Sins

*H*ere is the message we have heard from Christ and now announce to you: God is light, and in him there is no darkness at all. So if we say we have fellowship with God, but we continue living in darkness, we are liars and do not follow the truth. But if we live in the light, as God is in the light, we can share fellowship with each other. Then the blood of Jesus, God's Son, cleanses us from every sin.

If we say we have no sin, we are fooling ourselves, and the truth is not in us. But if we confess our sins, he will forgive our sins, because we can trust God to do what is right. He will cleanse us from all the wrongs we have done. If we say we have not sinned, we make God a liar, and we do not accept God's teaching.

Jesus Is Our Helper

*M*y dear children, I write this letter to you so you will not sin. But if anyone does sin, we have a helper in the presence of the Father—Jesus Christ, the One who does what is right. He is the way our sins are taken away, and not only our sins but the sins of all people.

We can be sure that we know God if we obey his commands. Anyone who says, "I know God," but does not obey God's commands is a liar, and the truth is not in that person. But if someone obeys God's teaching, then in that person God's love has truly reached its goal. This is how we can be sure we are living in God: Whoever says that he lives in God must live as Jesus lived.

The Command to Love Others

*M*y dear friends, I am not writing a new command to you but an old command you have had from the beginning. It is the teaching you have already heard. But also I am writing a new command to you, and you can see its truth in Jesus and in you, because the darkness is passing away, and the true light is already shining.

Anyone who says, "I am in the light," but hates a brother or sister, is still in the darkness. Whoever loves a brother or sister lives in the light and will not cause anyone to stumble in his faith. But whoever hates a brother or sister is in darkness, lives in darkness, and does not know where to go, because the darkness has made that person blind.

I write to you, dear children,
because your sins are forgiven
through Christ.
I write to you, parents,
because you know the One who
existed from the beginning.
I write to you, young people,
because you have defeated the Evil
One.
I write to you, children,
because you know the Father.
I write to you, parents,
because you know the One who
existed from the beginning.
I write to you, young people,
because you are strong;
the teaching of God lives in you,
and you have defeated the Evil One.

God Will Send His Light

*B*efore those people lived in darkness,
but now they have seen a great light.

They lived in a dark land,
but a light has shined on them.

Isaiah 9:2

*T*he LORD says, "I, the LORD, called you
to do right,
and I will hold your hand
and protect you.
You will be the sign of my agreement with the people,
a light to shine for all people.
You will help the blind to see.
You will free those who are in
prison,
and you will lead those who live in
darkness out of their prison."

Isaiah 42:6–7

The Joy of Those Who Live
in the Light

*S*end me your light and truth
to guide me.
Let them lead me to your holy mountain,
to where you live.
Then I will go to the altar of God,
to God who is my joy and happiness.
I will praise you with a harp,
God, my God.

Psalm 43:3–4

*T*he way of the good person is like the
light of dawn,
growing brighter and brighter until
full daylight.
But the wicked walk around in the
dark;
they can't even see what makes
them stumble.

Proverbs 4:18–19

The Hopelessness of Those
Who Do Evil

*L*isten and pay attention.
Don't be too proud,
because the LORD has spoken to you.
Give glory to the LORD your God
before he brings darkness
and before you slip and fall
on the dark hills.
You hope for light,

but he will turn it into thick darkness;
he will change it into deep gloom.

Jeremiah 13:15–16

*T*hose who fight against the light
do not know God's ways
or stay in his paths.

Job 24:13

*L*ight is not given to evil people.

Job 38:15a

INSIGHTS

*S*ervants of Christ shine with His light in a
society that is hopelessly lost. . . .
We pose a weird phenomenon to those in
darkness. They cannot figure us out! And that
is exactly as Jesus planned it. Think of some
distinctive characteristics of light:
• Light is silent. No noise, no big splash,
no banners—light simply shines. It's like a
single lighthouse along a rugged shoreline. All
it does is shine as it turns.
• Light gives direction. No words, no
sermon. Jesus says that others "see" our actions—but nothing is said of their hearing.
• Light attracts attention. You don't
have to ask people to look at you when you
turn a light on in a dark room. It happens
automatically. . . . If you are a Christian
family in a non-Christian neighborhood, you
are the light in that darkness. The same is
true if you are the only Christian nurse on
your floor, or student in your school, or professional in your firm or group, or salesman
in your district. You are a light in darkness—
a servant of God who is being watched, who
gives off a very distinct message . . . often
with hardly a word being said. . . . Let it
shine! Don't attempt to show off how bright
and sparkling you are, just shine!

Charles Swindoll

APPLICATION

*W*hat feelings does the God of light bring
into your life? Describe what it means for
you to "live in the light." What corners of
darkness in your life do you need to open up
to God's cleansing light?

FRIDAY:

You Have Been Forgiven, so Don't Love the World's Fleeting Pleasures

1 John 2:15—3:10

NEW TESTAMENT READING

*D*o not love the world or the things in the world. If you love the world, the love of the Father is not in you. These are the ways of the world: wanting to please our sinful selves, wanting the sinful things we see, and being too proud of what we have. None of these come from the Father, but all of them come from the world. The world and everything that people want in it are passing away, but the person who does what God wants lives forever.

Reject the Enemies of Christ

*M*y dear children, these are the last days. You have heard that the enemy of Christ is coming, and now many enemies of Christ are already here. This is how we know that these are the last days. These enemies of Christ were in our fellowship, but they left us. They never really belonged to us; if they had been a part of us, they would have stayed with us. But they left, and this shows that none of them really belonged to us.

You have the gift that the Holy One gave you, so you all know the truth. I do not write to you because you do not know the truth but because you do know the truth. And you know that no lie comes from the truth.

Who is the liar? It is the person who does not accept Jesus as the Christ. This is the enemy of Christ: the person who does not accept the Father and his Son. Whoever does not accept the Son does not have the Father. But whoever confesses the Son has the Father, too.

Be sure you continue to follow the teaching you heard from the beginning. If you continue to follow what you heard from the beginning, you will stay in the Son and in the Father. And this is what the Son promised to us—life forever.

I am writing this letter about those people who are trying to lead you the wrong way. Christ gave you a special gift that is still in you, so you do not need any other teacher. His gift teaches you about everything, and it is true, not false. So continue to live in Christ, as his gift taught you.

Yes, my dear children, live in him so that when Christ comes back, we can be without fear and not be ashamed in his presence. If you know that Christ is all that is right, you know that all who do right are God's children.

We Are God's Children

*T*he Father has loved us so much that we are called children of God. And we really are his children. The reason the people in the world do not know us is that they have not known him. Dear friends, now we are children of God, and we have not yet been shown what we will be in the future. But we know that when Christ comes again, we will be like him, because we will see him as he really is. Christ is pure, and all who have this hope in Christ keep themselves pure like Christ.

The person who sins breaks God's law. Yes, sin is living against God's law. You know that Christ came to take away sins and that there is no sin in Christ. So anyone who lives in Christ does not go on sinning. Anyone who goes on sinning has never really understood Christ and has never known him.

Dear children, do not let anyone lead you the wrong way. Christ is all that is right. So to be like Christ a person must do what is right. The devil has been sinning since the beginning, so anyone who continues to sin belongs to the devil. The Son of God came for this purpose: to destroy the devil's work.

Those who are God's children do not continue sinning, because the new life from God remains in them. They are not able to go on sinning, because they have become children of God. So we can see who God's children are and who the devil's children are: Those who do not do what is right are not God's children, and those who do not love their brothers and sisters are not God's children.

*I*f you hide your sins, you will not
succeed.
If you confess and reject them, you
will receive mercy.

Proverbs 28:13

*W*hen good people stop doing good and
do wrong, they will die because of it. They
will die, because they did wrong. When the
wicked stop being wicked and do what is
fair and right, they will save their lives. Because they thought about it and stopped
doing all the sins they had done, they will
surely live; they will not die.

"So I will judge you, people of Israel; I
will judge each of you by what you do, says
the Lord GOD. Change your hearts and stop all
your sinning so sin will not bring your ruin."

Ezekiel 18:26–28, 30

*G*od, you will be praised in Jerusalem.
We will keep our promises to you.
You hear our prayers.
All people will come to you.
Our guilt overwhelms us,
but you forgive our sins.

Psalm 65:1–3

Solomon Discovers the Futility
of All the World's Pleasures

I said to myself, "I will try having fun. I will
enjoy myself." But I found that this is also
useless.

I also gathered silver and gold for myself, treasures from kings and other areas.
I had male and female singers and all the
women a man could ever want. I became
very famous, even greater than anyone
who had lived in Jerusalem before me. My
wisdom helped me in all this.

Anything I saw and wanted, I got for
myself;
I did not miss any pleasure I desired.
I was pleased with everything I did,
and this pleasure was the reward for
all my hard work.
But then I looked at what I had done,
and I thought about all the hard
work.

Suddenly I realized it was useless, like
chasing the wind.
There is nothing to gain from
anything we do here on earth.

Ecclesiastes 2:1, 8–11

*N*ow, everything has been heard,
so I give my final advice:
Honor God and obey his commands,
because this is all people must do.
God will judge everything,
even what is done in secret,
the good and the evil.

Ecclesiastes 12:13–14

*W*hen I look back on my life nowadays,
which I sometimes do, what strikes me forc-
ibly about it is that what seemed at the time
most significant and seductive, seems now
most futile and absurd. For instance, success
in all of its various guises; being known and
being praised; ostensible pleasures, like ac-
quiring money or seducing women, or trav-
elling, going to and fro in the world and up
and down in it like Satan, exploring and experiencing whatever Vanity Fair has to offer.

In retrospect all these exercises in self-
gratification seem pure fantasy, what Pascal
called "licking the earth." They are diversions
designed to distract our attention from the
true purpose of our existence in this world,
which is, quite simply, to look for God, and,
in looking, to find Him, and having found
Him, to love Him, thereby establishing a
harmonious relationship with His purposes
for His creation.

Malcolm Muggeridge

*W*rite down what you believe to be your true
purpose in life. What things are important
according to that purpose? Pray that God will
help you focus on the important things and
put aside everything else—no matter how
tempting it may appear!

WEEKEND:

God's People Must Show Their Love for One Another

1 John 3:11—4:12

We Must Love Each Other

*T*his is the teaching you have heard from the beginning: We must love each other. Do not be like Cain who belonged to the Evil One and killed his brother. And why did he kill him? Because the things Cain did were evil, and the things his brother did were good.

Brothers and sisters, do not be surprised when the people of the world hate you. We know we have left death and have come into life because we love each other. Whoever does not love is still dead. Everyone who hates a brother or sister is a murderer, and you know that no murderers have eternal life in them. This is how we know what real love is: Jesus gave his life for us. So we should give our lives for our brothers and sisters. Suppose someone has enough to live and sees a brother or sister in need, but does not help. Then God's love is not living in that person. My children, we should love people not only with words and talk, but by our actions and true caring.

This is the way we know that we belong to the way of truth. When our hearts make us feel guilty, we can still have peace before God. God is greater than our hearts, and he knows everything. My dear friends, if our hearts do not make us feel guilty, we can come without fear into God's presence. And God gives us what we ask for because we obey God's commands and do what pleases him. This is what God commands: that we believe in his Son, Jesus Christ, and that we love each other, just as he commanded. The people who obey God's commands live in God, and God lives in them. We know that God lives in us because of the Spirit God gave us.

Warning Against False Teachers

*M*y dear friends, many false prophets have gone out into the world. So do not believe every spirit, but test the spirits to see if they are from God. This is how you can know God's Spirit: Every spirit who confesses that Jesus Christ came to earth as a human is from God. And every spirit who refuses to say this about Jesus is not from God. It is the spirit of the enemy of Christ, which you have heard is coming, and now he is already in the world.

My dear children, you belong to God and have defeated them; because God's Spirit, who is in you, is greater than the devil, who is in the world. And they belong to the world, so what they say is from the world, and the world listens to them. But we belong to God, and those who know God listen to us. But those who are not from God do not listen to us. That is how we know the Spirit that is true and the spirit that is false.

Love Comes from God

*D*ear friends, we should love each other, because love comes from God. Everyone who loves has become God's child and knows God. Whoever does not love does not know God, because God is love. This is how God showed his love to us: He sent his one and only Son into the world so that we could have life through him. This is what real love is: It is not our love for God; it is God's love for us in sending his Son to be the way to take away our sins.

Dear friends, if God loved us that much we also should love each other. No one has ever seen God, but if we love each other, God lives in us, and his love is made perfect in us.

*T*his is what the LORD All-Powerful says: 'Do what is right and true. Be kind and merciful to each other. Don't hurt widows and orphans, foreigners or the poor; don't even think of doing evil to somebody else.'

"But they refused to pay attention; they were stubborn and did not want to listen anymore. They made their hearts as hard as rock and would not listen to the teachings of the LORD All-Powerful. And they would not hear the words he sent by his Spirit through the earlier prophets. So the LORD All-Powerful became very angry."

Zechariah 7:9–12

*M*ordecai had a cousin named Hadassah, who had no father or mother, so Mordecai took care of her. Hadassah was also called Esther, and she had a very pretty figure and face. Mordecai had adopted her as his own daughter when her father and mother died.

Esther 2:7

*T*he king asked, "Is anyone left in Saul's family? I want to show God's kindness to that person."

Ziba answered the king, "Jonathan has a son still living who is crippled in both feet."

The king asked Ziba, "Where is this son?"

Ziba answered, "He is at the house of Makir son of Ammiel in Lo Debar."

Then King David had servants bring Jonathan's son from the house of Makir son of Ammiel in Lo Debar. Mephibosheth, Jonathan's son, came before David and bowed facedown on the floor.

David said, "Mephibosheth!"

Mephibosheth said, "I am your servant."

David said to him, "Don't be afraid. I will be kind to you for your father Jonathan's sake. I will give you back all the land of your grandfather Saul, and you will always eat at my table."

Mephibosheth bowed to David again and said, "You are being very kind to me, your servant! And I am no better than a dead dog!"

Then King David called Saul's servant Ziba. David said to him, "I have given your master's grandson everything that belonged to Saul and his family. You, your sons, and your servants will farm the land and harvest the crops. Then your family will have food to eat. But Mephibosheth, your master's grandson, will always eat at my table."

(Now Ziba had fifteen sons and twenty servants.)

2 Samuel 9:3–10

INSIGHTS

*T*here is more to becoming a Christian than accepting a set of doctrines and striving to live out a particular lifestyle. Being a Christian involves allowing God to become a living presence in your life. . . . A Christian is a person who is possessed by Christ in such a way that feelings, thoughts, and attitudes are all changed. For the Christian person, loving becomes a spiritual exercise because God is love, and the Christian knows that "every one that loveth is born of God." God wants to indwell you and affect your consciousness for many reasons, but above them all is His desire to be able to reach other people with His love through you. . . . If you will pray and ask Him to be an indwelling reality and if you are willing to yield to His will in all things, He will enter into your consciousness and begin to effect a transformation in your life. Most important, you will, little by little, begin to relate to other people as He would relate to them. You will recognize that being a Christian involves a commitment to treat others as He would treat them. . . .

If you want to do something that will cause you to become a more loving person, surrender yourself to Jesus. He has a way of making lovers out of people.

Tony Campolo

APPLICATION

*W*hy is love characteristic of God's children? What does a lack of love reveal about a person's heart? How much should God's children love each other? In what ways do God's children demonstrate their love? To whom can you show the kind of godly love that David showed Mephibosheth?

MONDAY:

God Listens to the Prayers of His People

1 John 4:13—5:21

*W*e know that we live in God and he lives in us, because he gave us his Spirit. We have seen and can testify that the Father sent his Son to be the Savior of the world. Whoever confesses that Jesus is the Son of God has God living inside, and that person lives in God. And so we know the love that God has for us, and we trust that love.

God is love. Those who live in love live in God, and God lives in them. This is how love is made perfect in us: that we can be without fear on the day God judges us, because in this world we are like him. Where God's love is, there is no fear, because God's perfect love drives out fear. It is punishment that makes a person fear, so love is not made perfect in the person who fears.

We love because God first loved us. If people say, "I love God," but hate their brothers or sisters, they are liars. Those who do not love their brothers and sisters, whom they have seen, cannot love God, whom they have never seen. And God gave us this command: Those who love God must also love their brothers and sisters.

Faith in the Son of God

*E*veryone who believes that Jesus is the Christ is God's child, and whoever loves the Father also loves the Father's children. This is how we know we love God's children: when we love God and obey his commands. Loving God means obeying his commands. And God's commands are not too hard for us, because everyone who is a child of God conquers the world. And this is the victory that conquers the world—our faith. So the one who wins against the world is the person who believes that Jesus is the Son of God.

Jesus Christ is the One who came by water and blood. He did not come by water only, but by water and blood. And the Spirit says that this is true, because the Spirit is the truth. So there are three witnesses that tell us about Jesus: the Spirit, the water, and the blood; and these three witnesses agree. We believe people when they say something is true. But what God says is more important, and he has told us the truth about his own Son. Anyone who believes in the Son of God has the truth that God told us. Anyone who does not believe makes God a liar, because that person does not believe what God told us about his Son. This is what God told us: God has given us eternal life, and this life is in his Son. Whoever has the Son has life, but whoever does not have the Son of God does not have life.

We Have Eternal Life Now

I write this letter to you who believe in the Son of God so you will know you have eternal life. And this is the boldness we have in God's presence: that if we ask God for anything that agrees with what he wants, he hears us. If we know he hears us every time we ask him, we know we have what we ask from him.

If anyone sees a brother or sister sinning (sin that does not lead to eternal death), that person should pray, and God will give the sinner life. I am talking about people whose sin does not lead to eternal death. There is sin that leads to death. I do not mean that a person should pray about that sin. Doing wrong is always sin, but there is sin that does not lead to eternal death.

We know that those who are God's children do not continue to sin. The Son of God keeps them safe, and the Evil One cannot touch them. We know that we belong to God, but the Evil One controls the whole world. We also know that the Son of God has come and has given us understanding so that we can know the True One. And our lives are in the True One and in his Son, Jesus Christ. He is the true God and the eternal life.

So, dear children, keep yourselves away from gods.

*A*ll of you who fear God, come and listen,

and I will tell you what he has done
for me.
I cried out to him with my mouth
and praised him with my tongue.
If I had known of any sin in my
heart,
the Lord would not have listened to
me.
But God has listened;
he has heard my prayer.
Praise God,
who did not ignore my prayer
or hold back his love from me.

Psalm 66:16–20

While there, Johanan son of Kareah and Jezaniah son of Hoshaiah went to Jeremiah the prophet. All the army officers and all the people, from the least important to the greatest, went along, too. They said to him, "Jeremiah, please listen to what we ask. Pray to the LORD your God for all the people left alive from the family of Judah. At one time there were many of us, but you can see that there are few of us now. So pray that the LORD your God will tell us where we should go and what we should do."

Then Jeremiah the prophet answered, "I understand what you want me to do. I will pray to the LORD your God as you have asked. I will tell you everything he says and not hide anything from you."

Then the people said to Jeremiah, "May the LORD be a true and loyal witness against us if we don't do everything the LORD your God sends you to tell us. It does not matter if we like the message or not. We will obey the LORD our God, to whom we are sending you. We will obey what he says so good things will happen to us."

Ten days later the LORD spoke his word to Jeremiah.

Jeremiah said to them, "You sent me to ask the LORD for what you wanted. This is what the God of Israel says: 'If you will stay in Judah, I will build you up and not tear you down. I will plant you and not pull you up, because I am sad about the disaster I brought on you. Now you fear the king of Babylon, but don't be afraid of him. Don't be afraid of him,' says the LORD, 'because I

am with you. I will save you and rescue you from his power.'"

Jeremiah 42:1–7, 9–11

INSIGHTS

PLEASE INTERRUPT

Sometimes I feel like an interruption,
and then I want to shrink
back into my shell
and never come out again.
I want to walk away and say,
"I'm sorry I took your time."

Being an interruption hurts.
It tells me
something is more important than I am.
It tells me
to hurry up and move along.
It tells me
you are looking
but don't see me.
It tells me
you are listening
but don't hear me.
And so I move along.

But, God says,
"Don't hurry away.
Stick around.
Tell me how it is with you.
Tell me what you're feeling
right this minute.
Tell me why you feel that way.
I want to know you.
You count with me.
I care about you.
Tell me what I can do for you."

And I go away feeling
He was glad I called.

Ruth Senter

PAUSE FOR REFLECTION

Who listens to you every time you speak? How do you know that God hears your prayers? What would you tell others that he has done for you?

TUESDAY:

Encourage and Support One Another in the Faith

2 John 1—3 John 15

*F*rom the Elder.

To the chosen lady and her children:

I love all of you in the truth, and all those who know the truth love you. We love you because of the truth that lives in us and will be with us forever.

Grace, mercy, and peace from God the Father and his Son, Jesus Christ, will be with us in truth and love.

I was very happy to learn that some of your children are following the way of truth, as the Father commanded us. And now, dear lady, this is not a new command but is the same command we have had from the beginning. I ask you that we all love each other. And love means living the way God commanded us to live. As you have heard from the beginning, his command is this: Live a life of love.

Many false teachers are in the world now who do not confess that Jesus Christ came to earth as a human. Anyone who does not confess this is a false teacher and an enemy of Christ. Be careful yourselves that you do not lose everything you have worked for, but that you receive your full reward.

Anyone who goes beyond Christ's teaching and does not continue to follow only his teaching does not have God. But whoever continues to follow the teaching of Christ has both the Father and the Son. If someone comes to you and does not bring this teaching, do not welcome or accept that person into your house. If you welcome such a person, you share in the evil work.

I have many things to write to you, but I do not want to use paper and ink. Instead, I hope to come to you and talk face to face so we can be full of joy. The children of your chosen sister greet you.

Help Christians Who Teach Truth

*F*rom the Elder.

To my dear friend Gaius, whom I love in the truth:

My dear friend, I know your soul is doing fine, and I pray that you are doing well in every way and that your health is good. I was very happy when some brothers and sisters came and told me about the truth in your life and how you are following the way of truth. Nothing gives me greater joy than to hear that my children are following the way of truth.

My dear friend, it is good that you help the brothers and sisters, even those you do not know. They told the church about your love. Please help them to continue their trip in a way worthy of God. They started out in service to Christ, and they have been accepting nothing from nonbelievers. So we should help such people; when we do, we share in their work for the truth.

I wrote something to the church, but Diotrephes, who loves to be their leader, will not listen to us. So if I come, I will talk about what Diotrephes is doing, about how he lies and says evil things about us. But more than that, he refuses to accept the other brothers and sisters; he even stops those who do want to accept them and puts them out of the church.

My dear friend, do not follow what is bad; follow what is good. The one who does good belongs to God. But the one who does evil has never known God.

Everyone says good things about Demetrius, and the truth agrees with what they say. We also speak well of him, and you know what we say is true.

I have many things I want to write you, but I do not want to use pen and ink. I hope to see you soon and talk face to face. Peace to you. The friends here greet you. Please greet each friend there by name.

*T*hen Moses called Joshua and said to him in front of the people, "Be strong and brave, because you will lead these people into the land the LORD promised to give their ancestors, and help them take it as their own. The LORD himself will go before you. He will be with you; he will not leave you or forget you.

Don't be afraid and don't worry."

Deuteronomy 31:7–8

Since it was almost time for David to die, he gave his son Solomon his last commands. David said, "My time to die is near. Be a good and strong leader. Obey the LORD your God. Follow him by obeying his demands, his commands, his laws, and his rules that are written in the teachings of Moses. If you do these things, you will be successful in all you do and wherever you go. And if you obey the LORD, he will keep the promise he made to me. He said: 'If your descendants live as I tell them and have complete faith in me, a man from your family will always be king over the people of Israel.'"

1 Kings 2:1–4

Ebed-Meiech said to him, "My master and king, these rulers have acted in an evil way. They have treated Jeremiah the prophet badly. They have thrown him into a well and left him there to die! When there is no more bread in the city, he will starve to death."

Then King Zedekiah commanded Ebed-Melech the Cushite, "Take thirty men from the palace and lift Jeremiah the prophet out of the well before he dies."

The men pulled Jeremiah up with the ropes and lifted him out of the well. And Jeremiah stayed under guard in the courtyard of the guard.

While Jeremiah was guarded in the courtyard, the LORD spoke his word to him: "Jeremiah, go and tell Ebed-Melech the Cushite this message: 'This is what the LORD All-Powerful, the God of Israel, says: Very soon I will make my words about Jerusalem come true through disaster, not through good times. You will see everything come true with your own eyes. But I will save you on that day, Ebed-Melech, says the LORD. You will not be handed over to the people you fear. I will surely save you, Ebed-Melech. You will not die from a sword, but you will escape and live. This will happen because you have trusted in me, says the LORD.'"

Jeremiah 38:8b–10, 13; 39:15–18

I decided to take a break and hit the slopes (emphasis on hit, since it was my first time in all my life to attempt to ski). . . .

It was unbelievable! You have heard of the elephant man? On skis, I'm the rhinoceros man. It is doubtful that anyone else on planet earth has ever come down any ski slope more ways than I did. Or landed in more positions. Or did more creative things in the air before landing. . . .

Working with me that humiliating day was the world's most encouraging ski instructor (yes, I had an instructor!) who set the new record in patience. . . .

Never once did she lose her cool.

Never once did she laugh at me.

Never once did she yell, scream, threaten, or swear.

Never once did she call me "dummy." . . .

. . . That day God gave me a living, never-to-be-forgotten illustration of the value of encouragement. . . .

What is true for a novice on the snow once a year is all the more true for the people we meet every day. Harassed by demands and deadlines; bruised by worry, adversity, and failure; broken by disillusionment; and defeated by sin, they live somewhere between dull discouragement and sheer panic. Even Christians are not immune! We may give off this "I've got it all together" air of confidence, much like I did when I first snapped on the skis. But realistically, we also struggle, lose our balance, slip and slide, tumble, and fall flat on our faces.

All of us need encouragement—somebody to believe in us. To reassure and reinforce us. To help us pick up the pieces and go on. To provide us with increased determination in spite of the odds.

Charles Swindoll

Describe the kinds of encouragement in faith revealed through these Scripture readings. When have you been blessed by spiritual encouragement? Who could use your encouragement today?

581

WEDNESDAY:

God Will Punish Everyone Who Is Against Him

Jude 1–13

*F*rom Jude, a servant of Jesus Christ and a brother of James.

To all who have been called by God. God the Father loves you, and you have been kept safe in Jesus Christ:

Mercy, peace, and love be yours richly.

God Will Punish Sinners

*D*ear friends, I wanted very much to write you about the salvation we all share. But I felt the need to write you about something else: I want to encourage you to fight hard for the faith that was given the holy people of God once and for all time. Some people have secretly entered your group. Long ago the prophets wrote about these people who will be judged guilty. They are against God and have changed the grace of our God into a reason for sexual sin. They also refuse to accept Jesus Christ, our only Master and Lord.

I want to remind you of some things you already know: Remember that the Lord saved his people by bringing them out of the land of Egypt. But later he destroyed all those who did not believe. And remember the angels who did not keep their place of power but left their proper home. The Lord has kept these angels in darkness, bound with everlasting chains, to be judged on the great day. Also remember the cities of Sodom and Gomorrah and the other towns around them. In the same way they were full of sexual sin and people who desired sexual relations that God does not allow. They suffer the punishment of eternal fire, as an example for all to see.

It is the same with these people who have entered your group. They are guided by dreams and make themselves filthy with sin. They reject God's authority and speak against the angels. Not even the archangel Michael, when he argued with the devil about who would have the body of Moses, dared to judge the devil guilty. Instead, he said, "The Lord punish you." But these people speak against things they do not understand. And what they do know, by feeling, as dumb animals know things, are the very things that destroy them. It will be terrible for them. They have followed the way of Cain, and for money they have given themselves to doing the wrong that Balaam did. They have fought against God as Korah did, and like Korah, they surely will be destroyed. They are like dirty spots in your special Christian meals you share. They eat with you and have no fear, caring only for themselves. They are clouds without rain, which the wind blows around. They are autumn trees without fruit that are pulled out of the ground. So they are twice dead. They are like wild waves of the sea, tossing up their own shameful actions like foam. They are like stars that wander in the sky. A place in the blackest darkness has been kept for them forever.

*B*ut God says to the wicked,
  "Why do you talk about my laws?
  Why do you mention my agreement?
You hate my teachings
  and turn your back on what I say.
When you see a thief, you join him.
  You take part in adultery.
You don't stop your mouth from
    speaking evil,
  and your tongue makes up lies.
You speak against your brother
  and lie about your mother's son.
I have kept quiet while you did these
    things,
  so you thought I was just like you.
But I will scold you
  and accuse you to your face.

"Think about this, you who forget God.
  Otherwise, I will tear you apart,
  and no one will save you.
Those people honor me
  who bring me offerings to show
    thanks.
And I, God, will save those who do that."

Psalm 50:16–23

Cry, because the LORD's day of
    judging is near;
    the Almighty is sending destruction.
People will be weak with fear,
    and their courage will melt away.
Everyone will be afraid.
    Pain and hurt will grab them;
    they will hurt like a woman giving
      birth to a baby.
They will look at each other in fear,
    with their faces red like fire.

Look, the LORD's day of judging is
    coming—
    a terrible day, a day of God's
      anger.
He will destroy the land
    and the sinners who live in it.
The stars will not show their light;
    the skies will be dark.
The sun will grow dark as it rises,
    and the moon will not give its light.

The LORD says, "I will punish the world
    for its evil
    and wicked people for their sins.
I will cause proud people to lose their
    pride,
    and I will destroy the pride of those
    who are cruel to others."

Isaiah 13:6–11

INSIGHTS

You have a "lake of fire and brimstone," and you see lost sinners thrown into its waves of rolling fire; and they lash its burning shore, and gnaw their tongues for pain. There the worm dieth not, and their fire is not quenched, and "not one drop of water" can reach them to "cool their tongues"—"tormented in that flame."

What think you? Has God said these things to frighten our poor souls? Did He mean to play on our fears for His own amusement? Can you think so? Nay, does it not rather grieve His heart that He must build such a hell, and must plunge therein the sinners who will not honour His law—will not embrace salvation from sinning through His grace? Ah, the waves of death roll darkly under the eye of the Holy and compassionate One! He has no pleasure in the death of the sinner!

But He must sustain His throne, and save His loyal subjects if He can. . . .

God would have us understand what an awful thing sin is, and what fearful punishment it deserves. He would fain show us by such figures how terrible must be the doom of the determined sinner.

Charles Finney

PAUSE   FOR   REFLECTION

Why must God punish those who are against him? List the sins of those who are against God. How can God's people stand strong against them? How are God's people to treat those who have doubts?

THURSDAY:
God Is a Merciful Judge
Jude 14–25

*E*noch, the seventh descendant from Adam, said about these people: "Look, the Lord is coming with many thousands of his holy angels to judge every person. He is coming to punish all who are against God for all the evil they have done against him. And he will punish the sinners who are against God for all the evil they have said against him."

These people complain and blame others, doing the evil things they want to do. They brag about themselves, and they flatter others to get what they want.

A Warning and Things to Do

*D*ear friends, remember what the apostles of our Lord Jesus Christ said before. They said to you, "In the last times there will be people who laugh about God, following their own evil desires which are against God." These are the people who divide you, people whose thoughts are only of this world, who do not have the Spirit.

But dear friends, use your most holy faith to build yourselves up, praying in the Holy Spirit. Keep yourselves in God's love as you wait for the Lord Jesus Christ with his mercy to give you life forever.

Show mercy to some people who have doubts. Take others out of the fire, and save them. Show mercy mixed with fear to others, hating even their clothes which are dirty from sin.

Praise God

*G*od is strong and can help you not to fall. He can bring you before his glory without any wrong in you and can give you great joy. He is the only God, the One who saves us. To him be glory, greatness, power, and authority through Jesus Christ our Lord for all time past, now, and forever. Amen.

Judgment Will Come to People Who Speak Falsely About God

*B*ut I said, "Oh, Lord GOD, the prophets keep telling the people, 'You will not suffer from an enemy's sword or from hunger. I, the LORD, will give you peace in this land.'"

Then the LORD said to me, "Those prophets are prophesying lies in my name. I did not send them or appoint them or speak to them. They have been prophesying false visions, idolatries, worthless magic, and their own wishful thinking. So this is what I say about the prophets who are prophesying in my name. I did not send them. They say, 'No enemy will attack this country with swords. There will never be hunger in this land.' So those prophets will die from hunger and from an enemy's sword. And the people to whom the prophets speak will be thrown into the streets of Jerusalem. There they will die from hunger and from an enemy's sword. And no one will be there to bury them, or their wives, or their sons, or their daughters. I will punish them."

Jeremiah 14:13–16

The Truth About Bragging

*T*his is what the LORD says:
"The wise must not brag about their
    wisdom.
  The strong must not brag about
    their strength.
  The rich must not brag about their
    money.
But if someone wants to brag, let him
    brag
  that he understands and knows me.
Let him brag that I am the LORD,
  and that I am kind and fair,
  and that I do things that are right on
    earth.
This kind of bragging pleases me," says
    the LORD.

Jeremiah 9:23–24

Those Who Have Faith in God Will Receive His Mercy

*G*ive happiness to me, your servant,
  because I give my life to you, Lord.

Lord, you are kind and forgiving
  and have great love for those who
    call to you.

LORD, teach me what you want me to do,
  and I will live by your truth.
Teach me to respect you completely.
Lord, my God, I will praise you with all
    my heart,
  and I will honor your name forever.
You have great love for me.
  You have saved me from death.

God, proud men are attacking me;
  a gang of cruel men is trying to kill
    me.
They do not respect you.
Turn to me and have mercy.

Psalm 86:4–5, 11–14, 16a

*T*he LORD's love never ends;
  his mercies never stop.
They are new every morning;
  LORD, your loyalty is great.
I say to myself, "The LORD is mine,
  so I hope in him."

The LORD is good to those who hope in
    him,
  to those who seek him.
It is good to wait quietly
  for the LORD to save.

Lamentations 3:22–26

who had just administered justice reached for
his big white handkerchief and wiped the tears
from his eyes. That day, justice and love were
forever linked in my mind.

My father's actions pointed me toward a
heavenly Father who sits in the hall of justice, calls His creation to accountability, but
weeps over waywardness even as He pro-
nounces sentence. "Oh, Jerusalem, Jerusalem . . . how often I have longed to gather
your children together, as a hen gathers her
chicks under her wings, but you were not
willing!" (Luke 13:34, NIV). Justice and love
exist in the same person.

. . . I can be at peace about God's system
of justice, for I have confidence in the Judge.
There will be no payoffs. He judges clean.

As a sinner who knew where to find grace,
I know God today not as my judge but as a
loving Father who continually calls me to
accountability. One day He was my judge. But
I can almost see a white handkerchief dab-
bing tears as He wept over my rebellion, is-
sued the sentence, and then took my penalty
upon Himself. I am acquitted. Justice has
been done. My debt has been paid. I can rest
my case. . . .

"God is fair," I said to myself, "whether or
not I understand His ways. For He is a God
of justice."

Ruth Senter

INSIGHTS

*G*od is a just God, One who shows no par-
tiality. Outside of grace, God's penalty falls
on all. "The wages of sin is death" (Romans
6:23). Sin is sin. The consequences have been
posted; He gives fair warning. No excuses accepted. No variations on the rules. Man is
accountable. Rebellion, be it active or passive,
calls for justice.

I understand God's justice because I remember rebellion—ten-year-old rebellion. My
father was the dispenser of justice. "No
swimming in the creek today," he said. I had
plenty of excuses: "Jimmy went in." "I was so
hot." "It isn't fair when everybody else's dad
lets them go."

Excuses didn't matter because the standard
had been violated. The penalty was swift and
sure. Justice was done. But then the father

APPLICATION

*H*ow does God want his people to treat those
who have doubts? Do you have complete trust
in God, who is both Judge and Savior? Are
you at rest in his love?

F R I D A Y:

God Is the Great I AM—
the Beginning and the End

Revelation 1:1–20

NEW TESTAMENT READING

John Tells About This Book

*T*his is the revelation of Jesus Christ, which God gave to him, to show his servants what must soon happen. And Jesus sent his angel to show it to his servant John, who has told everything he has seen. It is the word of God; it is the message from Jesus Christ. Happy is the one who reads the words of God's message, and happy are the people who hear this message and do what is written in it. The time is near when all of this will happen.

Jesus' Message to the Churches

*F*rom John.

To the seven churches in the country of Asia:

Grace and peace to you from the One who is and was and is coming, and from the seven spirits before his throne, and from Jesus Christ. Jesus is the faithful witness, the first among those raised from the dead. He is the ruler of the kings of the earth.

He is the One who loves us, who made us free from our sins with the blood of his death. He made us to be a kingdom of priests who serve God his Father. To Jesus Christ be glory and power forever and ever! Amen.

Look, Jesus is coming with the clouds, and everyone will see him, even those who stabbed him. And all peoples of the earth will cry loudly because of him. Yes, this will happen! Amen.

The Lord God says, "I am the Alpha and the Omega. I am the One who is and was and is coming. I am the Almighty."

I, John, am your brother. All of us share with Christ in suffering, in the kingdom, and in patience to continue. I was on the island of Patmos, because I had preached the word of God and the message about Jesus. On the Lord's day I was in the Spirit, and I heard a loud voice behind me

that sounded like a trumpet. The voice said, "Write what you see in a book and send it to the seven churches: to Ephesus, Smyrna, Pergamum, Thyatira, Sardis, Philadelphia, and Laodicea."

I turned to see who was talking to me. When I turned, I saw seven golden lampstands and someone among the lampstands who was "like a Son of Man." He was dressed in a long robe and had a gold band around his chest. His head and hair were white like wool, as white as snow, and his eyes were like flames of fire. His feet were like bronze that glows hot in a furnace, and his voice was like the noise of flooding water. He held seven stars in his right hand, and a sharp double-edged sword came out of his mouth. He looked like the sun shining at its brightest time.

When I saw him, I fell down at his feet like a dead man. He put his right hand on me and said, "Do not be afraid. I am the First and the Last. I am the One who lives; I was dead, but look, I am alive forever and ever! And I hold the keys to death and to the place of the dead. So write the things you see, what is now and what will happen later. Here is the secret of the seven stars that you saw in my right hand and the seven golden lampstands: The seven lampstands are the seven churches, and the seven stars are the angels of the seven churches.

OLD TESTAMENT READING

*P*eople of Jacob, listen to me.
    People of Israel, I have called you to
        be my people.
I am God;
    I am the beginning and the end.
I made the earth with my own hands.
    With my right hand I spread out the
        skies.
When I call them,
    they come together before me."

Isaiah 48:12–13

I have always been God.
No one can save people from my power;
    when I do something, no one can
        change it."

Isaiah 43:13

The LORD, the king of Israel,
    is the LORD All-Powerful, who saves
        Israel.
This is what he says: "I am the begin-
        ning and the end.
    I am the only God."

Isaiah 44:6

Then God said to Moses, "I AM WHO I AM.
When you go to the people of Israel, tell
them, 'I AM sent me to you.'"

Exodus 3:14

Praise the LORD, the God of Israel.
    He has always been,
    and he will always be.
                Amen and amen.

Psalm 41:13

In the beginning you made the earth,
    and your hands made the skies.
They will be destroyed, but you will
        remain.
    They will all wear out like clothes.
And, like clothes, you will change them
    and throw them away.
But you never change,
    and your life will never end.

Psalm 102:25–27

Lord, you have been our home
    since the beginning.
Before the mountains were born
        and before you created the earth and
        the world,
you are God.
    You have always been, and you will
        always be.

You turn people back into dust.
    You say, "Go back into dust, human
        beings."
To you, a thousand years
    is like the passing of a day,
    or like a few hours in the night.

Psalm 90:1–4

INSIGHTS

I am the beginning;
    I am the end.
You are very concerned with beginnings.

You hesitate to reach
    the end.
The Alpha/beginning,
    the Omega/end,
    means that I am your all-in-all.
Do you want to stay
    an Alpha person—
    always at the starting line of faith?
    That is a safe place—
    where you say you believe Me,
    where you champion truth,
    but you don't move.

Move, I say!
    Feel the wind of trials and
    victories in Me.
I am the Finisher, the Omega.
Lift your eyes from the starting line
    and focus on all that lies before you—
on the intelligent golden faith
    awaiting you at the finish.

Learn of me; digest My Word,
    always in communion with Me.
I am your health, your energy:
    I bring you to a "finish"
    that is not the end of all things;
    not a place where you collapse,
    emptied out, done.
It is the place where you
    allow Me freely
    to live through you.

My finish means new development,
    new discoveries,
    new victories,
    new holy charges.
My dearest and most effective servants
    are those who move
    in "finished" faith.

Marie Chapian

APPLICATION

As you read about the awesome power and greatness of God, the I AM, fear seems to be an appropriate response, doesn't it? Yet when John fell down in fear before God, God gently and compassionately reached out to him and told him what he was to do (Rev. 1:17–20). What is the great I AM moving you to do today?

WEEKEND:

Repent and Regain Your Love for Christ

Revelation 2:1–17

NEW TESTAMENT READING

To the Church in Ephesus

Write this to the angel of the church in Ephesus:

"The One who holds the seven stars in his right hand and walks among the seven golden lampstands says this: I know what you do, how you work hard and never give up. I know you do not put up with the false teachings of evil people. You have tested those who say they are apostles but really are not, and you found they are liars. You have patience and have suffered troubles for my name and have not given up.

"But I have this against you: You have left the love you had in the beginning. So remember where you were before you fell. Change your hearts and do what you did at first. If you do not change, I will come to you and will take away your lampstand from its place. But there is something you do that is right: You hate what the Nicolaitans do, as much as I.

"Every person who has ears should listen to what the Spirit says to the churches. To those who win the victory I will give the right to eat the fruit from the tree of life, which is in the garden of God.

To the Church in Smyrna

Write this to the angel of the church in Smyrna:

"The One who is the First and the Last, who died and came to life again, says this: I know your troubles and that you are poor, but really you are rich! I know the bad things some people say about you. They say they are Jews, but they are not true Jews. They are a synagogue that belongs to Satan. Do not be afraid of what you are about to suffer. I tell you, the devil will put some of you in prison to test you, and you will suffer for ten days. But be faithful, even if you have to die, and I will give you the crown of life.

"Everyone who has ears should listen to what the Spirit says to the churches. Those who win the victory will not be hurt by the second death.

To the Church in Pergamum

Write this to the angel of the church in Pergamum:

"The One who has the sharp, double-edged sword says this: I know where you live. It is where Satan has his throne. But you are true to me. You did not refuse to tell about your faith in me even during the time of Antipas, my faithful witness who was killed in your city, where Satan lives.

"But I have a few things against you: You have some there who follow the teaching of Balaam. He taught Balak how to cause the people of Israel to sin by eating food offered to idols and by taking part in sexual sins. You also have some who follow the teaching of the Nicolaitans. So change your hearts and lives. If you do not, I will come to you quickly and fight against them with the sword that comes out of my mouth.

"Everyone who has ears should listen to what the Spirit says to the churches.

"I will give some of the hidden manna to everyone who wins the victory. I will also give to each one who wins the victory a white stone with a new name written on it. No one knows this new name except the one who receives it."

OLD TESTAMENT READING

Jeremiah Delivers a Message of Repentance

The LORD spoke his word to me, saying: "Go and speak to the people of Jerusalem, saying: This is what the LORD says:

'I remember how faithful you were to
  me when you were a young
  nation.
You loved me like a young bride.
You followed me through the desert,
  a land that had never been planted.
The people of Israel were holy to the
  LORD,
  like the first fruits from his harvest.
Those who tried to hurt Israel were
  judged guilty.

Disasters struck them,'" says the LORD.

Hear the word of the LORD, family of
	Jacob,
	all you family groups of Israel.
This is what the LORD says:
"I was fair to your ancestors,
	so why did they turn away from me?
Your ancestors worshiped useless idols
	and became useless themselves.
Your ancestors didn't say,
	'Where is the LORD who brought us
		out of Egypt?
He led us through the desert,
	through a dry and rocky land,
through a dark and dangerous land.
	He led us where no one travels or
		lives.'
I brought you into a fertile land
	so you could eat its fruit and produce.
But you came and made my land
		unclean;
	you made it a hateful place.
The priests didn't ask,
	'Where is the LORD?'
The people who know the teachings
		didn't know me.
The leaders turned against me.
The prophets prophesied in the name
		of Baal
	and worshiped useless idols.

"So now I will again tell what I have
		against you," says the LORD.
	"And I will tell what I have against
		your grandchildren."
						Jeremiah 2:1–9

---

*A few years ago, in a commencement ad-
dress at Harvard University, Alexander
Solzhenitsyn tried to summarize the root
problem facing capitalism and Marxism. He
said that the trouble with both systems is that
men have forgotten God. One system does it
by its materialist philosophy; the other system
by its materialist economy.*

*But "the sin of forgetting God" is not just
the sin of economics and governments. It can
be the sin of religion as well. Religious people
forget God by setting up a religious system in
His place.*

*Stephen was up against such a system in
Acts 7. Stephen charged that the religion of
Jerusalem had turned bad. The supreme court
of that city did not take Stephen's words
lightly. They were furious. They tried to silence him by running him out of town, and
finally they killed him by stoning. Stephen's
hot piety was a threat to the council's cold
religion.*

*A fire dies unless it is fed. The most natu-
ral thing in this world is for a person to lose
his zeal, fervor, and drive. . . .*

*Each of us forgets too soon. We all have
the inherent tendency to drift from God.*

*The constant call of the Bible is to be on
guard—to remember! Continually we are told
to turn around, to repent, to draw near to
God and submit to Him. . . .*

*The first lesson we must learn is the one
Stephen tried to teach the Sanhedrin: "The
Most High does not dwell in houses [or
structures, or systems] made by human
hands" (v. 48). He is God, Maker of heaven
and earth, Alpha and Omega. He is the One
to whom every man shall one day give account.*

*The second lesson that Stephen preached,
by his words and life, is that God wants a
personal relationship with His people. He does
not want a system or a dead religion. He
wants you. He wants to be your God and your
friend. He wants a partnership with His
creatures. He wants them to love Him and
enjoy Him forever.*

						George Sweeting

---

*How much does God treasure the faithful
love of his followers? What does he promise
to those who love him faithfully? What is his
warning to those who forsake him? In what
ways have you forsaken God? How will you
regain your love for him?*

MONDAY:

God Calls Us to Get Rid of Sin and Walk with Him

Revelation 2:18—3:6

To the Church in Thyatira

*W*rite this to the angel of the church in Thyatira:

"The Son of God, who has eyes that blaze like fire and feet like shining bronze, says this: I know what you do. I know about your love, your faith, your service, and your patience. I know that you are doing more now than you did at first.

But I have this against you: You let that woman Jezebel spread false teachings. She says she is a prophetess, but by her teaching she leads my people to take part in sexual sins and to eat food that is offered to idols. I have given her time to change her heart and turn away from her sin, but she does not want to change. So I will throw her on a bed of suffering. And all those who take part in adultery with her will suffer greatly if they do not turn away from the wrongs she does. I will also kill her followers. Then all the churches will know I am the One who searches hearts and minds, and I will repay each of you for what you have done.

"But others of you in Thyatira have not followed her teaching and have not learned what some call Satan's deep secrets. I say to you that I will not put any other load on you. Only continue in your loyalty until I come.

"I will give power over the nations to everyone who wins the victory and continues to be obedient to me until the end.

'You will rule over them with an iron rod,
as when pottery is broken into
pieces.' *Psalm 2:9*

This is the same power I received from my Father. I will also give him the morning star. Everyone who has ears should listen to what the Spirit says to the churches.

To the Church in Sardis

*W*rite this to the angel of the church in Sardis:

"The One who has the seven spirits and the seven stars says this: I know what you do. People say that you are alive, but really you are dead. Wake up! Make yourselves stronger before what you have left dies completely. I have found that what you are doing is less than what my God wants. So do not forget what you have received and heard. Obey it, and change your hearts and lives. So you must wake up, or I will come like a thief, and you will not know when I will come to you. But you have a few there in Sardis who have kept their clothes unstained, so they will walk with me and will wear white clothes, because they are worthy. Those who win the victory will be dressed in white clothes like them. And I will not erase their names from the book of life, but I will say they belong to me before my Father and before his angels. Everyone who has ears should listen to what the Spirit says to the churches."

God Expects His People to Walk in Obedience to Him

*N*ow, Israel, this is what the LORD your God wants you to do: Respect the LORD your God, and do what he has told you to do. Love him. Serve the LORD your God with your whole being.

Deuteronomy 10:12

*T*oday you have said that the LORD is your God, and you have promised to do what he wants you to do—to keep his rules, commands, and laws. You have said you will obey him. And today the LORD has said that you are his very own people, as he has promised you. But you must obey his commands.

Deuteronomy 26:17–18

God Expects His People to Get Rid of the Sin Among Them

*P*rophets or those who tell the future with dreams might come to you and say they will show you a miracle or a sign. The miracle or sign might even happen, and then they might say, "Let's serve other gods" (gods you have not known) "and let's worship them." But you must not listen to those prophets or dreamers. The LORD your God is testing you, to find out if you love him with your whole being. Serve only the LORD your God. Respect him, keep his commands, and obey him. Serve him and be loyal to him. The prophets or dreamers must be killed, because they said you should turn against the LORD your God, who brought you out of Egypt and saved you from the land where you were slaves. They tried to turn you from doing what the LORD your God commanded you to do. You must get rid of the evil among you.

Deuteronomy 13:1–5

A man or woman in one of the towns the LORD gave you might be found doing something evil and breaking the Agreement. Take the man or woman who has done the evil thing to the city gates and throw stones at that person until he dies. There must be two or three witnesses that it is true before the person is put to death; if there is only one witness, the person should not be put to death. The witnesses must be the first to throw stones at the person, and then everyone else will follow. You must get rid of the evil among you.

Deuteronomy 17:2, 5–7

*I*f a man is found having sexual relations with another man's wife, both the woman and the man who had sexual relations with her must die. Get rid of this evil from Israel.

Deuteronomy 22:22

God Punishes Those Who Do Not Change Their Ways

*G*od protects me like a shield;
  he saves those whose hearts are
    right.
God judges by what is right,
  and God is always ready to punish
    the wicked.
If they do not change their lives,
  God will sharpen his sword;
  he will string his bow and take aim.
He has prepared his deadly weapons;
  he has made his flaming arrows.

Psalm 7:10–13

*T*he older I get and the better acquainted I am with Christ, the more I'm aware of His insistence on holiness. This seems to be a matter about which He's not open to negotiation even in the slightest.

I guess somebody could consider bringing up this subject for discussion, "Ah, Jesus, I feel You're a bit too stubborn on this righteousness issue. I mean, I figure I've made some pretty big concessions Your way. On the matter of this one pet sin, couldn't You compromise a little? Accommodate me? Maybe 3 or 4 percent darkness allowable, and all the rest light?"

I warn you, the Lord won't budge even one millimeter. . . .

The absolute truth is: Anyone who wants to be close friends with Christ needs to achieve this victory-over-sin mindset, needs to learn to keep short accounts with God, needs to refuse to allow sins of long standing to go unconfessed day after day, week after week, even year after year. . . .

The hour must come when the church as a body and the individuals who compose the corporate entity reach for holiness. We must ask God for determination to overcome sin; we must pray for conviction for our unrighteousness. We must understand that we will never experience that overwhelming sense of the presence of Christ if we are not intent on striving to be 100 percent light-walkers.

David Mains

*W*hat attitude do these readings say God's people must have toward sin? What action does he require? What does God promise to those who win the victory? How determined are you to overcome the sin in your life?

TUESDAY:

God Saves and Honors Those Who Follow Him Faithfully

Revelation 3:7—4:5

To the Church in Philadelphia

Write this to the angel of the church in Philadelphia:

"This is what the One who is holy and true, who holds the key of David, says. When he opens a door, no one can close it. And when he closes it, no one can open it. I know what you do. I have put an open door before you, which no one can close. I know you have a little strength, but you have obeyed my teaching and were not afraid to speak my name. Those in the synagogue that belongs to Satan say they are Jews, but they are not true Jews; they are liars. I will make them come before you and bow at your feet, and they will know that I have loved you. You have obeyed my teaching about not giving up your faith. So I will keep you from the time of trouble that will come to the whole world to test those who live on earth.

"I am coming soon. Continue strong in your faith so no one will take away your crown. I will make those who win the victory pillars in the temple of my God, and they will never have to leave it. I will write on them the name of my God and the name of the city of my God, the new Jerusalem, that comes down out of heaven from my God. I will also write on them my new name. Everyone who has ears should listen to what the Spirit says to the churches.

To the Church in Laodicea

Write this to the angel of the church in Laodicea:

"The Amen, the faithful and true witness, the beginning of all God has made, says this: I know what you do, that you are not hot or cold. I wish that you were hot or cold! But because you are lukewarm—neither hot, nor cold—I am ready to spit you out of my mouth. You say, 'I am rich, and I have

become wealthy and do not need anything.' But you do not know that you are really miserable, pitiful, poor, blind, and naked. I advise you to buy from me gold made pure in fire so you can be truly rich. Buy from me white clothes so you can be clothed and so you can cover your shameful nakedness. Buy from me medicine to put on your eyes so you can truly see.

"I correct and punish those whom I love. So be eager to do right, and change your hearts and lives. Here I am! I stand at the door and knock. If you hear my voice and open the door, I will come in and eat with you, and you will eat with me.

"Those who win the victory will sit with me on my throne in the same way that I won the victory and sat down with my Father on his throne. Everyone who has ears should listen to what the Spirit says to the churches."

John Sees Heaven

After the vision of these things I looked, and there before me was an open door in heaven. And the same voice that spoke to me before, that sounded like a trumpet, said, "Come up here, and I will show you what must happen after this." Immediately I was in the Spirit, and before me was a throne in heaven, and someone was sitting on it. The One who sat on the throne looked like precious stones, like jasper and carnelian. All around the throne was a rainbow the color of an emerald. Around the throne there were twenty-four other thrones with twenty-four elders sitting on them. They were dressed in white and had golden crowns on their heads. Lightning flashes and noises and thundering came from the throne. Before the throne seven lamps were burning, which are the seven spirits of God.

At that time I will call for my servant Eliakim son of Hilkiah. I will take your robe and put it on him and give him your belt. I will hand over to him the important job you have, and he will be like a father to the people of Jerusalem and the family of Judah. I will put the key to the house of David around his neck. If he opens a door, no one will be able to close it; if he closes a door, no one will be able to open it. He will be like an honored chair in his father's house. I will make him strong like a peg that is hammered into a strong board. All the honored and important things of his family will depend on him; all the adults and little children will depend on him. They will be like bowls and jars hanging on him.

"At that time," says the LORD All-Powerful, "the peg hammered into the strong board will weaken. It will break and fall, and everything hanging on it will be destroyed." The LORD says this.

Isaiah 22:20–25

The Horror of God's Time of Trouble

*T*he LORD's day of judging is coming
    soon;
  it is near and coming fast.
The cry will be very sad on the day of
    the LORD;
  even soldiers will cry.
That day will be a day of anger,
  a day of terror and trouble,
a day of destruction and ruin,
  a day of darkness and gloom,
  a day of clouds and blackness,
a day of alarms and battle cries."

Zephaniah 1:14–16a

God Will Save and Honor His People

*A*t that time Michael, the great prince who protects your people, will stand up. There will be a time of much trouble, the worst time since nations have been on earth, but your people will be saved. Everyone whose name is written in God's book will be saved. Many people who have already died will live again. Some of them will wake up to have life forever, but some will wake up to find shame and disgrace forever. The wise people will shine like the brightness of the sky. Those who teach others to live right will shine like stars forever and ever.

Daniel 12:1–3

*T*he LORD says, "Whoever loves me, I will save.
I will protect those who know me.

They will call to me, and I will answer
    them.
  I will be with them in trouble;
  I will rescue them and honor them.
I will give them a long, full life,
  and they will see how I can save."

Psalm 91:14–16

---

*R*ay *Stedman tells the story of an old missionary couple who had been working in Africa for many years and were returning to New York City to retire. With no pension and broken in health, they were discouraged, fearful of the future.*

They happened to be booked on the same ship as Teddy Roosevelt, who was returning from a big-game hunting expedition. They watched the passengers trying to glimpse the great man, the crew fussing over him. . . .

At the dock in New York a band was waiting to greet the President. . . . But the missionary couple slipped off the ship unnoticed.

That night, in a cheap flat they found on the East Side, the man's spirit broke. He said to his wife, "I can't take this; God is not treating us fairly." His wife suggested he go in the bedroom and tell the Lord.

A short time later he came out of the bedroom with a face completely changed. His wife asked, "Dear, what happened?"

"The Lord settled it with me," he said. "I told him how bitter I was that the President should receive this tremendous homecoming, when no one met us as we returned home. And when I finished, it seemed as though the Lord put his hand on my shoulder and simply said, 'But you're not home yet!'"

Donald McCullough

APPLICATION

*T*o *whom does Jesus promise salvation? What kind of a 'homecoming' does he promise to those who belong to him? Ask God to help you, like the old missionary, keep perspective on what is to come!*

WEDNESDAY:

A Glimpse of Heaven's Holiness

Revelation 4:6—6:2

*A*lso before the throne there was something that looked like a sea of glass, clear like crystal.

In the center and around the throne were four living creatures with eyes all over them, in front and in back. The first living creature was like a lion. The second was like a calf. The third had a face like a man. The fourth was like a flying eagle. Each of these four living creatures had six wings and was covered all over with eyes, inside and out. Day and night they never stop saying:

"Holy, holy, holy is the Lord God
　　Almighty.
　　He was, he is, and he is coming."

These living creatures give glory, honor, and thanks to the One who sits on the throne, who lives forever and ever. Then the twenty-four elders bow down before the One who sits on the throne, and they worship him who lives forever and ever. They put their crowns down before the throne and say:

"You are worthy, our Lord and God,
　　to receive glory and honor and power,
　because you made all things.
　　Everything existed and was made,
　　because you wanted it."

Then I saw a scroll in the right hand of the One sitting on the throne. The scroll had writing on both sides and was kept closed with seven seals. And I saw a powerful angel calling in a loud voice, "Who is worthy to break the seals and open the scroll?" But there was no one in heaven or on earth or under the earth who could open the scroll or look inside it. I cried hard because there was no one who was worthy to open the scroll or look inside. But one of the elders said to me, "Do not cry! The Lion from the tribe of Judah, David's descendant, has won the victory so that he is able to open the scroll and its seven seals."

Then I saw a Lamb standing in the center of the throne and in the middle of the four living creatures and the elders. The Lamb looked as if he had been killed. He had seven horns and seven eyes, which are the seven spirits of God that were sent into all the world. The Lamb came and took the scroll from the right hand of the One sitting on the throne. When he took the scroll, the four living creatures and the twenty-four elders bowed down before the Lamb. Each one of them had a harp and golden bowls full of incense, which are the prayers of God's holy people. And they all sang a new song to the Lamb:

"You are worthy to take the scroll
　　and to open its seals,
　because you were killed,
　　and with the blood of your death you
　　　　bought people for God
　　from every tribe, language, people,
　　　　and nation.
You made them to be a kingdom of
　　priests for our God,
　　and they will rule on the earth."

Then I looked, and I heard the voices of many angels around the throne, and the four living creatures, and the elders. There were thousands and thousands of angels, saying in a loud voice:

"The Lamb who was killed is worthy
　　to receive power, wealth, wisdom, and
　　　　strength,
　honor, glory, and praise!"

Then I heard all creatures in heaven and on earth and under the earth and in the sea saying:

"To the One who sits on the throne
　　and to the Lamb
　be praise and honor and glory and
　　　　power
　　forever and ever."

The four living creatures said, "Amen," and the elders bowed down and worshiped.

Then I watched while the Lamb opened the first of the seven seals. I heard one of the four living creatures say with a voice like thunder, "Come!" I looked, and there before me was a white horse. The rider on the horse held a bow, and he was given a crown, and he rode out, determined to win the victory.

Two of God's Prophets See
a Vision of God in Heaven

*I*n the year that King Uzziah died, I saw the Lord sitting on a very high throne. His long robe filled the Temple. Heavenly creatures of fire stood above him. Each creature had six wings: It used two wings to cover its face, two wings to cover its feet, and two wings for flying. Each creature was calling to the others:

"Holy, holy, holy is the LORD All-Powerful. His glory fills the whole earth."

Their calling caused the frame around the door to shake, as the Temple filled with smoke.

I said, "Oh, no! I will be destroyed. I am not pure, and I live among people who are not pure, but I have seen the King, the LORD All-Powerful."

One of the heavenly creatures used a pair of tongs to take a hot coal from the altar. Then he flew to me with the hot coal in his hand. The creature touched my mouth with the hot coal and said, "Look, your guilt is taken away, because this hot coal has touched your lips. Your sin is taken away."

Then I heard the Lord's voice, saying, "Whom can I send? Who will go for us?"

So I said, "Here I am. Send me!"

Isaiah 6:1–8

*T*he LORD spoke his word to Ezekiel son of Buzi in the land of the Babylonians by the Kebar River. There he felt the power of the LORD.

When I looked, I saw a stormy wind coming from the north. There was a great cloud with a bright light around it and fire flashing out of it. Something that looked like glowing metal was in the center of the fire. Inside the cloud was what looked like four living creatures, who were shaped like humans, but each of them had four faces and four wings.

Now, over the heads of the living creatures was something like a dome that sparkled like ice and was frightening.

Now above the dome there was something that looked like a throne. It looked like a sapphire gem. And on the throne was a shape like a human. Then I noticed that from the waist up the shape looked like glowing metal with fire inside. From the waist down it looked like fire, and a bright light was all around. The surrounding glow looked like the rainbow in the clouds on a rainy day. It seemed to look like the glory of the LORD. So when I saw it, I bowed facedown on the ground and heard a voice speaking.

Ezekiel 1:3–6, 22, 26–28

I N S I G H T S

*F*or this one moment in time, the old apostle was ushered into the presence of the Mystery behind the universe. There is no way to describe God. John could only describe the response to God. . . . Even as he stood before Him, God remained a mystery to John and to us—the Mystery who was and is and will always be, the Mystery behind our creation and our preservation, the Mystery worthy of our glory and honor and power.

The risen Christ had called John into the presence of God so that the old man could know, and through him we could know, this fact: Behind the universe there is a Power worthy of our praise and of our trust. In spite of rumors to the contrary, we are not creatures abandoned on a planet spinning madly through the universe. . . . We are the children of a great and wonderful God who even now sits in power accomplishing His purposes in His creation.

Billy Graham

A P P L I C A T I O N

*R*eread each detail John uses to describe heaven's holiness. Imagine the sights, the sounds, and magnitude of God's powerful holiness! Praise God for his holiness. Seek to live in his holiness.

THURSDAY:

Who Can Stand Against the Lord's Anger?

Revelation 6:3—7:8

NEW TESTAMENT READING

*W*hen the Lamb opened the second seal, I heard the second living creature say, "Come!" Then another horse came out, a red one. Its rider was given power to take away peace from the earth and to make people kill each other, and he was given a big sword.

When the Lamb opened the third seal, I heard the third living creature say, "Come!" I looked, and there before me was a black horse, and its rider held a pair of scales in his hand. Then I heard something that sounded like a voice coming from the middle of the four living creatures. The voice said, "A quart of wheat for a day's pay, and three quarts of barley for a day's pay, and do not damage the olive oil and wine!"

When the Lamb opened the fourth seal, I heard the voice of the fourth living creature say, "Come!" I looked, and there before me was a pale horse. Its rider was named death, and Hades was following close behind him. They were given power over a fourth of the earth to kill people by war, by starvation, by disease, and by the wild animals of the earth.

When the Lamb opened the fifth seal, I saw under the altar the souls of those who had been killed because they were faithful to the word of God and to the message they had received. These souls shouted in a loud voice, "Holy and true Lord, how long until you judge the people of the earth and punish them for killing us?" Then each one of them was given a white robe and was told to wait a short time longer. There were still some of their fellow servants and brothers and sisters in the service of Christ who must be killed as they were. They had to wait until all of this was finished.

Then I watched while the Lamb opened the sixth seal, and there was a great earthquake. The sun became black like rough black cloth, and the whole moon became red like blood. And the stars in the sky fell to the earth like figs falling from a fig tree when the wind blows. The sky disappeared as a scroll when it is rolled up, and every mountain and island was moved from its place.

Then the kings of the earth, the rulers, the generals, the rich people, the powerful people, the slaves, and the free people hid themselves in caves and in the rocks on the mountains. They called to the mountains and the rocks, "Fall on us. Hide us from the face of the One who sits on the throne and from the anger of the Lamb! The great day for their anger has come, and who can stand against it?"

The 144,000 People of Israel

*A*fter the vision of these things I saw four angels standing at the four corners of the earth. The angels were holding the four winds of the earth to keep them from blowing on the land or on the sea or on any tree. Then I saw another angel coming up from the east who had the seal of the living God. And he called out in a loud voice to the four angels to whom God had given power to harm the earth and the sea. He said to them, "Do not harm the land or the sea or the trees until we mark with a sign the foreheads of the people who serve our God." Then I heard how many people were marked with the sign. There were one hundred forty-four thousand from every tribe of the people of Israel.

From the tribe of Judah twelve thousand were marked with the sign,
from the tribe of Reuben twelve thousand,
from the tribe of Gad twelve thousand,
from the tribe of Asher twelve thousand,
from the tribe of Naphtali twelve thousand,
from the tribe of Manasseh twelve thousand,
from the tribe of Simeon twelve thousand,
from the tribe of Levi twelve thousand,
from the tribe of Issachar twelve thousand,
from the tribe of Zebulun twelve thousand,

from the tribe of Joseph twelve thousand,
and from the tribe of Benjamin twelve
thousand were marked with the
sign.

God Declares His Anger
Against Nineveh

The LORD is a jealous God who punishes;
the LORD punishes and is filled with
anger.
The LORD punishes those who are
against him,
and he stays angry with his enemies.
The LORD does not become angry
quickly,
and his power is great.
The LORD will not let the guilty go
unpunished.
Where the LORD goes, there are
whirlwinds and storms,
and the clouds are the dust beneath
his feet.
He speaks to the sea and makes it dry;
he dries up all the rivers.
The areas of Bashan and Carmel dry up,
and the flowers of Lebanon dry up.
The mountains shake in front of him,
and the hills melt.
The earth trembles when he comes;
the world and all who live in it shake
with fear.
No one can stay alive when he is angry;
no one can survive his strong anger.
His anger is poured out like fire;
the rocks are smashed by him.

Nahum 1:2–6

God Pours Out His Anger
Against Jerusalem

The LORD All-Powerful has a certain
day planned
when he will punish the proud and
those who brag,
and they will no longer be important.
He will bring down the tall cedar trees
from Lebanon

and the great oak trees of Bashan,
all the tall mountains
and the high hills,
every tall tower
and every high, strong wall,
all the trading ships
and the beautiful ships.
At that time proud people will be made
humble,
and they will bow low with shame.
At that time only the LORD will be
praised,
but all the idols will be gone.

People will run to caves in the rocky
cliffs
and will dig holes and hide in the
ground
from the anger of the LORD
and his great power,
when he stands to shake the earth.

Isaiah 2:12–19

*The Sixth Seal Judgment (Rev. 6:12–17)
. . . unleashes universal havoc on the
earth. . . .*

*These judgments will produce terror in the
hearts of all living men. Their hearts will be
filled with fear—not primarily because of the
physical disturbances or the awful wars and
pestilences, but because they will see God on
His throne. Men will plead to be hidden "from
the face of Him that sitteth on the throne, and
from the wrath of the Lamb." They will go to
any length to avoid facing their Creator and
Judge, even to seeking death under the rocks
and mountains in which they will try to hide.
All classes of people (v. 15) will be affected.
As has been true throughout history, there will
be no general or mass turning to God in repentance, but only a turning from God's face.*

Charles Ryrie

*What does God promise to those who are
guilty of sin? When their time of punishment
comes, how can they escape and who can save
them? Pray that you will be faithful so you
will not hide from God's presence.*

FRIDAY:

The Glorious Reward of Those Washed Clean by the Blood of the Lamb

Revelation 7:9—8:13

The Great Crowd Worships God

*A*fter the vision of these things I looked, and there was a great number of people, so many that no one could count them. They were from every nation, tribe, people, and language of the earth. They were all standing before the throne and before the Lamb, wearing white robes and holding palm branches in their hands. They were shouting in a loud voice, "Salvation belongs to our God, who sits on the throne, and to the Lamb." All the angels were standing around the throne and the elders and the four living creatures. They all bowed down on their faces before the throne and worshiped God, saying, "Amen! Praise, glory, wisdom, thanks, honor, power, and strength belong to our God forever and ever. Amen!"

Then one of the elders asked me, "Who are these people dressed in white robes? Where did they come from?"

I answered, "You know, sir."

And the elder said to me, "These are the people who have come out of the great distress. They have washed their robes and made them white in the blood of the Lamb. Because of this, they are before the throne of God. They worship him day and night in his temple. And the One who sits on the throne will be present with them. Those people will never be hungry again, and they will never be thirsty again. The sun will not hurt them, and no heat will burn them, because the Lamb at the center of the throne will be their shepherd. He will lead them to springs of water that give life. And God will wipe away every tear from their eyes."

The Seventh Seal

*W*hen the Lamb opened the seventh seal, there was silence in heaven for about half an hour. And I saw the seven angels who stand before God and to whom were given seven trumpets.

Another angel came and stood at the altar, holding a golden pan for incense. He was given much incense to offer with the prayers of all God's holy people. The angel put this offering on the golden altar before the throne. The smoke from the incense went up from the angel's hand to God with the prayers of God's people. Then the angel filled the incense pan with fire from the altar and threw it on the earth, and there were flashes of lightning, thunder and loud noises, and an earthquake.

The Seven Angels and Trumpets

*T*hen the seven angels who had the seven trumpets prepared to blow them.

The first angel blew his trumpet, and hail and fire mixed with blood were poured down on the earth. And a third of the earth, and all the green grass, and a third of the trees were burned up.

Then the second angel blew his trumpet, and something that looked like a big mountain, burning with fire, was thrown into the sea. And a third of the sea became blood, a third of the living things in the sea died, and a third of the ships were destroyed.

Then the third angel blew his trumpet, and a large star, burning like a torch, fell from the sky. It fell on a third of the rivers and on the springs of water. The name of the star is Wormwood. And a third of all the water became bitter, and many people died from drinking the water that was bitter.

Then the fourth angel blew his trumpet, and a third of the sun, and a third of the moon, and a third of the stars were struck. So a third of them became dark, and a third of the day was without light, and also the night.

While I watched, I heard an eagle that was flying high in the air cry out in a loud voice, "Trouble! Trouble! Trouble for those who live on the earth because of the remaining sounds of the trumpets that the other three angels are about to blow!"

Promises of God's Reward

*T*he LORD All-Powerful will prepare a
feast
on this mountain for all people.
It will be a feast with all the best food
and wine,
the finest meat and wine.
On this mountain God will destroy
the veil that covers all nations,
the veil that stretches over all peoples;
he will destroy death forever.
The Lord GOD will wipe away every tear
from every face.
He will take away the shame of his
people from the earth.
The LORD has spoken.

At that time people will say,
"Our God is doing this!
We have waited for him, and he has
come to save us.
This is the LORD. We waited for him,
so we will rejoice and be happy when
he saves us."

Isaiah 25:6–9

*T*he LORD makes me very happy;
all that I am rejoices in my God.
He has covered me with clothes of
salvation
and wrapped me with a coat of
goodness,
like a bridegroom dressed for his
wedding,
like a bride dressed in jewels.

Isaiah 61:10

*L*ook up to the heavens.
Look around you at the earth below.
The skies will disappear like clouds of
smoke.
The earth will become useless like
old clothes,
and its people will die like flies.
But my salvation will continue forever,
and my goodness will never end.

Isaiah 51:6

*T*hose who are still living in Jerusalem will
be called holy; their names are recorded
among the living in Jerusalem. The Lord

will wash away the filth from the women of
Jerusalem. He will wash the bloodstains out
of Jerusalem and clean the city with the
spirit of fairness and the spirit of fire. Then
the LORD will cover Mount Zion and the
people who meet there with a cloud of
smoke during the day and with a bright,
flaming fire at night. There will be a covering over every person. This covering will
protect the people from the heat of the sun
and will provide a safe place to hide from
the storm and rain.

Isaiah 4:3–6

INSIGHTS

*H*ow *many achievements and how many
blessings for men the Scripture ascribes to the
power of the Blood of the Lord Jesus! By the
power of His Blood peace is made between
man and God. By its power there is forgiveness of sins and eternal life for all who put
their faith in the Lord Jesus. By the power of
His Blood Satan is overcome. By its power
there is continual cleansing from all sin for
us. By the power of His Blood we may be set
free from the tyranny of an evil conscience to
serve the living God. By its infinite power
with God the most unworthy have liberty to
enter the Holy of Holies of God's presence and
live there all the day. . . .
. . . That which gives the precious Blood
its power with God for men is the lamb-like
disposition of the One who shed it. . . . The
title "the Lamb" so frequently given to the Lord
Jesus in Scripture is first of all descriptive of
His work—that of being a sacrifice for our
sin. . . . But the title "the Lamb" has a
deeper meaning. It describes His character.
He is the Lamb in that He is meek and lowly
in heart, gentle and unresisting, and all the
time surrendering His own will to the Father's
for the blessing and saving of men.*

Roy and Revel Hession

ACTION POINT

*W*ho *is the Lamb of God? What does the
blood of the Lamb do? List the ways God will
bless those who are washed clean by the blood
of the Lamb. Pray now and thank him for
such a glorious salvation!*

WEEKEND:

God Sends Punishment in Order to Turn People from Sin

Revelation 9:1—10:4

N E W   T E S T A M E N T   R E A D I N G

*T*hen the fifth angel blew his trumpet, and I saw a star fall from the sky to the earth. The star was given the key to the deep hole that leads to the bottomless pit. Then it opened up the hole that leads to the bottomless pit, and smoke came up from the hole like smoke from a big furnace. Then the sun and sky became dark because of the smoke from the hole. Then locusts came down to the earth out of the smoke, and they were given the power to sting like scorpions. They were told not to harm the grass on the earth or any plant or tree. They could harm only the people who did not have the sign of God on their foreheads. These locusts were not given the power to kill anyone, but to cause pain to the people for five months. And the pain they felt was like the pain a scorpion gives when it stings someone. During those days people will look for a way to die, but they will not find it. They will want to die, but death will run away from them.

The locusts looked like horses prepared for battle. On their heads they wore what looked like crowns of gold, and their faces looked like human faces. Their hair was like women's hair, and their teeth were like lions' teeth. Their chests looked like iron breastplates, and the sound of their wings was like the noise of many horses and chariots hurrying into battle. The locusts had tails with stingers like scorpions, and in their tails was their power to hurt people for five months. The locusts had a king who was the angel of the bottomless pit. His name in the Hebrew language is Abaddon and in the Greek language is Apollyon.

The first trouble is past; there are still two other troubles that will come.

Then the sixth angel blew his trumpet, and I heard a voice coming from the horns on the golden altar that is before God. The voice said to the sixth angel who had the trumpet, "Free the four angels who are tied at the great river Euphrates." And they let loose the four angels who had been kept ready for this hour and day and month and year so they could kill a third of all people on the earth. I heard how many troops on horses were in their army—two hundred million.

The horses and their riders I saw in the vision looked like this: They had breastplates that were fiery red, dark blue, and yellow like sulfur. The heads of the horses looked like heads of lions, with fire, smoke, and sulfur coming out of their mouths. A third of all the people on earth were killed by these three terrible disasters coming out of the horses' mouths: the fire, the smoke, and the sulfur. The horses' power was in their mouths and in their tails; their tails were like snakes with heads, and with them they hurt people.

The other people who were not killed by these terrible disasters still did not change their hearts and turn away from what they had made with their own hands. They did not stop worshiping demons and idols made of gold, silver, bronze, stone, and wood—things that cannot see or hear or walk. These people did not change their hearts and turn away from murder or evil magic, from their sexual sins or stealing.

The Angel and the Small Scroll

*T*hen I saw another powerful angel coming down from heaven dressed in a cloud with a rainbow over his head. His face was like the sun, and his legs were like pillars of fire. The angel was holding a small scroll open in his hand. He put his right foot on the sea and his left foot on the land. Then he shouted loudly like the roaring of a lion. And when he shouted, the voices of seven thunders spoke. When the seven thunders spoke, I started to write. But I heard a voice from heaven say, "Keep hidden what the seven thunders said, and do not write them down."

O L D   T E S T A M E N T   R E A D I N G

*B*low the trumpet in Jerusalem;
    shout a warning on my holy mountain.

Let all the people who live in the land
   shake with fear,
      because the Lord's day of judging is
         coming;
      it is near.
It will be a dark, gloomy day,
   cloudy and black.
Like the light at sunrise,
   a great and powerful army will
      spread over the mountains.
There has never been anything like it
   before,
      and there will never be anything like
         it again.

In front of them a fire destroys;
   in back of them a flame burns.
The land in front of them is like the
   garden of Eden;
      the land behind them is like an
         empty desert.
Nothing will escape from them.

When they see them, nations shake
   with fear,
      and everyone's face becomes pale.

Before them, earth and sky shake.
The sun and the moon become dark,
   and the stars stop shining.
The Lord shouts out orders
   to his army.
His army is very large!
   Those who obey him are very strong!
The Lord's day of judging
   is an overwhelming and terrible day.
      No one can stand up against it!

The Lord says, "Even now, come back
   to me with all your heart.
Go without food, and cry and be sad."

Tearing your clothes is not enough to
   show you are sad;
      let your heart be broken.
Come back to the Lord your God,
   because he is kind and shows mercy.
He doesn't become angry quickly,
   and he has great love.
He can change his mind about doing
   harm.

Joel 2:1–3, 6, 10–13

*S*o, say this to the people of Judah and
those who live in Jerusalem: 'This is what
the Lord says: I am preparing disaster for
you and making plans against you. So stop
doing evil. Change your ways and do what
is right.' But the people of Judah will answer, 'It won't do any good to try! We will
continue to do what we want. Each of us will
do what his stubborn, evil heart wants!'"

Jeremiah 18:11–12

*H*ow terrible it is to witness the approach
of a tempest: to note the forewarnings of the
storm; to mark the birds of heaven as they
droop their wings; to see the cattle as they lay
their heads low in terror; to discern the face
of the sky as it groweth black, and look to the
sun which shineth not, and the heavens which
are angry and frowning! . . . And yet, sinner, this is your present position. No hot drops
have as yet fallen, but a shower of fire is coming. No terrible winds howl around you, but
God's tempest is gathering its dread artillery.
As yet the water-floods are dammed up by
mercy, but the flood-gates shall soon be
opened: the thunderbolts of God are yet in His
storehouse, but lo! the tempest hastens, and
how awful shall that moment be when God,
robed in vengeance, shall march forth in fury!
Where, where, where, O sinner, wilt thou hide
thy head, or whither wilt thou flee? O that
the hand of mercy may now lead you to Christ!
He is freely set before you in the gospel: His
riven side is the rock of shelter. Thou knowest
thy need of Him; believe in Him, cast thyself
upon Him, and then the fury shall be overpast
for ever.

Charles Spurgeon

P A U S E   F O R   R E F L E C T I O N

*W*hat is the sole reason for the horrible
punishment that is promised on God's day of
judgment? What does God want from every
person? What do you learn about God's love
from these passages?

MONDAY:
God's Prophets Are Empowered to Deliver His Message
Revelation 10:5—11:14

*T*hen the angel I saw standing on the sea and on the land raised his right hand to heaven, and he made a promise by the power of the One who lives forever and ever. He is the One who made the skies and all that is in them, the earth and all that is in it, and the sea and all that is in it. The angel promised, "There will be no more waiting! In the days when the seventh angel is ready to blow his trumpet, God's secret will be finished. This secret is the Good News God told to his servants, the prophets."

Then I heard the same voice from heaven again, saying to me: "Go and take the open scroll that is in the hand of the angel that is standing on the sea and on the land."

So I went to the angel and told him to give me the small scroll. And he said to me, "Take the scroll and eat it. It will be sour in your stomach, but in your mouth it will be sweet as honey." So I took the small scroll from the angel's hand and ate it. In my mouth it tasted sweet as honey, but after I ate it, it was sour in my stomach. Then I was told, "You must prophesy again about many peoples, nations, languages, and kings."

The Two Witnesses

I was given a measuring stick like a rod, and I was told, "Go and measure the temple of God and the altar, and count the people worshiping there. But do not measure the yard outside the temple. Leave it alone, because it has been given to those who are not God's people. And they will trample on the holy city for forty-two months. And I will give power to my two witnesses to prophesy for one thousand two hundred sixty days, and they will be dressed in rough cloth to show their sadness."

These two witnesses are the two olive trees and the two lampstands that stand before the Lord of the earth. And if anyone tries to hurt them, fire comes from their mouths and kills their enemies. And if anyone tries to hurt them in whatever way, in that same way that person will die. These witnesses have the power to stop the sky from raining during the time they are prophesying. And they have power to make the waters become blood, and they have power to send every kind of trouble to the earth as many times as they want.

When the two witnesses have finished telling their message, the beast that comes up from the bottomless pit will fight a war against them. He will defeat them and kill them. The bodies of the two witnesses will lie in the street of the great city where the Lord was killed. This city is named Sodom and Egypt, which has a spiritual meaning. Those from every race of people, tribe, language, and nation will look at the bodies of the two witnesses for three and one-half days, and they will refuse to bury them. People who live on the earth will rejoice and be happy because these two are dead. They will send each other gifts, because these two prophets brought much suffering to those who live on the earth.

But after three and one-half days, God put the breath of life into the two prophets again. They stood on their feet, and everyone who saw them became very afraid. Then the two prophets heard a loud voice from heaven saying, "Come up here!" And they went up into heaven in a cloud as their enemies watched.

In the same hour there was a great earthquake, and a tenth of the city was destroyed. Seven thousand people were killed in the earthquake, and those who did not die were very afraid and gave glory to the God of heaven.

The second trouble is finished. Pay attention: The third trouble is coming soon.

Daniel and Zechariah Have Visions of the Two Prophets of Revelation

*T*hen I, Daniel, looked, and saw two other

men. One was standing on my side of the river, and the other was standing on the far side. The man who was dressed in linen was standing over the water in the river. One of the two men spoke to him and asked, "How long will it be before these amazing things come true?"

The man dressed in linen, who stood over the water, raised his hands toward heaven. And I heard him swear by the name of God who lives forever, "It will be for three and one-half years. The power of the holy people will finally be broken, and then all these things will come true."

I heard the answer, but I did not really understand, so I asked, "Master, what will happen after all these things come true?"

He answered, "Go your way, Daniel. The message is closed up and sealed until the time of the end."

Daniel 12:5–9

*T*hen I asked the angel, "What are the two olive trees on the right and left of the lampstand?"

I also asked him, "What are the two olive branches beside the two gold pipes, from which the olive oil flows to the lamps?"

He answered, "Don't you know what they are?"

"No, sir," I said.

So he said, "They are symbols of the two who have been appointed to serve the LORD of all the earth."

Zechariah 4:11–14

God Gave Miraculous Powers to Old Testament Prophets

*T*he LORD said to Moses, "Tell Aaron: 'Take the walking stick in your hand and stretch your hand over the rivers, canals, ponds, and pools in Egypt.' The water will become blood everywhere in Egypt, both in wooden buckets and in stone jars."

So Moses and Aaron did just as the LORD had commanded. In front of the king and his officers, Aaron raised his walking stick and struck the water in the Nile River. So all the water in the Nile changed into blood.

Exodus 7:19–21

*N*ow Elijah the Tishbite was a prophet from the settlers in Gilead. "I serve the LORD, the God of Israel," Elijah said to Ahab. "As surely as the LORD lives, no rain or dew will fall during the next few years unless I command it."

1 Kings 17:1

*D*uring the third year without rain, the LORD spoke his word to Elijah: "Go and meet King Ahab, and I will soon send rain." So Elijah went to meet Ahab.

By this time there was no food in Samaria.

1 Kings 18:1–2

INSIGHTS

*D*uring the darkest ages, men have been raised up to testify against the prevailing corruption of their time, and especially the corruption of the apostate church. Their opponents have endeavored to silence their voice and blacken their character, but God has ever vindicated them and given life out of death. Always when the enemies of the truth have deemed themselves triumphant, there has been a rekindling of gospel testimony. A few years before Luther appeared, a medal was struck to commemorate the extinction of so-called heresy. Such witness-bearing as is suggested by the comparison with Zechariah's vision is fed from the heart of Christ. He is the root of the martyr line; his Spirit is the life-breath of his witnesses. All through the centuries, commonly called Christian though generally very un-Christian, there has been an unbroken succession of pure and noble souls who have stood for Jesus Christ even unto death. Let us dare to stand with them and our Lord, that he may not be ashamed of us at his coming.

F. B. Meyer

ACTION POINT

*A*t what times does God call special prophets? What powers does he give them? Who controls their fate? What has God called you to do? Pray that you will trust him to care for you and enable you to accomplish his work.

TUESDAY:

*Satan Is Defeated
by Christ's Coming*

Revelation 11:15—12:12

The Seventh Trumpet

*T*hen the seventh angel blew his trumpet. And there were loud voices in heaven, saying:

"The power to rule the world
now belongs to our Lord and his
Christ,
and he will rule forever and ever."

Then the twenty-four elders, who sit on their thrones before God, bowed down on their faces and worshiped God. They said:

"We give thanks to you, Lord God
Almighty,
who is and who was,
because you have used your great
power
and have begun to rule!
The people of the world were angry,
but your anger has come.
The time has come to judge the
dead
and to reward your servants the
prophets
and your holy people,
all who respect you, great and small.
The time has come to destroy those
who destroy the earth!"

Then God's temple in heaven was opened. The Ark that holds the agreement God gave to his people could be seen in his temple. Then there were flashes of lightning, noises, thunder, an earthquake, and a great hailstorm.

The Woman and the Dragon

*A*nd then a great wonder appeared in heaven: A woman was clothed with the sun, and the moon was under her feet, and a crown of twelve stars was on her head. She was pregnant and cried out with pain, because she was about to give birth. Then another wonder appeared in heaven: There was a giant red dragon with seven heads and seven crowns on each head. He also had ten horns. His tail swept a third of the stars out of the sky and threw them down to the earth. He stood in front of the woman who was ready to give birth so he could eat her baby as soon as it was born. Then the woman gave birth to a son who will rule all the nations with an iron rod. And her child was taken up to God and to his throne. The woman ran away into the desert to a place God prepared for her where she would be taken care of for one thousand two hundred sixty days.

Then there was a war in heaven. Michael and his angels fought against the dragon, and the dragon and his angels fought back. But the dragon was not strong enough, and he and his angels lost their place in heaven. The giant dragon was thrown down out of heaven. (He is that old snake called the devil or Satan, who tricks the whole world.) The dragon with his angels was thrown down to the earth.

Then I heard a loud voice in heaven saying:

"The salvation and the power and the
kingdom of our God
and the authority of his Christ have
now come.
The accuser of our brothers and sisters,
who accused them day and night
before our God,
has been thrown down.
And our brothers and sisters defeated
him
by the blood of the Lamb's death
and by the message they preached.
They did not love their lives so much
that they were afraid of death.
So rejoice, you heavens
and all who live there!
But it will be terrible for the earth and
the sea,
because the devil has come down to
you!
He is filled with anger,
because he knows he does not have
much time."

*W*hy are the nations so angry?

Why are the people making useless
plans?
The kings of the earth prepare to fight,
and their leaders make plans
together
against the LORD
and his appointed one.
They say, "Let's break the chains that
hold us back
and throw off the ropes that tie us
down."
But the one who sits in heaven laughs;
the Lord makes fun of them.
Then the LORD warns them
and frightens them with his anger.
He says, "I have appointed my own
king
to rule in Jerusalem on my holy
mountain, Zion."

Now I will tell you what the LORD has
declared:
He said to me, "You are my son.
Today I have become your father.
If you ask me, I will give you the nations;
all the people on earth will be yours.
You will rule over them with an iron
rod.
You will break them into pieces like
pottery."

Psalm 2:1–9

*I*n my vision at night I saw in front of
me someone who looked like a human being coming on the clouds in the sky. He
came near God, who has been alive forever,
and he was led to God. He was given authority to rule, glory, and the strength of a
king. People of every tribe, nation, and
language will serve him. His rule will last
forever, and his kingdom will never be
destroyed.

"I, Daniel, was worried. The visions that
went through my mind frightened me. I
came near one of those standing there and
asked what all this meant.

"So he told me and explained to me what
these things meant: 'The four great animals
are four kingdoms that will come from the
earth. But the holy people who belong to
the Most High God will receive the power
to rule and will have the power to rule forever, from now on.'

"As I watched, the little horn began
making war against God's holy people and
was defeating them until God, who has been
alive forever, came. He judged in favor of
the holy people who belong to the Most
High God; then the time came for them to
receive the power to rule."

Daniel 7:13–18, 21–22

---

*W*hat is this celestial conflict all about? The
fact that Michael led God's angels to victory
is significant, because Michael is identified
with the nation Israel. . . . Apparently, the
devil's hatred of Israel will spur him to make
one final assault against the throne of God,
but he will be defeated by Michael and a
heavenly host. . . .

How does this future war apply to the
church today? The same serpent who accuses
the saints in heaven also deceives . . . the
nations into thinking that the people of God
are dangerous, deluded, even destructive. . . .
God's people in every age must expect the
world's opposition, but the church can always
defeat the enemy by being faithful to Jesus
Christ. . . .

. . . Satan is not equal to God; he is not
omnipotent, omnipresent, or omniscient. His
power is limited and his tactics must fail
when God's people trust the power of the blood
and of the Word. . . .

Believers in any age or situation can rejoice in this victory, no matter how difficult
their experiences may be. Our warfare is not
against flesh and blood, but against the
spiritual forces of the wicked one; and these
have been defeated by our Saviour (Eph.
6:10ff; note also 1:15–23).

Warren Wiersbe

ACTION   POINT

*W*hat persepective do you gain on your
struggles today from this account of ultimate
struggle in heaven? Thank God he has already won the battle! Pray that you will
remain faithful to him as you fight the battles
in your life.

WEDNESDAY:

God's People Must Fight Satan with Patience and Faith

Revelation 12:13—13:18

*W*hen the dragon saw he had been thrown down to the earth, he hunted for the woman who had given birth to the son. But the woman was given the two wings of a great eagle so she could fly to the place prepared for her in the desert. There she would be taken care of for three and one-half years, away from the snake. Then the snake poured water out of its mouth like a river toward the woman so the flood would carry her away. But the earth helped the woman by opening its mouth and swallowing the river that came from the mouth of the dragon. Then the dragon was very angry at the woman, and he went off to make war against all her other children—those who obey God's commands and who have the message Jesus taught.

And the dragon stood on the seashore.

The Two Beasts

*T*hen I saw a beast coming up out of the sea. It had ten horns and seven heads, and there was a crown on each horn. A name against God was written on each head. This beast looked like a leopard, with feet like a bear's feet and a mouth like a lion's mouth. And the dragon gave the beast all of his power and his throne and great authority. One of the heads of the beast looked as if it had been killed by a wound, but this death wound was healed. Then the whole world was amazed and followed the beast. People worshiped the dragon because he had given his power to the beast. And they also worshiped the beast, asking, "Who is like the beast? Who can make war against it?"

The beast was allowed to say proud words and words against God, and it was allowed to use its power for forty-two months. It used its mouth to speak against God, against God's name, against the place where God lives, and against all those who live in heaven. It was given power to make war against God's holy people and to defeat them. It was given power over every tribe, people, language, and nation. And all who live on earth will worship the beast—all the people since the beginning of the world whose names are not written in the Lamb's book of life. The Lamb is the One who was killed.

Anyone who has ears should listen:
If you are to be a prisoner,
 then you will be a prisoner.
If you are to be killed with the sword,
 then you will be killed with the sword.
This means that God's holy people must have patience and faith.

Then I saw another beast coming up out of the earth. It had two horns like a lamb, but it spoke like a dragon. This beast stands before the first beast and uses the same power the first beast has. By this power it makes everyone living on earth worship the first beast, who had the death wound that was healed. And the second beast does great miracles so that it even makes fire come down from heaven to earth while people are watching. It fools those who live on earth by the miracles it has been given the power to do. It does these miracles to serve the first beast. The second beast orders people to make an idol to honor the first beast, the one that was wounded by the deadly sword but sprang to life again. The second beast was given power to give life to the idol of the first one so that the idol could speak. And the second beast was given power to command all who will not worship the image of the beast to be killed. The second beast also forced all people, small and great, rich and poor, free and slave, to have a mark on their right hand or on their forehead. No one could buy or sell without this mark, which is the name of the beast or the number of its name. This takes wisdom. Let the one who has understanding find the meaning of the number, which is the number of a person. Its number is six hundred sixty-six.

*A*nd he explained this to me: 'The fourth

animal is a fourth kingdom that will come on the earth. It will be different from all the other kingdoms and will destroy people all over the world. It will walk on and crush the whole earth. The ten horns are ten kings who will come from this fourth kingdom. After those ten kings are gone, another king will come. He will be different from the kings who ruled before him, and he will defeat three of the other kings. This king will speak against the Most High God, and he will hurt and kill God's holy people. He will try to change times and laws that have already been set. The holy people that belong to God will be in that king's power for three and one-half years.

"'But the court will decide what should happen. The power of the king will be taken away, and his kingdom will be completely destroyed. Then the holy people who belong to the Most High God will have the power to rule. They will rule over all the kingdoms under heaven with power and greatness, and their power to rule will last forever. People from all the other kingdoms will respect and serve them.'"

Daniel 7:23–27

*A*t the right time the king of the North will attack the king of the South again, but this time he will not be successful as he was before. Ships from the west will come and fight against the king of the North, so he will be afraid. Then he will return and show his anger against the holy agreement. He will be good to those who have stopped obeying the holy agreement.

"The king of the North will send his army to make the Temple in Jerusalem unclean. They will stop the people from offering the daily sacrifice, and then they will set up the destroying terror. The king of the North will tell lies and cause those who have not obeyed God to be ruined. But those who know God and obey him will be strong and fight back.

"Those who are wise will help the others understand what is happening. But they will be killed with swords, or burned, or taken captive, or robbed of their homes and possessions. These things will continue for many days. When the wise ones are suffering, they will get a little help, but many who join the wise ones will not help them in their time of need. Some of the wise ones will be killed. But the hard times must come so they can be made stronger and purer and without faults until the time of the end comes. Then, at the right time, the end will come."

Daniel 11:29–35

I N S I G H T S

*W*e must be entrenched in the strength of the Lord. We must be enclosed "in the power of his might," or, as one has paraphrased it, "in the energy of him, the strong." It is in vain we engage in the conflict if that preliminary condition has not been fulfilled. In earthly warfare the soldier does not provide his own means of defense or weapons of assault. So in Christian conflict our whole equipment is divinely provided for us. He gives us a position that is impregnable—strength in the Lord; an armor that is impenetrable; and a weapon that is infallible—"the sword of the Spirit." We have by faith to take that position and continually to abide in it. We have by faith to put on that armor and wear it constantly.

Evan Hopkins

ACTION POINT

*W*hat difficulties will God's people face in the end times? How must they respond to Satan? What are their weapons, and what must they be prepared to give up? What will be accomplished by those who remain strong? Pray that your faith will be purified through the battles you face!

THURSDAY:
God Will Pour Out His Holy Anger Against the Wicked
Revelation 14:1–20

The Song of the Saved

*T*hen I looked, and there before me was the Lamb standing on Mount Zion. With him were one hundred forty-four thousand people who had his name and his Father's name written on their foreheads. And I heard a sound from heaven like the noise of flooding water and like the sound of loud thunder. The sound I heard was like people playing harps. And they sang a new song before the throne and before the four living creatures and the elders. No one could learn the new song except the one hundred forty-four thousand who had been bought from the earth. These are the ones who did not do sinful things with women, because they kept themselves pure. They follow the Lamb every place he goes. These one hundred forty-four thousand were bought from among the people of the earth as people to be offered to God and the Lamb. They were not guilty of telling lies; they are without fault.

The Three Angels

*T*hen I saw another angel flying high in the air. He had the eternal Good News to preach to those who live on earth—to every nation, tribe, language, and people. He preached in a loud voice, "Fear God and give him praise, because the time has come for God to judge all people. So worship God who made the heavens, and the earth, and the sea, and the springs of water."

Then the second angel followed the first angel and said, "Ruined, ruined is the great city of Babylon! She made all the nations drink the wine of the anger of her adultery."

Then a third angel followed the first two angels, saying in a loud voice: "If anyone worships the beast and his idol and gets the beast's mark on the forehead or on the hand, that one also will drink the wine of God's anger, which is prepared with all its strength in the cup of his anger. And that person will be put in pain with burning sulfur before the holy angels and the Lamb. And the smoke from their burning pain will rise forever and ever. There will be no rest, day or night, for those who worship the beast and his idol or who get the mark of his name." This means God's holy people must be patient. They must obey God's commands and keep their faith in Jesus.

Then I heard a voice from heaven saying, "Write this: Happy are the dead who die from now on in the Lord."

The Spirit says, "Yes, they will rest from their hard work, and the reward of all they have done stays with them."

The Earth Is Harvested

*T*hen I looked, and there before me was a white cloud, and sitting on the white cloud was One who looked like a Son of Man. He had a gold crown on his head and a sharp sickle in his hand. Then another angel came out of the temple and called out in a loud voice to the One who was sitting on the cloud, "Take your sickle and harvest from the earth, because the time to harvest has come, and the fruit of the earth is ripe." So the One who was sitting on the cloud swung his sickle over the earth, and the earth was harvested.

Then another angel came out of the temple in heaven, and he also had a sharp sickle. And then another angel, who has power over the fire, came from the altar. This angel called to the angel with the sharp sickle, saying, "Take your sharp sickle and gather the bunches of grapes from the earth's vine, because its grapes are ripe." Then the angel swung his sickle over the earth. He gathered the earth's grapes and threw them into the great winepress of God's anger. They were trampled in the winepress outside the city, and blood flowed out of the winepress as high as horses' bridles for a distance of about one hundred eighty miles.

*W*ake up, nations,

and come to attack in the Valley
  Where the LORD Judges.
There I will sit to judge
  all the nations on every side.
Swing the cutting tool,
  because the harvest is ripe.
Come, walk on them as you would walk
  on grapes to get their juice,
  because the winepress is full
  and the barrels are spilling over,
because these people are so evil!"

Joel 3:12–13

The LORD, the God of Israel, said this to me:
"My anger is like the wine in a cup. Take it
from my hand and make all the nations, to
whom I am sending you, drink all of my
anger from this cup. They will drink my
anger and stumble about and act like mad-
men because of the war I am going to send
among them."

So I took the cup from the LORD's hand
and went to those nations and made them
drink from it. I made all the kingdoms on
earth drink from the cup of the LORD's anger, but the king of Babylon will drink from
this cup after all the others.

Jeremiah 25:15–17, 26b

Someone asks, "Why are your clothes
  bright red
  as if you had walked on the grapes
    to make wine?"

The LORD answers, "I have walked in
    the winepress alone,
  and no one among the nations
    helped me.
I was angry and walked on the nations
  and crushed them because of my
    anger.
Blood splashed on my clothes,
  and I stained all my clothing.

"While I was angry, I walked on the
    nations.
  In my anger I punished them
  and poured their blood on the
    ground."

Isaiah 63:2–3, 6

God is the judge;
  he judges one person as guilty and
    another as innocent.

The LORD holds a cup of anger in his
    hand;
  it is full of wine mixed with spices.
He pours it out even to the last drop,
  and the wicked drink it all.

Psalm 75:7–8

I N S I G H T S

*The sinner's peace is that terribly prophetic
calm that the traveler occasionally experiences on the higher Alps. Everything is still.
The birds suspend their notes, fly low, and
cower down with fear. The hum of bees among
the flowers is hushed. A horrible stillness rules
the hour, as if death had silenced all things
by stretching his awful scepter over them. But
the tempest is preparing—the lightning will
soon cast abroad its flames of fire. Earth will
rock with thunder-blasts; granite peaks will
be dissolved. All nature will tremble beneath
the fury of the storm. That calm is what the
sinner is experiencing. He should not rejoice
in it, because the hurricane of wrath is coming, the whirlwind and the tribulation that
can sweep him away and utterly destroy him.*

Charles Spurgeon

P A U S E   F O R   R E F L E C T I O N

*In light of these Scripture readings, the
"sinner's peace" that Spurgeon refers to certainly is ominous, isn't it? What does God's
merciful forgiveness that he repeatedly offers
to all people, contrasted with his guarantee
of final, unchangeable punishment, teach you
about the divine nature?*

F R I D A Y:

God's People Praise Their Righteous and Faithful God

Revelation 15:1—16:11

The Last Troubles

*T*hen I saw another wonder in heaven that was great and amazing. There were seven angels bringing seven disasters. These are the last disasters, because after them, God's anger is finished.

I saw what looked like a sea of glass mixed with fire. All of those who had won the victory over the beast and his idol and over the number of his name were standing by the sea of glass. They had harps that God had given them. They sang the song of Moses, the servant of God, and the song of the Lamb:

"You do great and wonderful things,

Psalm 111:2

  Lord God Almighty.   *Amos 3:13*

Everything the Lord does is right and

  true,   *Psalm 145:17*

  King of the nations.

Everyone will respect you, Lord,

Jeremiah 10:7

  and will honor you.

  Only you are holy.

All the nations will come

  and worship you,   *Psalm 86:9–10*

because the right things you have

  done

  are now made known." *Deuteronomy 32:4*

After this I saw that the temple (the Tent of the Agreement) in heaven was opened. And the seven angels bringing the seven disasters came out of the temple. They were dressed in clean, shining linen and wore golden bands tied around their chests. Then one of the four living creatures gave to the seven angels seven golden bowls filled with the anger of God, who lives forever and ever. The temple was filled with smoke from the glory and the power of God, and no one could enter the temple until the seven disasters of the seven angels were finished.

The Bowls of God's Anger

*T*hen I heard a loud voice from the temple saying to the seven angels, "Go and pour out the seven bowls of God's anger on the earth."

The first angel left and poured out his bowl on the land. Then ugly and painful sores came upon all those who had the mark of the beast and who worshiped his idol.

The second angel poured out his bowl on the sea, and it became blood like that of a dead man, and every living thing in the sea died.

The third angel poured out his bowl on the rivers and the springs of water, and they became blood. Then I heard the angel of the waters saying:

"Holy One, you are the One who is and

  who was.

You are right to decide to punish

  these evil people.

They have poured out the blood of your

  holy people and your prophets.

So now you have given them blood

  to drink as they deserve."

And I heard a voice coming from the altar saying:

"Yes, Lord God Almighty,

  the way you punish evil people is

  right and fair."

The fourth angel poured out his bowl on the sun, and he was given power to burn the people with fire. They were burned by the great heat, and they cursed the name of God, who had control over these disasters. But the people refused to change their hearts and lives and give glory to God.

The fifth angel poured out his bowl on the throne of the beast, and darkness covered its kingdom. People gnawed their tongues because of the pain. They also cursed the God of heaven because of their pain and the sores they had, but they refused to change their hearts and turn away from the evil things they did.

*H*ear, heavens, and I will speak.
  Listen, earth, to what I say.

My teaching will drop like rain;
my words will fall like dew.
They will be like showers on the grass;
they will pour down like rain on
young plants.
I will announce the name of the LORD.
Praise God because he is great!
He is like a rock; what he does is perfect,
and he is always fair.
He is a faithful God who does no wrong,
who is right and fair.

They have done evil against him.
To their shame they are no longer
his children;
they are an evil and lying people.
This is not the way to repay the LORD,
you foolish and unwise people.
He is your Father and Maker,
who made you and formed you.

Israel grew fat and kicked;
they were fat and full and firm.
They left the God who made them
and rejected the Rock who saved
them.

The LORD saw this and rejected them;
his sons and daughters had made
him angry.
He said, "I will turn away from them
and see what will happen to them.
They are evil people,
unfaithful children.

"I will pile troubles upon them
and shoot my arrows at them.
They will be starved and sick,
destroyed by terrible diseases.
I will send them vicious animals
and gliding, poisonous snakes.
In the streets the sword will kill;
in their homes there will be terror.
Young men and women will die,
and so will babies and gray-haired
men."

"Now you will see that I am the one God!
There is no god but me.
I send life and death;
I can hurt, and I can heal.
No one can escape from me.
I raise my hand toward heaven and
make this promise:
As surely as I live forever,

I will sharpen my flashing sword,
and I will take it in my hand to judge.
I will punish my enemies
and pay back those who hate me."

Be happy, nations, with his people,
because he will repay you for the
blood of his servants.
He will punish his enemies,
and he will remove the sin of his
land and people.

Deuteronomy 32:1–6, 15, 19–20,
23–25, 39–41, 43

INSIGHTS

How glorious must He [Christ] have been in the eyes of seraphs, when a cloud received Him out of mortal sight, and He ascended up to heaven! Now He wears the glory which He had with God or ever the earth was, and yet another glory above all—that which He has well earned in the fight against sin, death, and hell. As victor He wears the illustrious crown. . . . He wears the glory of an Intercessor who can never fail, of a Prince who can never be defeated, of a Conqueror who has vanquished every foe, of a Lord who has the heart's allegiance of every subject. Jesus wears all the glory which the pomp of heaven can bestow upon Him, which ten thousand times ten thousand angels can minister to Him. You cannot with your utmost stretch of imagination conceive His exceeding greatness; yet there will be a further revelation of it when He shall descend from heaven in great power, with all the holy angels—"Then shall He sit upon the throne of His glory." Oh, the splendour of that glory! It will ravish His people's hearts. Nor is this the close, for eternity shall sound His praise, "Thy throne, O God, is for ever and ever!" Reader, if you would joy in Christ's glory hereafter, He must be glorious in your sight now. Is He so?

Charles Spurgeon

APPLICATION

Study the contrasts between the praises of God's people and the evil of those who reject God and his salvation. On which side of the battle will you stand firm? Do you delight to sing God's praises?

WEEKEND:

God Reveals His Holiness Through His Anger Against Evil

Revelation 16:12—17:8

*T*he sixth angel poured out his bowl on the great river Euphrates so that the water in the river was dried up to prepare the way for the kings from the east to come. Then I saw three evil spirits that looked like frogs coming out of the mouth of the dragon, out of the mouth of the beast, and out of the mouth of the false prophet. These evil spirits are the spirits of demons, which have power to do miracles. They go out to the kings of the whole world to gather them together for the battle on the great day of God Almighty.

"Listen! I will come as a thief comes! Happy are those who stay awake and keep their clothes on so that they will not walk around naked and have people see their shame."

Then the evil spirits gathered the kings together to the place that is called Armageddon in the Hebrew language.

The seventh angel poured out his bowl into the air. Then a loud voice came out of the temple from the throne, saying, "It is finished!" Then there were flashes of lightning, noises, thunder, and a big earthquake—the worst earthquake that has ever happened since people have been on earth. The great city split into three parts, and the cities of the nations were destroyed. And God remembered the sins of Babylon the Great, so he gave that city the cup filled with the wine of his terrible anger. Then every island ran away, and mountains disappeared. Giant hailstones, each weighing about a hundred pounds, fell from the sky upon people. People cursed God for the disaster of the hail, because this disaster was so terrible.

The Woman on the Animal

*T*hen one of the seven angels who had the seven bowls came and spoke to me. He said, "Come, and I will show you the punishment that will be given to the great prostitute, the one sitting over many waters. The kings of the earth sinned sexually with her, and the people of the earth became drunk from the wine of her sexual sin."

Then the angel carried me away by the Spirit to the desert. There I saw a woman sitting on a red beast. It was covered with names against God written on it, and it had seven heads and ten horns. The woman was dressed in purple and red and was shining with the gold, precious jewels, and pearls she was wearing. She had a golden cup in her hand, a cup filled with evil things and the uncleanness of her sexual sin. On her forehead a title was written that was secret. This is what was written:

THE GREAT BABYLON

MOTHER OF PROSTITUES

AND OF THE EVIL THINGS OF THE EARTH

Then I saw that the woman was drunk with the blood of God's holy people and with the blood of those who were killed because of their faith in Jesus.

When I saw the woman, I was very amazed. Then the angel said to me, "Why are you amazed? I will tell you the secret of this woman and the beast she rides—the one with seven heads and ten horns. The beast you saw was once alive but is not alive now. But soon it will come up out of the bottomless pit and go away to be destroyed. There are people who live on earth whose names have not been written in the book of life since the beginning of the world. They will be amazed when they see the beast, because he was once alive, is not alive now, but will come again.

Ezekiel Warns of God's Coming Judgement

*S*o this is what the Lord GOD says: Because you prophets spoke things that are false and saw visions that do not come true, I am against you, says the Lord GOD. I will punish the prophets who see false visions and prophesy lies. They will have no place among my people. Their names will not be written on the list of the people of Israel, and they will not enter the land of Israel. Then you will know that I am the Lord GOD.

"'It is because they lead my people the wrong way by saying, "Peace!" when there is no peace. When the people build a weak wall, the prophets cover it with whitewash to make it look strong. So tell those who cover a weak wall with whitewash that it will fall down. Rain will pour down, hailstones will fall, and a stormy wind will break the wall down. When the wall has fallen, people will ask you, "Where is the whitewash you used on the wall?"

"'So this is what the Lord GOD says: I will break the wall with a stormy wind. In my anger rain will pour down, and hailstones will destroy the wall. I will tear down the wall on which you put whitewash. I will level it to the ground so that people will see the wall's foundation. And when the wall falls, you will be destroyed under it. Then you will know that I am the LORD.'"

Ezekiel 13:8–14

*T*his is what will happen: On the day Gog attacks the land of Israel, I will become very angry, says the Lord GOD. With jealousy and great anger I tell you that at that time there will surely be a great earthquake in Israel. The fish of the sea, the birds of the sky, the wild animals, everything that crawls on the ground, and all the people on the earth will shake with fear before me. Also the mountains will be thrown down, the cliffs will fall, and every wall will fall to the ground. Then I will call for a war against Gog on all my mountains, says the Lord GOD. Everyone's sword will attack the soldier next to him. I will punish Gog with disease and death. I will send a heavy rain with hailstones and burning sulfur on Gog, his army, and the many nations with him. Then I will show how great I am. I will show my holiness, and I will make myself known to the many nations that watch. Then they will know that I am the LORD.'"

Ezekiel 38:18–23

INSIGHTS

*I*f men and women will not yield to the love

of God, and be changed by the grace of God, then there is no way for them to escape the wrath of God.

Rank and wealth will not deliver anyone in that terrible day. John's list included kings, captains, and slaves, the rich and the poor. "Who shall be able to stand?"

. . . We are so accustomed to emphasizing the meekness and gentleness of Christ (Matt. 11:28–30) that we forget His holiness and justice. The same Christ who welcomed the children in the temple also drove merchants from that same temple. God's wrath is not like a child's temper tantrum or punishment meted out by an impatient parent. God's wrath is the evidence of His holy love for all that is right and His holy hatred for all that is evil. Only a soft and sentimental person would want to worship a God who did not deal justly with evil in the world.

Warren Wiersbe

PAUSE FOR REFLECTION

*W*hat are God's purposes in punishing the evil nations? How will the people on earth respond when the last of God's angels pours out his anger? Pray that God will give you greater insight into his perfect holiness as you study these passages.

MONDAY:

God Calls His People to Run Away from Evil

Revelation 17:9—18:10

*Y*ou need a wise mind to understand this. The seven heads on the beast are seven mountains where the woman sits. And they are seven kings. Five of the kings have already been destroyed, one of the kings lives now, and another has not yet come. When he comes, he must stay a short time. The beast that was once alive, but is not alive now, is also an eighth king. He belongs to the first seven kings, and he will go away to be destroyed.

"The ten horns you saw are ten kings who have not yet begun to rule, but they will receive power to rule with the beast for one hour. All ten of these kings have the same purpose, and they will give their power and authority to the beast. They will make war against the Lamb, but the Lamb will defeat them, because he is Lord of lords and King of kings. He will defeat them with his called, chosen, and faithful followers."

Then the angel said to me, "The waters that you saw, where the prostitute sits, are peoples, races, nations, and languages. The ten horns and the beast you saw will hate the prostitute. They will take everything she has and leave her naked. They will eat her body and burn her with fire. God made the ten horns want to carry out his purpose by agreeing to give the beast their power to rule, until what God has said comes about. The woman you saw is the great city that rules over the kings of the earth."

Babylon Is Destroyed

*A*fter the vision of these things, I saw another angel coming down from heaven. This angel had great power, and his glory made the earth bright. He shouted in a powerful voice:

"Ruined, ruined is the great city of
    Babylon!

She has become a home for demons
and a prison for every evil spirit,
    and a prison for every unclean bird
      and unclean beast.
She has been ruined, because all the
    peoples of the earth
    have drunk the wine of the desire of
      her sexual sin.
She has been ruined also because the
    kings of the earth
    have sinned sexually with her,
and the merchants of the earth
    have grown rich from the great
      wealth of her luxury."

Then I heard another voice from heaven saying:
    "Come out of that city, my people,
      so that you will not share in her sins,
      so that you will not receive the
        disasters that will come to her.
Her sins have piled up as high as the
    sky,
    and God has not forgotten the
      wrongs she has done.
Give that city the same as she gave to
    others.
    Pay her back twice as much as she
      did.
Prepare wine for her that is twice as
    strong
    as the wine she prepared for others.
She gave herself much glory and rich
    living.
    Give her that much suffering and
      sadness.
She says to herself, 'I am a queen
    sitting on my throne.
    I am not a widow; I will never be sad.'
So these disasters will come to her in
    one day:
    death, and crying, and great hunger,
and she will be destroyed by fire,
    because the Lord God who judges
      her is powerful."

The kings of the earth who sinned sexually with her and shared her wealth will see the smoke from her burning. Then they will cry and be sad because of her death. They will be afraid of her suffering and stand far away and say:

"Terrible! How terrible for you, great
    city,

powerful city of Babylon,
because your punishment has come in
one hour!"

*T*he two men said to Lot, "Do you have any other relatives in this city? Do you have any sons-in-law, sons, daughters, or any other relatives? If you do, tell them to leave now, because we are about to destroy this city. The LORD has heard of all the evil that is here, so he has sent us to destroy it."

So Lot went out and said to his future sons-in-law who were pledged to marry his daughters, "Hurry and leave this city! The LORD is about to destroy it!" But they thought Lot was joking.

At dawn the next morning, the angels begged Lot to hurry. They said, "Go! Take your wife and your two daughters with you so you will not be destroyed when the city is punished."

Genesis 19:12–15

*R*un away from Babylon
and save your lives!
Don't stay and be killed because of
Babylon's sins.
It is time for the LORD to punish Babylon;
he will give Babylon the punishment
she deserves.

"Come out of Babylon, my people!
Run for your lives!
Run from the LORD's great anger.
Don't lose courage;
rumors will spread through the land,
but don't be afraid.
One rumor comes this year, and
another comes the next year.
There will be rumors of terrible
fighting in the country,
of rulers fighting against rulers.
The time will surely come
when I will punish the idols of
Babylon,
and the whole land will be disgraced.
There will be many dead people
lying all around.

"Babylon must fall, because she killed
people from Israel.

She killed people from everywhere
on earth.
You who have escaped being killed
with swords,
leave Babylon! Don't wait!
Remember the LORD in the faraway
land
and think about Jerusalem."

Jeremiah 51:6, 45–47, 49–50

*T*hrough our union with Christ in His death we are delivered from the dominion of sin. But we still find sin struggling to gain mastery over us. . . . We may not like the fact that we have this lifelong struggle with sin, but the more we realize and accept it, the better equipped we will be to deal with it. . . .

The Bible tells us that the heart is deceitful and unsearchable to any but God alone (Jeremiah 17:9–10). Even as believers we do not know our own hearts (1 Corinthians 4:3–5). . . .

Knowing that indwelling sin occupies a heart that is deceitful and unsearchable should make us extremely wary. . . .

. . . Though sin no longer has dominion over us, it wages its guerrilla warfare against us. If left unchecked, it will defeat us. Our recourse against this warfare is to deal swiftly and firmly with the first motions of indwelling sin. . . .

. . . We must never consider that our fight against sin is at an end. The heart is unsearchable, our evil desires are insatiable, and our reason is constantly in danger of being deceived. Well did Jesus say, "Watch and pray so that you will not fall into temptation" (Matthew 26:41).

Jerry Bridges

*W*hy is it important for God's people to do everything they can to separate themselves from sin? What punishment will come to those who linger when God tells them to run? Are you listening for his warning?

TUESDAY:
God Will Punish Babylon
Revelation 18:11–24

NEW TESTAMENT READING

*A*nd the merchants of the earth will cry and be sad about her, because now there is no one to buy their cargoes—cargoes of gold, silver, jewels, pearls, fine linen, purple cloth, silk, red cloth; all kinds of citron wood and all kinds of things made from ivory, expensive wood, bronze, iron, and marble; cinnamon, spice, incense, myrrh, frankincense, wine, olive oil, fine flour, wheat, cattle, sheep, horses, carriages, slaves, and human lives.

The merchants will say,
"Babylon, the good things you wanted
  are gone from you.
All your rich and fancy things have
  disappeared.
  You will never have them again."
The merchants who became rich from selling to her will be afraid of her suffering and will stand far away. They will cry and be sad and say:
"Terrible! How terrible for the great city!
  She was dressed in fine linen, purple
    and red cloth,
  and she was shining with gold,
    precious jewels, and pearls!
All these riches have been destroyed in
  one hour!"
Every sea captain, every passenger, the sailors, and all those who earn their living from the sea stood far away from Babylon. As they saw the smoke from her burning, they cried out loudly, "There was never a city like this great city!" And they threw dust on their heads and cried out, weeping and being sad. They said:
"Terrible! How terrible for the great city!
All the people who had ships on the sea
  became rich because of her wealth!
But she has been destroyed in one hour!
Be happy because of this, heaven!
  Be happy, God's holy people and
    apostles and prophets!
God has punished her because of what
  she did to you."

Then a powerful angel picked up a large stone, like one used for grinding grain, and threw it into the sea. He said:
"In the same way, the great city of
    Babylon will be thrown down,
  and it will never be found again.
The music of people playing harps and
    other instruments, flutes, and
    trumpets,
  will never be heard in you again.
No workman doing any job
  will ever be found in you again.
The sound of grinding grain
  will never be heard in you again.
The light of a lamp
  will never shine in you again,
and the voices of a bridegroom and
    bride
  will never be heard in you again.
Your merchants were the world's great
    people,
  and all the nations were tricked by
    your magic.
You are guilty of the death of the
    prophets and God's holy people
and all who have been killed on
    earth."

OLD TESTAMENT READING

*T*he LORD says,
"Babylon, you are a destroying mountain,
  and I am against you.
  You have destroyed the whole land.
I will put my hand out against you.
  I will roll you off the cliffs,
  and I will make you a burned-out
    mountain.
People will not find any rocks in
    Babylon big enough for corner-
    stones.
  People will not take any rocks from
    Babylon to use for the foundation
    of a building,
  because your city will be just a pile
    of ruins forever," says the LORD.

So this is what the LORD says:
"I will soon defend you, Judah,
  and make sure that Babylon is
    punished.
I will dry up Babylon's sea
  and make her springs become dry.

Babylon will become a pile of ruins,
a home for wild dogs.
People will be shocked by what
happened there.
No one will live there anymore.
Babylon's people roar like young lions;
they growl like baby lions.
While they are stirred up,
I will give a feast for them
and make them drunk.
They will shout and laugh.
And they will sleep forever and
never wake up!" says the LORD.
"I will take the people of Babylon to be
killed.
They will be like lambs,
like sheep and goats waiting to be
killed.

"How Babylon has been defeated!
The pride of the whole earth has
been taken captive.
People from other nations are shocked
at what happened to Babylon,
and the things they see make them
afraid.
The sea has risen over Babylon;
its roaring waves cover her.
Babylon's towns are ruined and empty.
It has become a dry, desert land,
a land where no one lives.
People do not even travel through
Babylon.
I will punish the god Bel in Babylon.
I will make him spit out what he has
swallowed.
Nations will no longer come to Babylon;
even the wall around the city will
fall."

Jeremiah 51:25–26, 36–44

INSIGHTS

In spite of what people often think, no one is getting away with anything. Payday someday! God's vengeance will be revealed, even against false religion in whose name and under whose influence millions have suffered and died. God's judgment will fall and vindicate His people. . . .

The extent of Babylon's payment: The law of retribution is applied; what we sow, we shall reap. It is doubled to emphasize the enormity of the woman's sins and the justice behind her judgment and fall. The "cup which she has mixed," containing the wine of her wrath against the people of God, is now mixed for her with a double portion of God's wrath (14:10).

The experience of Babylon's sorrow: Like so many unbelievers today, this woman believes she will never experience sorrow or torment for her lifestyle and luxurious living. She boasts "I sit as queen, and am no widow." After all, she reasons, the kings of the earth are her lovers. But she is a widow in that God has forsaken her. . . .

Two things characterize the harlot's lifestyle: self-glorification and sensuous living. For this, she will receive torment and sorrow. So will all who choose to follow her path. . . .

The hunger for achievement and accumulation of wealth remains as the dominant factor of people's lifestyles and desires. The "fools" of this world are found daily in every marketplace and place of business. . . . But judgment day is coming! The merchants of the world, along with the kings of the earth, will mourn the sudden destruction of the woman who helped them become prosperous.

David Hocking

PAUSE FOR REFLECTION

Why is God against Babylon? Why will the people of earth mourn the destruction of Babylon? What does her defeat symbolize? Where is your heart's loyalty? Will you shed even one tear over Babylon's loss?

WEDNESDAY:

All the People of Heaven Worship God!

Revelation 19:1–16

People in Heaven Praise God

*A*fter this vision and announcement I heard what sounded like a great many people in heaven saying:

"Hallelujah!

Salvation, glory, and power belong to our God,

because his judgments are true and right.

He has punished the prostitute

who made the earth evil with her sexual sin.

He has paid her back for the death of his servants."

Again they said:

"Hallelujah!

She is burning, and her smoke will rise forever and ever."

Then the twenty-four elders and the four living creatures bowed down and worshiped God, who sits on the throne. They said:

"Amen, Hallelujah!"

Then a voice came from the throne, saying:

"Praise our God, all you who serve him

and all you who honor him, both small and great!"

Then I heard what sounded like a great many people, like the noise of flooding water, and like the noise of loud thunder. The people were saying:

"Hallelujah!

Our Lord God, the Almighty, rules.

Let us rejoice and be happy

and give God glory,

because the wedding of the Lamb has come,

and the Lamb's bride has made herself ready.

Fine linen, bright and clean, was given to her to wear."

(The fine linen means the good things done by God's holy people.)

And the angel said to me, "Write this: Happy are those who have been invited to the wedding meal of the Lamb!" And the angel said, "These are the true words of God."

Then I bowed down at the angel's feet to worship him, but he said to me, "Do not worship me! I am a servant like you and your brothers and sisters who have the message of Jesus. Worship God, because the message about Jesus is the spirit that gives all prophecy."

The Rider on the White Horse

*T*hen I saw heaven opened, and there before me was a white horse. The rider on the horse is called Faithful and True, and he is right when he judges and makes war. His eyes are like burning fire, and on his head are many crowns. He has a name written on him, which no one but himself knows. He is dressed in a robe dipped in blood, and his name is the Word of God. The armies of heaven, dressed in fine linen, white and clean, were following him on white horses. Out of the rider's mouth comes a sharp sword that he will use to defeat the nations, and he will rule them with a rod of iron. He will crush out the wine in the winepress of the terrible anger of God the Almighty. On his robe and on his upper leg was written this name: KING OF KINGS AND LORD OF LORDS.

*A*re there any gods like you, LORD?

There are no gods like you.

You are wonderfully holy,

amazingly powerful,

a worker of miracles.

You reached out with your right hand,

and the earth swallowed our enemies.

You keep your loving promise

and lead the people you have saved.

With your strength you will guide them to your holy place.

You will lead your people and place them on your very own mountain,

the place that you, LORD, made for yourself to live,

the temple, Lord, that your hands
have made.
The LORD will be king forever!"

Exodus 15:11–13, 17–18

*M*ay the glory of the LORD be forever.
May the LORD enjoy what he has
made.
He just looks at the earth, and it
shakes.
He touches the mountains, and they
smoke.

I will sing to the LORD all my life;
I will sing praises to my God as long
as I live.
May my thoughts please him;
I am happy in the LORD.
Let sinners be destroyed from the
earth,
and let the wicked live no longer.

My whole being, praise the LORD.
Praise the LORD.

Psalm 104:31–35

*P*raise the LORD!

Praise the LORD from the skies.
Praise him high above the earth.
Praise him, all you angels.
Praise him, all you armies of
heaven.
Praise him, sun and moon.
Praise him, all you shining stars.
Praise him, highest heavens
and you waters above the sky.
Let them praise the LORD,
because they were created by his
command.
He put them in place forever and ever;
he made a law that will never
change.

Psalm 148:1–6

*P*raise the LORD!

Praise God in his Temple;
praise him in his mighty heaven.
Praise him for his strength;
praise him for his greatness.
Praise him with trumpet blasts;
praise him with harps and lyres.
Praise him with tambourines and
dancing;

praise him with stringed instruments
and flutes.
Praise him with loud cymbals;
praise him with crashing cymbals.
Let everything that breathes praise the
LORD.

Praise the LORD!

Psalm 150:1–6

INSIGHTS

*T*here is a party in heaven because the party
that meant destruction for so many has been
ended. A new celebration sponsored by God
has gotten under way. According to this
scripture, those allied with the Lamb of God
cannot help but shout, "Hallelujah!" at this
incredible turn of events. . . .

. . . Many of the most credible biblical
scholars have agreed that Babylon in the Book
of Revelation always refers to the dominant
society in which Christians have to live. . . .

. . . When our Babylon falls (and it, like
all Babylons, will one day fall), how will you
react? Will you react like the merchants described in Revelation 18:3 who "grew rich
from her excessive luxuries" and those politi-
cal potentates who conspired with her to ex-
ploit the weak and the poor? Or will you be
able to join the angels on that day and sing
praises to God?

. . . Have you given your time and energy to get those things that go with living in
Babylon so that, when it falls, all that you
have ever worked for will fall with it? Or have
you so invested your life in the Kingdom of
God that, even if heaven and earth shall pass
away, what is important to you will endure?
In the end, will you be able to shout and sing
in that eternal party that will be shared by
those who have laid up their treasures in
heaven (Matt. 6:19–21)?

Tony Campolo

PAUSE FOR REFLECTION

*R*eread the praises to God in these passages—several times, if you'd like. Can you
imagine anything more wonderful than
praising God in heaven? Have you accepted
your invitation to join his everlasting party?

THURSDAY:

God's Triumph over Satan and Sin Is Complete

Revelation 19:17—20:15

*T*hen I saw an angel standing in the sun, and he called with a loud voice to all the birds flying in the sky: "Come and gather together for the great feast of God so that you can eat the bodies of kings, generals, mighty people, horses and their riders, and the bodies of all people—free, slave, small, and great."

Then I saw the beast and the kings of the earth. Their armies were gathered together to make war against the rider on the horse and his army. But the beast was captured and with him the false prophet who did the miracles for the beast. The false prophet had used these miracles to trick those who had the mark of the beast and worshiped his idol. The false prophet and the beast were thrown alive into the lake of fire that burns with sulfur. And their armies were killed with the sword that came out of the mouth of the rider on the horse, and all the birds ate the bodies until they were full.

The Thousand Years

I saw an angel coming down from heaven. He had the key to the bottomless pit and a large chain in his hand. The angel grabbed the dragon, that old snake who is the devil and Satan, and tied him up for a thousand years. Then he threw him into the bottomless pit, closed it, and locked it over him. The angel did this so he could not trick the people of the earth anymore until the thousand years were ended. After a thousand years he must be set free for a short time.

Then I saw some thrones and people sitting on them who had been given the power to judge. And I saw the souls of those who had been killed because they were faithful to the message of Jesus and the message from God. They had not worshiped the beast or his idol, and they had not received the mark of the beast on their foreheads or on their hands. They came back to life and ruled with Christ for a thousand years. (The others that were dead did not live again until the thousand years were ended.) This is the first raising of the dead. Happy and holy are those who share in this first raising of the dead. The second death has no power over them. They will be priests for God and for Christ and will rule with him for a thousand years.

When the thousand years are over, Satan will be set free from his prison. Then he will go out to trick the nations in all the earth—Gog and Magog—to gather them for battle. There are so many people they will be like sand on the seashore. And Satan's army marched across the earth and gathered around the camp of God's people and the city God loves. But fire came down from heaven and burned them up. And Satan, who tricked them, was thrown into the lake of burning sulfur with the beast and the false prophet. There they will be punished day and night forever and ever.

People of the World Are Judged

*T*hen I saw a great white throne and the One who was sitting on it. Earth and sky ran away from him and disappeared. And I saw the dead, great and small, standing before the throne. Then books were opened, and the book of life was opened. The dead were judged by what they had done, which was written in the books. The sea gave up the dead who were in it, and Death and Hades gave up the dead who were in them. Each person was judged by what he had done. And Death and Hades were thrown into the lake of fire. The lake of fire is the second death. And anyone whose name was not found written in the book of life was thrown into the lake of fire.

*A*t that time the LORD will punish
   the powers in the sky above
   and the rulers on earth below.
They will be gathered together
   like prisoners thrown into a dungeon;

they will be shut up in prison.
After much time they will be punished.

Isaiah 24:21–22

*T*he LORD All-Powerful will come
with thunder, earthquakes, and great
noises,
with storms, strong winds, and a fire
that destroys.
Then all the nations that fight against
Jerusalem
will be like a dream;
all the nations that attack her
will be like a vision in the night.
They will be like a hungry man who
dreams he is eating,
but when he awakens, he is still
hungry.
They will be like a thirsty man who
dreams he is drinking,
but when he awakens, he is still
weak and thirsty.
It will be the same way with all the
nations
who fight against Mount Zion.

Isaiah 29:6–8

*H*uman, prophesy against Gog and say,
'This is what the Lord GOD says: I am
against you, Gog, chief ruler of Meshech
and Tubal. You, all your troops, and the nations with you will fall dead on the mountains of Israel. I will let you be food for every bird that eats meat and every wild animal. You will lie fallen on the ground, because I have spoken, says the Lord GOD. I
will send fire on Magog and those who live
in safety on the coastlands. Then they will
know that I am the LORD.

"'I will make myself known among my
people Israel, and I will not let myself be
dishonored anymore. Then the nations
will know that I am the LORD, the Holy One
in Israel. It is coming! It will happen, says
the Lord GOD. The time I talked about is
coming.'"

Ezekiel 39:1, 4–8

*T*hen there will be a fourth kingdom,
strong as iron. In the same way that iron
crushes and smashes things to pieces, the
fourth kingdom will smash and crush all the
other kingdoms.

"During the time of those kings, the God
of heaven will set up another kingdom that
will never be destroyed or given to another
group of people. This kingdom will crush
all the other kingdoms and bring them to
an end, but it will continue forever."

Daniel 2:40, 44

*F*or thousands of years, Satan has seduced
nations and people into thinking that they can
build a world of peace and love without
Christ. Sometimes he has deceived people into
thinking that education or money would solve
personal problems. But his dirty work is over,
for a time. At the end of the thousand years
"he must be set free for a short time" (Revelation 20:3).

During the Millennium, believers will
continue to populate the earth. However, their
offspring, living in an ideal environment with
King Jesus as the loving, benevolent ruler, can
still rebel against God, and some will.

When Satan is released for a time, he will
gather some of his old cohorts, Gog and
Magog, the nations that hated Israel, and
march on Jerusalem once more. This battle
will not last long, for fire will come down from
heaven and zap them. Then Satan will have
his final place of unrest; he will be thrown
"into the lake of burning sulfur, where the
beast and the false prophet had been thrown.
They will be tormented day and night for ever
and ever" (Revelation 20:10).

David Jeremiah

*W*hat amazing events are promised for future times in this portion of Scripture? What
is the penalty for those who are not faithful to
God? Pray that you, no matter what happens
in your lifetime, will remain faithful to your
Lord.

FRIDAY:

God Makes All Things New and Comes to Live with His People

Revelation 21:1–27

The New Jerusalem

Then I saw a new heaven and a new earth. The first heaven and the first earth had disappeared, and there was no sea anymore. And I saw the holy city, the new Jerusalem, coming down out of heaven from God. It was prepared like a bride dressed for her husband. And I heard a loud voice from the throne, saying, "Now God's presence is with people, and he will live with them, and they will be his people. God himself will be with them and will be their God. He will wipe away every tear from their eyes, and there will be no more death, sadness, crying, or pain, because all the old ways are gone."

The One who was sitting on the throne said, "Look! I am making everything new!" Then he said, "Write this, because these words are true and can be trusted."

The One on the throne said to me, "It is finished. I am the Alpha and the Omega, the Beginning and the End. I will give free water from the spring of the water of life to anyone who is thirsty. Those who win the victory will receive this, and I will be their God, and they will be my children. But cowards, those who refuse to believe, who do evil things, who kill, who sin sexually, who do evil magic, who worship idols, and who tell lies—all these will have a place in the lake of burning sulfur. This is the second death."

Then one of the seven angels who had the seven bowls full of the seven last troubles came to me, saying, "Come with me, and I will show you the bride, the wife of the Lamb." And the angel carried me away by the Spirit to a very large and high mountain. He showed me the holy city, Jerusalem, coming down out of heaven from God. It was shining with the glory of God and was bright like a very expensive jewel, like a jasper, clear as crystal. The city had a great high wall with twelve gates with twelve angels at the gates, and on each gate was written the name of one of the twelve tribes of Israel. There were three gates on the east, three on the north, three on the south, and three on the west. The walls of the city were built on twelve foundation stones, and on the stones were written the names of the twelve apostles of the Lamb.

The angel who talked with me had a measuring rod made of gold to measure the city, its gates, and its wall. The city was built in a square, and its length was equal to its width. The angel measured the city with the rod. The city was twelve thousand stadia long, twelve thousand stadia wide, and twelve thousand stadia high. The angel also measured the wall. It was one hundred forty-four cubits high, by human measurements, which the angel was using. The wall was made of jasper, and the city was made of pure gold, as pure as glass. The foundation stones of the city walls were decorated with every kind of jewel. The first foundation was jasper, the second was sapphire, the third was chalcedony, the fourth was emerald, the fifth was onyx, the sixth was carnelian, the seventh was chrysolite, the eighth was beryl, the ninth was topaz, the tenth was chrysoprase, the eleventh was jacinth, and the twelfth was amethyst. The twelve gates were twelve pearls, each gate having been made from a single pearl. And the street of the city was made of pure gold as clear as glass.

I did not see a temple in the city, because the Lord God Almighty and the Lamb are the city's temple. The city does not need the sun or the moon to shine on it, because the glory of God is its light, and the Lamb is the city's lamp. By its light the people of the world will walk, and the kings of the earth will bring their glory into it. The city's gates will never be shut on any day, because there is no night there. The glory and the honor of the nations will be brought into it. Nothing unclean and no one who does shameful things or tells lies will ever go into it. Only those whose names are written in the Lamb's book of life will enter the city.

*L*ook, I will make new heavens and a
  new earth,
  and people will not remember the
  past
  or think about those things.
My people will be happy forever
  because of the things I will make.
I will make a Jerusalem that is full of
  joy,
  and I will make her people a delight.
Then I will rejoice over Jerusalem
  and be delighted with my people.
There will never again be heard in that
  city
  the sounds of crying and sadness.
No more will one person build a house
  and someone else live there.
  One person will not plant a garden
  and someone else eat its fruit.
My people will live a long time,
  as trees live long.
My chosen people will live there
  and enjoy the things they make.
They will never again work for
  nothing.
  They will never again give birth to
  children who die young.
All my people will be blessed by the
  LORD;
  they and their children will be
  blessed.
I will provide for their needs before
  they ask,
  and I will help them while they are
  still asking for help."

Isaiah 65:17–19, 22–24

*T*here will be no more violence in your
  country;
  it will not be ruined or destroyed.
You will name your walls Salvation
  and your gates Praise.
The sun will no longer be your light
  during the day
  nor will the brightness from the
  moon be your light,
because the LORD will be your light
  forever,
  and your God will be your glory."

Isaiah 60:18–19

*S*hout and be glad, Jerusalem. I am coming, and I will live among you," says the
LORD. "At that time people from many nations will join with the LORD and will become my people. Then I will live among
you, and you will know that the LORD All-
Powerful has sent me to you. The LORD will
take Judah as his own part of the holy land,
and Jerusalem will be his chosen city again.
Be silent, everyone, in the presence of the
LORD. He is coming out of the holy place
where he lives."

Zechariah 2:10–13

INSIGHTS

*T*he longing for a future glorious city of God
can be traced back as far as the Old Testament patriarchs. Abraham ". . . was looking
forward to the city with foundations, whose
architect and builder is God" (Hebrews
11:10).

Paul mentioned this city in his letter to the
Galatians. He called it "the Jerusalem which
is above" (Galatians 4:26).

The "New Jerusalem" (Revelation 21:2;
3:12) is just one of the several names given
to this future city of God. It is also called The
Holy City, the Heavenly Jerusalem, and
Mount Zion. Whatever it is named, it will be
a holy and beautiful place, more perfect than
the Garden of Eden. . . .

Jesus is preparing the New Jerusalem for
us now. . . .

. . . His light will be among us forevermore.

In our eternal home there will be no sadness, no more tears. . . .

. . . For all eternity He will be with us
and we will know and see Him.

David Jeremiah

ACTION POINT

*S*tudy what God promises to his children in
the New Jerusalem. Do you have any doubts
that God deeply loves you and fully knows your
every pain and sorrow? Trust your heavenly
Father's promise. Thank him for his goodness.

WEEKEND:

Come to the Water of Life, for Jesus Is Coming Soon

Revelation 22:1–21

*T*hen the angel showed me the river of the water of life. It was shining like crystal and was flowing from the throne of God and of the Lamb down the middle of the street of the city. The tree of life was on each side of the river. It produces fruit twelve times a year, once each month. The leaves of the tree are for the healing of all the nations. Nothing that God judges guilty will be in that city. The throne of God and of the Lamb will be there, and God's servants will worship him. They will see his face, and his name will be written on their foreheads. There will never be night again. They will not need the light of a lamp or the light of the sun, because the Lord God will give them light. And they will rule as kings forever and ever.

The angel said to me, "These words can be trusted and are true." The Lord, the God of the spirits of the prophets, sent his angel to show his servants the things that must happen soon.

"Listen! I am coming soon! Happy is the one who obeys the words of prophecy in this book."

I, John, am the one who heard and saw these things. When I heard and saw them, I bowed down to worship at the feet of the angel who showed these things to me. But the angel said to me, "Do not worship me! I am a servant like you, your brothers the prophets, and all those who obey the words in this book. Worship God!"

Then the angel told me, "Do not keep secret the words of prophecy in this book, because the time is near for all this to happen. Let whoever is doing evil continue to do evil. Let whoever is unclean continue to be unclean. Let whoever is doing right continue to do right. Let whoever is holy continue to be holy."

"Listen! I am coming soon! I will bring my reward with me, and I will repay each one of you for what you have done. I am the Alpha and the Omega, the First and the Last, the Beginning and the End.

"Happy are those who wash their robes so that they will receive the right to eat the fruit from the tree of life and may go through the gates into the city. Outside the city are the evil people, those who do evil magic, who sin sexually, who murder, who worship idols, and who love lies and tell lies.

"I, Jesus, have sent my angel to tell you these things for the churches. I am the descendant from the family of David, and I am the bright morning star."

The Spirit and the bride say, "Come!" Let the one who hears this say, "Come!" Let whoever is thirsty come; whoever wishes may have the water of life as a free gift.

I warn everyone who hears the words of the prophecy of this book: If anyone adds anything to these words, God will add to that person the disasters written about in this book. And if anyone takes away from the words of this book of prophecy, God will take away that one's share of the tree of life and of the holy city, which are written about in this book.

Jesus, the One who says these things are true, says, "Yes, I am coming soon."

Amen. Come, Lord Jesus!

The grace of the Lord Jesus be with all. Amen.

*T*he LORD says, "All you who are thirsty,
   come and drink.
Those of you who do not have money,
   come, buy and eat!
Come buy wine and milk
   without money and without cost.
Why spend your money on something
   that is not real food?
Why work for something that
   doesn't really satisfy you?
Listen closely to me, and you will eat
   what is good;
   your soul will enjoy the rich food
     that satisfies.
Come to me and listen;

listen to me so you may live.
I will make an agreement with you that
    will last forever.
I will give you the blessings I
    promised to David."

Isaiah 55:1–3

*T*here is a river that brings joy to the
    city of God,
    the holy place where God Most High
    lives.
God is in that city, and so it will not be
    shaken.

Psalm 46:4–5a

*T*he man led me back to the door of the Temple, and I saw water coming out from under the doorway and flowing east. (The Temple faced east.) The water flowed down from the south side wall of the Temple and then south of the altar. As I went back, I saw many trees on both sides of the river. The man said to me, "This water will flow toward the eastern areas and go down into the Jordan Valley. When it enters the Dead Sea, it will become fresh. Everywhere the river goes, there will be many fish. Wherever this water goes the Dead Sea will become fresh, and so where the river goes there will be many living things. Fishermen will stand by the Dead Sea. From En Gedi all the way to En Eglaim there will be places to spread fishing nets. There will be many kinds of fish in the Dead Sea, as many as in the Mediterranean Sea. But its swamps and marshes will not become fresh; they will be left for salt. All kinds of fruit trees will grow on both banks of the river, and their leaves will not dry and die. The trees will have fruit every month, because the water for them comes from the Temple. The fruit from the trees will be used for food, and their leaves for medicine."

Ezekiel 47:1, 7–12

INSIGHTS

*C*ome celebrate the living water that *flows for you from an eternal spring. You need not fear stagnation. You need only draw nearer—put your roots down deep, settle in, and be at home in My love. Then every day*

will be a new day. Every day you will wonder at the richness of life that has come to you by My grace. Every day you will watch eagerly for My sunrise, search eagerly for My presence in the mundane activities of your world. Every day you will know Me better, and every day you will want to know Me more.

And every day you will live in joyful anticipation of My presence. You will think of My love for you as it is now, and as it will be on that day when I carry you across the threshold into the New Jerusalem—the home I am preparing for you.

Every day you will count the days until the wedding, when you and I will sit down together at the marriage supper of the Lamb. . . .

On that day, child, I will call you by a new name. You will be a crown of splendor in My hand, a royal diadem in the hand of your God. I will delight in you, I will rejoice over you as a bridegroom rejoices over his bride.

Come to the spring and drink deeply of My love. Let it flow over you, bringing a foretaste of that day when the river of life will flow for you through the New Jerusalem and love will be forever fresh.

Until then, turn from your fears and relax in My love. Here at the source you will find your renewal.

Ruth Senter

PAUSE   FOR   REFLECTION

*W*hat to you is the most meaningful aspect *of God's salvation, of his endless river of life? Meditate on this glorious gift. Thank him for what he has done for you and for anyone who will forsake sin and come to him.*

INDEX

ACKNOWLEDGMENTS

Alcorn, Randy C., taken from *Sexual Temptation*. © 1989 by Randy Alcorn. Used by permission of InterVarsity Press, P.O. Box 1400, Downers Grove, IL 60515.

Anderson, Lynn, *Finding the Heart to Go On,* Here's Life Publishers, San Bernadino, CA, © 1991.

Arnold, Duane W. H., taken from the book *Prayers of the Martyrs*. Copyright © 1991 by Duane W. H. Arnold. Used by permission of Zondervan Publishing House.

Augsburger, David W., taken from *Freedom of Forgiveness*. Copyright ©1970, 1988. Moody Bible Institute of Chicago. Moody Press. Used by permission.

Avila, St. Theresa of, from the book *A Life of Prayer,* copyright 1983 by Multnomah Press. Published by Multnomah Press, Portland, Oregon, 97206. Used by permission.

Babcock, Maltbie, *This Is My Father's World* in *The Hymnal for Worship and Celebration,* copyright © 1986, Word Music, Waco, Texas.

Barna, George, *The Frog in the Kettle,* copyright © 1990 by Regal Books, a division of Gospel Light Publications. Used by permission.

Baxter, J. Sidlow, taken from the book *Awake My Heart*. Copyright © 1959 by J. Sidlow Baxter. Used by permission of the Zondervan Publishing House.

Beals, Art, *Beyond Hunger,* copyright © 1985, Multnomah Press, Portland, Oregon 97266.

Beckwith, Mary, *Still Moments,* copyright © 1989 by Regal Books, a division of Gospel Light Publications. Used by permission.

Blue, Ron, *Master Your Money,* copyright © 1986, Thomas Nelson Publishers, Nashville, TN.

Boice, James Montgomery, taken from *The Parables of Jesus*. Copyright © 1983. Moody Bible Institute of Chicago. Moody Press. Used by permission.

Bridges, Jerry, *The Practice of Godliness,* copyright © 1983 by Jerry Bridges, NavPress, Colorado Springs, Colorado.

Bridges, Jerry, *The Pursuit of Holiness,* copyright © 1978 by the Navigators, NavPress, Colorado Springs, Colorado.

Bright, Bill, *Promises — A Daily Guide to Supernatural Living,* Here's Life Publishers, San Bernadino, CA, © 1983.

Bright, Bill, *The Secret: How to Live with Purpose and Power,* Here's Life Publishers, San Bernadino, CA, © 1989.

Briscoe, Jill, *Running on Empty,* copyright © 1988, Word, Inc., Dallas, Texas.

Bruce, F. F., taken from *The Hard Sayings of Jesus*. © 1983 by F. F. Bruce. Used by permission of InterVarsity Press, P.O. Box 1400, Downers Grove, IL 60515. Worldwide permission granted by Hodder & Stoughton Limited, England.

Bryant, Al, (Compiler) *Day By Day With C. H. Spurgeon,* copyright © 1980, Word, Inc., Dallas, Texas.

Bryant, Al, *Keep in Touch,* copyright © 1981, Word, Inc., Dallas, Texas.

Bryant, Al, *Strength for the Day: Daily Meditations with F. B. Meyer,* copyright © 1979, Word, Inc., Dallas, Texas.

Buechner, Frederick, excerpt from *Wishful Thinking*. Copyright © 1973 by Frederick Buechner. Reprinted by permission of HarperCollins Publishers.

Calkins, Ruth Harms, from *Tell Me Again Lord, I Forget,* © 1974. Used by permission of Tyndale House Publishers, Inc. All rights reserved.

Campolo, Anthony, *The Kingdom of God is a Party,* copyright © 1990, Word, Inc., Dallas, Texas.

Campolo, Anthony, *Who Switched the Price Tags?,* copyright © 1986, Word, Inc., Dallas, Texas.

Chapian, Marie, *Discovering Joy,* Bethany House Publishers, © 1990.

Chisholm, Thomas O. (Words) and Runyan, William M. (Music), *Great Is Thy Faithfulness* in *The Hymnal for Worship and Celebration,* copyright © 1923. Renewal 1951 by Hope Publishing Co., Carol Stream, IL 60188. All rights reserved. Used by permission.

Crabb, Rachael, *The Personal Touch,* copyright © 1990 by Rachael Crabb and Raeann Hart, NavPress, Colorado Springs, Colorado.

Evans, Anthony T., taken from *America's Only Hope*. Copyright © 1990. Moody Bible Institute of Chicago. Moody Press. Used by permission.

Fickett, Harold L., *Walking What You're Talking (Principles of James),* copyright © 1988 by Regal Books, a division of Gospel Light Publications. Used by permission.

Finney, Charles G., *God's Love for a Sinning World*. © 1966 by Kregel Publications: Grand Rapids, Michigan. Used by permission.

Finney, Charles G., *Principles of Consecration,* Bethany House Publishers, © 1990.

Finney, Charles Grandison, *Principles of Devotion,* Bethany House Publishers, © 1987.

Finney, Charles G., *Victory Over the World*. © 1966 by Kregel Publications: Grand Rapids, Michigan. Used by permission.

Fletcher, William M., *The Second Greatest Commandment*. Copyright © 1983. NavPress, Colorado Springs, Colorado. (Dr. William M. Fletcher is Minister-at-Large, Rocky Mountain Conservative Baptist Association.)

Foster, Richard J., excerpts from *Celebration of Discipline*. Copyright © 1978 by Richard J. Foster. Reprinted by permission of HarperCollins Publishers.

Foster, Richard J., excerpts from *Money, Sex and Power*. Copyright © 1985 by Richard J. Foster. Reprinted by permission of HarperCollins Publishers.

Fullham, Terry L., *Thirsting,* copyright © 1989, Thomas Nelson Publishers, Nashville, TN.

Gaither, Gloria, *We Have This Moment,* copyright © 1988, Word, Inc., Dallas, Texas.

Geisler, Norman L., (Editor), *What Augustine Says,* Baker Book House, © 1982.

Gillham, Bill, *Lifetime Guarantee,* Wolgemuth & Hyatt, Publishers, Inc. Used by permission.

Graham, Billy, *Answers to Life's Problems,* copyright © 1960, 1988, Word, Inc., Dallas, Texas.

Graham, Billy, *Approaching Hoofbeats,* copyright © 1983, Word, Inc., Dallas, Texas.

Graham, Billy, *The Holy Spirit,* copyright © 1978, 1988, Word, Inc., Dallas, Texas.

Graham, Billy, *Unto the Hills: A Devotional Treasury from Billy Graham,* copyright © 1986, Word, Inc., Dallas, Texas.

Gregory, Joel C., *Growing Pains of the Soul,* copyright © 1987, Word, Inc., Dallas, Texas.

Guiness, Os, taken from *The Devil's Gauntlet.* © 1989 by Os Guiness. Used by permission of InterVarsity Press, P.O. Box 1400, Downers Grove, IL 60515.

Halverson, Richard C., *No Greater Power,* copyright © 1986, Multnomah Press, Portland, Oregon 97266.

Harris, Madalene, *Climbing Higher,* Here's Life Publishers, San Bernadino, CA, © 1989.

Hayford, Jack, from *Daybreak,* © 1984. Used by permission of Tyndale House Publishers, Inc. All rights reserved.

Hendrichson, Walter A., Reprinted by permission from *Disciples are Made -- Not Born.* Published by Victor Books and © 1974 by SP Publications, Inc., Wheaton, IL.

Hendricks, Howard G. and Jeanne W., from the book *Footprints,* copyright © 1981, Multnomah Press, Portland, Oregon, 97266. (Howard Hendricks is a distinguished professor at Dallas Theological Seminary; Jeanne Hendricks is an author, mother of four, and grandmother of six.)

Hession, Roy, from *The Calvary Road,* copyright 1952 Christian Literature Crusade, London (Ft. Washington, PA and Alresford, Hants: Christian Literature Crusade). Used by permission.

Hocking, David L., from the book *The Coming World Leader,* copyright 1988 by Calvary Communications, Inc. Published by Multnomah Press, Portland, Oregon 97266. Used by permission.

Hughes, R. Kent, taken from *Ephesians,* copyright 1990. Used with permission by Good News Publishers/Crossway Books, Wheaton, IL.

Hybels, Bill, *Seven Wonders of the Spiritual World,* copyright © 1988, Word, Inc., Dallas, Texas.

Hybels, Bill, taken from *Too Busy Not to Pray.* © 1988 by Bill Hybels. Used by permission of InterVarsity Press, P.O. Box 1400, Downers Grove, IL 60515.

Jeremiah, David and Carlson, Carole C., *Escape the Coming Night,* copyright © 1990, Word, Inc., Dallas, Texas.

Johnson, Elliott and Schierbaum, Al, *Our Great and Awesome God: Meditations for Athletes.* Wolgemuth & Hyatt, Publishers, Inc. Used by permission.

Keller, W. Phillip, *A Gardener Looks at the Fruits of the Spirit,* copyright © 1986, Word, Inc., Dallas, Texas.

Keller, W. Phillip, *Salt for Society,* copyright © 1981, Word, Inc., Dallas, Texas.

Keller, W. Phillip, *Songs of My Soul,* copyright © 1989, Word, Inc., Dallas, Texas.

Keller, W. Phillip, *Taming Tension,* Baker Book House, © 1979.

Kempis, Thomas A, taken from *The Imitation of Christ.* Copyright © 1984. Moody Bible Institute of Chicago. Moody Press. Used by permission.

Kroll, Woodrow Michael, *Early in the Morning, Book Two.* Used by permission of Loizeaux Brothers, Inc., Neptune, New Jersey.

Lake, Vicki, reprinted by permission from *Firming Up Your Flabby Faith.* Published by Victor Books and © 1990 by SP Publications, Inc., Wheaton, IL.

Larson, Bruce, reprinted from *A Call to Holy Living,* copyright © 1988 Augsburg Publishing House. Used by permission of Augsburg Fortress.

Lee, Richard, *The Unfailing Promise,* copyright © 1988, Word, Inc., Dallas, Texas.

Lockerbie, Jeanette, taken from *Springtime of Faith.* Copyright © 1990. Moody Bible Institute of Chicago. Moody Press. Used by permission.

Lockyer, Herbert, *Satan: His Person and Power,* copyright © 1980, Word, Inc., Dallas, Texas.

Lucado, Max, *The Applause of Heaven,* copyright © 1990, Word, Inc., Dallas, Texas.

Lucado, Max, from the book *God Came Near,* copyright 1987 by Max Lucado. Published by Multnomah Press, Portland, Oregon 97266. Used by permission.

Lucado, Max, from *On the Anvil,* © 1985. Used by permission of Tyndale House Publishers, Inc. All rights reserved.

Luther, Martin, *A Mighty Fortress Is Our God* in *The Hymnal for Worship and Celebration,* copyright © 1986, Word Music, Waco, Texas.

MacArthur, John Jr., taken from the book *The Gospel According to Jesus.* Copyright © 1988 by John F. MacArthur, Jr. Used by permission of Zondervan Publishing House.

MacDonald, George, *Knowing the Heart of God,* Bethany House Publishers, © 1990.

MacDonald, Gordon, *Ordering Your Private World,* copyright © 1984, 1985, Thomas Nelson Publishers, Nashville, TN.

MacDonald, Gordon, *Rebuilding Your Broken World,* copyright © 1988, 1990, Thomas Nelson Publishers, Nashville, TN.

McClung, Floyd, *Holiness and the Spirit of the Age.* Copyright © 1990 by Harvest House Publishers, Eugene, OR 97402.

McClung, Floyd, taken from *Wholehearted.* © 1988, 1990 by Floyd McClung. Used by permission of InterVarsity Press, P.O. Box 1400, Downers Grove, IL 60515. Worldwide permission granted by HarperCollins Publishers, London, England.

McCullough, Donald W., taken from *Finding Happiness in the Most Unlikely Places.* © 1990 by Donald W. McCullough. Used by permission of InterVarsity Press, P.O. Box 1400, Downers Grove, IL 60515.

McKenna, David, from *Practical Christianity;* LaVonne Neff, Ron Beers, Bruce Barton, Linda Taylor, Dave Veerman, and Jim Galvin (Compilers and Editors), © 1987 by Youth for Christ/USA. Used by permission of Tyndale House Publishers. All rights reserved.

Magdalen, Margaret, taken from *Jesus, Man of Prayer.* © 1987 by Sister Margaret Magdalen. Used by permission of InterVarsity Press, P.O. Box 1400, Downers Grove, IL 60515. Worldwide permission granted by Hodder & Stoughton Limited, England.

Mains, David R., *The Sense of His Presence,* copyright © 1988, Word, Inc., Dallas, Texas.

Mains, Karen Burton, taken from the book *You Are What You Say.* Copyright © 1988 by Karen Burton Mains. Used by permission of the Zondervan Publishing House.

Merritt, James Gregory, reprinted by permission from *God's Prescription for a Healthy Christian.* Published by Victor Books and © 1990 by SP Publications, Inc., Wheaton, IL.

Meyer, F. B., from *Devotional Commentary by F. B. Meyer* (1989) Tyndale House Publishers, Inc. Used by permission. All rights reserved.

Meyer, F. B., taken from *Our Daily Walk.* Copyright © 1951, 1972 by the Zondervan Publishing House. Used by permission.

Miley, Jeanie, *Creative Silence: Keys to the Deeper Life,* copyright © 1989, Word, Inc., Dallas, Texas.

Mitchell, John G., from the book *An Everlasting Love,* copyright 1982 by Multnomah Press. Published by Multnomah Press, Portland, Oregon 97206. Used by permission.

Moody, D. L., taken from *The Way to God and How to Find It.* Copyright © 1983. Moody Bible Institute of Chicago. Moody Press. Used by permission.

Morley, Patrick, *I Surrender.* Wolgemuth & Hyatt, Publishers, Inc. Used by permission.

Mote, Edward, *The Solid Rock* in *The Hymnal for Worship and Celebration,* copyright © 1986, Word Music, Waco, Texas.

Muggeridge, Malcolm, from *The End of Christendom,* copyright 1980 by William B. Eerdmans Publishing Co., pp. 51-54. Used by permission.

Muggeridge, Malcolm, *A Twentieth Century Testimony,* copyright © 1978, Thomas Nelson Publishers, Nashville, TN.

Murray, Andrew, from *Abide in Christ* (Ft. Washington, PA: Christian Literature Crusade).

Murray, Andrew, *The Believer's Secret of Living Like Christ,* Bethany House Publishers, © 1985.

Murray, Andrew, *The Believer's Secret of Waiting on God,* Bethany House Publishers, © 1986.

Murray, Andrew, taken from *The True Vine.* Copyright © 1983. Moody Bible Institute of Chicago. Moody Press. Used by permission.

Murray, Andrew, and Edwards, Jonathan; Parkhurst, Louis Gifford (Compiler and Editor), *The Believer's Secret of Christian Love,* Bethany House Publishers, © 1990.

Murray, Andrew, and Finney, Charles G.; Parkhurst, L. G. (Compiler and Editor), *The Believer's Secret of Spiritual Power,* Bethany House Publishers, © 1987.

Myers, Warren and Ruth, *Pray: How to Be Effective in Prayer,* copyright © 1983, Navpress, Colorado Springs, Colorado.

Oatman, Johnson Jr., *Count Your Blessings* in *The Hymnal for Worship and Celebration,* copyright © 1986, Word Music, Waco, Texas.

Ogilvie, Lloyd, *Enjoying God,* copyright © 1989, Word, Inc., Dallas, Texas.

Ogilvie, Lloyd John, taken from *Silent Strength for My Life.* Copyright © 1990 by Harvest House Publishers, Eugene, OR 97402. Used by permission.

Ortlund, Anne, *Disciplines of the Home,* copyright © 1990, Word, Inc., Dallas, Texas.

Packer, J. I., taken from *Knowing God.* © 1973 by J. I. Packer. Used by permission of InterVarsity Press, P.O. Box 1400, Downers Grove, IL 60515. Worldwide permission granted by Hodder & Stoughton Limited, England.

Packer, James and Watson, Jean, reprinted from *Your Father Loves You,* © 1986. Used by permission of Harold Shaw Publishers, Wheaton, IL. Worldwide permission granted by Hodder & Stoughton Limited, England.

Palau, Luis, reprinted by permission from *Time to Stop Pretending.* Published by Victor Books and © 1985 by SP Publications, Inc., Wheaton, IL.

Pinnock, Clark H., from *Practical Christianity;* LaVonne Neff, Ron Beers, Bruce Barton, Linda Taylor, Dave Veerman, and Jim Galvin (Compilers and Editors), © 1987 by Youth for Christ/USA. Used by permission of Tyndale House Publishers. All rights reserved.

Pippert, Rebecca Manley, taken from *Out of the Saltshaker and Into the World.* © 1979 by Inter-Varsity Christian Fellowship of the USA. Used by permission of InterVarsity Press, P.O. Box 1400, Downers Grove, IL 60515.

Reid, David, *Devotions for Growing Christians.* Used by permission of Loizeaux Brothers, Inc., Neptune, New Jersey.

Ryrie, Charles C., reprinted by permission from *The Final Countdown.* Published by Victor Books and © 1982 by SP Publications, Inc., Wheaton, IL.

Sanders, J. Oswald, taken from *Enjoying Intimacy With God.* Copyright © 1980. Moody Bible Institute of Chicago. Moody Press. Used by permission.

Sanders, J. Oswald, taken from *Just Like Us.* Copyright © 1978. Moody Bible Institute of Chicago. Moody Press. Used by permission.

Sanders, J. Oswald, taken from *Shoe Leather Commitment.* Copyright © 1990. Moody Bible Institute of Chicago. Moody Press. Used by permission.

Schaeffer, Edith, from the book *Affliction,* copyright © 1978 by Edith Schaeffer. Used by permission of Fleming H. Revell Company.

Schaeffer, Edith, *Common Sense Christian Living,* copyright © 1983, Thomas Nelson Publishers, Nashville, TN.

Schmidt, Thomas E., taken from the book *Trying to Be Good.* Copyright © 1990 by Thomas E. Schmidt. Used by permission of the Zondervan Publishing House.

Senter, Ruth, taken from *The Attributes of God.* Copyright © 1987. Moody Bible Institute of Chicago. Moody Press. Used by permission.

Senter, Ruth, *Longing for Love,* copyright © 1991 by Ruth Senter, NavPress, Colorado Springs, Colorado.

Senter, Ruth, taken from the book *Startled by Silence.* Copyright © 1986 by Ruth Senter. Used by permission of the Zondervan Publishing House.

Shaw, Luci, reprinted from *Postcard from the Shore,* © 1985 by Luci Shaw. Used by permission of Harold Shaw Publishers, Wheaton, IL.

Sherman, Doug and Hendricks, William, *How to Succeed Where It Really Counts,* copyright © 1989 by Doug Sherman and William Hendricks, NavPress, Colorado Springs, Colorado.

Sider, Ronald J., *Rich Christians in an Age of Hunger,* copyright © 1990, Word, Inc., Dallas, Texas.

Simpson, A. B., taken from the book *Days of Heaven on Earth.* Copyright © 1984 by Christian Publications. Used by permission of the Zondervan Publishing House.

Smith, F. LaGard, *The Daily Gospels* (formerly *The Intimate Jesus*). Copyright © 1988 by Harvest House Publishers, Eugene, OR 97402.

Smith, Hannah Whitall, from the book *The Christian's Secret of a Happy Life.* Copyright © 1952 by Fleming H. Revell Company. Used by permission of Fleming H. Revell Company.

Sollenberger, Lucille Fern, *My Daily Appointment with God,* copyright © 1988, Word, Inc., Dallas, Texas.

Sproul, R. C., from *Effective Prayer,* © 1984. Used by permission of Tyndale House Publishers, Inc. All rights reserved.

Sproul, R. C., from *The Holiness of God,* © 1985. Used by permission of Tyndale House Publishers, Inc. All rights reserved.

Sproul, R. C., *One Holy Passion,* copyright © 1987, Thomas Nelson Publishers, Nashville, TN.

Spurgeon, C. H., taken from *All of Grace.* Copyright © 1984. Moody Bible Institute of Chicago. Moody Press. Used by permission.

Spurgeon, Charles H., taken from *Faith's Checkbook.* Copyright © 1987. Moody Bible Institute of Chicago. Moody Press. Used by permission.

Spurgeon, Charles H., *Morning and Evening,* copyright © 1991, Hendrickson Publishers, Inc. Peabody, MA.

Spurgeon, C. H., reprinted from *The Quotable Spurgeon,* © 1990 by Harold Shaw Publishers, Wheaton, IL. Used by permission.

Stamm, Mildred, taken from the book *Meditation Moments for Women.* Copyright © 1967 by the Zondervan Publishing House. Used by permission.

Stamm, Millie, taken from the book *Beside Still Waters.* Copyright © 1984 by Christian Women's Club. Used by permission of the Zondervan Publishing House.

Stamm, Millie, taken from the book *Be Still and Know.* Copyright © 1978 by Millie Stamm. Used by permission of the Zondervan Publishing House.

Stanley, Charles, *How to Handle Adversity,* copyright © 1989, Thomas Nelson Publishers, Nashville, TN.

Steer, Roger, reprinted from *Spiritual Secrets of George Müller,* © 1985 by Roger Steer. U.S.A. rights granted by permission of Harold Shaw Publishers, Wheaton, IL. Worldwide permission granted by Hodder & Stoughton Limited, England.

Steinberger, G., *In the Footprints of the Lamb,* Bethany House Publishers, © 1936.

Stoddard, William S., from the book *First Light,* copyright 1990 by Multnomah Press. Published by Multnomah Press, Portland, Oregon 97266. Used by permission.

Stott, John, from *Basic Christianity.* Copyright 1958, 1971. Inter-Varsity Press, London. Published in the U.S.A. by William B. Eerdmans Publishing Co. and in the U.K. by Inter-Varsity Press. Used by permission. Worldwide permission granted by InterVarsity Press, London, England. Second edition.

Sweeting, George, taken from *The Acts of God.* Copyright © 1986. Moody Bible Institute of Chicago. Moody Press. Used by permission.

Swindoll, Charles R., *The Grace Awakening,* copyright © 1990, Word, Inc., Dallas, Texas.

Swindoll, Charles R., *Improving Your Serve: The Art of Unselfish Living,* copyright © 1981, Word, Inc., Dallas, Texas.

Swindoll, Charles R., *Living Above the Level of Mediocrity: A Commitment to Excellence.* Copyright © 1987, Word, Inc., Dallas, Texas.

Swindoll, Charles R., from the book *Make Up Your Mind,* copyright 1981. Published by Multnomah Press, Portland, Oregon 97266. Used by permission.

Swindoll, Charles R., *Strengthening Your Grip: Essentials in an Aimless World,* copyright © 1982, Word, Inc., Dallas, Texas.

Tada, Joni Eareckson, from the book *Secret Strength,* copyright 1988 by Joni, Inc. Published by Multnomah Press, Portland, Oregon 97266. Used by permission.

Tamasy, Robert J., (General Editor), *The Complete Christian Businessman,* Wolgemuth & Hyatt, Publishers, Inc. Used by permission.

Tucker, Ruth A., taken from the book *Stories of Faith.* Copyright © 1989 by Ruth A. Tucker. Used by permission of Zondervan Publishing House.

Webber, Robert, *Worship is a Verb,* copyright © 1985, Word, Inc., Dallas, Texas. (Second edition soon to be released in 1991 by Abbott Martyn Press, Nashville, TN).

Wenham, David, taken from *The Parables of Jesus.* © 1989 by David Wenham. Used by permission of InterVarsity Press, P.O. Box 1400, Downers Grove, IL 60515. Worldwide permission granted by Hodder & Stoughton Limited, England.

White, John, taken from *The Fight.* © 1976 by Inter-Varsity Christian Fellowship of the U.S.A. Used by permission of InterVarsity Press, P.O. Box 1400, Downers Grove, IL 60515.

Wiersbe, Warren W., Reprinted by permission from *Be Alert.* Published by Victor Books and © 1984 by SP Publications, Inc., Wheaton, IL.

Wiersbe, Warren W., Reprinted by permission from *Be Victorious.* Published by Victor Books and © by 1985 SP Publications, Inc., Wheaton, IL.

Wiersbe, Warren W. (Compiler), *Classic Sermons on the Attributes of God.* © 1989 by Kregel Publications: Grand Rapids, Michigan. Used by permission.

Wiersbe, Warren W., taken from *Thoughts for Men on the Move.* Copyright © 1970, 1988. Moody Bible Institute of Chicago. Moody Press. Used by permission.

Wiersbe, Warren W., Reprinted by permission from *Windows on the Parables.* Published by Victor Books and © 1979 by SP Publications, Inc., Wheaton, IL.

Wirt, Sherwood E., *Your Mighty Fortress: Cultivating Your Inner Life With God,* Here's Life Publishers, San Bernadino, CA, © 1989.

Wright, H. Norman, *Quiet Times for Couples.* Copyright © 1990 by Harvest House Publishers, Eugene, OR 97402.

YFC Editors, from *Practical Christianity;* LaVonne Neff, Ron Beers, Bruce Barton, Linda Taylor, Dave Veerman, and Jim Galvin (Compilers and Editors), © 1987 by Youth for Christ/USA. Used by permission of Tyndale House Publishers. All rights reserved.

Yancey, Philip, taken from the book *Where is God When It Hurts?* Copyright © 1990, 1977 by Philip Yancey. Used by permission of the Zondervan Publishing House.

Yohn, Rick, *Finding Time,* copyright © 1984, Word, Inc., Dallas, Texas.

Zuck, Roy B. (Editor), reprinted by permission from *Devotions for Kindred Spirits.* Published by Victor Books and © 1990 by SP Publications, Inc., Wheaton, IL.